The Encyclopedia of Lost and Rejected Scriptures: The Pseudepigrapha and Apocrypha

By Joseph B. Lumpkin

The Encyclopedia of Lost and Rejected Scriptures:
The Pseudepigrapha and Apocrypha

First time or interested authors, contact Fifth Estate Publishers,
Post Office Box 116, Blountsville, AL 35031.

First Printing February 2010

Cover Design by An Quigley

Printed on acid-free paper

Library of Congress Control No: 2010922309

ISBN13: 9781936533558

Fifth Estate 2010

Table of Contents

Section One - Lost Scriptures of the Old Testament

Section Two - Apocalyptic Writings and the End of Days

Section Three - Lost Scriptures of the New Testament

Section Four - The Life and Times of Jesus

Section Five - The Apocrypha

INTRODUCTION

The study of scripture is a lifelong venture. Many times our search for deeper understanding of the holy book leads to questions beyond the Bible itself. As we encounter references to social conditions, cultural practices, and even other writings mentioned within the scriptures we are called to investigate and expand our knowledge in order to fully appreciate the context, knowledge base, and cultural significance of what is being taught. Thus, to fully understand the Bible, we are necessarily drawn to sources outside the Bible. These sources add to the historical, social, or theological understanding of Biblical times. As our view becomes more macrocosmic, we see the panoramic setting and further understand the full truth within the scriptures.

To point us to the sources we should be concerned with, we must know which books were popular and important at the time. There are several books mentioned in the Bible, which are not included in the Bible. They are not spiritual canon, either because they were not available at the time the canon was originally adopted, or at the time they were not considered "inspired." In cases when inspiration was questioned, one could argue that any book quoted or mentioned by a prophet or an apostle should be considered as spiritual canon, unfortunately this position would prove too simplistic.

Books and writings can fall under various categories such as civil records and laws, historical documents, or spiritual writings. A city or state census is not inspired, but it could add insight into certain areas of life. Spiritual writings which are directly quoted in the Bible serve as insights into the beliefs of the writer or what was considered acceptable by society at the time. As with any new discovery, invention, or belief, the new is interpreted based upon the structure of what came before. This was the way in the first century Christian church as beliefs were based upon the old Jewish understanding. Although, one should realize pagan beliefs were also added to the church as non-Jewish populations were converted, bringing with them the foundations of their beliefs on which they interpreted Christianity. In the case of Jude, James, Paul, and others, the Jewish past was giving way to the Christian present but their understanding and doctrine were still being influenced by what they had learned and experienced previously. It becomes obvious that to understand the Bible one should endeavor to investigate the books and doctrines that most influenced the writers of the Bible. Some of these doctrines evolved to become today's faith. Some diverged and competed as with orthodox doctrine, other simply faded away.

The Dead Sea Scrolls found in the caves of Qumran are of great interest in the venture of clarifying the history and doctrine in existence between biblical times and the fixing of canon. The scrolls were penned in the second century B.C. and were in use at least until the destruction of the second temple in 70 A.D. Similar scrolls to those found in the eleven caves of Qumran were also found at the Masada stronghold which fell in 73 A.D. Fragments of every book of the Old Testament except Esther were found in the caves of Qumran, but so were many other books. Some of these books are considered to have been of equal importance and influence to the people of Qumran and to the writers and scholars of the time. Some of those studying the scrolls found in Qumran were the writers of the New Testament.

Knowing this, one might ask which of the dozens of non-canonical books most influenced the writers of the New Testament. It is possible to ascertain the existence of certain influences within the Bible context by using the Bible itself. The Bible can direct us to other works in three ways. The work can be mentioned by name, as is the Book of Jasher. The work can be quoted within the Bible text, as is the case with the Book of Enoch. The existence of a work can be alluded to, as is the case of the missing letter from the apostle Paul to the Corinthians.

In the case of those books named in the Bible, one can set a list as the titles are named. The list is lengthier than one might at first suspect. Most of these works have not been found. Some have been unearthed but their authenticity is questioned. Others have been found and the link between scripture and scroll is generally accepted. Following is a list of books mentioned in the Holy Bible.

The Book of Jasher: There are two references to the book in the Old Testament:

2 Samuel 1:18 - Behold, it is written in the Book of Jasher. "So the sun stood still, and the moon stopped, until the nations avenged themselves of their enemies."

Joshua 10:13 - Is it not written in the Book of Jasher? And the sun stopped in the middle of the sky and did not hasten to go down for about a whole day.

There are several books which have come to us entitled, "Book of Jasher." One is an ethical treatise from the Middle Ages. It begins with a section on the Mystery of the Creation of the World: It is clearly unrelated to the Biblical Book of Jasher.

Another was published in 1829 supposedly translated by Flaccus Albinus Alcuinus. It opens with the Chapter 1 Verse 1 reading: "While it was the beginning, darkness overspread the face of nature." It is now considered a fake.

The third and most important is by Midrash, first translated into English in 1840. It opens with Chapter 1 Verse 1 reading: "And God said, Let us make man in our image, after our likeness, and God created man in his own image." A comparison of Joshua 10:13 with Jasher 88:63-64 and 2Sam. 1:18 with Jasher 56:9 makes it clear that this Book of Jasher at least follows close enough with the Bible to be the Book of Jasher mentioned in the Bible.

Other books mentioned by name in the Bible are:

1.   The Book of Wars of the Lord: "Therefore it is said in the Book of the Wars of the Lord." Num. 21:14
2.   The Annals of Jehu: "Now the rest of the acts of Jehoshaphat, first to last, behold, they are written in the annals of Jehu the son of Hanani, which is recorded in the Book of the Kings of Israel." 2 Chronicles 20:34
3.   The treatise of the Book of the Kings: "As to his sons and the many oracles against him and the rebuilding of the house of God, behold, they are written in the treatise of the Book of the Kings. Then Amaziah his son became king in his place." 2 Chronicles 24:27
4.   The Book of Records, Book of the Chronicles of Ahasuerus: "Now when the plot was investigated and found to be so, they were both hanged on a gallows; and it was written in the Book of the Chronicles in the king's presence." ... "During that night the king could not sleep so he gave an order to bring the book of records, the chronicles, and they were read before the king." Esther 2:23; 6:1
5.   The Acts of Solomon: "Now the rest of the acts of Solomon and whatever he did, and his wisdom, are they not written in the book of the Acts of Solomon?" 1 Kings 11:41
6.   The Sayings of Hozai: "His prayer also and how God was entreated by him, and all his sin, his unfaithfulness, and the sites on which he built high places and erected the Asherim and the carved images, before he humbled himself, behold, they are written in the records of the Hozai." 2 Chronicles 33:19
7.   The Chronicles of David: "Joab the son of Zeruiah had begun to count them, but did not finish; and because of this, wrath came upon Israel, and the number was not included in the account of the Chronicles of King David." 1 Chronicles 27:24
8.   The Chronicles of Samuel, Nathan, Gad: "Now the acts of King David, from first to last, are written in the Chronicles of Samuel the seer, in the Chronicles of Nathan the prophet and in the Chronicles of Gad the seer." 1 Chronicles 29:29
9.   Samuel's book: "Then Samuel told the people the ordinances of the kingdom, and wrote them in the book and placed it before the Lord." 1 Samuel 10:25
10.   The Records of Nathan the prophet: "Now the rest of the acts of Solomon, from first to last, are they not written in the Records of Nathan the prophet, and in the prophecy of Ahijah the Shilonite, and in the visions of Iddo the seer concerning Jeroboam the son of Nebat?" 2 Chronicles 9:29
11.   The Prophecy of Ahijah the Shilonite: "Now the rest of the acts of Solomon, from first to last, are they not written in the Records of Nathan the prophet, and in the prophecy of Ahijah the Shilonite, and in the visions of Iddo the seer concerning Jeroboam the son of Nebat?" 2 Chronicles 9:29
12. The Treatise of the Prophet Iddo: "Now the rest of the acts of Abijah, and his ways and his words are written in the treatise of the prophet Iddo." 2 Chronicles 13:22
13. The Book Of Jasher: "Is it not written in the book of Jasher? 2 Samuel 1:18 and   Joshua 10:13

The existence of a book can be inferred as well, this is clearly seen with several missing epistles. Paul's letter to the church at Laodicea: "When this letter is read among you, have it also read in the church of the Laodiceans; and you, for your part read my letter that is coming from Laodicea." Colossians 4:16 (Since three earlier manuscripts do not contain the words "at Ephesus" in Eph 1:1, some have speculated that the letter coming from Laodicea was in fact the letter of Ephesians. Apostolic fathers also debated this possibility.) In Paul's first letter to Corinth, he predated that letter by saying: "I wrote you in my letter not to associate with immoral people" (1 Corinthians 5:9) (This could merely be a reference to the present letter of 1 Corinthians.)

Many lost books have been discovered. Some books are considered to be part of the Apocrypha, while others are considered to be part of the Pseudepigrapha. The difference between the Apocrypha and Pseudepigrapha is at times a matter of opinion. Strictly speaking, the Pseudepigrapha are religious books, most of which were written between 200 B.C. and 200 A.D., which have authorship falsely attributed to a another person, usually a well known saint or patriarch. The Apocrypha refers to a body of hidden or esoteric work of questionable authenticity. It is the purpose of this work to bring into light the treasure trove of books attributed to both the Apocrypha and Pseudepigrapha. Here are over forty of the most sought after books written in the most ancient of times.

When reading through this tome and comparing book to book, it will be noticed that books in this volume are laid out in a slightly different style when compared to the one before or after. It was hoped that the variety would provide each reader with a preferred presentation.

SECTION ONE

LOST SCRIPTURES OF THE OLD TESTAMENT

The First Book of Adam and Eve:

The Conflict With Satan

The First Book of Adam and Eve is an apocryphal story, written in a midrash style, detailing the life of Adam and Eve from the time God planted the Garden of Eden to the time that Cain killed his brother, Abel.

The story is a fanciful embellishment of the Genesis story up to the point of the cursing of Cain for the murder of Abel.

Of the numerous apocryphal works that were written regarding Adam and Eve this text seems to have most influenced early theologians. This is evident in the widespread popularity of the book from the third to the thirteenth century. Even though the book was widely read in the Middle Ages, and considered to shine light on what actually took place in the time of creation, today it is considered fiction and thus relegated to a collection of texts called the Pseudepigrapha, or "false writings."

The text shows some cobbling together of various works, combined into a single storyline. Although the foundation of the text can be traced to combined oral traditions thousands of years old, the primary story was likely created around two or three hundred years before Christ. Additions and details were added over many years, leading to this version being penned around the 3rd century A.D.

The text presented here is an embellishment of the Jewish storyline from Genesis that is "Christianized" by additions of allusions and references to the New Testament. Quite often the details of the story are made to foreshadow the birth, death, and resurrection of Jesus. The result is the text before you.

The central part of the text focuses on the conflict between Good and Evil in the form of Satan's endeavor to destroy God's creations, Adam and Eve. The story begs the eternal question, how does one know whether God or Satan guides the opportunity, situation, or person confronting us. The fight between good and evil, as well as the question of who is influencing our surroundings, are eternal, and the story attempts to answer in metaphor.

The creation story and the tale of Adam and Eve pervaded the thoughts of writers throughout the ancient world. Evidence is seen in the large number of versions that exist in various languages and cultures. Indeed, it is due to the amazing popularity of the text that it has survived in six languages: Greek, Latin, Armenian, Georgian, and Slavonic, as well as a fragment in Coptic. The stories may also be traced through the writings of Greeks, Syrians, Egyptians, Abyssinians, Hebrews, and other ancient peoples.

Most scholars agree that the text was written originally in Greek and that all of the six versions show evidence of Greek linguistic roots. Those Greek manuscripts we posses seem to be no more accurate to the original than any of the other translations, having been so many generations removed from the source document.

The foundation of our modern English translation began with the work of, Vicar of Broadwindsor, Dr. S. C. Malan, who worked from the Ethiopic edition edited by, Professor at the University of Munich. Dr. Trumpp, who had the advantage of having an older version at his disposal.

From an ancient oral tradition, to a 3rd century codex, through the hands of Dr. E. Trumpp and Dr. S. C. Malan, to this modern English version, the First Book of Adam and Eve has survived, just as mankind has survived the struggles written of in the book itself.

The Malan translation of the text was penned in a rather stilted and formal style of English resembling that of the King James Bible. The Malan translation was then taken and re-written with word choices and sentence structure altered to make it more palatable and understandable to the modern reader, while keeping the poetic flow of the text.

Notes and references are added in italicized font. Alternate words or phrases that may add more depth or possibilities in translation are place in parentheses.

The First Book of Adam and Eve

Chapter I

1 On the third day, God planted the garden in the east of the earth, on the border of the world in the eastward direction toward and beyond the rising sun. There one finds nothing but water that encompasses the whole world and reaches to the borders of heaven. 2 And to the north of the garden there is a sea of water, clear and pure to the taste, unlike anything else; so that, through the clearness one may look into the depths of the earth. 3 And when a man washes himself in it, he becomes perfectly clean and perfectly white, even if he were dark. 4 And God created that sea of his own good pleasure, for He knew what would come of the man He would make; so that after he had left the garden, because of his transgression, men should be born in the earth. Among them are righteous ones who will die, whose souls God would raise at the last day when all of them will return to their flesh, bathe in the water of that sea, and repent of their sins. 5 But when God caused Adam go out of the garden, He did not place him on the border of it northward. This was so that he and Eve would not be able to go near to the sea of water where they could wash themselves in it and be cleansed from their sins and erase the transgression they had committed, so that they be no longer reminded of it in the thought of their punishment. 6 As to the southern side of the garden, God did not want Adam to live there either, because, when the wind blew from the north, it would bring to him, on that southern side, the delicious smell of the trees of the garden. 7 So God did not put Adam there. This was so that he would not be able to smell the sweet smell of those trees and forget his transgression, and find consolation for what he had done by taking delight in the smell of the trees and yet not be cleansed from his transgression. 8 Also, because God is merciful and of great pity, and governs all things in a way that He alone knows He made our father Adam to live in the western border of the garden because on that side the land is very wide. 9 And God commanded him to live there in a cave in a rock. This was the Cave of Treasures, which is below the garden.

Chapter II

1 But when our father Adam, and Eve, went out of the garden, they walked the ground on their feet, not knowing where they were going. 2 And when they came to the opening of the gate of the garden and saw the land spread before them widely, covered with stones large and small, and with sand, they feared and trembled, and fell on their faces from the fear that came over them and they were as though they were dead. 3 Until this time they had been in the garden land, beautifully planted with all manner of trees and they now saw themselves in a strange land, which they did not know and had never seen. 4 When they were in the garden they were filled with the grace of a bright nature, and they had hearts not turned toward earthly things. 5 Therefore God had pity on them; and when He saw them fallen before the gate of the garden, He sent His Word to our father Adam, and to Eve, and raised them from their fallen state.

Chapter III

1 God said to Adam, "I have ordained days and years on this earth, and you and your descendants shall live and walk in them until the days and years are fulfilled. Then I shall send the Word that created you and against which you have transgressed the Word that made you come out of the garden and that raised you when you were fallen. 2 Yes, this is the Word that will again save you when the five and a half days are fulfilled." 3 But when Adam heard these words from God, and of the great five and a half days he did not understand the meaning of them. 4 For Adam was thinking there would be only five and a half days for him until the end of the world. 5 And Adam cried and prayed to God to explain it to him. 6 Then God in his mercy for Adam who was made after His own image and likeness explained to him that these were 5,000 and 500 years and how (the) One would then come and save him and his descendants. 7 But before that, God had made this covenant with our father, Adam, in the same terms before he came out of the garden, when he was by the tree where Eve took of the fruit and gave it to him to eat. 8 Because, when our father, Adam, came out of the garden he passed by that tree and saw how God had changed the appearance of it into another form and how it had shriveled. 9 And as Adam went to it he feared, trembled, and fell down. But God in His mercy lifted him up and then made this covenant with him. 10 Also, when Adam was by the gate of the garden he saw the cherub with a sword of flashing fire in his hand, and the cherub grew angry and frowned at him. Both Adam and Eve became afraid of the cherub and thought he meant to put them to death. So they fell on their faces, trembling with fear. 11 But he had pity on them and showed them mercy. And turning from them, he went up to heaven and prayed to the Lord, and said; 12 "Lord, You sent me to watch at the gate of the garden, with a sword of fire. 13 But when Your servants, Adam and Eve, saw me, they fell on their faces, and were as dead. O my Lord, what shall we do to Your servants?" 14 Then God had pity on them, and showed them mercy, and sent His Angel to keep the garden. 15 And the Word of the Lord came to Adam and Eve, and raised them up. 16 And the Lord said to Adam, "I told you that at the end of the five and a half days I will send my Word and save you. 17 Therefore, strengthen your heart and stay in the Cave of Treasures, of which I have spoken to you before." 18 And when Adam heard this Word from God he was comforted with that

which God had told him. For He had told him how He would save him.

Author's note: The year 1740 equates to the Hebrew year 5500. It was around this time the Great Revival or the Great Awakening began in the United States and lasted until around 1750. Some sources have the religious revival at 1678 – 1745 while other sources have 1740 – 1750. However, the time between creation and Adam's fall must be accounted for. The author is suggesting that the time between the fall of Adam and the death of Christ is 5500 years.

Chapter IV

1 But Adam and Eve cried for having come out of the garden, which was their first home. 2 And indeed, when Adam looked at his flesh he saw that it was altered, and he cried bitterly, he and Eve cried, over what they had done. And they walked and went gently down into the Cave of Treasures. 3 And as they came to it, Adam cried over himself and said to Eve, "Look at this cave that is to be our prison in this world, and a place of punishment! 4 What is it compared with the garden? What is its narrowness compared with the space of the other? 5 What is this rock compared of those groves? What is the gloom of this cavern, compared with the light of the garden? 6 What is this overhanging ledge of rock that shelters us compared with the mercy of the Lord that overshadowed us? 7 What is the soil of this cave compared with the garden land? Does this earth, scattered with stones, compared to that garden planted with delicious fruit trees?" 8 And Adam said to Eve, "Look at your eyes, and at mine, which before beheld angels praising in heaven without ceasing. 9 Now we do not see as we did; our eyes have become of flesh; they cannot see like they saw before." 10 Adam said again to Eve, "What is our body today, compared to what it was in former days, when we lived in the garden?" 11 After this, Adam did not want to enter the cave under the overhanging rock. He never wanted to enter it again. 12 But he bowed to God's commands; and said to himself, "Unless I enter the cave, I shall again be a transgressor."

Chapter V

1 Then Adam and Eve entered the cave, and stood praying, in their own tongue, unknown to us, but which they knew well. 2 And as they prayed, Adam raised his eyes and saw the rock and the roof of the cave that covered him overhead. This prevented him from seeing either heaven or God's creatures. So he cried and beat his chest hard, until he dropped, and was as dead. 3 And Eve sat crying; for she believed he was dead. 4 Then she got up, spread her hands toward God, appealing to Him for mercy and pity, and said, "O God, forgive me my sin, the sin which I committed, and don't remember it against me. 5 For I alone caused Your servant to fall from the garden into this condemned land; from light into this darkness; and from the house of joy into this prison. 6 O God, look at this Your servant fallen in this manner, and bring him back to life, that he may cry and repent of his transgression which he committed through (because of) me. 7 Don't take away his soul at this time; but let him live so that he may stand after the measure of his repentance, and do Your will, as before his death. 8 But if You do not bring him back to life, then, O God, take away my own soul, so that I will be like him, and leave me not in this dungeon, alone; for I could not stand alone in this world, without him. 9 For You, O God, caused him to fall asleep, and took a bone from his side, and placed the flesh back in its place by Your divine power. 10 And You took me, the bone, and made me, a woman, bright like him, with heart, reason, and speech; and flesh like to his own; and You made me after the likeness of his looks, by Your mercy and power. 11 O Lord, I and he are one, and You, O God, are our Creator, You are He who made us both in one day. 12 Therefore, O God, give him life so that he may be with me in this strange land while we live in it due to our transgression. 13 But if You will not give him life, then take me, even me, like him; that we both may die the same day." 14 And Eve cried bitterly, and fell on our father, Adam, because of her great sorrow.

Chapter VI

1 But God looked at them, for they had killed themselves through great grief. 2 And He decided to raise them and comfort them. 3 Therefore, He sent His Word to them that they should stand and be raised immediately. 4 And the Lord said to Adam and Eve, "You transgressed of your own free will, until you came out of the garden in which I had placed you. 5 Of your own free will have you transgressed through your desire for divinity, greatness, and an exalted state, such as I have; therefore I deprived you of the bright nature which you had then, and I made you come out of the garden to this land, rough and full of trouble. 6 If only you had not transgressed My commandment and had kept My law, and had not eaten of the fruit of the tree which I told you not to come near! And there were fruit trees in the garden better than that one. 7 But the wicked Satan did not keep his faith and had no good intent towards Me, and although I had created him he considered Me to be useless, and he sought the Godhead for himself. For this I hurled him down from heaven so that he could not remain in his first estate. It was he who made the tree appear pleasant to your eyes until you ate of it by believing his words. 8 Thus have you transgressed My commandment, and therefore I have brought on you all these sorrows. 9 For I am God the Creator, who, when I created My creatures, did not intend to destroy them. But after they had greatly roused My anger I punished them with grievous plagues until they repent. 10 But, if on the contrary they still continue hardened in their transgression they shall be under a curse forever."

Chapter VII

1 When Adam and Eve heard these words from God, they cried and sobbed even more, but they strengthened their hearts in God because they now felt that the Lord was to them like a father and a mother; and for this very reason, they cried before Him, and sought mercy from Him. 2 Then God had pity on them, and said: "O Adam, I have made My covenant with you, and I will not turn from it; neither will I let you return to the garden, until My covenant of the great five and a half days is fulfilled." 3 Then Adam said to God, "O Lord, You created us, and made us fit to be in the garden; and before I transgressed, You made all beasts come to me, that I should name them. 4 Your grace was then on me; and I named every one according to Your mind; and you made them all subject to me. 5 But now, O Lord God, that I have transgressed Your commandment, all beasts will rise against me and will devour me, and Eve Your handmaid; and will cut off our life from the face of the earth. 6 I therefore beg you, O God, that since You have made us come out of the garden, and have made us be in a strange land, You will not let the beasts hurt us." 7 When the Lord heard these words from Adam, He had pity on him, and felt that he had truly said that the beasts of the field would rise and devour him and Eve, because He, the Lord, was angry with the two of them because of their transgressions. 8 Then God commanded the beasts, and the birds, and all that moves on the earth, to come to Adam and to be familiar with him, and not to trouble him and Eve; nor any of the good and righteous among their offspring. 9 Then all the beasts paid homage to Adam, according to the commandment of God except the serpent, against which God was angry. It did not come to Adam, with the beasts.

Chapter VIII

1 Then Adam cried and said, "O God, when we lived in the garden, and our hearts were lifted up, we saw the angels that sang praises in heaven, but now we can't see like we once saw. No. When we entered the cave all creation became hidden from us." 2 Then God the Lord said to Adam, "When you were under subjection to Me, you had a bright nature within you and for that reason could you see distant things. But after you transgressed your bright nature was taken out of you and it was not left in you to see distant things, but only things near to you, as is the ability of the flesh, for it is brutish." 3 When Adam and Eve had heard these words from God, they went their way, praising and worshipping Him with a sorrowful heart. 4 And God ceased communing with them.

Chapter IX

1 Then Adam and Eve came out of the Cave of Treasures, and came near to the garden gate. There they stood and looked at it and cried for having gone away from it. 2 And Adam and Eve went south of the gate of the garden to the side of it and found there the water that watered the garden, which came from the root of the Tree of Life, and they saw that the water was split from there into four rivers over the earth. 3 Then they came near to that water and looked at it and saw that it was the water that came up from under the root of the Tree of Life in the garden. 4 And Adam cried and wailed, and beat his chest for being cut out from the garden; and said to Eve: 5 "Why have you brought so many of these plagues and punishments on me, on yourself, and on our descendants?" 6 And Eve said to him, "What is it you have seen that has caused you to cry and to speak to me in this manner?" 7 And he said to Eve, "Do you not see this water that watered the trees of the garden, and flowed out from there that was with us in the garden? 8 And when we were in the garden we did not care about it, but since we came to this strange land we love it and turn it to use for our body." 9 But when Eve heard these words from him, she cried; and from the soreness of their crying, they fell into that water; and would have put an end to themselves in it so as never again to return and behold the creation for when they looked at the work of creation, they felt they must put an end to themselves.

Chapter X

1 Then God, merciful and gracious, looked at them as they were lying in the water, and close to death, and He sent an angel who brought them out of the water and laid them on the seashore as dead. 2 Then the angel went up to God and said, "O God, Your creatures have breathed their last breath." 3 Then God sent His Word to Adam and Eve, who raised them from their death. 4 And Adam said, after he was raised, "O God, while we were in the garden we did not require or care about this water, but since we came to this land we cannot do without it." 5 Then God said to Adam, "While you were under My command and were a bright angel you did not experience this water. 6 But now that you have transgressed My commandment, you can not do without water to wash your body and make it grow, for it is now like that of beasts, and is in want of water." 7 When Adam and Eve heard these words from God, they cried a bitter cry; and Adam entreated God to let him return into the garden and look at it a second time. 8 But God said to Adam, "I have made you a promise; when that promise is fulfilled, I will bring you back into the garden, you and your righteous descendants." 9 And God ceased to commune with Adam.

Authors note: Notice the text promises Adam and his righteous descendants will be returned to Eden after the 5,500 year term is completed. Thus, the righteous portion of mankind would be returned in the Hebrew year 5,500 plus the time between creation and Adam's fall. Adam must be kept alive or transfigured since resurrection of the body was not part of Jewish doctrine.

Chapter XI

1 Adam and Eve then felt themselves burning with thirst, and heat, and sorrow. 2 And Adam said to Eve, "We shall not drink of this water even if we were to die. O Eve, when this water comes into our inner parts it will increase our punishments and that of our descendants." 3 Both Adam and Eve then went away from the water, and drank none of it at all but came and entered the Cave of Treasures. 4 But when in it Adam could not see Eve he only heard the noise she made. Neither could she see Adam, but heard the noise he made. 5 Then Adam cried in deep affliction and beat his chest, and he got up and said to Eve, "Where are you?" 6 And she said to him, "Look, I am standing here in this darkness." 7 He then said to her, "Remember the bright nature in which we lived, when we lived in the garden! 8 O Eve! Remember the glory that rested on us in the garden. O Eve! Remember the trees that overshadowed us in the garden while we moved among them. 9 O Eve! Remember that while we were in the garden, we knew neither night nor day. Think of the Tree of Life. From below it flowed the water and that shed splendor over us! Remember, O Eve, the land of the garden and the brightness of it. 10 Think, oh think of that garden in which there was no darkness while we lived in it. 11 But no sooner did we come into this Cave of Treasures than darkness surrounded us all around until we can no longer see each other, and all the pleasure of this life has come to an end."

Chapter XII

1 Then Adam beat his chest, he and Eve, and they mourned the whole night until the first light of dawn, and they sighed over the length of the night in Miyazia. 2 And Adam beat himself, and threw himself on the ground in the cave, from bitter grief, and because of the darkness and lay there as dead. 3 But Eve heard the noise he made in falling on the ground. And she felt about for him with her hands and found him like a corpse. 4 Then she was afraid, speechless, and she remained by him. 5 But the merciful Lord looked on the death of Adam, and on Eve's silence from fear of the darkness. 6 And the Word of God came to Adam and raised him from his death, and opened Eve's mouth that she might speak. 7 Then Adam stood up in the cave and said, "O God, why has light departed from us and darkness covered us? Why did you leave us in this extensive darkness? Why do you plague us like this? 8 And this darkness, O Lord, where was it before it covered us? It is because of this that we cannot see each other. 9 For so long as we were in the garden we neither saw nor even knew what darkness was. I was not hidden from Eve, neither was she hidden from me, until now that she cannot see me and no darkness came over us to separate us from each other. 10 But she and I were both in one bright light. I saw her and she saw me. Yet now since we came into this cave darkness has covered us and separated us from each other so that I do not see her, and she does not see me. 11 O Lord, will You then plague us with this darkness?"

Author's note: Miyazia equates to a particular month in the Ethiopian calendar.

Chapter XIII

1 Then when God, who is merciful and full of pity, heard Adam's voice, He said to him: 2 "O Adam, so long as the good angel was obedient to Me, a bright light rested on him and on his hosts. 3 But when he transgressed My commandment, I dispossessed him of that bright nature, and he became dark. 4 And when he was in the heavens, in the realms of light, he knew nothing of darkness. 5 But he transgressed, and I made him fall from the heaven onto the earth; and it was this darkness that came over him. 6 And, O Adam, while in My garden and obedient to Me that bright light rest also on you. 7 But when I heard of your transgression, I took from you that bright light. Yet, of My mercy, I did not turn you into darkness but I made your body a body of flesh over which I spread this skin in order that it may bear cold and heat. 8 If I had let My wrath fall heavily on you I should have destroyed you and had I turned you into darkness it would have been as if I had killed you. 9 But in My mercy I have made you as you are when you transgressed My commandment, O Adam, I drove you from the garden, and made you come forth into this land and commanded you to live in this cave and darkness covered you, as it did over him who transgressed My commandment. 10 Thus, O Adam, has this night deceived you. It is not to last forever but is only of twelve hours when it is over daylight will return. 11 Do not sigh or be moved and do not say in your heart that this darkness is long and drags on wearily. Do not say in your heart that I plague you with it. 12 Strengthen your heart and be not afraid. This darkness is not a punishment. Adam, I have made the day and have placed the sun in it to give light in order that you and your children should do your work. 13 For I knew you would sin and transgress and come out into this land. Yet I wouldn't force you nor ride heard over you, nor shut up, nor doom you through your fall, nor through your coming out from light into darkness, nor yet through your coming from the garden into this land. 14 For I made you of the light and I willed to bring out children of light from you that were like you. 15 But you did not keep My commandment one day until I had finished the creation and blessed everything in it. 16 Then, concerning the tree, I commanded you not to

eat of it. Yet I knew that Satan, who deceived himself, would also deceive you. 17 So I made known to you by means of the tree, not to come near him. And I told you not to eat of the fruit thereof, nor to taste of it, nor yet to sit under it, nor to yield to it. 18 Had I not spoken to you, O Adam, concerning the tree and had I left you without a commandment and you had sinned it would have been an offence on My part, for not having given you any order you would turn around and blame Me for it. 19 But I commanded you, and warned you, and you fell. So that My creatures cannot blame Me; but the blame rests on them alone. 20 And, O Adam, I have made the day so that you and your descendants can work and toil in it. And I have made the night for them to rest in it from their work and for the beasts of the field to go forth by night and look for their food. 21 But little of darkness now remains, O Adam, and daylight will soon appear."

Chapter XIV

1 Then Adam said to God: "O Lord, take my soul and let me not see this gloom any more, or remove me to some place where there is no darkness." 2 But God the Lord said to Adam, " I say to you, indeed, this darkness will pass from you every day, I have determined for you until the fulfillment of My covenant when I will save you and bring you back again into the garden and into the house of light you long for, in which there is no darkness. I will bring you to it in the kingdom of heaven." 3 Again God said to Adam, "All this misery that you have been made to take on yourself because of your transgression will not free you from the hand of Satan and it will not save you. 4 But I will. When I shall come down from heaven and shall become flesh of your descendants, and take on Myself the infirmity from which you suffer then the darkness that covered you in this cave shall cover Me in the grave, when I am in the flesh of your descendants. 5 And I, who am without years, shall be subject to the reckoning of years of times of months, and of days, and I shall be reckoned as one of the sons of men in order to save you." 6 And God ceased to commune with Adam.

Author's Note: John 1:14And the Word was made flesh, and dwelt among us, (and we beheld his glory, the glory as of the only begotten of the Father,) full of grace and truth.
John 12:46 American King James Version: I am come a light into the world, that whoever believes on me should not abide in darkness.

Chapter XV

1 Then Adam and Eve cried and was sorrowful because of God's word to them, that they should not return to the garden until the fulfillment of the days decreed on them, but mostly because God had told them that He should suffer for their salvation.

Chapter XVI

1 After this, Adam and Eve continued to stand in the cave, praying and crying, until the morning dawned on them. 2 And when they saw the light returned to them they refrained from being afraid and strengthened their hearts. 3 Then Adam came out of the cave. And when he came to the mouth of it and stood and turned his face towards the east and saw the sunrise in glowing rays and felt the heat thereof on his body, he was afraid of it and thought in his heart that this flame came forth to plague him. 4 He then cried and beat his chest and he fell on the ground on his face and made his appeal saying: 5 "O Lord, plague me not, neither consume me, nor yet take away my life from the earth." 6 For he thought the sun was God. 7 Because while he was in the garden and heard the voice of God and the sound He made in the garden, and feared Him, Adam never saw the brilliant light of the sun, neither did its flaming heat touch his body. 8 Therefore he was afraid of the sun when flaming rays of it reached him. He thought God meant to plague him with it all the days He had decreed for him. 9 For Adam also said in his thoughts, that God did not plague them with darkness but He had caused this sun to rise and to plague them with burning heat. 10 But while he was thinking like this in his heart the Word of God came to him and said: 11 " Adam, get up on your feet. This sun is not God, but it has been created to give light by day that I spoke to you about in the cave saying, 'The dawn would come, and there would be light by day.' 12 But I am God who comforted you in the night." 13 And God ceased to commune with Adam.

Chapter XVII

1 Then, Adam and Eve came out at the mouth of the cave and went toward the garden. 2 But as they went near the western gate, from which Satan came when he deceived Adam and Eve, they found the serpent that became Satan coming at the gate, and it was sorrowfully licking the dust, and wiggling on its breast on the ground because of the curse that fell on it from God. 3 Before the curse the serpent was the most exalted of all beasts, now it was changed and become slippery and the meanest of them all, and it crept on its breast and went on its belly. 4 Before, it was the fairest of all beasts. It had been changed and became the most ugly of them all. Instead of feeding on the best food, now it turned to eat the dust. Instead of living as before, in the best places, now it lived in the dust. 5 It had been the most beautiful of all beasts, and all stood speechless at its beauty, it was now abhorred of them. 6 And, again, whereas it lived in a beautiful home, to which all other animals came

from everywhere; and where it drank, they drank also of the same; now, after it had become venomous, by reason of God's curse, all beasts fled from its home and would not drink of the water it drank, but fled from it.

Chapter XVIII

1 When the accursed serpent saw Adam and Eve it swelled its head, stood on its tail, and with eyes blood- red, it acted like it would kill them. 2 It made straight for Eve and ran after her while Adam stood by and yelled because he had no stick in his hand with which to hit the serpent, and did not know how to put it to death. 3 But with a heart burning for Eve, Adam approached the serpent and held it by the tail. When it turned towards him and said to him: 4 "O Adam, because of you and Eve I am slippery, and go on my belly." Then with its great strength it threw down Adam and Eve and squeezed them, and tried to kill them. 5 But God sent an angel who threw the serpent away from them, and raised them up. 6 Then the Word of God came to the serpent, and said to it, "The first time I made you slick, and made you to go on your belly but I did not deprive you of speech. 7 This time, however, you will be mute, and you and your race will speak no more because, the first time My creatures were ruined because of you, and this time you tried to kill them." 8 Then the serpent was struck mute, and it was no longer able to speak. 9 And a wind blew down from heaven by the command of God and carried away the serpent from Adam and Eve and threw it on the seashore where it landed in India.

Chapter XIX

1 But Adam and Eve cried before God. And Adam said to Him: 2 "O Lord, when I was in the cave I said this to you, my Lord, the beasts of the field would rise and devour me and cut off my life from the earth." 3 Then Adam, because of what had happened to him, beat his chest and fell on the ground like a corpse. Then the Word of God came to him, who raised him, and said to him, 4 "O Adam, not one of these beasts will be able to hurt you because I have made the beasts and other moving things come to you in the cave. I did not let the serpent come with them because it might have risen against you and made you tremble and the fear of it should fall into your hearts. 5 I knew that the accursed one is wicked; therefore I would not let it come near you with the other beasts. 6 But now strengthen your heart and fear not. I am with you to the end of the days I have determined for you."

Chapter XX

1 Then Adam cried and said, "O God, take us away to some other place, where the serpent can not come near us again and rise against us. For I fear that it might find your handmaid Eve alone and kill her, for its eyes are hideous and evil." 2 But God said to Adam and Eve, " Don't be afraid. From now on, I will not let it come near you. I have driven it away from you and from this mountain. I will not leave in it the ability to hurt you." 3 Then Adam and Eve worshipped before God and gave Him thanks and praised Him for having delivered them from death.

Chapter XXI

1 Then Adam and Eve went in search of the garden. 2 And the heat beat like a flame on their faces and they sweated from the heat. And they cried before the Lord. 3 But the place where they cried was close to a high mountain (top) that faced the western gate of the garden. 4 Then Adam threw himself down from the top of that mountain. His face was torn and his flesh was ripped and he lost much of his blood and was close to death. 5 Meanwhile Eve remained standing on the mountain crying over him lying as he was. 6 And she said, "I don't wish to live after him, for all that he did to himself was because of me." 7 Then she threw herself after him; and was torn and ripped by stones and remained lying as dead. 8 But the merciful God, who looks over His creatures, looked at Adam and Eve as they lay dead, and He sent His Word to them and raised them. 9 And said to Adam, "O Adam, all this misery, which you have brought on yourself, will have no affect on My ruling, neither will it alter the covenant of the five thousand and five hundred (5,500) years."

Chapter XXII

1 Then Adam said to God, "I dry up in the heat, I am faint from walking, and I don't want to be in this world. And I don't know when You will let me rest and take me out of it." 2 Then the Lord God said to him, "O Adam, it cannot be now, not until you have ended your days. Then I shall bring you out of this miserable land." 3 And Adam said to God, "While I was in the garden I knew neither heat, nor fatigue, neither transience, nor trembling, nor fear; but now since I came to this land, all this affliction has come over me. 4 Then God said to Adam, "So long as you were keeping My commandment, My light and My grace rested on you. But when you transgressed My commandment, sorrow and misery came to you in this land." 5 And Adam cried and said, "O Lord, do not cut me off for this, neither punish me with heavy plagues, nor yet repay me according to my sin; for we, of our own will, transgressed Your commandment and ignored Your law and tried to become gods like you when Satan the enemy deceived us." 6 Then God said again to Adam, "Because you have endured fear and trembling in

this land of fatigue and suffering, treading and walking about, going on this mountain, and dying from it, I will take all this on Myself in order to save you."

Author's note:
Isaiah 53
1 Who hath believed our report? and to whom is the arm of the LORD revealed?
2 For he shall grow up before him as a tender plant, and as a root out of a dry ground: he hath no form nor comeliness; and when we shall see him, there is no beauty that we should desire him.
3 He is despised and rejected of men; a man of sorrows, and acquainted with grief: and we hid as it were our faces from him; he was despised, and we esteemed him not.
4 Surely he hath borne our griefs, and carried our sorrows: yet we did esteem him stricken, smitten of God, and afflicted.
5 But he was wounded for our transgressions, he was bruised for our iniquities: the chastisement of our peace was upon him; and with his stripes we are healed.
6 All we like sheep have gone astray; we have turned every one to his own way; and the LORD hath laid on him the iniquity of us all.
7 He was oppressed, and he was afflicted, yet he opened not his mouth: he is brought as a lamb to the slaughter, and as a sheep before her shearers is dumb, so he openeth not his mouth.
8 He was taken from prison and from judgment: and who shall declare his generation? for he was cut off out of the land of the living: for the transgression of my people was he stricken.
9 And he made his grave with the wicked, and with the rich in his death; because he had done no violence, neither was any deceit in his mouth.
10 Yet it pleased the LORD to bruise him; he hath put him to grief: when thou shalt make his soul an offering for sin, he shall see his seed, he shall prolong his days, and the pleasure of the LORD shall prosper in his hand.
11 He shall see of the travail of his soul, and shall be satisfied: by his knowledge shall my righteous servant justify many; for he shall bear their iniquities.

Chapter XXIII

1 Then Adam cried more and said, "O God, have mercy on me and do not take on yourself that which I will do." 2 But God withdrew His Word from Adam and Eve. 3 Then Adam and Eve stood on their feet and Adam said to Eve, "Strengthen yourself, and I also will strengthen myself." And she strengthened herself as Adam told her. 4 Then Adam and Eve took stones and placed them in the shape of an altar and they took leaves from the trees outside the garden, with which they wiped from the face of the rock the blood they had spilled. 5 But that which had dropped on the sand they took together with the dust with which it was mixed and offered it on the altar as an offering to God. 6 Then Adam and Eve stood under the Altar and cried, praying to God, "Forgive us our offense and our sin, and look at us with Your eye of mercy. For when we were in the garden our praises and our hymns went up before you without ceasing. 7 But when we came into this strange land, pure praise was no longer ours, nor righteous prayer, nor understanding hearts, nor sweet thoughts, nor wise judgment, nor long discernment, nor upright feelings, neither was our bright nature left within us. But our body is changed from the likeness in which it was at first when we were created. 8 Yet now look at our blood which is offered on these stones and accept it at our hands as if it were the praise we used to sing to you at first when we were in the garden." 9 And Adam began to make more requests of God. Our Father, Who are in Heaven, be gracious unto us. O Lord, our God, hallowed be Your Name and let the remembrance of You be glorified in Heaven above and upon earth here below. Let Your kingdom reign over us now and forever. The Holy Men of old said remit and forgive unto all men whatsoever they have done unto me. And lead us not into temptation, but deliver us from the evil thing; for Your is the kingdom and You shall reign in glory forever and forevermore, AMEN.

Author's note: Verse 4 and continuing to the end of the chapter contain and present ideas that are of an obviously Christian era. There would have been no "men of old" at the time of Adam and Eve. The text parallels the Lord's Prayer. This, and other references to Christian symbols, makes the dating of the text at about the 3rd century A.D. likely.

Matthew 6: 9
9 After this manner therefore pray ye: Our Father which art in heaven, Hallowed be your name.
10 Thy kingdom come, Thy will be done in earth, as it is in heaven.
11 Give us this day our daily bread.
12 And forgive us our debts, as we forgive our debtors.
13 And lead us not into temptation, but deliver us from evil: For thine is the kingdom, and the power, and the glory, for ever. Amen.
14 For if ye forgive men their trespasses, your heavenly Father will also forgive you: 15 But if ye forgive not men their trespasses, neither will your Father forgive your trespasses.

Chapter XXIV

1 Then the merciful God, who is good and a lover of men, looked at Adam and Eve and at their blood, which they had held up as an offering to Him without an order from Him for so doing. But He wondered at them and accepted their offering. 2 And God sent from His presence a bright fire that consumed their offering. 3 He smelled the sweet savor of their offering and showed them mercy. 4 Then the Word of God came to Adam, and said to him, "O Adam, as you have shed your blood so will I shed My own blood when I become flesh of your descendants. And as you died, O Adam, so also will I die. And as you built an altar, so also will I make for you an altar of the earth. And as you offered your blood on it, so also will I offer My blood on an altar on the earth. 5 And as you appealed for forgiveness through that blood, so also will I make My blood forgiveness of sins and erase transgressions in it. 6 And now, behold, I have accepted your offering, O Adam, but the days of the covenant in which I have bound you are not fulfilled. When they are fulfilled, then will I bring you back into the garden. 7 Now, therefore, strengthen your heart. And when sorrow comes over you make Me an offering and I will be favorable to you."

Chapter XXV

1 But God knew that Adam believed he would frequently kill himself and make an offering to Him of his blood. 2 Therefore He said to him, "Adam, don't ever kill yourself like this again, by throwing yourself down from that mountain." 3 But Adam said to God, "I was thinking to put an end to myself right now for having transgressed Your commandments and for my having come out of the beautiful garden and for the bright light which You have taken from me, and for the praises which poured out from my mouth without ceasing, and for the light that covered me. 4 Yet because of Your goodness, O God, you did not get rid of me altogether, but you have been favorable to me every time I die and you bring me to life. 5 And thereby it will be made known that You are a merciful God who does not want anyone to perish, who would love it if no one should fall, and who does not condemn any one cruelly, badly, or by total destruction." 6 Then Adam remained silent. 7 And the Word of God came to him and blessed him and comforted him and covenanted with him that He would save him at the end of the days determined for him. 8 This, then, was the first offering Adam made to God and so it became his custom to do.

Chapter XXVI

1 Then Adam took Eve and they began to return to the Cave of Treasures where they lived. But when they got closer to it and saw it from a distance, heavy sorrow fell on Adam and Eve when they looked at it. 2 Then Adam said to Eve, "When we were on the mountain we were comforted by the Word of God that talked with us and the light that came from the east shown over us. 3 But now the Word of God is hidden from us and the light that shined over us has changed so much that it has disappeared and let darkness and sorrow cover us. 4 And we are forced to enter this cave that is like a prison, in which darkness covers us so that we are separated from each other. You cannot see me. I cannot see you." 5 When Adam had said these words, they cried and spread their hands before God because they were full of sorrow. 6 And they prayed to God to bring the sun for them to shine on them so that darkness would not return to them and that they wouldn't have to go under this covering of rock. They wanted to die rather than see the darkness. 7 Then God looked at Adam and Eve and at their great sorrow and all they had done with a fervent heart because of all the trouble they were in. When compared to their former state of well-being, all the misery that came over them did so in this strange land. 8 Therefore God was neither angry with them nor impatient, but he was patient and longsuffering toward them, as toward the children He had created. 9 Then the Word of God came to Adam and said to him, "Adam, regarding the sun, if I were to take it and bring it to you, days, hours, years and months would all stop and the covenant I have made with you, would never be fulfilled. 10 And you would be deserted and stuck in a perpetual plague and you would never be saved. 11 Yes, rather, bear up long, and calm your soul while you live night and day until the fulfillment of the days and the time of My covenant has come. 12 Then I shall come and save you, Adam. I do not wish for you to be afflicted. 13 And when I look at all the good things that you lived in before, and why you came out of them, then I am willing to show you mercy. 14 But I cannot alter the covenant that has gone out of My mouth, otherwise I would have brought you back into the garden. 15 However, when the covenant is fulfilled then I will show you and your descendants mercy, and bring you into a land of gladness where there is neither sorrow nor suffering but abiding joy and gladness, and light that never fails, and praises that never cease, and a beautiful garden that shall never pass away." 16 And God said again to Adam, "Be patient and enter the cave because of the darkness of which you were afraid shall only be twelve hours long. When it is over, light will come up." 17 Then when Adam heard these words from God, he and Eve worshipped before Him, and their hearts were comforted. They returned into the cave after their custom, while tears flowed from their eyes sorrow and wailing came from their hearts and they wished their soul would leave their body. 18 And Adam and Eve stood praying until the darkness of night covered them and Adam was hidden from Eve and she from him. 19 And they remained standing in prayer.

Chapter XXVII

1 Satan, the hater of all that is good, saw how they continued in prayer, and how God communed with them, and comforted them, and how He had accepted their offering. Then Satan made a phantasm. 2 He began by transforming his hosts. In his hands was a shining, glimmering fire, and they were in a huge light. 3 Then, he placed his throne near the mouth of the cave, because he could not enter it due to their prayers. And he shown light into the cave until the cave glistened over Adam and Eve while his hosts began to sing praises. 4 Satan did this so that when Adam saw the light he would think to himself that it was a heavenly light and that Satan's hosts were angels and that God had sent them to watch at the cave, and give him light in the darkness. 5 Satan planned that when Adam came out of the cave and saw them and Adam and Eve bowed to Satan, then he would overcome Adam and humble him before God a second time. 6 When, therefore, Adam and Eve saw the light, thinking it was real, they strengthened their hearts. Then, as they were trembling, Adam said to Eve: 7 "Look at that great light, and at those many songs of praise, and at that host standing outside who won't come into our cave. Why don't they tell us what they want or where they are from or what the meaning of this light is or what those praises are or why they have been sent to this place, and why they won't come in? 8 If they were from God, they would come into the cave with us and would tell us why they were sent." 9 Then Adam stood up and prayed to God with a burning heart and said: 10 "O Lord, is there in the world another god besides You who created angels and filled them with light, and sent them to keep us, who would come with them? 11 But, look, we see these hosts that stand at the mouth of the cave. They are in a great light and they sing loud praises. If they are of some other god(s) than You, tell me, and if they are sent by you, inform me of the reason for which You have sent them." 12 No sooner had Adam said this, than an angel from God appeared to him in the cave, who said to him, "O Adam, fear not. This is Satan and his hosts. He wishes to deceive you as he deceived you at first. For the first time, he was hidden in the serpent, but this time he is come to you in the likeness of an angel of light in order that, when you worshipped him, he might enslave you in the very presence of God." 13 Then the angel went from Adam and seized Satan at the opening of the cave, and stripped him of the false image (lie / pretense) he had assumed and brought him in his own hideous form to Adam and Eve who were afraid of him when they saw him. 14 And the angel said to Adam, "This hideous form has been his ever since God made him fall from heaven. He could not have come near you in it. Therefore, he transformed himself into an angel of light." 15 Then the angel drove Satan and his hosts away from Adam and Eve and said to them, "Fear not. God who created you will strengthen you." 16 And the angel left them. 17 But Adam and Eve remained standing in the cave and no consolation came to them as they were divided in their thoughts. 18 And when it was morning they prayed and then went out to seek the garden, for their hearts were seeking it, and they could get no consolation for having left it.

Chapter XXVIII

1 But when the crafty Satan saw that they were going to the garden he gathered together his host and came in appearance on a cloud, intent on deceiving them. 2 But when Adam and Eve saw him in a vision, they thought they were angels of God come to comfort them about having left the garden, or to bring them back again into it. 3 And Adam spread his hands before God, begged Him to make him understand what they were. 4 Then Satan, the hater of all that is good, said to Adam, "O Adam, I am an angel of the great God and, behold the hosts that surround me. 5 God has sent us to take you and bring you to the northern border of the garden to the shore of the clear sea, and bathe you and Eve in it, and raise you to your former joy, that you return to the garden once again." 6 These words sank into the heart of Adam and Eve. 7 Yet God withheld His Word from Adam, and did not make him understand at once but waited to see his strength and whether he would be overcome as Eve was when in the garden, or whether he would win this battle. 8 Then Satan called to Adam and Eve and said, "Behold, we go to the sea of water," and they began to go. 9 And Adam and Eve followed them at little distance. 10 But when they came to the mountain to the north of the garden which was a very high mountain without any steps to the top of it, the Devil came near to Adam and Eve, and made them go up to the top in reality and not in a vision, because he wished to throw them down and kill them, and to wipe their names from the earth, so that this earth should belong to him and his hosts alone.

Chapter XXIX

1 But when the merciful God saw that Satan wished to kill Adam with his many tricks, and saw that Adam was meek and without guile, God spoke to Satan in a loud voice, and cursed him. 2 Then he and his hosts fled, and Adam and Eve remained standing on the top of the mountain, from there they saw below them the wide world, high above which they were. But they saw none of the host which time after time were by them. 3 They cried, both Adam and Eve, before God, and begged for forgiveness of Him. 4 Then the Word from God came to Adam, and said to him, "You must know and understand concerning this Satan, that he seeks to deceive you and your descendants after you." 5 And Adam cried before the Lord God, and begged and prayed to Him to give him something from the garden, as a token to him, wherein to be comforted. 6 And God considered Adam's thought, and sent the angel Michael as far as the sea that reaches India, to take from there golden rods and bring them to Adam. 7 This God did in His wisdom in order that these golden rods, being with Adam in the cave, should shine forth with light in the night around him, and put an end to his fear of the darkness. 8 Then the angel Michael

went down by God's order, took golden rods, as God had commanded him, and brought them to God.

Author's note: God spoke to Adam concerning "this Satan," a turn of phrase that leads one to believe there are other Satans. Based on the meaning of the word satan, there is no limit to the number of satans one could have. Satan is derived from Hebrew, satan meaning "adversary". Satan, or the Devil, plays various evil roles in ancient and modern literature and in Jewish, Christian, Muslim and Zoroastrian religious traditions. Satan is an opponent of God and of those seeking to do God's will. He is often described as an angel named Lucifer who was cast out of heaven for rebelling against God, was condemned to roam the earth and rule hell, and who battles God for possession of souls and the earth. That legend is not found as such in the Bible but is based on interpretations of scattered Bible passages and later literary portrayals.
The English word "Satan" is from a Hebrew word meaning "to oppose" or "adversary." "Devil" is from the Greek diabolos , meaning "to slander or accuse." The name "Lucifer" appears in Isaiah 14 in the King James Version of the Bible

Chapter XXX

1 After these things, God commanded the angel Gabriel to go down to the garden and say to the cherub who kept it, "Behold, God has commanded me to come into the garden, and to take from it sweet smelling incense and give it to Adam." 2 Then the angel Gabriel went down by God's order to the garden and told the cherub as God had commanded him. 3 The cherub then said, "This is acceptable." And Gabriel went in and took the incense. 4 Then God commanded his angel Raphael to go down to the garden, and speak to the cherub about some myrrh to give to Adam. 5 And the angel Raphael went down and told the cherub as God had commanded him, and the cherub said, "This is acceptable." Then Raphael went in and took the myrrh. 6 The golden rods were from the Indian sea, where there are precious stones. The incense was from the eastern border of the garden, and the myrrh from the western border, from where bitterness came over Adam. 7 And the angels brought these things to God, by the Tree of Life, in the garden. 8 Then God said to the angels, "Dip them in the spring of water, then take them and sprinkle their water over Adam and Eve, that they should be a little comforted in their sorrow, and give them to Adam and Eve. 9 And the angels did as God had commanded them, and they gave all those things to Adam and Eve on the top of the mountain on which Satan had placed them, when he sought to make an end of them. 10 And when Adam saw the golden rods, the incense and the myrrh, he rejoiced and cried because he thought that the gold was a token of the kingdom from where he had come and the incense was a token of the bright light which had been taken from him, and that the myrrh was a token of the sorrow which he was in.

Chapter XXXI

1 After these things happened, God said to Adam, "You asked Me for something from the garden to be comforted with, and I have given you these three tokens as a consolation to you so that you trust in Me and in My covenant with you. 2 For I will come and save you and when I am in the flesh, kings shall bring me gold, incense, and myrrh. Gold is a token of My kingdom, incense is a token of My divinity, and myrrh is a token of My suffering and of My death. 3 But, Adam, put these by you in the cave, the gold so that it may shine light over you by night, the incense so that you smell its sweet savor, and the myrrh to comfort you in your sorrow." 4 When Adam heard these words from God, he worshipped before Him. He and Eve worshipped Him and gave Him thanks because He had dealt mercifully with them. 5 Then God commanded the three angels, Michael, Gabriel and Raphael each to bring what he had brought and give it to Adam. And they did so, one by one. 6 And God commanded Suriyel and Salathiel to bear up Adam and Eve, and bring them down from the top of the high mountain, and to take them to the Cave of Treasures. 7 There they laid the gold on the south side of the cave, the incense on the eastern side, and the myrrh on the western side. For the mouth of the cave was on the north side. 8 The angels then comforted Adam and Eve, and departed. 9 The gold was seventy rods. The incense was twelve pounds, and the myrrh was three pounds. 10 These remained by Adam in the Cave of Treasures, in the House of Treasures; therefore was it called 'Cave of Concealment.' And it was called the 'Cave of Treasures,' by reason of the bodies of righteous men that were in it. 11 God gave these three things to Adam on the third day after he had come out of the garden as a sign of the three days the Lord should remain in the heart of the earth. 12 And these three things, as they continued with Adam in the cave, gave him light by night, and by day they gave him a little relief from his sorrow.

Author's note: A rod is a unit of linear measure equal to approximately 5.5 yards and also a unit of area measure equivalent to approximately 30.25 square yards. Rod is also a description indicating a long, thin piece of unspecified size.

Author's note: Suriyel means "Command of God" and is one of the archangels from Judaic traditions. Other possible versions of his name are Suriel, Suriyel,(Some Dead Sea Scrolls translations), Esdreel, Sahariel, Juriel, Seriel, Sauriel, Surya, Jariel. The angel is mentioned in the Lost Book Of Enoch.
Salathiel means, "Whom I asked of God." The name is the son of Jeconiah (Matt. 1:12; 1 Chr. 3:17); also called the son of Neri (Luke

3:27) The probable explanation of the apparent discrepancy is that he was the son of Neri, the descendant of Nathan, and thus heir to the throne of David on the death of Jeconiah . See Jer. 22:30). The name acknowledges that the son is an answer to the parents' prayer to God (El) to help them conceive and birth a child. In 2 Esdras, the author claims to be "Ezra, who is also called Shealtiel" (3:1). For this reason, this work is also sometimes known as Ezra Shealtiel.

Chapter XXXII

1 And Adam and Eve remained in the Cave of Treasures until the seventh day. They neither ate of the fruit of the earth, nor drank water. 2 And on the eighth day, when it dawned, Adam said to Eve, " Eve, we prayed God to give us something from the garden and He sent his angels who brought us what we had desired. 3 But now, get up, and let us go to the sea of water we saw at first, and let us stand in it and pray that God will again be favorable to us and take us back to the garden, or give us something, or that He will give us comfort in some other land than this one we are in." 4 Then Adam and Eve came out of the cave and went and stood on the border of the sea in which they had thrown themselves before. 5 Then Adam said to Eve: "Come, go down into this place, and do not come out until the end of thirty days, when I shall come to you. And pray to God with burning heart and a sweet voice to forgive us. 6 And I will go to another place, and go down into it and do like you." 7 Then Eve went down into the water as Adam had commanded her. Adam also went down into the water, and they stood praying, and besought the Lord to forgive them their offense and to restore them to their former state. 8 And they stood like that praying until the end of the thirty-five days.

Author's note: There is a discrepancy between the 30 days mentioned first and the 35 days cited later in the chapter. The number 35 is a combination of 3, the number of spiritual completion, and 5, the number of grace.

Chapter XXXIII

1 But Satan, the hater of all that is good, sought them in the cave, but did not find them although he searched diligently for them. 2 But he found them standing in the water praying and thought within himself, "Adam and Eve are standing like that in that water praying to God to forgive them their transgression, and to restore them to their former state, and to take them from under my hand. 3 But I will deceive them so that they shall come out of the water, and not fulfill their vow." 4 Then the hater of all that is good, did not go to Adam, but he went to Eve, and took the form of an angel of God, praising and rejoicing, and he said to her: 5 "Peace be to you! Be glad and rejoice! God is favorable to you and He sent me to Adam. I have brought him the glad tidings of salvation and of his being filled with bright light as he was at first. 6 And Adam, in his joy for his restoration, has sent me to you so that you would come with me in order that I might crown you with light like him. 7 And he said to me, 'Speak to Eve; if she does not come with you, tell her of the sign when we were on the top of the mountain, how God sent his angels who took us and brought us to the Cave of Treasures; and laid the gold on the southern side, incense on the eastern side, and myrrh on the western side.' Now come to him." 8 When Eve heard these words from him, she rejoiced much. And thinking Satan's appearance was real; she came out of the sea. 9 He went first and she followed him until they came to Adam. Then Satan hid himself from her and she saw him no more. 10 She then came and stood before Adam, who was standing by the water and she rejoiced in God's forgiveness. 11 And as she called to him, he turned around and found her there and cried when he saw her and beat his chest from the bitterness of his grief. He sank into the water. 12 But God looked at him and at his misery and that he was about to breathe his last breath. And the Word of God came from heaven, raised him out of the water, and said to him, "Go up the high bank to Eve." And when he came up to Eve he said to her, "Who told you to come here?" 13 Then she told him the discourse of the angel who had appeared to her and had given her a sign. 14 But Adam grieved, and explained to her that it was Satan. He then took her and they both returned to the cave. 15 These things happened to them the second time they went down to the water seven days after their coming out of the garden. 16 They fasted in the water thirty-five days. It was altogether forty-two days since they had left the garden.

Chapter XXXIV

1 On the morning of the forty-third day, they came out of the cave, sorrowful and crying. Their bodies were lean, and they were parched from hunger and thirst, from fasting and praying, and from their heavy sorrow because of their transgression. 2 And when they had come out of the cave they went up the mountain to the west of the garden. 3 There they stood and prayed and asked God to grant them forgiveness of their sins. 4 And after their prayers Adam began to beg God, saying, "O my Lord, my God, and my Creator, You commanded the four elements to be gathered together, and they were gathered together by Your order. 5 Then You spread Your hand and created me out of one element, that of dust of the earth. You brought me into the garden at the third hour, on a Friday, and informed me of it in the cave. 6 Then, at first, I knew neither night nor day, because I had a bright nature so that the light in which I lived ever left me to know night or day. 7 Then, again, O Lord, in that third hour in which You created me, You brought to me all beasts, and lions, and ostriches, and fowls of the air, and all things that move in the earth, which You had created at the first hour before me of the Friday. 8 And Your will was that I should name them all, one by one, with a suitable name. But You gave me understanding and knowledge and a

pure heart and a right mind from you, that I should name them after Your own mind regarding the naming of them. 9 O God, You made them obedient to me and ordered that not one of them break from my control according to Your commandment and to the dominion which You had given me over them. But now they are all estranged from me. 10 Then it was in that third hour of Friday, in which You created me, and commanded me concerning the tree, to which I was neither to go near, nor to eat from; because You said to me in the garden, 'When you eat of it, from death you shall die.' 11 But if You had punished me as You said, with death, I should have died that very moment. 12 When You commanded me regarding the tree, that I was neither to approach nor to eat of it, Eve was not with me. You had not yet created her, neither had You yet taken her out of my side, so had she yet heard this order from you. 13 Then, at the end of the third hour of that Friday, O Lord, You caused a sleep to come over me, and I slept, and was overwhelmed in sleep. 14 Then You took a rib out of my side and You created her after my own likeness and image. Then I awoke and when I saw her and knew who she was, I said, 'This is bone of my bones, and flesh of my flesh. From now on she shall be called woman.' 15 It was of Your good will, O God, that You brought a sleep over me and that You quickly drew Eve out of my side until she was fully out, so that I did not see how she was made, neither could I witness. O my Lord, Your goodness and glory are awful and great. 16 And of Your goodwill, O Lord, You made us both with bodies of a bright nature, and You made the two of us one. You gave us Your grace and filled us with praises of the Holy Spirit that we should be neither hungry nor thirsty nor know what sorrow is, nor know faintness of heart, neither suffering, fasting nor weariness. 17 But now, O God, since we transgressed Your commandment and broke Your law, You have brought us out into a strange land, and have caused suffering, faintness, hunger and thirst to come over us. 18 Now, therefore, O God, we pray you, give us something to eat from the garden, to satisfy our hunger with it, and something wherewith to quench our thirst. 19 For, behold, many days, O God, we have tasted nothing and drunk nothing, and our flesh has dried up and our strength is wasted. Sleep is gone from our eyes from faintness and crying. 20 Then, O God, we dare not gather anything from the fruit of trees, from fear of you. For when we transgress the first time You spared us and did not make us die. 21 But now, we thought in our hearts that if we eat the fruit of the trees without God's order He will destroy us this time and will remove us from the earth. 22 And if we drink of this water without God's order He will make an end of us and root us up at once. 23 Now, therefore, O God, I have come to this place with Eve, and we beg You to give us some fruit from the garden so that we may be satisfied with it. 24 For we desire the fruit that is on the earth and all else that we lack in it."

Author's note: The four elements referred to are earth, air, fire, and water. Man was formed from dust, or earth.

Chapter XXXV

1 Then God looked again at Adam and his crying and groaning, and the Word of God came to him, and said to him: 2 "Adam, when you were in My garden, you knew neither eating nor drinking, faintness nor suffering, leanness of flesh, nor change; neither did sleep depart from your eyes. But since you transgressed and came into this strange land all these trials have come over you."

Author's note: It is unclear as to if this implies that Adam did not sleep or if he had no trouble sleeping while in the garden. Other verses seem to hint at the fact that his "bright nature and the perpetual glory of God shining in the garden provided no need nor place for sleep. While in the garden, Adam may not have needed sleep.

Chapter XXXVI

1 Then God commanded the cherub, who guarded the gate of the garden with a sword of fire in his hand, to take some of the fruit of the fig-tree and to give it to Adam. 2 The cherub obeyed the command of the Lord God and went into the garden and brought two figs on two twigs, each fig hanging to its leaf. They were from two of the trees among which Adam and Eve hid themselves when God went to walk in the garden and the Word of God came to Adam and Eve and said to them, "Adam! Adam! Where are you?" 3 And Adam answered, "O God, here I am. When I heard the sound of You and Your voice, I hid myself, because I am naked." 4 Then the cherub took two figs and brought them to Adam and Eve. But he threw the figs to them from a distance because they would not come near the cherub, for their flesh that could not come near the fire. 5 At first, angels trembled at the presence of Adam and were afraid of him. But now Adam trembled before the angels and was afraid of them. 6 Then Adam came closer and took one fig, and Eve also came in turn and took the other. 7 And as they took them up in their hands they looked at them and knew they were from the trees among which they had hidden themselves.

Chapter XXXVII

1 Then Adam said to Eve, "Do you not see these figs and their leaves with which we covered ourselves when we were stripped of our bright nature? But now, we do not know what misery and suffering may come to us from eating them. 2

Now, therefore, Eve, let us restrain ourselves and not eat them. Let us ask God to give us of the fruit of the Tree of Life." 3 So Adam and Eve restrained themselves and did not eat these figs. 4 But Adam began to pray to God and to beg Him to give him of the fruit of the Tree of Life, saying: "O God, when we transgressed Your commandment at the sixth hour of Friday, we were stripped of the bright nature we had, and did not continue in the garden after our transgression more than three hours. 5 But in the evening You made us come out of it. O God, we transgressed against You one hour and all these trials and sorrows have come over us until this day. 6 And those days together with this the forty-third days do not redeem that one hour in which we transgressed! 7 O God, look at us with an eye of pity, and do not avenge us according to our transgression of Your commandment in Your presence. 8 O God, give us of the fruit of the Tree of Life that we may eat it and live and turn not to see sufferings and other trouble in this earth, for You are God. 9 When we transgressed Your commandment You made us come out of the garden and sent a cherub to keep the Tree of Life so that we should not eat thereof and live and know nothing of faintness after we transgressed. 10 But now, O Lord, behold, we have endured all these days and have borne sufferings. Make these forty-three days an equivalent for the one hour in which we transgressed."

Author's note: The day begins at sundown, or about 6 P.M. This would mean that is the sin occurred in the sixth hour it would have been midnight in the garden. If Adam and Eve were removed three hours afterward it would have been 3 A.M.

Chapter XXXVIII

1 After these things the Word of God came to Adam, and said to him: 2 "Adam, as to the fruit on the Tree of Life that you have asked for, I will not give it to you now, but only when the 5,500 years are fulfilled. At that time I will give you fruit from the Tree of Life and you will eat and live forever, both you and Eve, and also your righteous descendants. 3 But these forty-three days cannot make amends for the hour in which you transgressed My commandment. 4 Adam, I gave you the fruit of the fig-tree in which you hid yourself for you to eat. So, you and Eve go and eat it. 5 I will not deny your request; neither will I disappoint your hope. Therefore, endure until the fulfillment of the covenant I made with you." 6 And God withdrew His Word from Adam.

Chapter XXXIX

1 Then Adam returned to Eve and said to her, "Get up, and take a fig for yourself, and I will take the other; and let us go to our cave." 2 Then Adam and Eve each took a fig and went toward the cave. The time was about the setting of the sun and their thoughts made them long to eat of the fruit. 3 But Adam said to Eve, "I am afraid to eat of this fig. I do not know what may come over me from it." 4 So Adam cried and stood praying before God saying, "Satisfy my hunger, without my having to eat this fig because after I have eaten it, what will it profit me? And what shall I desire and ask of you, O God, when it is gone?" 5 And he said again, "I am afraid to eat of it; for I do not know what will befall me through it."

Chapter XL

1 Then the Word of God came to Adam and said to him, "Adam, why didn't you have this trepidation, or this will to fast, or this care before now? And why didn't you have this fear before you transgressed? 2 But when you came to live in this strange land your animal body could not survive on earth without earthly food to strengthen it and to restore its powers." 3 And God withdrew His Word for Adam.

Chapter XLI

1 Then Adam took the fig and laid it on the golden rods. Eve also took her fig and put it on the incense. 2 And the weight of each fig was that of a water-melon; for the fruit of the garden was much larger than the fruit of this land. 3 But Adam and Eve remained standing and fasting the entirety of that night until the morning dawned. 4 When the sun rose they were still praying, but after they had finished praying Adam said to Eve: 5 "Eve, come, let us go to the border of the garden looking south to the place from where the river flows and is parted into four heads. There we will pray to God and ask Him to give us some of the Water of Life to drink. 6 For God has not fed us with the Tree of Life in order that we may not live. Therefore, we will ask him to give us some of the Water of Life to quench our thirst with it, rather than with a drink of water of this land." 7 When Eve heard these words from Adam she agreed, and they both got up and came to the southern border of the garden, at the edge of the river of water a short distance from the garden. 8 And they stood and prayed before the Lord, and asked Him to look at them and for this one time to forgive them, and to grant them their request. 9 After this prayer from both of them, Adam began to pray with his voice before God, and said; 10 "O Lord, when I was in the garden and saw the water that flowed from under the Tree of Life, my heart did not desire, neither did my body require to drink of it. I did not know thirst, because I was living, and above that which I am now. 11 So that in order to live I did not require any Food of

Life nor did I need to drink of the Water of Life. 12 But now, O God, I am dead and my flesh is parched with thirst. Give me of the Water of Life that I may drink of it and live. 13 O God, through Your mercy save me from these plagues and trials, and bring me into another land different from this. Let me live in Your garden."

Author's note: One could extrapolate the size of the fruit, knowing that the size of the fig leaves were large enough to fashion loincloths from them. (See Genesis 3:7) Later, we are told the size of a fig was that of a watermelon.

Chapter XLII

1 Then the Word of God came to Adam, and said to him: 2 "Adam, you said, 'Bring me into a land where there is rest.' Another land than this will not bring you rest. It is the kingdom of heaven alone where there is rest. 3 But you cannot enter into it at present, but only after your judgment is past and fulfilled. 4 Then will I make you go up into the kingdom of heaven, you and your righteous descendants; and I will give you and them the rest you ask for now. 5 And if you said, 'Give me of the Water of Life that I may drink and live,' it cannot be this day, but on the day that I shall descend into hell, and break the gates of brass, and crush into pieces the kingdoms of iron. 6 Then I will, through mercy, save your soul and the souls of the righteous, and thus give them rest in My garden. That shall be when the end of the world is come. 7 And the Water of Life you seek will not be granted you this day, but on the day that I shall shed My blood on your head in the land of Golgotha. 8 For My blood shall be the Water of Life to you at that time, and not to just you alone but to all your descendants who shall believe in Me. This will be rest to them for ever." 9 The Lord said again to Adam, "Adam, when you were in the garden these trials did not come to you. 10 But since you transgressed My commandment, all these sufferings have covered you. 11 Now, also, your flesh requires food and drink. So drink then of that water that flows by you on the face of the earth. 12 Then God withdrew His Word from Adam. 13 And Adam and Eve worshipped the Lord, and returned from the river of water to the cave. It was noon when they drew near to the cave, they saw a large fire by it.

Author's note: The kingdom of iron refers to Rome.
Jesus was fixed to the cross above the ground and the people, (raised up so that all would be brought to Him) and the blood flowed from above and fell on the people below on Golgotha (goal-goth-uh), which was the hill outside the walls of Jerusalem where Jesus was crucified. See John 6:25 and 7:38

Chapter XLIII

1 Then Adam and Eve were afraid, and stood still. And Adam said to Eve, "What is that fire by our cave? We have done nothing in it to cause this fire. 2 We neither have bread to bake, nor broth to cook there. We have never known anything like this fire, and we do not know what to call it. 3 But ever since God sent the cherub with a sword of fire that flashed in his hand and had lightning coming from it we fell down and were like corpses from fear and we have not seen the like. 4 But now, Eve, look, this is the same fire that was in the cherub's hand, which God has sent to keep the cave in which we live. 5 O Eve, it is because God is angry with us and will drive us from it. 6 Eve, we have transgressed His commandment again in that cave, so that He had sent this fire to burn around it and prevent us from going into it. 7 If this is really the case, Eve, where shall we live? And where shall we flee to be away from the face of the Lord? Since, like it is with the garden, He will not let us live in it, and He has deprived us of the good things of it. But He has placed us in this cave, in which we have endured darkness, tests and hardships until at last we have found comfort in it. 8 But now that He has brought us out into another land, who knows what may happen in it? And who knows but that the darkness of that land may be far greater than the darkness of this land? 9 Who knows what may happen in that land by day or by night? And who knows whether it will be far or near, Eve? Do you think it will please God to put us far from the garden, Eve? Where will God put us to prevent us from beholding Him, because we have transgressed His commandment, and because we have made requests of Him all the time? 10 Eve, if God will bring us into a strange land other than this, in which we find consolation, it must be to put our souls to death, and blot out our name from the face of the earth. 11 O Eve, if we are further alienated from the garden and from God, where shall we find Him again, and ask Him to give us gold, incense, myrrh, and some fruit of the fig-tree? 12 Where shall we find Him to comfort us a second time? Where shall we find Him so that He may think of us regarding the covenant He has made on our behalf?" 13 Then Adam said nothing else more. And they kept looking, he and Eve, towards the cave, and at the fire that flared up around it. 14 But that fire was from Satan. For he had gathered trees and dry grasses, and had carried and brought them to the cave, and had set fire to them, in order to consume the cave and what was in it. 15 So that Adam and Eve should be left in sorrow, and he should cut off their trust in God, and make them deny Him. 16 But by the mercy of God he could not burn the cave because God sent His angel to the cave to guard it from this fire, until it went out. 17 And this fire lasted from noon until the break of the next day. That was the forty-fifth day.

Chapter XLIV

1 Adam and Eve stood, looking at the fire and were unable to come near the cave from their fear of the fire. 2 And Satan kept on bringing trees and throwing them into the fire until the flames of the fire rose up very high and covered the entire cave, thinking in his mind, to consume the cave with the great fire. But the angel of the Lord was guarding it. 3 But he could not curse Satan nor wound him by word because he had no authority over him, neither did he attempt to do so with words from his mouth. 4 Therefore the angel tolerated him without uttering a bad word against him, until the Word of God came to Satan saying, "Go away from here at once before you deceive My servants, for this time you seek to destroy them. 5 Were it not for My mercy I would have destroyed you and your hosts from off the earth. But I have had patience with you until the end of the world." 6 Then Satan fled from before the Lord. But the fire went on burning around the cave like a coal-fire the entire day. This was the forty-sixth day that Adam and Eve had spent since they came out of the garden. 7 And when Adam and Eve saw that the heat of the fire had began to cool down, they started to walk toward the cave to get into it as they usually did but they could not because of the heat of the fire. 8 Then they both began crying because the fire separated them from the cave, and the fire came toward them, burning, and they were afraid. 9 Then Adam said to Eve, "See this fire of which we have a portion within us. It formerly obeyed us, but it no longer does so now, for we have violated the boundaries of creation and changed our condition and our nature has been altered. But the fire is not changed in its nature, nor altered from its creation. Therefore it now has power over us and when we come near it, it scorches our flesh."

Author's note: The Word of the Lord spoke to Satan stating, "I have had patience with you until the end of the world." This is a statement spoken in the future and recorded in the past. The precise meaning indicates that the statement was made at or after the end of the world.

Chapter XLV

1 Then Adam rose and prayed to God, saying, "This fire has separated us from the cave in which You have commanded us to live; and now, we cannot go into it." 2 Then God heard Adam, and sent him His Word, that said: 3 "Adam, see this fire! It is different from the flame and heat from the garden of delights and the good things in it! 4 When you were under My control all creatures yielded to you, but after you transgressed My commandment they all rose up over you." 5 God said again to him, "Adam, see how Satan has exalted you! He has deprived you of the Godhead and of an exalted state like Me, and has not kept his word to you but has ended up to become your enemy. He is the one who made this fire in which he meant to burn you and Eve. 6 Adam, why has he not kept his agreement with you even one day, but has deprived you of the glory that was on you when you obeyed his command? 7 Adam, do you think that he loved you when he made this agreement with you? Do you think that he loved you and wished to raise you on high? 8 No, Adam, he did not do anything out of love for you. He wished to force you to come out of light and into darkness, and from an exalted state to degradation, and from glory to this humble state, from joy to sorrow, and from rest to hunger and fainting." 9 God also said to Adam, "See this fire kindled by Satan around your cave? See this curious thing that surrounds you? Know that it will surround both you and your descendants when you obey his command and he will plague you with fire and you will go down into hell after you are dead. 10 Then, you will experience the burning of his fire that will surround you and your descendants. You will not be delivered from it until My coming. Just as you cannot go into your cave right now because of the great fire around it, a way for you will not be made for you until My Word comes on the day My covenant is fulfilled. 11 There is no way for you at present to come from this life to rest until he who is My Word comes. Then He will make a way for you, and you shall have rest." Then God called to the fire that burned around the cave with His Word, that it split itself in half until Adam passed through it. Then the fire parted itself by God's order and a way was made for Adam. 12 And God withdrew His Word from Adam.

Author's note: By God's word His servants passed through the fire, just as the waters were parted.
The "WORD" is made flesh in the form of the Messiah.

Chapter XLVI

1 Then Adam and Eve began again to come into the cave. And when they came to the passage in the midst of the fire, Satan blew into the fire like a whirlwind and caused the burning coal-fire to cover Adam and Eve so that their bodies were singed and the coal-fire burned their skin. 2 Adam and Eve screamed from the burning of the fire, and said, "O Lord, save us! Do not leave us to be consumed and plagued by this burning fire. Do not require us as the payment for having transgressed Your commandment." 3 Then God looked at their bodies on which Satan had caused fire to burn. God sent His angel that held back the burning fire. But the wounds remained on their bodies. 4 Then God said to Adam, "See Satan's love for you. He pretended to give you the Godhead and greatness and, now look, he burns you with fire and seeks to destroy you from off the earth. 5 Then look at Me, Adam. I created you, and how many times have I delivered you out of his hand? If not, wouldn't he have destroyed you?" 6 God spoke again, this time to Eve and said, "He promised you in the garden, saying, 'As soon as you eat from the tree, your eyes will be opened, and you shall become like gods, knowing good and evil.' But look!

He has burned your bodies with fire and has made you taste the taste of fire, in exchange for the taste of the garden. He has made you see the burning of fire, and the evil of it, and the power it has over you. 7 Your eyes have seen the good he has taken from you, and in truth he has opened your eyes. You have seen the garden in which you were with Me, and you have also seen the evil that has come over you from Satan. But as to the, Godhead he cannot give it to you, nor fulfill his promise to you. He was bitter against you and your descendants, that will come after you." 8 And God withdrew His Word form them.

Chapter XLVII

1 Then Adam and Eve came into the cave, still trembling because of the fire that had scorched them. So Adam said to Eve: 2 "Look, in this world the fire burns our flesh. How will it be when we are dead and Satan shall punish our souls? Is not our deliverance far off unless God comes in His mercy and fulfills His promise to us?" 3 Then Adam and Eve stepped into the cave blessing themselves for coming into it once more. For they thought that they would never enter it, when they saw the fire around it. 4 But as the sun was setting the fire was still burning and coming closer to Adam and Eve in the cave, so that they could not sleep in it. After the sunset they went out of the cave. This was the forty-seventh day after they came out of the garden. 5 Adam and Eve then came under the top of hill by the garden to sleep, as they were accustomed. 6 And they stood and prayed God to forgive them their sins, and then fell asleep under the top of the mountain. 7 But Satan, the hater of all that is good, thought to himself: "God has promised salvation to Adam by covenant, and promised that He would deliver him from all the hardships that have befallen him, but God has not promised me by covenant, and will not deliver me out of my hardships. He has promised Adam that He should make him and his descendants live in the kingdom that I once lived in. I will kill Adam. 8 The earth shall be rid of him. The earth shall be left to me alone. When he is dead he will not have any descendants left to inherit the kingdom and it will remain my own realm. God will then be wanting me, and He will restore it to me and my hosts."

Chapter XLVIII

1 After this Satan called to his hosts, all of which came to him, and said to him: 2 "Our lord, what will you do?" 3 Then he said to them, "This Adam, whom God created out of the dust, is the one who has taken our kingdom from us. Come, let us gather together and kill him. Hurl a rock at him and at Eve, and crush them under it." 4 When Satan's hosts heard these words they came to the part of the mountain where Adam and Eve were asleep. 5 Then Satan and his host took a huge rock, broad and smooth, and without blemish. He thought to himself, "If there should be a hole in the rock, when it fell on them the hole in the rock might align over them so they would escape and not die." 6 He then said to his hosts, "Take up this stone and drop it flat on them so that it doesn't roll off them to somewhere else. And when you have hurled it at them get away from there quickly." 7 And they did as he told them. But as the rock fell down from the mountain toward Adam and Eve, God commanded the rock to become a covering over them so that it did them no harm. And so it was by God's order. 8 But when the rock fell, the whole earth quaked because of it, and was shaken from the size of the rock. 9 And as it quaked and shook Adam and Eve awoke from sleep and found themselves under a covering of rock. But they didn't know what had happened because when they fell asleep they were under the sky and not under a covering, and when they saw it they were afraid. 10 Then Adam said to Eve, "How has the mountain bent itself and the earth quaked and shaken on our account? And why has this rock spread itself over us like a tent? 11 Does God intend to plague us and to shut us up in this prison? Or will He close the earth over us? 12 He is angry with us for our having come out of the cave without His permission and for our having done so of our own accord without asking Him when we left the cave and came to this place." 13 Then Eve said, "Adam, if indeed the earth shook for our sake and this rock formed a tent over us because of our transgression we will be sorry, because our punishment will be long. 14 But get up and pray to God to let us know concerning this, and what this rock is that is spread over us like a tent." 15 Then Adam stood up and prayed before the Lord to let him know what had brought about this difficult time. And Adam stood praying like that until the morning.

Chapter XLIX

1 Then the Word of God came and said: 2 "O Adam, who counseled you when you came out of the cave to come to this place?" 3 And Adam said to God, "Lord, we came to this place because of the heat of the fire that came over us inside the cave." 4 Then the Lord God said to Adam, "Adam, you dread the heat of fire for one night, but how will it be when you live in hell? 5 But Adam, do not be afraid and do not believe that I have placed this covering of rock over you to plague you. 6 It came from Satan, who had promised you the Godhead and majesty. It is he who threw down this rock to kill you under it, and Eve with you, and in this way to prevent you from living on the earth. 7 But, as that rock was falling down on you I was merciful. I commanded it to form a tent over you, and the rock under you to lower itself. 8 And this sign, O Adam, will happen to Me at My coming on earth: Satan will raise the people of the Jews to put Me to death and they will lay Me in a rock, and seal a large stone over Me, and I shall remain within that rock three days and three nights. 9 But on the third day I shall rise again, and it shall be salvation to you, O Adam, and to your descendants, so that you will believe in Me. But, Adam,

I will not bring you from under this rock until three days and three nights have passed." 10 And God withdrew His Word from Adam. 11 But Adam and Eve lived under the rock three days and three nights, as God had told them. 12 And God did so to them because they had left their cave and had come to this same place without God's permission. 13 But, after three days and three nights, God created an opening in the covering of rock and allowed them to get out from under it. Their flesh was dried up, and their eyes and hearts were troubled from crying and sorrow.

Author's note: Some translations have the rock forming a dome, but the text gives no shape. If one reads the text closely, it becomes obvious that the shape of the falling rock may not be as important as the fact that the ground Adam and Eve were sleeping on was made to form a depression between the tent or dome shape and the depression of the ground. This formed a cave shape, which mimicked the cave in which Jesus would be buried. It is less obvious but implied that Adam and Eve had some amount of light inside the cave. The text gives no explanation, whether there were gaps, cracks, or holes for air and light.

Chapter L

1 Then Adam and Eve went out and came into the Cave of Treasures and stood praying in it the entire day until the evening. 2 And this took place at the end of the fifty days after they had left the garden. 3 But Adam and Eve rose again and prayed to God in the cave the whole of that night, and begged for mercy from Him. 4 And when the day dawned, Adam said to Eve, "Come! Let us go and do some work for our bodies." 5 So they went out of the cave, and came to the northern border of the garden, and they looked for something to cover their bodies with. But they found nothing, and did not know how to do the work. But their bodies were stained, and they could not speak from cold and heat. 6 Then Adam stood and asked God to show him something with which to cover their bodies. 7 Then came the Word of God and said to him, "O Adam, take Eve and come to the seashore where you fasted before. There you will find skins of sheep that were left after lions ate the carcasses. Take them and make garments for yourselves, and clothe yourselves with them.

Author's Note: There is no direct explanation as to how Adam and Eve became naked again. One possibility is found in chapter XLVI, verse 1, which states that Satan blew into the fire and singed Adam and Eve. It is possible that the garments that the Lord had given them in Genesis 3:21 were burned away at this point, leaving Adam and Eve naked once more.

Chapter LI

1 When Adam heard these words from God, he took Eve and went from the northern side of the garden to the south of it, by the river of water where they once fasted. 2 But as they were on their way, and before they arrived, Satan, the wicked one, had heard the Word of God communing with Adam respecting his covering. 3 It distressed him, and he hurried to the place where the sheepskins were, with the intention of taking them and throwing them into the sea or of burning them so that Adam and Eve would not find them. 4 But as he was about to take them, the Word of God came from heaven and bound him by the side of those skins until Adam and Eve came near him. But as they got closer to him they were afraid of him and of his hideous appearance. 5 Then the Word of God came to Adam and Eve, and said to them, "This is he who was hidden in the serpent, who deceived you, and stripped from you your garment of light and glory. 6 This is he who promised you majesty and divinity. Where is the beauty that was on him? Where is his divinity? Where is his light? Where is the glory that rested on him? 7 Now his form is hideous. He has become abominable (offensive) among angels, and he has come to be called Satan. 8 Adam, he wished to steal from you this earthly garment of sheepskins so that he could destroy it not let you be covered with it. 9 What is his beauty that you should have followed him? And what have you gained by obeying him? See his evil works and then look at Me, your Creator. Look at the good deeds I do for you. 10 I bound him until you came and saw him and his weakness and that no power is left with him." 11 And God released him from his bonds.

Chapter LII

1 After this Adam and Eve said no more, but cried before God because of their creation, and their bodies that required an earthly covering. 2 Then Adam said to Eve, "Eve, this is the skin of beasts with which we shall be covered, but when we put it on we shall be wearing a sign of death on our bodies. Just as the owners of these skins have died and have decomposed, so also shall we die and pass away." 3 Then Adam and Eve took the skins and went back to the Cave of Treasures. When they were in it, they stood and prayed, as was their habit. 4 And they thought how they could make garments of those skins because they had no skill. 5 Then God sent to them His angel to show them how to accomplish this. And the angel said to Adam, "Go out and bring some palm-thorns." Then Adam went out, and brought some, as the angel had commanded him. 6 Then the angel began before them to work the skins, after the manner of one who prepares a shirt. And he took the thorns and stuck them into the skins before their eyes. 7 Then the angel again stood up and prayed God that the thorns in those skins should be hidden, so as to be as if it were sewn with one thread. 8 And so it was, by God's order, and they became garments for Adam and Eve. And He clothed them with the skins. 9 From that time the nakedness of their bodies was

covered from the sight of each other's eyes. 10 And this happened at the end of the fifty-first day. 11 Then when Adam's and Eve's bodies were covered they stood and prayed and sought mercy of the Lord and forgiveness, and gave Him thanks because He had mercy on them and had covered their nakedness. And they did not stop praying the entirety of that night. 12 Then, when the morning dawned at sunrise, they said their prayers, as was their custom, and then went out of the cave. 13 And Adam said to Eve, "Since we don't know what there is to the west of this cave, let us go out and see it today." Then they departed and went toward the western border.

Chapter LIII

1 They were not very far from the cave when Satan came toward them. He hid himself between them and the cave in the form of two ravenous lions that had been three days without food. And they came toward Adam and Eve as if to break them in pieces and devour them. 2 Then Adam and Eve cried out and begged God to deliver them from their paws. 3 Then the Word of God came to them and drove away the lions from them. 4 And God said to Adam, "Adam, what do you seek on the western border? And why have you left of your own will the eastern border which was your living place? 5 Now, turn back to your cave and remain in it, so that Satan won't deceive you or achieve his goal to overtake you. 6 In this western border, Adam, there will go from you a descendant that shall replenish it. And they will defile themselves with their sins, and with their yielding to the commands of Satan, and by following his works. 7 Therefore will I bring waters of a flood to cover them and overwhelm them all. But I will deliver what is left of the righteous among them and I will bring them to a distant land, but the land in which you live now shall remain desolate and without one inhabitant in it. 8 After God had spoken to them, they went back to the Cave of Treasures. But their flesh was dried up, and they were weak from fasting and praying, and from the sorrow they felt at having sinned against God.

Chapter LIV

1 Then Adam and Eve stood up in the cave and prayed the entire night until the morning dawned. And when the sun came up they both went out of the cave. Their minds were wandering from the heaviness of sorrow and they didn't know where they were going. 2 And they walked in that condition to the southern border of the garden. And they began to go up that border until they came to the eastern border, which was land's end. 3 And the cherub who guarded the garden was standing at the western gate to guard it from Adam and Eve in case they should attempt to suddenly come into the garden. 4 When Adam and Eve thought the cherub was not watching they came to the eastern border of the garden. But as they were standing by the gate, as if they desired to go in, the cherub turned around as if to put them to death according to the order God had given him. And the cherub suddenly came with a flashing sword of fire in his hand. When he saw them, he went toward them to kill them. For he was afraid that God would destroy him if they went into the garden without God's order. 5 And the sword of the cherub seemed to shoot flames a distance away from it. But when he raised it over Adam and Eve, the flame of the sword did not flash out at them. 6 Because of this the cherub thought that God was approving to them and was bringing them back into the garden. And the cherub stood wondering. 7 He could not go up to Heaven to ascertain God's order regarding Adam and Eve's entering the garden so continued to stand by them, unable to leave them because he was afraid that if they should enter the garden without permission God would destroy him. 8 When Adam and Eve saw the cherub coming towards them with a flaming sword of fire in his hand they fell on their faces from fear, and were as dead. 9 Then, the heavens and the earth shook, and another cherubim came down from heaven to the cherub who guarded the garden, and saw him amazed and silent. 10 Then, again, other angels came down close to the place where Adam and Eve were. And the cherubs were split between joy and sorrow. 11 They were joyous because they thought that God was approving to Adam, and wished him to return to the garden and wished to return him to the gladness he once enjoyed. 12 But they were sorrowful over Adam because he was fallen like a dead man, he and Eve. And they said to themselves, "Adam has not died in this place, but God has put him to death for coming to this place and wishing to enter the garden without His permission."

Chapter LV

1 Then the Word of God came to Adam and Eve, and raised them up from their dead state, saying to them, "Why did you come up here? Do you intend to go into the garden from which I brought you out? You cannot return today but only when the covenant I have made with you is fulfilled." 2 Then Adam, when he heard the Word of God, and the fluttering of the angels, which he only heard and did not see, he and Eve cried and said to the angels: 3 "O Spirits, who wait on God, look at me and at my inability to see you! When I was in my former bright nature I could see you. I sang praises as you do and my heart was far above you. 4 But now that I have transgressed, that bright nature is gone from me and I have come to this miserable state in which I cannot see you. You do not serve me like you used to do. For my flesh has become like that of the animals. 5 O angels of God, ask God to restore me to the state I was in formerly and ask him to rescue me from this misery, and to remove the sentence of death He passed on me for having trespassed against Him. Ask Him, as I ask Him to do these things." 6 Then, when the angels heard these words they all grieved over him and cursed Satan who had misled Adam until

he came from the garden to misery, and from life to death, and from peace to distress, and from gladness to a strange land. 7 Then the angels said to Adam, "You obeyed Satan and ignored the Word of God who created you. You believed that Satan would fulfill all he had promised you. 8 But now, Adam, we will make known to you what came over us though him, before his fall from heaven. 9 He gathered together his hosts and deceived them, promising to give them a great kingdom, a divine nature, and other promises he made them. 10 His hosts believed that his word was true, so they followed him, and renounced the glory of God. 11 He then ordered us, and some obeyed and under his command, and accepted his empty promises. But we would not obey and we did not take his orders. 12 Then, after he had fought with God and had dealt disrespectfully with Him, he gathered together his hosts and made war with us. And if it had not been for God's strength that was with us we could not have prevailed against him to hurl him from heaven. 13 But when he fell from among us there was great joy in heaven because of his descent from us. If he had remained in heaven, nothing, not even one angel would have remained in it. 14 But God in His mercy drove him from among us to this dark earth because he had become darkness itself and a performer of unrighteousness. 15 And Adam, he has continued to make war against you until he tricked you and made you come out of the garden to this strange land, where all these trials have come to you. And death, which God brought to him, he has also brought to you because you obeyed him and sinned against God." 16 Then all the angels rejoiced and praised God and asked Him not to destroy Adam for his having sought to enter the garden at this time, but to bear with him until the fulfillment of the promise, and to help him in this world until he was free from Satan's hand.

Chapter LVI

1 Then the Word of God came to Adam, and said to him: 2 "Adam, look at that garden of joy and at this earth of toil, and see, the garden is full of angels, but look at yourself alone on this earth with Satan whom you obeyed. 3 If you had submitted and been obedient to Me and had kept My Word, you would be with My angels in My garden. 4 But when you sinned and obeyed Satan, you became his guests among his angels, that are full of wickedness, and you came to this earth that produces thorns and thistles for you. 5 O Adam, ask the one who deceived you to give you the divine nature he promised you, or to make you a garden as I had made for you, or to fill you with that same bright nature with which I had filled you. 6 Ask him to make you a body like the one I made you, or to give you a day of rest as I gave you, or to create within you a wise (intelligent, sound, reasonable) soul, as I created for you; or to take you from here to some other earth than this one which I gave you. But, Adam, he will not fulfill even one of the things he told you. 7 Acknowledge My favor toward you, and My mercy on you, My creature. Acknowledge that I have not shown vengeance on you for your transgression against Me, but in My pity for you I have promised you that at the end of the great five and a half days I will come and save you." 8 Then God said again to Adam and Eve, "Get up, go down from here before the cherub with a sword of fire in his hand destroys you." 9 But Adam's heart was comforted by God's words to him, and he worshipped before Him. 10 And God commanded His angels to escort Adam and Eve to the cave with joy instead of the fear that had come over them. 11 Then the angels took up Adam and Eve and brought them down the mountain by the garden, with songs and praises and hymns until they arrived at the cave. There the angels began to comfort and to strengthen them, and then departed from them towards heaven to their Creator, who had sent them. 12 But after the angels had departed from Adam and Eve, Satan came with shamefacedness and stood at the entrance of the cave in which were Adam and Eve. He then called to Adam, and said, "O Adam, come, let me speak to you." 13 Then Adam came out of the cave, thinking he was one of God's angels that had come to give him some good counsel.

Chapter LVII

1 But when Adam came out and saw his hideous figure he was afraid of him, and said to him, "Who are you?" 2 Then Satan answered and said to him, "It is I, who hid myself within the serpent, and who spoke to Eve, and who enticed her until she obeyed my command. I am he who, using my deceitful speech, sent her to deceive you until you both ate of the fruit of the tree and rejected the command of God." 3 But when Adam heard these words from him, he said to him, "Can you make me a garden as God made for me? Or can you clothe me in the same bright nature in which God had clothed me? 4 Where is the divine nature you promised to give me? Where is that clever speech of yours that you had with us at first, when we were in the garden?" 5 Then Satan said to Adam, "Do you think that when I have promised someone something that I would actually deliver it to him or fulfill my word? Of course not. I myself have no hope of (never even thought of) obtaining what I promised. 6 Therefore I fell, and I made you fall for the same reason that I myself fell. Whoever accepts my counsel, falls. 7 But now, O Adam, because you fell you are under my rule and I am king over you because you have obeyed me and have sinned against your God. There will be no deliverance from my hands until the day promised you by your God." 8 Again he said, "Because we do not know the day agreed on with you by your God, nor the hour in which you shall be delivered, we will multiply wars and murders on you and your descendants after you. 9 This is our will and our good pleasure that we may not leave one of the sons of men to inherit our place in heaven. 10 Our home, Adam, is in burning fire and we will not stop our evil doing even a single day nor even a single hour. And I, O Adam, shall set you on fire when you come into the cave to live there." 11 When Adam heard these words he cried and mourned and said to Eve, "Did you hear what he said? He said that he would not fulfill any of what he promised you in the garden. Did he really, at that time, become king over us? 12

We will ask God, who created us, to deliver us out of his hands."

Chapter LVIII

1 Then Adam and Eve spread their hands before God, praying and begging Him to drive Satan away from them so that he could not harm them or force them to deny God. 2 Then, suddenly, God sent to them His angel who drove Satan away from them. This happened about sunset on the fifty-third day after they had come out of the garden. 3 Then Adam and Eve went into the cave, and stood up and lowered their faces to the ground to pray to God. 4 But before they prayed Adam said to Eve, "Look, you have seen what temptations have befallen us in this land. Come, let us get up and ask God to forgive us the sins we have committed and we will not come out until the end of the day before the fortieth day. And if we die in here He will save us." 5 Then Adam and Eve got up and joined together in entreating God. 6 They continued praying like this in the cave and did not come out of it in the night or day, until their prayers went up out of their mouths like a flame of fire.

Author's note: This little chapter has several details showing connections to customs of punishment and also to number symbolism. The day is the 53rd day. 5+3=8. Eight is the number of judgment. Adam and Eve elected to stay in the cave praying for 40 days minus 1. Forty is the number of testing and trails. The rains were to fall for 40 days. Jesus was in the desert for 40 days. The Israelites wondered in the desert for 40 years... However, when it came to punishment inflicted by the state, as was in the case of the flogging of Jesus, the punishment was 40 lashes minus 1.

Chapter LIX

1 But Satan, the hater of all that is good, did not allow them to finish their prayers. He called to his hosts and they all came. Then he said to them, "Since Adam and Eve, whom we deceived, have agreed together to pray to God night and day, and to beg Him to deliver them, and since they will not come out of the cave until the end of the fortieth day. 2 And since they will continue their prayers as they have both agreed to do, that He will deliver them out of our hands and restore them to their former state, let us see what we shall do to them." And his hosts said to him, "Power is yours, our lord, to do what you command." 3 Then Satan, great in wickedness, took his hosts and came into the cave on the thirtieth night of the forty day period, and he beat Adam and Eve until he thought they were dead and he left them as dead. 4 Then the Word of God came to Adam and Eve and raised them from their suffering, and God said to Adam, "Be strong, and do not be afraid of him who has just come to you." 5 But Adam cried and said, "Where were you, my God, that they should punish me with such blows and that this suffering should come over me and over Eve, your handmaiden?" 6 Then God said to him, "Adam, see, he is lord and master of all you have, he who said, he would give you divinity. Where is this love for you? And where is the gift he promised? 7 Did it please him just once, Adam, to come to you, comfort you, strengthen you, rejoice with you, or send his hosts to protect you, because you have obeyed him and have obeyed his counsel and have followed his commandment and transgressed Mine?" 8 Then Adam cried before the Lord, and said, "Lord because I transgressed a little, You have severely punished me in return. I ask You to deliver me out of his hands, or at least have pity on me and take my soul out of my body now in this strange land." 9 Then God said to Adam, "If only there had been this moaning and praying before you transgressed you would have rest from the trouble in which you are now." 10 But God had patience with Adam, and let him and Eve remain in the cave until they had fulfilled the forty days. 11 But the strength and flesh withered on Adam and Eve from fasting and praying, from hunger and thirst, because they had not tasted either food or drink since they left the garden, and their bodies functioned erratically because they had no strength left to continue in prayer from hunger until the end of the next day to the fortieth. They were fallen down in the cave, yet what speech escaped from their mouths, was only in praises.

Chapter LX

1 Then on the eighty-ninth day, Satan came to the cave, clad in a garment of light, and belted with a bright girdle. 2 In his hands was a staff of light, and he looked most frightening, but his face was pleasant and his speech was sweet. 3 He had transformed himself like this in order to deceive Adam and Eve and to make them come out of the cave before they had fulfilled the forty days. 4 He said to himself, "When they had fulfilled the forty days' fasting and praying, God would restore them to their former state but if He did not do this He would still be favorable to them, and even if He had no mercy on them would He still give them something from the garden to comfort them as He had already twice before." 5 Then Satan came near the cave in beautiful appearance and said: 6 "Adam, you and Eve arise and stand up and come along with me to a good land and don't be afraid. I am flesh and bones like you and at first I was a creature that God created. 7 It was like this when He had created me, He placed me in a garden in the north on the border of the world. 8 And He said to me, 'Stay here!' And I remained there according to His word and I did not violate His commandment. 9 Then He made a sleep to come over me and then He brought you, Adam, out of my side, but He did not make you stay with me. 10 But God took you in His holy hand and placed you in a garden to the east. 11 Then I worried about you, because even though God had taken you out of my side, He had not allowed you to stay with me. 12 But God said to me: 'Do not worry about Adam, whom I brought out of your

29

side, no harm will come to him. 13 For now I have brought out of his side a help-meet for him and I have given him joy by so doing.' " 14 Then Satan spoke again, saying, "I did not know how it is you came to be in this cave, nor anything about this trial that has come over you until God said to me, 'Behold, Adam has transgressed. He whom I had taken out of your side, and Eve also, whom I took out of his side have sinned and I have driven them out of the garden. I have made them live in a land of sorrow and misery because they transgressed against Me, and have obeyed Satan. And look, they are suffering to this day, the eightieth.' 15 Then God said to me, 'Get up, go to them, and make them come to your place, and do not permit Satan to come near them and afflict them. For they are now in great misery and lie helpless from hunger.' 16 He further said to me, 'When you have taken them to yourself, give them to eat of the fruit of the Tree of Life and give them to drink of the water of peace, and clothe them in a garment of light, and restore them to their former state of grace, and leave them not in misery, for they came from you. But grieve not over them, nor be sorry of that which has come over them. 17 But when I heard this, I was sorry and my heart could not bear it for your sake and I could not wait, my child. 18 But, Adam, when I heard the name of Satan I was afraid, and I said to myself, I will not come out because he might trap me as he did my children, Adam and Eve. 19 And I said, 'God, when I go to my children, Satan will meet me on the way and fight against me as he did against them.' 20 Then God said to me, 'Fear not; when you find him, hit him with the staff that is in your hand and don't be afraid of him, because you are old and established, and he shall not prevail against you.' 21 Then I said, 'O my Lord, I am old, and cannot go. Send Your angels to bring them.' 22 But God said to me, 'Angels are not like Adam and Eve; and they will not consent to come with them. But I have chosen you, because they are your offspring and are like you and they will listen to what you say.' 23 God said further to me, 'If you don't have enough strength to walk, I will send a cloud to carry you and set you down at the entrance of their cave, then the cloud will return and leave you there. 24 And if they will come with you, I will send a cloud to carry you and them.' 25 Then He commanded a cloud to carry me up and it brought me to you, and then it went back. 26 And now, my children, Adam and Eve, look at my old gray hair and at my feeble state, and at my coming from that distant place. Come with me to a place of rest." 27 Then he began to cry and to sob before Adam and Eve, and his tears poured on the ground like water. 28 And when Adam and Eve raised their eyes and saw his beard and heard his sweet talk, their hearts softened towards him and they obeyed him, because they believed he was true. 29 And it seemed to them that they were really his offspring when they saw that his face was like their own; and they trusted him.

Author note: This chapter is a cruel mockery. It represents the purpose of Christ turned upside down. Satan claims to be sent by God because he is in human form, in order to rescued Adam and Eve because he was made like them and they would listen and obey him. Adam and Eve believed Satan. When Jesus came we rejected the true savior.
Later in the chapter the word "helpmeet" is used. Meet, in the archaic usage, means to be fit, suitable, or proper. Thus, in the King James usage, the word helpmeet means someone who is a fit or suitable helper. It was only in the 17th century that the two words help and meet were mistaken for one word, helpmeet, and came to mean a wife. Later, in the 18th century a mistake in spelling along with a misunderstanding of the broader meaning of the word produced the word "helpmate" to mean a wife or sexual mate.

Chapter LXI

1 Then Satan took Adam and Eve by the hand started to lead them out of the cave. 2 But when they had gone a little way out of it God knew that Satan had overcome them and had brought them out before the forty days were ended in order to take them to some distant place and to destroy them. 3 Then the Word of the Lord God again came and cursed Satan and drove him away from them. 4 And God began to speak to Adam and Eve, saying to them, "What made you come out of the cave to this place?" 5 Then Adam said to God, "Did you create a man before us? Because, when we were in the cave there suddenly came to us a friendly old man who said to us, 'I am a messenger from God to you, to bring you back to some place of rest.' 6 And we believed that he was a messenger from you, O God, and we came out with him. We did not know where we should go with him." 7 Then God said to Adam, "This is the father of the evil arts who brought you and Eve out of the Garden of Delights. And when he saw that you and Eve both joined together in fasting and praying so that you did not come out of the cave before the end of the forty days, he wished to make your efforts wasted and break your mutual bond in order to take away all hope from you and to drive you to some place where he might destroy you. 8 Because he couldn't do anything to you unless he showed himself in the likeness of you. 9 Therefore he came to you with a face like your own and began to give you signs as if they were all true. 10 But because I am merciful and am favorable to you, I did not allow him to destroy you. Instead, I drove him away from you. 11 Now, Adam, take Eve and return to your cave and remain in it until the morning after the fortieth day. And when you come out, go toward the eastern gate of the garden." 12 Then Adam and Eve worshipped God, and praised and blessed Him for the deliverance that had come to them from Him. And they returned to the cave. This happened in the evening of the thirty-ninth day. 13 Then Adam and Eve stood up and with a fervent passion, prayed to God to give them strength, for they had become weak because of hunger and thirst and prayer. But they watched the entire night praying until morning. 14 Then Adam said to Eve, "Get up. Let us go toward the eastern gate of the garden as God told us." 15 And they said their prayers as they were accustomed to do every day, and they left the cave to go near to the eastern gate of the garden. 16 Then Adam and Eve stood up and prayed and appealed to God to strengthen them and to send them something to satisfy their hunger. 17 But after they finished their prayers they were too weak to move. 18 Then the

Word of God came again, and said to them, "Adam, get up, go and bring the two figs here." 19 Then Adam and Eve got up, and went until they came near to the cave.

Chapter LXII

1 But Satan, the wicked one, was envious because of the consolation God had given them. 2 So he prevented them from getting the figs and went into the cave and took the two figs and buried them outside the cave so that Adam and Eve should not find them. He also had thought to destroy them. 3 But by God's mercy, as soon as those two figs were in the ground God defeated Satan's wishes regarding the figs and made them into two fruit trees that grew higher than the cave and shaded the cave because Satan had buried them on the eastern side of it. 4 Then when the two trees were grown, and were covered with fruit, Satan grieved and mourned, and said, "It would have been better to have left those figs where they were, because now they have become two fruit trees that Adam will eat from all the days of his life. But I had in my mind that when I buried them it would destroy them entirely and hide them forever. 5 But God has overturned my plan and would not let that sacred fruit perish, and He has made known my intention, and has defeated the plan I had formed against His servants." 6 Then Satan went away ashamed because he hadn't thought his plans all the way through.

Chapter LXIII

1 As they got closer to the cave Adam and Eve saw two fig trees covered with fruit, and giving shade to the cave. 2 Then Adam said to Eve, "It seems to me that we have gone the wrong way. When did these two trees grow here? It seems to me that the enemy wishes to lead us the wrong way. Do you suppose that there is another cave in the earth besides this one? 3 But, Eve let us go into the cave and find the two figs because this is our cave we were in. But if we do not find the two figs in it then it cannot be our cave." 4 Then they went into the cave and looked into the four corners of it but did not find the two figs. 5 And Adam cried and said to Eve, "Did we go to the wrong cave, Eve? It seems to me the two figs should have been in the cave." And Eve said, "I, do not know." 6 Then Adam stood up and prayed and said, "O God, You commanded us to come back to the cave to take the two figs and return to you. 7 But now, we cannot find them. God, have you taken them and planted these two trees, or have we lost our way (gotten lost) in the earth, or has the enemy deceived us? If this is real then, O God, reveal the secret of these two trees (outside) and figs to us." 8 Then the Word of God came to Adam, and said to him, "Adam, when I sent you to bring back the figs, Satan went ahead of you to the cave and took the figs, and buried them outside, east of the cave, thinking to destroy them, by not sowing them with good intent. 9 It wasn't because of him that these trees have immediately grown up but I had mercy on you and I commanded them to grow. And they grew to be two large trees, that would give you shade by their branches, and you should find rest, and by this I made you see My power and My marvelous works. 10 And, also I showed you Satan's cruelty and his evil works. Ever since you came out of the garden he has not ceased for a single day from doing you harm in some way. But I have not given him power over you." 11 And God said, "From now on, Adam, rejoice because of the trees that you and Eve can rest under when you feel weary. But do not eat any of their fruit or come near them." 12 Then Adam cried, and said, "God, will You kill us again, or will You drive us away from Your face, and cut off our life from the face of the earth? 13 O God, I beg you, if You know that these trees bring either death or some other evil, as they did the first time, root them up from near our cave and leave us to die of the heat or hunger or thirst. 14 For we know Your marvelous works, O God, that they are great, and that by Your power You can bring one thing out of another without the thing's (person's) consent. For Your power can make rocks to become trees, and trees to become rocks."

Author's Note: They would have known it was their cave because the gold was still there. This verse brings up questions of Satan's power over Adam and Eve and the extent of any authority. In previous verses we were led to think Satan had gained power of them because of their sin. Now, in this verse we read," But I have not given him power over you." This seems to be a contradiction.

Chapter LXIV

1 Then God looked at Adam and at his strength of mind and at his ability to endure hunger, thirst, and heat. And He changed the two fig trees into two figs as they were at first. Then He said to Adam and Eve, "Each of you may take one fig." And they took them as the Lord commanded them. 2 And He said to them, "You must now go into the cave and eat the figs and satisfy your hunger or else you will die." 3 So, they went into the cave about sunset as God commanded them. And Adam and Eve stood up and prayed during the setting sun. 4 Then they sat down to eat the figs, but they did not know how to eat them because they were not accustomed to eating earthly food. They were afraid that if they ate, their stomach would become heavy and their flesh thickened, and their hearts would begin to crave earthly food. 5 But while they were seated, God sent them His angel, out of pity for them, so they wouldn't perish of hunger and thirst. 6 And the angel said to Adam and Eve, "God says to you that you do not have the strength that would be required to fast until death, so eat and strengthen

your bodies, for you are now animal flesh and cannot subsist without food and drink." 7 Then Adam and Eve took the figs and began to eat of them. But God had put into them a mixture as of savory bread and blood. 8 Then, the angel left Adam and Eve as they ate of the figs until they had satisfied their hunger. Then they put aside what was left over, but by the power of God the figs became whole again, because God blessed them. 9 After this Adam and Eve got up and prayed with a joyful heart and renewed strength, and praised and rejoiced much for the entire night. And this was the end of the eighty-third day.

Author's not: The meaning of the phrase, "God says to you that you do not have the strength that would be required to fast until death…" is not clear. It is likely that it simply is somewhat inverted and should be, "If you fast, you will not have the required strength and you will die." Although one could look at it as a spiritual strength and a warning the one does not have the required determination to endure death by fasting. But God saw Adam had the will.

Chapter LXV

1 And when it was day, they got up and prayed, after their custom, and then went out of the cave. 2 But they became sick from the food they had eaten because they were not used to it, so they went about in the cave saying to each other: 3 "What has our eating caused to happen to us, that we should be in such pain? We are in misery. We are going to die! It would have been better for us to have died keeping our bodies pure than to have eaten and defiled them with food." 4 Then Adam said to Eve, "This pain did not come to us in the garden, neither did we eat such bad food there. Eve, do you think that God will plague us through the food that is in us, or that our insides will come out, or that God intends to kill us with this pain before He has fulfilled His promise to us?" 5 Then Adam besought the Lord and said, "O Lord, let us not perish because of the food we have eaten. O Lord, don't punish us, but deal with us according to Your great mercy, and do not forsake us until the day of the promise You have made us." 6 Then God looked at them, and then equipped them to be able to eat (fitted them for eating) food at once, as it is to this day, so that they should not perish. 7 Then Adam and Eve came back into the cave sorrowful and crying because of the alteration of their bodies. And they both knew from that hour that they were altered beings and all hope of returning to the garden was now lost, and they could not enter it again. 8 For now their bodies had strange functions and all flesh that requires food and drink for its existence cannot be in the garden. 9 Then Adam said to Eve, "See, our hope is now lost and so is our faith that we will enter the garden. We no longer belong to the inhabitants of the garden but from now on we are earthy and of the dust, and of the inhabitants of the earth. We shall not return to the garden until the day in which God has promised to save us and to bring us again into the garden, as He promised us." 10 Then they prayed to God that He would have mercy on them. After this, their minds were quieted, their hearts were broken, and their longing was cooled down, and they were like strangers on earth. That night Adam and Eve spent in the cave, where they slept heavily because of the food they had eaten.

Chapter LXVI

1 When the morning of the day after they had eaten food came, Adam and Eve prayed in the cave, and Adam said to Eve, "Look, we asked God for food, and He gave it. But now let us also ask Him to give us a drink of water." 2 Then they got up, and went to the bank of the stream of water, that was on the south border of the garden, which they had thrown themselves in before. And they stood on the bank, and prayed to God that He would command them to drink the water. 3 Then the Word of God came to Adam, and said to him, "O Adam, your body has become brutish, and requires water to drink. Take some and drink it, you and Eve, then give thanks and praise." 4 Adam and Eve then went down to the stream and drank from it, until their bodies felt refreshed. After they drank, they praised God and then returned to their cave, as was their custom. This happened at the end of eighty-three days. 5 Then on the eighty-fourth day, they took the two figs and hung them in the cave together with the leaves of the figs. To them these were a sign and a blessing from God. And they placed them there so that if their descendants came there they would see the wonderful things God had done for them. 6 Then Adam and Eve stood outside the cave again and asked God to show them some food with which they could nourish their bodies. 7 Then the Word of God came and said to him, "Adam, go down west of the cave until you come to a land that has dark soil, and there you will find food." 8 And Adam obeyed the Word of God and took Eve, and went down to a land that had dark soil and found wheat growing ripe in the ear, and figs to eat; and Adam rejoiced over it. 9 Then the Word of God came again to Adam, and said to him, "Take some of this wheat and make yourselves some bread with it, to nourish your body." And God gave Adam's heart wisdom to work the corn until it became bread. 10 Adam accomplished it all until he grew very faint and weak. He then returned to the cave rejoicing at what he had learned what he had done with the wheat, until it was made into bread.

The word, "corn" is used to mean a seed. However, the sentence indicates it is a seed of wheat that is used to make bread. The words for corn, meaning a seed, and wheat, are used to mean the same thing. In Egypt there is a type of wheat called Durra. The seed (corn) of wheat was likely Durra.

Chapter LXVII

1 When Adam and Eve went down to the land of black earth (mud) and came near to the wheat God had showed them and saw that it was ripe and ready for reaping, they did not have a sickle to reap it with. So they put themselves to the task and began to pull up the wheat by hand until the task was complete. 2 They then heaped it into a pile. They were weak from heat and from thirst and went under a shady tree where the breeze fanned them to sleep. 3 But Satan saw what Adam and Eve had done and he called his hosts, and said to them, "God has shown to Adam and Eve all about this wheat to strengthen their bodies, and, look, they have come and made a big pile of it. Now they are weak from the toil are now asleep. Come, let us set fire to this heap of corn (wheat seed), and burn it. Let us take that bottle of water that is by them and empty it out, so that they may find nothing to drink, and we kill them with hunger and thirst. 4 Then, when they wake up from their sleep and seek to return to the cave, we will come to them along the way and lead them in the wrong direction (get them lost) so that they die of hunger and thirst. Then perhaps they will reject God, and He may destroy them. So, in this way we can be rid of them." 5 Then Satan and his hosts set the wheat on fire and burned it up. 6 But from the heat of the flame Adam and Eve awoke from their sleep and saw the wheat burning and the bucket of water by them was poured out. 7 Then they cried and began to go back to the cave. 8 But as they were going up from below the mountain, Satan and his hosts met them in the form of angels, praising God. 9 Then Satan said to Adam, "Adam, why are you so pained with hunger and thirst? It seems to me that Satan has burnt up the wheat." And Adam said to him, "Yes." 10 Satan said to Adam, "Come back with us. We are angels of God. God sent us to you to show you another field of corn (wheat) better than that, and beyond it is a fountain of good water and many trees, near where you shall live. And you shall work the corn field and make it better than that which Satan has consumed." 11 Adam thought that he was true, and that they were angels who talked with him and so he went back with them. 12 Then Satan began to lead Adam and Eve in the wrong direction for eight days, until they both fell down as if dead, from hunger, thirst, and weakness. Then he fled with his hosts, and left them.

Author's note: In this recurring theme of deceit by Satan, we are confronted by the age-old question in life; is the circumstance that confronts us an opportunity from God or a detour and trap of Satan. How are we to know?

Chapter LXVIII

1 Then God looked at Adam and Eve, and at what had befallen them from Satan, and how he killed them. 2 So, God sent His Word and raised Adam and Eve from of death. 3 Then, when he was raised, Adam said, "O God, You have burnt and taken the seeds which You had given us. You have emptied out the bucket of water. And You have sent Your angels, who have caused us to lose our way from the corn (wheat) field. Will You kill us? If this is from you, O God, then take away our souls but stop punishing us." 4 Then God said to Adam, "I did not burn down the wheat, and I did not pour the water out of the bucket, and I did not send My angels to lead you astray. 5 But it is Satan, your master who did it. It was he to whom you have subjected yourself, while setting my commandment aside. It is He who burnt down the corn (wheat), and poured out the water, and who has led you astray. All the promises he has made you were just a trick, a deception, and a lie. 6 But now, Adam, you shall acknowledge My good deeds done to you." 7 And God told His angels to take Adam and Eve, and to lift them up to the field of wheat, which they found as before with the bucket full of water. 8 There they saw a tree and found on it solid manna, and they were astonished at God's power. And the angels commanded them to eat of the manna when they were hungry. 9 And God admonished Satan with a curse, not to come again and destroy the field of corn (wheat). 10 Then Adam and Eve took of the corn (wheat / seeds), and made an offering of it, and took it and offered it up on the mountain, at the place where they had offered up their first offering of blood. 11 And they offered this offering again on the altar they had built at first. And they stood up and prayed, and besought the Lord saying, "O God, when we were in the garden, our praises went up to you like this offering, and our innocence went up to you like incense. But now, O God, accept this offering from us, and don't turn us away or deprive us of Your mercy." 12 Then God said to Adam and Eve, "Since you have made this offering and have offered it to Me, I shall make it My flesh when I come down on earth to save you. I shall cause it to be offered continually on an altar for forgiveness and mercy for those who partake of it appropriately." 13 Then God sent a bright fire over the offering of Adam and Eve and filled it with brightness, grace, and light. And the Holy Spirit came down on that offering. 14 Then God commanded an angel to take fire tongs, like a spoon, and take an offering and bring it to Adam and Eve. And the angel did so as God had commanded him, and offered it to them. 15 And the souls of Adam and Eve were brightened, and their hearts were filled with joy and gladness and with the praises of God. 16 And God said to Adam, "This shall be a custom to you to perform when affliction and sorrow should come over you. But your deliverance and your entrance in to the garden, shall not be until the days are fulfilled as agreed between you and Me. If it were not for this, I would bring you back to My garden and to My favor and My mercy and pity for you, for the sake of the offering you have just made to My name." 17 Adam rejoiced at these words, which he heard from God. And Adam and Eve worshipped before the altar, to which they bowed, and then went back to the Cave of Treasures. 18 And this took place at the end of the twelfth

day after the eighteenth day (92 days), from the time Adam and Eve came out of the garden. 19 And they stood up the entire night praying until morning. Then they went out of the cave. 20 Then Adam said to Eve, with joy in his heart, because of the offering they had made to God that had been accepted by Him, "Let us do this three times every week, on all the days of our life." 21 And as they agreed on these words and God was pleased with their thoughts and with the decision they made. 22 After this, the Word of God came to Adam, and said, "Adam, you have determined beforehand the days in which sufferings shall come over Me, when I am made flesh. They are the fourth day, which is Wednesday, and the preparation day, which is Friday. 23 But regarding the first day, I created all things in it, and I raised the heavens. Through My rising again on this day, will I create joy and raise them who believe in Me on high. Adam, make this offering all the days of your life." 24 Then the Word of God withdrew from Adam. 25 But Adam continued to make the offering as he had, every week, three times a week, until the end of seven weeks. And on the first day, which is the fiftieth, Adam made an offering as he was accustomed, and he and Eve took it and came to the altar before God, as He had taught them.

Author's note: The order and number of the days of the week are called out as follows, "the fourth day, Wednesday, on the preparation day Friday, and on the Sabbath Sunday." The Jewish Sabbath is from Friday at sundown to Saturday at sundown, wherein, Saturday is considered to be the Sabbath. The shift shows Christian influence and a dating later than the writer(s) would have us believe.

Chapter LXIX

1 Then Satan, the hater of all that is good, was envious of Adam the fact that his offering found favor with God. So Satan hurried and took a sharp stone from among the sharp ironstones, which were shaped in the form of a man. And Satan went and stood by Adam and Eve. 2 Adam was offering on the altar and had begun to pray with his hands spread before God. 3 Then Satan hurried with the sharp ironstone he had and pierced Adam on the right side, and blood and water flowed. Then Adam fell on the altar like a corpse, and Satan fled. 4 Then Eve came and took Adam and placed him below the altar. There she stayed, crying over him while a stream of blood flowed from Adam's side over his offering. 5 But God looked at the death of Adam. He then sent His Word and raised him up. And He said to him, "Fulfill your offering because, certainly Adam, it is worthy and there is no imperfection in it." 6 God continued speaking to Adam, "Thus will it also happen to Me while on the earth, when I shall be pierced and blood and water shall flow from My side and run over My body, which is the true offering, and which shall be offered on the altar as a perfect offering." 7 Then God commanded Adam to finish his offering. And when he had ended it he worshipped before God and praised Him for the signs He had showed him. 8 And God healed Adam in one day, which is the end of the seven weeks and is the fiftieth day. 9 Then Adam and Eve returned from the mountain and went into the Cave of Treasures, as they were used to do. This completed one hundred and forty days for Adam and Eve, since their coming out of the garden. 10 Then they both stood up that night and prayed to God. And when it was morning they went down to the west side of the cave, to the place where their wheat (corn) was, and there they rested under the shadow of a tree, as they were accustomed to do. 11 But when they were there, a multitude of beasts came all around them. It was Satan's wickedness and his way to wage war against Adam through marriage.

Author's note: The following chapter will explain how marriage fits into Satan's plan. The fact that Satan will use marriage against Adam and Eve indicates that the writer of this text viewed marriage in a less than positive light. It should also be stressed that the idea of a ceremony is not the point of marriage in this context. It is intercourse that establishes the state. The resulting children and complications were the point of Satan's plan.

Chapter LXX

1 After this Satan, the hater of all that is good, took the form of an angel, and two others with him. So, they looked like the three angels who had brought to Adam gold, incense, and myrrh. 2 They came to Adam and Eve while they were under the tree, and greeted Adam and Eve with friendly words that were full of deceit. 3 But when Adam and Eve saw their friendly countenance and heard their sweet speech, Adam rose, welcomed them, and brought them to Eve and they remained all together. Adam's heart was happy all the while because he thought that they were the same angels, who had brought him gold, incense, and myrrh. 4 This was because when they came to Adam the first time peace and joy came over him from them because they brought him good gifts. So Adam thought that they had come a second time to give him other gifts to make him rejoice. He did not know it was Satan, therefore he received them with joy and associated with them. 5 Then Satan, the tallest of them, said, "Rejoice, Adam, and be glad. Look, God has sent us to you to tell you something." 6 And Adam said, "What is it?" Then Satan said, "It is a simple thing, but it is the Word of God. Will you accept it from us and do it? If you will not accept it, we will return to God and tell Him that you would not receive His Word." 7 And Satan continued, saying to Adam, "Don't be afraid and don't shake. Don't you know us?" 8 But Adam said, "I do not know you." 9 Then Satan said to him, "I am the angel that brought you gold and took it to the cave. This other angel is the one that brought you incense. And that third angel is the one who brought you myrrh when you were on top of the mountain. It was he who carried you to the cave. 10 It was our other fellow angels who lifted you to the cave. God has not sent them with us this time because He said to us, 'You will be enough'. " 11 So when Adam heard these words he believed them, and said to the angels, "Speak the Word of God, and I

will receive it." 12 And Satan said to him, "Swear and promise me that you will receive it." 13 Then Adam said, "I do not know how to swear and promise." 14 And Satan said to him, "Hold out your hand and put it inside my hand." 15 Then Adam held out his hand, and put it into Satan's hand. Satan said to him, "Now say this; As God who raised the stars in heaven, and established the dry ground on the waters, and has created me out of the four elements, and out of the dust of the earth, and is logical and true does speak, I will not break my promise, nor abandon my word." 16 And Adam swore. 17 Then Satan said to him, "Look, some time has passed since you came out of the garden, and you do not know wickedness or evil. But now God says to you, to take Eve who came out of your side, and marry her so that she will bear you children to comfort you and to drive from you trouble and sorrow. This thing is not difficult and there is nothing morally wrong in it for you.

Chapter LXXI

1 But when Adam heard these words from Satan, he sorrowed much, because of his oath and his promise. And he said, "Shall I commit adultery with my flesh and my bones, and shall I sin against myself, so that God will destroy me blot me out from the face of the earth? 2 First, I ate of the tree and He drove me out of the garden into this strange land and deprived me of my bright nature, and brought my death. If I do this, He will cut off my life from the earth, and He will cast me into hell, and plague me there a long time. 3 But God never spoke the words that you have said and you are not God's angels. He did not send you. You are devils that have come to me under the false appearance of angels. Away from me, you cursed of God!" 4 Then the devils fled from Adam. And he and Eve got up and returned to the Cave of Treasures, and went into it. 5 Then Adam said to Eve, "If you saw what I did, don't tell anyone because I sinned against God in swearing by His great name, and I have placed my hand once again into that of Satan." Eve then held her peace as Adam told her. 6 Then Adam got up and spread his hands before God, beseeching and entreating Him with tears to forgive him of what he had done. And Adam remained standing and praying in that way for forty days and forty nights. He did not eat or drink until he dropped down on the ground from hunger and thirst. 7 Then God sent His Word to Adam, who raised him up from where he lay, and said to him, "Adam, why have you sworn by My name? Why have you made agreement with Satan again?" 8 But Adam cried and said, "O God, forgive me. I did this unwittingly because I believed they were God's angels." 9 And God forgave Adam and said to him, "Beware of Satan." 10 And He withdrew His Word from Adam. 11 Then Adam's heart was comforted, and he took Eve and they went out of the cave to prepare some food for their bodies. 12 But from that day Adam struggled in his mind about marrying Eve, because he was afraid that if he did it, God would be angry with him. 13 Then Adam and Eve went to the river of water, and sat on the bank, as people do when they enjoy themselves. 14 But Satan was jealous of them and planned to destroy them.

Author's note: Clearly, Adam viewed copulating with Eve as incest and therefore morally wrong, even though it was not yet law. The idea kindled his desire, which was in opposition to what Adam viewed as a moral issue. This issue will be visited again in other texts such as Jubliees and others as Cain's marriage to his sister is addressed.

Chapter LXXII

1 Then Satan, and ten from his hosts, transformed themselves into maidens, with more grace than any others in the entire world. 2 They came up out of the river in front of Adam and Eve, and they said among themselves, "Come, we will look at the faces of Adam and Eve who are of the men on earth. They are beautiful and their faces look different than ours." Then they came to Adam and Eve and greeted them, and they stood amazed at them. 3 Adam and Eve looked at them also, and wondered at their beauty, and said, "Is there another world under us with such beautiful creatures as these in it?" 4 And the maidens said to Adam and Eve, "Yes, indeed, many of us were created." 5 Then Adam said to them, "But how do you multiply?" 6 And they told him, "We have husbands who have married us and we bear them children, who grow up and in turn marry and are married and also bear children. Thus we increase. O Adam, you will not believe us, we will show you our husbands and our children." 7 Then they shouted over the river as if to call their husbands and their children. And men and children came up from the river, and every man came to his wife, and his children were with him. 8 But when Adam and Eve saw them, they stood speechless and were amazed at them. 9 Then they said to Adam and Eve, "See all our husbands and our children? You should marry Eve as we have married our husbands so that you will have children as we have." This was the way Satan was to deceive Adam. 10 Satan also thought to himself, "God at first commanded Adam concerning the fruit of the tree, saying to him, 'Do not eat of it or else you shall die.' But Adam ate of it but God did not kill him. He only gave him by law death, plagues, and trials, until the day he shall leave his body. 11 But if I deceive him to do this thing and marry Eve without God's permission, God will kill him." 12 Therefore Satan worked this apparition before Adam and Eve, because he sought to kill him, and to make him disappear from off the face of the earth. 13 Meanwhile the fire of immorality came over Adam and he thought of committing transgression. But he restrained himself, fearing that if he followed the advice of Satan, God would put him to death. 14 Then Adam and Eve got up and prayed to God, while Satan and his hosts went down into the river in front of Adam and Eve so they would see them going back to their own world. 15 Then Adam and Eve went back to the Cave of Treasures, as they usually did around evening time. 16 And they both got up and prayed to God that night.

Adam remained standing in prayer but did not know how to pray because of the thoughts in his heart about marrying Eve. And he continued this way until morning. 17 When light came up, Adam said to Eve, "Get up, let us go below the mountain where they brought us gold and let us ask the Lord concerning this matter." 18 Then Eve said, "What is that matter, Adam?" 19 And he answered her, "That I may request the Lord to inform me about marrying you because I will not do it without His permission or else He will kill you and me. For those devils have set my heart on fire with thoughts of what they showed us in their sinful visions. 20 Then Eve said to Adam, "Why do we need to go to the foot of the mountain? Let us rather stand up and pray in our cave to God to let us know whether this advice is good or not." 21 Then Adam rose up in prayer and said, "O God, you know that we transgressed against you, and from the moment we sinned we were stripped of our bright nature, and our body became brutish, requiring food and drink, and with animal desires. 22 Command us, O God, not to give way to them without Your permission, for fear that You will turn us into nothing. If you do not give us permission we will be overcome and follow that advice of Satan, and You will again kill us. 23 If not, then take our souls from us and let us be rid of this animal lust. And if You give us no order about this thing then separate Eve from me and me from her, and place us each far away from the other. 24 Then, O God, if You separate us from each other the devils will deceive us with their apparitions that resemble us, and destroy our hearts, and defile our thoughts towards each other. If our heart is not toward each other it will be toward them, through their appearance when the devils come to us in our likeness." Here Adam ended his prayer.

Chapter LXXIII

1 Then God considered the words of Adam that they were true, and that he could not wait long for His order, respecting the counsel of Satan. 2 And God approved Adam in what he had thought concerning this, and in the prayer he had offered in His presence; and the Word of God came to Adam and said to him, "O Adam, if only you had had this caution at first, before you came out of the garden into this land!" 3 After that, God sent His angel who had brought gold, and the angel who had brought incense, and the angel who had brought myrrh to Adam, that they should inform him respecting his marriage to Eve. 4 Then those angels said to Adam, "Take the gold and give it to Eve as a wedding gift, and promise to marry her; then give her some incense and myrrh as a present; and be you both will be one flesh." 5 Adam obeyed the angels, and took the gold and put it into Eve's bosom in her garment; and promised to marry her with his hand. 6 Then the angels commanded Adam and Eve to get up and pray forty days and forty nights; when that was done, then Adam was to have sexual intercourse with his wife; for then this would be an act pure and undefiled; so that he would have children who would multiply, and replenish the face of the earth. 7 Then both Adam and Eve received the words of the angels; and the angels departed from them. 8 Then Adam and Eve began to fast and pray, until the end of the forty days; and then they had sexual intercourse, as the angels had told them. And from the time Adam left the garden until he wedded Eve, were two hundred and twenty-three days, that is seven months and thirteen days. 9 This was how Satan's war with Adam was won by Adam and Satan was defeated.

Author's note: In the apocryphal book of Tobit, the main character goes into his new bride after praying to still his lust and was thus pure.
*   The word "replenish" indicates that the earth was once full or "plenished" and was to be "replenished" or filled again. This is the same word used in Genesis, leading two the Second Creation Theory.*

Chapter LXXIV

1 And they lived on the earth working so they could keep their bodies in good health. And they continued until the nine months of Eve's pregnancy were over and the time drew near when she would give birth. 2 Then she said to Adam, "The tokens placed in this cave since we left the garden show it to be a pure place. We will be praying in it again in a while. Because of this, it is not appropriate that I should give birth in it. Let us instead go to the sheltering rock cave that was formed by the command of God when Satan threw a big rock down on us in an attempt to kill us. 3 Adam then took Eve to that cave. When the time came for her to give birth she strained very much. Adam felt pity for her and he was very worried about her because she was close to death and the words of God to her were being fulfilled: " You shall bear a child in suffering, and in sorrow shall you bring forth a child." 4 But when Adam saw the distress Eve was in, he got up and prayed to God, and said, "O Lord, look at me with the eye of Your mercy, and deliver her out of her distress." 5 And God looked at His maid-servant Eve, and delivered her, and she gave birth to her first-born son, and with him a daughter. 6 Then Adam rejoiced at Eve's deliverance, and also over the children she had given him. And Adam ministered to Eve in the cave until the end of eight days, when they named the son Cain, and the daughter Luluwa. 7 The meaning of Cain is "hater," because he hated his sister in their mother's womb, before they were born. Because of this, Adam named him Cain. 8 But Luluwa means "beautiful," because she was more beautiful than her mother. 9 Then Adam and Eve waited until Cain and his sister were forty days old, when Adam said to Eve, "We will make an offering and offer it up in behalf of the children." 10 And Eve said, "We will first make one offering for the first-born son and then later we shall make one for the daughter."

Author's note: Jewish law says the woman is unclean for a time after giving birth. The act, having human blood present, makes the place unclean. The first cave served as home and temple. The second cave served as a place of safety and shelter.

It will be noted the each time Eve gave birth she did so with twins, symbolizing the replenishing or replacing of Adam and Eve.

Chapter LXXV

1 Then Adam prepared an offering. He and Eve brought it to the altar they had built at first and offered it up for their children. 2 And Adam offered up the offering, and asked God to accept his offering. 3 Then God accepted Adam's offering, and sent a light from heaven that shined down on the offering. Adam and his son drew near to the offering, but Eve and the daughter did not approach it. 4 Adam and his son were joyful as they came down from the altar. Adam and Eve waited until the daughter was eighty days old and then Adam prepared an offering and took it to Eve and to the children. They went to the altar where Adam offered it up, as he was accustomed, asking the Lord to accept his offering. 5 And the Lord accepted the offering of Adam and Eve. Then Adam, Eve, and the children gathered together and came down from the mountain, rejoicing. 6 But they did not return to the cave in which they were born. Instead they went to the Cave of Treasures, so that the children should live in it and be blessed with the tokens brought from the garden. 7 But after they had been blessed with the tokens they went back to the cave in which they were born. 8 But, before Eve had offered up the offering, Adam had taken her to the river of water in which they threw themselves at first. There they washed themselves. Adam washed his body and Eve washed hers clean also, after the suffering and distress that had come over them. 9 But after washing themselves in the river of water, Adam and Eve returned every night to the Cave of Treasures, where they prayed and were blessed, and then went back to their cave where their children were born. 10 Adam and Eve did this until the children had been weaned. After they were weaned, Adam made an offering for the souls of his children in addition to the three times every week he made an offering for them. 11 When the children were weaned, Eve conceived again, and when her pregnancy came to term, she gave birth to another son and daughter. They named the son Abel and the daughter Aklia. 12 Then at the end of forty days, Adam made an offering for the son, and at the end of eighty days he made another offering for the daughter, and treated them as he had previously treated Cain and his sister Luluwa. 13 He brought them to the Cave of Treasures, where they received a blessing and then returned to the cave where they were born. After these children were born, Eve stopped having children.

Author's note: To compare the purification ritual recounted here to those of the Old Testament we look to the book of the law. Leviticus 12 (RSV) 1 The LORD said to Moses, 2" Say to the people of Israel, If a woman conceives, and bears a male child, then she shall be unclean seven days; as at the time of her menstruation, she shall be unclean. 3 And on the eighth day the flesh of his foreskin shall be circumcised. 4 Then she shall continue for thirty-three days in the blood of her purifying; she shall not touch any hallowed thing, nor come into the sanctuary, until the days of her purifying are completed. 5 But if she bears a female child, then she shall be unclean two weeks, as in her menstruation; and she shall continue in the blood of her purifying for sixty-six days. 6 "And when the days of her purifying are completed, whether for a son or for a daughter, she shall bring to the priest at the door of the tent of meeting a lamb a year old for a burnt offering, and a young pigeon or a turtledove for a sin offering , 7 and he shall offer it before the LORD, and make atonement for her; then she shall be clean from the flow of her blood. This is the law for her who bears a child, either male or female. 8 And if she cannot afford a lamb, then she shall take two turtledoves or two young pigeons, one for a burnt offering and the other for a sin offering; and the priest shall make atonement for her, and she shall be clean."

Chapter LXXVI

1 As the children began to grow stronger and taller, Cain grew hard-hearted, and he ruled over his younger brother. 2 Often, when his father made an offering, Cain would remain behind and not go with them to make the offering. 3 But Abel had a meek heart, and was obedient to his father and mother. He frequently influenced them to make an offering because he loved it. He prayed and fasted much. 4 Then this sign came to Abel. As he was coming into the Cave of Treasures he saw the golden rods, the incense and the myrrh and he asked his parents, Adam and Eve, to tell him about them. Abel asked, "Where did you get these from?" 5 Then Adam told him all that had befallen them. And Abel felt deeply about what his father told him. 6 Then his father, Adam, told him about the works of God and of the garden. After hearing these things, Abel remained behind after his father left and stayed the entire of that night in the Cave of Treasures. 7 And that night, while he was praying, Satan appeared to him in the form of a man. And Satan said to him, "Often you have moved your father into making offerings, and to fast and pray. Because of this, I will kill you and make you perish from this world." 8 But Abel prayed to God and drove away Satan, and he did not believe the words of the devil. Then when it was day, an angel of God appeared to him, who said to him, "Do not stop your fasting, prayer, or offering to your God. For, look, the Lord has accepted your prayer. Be not afraid of the form which appeared to you in the night, and who cursed you to death." Then the angel departed from him. 9 Then Abel came to Adam and Eve when it was day, and told them about the vision he had seen. When they heard it they worried about it very much, but said nothing to him about it. They only comforted him. 10 But Satan came to the hard-hearted Cain by night and showed himself and said to him, "Since Adam and Eve love your brother Abel so much more than they love you, they wish to join him in marriage to your beautiful sister because they love him. However, they wish to join you in marriage to his ugly sister, because they hate you. 11 Now before they do that, I am telling you that you should kill your brother. That way your sister will be left for you and you can throw his sister away." 12 And Satan departed from him. But the devil remained behind in Cain's heart, and frequently prompted his ambition to kill his brother.

Author's note: Since the children were born in pairs, it seems more reasonable to have those that were not twins marry.

Note the word used in reference to Cain's heart. He was hard-hearted and the devil gave him ambition – or hope – or aspiration to kill. As if this were something to achieve as a noble end.

Chapter LXXVII

1 But when Adam saw that the older brother hated the younger brother, he attempted to soften their hearts. He said to Cain, "My son, take some of the fruits of your sowing and make an offering to God, so that He might forgive you for your wickedness and your sin." 2 He said also to Abel, "Take some of the fruit of your sowing and make an offering and bring it to God, so that He might forgive you for your wickedness and your sin." 3 Then Abel obeyed his father and took some of his sowing, and made a good offering, and said to his father, Adam, "Come with me and show me how to offer it up." 4 And they went, Adam and Eve with him, and they showed him how to offer up his gift on the altar. Then after that they stood up and prayed that God would accept Abel's offering. 5 Then God looked at Abel and accepted his offering. And God was more pleased with Abel than He was with his offering, because of his good heart and pure body. There was no trace of guile in him. 6 Then they came down from the altar and went to the cave in which they lived. But because of his joy felt at making his offering, Abel repeated it three times a week, following the example of his father Adam. 7 But Cain did not want to make an offering, but after his father became very angry, he offered up a gift once. He took the smallest of his sheep for an offering and when he offered it up, his eyes were on the lamb. 8 Because of this, God did not accept his offering, because his heart was full of murderous thoughts. 9 And they all lived together like this in the cave in which Eve had given birth, until Cain was fifteen years old, and Abel twelve years old.

Chapter LXXVIII

1 Then Adam said to Eve, "The children have grown up. We must think of finding wives for them." 2 Then Eve answered, "How can we do that?" 3 Then Adam said to her, "We will join Abel's sister in marriage to Cain, and Cain's sister to Abel. 4 Then Eve said to Adam, "I do not like Cain because he is hard-hearted. So, let them stay with us until we offer up (an offering) to the Lord in their behalf." 5 And Adam said no more. 6 Meanwhile Satan came to Cain in the form of a man of the field, and said to him, "Look. Adam and Eve have discussed together about the marriage of you two, and they have agreed to marry Abel's sister to you, and your sister to Abel. 7 But if it were not that I love you, I would not have told you this thing. So, if you will take my advice and obey me, I will bring beautiful robes, plenty of gold and silver, and my relations will attend you on your wedding day." 8 Then Cain said with joy, "Where are your relations?" 9 And Satan answered, "My relations are in a garden in the north, where I once meant to bring your father Adam, but he would not accept my offer. 10 But if you will receive my words and if you will come to me after your wedding, you shall rest from the misery in which you are; and you shall rest and be better off than your father Adam." 11 At these words, Satan got Cain's attention (opened his ears), and Cain inclined toward Satan to listen (leaned towards his speech). 12 After this, he did not remain in the field, but he went to Eve, his mother, and beat her and cursed her, and said to her, "Why are you planning to take my sister to marry her to my brother? Am I dead?" 13 But his mother quieted him and sent him back to the field where he had been. 14 Then when Adam came, she told him of what Cain had done. 15 Adam was very worried, but held his peace, and did not say a word. 16 Then, the next morning Adam said to Cain his son, "Take of your young and good sheep and offer them up to your God, and I will speak to your brother and have him make an offering of corn to his God." 17 They both obeyed their father Adam, and they took their offerings, and offered them up on the mountain by the altar. 18 But Cain behaved arrogantly (haughtily) toward his brother, and he shoved him from the altar, and would not let him offer up his gift on the altar, but he offered his own offering on it with a proud heart, full of guile and fraud. 19 But Abel set up stones that were near at hand and on that, he offered up his gift with a heart humble and free from guile. 20 Cain was then standing by the altar on which he had offered up his gift and he cried to God to accept his offering, but God did not accept it from Cain, nor did a divine fire come down to consume his offering. 21 But he remained standing over against the altar out of meanness, to make fun of his brother, and he glared at his brother Abel to see if God would accept his offering or not. 22 And Abel prayed to God to accept his offering. Then a divine fire came down and consumed his offering. And God smelled the sweet savor of his offering, because Abel loved Him and rejoice in Him. 23 And because God was well pleased with him, He sent him an angel of light in the form of a man to partake of his offering, because He had smelled the sweet savor of his offering, and he comforted Abel and strengthened his heart. 24 But Cain was looking on all that took place at his brother's offering, and was angry because of it. 25 Then he opened his mouth and blasphemed God because He had not accepted his offering. 26 But God said to Cain, "Why do you look sad? Be in right standing with Me so that I may accept your offering. You have not murmured against Me, but against yourself. 27 And God said this to Cain in rebuke, and because He hated him and his offering. 28 And Cain came down from the altar and his color changed and he had a sad face. And he came to his father and mother and told them all that had happened to him. And Adam grieved much because God had not accepted Cain's offering. 29 But Abel came down rejoicing, and with a glad heart, and told his father and mother how God had accepted his offering. And they rejoiced at it and kissed his face. 30 And Abel said to his father, "Because Cain shoved me from the altar, and would not allow me to offer

my gift on it, I made an altar for myself and offered my gift on it."

31 But when Adam heard this he was very sorry because it was the altar he had built at first, and on which he had offered his own gifts. 32 Cain was so resentful and so angry that he went into the field. There, Satan came to him and said to him, "Your brother Abel has taken refuge with your father Adam, because you shoved him from the altar. They have kissed his face and they rejoice over him far more than over you." 33 When Cain heard these words of Satan he was filled with rage but he let no one know. But he was laying in wait to kill his brother, until he brought him into the cave, and then said to him: 34 "Brother, the country is so beautiful and there are such beautiful and pleasurable trees in it, and charming to look at! But brother, you have never been one day in the field to take your pleasure in that place. 35 Today, my brother, I wish very much that you would come into the field with me, to enjoy yourself and to bless our fields and our flocks, for you are righteous, and I love you much, O my brother! But you have alienated yourself from me." 36 Then Abel agreed to go with his brother Cain into the field. 37 But before going out, Cain said to Abel, "Wait for me and I will fetch a staff because of wild beasts." 38 Then Abel stood innocently waiting. But Cain, the presumptuous, got a staff and went out. 39 And Cain and his brother Abel began to walk in the path. Cain was talking to him, and comforting him, to make him forget everything.

Chapter LXXIX

1 And so they walked on until they came to a place they were alone where there were no sheep. Then Abel said to Cain, "Look, my brother, we are tired from walking. We see none of the trees, or fruits, or the growing green plants, or the sheep, or any of the things of which you told me. Where are those sheep of yours that you told me to bless?" 2 Then Cain said to him, "Come on, and you shall see many beautiful things very soon, but go before me until I catch up to you." 3 Then Abel went on but Cain stayed behind him. 4 And Abel was innocently walking, without suspecting any craftiness, not thinking that his brother would kill him. 5 Then Cain came up to him, comforted him with his words while walking a little behind him. Then he ran up to him and beat him with the staff, blow after blow, until he was dazed. 6 But when Abel fell down on the ground and saw that his brother meant to kill him, he said to Cain, "O, my brother, have pity on me. By the breasts we have sucked, do not hit me! By the womb that bore us and that brought us into the world, do not beat me to death with that staff! If you are set on killing me, take one of these large stones and kill me outright." 7 Then Cain, the hard-hearted, and cruel murderer, took a large stone, and beat his brother's head with it until his brains oozed out, and he wallowed in his blood, before him. 8 And Cain was not sorry for what he had done. 9 But when the blood of righteous Abel fell on the earth, it trembled as it drank his blood, and would have destroyed Cain because of it. 10 And the blood of Abel cried mysteriously to God to avenge him of his murderer. 11 Then Cain began to dig furiously at the ground to bury his brother, because he was shaking from fear that came over him when he saw the earth tremble because of him. 12 He then threw his brother into the hole he made, and covered him with dust. But the ground would not receive him and it threw him up at once. 13 Again Cain dug the ground and covered his brother in it, but again the ground threw him up. Three times the ground threw up the body of Abel on itself. 14 The muddy ground threw him up the first time because he was not the first creation. It threw him up the second time and would not receive him because he was righteous and good and was killed without a cause. The ground threw him up the third time and would not receive him so that there might remain before his brother a witness against him. 15 And so the earth mocked Cain until the Word of God came to him concerning his brother. 16 Then God was angry and very much displeased at Abel's death. And He thundered from heaven, and lightning went out from Him, and the Word of the Lord God came from heaven to Cain, and said to him, "Where is Abel, your brother?" 17 Then Cain answered with a proud heart and a gruff voice, "How am I to know, O God? Am I my brother's keeper?" 18 Then God said to Cain, "Cursed be the earth that has drunk the blood of Abel, your brother. And as for you, you will always be trembling and shaking, and this will be a mark on you so that whoever finds you will kill you." 19 But Cain cried because God had said those words to him. And Cain said to Him, "O God, whosoever finds me shall kill me, and I shall be blotted out from the face of the earth." 20 Then God said to Cain, "Whoever finds you will not kill you," because before this, God had been saying to Cain, "I shall put seven punishments on anyone that kills Cain." For the word of God to Cain was, "Where is your brother?" God said it in mercy to him, to try and make him repent. 21 And if Cain had repented at that time, and had said, "O God, forgive me my sin, and the murder of my brother," God would then have forgiven him his sin. 22 But God said to Cain, "Cursed be the ground that has drunk the blood of your brother" That also, was God's mercy on Cain, because God did not curse him, but He cursed the ground, although it was not the ground that had killed Abel, and committed a wicked sin. 23 But it was fitting that the curse should fall on the murderer, and yet, in mercy did God managed His thoughts so that no one should know the extent of His anger for He turned it away from Cain. 24 And He said to him, "Where is your brother?" To which he answered and said, "I know not." Then the Creator said to him, "Be trembling and quaking." 25 Then Cain trembled and became terrified, and through this sign God made him an example before all the creation to show him as the murderer of his brother. Also God brought trembling and terror over him so that he might see the peace he had before and also see the trembling and terror he endured at the end, so that he might humble himself before God and repent of his sin, and seek the peace that he enjoyed at first. 26 The word of God said, "I will put seven punishments on anyone who kills Cain." So, God was not seeking to kill Cain with the sword, but He sought to make him die of fasting, and praying, and crying by His discipline, until the time that he was delivered from his sin. 27 And the seven punishments are the seven generations during which God awaited Cain for the murder of his brother. 28 But, ever since he had killed his brother, Cain could find no rest in any place, so he

went back to Adam and Eve, trembling, terrified, and defiled with blood.

This ends The First Book of Adam and Eve

Author's note: Wallowing in the blood of a kill coveys an extreme in animal behavior and state.

What is amazing about this chapter is the limits explored to explain the thoughts, actions, and strategy of God toward Cain. We are told that the enigmatic mark left on Cain as a curse is actually the physical trait of shaking and trembling in fear. One may ask if this is the mark of cowardice exhibited by a bully.

The explanation of God's first statement to kill Cain, then cursing anyone who would kill Cain, then "waiting for Cain seven generations is wordy, convoluted, and odd. The author seems to be attempting to put all of the pieces together in some reasonable manner. This could be due to the knitting together of several sources with the last man left with the task of tying the story together into a cohesive conclusion.

The Second Book of Adam and Eve

The Second Book of Adam and Eve expands on the time from Cain's act of murder to the time Enoch was taken by God. It is, above all, a continuation of the story of *The First Book of Adam and Eve*.

Like the first book, this book is also part of the "Pseudepigrapha", which is a collection of historical biblical works that are considered to be fiction. Although considered to be Pseudepigrapha, it carries significance in that it provides insight into what was considered acceptable religious writing and ideas of the time.

This book is a composite of oral versions of an account handed down by word of mouth, from generation to generation until an unknown author pieced the stories together into a written form.

This particular version is the work of unknown Egyptians. The lack of historical allusion makes it difficult to date the writing. Using other Pseudepigrapha works as a reference only slightly narrows the probable dates to a range of a few hundred years. Parts of the text were probably included in an oral tradition, two or three hundred years before the birth of Christ. Certainly, book two was written after book one.

Sections of the text are found in the Jewish Talmud, and the Islamic Koran. Although some think this shows how the books of Adam and Eve played a vital role in ancient literature, it could just as well expose the fact that the authors of the Adam and Eve stories borrowed heavily from accepted holy books.

The Egyptian author wrote in Arabic, but later translations were found written in Ethiopic. The present English translation was completed in the late 1800's by Dr. S. C. Malan and Dr. E. Trumpp. They translated the text into King James English from both the Arabic version and the Ethiopic version, which was then published in The Forgotten Books of Eden in 1927 by The World Publishing Company. The version presented here takes the 1927 version, written in King James style English, and renders it into wording more familiar to the modern reader. Tangled sentence structure and archaic words were replaced with a more clear, crisp, twenty-first century English.

Second Book of Adam and Eve

Chapter I.

1 When Luluwa heard Cain's words, she wept and went to call her father and mother, and told them how Cain had killed his brother Abel.
2 Then they all cried aloud and lifted up their voices, and slapped their faces, and threw dust upon their heads, and ripped their garments apart, and went out and came to the place where Abel was killed.
3 And they found him lying on the earth, killed, and beasts were around him. They wept and cried because he was a just person. Because his body was pure, from it went forth a smell of sweet spices.
4 And Adam carried him as Adam's tears streaming down his face; and he went to the Cave of Treasures, where he laid Abel, and Adam wound him up with sweet spices and myrrh.
5 And Adam and Eve continued in great grief by the burial site for a hundred and forty days. Abel was fifteen and a half years old, and Cain seventeen years and a half.
6 When the mourning for his brother was ended, Cain took his sister Luluwa and married her, without permission from his father and mother. Because of their heavy hearts they could not keep him from her.
7 He then went down to the foot of the mountain, away from the garden, near the place where he had killed his brother.
8 And in that place were many fruit trees and forest trees. His sister gave birth to his children, who in their turn began to multiply by degrees until they filled that place.
9 But Adam and Eve did not come together (have intercourse) for seven years after Abel's funeral. After this, however, Eve conceived. And while she was with child Adam said to her, "Come, let us take an offering and offer it up unto God and ask Him to give us a beautiful child in whom we may find comfort, and whom we may join in marriage to Abel's sister."
10 Then they prepared an offering and brought it up to the altar, and offered it before the Lord, and began to ask Him to accept their offering and to give them a good offspring.
11 And God heard Adam and accepted his offering. Then, Adam, Eve and their daughter worshipped, and came down to the Cave of Treasures and placed a lamp in it by the body of Abel to burn by the body, night and day.
12 Then Adam and Eve continued fasting and praying until Eve's time came that she should be delivered, when she said to Adam, "I wish to go to the cave in the rock, to give birth in it."
13 And he said, "Go, and take your daughter with you to wait on you; but I will remain in this Cave of Treasures before the body of my son Abel."
14 Then Eve listened to Adam, and she and her daughter left, but Adam remained by himself in the Cave of Treasures.

Chapter II.

1 And Eve gave birth to a son, perfectly beautiful in form and in demeanor. His beauty was like that of his father Adam, yet more beautiful.
2 Then Eve was comforted when she saw him, and remained eight days in the cave; then she sent her daughter unto Adam to tell him to come and see the child and name him. But the daughter stayed in his place by the body of her brother, until Adam returned.
3 But when Adam came and saw the child's good looks, his beauty, and his perfect form, he rejoiced over him, and was comforted for Abel. Then he named the child Seth, which means, "that God has heard my prayer, and has delivered me out of my affliction." But it means also "power and strength."
4 Then after Adam had named the child, he returned to the Cave of Treasures; and his daughter went back to her mother.
5 But Eve continued in her cave, until forty days were fulfilled, when she came to Adam, and brought with her the child and her daughter.
6 And they came to a river of water, where Adam and his daughter washed themselves, because of their sorrow for Abel; but Eve and the babe washed for purification.
7 Then they returned, and took an offering, and went to the mountain and offered it up for the babe; and God accepted their offering, and sent His blessing upon them, and upon their son Seth; and they came back to the Cave of Treasures.
8 As for Adam, he did not have intercourse again with his wife Eve, all the days of his life; neither was any more offspring born of them; but only those five, Cain, Luluwa, Abel, Aklia, and Seth alone.
9 But Seth waxed in stature and in strength; and began to fast and pray, fervently.

Author's note: Abel was fifteen and a half years old, and Cain seventeen years and a half when Abel was killed. Cain and Luluwa were twins. Abel and Aklia were twins. Cain married his twin sister. Aklia was fifteen and a half when Abel died. Adam and Eve did not come together (have intercourse) for seven years after Abel's funeral. Aklia would now be twenty-two and a half. Eve carried Seth for nine months. At the time of Seth's birth, Aklia would have been twenty-three years old.

Chapter III.

1 At the end of seven years from the day Adam had been separated from his wife Eve, Satan envied him, and when he saw Adam was separated from her, Satan strove to make him live with her again.

2 Then Adam arose and went up above the Cave of Treasures and continued to sleep there night by night. But every day as soon as it was light he came down to the cave to pray there and to receive a blessing from it.

3 But when it was evening he went up on the top of the cave, where he slept by himself, fearing that Satan could overcome him. And he continued apart in this way for thirty-nine days.

4 Then when Satan, the hater of all that is good, saw Adam alone, fasting and praying, he appeared unto him in the form of a beautiful woman who came and stood in front of him in the night of the fortieth day, and said to him:

5 "Adam, from the time you have dwelt in this cave, we have experienced great peace from you, and your prayers have reached us, and we have been comforted because of you.

6 "But now, Adam, that you have gone up over the roof of the cave to sleep, we have had doubts about you, and a great sorrow has come upon us because of your separation from Eve. Then again, when you are on the roof of this cave, your prayer is poured out, and your heart wanders from side to side.

7 "But when you were in the cave your prayer was like fire gathered together. It came down to us, and you found rest.

8 "Then I also worried over your children who are separated from you, and my sorrow is great about the murder of your son Abel because he was righteous, and over a righteous man every one will grieve.

9 "But I rejoiced over the birth of your son Seth. But after a little while I sorrowed greatly over Eve, because she is my sister. For when God sent a deep sleep over you, and drew her out of your side, He brought me out with her. But He raised her by placing her with you, while He lowered me.

10 "I rejoiced over my sister for her being with you. But God had made me a promise before, and said, 'Do not grieve; when Adam has gone up on the roof of the Cave of Treasures, and is separated from Eve his wife, I will send you to him and you shall join yourself to him in marriage, and bear five children for him, as Eve gave him five children.'

11 "And now, look! God's promise to me is fulfilled because it is He who has sent me to you for the wedding, because if you wed me I shall bear you finer and better children than those of Eve.

12 "You are still young. Do not end your youth in this world in sorrow. Spend the days of your youth in happiness and pleasure. Your days are few and your trials have been great. Be strong and end your days in this world in rejoicing. I shall take pleasure in you, and you shall rejoice with me in this way and without fear.

13 "Get up and fulfill the command of your God," she then came near Adam and embraced him.

14 But when Adam saw that he was going to be overcome by her, he prayed to God with a fervent heart to deliver him from her.

15 Then God sent His Word to Adam, saying, "Adam, that apparition is the one that promised you the Godhead, and majesty. He does not intend good for you, but shows himself to you at one time in the form of a woman and in another moment in the likeness of an angel, and on another occasions in the apparition of a serpent, and at another time in the semblance of a god. But he does all of this only to destroy your soul.

16 " Adam, now that you understand this in your heart you will see that I have delivered you many a time from his hands in order to show you that I am a merciful God. I wish you good and I do not wish your ruin."

Chapter IV.

1 Then God ordered Satan to show himself to Adam in his own hideous form, plainly.

2 But when Adam saw him he feared and trembled at the sight of him.

3 And God said to Adam, 'Look at this devil, and at his hideous sight, and know that he it is who made you fall from brightness into darkness, from peace and rest to toil and misery.

4 And look at him, Adam. He is the one who said that he is God! Can God be black? Would God take the form of a woman? Is there any one stronger than God? And can He be overpowered?

5 "See Adam. Look at him bound in your presence, in the air, unable to flee away! So, I say to you, do not be afraid of him. From now on, take care, and beware of him. He will try to do things to you."

6 Then God drove Satan away from Adam. And God strengthened Adam's heart and comforted him, saying, "Go down to the Cave of Treasures, and do not separate yourself from Eve. I will quiet all of your animal lust."

7 From that hour it left Adam and Eve, and they enjoyed rest by the commandment of God. But God did not do the same to any of Adam's seed (relations). God did this only to Adam and Eve.

8 Then Adam worshipped before the Lord for delivering him, and for having subdued his passions. And he came down from above the cave, and lived with Eve as had done before.

9 This ended the forty days of his separation from Eve.

Chapter V

1 When Seth was seven years old, he knew good and evil, and was consistent in fasting and praying, and spent all his nights in praying to God for mercy and forgiveness.
2 He also fasted when bringing up his offering every day. He fasted more than his father did because his demeanor was beautiful, like that of an angel of God. He also had a good heart, and his soul was precious; and for this reason he brought up his offering every day.
3 And God was pleased with his offering, but He was also pleased with his purity. And he continued doing the will of God, and of his father and mother until he was seven years old.
4 After that, as he was coming down from the altar after giving his offering, Satan appeared to him in the form of a beautiful angel, brilliant with light, with a staff of light in his hand, and wrapped with a girdle of light.
5 He greeted Seth with a beautiful smile, and began to beguile him with beautiful words, saying to him, "Seth, why do you live in this mountain? It is rough, full of stones and sand, and trees with no good fruit on them. It is a wilderness without houses or towns, no good place to live in. But everywhere there is heat, weariness, and trouble."
6 He said further, 'But we live in beautiful places, in a world other than this earth. Our world is one of light and we live in the best conditions. Our women are more beautiful than any others. Seth, I wish you to marry one of them, because I see that you are handsome to look at. In this land there is not one woman good enough for you and there are only five souls in it.
7 "But in our world there are many men and many young, unmarried women, all more beautiful one than the other. So, I wish to remove you from here so that you may see my relations and be wedded to which ever you like.
8 "You shall live by me and be at peace. You shall be filled with glory and light, just as we are.
9 "You shall remain in our world and rest from this world and its misery. You shall never again feel weak and weary. You shall never bring up an offering or appeal for mercy. You shall commit no more sin nor be swayed by passions.
10 "And if you will listen to what I say, you shall wed one of my daughters because to us it is not a sin and it is not considered animal lust.
11 "For in our world we have no God because we all are gods and we all are of the light and are heavenly, powerful, strong and glorious."

Chapter VI

1 When Seth heard these words he was amazed, and began to believe Satan's treacherous speech, and said to him, "You said there is another world created other than this one, and there are other creatures more beautiful than the creatures that are in this world?"
2 And Satan said, "Yes; you have heard me correctly, and I will tell you more good things about them and their ways."
3 But Seth said to him, "Your words have amazed me, and your beautiful description of it all."
4 "But I cannot go with you today, at least not until I have gone to my father Adam and to my mother Eve, and told them all you have said to me. Then if they give me permission to go with you, I will come."
5 Seth said, "I am afraid of doing any thing without my father's and mother's permission. I do not want to perish like my brother Cain, and like my father Adam, who transgressed the commandment of God. But, you know your way to this place, so come and meet me here tomorrow."
6 When Satan heard this, he said to Seth, "If you tell your father Adam what I have told you, he will not let you come with me.
7 But listen to me, do not tell your father and mother what I have said to you. Instead, come with me today. Come now to our world where you will see beautiful things and enjoy yourself there, and celebrate this day among my children, watching them and taking your fill of happiness; and have joy there. Then I shall bring you back to this place tomorrow. However, if you would rather stay there with me, so be it."
8 Then Seth answered, "The hope / love (spirit) of my father and of my mother, hangs on me and if I hide from them one day, they will die, and God will hold me guilty of sinning against them.
9 "And if they know that I have come to this place they assume it is to bring up my offering, and they would expect not to be separated from me one hour. Neither should I go to any other place unless they let me. But they treat me most kindly, because I always come back to them quickly."
10 Then Satan said to him, "What will happen to you if you were to disappear from them one night, and return to them at break of day?"

(Author's note: The assumption here is that he would sneak out after they fell asleep and not tell them.)

11 But Seth, when he saw how he kept on talking, and that he would not leave him alone, he ran and went up to the altar, and spread his hands to God, and sought deliverance from God.
12 Then God sent His Word, and cursed Satan, who fled from Him.
13 But Seth had gone up to the altar, saying in his heart. "The altar is the place of offering, and God is there. A divine fire

shall consume what is on it and so Satan will be unable to hurt me, and shall not take me away from here."

14 Then Seth came down from the altar and went to his father and mother, whom he found on his way and who were longing to hear his voice, because he had been missing a while.

15 He then began to tell them what had befallen him from Satan, under the form of an angel.

16 But when Adam heard his account, he kissed his face, and warned him against that angel, telling him it was Satan who appeared to him. Then Adam took Seth, and they went to the Cave of Treasures and rejoiced there.

17 But from that day on Adam and Eve were never separated from him wherever he went, whether for his offering or for any thing else.

18 This sign happened to Seth, when he was nine years old.

Chapter VII.

1 When our father Adam saw that Seth was of a perfect heart, he wished him to marry; lest the enemy should appear to him another time, and overcome him.

2 So Adam said to his son Seth, "I wish, 0 my son, that you wed your sister Aklia, Abel's sister, that she may bear you children, who shall replenish the earth, according to God's promise to us.

3 "Be not afraid, my son; there is no disgrace in it. I wish you to marry, from fear that if you do not the enemy could overcome you.'

4 Seth, however, did not wish to marry; but in obedience to his father and mother, he did not say a word.

5 So Adam married him to Aklia. And he was fifteen years old.

6 But when he was twenty years of age, he had a son, whom he called Enos (Enoch); and then had other children.

7 Then Enos grew up, married, and begat Cainan.

8 Cainan also grew up, married, and begat Mahalaleel.

9 Those fathers were born during Adam's lifetime, and dwelt by the Cave of Treasures.

10 Then were the days of Adam nine hundred and thirty years, and those of Mahalaleel one hundred. But Mahalaleel, when he was grown up, loved fasting, praying, and with hard work, until the end of our father Adam's days drew near.

Chapter VIII.

1 When our father Adam saw that his end was near, he called his son Seth, who came to him in the Cave of Treasures, and he said to him:

2 "Seth, my son, bring me your children and your children's children, so that I may shed my blessing on them before I die."

3 When Seth heard these words from his father Adam, he went from him, shed a flood of tears over his face, and gathered together his children and his children's children, and brought them to his father Adam.

4 But when our father Adam saw them around him, he wept at having to be separated from them.

5 And when they saw him weeping, they all wept together, and kissed his face saying, "How shall you be separated from us, father? And how shall the earth receive you and hide you from our eyes?" Thus they lamented with words like these.

6 Then our father Adam blessed them all, and said to Seth, after he had blessed them:

7 "Seth, my son, you know this world and that it is full of sorrow, and of weariness; and you know all that has come upon us from our trials in it. So, I command you in these words: I want you to keep being innocent, to be pure and just, and trusting in God; and do not believe the words of Satan, nor the apparitions in which he will show himself to you.

8 But keep the commandments that I give you this day; then give the same to your son Enos; and let Enos give it to his son Cainan; and Cainan to his son Mahalaleel; so that this commandment abide firm among all your children.

9 "Seth, my son, the moment I am dead take you my body and wrap it up with myrrh, aloes, and cassia, and leave me here in this Cave of Treasures in which are all the tokens which God gave us from the garden.

10 "My son, after a while a flood will come and overwhelm all creatures, and leave only eight souls out of it.

11 "But, my son, let those whom it will leave from among your children at that time, take my body with them out of this cave; and when they have taken it with them, let the oldest among them command his children to lay my body in a ship until the flood recedes, and they come out of the ship.

12 Then they shall take my body and lay it in the middle of the earth, shortly after they have been saved from the waters of the flood.

13 "The place where my body shall be laid is the middle of the earth and God shall come from that place and shall save all our kindred.

14 "But now, Seth, my son, place yourself at the head of your people. Tend to them and watch over them in the fear of God. Lead them in the good way. Command them to fast to God, and make them understand they should not to listen to Satan, or he will destroy them.

15 "I tell you again, separate your children and your children's children from Cain's children. Do not let them ever mix with them, nor come near them either to talk or to work."

16 Then Adam let his blessing descend upon Seth, and upon his children, and upon all his children's children.

17 He then turned to his son Seth, and to Eve his wife, and, said to them, "Preserve this gold, this incense, and this myrrh, that God has given us for a sign, because in days that are coming a flood will overwhelm the whole creation. But those who shall go into the ark shall take with them the gold, the incense, and the myrrh, together with my body, and will lay the gold, the incense, and the myrrh, with my body in the middle of the earth.

18 "Then, after a long time, the city in which the gold, the incense, and the myrrh are found with my body, shall be plundered. But when it is spoiled, the gold the incense, and the myrrh shall be taken care of with the spoil that is kept; and none of them shall perish, until the made man from the Word of God shall come. And kings shall take them, and shall offer to Him, gold in token of His being King; incense, in token of His being God of heaven and earth; and myrrh, in token of His passion.

19 "Gold also, as a token of His overcoming Satan, and all our foes; incense as a token that He will rise from the dead, and be exalted above things in heaven and things in the earth; and myrrh, in token that He will drink bitter gall; and feel the pains of hell from Satan.

20 "And now, Seth, my son, I have revealed to you hidden mysteries, which God had revealed to me. Keep my commandment for yourself and for your people."

Chapter IX

1 When Adam had ended his commandment to Seth, his limbs went limp, his hands and feet lost all strength, his voice became silent, and his tongue ceased to speak. He closed his eyes and gave up the ghost.

2 But when his children saw that he was dead, they threw themselves over him, men and women, old and young, weeping.

3 The death of Adam took place at the end of nine hundred and thirty years that he lived upon the earth; on the fifteenth day of Barmudeh, after the reckoning of an epact of the sun, at the ninth hour.

(Author's note: Barmudeh is the third month of the Egyptian calendar. The epact is the number of days into the moon's cycle that the solar calendar begins. Thus, it is the difference in days between the solar and lunar calendar.) (Adam had to die before his 1000th birthday so that he would fulfill the death curse from God. 1000 years is as one day.)

4 It was on a Friday, the very day on which he was created, and on which he rested. And the hour at which he died was the same as that at which he came out of the garden.

5 Then Seth wrapped him up well, and embalmed him with plenty of sweet spices, from sacred trees and from the Holy Mountain. And he laid his body on the eastern side of the inside of the cave, the side of the incense; and placed a lamp stand in front of him that kept burning.

6 Then his children stood before him weeping and wailing over him the entire night, until break of day.

7 Then Seth and his son Enos (Enoch), and Cainan, the son of Enos, went out and took good offerings to present to the Lord, and they came to the altar upon which Adam offered gifts to God.

8 But Eve said to them, "Wait until we have first asked God to accept our offering, and to keep the soul of Adam His servant by Him, and to take it up to rest."

9 And they all stood up and prayed.

Chapter X.

1 And when they had ended their prayer the Word of God came and comforted them concerning their father Adam.

2 After this, they offered their gifts for themselves and for their father.

3 And when they had ended their offering, the Word of God came to Seth, the eldest among them, saying to him, "Seth, Seth, Seth, three times. As I was with your father, so also shall I be with you, until the fulfillment of the promise I made your father saying, I will send My Word and save you and your seed.

4 "But as to your father Adam, keep you the commandment he gave you; and protect your seed (offspring) and keep them from that of Cain your brother."

5 And God withdrew His Word from Seth.

6 Then Seth, Eve, and their children, came down from the mountain to the Cave of Treasures.

7 But Adam was the first whose soul died in the land of Eden, in the Cave of Treasures; for no one died before him, but his son Abel, who died because he was murdered.

8 Then all the children of Adam rose up, and wept over their father Adam, and made offerings to him, one hundred and forty days.

Chapter XI.

1 After the death of Adam and of Eve, Seth separated his children, and his children's children, from Cain's children. Cain and his seed went down and lived to the west, below the place where he had killed his brother Abel.

2 But Seth and his children, lived to the north on the mountain of the Cave of Treasures, in order to be near to their father Adam.

3 And Seth the oldest (of his people), tall and good, with a worthy soul, and of a strong mind, stood at the head of his people; and tended to them in innocence, patience, and meekness, and did not allow even one of them to go down to Cain's children.

4 And because of their purity, they were named "Children of God," and they were with God instead of the hosts of angels who fell, for they continued in praises to God and in singing songs to Him in their cave, the Cave of Treasures.

5 Then Seth stood before the bodies of his father Adam and of his mother Eve, and he prayed night and day and asked for mercy for himself and his children, and that when he had some difficulty dealing with a child, God would give him counsel.

6 But Seth and his children did not like mundane work, but set themselves to do heavenly things, because they had no other thought other than praises, worship, and psalms to God.

7 Therefore did they at all times hear the voices of angels, praising and glorifying God; from within the garden, or when they were sent by God on an errand, or when they were going up to heaven.

8 Because of their own purity, Seth and his children heard and saw the angels. The garden was not far above them, only about fifteen spiritual (heavenly) cubits.

9 One spiritual cubit is equal to three cubits of man, altogether forty-five cubits.

10 Seth and his children lived on the mountain below the garden. They did not sow nor reap. They made no food for the body, not even wheat, but only enough for offerings. They ate the flavorful fruit of trees that grew on the mountain where they lived.

11 Seth often fasted for forty days, as did also his oldest children. The family of Seth smelled the smell of the trees in the garden when the wind blew that way.

12 They were happy, innocent, without sudden fear, there was no jealousy, no evil action, nor hatred among them. There was no animal passion. No one among them spoke either foul words or curse. There was neither evil intention nor fraud. The men of that time never swore, but when under hard circumstances, when men must swear, they swore by the blood of Abel the just.

13 But every day they compelled their children and their women to fast and pray, and to worship the most High God, in the cave. They blessed themselves by being near the body of their father Adam, and anointed themselves (with it).

14 And they did so until the end of Seth drew near.

(Author's note: It is unclear what the men anointed themselves with. It could be oil blessed by being left close to the body of Adam. To think that they anointed themselves with the oils from the dead body would violate religious laws that would be established latter than the story, yet far earlier than the writing of this 3rd century text.)

Chapter XII

1 Then Seth, the just, called his son Enos, and Cainan, the son of Enos, and Mahalaleel, the son of Cainan, and said he to them:

2 "My end is near, and I wish to build a roof over the altar on which gifts are offered."

3 They listened to his commandment and all of them, both old and young, went out and worked hard and built a beautiful roof over the altar.

4 And Seth's thought was that by doing this a blessing should come upon his children on the mountain. And he though he should present an offering for them before his death.

5 Then when the building of the roof was completed, he commanded them to make offerings. They worked diligently and brought them to Seth, their father, who took them and offered them upon the altar, and prayed God to accept their offerings, to have mercy on the souls of his children, and to keep them from the hand of Satan.

6 God accepted his offering and sent His blessing on him and on his children. Then God made a promise to Seth, saying, "At the end of the great five days and a half, which is the promise I have made to you and to your father, I will send My Word and save you and your seed." *(Author's note: A great day is 1000 years.)*

7 Then Seth and his children, and grandchildren met together and came down from the altar and went to the Cave of Treasures, where they prayed. And he blessed them in the body of our father Adam, and anointed them with it.

8 But Seth stayed in the Cave of Treasures, a few days, and then suffered - sufferings to death.

9 Then Enos, his first born son, came to him with Cainan, his son, and Mahalaleel, Cainan's son, and Jared, the son of Mahalaleel, and Enoch, Jared's son, and with their wives and children to receive a blessing from Seth.

10 Then Seth prayed over them, and blessed them, and earnestly requested them by the blood of Abel the just, saying, "I beg of you my children, not to let one of you go down from this Holy and pure Mountain.

11 Do not associate with the children of Cain the murderer and the sinner, who killed his brother. You know, my children, that we flee from him and from all his sin with all our might because he killed his brother Abel."

12 After having said this, Seth blessed Enos, his first-born son, and commanded him to minister continually in purity before the body of their father Adam, all the days of his life. He also made him promise to go at times to the altar, which he had built. And he commanded him to feed his people in righteousness, in judgment, and in purity all the days of his life.

13 Then Seth's limbs went limp. His hands and feet lost all strength. His voice became silent and unable to speak, and he gave up the ghost and died. Seth died the day after his nine hundred and twelfth year, on the twenty - seventh day of the month Abib; Enoch being then twenty years old.

(Author's note: There are three separate numbers of significance here. 27 is a gateway number to 9. 2+7=9. Nine is the number of endings. 912 reduces to the number 3, which is number of completeness. Abib is the seventh month of the year in the Hebrew calendar, corresponding to Nisan.)

14 Then they carefully wrapped up the body of Seth, and embalmed him with sweet spices, and laid him in the Cave Treasures, on the right side of our father Adam's body, and they mourned for him forty days. They offered gifts for him, as they had done for our father Adam.

15 After the death of Seth, Enos was raised to the head of his people, whom he fed in righteousness, and judgment, as his father had commanded him.

16 But by the time Enos was eight hundred and twenty years old, Cain had a very large number of offspring, because they had sex (married) often, being given to animal lusts, until the land below the mountain, was filled with them.

Chapter XIII

1 Lamech the blind lived in those days. He was one of the sons of Cain. He had a son whose name was Atun, and the two of them had many cattle.

2 Lamech was in the habit of sending them to graze with a young shepherd, who tended them. He was coming home in the evening when he went to his grandfather, his father Atun, and his mother Hazina, and he wept and he said to them, " I cannot feed those cattle alone, or someone may rob me of some of them, or kill me so they can take them." Because among the children of Cain there was a lot of robbery, murder, and sin.

3 Then Lamech pitied him, and he said, "You may be correct. When you are alone you might be overpowered by the men of this place."

4 So Lamech arose, took a bow he had kept ever since he was a youth, before he became blind, and he took large arrows, and smooth stones, and a sling, which he had, and he went to the field with the young shepherd, and placed himself behind the cattle while the young shepherd watched the cattle. Lamech did this for many days.

5 Meanwhile, ever since God had cast him off and had cursed him with trembling and fear, Cain could not be still (settle) nor find rest in any one place, so he wandered from place to place.

6 In his wanderings he came to Lamech's wives, and asked them about him. They said to him, "He is in the field with the cattle."

7 Then Cain went to look for him and as he came into the field, the young shepherd heard the noise he made, and the cattle herding together in front of him.

8 Then said he to Lamech, "My lord, is that a wild beast or a robber?"

9 And Lamech said to him, "Tell me where he is when he comes up."

10 Then Lamech bent his bow, placed an arrow on it, and fitted a stone in the sling, and when Cain came out from the open country, the shepherd said to Lamech, "Shoot, behold, he is coming."

11 Then Lamech shot at Cain with his arrow and hit him in his side. And Lamech struck him with a stone from his sling, and the stone struck his face and knocked out both his eyes. Then Cain fell dead instantly.

12 Then Lamech and the young shepherd came up to him and found him lying on the ground. And the young shepherd said to him, "It is Cain our grandfather, whom you have killed, my lord!"

18 Then Lamech grieved in bitterness and regret. And he clapped his hands together and struck the head of the youth with his flat palm, and the youth fell as if he were dead. But Lamech thought the youth was pretending, so he took up a stone and struck him, and smashed his head until he died.

Chapter XIV

1 When Enos was nine hundred years old, all the children of Seth, and of Cainan, and his first-born, with their wives and children, gathered around him, asking for a blessing from him.

2 Then he prayed over them and blessed them, and made them promise them by the blood of Abel the just, saying to them, "Do not let even one of your children go down from this Holy Mountain, and do not let them make friends with the children of Cain the murderer."

3 Then Enos called his son Cainan and said to him, "Look, my son, and set your heart on your people, and establish them in righteousness, and in innocence, and stand ministering before the body of our father Adam, all the days of your life."

4 After this Enos rested (died). He was nine hundred and eighty - five years old. Cainan wrapped him up, and laid him in the Cave of Treasures on the left of his father Adam, and made offerings for him, following the custom of his fathers.

Chapter XV

1 After the death of Enos, Cainan led his people in righteousness and innocence, as his father had commanded him. He also continued to minister before the body of Adam, in the Cave of Treasures.

2 Then when he had lived nine hundred and ten years, suffering and sickness came upon him. And when he was about to enter into rest (die), all the fathers with their wives and children came to him, and he blessed them, and earnestly urged them by the blood of Abel, the just, saying to them, "Let no one among you descend from this Holy Mountain; and do not make friends with the children of Cain the murderer."

3 Mahalaleel, his first - born son, received this commandment from his father, who blessed him and died.

4 Then Mahalaleel embalmed him with sweet spices, and laid him in the Cave of Treasures, with his fathers; and they made offerings for him, as was the custom of their fathers.

Chapter XVI

1 Then Mahalaleel led his people, and fed them in righteousness and innocence, and watched them to see they had no relationship with the children of Cain.

2 He also continued in the Cave of Treasures praying and ministering before the body of their father Adam, asking God for mercy on himself and on his people, until he was eight hundred and seventy years old, when he fell sick.

3 Then all his children gathered around him to see him, and to ask for his blessing on them all, before he left this world.

4 Then Mahalaleel arose and sat on his bed, his tears streaming down his face, and he called his eldest son Jared, who came to him.

5 He then kissed his face, and said to him, "Jared, my son, I solemnly urge you by Him who made heaven and earth, to watch over your people, and to feed them in righteousness and in innocence; and not to let even one of them go down from this Holy Mountain to the children of Cain, or he will perish with them.

6 "Hear, my son, there will come a great destruction upon this earth because of them. God will be angry with the world, and will destroy them with waters.

7 "But I also know that your children will not listen to you, and that they will go down from this mountain and have relations with the children of Cain, and that they shall perish with them.

8 " My son! Teach them, and watch over them, so that no guilt will be on you because of them."

9 Mahalaleel continued, saying to his son Jared, "When I die, embalm my body and lay it in the Cave of Treasures, by the bodies of my forefathers then stand by my body and pray to God, and take care of them, and fulfill your ministry before them, until you enter into rest yourself."

10 Mahalaleel then blessed all his children, then he laid down on his bed and entered into rest like his fathers.

11 But when Jared saw that his father Mahalaleel was dead, he wept and grieved, and embraced, and kissed his hands and his feet, and so did all his children.

12 And his children embalmed him carefully, and laid him by the bodies of his fathers. Then they stood and mourned for him forty days.

(Author's note: Mahalaleel's way of adjuring Jared, his son, was different in form from those before. He did not invoke the name of Abel, the just. The results were also different, in that it was at this time the children of Abel first began to have intercourse with the children of Cain.)

Chapter XVII

1 Then Jared kept his father's commandment, and arose like a lion over his people. He fed them in righteousness and innocence, and commanded them to do nothing without his consent. This was because he was afraid for them that they should go to the children of Cain.

2 He gave them orders repeatedly, and continued to do so until the end of the four hundred and eighty-fifth year of his life.

3 At the end of these years, there came to him a sign. As Jared was standing like a lion before the bodies of his fathers, praying and warning his people, Satan envied him and produced a beautiful specter because Jared would not let his children do anything without his counsel.

4 Satan appeared to him with thirty men of his hosts, in the form of handsome men. Satan himself was the oldest and tallest among them, with a fine beard.

5 They stood at the mouth of the cave, and called out Jared, who was in the cave.

6 He came out to them and found them looking like handsome men, full of light, and very beautiful. He was in awe of their beauty and their looks, and wondered to himself whether they might not be of the children of Cain.

7 He said also in his heart, " The children of Cain cannot come up to the height of this mountain, and none of them are this handsome as these appear to be, and among these men there is not one of my kindred, so they must be strangers."

8 Then Jared exchanged a greeting with them and he said to the oldest among them, " My father, tell me how you are so wonderful, and tell me who these are with you. They look to me like strange men."

9 Then the oldest began to weep and the rest wept with him, and he said to Jared, "I am Adam whom God made first, and this is Abel my son, who was killed by his brother Cain, whose heart was influenced by Satan to murder.

10 "And this is my son Seth, whom I asked Lord to give me to comfort me when I no longer had Abel.

11 "Then this one is my son Enos, son of Seth, and that other one is Cainan, son of Enos, and that other one is Mahalaleel, son of Cainan, your father."

12 But Jared remained wondering at their appearance and at the words of the elder to him.

13 Then the oldest said to him, "Do not stand there is awe, my son. We now live in the land north of the garden, which God created before the world. He would not let us live there, but placed us inside the garden, below which you are now living.

14 "After I transgressed, He made me come out of it and I was left to live in this cave. That was when great and horrible troubles came on me. And when the time of my death drew near, I commanded my son Seth to tend his people well. And my commandment is to be handed from one to another, to the end of the generations to come.

15 "But, Jared, my son, we live in beautiful regions while you live here in misery. Your father Mahalaleel informed me that a great flood would come and overwhelm the whole earth.

16 "Therefore, my son, fearing for your sakes, I rose and took my children with me, and came here to visit you and your children. I found you standing in this cave weeping, and your children scattered about this mountain in the heat and in misery.

17 "But, my son, as we missed our way, and came as far as this, we found other men below this mountain; who inhabit a beautiful country, full of trees and of fruits, and of all manner of lush, green vegetation. It is like a garden. When we found them we thought they were you, until your father Mahalaleel told me they were no such thing.

18 "Now, my son, listen to my advice, and go down to them, you and your children. You will rest from all this suffering you are in. If you will not go down to them then arise, take your children, and come with us to our garden. There, you shall live in our beautiful land, and you shall rest from all this trouble which you and your children are now living in."

19 But when he heard these words from the oldest, Jared was confused and went here and there, but at that moment he found none of his children.

20 Then he answered and said to the old one, "Why have you hidden yourselves until this day?"

21 And the oldest replied, "If your father had not told us, we would not have known it."

22 Then Jared believed his words were true.

23 So that oldest said to Jared, "Wherefore did you turn about, so and so?" And he said, "I was seeking one of my children, to tell him about my going with you, and about their coming down to those about whom you have spoken to me."

24 When the old one heard Jared's intention, he said to him, "Do not worry about that right now but come with us and you shall see our country. If the land in which we live pleases you, we shall all return here and take your family with us. But if our country does not please you, you shall come back to your own home."

25 And the old one urged Jared to go before one of his children came to talk him out of his decision.

26 Jared, then, came out of the cave and went with them, and among them. And they comforted him, until they came to the top of the mountain of the sons of Cain.

27 Then the old one said to one of his companions, "We have forgotten something by the mouth of the cave, and that is the chosen garment we had brought to clothe Jared with."

28 He then said to one of them, "One of you go back, and we will wait for you here until you come back. Then will we clothe Jared and he shall be like us, good, handsome, and fit to come with us into our country."

29 Then that one went back.

30 But when he was a short distance off, the old one called to him and said to him, "You stay there until I come up and speak to you."

31 Then he stood still and the old one went up to him and said to him, "One thing we forgot at the cave, it is this; we forgot to put out the lamp that burns inside the cave, above the bodies that are in there. Do it and come back to us, quickly."

32 That one went, and the old one came back to his fellows and to Jared. And they came down from the mountain, and Jared was with them. And they stayed by a fountain of water, near the houses of the children of Cain and waited for their companion until he brought the garment for Jared.

33 Then he who went back to the cave, put out the lamp, and came to them and brought an apparition with him and showed it them. And when Jared saw it he wondered at the beauty and grace thereof, and rejoiced in his heart believing it was all true.

34 But while they were staying there, three of them went into houses of the sons of Cain and said to them, "Bring us today some food by the fountain of water, for us and our companions to eat."

35 But when the sons of Cain saw them, they were in awe at them and thought: "These men are beautiful to look at. We have never seen such before." So they rose and came with them to the fountain of water, to see their companions.

36 They thought them so very handsome that they called aloud about their places for others to gather together and come and look at these beautiful beings. Then they gathered around them both men and women.

37 Then the old one said to them, "We are strangers in your land, bring us some good food and drink, and bring yourselves

and your women, so we can entertain (refresh) ourselves with you."

38 When those men heard these words of the old one, every one of Cain's sons brought his wife, and another brought his daughter, and so, many women came to them; every one calling out to Jared either for himself or for his wife.

39 But when Jared saw what they did, his very soul wrenched itself from them and he would not taste their food or their drink.

40 The old one saw him as he wrenched himself from them, and said to him, "Do not be sad. I am the great elder, as you shall see me do, do yourself in like manner."

41 Then he spread his hands and took one of the women, and five of his companions did the same in front of Jared, that he should do as they did.

42 But when Jared saw them doing their wickedness he wept, and said in his mind, "My fathers never acted like this."

43 He then spread his hands and prayed with a fervent heart, and with much weeping, and begged God to deliver him from their hands.

44 No sooner did Jared begin to pray than the old one fled with his companions; for they could not abide in a place of prayer.

45 Then Jared turned round but could not see them, but found himself standing in the midst of the children of Cain.

46 He then wept and said, "0 God, do not destroy me with this race, concerning which my fathers have warned me. For now, my Lord God, I was thinking that those who appeared to me were my forefathers, but I have found them out to be devils, who lured me by way of this beautiful apparition, until I believed them.

47 "But now I ask You, 0 God, to deliver me from this race, among whom I am now staying, as You did deliver me from those devils. Send Your angel to pull me out of the middle of them. I do not have the power within myself to escape from among them."

48 When Jared had ended his prayer, God sent His angel into the middle of them and he took Jared and set him up on the mountain, and showed him the way, and he gave him wise advice, and then departed from him.

Chapter XVIII

1 The children of Jared were in the habit of visiting him hour after hour, to receive his blessing and to ask his advice for every thing they did, and when he had work to do, they did it for him.

2 But this time when they went into the cave they did not find Jared, but they found the lamp put out, and the bodies of the fathers thrown about, and voices came from them by the power of God, that said, "Satan in an apparition has deceived our son, wishing to destroy him, as he destroyed our son Cain."

3 They said also, "Lord God of heaven and earth, deliver our son from the hand of Satan, who produced such a great and false specter before him." They also spoke of other matters, by the power of God.

4 But when the children of Jared heard these voices they feared, and stood weeping for their father because they did not know what had happened to him.

5 And they wept for him that day until the setting of the sun.

6 Then Jared come with a mournful expression, miserable in mind and body, and sorrowful at having been separated from the bodies of his fathers.

7 But as he came near the cave, his children saw him and ran to the cave, and hugged his neck, crying, and saying to him, "0 father, where have you been, and why have you left us because we know you did not want to?" And they spoke again saying, "Father, when you disappeared the lamp over the bodies of our fathers went out, and the bodies were thrown about, and voices came from them"

8 When Jared heard this he was sorry, and went into the cave; and there found the bodies thrown about, the lamp put out, and the fathers themselves praying for his deliverance from the hand of Satan.

9 Then Jared fell upon the bodies and embraced them, and said, "My fathers, through your intercession, God delivered me from the hand of Satan! I beg you to ask God to keep me and to hide me from him to the day of my death."

10 Then all the voices ceased except the voice of our father Adam, who spoke to Jared by the power of God, just as one would speak to his friend, saying, "Jared, my son, offer gifts to God for having delivered you from the hand of Satan. And when you bring those offerings, offer them on the same altar on which I gave offerings. Even then you must beware of Satan, for he deluded me many a time with his specters, wishing to destroy me, but God delivered me out of his hand.

11 "Command your people that they be on their guard against him, and never cease to offer up gifts to God."

12 Then the voice of Adam also became silent; and Jared and his children wondered at this. Then they laid the bodies as they were at first; and Jared and his children stood praying the entire night, until break of day.

13 Then Jared made an offering and offered it up on the altar, as Adam had commanded him. And as he went up to the altar, he prayed to God for mercy and for forgiveness of his sin concerning the lamp going out.

14 Then God appeared to Jared on the altar and blessed him and his children, and accepted their offerings; and commanded Jared to take of the sacred fire from the altar and light the lamp that shed light on the body of Adam.

Chapter XIX

1 Then God again revealed to him the promise He had made to Adam. He explained to him the 5500 years, and revealed to him the mystery of His coming to the earth.
2 And God said to Jared, "Let that fire you have taken from the altar to light the lamp abide with you to give light to the bodies. Do not let it come out of the cave until the body of Adam comes out.
3 But, Jared, take care of the fire, so that it burns brightly in the lamp. Do not go out of the cave again until you received an order through a vision, and not in an apparition, you see.

(Author's note: The distinction here is that a vision is internal and an apparition is external. Only God can guide us internally. Satan must entice and trick through external ploys.)

4 "Then command your people again not to have relations with the children of Cain, and not to learn their ways, for I am God who does not love hatred and works of iniquity."
5 God also gave many other commandments to Jared, and He blessed him. And then withdrew His Word from him.
6 Then Jared came near to his children, took some fire, and came down to the cave and lighted the lamp in front of the body of Adam. Then he gave his people the commandments just as God had told him to do.
7 This sign happened to Jared at the end of his four hundred and fiftieth year, as did many other wonders we did not record. But we record only this one for the sake of brevity to shorten our written account.
8 And Jared continued to teach his children eighty years, but after that they began to break the commandments he had given them, and to do many things without his permission. They began to go down from the Holy Mountain, one after another, and mix with the children of Cain, in obscene association.
9 Now the reason the children of Jared went down the Holy Mountain will now be revealed to you.

Chapter XX.

1 After Cain had gone down to the land of dark soil, and his children had multiplied, there was one of them, whose name was Genun, son of Lamech the blind who slew Cain.
2 Satan came to Genun in his childhood and made a variety trumpets and horns, and string instruments, cymbals and psalteries, and lyres and harps, and flutes. And Genun played them at all times and at every hour.
3 And when he played them, Satan came to them so that from among them were heard beautiful and sweet sounds that seized the heart with delight.
4 Then he gathered many crowds to play on them, and when they played it greatly pleased the children of Cain, who fanned themselves to flames of sin among themselves and they burned with fire while Satan inflamed their hearts with one another, and lust increased among them.
5 Satan also taught Genun to make strong drink out of corn. Genun used this to bring together crowd upon crowd in houses of drink, and brought into their hands all kinds of fruits and flowers, and they drank together.
6 Genun did this to multiply sin greatly. He also acted with pride, and taught the children of Cain to commit all manner of the grossest wickedness, which they did not know until then. And he put them up to all kinds of deeds, which they did not know of before.
7 Then, when Satan saw that they obeyed Genun and listened to him in every thing he told them, he rejoiced greatly, and he increased Genun's understanding until he took iron and with it made weapons of war.
8 Then when they were drunk, hatred and murder increased among them. One man would use violence against another and Satan would teach him evil in that one man would take the other man's children and defile them before him.
9 And when men saw they were vanquished and saw that others were not beaten, those who were beaten came to Genun and took refuge with him, and he made them part of his group.
10 Then sin increased among them greatly, until a man married his own sister, or daughter, or mother, and others, or the daughter of his father's sister (first cousin), so that there was no more distinction of relationship, and they could no longer discern what was sin and what was not, but always were wicked and the earth was defiled with sin. And they angered God the Judge, who had created them.
11 But Genun gathered together groups and groups, that played on horns and on all the other instruments we have already mentioned, at the foot of the Holy Mountain. They did that so the children of Seth who were on the Holy Mountain would hear it.
12 But when the children of Seth heard the noise, they wondered, and came by companies, and stood on the top of the mountain to look at those below. This went on an entire year.
13 At the end of that year, Genun saw that they were being won over to him little by little. Satan entered into him, and taught him to make the elements for dyeing garments of various patterns, and made him understand how to dye crimson and purple and what not.
14 And the sons of Cain who worked at all of this shone in beauty and gorgeous apparel. And they gathered together at the

foot of the mountain in splendor, with horns and gorgeous dresses, and horse races, and they were committing all manner of disgusting acts.

15 Meanwhile the children of Seth, who were on the Holy Mountain, prayed and praised God in the place of the hosts of angels who had fallen. God had called them 'angels," because He rejoiced over them greatly.

16 But after this time they no longer kept His commandment, nor were held by the promise He had made to their fathers. But they relaxed from their fasting and praying, and from the counsel of Jared their father. And they kept on gathering together on the top of the mountain to watch the children of Cain, from morning until evening. And they watched what they did and they looked at their beautiful dresses and ornaments.

17 Then the children of Cain looked up from below, and saw the children of Seth, standing in numbers on the top of the mountain, and they called to them to come down to them.

18 But from above them, the children of Seth said, "We don't know the way." Then Genun, the son of Lamech, heard them say they did not know the way, and he began to think to himself of ways he might bring them down.

19 Then Satan appeared to him by night, saying, "There is no way for them to come down from the part of the mountain on which they live, but when they come out tomorrow (to watch), say to them, 'Come to the western side of the mountain. There you will find a stream of water that comes down to the foot of the mountain, between two hills. That marks the way. Come down that way to us.'"

20 Then when it was day, Genun blew the horns and beat the drums below the mountain, as he was accustomed to do. The children of Seth heard it and came as they used to do.

21 Then Genun said to them from down below, "Go to the western side of the mountain, there you will find the way to come down."

22 But when the children of Seth heard these words from him, they went back into the cave to Jared to tell him all they had heard.

23 Then when Jared heard it, he was grieved because he knew that they would defy his wishes.

24 After this a hundred men of the children of Seth gathered together and said among themselves, "Come, let us go down to the children of Cain and see what they do, and enjoy ourselves with them."

25 But when Jared heard this of the hundred men his very soul was moved, and his heart was grieved. He then stood with great emotion in the middle of them, and earnestly compelled them by the blood of Abel the just and said, "Let no one of you go down from this holy and pure mountain, in which our fathers have ordered us to live."

26 But when Jared saw that they did not listen to his words, he said to them, "My good, innocent, and holy children, you must understand that once you go down from this holy mountain, God will not allow you to return to it again."

27 He again adjured them, saying, "I plead with you by the death of our father Adam, and by the blood of Abel, of Seth, of Enos, of Cainan, and of Mahalaleel, to listen to me. Do not go down from this holy mountain, because the moment you leave it, life and mercy will be taken from you; and you shall no longer be called 'children of God,' but 'children of the devil.'

28 But they would not listen to his words.

29 Enoch was already grown up at that time, and in his zeal for God, he stood and said, "Hear me, you large and small (young and old) sons of Seth! When you transgress the commandment of our fathers and go down from this holy mountain, you shall not come up here again for ever."

30 But they rose up against Enoch and would not listen to his words, but they went down from the Holy Mountain.

31 And when they looked at the daughters of Cain, at their beautiful figures, and at their hands and feet dyed with color, and the tattoos on their faces that ornamented them, the fire of sin was set ablaze in them.

32 Then Satan made them look most beautiful before the sons of Seth, as he also made the sons of Seth appear the most handsome in the eyes of the daughters of Cain, so that the daughters of Cain lusted after the sons of Seth like ravenous beasts, and the sons of Seth lusted after the daughters of Cain until they committed disgusting and disgraceful acts with them.

33 But after they had fallen into this defilement they returned by the way they had come, and tried to ascend the Holy Mountain. But they could not because the stones of that holy mountain were on fire flashing before them, and prevented them so that they could not go up again.

34 And God was angry with them, and turned from them because they had come down from glory, and because of this had lost and forsaken their own purity and innocence, and were fallen into the defilement of sin.

35 Then God sent His Word to Jared, saying, "These of your children, whom you once called 'My children,' have broken My commandment, and have gone down to the house of damnation and sin. Send a messenger to those that are left so that they will not go down, and be lost."

36 Then Jared wept before the Lord, and asked Him for mercy and forgiveness. But he wished that his soul might depart from his body rather than hear these words from God about his children that went down from the Holy Mountain.

37 But he followed God's order and preached to them not to go down from that holy mountain, and not to hold relations with the children of Cain.

38 But they did not listen to his message, and they would not obey his advice.

Chapter XXI

1 After this, another group gathered together and went to look after their brothers but they perished with them as well. And so it was, company after company, until only a few of them remained.

2 Then Jared was sickened with grief. And his sickness was such that the day of his death was near.

3 Then he called Enoch his eldest son, and Methuselah Enoch's son, and Lamech the son of Methuselah, and Noah the son of Lamech.

4 And when they came to him he prayed over them and blessed them, and said to them, "You are righteous, innocent sons. Do not go down from this holy mountain, because you have seen your children and your children's children have gone down from this holy mountain, and have alienated themselves from this holy mountain through their reprehensible lust and transgression of God's commandment.

5 But I know, through the power of God, that He will not leave you on this holy mountain. Your children have transgressed His commandment and that of our fathers, which we had received from them.

6 But, my sons, God will take you to a strange land, and you never shall return to see this garden and this holy mountain with your own eyes once again.

7 Therefore, my sons, set your hearts on your own selves, and keep the commandment of God which is with you. And when you go from this holy mountain into a strange land which you do not know, take the body of our father Adam with you, and with it take these three precious gifts and offerings, namely, the gold, the incense, and the myrrh; and let them be in the place where the body of our father Adam shall lay.

8 And, my sons, of you who are left, the Word of God will come, and when he goes out of this land he shall take with him the body of our father Adam, and shall lay it in the middle of the earth, the place in which salvation shall be worked out."

9 Then Noah said to him, "Who is he of us that shall be left?"

10 And Jared answered, "You are he that shall be left. And you shall take the body of our father Adam from the cave, and place it with you in the ark when the flood comes.

11 "And your son Shem, who shall come out of your loins, it is he who shall lay the body of our father Adam in the middle of the earth, in the place where salvation shall come."

12 Then Jared turned to his son Enoch, and said to him "My son, abide in this cave, and minister diligently before the body of our father Adam all the days of your life, and feed your people in righteousness and innocence."

13 And Jared said no more. His hands went limp, his eyes closed, and he entered into rest like his fathers. His death took place in the three hundred and sixtieth year of Noah, and in the nine hundred and eighty-ninth year of his own life; on the twelfth of Takhsas on a Friday.

(Author's note: In this year, the month of Takhsas was likely to be December.)

14 But as Jared died, tears streamed down his face by reason of his great sorrow, for the children of Seth, who had fallen in his days.

15 Then Enoch, Methuselah, Lamech and Noah, these four, wept over him; embalmed him carefully, and then laid him in the Cave of Treasures. Then they rose and mourned for him forty days.

16 And when these days of mourning were ended, Enoch, Methuselah, Lamech and Noah remained in sorrow of heart because their father had departed from them and could not see him again.

Chapter XXII

1 Enoch kept the commandment of Jared his father, and continued to minister in the cave.

2 Many wonders happened to this man, Enoch, and he also wrote a celebrated book; but those wonders may not be told in this place.

3 Then after this, the children of Seth, as well as their children and their wives went astray and fell. And when Enoch, Methuselah, Lamech and Noah saw them, their hearts suffered because of their fall, which filled them with doubt and unbelief. And they wept and sought of God mercy to preserve them, and to bring them out of that wicked generation.

4 Enoch continued in his ministry before the Lord three hundred and eighty-five years, and at the end of that time he became aware through the grace of God, that God intended to remove him from the earth.

5 He then said to his son, "0 my son, I know that God intends to bring the waters of the Flood on the earth, and destroy our (His) creation.

6 "And you are the last rulers over the people on this mountain. And I know that not one (woman) will be left for you to have children on this holy mountain. Not one of you will rule over the children of his people. No great number of you will be left on this mountain."

7 Enoch also said to them, "Watch over your souls, and hold tight to your fear of God and your service to Him, and worship Him in righteous faith, and serve Him in righteousness, innocence and judgment. Worship Him in repentance and in purity."

8 When Enoch had ended his commandments to them, God transported him from that mountain to the land of life, to the

mansions of the righteous and of the chosen ones, which is the abode of Paradise of joy, in light that reaches up to heaven. It is the light that is beyond the light of this world It is the light of God that fills the whole world and no place can contain.
9 Enoch was in the light of God and because of this he found himself out of the grasp of death, until God would have him die.
10 Altogether, not one of our fathers or of their children, remained on that holy mountain, except those three, Methuselah, Lamech, and Noah. All the rest went down from the mountain and fell into sin with the children of Cain. And they were forbidden to come back to that mountain. And none remained on it but those three men.
This completes The Second Book of Adam and Eve.

Author' Note:
In the pages we have read, we are confronted with the Genesis story, possibly embellished beyond recognition. Modern readers may find the story to be so fanciful as to be ridiculous. The story may appear to be repetitive and rife with storylines of Satanic deception and human frailty running in waves and cycles throughout the text. Yet, in this ancient script there is a central and universal question – How can we know if the circumstance, situation, or even the person in our life is an appointment of God or Satan?
According to the story, Satan may be able to manipulate the material world, but he cannot touch the spirit. Satan may give apparitions and illusions, but God gives visions. The world is Satan's, but the soul is the domain of God. The mystical vision is the terrain of God to tread. Look there for the answer.

The Book of 1 Enoch

Of all the books quoted, paraphrased, or referred to in the Bible, the Book of Enoch has influenced the writers of the Bible as few others have. Even more extensively than in the Old Testament, the writers of the New Testament were frequently influenced by other writings, including the Book of Enoch.

It is not the purpose of this work to make judgments as to the validity or worth of the Book of Enoch, but rather to simply put forth a meaningful question. Is not the non-canonical book that most influenced the thought and theology of the writers of the New Testament worth further research and contemplation?

Before we continue in our study of the Book of Enoch there are several questions we must keep in mind. If a book is mentioned or quoted in the Bible is it not worthy of further study? If it is worth investigating, is this the book of which the Bible speaks? What knowledge or insight does it add to our understanding of the Bible or the men who wrote it?

The Book of Enoch was once cherished by Jews and Christians alike. It is read in certain Coptic Christian Churches in Ethiopia. Two versions of the Book of Enoch exist today.

Most scholars date the Book of Enoch to sometime during the second century B.C. We do not know what earlier oral tradition, if any, the book contains. Enoch was considered inspired and authentic by certain Jewish sects of the first century B.C. and remained popular for at least five hundred years. The earliest Ethiopian text was apparently derived from a Greek manuscript of the Book of Enoch, which itself was a copy of an earlier text. The original was apparently written in the Semitic language, now thought to be Aramaic.

The Book of Enoch was discovered in the 18th century. It was assumed to have been penned after beginning of the Christian era. This theory was based upon the fact that it had quotes and paraphrases as well as concepts found in the New Testament. Thus, it was assumed that it was heavily influenced by writers such as Jude and Peter.

However, recent discoveries of copies of the book among the Dead Sea Scrolls found at Qumran prove the book was in existence before the time of Jesus Christ. These scrolls force a closer look and reconsideration. It becomes obvious that the New Testament did not influence the Book of Enoch; on the contrary, the Book of Enoch influenced the New Testament. The date of the original writing upon which the second century B.C. Qumran copies were based is shrouded in obscurity. Likewise lost are the sources of the oral traditions that came to be the Book of Enoch.

It has been largely the opinion of historians that the book does not really contain the authentic words of the ancient Enoch, since he would have lived several thousand years earlier than the first known appearance of the book attributed to him. However, the first century Christians accepted the Book of Enoch as inspired, if not authentic. They relied on it to understand the origin and purpose of many things, from angels to wind, sun, and stars. In fact, many of the key concepts used by Jesus Christ himself seem directly connected to terms and ideas in the Book of Enoch.

It is hard to avoid the evidence that Jesus not only studied the book, but also respected it highly enough to allude to its doctrine and content. Enoch is replete with mentions of the coming kingdom and other holy themes. It was not only Jesus who quoted phrases or ideas from Enoch, there are over one hundred comments in the New Testament which find precedence in the Book of Enoch.

Other evidence of the early Christians' acceptance of the Book of Enoch was for many years buried under the King James Bible's mistranslation of Luke 9:35, describing the transfiguration of Christ: "And there came a voice out of the cloud, saying, 'This is my beloved Son. Hear him.'" Apparently the translator here wished to make this verse agree with a similar verse in Matthew and Mark. But Luke's verse in the original Greek reads: "This is my Son, the Elect One (from the Greek ho eklelegmenos, lit., "This is mine, the elect one. Hear him."

The "Elect One" is a most significant term (found fourteen times) in the Book of Enoch. If the book was indeed known to the apostles of Christ, with its abundant descriptions of the Elect One who should "sit upon the throne of glory" and the Elect One who should "dwell in the midst of them;" then the great scriptural authenticity is justly accorded to the Book of Enoch when the "voice out of the cloud" tells the apostles, "This is my Son, the Elect One,"... the one promised in the Book of Enoch.

The Book of Jude tells us in Verse 14 that "Enoch, the seventh from Adam, prophesied." Jude also, in Verse 15, makes a direct reference to the Book of Enoch (2:1), where he writes, "to execute judgment on all, to convict all who are ungodly." As a matter of fact, it is a direct, word for word quote. Therefore, Jude's reference to the Enochian prophesies strongly leans toward the conclusion that these written prophesies were available to him at that time.

Fragments of ten Enoch manuscripts were found among the Dead Sea Scrolls. The number of scrolls indicate the Essenes (a Jewish commune or sect at the time of Christ) could well have used the Enochian writings as a community prayer book or teacher's manual and study text.

Many of the early church fathers also supported the Enochian writings. Justin Martyr ascribed all evil to demons whom he alleged to be the offspring of the angels who fell through lust for women; directly referencing the Enochian writings.

Athenagoras (170 A.D.), regarded Enoch as a true prophet. He describes the angels who "violated both their own nature and their office." In his writings, he goes into detail about the nature of fallen angels and the cause of their fall, which comes directly from the Enochian writings.

Since any book stands to be interpreted in many ways, Enoch posed problems for some theologians. Instead of reexamining their own theology, they sought to dispose of that which went counter to their beliefs. Some of the visions in Enoch are believed to point to the consummation of the age in conjunction with Christ's second coming which took place in A.D. 70 (in the destruction of Jerusalem).

This being the case, it should not surprise us that Enoch was declared a fake and was rejected by Hilary, Jerome, and Augustine. Enoch was subsequently lost to Western Christendom for over a thousand years.

Enoch's "seventy generations" was also a great problem. Many scholars thought it could not be made to stretch beyond the First Century. Copies of Enoch soon disappeared. Indeed, for almost two thousand years we knew only the references made to it in the Bible. Without having the book itself, we could not have known it was being quoted in the Bible, sometimes word for word by Peter and Jude.

"...the Lord, having saved a people out of the land of Egypt, afterward destroyed them that believed not. And angels that kept not their own principality, but left their proper habitation, he hath kept in everlasting bonds under darkness unto the judgment of the great day. Even as Sodom and Gomorrah, and the cities about them...in like manner...are set out as examples...." (Jude 5-7)

"For if God spared not the angels when they sinned, but cast them down into hell, and committed them to pits of darkness, to be reserved unto judgment." (2 Peter 2.4)

To what extent other New Testament writers regarded Enoch as scriptural canon may be determined by comparing their writings with those found in Enoch. A strong possibility of influence upon their thought and choice of wording is evidenced by a great many references found in Enoch which remind one of passages found in the New Testament.

The Book of Enoch had a profound impact on doctrines of both Jews and Christians. In short, the Book Of Enoch influenced and contributed to our modern day doctrine of angels, demons, hell, and jugement. Moreover, it set the stage for the Christology to come by expanding the reader's view of God's "Elect One." Later, the Enochian text (those books attributed to Enoch) spawned several divergent religions including the Order of Enochian Magick, The Hermetic Order of Sol, worship of the Enochian Angels, and others. These sects claim certain power derived by invoking the names and authority of the angels found in the Book Of Enoch.

The Book of Enoch seems to be a missing link between Jewish and Christian theology and is considered by many to be more Christian in its theology than Jewish. It was considered scripture by many early Christians. The literature of the church fathers is filled with references to this book. The early second century apocryphal book of the Epistle of Barnabus makes many references and quotes from the Book of Enoch. Second and third century church fathers like Justin Martyr, Irenaeus, Origin and Clement of Alexandria all seemed to have accepted Enoch as authentic. Tertullian (160-230 A.D.) even called the Book of Enoch, "Holy Scripture". The Ethiopian Coptic Church holds the Book of Enoch as part of its official spiritual canon. It was widely known and read the first three centuries after Christ. This and many other books became discredited after the Council of Laodicea. And being under ban of the authorities, it gradually disappeared from circulation.

In 1773, rumors of a surviving copy of the book drew Scottish explorer James Bruce to distant Ethiopia. He found the Book of Enoch had been preserved by the Ethiopian church, which put it right alongside the other books of the Bible.

Bruce secured not one, but three Ethiopian copies of the book and brought them back to Europe and Britain. In 1773 Bruce returned from six years in Abyssinia. In 1821 Richard Laurence published the first English translation. The famous R.H. Charles edition was published in 1912. In the following years several portions of the Greek text surfaced. Then with the discovery of cave 4 at Qumran, seven fragmentary copies of the Aramaic text were discovered.

Even in its complete form, the Book of Enoch is not one manuscript. It is a composite of several manuscripts written by several authors. Enoch and Noah each have pieces of the book ascribed to them. Yet still today the most complete text of the multifaceted book is the Ethiopian copy.

Later, another "Book of Enoch" surfaced. This text, dubbed "2 Enoch" and commonly called "the Slavonic Enoch," was discovered in 1886 by Professor Sokolov in the archives of the Belgrade Public Library. It appears that just as the Ethiopian Enoch ("1 Enoch") escaped the sixth-century Church suppression of Enoch texts in the Mediterranean area, so a Slavonic Enoch survived far away, long after the originals from which it was copied were destroyed or hidden.

Specialists in the Enochian texts believe that the missing original from which the Slavonic was copied was probably a Greek manuscript, which itself may have been based on a Hebrew or Aramaic manuscript.

The Slavonic text is evidence of many later additions to the original manuscript. Unfortunately, later additions and the deletion of teachings considered "erroneous," rendered the text unreliable.

Because of certain references to dates and data regarding certain calendar systems in the Slavonic Enoch, some claim the text cannot be earlier than the seventh century A.D. Some see these passages not as evidence of Christian authorship, but as later Christian interpolations into an earlier manuscript. Enochian specialist R.H. Charles, for instance, believes that even the better of the two Slavonic manuscripts contains interpolations and is, in textual terms, "corrupt." It is for the reasons above; we will look only at the book referred to as 1 Enoch. We will leave the inferior manuscript of 2 Enoch for another day.

The translations used for this work are taken from both the Richard Laurence and R.H. Charles manuscripts in addition to numerous sources and commentaries. The texts were compared and, in some cases, transliterated for easier reading by the modern "American" English reader as some phrasing from the 18th and 19th centuries may seem somewhat clumsy to our 21st century eyes. When there are clear differences, a word is added in parentheses to show both paths of translations.

In addition to the translation notes there are Biblical references showing how the Book of Enoch contains various Old Testament sources or how the Book of Enoch was quoted, referenced, or was possibly used as a source document for New Testament writers. These Biblical references are italicized and the chapters and verses are noted. Author's notes and comments are noted and separated from the scripture text.

THE BOOK OF 1 ENOCH

[Chapter 1]

1 The words of the blessing of Enoch, with which he blessed the elect and righteous, who will be living in the day of tribulation, when all the wicked and godless are to be removed.

2 And he began his story saying: Enoch a righteous man, whose eyes were opened by God, saw the vision of the Holy One in heaven, which the angels showed me, and I heard everything from them, and I saw and understood, but it was not for this generation, but for a remote one which is to come.

3 Concerning the elect I said, as I began my story concerning them: The Holy Great One will come out from His dwelling,

4 And the eternal God will tread on the earth, (even) on Mount Sinai, and appear in the strength of His might from heaven.

5 And all shall be very afraid, And the Watchers shall shake, And great fear and trembling shall seize them to the ends of the earth.

6 And the high mountains shall be shaken, and the high hills shall be laid low, and shall melt like wax in the flame.

7 And the earth shall be wholly torn apart, and all that is on the earth shall be destroyed, And there shall be a judgment on all.

8 But with the righteous He will make peace; and will protect the elect and mercy shall be on them. And they shall all belong to God, and they shall prosper, and they shall be blessed. And the light of God shall shine on them.

9 And behold! He comes with ten thousand of His holy ones (saints) to execute judgment on all, and to destroy all the ungodly (wicked); and to convict all flesh of all the works of their ungodliness, which they have ungodly committed, and of all the hard things which ungodly sinners have spoken against Him.

JUD 1:14 And Enoch also, the seventh from Adam, prophesied of these, saying, Behold, the Lord cometh with ten thousands of his saints, 15 To execute judgment upon all, and to convince all that are ungodly among them of all their ungodly deeds which they have ungodly committed, and of all their hard speeches which ungodly sinners have spoken against him.

[Chapter 2]

1 Observe everything that takes place in the sky, how the lights do not change their orbits, and the luminaries which are in heaven, how they all rise and set in order each in its season (proper time), and do not transgress against their appointed order.

2 Consider the earth, and give understanding to the things, which take place on it from start to finish, how steadfast they are, how none of the things on the earth change, but all the works of God appear to you.

3 Behold the summer and the winter, how the whole earth is filled with water, and clouds and dew and rain lie on it.

[Chapter 3]

1 Observe and see how (in the winter) all the trees seem as though they had withered and shed all their leaves, except fourteen trees, which do not lose their foliage but retain the old foliage from two to three years until the new comes.

[Chapter 4]

1 And again, observe the days of summer how the sun is above the earth. And you seek shade and shelter because of the heat of the sun, and the earth also burns with growing heat, and so you cannot walk on the earth, or on a rock because of its heat.

[Chapter 5]

1 Observe how the trees are covered with green leaves and how they bear fruit. Understand, know, and recognize that He that lives forever made them this way for you.

2 And all His works go on before Him from year to year forever, and all the work and the tasks which they accomplish for Him do not change, and so is it done.

3 Consider how the sea and the rivers in like manner accomplish their course do not change because of His commandments.

4 But you, you have neither held to nor have you done the commandments of the Lord, But you have turned away and spoken proud and hard words with your unclean mouths against His greatness. Oh, you hard-hearted, you shall find no peace.

5 Therefore shall you curse your days, and the years of your life shall perish, and the years of your destruction shall be multiplied and in an eternal curse you shall find no mercy.

6 In those days you shall make your names an eternal curse to all the righteous, and by you shall all who curse, curse, and all the sinners and godless shall curse you forever. And for you the godless there shall be a curse.

7 And all the elect shall rejoice, and there shall be forgiveness of sins, and mercy and peace and forbearance and joy. There shall be salvation for them, (like/and) a good light. And for all of you sinners there shall be no salvation, but on you all shall abide a curse. But for the elect there shall be light and joy and peace, and they shall inherit the earth.

8 And then wisdom shall be given to the elect, and they shall all live and never again sin, either through forgetfulness or through pride: But those who are given wisdom shall be humble.

9 And they shall not again transgress, Nor shall they sin all the days of their life, Nor shall they die of the anger or wrath of God, But they shall complete the number of the days of their lives. And their lives shall be increased in peace, and their years will grow in joy and eternal gladness and peace, all the days of their lives.

[Chapter 6]

1 And it came to pass when the children of men had multiplied that in those days were born to them beautiful and fair daughters.

GEN 6:1 And it came to pass, when men began to multiply on the face of the earth, and daughters were born unto them, 2 That the sons of God saw the daughters of men that they were fair; and they took them wives of all which they chose. 3 And the LORD said, My spirit shall not always strive with man, for that he also is flesh: yet his days shall be an hundred and twenty years.

2 And the angels, the sons of heaven, saw and lusted after them, and said to one another: 'Come, let us choose us wives from among the children of men

3 And have children with them.' And Semjaza, who was their leader, said to them: 'I fear you will not agree to do this deed,

4 And I alone shall have to pay the penalty of this great sin.'

5 And they all answered him and said: 'Let us all swear an oath, and all bind ourselves by mutual curses so we will not abandon this plan but to do this thing.' Then they all swore together and bound themselves by mutual curses.

6 And they were in all two hundred who descended in the days of Jared in the summit of Mount Hermon, and they called it Mount Hermon, because they had sworn and bound themselves by mutual curses on the act.

JUD 1:5 I will therefore put you in remembrance, though ye once knew this, how that the Lord, having saved the people out of the land of Egypt, afterward destroyed them that believed not. 6 And the angels who kept not their first estate, but left their own habitation, he hath reserved in everlasting chains under darkness unto the judgment of the great day.

7 And these are the names of their leaders: Samlazaz, their leader, Araklba, Rameel, Kokablel, Tamlel, Ramlel, Danel, Ezeqeel, Baraqijal,

(Author's note: Samlazaz could be another spelling of Semjaza, and possibly be the same entity.)

8 Asael, Armaros, Batarel, Ananel, Zaqiel, Samsapeel, Satarel, Turel, Jomjael, Sariel. These are their chiefs of tens.

[Chapter 7]

1 And all of them together went and took wives for themselves, each choosing one for himself, and they began to go in to them and to defile themselves with sex with them,

GEN 5:32 And Noah was five hundred years old: and Noah begat Shem, Ham, and Japheth. 6:1 And it came to pass, when men began to multiply on the face of the earth, and daughters were born unto them, 2 That the sons of God saw the daughters of men that they were fair; and they took them wives of all which they chose. 3 And the LORD said, My spirit shall not always strive with man, for that he also is flesh: yet his days shall be an hundred and twenty years. 4 There were giants in the earth in those days; and also after that, when the sons of God came in unto the daughters of men, and they bare children to them, the same became mighty men which were of old, men of renown. 5 And GOD saw that the wickedness of man was great in the earth, and that every imagination of the thoughts of his heart was only evil continually. 6 And it repented the LORD that he had made man on the earth, and it grieved him at his heart.

2 And the angels taught them charms and spells, and the cutting of roots, and made them acquainted with plants.

3 And the women became pregnant, and they bare large giants, whose height was three thousand cubits (ells).

4 The giants consumed all the work and toil of men. And when men could no longer sustain them, the giants turned against them and devoured mankind.

5 And they began to sin against birds, and beasts, and reptiles, and fish, and to devour one another's flesh, and drank the blood.

6 Then the earth laid accusation against the lawless ones.

[Chapter 8]

1 And Azazel taught men to make swords, and knives, and shields, and breastplates, and taught them about metals of the earth and the art of working them, and bracelets, and ornaments, and the use of antimony, and the beautifying of the eyelids, and all kinds of precious stones, and all coloring and dyes.

2 And there was great impiety, they turned away from God, and committed fornication, and they were led astray, and became corrupt in all their ways.

3 Semjaza taught the casting of spells, and root-cuttings, Armaros taught counter-spells (release from spells), Baraqijal taught astrology, Kokabel taught the constellations (portents), Ezeqeel the knowledge of the clouds, Araqiel the signs of the earth, Shamsiel the signs of the sun, and Sariel the course of the moon. And as men perished, they cried, and their cry went up to heaven.

[Chapter 9]

1 And then Michael, Uriel, Raphael, and Gabriel looked down from heaven and saw much blood being shed on the earth, and all lawlessness being done on the earth.

2 And they said to each other: 'Let the cries from the destruction of Earth ascend up to the gates of heaven.

3 And now to you, the holy ones of heaven, the souls of men make their petition, saying, "Bring our cause before the Most High."'

4 And they said to the Lord of the ages: 'Lord of lords, God of gods, King of kings, and God of the ages, the throne of your glory endures through all the generations of the ages, and your name holy and glorious and blessed to all the ages!

1TI 6:15 Which in his times he shall shew, who is the blessed and only Potentate, the King of kings, and Lord of lords; 16 Who only hath immortality, dwelling in the light which no man can approach unto; whom no man hath seen, nor can see: to whom be honour and power everlasting. Amen.

5 You have made all things, and you have power over all things: and all things are revealed and open in your sight, and you see all things, and nothing can hide itself from you.

6 Look at what Azazel has done, who hath taught all unrighteousness on earth and revealed the eternal secrets which were made and kept in heaven, which men were striving to learn:

7 And Semjaza, who taught spells, to whom you gave authority to rule over his associates.

8 And they have gone to the daughters of men on the earth, and have had sex with the women, and have defiled themselves, and revealed to them all kinds of sins.

GEN 6:4 There were giants in the earth in those days; and also after that, when the sons of God came in unto the daughters of men, and they bare children to them, the same became mighty men which were of old, men of renown.

9 And the women have borne giants, and the whole earth has thereby been filled with blood and unrighteousness.

GEN 6:5 And GOD saw that the wickedness of man was great in the earth, and that every imagination of the thoughts of his heart was only evil continually. 6 And it repented the LORD that he had made man on the earth, and it grieved him at his heart.

10 And now, behold, the souls of those who have died are crying out and making their petition to the gates of heaven, and their lament has ascended and cannot cease because of the lawless deeds which are done on the earth.

11 And you know all things before they come to pass, and you see these things and you have permitted them, and say nothing to us about these things. What are we to do with them about these things?'

[Chapter 10]

1 Then said the Most High, the Great and Holy One, Uriel go to the son of Lamech.

2 Say to him: 'Go to Noah and tell him in my name "Hide yourself!" and reveal to him the end that is approaching: that the whole earth will be destroyed, and a flood is about to come on the whole earth, and will destroy everything on it.'

GEN 7:4 For yet seven days, and I will cause it to rain upon the earth forty days and forty nights; and every living substance that I have made will I destroy from off the face of the earth.

3 'And now instruct him as to what he must do to escape that his offspring may be preserved for all the generations of the world.'

GEN 6:13 And God said unto Noah, The end of all flesh is come before me; for the earth is filled with violence through them; and, behold, I will destroy them with the earth. 14 Make thee an ark of gopher wood; rooms shalt thou make in the ark, and shalt pitch it within and without with pitch.

4 And again the Lord said to Raphael: 'Bind Azazel hand and foot, and cast him into the darkness and split open the desert, which is in Dudael, and cast him in.

5 And fill the hole by covering him rough and jagged rocks, and cover him with darkness, and let him live there for ever, and cover his face that he may not see the light.

6 And on the day of the great judgment he shall be hurled into the fire.

7 And heal the earth which the angels have ruined, and proclaim the healing of the earth, for I will restore the earth and heal the plague, that not all of the children of men may perish through all the secret things that the Watchers have disclosed and have taught their sons.

ROM 8:18 For I reckon that the sufferings of this present time are not worthy to be compared with the glory which shall be revealed in us. 19 For the earnest expectation of the creature waiteth for the manifestation of the sons of God. 20 For the creature was made subject to vanity, not willingly, but by reason of him who hath subjected the same in hope, 21 Because the creature itself also shall be delivered from the bondage of corruption into the glorious liberty of the children of God.

8 The whole earth has been corrupted through the works that were taught by Azazel: to him ascribe ALL SIN.'

9 To Gabriel said the Lord: 'Proceed against the bastards and the reprobates, and against the children of fornication and destroy the children of fornication and the children of the Watchers. Cause them to go against one another that they may destroy each other in battle: Shorten their days.

GEN 6:7 And the LORD said, I will destroy man whom I have created from the face of the earth; both man, and beast, and the creeping thing, and the fowls of the air; for it repenteth me that I have made them. 8 But Noah found grace in the eyes of the LORD.

10 No request that (the Watchers) their fathers make of you shall be granted them on their behalf; for they hope to live an eternal life, and that each one of them will live five hundred years.'

11 And the Lord said to Michael: 'Go, bind Semjaza and his team who have associated with women and have defiled themselves in all their uncleanness.

12 When their sons have slain one another, and they have seen the destruction of their beloved ones, bind them fast for seventy generations under the hills of the earth, until the day of the consummation of their judgment and until the eternal judgment is accomplished.

(Author's note: 70 generations of 500 years = 3500 years.)

13 In those days they shall be led off to the abyss of fire and to the torment and the prison in which they shall be confined for ever.'

14 Then Semjaza shall be burnt up with the condemned and they will be destroyed, having been bound together with them to the end of all generations.

15 Destroy all the spirits of lust and the children of the Watchers, because they have wronged mankind.

16 Destroy all wrong from the face of the earth and let every evil work come to an end and let (the earth be planted with righteousness) the plant of righteousness and truth appear; and it shall prove a blessing, the works of righteousness and truth shall be planted in truth and joy for evermore.

GEN 6:7 And the LORD said, I will destroy man whom I have created from the face of the earth; both man, and beast, and the creeping thing, and the fowls of the air; for it repenteth me that I have made them.

17 And then shall all the righteous survive, and shall live until they beget thousands of children, and all the days of their youth and their old age shall they complete in peace.

GEN 8:22 While the earth remaineth, seedtime and harvest, and cold and heat, and summer and winter, and day and night shall not cease.

GEN 9:1 And God blessed Noah and his sons, and said unto them, Be fruitful, and multiply, and replenish the earth.

18 And then shall the whole earth be untilled in righteousness and shall be planted with trees and be full of blessing. And all desirable trees shall be planted on it, and they shall plant vines on it.

19 And the vine which they plant shall yield fruit in abundance, and as for all the seed which is sown, each measurement (of it) shall bear a thousand, and each measurement of olives shall yield ten presses of oil.

20 You shall cleanse the earth from all oppression, and from all unrighteousness, and from all sin, and from all godlessness, and all the uncleanness that is brought on the earth you shall destroy from off the earth.

21 All the children of men shall become righteous, and all nations shall offer adoration and shall praise Me,

22 And all shall worship Me. And the earth shall be cleansed from all defilement, and from all sin, and from all punishment, and from all torment, and I will never again send another flood from this generation to all generations and for ever.

[Chapter 11]

1 And in those days I will open the storehouse of blessings in heaven, and rain down blessings on the earth and over the work and labor of the children of men.

2 Truth and peace shall be united throughout all the days of the world and throughout all the generations of men.'

[Chapter 12]

1 Then Enoch disappeared and no one of the children of men knew where he was hidden, and where he abode;

GEN 5:21 And Enoch lived sixty and five years, and begat Methuselah: 22 And Enoch walked with God after he begat Methuselah three hundred years, and begat sons and daughters: 23 And all the days of Enoch were three hundred sixty and five years: 24 And Enoch walked with God: and he was not; for God took him.

2 And what had become of him. And his activities were with the Holy Ones and the Watchers.

3 And I, Enoch, was blessing the Lord of majesty and the King of the ages, and lo! the Watchers called me, Enoch the scribe, and said to me:

4 'Enoch, you scribe of righteousness, go, tell the Watchers of heaven who have left the high heaven, the holy eternal place, and have defiled themselves with women, and have done as the children of earth do, and have taken to themselves wives:

5 "You have done great destruction on the earth: And you shall have no peace nor forgiveness of sin:

6 Since they delight themselves in their children, They shall see the murder of their beloved ones, and the destruction of their children shall and they shall lament, and shall make supplication forever, you will receive neither mercy or peace."

[Chapter 13]

1 And Enoch went and said: 'Azazel, you shall have no peace: a severe sentence has been passed against you that you should be bound:

2 And you shall not have rest or mercy (toleration nor request granted), because of the unrighteousness which you have taught, and because of all the works of godlessness,

3 And unrighteousness and sin which you have shown to men.

4 Then I went and spoke to them all together, and they were all afraid, and fear and trembling seized them.

5 And they asked me to write a petition for them that they might find forgiveness, and to read their petition in the presence of the Lord of heaven. They had been forbidden to speak (with Him) nor were they to lift up their eyes to heaven for shame of their sins because they had been condemned.

6 Then I wrote out their petition, and the prayer in regard to their spirits and their deeds individually and in regard to their requests that they should obtain forgiveness and forbearance.

7 And I went off and sat down at the waters of Dan, in the land of Dan, to the southwest of Hermon: I read their petition until I fell asleep.

8 And I had a dream, and I saw a vision of their chastisement, and a voice came to me that I would reprimand (reprove) them.

9 And when I awoke, I came to them, and they were all sitting gathered together, weeping in Abelsjail, which is between Lebanon and Seneser, with their faces covered.

10 And I recounted to them all the visions which I had seen when I was asleep, and I began to speak the words of righteousness, and to reprimand heavenly Watchers.

[Chapter 14]

1 This is the book of the words of righteousness, and of the reprimand of the eternal Watchers in accordance with the command of the Holy Great One in that vision I saw in my sleep.

2 What I will now say with a tongue of flesh and with the breath of my mouth: which the Great One has given to men to speak with it and to understand with the heart.

3 As He has created and given to man the power of understanding the word of wisdom, so has He created me also and given me the power of reprimanding the Watchers, the children of heaven.

4 I wrote out your petition, and in my vision it appeared that your petition will not be granted to you throughout all the days of eternity, and that judgment has been finally passed on you:

5 Your petition will not be granted. From here on you shall not ascend into heaven again for all eternity, and you will be bound on earth for all eternity.

6 Before this you will see the destruction of your beloved sons and you shall have no pleasure in them, but they shall fall before you by the sword.

7 Your petition shall not be granted on their behalf or on yours, even though you weep and pray and speak all the words contained in my writings.

8 In the vision I saw clouds that invited me and summoned me into a mist, and the course of the stars and the flashes of lightning and hurried me and drove me,

9 And the winds in the vision caused me to fly and lifted me up, and bore me into heaven. And I went in until I drew near to a wall which was built out of crystals and surrounded by tongues of fire, and it began to frighten me.

10 I went into the tongues of fire and drew near a large house which was built of crystals: and the walls of the house were like a mosaic of hailstones and the floor was made of crystals like snow.

11 Its ceiling was like the path of the stars and lightning flashes, and between them were fiery cherubim,

12 Their sky was clear as water. A flaming fire surrounded the walls, and its doors blazed with fire.

13 I entered that house, and it was hot as fire and cold as ice; there were no pleasures or life therein: fear covered me, and trembling got hold of me.

14 As I shook and trembled, I fell on my face.

15 And I saw a vision, And lo! there was a second house, greater than the first,

16 And the all the doors stood open before me, and it was built of flames of fire. And in every respect it was splendid and magnificent to the extent that I cannot describe it to you.

17 Its floor was of fire, and above it was lightning and the path of the stars, and its ceiling also was flaming fire.

18 And I looked and saw a throne set on high, its appearance was like crystal, and its wheels were like a shining sun, and there was the vision of cherubim.

1TI 6:16 Who only hath immortality, dwelling in the light which no man can approach unto; whom no man hath seen, nor can see: to whom be honour and power everlasting. Amen.

19 And from underneath the throne came rivers of fire so that I could not look at it.

20 And He who is Great in Glory sat on the throne, and His raiment shone more brightly than the sun and was whiter than any snow.

MAT 25:31 When the Son of man shall come in his glory, and all the holy angels with him, then shall he sit upon the throne of his glory:

21 None of the angels could enter or could behold His face because of the magnificence and glory and no flesh could behold Him.

22 The sea of fire surrounded Him, and a great fire stood in front of Him, and no one could draw close to Him: ten thousand times ten thousand stood before Him, but He needed no Holy council.

23 The most Holy Ones who were near to Him did not leave night or day.

24 And until then I had been prostrate on my face, trembling, and the Lord called me with His own mouth, and said to me:

25' Come here, Enoch, and hear my word.' And one of the Holy Ones came to me picked me up and brought me to the door: and I bowed down my face.

[Chapter 15]

1 And He answered and said to me, and I heard His voice: 'Do not be afraid, Enoch, you righteous man and scribe of righteousness.

2 Approach and hear my voice. Go and say to the Watchers of heaven, for whom you have come to intercede: "You should intercede for men, and not men for you."

3 Why and for what cause have you left the high, holy, and eternal heaven, and had sex with women, and defiled yourselves with the daughters of men and taken to yourselves wives, and done like the children of earth, and begotten giants (as your) sons?

4 Though you were holy, spiritual, living the eternal life, you have defiled yourselves with the blood of women, and have begotten children with the blood of flesh, and, as the children of men, you have lusted after flesh and blood like those who die and are killed.

5 This is why I have given men wives, that they might impregnate them, and have children by them, that deeds might continue on the earth.

6 But you were formerly spiritual, living the eternal life, and immortal for all generations of the world.

7 Therefore I have not appointed wives for you; you are spiritual beings of heaven, and in heaven was your dwelling place.

LUK 20:34 And Jesus answering said unto them, The children of this world marry, and are given in marriage: 35 But they which shall be accounted worthy to obtain that world, and the resurrection from the dead, neither marry, nor are given in marriage: 36 Neither can they die any more: for they are equal unto the angels; and are the children of God, being the children of the resurrection.

8 And now, the giants, who are produced from the spirits and flesh, shall be called evil spirits on the earth,

9 And shall live on the earth. Evil spirits have come out from their bodies because they are born from men and from the holy Watchers, their beginning is of primal origin;

10 They shall be evil spirits on earth, and evil spirits shall they be called spirits of the evil ones. [As for the spirits of heaven, in heaven shall be their dwelling, but as for the spirits of the earth which were born on the earth, on the earth shall be their dwelling.] And the spirits of the giants afflict, oppress, destroy, attack, war, destroy, and cause trouble on the earth.

11 They take no food, but do not hunger or thirst. They cause offences but are not observed.

12 And these spirits shall rise up against the children of men and against the women, because they have proceeded from them in the days of the slaughter and destruction.'

[Chapter 16]

1 'And at the death of the giants, spirits will go out and shall destroy without incurring judgment, coming from their bodies their flesh shall be destroyed until the day of the consummation, the great judgment in which the age shall be consummated, over the Watchers and the godless, and shall be wholly consummated.'

MAT 8:28 And when he was come to the other side into the country of the Gergesenes, there met him two possessed with devils, coming out of the tombs, exceeding fierce, so that no man might pass by that way. 29 And, behold, they cried out, saying, What have we to do with thee, Jesus, thou Son of God? art thou come here to torment us before the time?

2 And now as to the Watchers who have sent you to intercede for them, who had been in heaven before,

3 (Say to them): "You were in heaven, but all the mysteries of heaven had not been revealed to you, and you knew worthless ones, and these in the hardness of your hearts you have made known to the women, and through these mysteries women and men work much evil on earth."

4 Say to them therefore: " You have no peace."'

[Chapter 17]

1 And they took me to a place in which those who were there were like flaming fire,

2 And, when they wished, they made themselves appear as men. They brought me to the place of darkness, and to a mountain the point of whose summit reached to heaven.

3 And I saw the lighted places and the treasuries of the stars and of the thunder and in the uttermost depths, where were a fiery bow and arrows and their quiver, and a fiery sword and all the lightning.

4 And they took me to the waters of life, and to the fire of the west, which receives every setting of the sun.

5 And I came to a river of fire in which the fire flows like water into the great sea towards the west.

6 I saw the great rivers and came to the great darkness, and went to the place where no flesh walks.

7 I saw the mountains of the darkness of winter and the place from where all the waters of the deep flow.

8 I saw the mouths of all the rivers of the earth and the mouth of the deep.

[Chapter 18]

1 I saw the storehouse of all the winds: I saw how He had adorned the whole creation with them and the firm foundations of the earth.

2 And I saw the corner-stone of the earth: I saw the four winds which support the earth and the firmament of the heaven.

3 I saw how the winds stretch out the height of heaven, and have their station between heaven and earth; these are the pillars of heaven.

4 I saw the winds of heaven which turn and bring the sky and the sun and all the stars to their setting place.

5 I saw the winds on the earth carrying the clouds: I saw the paths of the angels. I saw at the end of the earth the firmament of heaven above.

6 And I continued south and saw a place which burns day and night, where there are seven mountains of magnificent stones, three towards the east, and three towards the south.

7 And as for those towards the east, they were of colored stone, and one of pearl, and one of jacinth (a stone of healing), and those towards the south of red stone.

8 But the middle one reached to heaven like the throne of God, and was made of alabaster.

9 And the summit of the throne was of sapphire.

10 And I saw a great abyss of the earth, with pillars of heavenly fire, and I saw among them fiery pillars of Heaven, which were falling,

11 And as regards both height and depth, they were immeasurable.

12 And beyond that abyss I saw a place which had no firmament of heaven above, and no firmly founded earth beneath it: there was no water on it, and no birds,

13 But it was a desert and a horrible place. I saw there seven stars like great burning mountains,

14 And an angel questioned me regarding them. The angel said: 'This place is the end of heaven and earth.

15 This has become a prison for the stars and the host of heaven. And the stars which roll over the fire are they which have transgressed the commandment of the Lord in the beginning of their rising, because they did not come out at their proper times.

16 And He was angry with them, and bound them until the time when their guilt should be consummated even for ten thousand years.'

[Chapter 19]

1 And Uriel said to me: 'The angels who have had sex with women shall stand here, and their spirits, having assumed many different forms, are defiling mankind and shall lead them astray into sacrificing to demons as gods, here shall they stand, until the day of the great judgment in which they shall be judged and are made an end of.

2 And the women also of the angels who went astray shall become sirens (other versions read 'shall become peaceful' also, another version reads, 'shall salute them').'

3 And I, Enoch, alone saw the vision, the ends of all things: and no man shall see as I have seen.

1PE 4:7 But the end of all things is at hand: be ye therefore sober, and watch unto prayer.

[Chapter 20]

1 These are the names of the holy angels who watch.

2 Uriel, one of the holy angels, who is over the world, turmoil and terror.

3 Raphael, one of the holy angels, who is over the spirits of men.

4 Raguel, one of the holy angels who takes vengeance on the world of the luminaries.

5 Michael, one of the holy angels, set over the virtues of mankind and over chaos.

6 Saraqael, one of the holy angels, who is set over the spirits, who sin in the spirit.

7 Gabriel, one of the holy angels, who is over Paradise and the serpents and the Cherubim.

8 Remiel, one of the holy angels, whom God set over those who rise.

[Chapter 21]

1 Then, I proceeded to where things were chaotic and void.

2 And I saw there something horrible:

3 I saw neither a heaven above nor a firmly founded earth, but a place chaotic and horrible.

4 And there I saw seven stars of heaven bound together in it, like great mountains and burning with fire.

5 Then I said: 'For what sin are they bound, and on why have they been cast in here?' Then said Uriel, one of the holy angels, who was with me, and was chief over them: 'Enoch, why do you ask, and why art you eager for the truth?

6 These are some of the stars of heaven, which have transgressed the commandment of the Lord, and are bound here until ten thousand years, the time entailed by their sins, are consummated.'

7 And I went out from there to another place, which was still more horrible than the former, and I saw a terrible thing: a great fire there which burnt and blazed, and the place was cleft as far as the abyss, full of great falling columns of fire:

8 Neither its width or breadth could I see, nor could I see its source.

9 Then I said: 'I am afraid of this place and cannot stand to look at it.!' Then Uriel, one of the holy angels who was with me, answered and said to me: 'Enoch, why are you so afraid?'

10 And I answered: 'Because of this fearful place, and because of the spectacle of the pain.' And he said to me: 'This place is the prison of the angels, and here they will be imprisoned for ever.'

[Chapter 22]

1 And I went out to another place west where there was a mountain and hard rock.

2 And there was in it four hollow places, deep and wide and very smooth. How smooth are the hollow places and looked deep and dark.

3 Then Raphael answered, one of the holy angels who was with me, and said to me: 'These hollow places have been created for this very purpose, that the spirits of the souls of the dead should be gathered here, that all the souls of the children of men should brought together here. And these places have been made to receive them until the day of their judgment and until the period appointed, until the great judgment comes on them.'

4 I saw the spirit of a dead man, and his voice went out to heaven and made petitions.

5 And I asked Raphael the angel who was with me, and I said to him: 'This spirit which petitions,

6 Whose is it, whose voice goes up and petitions heaven?'

7 And he answered me saying: 'This is the spirit which went out from Abel, whom his brother Cain slew, and he makes his suit against him until his offspring is destroyed from the face of the earth, and his offspring are annihilated from among the children of men.'

GEN 4:8 And Cain talked with Abel his brother: and it came to pass, when they were in the field that Cain rose up against Abel his brother, and slew him. 9 And the LORD said unto Cain, Where is Abel thy brother? And he said, I know not: Am I my brother's keeper? 10 And he said, What hast thou done? the voice of thy brother's blood crieth unto me from the ground. 11 And now art thou cursed from the earth, which hath opened her mouth to receive thy brother's blood from thy hand; 12 When thou tillest the ground, it shall not henceforth yield unto thee her strength; a fugitive and a vagabond shalt thou be in the earth.

8 Then I asked, regarding all the hollow places: 'Why is one separated from the other?'

9 And he answered me and said to me: 'These three have been made that the spirits of the dead might be separated. Divisions have been made for the spirits of the righteous, in which there is the bright spring of water.

10 And one for sinners when they die and are buried in the earth and judgment has not been executed on them in their lifetime.

11 Here their spirits shall be set apart in this great pain until the great day of judgment and punishment and torment of those who curse for ever and retribution for their spirits.

12 There He shall bind them for ever. And such a division has been made for the spirits of those who make their petitions, who make disclosures concerning their destruction, when they were slain in the days of the sinners.

13 Such has been made for the spirits of men who were not righteous but sinners, who were complete in transgression, and of the transgressors they shall be companions, but their spirits shall not be destroyed in the day of judgment nor shall they be raised from here.'

14 Then I blessed the Lord of glory and said: 'Blessed be my Lord, the Lord of righteousness, who rules for ever.'

[Chapter 23]

1 From here I went to another place to the west of the ends of the earth.

2 And I saw a burning fire which ran without resting, and never stopped from its course day or night but flowed always in the same way.

3 And I asked saying: 'What is this which never stops?'

4 Then Raguel, one of the holy angels who was with me, answered me and said to me: 'This course of fire which you have seen is the fire in the west and is the fire of all the lights of heaven.'

[Chapter 24]

1 And from here I went to another place on the earth, and he showed me a mountain range of fire which burned day and night.

2 And I went beyond it and saw seven magnificent mountains, all differing from each other, and their stones were magnificent and beautiful, and their form was glorious: three towards the east, one founded on the other, and three towards the south, one on the other, and deep rough ravines, no one of which joined with any other.

3 And the seventh mountain was in the midst of these, and it was higher than them, resembling the seat of a throne.

4 And fragrant trees encircled the throne. And among them was a tree such as I had never smelled, nor was any among them or were others like it; it had a fragrance beyond all fragrance, and its leaves and blooms and wood would not ever wither:

5 And its fruit is beautiful, and its fruit resembles the dates of a palm. Then I said: 'How beautiful is this tree, and fragrant, and its leaves are fair, and its blooms very delightful in appearance.'

6 Then Michael, one of the holy and honored angels who was with me, and was their leader, spoke.

[Chapter 25]

1 And he said to me: 'Enoch, why do you ask me about the fragrance of the tree, and why do you wish to learn the truth?'

2 Then I answered him saying: 'I wish to know about everything, but especially about this tree.'

3 And he answered saying: 'This high mountain which you have seen, whose summit is like the throne of God, is His throne, where the Holy Great One, the Lord of Glory, the Eternal King, will sit, when He shall come down to visit the earth with goodness.

4 And as for this fragrant tree, no mortal is permitted to touch it until the great judgment, when He shall take vengeance on all and bring everything to its completion for ever.

5 It shall then be given to the righteous and holy. Its fruit shall be for food to the Elect: it shall be transplanted to the holy place, to the temple of the Lord, the Eternal King.

REV 22:1 And he shewed me a pure river of water of life, clear as crystal, proceeding out of the throne of God and of the Lamb. 2 In the midst of the street of it, and on either side of the river, was there the tree of life, which bare twelve manner of fruits, and yielded her fruit every month: and the leaves of the tree were for the healing of the nations. 3 And there shall be no more curses: but the throne of God and of the Lamb shall be in it; and his servants shall serve him.

6 Then they shall rejoice and be glad, and enter into the holy place; And its fragrance shall enter into their bones, And they shall live a long life on earth, as your fathers lived. And in their days there will be no sorrow or pain or torment or toil.'

7 Then I blessed the God of Glory, the Eternal King, who has prepared such things for the righteous, and has created them and promised to give to them.

[Chapter 26]

1 And I went from there to the middle of the earth, and I saw a blessed place in which there were trees with branches alive and blooming on a tree that had been cut down.

2 And there I saw a holy mountain,

3 And underneath the mountain to the east there was a stream and it flowed towards the south. And I saw towards the east another mountain higher than this, and between them a deep and narrow valley.

4 In it ran a stream underneath the mountain. And to the west of it there was another mountain, lower than the former and of small elevation, and a dry, deep valley between them; and another deep and dry valley was at the edge of the three mountains.

5 And all the valleys were deep and narrow, being formed from hard rock, and there were no trees planted on them.

6 And I was very amazed at the rocks in the valleys.

[Chapter 27]

1 Then I said: 'What is the purpose of this blessed land, which is entirely filled with trees, and what is the purpose of this accursed valley between them?'

2 Then Uriel, one of the holy angels who was with me, answered and said: 'This accursed valley is for those who are cursed for ever: Here shall all the accursed be gathered together who utter with their lips words against the Lord not befitting His glory or say hard things against Him. Here shall they be gathered together, and here shall be their place of judgment.

3 In the last days there shall be the spectacle of righteous judgment on them in the presence of the righteous for ever: here shall the merciful bless the Lord of glory, the Eternal King.

4 In the days of judgment they shall bless Him for the mercy in that He has shown them.'

5 Then I blessed the Lord of Glory and set out His glory and praised Him gloriously.

[Chapter 28]

1 Then, I went towards the east, into the midst of the mountain range in the desert, and I saw a wilderness.

2 And it was solitary, full of trees and plants. And water gushed out from above.

3 Rushing like a torrent which flowed towards the north-west it caused clouds and dew to fall on every side.

[Chapter 29]

1 Then I went to another place in the desert, and approached to the east of this mountain range.

2 And there I saw aromatic trees exuding the fragrance of frankincense and myrrh, and the trees also were similar to the almond tree.

[Chapter 30]

1 Beyond these, I went far to the east,

2 And I saw another place, a valley full of water like one that would not run dry.

3 And there was a tree, the color of fragrant trees was that of mastic. And on the sides of those valleys I saw fragrant cinnamon. And beyond these I proceeded to the east.

[Chapter 31]

1 And I saw other mountains, and among them were groves of trees, and there was nectar that flowed from them, which is named Sarara and Galbanum.

2 And beyond these mountains I saw another mountain to the east of the ends of the earth, on which there were aloe trees, and all the trees were full of fruit, being like almond trees.

3 And when it was burned it smelled sweeter than any fragrant odor.

[Chapter 32]

1 And after I had smelled these fragrant odors, I looked towards the north over the mountains I saw seven mountains full of fine nard and fragrant trees of cinnamon and pepper.

2 And then I went over the summits of all these mountains, far towards the east of the earth, and passed over the Red Sea and went far from it, and passed over the angel Zotiel.

3 And I came to the Garden of Righteousness. I saw far beyond those trees more trees and they were numerous and large. There were two trees there, very large, beautiful, glorious, and magnificent. The tree of knowledge, whose holy fruit they ate and acquired great wisdom.

4 That tree is in height like the fir, and its leaves are like those of the Carob tree,

5 And its fruit is like the clusters of the grapes, very beautiful: and the fragrance of the tree carries far.

6 Then I said: 'How beautiful is the tree, and how attractive is its look!' Then Raphael the holy angel, who was with me, answered me and said: 'This is the tree of wisdom, of which your father of old and your mother of old, who were your progenitors, have eaten, and they learned wisdom and their eyes were opened, and they knew that they were naked and they were driven out of the garden.'

[Chapter 33]

1 And from there I went to the ends of the earth and saw there large beasts, and each differed from the other; and I saw birds also differing in appearance and beauty and voice, the one differing from the other.

2 And to the east of those beasts I saw the ends of the earth where heaven rests on it, and the doors of heaven open. And I saw how the stars of heaven come out, and I counted the gates from which they came out,

3 And wrote down all their outlets, of each individual star by their number and their names, their courses and their positions, and their times and their months, as Uriel the holy angel who was with me showed me.

4 He showed me all things and wrote them down for me; also their names he wrote for me, and their laws and their functions.

[Chapter 34]

1 From there I went towards the north to the ends of the earth, and there I saw a great and glorious device at the ends of the whole earth.

2 And here I saw three gates of heaven open : through each of them proceed north winds: when they blow there is cold, hail, frost, snow, dew, and rain.

3 And out of one gate they blow for good: but when they blow through the other two gates, it is for violence and torment on the earth, and they blow with force.

[Chapter 35]

1 Then I went towards the west to the ends of the earth, and saw there three gates of heaven open such as I had seen in the east, the same number of gates, and the same number of outlets.

[Chapter 36]

1 And from there I went to the south to the ends of the earth, and saw there three open gates of heaven.

2 And from them come dew, rain, and wind. And from there I went to the east to the ends of heaven, and saw here the three eastern gates of heaven open and small gates above them.

3 Through each of these small gates pass the stars of heaven and they run their course to the west on the path which is shown to them.

4 And as often as I saw I blessed always the Lord of Glory, and I continued to bless the Lord of Glory who has done great and glorious wonders, who has shown the greatness of His work to the angels and to spirits and to men, that they might praise His work and all His creation: that they might see the power of His might and praise the great work of His hands and bless Him for ever.

[Chapter 37]

1 The second vision which he saw, the vision of wisdom which Enoch the son of Jared, the son of Mahalalel,

2 The son of Cainan, the son of Enos, the son of Seth, the son of Adam, saw. And this is the beginning of the words of wisdom which I lifted up my voice to speak and say to those which dwell on earth: Hear, you men of old time, and see, you that come after, the words of the Holy One which I will speak before the Lord of spirits.

3 The words are for the men of old time, and to those that come after. We will not withhold the beginning of wisdom from this present day. Such wisdom has never been given by the Lord of spirits as I have received according to my insight, according to the good pleasure of the Lord of spirits by whom the lot of eternal life has been given to me.

4 Now three Parables were imparted to me, and I lifted up my voice and recounted them to those that dwell on the earth.

[Chapter 38]

1 The first Parable: When the congregation of the righteous shall appear, and sinners shall be judged for their sins, and shall be driven from the face of the earth;

2 And when the Righteous One shall appear before the eyes of the elect righteous ones, whose works are weighed by the Lord of spirits, light shall appear to the righteous and the elect who dwell on the earth. Where will there be the dwelling for

sinners, and where will there be a resting-place for those who have denied the Lord of spirits? It had been good for them if they had not been born.

JOHN 1:1 In the beginning was the Word, and the Word was with God, and the Word was God. 2 The same was in the beginning with God. 3 All things were made by him; and without him was not any thing made that was made. 4 In him was life; and the life was the light of men. 5 And the light shineth in darkness; and the darkness comprehended it not.

3 When the secrets of the righteous shall be revealed and the sinners judged, and the godless driven from the presence of the righteous and elect,

4 From that time those that possess the earth shall no longer be powerful and mighty: And they shall not be able to look at the face of the holy ones, because the Lord of spirits has caused His light to appear on the face of the holy, righteous, and elect.

2CO 3:18 But we all, with open face beholding as in a glass the glory of the Lord, are changed into the same image from glory to glory, even as by the Spirit of the Lord.

5 Then the kings and the mighty shall be destroyed and be turned over into the hands of the righteous and holy.

6 And from then on none shall seek mercy from the Lord of spirits for themselves for their life is at an end.

[Chapter 39]

1 And it shall come to pass in those days that elect and holy children will descend from the high heaven, and their offspring will become one with the children of men.

2 And in those days Enoch received books of indignation and wrath, and books of turmoil and confusion. There will be no mercy for them, says the Lord of spirits.

3 And in those days a whirlwind carried me off from the earth, And set me down at the end of heaven.

4 There I saw another vision, the dwelling-places of the holy, and the resting-places of the righteous.

5 Here my eyes saw the dwelling places of His righteous angels, and the resting-places of the Holy Ones. And they petitioned and interceded and prayed for the children of men, and righteousness flowed before them like water, and mercy fell like dew on the earth: Thus it is among them for ever and ever.

6 And in that place my eyes saw the Elect One of righteousness and of faith,

7 And I saw his dwelling-place under the wings of the Lord of spirits.

6 And righteousness shall prevail in his days, and the righteous and elect shall be innumerable and will be before Him for ever and ever.

7 And all the righteous and elect ones before Him shall be as bright as fiery lights, and their mouth shall be full of blessing, and their lips shall praise the name of the Lord of spirits. Righteousness and truth before Him shall never fail.

8 There I wished to dwell, and my spirit longed for that dwelling-place; and thus it was decided and my portion was assigned and established by the Lord of spirits.

9 In those days I praised and exalted the name of the Lord of spirits with blessings and praises, because He had destined me for blessing and glory according to the good pleasure of the Lord of spirits.

10 For a long time my eyes looked at that place, and I blessed Him and praised Him, saying: 'Blessed is He, and may He be blessed from the beginning and for evermore. And in His presence there is no end.

11 He knows before the world was created what is for ever and what will be from generation to generation.

12 Those who do not sleep bless you, they stand before your glory and bless, praise, and exalt you, saying: "Holy, holy, holy, is the Lord of spirits: He fills the earth with spirits."'

13 And here my eyes saw all those who do not sleep: they stand before Him and bless Him saying: 'Blessed be you, and blessed be the name of the Lord for ever and ever.'

14 And my face was changed; for I could no longer see.

[Chapter 40]

1 And after that I saw thousands of thousands and ten thousand times ten thousand,

2 I saw a multitude beyond number and reckoning, who stood before the Lord of spirits. And on the four sides of the Lord of spirits I saw four figures, different from those that did not sleep, and I learned their names; for the angel that went with me told me their names, and showed me all the hidden things.

3 And I heard the voices of those four presences as they uttered praises before the Lord of glory.

4 The first voice blessed the Lord of spirits for ever and ever.

5 The second voice I heard blessing the Elect One and the elect ones who depend on the Lord of spirits.

6 And the third voice I heard pray and intercede for those who live on the earth and pray earnestly in the name of the Lord of spirits.

7 And I heard the fourth voice fending off the Satans (advisories or accusers) and forbidding them to come before the Lord of spirits to accuse them who dwell on the earth.

8 After that I asked the angel of peace who went with me, who showed me everything that is hidden: 'Who are these four figures which I have seen and whose words I have heard and written down?'

9 And he said to me: 'This first is Michael, the merciful and long-suffering; and the second, who is set over all the diseases and all the wounds of the children of men, is Raphael; and the third, who is set over all the powers, is Gabriel' and the fourth, who is set over the repentance and those who hope to inherit eternal life, is named Phanuel.'

10 And these are the four angels of the Lord of spirits and the four voices I heard in those days.

[Chapter 41]

1 And after that I saw all the secrets of heavens, and how the kingdom is divided, and how the actions of men are weighed in the balance.

2 And there I saw the mansions of the elect and the mansions of the holy, and my eyes saw all the sinners being driven from there which deny the name of the Lord of spirits, and they were being dragged off; and they could not live because of the punishment which proceeds from the Lord of spirits.

JOHN 14:2 In my Father's house are many mansions: if it were not so, I would have told you. I go to prepare a place for you. 3 And if I go and prepare a place for you, I will come again, and receive you unto myself; that where I am, there ye may be also.

3 And there my eyes saw the secrets of the lightning and of the thunder, and the secrets of the winds, how they are divided to blow over the earth, and the secrets of the clouds and dew,

4 And there I saw where they came from and how they saturate the dusty earth.

5 And there I saw closed storehouses out of which the winds are divided, the storehouse of the hail and winds, the storehouse of the mist, and of the clouds, and the cloud thereof hovers over the earth from the beginning of the world.

6 And I saw the storehouses of the sun and moon, where they go and where they come, and their glorious return, and how one is superior to the other, and their stately orbit, and how they do not leave their orbit, and they add nothing to their orbit

and they take nothing from it, and they keep faith with each other, in accordance with the oath by which they are bound together.

7 And first the sun goes out and traverses his path according to the commandment of the Lord of spirits, and mighty is His name for ever and ever. And after that I saw the invisible and the visible path of the moon, and she accomplishes the course of her path in that place by day and by night-the one holding a position opposite to the other before the Lord of spirits. And they give thanks and praise and rest not; but their thanksgiving is for ever and ever.

8 For the sun makes many revolutions for a blessing or a curse, and the course of the path of the moon is light to the righteous and darkness to the sinners in the name of the Lord, who made a separation between the light and the darkness, and divided the spirits of men and strengthened the spirits of the righteous, in the name of His righteousness.

9 For no angel hinders and no power is able to hinder; for He appoints a judge for them all and He judges them all Himself.

[Chapter 42]

1 Wisdom found no place where she might dwell; then a dwelling-place was assigned her in heavens.

2 Wisdom went out to make her dwelling among the children of men, and found no dwelling-place. Wisdom returned to her place, and took her seat among the angels.

3 And unrighteousness went out from her storehouses. She found those she did not seek, and dwelt with them, (she sought no one in particular but found a place...); as rain in a desert and dew on a thirsty land.

[Chapter 43]

1 And I saw other lightning and the stars of heaven, and I saw how He called them all by their names and they obeyed Him.

2 And I saw how they are weighed in a righteous balance according to their proportions of light: I saw the width of their spaces and the day of their appearing, and how their revolution produces lightning:

3 And I saw their revolution according to the number of the angels, and how they keep faith with each other. And I asked the angel who went with me who showed me what was hidden:

4 'What are these?' And he said to me: 'The Lord of spirits has shown you their parable: these are the names of the holy who dwell on the earth and believe in the name of the Lord of spirits for ever and ever.'

[Chapter 44]

1 Also another phenomenon I saw in regard to the lightning: how some of the stars arise and become lightning and cannot part with their new form.

[Chapter 45]

1 And this is the second Parable: concerning those who deny the name of the dwelling of the holy ones and the Lord of spirits.

2 They shall not ascend to heaven, and they shall not come on the earth: Such shall be the lot of the sinners who have denied the name of the Lord of spirits, who are preserved for the day of suffering and tribulation.

3 On that day My Elect One shall sit on the throne of glory and shall try the works of the righteous, and their places of rest shall be innumerable. And their souls shall grow strong within them when they see My Elect One, And those who have called on My glorious name:

4 Then will I cause My Elect One to dwell among them. I will transform heaven and make it an eternal blessing and light,

5 And I will transform the earth and make it a blessing, and I will cause My elect ones to dwell on it. But the sinners and evil-doers shall not set foot on it.

6 For I have seen and satisfied My righteous ones with peace and have caused them to dwell before Me, but for the sinners there is judgment impending with Me, so that I shall destroy them from the face of the earth.

[Chapter 46]

1 And there I saw One whose face looked ancient. His head was white like wool, and with Him was another being whose countenance had the appearance of a man, and his face was full of graciousness, like one of the holy angels.

2 And I asked the angel who went with me and showed me all the hidden things, concerning that Son of Man, who he was, and where came from, and why he went with the Ancient One? And he answered and said to me:

3 "This is the son of Man who hath righteousness, with whom dwells righteousness, and who reveals all the treasures of that which is hidden, because the Lord of spirits hath chosen him, and whose lot has preeminence before the Lord of spirits in righteousness and is for ever.

4 And this Son of Man whom you have seen shall raise up the kings and the mighty from their seats, and the strong from their thrones and shall loosen the reins of the strong, and break the teeth of the sinners.

5 And he shall put down the kings from their thrones and kingdoms because they do not exalt and praise Him, nor humbly acknowledge who bestowed their kingdom on them.

6 And he shall make the strong hang their heads, and shall fill them with shame. And darkness shall be their dwelling, and worms shall be their bed, and they shall have no hope of rising from their beds, because they do not exalt the name of the Lord of spirits."

7 They raise their hands against the Most High and tread on the earth and dwell on it and all their deeds manifest unrighteousness. Their power rests on their riches, and their faith is in the gods which they have made with their hands. They deny the name of the Lord of spirits,

8 And they persecute the houses of His congregations, and the faithful who depend on the name of the Lord of Spirits.

[Chapter 47]

1 In those days the prayer of the righteous shall have ascended, and the blood of the righteous from the earth shall be before the Lord of spirits.

2 In those days the holy ones who dwell above in heavens shall unite with one voice and supplicate and pray and praise, and give thanks and bless the name of the Lord of spirits on behalf of the blood of the righteous which has been shed, that the prayer of the righteous may not be in vain before the Lord of spirits, that they may have justice, and that they may not have to wait for ever.

3 In those days I saw the "Head of Days" when He seated himself on the throne of His glory, and the books of the living were opened before Him; and all His host which is in heaven above and His counselors stood before Him,

4 And the hearts of the holy were filled with joy because the number of the righteous had been offered, and the prayer of the righteous had been heard, and the blood of the righteous not been required before the Lord of spirits.

[Chapter 48]

1 And in that place I saw the spring of righteousness, which was inexhaustible. And around it were many springs of wisdom. And all the thirsty drank of them, and were filled with wisdom, and their dwellings were with the righteous and holy and elect.

2 And at that hour that Son of Man was named in the presence of the Lord of spirits. And his name was brought before the Head of Days.

3 Even before the sun and the signs were created, before the stars of heaven were made, His name was named before the Lord of spirits.

4 He shall be a staff to the righteous and they shall steady themselves and not fall. And he shall be the light of the Gentiles, and the hope of those who are troubled of heart.

5 All who dwell on earth shall fall down and worship before him, and will praise and bless and sing and celebrate the Lord of spirits.

6 And for this reason he has been chosen and hidden in front of (kept safe by) Him, before the creation of the world and for evermore.

7 And the wisdom of the Lord of spirits has revealed him to the holy and righteous; For he hath preserved the lot of the righteous, because they have hated and rejected this world of unrighteousness, and have hated all its works and ways in the name of the Lord of spirits. For in his name they are saved, and according to his good pleasure and it is He who has regard to their life.

8 In these days the kings of the earth and the strong who possess the land because of the works of their hands will be shamed, because on the day of their anguish and affliction they shall not be able to save themselves. And I will give them over into the hands of My elect.

9 As straw in the fire so shall they burn before the face of the holy; as lead in the water shall they sink before the face of the righteous, and no trace of them shall be found anymore.

10 And on the day of their affliction there shall be rest on the earth (because the evil ones will be destroyed), and before Him they shall fall down and not rise again, and there shall be no one to take them with his hands and raise them up; for they have denied the Lord of spirits and His Anointed. The name of the Lord of spirits be blessed.

[Chapter 49]

1 For wisdom is poured out like water, and glory will not fail before him ever.

2 For he is mighty in all the secrets of righteousness, and unrighteousness shall disappear like a shadow, and will no longer exist; because the Elect One stands before the Lord of spirits, and his glory is for ever and ever, and his might for all generations.

3 In him dwells the spirit of wisdom, and the spirit which gives insight, and the spirit of understanding and of might, and the spirit of those who have fallen asleep in righteousness.

4 And he shall judge the secret things, and no one shall be able to utter a lying or idle word before him, for he is the Elect One before the Lord of spirits according to His good pleasure.

[Chapter 50]

1 And in those days a change shall take place for the holy and elect, and the light of days shall abide on them, and glory and honor shall turn to the Holy.

2 On the day of trouble, affliction will be heaped on the evil. And the righteous shall be victorious in the name of the Lord of spirits. For He will do this to others that they may repent and turn away from the works of their hands.

3 They shall have no honor through the name of the Lord of spirits, but through His name they shall be saved, and the Lord of spirits will have compassion on them, for His mercy is great.

4 He is righteous also in His judgment, and in the presence of His glory unrighteousness also shall not stand: At His judgment the unrepentant shall perish before Him.

5 And from now on I will have no mercy on them, says the Lord of spirits.

[Chapter 51]

1 And in those days shall the earth also give back that which has been entrusted to it, and Sheol (the grave) also shall give back that which it has received, and hell shall give back that which it owes. For in those days the Elect One shall arise,

2 And he shall choose the righteous and holy from among them. For the day has drawn near that they should be saved.

3 And in those days the Elect One shall sit on His throne, and all the secrets of wisdom and counsel shall pour from His mouth, for the Lord of spirits hath given them to Him and has glorified Him.

4 In those days shall the mountains leap like rams, and the hills shall skip like lambs satisfied with milk, and the faces of all the angels in heaven shall be lighted up with joy.

5 And the earth shall rejoice, and the righteous shall dwell on it, and the elect shall walk on it.

[Chapter 52]

1 And after those days in that place where I had seen all the visions of that which is hidden, for I had been carried off in a whirlwind and they had borne me towards the west.

2 There my eyes saw all the secret things of heaven that shall be, a mountain of iron, and a mountain of copper, and a mountain of silver, and a mountain of gold, and a mountain of soft metal, and a mountain of lead.

3 And I asked the angel who went with me, saying, 'What things are these which I have seen in secret?'

4 And he said to me: 'All these things which you have seen shall serve the authority of His Messiah that he may be powerful and mighty on the earth.'

5 The angel of peace answered me saying: 'Wait a little while, and all secret things shall be revealed to you, things which surround the Lord of spirits.

6 And these mountains which your eyes have seen, the mountain of iron, and the mountain of copper, and the mountain of silver, and the mountain of gold, and the mountain of soft metal, and the mountain of lead, all of these shall be like wax before a fire in the presence of the Elect One. Like the water which streams down from above on those mountains, and they shall be weak under his feet.

7 And it shall come to pass in those days that none shall be saved, either by gold or by silver, and none will be able to save themselves or escape.

8 And there shall be no iron for war, nor materials for breastplates. Bronze shall be of no use, tin shall be worthless, and lead shall not be desired.

9 All these things shall be destroyed from the face of the earth, when the Elect One appears before the Lord of spirits.'

[Chapter 53]

1 There my eyes saw a deep valley with its mouth open, and all who dwell on the earth and sea and islands shall bring gifts and presents and tokens of homage to Him, but that deep valley shall not become full.

2 And their hands commit lawless deeds, and everything the righteous work at the sinners devour. The sinners shall be destroyed in front of the face of the Lord of spirits, and they shall be banished from off the face of His earth, and they shall perish for ever and ever.

3 For I saw all the angels of punishment abiding there and preparing all the instruments of Satan.

4 And I asked the angel of peace who went with me: 'For whom are they preparing these instruments?'

5 And he said to me: 'They prepare these for the kings and the powerful of this earth, that they may with them they be destroyed.

6 After this the Righteous and Elect One shall cause the house of His congregation to appear and from then on they shall hinder no more, in the name of the Lord of spirits.

7 And these mountains shall not stand as solid ground before His righteousness, but the hills shall be like springs of water, and the righteous shall have rest from the oppression of sinners.'

[Chapter 54]

1 And I looked and turned to another part of the earth, and saw there a deep valley with burning fire.

2 And they brought the kings and the powerful, and began to cast them into this deep valley.

3 And there my eyes saw how they made their instruments for them, iron chains of immeasurable weight.

4 And I asked the angel of peace who was with me, saying: 'For whom are these chains being prepared ?'

5 And he said to me: 'These are being prepared for the hosts of Azazel, so that they may take them and throw them into the bottom of the pit of hell, and they shall cover their jaws with rough stones as the Lord of spirits commanded.

6 And Michael, and Gabriel, and Raphael, and Phanuel shall take hold of them on that great day, and throw them into the burning furnace on that day, that the Lord of spirits may take vengeance on them for their unrighteousness in becoming servants to Satan and for leading astray those who live on the earth.'

7 And in those days, punishment will come from the Lord of spirits, and he will open all the storehouses of waters above heavens, and of the fountains which are under the surface of the earth.

8 And all the waters shall be come together (flow into or be joined) with the waters of heaven (above the sky), that which is above heavens is the masculine, and the water which is beneath the earth is the feminine.

9 And they shall destroy all who live on the dry land and those who live under the ends of heaven.

(Author's note: The previous verse refers to Noah's flood).

10 And when they have acknowledged the unrighteousness which they have done on the earth, by these they shall perish.

[Chapter 55]

1 And after that the Head of Days repented and said: 'I have destroyed all who dwell on the earth to no avail.'

2 And He swore by His great name: 'From now on I will not do this to all who dwell on the earth again, and I will set a sign in heaven: and this shall be a covenant of good faith between Me and them for ever, so long as heaven is above the earth. And this is in accordance with My command.

(Author's note: The previous verse refers to the rainbow).

3 When I have desired to take hold of them by the hand of the angels on the day of tribulation, anger, and pain because of this, I will cause My punishment and anger to abide on them, says God, the Lord of spirits.

4 You mighty kings who live on the earth, you shall have to watch My Elect One, sit on the throne of glory and judge Azazel, and all his associates, and all his hosts in the name of the Lord of spirits.'

[Chapter 56]

1 And I saw there the hosts of the angels of punishment going, and they held scourges and chains of iron and bronze.

2 And I asked the angel of peace who went with me, saying: 'To whom are these who hold the scourges going?'

3 And he said to me: 'Each one to the ones they have chosen and to their loved ones, that they may be cast into the chasm of the abyss in the valley.

4 And then that valley shall be filled with ones they chose and their loved ones, and the days of their lives shall be at an end, and the days of their leading astray shall no longer be remembered (counted).

5 In those days the angels shall return and gather together and throw themselves to the east on the Parthians and Medes. They shall stir up the kings, so that a spirit of unrest and disturbance will come on them, and they shall drive them from their thrones, that they may rush out like lions from their lairs, and as hungry wolves among their flocks.

(Author's note: The names of certain countries help set the date of the manuscript. Scholars believe, based on the names of the countries mentioned in Enoch that the book could not have been written prior to 250 B.C. since some countries did not exist before that date. One could add that the particular part of Enoch is the only thing dated, since the book consists of several disjointed parts.)

6 And they shall go up and trample the lands of My elect ones, and the land of His elect ones shall be before them a threshing-floor (trampled, barren ground and a highway).

7 But the city of my righteous ones shall be a hindrance to their horses, and they shall begin to fight among themselves, and their own right hand shall be strong against themselves, and a man shall not know his brother, nor a son his father or his mother, until there will be innumerable corpses because of their slaughter, and their punishment shall be not in vain.

8 In those days hell (Sheol) shall open its jaws, and they shall be swallowed up. Their destruction shall be final. Hell (Sheol) shall devour the sinners in the presence of the elect.'

REV 20:1 And I saw an angel come down from heaven, having the key of the bottomless pit and a great chain in his hand. 2 And he laid hold on the dragon, that old serpent, which is the Devil, and Satan, and bound him a thousand years.

[Chapter 57]

1 And it came to pass after this that I saw another host of chariots, and men riding on them. They were coming on the winds from the east, and from the west to the south.

2 The noise of their chariots was heard, and when this turmoil took place the holy ones from heaven watched it, and the pillars of the earth were shaken and moved, and the sound of it was heard from the one end of heaven to the other, in one day.

3 And all shall fall down and worship the Lord of spirits. This is the end of the second Parable.

[Chapter 58]

1 And I began to speak the third Parable concerning the righteous and elect.

2 Blessed are you, you righteous and elect, for glorious shall be your lot.

3 And the righteous shall be in the light of the sun, and the elect will be in the light of eternal life. The days of their life shall be unending, and the days of the holy will be without number.

4 And they shall seek the light and find righteousness with the Lord of spirits. Peace to the righteous in the name of the Eternal Lord!

5 And after this it shall be said to the holy in heaven that they should seek secrets of righteousness, and the destiny of faith. For it has become bright as the sun on earth, and the darkness is passed away.

6 And there shall be a light that never ends, and to a number of days they shall not come, for the darkness shall first have been destroyed, [And the light established before the Lord of spirits] and the light of righteousness established for ever before the Lord of spirits.

[Chapter 59]

1 In those days my eyes saw the secrets of the lightning, and of the lights, and they judge and execute their judgment, and they illuminate for a blessing or a curse as the Lord of spirits wills.

2 And there I saw the secrets of the thunder, and how when it resounds above in heaven, the sound thereof is heard, and he caused me to see the judgments executed on the earth, whether they are for well-being and blessing, or for a curse according to the word of the Lord of spirits.

3 And after that all the secrets of the lights and lightning were shown to me, and they lighten for blessing and for satisfying.

[Chapter 60] - Noah's Vision

1 In the year 500, in the seventh month, on the fourteenth day of the month in the life of Enoch, in that parable I saw how a mighty quaking made the heaven of heavens to quake, and the host of the Most High, and the angels, a thousand thousands and ten thousand times ten thousand, were disquieted with great foreboding.

2 And the Head of Days sat on the throne of His glory, and the angels and the righteous stood around Him.

3 And a great trembling seized me, and fear took hold of me, and my legs gave way, and I melted with weakness and I fell on my face.

4 And Michael sent another angel from among the holy ones and he raised me up, and when he had raised me up my spirit returned; for I had not been able to endure the look of this host, and the disturbance and the shaking of heaven.

5 And Michael said to me: 'Why are you upset with such a vision? Until this day, His mercy, and long-suffering has lasted toward those who dwell on the earth.'

6 And when the day, and the power, and the punishment, and the judgment come, which the Lord of spirits hath prepared for those who worship not the righteous law, and for those who deny the righteous judgment, and for those who take His name in vain, that day is prepared. It will be a covenant for the elect, but for sinners an inquisition. When the punishment of the Lord of spirits shall rest on them, it will not come in vain, and it shall slay the children with their mothers and the children with their fathers.

7 And on that day two monsters were separated from one another, a female monster named Leviathan, to dwell in the abyss of the ocean over the fountains of the waters;

8 And the male is named Behemoth, who occupied with his breast a wasted wilderness named Duidain, on the east of the garden where the elect and righteous dwell, where my (great) grandfather was taken up, the seventh from Adam, the first man whom the Lord of spirits created.

9 And I asked the other angel to show me the might of those monsters, how they were separated on one day and thrown, the one into the abyss of the sea, and the other to the earth's desert.

10 And he said to me: ' Son of man, you wish to know what is kept secret.'

11 And the other angel who went with me and showed me what was kept secret; told me what is first and last in heaven in the sky, and beneath the earth in the depth, and at the ends of heaven, and on the foundation of heaven.

12 And the storehouse of the winds, and how the winds are divided, and how they are weighed, and how the doors of the winds are calculated for each according to the power of the wind, and the power of the lights of the moon according to the power that is fitting; and the divisions of the stars according to their names, and how all the divisions are divided.

13 And the thunder according to the places where they fall, and all the divisions that are made among the lightning that it may light, and their host that they may at once obey.

14 For the thunder has places of rest which are assigned while it is waiting for its peal; and the thunder and lightning are inseparable, and although not one and undivided, they both go together in spirit and are not separate.

15 For when the lightning flashes, the thunder utters its voice, and the spirit enforces a pause during the peal, and divides equally between them; for the treasury of their peals is like the sand (of an hourglass), and each one of them as it peals is held in with a bridle, and turned back by the power of the spirit, and pushed forward according to the many parts of the earth.

16 And the spirit of the sea is masculine and strong, and according to the might of His strength He draws it back with a rein, and in like manner it is driven forward and disperses in the midst of all the mountains of the earth.

17 And the spirit of the hoar-frost is his own angel, and the spirit of the hail is a good angel. And the spirit of the snow has forsaken his storehouse because of his strength.

18 There is a special spirit there, and that which ascends from it is like smoke, and its name is frost. And the spirit of the mist is not united with them in their storehouse, but it has a special storehouse; for its course is glorious both in light and in darkness, and in winter and in summer, and in its storehouse is an angel.

19 And the spirit of the dew has its dwelling at the ends of heaven, and is connected with the storehouse of the rain, and its course is in winter and summer; and its clouds and the clouds of the mist are connected, and the one gives to the other.

20 And when the spirit of the rain goes out from its storehouse, the angels come and open the storehouse and lead it out, and when it is diffused over the whole earth it unites with the water on the earth.

21 And whenever it unites with the water on the earth, (for the waters are for those who live on the earth), they are (become) nourishment for the earth from the Most High who is in heaven.

22 Therefore there is a measurement for the rain, and the angels are in charge of it. And these things I saw towards the Garden of the Righteous.

23 And the Angel of Peace who was with me, said to me:

24 'These two monsters, prepared in accordance with the greatness of the Lord, will feed them the punishment of the Lord. And children will be killed with their mothers, and sons with their fathers.'

[Chapter 61]

1 And I saw in those days that long cords were given to those angels, and they took to themselves wings and flew, and they went towards the north.

2 I asked the angel, saying to him: 'Why have those angels who have cords taken flight?' And he said to me: 'They have gone to take measurements.'

3 And the angel who went with me said to me: 'These shall bring the measurements of the righteous, and the cords of the righteous to the righteous, that they may rely on the name of the Lord of spirits for ever and ever.

4 The elect shall begin to dwell with the elect, and those are the measurements which shall be given to faith and which shall strengthen righteousness.

5 And these measurements shall reveal all the secrets of the depths of the earth, and those who have been destroyed by the desert, and those who have been devoured by the beasts, and those who have been devoured by the fish of the sea, that they may return and rely on the day of the Elect One. For none shall be destroyed before the Lord of spirits, and none can be destroyed.

6 And all who dwell in heaven received a command and power and one voice and one light like to fire.

7 And they blessed Him with their first words and exalted and praised Him in their wisdom. And they were wise in utterance and in the spirit of life.

8 And the Lord of spirits placed the Elect One on the throne of glory. And he shall judge all the works of the holy above in heaven, and in the balance their deeds shall be weighed.

9 And when he shall lift up his face to judge their secret ways according to the word of the name of the Lord of spirits, and their path according to the way of the righteous judgment of the Lord of spirits; then they shall all speak with one voice and bless and glorify and exalt the name of the Lord of spirits.

10 And He will summon all the host of heavens, and all the holy ones above, and the host of God, the cherubim, seraphim and ophannim, and all the angels of power, and all the angels of principalities (angels that rule over other angels), and the Elect One, and the other powers on the earth and over the water.

11 On that day shall raise one voice, and bless and glorify and exalt in the spirit of faith, and in the spirit of wisdom, and in the spirit of patience, and in the spirit of mercy, and in the spirit of judgment and of peace, and in the spirit of goodness, and shall all say with one voice: "Blessed is He, and may the name of the Lord of spirits be blessed for ever and ever."

12 All who do not sleep above in heaven shall bless Him. All the holy ones who are in heaven shall bless Him; and all the elect who dwell in the garden of life, and every spirit who is able to bless, and glorify, and exalt, and praise Your blessed name, and to the extent of its ability all flesh shall glorify and bless Your name for ever and ever.

13 For great is the mercy of the Lord of spirits. He is long-suffering, and all His works and all that He has created He has revealed to the righteous and elect, in the name of the Lord of spirits.

[Chapter 62]

1 Thus the Lord commanded the kings and the mighty and the exalted, and those who dwell on the earth, and said: 'Open your eyes and lift up your horns if you are able to recognize the Elect One.'

2 And the Lord of spirits seated Him on the throne of His glory, and the spirit of righteousness was poured out on Him, and the word of His mouth slays all the sinners, and all the unrighteous are destroyed from in front of His face.

REV 19:15 And out of his mouth goeth a sharp sword, that with it he should smite the nations: and he shall rule them with a rod of iron: and he treadeth the winepress of the fierceness and wrath of Almighty God. 16 And he hath on his vesture and on his thigh a name written, KING OF KINGS, AND LORD OF LORDS.

3 And in that day all the kings and the mighty, and the exalted and those who hold the earth shall stand up and shall see and recognize that He sits on the throne of His glory, and that righteousness is judged before Him, and no lying word is spoken before Him.

4 Then pain will come on them as on a woman in labor, and she has pain in giving birth when her child enters the mouth of the womb, and she has pain in childbirth.

5 And one portion of them shall look at the other, and they shall be terrified, and they shall look downcast, and pain shall seize them, when they see that Son of Man sitting on the throne of His glory.

MAT 25:31 When the Son of Man shall come in His glory, and all the holy angels with Him, then shall He sit upon the throne of His glory:

6 And the kings and the mighty and all who possess the earth shall bless and glorify and exalt Him who rules over all, who was hidden.

7 For from the beginning the Son of Man was hidden, and the Most High preserved Him in the presence of His might, and revealed Him to the elect.

8 And the congregation of the elect and holy shall be sown, and all the elect shall stand before Him on that day.

9 And all the kings and the mighty and the exalted and those who rule the earth shall fall down before Him on their faces, and worship and set their hope on that Son of Man, and petition Him and supplicate for mercy at His hands.

10 Nevertheless that Lord of spirits will so press them that they shall heavily go out from His presence, and their faces shall be filled with shame, and the darkness grows deeper on their faces.

11 And He will deliver them to the angels for punishment, to execute vengeance on them because they have oppressed His children and His elect.

12 And they shall be a spectacle for the righteous and for His elect. They shall rejoice over them, because the wrath of the Lord of spirits rests on them, and His sword is drunk with their blood.

13 The righteous and elect shall be saved on that day, and they shall never again see the face of the sinners and unrighteous.

14 And the Lord of spirits will abide over them, and they shall eat, lie down and rise up with the Son of Man for ever and ever.

15 The righteous and elect shall have risen from the earth, and ceased to be downcast and they will have been clothed with garments of life.

16 And these shall be the garments of life from the Lord of spirits; they shall not wear out nor will your glory pass away from before the Lord of spirits.

[Chapter 63]

1 In those days shall the mighty and the kings who possess the earth beg Him to grant them a little respite from His angels of punishment to whom they were delivered, that they might fall down and worship before the Lord of spirits, and confess their sins before Him.

2 And they shall bless and glorify the Lord of spirits, and say: 'Blessed is the Lord of spirits and the Lord of kings, and the Lord of the mighty and the Lord of the rich, and the Lord of glory and the Lord of wisdom,

3 And every secret is revealed in front of you. Your power is from generation to generation, and your glory for ever and ever. Deep and innumerable are all your secrets, and your righteousness is beyond reckoning.

4 We have now learned that we should glorify and bless the Lord of kings and Him who is King over all kings.'

5 And they shall say: 'Would that we had a respite to glorify and give thanks and confess our faith before His glory!

6 And now we long for a little respite but find it not. We are driven away and obtain it not: And light has vanished from before us, and darkness is our dwelling-place for ever and ever;

7 Because we have not believed in Him nor glorified the name of the Lord of spirits, but our hope was in the scepter of our kingdom, and in our own glory.

8 In the day of our suffering and tribulation He does not save and we find no respite for confession that our Lord is true in all His works, and in His judgments and His justice, and His judgments have no respect of persons. We pass away from before His face on account of our works, and all our sins are judged in (in comparison to) righteousness.'

10 Now they shall say to themselves: 'Our souls are full of unrighteous gain, but what we have gained does not prevent us from descending from the midst of our worldly gain into the torment (burden) of Hell (Sheol).'

11 And after that their faces shall be filled with darkness and shame before that Son of Man, and they shall be driven from His presence, and the sword shall abide before His face in their midst.

12 Thus spoke the Lord of spirits: 'This is the ordinance and judgment with respect to the mighty and the kings and the exalted and those who possess the earth before the Lord of spirits.'

[Chapter 64]

1 And other forms I saw hidden in that place.

2 I heard the voice of the angel saying: 'These are the angels who descended to the earth, and revealed what was hidden to the children of men and seduced the children of men into committing sin.'

[Chapter 65]

1 And in those days Noah saw the earth that it had sunk down and its destruction was near.

2 And he arose from there and went to the ends of the earth, and cried aloud to his grandfather, Enoch.

3 And Noah said three times with an embittered voice: "Hear me, hear me, hear me." And I said to him: 'Tell me what it is that is falling out on the earth that the earth is in such evil plight and shaken, lest perchance I shall perish with it?'

4 And there was a great disturbance on the earth, and a voice was heard from heaven, and I fell on my face. And Enoch my grandfather came and stood by me, and said to me: 'Why have you cried to me with a bitter cry and weeping?'

5 A command has gone out from the presence of the Lord concerning those who dwell on the earth that their ruin is accomplished because they have learned all the secrets of the angels, and all the violence of the Satans (deceivers, accusers);

6 And all their powers - the most secret ones - and all the power of those who practice sorcery, and the power of witchcraft, and the power of those who make molten images for the whole earth.

7 And how silver is produced from the dust of the earth, and how soft metal originates in the earth.

8 For lead and tin are not produced from the earth like the first; it is a fountain that produces them;

9 And an angel stands in it, and that angel is preeminent.' And after that my grandfather Enoch took hold of me by my hand and lifted me up, and said to me:

10 'Go, for I have asked the Lord of spirits about this disturbance on the earth.' And He said to me: "Because of their unrighteousness their judgment has been determined and shall not be withheld by Me for ever. Because of the sorceries which they have searched out and learned, the earth and those who dwell on it shall be destroyed."

11 And from these, they have no place of repentance for ever, because they have shown them what was hidden, and they are the damned. But as for you, my son, the Lord of spirits knows that you are pure and guiltless of this reproach concerning the secrets.

12 And He has destined your name to be among the holy, and will preserve you among those who dwell on the earth; and has destined your righteous seed both for kingship and for great honors, and from your seed shall proceed a fountain of the righteous and holy without number for ever.

[Chapter 66]

1 And after that he showed me the angels of punishment who are prepared to come and let loose all the powers of the waters which are beneath in the earth in order to bring judgment and destruction on all who dwell on the earth.

2 And the Lord of spirits gave commandment to the angels who were going out, that they should not cause the waters to rise but should hold them in check; for those angels were in charge of the forces of the waters.

3 And I went away from the presence of Enoch.

[Chapter 67]

1 And in those days the word of God came to me, and He said to me: 'Noah, your lot has come up before Me, a lot without blame, a lot of love and righteousness.

2 And now the angels are making a wooden structure, and when they have completed that task I will place My hand on it and preserve it (keep it safe), and there shall come out of it the seed of life, and a change shall set in so that the earth will not remain without inhabitants.

3 And I will establish your seed before me for ever and ever, and I will spread abroad those who dwell with you; and the face of the earth will be fruitful. They shall be blessed and multiply on the earth in the name of the Lord.'

4 And He will imprison those angels, who have shown unrighteousness, in that burning valley which my grandfather Enoch had formerly shown to me in the west among the mountains of gold and silver and iron and soft metal and tin.

5 And I saw that valley in which there was a great earth quake and a tidal waves of the waters.

6 And when all this took place, from that fiery molten metal and from the convulsion thereof in that place, there was a smell of sulfur produced, and it was connected with those waters, and that valley of the angels who had led mankind astray burned beneath that ground.

7 And there were streams of fire throughout the valley, where these angels are punished who had led astray those who dwell on the earth.

8 But those waters shall in those days serve for the kings and the mighty and the exalted, and those who dwell on the earth, for the healing of the body, but for the punishment of the spirit. Their spirit is full of lust, that they will be punished in their body, for they have denied the Lord of spirits. They will see their punishment daily, and yet, they believe not in His name.

9 There will be a relationship between the punishment and change. As their bodies burn, a change will take place in their spirit for ever and ever; for before the Lord of spirits none shall utter an idle word.

10 For the judgment shall come on them, because they believe in the lust of their body and deny the Spirit of the Lord.

11 And the waters will change in those days; for when those angels are punished in these waters, the springs shall change, and when the angels ascend, this water of the springs shall change their temperature and become cold.

12 And I heard Michael answering and saying: 'This judgment in which the angels are judged is a testimony for the kings and the mighty who possess the earth.'

13 Because these waters of judgment minister to the healing of the body of the kings and the lust of their bodies; therefore they will not see and will not believe that those waters will change and become a fire which burns for ever.

[Chapter 68]

1 And after that my grandfather Enoch gave me the explanations of all the secrets in the book of the Parables which had been given to him, and he put them together for me in the words of the book of the Parables.

2 And on that day Michael answered Raphael and said: 'The power of the spirit grips me and makes me tremble because of the severity of the judgment of the secrets, and the judgment of the angels. Who can endure the severe judgment which has been executed, and before which they melt away?'

3 And Michael answered again, and said to Raphael: 'Who would not have a softened heart concerning it, and whose mind would not be troubled by this judgment against them because of those who have led them out?'

4 And it came to pass when he stood before the Lord of spirits, Michael said thus to Raphael: 'I will not defend them under the eye of the Lord; for the Lord of spirits has been angry with them because they act as if they were the Lord.'

5 Therefore all that is hidden shall come on them for ever and ever; for no other angel or man shall have his portion in this judgment, but they alone have received their judgment for ever and ever.

[Chapter 69]

1 And after this judgment I will terrify and make them tremble because they have shown this to those who dwell on the earth.

2 And behold the names of those angels: the first of them is Samjaza; the second Artaqifa; and the third Armen, the fourth Kokabe, the fifth Turael; the sixth Rumjal; the seventh Danjal; the eighth Neqael; the ninth Baraqel; the tenth Azazel; the eleventh Armaros; the twelfth Batarjal; the thirteenth Busasejal; the fourteenth Hananel; the fifteenth Turel; and the sixteenth Simapesiel; the seventeenth Jetrel; the eighteenth Tumael; the nineteenth Turel; the twentieth Rumael; the twenty-first Azazyel;

3 And these are the chiefs of their angels and their names, and their leaders over hundreds, and leaders over fifties, and leaders over tens.

4 The name of the first Jeqon, that is, the one who led astray the sons of God, and brought them down to the earth, and led them astray through the daughters of men.

5 And the second was named Asbeel; he imparted to the holy sons of God evil counsel, and led them astray so that they defiled their bodies with the daughters of men.

6 And the third was named Gadreel; it is he who showed the children of men all the blows of death, and he led astray Eve, and showed the weapons of death to the sons of men; the shield and the coat of mail, and the sword for battle, and all the weapons of death to the children of men.

7 And from his hand they have proceeded against those who dwell on the earth from that day and for evermore.

8 And the fourth was named Penemue; he taught the children of men the bitter and the sweet, and he taught them all the secrets of their wisdom.

9 And he instructed mankind in writing with ink and paper, and thereby many sinned from eternity to eternity and until this day.

10 For men were not created for the purpose of confirming their good faith with pen and ink.

11 For men were created exactly like the angels, to the intent that they should continue pure and righteous; and death, which destroys everything, should not have taken hold of them, but through their knowledge they are perishing, and through this, the power of death consumes them.

12 And the fifth was named Kasdeja; this is he who showed the children of men all the wicked smitings (blows) of spirits and demons, and the smitings (blows) of the embryo in the womb, that it may pass away, and the smitings (blows) of the soul the bites of the serpent, and the smitings (blows) which befall through the midday heat, the son of the serpent named Taba'et.

13 And this is the task of Kasbeel, the chief of the oath which he showed to the holy ones when he dwelt high above in glory, and its name is Biqa.

14 This (angel) requested Michael to show him the hidden name, that he might enunciate it in the oath,

15 So that those might quake before that name and oath who revealed all that was in secret to the children of men. And this is the power of this oath, for it is powerful and strong, and he placed this oath Akae in the hand of (under the control of) Michael.

16 And these are the secrets of this oath (God's promise, word) that heaven was suspended before the world was created, and for ever, and they are strong through his oath (word, promise).

17 And through it the earth was founded on the water, and from the secret recesses of the mountains come beautiful waters, from the creation of the world and to eternity.

18 And through that oath the sea was created, and as its foundation He set for it the sand against the time of its anger (rage) that it dare not pass beyond it from the creation of the world to eternity.

19 And through that oath are the depths made fast, and abide and stir not from their place from eternity to eternity.

20 And through that oath the sun and moon complete their course, and deviate not from their ordinance from eternity to eternity.

21 And through that oath the stars complete their course, and He calls them by their names, and they answer Him from eternity to eternity.

22 [And in like manner the spirits of the water, and of the winds, and of all kinds of spirits, and (their) paths from all the quarters of the winds respond to His command.]

(Author's note: Verse 22 is not complete in some translations.)

23 And there are preserved the voices of the thunder and the light of the lightning: and there are preserved the storehouses of the hail and the storehouses of the hoarfrost,

24 And the storehouses of the mist, and the storehouses of the rain and the dew. And all these believe and give thanks before the Lord of spirits, and glorify (Him) with all their power, and their food is in every act of thanksgiving; they thank and glorify and exalt the name of the Lord of spirits for ever and ever.

25 And this oath is mighty over them and through it they are preserved and their paths are preserved, and their course is not destroyed.

26 And there was great joy among them, and they blessed and glorified and exalted because the name of that Son of Man had been revealed to them.

27 And he sat on the throne of his glory, and the sum of judgment was given to the Son of Man. And he caused the sinners and all those who led the world astray to pass away and be destroyed from off the face of the earth.

28 They shall be bound with chains, and shut up and imprisoned in their place of assembly, and all their works vanish from the face of the earth.

29 And from that time forward, there shall be nothing corruptible; for that Son of Man has appeared, and has seated himself on the throne of his glory. And all evil shall pass away before his face, and the word of that Son of Man shall go out and be strong before the Lord of spirits.

[Chapter 70]

1 And it came to pass after this that during His lifetime His name was raised up to the Son of Man,

2 And to the Lord of spirits from among those who dwell on the earth.

3 And He was raised aloft on the chariots of the spirit and His name vanished among them. And from that day I was no longer numbered among them; and He placed me between the two winds, between the North and the West, where the angels took the cords to measure the place for the elect and righteous for me.

4 And there I saw the first fathers and the righteous who dwell in that place from the beginning.

[Chapter 71]

1 And it came to pass after this that my spirit was translated (carried off) and it ascended into heaven; and I saw the sons of the holy angels (sons) of God. They were walking on flames of fire; their garments were white, and their faces shone like snow.

2 And I saw two rivers of fire, and the light of that fire shone like hyacinth, and I fell on my face before the Lord of spirits.

3 And the angel Michael, one of the archangels, seized me by my right hand, and lifted me up and led me out into all the secrets, and he showed me all the secrets of righteousness.

4 And he showed me all the secrets of the ends of heaven, and all the storehouses of all the stars, and all the lights, from where they proceed before the face of the holy ones.

5 And he translated (carried) my spirit into heaven of heavens, and I saw there as it were built of crystals, and between those crystals tongues of living fire.

REV 21:10 And he carried me away in the spirit to a great and high mountain, and shewed me that great city, the holy Jerusalem, descending out of heaven from God, 11 Having the glory of God: and her light was like unto a stone most precious, even like a jasper stone, clear as crystal.

6 My spirit saw circle of fire binding around the house of fire, and on its four sides were rivers full of living fire, and they encircled that house.

7 And round about were seraphim, cherubim, and ophannim; and these are they who sleep not and guard the throne of His glory.

8 And I saw angels who could not be counted, a thousand thousands, and ten thousand times ten thousand, encircling that house. And Michael, and Raphael, and Gabriel, and Phanuel, and the holy angels who are in heaven above, go in and out of that house.

9 And they came out from that house, and Michael and Gabriel, Raphael and Phanuel, and many holy angels without number.

10 And with them the Head of Days, His head white and pure as wool, and His raiment indescribable.

11 And I fell on my face, and my whole body melted, and my spirit was (transformed) transfigured. And I cried with a loud voice in the spirit of power, and I blessed and glorified and exalted.

12 And these blessings which came from my mouth were very pleasing before that Head of Days.

13 And the Head of Days came with Michael and Gabriel, Raphael and Phanuel, and thousands and ten thousands of angels without number.

14 And the angel came to me and greeted me with his voice, and said to me 'This is the Son of Man who is born to righteousness, and righteousness abides over him, and the righteousness of the Head of Days forsakes him not.'

15 And he said to me: 'He proclaims to you peace in the name of the world to come; for from there peace has proceeded since the creation of the world, and it shall be with you for ever and for ever and ever.

JOHN 17:24 Father, I will that they also, whom thou hast given me, be with me where I am; that they may behold my glory, which thou hast given me: for thou lovest me before the foundation of the world.

16 And all shall walk in His ways since righteousness never forsook Him. Their dwelling-place shall be with Him and it will be their heritage, and they shall not be separated from Him forever and ever and ever.

17 And so there shall be length of days with the Son of Man, and the righteous shall have peace and an upright way in the name of the Lord of spirits for ever and ever.'

HEB 4:3 For we which have believed do enter into rest, as he said, As I have sworn in my wrath, if they shall enter into my rest: although the works were finished from the foundation of the world.

[Chapter 72]

1 The book of the courses of the luminaries of heaven, the relations of each, according to their name, origin, and months (dominion and seasons) which Uriel, the holy angel who was with me, who is their guide, showed me; and he showed me all their laws (regulations) exactly as they are, and how it is with each of the years of the world and to eternity, until the new creation is accomplished which endures until eternity.

2 And this is the first law of the luminaries: the luminary the Sun has its rising in the eastern doors of heaven, and its setting in the western doors of heaven.

3 And I saw six doors in which the sun rises, and six doors in which the sun sets and the moon rises and sets in these doors, and the leaders of the stars and those whom they lead: six in the east and six in the west, and all following each other in accurately corresponding order.

4 There were also many windows to the right and left of these doors. And first there goes out the great luminary, named the Sun, and his sphere (orbit, disc) is like the sphere (orbit, disc) of heaven, and he is quite filled with illuminating and heating fire.

5 The chariot on which he ascends, the wind drives, and the sun goes down from heaven and returns through the north in order to reach the east, and is so guided that he comes to the appropriate door and shines in the face of heaven.

6 In this way he rises in the first month in the great door, which is the fourth.

7 And in that fourth door from which the sun rises in the first month are twelve windows, from which proceed a flame when they are opened in their season.

8 When the sun rises in heaven, he comes out through that fourth door, thirty mornings in succession, and sets accurately in the fourth door in the west of the heaven.

9 And during this period the day becomes daily longer and nights grow shorter to the thirtieth morning.

10 On that day the day is longer than the night by a ninth part, and the day amounts exactly to ten parts and the night to eight parts.

11 And the sun rises from that fourth door, and sets in the fourth and returns to the fifth door of the east thirty mornings, and rises from it and sets in the fifth door.

12 And then the day becomes longer by two parts and amounts to eleven parts, and the night becomes shorter and amounts to seven parts.

13 And it returns to the east and enters into the sixth door, and rises and sets in the sixth door one-and-thirty mornings on account of its sign.

14 On that day the day becomes longer than the night, and the day becomes double the night, and the day becomes twelve parts, and the night is shortened and becomes six parts.

15 And the sun mounts up to make the day shorter and the night longer, and the sun returns to the east and enters into the sixth door, and rises from it and sets thirty mornings.

16 And when thirty mornings are accomplished, the day decreases by exactly one part, and becomes eleven parts, and the night seven.

17 And the sun goes out from that sixth door in the west, and goes to the east and rises in the fifth door for thirty mornings, and sets in the west again in the fifth western door.

18 On that day the day decreases by two parts, and amounts to ten parts and the night to eight parts.

19 And the sun goes out from that fifth door and sets in the fifth door of the west, and rises in the fourth door for one-and-thirty mornings on account of its sign, and sets in the west.

20 On that day the day becomes equal with the night in length, and the night amounts to nine parts and the day to nine parts.

21 And the sun rises from that door and sets in the west, and returns to the east and rises thirty mornings in the third door and sets in the west in the third door.

22 And on that day the night becomes longer than the day, and night becomes longer than night, and day shorter than day until the thirtieth morning, and the night amounts exactly to ten parts and the day to eight parts.

23 And the sun rises from that third door and sets in the third door in the west and returns to the east, and for thirty mornings rises in the second door in the east, and in like manner sets in the second door in the west of heaven.

24 And on that day the night amounts to eleven parts and the day to seven parts.

25 And the sun rises on that day from that second door and sets in the west in the second door, and returns to the east into the first door for one-and-thirty mornings, and sets in the first door in the west of heaven.

26 And on that day the night becomes longer and amounts to the double of the day: and the night amounts exactly to twelve parts and the day to six.

(Author's note: The day is divided into 18 sections of 90 minutes each.)

27 And the sun has traversed the divisions of his orbit and turns again on those divisions of his orbit, and enters that door thirty mornings and sets also in the west opposite to it.

28 And on that night has the night decreased in length by a ninth part, and the night has become eleven parts and the day seven parts.

29 And the sun has returned and entered into the second door in the east, and returns on those his divisions of his orbit for thirty mornings, rising and setting.

30 And on that day the night decreases in length, and the night amounts to ten parts and the day to eight.

31 And on that day the sun rises from that door, and sets in the west, and returns to the east, and rises in the third door for one-and-thirty mornings, and sets in the west of heaven.

32 On that day the night decreases and amounts to nine parts, and the day to nine parts, and the night is equal to the day and the year is exactly as to its days three hundred and sixty-four.

33 And the length of the day and of the night, and the shortness of the day and of the night arise through the course of the sun these distinctions are separated.

34 So it comes that its course becomes daily longer, and its course nightly shorter.

35 And this is the law and the course of the great luminary which is named the sun, and his return as often as he returns sixty times and rises, for ever and ever.

36 And that which rises is the great luminary, and is so named according to its appearance, according as the Lord commanded.

37 As he rises, so he sets and decreases not, and rests not, but runs day and night, and his light is sevenfold brighter than that of the moon; but in regard to size, they are both equal.

[Chapter 73]

1 And after this law I saw another law dealing with the smaller luminary, which is named the Moon.

2 And her orbit is like the sphere (orbit, disc) of heaven, and her chariot in which she rides is driven by the wind, and light is given to her in measurement.

3 And her rising and setting change every month and her days are like the days of the sun, and when her light is uniformly (completely) full it amounts to the seventh part of the light of the sun.

4 And thus she rises. And her first phase in the east comes out on the thirtieth morning and on that day she becomes visible, and constitutes for you the first phase of the moon on the thirtieth day together with the sun in the door where the sun rises.

5 And the one half of her goes out by a seventh part, and her whole disc is empty, without light, with the exception of one-seventh part of it, and the fourteenth part of her light.

6 And when she receives one-seventh part of the half of her light, her light amounts to one-seventh part and the half thereof.

7 And she sets with the sun, and when the sun rises the moon rises with him and receives the half of one part of light, and in that night in the beginning of her morning in the beginning of the lunar day the moon sets with the sun, and is invisible that night with the fourteen parts and the half of one of them.

8 And she rises on that day with exactly a seventh part, and comes out and recedes from the rising of the sun, and in her remaining days she becomes bright in the remaining thirteen parts.

[Chapter 74]

1 And I saw another course, a law for her, and how according to that law she performs her monthly revolution.

2 And all these Uriel, the holy angel who is the leader of them all, showed to me, and their positions, and I wrote down their positions as he showed them to me, and I wrote down their months as they were, and the appearance of their lights until fifteen days were accomplished.

3 In single seventh parts she accomplishes all her light in the east, and in single seventh parts accomplishes all her darkness in the west.

4 And in certain months she alters her settings, and in certain months she pursues her own peculiar course.

5 In two months the moon sets with the sun: in those two middle doors the third and the fourth.

6 She goes out for seven days, and turns about and returns again through the door where the sun rises, and all her light is full; and she recedes from the sun, and in eight days enters the sixth door from which the sun goes out.

7 And when the sun goes out from the fourth door she goes out seven days, until she goes out from the fifth and turns back again in seven days into the fourth door and accomplishes all her light; and she recedes and enters into the first door in eight days.

8 And she returns again in seven days into the fourth door from which the sun goes out.

9 Thus I saw their positions, how the moons rose and the sun set in those days.

10 And if five years are added together the sun has an excess of thirty days, and all the days which accrue to it for one of those five years, when they are full, amount to 364 days.

11 And an excess of the sun and of the stars amounts to six days; in five years six days every year come to 30 days, and the moon falls behind the sun and stars to the number of 30 days.

12 And the sun and the stars bring in all the years exactly, so that they do not advance or delay their position by a single day to eternity; but complete the years with perfect justice in 364 days.

13 In three years there are 1,092 days, and in five years 1,820 days, so that in eight years there are 2,912 days.

14 For the moon alone the days amount in three years to 1,062 days, and in five years she falls 50 days behind to the sum of 1,770 there is five to be added 1,000 and 62 days.

15 And in five years there are 1,770 days, so that for the moon the days six in eight years amount to 21,832 days.

16 For in eight years she falls behind to the amount of 80 days, all the days she falls behind in eight years are 80.

17 And the year is accurately completed in conformity with their world-stations and the stations of the sun, which rise from the doors through which the sun rises and sets 30 days.

[Chapter 75]

1 And the leaders of the heads of the (ten) thousands, who are in charge of the whole creation and over all the stars, have also to do with the four days of the year which are not counted in the yearly calendar, being not separated from their office, according to the reckoning of the year, and these render service on the four days which are not counted in the reckoning of the year.

2 And because of them men go wrong in them, for those luminaries truly render service to the stations of the world, one in the first door, one on the third door of heaven, one in the fourth door, and one in the sixth door, and the exactness of the year is accomplished through its separate three hundred and sixty-four stations.

3 For the signs and the times and the years and the days the angel Uriel showed to me, whom the Lord of glory hath set for ever over all the luminaries of heaven, in heaven and in the world, that they should rule on the face of heaven and be seen on the earth, and be leaders for the day via the sun and the night via the moon, and stars, and all the ministering creatures which make their revolution in all the chariots of heaven.

4 In like manner, twelve doors Uriel showed me, open in the sphere (disc) of the sun's chariot in heaven, through which the rays of the sun break out; and from them is warmth diffused over the earth, when they are opened at their appointed seasons.

5 And there are openings for the wind and the spirit of dew that when they are opened, stand open in heaven at the ends of the earth.

6 As for the twelve doors in the heaven, at the ends of the earth, out of which go out the sun, moon, and stars, and all the works of heaven in the east and in the west; there are many windows open to the left and right of them,

7 And one window at its appointed season produces warmth, corresponding to the doors from which the stars come out as He has commanded them; and in which they are set, corresponding to their number.

8 And I saw chariots in heaven, running in the world, above those doors in which the stars that never set.

9 And one is larger than all the rest, and it is that that makes its course through the entire world.

[Chapter 76]

1 At the ends of the earth I saw twelve doors open to all quarters of heaven, from which the winds go out and blow over the earth.

2 Three of them are open on the face of heaven, and three in the west; and three on the right of heaven, and three on the left.

3 And the three first are those of the east, and three are of the north, and three, after those on the left, of the south, and three of the west.

4 Through four of these come winds of blessing and prosperity (peace), and from those eight come hurtful winds; when they are sent, they bring destruction on all the earth and the water on it, and on all who dwell on it, and on everything which is in the water and on the land.

5 And the first wind from those doors, called the east wind, comes out through the first door which is in the east, inclining towards the south; from it desolation, drought, heat, and destruction come out .

6 And through the second door in the middle comes what is fitting (right, correct), and there come rain and fruitfulness and prosperity and dew. And through the third door which lies toward the north comes cold and drought.

7 And after these, comes out the south winds through three doors; through the first door of them inclining to the east comes out a hot wind.

8 And through the middle door next to it there comes out fragrant smells, and dew and rain, and prosperity and health.

9 And through the third door which lies to the west dew comes out and also rain, locusts and desolation.

10 And from the seventh door in the east comes the north winds, and dew, rain, locusts and desolation.

11 And from the center door come health and rain and dew and prosperity; and through the third door in the west come cloud and hoar-frost, and snow and rain, and dew and locusts.

12 And after these came the four west winds; through the first door adjoining the north come out dew and hoar-frost, and cold and snow and frost.

13 And from the center door come out dew and rain, and prosperity and blessing.

14 And through the last door which adjoins the south, come drought and desolation, and burning and destruction. And the twelve doors of the four quarters of heaven are therewith completed, and all their laws and all their plagues and all their benefactions have I shown to you, my son Methuselah.

[Chapter 77]

1 And the first quarter is called the east, because it is the first; and the second, the south, because the Most High will descend there. From there will He who is blessed for ever descend.

2 And the west quarter is named the diminished, because there all the luminaries of the heaven wane and go down.

3 And the fourth quarter, named the north, is divided into three parts: the first of them is for the dwelling of men; and the second contains seas of water, and the abyss (deep) and forests and rivers, and darkness and clouds; and the third part contains the garden of righteousness.

4 I saw seven high mountains, higher than all the mountains which are on the earth: and from here comes hoar-frost, and days, seasons, and years pass away.

5 I saw seven rivers on the earth larger than all the rivers. One of them coming from the west pours its waters into the Great Sea.

6 And these two come from the north to the sea and pour their waters into the Erythraean Sea in the east.

7 And the remaining four come out on the side of the north to their own sea, two of them to the Erythraean Sea, and two into the Great Sea and some say they discharge themselves there into the desert.

8 I saw seven great islands in the sea and in the mainland, two in the mainland and five in the Great Sea.

[Chapter 78]

1 And the names of the sun are the following: the first Orjares, and the second Tomas.

2 And the moon has four names: the first name is Asonja, the second Ebla, the third Benase, and the fourth Erae.

3 These are the two great luminaries; their spheres (disc) are like the sphere (disc) of the heaven, and the size of the spheres (disc) of both is alike.

4 In the sphere (disc) of the sun there are seven portions of light which are added to it more than to the moon, and in fixed measurements it is transferred until the seventh portion of the sun is exhausted.

5 And they set and enter the doors of the west, and make their revolution by the north, and come out through the eastern doors on the face of heaven.

6 And when the moon rises one-fourteenth part appears in heaven, and on the fourteenth day the moon's light becomes full.

7 And fifteen parts of light are transferred to her until the fifteenth day when her light is full, according to the sign of the year, and she becomes fifteen parts, and the moon grows by an additional fourteenth parts.

8 And as the moon's waning decreases on the first day to fourteen parts of her light, on the second to thirteen parts of light, on the third to twelve, on the fourth to eleven, on the fifth to ten, on the sixth to nine, on the seventh to eight, on the eighth to seven, on the ninth to six, on the tenth to five, on the eleventh to four, on the twelfth to three, on the thirteenth to two, on the fourteenth to the half of a seventh, and all her remaining light disappears wholly on the fifteenth.

9 And in certain months the month has twenty-nine days and once twenty-eight.

10 And Uriel showed me another law: when light is transferred to the moon, and on which side it is transferred to her by the sun.

11 During all the period during which the moon is growing in her light, she is transferring it to herself when opposite to the sun during fourteen days her light is full in heaven, and when she is ablaze throughout, her light is full in heaven.

12 And on the first day she is called the new moon, for on that day the light rises on her.

13 She becomes full moon exactly on the day when the sun sets in the west, and from the east she rises at night, and the moon shines the whole night through until the sun rises over against her and the moon is seen over against the sun.

14 On the side whence the light of the moon comes out, there again she wanes until all the light vanishes and all the days of the month are at an end, and her sphere (disc) is empty, void of light.

15 And three months she makes of thirty days, and at her time she makes three months of twenty-nine days each, in which she accomplishes her waning in the first period of time, and in the first door for one hundred and seventy-seven days.

16 And in the time of her going out she appears for three months consisting of thirty days each, and she appears for three months consisting of twenty-nine each.

17 By night she looks like a man for twenty days each time, and by day she appears like heaven, and there is nothing else in her save her light.

[Chapter 79]

1 And now, my son Methuselah, I have shown you everything, and the law of all the stars of heaven is completed.

2 And he showed me all the laws of these for every day, and for every season of every rule, and for every year, and for its going out, and for the order prescribed to it every month and every week.

3 And the waning of the moon which takes place in the sixth door, for in this sixth door her light is accomplished, and after that there is the beginning of the waning.

4 And the waning which takes place in the first door in its season, until one hundred and seventy-seven days are accomplished, calculated according to weeks, twenty-five weeks and two days.

5 She falls behind the sun and the order of the stars exactly five days in the course of one period, and when this place which you see has been traversed.

6 Such is the picture and sketch of every luminary which Uriel the archangel, who is their leader, showed to me.

[Chapter 80]

1 And in those days the angel Uriel answered and said to me: 'Behold, I have shown you everything, Enoch, and I have revealed everything to you that you should see this sun and this moon, and the leaders of the stars of heaven and all those who turn them, their tasks and times and departures.

2 And in the days of the sinners the years shall be shortened, and their seed shall be tardy on their lands and fields, and all things on the earth shall alter, and shall not appear in their time. And the rain shall be kept back, and heaven shall withhold it.

3 And in those times the fruits of the earth shall be backward, and shall not grow in their time, and the fruits of the trees shall be withheld in their time.

4 And the moon shall alter her customs, and not appear at her time.

5 And in those days the sun shall be seen and he shall journey in the evening on the extremity of the great chariot in the west and shall shine more brightly than accords with the order of light.

6 And many rulers of the stars shall transgress their customary order. And these shall alter their orbits and tasks, and not appear at the seasons prescribed to them.

7 And the whole order of the stars shall be concealed from the sinners, and the thoughts of those on the earth shall err concerning them, and they shall be altered from all their ways, they shall err and take them to be gods.

8 And evil shall be multiplied on them, and punishment shall come on them so as to destroy all.'

[Chapter 81]

1 And he said to me: 'Enoch, look at these heavenly tablets and read what is written on them, and mark every individual fact.'

2 And I looked at the heavenly tablets, and read everything which was written on it and understood everything, and read the book of all the deeds of mankind, and of all the children of flesh; that shall be on the earth to the end of generations.

3 And I blessed the great Lord the King of glory for ever, in that He has made all the works of the world, and I exalted the Lord because of His patience, and blessed Him because of the children of men (sons of Abraham).

4 And then I said: 'Blessed is the man who dies in righteousness and goodness, concerning whom there is no book of unrighteousness written, and against whom no day of judgment shall be found.'

5 And the seven holy ones brought me and placed me on the earth before the door of my house, and said to me: 'Declare everything to your son Methuselah, and show to all your children that no flesh is righteous in the sight of the Lord, for He is their Creator.

6 For one year we will leave you with your son, until you give your last commands, that you may teach your children and record it for them, and testify to all your children; and in the second year they shall take you from their midst.

7 Let your heart be strong, for the good shall proclaim righteousness to the good; the righteous shall rejoice with the righteous, and shall wish one another well.

8 But the sinners shall die with the sinners, and the apostate shall go down with the apostate.

9 And those who practice righteousness shall die on account of the deeds of men, and be taken away on account of the deeds of the godless.'

10 And in those days they finished speaking to me, and I came to my people, blessing the Lord of the world.

[Chapter 82]

1 And now, my son Methuselah, all these things I am recounting to you and writing down for you! And I have revealed to you everything, and given you books concerning all these; so, my son Methuselah, preserve the books from your father's hand, and see that you deliver them to the generations of the world.

2 I have given wisdom to you and to your children, and those children to come, that they may give it to their children for generations. This wisdom namely that passes their understanding.

3 And those who understand it shall not sleep, but shall listen that they may learn this wisdom, and it shall please those that eat thereof better than good food.

4 Blessed are all the righteous, blessed are all those who walk in the way of righteousness and sin not as the sinners, in the numbering of all their days in which the sun traverses heaven, entering into and departing from the doors for thirty days with the heads of thousands of the order of the stars, together with the four which are within the calendar which divide the four portions of the year, which lead them and enter with them four days.

5 Owing to them men shall be at fault and not count them in the whole number of days of the year. Men shall be at fault, and not recognize them accurately.

6 For they belong to the calculations of the year and are truly recorded therein for ever, one in the first door and one in the third, and one in the fourth and one in the sixth, and the year is completed in three hundred and sixty-four days.

7 And the account of it is accurate and the recorded counting thereof is exact; for the luminaries, and months and festivals, and years and days, has Uriel shown and revealed to me, to whom the Lord of the whole creation of the world hath subjected the host of heaven.

8 And he has power over night and day in heaven to cause the light to shine on men via the sun, moon, and stars, and all the powers of the heaven which revolve in their circular chariots.

9 And these are the orders of the stars, which set in their places, and in their seasons and festivals and months.

10 And these are the names of those who lead them, who watch that they enter at their times, in their orders, in their seasons, in their months, in their periods of dominion, and in their positions.

11 Their four leaders who divide the four parts of the year enter first; and after them the twelve leaders of the orders who divide the months; and for the three hundred and sixty days there are heads over thousands who divide the days; and for the four days in the calendar there are the leaders which divide the four parts of the year.

12 And these heads over thousands are interspersed between leader and leader, each behind a station, but their leaders make the division.

13 And these are the names of the leaders who divide the four parts of the year which are ordained:

14 Milki'el, Hel'emmelek, and Mel'ejal, and Narel. And the names of those who lead them: Adnar'el, and Ijasusa'el, and 'Elome'el.

15 These three follow the leaders of the orders, and there is one that follows the three leaders of the orders which follow those leaders of stations that divide the four parts of the year. In the beginning of the year Melkejal rises first and rules, who is named Tam'aini and sun, and all the days of his dominion while he bears rule are ninety-one days.

16 And these are the signs of the days which are to be seen on earth in the days of his dominion: sweat, and heat; and calms; and all the trees bear fruit, and leaves are produced on all the trees, and the harvest of wheat, and the rose-flowers, and all the flowers which come out in the field, but the trees of the winter season become withered.

17 And these are the names of the leaders which are under them: Berka'el, Zelebs'el, and another who is added a head of a thousand, called Hilujaseph: and the days of the dominion of this leader are at an end.

18 The next leader after him is Hel'emmelek, whom one names the shining sun, and all the days of his light are ninety-one days.

19 And these are the signs of his days on the earth: glowing heat and dryness, and the trees ripen their fruits and produce all their fruits ripe and ready, and the sheep pair and become pregnant, and all the fruits of the earth are gathered in, and everything that is in the fields, and the winepress: these things take place in the days of his dominion.

20 These are the names, and the orders, and the leaders of those heads of thousands: Gida'ljal, Ke'el, and He'el, and the name of the head of a thousand which is added to them, Asfa'el: and the days of his dominion are at an end.

[Chapter 83]

1 And now, my son Methuselah, I will show you all my visions which I have seen, recounting them before you.

2 I saw two visions before I got married (took a wife), and the one was quite unlike the other: the first when I was learning to write: the second before I married (took) your mother, was when I saw a terrible vision.

3 And regarding them I prayed to the Lord. I had laid down in the house of my grandfather Mahalalel, when I saw in a vision how heaven collapsed and was carried off (removed, torn down) and fell to the earth.

4 And when it fell to the earth I saw how the earth was swallowed up in a great abyss, and mountains were suspended on mountains, and hills sank down on hills, and high trees were ripped from their stems, and hurled down and sunk in the abyss.

5 And then a word fell into my mouth, and I lifted up my voice to cry aloud, and said:

6 'The earth is destroyed.' And my grandfather Mahalalel woke me as I lay near him, and said to me: 'Why do you cry so, my son, and why do you make such moaning (lamentation)?'

7 And I recounted to him the whole vision which I had seen, and he said to me: 'You have seen a terrible thing , my son. Your dream (vision) is of a grave time and concerns the secrets of all the sin of the earth: it must sink into the abyss and be totally destroyed.

8 And now, my son, arise and pray to the Lord of glory, since you are a believer, that a remnant may remain on the earth, and that He may not destroy the whole earth.

9 My son, from heaven all this will come on the earth, and on the earth there will be great destruction.

10 After that I arose and prayed and implored and besought (God), and wrote down my prayer for the generations of the world, and I will show everything to you, my son Methuselah.

11 And when I had gone out below and seen the heaven, and the sun rising in the east, and the moon setting in the west, and a few stars, and the whole earth, and everything as He had known it in the beginning, then I blessed the Lord of judgment and exalted Him because He had made the sun to go out from the windows of the east, and he ascended and rose on the face of heaven, and set out and kept traversing the path shown to it.

[Chapter 84]

1 And I lifted up my hands in righteousness and blessed the Holy and Great One, and spoke with the breath of my mouth, and with the tongue of flesh, which God has made for the children of the flesh of men, that they should speak therewith, and He gave them breath and a tongue and a mouth that they should speak therewith:

2 Blessed be you, O Lord, King, Great and mighty in your greatness, Lord of the whole creation of heaven, King of kings and God of the whole world. And your power and kingship and greatness abide for ever and ever, and throughout all generations your dominion and all heavens are your throne for ever, and the whole earth your footstool for ever and ever.

3 For you have made and you rule all things, and nothing is too hard for you, wisdom never departs from the place of your throne, nor turns away from your presence. You know and see and hear everything, and there is nothing hidden from you for you see everything.

4 And now the angels of your heavens are guilty of trespass, and on the flesh of men abide your wrath until the great day of judgment.

5 And now, O God and Lord and Great King, I implore and beseech you to fulfill my prayer, to leave me a posterity on earth, and not destroy all the flesh of man, and make the earth without inhabitant, so that there should be an eternal destruction.

6 And now, my Lord, destroy from the earth the flesh which has aroused your wrath, but the flesh of righteousness and uprightness establish as an eternal plant bearing seed forever, and hide not your face from the prayer of your servant, O Lord.'

[Author's note: In chapter 85 and following, a series of animals is mentioned. These seem to refer to nations or ethnicities. For example, the eagles may refer to the Roman empire, the Islamic nation is represented by the asses, Abraham may be the white bull, Jacob is a sheep, Egyptians are wolves, and so on. See Daniel Chapter 10 for other like imagery.

Other writers have attempted to be more specific. Starting with the concept of Noah's three sons, Shem, Ham and Japheth, giving rise to all the animals or nations in Chapter 89, they link the white bull to Abraham; Abraham's son, Ishmael, to the wild ass; Isaac to the white bull; Esau to the wild boar; Jacob to the white sheep; the Assyrians to lions; The small lambs with open eyes to the Essenes; Jesus to the "sheep with the big horn"; and in 90.17, the final twelve shepherds represent the Christian era.]

[Chapter 85]

1 And after this I saw another dream, and I will show the whole dream to you, my son.

2 And Enoch lifted up his voice and spoke to his son Methuselah: 'I will speak to you, my son, hear my words. Incline your ear to the dream (vision) of your father.

3 Before I married (took) your mother Edna, I saw in a vision on my bed, and behold a bull came out from the earth, and that bull was white.

4 And after it came out a heifer, and along with this later came out two bulls, one of them black and the other red.

5 And that black bull gored the red one and pursued him over the earth, and then I could no longer see that red bull. But that black bull grew and that heifer went with him, and I saw that many oxen proceeded from him which resembled and followed him.

6 And that cow, that first one, went from the presence of that first bull in order to seek that red one, but found him not, and mourned with a great lamentation and sought him.

7 And I looked until that first bull came to her and quieted (calmed) her, and from that time onward she cried no more.

8 And after that she bore another white bull, and after him she bore many bulls and black cows.

9 And I saw in my sleep that white bull likewise grew and became a great white bull, and from him proceeded many white bulls, and they resembled him. And they began to father many white bulls, which resembled them, one following another.

[Chapter 86]

1 And again I looked with my eyes as I slept, and I saw the heaven above, and behold a star fell from heaven, and it arose and ate and pastured among those oxen (bulls).

2 And after that I saw the large and the black oxen (bulls), and behold they all changed their stalls and pastures and their heifers (cattle) , and began to live with each other.

3 And again I saw in the vision, and looked towards heaven, and behold I saw many stars descend and cast themselves down from heaven to that first star, and they became bulls among those cattle and pastured with them.

4 And I looked at them and saw they all let out their private (sexual) members, like horses, and began to mount the cows of the bulls (oxen), and they all became pregnant and bore elephants, camels, and asses.

5 And all the bulls (oxen) feared them and were frightened of them, and began to bite with their teeth and to devour, and to gore with their horns.

6 And, moreover, they began to devour those oxen; and behold all the children of the earth began to tremble and shake before them and to flee from them.

[Chapter 87]

1 And again I saw how they began to gore each other and to devour each other, and the earth began to cry aloud.

2 And I raised my eyes again to heaven, and I saw in the vision, and behold there came out from heaven beings who were like white men, and four went out from that place and three others with them.

3 And those three that had come out last grasped me by my hand and took me up, away from the generations of the earth, and raised me up to a high place, and showed me a tower raised high above the earth, and all the hills were lower.

4 And one said to me: 'Remain here until you see everything that befalls those elephants, camels, and asses, and the stars and the oxen, and all of them.'

[Chapter 88]

1 And I saw one of those four who had come out first, and he seized that first star which had fallen from heaven, and bound it hand and foot and cast it into an abyss; now that abyss was narrow and deep, and horrible and dark.

2PE 2:4 For if God spared not the angels that sinned, but cast them down to hell, and delivered them into chains of darkness, to be reserved unto judgment;

2 And one of them drew a sword, and gave it to those elephants and camels and asses then they began to smite each other, and the whole earth shook because of them.

3 And as I was beholding in the vision one of those four who had come out stoned them from heaven, and gathered and took all the great stars whose private (sexual) members were like those of horses, and bound them all hand and foot, and threw them in an abyss of the earth.

[Chapter 89]

1 And one of those four went to that white bull and instructed him in a secret, and he was terrified: he was born a bull and became a man, and built for himself a great vessel and dwelt on it.

2 And three bulls dwelt with him in the vessel and they were covered over. And again I raised my eyes towards heaven and saw a high roof, with seven water torrents on it, and those torrents flowed with much water into an enclosure.

3 And I looked again, and behold fountains were opened on the surface of that great enclosure, and the water began to bubble and swell and rise on the surface, and I saw that enclosure until all its surface was covered with water.

4 And the water, the darkness, and mist increased on it; and as I looked at the height of that water, the water had risen above the height of the enclosure, and was streaming over the enclosure, and it stood on the earth.

5 And all the cattle of the enclosure were gathered together until I saw how they sank and were swallowed up and perished in that water.

6 But that vessel floated on the water, while all the oxen (bulls) and elephants and camels and asses sank to the bottom with all the animals, so that I could no longer see them, and they were not able to escape, but perished and sank into the depths.

7 And again I watched in the vision until those water torrents were removed from that high roof, and the chasms of the earth were leveled up and other abysses were opened.

8 Then the water began to run down into these abysses, until the earth became visible; but that vessel settled on the earth, and the darkness retired and light appeared.

9 But that white bull which had become a man came out of that vessel, and the three bulls with him, and one of those three was white like that bull, and one of them was red as blood, and one black; and that white bull departed from them.

10 And they began to bring out beasts of the field and birds, so that there arose different genera: lions, tigers, wolves, dogs, hyenas, wild boars, foxes, squirrels, swine, falcons, vultures, kites, eagles, and ravens; and among them was born a white bull.

11 And they began to bite one another; but that white bull which was born among them fathered a wild ass and a white bull with it, and the wild asses multiplied.

12 But that bull which was born from him fathered a black wild boar and a white sheep; and the former fathered many boars, but the sheep gave birth to twelve sheep.

13 And when those twelve sheep had grown, they gave up one of them to the asses, and the asses again gave up that sheep to the wolves, and that sheep grew up among the wolves.

14 And the Lord brought the eleven sheep to live with it and to pasture with it among the wolves and they multiplied and became many flocks of sheep.

15 And the wolves began to fear them, and they oppressed them until they destroyed their little ones, and they threw their young into a deep river, but those sheep began to cry aloud on account of their little ones, and to complain to their Lord.

16 And a sheep which had been saved from the wolves fled and escaped to the wild asses; and I saw the sheep how they lamented and cried, and besought their Lord with all their might, until that Lord of the sheep descended at the voice of the sheep from a high abode, and came to them and pastured them.

17 And He called that sheep which had escaped the wolves, and spoke with it concerning the wolves that it should admonish them not to touch the sheep.

18 And the sheep went to the wolves according to the word of the Lord, and another sheep met it and went with it, and the two went and entered together into the assembly of those wolves, and spoke with them and admonished them not to touch the sheep from then on.

19 And on it I saw the wolves, and how they more harshly oppressed the sheep with all their power; and the sheep cried aloud.

20 And the Lord came to the sheep and they began to beat those wolves, and the wolves began to make lamentation; but the sheep became quiet and ceased to cry out.

21 And I saw the sheep until they departed from among the wolves; but the eyes of the wolves were blinded, and the wolves departed in pursuit of the sheep with all their power.

22 And the Lord of the sheep went with them, as their leader, and all His sheep followed Him.

23 And his face was dazzling and glorious and terrible to behold. But the wolves began to pursue those sheep until they reached a sea of water.

24 And that sea was divided, and the water stood on this side and on that before their face, and their Lord led them and placed Himself between them and the wolves.

25 And as those wolves had not yet seen the sheep, they proceeded into the midst of that sea, and the wolves followed the sheep, and those wolves ran after them into that sea.

26 And when they saw the Lord of the sheep, they turned to flee before His face, but that sea gathered itself together, and became as it had been created, and the water swelled and rose until it covered the wolves.

27 And I watched until all the wolves who pursued those sheep perished and were drowned.

28 But the sheep escaped from that water and went out into a wilderness, where there was no water and no grass; and they began to open their eyes and to see;

29 And I saw the Lord of the sheep pasturing them and giving them water and grass, and that sheep going and leading them.

30 And the sheep ascended to the summit of that high rock, and the Lord of the sheep sent it to them. And after that I saw the Lord of the sheep who stood before them, and His appearance was great and terrible and majestic, and all those sheep saw Him and were afraid before His face.

31 And they all feared and trembled because of Him, and they cried to that sheep which was among them:

32 'We are not able to stand before our Lord or to behold Him.' And that sheep which led them again ascended to the summit of that rock, but the sheep began to be blinded and to wander from the way which he had showed them, but that sheep did not realize it.

34 And the Lord of the sheep was very angry with them, and that sheep discovered it, and went down from the summit of the rock, and came to the sheep, and found the greatest part of them blinded and fallen away.

35 And when they saw it they feared and trembled at its presence, and desired to return to their folds. And that sheep took other sheep with it, and came to those sheep which had fallen away, and began to slay them; and the sheep feared its presence, and thus that sheep brought back those sheep that had fallen away, and they returned to their folds.

36 And I saw in this vision until that sheep became a man and built a house for the Lord of the sheep, and placed all the sheep in that house.

37 And I saw until this sheep which had met that sheep which led them fell asleep (died); and I saw until all the great sheep perished and little ones arose in their place, and they came to a pasture, and approached a stream of water.

38 Then that sheep, their leader which had become a man, withdrew from them and fell asleep (died), and all the sheep looked for it (sought it) and cried over it with a great crying.

39 And I saw until they left off crying for that sheep and crossed that stream of water, and there arose the two sheep as leaders in the place of those which had led them and fallen asleep.

40 And I saw until the sheep came to a good place, and a pleasant and glorious land, and I saw until those sheep were satisfied; and that house stood among them in the (green) pleasant land.

41 And sometimes their eyes were opened, and sometimes blinded, until another sheep arose and led them and brought them all back, and their eyes were opened.

42 And the dogs and the foxes and the wild boars began to devour those sheep until the Lord of the sheep raised up another sheep, a ram from their midst, which led them.

43 And that ram began to butt on either side those dogs, foxes, and wild boars until he had destroyed them all.

44 And that sheep whose eyes were opened saw that ram, which was among the sheep, until it forsook its glory and began to butt those sheep, and trampled on them, and behaved itself unseemly.

45 And the Lord of the sheep sent the lamb to another lamb and raised it to being a ram and leader of the sheep instead of that ram which had forsaken its glory.

46 And it went to it and spoke to it alone, and raised it to being a ram, and made it the prince and leader of the sheep; but during all these things those dogs oppressed the sheep.

47 And the first ram pursued the second ram, and the second ram arose and fled before it; and I saw until those dogs pulled down the first ram.

48 And that second ram arose and led the little sheep. And those sheep grew and multiplied; but all the dogs, and foxes, and wild boars feared and fled before it, and that ram butted and killed the wild beasts, and those wild beasts had no longer any power among the sheep and robbed them no more of anything.

49 And that ram fathered many sheep and fell asleep; and a little sheep became ram in its place, and became prince and leader of those sheep.

50 And that house became great and broad, and it was built for those sheep: and a high and great tower was built on the house for the Lord of the sheep, and that house was low, but the tower was elevated and high, and the Lord of the sheep stood on that tower and they offered a full table before him.

51 And again I saw those sheep that they again erred and went many ways, and forsook that their house, and the Lord of the sheep called some from among the sheep and sent them to the sheep, but the sheep began to slay them.

52 And one of them was saved and was not slain, and it sped away and cried aloud over the sheep; and they sought to slay it, but the Lord of the sheep saved it from the sheep, and brought it up to me, and caused it to live there.

53 And many other sheep He sent to those sheep to testify to them and lament over them.

54 And after that I saw that when they forsook the house of the Lord and His tower they fell away entirely, and their eyes were blinded; and I saw the Lord of the sheep how He worked much slaughter among them in their herds until those sheep invited that slaughter and betrayed His place.

55 And He gave them over into the hands of the lions and tigers, and wolves and hyenas, and into the hand of the foxes, and to all the wild beasts, and those wild beasts began to tear in pieces those sheep.

56 And I saw that He forsook their house and their tower and gave them all into the hand of the lions, to tear and devour them, into the hand of all the wild beasts.

57 And I began to cry aloud with all my power, and to appeal to the Lord of the sheep, because the sheep were being devoured by all the wild beasts.

58 But He remained unmoved, though He saw it, and rejoiced that they were devoured and swallowed and robbed, and left them to be devoured in the hand of all the beasts.

59 And He called seventy shepherds, and gave those sheep to them that they might pasture them, and He spoke to the shepherds and their companions: 'Let each individual of you pasture the sheep from now on, and everything that I shall command you that do you.

60 And I will deliver them over to you duly numbered, and tell you which of them are to be destroyed-and them you will destroy.' And He gave over to them those sheep.

61 And He called another and spoke to him: 'Observe and mark everything that the shepherds will do to those sheep; for they will destroy more of them than I have commanded them.

62 And every excess and the destruction which will be done through the shepherds, record how many they destroy according to my command, and how many according to their own caprice; record against every individual shepherd all the destruction he effects.

63 And read out before me by number how many they destroy, and how many they deliver over for destruction, that I may have this as a testimony against them, and know every deed of the shepherds, that I may comprehend and see what they do, whether or not they abide by my command which I have commanded them.

64 But they shall not know it, and you shall not declare it to them, nor admonish them, but only record against each individual all the destruction which the shepherds effect each in his time and lay it all before me.'

65 And I saw until those shepherds pastured in their season, and they began to slay and to destroy more than they were bidden, and they delivered those sheep into the hand of the lions.

66 And the lions and tigers ate and devoured the greater part of those sheep, and the wild boars ate along with them; and they burned that tower and demolished that house.

67 And I became very sorrowful over that tower because that house of the sheep was demolished, and afterwards I was unable to see if those sheep entered that house.

68 And the shepherds and their associates delivered over those sheep to all the wild beasts, to devour them, and each one of them received in his time a definite number, it was written by the other in a book how many each one of them destroyed of them.

69 And each one slew and destroyed many more than was prescribed; and I began to weep and lament on account of those sheep.

70 And thus in the vision I saw that one who wrote, how he wrote down every one that was destroyed by those shepherds, day by day, and carried up and laid down and showed actually the whole book to the Lord of the sheep - everything that they had done, and all that each one of them had made away with, and all that they had given over to destruction.

71 And the book was read before the Lord of the sheep, and He took the book from his hand and read it and sealed it and laid it down.

72 And I saw how the shepherds pastured for twelve hours, and behold three of those sheep turned back and came and entered and began to build up all that had fallen down of that house; but the wild boars tried to hinder them, but they were not able.

73 And they began again to build as before, and they raised up that tower, and it was named the high tower; and they began again to place a table before the tower, but all the bread on it was polluted and not pure.

74 And as touching all this the eyes of those sheep were blinded so that they saw not, and the eyes of their shepherds likewise were blinded; and they delivered them in large numbers to their shepherds for destruction, and they trampled the sheep with their feet and devoured them.

75 And the Lord of the sheep remained unmoved until all the sheep were dispersed over the field and mingled with the beasts, and the shepherds did not save them out of the hand of the beasts.

76 And this one who wrote the book carried it up, and showed it and read it before the Lord of the sheep, and implored Him on their account, and besought Him on their account as he showed Him all the doings of the shepherds, and gave testimony before Him against all the shepherds.

77 And he took the actual book and laid it down beside Him and departed.

[Chapter 90]

1 And I saw until that in this manner thirty-five shepherds undertook the pasturing of the sheep, and they completed their periods as did the first; and others received them into their hands, to pasture them for their period, each shepherd in his own period.

2 And after that I saw in my vision all the birds of heaven coming, the eagles, the vultures, the kites, the ravens; but the eagles led all the birds; and they began to devour those sheep, and to pick out their eyes and to devour their flesh.

3 And the sheep cried out because their flesh was being devoured by the birds, and as for me I looked and lamented in my sleep over that shepherd who pastured the sheep.

4 And I saw until those sheep were devoured by the dogs and eagles and kites, and they left neither flesh nor skin nor sinew remaining on them until only their bones stood there; and their bones too fell to the earth and the sheep became few.

5 And I saw until that twenty-three had undertaken the pasturing and completed in their many periods fifty-eight times.

6 But behold lambs were borne by those white sheep, and they began to open their eyes and to see, and to cry to the sheep.

7 They cried to them, but they did not hearken to what they said to them, but were very deaf, and their eyes were very blinded.

8 And I saw in the vision how the ravens flew on those lambs and took one of those lambs, and dashed the sheep in pieces and devoured them.

9 And I saw until horns grew on those lambs, and the ravens cast down their horns; and I saw until there sprouted a great horn of one of those sheep, and their eyes were opened.

10 And it looked at them and their eyes opened, and it cried to the sheep, and the rams saw it and all ran to it.

11 And notwithstanding all this, those eagles and vultures and ravens and kites kept on tearing the sheep and swooping down on them and devouring them until the sheep remained silent, but the rams lamented and cried out.

12 And those ravens fought and battled with it and sought to lay low its horn, but they had no power over it.

13 All the eagles and vultures and ravens and kites were gathered together, and there came with them all the sheep of the field, they all came together, and helped each other to break that horn of the ram.

14 And I saw that man, who wrote down the names of the shepherds and brought them up before the Lord of the sheep, came, and he helped that ram and showed it everything; its help was coming down.

15 And I looked until that Lord of the sheep came to them angry, all those who saw him ran, and they all fell into the shadow in front of Him.

16 All the eagles and vultures and ravens and kites, gathered together and brought with them all the wild sheep, and they all came together and helped one another in order to dash that horn of the ram in pieces.

17 And I looked at that man, who wrote the book at the command of the Lord, until he opened that book of the destruction that those last twelve shepherds had done. And he showed, in front of the Lord of the sheep, that they had destroyed even more than those before them had.

18 And I looked and the Lord of the sheep came to them and took the Staff of His Anger and struck the Earth. And the Earth was split. And all the animals, and the birds of the sky, fell from those sheep and sank in the earth, and it closed over them.

19 And I saw until a great sword was given to the sheep, and the sheep proceeded against all the beasts of the field to slay them, and all the beasts and the birds of the heaven fled before their face. And I saw that man, who wrote the book according to the command of the Lord, until he opened that book concerning the destruction which those twelve last shepherds had wrought, and showed that they had destroyed much more than their predecessors, before the Lord of the sheep. And I saw until the Lord of the sheep came to them and took in His hand the staff of His wrath, and smote the earth, and the earth clave asunder, and all the beasts and all the birds of heaven fell from among those sheep, and were swallowed up in the earth and it covered them.

20 And I saw until a throne was erected in the pleasant land, and the Lord of the sheep sat Himself on it, and the other took the sealed books and opened those books before the Lord of the sheep.

21 And the Lord called those men, the seven first white ones, and commanded that they should bring before Him, beginning with the first star which led the way, all the stars whose private members were like those of horses, and they brought them all before Him.

22 And He said to that man who wrote before Him, being one of those seven white ones, and said to him: 'Take those seventy shepherds to whom I delivered the sheep, and who taking them on their own authority slew more than I commanded them.'

23 And behold they were all bound, I saw, and they all stood before Him.

24 And the judgment was held first over the stars, and they were judged and found guilty, and went to the place of condemnation, and they were cast into an abyss, full of fire and flaming, and full of pillars of fire.

25 And those seventy shepherds were judged and found guilty, and they were cast into that fiery abyss.

26 And I saw at that time how a like abyss was opened in the midst of the earth, full of fire, and they brought those blinded sheep, and they were all judged and found guilty and cast into this fiery abyss, and they burned; now this abyss was to the right of that house.

27 And I saw those sheep burning and their bones burning.

28 And I stood up to see until they folded up that old house; and carried off all the pillars, and all the beams and ornaments of the house were at the same time folded up with it, and they carried it off and laid it in a place in the south of the land.

29 And I saw until the Lord of the sheep brought a new house greater and loftier than that first, and set it up in the place of the first which had been folded up; all its pillars were new, and its ornaments were new and larger than those of the first, the old one which He had taken away, and all the sheep were within it.

HEB 13:14 For here have we no continuing city, but we seek one to come.

30 And I saw all the sheep which had been left, and all the beasts on the earth, and all the birds of heaven, falling down and doing homage to those sheep and making petition to and obeying them in every thing.

31 And thereafter those three who were clothed in white and had seized me by my hand [who had taken me up before], and the hand of that ram also seizing hold of me, they took me up and set me down in the midst of those sheep before the judgment took place.

32 And those sheep were all white, and their wool was abundant and clean.

33 And all that had been destroyed and dispersed, and all the beasts of the field, and all the birds of heaven, assembled in that house, and the Lord of the sheep rejoiced with great joy because they were all good and had returned to His house.

34 And I saw until they laid down that sword, which had been given to the sheep, and they brought it back into the house, and it was sealed before the presence of the Lord, and all the sheep were invited into that house, but it held them not.

35 And the eyes of them all were opened, and they saw the good, and there was not one among them that did not see.

36 And I saw that the house was large and broad and very full.

37 And I saw that a white bull was born, with large horns and all the beasts of the field and all the birds of the air feared him and made petition to him all the time.

38 And I saw until all their generations were transformed, and they all became white bulls; and the first among them became a lamb, and that lamb became a great animal and had great black horns on its head; and the Lord of the sheep rejoiced over it and over all the oxen.

39 And I slept in their midst: And I awoke and saw everything.

40 This is the vision which I saw while I slept, and I awoke and blessed the Lord of righteousness and gave Him glory.

41 Then I wept greatly and my tears ceased not until I could no longer endure it; when I saw, they flowed on account of what I had seen; for everything shall come and be fulfilled, and all the deeds of men in their order were shown to me.

42 On that night I remembered the first dream, and because of it I wept and was troubled--because I had seen that vision.

[Author's note: As this section was interpreted from a Jewish point of reference, many have assumed the 'large horn' was Judas Maccabee. In the Christian frame of reference, the same symbol was Jesus Christ.]

[Author's note: At this point, the time frame and text flow becomes non sequitur. It appears the codex was not kept in sequence here. Thus, the translated pages are out of sequence. The flow of time and occurrences seems to follow the pattern listed:

91:6 to 92.1 through 92:5 then jumps to 93:1. The flow then continues from 93:1 to 93:10 and then jumps to 91:7. From 91:7 the text continues to 91:19. It then picks up again at 93:11 and continues.

If one were to attempt to put this section into a time line, the interval would link together in some fashion resembling the following:

Ten Weeks of Judgment

WEEK 1 Judgment & righteousness 93.3 Enoch's time Antediluvian		
WEEK 2	Judgment & cleansing 93.4 Noah's time and the great flood	
WEEK 3	Righteousness is planted 93.5 Abraham's time	
WEEK 4 Law for all generations 93.6 Moses' time		
WEEK 5	House of Glory 93.7 Solomon's time	
WEEK 6 Jesus ascends, temple burned, elect scattered 93.8 Jesus' time		
WEEK 7	Apostate generation Judgment of Fire 93.9 - 91.11 Our time	
WEEK 8	A sword 91.12–13 New house, new heaven & earth Future time	
WEEK 9 The righteous judgment revealed 91.14 The judgment time		
WEEK 10	God's power is forever 91.15-16 Eternal time	

When reading the text from this point to the end of chapter 93 one should keep this flow in mind.]

[Chapter 91]

1 And now, my son Methuselah, call to me all your brothers and gather together to me all the sons of your mother; for the word calls me, and the spirit is poured out on me, that I may show you everything that shall befall you for ever.'

2 And thereon Methuselah went and summoned to him all his brothers and assembled his relatives.

3 And he spoke to all the children of righteousness and said: 'Hear, you sons of Enoch, all the words of your father, and hearken, as you should, to the voice of my mouth; for I exhort you and say to you, beloved:

4 Love righteousness and walk in it, and draw near to righteousness without a double heart, and do not associate with those of a double heart, but walk in righteousness, my sons. And it shall guide you on good paths. And righteousness shall be your companion.'

JAM 1:6 But let him ask in faith, nothing wavering. For he that wavereth is like a wave of the sea driven with the wind and tossed. 7 For let not that man think that he shall receive any thing of the Lord. 8 A double minded man is unstable in all his ways.

5 'For I know that violence must increase on the earth, and a great punishment will be executed on the earth, it shall be cut off from its roots, and its whole construct will be destroyed.

6 And unrighteousness shall again be complete on the earth, and all the deeds of unrighteousness and of violence and sin shall prevail a second time.

7 And when sin and unrighteousness and blasphemy and violence in all kinds of deeds increase, and apostasy and transgression and uncleanness increase; a great chastisement shall come from heaven on all these, and the holy Lord will come out with wrath and chastisement to execute judgment on earth.

2TH 2:3 Let no man deceive you by any means: for that day shall not come, except there come a falling away first, and that man of sin be revealed, the son of perdition.

8 In those days violence shall be cut off from its roots, and the roots of unrighteousness together with deceit, and they shall be destroyed from under heaven.

9 And all the idols of the heathen shall be abandoned. And the temples burned with fire, and they shall remove them from the whole earth; and the heathen shall be cast into the judgment of fire, and shall perish in wrath and in grievous judgment for ever.

10 And the righteous shall arise from their sleep, and wisdom shall arise and be given to them.

11 And after that the roots of unrighteousness and those who plan violence and those who commit blasphemy shall be cut off, and the sinners shall be destroyed by the sword.

12 And after this there will be another week; the eighth, that of righteousness, and a sword will be given to it so that the Righteous Judgment may be executed on those who do wrong, and the sinners will be handed over into the hands of the righteous.

13 And, at its end, they will acquire Houses because of their righteousness, and a House will be built for the Great King in Glory, forever.

14 And after this, in the ninth week, the Righteous Judgment will be revealed to the whole world. And all the deeds of the impious will vanish from the whole Earth. And the world will be written down for destruction and all men will look to the Path of Uprightness.

15 And, after this, in the tenth week, in the seventh part, there will be an Eternal Judgment that will be executed on the Watchers and the Great Eternal Heaven that will spring from the midst of the Angels.

16 And the First Heaven will vanish and pass away and a New Heaven will appear, and all the Powers of Heaven will shine forever, with light seven times as bright.

17 And after this, there will be many weeks without number, forever, in goodness and in righteousness. And from then on sin will never again be mentioned.

18 And now I tell you, my sons, and show you, the paths of righteousness and the paths of violence. I will show them to you again that you may know what will come to pass.

19 And now, hearken to me, my sons, and walk in the paths of righteousness, and walk not in the paths of violence; for all who walk in the paths of unrighteousness shall perish for ever.'

[Chapter 92]

1 The book written by Enoch {Enoch indeed wrote this complete doctrine of wisdom, (which is) praised of all men and a judge of all the earth} for all my children who shall live on the earth. And for the future generations who shall observe righteousness and peace.

2 Let not your spirit be troubled on account of the times; for the Holy and Great One has appointed days for all things.

3 And the righteous one shall arise from sleep, [Shall arise] and walk in the paths of righteousness, and all his path and conversation shall be in eternal goodness and grace.

4 He will be gracious to the righteous and give him eternal righteousness, and He will give him power so that he shall be (endowed) with goodness and righteousness. And he shall walk in eternal light.

5 And sin shall perish in darkness for ever, and shall no more be seen from that day for evermore.

[Chapter 93]

(Author's Note: Chapters 91 – 93 recount and expand on the events listed in the following weeks of prophecy. The explanation of the event are scattered in chapters 91 – 93, however, the list of events are stated clearly in the following list of weeks in chapter 93).

1 And after that Enoch both gave and began to recount from the books. And Enoch said:

2 'Concerning the children of righteousness and concerning the elect of the world, and concerning the plant of righteousness, I will speak these things. I Enoch will declare (them) to you, my sons, according to that which appeared to me in heavenly vision, and which I have known through the word of the holy angels, and have learned from heavenly tablets.'

3 And Enoch began to recount from the books and said: 'I was born the seventh in the first week, able judgment and righteousness still endured.

4 And after me there shall arise in the second week great wickedness, and deceit shall have sprung up; and in it there shall be the first end.

5 And in it a man shall be saved; and after it is ended unrighteousness shall grow up, and a law shall be made for the sinners. And after that in the third week at its close a man shall be elected as the plant of righteous judgment, and his posterity shall become the plant of righteousness for evermore.

6 And after that in the fourth week, at its close, visions of the holy and righteous shall be seen, and a law for all generations and an enclosure shall be made for them.

7 And after that in the fifth week, at its close, the house of glory and dominion shall be built for ever.

8 And after that in the sixth week, all who live in it shall be blinded, and the hearts of all of them shall godlessly forsake wisdom. And in it a man shall ascend; and at its close the house of dominion shall be burned with fire, and the whole race of the chosen root shall be dispersed.

9 And after that in the seventh week shall an apostate generation arise, and many shall be its deeds, and all its deeds shall be apostate.

10 And at its end shall be elected, the elect righteous of the eternal plant of righteousness shall be chosen to receive sevenfold instruction concerning all His creation.

11 For who is there of all the children of men that is able to hear the voice of the Holy One without being troubled? And who can think His thoughts? Who is there that can behold all the works of heaven?

12 And how should there be one who could behold heaven, and who is there that could understand the things of heaven and see a soul or a spirit and could tell of it, or ascend and see all their ends and think them or do like them?

13 And who is there of all men that could know what is the breadth and the length of the earth, and to whom has the measurement been shown of all of them?

14 Or is there any one who could discern the length of the heaven and how great is its height, and on what it is founded, and how great is the number of the stars, and where all the luminaries rest?

[Chapter 94]

1 And now I say to you, my sons, love righteousness and walk in it; because the paths of righteousness are worthy of acceptation, but the paths of unrighteousness shall suddenly be destroyed and vanish.

2 And to certain men of a generation shall the paths of violence and of death be revealed, and they shall hold themselves afar from them, and shall not follow them.

3 And now I say to you, the righteous, walk not in the paths of wickedness, nor in the paths of death, and draw not near to them, lest you be destroyed.

4 But seek and choose for yourselves righteousness and an elect life, and walk in the paths of peace, and you shall live and prosper.

5 And hold (keep) my words in the thoughts of your hearts, and permit them not to be erased from your hearts; for I know that sinners will tempt men to evilly entreat wisdom, so that no place may be found for her, and temptation will increase.

6 Woe to those who build unrighteousness and oppression and lay deceit as a foundation; for they shall be suddenly overthrown, and they shall have no peace.

7 Woe to those who build their houses with sin; for from all their foundations shall they be overthrown, and by the sword shall they fall. And those who acquire gold and silver shall suddenly perish in the judgment.

8 Woe to you, you rich, for you have trusted in your riches, and from your riches shall you depart, because you have not remembered the Most High in the days of your riches.

9 You have committed blasphemy and unrighteousness, and have become ready for the day of slaughter, and the day of darkness and the day of the great judgment.

10 Thus I speak and tell you: He who hath created you will overthrow you, and for your fall there shall be no compassion, and your Creator will rejoice at your destruction.

11 And your righteousness shall be a reproach to the sinners and the godless in those days.

JAM 5:1 Go to now, ye rich men, weep and howl for your miseries that shall come upon you. 2 Your riches are corrupted, and your garments are moth-eaten. 3 Your gold and silver is cankered; and the rust of them shall be a witness against you, and shall eat your flesh as it were fire. Ye have heaped treasure together for the last days. 4 Behold, the hire of the labourers who have reaped down your fields, which is of you kept back by fraud, crieth: and the cries of them which have reaped are entered into the ears of the Lord of sabaoth. 5 Ye have lived in pleasure on the earth, and been wanton; ye have nourished your hearts, as in a day of slaughter. 6 Ye have condemned and killed the just; and he doth not resist you.

(Author's note: In the above biblical verses from James, "sabaoth" is from the Hebrew, plural form of "host" or "army". The word is used almost exclusively in conjunction with the Divine name as a title of majesty: "the Lord of Hosts", or "the Lord God of Hosts".)

[Chapter 95]

1 Would that my eyes were rain clouds of water that I might weep over you, and pour down my tears as a cloud of water, that I might rest from my trouble of heart!

2 Who has permitted you to practice reproaches and wickedness? And so judgment shall overtake you, sinners.

3 You, righteous! Fear not the sinners, for again the Lord will deliver them into your hands, that you may execute judgment on them according to your desires.

4 Woe to you who speak against God (fulminate anathemas) which cannot be removed (reversed) - healing shall be far from you because of your sins.

5 Woe to you who repay your neighbor with evil; for you shall be repaid according to your works.

6 Woe to you, lying witnesses, and to those who weigh out injustice, for you shall suddenly perish.

7 Woe to you, sinners, for you persecute the righteous; for you shall be delivered up and persecuted because of injustice, and your yoke shall be heavy on you.

[Chapter 96]

1 Be hopeful, you righteous; for suddenly shall the sinners perish before you, and you shall have lordship over them, according to your desires.

2 And in the day of the tribulation of the sinners, your children shall mount and rise as eagles, and your nests shall be higher than the vultures'. You shall ascend as badgers and enter the crevices of the earth, and the clefts of the rock for ever before the unrighteous. And the satyrs (sirens) shall sigh and weep because of you.

3 Wherefore fear not, you that have suffered, for healing shall be your portion, and a bright light shall enlighten you, and the voice of rest you shall hear from heaven.

4 Woe to you, you sinners, for your riches make you appear like the righteous, but your hearts convict you of being sinners, and this fact shall be a testimony against you for a memorial of your evil deeds.

5 Woe to you who devour the finest of the wheat, and drink wine in large bowls (the best of waters), and tread under foot the lowly (humble) with your might.

6 Woe to you who drink water from every fountain (drink water all the time), for suddenly shall you be consumed and wither away, because you have forsaken the fountain of life.

(Author's note: The above reference is a euphemism for promiscuity.)

7 Woe to you who work unrighteousness and deceit and blasphemy; it shall be a memorial against you for evil.

8 Woe to you, you mighty, who with might oppress the righteous; for the day of your destruction is coming. Many and good days shall come to the righteous in those days - in the day of your judgment.

[Chapter 97]

1 Believe, you righteous, that the sinners will become a shame and perish in the day of unrighteousness.

2 Be it known to you, you sinners, that the Most High is mindful of your destruction, and the angels of heaven rejoice over your destruction.

3 What will you do, you sinners, and where shall you flee on that day of judgment, when you hear the voice of the prayer of the righteous?

4 You shall fare like to them, against whom these words shall be a testimony: "You have been companions of sinners."

5 And in those days the prayer of the righteous shall reach to the Lord, and for you the days of your judgment shall come.

6 And all the words of your unrighteousness shall be read out before the Great Holy One, and your faces shall be covered with shame, and He will reject every work which is grounded on unrighteousness.

7 Woe to you, you sinners, who live on the middle of the ocean and on the dry land, whose remembrance is evil against you.

8 Woe to you who acquire silver and gold in unrighteousness and say: "We have become rich with riches and have possessions; and have acquired everything we have desired.

9 And now let us do what we purposed, for we have gathered silver, and many are the servants in our houses and our granaries are full to the brim as if with water."

10 Yea, and like water your lies shall flow away; for your riches shall not abide but quickly depart (go up) from you, for you have acquired it all in unrighteousness, and you shall be given over to a great curse.

[Chapter 98]

1 And now I swear to you, to the wise and to the foolish, that you shall see (have) many experiences on the earth.

2 For you men shall put on more adornments than a woman, and colored garments more than a young woman, like royalty and in grandeur and in power, and in silver and in gold and in purple, and in splendor and in food they shall be poured out as water.

3 Therefore they shall have neither knowledge nor wisdom, and because of this they shall die together with their possessions; and with all their glory and their splendor, and in shame and in slaughter and in great destitution, their spirits shall be thrown into the furnace of fire.

4 I have sworn to you, you sinners, as a mountain has not become a slave, and a hill does not become the servant of a woman, even so sin has not been sent on the earth, but man of himself has created it, and they that commit it shall fall under a great curse.

5 And barrenness has not been given to the woman, but on account of the deeds of her own hands she dies without children.

6 I have sworn to you, you sinners, by the Holy Great One, that all your evil deeds are revealed in heaven, and that none of your wrong deeds (of oppression) are covered and hidden.

7 And do not think in your spirit nor say in your heart that you do not know and that you do not see that every sin is recorded every day in heaven in the presence of the Most High.

8 From now on, you know that all your wrongdoing that you do will be written down every day, until the day of your judgment.

9 Woe to you, you fools, for through your folly you shall perish; and you do not listen to the wise so no good will come to you against the wise,

10 And so and now, know you that you are prepared for the day of destruction. Therefore do not hope to live, you sinners, but you shall depart and die; for there will be no ransom for you; because you are prepared for the day of the great judgment, for the day of tribulation and great shame for your spirits.

11 Woe to you, you obstinate of heart, who work wickedness and eat blood. Where do you have good things to eat and to drink and to be filled? From all the good things which the Lord the Most High has placed in abundance on the earth; therefore you shall have no peace.

(Author's note: The above reference to eating blood may indicate cannibalism.)

GEN 9:3 *Every moving thing that liveth shall be meat for you; even as the green herb have I given you all things. 4 But flesh with the life thereof, which is the blood thereof, shall ye not eat. 5 And surely your blood of your lives will I require; at the hand of every beast will I require it, and at the hand of man; at the hand of every man's brother will I require the life of man. 6 Whoso sheddeth man's blood, by man shall his blood be shed: for in the image of God made he man.*

12 Woe to you who love the deeds of unrighteousness; wherefore do you hope for good for yourselves? You know that you shall be delivered into the hands of the righteous, and they shall cut off your necks and slay you, and have no mercy on you.

13 Woe to you who rejoice in the distress of the righteous; for no grave shall be dug for you.

14 Woe to you who say the words of the wise are empty; for you shall have no hope of life.

15 Woe to you who write down lying and godless words; for they write down their lies so that men may hear them and act godlessly towards their neighbor. Therefore they shall have no peace but die a sudden death.

[Chapter 99]

1 Woe to you who do godless acts, and praise and honor lies; you shall perish, and no happy life shall be yours.

2 Woe to them who pervert the words of righteousness, and transgress the eternal law, and count themselves as sinless. They shall be trodden under foot on the earth.

3 In those days make ready, you righteous, to raise your prayers as a memorial, and place them as a testimony before the angels, that they may place the sin of the sinners for a reminder before the Most High.

4 In those days the nations shall be stirred up, and the families of the nations shall arise on the day of destruction.

5 And in those days the destitute shall go and throw their children out, and they shall abandon them, so that their children shall perish because of them. They shall abandon their children that are still babies (sucklings), and not return to them, and shall have no pity on their loved ones.

6 Again, I swear to you, you sinners, that sin is prepared for a day of unceasing bloodshed.

MAT 24:6 And ye shall hear of wars and rumours of wars: see that ye be not troubled: for all these things must come to pass, but the end is not yet. 7 For nation shall rise against nation, and kingdom against kingdom: and there shall be famines, and pestilences, and earthquakes, in diverse places. 8 All these are the beginning of sorrows.

7 And they who worship stones, and carved images of gold and silver and wood and stone and clay, and those who worship impure spirits and demons, and all kinds of idols not according to knowledge, shall get no manner of help from them.

8 And they shall become godless by reason of the folly of their hearts, and their eyes shall be blinded through the fear of their hearts and through visions in their ambitions (dreams).

9 Through these they shall become godless and fearful; for they shall have done all their work with lies, and shall have worshiped a stone, therefore in an instant shall they perish.

10 But in those days blessed are all they who accept the words of wisdom, and understand them, and observe the paths of the Most High, and walk in the path of His righteousness, and become not godless with the godless, for they shall be saved.

11 Woe to you who spread evil to your neighbors, for you shall be slain in Hell.

12 Woe to you who make your foundation that of deceitful (sin) and lies, and who cause bitterness on the earth; for they shall thereby be utterly consumed.

13 Woe to you who build your houses through the hard labor of others, and all their building materials are the bricks and stones of sin; I tell you, you shall have no peace.

14 Woe to them who reject the measure and eternal inheritance of their fathers and whose souls follow after idols; for they shall have no rest.

15 Woe to them who do unrighteous acts and help oppression, and kill their neighbors until the day of the great judgment, for He will throw down your glory.

16 For He shall throw down your glory, and bring affliction on your hearts, and shall arouse His fierce anger, and destroy you all with the sword; and all the holy and righteous shall remember your sins.

[Chapter 100]

1 And in those days in one place the fathers together with their sons shall kill one another and brothers shall fall in death together until the streams flow with their blood.

2 For a man shall not withhold his hand from killing his sons and his sons' sons, and the sinner shall not withhold his hand from his honored brother, from dawn until sunset they shall kill one another.

MAR 13:12 Now the brother shall betray the brother to death, and the father the son; and children shall rise up against their parents, and shall cause them to be put to death.

3 And the horse shall walk up to the breast in the blood of sinners, and the chariot shall be submerged to its height.

REV 14:20 And the winepress was trodden without the city, and blood came out of the winepress, even unto the horse bridles, by the space of a thousand and six hundred furlongs.

4 In those days the angels shall descend into the secret places and gather together into one place all those who brought down sin and the Most High will arise on that day of judgment to execute great judgment among sinners.

5 And over all the righteous and holy He will appoint guardians from among the holy angels to guard them as the apple of an eye, until He makes an end of all wickedness and all sin, and even if the righteous sleep a long sleep, they have nothing to fear.

6 And the wise men will seek the truth and they and their sons will understand the words of this book, and recognize that their riches shall not be able to save them or overcome their sins.

7 Woe to you sinners, on the day of strong anguish, you who afflict the righteous and burn them with fire; you shall be requited according to your works.

8 Woe to you, you obstinate of heart, who watch in order to devise wickedness; therefore shall fear come on you and there shall be none to help you.

9 Woe to you, you sinners, on account of the words of your mouth, and on account of the deeds of your hands which your godlessness has caused, in blazing flames burning worse than fire shall you burn.

2TH 1:7 And to you who are troubled rest with us, when the Lord Jesus shall be revealed from heaven with his mighty angels, 8 In flaming fire taking vengeance on them that know not God, and that obey not the gospel of our Lord Jesus Christ: 9 Who shall be punished with everlasting destruction from the presence of the Lord, and from the glory of his power?

10 And now, know that the angels will ask Him in heaven about your deeds and from the sun and from the moon and from the stars they will ask about your sins because on the earth you execute judgment on the righteous.

11 And He will summon to testify against you every cloud and mist and dew and rain; for they shall all be withheld from falling on you, and they shall be mindful of your sins.

12 And now give gifts to the rain that it cease not from falling on you, nor the dew, when it has received gold and silver from you that it may fall. When the hoar-frost and snow with their chilliness, and all the snow storms with all their plagues fall on you, in those days you shall not be able to stand before them.

[Chapter 101]

1 Observe heaven, you children of heaven, and every work of the Most High, and fear Him and work no evil in His presence.

2 If He closes the windows of heaven, and withholds the rain and the dew from falling on the earth on your account, what will you do then?

3 And if He sends His anger on you because of your deeds, you cannot petition Him; for you spoke proud and arrogant words against His righteousness, therefore you shall have no peace.

4 Don't you see the sailors of the ships, how their ships are tossed back and forth by the waves, and are shaken by the winds, and are in great trouble?

5 And therefore they are afraid because all their nice possessions go on the sea with them, and they have bad feelings in their heart that the sea will swallow them and they will perish therein.

6 Are not the entire sea and all its waters, and all its movements, the work of the Most High, and has He not set limits to its actions, and confined it throughout by the sand?

7 And at His reproof it fears and dries up, and all its fish die and all that is in it; but you sinners that are on the earth fear Him not.

8 Has He not made heaven and the earth, and all that is in it? Who has given understanding and wisdom to everything that moves on the earth and in the sea?

9 Do not the sailors of the ships fear the sea? Yet you sinners do not fear the Most High.

[Chapter 102]

1 In those days if He sent a horrible fire on you, where will you flee, and where will you find deliverance? And when He launches out His Word against you will you not be shaken and afraid?

2 And all the luminaries shall be shaken with great fear, and all the earth shall be afraid and tremble and be alarmed.

3 And all the angels shall execute their commands and shall seek to hide themselves from the presence of He who is Great in Glory, and the children of earth shall tremble and shake; and you sinners shall be cursed for ever, and you shall have no peace.

4 Fear you not, you souls of the righteous, and fear not you who have died in righteousness.

5 And don't grieve if your soul has descended in to the grave in grief, and that in your life you were not rewarded according to your goodness, but wait for the day of the judgment of sinners and for the day of cursing and chastisement.

6 And when you die the sinners will say about you: "As we die, so die the righteous, and what benefit do they reap for their deeds?

7 See, even as we, so do they die in grief and darkness, and what have they more than we? From now on we are equal.

8 And what will they receive and what will they see for ever? Look, they too have died, and from now on for ever shall they see no light."

9 I tell you, you sinners, you are content to eat and drink, and rob and sin, and strip men naked, and acquire wealth and see good days.

10 Have you seen the righteous how their end was peace, that no violence is found in them until their death?

11 Nevertheless they died and became as though they had not been, and their spirits descended into Hell in tribulation.

[Chapter 103]

1 Now, therefore, I swear to the righteous, by the glory of the Great and Honored and Mighty One who reigns, I swear to you, I know this mystery.

2 I have read the heavenly tablets, and have seen the holy books, and have found written in it and inscribed regarding them.

3 That all goodness and joy and glory are prepared for them, and written down for the spirits of those who have died in righteousness, and that much good shall be given to you in reward for your labors, and that your lot is abundant beyond the lot of the living.

4 And the spirits of you who have died in righteousness shall live and rejoice, and your spirits shall not perish, nor shall your memory from before the face of the Great One to all the generations of the world, therefore no longer fear their abuse.

5 Woe to you, you sinners, when you have died, if you die in the abundance of your sins, and woe to those who are like you and say regarding you: "Blessed are the sinners, they have seen all their days.

6 And how they have died in prosperity and in wealth, and have not seen tribulation or murder in their life; and they have died in honor, and judgment has not been executed on them during their life."

7 You know that their souls will be made to descend into Hell and they shall be wracked in great tribulation.

8 And into darkness and chains and a burning flame where there is harsh judgment your spirits shall enter, and the great judgment shall be for all the generations of the world. Woe to you, for you shall have no peace.

9 The righteous and good who are alive, do not say: "In our troubled days we have worked hard and experienced every trouble, and met with much evil and been afflicted, and have become few and our spirit small.

10 And we have been destroyed and have not found any to help us even with a word. We have been tortured and destroyed, and not expect to live from day to day.

11 We hoped to be the head and have become the tail. We have worked hard and had no satisfaction in our labor; and we have become the food of the sinners and the unrighteous, and they have laid their yoke heavily on us.

12 They have ruled over us and hated us and hit us, and to those that hated us we have bowed our necks but they pitied us not.

13 We desired to get away from them that we might escape and be at rest, but found no place where we should flee and be safe from them.

14 We complained to the rulers in our tribulation, and cried out against those who devoured us, but they did not pay attention to our cries and would not listen to our voice.

15 And they helped those who robbed us and devoured us and those who made us few; and they concealed their oppression (wrongdoing), and they did not remove from us the yoke of those that devoured us and dispersed us and murdered us, and they concealed their murder, and did not remember that they had lifted up their hands against us."

[Chapter 104]

1 I swear to you, that in heaven the angels remember you for good before the glory of the Great One.

2 And your names are written before the glory of the Great One. Be hopeful; for before you were put to shame through sickness and affliction; but now you shall shine as the lights of heaven,

3 You shall shine and you shall be seen, and the doors of heaven shall be opened to you. And in your cry, cry for judgment, and it shall appear to you; for all your tribulation shall be visited on the rulers, and on all who helped those who plundered you.

4 Be hopeful, and do not throw away your hopes for you shall have great joy as the angels of heaven.

5 What will you have to do? You shall not have to hide on the day of the great judgment and you shall not be found as sinners, and the eternal judgment shall not come to you for all the generations, eternally.

6 And now fear not, you righteous, when you see the sinners growing strong and prospering in their ways; do not be their companions, but keep away from their violence.

7 For you shall become companions of the hosts of heaven. And, although you sinners say: "All our sins shall not be found out and be written down," nevertheless they shall write down all your sins every day.

8 And now I show to you that light and darkness, day and night, see all your sins.

9 Do not be godless in your hearts, and do not lie and do not change the words of righteousness, nor say that the words of the Holy Great One are lies, nor praise or rely on your idols; for all your lying and all your godlessness (leads not to) come not from righteousness but (leads to) from great sin.

10 And now I know this mystery, that sinners will alter and pervert the words of righteousness in many ways, and will speak wicked words, and lie, and practice great deceits, and write books concerning their words.

11 But when they write down all my words truthfully in their languages, and do not change or omit any of my words but write them all down truthfully - all that I first testified concerning them.

12 Then, I know another mystery, that books will be given to the righteous and the wise to produce joy and righteousness and much wisdom.

13 And to them the books shall be given, and they shall believe them and rejoice over them, and then all the righteous who have learned from them all the paths of righteousness shall be paid back.'

[Chapter 105]

1 In those days the Lord called them (the wise and righteous) to testify to the children of earth concerning their wisdom: Show it to them; for you are their guides, and a recompense over the whole earth.

2 For I and my son will be united with them for ever in the paths of righteousness in their lives; and you shall have peace: rejoice, you children of righteousness. Amen.

[Chapter 106]

Fragment of the Book of Noah

1 And after some days my son Methuselah took a wife for his son, Lamech, and she became pregnant by him and bore a son. And his body was white as snow and red as the blooming of a rose, and the hair of his head and his long curls were white as wool, and his eyes beautiful.

2 And when he opened his eyes, he lit up the whole house like the sun, and the whole house was very bright.

3 And on it he levitated (arose) in the hands of the midwife, opened his mouth, and conversed with the Lord of righteousness.

4 And his father, Lamech, was afraid of him and fled, and came to his father Methuselah. And he said to him: 'I have begotten a strange son, different and unlike man, and resembling the sons of the God of heaven; and his nature is different and he is not like us, and his eyes are as the rays of the sun, and his face is glorious.

6 And it seems to me that he did not spring from me but from the angels, and I fear that in his days a wonder may be performed on the earth.

7 And now, my father, I am here to ask you and beg you that you may go to Enoch, our father, and learn from him the truth, for his dwelling-place is among the angels."

8 And when Methuselah heard the words of his son, he came to me to the ends of the earth; for he had heard that I was there, and he cried aloud, and I heard his voice and I came to him. And I said to him: 'Behold, here am I, my son, why have you come to me? '

9 And he answered and said: 'Because of a great cause of anxiety have I come to you, and because of a disturbing vision have I approached.

10 And now, my father, hear me. To Lamech, my son, there has been born a son, the like of whom there is none other, and his nature is not like man's nature, and the color of his body is whiter than snow and redder than the bloom of a rose, and the hair of his head is whiter than white wool, and his eyes are like the rays of the sun, and he opened his eyes and the whole house lit up.

11 And he levitated (arose) in the hands of the midwife, and opened his mouth and blessed the Lord of heaven.

12 And his father Lamech became afraid and fled to me, and did not believe that he was sprung from him, but that he was in the likeness of the angels of heaven; and now I have come to you that you may make known to me the truth.'

13 And I, Enoch, answered and said to him: 'The Lord will do a new thing on the earth, and this I have already seen in a vision, and make known to you that in the generation of my father Jared some of the angels of heaven violated the word of

the Lord. And they commit sin and broke the law, and have had sex (united themselves) with women and committed sin with them, and have married some of them, and have had children by them.

14 And they shall produce on the earth giants not according to the spirit, but according to the flesh, and there shall be a great punishment on the earth, and the earth shall be cleansed from all impurity.

15 There shall come a great destruction over the whole earth, and there shall be a flood (deluge) and a great destruction for one year.

16 And this son who has been born to you shall be left on the earth, and his three children shall be saved with him: when all mankind that are on the earth shall die, he and his sons shall be saved.

17 And now make known to your son, Lamech, that he who has been born is in truth his son, and call his name Noah; for he shall be left to you, and he and his sons shall be saved from the destruction, which shall come on the earth on account of all the sin and all the unrighteousness, which shall be full (completed) on the earth in his days.

18 And after that (flood) there shall be more unrighteousness than that which was done before on the earth; for I know the mysteries of the holy ones; for He, the Lord, has showed me and informed me, and I have read (them) in heavenly tablets.

[Chapter 107]

1 And I saw written about them that generation after generation shall transgress, until a generation of righteousness arises, and transgression is destroyed and sin passes away from the earth, and all manner of good comes on it.

2 And now, my son, go and make known to your son Lamech that this son, which has been born, is in truth his son, and this is no lie.'

3 And when Methuselah had heard the words of his father Enoch, for he had shown to him everything in secret, he returned and showed those things to him and called the name of that son Noah; for he will comfort the earth after all the destruction.

[Chapter 108]

1 Another book which Enoch wrote for his son Methuselah and for those who will come after him, and keep the law in the last days.

2 You who have done good shall wait for those days until an end is made of those who work evil; and an end of the power of the wrongdoers.

3 And wait until sin has passed away indeed, for their names shall be blotted out of the book of life and out of the holy books, and their (children) seed shall be destroyed for ever, and their spirits shall be killed, and they shall cry and lament in a place that is a chaotic desert, and they shall be burned in the fire; for there is no earth there.

4 I saw something there like an invisible cloud; because it was so deep I could not look over it, and I saw a flame of fire blazing brightly, and things like shining mountains circling and sweeping back and forth.

5 And I asked one of the holy angels who was with me and said to him: 'What is this bright thing (shining)? For it is not heaven but there was only the flame of a blazing fire, and the voice of weeping and crying and moaning, lamenting, and agony.'

6 And he said to me: 'This place which you see are where the spirits of sinners and blasphemers, and of those who work wickedness, are cast and the spirits of those who pervert everything that the Lord hath spoken through the mouth of the prophets and even the prophecies (things that shall be).

7 For some of them are written and inscribed above in heaven, in order that the angels may read them and know that which shall befall the sinners, and the spirits of the humble, and of those who have afflicted their bodies, and been recompensed by God; and of those who have been abused (put to shame) by wicked men:

8 Who love God and loved neither gold nor silver nor any of the good things which are in the world, but gave over their bodies to torture.

9 Who, since they were born, longed not after earthly food, but regarded everything as a passing breath, and lived accordingly, and the Lord tried them much, and their spirits were found pure so that they should bless His name.

10 And all the blessings destined for them I have recounted in the books. And he has assigned them their reward, because they have been found to love heaven more than their life in the world, and though they were trodden under foot by wicked men, and experienced abuse and reviling from them and were put to shame, they blessed Me.

11 And now I will summon the spirits of the good who belong to the generation of light, and I will transform those who were born in darkness, who in the flesh were not rewarded with such honor as their faithfulness deserved.

12 And I will bring out in shining light those who have loved My holy name, and I will seat each on the throne of his honor.

MAT 19:28 And Jesus said unto them, Verily I say unto you, That ye which have followed me, in the regeneration when the Son of man shall sit in the throne of his glory, ye also shall sit upon twelve thrones, judging the twelve tribes of Israel.

13 And they shall shine for time without end; for righteousness is the judgment of God; because to the faithful He will give faithfulness in the habitation of upright paths.

14 And they shall see those who were born in darkness led into darkness, while the righteous shall shine. And the sinners shall cry aloud and see them shining, and they indeed will go where days and seasons are written down (prescribed) for them.'

The End

Introduction to The Second Book of Enoch:
Slavonic Enoch

As part of the Enochian literature, The Second Book of Enoch is included in the pseudepigraphal corpus.

Pseudepigrapha : Spurious or pseudonymous writings, especially Jewish writings ascribed to various biblical patriarchs and prophets but composed within approximately 200 years of the birth of Jesus Christ.

In 1773, rumors of a surviving copy of an ancient book drew Scottish explorer James Bruce to distant Ethiopia. There, he found the "First Book of Enoch." Later, another "Book of Enoch" surfaced. The text, which is known as "Second Enoch," was discovered in 1886 by Professor Sokolov in the archives of the Belgrade Public Library. The Second Book of Enoch was written in the latter half of the first century A.D. The text was preserved only in Slavonic and consequently bears the designation, "Slavonic Enoch." The text has also been known by the titles of "2 Enoch", and "The Secrets of Enoch." 2 Enoch is basically an expansion of Genesis 5:21-32, taking the reader from the time of Enoch to the onset of the great flood of Noah's day.

The main theme of the book is the ascension of Enoch progressively through multiple heavens. During the ascension Enoch is transfigured into an angel and granted access to the secrets of creation. Enoch is then given a 30 day grace period to return to earth and instruct his sons and all the members of his household regarding everything God had revealed to him. The text reports that after period of grace an angel will then come to retrieve him to take him from the earth.

Many credible versions end with chapter 68, however there is a longer version of 2 Enoch, which we will examine. In this version the wisdom and insights given to the family of Enoch is passed from family members to Melchizedek, whom God raises up as an archpriest. Melchizedek then fulfills the function of a prophet-priest. To pave the way to Melchizedek, Methuselah functions as a priest for ten years and then passed his station on to Nir, Noah's younger brother. Nir's wife, Sopanim, miraculously conceives without human intercourse while about to die and posthumously gives birth to Melchizedek, who is born with the appearance and maturity of a three-year old child and the symbol of the priesthood on his chest.

The world is doomed to suffer the flood but Michael the archangel promises Melchizedek salvation. This establishes his priesthood for all of eternity. The text goes on to report that in the last generation, there will be another Melchizedek who will be "the head of all, a great archpriest, the Word and Power of God, who will perform miracles, greater and more glorious than all the previous ones".

The manuscripts, which contain and preserve this document, exist only in Old Slavonic. Of the twenty or more manuscripts dating from the 13th century A.D. no single one contains the complete text of 2 Enoch. When pieced together there appears to be two versions. These we will refer to as the long and short version.

The difference in length between the two is due to two quite different features. There are blocks of text found only in the longer manuscripts; but even when the passages are parallel, the longer manuscripts tend to be more full and detailed. At the same time there is so much verbal similarity when the passages correspond that a common source must be supposed.

The form of 2 Enoch is what one finds in Jewish Wisdom literature and Jewish Apocalyptic literature. It has been suggested that the longer version is characterized by editorial expansions and Christian interpolations. Hence, the shorter version contains fewer Christian elements. The author of 2 Enoch speaks much of the Creator and final judgment, but he speaks very little, about redemption, which seems to be absent from the thoughts of the author. Indeed, there seems to be a total lack of a Savior or Redeemer in 2 Enoch. What is noteworthy is that 2 Enoch has no reference to the mercy of God.

In the long version presented here, it appears that the last portion of the text was added as an afterthought. It contains the rise of Melchizedek. The appearance of Melchizedek ties 2 Enoch to several other texts forming a Melchizedkian tradition. The author of 2 Enoch follows a tradition in which an aged mother, who had been barren up to her deathbed, miraculously conceived Melchizedek without human intervention. Before she was able to give birth to the baby she died. The baby then emerged from her dead body with the maturity of a three-year-old boy. His priesthood will be perpetuated throughout the generations until "another Melchizedek" appears. If the last Melchizedek serves as the archpriest for the last generation, it indicates that in the mind of this Jewish writer, the Temple was to be rebuilt and would be the place were God would meet His people when the heathen nations were destroyed. The continuation and victory of the Jews as the selected and blessed people of God is implied. In this vein, 2 Enoch follows certain apocalyptic writings.

(For more information on apocalyptic writings see "End of Days" by Joseph Lumpkin.)

The Slavonic version is translated from a Greek source. Most scholars agree that there was either a Hebrew or Aramaic original lying behind the Greek source from which the Slavonic manuscripts were produced. The Hebrew origins are indicated by "Semitisms" in the work, but there are also Greek words and expressions, such as the names of the planets in chapter 30.

Proof that The Slavonic Enoch was written in Greek is shown by the derivation of Adam's name, and by several coincidences with the Septuagint. The origin of the story is perhaps based on Hebrew traditions and certain Semitic turns of language show up in the text. This tends to indicate that there was at one time a Hebrew or Aramaic text that preceded the Greek. From the Greek it was translated into Slavonic. Of this version there are five manuscripts or pieces thereof found.

The short version or the Slavonic Enoch was probably written by a single author in an attempt to bring all the current traditions about Enoch of his time into a central storyline and system. The schema to accomplish the unity of traditions implements Enoch's ascension through multiple heavens. This author was probably a Jew living in Egypt. There are several elements in the book, which betray Egyptian origin. The longer version of 2 Enoch was seeded with Christian elements and appended with an ending that does not fit well, illuminating the fact that there were several authors involved in the longer version.

Parts of the book was probably written in the late first century A.D. The first date is a limit set by the fact that Ethiopic Enoch, Ecclesiasticus, and Wisdom of Solomon are used as sources or references within the text; the second date is a limit set by the fact that the destruction of the Temple is not mentioned at all.

The Slavonic Enoch furnishes new material for the study of religious thought in the beginning of the Common Era. The ideas of the millennium and of the multiple heavens are the most important in this connection. Another very interesting feature is the presence of evil in heaven, the fallen angels in the second heaven, and hell in the third. The idea of evil in heaven may be a nod to the book of Job and the dialog between God and Satan, who was coming and going between heaven and earth. The idea of hell in the third heaven may have been derived from ideas expressed in the Old Testament book of Isaiah, which mentions that the sufferings of the wicked will be witnessed by the righteous in paradise.

Chapter 21 and forward for several chapters shows a heavy influence of Greek mythology. The Zodiac is mentioned along with celestial bodies with names such as Zeus, Cronus, Aphrodite, and others. The part of the text containing names and astrological descriptions could have been tampered with as late as the seventh century A.D.

By far, the most interesting and confusing section begins around chapter 25 and runs for several chapters. Here the text takes a turn toward Gnostic theology and cosmology. The Gnostics were a Christian sect, which formed and grew in the first century A.D. and thrived in the second century A.D.

Although Gnostic borrowed from Plato's (428 B.C. – 348 B.C.) creation myth, the maturity and construction of the story shows it to be of Gnostic Christian origin, placing it no earlier than the last part of the first century A.D. and no later than the end of the Second century. Add to the dating question the fact that the destruction of the Temple in Jerusalem is not mentioned, which leads to a date just before 70 A.D., if one assumes the Gnostic flavor was not added later.

The history of the text is obviously long and varied. It probably began as a Jewish oral tradition with pieces taken from several Enochian stories. It was first penned in Hebrew or Aramaic. The date of this incarnation of the text is unknown. Later, the story was expanded and embellished by Greek influences. Lastly, Christians and Gnostics commandeered the book and added their own matter. Thus 2 Enoch exhibits a kaleidoscope of cultural and religious contributions over a great scope of time from the first century B.C. (assuming it came after 1 Enoch) and ending as late as the seventh century A.D. These additions would allow any serious student insight into how ancient texts evolve.

Second Enoch was rediscovered and published in the early 19th century A.D The text before you uses the R. H. Charles and W. R. Morfill translation of 1896 with additions from other sources. Archaic terms and sentence structure were revised or explained to convey a more modern rendering for the twenty-first century readers.

2 Enoch
Slavonic Enoch
The Book of the Secrets of Enoch

Chapter 1
1 There was a wise man and a great craftsman, and the Lord formed a love for him and received him, so that he should see the highest dwellings and be an eye-witness of the wise and great and inconceivable and unchanging realm of God Almighty, and of the very wonderful and glorious and bright and manifold vision of the position of the Lord's servants, and of the inaccessible throne of the Lord, and of the degrees and manifestations of the spiritual (non-physical) hosts, and of the unspeakable ministration of the multitude of the elements, and of the various apparition and singing of the host of Cherubim which is beyond description, and of the limitless light.
2 At that time, he said, when my one hundred and sixty-fifth year was completed, I begat my son Methuselah.
3 After this I lived two hundred years and finished of all the years of my life three hundred and sixty-five years.
4 On the first day of the month I was in my house alone and was resting on my bed and slept.
5 And when I was asleep, great distress came up into my heart, and I was weeping with my eyes in sleep, and I could not understand what this distress was, or what was happening to me.
6 And there appeared to me two very large men, so big that I never saw such on earth. Their faces were shining like the sun, their eyes were like a burning light, and from their lips fire was coming out. They were singing. Their clothing was of various kinds in appearance and was purple. Their wings were brighter than gold, and their hands whiter than snow.
7 They were standing at the head of my bed and began to call me by my name.
8 And I arose from my sleep and clearly saw the two men standing in front of me.
9 And I greeted them and was seized with fear and the appearance of my face was changed to terror, and those men said to me:
10 Enoch, have courage and do not fear. The eternal God sent us to you, and you shall ascend today with us into heaven, and you shall tell your sons and all your household all that they shall do without you on earth in your house, and let no one seek you until the Lord returns you to them.
11 And I hurried to obey them and went out of my house, and went to the doors, as I was ordered, and I summoned my sons Methuselah and Regim and Gaidad and explained to them all the marvels the men had told me.

Chapter 2
1 Listen to me, my children, I do not know where I will go, or what will befall me. So now, my children, I tell you, do not turn from God in the face of that which is empty or prideful, which did not make heaven and earth, for these shall perish along with those who worship them, and may the Lord make your hearts confident in the fear (respect) of him. And now, my children, let no one consider seeking me, until the Lord returns me to you.

Chapter 3
1 (It came to pass, when Enoch had finished speaking to his sons, that the angels took him on to their wings and lifted him up on to the first heaven and placed him on the clouds.)
And there I (Enoch) looked, and again I looked higher, and saw the ether, and they placed me on the first heaven and showed me a very large sea, bigger than the earthly sea.

Chapter 4
1 They brought the elders and rulers of the stellar orders in front of me, and showed me two hundred angels, who rule the stars and services of the stars to the heavens, and fly with their wings and come round all those who sail.

Chapter 5
1 And here I looked down and saw the storehouses of snow, and the angels who keep their amazing storehouses, and the clouds where they come out of and into which they go.

Chapter 6
1 They showed me the storehouse of the dew, like olive oil in its appearance and its form, as of all the flowers of the earth. And they also showed me many angels guarding the storehouses of these things, and how they are made to shut and open.

Chapter 7

1 And those men took me and led me up on to the second heaven, and showed me darkness, greater than earthly darkness, and there I saw prisoners hanging, watched, (guarded,) awaiting the great and limitless judgment, and the spirits were dark in appearance, more than earthly darkness, and perpetually weeping through all hours.

2 And I said to the men who were with me: Why are these being unceasingly tortured? They answered me: These are God's apostates, who did not obey God's commands, but took counsel with their own will, and turned away with their prince, who is also held captive in the fifth heaven.

3 And I felt great pity for them, and they greeted me, and said to me: Man of God, pray to the Lord for us. And I answered them: I am just a mortal man. Who am I that I should pray for spirits? Who knows where I go or what will become of me? Or who will pray for me?

Chapter 8

1 And those men took me from there and led me up on to the third heaven, and placed me there. I looked down and saw what this place produces and that it was so good that such as has never been known.

2 And I saw all the sweet, flowering trees and I saw their fruits, which were sweet smelling, and I saw all the foods that came from them and that the food was bubbling with fragrant vapors.

3 And in the middle of the trees was the tree of life, in that place where the Lord rests when he goes up into paradise. And this tree is of indescribable goodness and fragrance, and adorned more than anything existing. And all sides of its form were golden and brilliant red and fire-like and it was completely covered, and it produced all fruits.

4 Its root is in the garden at the earth's end.

5 And paradise resides between spiritual and physical.

6 And two springs come out which send forth honey and milk, and their springs send forth oil and wine, and they separate into four parts, and flow quietly around, and go down into the paradise of Eden, between the mutable and the eternal.

7 And there they go forth along the earth, and have a circular flow even as other elements.

8 And there is no unfruitful tree here, and every place is blessed.

9 Three hundred angels, which are very bright, are there to keep the garden, and with incessant sweet singing with voices, which are never silent, serve the Lord throughout all the hours of days.

10 And I said: How very sweet is this place, and those men said to me:

Chapter 9

1 This place, O Enoch, is prepared for the righteous, who endure all manner of offence from those that exasperate their souls, who avert their eyes from iniquity, and make righteous judgment, and give bread to the hungering, and cover the naked with clothing, and raise up the fallen, and help injured orphans, and who walk without fault before the face of the Lord, and serve him alone, and for them is prepared this place for eternal inheritance.

Chapter 10

1 And those two men led me up on to the Northern side, and showed me there a very terrible place, and there were every kind of tortures in that place: cruel darkness and gloom, and there was absolutely no light at all there, but murky fire constantly flaming above, and there is a fiery river coming out, and everywhere in that entire place is fire, and everywhere there is frost and ice, thirst and shivering, while the physical restraints are very cruel, and the spirits were fearsome and merciless, bearing angry weapons, torturing without mercy.

2 And I said: Woe, woe! This place is so terrible.

3 And those men said to me: This place, O Enoch, is prepared for those who dishonor God, who on earth practice sin against nature, which is sodomy of a child, corruption of children, performing magic, enchantments and devilish witchcrafts, and who boast of their wicked deeds, stealing, lying, slander, envy, resentment, fornication, murder, and who are accursed and steal the souls of men, and those who see the poor and still take away their goods so they grow rich, and injure them for other men's goods. And this is reserved for those who satisfy their own emptiness made the hungering die; those who clothe themselves by stripping the naked; and who did not know their creator, but instead bowed to lifeless gods who have no soul who cannot see nor hear, empty, who built carved images and bow down to unclean fashioning of useless gods, this place is prepared for these as an eternal inheritance.

Chapter 11

1 Those men took me, and led me up on to the fourth heaven, and showed me the entire succession of activities, and all the rays of the light of sun and moon.

2 And I measured their progression, and compared their light, and saw that the sun's light is greater than the moon's.

3 Its circle and the wheels on which it goes always is like the wind passing with very amazing speed with no rest day or night.

4 Its egress and ingress are accompanied by four huge stars, and each star has a thousand stars under it, to the right of the sun's wheel there are four thousand stars and to the left are four thousand, altogether eight thousand, going out with the sun continually.

5 And by day fifteen groups of ten thousand angels attend it, and by night there were a thousand.

6 And six-winged ones go fourth with the angels before the sun's wheel into the fiery flames, and a hundred angels kindle the sun and set it alight.

Chapter 12

1 And I looked and saw other flying elements of the sun, whose names are Phoenixes and Chalkydri, which are marvelous and wonderful, with feet and tails of a lion, and a crocodile's head, they appear to be purple in color like that in the rainbow; their size is nine hundred measures, their wings are like those of angels, each has twelve wings, and they attend and accompany the sun, bearing heat and dew, as it is ordered them from God.

(Note: The word CHALKYDRI means "serpents". It appears that the Slavonic translators rendered the Hebrew word SERAPHIM differently in various places in the text. The word was translated "Serpent" in some places and SERAPHIM in others.)

2 This is how the sun revolves and goes, and rises under the heaven, and its course goes under the earth with the light of its rays continually.

Chapter 13

1 Then those men carried me away to the east, and placed me at the sun's gates, where the sun has egress according to the seasons circuit and regulation of the months of the whole year, and the number of the hours day and night.

2 And I saw six gates open, each gate having sixty-one stadia (185 meters) and A quarter of one stadium (46.25 meters), and I measured them accurately, and knew their size. Through the gates the sun goes out, and goes to the west, and is made even, and rises throughout all the months, and turns back again from the six gates according to the succession of the seasons. In this way the period of the entire year is finished after the return of the four seasons.

(Note: 6 X 61=366 With the quarter day added, this is the length of the leap year.)

Chapter 14

1 And again those men led me away to the western parts, and showed me six great open gates corresponding to the eastern gates, opposite to where the sun sets, according to the number of the days three hundred and sixty-five and a quarter.

(Note that this is a solar calendar of the same length as our modern calendar.)

2 Again it goes down to the western gates, and diminishes (pulls away) its light with the prominent brightness, under the earth. The crown of its glory is in heaven with the Lord, and it is guarded by four hundred angels while the sun goes round on wheel under the earth. And it stands seven great hours in night, and spends half its course under the earth. And when it comes to the eastern approach in the eighth hour of the night it brings its lights and the crown of glory, and the sun burns (flames) outwardly more than fire.

Chapter 15

1 Then the elements of the sun, called Phoenixes and Chalkydri (Seraphim) break into song, therefore every bird flutters its wings, rejoicing at the giver of light, and they brake into song at the command of the Lord.

2 The giver of light comes to illuminate the entire world, and the morning guard takes shape, which is the rays of the sun, and the sun of the earth goes out, and receives its luminance to light up the entire face of the earth, and they showed me this calculation of the sun's going.

3 And the great gates, which it enters into, are for the calculation of the hours of the year. For this reason the sun is a great creation, whose circuit lasts twenty-eight years, and begins again from the beginning.

(Note: For 29 February, which is the leap year day, to fall on a particular weekday, there is a 28-year (2 x 14 year) cycle. This forms a type of perpetual calendar.)

Chapter 16

1 Those men showed me the great course of the moon. There are twelve great gates that are crowned from west to east, by which the moon comes and goes in its customary times.

2 It goes in at the first gate to the western places of the sun, by the first gates with thirty-one days exactly, by the second gates with thirty-one days exactly, by the third with thirty days exactly, by the fourth with thirty days exactly, by the fifth with thirty-one days exactly, by the sixth with thirty-one days exactly, by the seventh with thirty days exactly, by the eighth with thirty-one days perfectly, by the ninth with thirty-one days exactly, by the tenth with thirty days perfectly, by the eleventh with thirty-one days exactly, by the twelfth with twenty-eight days exactly.

(Note: The sum of the days total 365 with the year beginning in March.)

3 And it goes through the western gates in the order and number of the eastern, and accomplishes the three hundred and sixty-five and a quarter days of the solar year, while the lunar year has three hundred fifty-four, and there twelve days lacking of the solar circle, which are the lunar epacts of the whole year.

(Note: epact | The number of days by which the solar year differs from the lunar year.
• the number of days into the moon's phase cycle at the beginning of the solar (calendar) year.
Origin - mid 16th century. (Denoting the age of the moon in days at the beginning of the calendar year): from French épacte, via late Latin from Greek epaktai (h merai) 'intercalated (days).

4 The great circle also contains five hundred and thirty-two years.

(Note: The 532-year cycle is calculated from the creation of Adam, which, as we know, took place on Friday, March 1, 5508 B.C., which is the base date on which the entire calendar system of the Orthodox Church is founded. The final sections of the Typikon, which is the book that dictates the services, are the Paschalion Calendar sections. Here, there are tables reflecting the 532 year cycle of the Church services, which consists of 19-year solar cycles multiplied by 28-day lunar cycles. There is a table that consists of 19 columns by 28 rows, giving the Paschal Key number or letter for each of the years of the 532-year cycle. Once you know the Paschal Key, you look up the details in the following section, which consists of 35 brief calendar synopses, one for each possible day that Pascha can fall. Each of these synopses actually consists of two services; one for regular years, and one for leap years.

5 The quarter (of a day) is omitted for three years, the fourth fulfills it exactly.

6 Because of this, they are taken outside of heaven for three years and are not added to the number of days, because they change the time of the years to two new months toward completion, to two others toward the decrease.

7 And when the course through the western gates is finished, it returns and goes to the eastern to the lights, and goes this way day and night in its heavenly circles, below all circles, swifter than the heavenly winds, and spirits and elements and flying angels. Each angel has six wings.

8 In nineteen years it travels the course seven times.

Chapter 17

1 In the midst of the heavens I saw armed soldiers, serving the Lord, with drums and organs, with constant voice, with sweet voice, with sweet and unceasing voice and various singing, which it is impossible to describe, and which astonishes every mind, so wonderful and marvelous is the singing of those angels, and I was delighted listening to it.

Chapter 18

1 The men took me on to the fifth heaven and placed me, and there I saw many and countless soldiers, called Grigori, of human appearance, and their size (was) greater than that of great giants and their faces withered, and the silence of their mouths perpetual, and their was no service on the fifth heaven, and I said to the men who were with me:

(Note: The Greek transliteration egegoroi are the Watchers; a group of fallen angels who mated with mortal women and produced the Nephilim mentioned in the books of Jubilees, 1Enoch, and Genesis 6:4.)

2 Why are they so very withered and their faces melancholy, and their mouths silent, and why is there no service in this heaven?

3 And they said to me: These are the Grigori, who with their prince Satanail (Satan) rejected the Lord of Light. After them are those who are held in great darkness in the second heaven, and three of them went down on to earth from the Lord's throne, to the place Ermon, and broke through their vows on the shoulder of the hill Ermon and saw the daughters of men how good they are, and took to themselves wives, and fouled the earth with their deeds, who broke the law and mixing (with the women), giants are born and amazingly large men with great hatred.

(Note: The Hill of Ermon could be Mount Hermon, which is mentioned over a dozen times in the Bible.)

4 And therefore God judged them with great judgment, and they weep for their brethren and they will be punished on the Lord's great day.

5 And I said to the Grigori: I saw your brethren and their works, and their great torments, and I prayed for them, but the Lord has condemned them to be under earth until this heaven and this earth shall end for ever.

6 And I said: Why do you stand there, brethren, and do not serve before the Lord's face, and have not put your services before the Lord's face? You could anger your Lord completely.

7 And they listened to my advice, and spoke to the four ranks in heaven. As I stood with those two men four trumpets sounded together with a loud voice, and the Grigori broke into song with one voice, and their voice went up before the Lord pitifully and touchingly.

Chapter 19

1 From there, those men took me and lifted me up on to the sixth heaven, and there I saw seven bands of angels, very bright and very glorious, and their faces shining more than the sun's shining, glistening, and there is no difference in their faces, or behavior, or manner of dress; and these make the orders, and learn the goings of the stars, and the alteration of the moon, or revolution of the sun, and the good administration of the world.

2 And when they see evildoing they make commandments and instruction, and make sweet and loud singing, and all (songs) of praise.

3 These are the archangels who are above angels, and they measure all life in heaven and on earth, and the angels who are (appointed) over seasons and years, the angels who are over rivers and sea, and who are over the fruits of the earth, and the angels who are over every grass, giving food to every and all living things, and the angels who write down all the souls of men, and all their deeds, and their lives before the Lord's face. In their midst are six Phoenixes and six Cherubim and six six-winged ones continually singing with one voice, and it is not possible to describe their singing, and they rejoice before the Lord at his footstool.

Chapter 20

1 And those two men lifted me up from there on to the seventh heaven, and I saw there a very great light, and fiery troops of great archangels, incorporeal forces, and dominions, orders and governments, Cherubim and Seraphim, thrones and many-eyed ones, nine regiments, the Ioanit stations of light, and I became afraid, and began to tremble with great terror, and those men took me, and led me after them, and said to me:

2 Have courage, Enoch, do not fear, and showed me the Lord from afar, sitting on His very high throne. For what is there on the tenth heaven, since the Lord dwells there?

3 On the tenth heaven is God, in the Hebrew tongue he is called Aravat.

(Note: The meaning of Ioanit is not clear. However, it may be derived from the transliteration of the name John. John means, "The Lord is Gracious." The meaning of Aravat is equally unclear but seems to mean, "Father of Creation."
Each level of heaven represents or demonstrates a personality or part of the Godhead. One of the highest demonstrations of God's power and divinity is the power of Creation. It is found on the tenth level of heaven.)

4 And all the heavenly soldiers would come and stand on the ten steps according to their rank, and would bow down to the Lord, and would then return to their places in joy and bliss, singing songs in the unlimited light with soft and gentle voices, gloriously serving him.

(Note: Strong and fierce soldiers sing with soft, gentle voices, bowing and serving in bliss.)

Chapter 21

1 And the Cherubim and Seraphim standing around the throne, and the six-winged and many-eyed ones do not depart, standing before the Lord's face doing his will, and cover his whole throne, singing with gentle voice before the Lord's face: Holy, holy, holy, Lord Ruler of Sabaoth (Host / army), heavens and earth are full of Your glory.

2 When I saw all these things, the men said to me: Enoch, thus far we were commanded to journey with you, and those men went away from me and after that I did not see them.

3 And I remained alone at the end of the seventh heaven and became afraid, and fell on my face and said to myself: Woe is me. What has befallen me?

4 And the Lord sent one of his glorious ones, the archangel Gabriel, and he said to me: "Have courage, Enoch, do not fear, arise before the Lord's face into eternity, arise and come with me."

5 And I answered him, and said within myself: My Lord, my soul has departed from me from terror and trembling, and I called to the men who led me up to this place. I relied on them, and it is with them that I can go before the Lord's face.

(Note: When speaking to God, Enoch "said within himself." He did not have to speak aloud.)

6 And Gabriel lifted me up like a leaf caught up by the wind, and he placed me before the Lord's face.

7 And I saw the eighth heaven, which is called in the Hebrew tongue Muzaloth, (Zodiac) changer of the seasons, of drought, and of wet, and of the twelve constellations of the circle of the firmament, which are above the seventh heaven.

8 And I saw the ninth heaven, which is called in Hebrew Kuchavim, where are the heavenly homes of the twelve constellations of the circle of the firmament.

Chapter 22

1 On the tenth heaven, which is called Aravoth, I saw the appearance of the Lord's face, like iron made to glow in fire, and it shone forth and casted out, emitting sparks, and it burned.

(Note: One possible meaning of Aravoth is "three times holy" or "holy, holy, holy."

2 In a moment of eternity I saw the Lord's face, but the Lord's face is indescribable, marvelous and very amazing, and very, very terrible.

3 And who am I to tell of the Lord's unspeakable being, and of his very wonderful face? I cannot tell the amount of his instructions, and the variety of voices. The Lord's throne is very great and not made with hands, and I cannot tell the number of those standing around him. There were troops of Cherubim and Seraphim, and they sang unceasingly. I cannot tell of his unchanging beauty. Who shall tell of the unpronounceable greatness of his glory?

4 And I fell prone and bowed down to the Lord, and the Lord with his lips said to me:

5 Have courage, Enoch, do not fear, arise and stand before my face into eternity (stand before my face eternally / stand before my eternal face.)

(Note: Enoch is out of and above time-space. Eternity is now and he can feel the timelessness of where he is. The language struggles to convey this fact.)

6 And the archangel Michael lifted me up, and led me to the Lord's face.

7 And the Lord said to his servants, testing them: Let Enoch stand before my face into eternity, and the glorious ones bowed down to the Lord, and said: Let Enoch go according to Your word.

8 And the Lord said to Michael: Go and take Enoch and remove his earthly garments, and anoint him with my sweet ointment, and put him into the garments of My glory.

9 And Michael did as the Lord told him. He anointed me, and dressed me, and the appearance of that ointment is more than the great light, and his ointment is like sweet dew, and its smell mild, shining like the sun's ray, and I looked at myself, and I was transformed into one of his glorious ones.

(Note: The number symbolism of ten is that of new starts at a higher level, new beginnings, and re-creation.)

10 And the Lord summoned one of his archangels, whose name is Pravuil, whose knowledge was quicker in wisdom than the other archangels, who wrote all the deeds of the Lord; and the Lord said to Pravuil: Bring out the books from my store-houses, and a reed of quick-writing, and give it to Enoch, and deliver to him the best and comforting books out of your hand.

(Note: Enoch is now an angel. He now has access to the heavenly records and the understanding to use the knowledge. A reed was used in writing much like a quill was used.)

Chapter 23

1 And he was explaining to me all the works of heaven, earth and sea, and all the elements, their passages and goings, and the sounding of the thunders, the sun and moon, the progression and changes of the stars, the seasons, years, days, and hours, as well as the risings of the wind, the numbers of the angels, and the formation of their songs, and all human things, the tongue of every human song and life, the commandments, instructions, and sweet-voiced singings, and all things that are fitting to learn.

2 And Pravuil told me: All the things that I have told you, we have written. Sit and write all the souls of mankind, however many of them are born, and the places prepared for them to eternity. And he said, all souls are prepared for eternity, before the formation of the world.

3 And for both thirty days and thirty nights, and I wrote out all things exactly, and wrote three hundred and sixty-six books.

(Note: If all things were created in six days, then the souls of all people were created at that time. In Jewish mythology, the place that the souls were houses until birth was called the Guf. Each soul was created for a certain place, time, and destiny. According to one version of

the myth, when the Guf is emptied of souls, time ceases. In another version, when the last soul dies and returns to God, time will end. Enoch wrote 366 book in a 720 hour period containing information on all things, including, "all souls (who) are prepared for eternity, before the formation of the world.")

Chapter 24
1 And the Lord summoned me, and said to me: Enoch, sit down on my left with Gabriel.
2 And I bowed down to the Lord, and the Lord spoke to me: Enoch, beloved, all that you see, all things that are standing finished, I tell you even before the very beginning, I created all things from non-being. I created the visible, physical things from the invisible, spiritual (world).
3 Hear, Enoch, and take in my words, for I have not told My angels My secret, and I have not told them their rise (beginnings), nor My endless realm, nor have they understood my creating, which I tell you today.
4 For before all things were visible, physical, I alone used to go about in the invisible, spiritual things, like the sun from east to west, and from west to east.
5 But even the sun has peace in itself, while I found no peace, because I was creating all things, and I conceived the thought of placing foundations, and of creating the visible, physical creation.

(Note: Overview of the heavens:
First heaven - , Enoch arrives on angel's wings. There are storehouses of snow and dew.
Second heaven - , Enoch finds a group of fallen angels. There is darkness and torture.
Third heaven - There are sweet flowers, trees, and fruit.
Fourth heaven – There are soldiers, heaven's army, and the progression of sun and moon.
Fifth heaven - The leaders of the fallen angels, the "Grigori" (Greek "Gregoroi," translating Mearim, the Hebrew word for watchers.)
Three of them went down and had intercourse with the daughters of men, yielding giants, who became the source of enmity on earth.
Sixth heaven – Seven bands of angels and the ordering of the stars.
Seventh heaven, shows something unusual happening to Enoch when Gabriel puts Enoch in front of the throne of the Lord.
The Eighth, Ninth, and Tenth Heavens are thought to be later additions and not part of the original text.
Eighth heaven - "Muzaloth" -- Zodiac
Ninth heaven - "Kuchavim" -- heavenly bodies (stars).
Tenth heaven - "Aravoth" -- descriptions of God's face like that of iron made to glow in fire.
Enoch sees the "appearance of the Lord's face," but describes it as indescribable.
Pravuil, the archangel, is commanded to write down secret information about astronomy, climate, and language and give it over to Enoch.
In other Enochian writings the same angel, also spelled "Penemue", is criticized for teaching humans to write.

Chapter 25
1 I commanded in the very lowest parts, that the visible, physical things should come down from the invisible, spiritual (realm), and Adoil came down very great, and I beheld him, and he had a belly of great light.
2 And I said to him: Become undone, Adoil, and let the visible, physical (universe) come out of you.
3 And he came undone, and a great light came out. And I was in the midst of the great light, and as there is born light from light, there came forth a great age (eon / space of time), and showed all creation, which I had thought to create.
4 And I saw that it was good.
5 And I placed for myself a throne, and took my seat on it, and said to the light: Go up higher from here and station yourself high above the throne, and be a foundation to the highest things.
6 And above the light there is nothing else, and then I rose up and looked up from my throne.

(Note: Beginning with chapters 25 and 26, the book of 2 Enoch takes a rather Gnostic diversion. The Gnostics were a Christian sect that flourished around the 3rd century A.D. The Gnostic view of the Godhead borrowed heavily from the creation saga preached by Plato (circa 428 B.C. to 348 B.C.) The story of Adoil and the emanation of pure light from God, which brings about creation of the physical world, is similar to other Gnostic works. Gnosticism teaches that in the beginning a Supreme Being called The Father, The Divine All, The Origin, The Supreme God, or The Fullness, emanated the element of existence, both visible and invisible. His intent was not to create but, just as light emanates from a flame, so did creation shine forth from God. This manifested the primal element needed for creation.

This was the creation of Barbelo, who is the "Thought of God."
The Father's thought performed a deed and she was created from it. It is she who had appeared before him in the shining of his light. This is the first power which was before all of them and which was created from his mind. She is the Thought of the All and her light shines like his light. It is the perfect power, which is the visage of the invisible. She is the pure, undefiled Spirit who is perfect. She is the first power. Adoil has that place is this myth.

It could be said that Barbelo was the creative emanation and, like the Divine All, is both male and female. It was the "agreement" of Barbelo and the Divine All, representing the union of male and female, that created the Christ Spirit and all the Aeons. In some renderings the word "Aeon" is used to designate an ethereal realm or kingdom. In other versions "Aeon" indicates the ruler of the realm. The Aeons of this world are merely reflections of the Aeons of the eternal realm. The reflection is always inferior to real.

In several Gnostic cosmologies the "living" world is under the control of entities called Aeons, of which Sophia is head. This means the Aeons influence or control the soul, life force, intelligence, thought, and mind. Control of the mechanical or inorganic world is given to the Archons.

The Archons were created by Sophia. Sophia, probably out of pride, tried to emulate the creative force of God by created an image of herself. Meaning that she wanted to produce an offspring, without either consort or the approval of her Father, God. As an aeon, she did have the power to do so, but she wasn't perfect like the Great Spirit, or like the other two perfect aeons, Barbelo and the Autogenes. Nevertheless, in her arrogance, she attempted to create and failed. She was horrified when she saw her creation, imperfect, bruthish creature with a lion-faced serpent with eyes of fire, whom she called Yaldabaoth.
Sophia cast her offspring out of pleroma (heaven), and hid her child within a thick cloud from the other aeons, because of her embarrassment and shame.
Yaldabaoth was the first of the archon ("ruler") and he stole his mother's power, so that she wasn't able to escape from the cloud. Despite gaining Sophia's aeonic power, he was weak, but prideful, ambitious and power hungry.
Since the archons, including Yaldabaoth, were androgynous beings, Yaldabaoth fathered twelve archons, giving each a bit of his power. They were named Athoth, Harmas, Kalila-Oumbri, Yabel, Adonaiou (or Sabaoth), Cain, Abel, Abrisene, Yobel, Armoupieel, Melceir-Adonein and Belias. Seven archons would rule seven heavens and five in the abyss, which Yaldabaoth and the archons created. Each archon would rule a heaven (or the abyss), and created 365 angels to help them.

The archons rule the physical aspects of systems, regulation, limits, and order in the world. Both the ineptitude and cruelty of the Archons are reflected in the chaos and pain of the material realm.
(See the book, The Gnostic Scriptures, by Joseph Lumpkin, published by Fifth Estate.)

Although the above may be a digression from the text of 2 Enoch, it adds insight into the time frame and origins of its production. Gnostic influences were felt from the late first century to the early fourth century A.D. If the writer of this section of 2 Enoch was exposed to the Gnostic sect, it would conclusively make 2 Enoch a text with Christian influences.)

Chapter 26

1 And I summoned the very lowest a second time, and said: Let Archas come forth hard, and he came forth hard from the invisible, spiritual.
2 And Archas came forth, hard, heavy, and very red.
3 And I said: Be opened, Archas, and let there be born from you, and he came apart, and an age came forth, very great and very dark, bearing the creation of all lower things, and I saw that it was good and said to him:
4 Go down below, and make yourself solid, and be a foundation for the lower things, and it happened and he went down and stationed himself, and became the foundation for the lower things, and below the darkness there is nothing else.

(Note: Hard and heavy could be terms for "gravid" or pregnant, with birth being imminent. Archas could equate to "The Archons.")

Chapter 27

1 And I commanded that there should be taken from light and darkness, and I said: Be thick, and it became thick, and I spread it out with the light, and it became water, and I spread it out over the darkness, below the light, and then I made firm the waters, that is to say the bottomless (abyss), and I made foundation of light around the water, and created seven circles from inside, and made the water look like crystal, wet and dry, so it was like glass, and the circles were around the waters and the other elements, and I showed each one of them its path, and the seven stars each one of them in its heaven, that they go that way, and I saw that it was good.
2 And I made separations between light and darkness in the midst of the water here and there, and I said to the light, that it should be the day, and to the darkness, that it should be the night, and there was evening and there was morning on the first day.

(Note: The foundation of light around the water that is like crystal is likely a reference to the sky. One belief of the time was that the sky was an expanse of water like an endless sea.)

Chapter 28

1 And then I made firm the heavenly circle, and made that the lower water which is under heaven collect itself together into one whole, and that the chaos become dry, and it became so.

2 Out of the waves I created hard and large rock, and from the rock I piled up the dry (land), and the dry (land) I called earth, and the middle of the earth I called the abyss, or the bottomless. I collected the sea in one place and bound it together with a yoke. *(Note: This is the bank or shoreline.)*

3 And I said to the sea: Behold I give you eternal limits, and you shall not break loose from your integral parts.

4 Thus I made the firmament hold together. This day I called me the first-created, Sunday. (This, I call the first day of creation.)

Chapter 29

1 And for all the heavenly soldiers I made them the image and essence of fire, and my eye looked at the very hard, firm rock, and from the gleam of my eye the lightning received its wonderful nature, (which) is both fire in water and water in fire, and one does not put out the other, nor does the one dry up the other, therefore the lightning is brighter than the sun, softer than water and firmer than hard rock.

(Note: If the sky is made of water and lightning, which is fire, issues from the sky, then water and fire must exist together in a heavenly form.)

2 And from the rock I cut off a great fire, and from the fire I created the orders of the incorporeal (spiritual / non-physical) ten troops of angels, and their weapons are fiery and their raiment a burning flame, and I commanded that each one should stand in his order.

3 And one from out the order of angels, having violated the command he was given, conceived an impossible thought, to place his throne higher than the clouds above the earth so that he might become equal in rank to my power.

4 And I threw him out from the height with his angels, and he was flying in the air continuously above the bottomless (abyss).

(Note: We assume this ends the second day, although it is not mentioned.)

Chapter 30

1 On the third day I commanded the earth to make grow great and fruitful trees, and hills, and seed to sow, and I planted Paradise, and enclosed it, and placed armed guards in the form of my flaming angels, and in this way I created renewal.

2 Then came evening, and morning came of the fourth day.

3 On Wednesday, the fourth day, I commanded that there should be great lights on the heavenly circles.

4 On the first uppermost circle I placed the stars, Cronus, and on the second Aphrodite, on the third Ares, on the fifth Zeus, on the sixth Ermis (Hermes), on the seventh lesser the moon, and adorned it with the lesser stars.

(Note: The fourth heavenly circle is vacant. The Greek names for the heavenly bodies leave no doubt as to the influence of Greek words and ideas within this section of the text.)

5 And on the lower (parts) I placed the sun for the illumination of day, and the moon and stars for the illumination of night.

6 (And I set) the sun that it should go according to each of the twelve constellations , and I appointed the succession of the months and their names and lives, their thundering, and how they mark the hours, and how they should proceed.

7 Then evening came and morning came of the fifth day.

8 On Thursday, the fifth day, I commanded the sea, that it should bring forth fishes, and feathered birds of many varieties, and all animals creeping over the earth, going forth over the earth on four legs, and soaring in the air, of male and female sex, and every soul breathing the spirit of life.

(Note: Verse eight proclaims the creation of all souls breathing (inspired by) the spirit of life. The next verse proclaims the creation of man. This day filled the Guf and incarnation begins in next.)

9 And there came evening, and there came morning of the sixth day.

10 On Friday, the sixth day, I commanded my wisdom to create man from seven consistent applications: one, his flesh from the earth; two, his blood from the dew; three, his eyes from the sun; four, his bones from stone; five, his intelligence from the swiftness of the angels and cloud; six, his veins and his hair from the grass of the earth; seven, his soul from my breath and from the wind.

11 And I gave him seven natures: to the flesh - hearing, the eyes for sight, to the soul - smell, the veins for touch, the blood for taste, the bones for endurance, to the intelligence - enjoyment.

12 I created a saying (speech) from knowing. I created man from spiritual and from physical nature, from both come his death and life and appearance. He knows speech like some created thing. He is small in greatness and great in smallness, and I placed him on earth, like a second angel, to be honorable, great and glorious. And I appointed him as ruler to rule on earth and to have my wisdom, and there was none like him on earth of all my existing creatures.

13 And I appointed him a name made from the four components, from east, from west, from south, and from north. And I appointed for him four special stars, and I called his name Adam, and showed him the two ways, the light and the darkness, and I told him:

14 This is good, and that bad, so that I should learn whether he has love towards me, or hatred, and so that it would be clear who in his race loves me.

(Note: The Hebrew name of Adam means "man.)

15 For I have seen his nature, but he has not seen his own nature, and therefore by not seeing it he will sin worse, and I said, "After sin is there nothing but death?"

16 And I put sleep into him and he fell asleep. And I took from him a rib, and created him a wife, so that death should come to him by his wife, and I took his last word and called her name mother, that is to say, Eve.

Chapter 31

1 Adam has life on earth, and I created a garden in Eden in the east, so that he should observe the testament and keep the command.

2 I made the heavens open to him, so that he would see the angels singing the song of victory, and the light without shadow.

3 And he was continuously in paradise, and the devil understood that I wanted to create another world, because Adam was lord on earth, to rule and control it.

4 The devil is the evil spirit of the lower places, he made himself a fugitive from the heavens as the devil and his name was Satan. Thus he became different from the angels, but his nature did not change his intelligence as it applied to his understanding of righteous and sinful things.

5 And he understood his condemnation and the sin that he had committed before. Therefore he devised a thought against Adam, in which he entered and seduced Eve, but did not touch Adam.

6 But I cursed ignorance. However, what I had blessed before I did not curse. I did not curse man, nor the earth, nor other creatures. But I cursed man's evil results, and his works.

Chapter 32

1 I said to him: You are earth (dirt), and into the earth from where I took you, you shall go, and I will not destroy you, but send you back from where I took you.

2 Then I can again receive you at My second presence.

3 And I blessed all my creatures, both physical and spiritual. And Adam was five and half hours in paradise.

4 And I blessed the seventh day, which is the Sabbath, on which he rested from all his works.

(Note: The five and a half hours is tied to the 5500 years of punishment mentioned in the Books of Adam and Eve. Se "The First and Second Books of Adam and Eve" by Joseph Lumpkin.)

Chapter 33

1 And I appointed the eighth day also, that the eighth day should be the first-created after my work, and that the first seven revolve in the form of the seventh thousand, and that at the beginning of the eighth thousand there should be a time of not-counting, endless, with neither years nor months nor weeks nor days nor hours.

(Note: A day is as a thousand years. This is a prophecy seems to indicate that after six thousand years there will be a thousand years of rest, then there will be timelessness.)

2 And now, Enoch, all that I have told you, all that you have understood, all that you have seen of heavenly things, all that you have seen on earth, all that I have written in books by my great wisdom, and all these things I have devised and created from the uppermost foundation to the lower and to the end, and there is no counselor nor inheritor to my creations.

3 I am eternal unto myself, not made with hands, and without change.

4 My thought is my own counselor, my wisdom and my word creates, and my eyes observe how all things stand here and tremble with terror.

5 If I turn away my face, then all things will be destroyed.

6 Apply your mind, Enoch, and know him who is speaking to you, and take the books there, which you yourself have written.

7 I give you Samuil and Raguil, who led you upward with the books, and go down to earth, and tell your sons all that I have told you, and all that you have seen, from the lower heaven up to my throne, and all the troops.

8 For I created all forces, and there is none that resists me and none that does not subject himself to me. For all subject themselves to my kingdom, and labor for my complete rule.

9 Give them the books of the handwriting, and they will read them and will know that I am the creator of all things, and will understand how there is no other God but me.

10 And let them distribute the books of your handwriting from children to children, generation to generation, nation to nation.

11 And Enoch, I will give you, my intercessor, the archangel Michael, for the writings of your fathers Adam, Seth, Enos, Cainan, Mahaleleel, and Jared your father.

Chapter 34

1 They have rejected my commandments and my yoke, therefore worthless seed has come up, not fearing God, and they would not bow down to me, but have begun to bow down to empty gods, and rejected my unity (oneness / sovereignty), and have piled the whole earth up with lies, offences, abominable lust with one another, and all manner of other unclean wickedness, which are disgusting to even mention.

2 And therefore I will bring down a deluge upon the earth and will destroy all men, and the whole earth will crumble together into great darkness.

Chapter 35

1 You will see that from their seed shall arise another generation, long afterward, but of them many will be full of very strong desires that are never satisfied.

2 He who raises that generation shall reveal the books of your writing of your fathers to them. And He must point out the guardianship of the world to the faithful men and workers of my pleasure, who do not acknowledge my name in empty words.

3 And they shall tell another generation, and those others who, having read, shall afterward be glorified more than the first.

Chapter 36

1 Now, Enoch, I give you a period of thirty days to spend in your house, and tell your sons and all your household, so that all may hear from you what was spoken by my face, so that they may read and understand that there is no other God but me.

2 And that they may always keep my commandments, and begin to read and absorb the books of your writing.

3 And after thirty days I shall send my angel for you, and he will take you from earth and from your sons and bring you to me.

Chapter 37

1 And the Lord called upon one of the older angels who was terrible and menacing, and He placed him by me. He appeared white as snow, and his hands were like ice, having the appearance of great frost, and he froze my face, because I could not endure the terror of the Lord, just as it is not possible to endure a stove's fire or the sun's heat, or the frost of the air.

2 And the Lord said to me: Enoch, if your face is not frozen here, no man will be able to look at your face.

Chapter 38

1 And the Lord said to those men who first led me up: "Let Enoch go down on to earth with you, and await him until the determined day."

2 And by night they placed me on my bed.

3 But Methuselah was expecting my return and was keeping watch at my bed by day and night. And he was filled with awe when he heard my return, and I told him, "Let all my household come together, so that I may tell them everything."

Chapter 39

1 Oh my children, my loved ones, hear the advice of your father, as much as is according to the Lord's will.

2 I have been allowed to come to you today, and preach to you, not from my lips, but from the Lord's lips, all that is now, and was, and all that will be until judgment day.

3 For the Lord has allowed me to come to you so that you could hear the words of my lips, of a man made great for you, but I am one who has seen the Lord's face, and it was like iron made to glow from fire it sends forth sparks and burns.

4 You look upon my eyes now. They are the eyes of a man enlarged with meaning for you, but I have seen the Lord's eyes, shining like the sun's rays and filling the eyes of man with awe.

5 You see now, my children, the right hand of a man that helps you, but I have seen the Lord's right hand filling heaven as he helped me.

6 You see the scope of my work is like your own, but I have seen the Lord's limitless and perfect scope, which has no end.

7 You hear the words of my lips, as I heard the words of the Lord, and they are like constant and great thunder with hurling of clouds.

8 And now, my children, hear the lecture of the father of the earth. I will tell you how fearful and awful it is to come before the face of the ruler of the earth, and how much more terrible and awful it is to come before the face of the ruler of heaven, who is the judge of the quick and the dead, and of the controller of the heavenly troops. Who (of us) can endure that endless pain?

Chapter 40

1 And now, my children, I know all things, for this is from the Lord's lips, and my eyes have seen this, from beginning to end.

2 I know all things, and have written all things in the books, the heavens and their end, and their abundance, and all the armies and their marching.

3 I have measured and described the stars, the great innumerable multitude of them.

4 What man has seen their revolutions and their entrances? For not even the angels see their number, but I have written all their names.

5 And I measured the sun's circumference, and measured its rays, and counted the hours. I also wrote down all things that go over the earth. I have written the things that are nourished, and all seed sown and unsown, which the earth produces, and all plants, and every grass and every flower, and their sweet smells, and their names, and the dwelling-places of the clouds, and their composition, and their wings, and how they carry rain and raindrops.

6 And I investigated all things, and described the road of the thunder and of the lightning, and they showed me the keys and their guardians, their rise, and the way they precede. They are let out gradually, in measure, by a chain. If they were not let out at a measured rate by a heavy chain their violence would hurl down the angry clouds and destroy all things on earth.

7 I described the treasure houses of the snow, and the storehouses of the cold and the frosty airs, and I observed the key-holders of the seasons. He fills the clouds with them, and it does not exhaust the treasure houses.

8 And I wrote down the resting places of the winds and observed and saw how their key-holders bear weighing-scales and measures. First, they put them in one side of the weighing-scale, then in the other side they place the weights and let them out according to measure skillfully, over the whole earth, to keep the heavy winds from making the earth rock.

9 And I measured out the whole earth, its mountains, and all hills, fields, trees, stones, rivers, all existing things I wrote down, the height from earth to the seventh heaven, and downwards to the very lowest hell, and the judgment-place, and the very great, open and weeping (gaping) hell.

10 And I saw how the prisoners are in pain, expecting the limitless judgment.

11 And I wrote down all those being judged by the judge, and all their judgment and sentences and all their works.

Chapter 41

1 And I saw throughout all time all the forefathers from Adam and Eve, and I sighed and broke into tears and spoke of the ruin and their dishonor.

2 And I sad, "Woe is me for my infirmity and for that of my forefathers," and thought in my heart and said:

3 "Blessed is the man who has not been born or who has been born and shall not sin before the Lord's face, because he will not come into this place, nor bear the yoke of this place on himself.

Chapter 42

1 I saw the key-holders and guards of the gates of hell standing like great serpents. And their faces were glowing like extinguishing lamps, and I saw their eyes of fire, and their sharp teeth. And I saw all of the Lord's works, how they are right, while some of the works of man are of limited good, and others bad, and in their works are those who are known to speak evil lies.

Chapter 43

1 My children, I measured and wrote out every work and every measure and every righteous judgment.

2 As one year is more honorable than another, so is one man more honorable than another. Some men are honored for great possessions, some for wisdom of heart, some for particular intellect, some for skillfulness, one for silence of lip, another for cleanliness, one for strength, another for beauty, one for youth, another for sharp wit, one for shape of body, another for sensibility, but let it be heard everywhere: There is none better than he who fears God. He shall be more glorious in time to come.

Chapter 44

1 The Lord created man with his hands in the likeness of his own face. The Lord made him small and great.

2 Whoever reviles the ruler's face hates the Lord's face, and has contempt for the Lord's face, and he who vents anger on any man without having been injured by him, the Lord's great anger will cut him down, he who spits on the face of man reproachfully will be cut down at the Lord's great judgment.

3 Blessed is the man who does not direct his heart with malice against any man, and helps the injured and condemned, and raises up the broken down, and shall do charity to the needy, because on the day of the great judgment every weight, every measure and every makeweight will be as in the market, so they are hung on scales and stand in the market, and every one shall learn his own measure, and according to his measure shall take his reward.

(Note: Makeweight is something put on a scale to make up the required weight for a more precise measurement.)

Chapter 45

1 Whoever hurries to make offerings before the Lord's face, the Lord will hasten that offering by giving of His work.

2 But whoever increases his lamp before the Lord's face and makes a judgment that is not true, the Lord will not increase his treasure in the realm of the highest.

(Note: Whoever makes himself out to be more than he is and whoever judges others without truth or cause, the Lord will not reward in heaven.)

3 When the Lord demands bread, or candles, or the flesh of beasts, or any other sacrifice, it is nothing; but God demands pure hearts, and with all He does it is only the tests of man's heart.

Chapter 46

1 Hear, my people, and take in the words of my lips.

2 If any one brings any gifts to an earthly ruler, and has disloyal thoughts in his heart, and the ruler know this, will the ruler not be angry with him, and refuse his gifts, and give him over to judgment?

3 Or if one man makes himself appear good to another by deceit of the tongue, but has evil in his heart, then will the other person not understand the treachery of his heart, and condemned him, since his lie was plain to all?

4 And when the Lord shall send a great light, then there will be judgment for the just and the unjust, and no one shall escape notice.

Chapter 47

1 And now, my children, with your minds and your hearts, mark well the words of your father, which all have come to you from the Lord's lips.

2 Take these books of your father's writing and read them.

3 For there are many books, and in them you will learn all the Lord's works, all that has been from the beginning of creation, and will be until the end of time.

4 And if you will observe my writing, you will not sin against the Lord; because there is no other except the Lord in heaven, nor in earth, nor in the very lowest places, nor in the foundation.

5 The Lord has placed the foundations in the unknown, and has spread out heavens, both physical and spiritual; he anchored the earth on the waters, and created countless creatures. Who has counted the water and the foundation of the mutable, or the dust of the earth, or the sand of the sea, or the drops of the rain, or the morning dew, or the wind's blowing (breathing)? Who has filled earth and sea, and the indestructible winter?

6 I (The Lord) cut the stars out of fire, and decorated heaven, and put it in their midst.

Chapter 48

1 The sun goes along the seven heavenly circles, which are the appointment of one hundred and eighty-two thrones. It goes down on a short day, and again one hundred and eighty-two. It goes down on a long day, and he has two thrones on which he rests, revolving here and there above the thrones of the months, from the seventeenth day of the month Tsivan it goes down to the month Thevan, from the seventeenth of Thevan it goes up.

(Note: The words Tsivan and Thevan refer to the summer and winter solstice, dividing the lengthening and shortening of days. The sun goes in a sinusoidal wave, decreasing daylight time for 182 days and growing longer in daylight hours for 182 days, with an extra day, which is a long day. The total is 365 days.)

2 When it goes close to the earth, then the earth is glad and makes its fruits grow, and when it goes away, then the earth is sad, and trees and all fruits will not flower.

3 All this He measured, with good measurement of hours, and predetermined a measure by his wisdom, of the physical and the spiritual (realms).

4 From the spiritual realm he made all things that are physical, himself being spiritual.

5 So I teach you, my children, and tell you to distribute the books to your children, into all your generations, and among the nations who shall have the sense to fear God. Let them receive them, and may they come to love them more than any food or earthly sweets, and read them and apply themselves to them.

6 And those who do not understand the Lord, who do not fear God, who do not accept, but reject, who do not receive the books, a terrible judgment awaits these.

7 Blessed is the man who shall bear their yoke and shall drag them along, for he shall be released on the day of the great judgment.

Chapter 49

1 I swear to you, my children, but I do not swear by any oath, neither by heaven nor by earth, nor by any other creature created by God.

2 The Lord said: "There is no oath in Me, nor injustice, but only truth."

3 But there is no truth in men, so let them swear by the words, Yea, yea, or else, Nay, nay.

4 And I swear to you, yea, yea, that every man that has been in his mother's womb has had a place prepared for the repose of that soul, and a measure predetermined of how much it is intended that a man be tried (tested) in this world.

5 Yea, children, do not deceive yourselves, for there has been a place previously prepared for the soul of every man.

Chapter 50

1 I have put every man's work in writing and none born on earth can remain hidden nor his works remain concealed.

2 I see all things.

3 Therefore, my children, spend the number of your days in patience and meekness so that you may inherit eternal life.

4 For the sake of the Lord, endure every wound, every injury, every evil word, and every attack.

5 If your good deeds are not rewarded but returned for ill to you, do not repay them to neither neighbor nor enemy, because the Lord will return them for you and be your avenger on the day of great judgment, so that there should be no vengeance here among men.

6 Whoever of you spends gold or silver for his brother's sake, he will receive ample treasure in the world to come.

7 Do not injure widows or orphans or strangers, for if you do God's wrath will come upon you.

Chapter 51

1 Stretch out your hands to the poor according to your strength.

2 Do not hide your silver in the earth.

3 Help the faithful man in affliction, and affliction will not find you in the time of your trouble.

4 And bear every grievous and cruel yoke that comes upon you, for the sake of the Lord, and thus you will find your reward in the Day of Judgment.

5 It is good to go morning, midday, and evening into the Lord's house, for the glory of your creator.

6 Because every breathing thing glorifies him, and every creature, both physical and spiritual, gives him praise. (Gives His praise back to Him.)

Chapter 52

1 Blessed is the man who opens his lips in praise of God of Sabaoth (Host / army) and praises the Lord with his heart.

2 Cursed is every man who opens his lips for the purpose of bringing contempt and slander to (of) his neighbor, because he brings God into contempt.

3 Blessed is he who opens his lips blessing and praising God.

4 Cursed before the Lord all the days of his life, is he who opens his lips to curse and abuse.

5 Blessed is he who blesses all the Lord's works.

6 Cursed is he who brings the Lord's creation into contempt.

7 Blessed is he who looks down and raises the fallen.

8 Cursed is he who looks to and is eager for the destruction of what is not his.

9 Blessed is he who keeps the foundations of his fathers that were made firm from the beginning.

10 Cursed is he who corrupts the doctrine of his forefathers.

11 Blessed is he who imparts peace and love.

12 Cursed is he who disturbs those that love their neighbors.

13 Blessed is he who speaks with humble tongue and heart to all.

14 Cursed is he who speaks peace with his tongue, while in his heart there is no peace but a sword.

15 For all these things will be laid bare in the scales of balance and in the books, on the day of the great judgment.

Chapter 53

1 And now, my children, do not say: "Our father is standing before God, and is praying for our sins. For there is there no helper for any man who has sinned.

2 You see how I wrote down all of the works of every man, before his creation, all that is done among all men for all time, and none can tell or relate my writing, because the Lord sees all imaginings of man, and how they are empty and prideful, where they lie in the treasure houses of the heart.

3 And now, my children, mark well all the words of your father that I tell you, or you will be regretful, saying: Why did our father not tell us?

(Note: although chapters 51 and 52 seem similar to the Sermon on the Mount, Chapter 53 offers no balance between mercy and justice. "There is no helper for any man who has sinned," is a statement excluding a savior. Scholars point to this verse to conclude 2 Enoch is a Jewish text. As stated before, 2 Enoch seems to be a Jewish text that was Christianized by additions and embellishment of the core text. Chapter 53 is part of the core Jewish text, likely written before the Christian sect.)

Chapter 54
1 Let these books, which I have given you, be for an inheritance of your peace in that time that you do not understand this.
2 Hand them to all who want them, and instruct them, that they may see the Lord's very great and marvelous works.

Chapter 55
1 My children, behold, the day of my determined period (term and time) has approached.
2 For the angels who shall go with me are standing before me and urge me to my departure from you. They are standing here on earth, awaiting what has been told them.
3 For tomorrow I shall go up to heaven, to the uppermost Jerusalem, to my eternal inheritance.
4 Therefore I bid you to do the Lord's good pleasure before his face at all times.

(Note: The Jerusalem spoken of here is the spiritual Jerusalem, spoken of by John, coming down from heaven. The name, "Jerusalem" refers to the components of the actual name, which break down to mean "provision" and "peace".)

Chapter 56"
1 Methuselah answered his father Enoch, and said: What (food) is agreeable to your eyes, father, that I may prepare before your face, that you may bless our houses, and your sons, and that your people may be made glorious through you, and then that you may depart, as the Lord said?"
2 Enoch answered his son Methuselah and said: "Hear me, my child. From the time when the Lord anointed me with the ointment of his glory, there has been no food in me, and my soul remembers not earthly enjoyment, neither do I want anything earthly."

Chapter 57
1 My child Methuselah, summon all your brethren and all of your household and the elders of the people, that I may talk to them and depart, as is planned for me.
2 And Methuselah hurried, and summoned his brethren, Regim, Riman, Uchan, Chermion, Gaidad, and all the elders of the people before the face of his father Enoch; and he blessed them, and said to them:

Chapter 58
1 "Listen to me, my children, today.
2 In those days when the Lord came down to earth for Adam's sake, and visited all his creatures, which he created himself, after all these he created Adam, and the Lord called all the beasts of the earth, all the reptiles, and all the birds that soar in the air, and brought them all before the face of our father Adam.
3 And Adam gave names to all things living on earth.
4 And the Lord appointed him ruler over all, and subjected all things to him under his hands, and made them dumb and made them dull that they would be commanded by man, and be in subjection and obedience to him.
5 The Lord also created every man lord over all his possessions.
6 The Lord will not judge a single soul of beast for man's sake, but He judges the souls of men through their beasts in this world, for men have a special place.
7 And as every soul of man is according to number, similarly beasts will not perish, nor all souls of beasts which the Lord created, until the great judgment, and they will accuse man, if he did not feed them well.

Chapter 59
1 Whoever defiles the soul of beasts, defiles his own soul.
2 For man brings clean animals to make sacrifice for sin, that he may have cure for his soul.
3 And if they bring clean animals and birds for sacrifice, man has a cure. He cures his soul.
4 All is given you for food, bind it by the four feet, to make good the cure.
5 But whoever kills beast without wounds, kills his own souls and defiles his own flesh.

6 And he who does any beast any injury whatsoever, in secret, it is evil practice, and he defiles his own soul.

(Note: To kill without a wound is to inflict blunt force trauma - to beat them to death.)

Chapter 60

1 He who works the killing of a man's soul (he who murders), kills his own soul, and kills his own body, and there is no cure for him for all time.

2 He who puts a man in any snare (moral entrapment), shall stick himself in it, and there is no cure for him for all time.

3 He who puts a man in any vessel, his retribution will not be wanting at the great judgment for all time.

4 He who works dishonestly or speaks evil against any soul, will not make justice for himself for all time.

Chapter 61

1 And now, my children, keep your hearts from every injustice, which the Lord hates. Just as a man asks something for his own soul from God, so let him do the same to every living soul, because I know all things, how in the great time to come there is a great inheritance prepared for men, good for the good, and bad for the bad, no matter the number.

2 Blessed are those who enter the good houses, for in the bad houses there is no peace or return from them.

3 Hear, my children, small and great! When man puts a good thought in his heart, it brings gifts from his labors before the Lord's face. But if his hands did not make them, then the Lord will turn away his face from the labor of his hand, and (that) man cannot find the labor of his hands.

4 And if his hands made it, but his heart murmurs (complains), and his heart does not stop murmurs incessantly, he does not have (gain) any advantage.

Chapter 62

1 Blessed is the man who, in his patience, brings his gifts with faith before the Lord's face, because he will find forgiveness of sins.

2 But if he takes back his words before the time, there is no repentance for him; and if the time passes and he does not of his own will perform what is promised, there is no repentance after death.

3 Because every work which man does before the time (outside the time he has promised it), is all deceit before men, and sin before God.

Chapter 63

1 When man clothes the naked and fills the hungry, he will find reward from God.

2 But if his heart complains, he commits a double evil; ruin of himself and of that which he gives; and for him there will be no finding of reward because of that.

3 And if his own heart is filled with his food and his own flesh is clothed with his own clothing, he commits contempt, and will forfeit all his endurance of poverty, and will not find reward of his good deeds. (If he is selfish and does not add to the economy of others…)

4 Every proud and pontificating man is hateful to the Lord, and every false speech is clothed in lies. It will be cut with the blade of the sword of death, and thrown into the fire, and shall burn for all time.

Chapter 64

1 When Enoch had spoken these words to his sons, all people far and near heard how the Lord was calling Enoch. They took counsel together:

2 Let us go and kiss Enoch, and two thousand men came together and came to the place called Achuzan, where Enoch was with his sons.

3 And the elders of the people with the entire assembly came and bowed down and began to kiss Enoch and said to him:

4 "Our father Enoch, may you be blessed by the Lord, the eternal ruler, and now bless your sons and all the people, that we may be glorified today before your face.

5 For you shall be glorified before the Lord's face for eternity, since the Lord chose you from among all men on earth, and designated you as the writer of all his creation, both physical and spiritual, and you are redeemed from the sins of man, and are the helper of your household."

Chapter 65

1 And Enoch said to all his people: "Hear me, my children. Before all creatures were created, the Lord created the physical and spiritual things.

2 And then a long term passed. Then after all of that he created man in the likeness of his own form, and put eyes into him to see, and ears into him to hear, and a heart to reflect, and intellect to enable him to deliberate.

3 And the Lord saw all the works of man, and created all his creatures, and divided time. From time he determined the years, and from the years he appointed the months, and from the months he appointed the days, and of days he appointed seven.
4 And in those he appointed the hours, measured them out exactly, that man might reflect on time and count years, months, and hours, as they alternate from beginning to end, so that he might count his own life from the beginning until death, and reflect on his sin and write his works, both bad and good. No work is hidden from the Lord, so that every man might know his works and never transgress all his commandments, and keep my writing from generation to generation.
5 When all creation, both physical and spiritual, as the Lord created it, shall end, then every man goes to the great judgment, and then all time shall be destroyed along with the years. And from then on there will be neither months nor days nor hours. They will run together and will not be counted.
6 There will be one eon, and all the righteous who shall escape the Lord's great judgment, shall be collected in the great eon. For the righteous the great eon will begin, and they will live eternally, and there will be no labor, nor sickness, nor humiliation, nor anxiety, nor need, nor brutality, nor night, nor darkness, but great light among them.
7 And they shall have a great indestructible wall, and a paradise that is bright and eternal, for all mortal things shall pass away, and there will be eternal life.

(Note: an eon is one billion years but is used to mean a very long but indefinite period of time. The word "eternal" means "unchanging, incorruptible, immortal." The word used for "mortal" is the opposite of "eternal", thus, "mortal, corruptible, changing.")

Chapter 66
1 And now, my children, keep your souls from all injustice the Lord hates.
2 Walk before his face with great fear (respect) and trembling and serve him only.
3 Bow down to the true God, not to dumb idols, but bow down to his likeness, and bring all just offerings before the Lord's face. The Lord hates what is unjust.

(Note: This is an odd command issued by Enoch, that the people are not to bow to dumb idols but are to bow to the likeness or similitude of God.)

4 For the Lord sees all things; when man takes thought in his heart, then he counsels the intellects, and every thought is always before the Lord, who made firm the earth and put all creatures on it.
5 If you look to heaven, the Lord is there; if you take thought of the sea's deep and all under the earth, the Lord is there.
6 For the Lord created all things. Bow not down to things made by man, leaving the Lord of all creation, because no work can remain hidden before the Lord's face.
7 Walk, my children, in long-suffering, in meekness, honesty, in thoughtfulness, in grief, in faith and in truth. Walk in (rely on) promises, in (times of) illness, in abuse, in wounds, in temptation, in nakedness, in privation, loving one another, until you go out from this age of ills, that you become inheritors of endless time.
8 Blessed are the just who shall escape the great judgment, for they shall shine forth more than the sun sevenfold, for in this world the seventh part is taken off from all, light, darkness, food, enjoyment, sorrow, paradise, torture, fire, frost, and other things; he put all down in writing, that you might read and understand.

Chapter 67
1 When Enoch had talked to the people, the Lord sent out darkness on to the earth, and there was darkness, and it covered those men standing with Enoch, and they took Enoch up on to the highest heaven, where the Lord is. And there God received him and placed him before His face, and the darkness went off from the earth, and light came again.
2 And the people saw and did not understand how Enoch had been taken, and they glorified God, and found a scroll in which was written "The God of the Spiritual." Then all went to their dwelling places.

Chapter 68
1 Enoch was born on the sixth day of the month Tsivan (the first month of the year), and lived three hundred and sixty-five years.
2 He was taken up to heaven on the first day of the month Tsivan and remained in heaven sixty days.
3 He wrote all these signs of all creation, which the Lord created, and wrote three hundred and sixty-six books, and handed them over to his sons and remained on earth thirty days, and was again taken up to heaven on the sixth day of the month Tsivan, on the very day and hour when he was born.
4 As every man's nature in this life is dark, so are also his conception, birth, and departure from this life.
5 At what hour he was conceived, at that hour he was born, and at that hour too he died.
6 Methuselah and his brethren, all the sons of Enoch, made haste, and erected an altar at that place called Achuzan, where Enoch had been taken up to heaven.
7 And they took sacrificial oxen and summoned all people and sacrificed the sacrifice before the Lord's face.
8 All people, the elders of the people and the whole assembly came to the feast and brought gifts to the sons of Enoch.

9 And they made a great feast, rejoicing and making merry three days, praising God, who had given them such a sign through Enoch, who had found favor with him, and that they should hand it on to their sons from generation to generation, from age to age.   Amen.

(Note: Enoch was born on the 6th day of Tsivan. Tsivan is the first month of the year. The sum is seven, one of the holy numbers. He lived 365 years. One year of years. He remained in heaven 60 days. Six is the number of man, which always falls short of God.)

The Short Version Ends Here

The wife of Nir was Sopanim. She was sterile and never had at any time given birth to a child by Nir.
Sopanim was in her old age and in the last days (time) of her death. She conceived in her womb, but Nir the priest had not slept with her from the day that that the Lord had appointed him to conduct the liturgy in front of the face of the people.

When Sopanim saw her pregnancy, she was ashamed and embarrassed, and she hid herself during all the days until she gave birth. Not one of the people knew about it. When 282 days had been completed, and the day of birth had begun to approach, Nir thought about his wife, and he called her to come to him in his house, so that he might converse with her.

Sopanim came to Nir, her husband; and, behold, she was pregnant, and the day appointed for giving birth was drawing near. Nir saw her and became very ashamed. He said to her, "What is this that you have done, O wife? Why have you disgraced me in front of the face of these people? Now, depart from me and go back to where you began this disgrace of your womb, so that I might not defile my hands in front of The Face of The Lord on account of you and sin."

Sopanim spoke to her husband, Nir, saying, "O my lord! Look at me. It is the time of my old age, the day of my death has arrived. I do not understand how my menopause and the barrenness of my womb have been reversed." But Nir did not believe his wife, and for the second time he said to her, "Depart from me, or else I might assault you, and commit a sin in front of the face of The Lord."

And after Nir had spoken to his wife, Sopanim, she fell down at Nir's feet and died. Nir was extremely distressed and said to himself, "Could this have happened because of my words? And now, merciful is The Eternal Lord, because my hand was not upon her."

The archangel Gabriel appeared to Nir, and said to him, "Do not think that your wife Sopanim has died due to your error? This child, which is to be born from her, is a righteous fruit, and one whom I shall receive into paradise so that you will not be the father of a gift of God."

Nir hurried and shut the door of his house. He went to Noah, his brother, and he reported to him everything that had happened in connection with his wife. Noah hurried to the room of his brother. The appearance of his brother's wife was as if she were dead but her womb was at the same time giving birth.

Noah said to Nir, "Don't let yourself be sorrowful, Nir, my brother! Today the Lord has covered up our scandal, because nobody from the people knows this. Now let us go quickly and bury her, and the Lord will cover up the scandal of our shame." They placed Sopanim on the bed, wrapped her around with black garments, and shut the door. They dug a grave in secret.

When they had gone out toward the grave, a child came out from Sopanim's dead body and sat on the bed at her side. Noah and Nir came in to bury Sopanim and they saw the child sitting beside Sopanim's dead body and he was wiping his clothing. Noah and Nir were very terrified with a great fear, because the child was physically fully developed. The child spoke with his lips and blessed The Lord.
Noah and Nir looked at him closely, saying, "This is from the Lord, my brother." The badge of priesthood is on his chest, and it is glorious in appearance. Noah said to Nir, "God is renewing the priesthood from blood related to us, just as He pleases."

Noah and Nir hurried and washed the child, they dressed him in the garments of the priesthood, and they gave him bread to eat and he ate it. And they called him Melchizedek.

Noah and Nir lifted up the body of Sopanim, and took the black garment off of her and washed her. They clothed her in exceptionally bright garments and built a grave for her. Noah, Nir, and Melchizedek came and they buried her publicly. Then Noah said to his brother Nir, "Take care of this child in secret until the proper time comes, because all of the people on earth will become treacherous and they will begin to turn away from God. Having become completely ignorant (of God), when they see him, they will put him to death in some way."

Then Noah went away to his own place, and there came great lawlessness that began to become abundant over all the earth in the days of Nir. And Nir began to worry greatly about the child saying, "What will I do with him?" And stretching out his hands toward heaven, Nir called out to The Lord, saying, " It is miserable for me, Eternal Lord, that all of this lawlessness has begun to become abundant over all the earth in my lifetime! I realize how much nearer our end is because of the lawlessness of the people. And now, Lord, what is the vision about this child, and what is his destiny, or what will I do for him, so that he will not be joined along with us in this destruction?"

The Lord took notice of Nir and appeared to him in a night vision. And He said to him, "Nir, the great lawlessness which has come about on the earth I shall not tolerate anymore. I plan to send down a great destruction onto the earth. But do not worry about the child, Nir. In a short while I will send My archangel Gabriel and he will take the child and put him in the paradise of Edem. He will not perish along with those who must perish. As I have revealed it, Melchizedek will be My priest to all holy priests, I will sanctify him and I will establish him so that he will be the head of the priests of the future."

(Note: Edem means, "God will save." It is assumed Edem is Eden.)

Then Nir arose from his sleep and blessed The Lord, who had appeared to him saying: "Blessed be The Lord, The God of my fathers, who has approved of my priesthood and the priesthood of my fathers, because by His Word, He has created a great priest in the womb of Sopanim, my wife. For I have no descendants. So let this child take the place of my descendants and become as my own son. You will count him in the number of your servants."

"Therefore honor him together with your servants and great priests and me your servant, Nir. And behold, Melchizedek will be the head of priests in another generation. I know that great confusion has come and in confusion this generation will come to an end, and everyone will perish, except that Noah, my brother, will be preserved for procreation. From his tribe, there will arise numerous people, and Melchizedek will become the head of priests reigning over a royal people who will serve you, O Lord."

It happened when the child had completed 40 days in Nir's tent, The Lord said to the archangel Gabriel, "Go down to the earth to Nir the priest, and take the child Melchizedek, who is with him. Place him in the paradise of Edem for preservation. For the time is already approaching, and I will pour out all the water onto the earth, and everything that is on the earth will perish. And I will raise it up again, and Melchizedek will be the head of the priests in that generation." And Gabriel hurried, and came flying down when it was night when Nir was sleeping on his bed that night.

Gabriel appeared to him and said to him, "The Lord says: "Nir! Restore the child to me whom I entrusted to you." But Nir did not realize who was speaking to him and he was confused. And he said, "When the people find out about the child, they will seize him and kill him, because the heart of these people are deceitful before The Lord." And he answered Gabriel and said, "The child is not with me, and I don't know who is speaking to me."

Gabriel answered him, " Nir, do not be afraid. I am the archangel Gabriel. The Lord sent me to take your child today. I will go with him and I will place him in the paradise of Edem." Then Nir remembered the first dream and believed it. He answered Gabriel, "Blessed be The Lord, who has sent you to me today! Now bless your servant Nir! Take the child and do to him all that has been said to you." And Gabriel took the child, Melchizedek on his wings in that same night, and he placed him in the paradise of Edem. Nir got up in the morning, and he went into his tent and did not find the child. There was great joy and grief for Nir because he felt the child had the place of a son.

The Lord said to Noah, "Make an ark that is 300 cubits in length, 50 cubits in width and in 30 cubits height. Put the entrance to the ark in its side; and make it with two stories in the middle" The Lord God opened the doors of heaven. Rain came onto the earth and all flesh died.

Noah fathered 3 sons: Shem, Ham and Japheth. He went into the ark in his six hundredth year. After the flood, he lived 350 years. He lived in all 950 years, according to The Lord our God.
To our God be Glory always, now and eternally. AMEN.

Introduction of 3 Enoch

Author's Note: It was not until the early 1900's that The Hebrew Book of Enoch, or 3 Enoch, could be reconstructed. Although the text claims to be written around 100 A.D. it was likely written by a highly educated Rabbi around 300 to 400 A.D. and preserved only in fragments, here and there. Then, in 1928 Dr. Hugo Odeberg PhD. gathered the various fragmentary sources and published the first full translation along with copious scholarly notes and the source Hebrew material. The University Press at Cambridge, in the United Kingdom, published the book. A photocopy of the book made its way to the United State and into the University of Chicago library, where it was kept for many years. It was from this body of work and from this photocopied and preserved manuscript that the majority of this work was compiled.

3 Enoch purports to have been written around 100 A.D., but its origins can only be traced to the late fourth or early fifth centuries. Other names for 3 Enoch include "The Third Book of Enoch" and "The Book of the Palaces." The angelology and description of heaven in 1 Enoch is built upon and greatly expanded in 3 Enoch.

The book is rife with Hebrew words, which have no single English equivalent. Even though care was taken to define the majority of these words when first they appear in the text, the reader should expect only keywords to replace or augment meanings thereafter. To do otherwise would either leave the reader to remember the meanings of all Hebrew words or bloat the book to the point of making it difficult to follow.

Modern scholars describe this book as belonging to a body of work called the pseudepigraphia. 3 Enoch claims to be written by a Rabbi, who became a 'high priest' after he had visions of an ascension to Heaven, 90 AD - 135 AD. Rabbi Ishmael is a leading figure of Merkabah literature; however, a number of scholars suggest that it was in fact written by a number of people over a prolonged period of time.

Merkabah writings had to do with the theme of ascension into heaven. The name is derived from a Hebrew word meaning "chariot," referring to Ezekiel's vision beginning in Ezekiel 1:4. Enoch's contents and ideas are unique and newer than those shown in other Merkabah texts, suggesting the book may be among the first in the Merkabah movement or that it is derived through unique influences.

As the other name of this book implies, 3 Enoch is also part of the Temple or Hekalot body of literature. The name Sefer Hekhalot means, "Palaces" or "Temples."

As with 1 Enoch, the exact dating of this book is a difficult task, but some scholars believe it was completed around the time of the Babylonian Talmud, which was around the early 5th century A.D.

3 Enoch was originally written in Hebrew, although it contains a number of words from both Greek and Latin. Parts of the book seem to have been influenced by 1 Enoch, showing the author was familiar with the Mystical Enochian Tradition.

Similar points appearing in 1 Enoch and 3 Enoch are:
  Enoch ascends to Heaven in a storm chariot (3 Enoch 6:1; 7:1)
  Enoch is translated into an angel (3 Enoch 9:1-5; 15:1-2)
  Enoch, as an angel, is given authority in Heaven (3 Enoch 10:1- 3; 16:1)
  Enoch receives an explanation or vision of creation and cosmology. (3 Enoch 13:1-2)
  Enoch sees a hostile angel named Azazel (3 Enoch 4:6; 5:9)

The main theme, throughout the book is the "transubstantiation" or change of Enoch into the angel Metatron.

Metatron appears in various Jewish, Christian, and Islamic works but was a central focus in medieval Jewish mystical texts and occult sources. Rabbinical texts point to Metatron as the angel who stilled the hand of Abraham, preventing him from sacrificing Isaac.

The place and authority of Metatron has been hotly debated, and is seen even within the book. He is seen as sitting in heaven. This is only permitted if one is a deity. He is referred to in the text as "The Lesser YHWH."

YHWH makes up the Tetragrammaton forming the name we pronounce as "Yahweh" or "Jehovah." The four letters making up the divine name are Yodh, He Waw, He, having the sounds of "Y", "H", "W, O, U or a place holder", and "H." When "He" ends a word it is often silent. Due to the fact that German theologians were heavily involved in theological research and study, one may also find the Tetragrammaton rendered as YHVH, since the V in German has a W sound.

There is a very personal attack within the text, which should be explained. A curse is placed on a man known only as Acher.

In Hebrew the name means, "the other," and is used as a term of alienation from the rabbinic community. The Talmud tells us that Elisha be Abuyah entered Paradise in a vision and saw Metatron sitting down (an action that in heaven is permitted only to God himself). Elishah ben Abuyah therefore looked to Metatron as a deity and proclaimed, "There are indeed two powers in heaven!" The other rabbis explain that Metatron was allowed to sit because he was the Heavenly Scribe, writing down the deeds of Israel (Babylonian Talmud, Hagiga 15a).

The intense hatred for any idea hinting at dualism or polytheism, as opposed to monotheism, caused such a reaction within the Rabbinical community that they labeled Elisha be Abuyah a heretic. In 3 Enoch this point is driven home when the entire nation of Israel is to be reconciled to God, except for Acher, whose name is blotted out.

In spite of the disagreements within the ancient Jewsih community, the reader is still left to wonder what position Metatron occupies in heaven. Metatron is described in two ways: as a primordial angel (9:2–13:2) and as the transformation of Enoch after he was assumed into Heaven, and he is called "The Lesser YHWH."

Enoch walked with God; then he was no more, because God took him away. [Genesis 5:24 NIV.]
This Enoch, whose flesh was turned to flame, his veins to fire, his eye-lashes to flashes of lightning, his eye-balls to flaming torches, and whom God placed on a throne next to the throne of glory, received after this heavenly transformation the name Metatron. [3 Enoch]

As the Christian community came in contact with the Jewish book of 3 Enoch, they had little trouble reconciling the names and position of Metatron. To those Christians a person who may sit in heaven and who judges, and who is called by the same name taken by God must be Yeshua (Jesus.)

It may be of help if the meaning of the name, Metatron, could be ascertained, but it is not clear. Suggestions are that the name originated from the root words of such phrases as, "keeper of the watch," "guard," "to protect," "one who serves behind the throne," "one who occupies the throne next to the throne of glory," "to lead," or " to measure." None of these suggestions can be proven. From the text itself we know only that Metatron is referred to as "the youth," likely because he would be the newest and youngest angel. He is also called, "the prince of the presence (of God)." His purpose in heaven was to be a witness against mankind.

A type of numerology is used and referred to within the text. Temurah is one of the three ancient methods used by Cabbalist to rearrange words and sentences in the Torah, in the belief that by this method they can derive the deeper, hidden spiritual meaning of the words. Temurah may be used to change letters in certain words to create a new meaning for a Biblical statement. Another method is called Gematria. In this method letters are substituted for numbers and the meaning of words with the same value are compared along with the numerical meaning of the words.

A preparatory summery of the first section of the book may be framed as a revelation from Metatron, or the Prince of the Presence, to Rabbi Ishmael. Metatron, as it turns out, is Enoch and this is why the title of this book has come to be called, "3 Enoch." Any question as to who Metatron may be is answered clearly in CHAPTER IV, where it is written, "Rabbi Ishmael said: I asked Metatron and said to him: " why are you called by the name of your Creator, by seventy names? You are greater than all the princes, higher than all the angels, beloved more than all the servants, honored above all the mighty ones in kingship, greatness and glory: why do they call you 'Youth' in the high heavens?" He answered and said to me: "Because I am Enoch, the son of Jared. For when the generation of the flood sinned and were confounded in their deeds, saying unto God: Depart from us, for we desire not the knowledge of your ways (Job 21:14), then the Holy One, blessed be He, removed me from their midst to be a witness against them in the high heavens to all the inhabitants of the world, that they may not say: 'The Merciful One is cruel'.

The following text begins the book of 3 Enoch. Notes and explanations are italicized. Words placed in parentheses are alternate renderings of a word of phrase.

BOOK OF 3 ENOCH
or the Hebrew Book of Enoch
By Rabbi ISHMAEL BEN ELISHA
THE HIGH PRIEST

CHAPTER I

INTRODUCTION: Rabbi Ishmael ascends to heaven to witness the vision of the Merkaba (chariot). He is given to Metatron

AND ENOCH WALKED WITH GOD: AND HE WAS NOT;
FOR GOD TOOK HIM.

(1) I ascended on high to witness the vision of the Merkaba (the divine chariot) and I had entered the six Halls, which were situated within one another.

The halls were in concentric circles, one within the other.

(2) As soon as I reached the door of the Seventh Hall I stood still in prayer before the Holy One, blessed be He. I lifted up my eyes on high towards the Divine Majesty and I said: (3) " Lord of the Universe, I pray you, that the worthiness of Aaron, the son of Amram, who loves and pursues peace, and who received the crown of priesthood from Your Glory on Mount Sinai, be upon me in this hour, so that Khafsiel, (Qafsiel) the prince, and the angels with him may not overcome (overpower) me nor cast me down from the heavens."

Qafsiel or Qaphsiel is an angel of a high order set to guard the seventh hall of heaven

(4) At that moment the Holy One, blessed be He, sent Metatron, his Servant, also called Ebed, to me. He is the angel, the Prince of the Presence. With great joy he spread his wings as he came to meet me in order to save me from their hand. (5) And by his hand he took me so that they could see us, and he said to me: "Enter in peace before the high and exalted King and see the picture of Merkaba (chariot)."

Merkaba (chariot) – Chariot of fire, Chariot of light - Pulled by four Chayot or living creatures, each of which has four wings and the four faces of a man, lion, ox, and eagle.. See Ezekiel 1:4-26. The Bible makes mention of three types of angel found in the Merkaba (chariot). The first is the "Seraphim" (lit. "burning") angels. These angels appear like flashes of fire continuously ascending and descending. These "Seraphim" angels powered the movement of the chariot. In the hierarchy of these angels, "Seraphim" are the highest, that is, closest to God, followed by the "Chayot", which are followed by the "Ophanim." The chariot is in a constant state of motion, and the energy behind this movement runs according to this hierarchy. The movement of the "Ophanim" are controlled by the "Chayot" while the movement of the "Chayot" is controlled by the "Seraphim." The movement of all the angels of the chariot are controlled by the "Likeness of a Man" on the Throne.

(6) Then I entered the seventh Hall, and he led me to the camps of Shekina (understanding) and stood me in front of the Holy One, blessed be He, to see the Merkaba (chariot).

Shekina - Shekhinah is derived from a Hebrew verb literally meaning "to settle, inhabit, or dwell." (See Exodus 40:35, "Moses could not enter the Tent of Meeting, for the cloud rested [shakhan] upon it, and the glory of the Lord filled the Tabernacle." See also Genesis 9:27, 14:13, Psalms 37:3, Jeremiah 33:16), as well as the weekly Shabbat blessing recited in the Temple ("May He who causes His name to dwell [shochan] in this House, cause to dwell among you love and brotherliness, peace and friendship"). Also see Talmud Ketubot 85b). Shekina can also mean royalty or royal residence. Shekina has come to mean the effect or manifestation caused by the presence or inhabitation of God. The manifestation is glory, creativity, and understanding. These words may be used to explain "Shekina."

(7) As soon as the princes of the Merkaba (chariot) and the flaming Seraphim knew I was there, they fixed their gaze on me. Trembling and shuddering seized me at once and I fell down and was numbed by the brightness of the vision of their faces; until the Holy One, blessed be He, chastised them, saying: (8)" My servants, my Seraphim, my Cherubim and my Ophannim! Cover your eyes before Ishmael, my son, my friend, my beloved one and (my) glory, so that he ceases trembling and shaking! "

The root of Seraphim comes either from the Hebrew verb saraph ('to burn') or the Hebrew noun saraph (a fiery, flying serpent). Because the term appears several times with reference to the serpents encountered in the wilderness (Num. 21.8, Deut. 8.15; Isa. 14.29; 30.6), it has often been understood to refer to "fiery serpents." From this it has also often been proposed that the seraphim were serpentine in form and in some sense "fiery" creatures or associated with fire.
It is said that whoever lays eyes on a Seraph, he would instantly be incinerated due to the immense brightness of the Seraph.

Cherubs are described as winged beings. The biblical prophet Ezekiel describes the cherubim as a tetrad of living creatures, each having four faces: of a lion, an ox, an eagle, and a man. They are said to have the stature and hands of a man, the feet of a calf, and four wings. Two of the wings extended upward, meeting above and sustaining the throne of God; while the other two stretched downward and covered the creatures themselves.

Ophanim are described in 1 Enoch as never sleeping. They watch and guard the throne of God.The word ophan means "wheel" in Hebrew. For this reason the Ophanim have been associated with the chariot in Ezekiel and Daniel. It is mentioned as gagal, traditionally "the wheels of gagallin", in "fiery flame" and "burning fire" of the four, eye-covered wheels, each composed of two nested wheels, that move next to the winged Cherubim, beneath the throne of God. The four wheels move with the Cherubim because the spirit of the Cherubim is in them. These are also referred to as the "many-eyed ones" in 2 Enoch. The Ophanim are also equated as the "Thrones", and associated with the "Wheels", in the vision of Daniel 7:9. They carry the throne of God, hence the name.

This may be a good time to explain the singular and plural in Hebrew. Whereas in English we add an "s" to denote a plural, in Hebrew an "im" is added. Thus, there is one Cherub but many Cherubim. There is one Seraph but many Seraphim. Knowing this fact may make the text easier to follow.

(9) Then Metatron, the Prince of the Presence, came and placed my spirit in me again and he stood me up on my feet. (10) After that (moment) for an hour I did not have enough strength to sing a song before the Throne of Glory of the Glorious King, the mightiest of all kings, the most excellent of all princes. (11) After an hour had passed the Holy One, blessed be He, opened the gates of Shekina (understanding) to me. These are the gates of Peace, and of Wisdom, and of Strength, and of Power, and of Speech (Dibbur), and of Song, and of Kedushah (Sacred Salutation of Holy, Holy, Holy), and the gates of Chanting. (12) And he opened and shined His light in my eyes and my heart by words of psalm, song, praise, exaltation, thanksgiving, extolment, glorification, hymn and eulogy (to speak well of). And as I opened my mouth, singing a song before the Holy One, blessed be He the Holy Chayoth beneath and above the Throne of Glory answered and said (chanted the prayer): "HOLY!" "BLESSED BE THE GLORY OF YHWH FROM HIS PLACE!."

The Chayot (or Chayyot) are a class of Merkabah, or Jewish Mystical Angels, reported in Ezekeil's vision of the Merkabah and its surrounding angels as recorded in the first chapter of the Book of Ezekiel describing his vision by the river Chebar.

Kedushah (Sacred Salutation of Holy, Holy, Holy) is a call to greet and glorify God. KODOISH, KODOISH, KODOISH ADONAI 'TSEBAYOTH: "Holy, Holy, Holy, is the Lord God of Hosts."
This is the Sacred Salutation, the Kedushah (Sacred Salutation of Holy, Holy, Holy) , which is used by all the heavenly hosts to worship The Father before His Throne.

CHAPTER 2
The highest classes of angels make inquiries about Rabbi Ishmael, which are answered by Metatron

Rabbi Ishmael said:
(1) Within the hour the eagles of The Chariot (Merkaba), the flaming Ophannim and the Seraphim of consuming fire asked Metatron: (2) "Youth! Why do you permit one born of woman to enter and see the chariot (Merkaba)? From which nation and from which tribe is this one? What is his nature?" (3) Metatron answered and said to them: "From the nation of Israel whom the Holy One, blessed be He, chose for his people from among seventy tongues (nations of the world). He is from the tribe of Levi, whom He set aside as a contribution to his name. He is from the seed of Aaron whom the Holy One, blessed be He, chose for his servant and He put upon him the crown of priesthood on Sinai." (4) Then they spoke and said: "Happy is the people (nation) that is in that position!" (Ps. 144:15).

CHAPTER 3
Metatron has 70 names, but God calls him 'Youth'

Rabbi Ishmael said:
(1) In that hour I asked Metatron, the angel, the Prince of the Presence: "What is your name?" (2) He answered me: "I have seventy names, corresponding to the seventy nations of the world and all of them are based upon the name Metatron, angel of the Presence; but my King calls me 'Youth' (Naar)."

Seventy tongues represent the seventy nations or the entirety of the known world.
It is likely the word "youth" is used because Metatron is the newest and youngest being in heaven.
The seventy names are derived from the divine name or the Tetragrammaton – YHWH. Yah is a shortened version of this, meaning "God."

CHAPTER 4
Metatron is Enoch who was translated to heaven at the time of the flood.

Rabbi Ishmael said:

(1) I asked Metatron and said to him: "why does your Creator call you by seventy names? You are greater than all the princes, higher than all the angels, beloved more than all the servants, honored above all the mighty ones in kingship, greatness and glory, so why do they in the high heavens call you 'Youth'? (2) He answered and said to me: "Because I am Enoch, the son of Jared. (3) When the generation of the flood sinned and were twisted and contorted in their deeds, saying unto God: "Depart from us! We do not want the knowledge of your ways," (See Job 21:14), then the Holy One, blessed be He, removed me from their midst so that I could be a witness against them in the high heavens to all the inhabitants of the world, so that they can not say: 'The Merciful One is cruel'. (4) "What sin did all those throngs of their wives, their sons and their daughters, their horses, their mules and their cattle and their property, and all the birds of the world commit so that the Holy One, blessed be He, destroyed the world, together with them in the waters of the flood?" They cannot say: "What in the generation of the flood sinned and what sin did they do so that the beasts and the birds should perish with them?" (5) Then the Holy One, blessed be He, lifted me up in their lifetime in their sight to be a witness against them to the future world. And the Holy One, blessed be He, assigned me to be a prince and a ruler among the ministering angels.

This chapter lays out the purpose of 3 Enoch and why it is so named. Metatron confirms that he is indeed Enoch, who was taken to heaven, translated into the being, Metatron, His primary purpose was to be a witness against man's sin on earth. When man or angel asked what sin was committed that all on earth should be destroyed, Enoch, now known as Metatron, would be a witness.

(6) In that hour three of the ministering angels, UZZA, 'AZZA and AZZAEL came out and accused me in the high heavens in front of the Holy One, blessed be He: And they said, "The Progenitors, The Ancient Ones, said before You with justification: Do not create man! The Holy One, blessed be He, answered and said unto them: "I have made and I will bear, and yes, I will carry and will deliver." (7) As soon as they saw me, they said before Him: "Lord of the Universe! What is this one that he should ascend to the highest heights? Is he not one from among the sons of those who perished in the days of the Flood? What is he doing in the Raqia (firmament / heavens)." What business does he have being in heaven?

Some sources have the names of the angels include Mal'aki or Mamlaketi. Azzael is one of the ten heads of the heavenly Sanhedrin. Rabbinical sources have Azza and Azzael as giants. All three are said to be agents of evil who accuse man of sins. These are the fallen angels. Another theory is that Azza and Azzael are not individual angels but are orders of angels.

Raquia is a key Hebrew word in Genesis 1:6–8a. It is translated "firmament" in the King James Version and "expanse" in most Hebrew dictionaries and modern translations. Raqa means to spread out, beat out, or hammer as one would a malleable metal. It can also mean "plate." The Greek Septuagint translated raqia 16 out of 17 times with the Greek word stereoma, which means "a firm or solid structure." The Latin Vulgate (A.D. 382) used the Latin term "firmamentum," which also denotes solidness and firmness. The King James translators coined the word "firmament" because there was no single word equivalent in English. Today, "firmament" is usually used poetically to mean sky, atmosphere, or heavens. In modern Hebrew, raqia means sky or heavens. However, originally it probably meant something solid or firm that was spread out.
Azzael is likely the same being as Azazel, the accuser angel who was the leader of the fallen ones. Etymology connects the word with the mythological "Uza" and "Azael", the fallen angels, to whom a reference is believed to be found in Gen. 6:2,4. In accordance with this etymology, the sacrifice of the goat atones for the sin of fornication of which those angels were guilty. (See 1 Enoch.) Leviticus 16:8-10: "and Aaron shall cast lots upon the two goats, one lot for the Lord and the other lot for Azazel. And Aaron shall present the goat on which the lot fell for the Lord, and offer it as a sin offering; but the goat on which the lot fell for Azazel shall be presented alive before the Lord to make atonement over it, that it may be sent away into the wilderness to Azazel."

(8) Again, the Holy One, blessed be He, answered and said to them: "What are you, that you enter and speak in my presence? I delight more in this one than in all of you put together, and therefore he will be a prince and a ruler over you in the high heavens." (9) Then they all stood up and went out to meet me, and bowed themselves down before me and said: "Happy are you and happy is your father for your Creator favors you." (10) And because I am small and a youth among them in days, months and years, therefore they call me "Youth" (Na'ar).

CHAPTER 5
The idolatry of the generation of Enosh causes God to remove the Shekina from earth. Idolatry was inspired by Azza, Uzza and Azzael.

Rabbi Ishmael said: Metatron, the Prince of the Presence, said to me:
(1) From the day when the Holy One, blessed be He, evicted the first Adam from the Garden of Eden, and continuing from that day, the Shekina (glory) was dwelling upon a Cherub under the Tree of Life. (2) And the ministering angels were gathering together and going down from heaven in groups. From the Raqia (heaven) they went in companies from the heavens in camps to perform His will in the entire world. (3) And the first man and his children were sitting outside the gate of the Garden to see the glowing, bright appearance of the Shekina (glory). (4) For the splendor of the Shekina (glory) enfolds the world from end to end with its splendor 365,000 times that of the orb of the sun. And everyone who made use of the splendor of the Shekina, on him no flies and no gnats lit, and he was not ill and he suffered no pain. No demons could overpower him, neither were they able to injure him. (5) When the Holy One, blessed be He, went out and went in from the Garden to Eden, from Eden to the Garden, from the Garden to Raqia (heaven) and from Raqia (heaven) to the Garden of Eden then everything and everyone saw His magnificent Shekina and they were not injured; (6) until the time of the generation of Enosh who was the head of all idol worshippers of the world.

The Shekina was an energy or substance that was protecting those who used it from illness, demons, and even bugs.

(7) And what did the generation of Enosh do? They went from one end of the world to the other, and each person brought silver, gold, precious stones and pearls in heaps the size of mountains and hills to make idols out of them throughout the entire world. And they erected the idols in every corner of the world: the size of each idol was 1000 parasangs.

The generations of Enoch are as follows: Adam, Seth, Enosh, Kenan, Mahalalel, Jared, Enoch.
The highest (worst) sins, according to Rabbis, are idolatry, adultery, bloodshed, and sorcery and calling God's name in vain.
A parasang is a length or measurement of distance used in what is now Iran. It varied according to the region. The north-eastern parasang was about 15,000 paces, the north-western parasang was 18,000 paces, and the one of the south-west was merely 6,000 paces. The measurement called the "true parasang" was about 9,000 paces.

(8) And they brought down the sun, the moon, planets and constellations, and placed them in front of the idols on the right side and on the left side of the idols, to attend to them just like they attend the Holy One, blessed be He, for it is written (I Kings 22:19): "And all the hosts of heaven were standing by him on his right hand and on his left." (9) What power was in them to enable to bring them down? They would not have been able to bring them down, if it had not been for the fact that UZZA, and AZZIEL (other sources have Azzael) taught them sorceries by which they brought them down and enslaved them.

It is obvious that the actual sun and stars were not brought down, but the angelic powers controlling them were summoned. Also, keep in mind that some cultures thought stars to be evil angels who flew across the sky. These agents were summoned and used.

(10) In that time the ministering angels accused them before the Holy One, blessed be He, saying: "Master of the World! Why do you bother with the children of men? As it is written (Ps. 8:4) 'What is man (Adam) that you are mindful of him?' But it was not about Adam that this was written but about Enosh, for he is the head of the idol worshippers. (11) Why have you left the highest of the high heavens which are filled with the majesty of your glory and are high, lifted up, and exalted on the high and exalted throne in the Raqia (heaven) of Araboth (highest heaven) and are gone and dwell with the children of men who worship idols and equate you to (place you on the same level as) the idols.

The word "Araboth (highest heaven)" occurs in Psalm 68:4 'Extol him who rides upon the Araboth (highest heaven)' in which it is usually translated simply as the highest heaven. In the case of 3 Enoch, this would be the throne of God. In the Zoharic commentary on Exodus it is referred to thus: 'Be glad in the presence of him who rides upon that concealed heaven which is supported by the Chayoth.' The Zohar also interprets the word to mean 'mixture' because, it says, this heaven is a mixture of fire and water. This is a mystical statement of a place containing opposites, and thus everything.

(12) Now you are on earth just like the idols. What have you to do with the inhabitants of the earth who worship idols? (13) Then the Holy One, blessed be He, lifted up His Shekina from the earth, from their midst (14) In that moment the ministering angels came. They are troops of the host and the armies of Araboth (highest heaven) in thousand camps and ten thousand host. They brought trumpets and took the horns in their hands and surrounded the Shekina with all kinds of songs. And He ascended to the high heavens, for it is written (Ps. 47:5) "God is gone up with a shout, the Lord with the sound of a trumpet."

Here the presence and dwelling of God is the Shekina. When the Shekina was taken, God himself left them and took his glory because of idolatry.

CHAPTER 6
Enoch is lifted up to heaven together with the Shekina.

Rabbi Ishmael said: Metatron, the Angel, the Prince of the Presence, said to me:
(1) When the Holy One, blessed be He, wanted to lift me up on high, He first sent Anaphiel YHWH, the Prince, and he took me from their company out of their sight and carried me away in great glory on a chariot of fire pulled by horses of fire, and servants of glory. And he lifted me up to the high heavens together with the Shekina. (2) As soon as I reached the high heavens, the Holy Chayoth, the Ophannim, the Seraphim, the Cherubim, the Wheels of the Merkaba (chariot) (the Galgallim), and the ministers of the consuming fire, all smelled my scent from a distance of 365,000 myriads of parasangs, and said: "What smells like one born woman and what tastes like a white drop? Who is this that ascends on high. He is merely a gnat among those who can divide flames of fire?"

Chayot are considered angels of fire, who hold up the throne of God and the earth itself.
The angel smells the scent of human, which he finds revolting. He can taste it is the air. The white drop refers to semen. This is an extremely hateful and distasteful statement for the angel to make.

The Holy One, blessed be He, answered and spoke to them: "My servants, my host, my Cherubim, my Ophannim, my Seraphim! Do not be displeased on account of this! Since all the children of men have denied me and my great Kingdom and have all gone worshipping idols, I have removed my Shekina from among them and have lifted it up on high. But this one whom I have taken from among them is an Elect One among (the inhabitants of) the world and he is equal to all of them (put together) in his faith, righteousness and perfection of deed and I have taken him as a tribute from my world under all the heavens.

The statement of "taking a tribute" can be better understood if one looks at Enoch as the best mankind has to offer and God took him as a an act of admiration indicating the intended worth of mankind, had they not turned away from him. The term "Elect One" is very important. It occurs in 1 Enoch and in certain scripture regarding Christ.

CHAPTER 7
Enoch is raised upon the wings of Shekina to the place of the Throne

Rabbi Ishmael said: Metatron, the Angel, the Prince of the Presence, said to me: When the Holy One, blessed be He, took me away from the generation of the Flood, he lifted me on the wings of the wind of Shekina (his glory/understanding) to the highest heaven and brought me to the great palaces of the Araboth (highest heaven) in Raqia (heaven), where the glorious Throne of Shekina, the Merkaba (chariot), the troops of anger, the armies of vehemence, the fiery Shin'anim (accusers), and the flaming Cherubim, the burning Ophanim, the flaming servants, the flashing Chashmallin, the lightning Seraphim live. And he placed me (there) to attend daily to the Throne of Glory.

In some Jewish mystical writings the attributes of Elijah and those of Enoch are interchangeable. Here Enoch takes the same trip to heaven on a fiery chariot.
Here we have various classes of angels, on which we have little information. The Chashmallin are one of the ten classes, which are sometimes silent for a time in heaven. They cease speaking or singing when "The Word" emanates from the throne.
Shin'anim are a class of angel seen in lists of angelic orders. Their name seems to come from a word for "accuser" and thus could be the satans in heaven.

CHAPTER 8
The gates of heaven opened to Metatron

Rabbi Ishmael said: Metatron, the Prince of the presence, said to me:
(1) Before he appointed me to attend the Throne of Glory, the Holy One, blessed be He, opened to me
three hundred thousand gates of Understanding
three hundred thousand gates of Wisdom
three hundred thousand gates of Life
three hundred thousand gates of Grace and Loving-kindness
three hundred thousand gates of Love
three hundred thousand gates of The Torah
three hundred thousand gates of Meekness

three hundred thousand gates of Steadfastness
three hundred thousand gates of Mercy
three hundred thousand gates of Respect for heaven

Other readings add three hundred thousand gates of Shekina,
three hundred thousand gates of fear of sin,
three hundred thousand gates of power. The gates of steadfastness is also rendered as maintenance and refers to the sustenance to
maintain life. All of man's needs come from heaven. Subtlety is rendered as wisdom but includes diplomacy, and craftiness.

(2) Within the hour the Holy One, blessed be He, gave me additional wisdom and to wisdom He added understanding unto understanding, cunning unto cunning, knowledge unto knowledge, mercy unto mercy, instruction unto instruction, love unto love, loving-kindness unto loving-kindness, goodness unto goodness, meekness unto meekness, power unto power, strength unto strength, might unto might, brightness unto brightness, beauty unto beauty, splendor unto splendor, and I was honored and adorned with all these good praiseworthy things more than all the children of heaven.

Enoch has become more blessed or equipped than "all the children of heaven. Loving-kindness equates to "Grace" of the New Testament.

CHAPTER 9
Enoch receives blessings from the Most High and is adorned with angelic attributes.

Rabbi Ishmael said: Metatron, the Prince of the Presence, said to me: (1) After all these things the Holy One, blessed be He, put His hand on me and blessed me with 5360 blessings. (2) And I was raised up and grew to the size of the length and width of the world. (3) And he caused 72 wings to grow on me, 36 on each side. And each wing covered the entire world. (4) And He attached to me 365 eyes: each eye was as the great luminary (moon?). (5) And He left no kind of splendor, brilliance, radiance, beauty of all the lights of the universe that He did not affix to me.

There is no direct correlation for the number 5360. It is not evenly divisible by any other number in the chapter, but it is thought to reflect
the number 365, the number of days in a solar year. The number 72 is used to reflect the number of the nations of the world and represents
the known world. This is backed up by the phrase stating the wings cover the world.

CHAPTER 10
God places Metatron on a throne as ruler in the seventh Hall.

Rabbi Ishmael said: Metatron, the Prince of the Presence, said to me: (1) All these things the Holy One, blessed be He, made for me. He made me a Throne, similar in form and substance to the Throne of Glory. And He spread a curtain of magnificently bright appearance over me. And it was of beauty, grace, and mercy, similar to the curtain of the Throne of the Glory; and on it were affixed all kinds of lights in the universe.

The idea of a curtain could represent the divine secrets and processes unknown and not available to others.

(2) And He placed the curtain at the door of the Seventh Hall and sat me down on it. (3) And the announcement went forth into every heaven, saying: "This is Metatron, my servant. I have made him a prince and ruler over all the princes of my kingdoms and over all the children of heaven, except the eight great, honored, and revered princes who are the ones called YHWH, by the name of their King."

The eight beings who are called YHWH may refer to those angels who have the Tetragrammaton as part of their name. These are highly
ranked angels that are outside the normal system of authority. They are the ones God uses as his counsel.

(4) "And every angel and prince who has a word to speak to me shall now go before him and they shall speak to him instead of Me. (5) And every command that he speaks to you in my name, you will obey, carry out, and fulfill. (Some sources add "Beware of him and do not provoke him.") For the Prince of Wisdom and the Prince of Understanding have I committed to him to instruct him in the wisdom of heavenly things and earthly things, in the wisdom of this world and of the world to come. (6) Moreover, I have set him over all the storehouses of the palaces of Araboth (highest heaven) and over all the storehouses (reserves) of life that I have in the high heavens."

CHAPTER 11
God reveals all of the great mysteries to Metatron

Rabbi Ishmael said: Metatron, the angel, the Prince of the Presence, said to me:
(1) The Holy One, blessed be He, began revealing to me all the mysteries of Torah and all the secrets of wisdom and the deep mysteries of the Perfect Law. He revealed the thoughts of all living beings and their feelings and all the secrets of the universe and all the secrets of creation. All these were revealed to me just as they are known to the Maker of Creation. (2) And I watched intently to see and understand the secrets and depths of the wonderful mystery. Before a man thought a thought in secret, I saw it and before a man made a thing I watched it. (3) And there was nothing on high or in the depth of the world that was hidden from me.

Here Metatron is given the omniscient power of God.

CHAPTER 12
God puts a crown on him and calls him "the Lesser YHWH"

Rabbi Ishmael said: Metatron, the Prince of the Presence, said to me: (1) Because of the love that the Holy One, blessed be He, loved me with, was more than all the children of heaven, He made me a garment of glory on which were affixed lights of all varieties, and He clothed me in it. (2) And He made me a robe of honor on which were affixed beauty, magnificent brilliance and majesty of all sorts. (3) And he made me a crown of royalty on which were affixed forty-nine stones of worth, which were like the light of the orb of the sun.

Forty-nine is a mystical number of seven sevens. The number seven represents spiritual perfection.

(4) Its splendor went out into the four coners of the Araboth (highest heaven) of Raqia (heaven), and through the seven heavens, and throughout the four corners of the world. He placed it on my head. (5) And He called me THE LESSER YHWH in the presence of all His heavenly household; for it is written (Ex. 22: 21): " For my name is in him."

Without delving too deeply into Jewish mysticism, it should be pointed out that the numerical value (gematria) of the name Metatron and that of Shahhdai are the same.

CHAPTER 13
God writes with a flaming pen on Metatron's crown the letters by which heaven and earth were created

Rabbi Ishmael said: Metatron, the angel, the Glory of all heavens and the Prince of the Presence, , said to me: (1) Holy One, blessed be He, loved and cherished me with great love and mercy, more than all the children of heaven. Thus, He wrote with his finger with a flaming pen on the crown upon my head the letter by which heaven and earth, the seas and rivers, the mountains and hills, the planets and constellations, the lightning, winds, earthquakes and thunders, the snow and hail, the wind of the storm and the tempest were created. These are the letters by which all the needs of the world and all the orders of Creation were created. (2) And every single letter flashed out time after time like lightning, and time after time like lanterns, time after time like flames of fire, time after time rays like those of the rising of the sun and the moon and the planets.

There are 22 letters in the Hebrew alphabet. It is thought that all things were created when God spoke the words in the Hebrew tongue. These words are symbolized by the combinations of the 22 letters.

CHAPTER 14
All the highest of the princes and lowest angels fear and tremble at the sight of Metatron crowned.

Rabbi Ishmael said: Metatron, the Angel, the Prince of the Presence, said to me: (1) When the Holy One, blessed be He, put this crown on my head, all the Princes of Nations who are in the height of Araboth (highest heaven) of Raqia (heaven) and all the host of every heaven and even the prince of the Elim, the princes of the 'Er'ellim and the princes of the Tafsarim, who are greater than all the ministering angels who minister before the Throne of Glory, trembled before me. They shook, feared and trembled before me when they looked at me.

This is a very interesting list of angels and princes. According to Jewish mystical sources, such as the Zohar, there are ten classes of angels under Mikael (Michael). The Er'ellim denotes a general class of angels, while the Elim minster before God in the high heavens. The Tafsarim are the princes of the Elim.

(2) Even Sammael, the Prince of the Accusers, who is greater than all the princes of Nations on high, feared me and shook before me.

Sammael is the head of the satans or accusers. He is also the ruling angel over Rome, the archenemy of Israel.

(3) And even the angel of fire, and the angel of hail, and the angel of wind, and the angel of the lightning, and the angel of wrath, and the angel of the thunder, and the angel of the snow, and the angel of the rain; and the angel of the day, and the angel of the night, and the angel of the sun, and the angel of the moon, and the angel of the planets, and the angel of the constellations whose hands rule the world, all of them feared and shook and were frightened when they looked at me. (4) These are the names of the rulers of the world: Gabriel, the angel of fire, Baradi-el, the angel who controls hail, Ruchi-el who controls the wind, Baraqi-el who controls the lighting, Zahafi-el who controls the winds of the storm, Rahami-el who controls the thunders, Rahashi-el who controls the earthquake, Shalgiel who controls the snow, Matari-el who controls the rain, Shimshi-el who controls the planets, Rahati-el who controls the constellations. (5) And they all fell to the ground and bowed, when they saw me. And they were not able to look at me because of the majestic glory of the crown on my head.

CHAPTER 15
Metatron is transformed into fire

Rabbi Ishmael said: Metatron, the angel, the Prince of the Presence, and the Glory of all heavens, said to me: (1) As soon as the Holy One, blessed be He, took me into (His) service to attend the Throne of Glory and the Wheels (Galgallim) of the Merkaba (chariot) and the service of Shekina, suddenly my flesh was changed into flames, my muscles into flaming fire, my bones into coals of juniper wood, the light of my eye-lids into hot flames, and all of my limbs into wings of burning fire and my entire body into glowing fire.

Galgallim (sometimes spelled Galgalim) are a high-ranking order of angels, the equivalent of Seraphim. They are metaphorically called "the wheels of the Merkabah" (the 'divine chariot' used to connect people to the divine) and are considered the equivalent of the Orphanim (Cherubim). Galgalim is Hebrew for "wheels."

(2) And on my right flames were burning and dividing, on my left staves of wood (burning staves) were burning, around me the winds of storms and tempests were blowing and in front of me and behind me was roaring thunder accompanied by earthquakes.

CHAPTER 15 - B
This chapter does not occur in all manuscripts. It seems to be a later addition.

Rabbi Ishmael said me: Metatron, the Prince of the Presence and the prince ruling over all the princes, stands before Him who is greater than all the Elohim. And he enters in under the Throne of Glory. And he has a great dwelling of light on high. And he brings into existence the fire of deafness and places it in the ears of the Holy Chayoth, so that they cannot hear the voice of the Word that sounds from the mouth of the Divine Majesty.

This may indicate that he goes into the holy of holies where he worships and has his own sanctuary.
The idea of more than one Elohim is not new. It is addressed in Psalm 82:
1, The Psalm of Asaph. God stands in the council of the gods; he judges among the gods. 2. How long will you judge unjustly, and show preference to the wicked? Selah. 3. Judge the poor and the orphans; do righteousness to the afflicted and dispossessed. 4. Deliver the poor and oppressed; save them from the hand of the evil. 5. They do not know and they have no understanding; they walk about in darkness. All the foundations of the earth are shaken. 6. I said, "You are gods, and children of Elyon, every one of you." 7. But you will die like mortals, and fall like one of the princes. 8. Rise up, O God, and judge the earth, for you have inherited all the nations.

This section seems to preserve a fragment of a book called, "The Ascension of Moses." The chashmal is the highest point of heaven. It is like a zenith line out of which a window opens.

(2) And when Moses ascended on high, he fasted 121 fasts, until the places where the chashmal live were opened to him; and he saw that the place was as white as a Lion's heart and he saw the companies of the host round about him, which could not

be counted. And they wished to burn him. But Moses prayed for mercy, first for Israel and then for himself: and He who was sitting on the Merkaba (chariot) opened the windows above the heads of the Cherubim. And a host of 1800 helpers along with the Prince of the Presence, Metatron, all went out to meet Moses. They took the prayers of Israel and placed them like a crown on the head of the Holy One, blessed be He.

(3) The they said (Deut. 6:4): "Hear, O Israel; the Lord our God is one Lord." And their face were shining and they rejoiced over Shekina and they said to Metatron: "What are these? And to whom do they give all honor and glory?" And they answered: "To the Glorious Lord of Israel." And they spoke: Hear, O Israel: the Lord, our God is one Lord. To Who else shall be given this abundance of honor and majesty but to You YHWH, the Divine Majesty, the King, the living and eternal one."

(4) In that moment Akatriel Ya Yehod Sebaoth (a name of the most high) spoke and said to Metatron, the Prince of the Presence and said, "Let no prayer that he prays before me return to him empty (not done). Hear his prayer and fulfill his desire whether it is great or small (5) Then Metatron, the Prince of the presence, said to Moses, "Son of Amram! Do not be afraid. God delights in you. He asks you what you desire from the Glory and Majesty. Your face shines from one end of the world to the other." But Moses answered him: "I fear that I should bring guiltiness upon myself." Metatron said to him, "Receive the letters of the oath, which makes a covenant that cannot be broken."

Metatron is moving through time to and from the time of Moses.
The letters make up the divine names, which are eternal.

CHAPTER 16
This continues the additional material.
His privilege of presiding on a Throne are taken.

Rabbi Ishmael said: Metatron, the Angel, the Prince of the Presence, the Glory of all heaven, said to me: (1) At first I was sitting on a large Throne at the door of the Seventh Hall. There, by authority of the Holy One, blessed be He, I was judging the children of heaven and the servants on high. And I judged Greatness, Kingship, Dignity, Rulership, Honor and Praise, and the Diadem and Crown of Glory for all the princes of kingdoms. While I was presiding in the Court of the Sky (Yeshiba), the princes of nations were standing before me, on my right and on my left, by authority of the Holy One, blessed be He. (2) But when Acher came to see the vision of the Merkaba (chariot) and locked his eyes on me, he was afraid and shook before me so much that his soul was departing from him, because of fear, horror and dread of me, when he saw me sitting upon a throne like a king with all the ministering angels standing by my side serving me and all the princes of kingdoms adorned with crowns all around me. (3) At that moment he opened his mouth and said, "Surely there are two Divine Powers in heaven!" (4) Then the Divine Voice went out from heaven from the Shekina and said: "Return, you backsliding children (Jer.3:22), except for Acher!" (5) Then Anieyel came (Other sources have "Anaphiel YHWH), the Prince, the honored, glorified, beloved, wonderful, revered and fearful one, as ordered by the Holy One, blessed be He and beat me sixty times with whips of fire and made me stand to my feet.

Anieyel , or Anaphiel YHWH is higher in status than Metatron. It is possible the Anieyel is the angel who punishes. The purpose of this chapter is to refute the heresy of the Rabbi called Acher, who believed that there were now two deities in heaven, God and Metatron. To show Metatron is not a deity God sends in a higher angel to take him off his throne and beat him, proving Metatron is not God, nor is he a god. The chapter goes on to call all of Israel to return to God, except for Acher, who has committed an unforgivable sin against the monotheists and against God.

CHAPTER 17
The princes of the seven heavens, and of the sun, moon, planets and constellations.

Rabbi Ishmael said: Metatron, the angel, the Prince of the Presence, the glory of all heavens, said to me: (1) The number of princes are seven. They are the great, beautiful, wonderful, honored, and revered ones. They are assigned over the seven heavens, And these are they: MIKAEL (Michael), GABRIEL, SHATQIEL, BAKARIEL, BADARIEL, PACHRIEL. (Some sources omit Parchriel and add Sidriel.) (2) And every one of them is the prince of the host of one heaven. And each one of them is accompanied by 496,000 groups of ten-thousand ministering angels.

496 is the numerical value of the word Malkut (kingdom). These 496,000 angels are the ones who sing of the glory of God, singing "Holy, Holy. Holy."

(3) MIKAEL is the great prince assigned to ruler over the seventh heaven, the highest one, which is in the Araboth (highest heaven). Gabriel is the prince of the host assigned to rule over the sixth heaven which is in Makon. SHATAQIEL is the prince of the host assigned to rule over the fifth heaven which is in Makon. SHAHAQIEL is the prince of the host assigned to rule

over the fourth heaven which is in Zebul. BADARIEL is the prince of the host assigned to rule over the third heaven which is in Shehaqim. BARAKIEL is the prince of the host assigned to rule over the second heaven which is in the height of Raqia (heaven). PAZRIEL is the prince of the host assigned to rule over the first heaven which is in Wilon (or Velum, as the first heaven is called), which is in Shamayim. (4) Under them in GALGALLIEL, the prince who is assigned as ruler over the orb (galgal) of the sun, and with him are 96 great and revered angels who moves the sun in Raqia (heaven) a distance of 365,000 parasangs each day. (5) Under them is OPHANNIEL, the prince who is set the globe (Ophan) of the moon. And with him are 88 (some have it as 68) angels who move the globe of the moon 354 thousand parasangs every night at the time when the moon stands in the East at its turning point. And the moon is situated in the East at its turning point in the fifteenth day of every month. (6) Under them is RAHATIEL, the prince who is appointed to rule over the constellations. He is accompanied by 72 great and revered angels. And why is he called RAHATIEL? Because he makes the stars run (marhit) in their orbits and courses, which is 339 thousand parasangs every night from the East to West, and from West to East. The Holy One, blessed be He, has made a tent for all of them, for the sun, the moon, the planets and the stars, and they travel in it at night from the West to the East. (7) Under them is KOKBIEL, the prince who is assigned to rule over all the planets. And with him are 365,000 groups of ten-thousand ministering angels, great and revered ones who move the planets from city to city and from province to province in Raqia (the heaven) of heavens. (8) And ruling over them are seventy-two princes of nations (kingdoms) on high corresponding to the 72 nations of the world. And all of them are crowned with crowns of royalty and clothed in royal clothes and wrapped in royal robes. And all of them are riding on royal horses and holding royal scepters in their hands. In front of each of them when he is traveling in Raqia (heaven), royal servants are running with great glory and majesty just as on earth the Princes are traveling in chariots with horsemen and great armies and in glory and greatness with praise, song and honor.

CHAPTER 18
The order of ranks of the angels is established by the homage.

Rabbi Ishmael said: Metatron, the Angel, the Prince of the Presence, the glory of all heaven, said to me: (1) THE ANGELS OF THE FIRST HEAVEN, when (ever) they see their prince, they dismount from their horses and bow themselves. And THE PRINCE OF THE FIRST HEAVEN, when he sees the prince of the second heaven, he dismounts, removes the glorious crown from his head and bows himself to the ground. AND THE PRINCE OF THE SECOND HEAVEN, when he sees the prince of the third heaven, he removes the glorious crown form his head and bows himself to the ground. AND THE PRINCE OF THE THIRD HEAVEN, when he sees the prince of the fourth heaven, he removes the glorious crown form his head and bows himself to the ground. AND THE PRINCE OF THE FOURTH HEAVEN, when he sees the prince of the fifth heaven, he removes the glorious crown form his head and bows himself to the ground. AND THE PRINCE OF THE FIFTH HEAVEN, when he sees the prince of the sixth heaven, he removes the glorious crown from his head and bows himself to the ground. AND THE PRINCE OF THE SIXTH HEAVEN, when he sees the prince of the seventh heaven he removes the glorious crown from his head and bows himself to the ground. (2) AND THE PRINCE OF THE SEVENTH HEAVEN, when he sees THE SEVENTY-TWO PRINCES OF KINGDOMS, he removes the glorious crown from his head and bows himself to the ground.

The number 70 appears as does the number 72. It is possible the difference can be explained by the 70 angels along with two leaders, such as Mikael (Michael) and Sammael. In the following section the names of the angels do not follow their function, as in the prior portion of the book. The names are obscure and it is difficult to understand their meanings. The expression "bows himself to the ground" and "bow themselves" likely indicates a complete kneeling position with the head touching the earth.

(3) And the seventy two princes of kingdoms, when they see The door keepers of the first hall in the ARABOTH RAQIA in the highest heaven, they remove the royal crown from their head and bow themselves. And The door keepers of the first hall, when they see the doorkeepers of the second Hall, they remove the glorious crown form their head and bow themselves. The door keepers of the second hall, when they see the door keepers of the third hall, they remove the glorious crown from their head and bow themselves. The door keepers of the third hall, when they see the door keepers of the fourth Hall, they remove the crown from their head and bow themselves. The door keepers of the fourth hall, when they see the door keepers of the fifth Hall, they remove the glorious crown from their head and bow themselves. The door keepers of the fifth hall, when they see the doorkeepers of the sixth Hall, they remove the crown from their head and fall to their face. The door keepers of the sixth hall, when they see the The door keepers of the seventh hall, they remove the glorious crown from their head and bow themselves. (4) And the door keepers of the seventh Hall, when they see The Four Great Princes, the honored ones, who are appointed over the four Camps Of SHEKINA, they remove the crowns of glory from their head and bow themselves. (5) And the four great prince, when they see TAGHAS, the prince, great and honored with song (and) praise, at the head of all the children of heaven, they remove the glorious crown from their head and bow themselves. (6) And Taghas, the great and honored prince, when he sees BARATTIEL, the great prince of three fingers in the height of Araboth, the highest heaven, he removes the glorious crown from his head and bows himself to the ground.

Three fingers in height – Hold your hand out at arm's length with three fingers held out horizontally in front of your eyes. This is the measurement.

(7) And Barattiel, the great prince, when he sees HAMON, the great prince, the fearful and honored, beautiful and terrible, he who makes all the children of heaven to shake, when the time draws near that is set for the saying of the 'Thrice Holy', he removes the glorious crown form his head and bows himself to the ground. For it is written (Isa.33:3): " At noise of the confusion at the anxious preparation of the salutation of "Holy, Holy, Holy" the people are fled; at the lifting up of yourself the nations are scattered," (8) And Hamon, the great prince, when he sees TUTRESSIEL, the great prince he removes the glorious crown from his head and bows himself to the ground. (9) And Tutresiel YHWH, the great prince, when he sees ATRUGIEL, the great prince, he removes the glorious crown from his head and bows himself to the ground. (10) And Aatrugiel the great prince, when he sees NA'ARIRIEL YHWH, the great prince, he removes the glorious crown from his head and bows himself to the ground. (11) And Na'aririel YHWH, the great prince when he see SAANIGIEL, the great prince, he removes the glorious crown from his head and bows himself to the ground. (12) And Sasnigiel YHWH, when he sees ZAZRIEL YHWH, the great prince, he removes the glorious crown from his head and bows himself to the ground. (13) And Zazriel YHWH, the prince, when he sees GEBURATIEL YHWH, the prince, he removes the glorious crown from his head and bows himself to the ground. (14) And Geburatiel YHWH, the prince, when he sees ARAPHIEL YHWH, the prince, he removes the glorious crown from his head and bows himself to the ground. (15) And Araphiel YHWH, the prince, when he sees ASHRUYLU, the prince, who presides in all the sessions of the children of heaven, he removes the glorious crown from his head and bows himself to the ground. (16) And Ashruylu YHWH, the prince, when he sees GALLISUR YHWH, THE PRINCE, WHO REVEALS ALL THE SECRETS OF THE LAW (Torah), he removes the glorious crown from his head and bows himself to the ground. (17) And Gallisur YHWH, the prince, when he sees ZAKZAKIEL YHWH , the prince who is appointed to write down the merits of Israel on the Throne of Glory, he removes the glorious crown form his head and bows himself to the ground. (18) And Zakzakiel YHWH, the great prince, when he sees ANAPHIEL YHWH, the prince who keeps the keys of the heavenly Halls, he removes the glorious crown from his head and bows himself to the ground. Why is he called by the name of Anaphiel? Because the shoulders of his honor and majesty and his crown and his splendor and his brilliance overshadows all the chambers of Araboth (highest heaven) of Raqia (heaven) on high even as the Maker of the World overshadows them. Regarding the Maker of the world, it is written that His glory covered the heavens, and the earth was full of His praise. The honor and majesty of Anaphiel cover all the glories of Araboth (highest heaven) the highest.

Araphiel means "Neck or Strength of God." Ashruylu means "To cause to rest / dwell." It is one of the names of the Godhead. Gallisur means, "reveal the secrets of the Law. " He reveals the reasons and secrets of the Creator. Raziel means, "Secrets of God." He hears the divine decrees. Anaphiel means "Branch of God." Zakzakiel means, "Merit of God." The glorious crowns signify honor and status.

(19) And when he sees SOTHER ASHIEL YHWH, the prince, the great, fearful and honored one, he removes the glorious crown from his head and bows himself to the ground. Why is he called Sother Ashiel? Because he is assigned to rule over the four heads of the river of fire, which are beside the Throne of Glory; and every single prince who goes out or enters before the Shekina, goes out or enters only by his permission. For the seals of the river of fire are entrusted to him. And furthermore, his height is 7000 groups of ten-thousand parasangs. And he stirs up the fire of the river; and he goes out and enters before the Shekina to expound what is recorded concerning the inhabitants of the world. According for it is written (Dan. 7:10): "the judgment was set, and the books were opened." (20) And Sother Ashiel the prince, when he sees SHOQED CHOZI, the great prince, the mighty, terrible and honored one, he removes the glorious crown from his head and falls upon his face. And why is he called Shoqed Chozi? Because he weighs all the merits of man on a scale in the presence of the Holy One, blessed be He. (21) And when he sees ZEHANPURYU YHWH, the great prince, the mighty and terrible one, honored, glorified and feared in the entire heavenly household, he removes the glorious crown from his head and bows himself to the ground. Why is he called Zehanpuryu? Because he commands the river of fire and pushes it back to its place. (22) And when he sees AZBUGA YHWH, the great prince, glorified, revered, honored, adorned, wonderful, exalted, loved and feared among all the great princes who know the mystery of the Throne of Glory, he removes the glorious crown from his head and bows himself to the ground. Why is he called Azbuga? Because in the future he will clothe the righteous and pious of the world with garments of life and wrap them in the cloak of life, so that they can live an eternal life in them. (23) And when he sees the two great princes, the strong one and the glorified one who are standing above him, he removes the glorious crown from his head and bows himself to the ground. And these are the names of the two princes: SOPHERIEL YHWH (Sopheriel YHWH the Killer), the great prince, the honored, glorified, blameless, venerable, ancient and mighty one. (24) Why is he called Sopheriel YHWH who kills (Sopheriel YHWH the Killer)? Because he is assigned to control the books of the dead, so that everyone, when the day of his death draws near, is written by him in the books of the dead. Why is he called Sopheriel YHWH who makes alive (Sopheriel YHWH the Lifegiver)? Because he is assigned control over the books of life, so that every one whom the Holy One, blessed be He, will bring into life, he writes him in the book of life, by authority of The Divine Majesty. Perhaps he might say: "Since the Holy One, blessed be He, is sitting on a throne, they are also sitting when writing." The Scripture teaches us (I Kings 22:19, 2 Chron. 28:18): "And all the host of heaven are standing by him." They are called "The host of heaven" in order

to show us that even the Great Princes and all like them in the high heavens, fulfill the requests of the Shekina in no other way than standing. But how is it possible that they are able to write, when they are standing?

This section is very important to Jewish mystics and Cabbalists in that it sets the balance within the act of judgment between mercy and justice. If one were to strip down to the barest essentials the spiritual life of a person some may conclude it is to find balance between mercy and justice. The books of life and death are records of the birth and death of individuals. This is not the same as the Book of Life referred to in the Bible, which contains the names of the righteous.

(25) It is done thusly. One is standing on the wheels of the tempest and the other is standing on the wheels of the wind of the storm. The one is clothed in kingly garments, the other is clothed in kingly garments. The one is wrapped in a mantle of majesty and the other is wrapped in a mantle of majesty. One is crowned with a royal crown, and the other is crowned with a royal crown. The one's body is full of eyes, and the other's body is full of eyes. One is looks like lightning, and the other looks like lightning. The eyes of the one are like the sun in its power, and the eyes of the other are like the sun in its power. The one's height is the height of the seven heavens, and the other's height is the height of the seven heavens. The wings of the one are as many as the days of the year, and the wings of the other are as many as the days of the year. The wings of one reach over the width of Raqia (heaven), and the wings of the other reach over the width of Raqia (heaven). The lips of one look like the gates of the East, and the lips of the other look like the gates of the East. The tongue of the one is as high as the waves of the sea, and the tongue of the other is as high as the waves of the sea. From the mouth of the one a flame proceeds, and from the mouth of the other a flame proceeds. From the mouth of the one lightning is emitted and from the mouth of the other lightning is emitted. From the sweat of one fire is kindled, and from the sweat of the other fire is kindled. From the one's tongue a torch is burning, and from the tongue of the other a torch is burning. On the head of the one there is a sapphire stone, and upon the head of the other there is a sapphire stone. On the shoulders of the one there is a wheel of a swift cherubim, and on the shoulders of the other there is a wheel of a swift cherubim. One has in his hand a burning scroll; the other has his hand a burning scroll. The length of the scroll is 3000 times ten-thousand parasangs; the size of the pen is 3000 times ten-thousand of parasangs; the size of every single letter that they write is 365 parasangs.

Sopheriel is the prince appointed over the book of life. The name means "Scribe of God." Azbuga is a messenger. The name denoted strength, as many angelic names do. Zehanpuryu means "the face of fear." To be full of eyes is a symbol of omniscience. Eastern gates were large, tall structures. The two symbolic uses of fire are destruction and purification.

CHAPTER 19
Rikbiel, the prince of the wheels of the Merkaba (chariot). And the Sacred Salutation of Holy, Holy, Holy

Rabbi Ishmael said: Metatron, the Angel, the Prince of the Presence, said to me: (1) Above these three angels, who are these great princes, there is one Prince, distinguished, revered, noble, glorified, adorned, fearful, fearless, mighty, great, uplifted, glorious, crowned, wonderful, exalted, blameless, loved, like a ruler, he is high and lofty, ancient and mighty, there is none among the princes like him. His name is RIKBIEL YHWH, the great and revered prince who is standing by Merkaba (chariot). (2) And why is he called RIKBIEL? Because he is assigned to rule over the wheels of the Merkaba (chariot), and they are given to his authority. (3) And how many are the wheels? Eight; two in each direction. And there are four winds compassing them round about. And these are their names: "the Winds of the Storm", "the Tempest", "the Strong Wind", and "the Wind of Earthquake." (4) And under them four rivers of fire are constantly running and there is one river of fire on each side. And around them, between the rivers, four clouds are affixed. They are "clouds of fire", "clouds of torches", "clouds of coal", "clouds of brimstone" and they are standing by their wheels.

There is much number symbolism here. Some Eastern cultures believe there are only eight possible directions of movement. They could be looked at as north, south, east, west, up, down, in, out. Anything else must be a combination of these. Four is the number of limits and testing. Two is the number of assistance, witness, or duplicity.

(5) And the feet of the Chayoth are resting on the wheels. And between two wheels an earthquake is roaring and thunder is sounding. (6) And when the time draws near for the recital of the Song, numerous wheels are moved, the numerous clouds tremble, all the chieftains (shallishim) become afraid, and all the horsemen (parashim) become angry, and all the mighty ones (gibborim) are excited, all the host (seba'im) are frightened, and all the troops (gedudim) are fearful, all the appointed ones (memunnim) hurry away, all the princes (sarim) and armies (chayelim) are confused, all the servants (mesharetim) faint and all the angels (mal'akim) and divisions (degalim) suffer with pain. (7) And one wheel makes a sound to be heard by the other and one Cherub speaks to another, one Chayya to another, one Seraph to another (saying) (Ps. 68:5) "Extol to him that rides in Araboth (highest heaven), by his name Jah (Yah) and rejoice before him!"

The name Jah (Yah) is a shortened and "speakable" version of YHWH or Jehovah.

CHAPTER 20
CHAYYLIEL, the prince of the Chayoth

Rabbi Ishmael said: Metatron, the angel, the Prince of the Presence, said to me: (1) Above these there is one great and mighty prince. His name is CHAYYLIEL YHWH, a noble and honorable prince, a prince before whom all the children of heaven tremble, a prince who is able to swallow up the entire earth in one moment at a single mouthful. (2) And why is he called CHAYYLIEL YHWH? Because he is assigned to rule over the Holy Chayoth and he strikes the Chayoth with lashes of fire: and glorifies them, when they give praise and glory and rejoicing and he causes them to hurry and say "Holy" "Blessed be the Glory of YHWH from His place!" (The Kedushah - Sacred Salutation of Holy, Holy, Holy).

CHAPTER 21
The Chayoth

Rabbi Ishmael said: Metatron, the angel, the Prince of the Presence, said to me: (1) The Four Chayoth correspond to the four winds. Each Chayya is as big as the space of the entire world. And each one has four faces; and each face is like the face of the East (sunrise). (2) Each one has four wings and each wing is like the tent (ceiling) of the universe. (3) And each one has faces in the middle of faces and wings in the middle of wings. The size of the faces is 248 faces, and the size of the wings is 365 wings. (4) And every one is crowned with 2000 crowns on his head. And each crown is like the rainbow in the cloud. And its splendor is like the magnificence of the circle of the sun. And the sparks that go out from every one are like the glory of the morning star (planet Venus) in the East.

CHAPTER 22
KERUBIEL, the Prince of the Cherubim.
Description of the Cherubim

Rabbi Ishmael said: Metatron, the angel, the Prince of the Presence, said to me: (1) Above these there is one prince, noble, wonderful, strong, and praised with all kinds of praise. His name is CHERUBIEL YHWH, a mighty prince, full of power and strength, a prince of highness, and Highness (is) with him, a righteous Prince, and Righteousness (is) with him, a holy prince, and holiness (is) with him, a prince of glorified in (by) thousand host, exalted by ten thousand armies (2) At his anger the earth trembles, at his anger the camps (of armies) are moved, from fear of him the foundations are shaken, at his chastisement the Araboth (highest heaven) trembles. (3) His stature is full of (burning) coals. The height is that of the seven heavens and the breadth of his stature is like the sea. (4) The opening of his mouth is like a lamp of fire. His tongue is a consuming fire. His eyebrows are like the splendor of the lightning. His eyes are like sparks of bright light. His face is like a burning fire. (5) And there is a crown of holiness upon his head on which the Explicit Name is graven, and lightning proceeds from it. And the bow of the Shekina is between his shoulders. And his sword is like lightning; and on his thighs there are arrows like flames, and upon his armor and shield there is a consuming fire, and on his neck there are coals of burning juniper wood and (also) around him (there are coals of burning juniper).

The bow can represent a rainbow but it is certainly a weapon of great power. Juniper is a symbol of strength and longevity. It was said to shelter the prophet Elijah from Queen Jezebel's pursuit. Tales in the apocryphal books tell of how the infant Jesus and his parents were hidden from King Herod's soldiers by a juniper during their flight into Egypt.

(7) And the splendor of Shekina is on his face; and the horns of the majesty on his wheels; and a royal diadem upon his head. (8) And his body is full of eyes. And wings are covering the entire of his high stature (lit. the height of his stature is all wings). (9) On his right hand a flame is burning, and on his left a fire is glowing; and coals are burning from it. And burning staves go forth from his body. And lightning is projected from his face. With him there is always thunder within thunder, and by his side there is a never ending earthquake within an earthquake. (10) And the two princes of the Merkaba (chariot) are together with him. (11) Why is he called CHERUBIEL YHWH, the Prince. Because he is assigned to rule over the chariot of the Cherubim. And the mighty Cherubim are given into his authority. And he adorns the crowns on their heads and polishes the diadem upon their heads (skulls). (12) He increases the glory of their appearance. And he glorifies the beauty of their majesty. And he expands the greatness of their honor. He makes their songs of praise to be sung. He makes the strength of their beauty increase. He causes the brightness of their glory to shine forth. He makes their goodness, mercy, and lovingkindess to grow. He separates their radiance so it show even more. He makes the beauty of their mercy even more beautiful. He glorifies their upright majesty. He sings the order of their praise to establish the dwelling place of Him who dwells on the Cherubim. (13) And the Cherumim are standing by the Holy Chayoth, and their wings are raised up to their

heads (are as the height of their heads) and Shekina is (resting) upon them and the bright Glory is upon their faces and songs of praise are in their mouth and their hands are under their wings and their feet are covered by their wings and horns of glory are upon their heads and the splendor of Shekina on their face and Shekina is resting on them and sapphire stones surround them and columns of fire are on their four sides and columns of burning staves are beside them. (14) There is one sapphire on one side and another sapphire on the other side and under the sapphires there are coals of burning juniper wood. (15) And a Cherub is standing in each direction but the wings of the Cherubim surround each other above their heads in glory; and they spread them to sing with them a song to him that inhabits the clouds and to praise the fearful majesty of the king of kings with their wings.

The sound coming from their wings is heard as a song. This hearkens back to a description of Lucifer, before the fall. It was said that his body had instruments made within it, which made beautiful music.

(16) And CHERUBIEL YHWH, is the prince who is assigned to rule over them. He arrays them in proper, beautiful and pleasant orders and he exalts them in all manner of exaltation, dignity and glory. And he hurries them in glory and might to do the will of their Creator every moment. Above their high heads continually dwells the glory of the high king "who dwells on the Cherubim."

Names in this section are related to the station of the angels. Chayyliel is the prince of the Chayyoth, Cherubiel or Kerubiel is the prince of the Kerubim or Cherubim, and so on.

CHAPTER 22-B

Rabbi Ishmael said to me: Metatron, the angel, the Prince of the Presence, said to me: (1) How are the angels standing on high? He said: A bridge is placed from the beginning of the doorway to the end, like a bridge that is placed over a river for every one to pass over it. And three ministering angels surround it and sing a song before YHWH, the God of Israel. And standing before it are the lords of dread and captains of fear, numbering a thousand times thousand and ten thousand times ten thousand, and they sing praises and hymns before YHWH, the God of Israel. (3) Many bridges are there. There are bridges of fire and many bridges of hail. Also many rivers of hail, numerous storehouses of snow, and many wheels of fire. (4) And how many are the ministering angels are there? 12,000 times ten-thousand: six-thousand time ten-thousand above and six (thousand times ten-thousand) below. And 12,000 are the storehouses of snow, six above and six below. And 24 times ten-thousand wheels of fire, 12 times ten-thousand above and 12 times ten-thousand below. And they surround the bridges and the rivers of fire and the rivers of hail. And there are numerous ministering angels, forming entries, for all the creatures that are standing in the midst thereof, over against the paths of Raqia (heaven) Shamayim. (5) What does YHWH, the God of Israel, the King of Glory do? The Great and Fearful God, mighty in strength, covers His face. (6) In Araboth (highest heaven) are 660,000 times ten-thousand angels of glory standing over against the Throne of Glory and the divisions of flaming fire. And the King of Glory covers His face; for else the Araboth (highest heaven) of Raqia (heaven) would be torn apart from its center because of the majesty, splendor, beauty, radiance, loveliness, brilliancy, brightness and Excellency of the appearance of (the Holy One,) blessed be He. (7) There are innumerable ministering angels carrying out his will, many kings and princes in the Araboth (highest heaven) of His delight. They are angels who are revered among the rulers in heaven, distinguished, adorned with song and they bring love to the minds of those who are frightened by the splendor of Shekina, and their eyes are dazzled by the shining beauty of their King, their faces grow black and their strength fails. (8) There are rivers of joy, streams of gladness, rivers of happiness, streams of victory, rivers of life, streams of friendship and they flow over and go out from in front of the Throne of Glory and grow large and wend their way through the gates on the paths to Araboth (highest heaven) of Raqia (heaven) at the voice of shouting and music of the CHAYYOTH, at the voice of the rejoicing of the cymbals of his OPHANNIM and at the melody of the cymbals of His Cherubim. And they grow great and go out with noise and with the sound of the hymn: "HOLY, HOLY, HOLY, IS THE LORD OF HOST; THE WHOLE EARTH IS FULL OF HIS GLORY!"

CHAPTER 22 -C

Rabbi Ishmael said: Metatron, the Prince of the Presence said to me: (1) What is the distance between one bridge and another? Tens of thousands of parasangs. They rise up tens of thousands of parasangs , and the go down tens of thousands of parasangs. (2) The distance between the rivers of dread and the rivers of fear is 22 times ten-thousand parasangs; between the rivers of hail and the rivers of darkness 36 times ten-thousand paragangs; between the chambers of lightnings and the clouds of compassion 42 times ten-thousand parasangs; between the clouds of compassion and the Merkaba (chariot) 84 times ten-thousand parasangs; between the Merkaba (chariot) and the Cherubim 148 times ten-thousand parasangs; between the Cherubim and the Ophannim 24 times ten-thousand parasangs; between the chambers of chambers and the Holy Chayoth 40,000 times ten-thousand parasangs; between one wing (of the Chayoth) and another 12 times ten-thousand parasangs; and the breadth of each one wing is of that same measure; and the distance between the Holy Chayoth and the Throne of Glory is 30,000 times ten-thousand parasangs. (3) And from the foot of the Throne to the seat there are 40,000 times ten-thousand parasangs. And the name of Him that sits on it: let the name be sanctified! (4) And the arches of the Bow are set above the Araboth (highest heaven), and they are 1000 thousands and 10,000 times ten thousands of parasangs high. Their measure is after the measure of the 'Irin and Qaddishin (the Watchers and the Holy Ones). As it is written, (Gen. 9:13) "My bow I have set in the cloud." It is not written here "I will set" but "I have set," that is to say; I have already set it in the clouds that surround the Throne of Glory. As His clouds pass by, the angels of hail turn into burning coal. (5) And a voice of fire goes down from the Holy Chayoth. And because of the breath of that voice they run (Ezek. 1:14) to another place, fearing that it could command them to go; and they return for fear that it may injure them from the other side. Therefore "they run and return." (6) And these arches of the Bow are more beautiful and radiant than the radiance of the sun during the summer solstice. And they are brighter (whiter) than a flaming fire and they are large and beautiful. (7) Above the arches of the Bow are the wheels of the Ophannim. Their height is 1000 thousand and 10,000 times 10,000 units of measure after the measure of the Seraphim and the Troops (Gedudim).

The Irin and Qaddishin are the highest ranked of all the angels. They constitute the supreme council of heaven. These angels are the twin sentinels. The Irin decrees while the Qaddishin sentences every case in the court of heaven. In Daniel 4:14 we find references. "By decree of the sentinels is this decided, by order of the holy ones, this sentence, that all who live may know that the most High rules over the kingdom of men: he can give it to whom he will, or set over it the lowliest of men. For the words rendered, "of the holy god," we read in Chaldee (in which Daniel was composed) the words elain cadisin ('-l-h-y-n q-d-y-sh-y-n) [vocalized this would be 'elahin qaddishin], which means "holy gods," not "holy God," (St. Jerome, Commentary on Daniel (1958). pp. 15-157)

CHAPTER 23
The winds are blowing under the wings of the Cherubim

Rabbi Ishmael said: Metatron, the Angel, the Prince of the Presence, said to me: (1) There are numerous winds blowing under the wings of the Cherubim. There blows "the Brooding Wind", for it is written (Gen. 1: 2): "and the wind of God was brooding upon the face of the waters." (2) There blows "the Strong Wind", as it is said (Ex.14: 21): "and the Lord caused the sea to go back by a strong east wind all that night." (3) There blows "the East Wind" for it is written (Ex. 10: 13): "the east wind brought the locusts." (4) There blows "the Wind of Quails for it is written (Num. 9: 31): "And there went forth a wind from the Lord and brought quails." (5) There blows "the Wind of Jealousy" for it is written (Num. 5:14): "And the wind of jealousy came upon him." (6) There blows the "Wind of Earthquake" and it is written (I Kings. 19: 11): "and after that the wind of the earthquake; but the Lord was not in the earthquake." (7) There blows the "Wind of YHWH" for it is written (Ex. 37: 1): "and he carried me out by the wind of YHWH and set me down." (8) There blows the "Evil Wind" for it is written (I Sam. 14: 23): "and the evil wind departed from him." (9) There blows the "Wind of Wisdom" and the "Wind of Understanding" and the "Wind of Knowledge" and the "Wind of the Fear of YHWH" for it is written (Is. 11: 2): "And the wind of YHWH shall rest upon him; the wind of wisdom and understanding, the wind of counsel and might, the wind of knowledge and the fear of YHWH." (10) There blows the "Wind of Rain", for it is written (Prov. 25: 23) "the north wind brings forth rain." (11) There blows the "Wind of Lightning", for it is written (Jer. 10: 13): "he makes lightning for the rain and brings forth the wind out of his storehouses." (12) There blows the "Wind, Which Breaks the Rocks", for it is written (1 Kings 19: 11): "the Lord passed by and a great and strong wind (rent the mountains and break in pieces the rocks before the Lord.) (13) There blows the Wind of Assuagement of the Sea", for it is written (Gen. 7:1): "and God made a wind to pass over the earth, and the waters assuaged." (14) There blows the "Wind of Wrath", for it is written (Job1: 19): 'and behold there came a great wind from the wilderness and smote the four corners of the house and it fell." (15) There blows the "Wind of Storms", for it is written (Ps. 148: 8): "Winds of the storm, fulfilling his word." (16) And Satan is standing among these winds, for "the winds of the storm" is nothing else but "Satan" and all these winds do not blow but under the wings of Cherubim, for it is written (Ps. 18.11): "and he rode upon a cherub and flew, yes, and he flew with speed upon wings of the wind." (17) And where do all these winds go? The Scripture teaches us, that they go out from under the wings of the Cherubim and descend on the globe of the sun, for it is written (Eccl. 1:6): "The wind goes toward the south and turns around to the north; it turns around over and over in its course and the wind returns again to its route." And from the orb of the sun they return and go down on to the rivers and the seas, then up on the mountains and up on the hills, for it is written (Am. 55:13): "For lo, he that forms the mountains and creates the wind." (18) And from the mountains and the hills they return and go down again to the seas and the rivers; and from the seas and the rivers they return and go up to the cities and provinces: and from the cities and provinces they return and go down into the Garden, and from the Garden they return and descend to Eden, for it is written (Gen. 3: 8) "walking in the Garden in the wind (cool) of day." In the middle of the Garden they come together and blow from one side to the other. In the Garden they are perfumed with spices from the Garden in its most remote parts, until the winds again separate from each other. Filled with the odor of the pure spices, the winds bring the aroma from the most remote parts of Eden. They carry the spices of the Garden to the righteous and godly who in time to come will inherit the Garden of Eden

158

and the Tree of life, for it is written (Cant 45: 16): "Awake, O north wind; and come you south; blow upon my garden and eat his precious fruits."

The same word used for "wind" is also used for "spirit." It is interesting to read the same verses using the word "spirit." It should also be noted that when certain attributes are associated with "wind," such as the wind of jealousy, it could be seen to be an agent of God, such as an angel or demon.

CHAPTER 24
The different chariots of the Holy One, blessed be He

Rabbi Ishmael said: Metatron, the Angel, the Prince of the Presence, the glory of all heaven, said to me: (1) The Holy One blessed be He, has innumerable chariots. He has the "Chariots of the Cherubim", for it is written (Ps. 18:11, 2 Sam 22: 11): " And he rode upon a cherub and did fly." (2) He has the "Chariots of Wind", for it is written: "and he flew swiftly upon the wings of the wind." (3) He has the "Chariots of the Swift Cloud", for it is written (Is.19:1): "Behold, the Lord rides upon a swift cloud:. (4) He has "Chariots of Clouds", for it is written (Ex. 19:9): "Lo, I come unto you in a cloud." (5) He has the "Chariots of the Altar", for it is written, " I saw the Lord standing upon the Altar." (6) He has the "Chariots of Ribbotaim", for it is written (Ps. 68:18): "The chariots of God are Ribbotaim; thousands of angels."

Ribbotaim appear to be used as the chariot and are a type of Cherub.

(7) He has the "Chariots of the Tent", for it is written (Deut. 31:15): "And the Lord appeared in the Tent in a pillar of cloud." (8) He has the "Chariots of the Tabernacle", for it is written (Lev. 1:1): "And the Lord spoke unto him out of the tabernacle." (9) He has the "Chariots of the Mercy-Seat", for it is written (Num. 7:89): "then he heard the Voice speaking unto him from upon the mercy-seat." (10) He has the "Chariots of Sapphire", for it is written (Ex. 24:10): "and there was under his feet a paved street of sapphires." (11) He has the "Chariots of Eagles", for it is written (Ex. 19:4): "I bare you on eagles' wings." It is not Eagles that are not meant here but "they that fly as swiftly as the eagles." (12) He has the "Chariots of a Shout", for it is written: "God is gone up with a shout." (13) He has the "Chariots of Araboth (highest heaven)," for it is written (Ps 68 :5): " Praise Him that rides upon the Araboth (highest heaven)." (14) He has the "Chariots of Thick Clouds", for it is written (Ps. 106:3): "who makes the thick clouds His chariot." (15) He has the "Chariots of the Chayoth," for it is written (Ezek. 1:14): "and the Chayoth ran and returned." They run by permission and return by permission, for Shekina is above their heads. (16) He has the "Chariots of Wheels (Galgallim)", for it is written (Ezek. 10: 2): "And he said: Go in between the whirling wheels." (17) He has the "Chariots of a Swift Cherub," for it is written, "riding on a swift cherub." And at the time when He rides on a swift cherub, as he sets one of His feet upon his back, and before he sets the other foot upon his back, he looks through eighteen thousand worlds at one glace. And he perceives and understands and sees into them all and knows what is in all of them, and then he sets down the other foot upon the cherub, for it is written (Ezek. 48:35): " Round about eighteen thousand." How do we know that He looks through every one of them every day? It is written (Ps. 14: 2): "He looked down from heaven upon the children of men to see if there were any that understand, that seek after God." (18) He has the "Chariots of the Ophannim", for it is written (Ezek. 10:12): "and the Ophannim were full of eyes round about." (19) He has the "Chariots of His Holy Throne", for it is written (Ps. 67:8): "God sits upon his holy throne" (20) He has the "Chariots of the Throne of Yah (Jah)", for it is written (Ex. 17:16): "Because a hand is lifted up upon the Throne of Jah (Yah)." (21) He has the "Chariots of the Throne of Judgment," for it is written (Is. 5: 16): "but the Lord of hosts shall be exalted in judgment." (22) He has the "Chariots of the Throne of Glory", for it is written (Jer. 17:12): "The Throne of Glory, set on high from the beginning, is the place of our sanctuary." (23) He has the "Chariots of the High and exalted Throne", for it is written (Is. 6: 1): "I saw the Lord sitting upon the high and exalted throne."

CHAPTER 25
Ophphanniel, the Prince of the Ophannim and a description of the Ophannim

Rabbi Ishmael said: Metatron, the Angel, the Prince of the Presence, said to me: (1) Above these there is one great prince, highly honored, fit to rule, fearful, ancient and powerful. OPHAPHANNIEL YHWH is his name. (2) He has sixteen faces, four faces on each side, also a hundred wings on each side. And he has 8466 eyes, corresponding to the days of the year and sixteen on each side. (Other sources have it as: corresponding to the hours in a year.)

The number of 8466 is difficult to understand in a 365 day year. The lunar year was calculated to be 352.5 days at the time of the righting of 3 Enoch. 8466 is the number of hours in a lunar year. This makes sense and makes the alternate rendering the correct one. However, other places in the texts may refer to the number 8766, which is exact number of hours is a solar year of 365.25 days.

(3) And in those two eyes of his face, in each one of them lightning is flashing, and from each one of them burning staves are burning; and no creature is able to look at them: for anyone who looks at them is burned up instantly. (4) His height is the distance of 2500 years' journey. No eye can see and no mouth can tell of the mighty power of his strength except the King of kings, the Holy One, blessed be He. He alone can tell.

The number 2500 yields the number 7, as the digits are added together. This pattern will occur again is these types of measurements. It is a way Jewish mystics re-enforce the perfection of the template of heaven.

(5) Why is he called OPHPHANNIEL? Because he rules over the Ophannim and the Ophannim are given over to his authority. He stands every day and attends to them and makes them beautiful. And he raises them up and determines their activity. He polishes the place where they stand and makes their dwelling place bright. He even makes the corners of their crowns and their seats spotless. And he waits upon them early and late, by day and by night, in order to increase their beauty and make their dignity grow. He keeps them diligent in the praise of their Creator. (6) And all the Ophannim are full of eyes, and they are full of brightness; seventy-two sapphires are fastened to their garments on their right side and seventy-two sapphire are fastened to their garments on their left side.

Note the number 72 again, representing the nations of the world.

(7) And four carbuncle stones are fastened to the crown of every single one, the splendor of which shines out in the four directions of Araboth (the highest heaven) even as the splendor of the orb of the sun shines out in all the directions of the universe. And why is it called Carbuncle (Bare'qet)? Because its splendor is like the appearance of a lightning (Baraq). And tents of splendor, tents of brilliance, tents of brightness as of sapphire and carbuncle enclose them because of the shining appearance of their eyes.

Carbuncle is an archaic name given to red garnet. The word occurs in four places in most English translations of the Bible. Each use originates from the Greek term Anthrax – meaning coal, in reference to the color of burning coal. A carbuncle is usually taken to mean a gem, particularly a deep-red garnet, which has no facet and is convex. In the same place in the masoretic text is the Hebrew word "nofech (no'-fekh)." In Exdodus 28:17 and again is Exodus 39:10 the carbuncle is used as the third stone in the breastplate of the Hoshen. Ezekiel 28:13 refers to the carbuncle's presence in the Garden of Eden.

CHAPTER 26
The Prince of the Seraphim.
Description of the Seraphim

Rabbi Ishmael said: Metatron, the Angel, the Prince of the Presence, said to me: (1) Over them there is one prince, who is wonderful, noble, of great honor, powerful and terrible, a chief leader and a fast scribe. He is glorified, honored and loved. (2) He is completely filled with splendor, and full of praise. He shines and he is totally full of the brightness of light and beauty. He is full of goodness and greatness. (3) His face is identical to that of angels, but his body is like an eagle's body. (4) His is magnificent like lightning, his appearance like burning staves. His beauty like sparks. His honor burns bright like glowing coal. His majesty like chashmals, His radiance like the light of the planet Venus. His image is like the Sun. His height is as high as the seven heavens. The light from his eyebrows is seven times as bright.

Chasmal is the fiery substance, which makes up the pillars on which the world rests. It is a mysterious substance or entity illuminating the heart of Ekekiel's chariot vision. Midrash Konen designated chashmal another class of angelic being.

(5) The sapphire on his head is as large as the entire universe and as splendid as the great heavens in radiance. (6) His body is full of eyes like the stars of the sky, innumerable and cannot be known. Every eye is like the planet Venus. But there are some of them like the Moon and some of them like the Sun. From His ankles to his knees they are like stars twinkling (of lightning). From his knees to his thighs is like the planet Venus, across his thighs like the moon, from his thighs to his neck is like the sun. From his neck to his head is like the Eternal Light. (7) The crown on his head is like the splendor of the Throne of Glory. The size of the crown is the distance of 502 years' journey. There is no kind of splendor, no kind of brilliance, no kind of radiance, no kind of light in the universe that is not affixed to the crown.

As in the prior chapter, the number seven is the result of the addition of the digits in the measurement, which\in this case is 502.

(8) The name of that prince is SERAPHIEL YHWH. And the crown on his head, its name is "the Prince of Peace." And why is he called by the name of SERAPHIEL YHWH? Because he is assigned to rule over the Seraphim. And the flaming

Seraphim are under his authority. And he presides over them by day and night and teaches them to sing, praise, and proclaim the beauty, power and majesty of their King. They proclaim the beauty of their King through all types of Praise and Sanctification. (Kedushah - Sacred Salutation of Holy, Holy, Holy). (9) How many Seraphim are there? Four, equating to the four winds of the world. And how many wings have each one of them? Six, relating to the six days of Creation. And how many faces do they have? Each one of them have four faces. (10) The height measurement of the Seraphim is the height of the seven heavens. The size of each wing is like the span of all Raqia (heaven). The size of each face is like the face of the East. (11) And each one of them gives out light, adding to the splendor of the Throne of Glory, so that not even the Holy Chayoth, the honored Ophannim, nor the majestic Cherubim are able to look on it. Anyone who gazes at it would be blinded because of its great splendor. (12) Why are they called Seraphim? Because they burn (saraph) the writing tables of Satan: Every day Satan sits together with SAMMAEL, the Prince of Rome, and with DUBBIEL, the Prince of Persia, and they write down the sins of Israel on their writing tables, which they hand over to the Seraphim, so that the Seraphim can present them to the Holy One, blessed be He, so that He should eliminate (destroy) Israel from the world. But the Seraphim know the secrets of the Holy One, blessed be He. They know that He does not want the people Israel to perish. What do the Seraphim do about this? Every day they receive the tablets from the hand of Satan and they burn them in the burning fire, which is near the high and exalted Throne. They do this in order that the tablet should not come before the Holy One, blessed be He, when he is sitting upon the Throne of Judgment, judging the entire world in truth.

Satan and Sammael are not allowed to approach the throne of God, but their accusations are taken by a Seraph, who destroys the tablet with the accusations against Israel and burns it. The tablet is not given to God, who would have to judge Israel, since the Seraph knows God does not wish to judge or punish Israel.
Dubbiel is the guardian angel of Persia and one of the special accusers of Israel. Dubbiel is an angel who was ranked among angels who were said to act as guardians over the seventy nations. Dubbiel was counted as the protector of Persia and as such defended its interests against its enemy Israel, a role that naturally put him at odds with the Chosen People and their special patron, St. Michael the Archangel. Sammael is an angel whose name has been interpreted as meaning "angel" or "god" (el) of "poison" (sam). He is the guardian angel of Rome, another enemy of Israel. He is considered in legend a member of the heavenly host who fell. He is equated with Satan and the chief of the evil spirits. He is the angel of death. In this capacity he is a fallen angel but remains the Lord's servant, or at least under His control. As a good angel, Sammael resided in the seventh heaven, although he is declared to be the chief angel of the fifth heaven. Seraphim are among the highest and most splendid of the nine accepted angelic orders as developed by the sixth-century theologian Dionysius. They are the closest in all of heaven to the throne of God. They are said to glow as if they are on fire so brightly they no mortal can endure the sight..

CHAPTER 27
RADWERIEL, the keeper of the Book of Records.

Rabbi Ishmael said: Metatron, the Angel of YHWH, the Prince of the Presence, said to me: (1) Above the Seraphim there is one prince, exalted above all princes. He is more wonderful than all the servants. His name is RADWERIEL YHWH who is assigned to rule over the treasuries of the books.

Radweriel is appointed over the treasury of book of records or remembrances. (See Mal.3:16). He is an angelic scribe, fluent in reading and writing. He reads the records in the Beth Din, (house/court) of justice. This is another name for the Sanhedrin.

(2) He couriers the Case of Writings, which has the Books of Records in it, and he brings it to the Holy One, blessed be He. And he breaks the seals of the case, opens it, and takes out the books and delivers them before the Holy One, blessed be He. And the Holy One, blessed be He, receives them out of his hand and gives them to the Scribes to see so they may read them in the Great Beth (house) Din in the height of Araboth (highest heaven) of Raqia (heaven), before the household of heaven. (3) And why is he called RADWERIEL? Because from every word going out of his mouth an angel is created. He stands in the service of the company of the ministering angels and sings a song before the Holy One, blessed be He, as the time draws near for the recitation of the Thrice Holy One.

CHAPTER 28
The 'Irin and Qaddishin (Watchers and Holy Ones)

Rabbi Ishmael said: Metatron, the Angel, the Prince of the Presence, said to me: (1) Above all these there are four great princes. Their names are Irin and Qaddishin. They are highly honored, revered, loved, wonderfully glorious, and greater than any of the heavenly children. There is none like them among all the princes of heaven (sky). There are none equal to them among any Servants. Each one is equal to all the rest of the heavenly servants put together. (2) And their dwelling is near the Throne of Glory and their standing place near the Holy One, blessed be He. The brightness of their dwelling is a reflection from the brightness from the Throne of Glory. Their face is magnificent and is a reflection of the magnificence of Shekina. (3) They are elevated by the glory of the Divince Majesty (Gebura) and praised by (through) the praise of Shekina. (4) And not only that, but the Holy One, blessed be He, does nothing in his world without first consulting them. Only after He consults them does He perform it. As it is written (Dan. 4: 17): "The sentence is by the decree of the Irin and the demand by the word of the Qaddishin." (5) The Irin are two (twins) and the Qaddishin are two (twins). In what fashions standing before the Holy One, blessed be He? We should understood, that one Ir is standing on one side and the other 'Ir on the other side. Also, one Qaddish is standing on one side and the other on the other side. (6) And they exalt the humble forever, and they humble and bring to the ground those that are proud. They exalt to the heights those that are humble. (7) And every day, as the Holy One, blessed be He, is sitting upon the Throne of Judgment and judges the entire world, and the Books of the Living and the Books of the Dead are opened in front of Him all the children of heaven are standing before Him in fear and dread. They are in awe and they shake. When the Holy One, blessed be He, is sitting on the Throne of Judgment to execute His judgment , His garment is white as snow, the hair on his head is like pure wool and the His entire cloak is shining with light. He is covered with righteousness all over, like He is wearing a coat of mail. (8) And those Irin and Qaddishin (Watchers and Holy Ones) are standing before Him like court officers before the judge. And constantly they begin and argue a case and close the case that comes before the Holy One, blessed be He, in judgment, according for it is written (Dan. 4. 17): "The sentence is by the decree of the 'Irin and the demand by the word of Qaddishin."

This section explains the function of the Irin and Qaddishin. They are two pairs of angels forming the apex of angelic power. They are the holy councilors and they have authority over all things terrestrial. They are judge and executioner. Another tradition has the Irin and Qaddishin as two classes of angels but many in number. Yet, they seem to come in sets of two each, like twins. Again, this may represent the balance of mercy and justice always sought in heaven.

(9) Some of them argue the case and others pass the sentence in the Great Beth Din (Great House of the Sanhedrin) in Araboth (the highest heaven). Some of them make requests in the presence of the Divine Majesty and some close the cases before the Most High. Others finish by going down and confirming the judgement and executing the sentences on earth below. According for it is written (Dan. 4. 13, 14): "Behold an Ir and a Qaddish came down from heaven and cried aloud and said , "Chop down the tree, and cut off his branches, shake off his leaves, and scatter his fruit: let the beasts escape from under it, and the fowls from his branches." (10) Why are they called Irin and Qaddishin (Watchers and Holy Ones)? Because they sanctify the body and the spirit with beatings with fire on the third day of the judgment, for it is written (Hos. 6: 2): "After two days will he revive us: on the third he will raise us up, and we shall live before him."

Irin and Qaddishin or ministering spirits receive men from the angel of death. They judge him with angels arguing for him. This takes two days. On the third day they pass judgment. The sentence is based on the man's character and how closely he followed the Torah. They beat them accordingly.

CHAPTER 29
Description of a class of angels

Rabbi Ishmael said: Metatron, the Angel, the Prince of the Presence, said to me: (1) Each one of the Angels has seventy names corresponding to the seventy languages (nations) of the world. And all of them are based upon the name of the Holy One, blessed be He. And every several name is written with a flaming pen of iron on the Fearful Crown (Kether Nora), which is on the head of the high and exalted King.

Metatron was said to have names based upon the names of God. Fearful Crown refers to the crown of a sitting king, thus God.

(2) And each one of them projects sparks and lightning. Each one of them is covered with horns of splendor all over. Lights shine from each of them, and each one is surrounded by tents of brilliance so that not even the Seraphim and the Chayoth who are greater than all the children of heaven are able to look at them.

CHAPTER 30
The 72 princes of Kingdoms and the Prince of the World are at the Great Sanhedrin.

Rabbi Ishmael said: Metatron, the Angel, the Prince of the Presence, said to me: (1) Whenever the Great Beth Din (House of the Sanhedrin) is seated in the Araboth (highest heaven) of Raqia (heaven) there no one speaks. No mouth opens for anyone in the world except those great princes who are called YHWH by the name of the Holy One, blessed be He. (2) How many are those Princes are there? Seventy-two princes of the kingdoms of the world besides the Prince of the World who pleads in favor of the world before the Holy One, blessed be He. Every day at the appointed hour the book with the records of all the deeds of the world is opened. For it is written (Dan. 7:10): " The judgment was set and the books were opened."

The highest classes of angels are marked with the Tetragrammaton. Each nation has its own angel appointed to guard and plea for its cause. What is odd about this is the equal and universal appeal to justice. There is no difference in how the court is conducted between Gentile or Jew. In this scenario, Metatron is the Prince of the world.

CHAPTER 31
The attributes of Justice, Mercy and Truth

Rabbi Ishmael said: Metatron, the Angel, the Prince of the Presence, said to me: (1) At the time when the Holy One, blessed be He, is sitting on the Throne of Judgment, Justice is standing on His right and Mercy on His left and Truth in front of His face, (2) then man (Some sources say "wicked man" but this is to be read as mankind) enters before Him for judgment, then , a staff comes out from the splendor of Mercy towards him and it stands in front of the man. Then man falls upon his face, and all the angels of destruction are fearful and they shake before him. For it is written (Is. 16:5): "And with mercy shall the throne be established, and he shall sit upon it in truth."

The fundamental balance of justice and mercy is only possible through truth, including the truth of what the real intent of the person being judged was. This is only possible with God. The angels of destruction are there to execute man but Mercy stops them and makes the angels fear. The wording of the verse makes this point unclear.

CHAPTER 32
The execution of judgment on the wicked. God's sword

Rabbi Ishmael said: Metatron, the Angel, the Prince of the Presence, said to me: (1) When the Holy One, blessed be He, opens the Book, half of it is fire and half of it is flames. Then the angels of destruction go out from Him continually to execute the judgment on the wicked by His sword, which is drawn from its sheath and it shines like magnificent lightning and pervades the world from one end to the other. For it is written (Is. 66:16): "For by fire will the Lord plead by His sword with all flesh." (2) And all those who come into the world fear and shake before Him, when they behold His sharpened sword like lightning from one end of the world to the other, and sparks and flashes of the size of the stars of Raqia (heaven) going out from it; according for it is written (Deut. 32: 41): If I whet the lightning of my sword."

CHAPTER 33
The angels of Mercy, of Peace, and of Destruction are by the Throne of Judgment.

Rabbi Ishmael said: Metatron, the Angel, the Prince of the Presence, said to me: (1) At the time that the Holy One, blessed be He, is sitting on the Throne of Judgment, then the angels of Mercy are standing on His right, the angels of Peace are standing on His left and the angels of Destruction are standing in front of Him. (2) And there is one scribe standing beneath Him, and another scribe standing above Him. (3) And the glorious Seraphim surround the Throne on all four of its sides with walls of lightning. And the Ophannim surround them with burning staves all around the Throne of Glory. And clouds of fire and clouds of flames surround them to the right and to the left. The Holy Chayoth carry the Throne of Glory from below. Each one uses only three fingers. The length of each fingers is 800,000 and 700 times one hundred, and 66,000 parasangs. (4) And underneath the feet of the Chayoth there are seven rivers of fire running and flowing. And the distance across of each river is 365 thousand parasangs and its depth is 248 thousand times ten-thousand parasangs. Its length cannot be known and is immeasurable. (5) And each river turns round in a bow in the four directions of Araboth (the highest heaven) of Raqia (heaven), and from there it falls down to Maon and is stopped, and from Maon (some sources have "Velum") to Zebul, from Zegul to Shechaqim, from Shechaqim to Raqia (heaven) to Shamayim and from Shamayim it fows on the heads of the wicked who are in Gehenna, for it is written (Jer. 23:19): "Behold a whirlwind of the Lord, even His fury, is gone, yes, a whirling tempest; it shall burst upon the head of the wicked."

Maon or Velum is the name of the first heaven. The river flows down from heaven and all of its levels, to Gehenna, which is the burning hell. Speculation on the meaning of the numbers contained in this chapter are random. In general, 3 is the number of spiritual completeness, and 8 is the number of judgment. The number of man and his shortcomings is 6. The number 7 represents spiritual perfection. 5 represents grace and spirit.

CHAPTER 34
The different concentric circles around the Chayoth consist of fire, water, hailstones.

Rabbi Ishmael said: Metatron; the Angel, the Prince of the Presence, said to me: (1) The hoofs of the Chayoth are surrounded by seven clouds of burning coals. The clouds of burning coals are surrounded on the outside by seven walls of flames. The seven walls of flames are surrounded on the outside by seven walls of hailstones (stones of El-gabish, Ezek.13: 11, 13, 28: 22). The hailstones are surrounded on the outside by boulders (stones) of hail. The boulders (stones) of hail are surrounded on the outside by stones of "the wings of the tempest." The stones of "the of the winged tempest" are surrounded by the outside by flames of fire. The chambers of the whirlwind are surrounded on the outside by the fire and water. (2) Around the fire and the water are those who sing the "Holy." Around about those who sing the "Holy" are those who sing the "Blessed." Around about those who sing the "Blessed" are the bright clouds. The bright clouds are surrounded on the outside by coals of burning juniper wood. There are thousands of camps of fire and ten thousand hosts of flames. And between every camp and every host there is a cloud, so that they may not be burned by the fire.

The stones of hail are made of the two opposite substances of fire and ice. This, like the reference to fire and water, represent a balance of forces which, if applied within the spiritual realm, brings blessings.

CHAPTER 35
The camps of angels in Araboth (the highest heaven) of Raqia (heaven). Angels performing the Kedushah (Sacred Salutation of Holy, Holy, Holy)

Rabbi Ishmael said: Metatron, the Angel, the Prince of the Presence, said to me: (1) 506 (Other sources have 496) thousand times ten-thousand camps has the Holy One, blessed be He, in the height of Araboth (the highest heaven) of Raqia (heaven). And each camp is composed of 496 thousand angels.

The Gematria for 506 is "kingdom" and for 496 it is "kingdoms."

 (2) And every single angel is as tall as the width of the great sea; and the appearance of their face is like the appearance of lightning. Their eyes are like lamps of fire, and their arms and their feet were the color of polished brass and when they spoke words their voice roared and sounded like the voice of a multitude of them. (3) They all stand before the Throne of Glory in four rows. And the princes of the army are standing at the beginning of each row. (4) Some of them sing the "Holy" and others sing the "Blessed." Some run as messengers while others stand in attendance. For it is written (Dan. 7: 10): "Thousands of thousands ministered unto Him, and ten thousand times ten thousand stood before Him. The judgment was set and the books were opened."

The singing or chanting of "Holy, Holy, Holy" is returned by the phrase, "Blessed be Thou and blessed is the name of the Lord for ever and ever."

(5) When the time nears and the hour comes to say the "Holy", first a whirlwind from before the Holy One, blessed be He, goes out and bursts on the camp of Shekina and there arises a great noise and confusion among them. For it is written (Jer. 30: 23): "Behold, the whirlwind of the Lord goes forth with fury, a continuing commotion." (6) At that moment thousands of thousands of them are changed into sparks, thousands of thousands of them ignite into burning staves, thousands of thousands flashes, thousands of thousands burst into flames, thousands of thousands change into males, thousands of thousands change into females, thousands of thousands burst into winds, thousands of thousands burst into burning fires, thousands of thousands burst into flames, thousands of thousands turn into sparks, thousands of thousands turn into chashmals of light; until they take upon themselves the yoke of the kingdom of heaven, the high and lifted up, of the Creator of them all with fear, dread, awe, and trembling, with commotion, anguish, terror and trepidation. Then they are changed again into their former shape to have the fear of their King before them always, as they have set their hearts on saying the Song continually, for it is written (Is. 6:3): "And one cried unto another and said Holy, Holy, Holy."

The phrase, "…thousands of thousands change into males, thousands of thousands change into females …" is suspect and may have been added later. The idea of taking onto oneself the yoke of heaven may refers to the fact that the angels are reciting the "Holy" and "Blessed" discourse, which means they understand and acknowledge the ways of heaven and the place and power of God. Judgment comes accordingly.

CHAPTER 36
The angels bathe in the river of fire before they recite the Song

Rabbi Ishmael said: Metatron, the Angel, the Prince of Presence, said to me: (1) At the time when the ministering angels desire to sing (the) Song, (then) Nehar di-Nur (the stream of fire) rises with many "thousand thousands and ten-thousand ten-thousands" (of angels) of power and strength of fire (the intensity of the radiant fire of the angels flows) and it runs and passes under the Throne of Glory, between the camps of the ministering angels and the troops of Araboth (highest heaven). (2) And all the ministering angels first go down into Nehar di-Nur (stream of fire), and they dip themselves in the fire and dip their tongue and their mouth seven times; (2Kings 5:14) and after that they go up and put on the garment of Machaqe Samal and cover themselves with cloaks of chashmal (the zenith of heaven) and stand in four rows over near the side of the Throne of Glory, in all the heavens.

No meaning for the term Machaqe Samal could be found.

CHAPTER 37
The four camps of Shekina and their surroundings

Rabbi Ishmael said: Metatron, the Angel, the Prince of the Presence, said to me: (1) In the seven Halls four chariots of Shekina are standing. Before each one stands the four camps of Shekina. Between (or behind) each camp a river of fire is continually flowing. (2) Between (or behind) each river there are bright clouds surrounding them, and between (or behind) each cloud there are pillars of brimstone erected. Between one pillar and another there stands flaming wheels, which surround them. And between one wheel and another there are flames of fire all around. Between the flames there are storehouses of lightning. Behind the storehouses of lightning there are the wings of the Wind of the Storm. Behind the wings of the Wind of the Storm are the chambers of the tempest. Behind the chambers of the tempest there are winds, voices, thunder, and sparks emitting from sparks and earthquakes within earthquakes.

The original intent of the verse may have been to draw a picture of the rivers running in concentric circles through the heavens and beside the river, in rows are clouds, lightning, and wind.

CHAPTER 38
The fear in heavens at the sound of the "Holy" is appeased by the Prince of the World

Rabbi Ishmael said: Metatron, the Angel, the Prince of the Presence, said to me: (1) At the time, when the ministering angels sing (the Thrice) Holy, then all the pillars of the heavens and their sockets shake, and the gates of the Halls of Araboth (the highest heaven) of Raqia (heaven) are shaken and the foundations of Shechaqim and the universe are moved, and the orders (secrets) of Maon and the chambers of Makon quiver, and all the orders of Raqia (heaven) and the constellations and the planets are distressed. The orbs of the sun and the moon rush away and run out of their pattens and run 12,000 parasangs and the wish to throw themselves down from heaven, (2) because of the roaring voice (sound) of their song, and the noise of their praise and the sparks and lightning that proceed from their faces. For it is written (Ps. 77: 18): "The voice of your thunder was in the heaven (the lightning illuminated the world, the earth trembled and shook)." (3) Until the Prince of the World calls them, saying; Be quiet in your place! Do not fear because of the ministering angels who sing the Song before the Holy One, blessed be He." As it is written (Job. 38: 7): "When the morning stars sang together and all the children of heaven shouted for joy."

As the appointed times approached to sing the Holy, Holy, Holy, all of heaven became anxious. Metatron quieted them and gave them focus.

CHAPTER 39
The explicit names fly from the Throne.

Rabbi Ishmael said: Metatron, the Angel, the Prince of the Presence, said to me: (1) When the ministering angels sing the "Holy" then all the explicit names that are engraved with a flaming iron pen on the Throne of Glory go flying off like eagles, each with sixteen wings. And they surround and hover around the Holy One, blessed be He, on all four sides of the place of His Shekina. (2) And the angels of the host, and the flaming Servants, the mighty Ophannim, the Cherubim of the Shekina, the Holy Chayoth, the Seraphim, the Er'ellim, the Taphsarim, the troops of burning fire, the armies of fire, the flaming hosts, and the holy princes, adorned with crowns, clothed in kingly majesty, wrapped in glory, tied with high honor, fall on their faces three times, saying: "Blessed be the name of His glorious kingdom for ever and ever."
Taphsarim are the troupes of flames. Er'el, more commonly referred to in the plural as "the Erelim", are a rank of angels in Jewish Kabbala (Cabbalah) and mythology. The name is seen to mean "the valiant/courageous." They are generally seen as the third highest rank

of divine beings/angels below God. The description in the verse seems to say that letters fly off of the Torah like eagles when it is burned.

CHAPTER 40
The ministering angels rewarded and punished.

Rabbi Ishmael said: Metatron, the Angel, the Prince of the Presence, said to me: (1) When the ministering angels say "Holy" before the Holy One, blessed be He, in the proper way, then the servants of His Throne, the attendants of His Glory, go out with much happiness from under the Throne of Glory. (2) And each one carries in their hands thousands and ten thousand times ten thousand crowns of stars, similar in appearance to the planet Venus, and put them on the ministering angels and the great prince who sing the "Holy." They place three crowns on each one of them: one crown because they say "Holy", and another crown, because they say "Holy, Holy", and a third crown because they say "Holy, Holy, Holy, is the Lord of Hosts." (3) But in the moment that they do not sing the "Holy" in the right order, a consuming fire flashes out from the little finger of the Holy One, blessed be He, and descends into the middle of their ranks, which is divided into 496 thousand parts corresponding to the four camps of the ministering angels, and the fire burns up in a single moment those who did not say the "Holy" correctly. For it is written (Ps. 92:3): "A fire goes before him and burns up his adversaries round about." (4) After that the Holy One, blessed be He, opens His mouth and speaks one word and creates other new ones like them to replace them. And each one stands before His Throne of Glory, signing the "Holy", as it written (Lam. 12:23): "They are new every morning; great is your faithfulness."

Here we see the full extent of the phrase, "taking on the yoke of heaven." One is rewarded for proper worship and ceremony or annihilated if God disapproves. The text indicates that all of the angels in the offending group are destroyed. Angels are created, nullifying the six days of the creation of everything.

CHAPTER 41
Letters engraved on the Throne of Glory created everything.

Rabbi Ishmael said: Metatron, the Angel, the Prince of the Presence, said to me: (1) Come and see the letters by which the heaven and earth were created. These are the letters by which were created the mountains and hills. These are the letters by which were created the seas and rivers, these are the letters by which were created the trees and herbs, these are the letters by which were created the planets and the constellations, these are the letters by which were created the globe of the earth and the orb of the moon and the orb of the sun, as well as Orion, the Pleiades and all the different luminaries of Raqia (heaven) were created. (2) These are the letters by which were created the Throne of Glory and the Wheels of the Merkaba (chariot) , the letters by which were created the necessities of the worlds, (3) the letters by which were created wisdom, understanding, knowledge, prudence, meekness and righteousness by which the entire world is sustained. (4) And I walked by his side and he took me by his hand and raised me up on his wings and showed me those letters, all of them, that are engraved with a flaming iron pen on the Throne of Glory. Sparks go out from them and cover all the chambers of Araboth (the highest heaven).

Jewish tradition has it that God and angels spoke Hebrew, and thus all things came into existence when God spoke them into existence in Hebrew. It is a very short leap of logic to assume the written word would have the same power and effect. This means within the various combinations of the 22 Hebrew letters all things were created and are sustained.

CHAPTER 42
Opposites kept in balance by several Divine Names

Rabbi Ishmael said: Metatron, the Angel, the Prince of the Presence, said to me: (1) Come and I will show you, where the waters are suspended in the highest place, where fire is burning in the midst of hail, where lightning flashes forth from out of the middle of snowy mountains, where thunder is roaring in the heights of the skies, where a flame is burning in the burning fire, and where voices make themselves heard within (in spite of) thunder and earthquake.

The balance indicated herein reminds one of a Zen koan – "See the sun in the midst of the rain. Scoop clear water from the heart of the fire." This chapter reveals a fundamental truth. All things are created in heaven by His word, sustained by His word, and reflected in the lower world where we live only after being created in heaven.

(2) Then I went to his side and he took me by his hand and lifted me up on his wings and showed me all those things. I saw the waters suspended on high in Araboth (the highest heaven) of Raqia (heaven) by the power of the name YAH EHYE ASHER EHYE (Jah, I am that I am), and their fruits (rain) was falling down from heaven and watering the face of the world, for it is written (Ps. 104:13): "(He waters the mountains from his chambers:) the earth is satisfied with the fruit of your work." (3) And I saw fire and snow and hail that were mingled together within each other and yet were undamaged. This was accomplished by the power of the name ESH OKELA (consuming fire). For it is written (Deut. 55: 24): "For the Lord, your God, is a consuming fire." (4) And I saw lightning flashing out of mountains of snow and yet the lightning was not extinguished, by the power of the name YA SUR OLAMIM (Jah, the everlasting rock). For it is written (Is. 26: 4): "For Jah, YHWH is the everlasting rock." (5) And I saw thunder and heard voices that were roaring within flames of fire and they were not silenced. This is accomplished by the power of the name EL-SHADDAI RABBA (the Great God Almighty) for it is written (Gen. 17:1): "I am God Almighty." (6) And I saw a flame glowing in the middle of burning fire, and yet it was not devoured. This was done by the power of the name YAD AL KES YAH (the hand upon the Throne of the Lord.) For it is written (Ex. 17: 16): " And he said: for the hand is upon the Throne of the Lord." (7) And I looked and saw rivers of fire within of rivers of water and they were not extinguished. All of this was done by the power of the name OSE SHAIOM (Maker of Peace) for it is written (Job 25: 2): "He makes peace in high places." For he makes peace between fire and water, and between hail and fire, and between the wind and cloud, and between earthquakes and sparks.

CHAPTER 43
The abode of the unborn spirits and of the spirits of the righteous dead

Rabbi Ishmael said: Metatron said to me: (1) Come and I will show you where the spirits of the righteous are that have been created and those that have returned, and the spirits of the righteous that have not yet been created (born). (2) And he lifted me up to his side, took me by his hand and sat me near the Throne of Glory by the place of the Shekina; and he revealed the Throne of glory to me, and he showed me the spirits that have been created and had returned as well as those who were flying above the Thorne of Glory in front of the Holy One, blessed be He. (3) After that I went to interpret the following verse of Scripture and I found what is written (Isa. 57: 16: "for the spirit clothed itself before me .") It refers to the spirits that have been created in the chamber of creation of the righteous and that have returned before the Holy One, blessed be He; (and the (His) words.) "The souls I have made" refers to the spirits of the righteous that have not yet been created in the chamber (GUPH).

Within the entire book of 3 Enoch, this chapter could be the most important to all "Children of the book," Jews, Christians, and Moslems. The story of creation has God creating everything in six days. Everything must also include all of the souls that are ever to be born. These souls are housed in a chamber near the throne of God, called the Guph (Guf). This chapter tells us the souls of the righteous are housed. The righteous souls are housed in the Guph, waiting to be clothed in flesh for their incarnation. But if the righteous souls are here, where are the unrighteous souls kept? If there were another place where the unrighteous souls are kept the distinction would indicate predestination. If the character of the soul is already determined and they are stored accordingly then how is the determination made? Are we created as righteous and unrighteous beings? Does God simply look ahead and see us as we are to be?
As the next two chapters unfold, we see hints that the Guph may not be the place where all of the souls are housed but possibly it is where the souls of the righteous are conducted to be clothed in flesh and dispatched to earth through birth. The wicked soul finds his home in Sheol. If this were true it would still indicate predestination or foreknowledge are at work.
Mystical writings, such as the Zohar, describe God as a burning flame from where sparks fly outward. These sparks are the souls of the Jewish people. When these sparks return to the primal flame, time will come to an end. Another tradition states that when the Guph is emptied time will end.
Souls leaving the Guph are born and return to God after death.

CHAPTER 44
Metatron shows Rabbi Ishmael the abode of the wicked and the intermediate in Sheol.

Rabbi Ishmael said: Metatron, the Angel, the Prince of the Presence, said to me: (1) Come and I will show you the spirits of the wicked and the spirits of those in between (intermediate) where they are standing, and the spirits of those in between (intermediate), where they go down, and the spirits of the wicked, where they go down.

Now we know there are three classes of souls: the righteous, the intermediate – those in between, and the unrighteous. The obvious questions are, where were the souls of the "intermediates" kept and from where were they dispatched? Are these the souls of the "lukewarm?"

(2) And he said to me: The spirits of the wicked go down to Sheol by the hands of two angels of destruction: ZAAPHIEL and SIMKIEL. (3) SIMKIEL is assigned to rule over the intermediate to support them and purify them because of the great mercy

of the Prince of the Place (The Divine Majesty). ZAAPHIEL is assigned to rule over the spirits of the wicked in order to cast them down from the presence of the Holy One, blessed be He, and from the magnificence of the Shekina, and he casts them into Sheol, to punish them in the fire of Gehenna with rods of burning coal. (4) And I went by his side, and he took me by his hand and pointed them all out to me. (5) And I saw the faces of children of men and the way they looked. Their bodies were like eagles. And not only that but the color of the complexion of the intermediate was like pale grey because of their deeds. They were stained until they become cleansed from their iniquity in the fire.

It is interesting to note this indirect reference to Purgatory in a Jewish book written between the second and fifth centuries A.D.

(6) And the color of the wicked was like the bottom of a pot (burned black) because of the wickedness of their deeds. (7) And I saw the spirits of the Patriarchs Abraham, Isaac, and Jacob and the rest of the righteous, whom they have brought up out of their graves and who have ascended to Heaven. And they were praying before the Holy One, blessed be He, saying in their prayer: "Lord of the Universe! How long will you sit upon your Throne like a mourner in the days of his mourning with your right hand behind you and not deliver your children and reveal your Kingdom in the world? And how long will you have no pity upon your children who are made slaves among the nations of the world? Your right hand is behind you. Why do you not stretch out the heavens and the earth and the heavens of the highest heavens? When will you have compassion?"

The right hand is the symbol of power and authority. To have the right hand behind your back means you are not using the power or authority available to you.

(8) Then the Holy One, blessed be He, answered every one of them, saying: "Since these wicked commit sins on and on, and transgress with sins again and again against Me, how could I deliver my great Right Hand when it would mean their downfall would be caused by their own hands.

The reason God does not bring judgment upon the world is because many Jews were among the unrepentant sinners. He wishes to await their return to him before judging them. This is the ultimate mercy.

(9) In that moment Metatron called me and spoke to me: "My servant! Take the books, and read their evil deeds!" Then I took the books and read their deeds and there were 36 transgressions to be found written down regarding each wicked one and besides that they have transgressed all the letters in Torah, for it is written (Dan. 55: 11): "Yea, all Israel have transgressed your Law." It is not written, "for they have transgressed from Aleph to Taw (A to Z) 36 (40) statutes have they transgressed for each letter?

Some sources have "40 statues." The number "40" is the number of severe trials and testing. The implication of the verse is that the souls have broken 40 major laws and many minor ones.

(10) Then Abraham, Isaac and Jacob wept. Then the Holy One, blessed be He said to them: "Abraham, my beloved, Isaac, my Elect one, Jacob, my firstborn, how can I deliver them from among the nations of the world at this time?" And immediately MIKAEL (Michael), the Prince of Israel, cried and wept with a loud voice and said (Ps. 10:1): "Why stand you afar off, O Lord?"

CHAPTER 45
Past and future events recorded on the Curtain of the Throne.

Rabbi Ishmael said: Metatron said to me: (1) Come, and I will show you the Curtain of The Divine Majesty which is spread before the Holy One, blessed be He. On it are written all the generations of the world and all their deeds (actions/doings), both what they have done and what they will do until the end of all generations. (2) And I came, and he showed it to me pointing it out with his fingers like a father who teaches his children the letters of Torah. And I saw each generation and within the generations I saw the rulers, the leaders, the shepherds, the oppressors (despots), the keepers, the punisher, the counselors, the teachers, the supporters, the bosses, the presidents of academies, the magistrates, the princes, the advisors, the noblemen, and the warriors, the elders, and the guides of each generation.

In the ancient world, these represent all major groups that have influence over the lives of people.

(3) And I saw Adam, his generation, their deeds (actions/doings) and their thoughts, Noah and his generation, their deeds and their thoughts, and the generation of the flood, their deeds and their thoughts, Shem and his generation, their deeds and their thoughts, Nimrod and the generation of the confusion of tongues, and his generation, their deeds and their thoughts, Abraham and his generation, their deeds and their thoughts, Isaac and his generation, their deeds and their thoughts,

Ishmael and his generation, their deeds and their thoughts, Jacob and his generation, their deeds and their thoughts, Joseph and his generation , their deeds and their thoughts, the tribes and their generation, their deeds and their thoughts, Amram and his generation, their deeds and their thoughts , Moses and his generation, their deeds and their thoughts, (4) Aaron and Mirjam their accomplishments and actions, the princes and the elders, their works and deeds, Joshua and his generation, their works and deeds, the judges and their generation, their works and deeds, Eli and his generation, their works and deeds, Phinehas, their works and deeds, Elkanah and his generation, their accomplishments and actions, Samuel and his generation, their works and deeds, the kings of Judah with their generations, their works and their doing, the kings of Israel and their generation, their accomplishments and actions, the princes of Israel, their accomplishments and actions; the princes of the nations of the world, their accomplishments and actions, the heads of the councils of Israel, their accomplishments and actions; the heads of the councils in the nations of the world, their generations, their accomplishments and actions; the rulers of Israel and their generation, their accomplishments and actions; the noblemen of Israel and their generation, their works and their deeds; the noblemen of the nations of the world and their generations, their accomplishments and actions; the men of reputation in Israel, their generation, their accomplishments and actions; the judges of Israel, their generation, their accomplishments and actions; the judges of the nations of the world and their generation, their accomplishments and actions; the teachers of children in Israel, their generations, their accomplishments and actions: the teachers of children in the nations of the world, their generation, their accomplishments and actions; the interpreters) of Israel, their generation, their accomplishments and actions; the interpreters of the nations of the world, their generation, their accomplishments and actions; (5) and all the fights and wars that the nations of the world worked against the people of Israel in the time of their kingdom. And I saw Messiah, the son of Joseph, and his generation and their accomplishments and actions that they will do against the nations of the world. And I saw Messiah, the son of David, and his generation, and all the fights and wars, and their accomplishments and actions that they will do with Israel both for good and evil. And I saw all the fights and wars that Gog and Magog will fight with Israel in the days of Messiah, and all that the Holy One, blessed be He, will do with them in the time to come.

This is the first mention of two Messiahs. However, the dual functions of the Messiah can be seen as the impetus to this idea. The Messiah is seen as a peacemaker and teacher, who brings mercy. The Messiah is also seen as a warrior, destroyer, and bringer of justice. One comes in peace and the other is determined to do war to avenge God and Israel. It appears the Messiah, son of David, is truculent compared to the son of Joseph, who will be killed for his attempt to make peace. Christians believe the same Messiah will perform both functions because he came as peacemaker and teacher but will return from heaven as the warrior of God. The text here indicates there will be two separate Messiahs.

(6) And all the rest of all the leaders of the generations and all the works of the generations both in Israel and in the nations of the world, both what is done and what will be done hereafter to all generations until the end of time all were written on the Curtain of The Divine Majesty. And I saw all these things with my eyes; and after I had seen it, I opened my mouth in praise of The Divine Majesty saying, (Eccl. 8:4, 5): "For the King's word has power and who may say unto Him, What do you do? Whoever keeps the commandments shall know no evil thing." And I said: (Ps. 104: 24) "O Lord how manifold (multi-colored/multifaceted) are your works!"

Rabbi Ishmael was shown all of the deeds and works of mankind for all generations. This implies predestination or foreknowledge. The reader must decide for himself or herself.

CHAPTER 46
The place of the stars shown to Rabbi Ishmael

Rabbi Ishmael said: Metatron said to me: (1) Come and I will show you the distance between the stars that are standing in the Raqia (heaven), for they stand there night after night in fear of the Almighty and The Divine Majesty. I will show you where they go and where they stand. (2) I walked by his side, and he took me by his hand and pointed out all of them to me with his finger. And they were standing on sparks of flames around the Merkaba (chariot) of the Almighty, The Divine Majesty. What did Metatron do? At that moment he clapped his hands and chased them off from their place. Then they flew off on flaming wings, rose and fled from the four sides of the Throne of Merkaba (chariot), and as they flew he told me the names of ever-single one. As it is written, (Ps. 137:4) "He tells the number of the stars; he gives them all their names", teaching, that the Holy One, blessed be He, has given a name to each one of them. (3) And by the authority of RAHATIEL they enter in a numbered order to Raqia (heaven) ha-shamayim (the second of the seven heavens) to serve the world. And they go out in numbered order to praise the Holy One, blessed be He, with songs and hymns, for it is written (Ps. 19: 1): "The heavens declare the glory of God." (4) But in the age to come the Holy One, blessed be He, will create them anew. For it is written (Lam. 52: 23): "They are new every morning." And they open their mouth and sing a song. Which is the song that they sing? (Ps. 8:3): "When I consider your heavens."

Rahatiel is the angelic ruler of the stars and constellations. The Ophannim is the class of angels that move the celestial sphere. Stars were considered by many cultures to be spiritual entities, or angels. This was a Babylonian concept that was absorbed. It is in this light that the stars would sing. They leave the second heaven and proceed through the heavens to the seventh heaven where they end their journey at the throne.

CHAPTER 47
Metatron shows Rabbi Ishmael the spirits of punished angels.

Rabbi Ishmael said: Metatron said to me: (1) Come and I will show you the souls of the angels and the spirits of the servants that served, whose bodies have been burned up in the fire of The Divine Majesty of the Almighty, that projects from his little finger. And they have been made into burning and glowing coals in the midst of the river of fire (Nehar di-Nur). But their spirits and their souls are standing behind the Shekina. (2) Whenever the angel servants sing a song at a wrong time or they sing what was not appointed to be sung they are burned and consumed by the fire of their Creator and by a flame from their Maker from the rooms of the whirlwind. The fire blows on them and drives them into the river of fire (Nehar di-Nur). There they become mountains of burning coal. But their spirit and their soul return to their Creator, and all are standing behind their Master. (3) And I went by his side and he took me by his hand, and he showed me all the souls of the angels and the spirits of the attending servants who were standing behind the Shekina and were standing on the wings of a whirlwind with walls of fire all around them. (4) At that moment Metatron opened the gates of the walls within which they were standing behind the Shekina for me to see. And I raised my eyes and I saw them. I saw what of every one of the angels looked like and I saw their wings were like birds made out of flames. And it looked as if they were fashioned from burning fire. In that moment I opened my mouth in praise of The Divine Majesty and said (Ps. 92: 5): "How great are your works, O Lord."

The river of fire or Nehar di-Nur is presented here as a place of resurrection of the angels since their bodies were burnt but the spirit continues and ends up again with God. However, this idea is contradicted in most Jewish mystic writings. It is possible the text here is somehow corrupted or missunderstood.

CHAPTER 48 - A
Rabbi Ishmael sees the Right Hand of the Most High

Rabbi Ishmael said: Metatron said to me: (1) come, and I will show you the Right Hand of The Divine Majesty, which He keeps behind Him because of the destruction of the Holy Temple; from which all kinds of splendor and light shine forth and by which the 955 heavens were created; and whom not even the Seraphim and the Ophannim are permitted to experience until the day that salvation shall arrive.

God became inactive because of the destruction of the temple between March and September of 70 A.D. and onward. Why God would choose the sacking of his temple to mark his quiescence might be understood by looking at the reason given for the destruction. If the Jewish people believed themselves to be the only chosen people of God then God must be their protector. To have a heathen army come in and defeat them so soundly, looting and destroying the temple of the God that was supposed to protect them brought into question their position in the divine scheme. Since the fault could not be with God, it must have been with his people. The Jewish nation must have failed God by falling away from Him or sinning badly enough to cause God to turn them over to their enemy. Since this would be a great and grievous sin, God has chosen not to become active, since that would mean having to judge His apostate people. He awaits his people to return to Him in a righteous state.

(2) and I went by his side and he took me by his hand and showed me the Right Hand of The Divine Majesty, with all types of praises, joyous singing. No mouth can articulate its worth, and no eye can look at it because of its greatness, and dignity and its majesty, and splendid beauty. (3) Not only that, but all the souls of the righteous who are counted worthy to see the joy of Jerusalem are standing by it, praising and praying before it three times every day, saying (Is. 51: 9): "Awake, awake, put on strength, O arm of the Lord" according for it is written (Is. 63: 12): "He caused his glorious arm to go at the right hand of Moses." (4) In that moment the Right Hand of The Divine Majesty was weeping. And there flew out from its five fingers, five rivers of tears and fell they flowed down into the great sea and it shook the entire world. For it is written (Is. 24: 19,20): "The earth is utterly broken, the earth is totally dissolved, the earth is moved greatly, the earth shall stagger like a drunken man and shall be moved back and froth like a hut, five times corresponding to the fingers of His Great Right Hand. " (5) But when the Holy One, blessed be He, saw that there is not a righteous man in that generation, and no pious man on the entire earth, and no men doing justice, and that there is no one like Moses, and no intercessor like Samuel who could pray before The Divine Majesty for the salvation and deliverance of His Kingdom, His great Right Hand was revealed in the entire world that that He put it out from Himself again to work great salvation by it for Israel, (6) then the Holy One, blessed be He, will remember His own justice, favor, mercy and grace, and He will deliver His great Arm by himself, and His righteousness will

support Him. For it is written (Is. 59: 16): "And he saw, that there was no man" that is like Moses who prayed countless times for Israel in the desert and averted the Divine decrees from them – "and he wondered why there was no intercessor" – like Samuel who entreated the Holy One, blessed be He, and called unto Him and He answered him and fulfilled his desire, even if it did not fit into the Divine plan. For it is written (I Sam. 12: 17): "Is it not wheat-harvest today? I will call unto the Lord." (7) And not only that, but He joined fellowship with Moses in every place, for it is written (Ps. 99: 6): "Moses and Aaron among His priest." And again it is written, (Jer. 15: 1) "Though Moses and Samuel stood before Me" (Is. 63: 5): "Mine own arm brought salvation unto Me." (8) The Holy One, blessed be He said at that time, "How long do I have to wait for the children of men to obtain salvation according to their righteousness for My power and authority? For My own sake and for the sake of My worthiness and righteousness will I deliver My power and authority and by it I will redeem my children from among the nations of the world. For it is written (Is. 48: 11): "For My own sake will I do it. For how should My name be profaned."

At this point, God has waited as long as he wished for Israel to come back to Him in righteousness by their own power. He has decided to take them back from the heathen nations.

(9) In that moment the Holy One, blessed be He, will reveal His Great Power and Authority (Arm) and show it to the nations of the world. Its length is the length of the entire world and its width is the width of the world. And its splendor looks like the splendor of the sunshine in its power in the summer solstice. (10) Then Israel will be saved from among the nations of the world. And Messiah will appear unto them and He will bring them up to Jerusalem with great joy. And not only that but they will eat and drink for they will glorify the Kingdom of Messiah, of the house of David, in the four corners of the world.

This is the time, not for the Messiah of the house of Joseph, but for the Messiah of the house of David. This is the time of war and leadership of the nation in a physical sense.

And the nations of the world will not prevail against them, for it is written (Is. 52: 10): "The Lord has made bare His holy arm in the eyes of all the nations; and all the ends of the earth shall see the salvation of our God." And again (Deut. 32: 12): "The Lord alone did lead him, and there was no strange god with him." (Zech. 14: 9): "And the Lord shall be king over all the earth."

"Heaven" is the number 955 using Gematria. The meaning seems to be that of all heavens and all worlds.

CHAPTER 48 - B
The Divine Names that go forth from the Throne of Glory and pass through the heavens and back again to the Throne.

Many of the names are not decipherable. Attempting to place the letters into any kind of Latinized form or alphabet made the meanings even more obscure. For this reason, the names that could be interpreted with any certainty were listed. Those that yielded only meaningless letters were marked with only a dash.

These are the seventy-two names written on the heart of the Holy One, Blessed be He: Righteousness, - , Righteous (one) -, Lord of Host, God Almighty, God, YHWH - - - Living (one) - Riding upon the Araboth (highest heaven), - Life Giver - King of Kings, Holy One - - Holy, Holy, Holy, - - - Blessed be the Name of His glorious kingdom for ever and ever, - - Complete, King of the Universe, - - The beginning of Wisdom for the children of men, - -. Blessed be He who gives strength to the weary and increases strength to them that have no might, (Is. 40:29) that go forth adorned with many flaming crowns with many flames, with innumerable crowns of chashmal (celestial substance), with many, many crowns of lightning from before the Throne of Glory. And with them there are hundreds of hundreds of powerful angels who escort them like a king with trembling and dread, with amazement and shivering, with honor and majesty and fear, terror, greatness and dignity, and with glory and power, with wisdom and knowledge and with a pillar of fire and flame and lightning – and their light is as lightning flashes of light – and with the likeness of the chashmal (the substance of heaven). (2) And they give glory to them and they answer and cry before them, " Holy, Holy, Holy." And they lead them in a single line through every heaven as powerful and honorable princes. And when they bring them all back to the place of the Throne of Glory, then all the Chayoth by the Merkaba (chariot) open their mouth in praise of His glorious name, saying: "Blessed be the name of His glorious kingdom for ever and ever."

CHAPTER 48 - C
An Enoch-Metatron piece.

(1)"I seized him, and I took him and I appointed him" — that is Enoch, the son of Jared, whose name is Metatron (2) and I took him from among the children of men (5) and made him a Throne over near and beside My Throne. What is the size of that Throne? Seventy-thousand parasangs all of fire. (9) I committed to him 70 angels symbolizing the nations of the world and I gave into his authority all the household above and below. (7) And I imparted to him Wisdom and Intelligence more than all the angels. And I called his name "the LESSER YAH", whose name is by Gematria 71.

To refresh memory, Gematria was the ancient art of numerology. Each letter is given a number, usually determined by where it occurs in the alphabet. Numbers go from one to nine, then from ten to ninety, and, if there were enough letters, from one hundred to nine hundred. However, there are only 22 letters. Numbers are then summed. When the numbers are added they total seventy-one.

And I arranged all the works of creation for him. And I made him more powerful than all the ministering angels. (3) He gave Metatron — that is Enoch, the son of Jared — the authority over all the storehouses and treasuries, and appointed him over all the stores (reserves) in every heaven. And I assigned the keys of each store into him. (4) I made him the prince over all the princes and a minister of the Throne of Glory and the Halls of Araboth (the highest heaven). I appointed him over the Holy Chayoth for him to open their doors of the Throne of Glory to me, to exalt and arrange it, and I gave to him wreathe crowns to place upon their heads. I sent him to the majestic Ophannim, to crown them with strength and glory. I sent him to the honored Cherubim, to clothe them in majesty covered with radiant sparks, to make them to shine with splendor and bright light over the flaming Seraphim, to cover them with highness. I sent him to the Chashmallim of light, to make them radiant with light and to prepare the seat for me every morning as I sit upon the Throne of Glory. I have given him the secrets above and below, which are the heavenly secrets and earthly secrets so that he can praise and magnify my glory in the height of my power). (5) I made him higher than all. The height of his stature stood out in the midst of all who are of high of stature. I made seventy thousand parasangs. I made his Throne great by the majesty of my Throne. And I increased its glory by the honor of My glory. (6) I transformed his flesh into torches of fire, and all the bones of his body into burning coals; and I made his eyes look like lightning, and the light of his eyebrows as a light that will never be quenched. I made his face as bright as the splendor of the sun, and his eyes like the splendor of the Throne of Glory.

The description of Metatron is that of an angel and specifically a Seraphim, who is a fiery creature. A wreathe means victory.

(7) I made his clothing honor and majesty, beauty and highness. I covered him with a cloak and a crown of a size of 500 by 500 parasangs and this was his diadem. And I put My honor, My majesty and the splendor of My glory that is on My Throne of Glory upon him. I called him the "LESSER YHWH," the Prince of the Presence, the Knower of Secrets:. I revealed every secret to him as a father and as a friend, and all mysteries I spoke to him in truth. (8) I set up his throne at the door of My Hall that he may sit and judge the heavenly household on high. And I made every prince subject to him, so that they will receive his authority and perform his will. (9) I took Seventy names from my names and called him by them to enhance his glory. I placed Seventy princes into his hand so that he can command them to do my laws and obey my words in every language. And the proud will be brought to the ground by his word, and by the speech of his mouth he will exalt the humble to high places. He is to strike kings by his speech, to turn kings away from their own plans, and he is to set up the rulers over their dominion for it is written (Dan. 51: 21): "and he changes the times and the seasons, "and to give wisdom unto all the wise of the world and understanding and knowledge to all who understand (Dan. 51: 21): "and knowledge to them that know understanding." He is to reveal to them the secrets of my words and to teach them the command of my judgment in righteousness.

God is the God of the universe. He is the God of all. His names are infinite. Names reveal power, authority, personality traits, and character. Metatron is given authority over the nations. There are 70 nations and Metatron has 70 names.

(10) It is written (Is. 55: 11): "so shall My word be that goes forth out of my mouth; it shall not return unto me void but shall accomplish that which I please." I shall accomplish that which is not written here, but " he shall accomplish. Every word and every speech that goes out from the Holy One, blessed be He, Metatron stands and carries out. And he establishes the orders of the Holy One, blessed be He. (11) "And he shall make to prosper that which I sent." I will make to prosper what is not written here but he shall make to prosper teaching, that whatever decree proceeds from the Holy One, blessed be He, concerning a man, as soon as he makes repentance, they do not execute it upon him but they execute it upon another wicked man, for it is written (Prov. 9:8): "The righteous is delivered out of trouble, and the wicked comes in his place."

If a man repents and is no longer wicked, the angels inflicts his punishment on a person who is still wicked and has not repented

(12) And not only that but Metatron sits three hours every day in the high heavens, and he gathers all the souls of those dead who died in their mothers womb, and the nursing baby who died on their mother's breast, and of the scholars who died over the five books of the Law. And he brings them under the Throne of Glory and places them in companies, divisions and classes round the Presence, and there he teaches them the Law, and the books of Wisdom, and Haggada and Tradition and completes their education for them. It is written (Is. 28: 9) "Whom will he teach knowledge? And whom will he make to understand tradition? Them that are weaned from the milk and draw from the breast."

Ancient Jews viewed learning as one way to approach God. To study the Torah is almost as good as worship and prayer. Unborn, sucklings, those who die while studying the Torah are guiltless.

CHAPTER 48 - D

The names of Metatron.

The names fall into three major categories, those which are built upon the name "El," those that are based on the name "Metatron," and those based on the name "Yah." The reader will notice the letters EL, ON, and YAH or YA in the names. Although the text states there are 70 names, there are in fact 105 names listed. The Latinized version of the 1928 work is referenced in this list however the parsing and pronunciations are unique to this work in order to accent the holy names found within most of the 105 names..

(1)Seventy names has Metatron which the Holy One, blessed be He, took from His own name and put upon him. And these they are: 1 Yeho-EL Yah, 2 Yeho-EL, 3 Yofi-EL and 4 Yophphi-EL, and 5 Hafifi-EL and 6 Margezi-EL, 7 Gippyu-EL, 8 Pahazi-EL, 9 Hahah, 10 Pepri-EL, 11 Tatri-EL, 12 Tabki-EL, 13 Haw, 14 YHWH, 15 Dah 16, WHYH, 17 Hebed, 18 DiburiEL, 19 Hafhapi-EL, 20 Spi-EL, 21 Paspasi-EL, 22 Senetron, 23 Metatron, 24 Sogdin, 25 HadriGon, 26 Asum, 27 Sakhpam, 28 Sakhtam, 29 Mig-on, 30 Mitt-on, 31 Mot-tron, 32 Rosfim, 33 Khinoth, 34 KhataTiah, 35 Degaz-Yah, 36 Pisf-YaH, 37 Habiskin-Yah, 38 Mixar, 39 Barad, 40 Mikirk, 41 Mispird, 42 Khishig, 43 Khishib, 44 Minret, 45 Bisyrym, 46 Mitmon, 47 Titmon 48 Piskhon, 49 SafsafYah, 50 Zirkhi, 51 ZirkhYah 52 'B', 53 Be-Yah, 54 HiBhbe-Yah, 55 Pelet, 56 Pit-Yah, 57 Rabrab-YaH, 58 Khas, 59 Khas-Yah, 60 Tafaf-Yah, 61 Tamtam-Yah, 62 Sehas-Yah, 63 Hirhur-Yah, 64 Halhal-Yah, 65 BazrId-Yah, 66 Satsatk-Yah, 67 Sasd-Yah, 68 Razraz-Yah, 69 BaZzraz-Yah, 70 Harim-Yah, 71 Sibh-Yah, 72 Sibibkh-Yah, 73 Simkam, 74 Yah-Se-Yah, 75 Sibib-Yah, 76 Sabkasbe-Yah, 77 khelil-khil-Yah, 78 Kih, 79 HHYH, 80 WH, 81 WHYH, (letters in the holy YHWH) 82 Zakik-Yah, 83 Turtis-Yah, 84 Sur-Yah, 85 Zeh, 86 Penir-Yah, 87 ZihZih, 88 Galraza-Yah, 89 Mamlik-Yah, 90 Hitt-Yah, 91 Hemekh, 92 Kham-Yah, 93 Mekaper-Yah, 94 Perish-Yah, 95 Sefam, 96 Gibir, 97 Gibor-Yah, 98 Gor, 99 Gor-Yah, 100 Ziw, 101 Hokbar, the 102 LESSER YHWH, after the name of his Master, (Ex. 23: 21) "for My name is in him",103 Rabibi-EL, 104 TUMIEL, 105 Segansakkiel, the Prince of Wisdom.

(2) And why is he called by the name Sagnesakiel? Because all the storehouses of wisdom are committed in to his hand. (3) And all of them were opened to Moses on Sinai, so that he learned them during the forty days, while he remained. He learned the Torah in the seventy ways it applies to the seventy nations, and the Prophets and the seventy application of the seventy tongues, the writings in the seventy variations of the seventy tongues, the Halakas (Jewish law and ritual) in the seventy applications of the seventy nations, the Traditions in the seventy aspects of the seventy nations, the Haggadas (Passover Seder) in the seventy aspects of the seventy tongues and the Toseftas (Secondary compilation of Jewish oral laws) in the seventy aspects of the seventy tongues. (4) But as soon as the forty days were completed, he forgot all of them in one moment. Then the Holy One, blessed be He, called Yephiphyah, the Prince of the Law, and (through him) they were given to Moses as a gift, for it is written (Deut. 10:4): "and the Lord gave them to me." And after that it remained with him. And how do we know that it remained in his memory? Because it is written (Mal. 55: 4): "Remember the Law of Moses my servant which I commanded unto him in Horeb for all Israel, even my statues and judgments." 'The Law of Moses': that is the Torah, the Prophets and the Writings, 'statues': that is the Halakas and Traditions, 'judgments'; that is the Haggadas and the Toseftas. And all of them were given to Moses on high on Sinai. (5) These seventy names are a reflection of the Explicit names and given to the name of Metatron: seventy Names of His by which the ministering angels call the King of the kings of kings, blessed be He, in the high heavens, and twenty-two letters (of the Hebrew alphabet) that are on the ring placed on his finger with which are sealed the destinies of the high, powerful and great princes of kingdoms and with which are sealed along with the future of the Angel of Death, and the destinies of every nation and tongue. (6) Metatron, the Angel, the Prince of the Presence said; the Angel who is the Prince of the Wisdom and the Angel who the Prince of the Understanding, and the Angel who the Prince of the Kings, and the Angel who the Prince of the Rulers, and the angel who is the Prince of the Glory, and the angel who is the Prince of the high ones and of the princes, all of which are the exalted, greatly honored ones in heaven and on earth: (7) "YHWH, the God of Israel, is my witness that I revealed this secret to Moses and when I did all the host all the high heavens were enraged against me. (8) They asked me, saying, "Why do you reveal this secret to a son of man, born of woman, who is tainted and unclean, a man of the putrefying drop? You gave him the secret by which heaven and earth, sea and land, mountains and hills, rivers and springs, Gehenna of fire and hail, the Garden of Eden and the Tree of Life were all created and by which Adam and Eve, and the cattle, and the wild beasts, the birds of the air, and the fish of the sea, and

Behemoth and Leviathan, and the crawling things, the snakes, the dragons of the sea, and the creeping things of the deserts; and Torah and Wisdom and Knowledge and Thought and the imparted knowledge and the Gnosis of things above and of heaven and the fear of heaven were all created. Why did you reveal this to flesh and blood? I answered them: Because the Holy One, blessed be He, has given me authority. And furthermore, I have obtained permission from the high and exalted throne, from which all the Explicit names go forth with lightning and fire and flaming chashmallim.

Verse 7 makes a statement that when the complete gnosis or revealed knowledge was given to Moses (through Metatron) all the heavenly host was enraged at the act. This Knowledge was not even available to all the host of heaven but was given to a human. Verse 8 asks the question in a direct and insulting way. To slightly paraphrase, it asked, "Why did You give the secrets of creation to this human who was conceived by a woman, through the transfer of semen, which spoils and putrefies and then gives birth, when blood from birth and menses is considered unclean, as is the woman herself for a time after a ritual cleansing. In light of this, all the heavenly hosts consider humans to be inferior, unclean, animals. Still, God chose to transmit to Moses the secret gnosis of creation.
Behemoth is the primal unconquerable monster of the land. Leviathan is the primal monster of the waters of the sea. Ziz is their counterpart in the sky. There is a legend that the Leviathan and the Behemoth shall hold a battle at the end of the world. The two will finally kill each other, and the surviving men will feast on their meat. Behemoth also appears in the 1 Enoch, giving a description of this monster's origins there mentioned as being male, as opposed to the female Leviathan. See Job, chapter 40 for further information.

(9) But they (the hosts) were not appeased or satisfied, until the Holy One, blessed be He, scorned them and drove them away from Him with contempt and said to them: "I delight in him, and have set my love on him, and have entrusted to him and given unto Metatron, my Servant, and I have given to him alone, for he is Unique among all the children of heaven. (10) And Metatron brought them out from his house and storehouses and gave these secrets to Moses, and Moses gave them to Joshua, and Joshua gave them to the elders, and the elders to gave them the prophets and the men of the Great Synagogue, and the men of the Great Synagogue gave them to Ezra and Ezra the Scribe gave them to Hillel the elder, and Hillel the elder gave them to Rabbi Abbahu and Rabbi Abbahu to Rabbi Zera, and Rabbi Zera to the men of faith, and the men of faith gave them to give warning and to heal by them all disease that ravaged the world, for it is written (Ex. 15: 26): "If you will diligently hearken to the voice of the Lord, your God, and will do that which is right in His eyes, and will give ear to His commandments, and keep all his statues, I will put none of the disease upon you, which I have put on the Egyptians: for I am the Lord, that heals you."

(Ended and finished. Praise be unto the Creator of the World.)

Hillel was said to be one of the greatest and wisest Rabbis.

The Book of Jubilees
The Little Genesis, The Apocalypse of Moses

INTRODUCTION

The Book of Jubilees, also known as The Little Genesis and The Apocalypse of Moses, opens with an extraordinary claim of authorship. It is attributed to the very hand of Moses; penned while he was on Mount Sinai, as an angel of God dictated to him regarding those events that transpired from the beginning of the world. The story is written from the viewpoint of the angel. The angelic monolog takes place after the exodus of the children of Israel out of Egypt. The setting is atop Mount Sinai, where Moses was summoned by God. The text then unfolds as the angel reveals heaven's viewpoint of history. We are led through the creation of man, Adam's fall from grace, the union of fallen angels and earthly women, the birth of demonic offspring, the cleansing of the earth by flood, and the astonishing claim that man's very nature was somehow changed, bringing about a man with less sinful qualities than his antediluvian counterpart. The story goes on to fill in many details in Israel's history, ending at the point in time when the narrative itself takes place, after the exodus.

Scholars believe Jubilees was composed in the second century B.C. The Hebrew fragments found at Qumran are part of a Jewish library that contained other supporting literature such as the Book of Enoch and others. An analysis of the chronological development in the shapes of letters in the manuscripts confirms that Jubilees is pre-Christian in date and seems to have been penned between 100 and 200 B.C. Based on records of the High Priests of the time, the date of authorship is probably 140 – 100 B.C. The book of Jubilees is also cited in the Qumran Damascus Document in pre-Christian texts.

The Book of Jubilees was originally written in Hebrew. The author was a Pharisee (a doctor of the law), or someone very familiar with scripture and religious law. Since the scrolls were found in what is assumed to be an Essene library, and were dated to the time the Essene community was active, the author was probably a member of that particular religious group. Jubilees represents a hyper-legalistic and midrashic tendency, which was part of the Essene culture at the time.

"Midrash" – refers to writings containing extra-legal material of anecdotal or allegorical nature, designed either to clarify historical material, or to teach a moral point.

Jubilees represents a midrash on Genesis 1:1 through Exodus 12:50 which depicts the episodes from creation with the observance of the Sabbath by the angels and men to Israel's escape from Egyptian bondage.

Although originally written in Hebrew, the Hebrew texts were completely lost until the find at Qumran. Fragments of Jubilees were discovered among the Dead Sea Scrolls. At least fourteen copies of the Book of Jubilees have been identified from caves 1, 2, 3 and 11 at Qumran. This makes it clear that the Book of Jubilees was a popular and probably authoritative text for the community whose library was concealed in the caves. These fragments are actually generations closer to the original copies than many books in our accepted Bible. Unfortunately, the fragments found at Qumran were only pieces of the texts and offered the briefest of glimpses of the entire book. The only complete versions of the Book of Jubilees are in Ethiopic, which in turn were translations of a Greek version.

Four Ethiopian manuscripts of Jubilees were found to be hundreds of years old. Of these, the fifteenth and sixteenth century texts are the truest and least corrupted when compared to the fragments found at Qumran. There are also citations of Jubilees in Syriac literature that may reflect a lost translation from Hebrew. Pieces of Latin translations have also been found.

Other fragments of a Greek version are quoted or referenced by Justin Martyr, Origen, Diodorus of Antioch, Isidore of Alexandria, Isidore of Seville, Eutychius, Patriarch of Alexandria, John of Malala, and Syncellus. This amount of various information and translations is enough to allow us to reconstruct the original to a great degree. The internal evidence of Jubilees shows very little tampering by Christians during its transmission and subsequent translations, thus allowing a clear view of certain Jewish beliefs being propagated at the time of its origin. By removing certain variances, we can isolate Christian alterations and mistakes in translations with a reasonable degree of confidence. Due to the poor condition of the fragments of Qumran, we may never be able to confirm certain key phrases in Hebrew. Thus, as with many texts, including those of our own Bible, in the end we must trust in the accuracy of the ancient scribes and translators.

It should be noted that the books of Jubilees, Enoch, and Jasher present stories of "The Watchers"; a group of angels sent to earth to record and teach, but who fell by their own lust and pride into a demonic state. Both Enoch and Jubilees refer to a solar-based calendar. This may show a conflict or transition at the time of their penning since Judaism now uses a lunar-based calendar   Laws, rites, and functions are observed and noted in Jubilees. Circumcision is emphasized in both humans and angels. Angelic observance of Sabbath laws as well as parts of Jewish religious laws are said to have been observed in heaven before they were revealed to Moses.

To the Qumran community, complete obedience to the Laws of Moses entailed observing a series of holy days and festivals at a particular time according to a specific calendar. The calendar described in Jubilees is one of 364 days, divided into four seasons of three months each with thirteen weeks to a season. Each month had 30 days with one day added at certain times for each of the four seasons. With 52 weeks in a year, the festival and holy days recur at the same point each year. This calendar became a hallmark of an orthodox Qumran community.

The adherence to a specific calendar is one of many ways the Book of Jubilees shows the devotion to religious law. The law had been placed at the pinnacle of importance in the lives of the community at Qumran. All aspects of life were driven by a seemingly obsessive compliance to every jot and tittle of the law. The Book Of Jubilees confirms what can only be inferred from the books of Ezra, Nehemiah, and Zechariah, that the law and those who carried it out were supreme.

As the law took hold, by its nature, it crystallized the society. Free expression died, smothered under a mantle of hyperorthodoxy. Since free thought invited accusations of violations of the law or claims of heresy, prudence, a closed mind, and a silent voice prevailed. Free thought was limited to religious or apocryphal writings, which upheld the orthodox positions of the day. The silent period between Malachi and Mark may be a reflection of this stasis. Jubilees, Enoch, and other apocryphal books found in the Qumran caves are a triumph over the unimaginative mindset brought on by making religious law supreme and human expression contrary to law punishable by death. It may be an odd manifestation that such a burst of creativity was fueled by the very search for order that suppressed free thought in the first place.

The Book of Jubilees seems to be an attempt to answer and explain all questions left unanswered in the Book of Genesis as well as to bolster the position of the religious law. It attempts to trace the source of religious laws back to an ancient beginning thereby adding weight and sanction.

In the Book of Jubilees, we discover the origin of the wife of Cain. There is information offered about angels and the beginnings of the human race, how demons came into existence, and the place of Satan in the plans of God. Information is offered in an attempt to make perfect sense of the vagaries left in Genesis. For the defense of order and law and to maintain religious law as the center point of Jewish life, Jubilees was written as an answer to both pagan Greeks and liberal Jews. From the divine placement of law and order to its explanation of times and events, Jubilees is a panorama of legalism.

The name "Jubilees" comes from the division of time into eras known as Jubilees. One Jubilee occurs after the equivalent of forty-nine years, or seven Sabbaths or weeks of years has passed. It is the numerical perfection of seven sevens. In a balance and symmetry of years, the Jubilee occurs after seven cycles of seven or forty-nine years have been completed. Thus, the fiftieth year is a Jubilee year. Time is told by referencing the number of Jubilees that have transpired from the time the festival was first kept. For example, Israel entered Canaan at the close of the fiftieth jubilee, which is about 2450 BCE.

The obsession with time, dates, and the strict observance of festivals are all evidence of legalism taken to the highest level.

Based on the approximate time of writing, Jubilees was created in the time of the Maccabees, in the high priesthood of Hyrcanus. In this period of time the appearance of the Messiah and the rise of the Messianic kingdom were viewed as imminent. Followers were preparing themselves for the arrival of the Messiah and the establishment of His eternal kingdom.

Judaism was in contact with the Greek culture at the time. The Greeks were known to be philosophers and were developing processes of critical thinking. One objective of Jubilees was to defend Judaism against the attacks of the Hellenists and to prove that the law was logical, consistent, and valid. Attacks against paganism and non-believers are embedded in the text along with defense of the law and its consistency through proclamations of the law being observed by the angels in heaven from the beginning of creation.

Moral lessons are taught by use of the juxtaposition of the "satans" and their attempts to test and lead mankind into sin against the warning and advice of scriptural wisdom from Moses and his angels.

Mastema is mentioned only in The Book of Jubilees and in the Fragments of a Zadokite Work. Mastema is Satan. The name Mastema is derived from the Hebrew, "Mastim," meaning "adversary." The word occurs as singular and plural. The word is equivalent to Satan (adversary or accuser). This is similar to the chief Satan and his class of "satans" in 1 Enoch 40:7.

Mastema is subservient to God. His task is to tempt men to sin and if they do, he accuses them in the presence of the Throne of God. He and his minions lead men into sin but do not cause the sin. Once men have chosen to sin, they lead them from sin to destruction. Since man is given free will, sin is a choice, with Mastema simply encouraging and facilitating the decision. The choice, we can assume, is our own and the destruction that follows is "self-destruction."

Beliar is also mentioned. Beliar is the Greek name for Belial or Beliaal. The name in its Hebrew equivalent means "without value." This was a demon known by the Jews as the chief of all the devils. Belial is the leader of the Sons of Darkness. Belial is mentioned in the Fragments of a Zadokite fragment along with Mastema, which states that at the time of the Antichrist, Belial shall be let loose against Israel, as God spoke through Isaiah the prophet. Belial is sometimes presented as an agent of God's punishment although he is considered a "satan."

Although it is impossible to explore here in any detail the ramification of superhuman entities and their culpability in man's sin, it is important to mention that Judaism had no doctrine of original sin. The fall of Adam and Eve may have removed man from the perfect environment and the curses that followed may have shortened his lifespan, but propagation of sin through the bloodline was not considered. Sin seemed to affect only man and the animals he was given dominion over. Yet, man continued to sin, and to increase in his capacity and modes of sin. The explanation offered for man's inability to resist is the existence of fallen angels; spiritual, superhuman creations whose task it was to teach us but who now tempt and mislead men. In the end, the world declines and crumbles under the evil influence of the fallen angels turned demons called, "The Watchers."

With the establishment of the covenant between Abraham and God, we are told that God had appointed spirits to "mislead" all the nations but would not assign a spirit to lead or mislead the children of Isaac but God himself would be leading them.

Within the text are recurring numbers. Seven, being the number of perfection, is the most common. The number three is cited, being the number of completion. However, the number twenty-two occurs in the accounts of creation and lineage. It is worth noting that there are twenty-two letters in the Hebrew alphabet. The number twenty-two represents a type of Godly assignment or appointment. It is also the number of the perfect foundation and of the God-given language. It is presented within the text as a reminder that God established the ways of the Jews and gave the Hebrew language and writing first and only to the Jews.

The angels converse in Hebrew and it is the heavenly tongue. The law is written by God using this alphabet thus the law is also holy. All men spoke Hebrew until the time of Babel when it was lost. However, when Abraham dedicated himself to God, his ears were opened and his tongue was sanctified and Hebrew was again spoken and understood.

Finally, the entire text is based on the numbers of forty-nine and fifty. Forty-nine represents the pinnacle of perfection, being made up of seven times seven. The number fifty, which is the number of the Jubilee, is the number of grace. In this year slaves were to be set free, debts were forgiven, and grace filled the land and people.

Drawing from the theology and myths at the time, the book of Jubilees expands and embellishes on the creation story, the fall of Adam and Eve, and the fall of the angels. The expanded detail written into the text may have been one reason it was eventually rejected. However, the effects of the book can still be seen throughout the Judeo-Christian beliefs of today. The theology espoused in Jubilees can be seen in the angelology and demonology taught in the Christian churches of today and widely held by many Jews.

In an attempt to answer questions left unaddressed in Genesis the writer confronts the origin and identification of Cain's wife. According to The Book Of Jubilees, Cain married his sister, as did all of the sons of Adam and Eve, except Abel, who was murdered. This seemed offensive to some, since it flies in the face of the very law it was written to defend. Yet, this seemed to the writer to be the lesser of evils, given the problematic questions. Inbreeding is dismissed with the observation that the law was not fully given and understood then. The effects of the act were mute due to the purity of the newly created race.

The seeming discrepancy between divine command of Adam's death decree and the timing of his death is addressed. Seeing that Adam continued to live even after he ate the fruit, which was supposed to bring on his death, the writer set about to clarify God's actions. The problem is explained away in a single sentence. Since a day in heaven is as a thousand years on earth and Adam died having lived less than a thousand years this meant he died in the same heavenly day. Dying within the same day of the crime was acceptable.

In an astonishing parallel to the Book Of Enoch, written at about the same time as Jubilees, the Watchers, or sons of God mentioned in Genesis 6, fell from grace when they descended to earth and had sex with the daughters of men. In the Book of Enoch, the angels descended for the purpose of seducing the women of earth. However, in The Book Of Jubilee the angels were sent to teach men, but after living on earth for a while, were tempted by their own lust and fell. The offspring of this unholy union were bloodthirsty and cannibalistic giants. The Book of Jubilees indicates that each of the offspring were somehow different, yet they are divided into categories of the Naphidim, (or Naphilim, depending on the transliteration), the Giants, and the Eljo. (Naphil are also mentioned, however, this word is the singular of Naphilim.)

As sin spread throughout the world and the minds of men were turned toward evil, God saw no alternative but to cleanse the earth with a flood and establish a "new nature" in man that does not have to sin. It is this new nature that the messiah will meet in mankind when He comes. As far as this author is aware, the re-creation of man's nature is mentioned in no other book. This idea of human nature being altered as it exited before the flood is found nowhere else but in Jubilees.

The angelic narrator tells us there were times in Israel's history when no evil existed and all men lived in accord. We are also told when and where the satans were allowed to attack and confound Israel. In this narrative, God uses his satans to harden the hearts of the Egyptians compelling them to pursue Israel and be destroyed.

The Book of Jubilees had other names throughout its history and propagation. "The Little Genesis" is another name given to this text. The description of "Little" does not refer to the size of the book, but to its canonical disposition.

"The Apocalypse of Moses" is another name denoting the same work. This title seems to have been used for only a short period of time. It refers to the revelation given to Moses as the recipient of all the knowledge disclosed in the book. The term "Apocalypse" means to make known or to reveal. With the exception of minor differences picked up through translation and copying, the three titles represent the same text.

About the Translation

The translation presented herein is based in part on that of R.H. Charles and his works of 1902 through 1913. Although the translation seems to be a faithful one, his scholarly tone, pedantry, and quasi-Elizabethan language made the text less than accessible. The pleonasm of the text as well as the ancient writer's tendency to repeat phrases for the sake of emphasis added to the general lack of readability. Furthermore, many of the verse breaks occurred in mid-sentence and certainly in mid-thought, adding confusion when viewing the text. All of these difficulties were corrected.

To aid in comprehension, it was decided that the text would be put through three phases of change. First, all verse breaks would be aligned with sentence breaks and with complete streams of thought when possible. Next, all archaic words and phrases would be replaced with their modern equivalent. Lastly, convoluted sentence structure would be clarified and rewritten. Notes of explanation and clarification are added in parentheses.

Due to the vast differences in societal structure and rules, certain phrases remained in their archaic form, seeing that they had no direct equivalence in our western culture. One such phrase is "uncovered the skirt." This phrase indicates the person was seen naked. In most cases it carries a connotation of intercourse. If one were to "uncover his father's skirt" it indicates the father's wife or concubine has been seen naked, usually with the intent of having sex with her.

When possible, the poetic flow of the text would be kept, but not at the expense of understanding. Various translations of each verse were referenced in order to compare and contrast differing viewpoints. The best rendering of the text was chosen and written into a more modern and readable format.

Since the book of Jubilees is written from the viewpoint of the angel narrating or dictating the text, when the words "I," "we," and "us" appear and the words are not readily connected to anyone within the sentence, it can be assumed the angel is referring to himself or the angelic host to which he belongs. When the narrator uses the word "you" he is referring to Moses, to whom the angel is speaking and dictating.

For simplicity's sake, it was decided to keep the word "soul" in the translation as related to the blood of animal and man. The phrase, "The soul is in the blood," will occur several times in the texts. It should be noted that the soul is the "life force," which came from God and belongs to God. It was considered sacred. It did not belong to man and was to be offered to God alone. Since blood represented life itself, it must be the centerpiece of any animal sacrifice. Sin or transgression of the law was punishable by death. Life must be offered as payment. The life force of an animal was offered in place of the life of the sinner. The blood of the animal represents this life.

Now, let us delve into this fascinating and illuminating book.

THE BOOK OF JUBILEES
THE LITTLE GENESIS, THE APOCALYPSE OF MOSES

This is the history of how the days were divided and of the days of the law and of the testimony, of the events of the years, and of the weeks of years, of their Jubilees throughout all the years of the world, as the Lord spoke to Moses on Mount Sinai when he went up to receive the tablets of the law and the commandment, according to the voice of God when he said to him, "Go up to the top of the Mount."

[Chapter 1]

1 It happened in the first year of the exodus of the children of Israel out of Egypt, in the third month, on the sixteenth day of the month, that God spoke to Moses, saying, "Come up to Me on the Mountain, and I will give you two tablets of stone of the law and the commandment, which I have written, that you may teach them."
2 Moses went up into the mountain of God, and the glory of the Lord rested on Mount Sinai, and a cloud overshadowed it six days.
3 He called to Moses on the seventh day out of the middle of the cloud, and the appearance of the glory of the Lord was like a flame on the top of the mountain.
4 Moses was on the mountain forty days and forty nights, and God taught him the earlier and the later history of the division of all the days of the law and of the testimony.
5 He said, "Open your heart to every word which I shall speak to you on this mountain, and write them in a book in order that their generations may see how I have not forsaken them for all the evil which they have committed when they transgressed the covenant which I establish between Me and you for their generations this day on Mount Sinai.
6 It will come to pass when all these things come on them, that they will recognize that I am more righteous than they in all their judgments and in all their actions, and they will recognize that I have truly been with them.
7 Write all these words for yourself which I speak to you today, for I know their rebellion and their stubbornness, before I brought them into the land of which I swore to their fathers, to Abraham and to Isaac and to Jacob, saying, " Unto your offspring will I give a land flowing with milk and honey.
8 They will eat and be satisfied, and they will turn to strange gods, to gods that cannot deliver them from any of their tribulation, and this witness shall be heard for a witness against them.
9 They will forget all My commandments, even all that I command them, and they will walk in the ways of the Gentiles, and after their uncleanness, and after their shame, and will serve their gods, and these will prove to them an offence and a tribulation and an sickness and a trap.
10 Many will perish and they will be taken captive, and will fall into the hands of the enemy, because they have forsaken My laws and My commandments, and the festivals of My covenant, and My sabbaths, and My holy place which I have made holy for Myself in their presence, and My tabernacle, and My sanctuary, which I have made holy for Myself in the midst of the land, that I should set My name on it, that it should reside there.
11 They will make themselves high places and places of worship and graven images. Each will worship graven images of his own making, Thus they will go astray. They will sacrifice their children to demons, and to all errors their hearts can work.
12 I will send witnesses to them that I may testify against them, but they will not hear. They will kill the witnesses. They will persecute those who seek the law, and they will abolish and change everything (in the Law) so as to work evil before My eyes.
13 I will hide My face from them. I will deliver them into the hand of the Gentiles. They will be captured like prey for their eating. I will remove them from the out of the land. I will scatter them among the Gentiles.
14 And they will forget My law and all My commandments and all My judgments. They will go astray regarding the observance of new moons, and sabbaths, and festivals, and jubilees, and laws.
15 After this they will turn to Me from among the Gentiles with all their heart and with all their soul and with all their strength, and I will gather them from among all the Gentiles, and they will seek me. I shall be found by them when they seek me with all their heart and with all their soul.
16 I will allow them to see abounding peace with righteousness. I will remove them, the plant of uprightness, with all My heart and with all My soul, and they shall be for a blessing and not for a curse, and they shall be the head and not the tail.
17 I will build My sanctuary among them, and I will dwell with them, and I will be their God and they shall be My people in truth and righteousness.
18 I will not forsake them nor fail them; for I am the Lord their God."
19 Moses fell on his face and prayed and said, 'O Lord my God, do not forsake Your people and Your inheritance, so that they should wander in the error of their hearts, and do not deliver them into the hands of their enemies, the Gentiles, so that they should rule over them and cause them to sin against You.
20 Let your mercy, O Lord, be lifted up on Your people, and create in them an upright spirit, and let not the spirit of Beliar rule over them to accuse them before You, and to ensnare them from all the paths of righteousness, so that they may perish from before Your face.

21 But they are Your people and Your inheritance, which You have delivered with Your great power from the hands of the Egyptians, create in them a clean heart and a holy spirit, and let them not be ensnared in their sins from now on until eternity."

22 The Lord said to Moses, "I know their contrariness and their thoughts and their stubbornness, and they will not be obedient until they confess their own sin and the sin of their fathers.

23 After this they will turn to Me in all uprightness and with all their heart and with all their soul, and I will circumcise the foreskin of their heart and the foreskin of the heart of their offspring, and I will create in them a holy spirit, and I will cleanse them so that they shall not turn away from Me from that day to eternity.

24 And their souls will cling to Me and to all My commandments, and they will fulfill My commandments, and I will be their Father and they shall be My children.

25 They all shall be called children of the living God, and every angel and every spirit shall know, yes, they shall know that these are My children, and that I am their Father in uprightness and righteousness, and that I love them.

26 Write down for yourself all these words which I say to you on this mountain, from the first to the last, which shall come to pass in all the divisions of the days in the law and in the testimony and in the weeks and the jubilees to eternity, until I descend and dwell with them throughout eternity."

27 He said to the angel of the presence (of the Lord), "Write for Moses from the beginning of creation until My sanctuary has been built among them for all eternity.

28 The Lord will appear to the eyes of all, and all shall know that I am the God of Israel and the Father of all the children of Jacob, and King on Mount Zion for all eternity. And Zion and Jerusalem shall be holy."

29 The angel of the presence (of the Lord) who went before the camp of Israel took the tables of the divisions of the years, written from the time of the creation, concerning the law and the testimony of the weeks of the jubilees, according to the individual years, according to the numbering of all the jubilees, from the day of the new creation when the heavens and the earth shall be renewed and all their creation according to the powers of the heaven, and according to all the creation of the earth, until the sanctuary of the Lord shall be made in Jerusalem on Mount Zion, and all the stars and planets be renewed for healing, peace, and blessing for all the elect of Israel, and that this is the way it may be from that day and to all the days of the earth.

[Chapter 2]

1 The angel of the presence (of the Lord) spoke to Moses according to the word of the Lord, saying, "Write the complete history of the creation, how in six days the Lord God finished all His works and all that He created, and kept Sabbath on the seventh day and made it holy for all ages, and appointed it as a sign for all His works.

2 For on the first day He created the heavens which are above and the earth and the waters and all the spirits which serve before him which are the angels of the presence (of the Lord), and the angels of sanctification, and the angels of the spirit of fire, and the angels of the spirit of the winds, and the angels of the spirit of the clouds, and of darkness, and of snow and of hail and of white frost, and the angels of the voices and of the thunder and of the lightning, and the angels of the spirits of cold and of heat, and of winter and of spring and of autumn and of summer and of all the spirits of his creatures which are in the heavens and on the earth, He created the bottomless pit and the darkness, evening and night, and the light, dawn and day, which He has prepared in the knowledge of His heart.

3 When we saw His works, we praised Him, and worshiped before Him because of all His works; for seven great works did He create on the first day.

4 On the second day He created the sky between the waters (above and below), and the waters were divided on that day. Half of them went up above the sky and half of them went down below the sky that was in the middle over the face of the whole earth. And this was the only work God created on the second day.

5 On the third day He commanded the waters to pass from off the face of the whole earth into one place, and the dry land to appear.

6 The waters did as He commanded them, and they receded from off the face of the earth into one place, and the dry land appeared.

7 On that day He created for them all the seas according to their separate gathering-places, and all the rivers, and the gatherings of the waters in the mountains and on all the earth, and all the lakes, and all the dew of the earth, and the seed which is sown, and all sprouting things, and fruit-bearing trees, and trees of the wood, and the garden of Eden, in Eden and throughout. These four great works God created on the third day.

8 On the fourth day He created the sun and the moon and the stars, and set them in the sky of the heaven, to give light on all the earth, and to rule over the day and the night, and divide the light from the darkness.

9 God appointed the sun to be a great sign on the earth for days and for sabbaths and for months and for feasts and for years and for sabbaths of years and for jubilees and for all seasons of the years.

10 And it divides the light from the darkness for prosperity that all things may prosper which sprout and grow on the earth. These three kinds He made on the fourth day.

11 On the fifth day He created great sea monsters in the depths of the waters, for these were the first things of flesh that were created by his hands, the fish and everything that moves in the waters, and everything that flies, the birds and all their kind.

12 And the sun rose above them to make them prosper, and the sun rose above everything that was on the earth, everything that sprouts out of the earth, and all fruit-bearing trees, and all flesh.

13 He created these three kinds on the fifth day. On the sixth day He created all the animals of the earth, and all cattle, and everything that moves on the earth.

14 After all this He created mankind. He created a man and a woman, and gave him dominion over all that is on the earth, and in the seas, and over everything that flies, and over beasts, and over cattle, and over everything that moves on the earth, and over the whole earth, and over all this He gave him dominion.

15 He created these four kinds on the sixth day. And there were altogether two and twenty kinds.

16 He finished all his work on the sixth day. That is all that is in the heavens and on the earth, and in the seas and in the abysses, and in the light and in the darkness, and in everything.

17 He gave us a great sign, the Sabbath day, that we should work six days, but keep Sabbath on the seventh day from all work.

18 All the angels of the presence (of the Lord), and all the angels of sanctification, these two great types of angels He has told to tell us to keep the Sabbath with Him in heaven and on earth.

19 And He said to us, "Look, I will separate to Myself a people from among all the peoples, and these shall keep the Sabbath day, and I will sanctify them to Myself as My people, and will bless them; as I have sanctified the Sabbath day and do sanctify it to Myself, even so will I bless them, and they shall be My people and I will be their God.

20 I have chosen the offspring of Jacob from among all that I have seen, and have written him down as My first-born son, and have sanctified him to Myself forever and ever; and I will teach them the Sabbath day, that they may keep Sabbath on it from all work."

21 He created in it a sign in accordance with which they should keep Sabbath with us on the seventh day, to eat and to drink, and to bless Him who has created all things as He has blessed and sanctified to Himself a particular, exclusive people above all peoples, and that they should keep Sabbath together with us.

22 He caused His commands to rise up as a sweet odor acceptable before Him all the days.

23 There were two and twenty heads (representatives) of mankind from Adam to Jacob, and two and twenty kinds of work (creation) were made until the seventh day; this is blessed and holy; and the former also is blessed and holy; and this one serves with that one for sanctification and blessing.

24 Jacob and his offspring were granted that they should always be the blessed and holy ones of the first testimony and law, even as He had sanctified and blessed the Sabbath day on the seventh day.

25 He created heaven and earth and everything that He created in six days, and God made the seventh day holy, for all His works; therefore He commanded on its behalf that, whoever does any work on it shall die, and that he who defiles it shall surely die.

26 Because of this, command the children of Israel to observe this day that they may keep it holy and not do on it any work, and not to defile it, as it is holier than all other days.

27 And whoever profanes it shall surely die, and whoever does any work on it shall surely die eternally, that the children of Israel may observe this day throughout their generations, and not be rooted out of the land; for it is a holy day and a blessed day.

28 Every one who observes it and keeps Sabbath on it from all his work will be holy and blessed throughout all days as we are blessed.

29 Declare and say to the children of Israel the law of this day that they should keep Sabbath on it, and that they should not forsake it in the error of their hearts; and that it is not lawful to do any work on it which is not suitable, to do their own pleasure on it, and that they should not prepare anything to be eaten or drunk on it, and that it is not lawful to draw water, or bring in or take out through their gates any burden which they had not prepared for themselves on the sixth day in their dwellings.

30 They shall not bring or take anything from house to house on that day; for that day is more holy and blessed than any jubilee day of the jubilees; on this we kept Sabbath in the heavens before it was made known to any flesh to keep Sabbath on the earth.

31 The Creator of all things blessed it, but He did not sanctify all peoples and nations to keep Sabbath, but Israel alone, them alone He permitted to eat and drink and to keep Sabbath on the earth.

32 And the Creator of all things blessed this day which He had created for blessing and holiness and glory above all days.

33 This law and testimony was given to the children of Israel as a law forever to their generations.

[Chapter 3]

1 On the sixth day of the second week, according to the word of God, we brought to Adam all the beasts, and all the cattle, and all the birds, and everything that moves on the earth, and everything that moves in the water, according to their kinds,

and according to their types, the beasts on the first day; the cattle on the second day; the birds on the third day; and all that moves on the earth on the fourth day; and that moves in the water on the fifth day.

2 And Adam named them all by their respective names. As he called them, so was their name.

3 On these five days Adam saw all these, male and female, according to every kind that was on the earth, but he was alone and found no helpmate.

4 The Lord said to us, "It is not good that the man should be alone, let us make a helpmate for him."

5 And the Lord our God caused a deep sleep to fall on him, and he slept, and He took from Adam a rib from among his ribs for the woman, and this rib was the origin of the woman. And He built up the flesh in its place, and built the woman.

6 He awakened Adam out of his sleep and on awakening he rose on the sixth day, and He brought her to him, and he knew her, and said to her, "This is now bone of my bones and flesh of my flesh; she shall be called my wife; because she was taken from her husband."

7 Therefore shall man and wife become one and therefore shall a man leave his father and his mother, and cling to his wife, and they shall be one flesh.

8 In the first week Adam was created, and from his rib, his wife. In the second week God showed her to him, and for this reason the commandment was given to keep in their defilement. A male should be purified in seven days, and for a female twice seven days.

9 After Adam had completed forty days in the land where he had been created, we brought him into the garden of Eden to till and keep it, but his wife we brought in on the eightieth day, and after this she entered into the garden of Eden.

10 And for this reason the commandment is written on the heavenly tablets in regard to her that gives birth, "If she bears a male, she shall remain unclean for seven days according to the first week of days, and thirty-three days shall she remain in the blood of her purifying, and she shall not touch any holy thing, nor enter into the sanctuary, until she completes these days which are decreed in the case of a male child.

11 But in the case of a female child she shall remain unclean two weeks of days, according to the first two weeks, and sixty-six days in the blood of her purification, and they will be in all eighty days."

12 When she had completed these eighty days we brought her into the Garden of Eden, for it is holier than all the earth besides and every tree that is planted in it is holy.

13 Therefore, there was ordained regarding her who bears a male or a female child the statute of those days that she should touch no holy thing, nor enter into the sanctuary until these days for the male or female child are completed.

14 This is the law and testimony that was written down for Israel, in order that they should observe it all the days.

15 In the first week of the first jubilee, Adam and his wife were in the garden of Eden for seven years tilling and keeping it, and we gave him work and we instructed him to do everything that is suitable for tillage.

16 And he tilled the garden, and was naked and did not realize it, and was not ashamed. He protected the garden from the birds and beasts and cattle. He gathered its fruit, and ate, and put aside that which was left over for himself and for his wife.

17 After the completion of exactly seven years there, and in the second month, on the seventeenth day of the month, the serpent came and approached the woman, and the serpent said to the woman, "Has God commanded you saying, you shall not eat of every tree of the garden?"

18 She said to it, God said to us, of all the fruit of the trees of the garden, eat; but of the fruit of the tree which is in the middle of the garden God said to us, you shall not eat of it, neither shall you touch it, or you shall die."

19 The serpent said to the woman, "You shall not surely die. God does know that on the day you shall eat of it, your eyes will be opened, and you will be as gods, and you will know good and evil.

20 And the woman saw the tree that it was beautiful and pleasant to the eye, and that its fruit was good for food, and she took of it and ate.

21 First, she covered her shame with fig leaves and then she gave the fruit to Adam and he ate, and his eyes were opened, and he saw that he was naked.

22 He took fig leaves and sewed them together, and made an apron for himself, and covered his shame.

23 God cursed the serpent, and was very angry at it forever.

24 And He was very angry with the woman, because she listened to the voice of the serpent, and ate; and He said to her, "I will vastly multiply your sorrow and your pains, in sorrow you will bring forth children, and your master shall be your husband, and he will rule over you."

25 To Adam also he said, " Because you have listened to the voice of your wife, and have eaten of the tree of which I commanded you not to eat, cursed be the ground for your sake, thorns and thistles shall it produce for you, and you will eat your bread in the sweat of your face, untill you return to the earth from where you were taken; for earth you are, and to earth will you return."

26 And He made for them coats of skin, and clothed them, and sent them out from the Garden of Eden.

27 On that day on which Adam went out from the Garden, he offered as a sweet odor an offering, frankincense, incense, and sweet spice, and spices in the morning with the rising of the sun from the day when he covered his shame.

28 On that day was closed the mouth of all beasts, and of cattle, and of birds, and of whatever walks, and of whatever moves, so that they could no longer speak, for they had all spoken one with another with one dialect and with one language.

29 All flesh that was in the Garden of Eden He sent out of the Garden of Eden, and all flesh was scattered according to its kinds, and according to its types to the places that had been created for them.

30 Of all the beasts and cattle only to Adam alone He gave the ability to cover his shame.

31 Because of this, it is prescribed on the heavenly tablets as touching all those who know the judgment of the law, that they should cover their shame, and should not uncover themselves as the Gentiles uncover themselves.

32 On the new moon of the fourth month, Adam and his wife went out from the Garden of Eden, and they dwelt in the land of Elda in the land of their creation.

33 And Adam called the name of his wife Eve.

34 And they had no son until the first jubilee, and after this he knew her.

35 Now he tilled the land as he had been instructed in the Garden of Eden.

[Chapter 4]

1 In the third week in the second jubilee she gave birth to Cain, and in the fourth week she gave birth to Abel, and in the fifth week she gave birth to her daughter Awan. (A week is seven years.)

2 In the first year of the third jubilee, Cain killed Abel because God accepted the sacrifice of Abel, and did not accept the offering of Cain.

3 And he killed him in the field, and his blood cried from the ground to heaven, complaining because he had killed him.

4 The Lord blamed Cain, because he had killed Abel, and He made him a fugitive on the earth because of the blood of his brother, and He cursed him on the earth.

5 Because of this it is written on the heavenly tablets, "Cursed is he who kills his neighbor treacherously, and let all who have seen and heard say, 'So be it', and the man who has seen and not reported it, let him be accursed as the one committing it."

6 For this reason we announce when we come before the Lord our God all the sin that is committed in heaven and on earth, and in light and in darkness, and everywhere.

7 And Adam and his wife mourned for Abel four weeks of years, and in the fourth year of the fifth week they became joyful, and Adam knew his wife again, and she gave birth to a son, and he called his name Seth, for he said "God has raised up a second offspring to us on the earth instead of Abel; for Cain killed him."

8 In the sixth week he begat his daughter Azura.

9 And Cain took Awan his sister to be his wife and she gave birth to Enoch at the close of the fourth jubilee.

10 In the first year of the first week of the fifth jubilee, houses were built on the earth, and Cain built a city, and called its name after the name of his son Enoch.

11 Adam knew Eve his wife and she gave birth to a total of nine sons. In the fifth week of the fifth jubilee Seth took Azura his sister to be his wife, and in the fourth year of the sixth week she gave birth to Enos.

12 He began to call on the name of the Lord on the earth.

13 In the seventh jubilee in the third week Enos took Noam his sister to be his wife, and she gave birth to a son in the third year of the fifth week, and he called his name Kenan.

14 At the close of the eighth jubilee Kenan took Mualeleth his sister to be his wife, and she gave birth to a son in the ninth jubilee, in the first week in the third year of this week, and he called his name Mahalalel.

15 In the second week of the tenth jubilee Mahalalel took to him to wife Dinah, the daughter of Barakiel the daughter of his father's brother, and she gave birth to a son in the third week in the sixth year, and he called his name Jared, for in his days the angels of the Lord descended on the earth, those who are named the Watchers, that they should instruct the children of men, and that they should do judgment and uprightness on the earth.

16 In the eleventh jubilee Jared took to himself a wife, and her name was Baraka, the daughter of Rasujal, a daughter of his father's brother, in the fourth week of this jubilee, and she gave birth to a son in the fifth week, in the fourth year of the jubilee, and he called his name Enoch.

17 He was the first among men that are born on earth who learned writing and knowledge and wisdom and who wrote down the signs of heaven according to the order of their months in a book, that men might know the seasons of the years according to the order of their separate months.

18 He was the first to write a testimony and he testified to the sons of men among the generations of the earth, and recounted the weeks of the jubilees, and made known to them the days of the years, and set in order the months and recounted the Sabbaths of the years as we made them, known to him.

19 And what was and what will be he saw in a vision of his sleep, as it will happen to the children of men throughout their generations until the day of judgment; he saw and understood everything, and wrote his testimony, and placed the testimony on earth for all the children of men and for their generations.

20 In the twelfth jubilee, in the seventh week of it, he took to himself a wife, and her name was Edna, the daughter of Danel, the daughter of his father's brother, and in the sixth year in this week she gave birth to a son and he called his name Methuselah.

21 He was with the angels of God these six jubilees of years, and they showed him everything that is on earth and in the heavens, the rule of the sun, and he wrote down everything.

22 And he testified to the Watchers, who had sinned with the daughters of men; for these had begun to unite themselves, so as to be defiled with the daughters of men, and Enoch testified against them all.

23 And he was taken from among the children of men, and we conducted him into the Garden of Eden in majesty and honor, and there he wrote down the condemnation and judgment of the world, and all the wickedness of the children of men.

24 Because of it God brought the waters of the flood on all the land of Eden; for there he was set as a sign and that he should testify against all the children of men, that he should recount all the deeds of the generations until the day of condemnation.

25 He burnt the incense of the sanctuary, even sweet spices acceptable before the Lord on the Mount.

26 For the Lord has four places on the earth, the Garden of Eden, and the Mount of the East, and this mountain on which you are this day, Mount Sinai, and Mount Zion which will be sanctified in the new creation for a sanctification of the earth; through it will the earth be sanctified from all its guilt and its uncleanness throughout the generations of the world.

27 In the fourteenth jubilee Methuselah took to himself a wife, Edna the daughter of Azrial, the daughter of his father's brother, in the third week, in the first year of this week, and he begat a son and called his name Lamech.

28 In the fifteenth jubilee in the third week Lamech took to himself a wife, and her name was Betenos the daughter of Baraki'il, the daughter of his father's brother, and in this week she gave birth to a son and he called his name Noah, saying, "This one will comfort me for my trouble and all my work, and for the ground which the Lord has cursed."

29 At the close of the nineteenth jubilee, in the seventh week in the sixth year of it, Adam died, and all his sons buried him in the land of his creation, and he was the first to be buried in the earth.

30 He lacked seventy years of one thousand years, because one thousand years are as one day in the testimony of the heavens. Therefore was it written concerning the tree of knowledge, "On the day that you eat of it you shall die." Because of this he did not complete the one thousand years but instead he died during it.

31 At the close of this jubilee Cain was killed after him in the same year; because his house fell on him and he died in the middle of his house, and he was killed by its stones. With a stone he had killed Abel, and by a stone he was killed in righteous judgment.

32 For this reason it was ordained on the heavenly tablets, with the instrument with which a man kills his neighbor with the same shall he be killed. In the same manner that he wounded him, in like manner shall they deal with him."

33 In the twenty-fifth jubilee Noah took to himself a wife, and her name was Emzara, the daughter of Rake'el, the daughter of his father's brother, in the first year in the fifth week, and in the third year of it she gave birth to Shem, in the fifth year of it she gave birth to Ham, and in the first year in the sixth week she gave birth to Japheth.

[Chapter 5]

1 When the children of men began to multiply on the face of the earth and daughters were born to them, and the angels of God saw them on a certain year of this jubilee, that they were beautiful, and they took themselves wives of all whom they chose, and they gave birth to their sons and they were giants.

2 Because of them lawlessness increased on the earth and all flesh corrupted its way. Men and cattle and beasts and birds and everything that walked on the earth were all corrupted in their ways and their orders, and they began to devour each other. Lawlessness increased on the earth and the imagination and thoughts of all men were continually, totally evil.

3 God looked on the earth, and saw it was corrupt, and all flesh had corrupted its orders, and all that were on the earth had committed all manner of evil before His eyes.

4 He said that He would destroy man and all flesh on the face of the earth that He had created.

5 But Noah found grace before the eyes of the Lord.

6 And against the angels whom He had sent on the earth, He had boiling anger, and He gave commandment to root them out of all their dominion, and He commanded us to bind them in the depths of the earth, and look, they are bound in the middle of the earth, and are kept separate.

7 And against their sons went out a command from His mouth that they should be killed with the sword, and be left under heaven.

8 He said, "My spirit shall not always abide on man; for they also are flesh and their days shall be one hundred and twenty years."

9 He sent His sword into their presence that each should kill his neighbor, and they began to kill each other until they all fell by the sword and were destroyed from the earth.

10 And their fathers were witnesses of their destruction, and after this they were bound in the depths of the earth forever, until the day of the great condemnation, when judgment is executed on all those who have corrupted their ways and their works before the Lord.

11 He destroyed all wherever they were, and there was not one left of them whom He judged according to all their wickedness.

184

12 Through His work He made a new and righteous nature, so that they should not sin in their whole nature forever, but should be all righteous each in his own way always.

13 The judgment of all is ordained and written on the heavenly tablets in righteousness, even the judgment of all who depart from the path that is ordained for them to walk; and if they do not walk it, judgment is written down for every creature and for every kind.

14 There is nothing in heaven or on earth, or in light or in darkness, or in the abode of the dead or in the depth, or in the place of darkness that is not judged. All their judgments are ordained and written and engraved.

15 He will judge all, the great according to his greatness, and the small according to his smallness, and each according to his way.

16 He is not one who will regard the position of any person, nor is He one who will receive gifts, if He says that He will execute judgment on each.

17 If one gave everything that is on the earth, He will not regard the gifts or the person of any, nor accept anything at his hands, for He is a righteous judge.

18 Of the children of Israel it has been written and ordained, if they turn to him in righteousness He will forgive all their transgressions and pardon all their sins. It is written and ordained that He will show mercy to all who turn from all their guilt once each year.

19 And as for all those who corrupted their ways and their thoughts before the flood, no person was acceptable to God except Noah. His sons were saved in deference to him, and these God kept from the waters of the flood on his account; for Noah's heart was righteous in all his ways. He upheld the laws and did as God commanded him and he had not departed from anything that was ordained for him.

20 The Lord said that he would destroy everything on the earth, both men and cattle, and beasts, and birds of the air, and that which moves on the earth.

21 And He commanded Noah to make an ark, so that he might save himself from the waters of the flood.

22 And Noah made the ark in all respects as He commanded him, in the twenty-seventh jubilee of years, in the fifth week in the fifth year on the new moon of the first month.

23 He entered in the sixth year of it, in the second month, on the new moon of the second month, until the sixteenth; and he entered, and all that we brought to him, into the ark, and the Lord closed it from the outside on the seventeenth evening.

24 And the Lord opened seven floodgates of heaven, and He opened the mouths of the fountains of the great deep, seven mouths in number.

25 And the floodgates began to pour down water from the heaven forty days and forty closets, And the fountains of the deep also sent up waters, until the whole world was full of water.

26 The waters increased on the earth, by fifteen cubits (a cubit is about 18 inches) the waters rose above all the high mountains. And the ark was lift up from the earth. And it moved on the face of the waters.

27 And the water covered the face of the earth five months, which is one hundred and fifty days.

28 And the ark went and rested on the top of Lubar, one of the mountains of Ararat.

29 On the new moon in the fourth month the fountains of the great deep were closed and the floodgates of heaven were restrained; and on the new moon of the seventh month all the mouths of the bottomless gulfs of the earth were opened, and the water began to flow down into the deep below.

30 On the new moon of the tenth month the tops of the mountains were seen, and on the new moon of the first month the earth became visible.

31 The waters disappeared from the earth in the fifth week in the seventh year of it, and on the seventeenth day in the second month the earth was dry.

32 On the twenty-seventh of it he opened the ark, and sent out beasts, and cattle, and birds, and every moving thing.

[Chapter 6]

1 On the new moon of the third month he went out of the ark, and built an altar on that mountain.

2 And he made atonement for the earth, and took a kid and made atonement by its blood for all the guilt of the earth; for every thing that had been on it had been destroyed, except those that were in the ark with Noah.

3 He placed the fat of it on the altar, and he took an ox, and a goat, and a sheep and kids, and salt, and a turtle-dove, and the young of a dove, and placed a burnt sacrifice on the altar, and poured on it an offering mingled with oil, and sprinkled wine and sprinkled frankincense over everything, and caused a good and pleasing odor to arise, acceptable before the Lord.

4 And the Lord smelled the good and pleasing odor, and He made a covenant with Noah that there should not be any more floods to destroy the earth; that all the days of the earth seed-time and harvest should never cease; cold and heat, and summer and winter, and day and night should not change their order, nor cease forever.

5 "Increase and multiply on the earth, and become many, and be a blessing on it. I will inspire the fear of you and the dread of you in everything that is on earth and in the sea.

6 Look, I have given you all beasts, and all winged things, and everything that moves on the earth, and the fish in the waters, and all things for food; as the green herbs, I have given you all things to eat.

7 But you shall not eat anything live or with blood in it, for the life of all flesh is in the blood, or your blood of your lives will be required. At the hand of every man, at the hand of every beast will I require the blood of man.

8 Whoever sheds man's blood by man shall his blood be shed, for in the image of God He made man.

9 Increase, and multiply on the earth."

10 Noah and his sons swore that they would not eat any blood that was in any flesh, and he made a covenant before the Lord God forever throughout all the generations of the earth in this month.

11 Because of this He spoke to you that you should make a covenant with the children of Israel with an oath. In this month, on the mountain you should sprinkle blood on them because of all the words of the covenant, which the Lord made with them forever.

12 This testimony is written concerning you that you should observe it continually, so that you should not eat on any day any blood of beasts or birds or cattle during all the days of the earth, and the man who eats the blood of beast or of cattle or of birds during all the days of the earth, he and his offspring shall be rooted out of the land.

13 And you will command the children of Israel to eat no blood, so that their names and their offspring may be before the Lord our God continually.

14 There is no limit of days, for this law. It is forever. They shall observe it throughout their generations, so that they may continue supplicating on your behalf with blood before the altar; every day and at the time of morning and evening they shall seek forgiveness on your behalf perpetually before the Lord that they may keep it and not be rooted out.

15 And He gave to Noah and his sons a sign that there should not again be a flood on the earth.

16 He set His bow (a rainbow) in the cloud as a sign of the eternal covenant that there should never again be a flood on the earth to destroy it for all the days of the earth.

17 For this reason it is ordained and written on the heavenly tablets, that they should celebrate the feast of weeks in this month once a year, to renew the covenant every year.

18 This whole festival was celebrated in heaven from the day of creation until the days of Noah, which were twenty-six jubilees and five weeks of years. Noah and his sons observed it for seven jubilees and one week of years, until the day of Noah's death. From the day of Noah's death his sons did away with it until the days of Abraham, and they ate blood.

19 But Abraham observed it, and Isaac and Jacob and his children observed it up to your days, and in your days the children of Israel forgot it until you celebrated it anew on this mountain.

20 Command the children of Israel to observe this festival in all their generations for a commandment to them, one day in the year in this month they shall celebrate the festival.

21 For it is the feast of weeks and the feast of first-fruits, this feast is twofold and of a double nature, according to what is written and engraved concerning it, celebrate it.

22 For I have written in the book of the first law, in that which I have written for you, that you should celebrate it in its season, one day in the year, and I explained to you its sacrifices that the children of Israel should remember and should celebrate it throughout their generations in this month, the same day in every year.

23 On the new moon of the first month, and on the new moon of the fourth month, and on the new moon of the seventh month, and on the new moon of the tenth month are the days of remembrance, and the days of the seasons in the four divisions of the year. These are written and ordained as a testimony forever.

24 Noah ordained them for himself as feasts for the generations forever, so that they have become a memorial to him.

25 On the new moon of the first month he was told to make for himself an ark, and on that day the earth was dry and he saw from the opened ark, the earth. On the new moon of the fourth month the mouths of the depths of the bottomless pit beneath were closed.

26 On the new moon of the seventh month all the mouths of the abysses of the earth were opened, and the waters began to descend into them.

27 On the new moon of the tenth month the tops of the mountains were seen, and Noah was glad.

28 Because of this he ordained them for himself as feasts for a memorial forever, and thus are they ordained.

29 And they placed them on the heavenly tablets, each had thirteen weeks; from one to another passed their memorial, from the first to the second, and from the second to the third, and from the third to the fourth.

30 All the days of the commandment will be two and fifty weeks of days, and these will make the entire year complete. Thus it is engraved and ordained on the heavenly tablets.

31 And there is no neglecting this commandment for a single year or from year to year.

32 Command you the children of Israel that they observe the years according to this counting, three hundred and sixty-four days, and these will constitute a complete year, and they will not disturb its time from its days and from its feasts; for every thing will fall out in them according to their testimony, and they will not leave out any day nor disturb any feasts.

33 But if they neglect and do not observe them according to His commandment, then they will disturb all their seasons and the years will be dislodged from this order, and they will neglect their established rules.

34 And all the children of Israel will forget and will not find the path of the years, and will forget the new moons, and seasons, and sabbaths and they will wrongly determine all the order of the years.

35 For I know and from now on will I declare it to you, and it is not of my own devising; for the book lies written in the presence of me, and on the heavenly tablets the division of days is ordained, or they forget the feasts of the covenant and walk according to the feasts of the Gentiles after their error and after their ignorance.

36 For there will be those who will assuredly make observations of the moon and how it disturbs the seasons and comes in from year to year ten days too soon.

37 For this reason the years will come upon them when they disturb (misinterpret) the order, and make an abominable day the day of testimony, and an unclean day a feast day, and they will confound all the days, the holy with the unclean, and the unclean day with the holy; for they will go wrong as to the months and sabbaths and feasts and jubilees.

38 For this reason I command and testify to you that you may testify to them; for after your death your children will disturb them, so that they will not make the year three hundred and sixty-four days only, and for this reason they will go wrong as to the new moons and seasons and sabbaths and festivals, and they will eat all kinds of blood with all kinds of flesh.

[Chapter 7]

1 In the seventh week in the first year of it, in this jubilee, Noah planted vines on the mountain on which the ark had rested, named Lubar, one of the Ararat Mountains, and they produced fruit in the fourth year, and he guarded their fruit, and gathered it in that year in the seventh month.

2 He made wine from it and put it into a vessel, and kept it until the fifth year, until the first day, on the new moon of the first month.

3 And he celebrated with joy the day of this feast, and he made a burnt sacrifice to the Lord, one young ox and one ram, and seven sheep, each a year old, and a kid of the goats, that he might make atonement thereby for himself and his sons.

4 He prepared the kid first, and placed some of its blood on the flesh that was on the altar that he had made, and all the fat he laid on the altar where he made the burnt sacrifice, and the ox and the ram and the sheep, and he laid all their flesh on the altar.

5 He placed all their offerings mingled with oil on it, and afterwards he sprinkled wine on the fire which had previously been made on the altar, and he placed incense on the altar and caused a sweet odor to rise up which was acceptable before the Lord his God.

6 And he rejoiced and he and his children drank the wine with joy.

7 It was evening, and he went into his tent, and being drunken he lay down and slept, and was uncovered in his tent as he slept.

8 And Ham saw Noah his father naked, and went out and told his two brothers (ridiculed his father to his two brothers) who were outside.

9 Shem took his garment and arose, he and Japheth, and they placed the garment on their shoulders and went backward and covered the shame of their father, and their faces were backward.

10 Noah awoke from his sleep and knew all that his younger son had done to him, and he cursed his son and said, "Cursed be Canaan; an enslaved servant shall he be to his brothers."

11 And he blessed Shem, and said, "Blessed be the Lord God of Shem, and Canaan shall be his servant.

12 God shall enlarge Japheth, and God shall dwell in the dwelling of Shem, and Canaan shall be his servant."

13 Ham knew that his father had cursed, him, his younger son, and he was displeased that he had cursed him, his son. And Ham parted from his father, he and his sons with him, Cush and Mizraim and Put and Canaan.

14 And he built for himself a city and called its name after the name of his wife Ne'elatama'uk.

15 Japheth saw it, and became envious of his brother, and he too built for himself a city, and he called its name after the name of his wife Adataneses.

16 Shem dwelt with his father Noah, and he built a city close to his father on the mountain, and he too called its name after the name of his wife Sedeqetelebab.

17 These three cities are near Mount Lubar; Sedeqetelebab in front of the mountain on its east; and Na'eltama'uk on the south; Adatan'eses towards the west.

18 These are the sons of Shem, Elam, and Asshur, and Arpachshad who was born two years after the flood, and Lud, and Aram.

19 The sons of Japheth, Gomer, Magog, Madai , Javan, Tubal and Meshech and Tiras, these are the descendants of Noah.

20 In the twenty-eighth jubilee Noah began to direct his sons in the ordinances and commandments, and all the judgments that he knew, and he exhorted his sons to observe righteousness, and to cover the shame of their flesh, and to bless their Creator, and honor father and mother, and love their neighbor, and guard their souls from fornication and uncleanness and all iniquity.

21 Because of these three things came the flood on the earth, namely, the fornication that the Watchers committed against the law of their ordinances when they went whoring after the daughters of men, and took themselves wives of all they chose, and they made the beginning of uncleanness.

22 And they begat sons, the naphilim (Naphidim), and they were all dissimilar, and they devoured one another, and the Giants killed the Naphil, and the Naphil killed the Eljo, and the Eljo killed mankind, and one man killed one another.

23 Every one committed himself to crime and injustice and to shed much blood, and the earth was filled with sin.

24 After this they sinned against the beasts and birds, and all that moved and walked on the earth, and much blood was shed on the earth, and men continually desired only what was useless and evil.

25 And the Lord destroyed everything from the face of the earth. Because of the wickedness of their deeds, and because of the blood they had shed over all the earth, He destroyed everything. "

26 We were left, I and you, my sons, and everything that entered with us into the ark, and behold I see your works before me that you do not walk in righteousness, for in the path of destruction you have begun to walk, and you are turning one against another, and are envious one of another, and so it comes that you are not in harmony, my sons, each with his brother.

27 For I see the demons have begun their seductions against you and against your children and now I fear on your behalf, that after my death you will shed the blood of men on the earth, and that you, too, will be destroyed from the face of the earth.

28 For whoever sheds man's blood, and who ever eats the blood of any flesh, shall all be destroyed from the earth.

29 There shall be no man left that eats blood, or that sheds the blood of man on the earth, nor shall there be left to him any offspring or descendants living under heaven. Into the abode of the dead shall they go, and into the place of condemnation shall they descend, and into the darkness of the deep shall they all be removed by a violent death.

30 Do not smear blood on yourself or let it remain on you. Out of all the blood there shall be shed and out of all the days in which you have killed any beasts or cattle or whatever flies on the earth you must do a good work to your souls by covering that which has been shed on the face of the earth.

31 You shall not be like him who eats blood, but guard yourselves that none may eat blood before you, cover the blood, for thus have I been commanded to testify to you and your children, together with all flesh.

32 Do not permit the soul (life) to be eaten with the flesh, that your blood, which is your life, may not be required at the hand of any flesh that sheds it on the earth.

33 For the earth will not be clean from the blood that has been shed on it, for only through the blood of him that shed it will the earth be purified throughout all its generations.

34 Now, my children, listen, have judgment and righteousness that you maybe planted in righteousness over the face of the whole earth, and your glory lifted up in the presence of my God, who spared me from the waters of the flood.

35 Look, you will go and build for yourselves cities, and plant in them all the plants that are on the earth, and moreover all fruit-bearing trees.

36 For three years the fruit of everything that is eaten will not be gathered, and in the fourth year its fruit will be accounted holy, offered as first fruit, acceptable before the Most High God, who created heaven and earth and all things.

37 Let them offer in abundance the first of the wine and oil as first-fruits on the altar of the Lord, who receives it, and what is left let the servants of the house of the Lord eat before the altar which receives it.

38 In the fifth year make the release so that you release it in righteousness and uprightness, and you shall be righteous, and all that you plant shall prosper. For this is how Enoch did it, the father of your father commanded Methuselah, his son, and Methuselah commanded his son Lamech, and Lamech commanded me all the things that his fathers commanded him.

39 I also will give you commandment, my sons, as Enoch commanded his son in the first jubilees, while still living, the seventh in his generation, he commanded and testified to his son and to his son's sons until the day of his death.

[Chapter 8]

1 In the twenty-ninth jubilee, in the beginning of first week, Arpachshad took to himself a wife and her name was Rasu'eja, the daughter of Susan, the daughter of Elam, and she gave birth to a son in the third year in this week, and he called his name Kainam.

2 The son grew, and his father taught him writing, and he went to seek for himself a place where he might seize a city for himself.

3 He found writing which former generations had carved on a rock, and he read what was on it, and he transcribed it and sinned because of it, for it contained the teaching of the Watchers, which they had used to observe the omens of the sun and moon and stars in all the signs of heaven.

4 He wrote it down and said nothing of it, for he was afraid to speak to Noah about it or he would be angry with him because of it.

5 In the thirtieth jubilee, in the second week, in the first year of it, he took to himself a wife, and her name was Melka, the daughter of Madai, the son of Japheth, and in the fourth year he begat a son, and called his name Shelah; for he said, "Truly I have been sent."

6 Shelah grew up and took to himself a wife, and her name was Mu'ak, the daughter of Kesed, his father's brother, in the one and thirtieth jubilee, in the fifth week, in the first year of it.

7 And she gave birth to a son in the fifth year of it, and he called his name Eber, and he took to himself a wife, and her name was Azurad, the daughter of Nebrod, in the thirty-second jubilee, in the seventh week, in the third year of it.

8 In the sixth year of it, she gave birth to a son, and he called his name Peleg, for in the days when he was born the children of Noah began to divide the earth among themselves, for this reason he called his name Peleg.

9 They divided it secretly among themselves, and told it to Noah.

10 In the beginning of the thirty-third jubilee they divided the earth into three parts, for Shem and Ham and Japheth, according to the inheritance of each, in the first year in the first week, when one of us (angels) who had been sent, was with them.

11 He called his sons, and they drew close to him, they and their children, and he divided the earth into the lots, which his three sons were to take in possession, and they reached out their hands, and took the writing out of the arms of Noah, their father.

12 There came out on the writing as Shem's lot the middle of the earth that he should take as an inheritance for himself and for his sons for the generations of eternity. From the middle of the mountain range of Rafa, from the mouth of the water from the river Tina, and his portion goes towards the west through the middle of this river, and it extends until it reaches the water of the abysses, out of which this river goes out and pours its waters into the sea Me'at, and this river flows into the great sea.

13 All that is towards the north is Japheth's, and all that is towards the south belongs to Shem. And it extends until it reaches Karaso, this is in the center of the tongue of land that looks towards the south.

14 His portion extends along the great sea, and it extends in a straight line until it reaches the west of the tongue that looks towards the south, for this sea is named the tongue of the Egyptian Sea.

15 And it turns from here towards the south towards the mouth of the great sea on the shore of its waters, and it extends to the west to Afra, and it extends until it reaches the waters of the river Gihon, and to the south of the waters of Gihon, to the banks of this river.

16 It extends towards the east, until it reaches the Garden of Eden, to the south of it and from the east of the whole land of Eden and of the whole east, it turns to the east and proceeds until it reaches the east of the mountain named Rafa, and it descends to the bank of the mouth of the river Tina.

17 This portion came out by lot for Shem and his sons, that they should possess it forever to his generations forever.

18 Noah rejoiced that this portion came out for Shem and for his sons, and he remembered all that he had spoken with his mouth in prophecy; for he had said, "Blessed be the Lord God of Shem and may the Lord dwell in the dwelling of Shem."

19 He knew that the Garden of Eden is the holy of holies, and the dwelling of the Lord, and Mount Sinai the center of the desert, and Mount Zion which is the center of the navel of the earth, these three were created as holy places facing each other.

20 And he blessed the God of gods, who had put the word of the Lord into his mouth, and the Lord forever.

21 And he knew that a blessed portion and a blessing had come to Shem and his sons and to their generations forever which was the whole land of Eden and the whole land of the Red Sea, and the whole land of the east and India, and on the Red Sea and the mountains of it, and all the land of Bashan, and all the land of Lebanon and the islands of Kaftur, and all the mountains of Sanir and Amana, and the mountains of Asshur in the north, and all the land of Elam, Asshur, and Babel, and Susan and Ma'edai, and all the mountains of Ararat, and all the region beyond the sea, which is beyond the mountains of Asshur towards the north, a blessed and spacious land, and all that is in it is very good.

22 Ham received the second portion, beyond the Gihon towards the south to the right of the Garden, and it extends towards the south and it extends to all the mountains of fire, and it extends towards the west to the sea of 'atel and it extends towards the west until it reaches the sea of Ma'uk which was that sea into which everything that is not destroyed descends.

23 It goes out towards the north to the limits of Gadir, and it goes out to the coast of the waters of the sea to the waters of the great sea until it draws near to the river Gihon, and goes along the river Gihon until it reaches the right of the Garden of Eden.

24 This is the land that came out for Ham as the portion which he was to occupy forever for himself and his sons to their generations forever.

25 Japheth received the third portion beyond the river Tina to the north of the outflow of its waters, and it extends north-easterly to the whole region of Gog, and to all the country east of it.

26 It extends northerly, and it extends to the mountains of Qelt towards the north, and towards the sea of Ma'uk, and it goes out to the east of Gadir as far as the region of the waters of the sea.

27 It extends until it approaches the west of Fara and it returns towards Aferag, and it extends easterly to the waters of the sea of Me'at.

28 It extends to the region of the river Tina in a northeasterly direction until it approaches the boundary of its waters towards the mountain Rafa, and it turns round towards the north.

29 This is the land that came out for Japheth and his sons as the portion of his inheritance that he should possess five great islands, and a great land in the north, for himself and his sons, for their generations forever.

30 But it is cold, and the land of Ham is hot, and the land of Shem is neither hot nor cold, but it is of blended cold and heat.

[Chapter 9]

1 Ham divided among his sons, and the first portion came out for Cush towards the east, and to the west of him for Mizraim, and to the west of him for Put, and to the west of him on the sea for Canaan.

2 Shem also divided among his sons, and the first portion came out for Elam and his sons, to the east of the river Tigris until it approaches the east, the whole land of India, and on the Red Sea on its coast, and the waters of Dedan, and all the mountains of Mebri and Ela, and all the land of Susan and all that is on the side of Pharnak to the Red Sea and the river Tina.

3 Asshur received the second Portion, all the land of Asshur and Nineveh and Shinar and to the border of India, and it ascends and skirts the river.

4 Arpachshad received the third portion, all the land of the region of the Chaldees to the east of the Euphrates, bordering on the Red Sea, and all the waters of the desert close to the tongue of the sea which looks towards Egypt, all the land of Lebanon and Sanir and Amana to the border of the Euphrates.

5 Aram received the fourth portion, all the land of Mesopotamia between the Tigris and the Euphrates to the north of the Chaldees to the border of the mountains of Asshur and the land of Arara.

6 Lud got the fifth portion, the mountains of Asshur and all surrounding to them until it reaches the Great Sea, and until it reaches the east of Asshur his brother.

7 Japheth also divided the land of his inheritance among his sons.

8 The first portion came out for Gomer to the east from the north side to the river Tina, and in the north there came out for Magog all the inner portions of the north until it reaches to the sea of Me'at.

9 Madai received as his portion that he should possess from the west of his two brothers to the islands, and to the coasts of the islands.

10 Javan got the fourth portion, every island and the islands that are towards the border of Lud.

11 For Tubal there came out the fifth portion in the middle of the tongue that approaches towards the border of the portion of Lud to the second tongue, to the region beyond the second tongue to the third tongue.

12 Meshech received the sixth portion, that is the entire region beyond the third tongue until it approaches the east of Gadir.

13 Tiras got the seventh portion, four great islands in the middle of the sea, which reach to the portion of Ham, and the islands of Kamaturi came out by lot for the sons of Arpachshad as his inheritance.

14 Thus the sons of Noah divided to their sons in the presence of Noah their father, and he bound them all by an oath, and invoked a curse on every one that sought to seize any portion which had not fallen to him by his lot.

15 They all said, 'so be it; so be it " (amen and amen) for themselves and their sons forever throughout their generations until the day of judgment, on which the Lord God shall judge them with a sword and with fire for all the unclean wickedness of their errors, that they have filled the earth with, which are transgression, uncleanness and fornication and sin.

[Chapter 10]

1 In the third week of this jubilee the unclean demons began to lead astray the children of the sons of Noah, and to make them sin and to destroy them.

2 The sons of Noah came to Noah their father, and they told him about the demons that were leading astray and blinding and slaying his sons' sons.

3 And he prayed before the Lord his God, and said,
"God of the spirits of all flesh, who have shown mercy to me and have spared me and my sons from the waters of the flood, and have not caused me to die as You did the sons of perdition; For Your grace has been great toward me, and great has been Your mercy to my soul. Let Your grace be lifted up on my sons, and do not let the wicked spirits rule over them or they will destroy them from the earth.

4 But bless me and my sons, so that we may increase and multiply and replenish the earth.

5 You know how Your Watchers, the fathers of these spirits, acted in my day, and as for these spirits which are living, imprison them and hold them fast in the place of condemnation, and let them not bring destruction on the sons of your servant, my God; for these are like cancer and are created in order to destroy.

6 Let them not rule over the spirits of the living; for You alone can exercise dominion over them. And let them not have power over the sons of the righteous from now and forever."

7 And the Lord our God commanded us (angels) to bind all of them.

8 The chief of the spirits, Mastema, came and said, "Lord, Creator, let some of them remain before me, and let them listen to my voice, and do all that I shall say to them; for if some of them are not left to me, I shall not be able to execute the power of my will on the sons of men, for these are for corruption and leading astray before my judgment, for great is the wickedness of the sons of men."

9 He said, "Let one-tenth of them remain before him, and let nine-tenths of them descend into the place of condemnation."

10 He commanded one of us to teach Noah all their medicines, for He knew that they would not walk in uprightness, nor strive in righteousness.

11 We did according to all His words, all the malignant evil ones we bound in the place of condemnation and a tenth part of them we left that they might be subject in the presence of Satan on the earth.

12 We explained to Noah all the medicines of their diseases, together with their seductions, how he might heal them with herbs of the earth.

13 Noah wrote down all things in a book as we instructed him concerning every kind of medicine. Thus the evil spirits were precluded from hurting the sons of Noah.

14 He gave all that he had written to Shem, his eldest son, for he loved him greatly above all his sons.

15 And Noah slept with his fathers, and was buried on Mount Lubar in the land of Ararat.

16 Nine hundred and fifty years he completed in his life, nineteen jubilees and two weeks and five years.

17 In his life on earth he was greater than all the children of men except Enoch because of his righteousness he was perfect. For Enoch's office was ordained for a testimony to the generations of the world, so that he should recount all the deeds of generation to generation, until the day of judgment.

18 In the three and thirtieth jubilee, in the first year in the second week, Peleg took to himself a wife, whose name was Lomna the daughter of Sina'ar, and she gave birth to a son for him in the fourth year of this week, and he called his name Reu, for he said, "Look the children of men have become evil because the building a city and a tower in the land of Shinar was for an evil purpose."

19 For they departed from the land of Ararat eastward to Shinar, for in his days they built the city and the tower, saying, "Go to, let us rise up thereby into heaven."

20 They began to build, and in the fourth week they made brick with fire, and the bricks served them for stone, and the clay with which they cemented them together was asphalt which comes out of the sea, and out of the fountains of water in the land of Shinar.

21 They built it, forty-three years were they building it. Its breadth was 203 bricks, and the height of a brick was the third of one; its height amounted to 5433 cubits and 2 palms, and the extent of one wall was thirteen times 600 feet and of the other thirty times 600 feet.

22 And the Lord our God said to us, "Look, they are one people, and they begin to do this, and now nothing will be withheld from them. Let us go down and confound their language, that they may not understand one another's speech, and they may be dispersed into cities and nations, and they will not be in agreement together with one purpose until the day of judgment."

23 And the Lord descended, and we descended with him to see the city and the tower that the children of men had built.

24 He confounded their language, and they no longer understood one another's speech, and they then ceased to build the city and the tower.

25 For this reason the whole land of Shinar is called Babel, because the Lord confounded all the language of the children of men there, and from that place they were dispersed into their cities, each according to his language and his nation.

26 Then, the Lord sent a mighty wind against the tower and it fell to the earth, and behold it was between Asshur and Babylon in the land of Shinar, and they called its name "Overthrow."

27 In the fourth week in the first year in the beginning of it in the four and thirtieth jubilee, were they dispersed from the land of Shinar.

28 Ham and his sons went into the land that he was to occupy, which he acquired as his portion in the land of the south.

29 Canaan saw the land of Lebanon to the river of Egypt was very good, and he did not go into the land of his inheritance to the west that is to the sea, and he dwelt in the land of Lebanon, eastward and westward from the border of Jordan and from the border of the sea.

30 Ham, his father, and Cush and Mizraim, his brothers, said to him, "You have settled in a land which is not yours, and which did not fall to us by lot, do not do so. If you do you and your sons will be conquered in the land and be accursed through a war. By war you have settled, and by war will your children fall, and you will be rooted out forever.

31 Do not live in the land of Shem, for to Shem and to his sons did it come by their lot.

32 Cursed are you, and cursed will you be beyond all the sons of Noah, by the curse by which we bound ourselves by an oath in the presence of the holy judge, and in the presence of Noah our father."

33 But he did not listen to them, and settled in the land of Lebanon from Hamath to the border of Egypt, he and his sons until this day. For this reason that land is named Canaan. And Japheth and his sons went towards the sea and settled in the land of their portion, and Madai saw the land of the sea and it did not please him, and he begged Ham and Asshur and Arpachshad, his wife's brother for a portion, and he dwelt in the land of Media, near to his wife's brother until this day.

34 And he called his and his son's dwelling-place, Media, after the name of their father Madai.

[Chapter 11]

1 In the thirty-fifth jubilee, in the third week, in the first year of it, Reu took to himself a wife, and her name was 'Ora, the daughter of 'Ur, the son of Kesed, and she gave birth to a son, and he called his name Seroh, in the seventh year of this week in this jubilee.

2 The sons of Noah began to war with each other, to take captives and kill each other, and to shed the blood of men on the earth, and to eat blood, and to build strong cities, and walls, and towers, and individuals began to exalt themselves above the nation, and to establish kingdoms, and to go to war, people against people, and nation against nation, and city against city, and all began to do evil, and to acquire arms, and to teach their sons war, and they began to capture cities, and to sell male and female slaves.

3 Ur, the son of Kesed, built the city of Ara of the Chaldees, and called its name after his own name and the name of his father.

4 And they made themselves molten images, and they worshipped the idols and the molten image they had made for themselves, and they began to make graven images and unclean and shadowy presence, and malevolent and malicious spirits assisted and seduced them into committing transgression and uncleanness.

5 Prince Mastema exerted himself to do all this, and he sent out other spirits, which were put under his control, to do all manner of wrong and sin, and all manner of transgression, to corrupt and destroy, and to shed blood on the earth.

6 For this reason he called the name of Seroh, Serug, for every one turned to do all manner of sin and transgression.

7 He grew up, and dwelt in Ur of the Chaldees, near to the father of his wife's mother, and he worshipped idols, and he took to himself a wife in the thirty-sixth jubilee, in the fifth week, in the first year of it, and her name was Melka, the daughter of Kaber, the daughter of his father's brother.

8 She gave birth to Nahor, in the first year of this week, and he grew and dwelt in Ur of the Chaldees, and his father taught him the sciences of the Chaldees to divine and conjure, according to the signs of heaven.

9 In the thirty-seventh jubilee in the sixth week, in the first year of it, he took to himself a wife, and her name was 'Ijaska, the daughter of Nestag of the Chaldees.

10 And she gave birth to Terah in the seventh year of this week.

11 Prince Mastema sent ravens and birds to devour the seed that was sown in the land, in order to destroy the land, and rob the children of men of their labors. Before they could plow in the seed, the ravens picked it from the surface of the ground.

12 This is why he called his name Terah because the ravens and the birds reduced them to destitution and devoured their seed.

13 The years began to be barren, because of the birds, and they devoured all the fruit of the trees from the trees, it was only with great effort that they could harvest a little fruit from the earth in their days.

14 In this thirty-ninth jubilee, in the second week in the first year, Terah took to himself a wife, and her name was 'Edna, the daughter of Abram, the daughter of his father's sister.

15 In the seventh year of this week she gave birth to a son, and he called his name Abram, by the name of the father of his mother, for he had died before his daughter had conceived a son.

16 And the child began to understand the errors of the earth that all went astray after graven images and after uncleanness, and his father taught him writing, and he was two weeks of years old, and he separated himself from his father, that he might not worship idols with him.

17 He began to pray to the Creator of all things that He might spare him from the errors of the children of men, and that his portion should not fall into error after uncleanness and vileness.

18 The time came for the sowing of seed in the land, and they all went out together to protect their seed against the ravens, and Abram went out with those that went, and the child was a lad of fourteen years.

19 A cloud of ravens came to devour the seed, and Abram ran to meet them before they settled on the ground, and cried to them before they settled on the ground to devour the seed, and said, "Descend not, return to the place from where you came," and they began to turn back.

20 And he caused the clouds of ravens to turn back that day seventy times, and of all the ravens throughout all the land where Abram was there settled not so much as one.

21 All who were with him throughout all the land saw him cry out, and all the ravens turn back, and his name became great in all the land of the Chaldees.

22 There came to him this year all those that wished to sow, and he went with them until the time of sowing ceased, and they sowed their land, and that year they brought enough grain home to eat and they were satisfied.

23 In the first year of the fifth week Abram taught those who made implements for oxen, the artificers in wood, and they made a vessel above the ground, facing the frame of the plow, in order to put the seed in it, and the seed fell down from it on the share of the plow, and was hidden in the earth, and they no longer feared the ravens.

24 After this manner they made vessels above the ground on all the frames of the plows, and they sowed and tilled all the land, according as Abram commanded them, and they no longer feared the birds.

[Chapter 12]

1 In the sixth week, in the seventh year of it, that Abram said to Terah his father, saying, "Father!"

2 He said, "Look, here am I, my son." He said, "What help and profit have we from those idols which you worship, and in the presence of which you bow yourself?

3 For there is no spirit in them. They are dumb forms, and they mislead the heart.

4 Do not worship them, Worship the God of heaven, who causes the rain and the dew to fall on the earth and does everything on the earth, and has created everything by His word, and all life is from His presence.

5 Why do you worship things that have no spirit in them?

For they are the work of men's hands, and you bear them on your shoulders, and you have no help from them, but they are a great cause of shame to those who make them, and they mislead the heart of those who worship them. Do not worship them."

6 His father said to him, "I also know it, my son, but what shall I do with a people who have made me serve them?

7 If I tell them the truth, they will kill me, because their soul clings to them so they worship them and honor them.

8 Keep silent, my son, or they will kill you." And these words he spoke to his two brothers, and they were angry with him and he kept silent.

9 In the fortieth jubilee, in the second week, in the seventh year of it, Abram took to himself a wife, and her name was Sarai, the daughter of his father, and she became his wife.

10 Haran, his brother, took to himself a wife in the third year of the third week, and she gave birth to a son in the seventh year of this week, and he called his name Lot.

11 Nahor, his brother, took to himself a wife.

12 In the sixtieth year of the life of Abram, that is, in the fourth week, in the fourth year of it, Abram arose in the night and burned the house of the idols, and he burned all that was in the house and no man knew it.

13 And they arose and sought to save their gods from the fire.

14 Haran hasted to save them, but the fire flamed over him, and he was burnt in the fire, and he died in Ur of the Chaldees before Terah his father, and they buried him in Ur of the Chaldees.

15 Terah went out from Ur of the Chaldees, he and his sons, to go into the land of Lebanon and into the land of Canaan, and he dwelt in the land of Haran, and Abram dwelt with Terah his father in Haran two weeks of years.

16 In the sixth week, in the fifth year of it, Abram sat up all night on the new moon of the seventh month to observe the stars from the evening to the morning, in order to see what would be the character of the year with regard to the rains, and he was alone as he sat and observed.

17 And a word came into his heart and he said, "All the signs of the stars, and the signs of the moon and of the sun are all in the hand of the Lord. Why do I search them out?

18 If He desires, He causes it to rain, morning and evening, and if He desires, He withholds it, and all things are in his hand."

19 He prayed in the night and said, "My God, God Most High, You alone are my God, and You and Your dominion have I chosen. And You have created all things, and all things that are the work of Your hands.

20 Deliver me from the hands of evil spirits who have dominion over the thoughts of men's hearts, and let them not lead me astray from You, my God. And establish me and my offspring forever so that we do not go astray from now and forever."

21 He said, "Shall I return to Ur of the Chaldees who are trying to find me? Should I return to them? Am I to remain here in this place? The right path is before You. Make it prosper in the hands of your servant that he may fulfill it and that I may not walk in the deceitfulness of my heart, O my God."

22 He stopped speaking and stopped praying, and then the word of the Lord was sent to him through me, saying, "Get out of your country, and from your kindred and from the house of your father and go to a land which I will show you, and I shall make you a great and numerous nation.

23 And I will bless you and I will make your name great,

and you will be blessed in the earth, and in You shall all families of the earth be blessed, and I will bless them that bless you, and curse them that curse you.

24 I will be a God to you and your son, and to your son's son, and to all your offspring, fear not, from now on and to all generations of the earth I am your God."

25 The Lord God said, "Open his mouth and his ears, that he may hear and speak with his mouth, with the language which has been revealed," for it had ceased from the mouths of all the children of men from the day of the overthrow of Babel.

26 And I opened his mouth, and his ears and his lips, and I began to speak with him in Hebrew in the tongue of the creation.

27 He took the books of his fathers, and these were written in Hebrew, and he transcribed them, and he began from then on to study them, and I made known to him that which he could not understand, and he studied them during the six rainy months.

28 In the seventh year of the sixth week he spoke to his father and informed him, that he would leave Haran to go into the land of Canaan to see it and return to him.

29 Terah his father said to him; "Go in peace. May the eternal God make your path straight. And the Lord be with you, and protect you from all evil, and grant to you grace, mercy and favor before those who see you, and may none of the children of men have power over you to harm you. Go in peace.

30 If you see a land pleasant to your eyes to dwell in, then arise and take me with you and take Lot with you, the son of Haran your brother as your own son, the Lord be with you.

31 Nahor your brother leave with me until you return in peace, and we go with you all together."

[Chapter 13]

1 Abram journeyed from Haran, and he took Sarai, his wife, and Lot, his brother Haran's son and they went to the land of Canaan, and he came into Asshur, and proceeded to Shechem, and dwelt near a tall oak.

2 He saw the land was very pleasant from the border of Hamath to the tall oak.

3 The Lord said to him, "To you and to your offspring I will give this land."

4 He built an altar there, and he offered on it a burnt sacrifice to the Lord, who had appeared to him.

5 He left from that place and went to the mountain Bethel on the west and Ai on the east, and pitched his tent there.

6 He saw the land was very wide and good, and everything grew on it, vines, and figs, and pomegranates, oaks, and ilexes, and turpentine and oil trees, and cedars and cypresses, and date trees, and all trees of the field, and there was water on the mountains.

7 And he blessed the Lord who had led him out of Ur of the Chaldees, and had brought him to this land.

8 In the first year, in the seventh week, on the new moon of the first month, he built an altar on this mountain, and called on the name of the Lord and said, "You, the eternal God, are my God."

9 He offered on the altar a burnt sacrifice to the Lord that He should be with him and not forsake him all the days of his life.

10 He left that place and went toward the south, and he came to Hebron and Hebron was built at that time, and he lived there two years, and he went from that place into the land of the south, to Bealoth, and there was a famine in the land.

11Abram went into Egypt in the third year of the week, and he dwelt in Egypt five years before his wife was torn away from him.

12 Now, Tanais in Egypt was built seven years after Hebron.

13 When Pharaoh seized Sarai, the wife of Abram the Lord plagued Pharaoh and his house with great plagues because of Sarai, Abram's wife.

14 Abram was celebrated and admired because of his great possessions of sheep, and cattle, and donkeys, and horses, and camels, and menservants, and maidservants, and in silver and gold. Lot and his brother's son were also wealthy.

15 Pharaoh gave back Sarai, the wife of Abram, and he sent him out of the land of Egypt, and he journeyed to the place where he had pitched his tent at the beginning, to the place of the altar, with Ai on the east, and Bethel on the west, and he blessed the Lord his God who had brought him back in peace.

16 In the forty-first jubilee in the third year of the first week, that he returned to this place and offered on it a burnt sacrifice, and called on the name of the Lord, and said, "You, the most high God, are my God forever and ever."

17 In the fourth year of this week Lot parted from him, and Lot lived in Sodom, and the men of Sodom sinned greatly.

18 It grieved him in his heart that his brother's son had parted from him because Abram had no children.

19 After Lot had parted from him, in the fourth year of this week. In that year when Lot was taken captive, the Lord said to Abram, "Lift up your eyes from the place where you are dwelling, northward and southward, and westward and eastward.

20 All the land that you see I will give to you and to your offspring forever, and I will make your offspring as the sand of the sea, though a man may number the dust of the earth, yet your offspring shall not be numbered.

21 Arise, walk through the land in the length of it and the breadth of it, and see it all. To your offspring will I give it." And Abram went to Hebron, and lived there.

22 And in this year came Chedorlaomer, king of Elam, and Amraphel, king of Shinar, and Arioch king of Sellasar, and Tergal, king of nations, and killed the king of Gomorrah, and the king of Sodom fled, and many fell through wounds in the valley of Siddim, by the Salt Sea.

23 They took captive Sodom and Adam and Zeboim, and they took Lot captive, the son of Abram's brother, and all his possessions, and they went to Dan.

24 One who had escaped came and told Abram that his brother's son had been taken captive.

25 And Abram equipped his household servants for Abram, and for his offspring, a tenth of the first-fruits to the Lord, and the Lord ordained it as a law forever that they should give it to the priests who served before Him, that they should possess it forever.

26 There is no limit of days to this law, for He has ordained it for the generations forever that they should give to the Lord the tenth of everything, of the seed and of the wine and of the oil and of the cattle and of the sheep.

27 He gave it to His priests to eat and to drink with joy before Him.

28 The king of Sodom came and bowed down to him, and said, "Our Lord Abram, give to us the souls which you have rescued, but let the booty be yours."

29 And Abram said to him, "I lift up my hands to the Most High God, that from a thread to a shoe-latchet I shall not take anything that is yours so that you could never say, I have made Abram rich, except only what the young men, Aner and Eschol, and Mamre have eaten, and the portion of the men who went with me. These shall take their portion."

[Chapter 14]

1 After these things, in the fourth year of this week, on the new moon of the third month, the word of the Lord came to Abram
in a dream, saying, "Fear not, Abram, I am your defender, and your reward will be very great."
2 He said, "Lord, Lord, what will you give me, seeing I go from here childless, and the son of Maseq, the son of my handmaid, Eliezer of Damascus, he will be my heir, and to me you have given no offspring."
3 He said to him, "This man will not be your heir, but one that will come out of your own bowels. He will be your heir."
4 And He brought him out abroad, and said to him, "Look toward heaven and number the stars if you are able to number them."
5 He looked toward heaven, and beheld the stars. And He said to him, "so shall your offspring be."
6 And he believed in the Lord, and it was counted to him as righteousness.
7 God said to him, "I am the Lord that brought you out of Ur of the Chaldees, to give you the land of the Canaanites to possess it forever, and I will be God to you and to your offspring after you."
8 He said, "Lord, Lord, how shall I know that I shall inherit it?"
9 God said to him, "Take Me a heifer of three years, and a goat of three years, and a sheep of three years, and a turtle-dove, and a pigeon."
10 And he took all these in the middle of the month and he dwelt at the oak of Mamre, which is near Hebron.
11 He built an altar there, and sacrificed all these. He poured their blood on the altar, and divided them in half, and laid them over against each other, but the birds he did not divide.
12 Birds came down on the pieces, and Abram drove them away, and did not permit the birds to touch them.
13 It happened, when the sun had set, that an ecstasy fell on Abram, and such a horror of great darkness fell on him, and it was said to Abram, "Know of a surety that your offspring shall be a stranger in a land that is not theirs, and they shall be brought into bondage, and afflicted for four hundred years.
14 The nation also to whom they will be in bondage will I judge, and after that they shall come out from that place with many possessions.
15 You will go to your fathers in peace, and be buried in a good old age.
16 But in the fourth generation they shall return here, for the iniquity of the Amorites is not yet full."
17 And he awoke from his sleep, and he arose, and the sun had set; and there was a flame, and a furnace was smoking, and a flame of fire passed between the pieces.
18 On that day the Lord made a covenant with Abram, saying, "To your offspring will I give this land, from the river of Egypt to the great river, the river Euphrates, the Kenites, the Kenizzites, the Kadmonites, the Perizzites, and the Rephaim, the Phakorites, and the Hivites, and the Amorites, and the Canaanites, and the Girgashites, and the Jebusites.
19 The day passed, and Abram offered the pieces, and the birds, and their fruit offerings, and their drink offerings, and the fire devoured them.
20 On that day we made a covenant with Abram, in the same way we had covenanted with Noah in this month; and Abram renewed the festival and laws for himself forever.
21 Abram rejoiced, and made all these things known to Sarai his wife. He believed that he would have offspring, but she did not bear.
22 Sarai advised her husband Abram, and said to him, "Go in to Hagar, my Egyptian maid, it may be that I shall build up offspring to you by her."
23 Abram listened to the voice of Sarai his wife, and said to her, "Do so." And Sarai took Hagar, her maid, the Egyptian, and gave her to Abram, her husband, to be his wife.
24 He went in to her, and she conceived and gave birth to a son, and he called his name Ishmael, in the fifth year of this week; and this was the eighty-sixth year in the life of Abram.

[Chapter 15]

1 In the fifth year of the fourth week of this jubilee, in the third month, in the middle of the month, Abram celebrated the feast of the first-fruits of the grain harvest.
2 And he made new offerings on the altar, the first-fruits of the produce to the Lord, a heifer, and a goat, and a sheep on the altar as a burnt sacrifice to the Lord; their fruit offerings and their drink offerings he offered on the altar with frankincense.
3 The Lord appeared to Abram, and said to him, "I am God Almighty. Examine yourself and demonstrate yourself before me and be perfect.
4 I will make My covenant between Me and you, and I will multiply you greatly."
5 Abram fell on his face, and God talked with him, and said, "My law is with you, and you will be the father of many nations.
6 Neither shall your name any more be called Abram, but your name from now on, even forever, shall be Abraham.
7 For I have made you the father of many nations.

8 I will make you very great, and I will make you into nations, and kings shall come forth from you.

9 I shall establish My covenant between Me and you, and your offspring after you, throughout their generations, for an eternal covenant, so that I may be a God to you, and to your offspring after you.

10 You may possess the land where you have been a sojourner, the land of Canaan, and you will possess it forever, and I will be their God."

11 The Lord said to Abraham, "Keep my covenant, you and your offspring after you, and circumcise every male among you, and circumcise your foreskins, and it shall be a token of an eternal covenant between Me and you.

12 And the eighth day you shall circumcise the child, every male throughout your generations, him that is born in the house, or whom you have bought with money from any stranger, whom you have acquired who is not of your offspring.

13 He that is born in your house shall surely be circumcised, and those whom you have bought with money shall be circumcised, and My covenant shall be in your flesh for an eternal ordinance.

14 The uncircumcised male who is not circumcised in the flesh of his foreskin on the eighth day, that soul shall be cut off from his people, for he has broken My covenant."

15 God said to Abraham, "As for Sarai your wife, her name shall no more be called Sarai, but Sarah shall be her name.

16 I will bless her, and give you a son by her, and I will bless him, and he shall become a nation, and kings of nations shall proceed from him."

17 Abraham fell on his face, and rejoiced, and said in his heart, "Shall a son be born to him that is a hundred years old, and shall Sarah, who is ninety years old, bring forth?"

18 Abraham said to God, "Oh, that Ishmael might live before you!"

19 God said, "Yea, and Sarah also shall bear you a son, and you will call his name Isaac, and I will establish My covenant with him, an everlasting covenant, and for his offspring after him.

20 And as for Ishmael also have I heard you, and behold I will bless him, and make him great, and multiply him greatly, and he shall beget twelve princes, and I will make him a great nation.

21 But My covenant will I establish with Isaac, whom Sarah shall bear to you this time next year."

22 God ceased speaking with him, and God went up from Abraham.

23 Abraham did according as God had said to him, and he took Ishmael his son, and all that were born in his house, and whom he had bought with his money, every male in his house, and circumcised the flesh of their foreskin.

24 On that same day was Abraham circumcised, and all the men of his house, and all those whom he had bought with money from the children of the stranger were circumcised with him.

25 This law is for all the generations forever, and there is no variance of days, and no omission of one day out of the eight days, for it is an eternal law, ordained and written on the heavenly tablets.

26 Every one that is born, the flesh of whose foreskin is not circumcised on the eighth day, does not belong to the children of the covenant which the Lord made with Abraham, but instead they belong to the children of destruction; nor is there any other sign on him that he is the Lord's, but he is destined to be destroyed and killed from the earth, and to be rooted out of the earth, for he has broken the covenant of the Lord our God.

27 All the angels of the presence (of the Lord) and all the angels of sanctification have been created already circumcised from the day of their creation, and before the angels of the presence (of the Lord) and the angels of sanctification He has sanctified Israel, that they should be with Him and with His holy angels.

28 Command the children of Israel and let them observe the sign of this covenant for their generations as an eternal law, and they will not be rooted out of the land.

29 For the command is ordained for a covenant, that they should observe it forever among all the children of Israel.

30 For Ishmael and his sons and his brothers, and Esau, the Lord did not cause them to come to Him, and he did not choose them. Although they are the children of Abraham, He knew them, but He chose Israel to be His people.

31 He sanctified them, and gathered them from among all the children of men; for there are many nations and many peoples, and all are His, and over all nations He has placed spirits in authority to lead them astray from Him.

32 But over Israel He did not appoint any angel or spirit, for He alone is their ruler, and He will preserve them and require them at the hand of His angels and His spirits, and at the hand of all His powers in order that He may preserve them and bless them, that they may be His and He may be theirs from now on forever.

33 I announce to you that the children of Israel will not keep true to this law, and they will not circumcise their sons according to all this law; for in the flesh of their circumcision they will omit this circumcision of their sons, and all of the sons of Beliar will leave their sons uncircumcised as they were born.

34 There will be great wrath from the Lord against the children of Israel because they have forsaken His covenant and turned aside from His word, and provoked (God) and blasphemed, because they do not observe the ordinance of this law; for they have treated their genitalia like the Gentiles, so that they may be removed and rooted out of the land. And there will no more be pardon or forgiveness to them for all the sin of this eternal error.

[Chapter 16]

1 On the new moon of the fourth month we appeared to Abraham, at the oak of Mamre, and we talked with him, and we announced to him that Sarah, his wife, would give him a son.

2 And Sarah laughed, for she heard that we had spoken these words to Abraham. We warned her, and she became afraid, and denied that she had laughed because of the words.

3 We told her the name of her son, as his name is ordained and written in the heavenly tablets and it is Isaac.

4 We told her that when we returned to her at a set time, she would have conceived a son.

5 In this month the Lord executed his judgments on Sodom, and Gomorrah, and Zeboim, and all the region of the Jordan, and He burned them with fire and brimstone, and destroyed them and they are destroyed until this day, because of all their works. They are wicked and vast sinners, and they defile themselves and commit fornication in their flesh, and work uncleanness on the earth as I have told you.

6 In like manner, God will execute judgment on the places where they have done similar to the uncleanness of the Sodomites, and they will suffer a judgment like that of Sodom.

7 But for Lot, we made an exception, for God remembered Abraham, and sent him out from the place of the overthrow.

8 And he and his daughters committed sin on the earth, such as had not been on the earth since the days of Adam until his time, for the man had sex with his daughters.

9 It was commanded and engraved concerning all his offspring, on the heavenly tablets, to remove them and root them out, and to execute judgment on them like the judgment of Sodom, and to leave no offspring of that man on earth on the day of condemnation.

10 In this month Abraham moved from Hebron, and departed and lived between Kadesh and Shur in the mountains of Gerar.

11 In the middle of the fifth month he moved from that place, and lived at the Well of the Oath.

12 In the middle of the sixth month the Lord visited Sarah and did to her as He had spoken and she conceived.

13 And she gave birth to a son in the third month. In the middle of the month, at the time of which the Lord had spoken to Abraham, on the festival of the first-fruits of the harvest, Isaac was born.

14 Abraham circumcised his son on the eighth day, he was the first that was circumcised according to the covenant that is ordained forever.

15 In the sixth year of the fourth week we came to Abraham at the Well of the Oath, and we appeared to him.

16 We returned in the seventh month, and found Sarah with child before us and we blessed him, and we announced to him all the things that had been decreed concerning him, so that he should not die until he should beget six more sons and saw them before he died.

17 But in Isaac should his name and offspring be called, and that all the offspring of his sons should be Gentiles, and be counted with the Gentiles; but from the sons of Isaac one should become a holy offspring, and should not be counted among the Gentiles.

18 For he should become the portion (dowry) of the Most High, and all his offspring had fallen into the possession of God, that they should be to the Lord a people for His possession above all nations and that they should become a kingdom and priests and a holy nation.

19 We went our way, and we announced to Sarah all that we had told him, and they both rejoiced with very great joy.

20 He built there an altar to the Lord who had delivered him, and who was causing him to rejoice in the land of his sojourning, and he celebrated a festival of joy in this month for seven days, near the altar which he had built at the Well of the Oath.

21 He built tents for himself and for his servants on this festival, and he was the first to celebrate the feast of tabernacles on the earth.

22 During these seven days he brought a burnt offering to the Lord each day to the altar consisting of two oxen, two rams, seven sheep, one male goat, for a sin offering that he might atone thereby for himself and for his offspring.

23 As an offering of thanks he brought, seven rams, seven kids, seven sheep, and seven male goats, and their fruit offerings and their drink offerings; and he burnt all the fat of it on the altar, a chosen offering to the Lord for a sweet smelling odor.

24 Morning and evening he burnt fragrant substances, frankincense and incense, and sweet spice, and nard, and myrrh, and spice, and aromatic plants; all these seven he offered, crushed, mixed together in equal parts and pure.

25 And he celebrated this feast during seven days, rejoicing with all his heart and with all his soul, he and all those who were in his house, and there was no stranger with him, nor any that was uncircumcised.

26 He blessed his Creator who had created him in his generation, for He had created him according to His good pleasure. God knew and perceived that from him would arise the plant of righteousness for the eternal generations, and from him a holy offspring, so that it should become like Him who had made all things.

27 He blessed and rejoiced, and he called the name of this festival the festival of the Lord, a joy acceptable to the Most High God.

28 And we blessed him forever, and all his offspring after him throughout all the generations of the earth, because he celebrated this festival in its season, according to the testimony of the heavenly tablets.

29 For this reason it is ordained on the heavenly tablets concerning Israel, that they shall celebrate the feast of tabernacles seven days with joy, in the seventh month, acceptable before the Lord as a statute forever throughout their generations every year.

30 To this there is no limit of days; for it is ordained forever regarding Israel that they should celebrate it and dwell in tents, and set wreaths on their heads, and take leafy boughs, and willows from the brook.

31 Abraham took branches of palm trees, and the fruit of good and pleasing trees, and every day going round the altar with the branches seven times a day in the morning, he praised and gave thanks to his God for all things in joy.

[Chapter 17]

1 In the first year of the fifth week Isaac was weaned in this jubilee, and Abraham made a great banquet in the third month, on the day his son Isaac was weaned.

2 Ishmael, the son of Hagar, the Egyptian, was in front of Abraham, his father, in his place, and Abraham rejoiced and blessed God because he had seen his sons and had not died childless.

3 He remembered the words which He had spoken to him on the day that Lot had departed from him, and he rejoiced because the Lord had given him offspring on the earth to inherit the earth, and he blessed with all his mouth the Creator of all things.

4 Sarah saw Ishmael playing and dancing, and Abraham rejoicing with great joy, and she became jealous of Ishmael and said to Abraham, "Throw out this bondwoman and her son. The son of this bondwoman will not be heir with my son, Isaac."

5 And the situation was troubling to Abraham, because of his maidservant and because of his son, because he did not want to drive them from him.

6 God said to Abraham "Let it not be troubling in your sight, because of the child and because of the bondwoman. Listen to Sarah and to all her words and do them, for in Isaac shall your name and offspring be called.

7 But as for the son of this bondwoman I will make him a great nation, because he is of your offspring."

8 Abraham got up early in the morning, and took bread and a bottle of water, and placed them on the shoulders of Hagar and the child, and sent her away.

9 And she departed and wandered in the wilderness of Beersheba, and the water in the bottle was spent, and the child was thirsty, and was not able to go on, and fell down.

10 His mother took him and laid him under an olive tree, and went and sat her down over away from him at the distance of a bow-shot; for she said, "Let me not see the death of my child," and she sat and wept.

11 An angel of God, one of the holy ones, said to her, "Why do you weep, Hagar? Stand. Take the child, and hold him in your hand, for God has heard your voice, and has seen the child."

12 She opened her eyes, and she saw a well of water, and she went and filled her bottle with water, and she gave her child a drink, and she arose and went towards the wilderness of Paran.

13 And the child grew and became an archer, and God was with him, and his mother took him a wife from among the daughters of Egypt.

14 She (the wife) gave birth to a son, and he called his name Nebaioth; for she said, "The Lord was close to me when I called on him."

15 In the seventh week, in the first year of it, in the first month in this jubilee, on the twelfth of this month, there were voices in heaven regarding Abraham, that he was faithful in all that He told him, and that he loved the Lord, and that in every affliction he was faithful.

16 Prince Mastema came and said before God, "Look, Abraham loves Isaac his son, and he delights in him above all things, tell him to offer him as a burnt-offering on the altar, and You will see if he will do this command, and You will know if he is faithful in everyway that You test him.

17 The Lord knew that Abraham was faithful throughout all his afflictions, for He had tried him through his country and with famine, and had tried him with the wealth of kings, and had tried him again through his wife, when she was torn from him, and with circumcision; and had tried him through Ishmael and Hagar, his maid-servant, when he sent them away.

18 In everything that He had tried him, he was found faithful, and his soul was not impatient, and he was not slow to act, because he was faithful and a lover of the Lord.

[Chapter 18]

1 God said to him, "Abraham. Abraham." and he said, "Look, here am I."

2 He said, "Take your beloved son, Isaac, whom you love, and go to the high country, and offer him on one of the mountains which I will point out to you."

3 He got early in the morning and saddled his donkey, and took two young men with him, and Isaac his son, and split the wood of the burnt offering, and he went to the place on the third day, and he saw the place afar off.

4 He came to a well of water (near Mount Moriah), and he said to his young men, "You stay here with the donkey, and I and the lad shall go yonder, and when we have worshipped we shall come back to you."

5 He took the wood of the burnt-offering and laid it on Isaac his son, and he took the fire and the knife, and they went both of them together to that place.

6 Isaac said to his father, "Father" and he said, "Here am I, my son." He said to him, "Look, we have the fire, and the knife, and the wood, but where is the sheep for the burnt-offering, father?"

7 He said, "God will provide for himself a sheep for a burnt-offering, my son." And he neared the place of the mountain of God.

8 He built an altar, and he placed the wood on the altar, and bound Isaac his son, and placed him on the wood that was on the altar, and stretched out his hand to take the knife to kill Isaac, his son.

9 I stood in the presence of him, and before prince Mastema, (and the holy angels stood and wept over the altar as prince Mastema and his angels rejoiced and said "Isaac will be destroyed and we will see if Abraham is faithful), and the Lord said, "Command him not to lay his hand on the lad, nor to do anything to him, for I have shown that he fears the Lord."

10 I called to him from heaven, and said to him, "Abraham, Abraham." and he was terrified and said, "Here am I."

11 I said to him, "Lay not your hand on the lad, neither do anything to him; for now I have shown that you fear the Lord, and have not withheld your son, your first-born son, from me."

12 Prince Mastema was put to shame (and was bound by the angels); and Abraham lifted up his eyes and looked and saw a ram caught by his horns, and Abraham went and took the ram and offered it as a burnt-offering in place of his son.

13 Abraham called that place "The Lord has seen," so that it is said the Lord has seen. This is Mount Zion.

14 The Lord called Abraham by his name a second time from heaven, as he caused us to appear to speak to him in the name of the Lord.

15 He said, "By Myself have I sworn," said the Lord, "Because you have done this thing, and have not withheld your son, your beloved son, from Me, that in blessing I will bless you, and in multiplying I will multiply your offspring as the stars of heaven, and as the sand which is on the seashore.

16 Your offspring shall inherit the cities of its enemies, and in your offspring shall all nations of the earth be blessed. Because you have obeyed My voice, and I have shown to all that you are faithful to Me in all that I have said to you, "Go in peace."

17 Abraham went back to his young men, and they stood and went back together to Beersheba, and Abraham lived by the Well of the Oath.

18 And he celebrated this festival every year, seven days with joy, and he called it the festival of the Lord according to the seven days during which he went and returned in peace.

19 Accordingly, it has been ordained and written on the heavenly tablets regarding Israel and its children that they should observe this festival seven days with the joy of festival.

[Chapter 19]

1 In the first year of the first week in the forty-second jubilee, Abraham returned and lived across from Hebron, in Kirjath Arba for two weeks of years.

2 In the first year of the third week of this jubilee the days of the life of Sarah were completed, and she died in Hebron.

3 Abraham went to mourn over her and bury her, and we tested him to see if his spirit was patient and he had neither anger nor contempt in the words of his mouth, and he was found patient in this and was not disturbed.

4 In patience of spirit he discussed with the children of Heth that they should give him a place in which to bury his dead.

5 And the Lord gave him grace before all who saw him, and he asked the sons of Heth in gentleness, and they gave him the land of the double cave over beside Mamre, that is Hebron, for four hundred pieces of silver.

6 They said to him, "We shall give it to you for nothing," but he would not take it from them for nothing, for he gave the price of the place and paid the money in full. And he bowed down before them twice, and after this he buried his dead in the double cave.

7 All the days of the life of Sarah were one hundred and twenty-seven years, that is, two jubilees and four weeks and one year, these are the days of the years of the life of Sarah.

8 This is the tenth trial with which Abraham was tested, and he was found faithful and patient in spirit.

9 He did not say a single word regarding the rumor in the land of how God had said that He would give it to him and to his offspring after him, but instead he begged for a place there to bury his dead. Because he was found faithful, it was recorded on the heavenly tablets that he was the friend of God.

10 In the fourth year of it (this jubilee) he took a wife for his son Isaac and her name was Rebecca the daughter of Bethuel, the son of Nahor, the brother of Abraham the sister of Laban and daughter of Bethuel; and Bethuel was the son of Melca, who was the wife of Nahor, the brother of Abraham.

11 Abraham took to himself a third wife from among the daughters of his household servants, for Hagar had died before Sarah, and her name was Keturah,. And she gave birth to six sons, Zimram, and Jokshan, and Medan, and Midian, and Ishbak, and Shuah, in the two weeks of years.

12 In the sixth week, in the second year of it, Rebecca gave birth to two sons of Isaac, Jacob and Esau.

13 And Jacob had no beard and was a straight and tall man who dwelt in tents, and Esau was a powerful a man of the field, and was hairy.

14 The youths grew, and Jacob learned to write, but Esau did not learn, for he was a man of the field and a hunter, and he learned war, and all his deeds were fierce.

15 Abraham loved Jacob, but Isaac loved Esau.

16 And Abraham saw the deeds of Esau, and he knew that in Jacob should his name and offspring be called. He called Rebecca and gave commandment regarding Jacob, for he knew that she too loved Jacob much more than Esau.

17 He said to her, "My daughter, watch over my son Jacob, for he shall take my place on the earth. He shall be a blessing throughout the children of men and for the glory of all the offspring of Shem.

18 I know that the Lord will choose him to be a people (nation) and a possession to Himself, above all peoples that are on the face of the earth.

19 Isaac, my son, loves Esau more than Jacob, but I see that you truly love Jacob.

20 Add still further to your kindness to him, and regard him in love, for he shall be a blessing to us on the earth from now on to all generations of the earth.

21 Let your hands be strong and let your heart rejoice in your son Jacob, for I have loved him far beyond all my sons. He shall be blessed forever, and his offspring shall fill the whole earth.

22 If a man can number the sand of the earth, his offspring also shall be numbered.

23 And all the blessings with which the Lord has blessed me and my offspring shall belong to Jacob and his offspring always.

24 In his offspring shall my name be blessed, and the name of my fathers, Shem, Noah, Enoch, Mahalalel, Enos, Seth, and Adam. And these shall serve to lay the foundations of the heaven, and to strengthen the earth, and to renew all the stars and planets which are in the sky.

27 He called Jacob and kissed him in front of Rebecca, his mother, and blessed him, and said, "Jacob, my beloved son, whom my soul loves, may God bless you from above the sky, and may He give you all the blessings with which He blessed Adam, Enoch, Noah, and Shem; and all the things of which He told me, and all the things which He promised to give me, may He cause to be yours and your offspring forever, according to the days of heaven above the earth.

28 And the Spirits of Mastema shall not rule over you or over your offspring or turn you from the Lord, who is your God from now on forever.

29 May the Lord God be a father to you and may you be like His first-born son, and to the people always. Go in peace, my son."

30 And they both went out together from Abraham.

31 Rebecca loved Jacob, with all her heart and with all her soul, very much more than Esau, but Isaac loved Esau much more than Jacob.

[Chapter 20]

1 In the forty-second jubilee, in the first year of the seventh week, Abraham called Ishmael, and his twelve sons, and Isaac and his two sons, and the six sons of Keturah, and their sons.

2 And he commanded them that they should observe the way of the Lord, that they should work righteousness, and love each his neighbor, and act in this manner among all men, that they should each walk with regard to the ways of the Lord to do judgment and righteousness on the earth.

3 He also commanded them that they should circumcise their sons, according to the covenant, which God had made with them, and not deviate to the right or the left of all the paths which the Lord had commanded us, and that we should keep ourselves from all fornication and uncleanness.

4 He said, "If any woman or maid commits fornication among you, burn her with fire. And do not let them commit fornication with her with their eyes or their heart; and do not let them take to themselves wives from the daughters of Canaan, because the offspring of Canaan will be rooted out of the land."

5 He told them about the judgment on the giants, and the judgment on the Sodomites, how they had been judged because of their wickedness, and had died because of their fornication and uncleanness, and corruption through fornication together.

6 He said, "Guard yourselves from all fornication and uncleanness, and from all pollution of sin, or you will make our name a curse, and your whole life a shame, and all your sons to be destroyed by the sword, and you will become accursed like Sodom, and all that is left of you shall be as the sons of Gomorrah.

7 I implore you, my sons, love the God of heaven and cling to all His commandments.

8 Do not walk after their idols and after their ways of uncleanness, and do not make yourselves molten or graven gods. They are empty, and there is no spirit in them, for they are work of men's hands, and all who trust in them, trust in nothing.

9 Do not serve them, nor worship them, but serve the most high God, and worship Him continually, and hope for His presence always, and work uprightness and righteousness before Him, that He may have pleasure in you and grant you His mercy, and send rain on you morning and evening, and bless all your works which you have performed on the earth, and bless your bread and your water, and bless the fruit of your womb and the fruit of your land, and the herds of your cattle, and the flocks of your sheep.

10 You will be for a blessing on the earth, and all nations of the earth will desire you, and bless your sons in my name, that they may be blessed as I am."

11 He gave to Ishmael and to his sons, and to the sons of Keturah, gifts, and sent them away from Isaac his son, and he gave everything to Isaac his son.

12 Ishmael and his sons, and the sons of Keturah and their sons, went together and settled from Paran to the border of Babylon in all the land that is toward the East facing the desert.

13 These mingled (intermarried) with each other, and their names were called Arabs, and Ishmaelites.

[Chapter 21]

1 In the sixth year of the seventh week of this jubilee Abraham called Isaac his son, and commanded him, saying, "I have become old. I do not know the day of my death but I am full of my days.

2 I am one hundred and seventy-five years old, and throughout all the days of my life I have remembered the Lord, and sought with all my heart to do His will, and to walk uprightly in all His ways.

3 My soul has hated idols. I have given my heart and spirit to the observance of the will of Him who created me.

4 For He is the living God, and He is holy and faithful, and He is righteous beyond all, and He is no respecter of men or of their gifts, for God is righteous, and executes judgment on all those who transgress His commandments and despise His covenant.

5 My son, observe His commandments and His law and His judgments, and do not walk after the abominations and after the graven images and after the molten images.

6 And eat no blood at all of animals or cattle, or of any bird that flies in the heaven.

7 If you kill a sacrificial animal as an acceptable peace offering, kill it, and pour out its blood on the altar. Place all the fat of the offering on the altar with fine flour and the meat offering mingled with oil with its drink offering. Place them all together on the altar of burnt offering. It is a sweet odor before the Lord.

8 You will offer the fat of the sacrifice of thanks offerings on the fire which is on the altar, and the fat which is on the belly, and all the fat on the inside, behind the two kidneys, and all the fat that is on them, and lobes of the liver you will remove, together with the kidneys.

9 Offer all these for a sweet odor acceptable before the Lord, with its meat-offering and with its drink-offering, and the bread of the offering to the Lord.

10 Eat its meat on that day and on the second day, but do not let the sun go down on it until it is eaten. Let nothing be left over for the third day, for it is not acceptable. Let it no longer be eaten, and all who eat of it will bring sin on themselves, for thus I have found it written in the books of my forefathers, and in the words of Enoch, and in the words of Noah.

11 On all your offerings you will scatter salt, and do not let the salt of the covenant be lacking in all your offerings before the Lord.

12 As regards the wood of the sacrifices, beware to bring only these and no other wood to the altar in addition to these, cypress, bay, almond, fir, pine, cedar, savin, fig, olive, myrrh, laurel, aspalathus.

13 Of these kinds of wood lay on the altar under the sacrifice, such as have been tested as to their appearance, and do not lay on it any split or dark wood, but hard and clean, without fault, a healthy and new growth. Do not lay old wood on it, because there is no longer fragrance in it as before.

14 Besides these kinds of wood there is none other that you will place on the altar, for the fragrance is dispersed, and the smell of its fragrance will not go up to heaven.

15 Observe this commandment and do it, my son, that you may be upright in all your deeds.

16 Be clean in your body at all times. Wash yourself with water before you approach to offer on the altar. Wash your hands and your feet before you draw near to the altar, and when you are done sacrificing, wash your hands and your feet again.

17 Let no blood appear on you or on your clothes. Be on your guard against blood, my son. Be on your guard continually and cover it with dust.

18 Do not eat any blood for it is the soul. Eat no blood whatsoever.

19 Take no payment for shedding the blood of man, or it will cause it to be shed without fear of punishment, without judgment. It is the blood that is shed that causes the earth to sin, and the earth cannot be cleansed from the blood of man except by the blood of he who shed it.

20 Take no present or gift for the blood of man, blood for blood, that you may be accepted before the Lord, the Most High God. He is the defense of the good, so that you may be preserved from all evil, and that He may withhold you from every kind of death.

21 I see, my son, all the works of the children of men are sin and wickedness, and all their deeds are uncleanness and an abomination and a pollution, and there is no righteousness in them.

22 Beware, or you will walk in their ways and tread in their paths, and commit a sin worthy of death before the Most High God. He will hide His face from you and give you back into the hands of your transgression, and root you out of the land, and your offspring likewise from under heaven, and your name and your offspring shall perish from the whole earth.

23 Turn away from all their deeds and all their uncleanness, and observe the laws of the Most High God, and do His will and be upright in all things.

24 If you do this, He will bless you in all your deeds, and will raise up from you a plant of righteousness through all the earth, throughout all generations of the earth, and my name and your name shall not be forgotten under heaven forever.

25 Go, my son in peace. May the Most High God, my God and your God, strengthen you to do His will, and may He bless all your offspring and the remainder of your offspring for the generations forever, with all righteous blessings, that you may be a blessing on all the earth."

26 And he went out from him rejoicing.

[Chapter 22]

1 In the first week in the forty-fourth jubilee, in the second year, that is, the year in which Abraham died, Isaac and Ishmael came from the Well of the Oath to celebrate the feast of weeks which is the feast of the first-fruits of the harvest to Abraham, their father, and Abraham rejoiced because his two sons had come.

2 Isaac had many possessions in Beersheba, and Isaac desired to go and see his possessions and to return to his father.

3 In those days Ishmael came to see his father, and they both came together, and Isaac offered a sacrifice for a burnt offering, and presented it on the altar of his father that he had made in Hebron.

4 He offered a thanks offering and made a feast of joy in the presence of Ishmael, his brother, and Rebecca made new cakes from the new grain, and gave them to Jacob, her son, to take them to Abraham, his father, from the first-fruits of the land, that he might eat and bless the Creator of all things before he died.

5 Isaac, also, sent Jacob to Abraham with an offering of his best for thanks so that he might eat and drink.

6 He ate and drank, and blessed the Most High God, who has created heaven and earth, who has made all the fat things of the earth, and given them to the children of men that they might eat and drink and bless their Creator.

7 "And now I give thanks to You, my God, because you have caused me to see this day, behold, I am one hundred three score and fifteen years, an old man and full of days, and all my days have been peace to me.

8 The sword of the adversary has not overcome me in all that You have given me and my children all the days of my life until this day.

9 My God, may Your mercy and Your peace be on Your servant, and on the offspring of his sons, that they may be to You a chosen nation and an inheritance from among all the nations of the earth from now on to all the days of the generations of the earth, to all the ages."

10 He called Jacob and said, "My son Jacob, may the God of all bless you and strengthen you to do righteousness, and His will before Him, and may He choose you and your offspring that you may become a people for His inheritance according to His will always.

11 My son, Jacob, draw near and kiss me." And he drew near and kissed him, and he said, "Blessed be my son Jacob and all the sons of God Most High, to all the ages. May God give to you an offspring of righteousness; and some of your sons may He sanctify throughout the whole earth. May nations serve you, and all the nations bow themselves before your offspring.

12 Be strong in the presence of men, and exercise authority over all the offspring of Seth. Then your ways and the ways of your sons will be justified, so that they shall become a holy nation.

13 May the Most High God give you all the blessings with which He has blessed me and He blessed Noah and Adam. May they rest on the sacred head of your offspring from generation to generation forever.

14 May He cleanse you from all unrighteousness and impurity so that you may be forgiven all the transgressions, which you have committed ignorantly. May He strengthen you, and bless you.

15 May you inherit the whole earth, and may He renew His covenant with you so that you may be to Him a nation for His inheritance for all the ages, and so that He may be to you and to your offspring a God in truth and righteousness throughout all the days of the earth.

16 My son Jacob, remember my words. Observe the commandments of Abraham, your father, separate yourself from the nations (gentiles), and do not eat with them. Do not emulate their works, and do not associate with them because their works are unclean, and all their ways are a pollution and an abomination and uncleanness.

17 They offer their sacrifices to the dead and they worship evil spirits, and they eat over the graves, and all their works are empty and nothingness.

18 They have no heart to understand and their eyes do not see what their works are, and how they go astray by saying to a piece of wood, "You are my God," and to a stone, "You are my Lord and you are my deliverer," because the stone and wood have no heart.

19 And as for you, my son Jacob, may the Most High God help you and the God of heaven bless you and remove you from their uncleanness and from all their error.

20 Jacob, be warned. Do not take a wife from any offspring of the daughters of Canaan, for all his offspring are to be rooted out of the earth.

21 Because of the transgression of Ham, Canaan erred, and all his offspring shall be destroyed from the earth including any remnant of it, and none springing from him shall exist except on the day of judgment.

22 And as for all the worshippers of idols and the profane, there shall be no hope for them in the land of the living, and no one on earth will remember them, for they shall descend into the abode of the dead, and they shall go into the place of condemnation. As the children of Sodom were taken away from the earth, so will all those who worship idols be taken away.

23 Fear not, my son Jacob. Be not dismayed, son of Abraham. May the Most High God preserve you from destruction, and may He deliver you from all the paths of error.

24 This house have I built for myself that I might put my name on it in the earth. It is given to you and to your offspring forever, and it will be named the house of Abraham. It is given to you and your offspring forever, for you will build my house and establish my name before God forever. Your offspring and your name will stand throughout all generations of the earth."

25 He ceased commanding him and blessing him.

26 The two lay together on one bed, and Jacob slept in the embracing arms of Abraham, his father's father, and he kissed him seven times, and his affection and his heart rejoiced over him.

27 He blessed him with all his heart and said, "The Most High God, the God of all, and Creator of all, who brought me out from Ur of the Chaldees that He might give me this land to inherit forever, that I might establish a holy offspring.

28 Blessed be the Most High forever."

29 And he blessed Jacob and said, "May Your grace and Your mercy be lift up on my son, over whom I rejoice with all my heart and my affection and on his offspring always.

30 Do not forsake him, nor diminish him from now to the days of eternity, and may Your eyes be opened on him and on his offspring, that You may preserve him, and bless him, and may sanctify him as a nation for Your inheritance. Bless him with all Your blessings from now to all the days of eternity, and renew Your covenant and Your grace with him and with his offspring according to all Your good pleasure to all the generations of the earth."

[Chapter 23]

1 He placed Jacob's two fingers on his eyes, and he blessed the God of gods, and he covered his face and stretched out his feet and slept the sleep of eternity, and was gathered to his fathers.

2 In spite of all this, Jacob was lying in his embracing arms, and knew not that Abraham, his father's father, was dead.

3 Jacob awoke from his sleep, and realized Abraham was cold as ice, and he said, "Father, father," but there was no answer, and he knew that he was dead.

4 He arose from his embracing arms and ran and told Rebecca, his mother, and Rebecca went to Isaac in the night, and told him and they went together, and Jacob with them, and a lamp was in his hand, and when they had gone in they found Abraham lying dead.

5 Isaac fell on the face of his father and wept and kissed him.

6 Ishmael, his son, heard the voices in the house of Abraham, and he arose, and went to Abraham his father, and wept over Abraham his father, he and all the house of Abraham, and they wept greatly.

7 His sons, Isaac and Ishmael, buried him in the double cave, near Sarah his wife, and all the men of his house, and Isaac and Ishmael, and all their sons, and all the sons of Keturah in their places wept for him forty days and then the days of weeping for Abraham were ended.

8 He lived three jubilees and four weeks of years, one hundred and seventy-five years, and completed the days of his life, being old and full of days.

9 For the days of the lives of their forefathers were nineteen jubilees; and after the Flood they began to grow less than nineteen jubilees, and to decrease in jubilees, and to grow old quickly, and to be full of their days because of the many types of hardships and the wickedness of their ways, with the exception of Abraham.

10 For Abraham was perfect in all his deeds with the Lord, and well-pleasing in righteousness all the days of his life. Yet, he did not complete four jubilees in his life, when he had grown old because of the wickedness in the world, and was full of his days.

11 All the generations which shall arise from this time until the day of the great judgment shall grow old quickly, before they complete two jubilees, and their knowledge shall forsake them because of their old age and all their knowledge shall vanish away.

12 In those days, if a man lives a jubilee and a-half of years, they shall say regarding him, "He has lived long," and the greater part of his days are pain and sorrow and hardship, and there is no peace. For calamity follows on calamity, and wound on wound, and hardship on hardship, and evil deeds on evil deeds, and illness on illness, and all judgments of destruction such

as these, piled one on another, illness and overthrow, and snow and frost and ice, and fever, and chills, and mental and physical incapacity, and famine, and death, and sword, and captivity, and all kinds of calamities and pains.

13 All of these shall come on an evil generation, which transgresses on the earth. Their works are uncleanness and fornication, and pollution and abominations.

14 Then they shall say, "The days of the forefathers were many, lasting a thousand years, and were good; but the days of our lives, if a man lives a long life are three score years and ten, and, if he is strong, four score years, and those evil, and there is no peace in the days of this evil generation."

15 In that generation the sons shall convict their fathers and their elders of sin and unrighteousness, and of the words of their mouths and the great wickedness which they perform, and concerning their forsaking the covenant which the Lord made between them and Him. They should observe and do all His commandments and His ordinances and all His laws, without departing either to the right hand or the left.

16 For all have done evil, and every mouth speaks sinfully and all their works are unclean and an abomination, and all their ways are pollution, uncleanness, and destruction.

17 The earth shall be destroyed because of all their works, and there shall be no fruit (seed) of the vine, and no oil; for their actions are altogether faithless, and they shall all perish together, beasts and cattle and birds, and all the fish of the sea, because of the children of men.

18 They shall quarrel with one another, the young with the old, and the old with the young, the poor with the rich, the lowly with the great, and the beggar with the prince, because of the law and the covenant; for they have forgotten the commandments, and covenant, and feasts, and months, and Sabbaths, and jubilees, and all judgments.

19 They shall use swords and war to turn them back to the way, but they shall not return until much blood has been shed on the earth, one by another.

20 Those who have escaped shall not return from their wickedness to the way of righteousness, but they shall all raise themselves to a high status through deceit and wealth, that they may each steal all that belongs of his neighbor, and they shall name the great name (of God), but not in truth and not in righteousness, and they shall defile the holy of holies with their uncleanness and the corruption of their pollution.

21 A great punishment shall come because of the deeds of this generation, and the Lord will give them over to the sword and to judgment and to slavery, and to be plundered and consumed.

22 And He will arouse the Gentile sinners against them, who have neither mercy nor compassion, and who shall respect no one, neither old nor young, nor any one, for they are more wicked, strong, and evil than all the children of men.

23 They shall use violence against Israel and shall violate Jacob, and much blood shall be shed on the earth, and there shall be none to gather the dead and none to bury them.

24 In those days they shall cry aloud, and call and pray that they may be saved from the hand of the sinners, the Gentiles. But none shall be excluded (none shall be saved).

25 The heads of the children shall be white with grey hair, and a child of three weeks shall appear old like a man of one hundred years, and their work and worth shall be destroyed by hardship and oppression.

26 In those days the children shall begin to study the laws, and to seek the commandments, and to return to the path of righteousness.

27 The days shall begin to grow many and increase among those children of men until their days draw close to one thousand years, and to a greater number of years than before age was recorded.

28 There shall be neither old man nor one who is aged, for all shall be as children and youths.

29 All their days shall be full and they shall live in peace and in joy, and there shall be neither Satan nor any evil destroyer because all their days shall be days of blessing and healing.

30 And at that time the Lord will heal His servants, and they shall rise up and see great peace, and drive out their adversaries. The righteous shall understand and be thankful, and rejoice with joy forever and ever, and they shall see all their judgments and all their curses enacted on their enemies.

31 Their bones shall rest in the earth, and their spirits shall have much joy, and they shall know that it is the Lord who executes judgment, and shows mercy to hundreds and thousands and to all that love Him.

32 Moses, write down these words. Write them and record them on the heavenly tablets for a testimony for the generations forever.

[Chapter 24]

1 It happened after the death of Abraham, that the Lord blessed Isaac his son, who arose from Hebron and went and dwelt at the Well of the Vision in the first year of the third week of this jubilee, seven years.

2 In the first year of the fourth week a famine began in the land, besides the first famine, which had been in the days of Abraham.

3 Jacob made lentil soup, and Esau came from the field hungry. He said to Jacob his brother, "Give me some of this red soup."

4 Jacob said to him, "Sell to me your birthright and I will give you bread, and also some of this lentil soup." And Esau said in his heart, "If I shall die what good is my birthright to me?"

5 He said to Jacob, "I give it to you." And Jacob said, "Swear to me, this day," and he swore to him.

6 And Jacob gave his brother Esau bread and soup, and he ate until he was satisfied, and Esau despised his birthright. For this reason was Esau's name called Edom (red), because of the red soup which Jacob gave him for his birthright.

7 And Jacob became the elder, and Esau was brought down from his dignity.

8 The famine covered the land, and Isaac departed to go down into Egypt in the second year of this week, and went to the king of the Philistines to Gerar, into the presence of Abimelech.

9 The Lord appeared to him and said to him, "Do not go down into Egypt. Dwell in the land that I shall tell you of, and sojourn in this land, and I will be with you and bless you.

10 For to you and to your offspring will I give all this land, and I will establish My oath which I swore to Abraham your father, and I will multiply your offspring as the stars of heaven, and will give to your offspring all this land.

11 And in your offspring shall all the nations of the earth be blessed, because your father obeyed My voice, and kept My ways and My commandments, and My laws, and My ordinances, and My covenant; and now do as you are told and dwell in this land."

12 And he dwelt in Gelar three weeks of years. And Abimelech commanded concerning him, and concerning all that was his, saying, "Any man that shall touch him or anything that is his shall surely die."

13 Isaac grew strong among the Philistines, and he got many possessions, oxen and sheep and camels and donkeys and a great household.

14 He sowed in the land of the Philistines and brought in a hundred-fold, and Isaac became very great, and the Philistines envied him.

15 Now all the wells that the servants of Abraham had dug during the life of Abraham, the Philistines had stopped them after the death of Abraham, and filled them with dirt.

16 Abimelech said to Isaac, "Go from us, for you are much mightier than we." Isaac departed from that place in the first year of the seventh week, and sojourned in the valleys of Gerar.

17 And they dug the wells of water again which the servants of Abraham, his father, had dug, and which the Philistines had filled after the death of Abraham his father, and he called their names as Abraham his father had named them.

18 The servants of Isaac dug a well in the valley, and found fresh, flowing water, and the shepherds of Gerar bickered with the shepherds of Isaac, saying, "The water is ours." Isaac called the name of the well "Perversity," because they had been perverse with us.

19 And they dug a second well, and they fought for that also, and he called its name "Enmity."

20 He left that place and they dug another well, and for that they did not fight, and he called the name of it "Room," and Isaac said, "Now the Lord has made room for us, and we have increased in the land."

21 And he went up from that place to the Well of the Oath in the first year of the first week in the forty-fourth jubilee.

22 The Lord appeared to him in the night of the new moon of the first month, and said to him, "I am the God of Abraham your father; fear not, for I am with you, and shall bless you and shall surely multiply your offspring as the sand of the earth, for the sake of Abraham my servant."

23 And he built an altar there, which Abraham his father had first built, and he called on the name of the Lord, and he offered sacrifice to the God of Abraham his father.

24 They dug a well and they found fresh, flowing water.

25 The servants of Isaac dug another well and did not find water, and they went and told Isaac that they had not found water, and Isaac said, "I have sworn this day to the Philistines and this thing has been announced to us."

26 And he called the name of that place the Well of the

Oath, because there he had sworn to Abimelech and Ahuzzath ,his friend, and also to Phicol, who was the commander and his host.

27 Isaac knew that day that he had sworn to them under pressure to make peace with them.

28 On that day Isaac cursed the Philistines and said, "Cursed be the Philistines to the day of wrath and indignation from among all nations. May God make them a disdain and a curse and an object of anger and indignation in the hands of the Gentile sinners and in the hands of the Kittim.

29 Whoever escapes the sword of the enemy and the Kittim, may the righteous nation root them out in judgment from under heaven. They shall be the enemies and foes of my children throughout their generations on the earth.

30 No part of them will remain. Not even one shall be spared on the day of the wrath of judgment. The offspring of the Philistines will experience destruction, rooting out, and expulsion from the earth and this is all that is in store for them. There shall not be a name or an offspring left on the earth for these Caphtorim (the seat of the Philistine state).

31 For though he rises up to heaven, he shall be brought down, and though he makes himself strong on earth, from there shall he be dragged out, and though he hide himself among the nations, even from that place shall he be rooted out.

32 Though he descends into the abode of the dead, his condemnation shall be great, and he shall have no peace there.

33 If he goes into captivity by the hands of those that seek his life they shall kill him on the way (to his imprisonment), and neither his name nor offspring shall be left on all the earth. Into an eternal curse shall he depart."

34 It is written and engraved concerning him on the heavenly tablets, that on the day of judgment he will be rooted out of the earth.

[Chapter 25]

1 In the second year of this week in this jubilee, Rebecca called Jacob her son, and spoke to him, saying, "My son, do not take a wife from the daughters of Canaan as Esau, your brother, who took two wives of the daughters of Canaan, and they have made my soul bitter with all their unclean acts, for all their actions are fornication and lust, and there is no righteousness in them, because their deeds are evil.

2 I love you greatly, my son, and my heart and my affection bless you every hour of the day and in every night.

3 Now, my son, listen to my voice, and do the will of your mother, and do not take a wife of the daughters of this land, but only from the house of my father, and of those related to my father.

4 If you will take you a wife of the house of my father, the Most High God will bless you, and your children shall be a righteous generation and a holy offspring." And then spoke Jacob to Rebecca, his mother, and said to her, "Look, mother, I am nine weeks of years old, and I have neither been with nor have I touched any woman, nor have I engaged myself to any, nor I have even thought of taking me wife of the daughters of Canaan.

5 For I remember, mother, the words of Abraham, our father, for he commanded me not to take a wife of the daughters of Canaan, but to take me a wife from the offspring of my father's house and from my kind folks.

6 I have heard before that daughters have been born to Laban, your brother, and I have set my heart on them to take a wife from among them.

7 For this reason I have guarded myself in my spirit against sinning or being corrupted in any way throughout all the days of my life; for with regard to lust and fornication, Abraham, my father, gave me many commands.

8 Despite all that he has commanded me, these two and twenty years my brother has argued with me, and spoken frequently to me and said, "My brother, take a wife that is a sister of my two wives," but I refused to do as he has done.

9 I swear before you mother, that all the days of my life I will not take me a wife from the daughters of the offspring of Canaan, and I will not act wickedly as my brother has done.

10 Do not be afraid mother, be assured that I shall do your will and walk in uprightness, and not corrupt my ways forever."

11 When she heard this, she lifted up her face to heaven and extended the fingers of her hands, and opened her mouth and blessed the Most High God, who had created the heaven and the earth, and she gave Him thanks and praise.

12 She said, "Blessed be the Lord God, and may His holy name be blessed forever and ever. He has given me Jacob as a pure son and a holy offspring; for he is Yours, and Yours shall his offspring be continually, throughout all the generations forever.

13 Bless him, O Lord, and place in my mouth the blessing of righteousness, that I may bless him."

14 At that hour, when the spirit of righteousness descended into her mouth, she placed both her hands on the head of Jacob, and said, "Blessed are You, Lord of righteousness and God of the ages, and may You bless him beyond all the generations of men.

15 My Son, may He give you the path of righteousness, and reveal righteousness to your offspring.

16 May He make your sons many during your life, and may they arise according to the number of the months of the year. And may their sons become many and great beyond the stars of heaven, and may their numbers be more than the sand of the sea.

17 May He give them this good and pleasing land, as He said He would give it to Abraham and to his offspring after him always, and may they hold it as a possession forever.

18 My son, may I see blessed children born to you during my life, and may all your offspring be blessed and holy.

19 And as you have refreshed your mother's spirit during her life, the womb of her that gave birth to you blesses you now. My affection and my heart (breasts) bless you and my mouth and my tongue greatly praise you.

20 Increase and spread over the earth. May your offspring be perfect in the joy of heaven and earth forever. May your offspring rejoice, and on the great day of peace may they have peace.

21 May your name and your offspring endure to all the ages, and may the Most High God be their God, and may the God of righteousness dwell with them, and may His sanctuary be built by you all the ages.

22 Blessed be he that blesses you, and all flesh that curses you falsely, may it be cursed."

23 And she kissed him, and said to him, "May the Lord of the world love you as the heart of your mother and her affection rejoice in you and bless you." And she ceased from blessing.

[Chapter 26]

1 In the seventh year of this week Isaac called Esau, his elder son, and said to him, " I am old, my son, and my sight is dim, and I do not know the day of my death.

2 Now, take your hunting weapons, your quiver, and your bow, and go out to the field, and hunt and catch me venison, my son, and make me flavorful meat, like my soul loves, and bring it to me that I may eat, and that my soul may bless you before I die."

3 But Rebecca heard Isaac speaking to Esau.

4 Esau went out early to the field to hunt and catch and bring home meat to his father.

5 Rebecca called Jacob, her son, and said to him, "Look, I heard Isaac, your father, speak to Esau, your brother, saying, "Hunt for me, and make me flavorful meat, and bring it to me that I may eat and bless you before the Lord before I die."

6 Now, my son, do as you are told and do as I command you. Go to your flock and fetch me two good kids of the goats, and I will make them good tasting meat for your father, like he loves, and you will bring it to your father that he may eat and bless you to the Lord before he dies."

7 Jacob said to Rebecca his mother, "Mother, I shall not withhold anything which my father would eat and which would please him, but I am afraid that he will recognize my voice and wish to touch me.

8 And you know that I am smooth, and Esau, my brother, is hairy, and I he will see me an evildoer because I am doing something that he has not told me to do and he will be very angry with me, and I shall bring on myself a curse, and not a blessing."

9 Rebecca, his mother, said to him, "Your curse be on me, my son, just do as you are told."

10 Jacob obeyed the voice of Rebecca, his mother, and went and brought back two good and fat goat kids, and brought them to his mother, and his mother made them tasty meat like he loved.

11 Rebecca took the good and pleasing clothes of Esau, her elder son, which was with her in the house, and she clothed Jacob, her younger son, with them, and she put the skins of the kids on his hands and on the exposed parts of his neck.

12 And she gave the meat and the bread, which she had prepared, to her son Jacob.

13 Jacob went in to his father and said, "I am your son. I have done as you asked me. Arise and sit and eat of that which I have caught, father, that your soul may bless me."

14 Isaac said to his son, "How have you found game so quickly, my son?"

15 Jacob said, "Because the Lord your God caused me to find."

16 Isaac said to him, "Come closer, that I may feel you, my son, and know if you are my son Esau or not."

17 Jacob went near to Isaac, his father, and he felt him and said, "The voice is Jacob's voice, but the hands are the hands of Esau," and he did not recognize him, because it was a decision from heaven to remove his power of perception and Isaac discerned not, because his hands were hairy as his brother Esau's, so Isaac blessed him.

18 He said, "Are you my son Esau? " and Jacob said, "I am your son," and Isaac said, "Bring it to me that I may eat of that which you have caught, my son, that my soul may bless you."

19 And Jacob brought it to him, and he ate, and Jacob brought him wine and he drank.

20 Isaac, his father, said to him, "Come close and kiss me, my son."

21 He came close and kissed Isaac. And he smelled the smell of his raiment, and he blessed Jacob and said, "Look, the smell of my son is as the smell of a full field which the Lord has blessed.

22 May the Lord give you of the dew of heaven and of the dew of the earth, and plenty of corn and oil. Let nations serve you and peoples bow down to you.

23 Be ruler over your brothers, and let your mother's sons bow down to you; and may all the blessings that the Lord has blessed me and blessed Abraham, my father be imparted to you and to your offspring forever. Cursed be he that curses you, and blessed be he that blesses you."

24 It happened as soon as Isaac had made an end of blessing his son Jacob, that Jacob had went away from Isaac his father and hid himself.

25 Esau, his brother, came in from his hunting. And he also made flavorful meat, and brought it to his father and Esau said to his father, "Let my father arise, and eat of my venison that your soul may bless me."

26 Isaac, his father, said to him, "Who are you?" Esau said to him, "I am your first born, your son Esau. I have done as you have commanded me."

27 Isaac was very greatly surprised, and said, "Who is he that has hunted and caught and brought it to me, and I have eaten of all before you came, and have blessed him, and he shall be blessed, and all his offspring forever."

28 It happened when Esau heard the words of his father Isaac that he cried with a very loud and bitter cry, and said to his father, "Bless me also, father!"

29 Isaac said to him, "Your brother came with trickery, and has taken away your blessing."

30 He said, "Now I know why his name is Jacob. Behold, he has supplanted me these two times, he took away my birth-right, and now he has taken away my blessing."

31 Esau said, "Have you not reserved a blessing for me, father?" and Isaac answered and said to Esau, "Look, I have made him your lord, and all his brothers have I given to him for servants. I have strengthened him with plenty of corn and wine and oil. Now what shall I do for you, my son?"

32 Esau said to Isaac, his father, "Have you only one blessing, father? Please. Bless me, also, father. "

33 Esau lifted up his voice and wept. And Isaac answered and said to him, "Far from the dew of the earth shall be your dwelling, and far from the dew of heaven from above.

34 By your sword will you live, and you will serve your brother.

35 It shall happen that when you become great, and do shake his yoke from off your neck, you will sin completely and commit a sin worthy of death, and your offspring shall be rooted out from under heaven."

36 Esau kept threatening Jacob because of the blessing his father blessed him with, and he said in his heart, "May the days of mourning for my father come now, so that I may kill my brother Jacob."

[Chapter 27]

1 Rebecca was told Esau's words in a dream, and Rebecca sent for Jacob her younger son, and said to him, "Look Esau, your brother, will take vengeance on you and kill you.

2 Now, therefore, my son, do as you are told, and get up and flee to Laban, my brother, to Haran, and stay with him a few days until your brother's anger fades away, and he removes his anger from you, and forgets all that you have done. Then I will send for you to come from that place."

3 Jacob said, "I am not afraid. If he wishes to kill me, I will kill him."

4 But she said to him, "Let me not be bereft of both my sons on one day."

5 Jacob said to Rebecca, his mother, "Look, you know that my father has become old, and does not see because his eyes are dull. If I leave him he will think it is wrong. If I leave him and go away from you, my father will be angry and will curse me.

6 I will not go. When he sends me, only then will I go."

7 Rebecca said to Jacob, "I will go in and speak to him, and he will send you away."

8 Rebecca went in and said to Isaac, "I hate my life because of the two daughters of Heth, whom Esau has taken as wives. If Jacob take a wife from among the daughters of the land such as these, I could not live with it, because the daughters of Canaan are evil."

9 Isaac called Jacob and blessed him, and warned him and said to him, "Do not take you a wife of any of the daughters of Canaan. Arise and go to Mesopotamia, to the house of Bethuel, your mother's father, and take a wife from that place of the daughters of Laban, your mother's brother.

10 And God Almighty bless you and increase and multiply you that you may become a company of nations, and give you the blessings of my father, Abraham, to you and to your offspring after you, that you may inherit the land that you travel in and all the land which God gave to Abraham. Go in peace, my son."

11 Isaac sent Jacob away, and he went to Mesopotamia, to Laban the son of Bethuel the Syrian, the brother of Rebecca, Jacob's mother.

12 It happened after Jacob had departed to Mesopotamia that the spirit of Rebecca was grieved for her son, and she wept.

13 Isaac said to Rebecca, "My sister, weep not because of Jacob, my son, for he goes in peace, and in peace will he return.

14 The Most High God will preserve him from all evil and will be with him. He will not forsake him all his days, for I know that his ways will be made to prosper in all things wherever he goes, until he return in peace to us, and we see him in peace. Fear not on his account, my sister, for he is on the upright path and he is a perfect man, and he is faithful and will not perish. Weep not."

15 Isaac comforted Rebecca because of her son Jacob, and blessed him.

16 Jacob went from the Well of the Oath to go to Haran on the first year of the second week in the forty-fourth jubilee, and he came to Luz on the mountains, that is, Bethel, on the new moon of the first month of this week, and he came to the place at dusk and turned from the way to the west of the road that is close, and that night he slept there, for the sun had set.

17 He took one of the stones of that place (as a pillow) and laid down under the tree, and he was journeying alone, and he slept.

18 Jacob dreamt that night, and saw a ladder set up on the earth, and the top of it reached to heaven, and he saw the angels of the Lord ascended and descended on it, and behold, the Lord stood on it.

19 And He spoke to Jacob and said, "I am the Lord God of Abraham, your father, and the God of Isaac. The land you are sleeping on I will give to you and to your offspring after you.

20 Your offspring shall be as the dust of the earth, and you will increase to the west and to the east, to the north and the south, and in you and in your offspring shall all the families of the nations be blessed.

21 Behold, I will be with you, and will keep you wherever you go. I will bring you into this land again in peace. I will not leave you until I do everything that I told you."

22 Jacob awoke from his sleep and said, "Truly this place is the house of the Lord, and I did not know it."

23 He was afraid and said, "I am afraid because this place is none other than the house of God, and this is the gate of heaven, and I did not know it."

24 Jacob got up early in the morning, and took the stone that he had placed under his head and set it up as a pillar for a sign. And he poured oil on the top of it. And he called the name of that place Bethel, but the name of the place was previously Luz.

25 And Jacob vowed a vow to the Lord, saying, "If the Lord will be with me, and will keep me in the way that I go, and give me bread to eat and clothes to put on, so that I come again to my father's house in peace, then the Lord shall be my God, and

this stone which I have set up as a pillar for a sign in this place shall be the Lord's house, and of all that you gave me, I shall give the tenth to you, my God."

[Chapter 28]

1 He went on his journey, and came to the land of the east, to Laban, the brother of Rebecca, and he was with him, and Jacob served Laban for Rachel his daughter one week of years. In the first year of the third week of years he said to him, "Give me my wife, for whom I have served you seven years ," and Laban said to Jacob, "I will give you your wife."
2 Laban made a feast, and took Leah his elder daughter, and gave her to Jacob as a wife, and gave Leah Zilpah for a handmaid; and Jacob did not know, for he thought that she was Rachel.
3 He went in to her, and saw she was Leah; and Jacob was angry with Laban, and said to him, "Why have you done this to me?
4 Did I not serve you for Rachel and not for Leah? Why have you wronged me?
5 Take your daughter, and I will go. You have done evil to me." For Jacob loved Rachel more than Leah because Leah's eyes were weak, but her form was very beautiful. Rachel had beautiful eyes and a beautiful and very voluptuous form.
6 Laban said to Jacob, "It is not done that way in our country, we do not to give the younger before the elder." And it is not right to do this; for thus it is ordained and written in the heavenly tablets, that no one should give his younger daughter before the elder; but the elder one is given first and after her the younger. The man who does so will have guilt placed against him in heaven, and none is righteous that does this thing, for this deed is evil before the Lord.
7 Command the children of Israel that they not do this thing. Let them neither take nor give the younger before they have given the elder, for it is very wicked.
8 And Laban said to Jacob, "Let the seven days of the feast pass by, and I shall give you Rachel, that you may serve me another seven years, that you may pasture my sheep as you did in the former week (of years)."
9 On the day when the seven days of the feast of Leah had passed, Laban gave Rachel to Jacob, that he might serve him another seven years, and he gave Rachel, Bilhah, the sister of Zilpah, as a handmaid.
10 He served yet other seven years for Rachel, for Leah had been given to him for nothing, since it was Rachel he wanted.
11 And the Lord opened the womb of Leah, and she conceived and gave birth to a son for Jacob, and he called his name Reuben, on the fourteenth day of the ninth month, in the first year of the third week.
12 But the womb of Rachel was closed, for the Lord saw that Leah was hated and Rachel loved.
13 Again Jacob went in to Leah, and she conceived, and gave birth to a second son for Jacob, and he called his name Simeon, on the twenty-first of the tenth month, and in the third year of this week.
14 Again Jacob went in to Leah, and she conceived, and gave birth to a third son, and he called his name Levi, in the new moon of the first month in the sixth year of this week.
15 Again Jacob went in to her, and she conceived, and gave birth to a fourth son, and he called his name Judah, on the fifteenth of the third month, in the first year of the fourth week.
16 Because of all this Rachel envied Leah, for she did not bear a child, and she said to Jacob, "Give me children;" and Jacob said, "Have I withheld from you the fruits of your womb? Have I left you?"
17 And when Rachel saw that Leah had given birth to four sons for Jacob: Reuben and Simeon and Levi and Judah, she said to him, "Go in to Bilhah my handmaid, and she will conceive, and bear a son for me."
18 She gave him Bilhah, her handmaid, to wife. And he went in to her, and she conceived, and gave birth to a son, and he called his name Dan, on the ninth of the sixth month, in the sixth year of the third week.
19 Jacob went in again to Bilhah a second time, and she conceived, and gave birth to another son for Jacob, and Rachel called his name Napthali, on the fifth of the seventh month, in the second year of the fourth week.
20 When Leah saw that she had become sterile and could no longer have children, she envied Rachel, and she also gave her handmaid Zilpah to Jacob to wife, and she conceived, and gave birth to a son, and Leah called his name Gad, on the twelfth of the eighth month, in the third year of the fourth week.
21 He went in to her again, and she conceived and gave birth to a second son, and Leah called his name Asher, on the second of the eleventh month, in the fifth year of the fourth week.
22 Jacob went in to Leah, and she conceived, and gave birth to a son, and she called his name Issachar, on the fourth of the fifth month, in the fourth year of the fourth week, and she gave him to a nurse.
23 Jacob went in again to her, and she conceived, and gave birth to two children, a son and a daughter, and she called the name of the son Zabulon, and the name of the daughter Dinah, in the seventh day of the seventh month, in the sixth year of the fourth week.
24 The Lord was gracious to Rachel, and opened her womb, and she conceived, and gave birth to a son, and she called his name Joseph, on the new moon of the fourth month, in the sixth year in this fourth week.
25 In the days when Joseph was born, Jacob said to Laban, "Give me my wives and sons, and let me go to my father Isaac, and let me make household for myself; for I have completed the years in which I have served you for your two daughters, and I will go to the house of my father."
26 Laban said to Jacob, "Stay with me and I will pay you wages, and pasture my flock for me again, and take your wages."

27 They agreed with one another that he should give him as his wages those of the lambs and kids which were born spotted black and white, these were to be his wages.

28 All the sheep brought out spotted and speckled and black, variously marked, and they brought out again lambs like themselves, and all that were spotted were Jacob's and those which were not spotted were Laban's.

29 Jacob's possessions multiplied greatly, and he possessed oxen and sheep and donkeys and camels, and men-servants and maid-servants.

30 Laban and his sons envied Jacob, and Laban took back his sheep from him, and he envied him and watched him for an opportunity to do evil.

[Chapter 29]

1 It happened when Rachel had given birth to Joseph, that Laban went to shear his sheep; for they were distant from him, a three-day journey.

2 Jacob saw that Laban was going to shear his sheep, and Jacob called Leah and Rachel, and spoke sweetly to them in order to convince them to come with him to the land of Canaan.

3 For he told them how he had seen everything in a dream. All that God had spoken to him that he should return to his father's house, and they said, "To every place where you go we will go with you."

4 Jacob blessed the God of Isaac his father, and the God of Abraham his father's father, and he arose and placed his wives and his children on donkeys, and took all his possessions and crossed the river, and came to the land of Gilead, and Jacob hid his intention from Laban and did not tell him.

5 In the seventh year of the fourth week Jacob turned his face toward Gilead in the first month, on the twenty-first of it.

6 Laban pursued and overtook Jacob in the mountain of Gilead in the third month, on the thirteenth of it. And the Lord did not permit him to injure Jacob for he appeared to him in a dream by night.

7 Laban spoke to Jacob. On the fifteenth of those days Jacob made a feast for Laban, and for all who came with him, and Jacob swore to Laban that day, and Laban also swore to Jacob, that neither should cross the mountain of Gilead to do evil to the other.

8 He made a heap (of stones) for a witness there; wherefore the name of that place is called, "The Heap of Witness," after this heap.

9 But before they used to call the land of Gilead the land of the Rephaim. The Rephaim were born giants whose height was ten, nine, eight, down to seven cubits.

10 Their dwelling place was from the land of the children of Ammon to Mount Hermon, and the seats of their kingdom were Karnaim and Ashtaroth, and Edrei, and Misur, and Beon.

11 The Lord destroyed them because of the evil of their deeds, for they were malevolent, and the Amorites were wicked and sinful. There is no people today which has committed the full range of their sins, and their life on the earth was shortened.

12 Jacob sent Laban away, and he departed into Mesopotamia, the land of the East, and Jacob returned to the land of Gilead.

13 He passed over the Jabbok in the ninth month, on the eleventh of it. On that day Esau, his brother, came to him, and he was reconciled to him, and departed from him to the land of Seir, but Jacob dwelt in tents.

14 In the first year of the fifth week in this jubilee he crossed the Jordan, and dwelt beyond the Jordan. He pastured his sheep from the sea of the heap to Bethshan, and to Dothan and to the forest of Akrabbim.

15 He sent his father Isaac all of his possessions such as clothing, and food, and meat, and drink, and milk, and butter, and cheese, and some dates of the valley.

16 Four times a year, he sent gifts to his mother Rebecca who was living at the tower of Abraham. He sent the gifts between the times of the months between plowing and reaping, and between autumn and the rain season, and between winter and spring.

17 For Isaac had returned from the Well of the Oath and gone up to the tower of his father Abraham, and he dwelt there apart from his son Esau.

18 For in the days when Jacob went to Mesopotamia, Esau took to himself a wife Mahalath, the daughter of Ishmael,

and he gathered together all the flocks of his father and his wives, and went up and dwelt on Mount Seir, and left Isaac his father at the Well of the Oath alone.

19 And Isaac went up from the Well of the Oath and dwelt in the tower of Abraham his father on the mountains of Hebron, and that is where Jacob sent all that he did send to his father and his mother from time to time, all they needed, and they blessed Jacob with all their heart and with all their soul.

[Chapter 30]

1 In the first year of the sixth week he went up to Salem, to the east of Shechem, in the fourth month, and he went in peace. Shechem, the son of Hamor, the Hivite, the prince of the land carried off Dinah, the daughter of Jacob, into the house, and he had sex with her and defiled her. She was a little girl, a child of twelve years.

2 He begged his father and her brothers that she might be given to him as a wife.

3 Jacob and his sons were very angry because of the men of Shechem, for they had defiled Dinah, their sister. They spoke to them while planning evil acts and they dealt deceitfully with them and tricked them.

4 Simeon and Levi came unexpectedly to Shechem and executed judgment on all the men of Shechem, and killed all the men whom they found in it. They did not leave a single one remaining in it. They killed all in hand to hand battle because they had dishonored their sister Dinah.

5 Let it not again be done from now on that a daughter of Israel be defiled. Judgment is ordained in heaven against them that they should destroy all the men of the Shechemites with the sword because they had committed shame in Israel.

6 The Lord delivered them into the hands of the sons of Jacob that they might exterminate them with the sword and execute judgment on them. That it might not again be done in Israel that a virgin of Israel should be defiled.

7 If there is any man in Israel who wishes to give his daughter or his sister to any man who is of the offspring of the Gentiles he shall surely die. They shall stone him, for he has committed shame in Israel. They shall burn the woman with fire, because she has dishonored the name of the house of her father, and she shall be rooted out of Israel.

8 Do not let an adulteress and let no uncleanness be found in Israel throughout all the days of the generations of the earth. For Israel is holy to the Lord, and every man who has defiled it shall surely die. They shall stone him.

9 For it has been ordained and written in the heavenly tablets regarding all the offspring of Israel. He who defiles it shall surely die. He shall be killed by stoning. There is no limit of days for this law. There is no remission, and no atonement.

10 The man who has defiled his daughter shall be rooted out from every corner of all Israel, because he has given of his offspring to Moloch (a pagan God, the worship of which involved burning the child alive), and committed impurity and defiled his child.

11 Moses, command the children of Israel and exhort them not to give their daughters to the Gentiles, and not to take for their sons any of the daughters of the Gentiles, for this is abominable before the Lord.

12 It is because of this that I have written all the deeds of the Shechemites, which they committed against Dinah, and placed them in the words of the Law for you. I have also written how the sons of Jacob spoke, saying, "We will not give our daughter to a man who is uncircumcised, for that is a reproach to us."

13 It is a reproach to Israel that anyone take the daughters of the Gentiles, for this is unclean and abominable to Israel.

14 Israel will not be free from this uncleanness if it has a wife of the daughters of the Gentiles, or has given any of its daughters to a man who is of any of the Gentiles.

15 There will be plague upon plague, and curse upon curse, and every judgment and plague and curse will come if he does this thing, or if they ignore those who commit uncleanness, or defile the sanctuary of the Lord, or those who profane His holy name. If any of these happen the whole nation together will be judged for all the uncleanness and profanation of this man.

16 There will be no judging people by their position and no receiving fruits, or offerings, or burnt-offerings, or fat, or the fragrance of sweet odor from his hands. It will be unacceptable and so warn every man and woman in Israel who defiles the sanctuary.

17 For this reason I have commanded you, saying, "Give this testimony to Israel, see how the Shechemites and their sons fared? See how they were delivered into the hands of two sons of Jacob, and they killed them under torture? It was counted to them for righteousness, and it is written down to them for righteousness.

18 The offspring of Levi were chosen for the priesthood, and to be Levites, that they might minister before the Lord, as we do, continually. Levi and his sons will be blessed forever, for he was zealous to execute righteousness and judgment and vengeance on all those who arose against Israel.

19 So they wrote a testimony in his favor of blessing and righteousness on the heavenly tablets in the presence of the God of all.

20 We remember the righteousness that the man fulfilled during his life, throughout the years, until a thousand generations they will record it. It will come to him and to his descendants after him, and he has been recorded on the heavenly tablets as a friend and a righteous man.

21 All this account I have written for you, and have commanded you to tell the children of Israel, so that they will not commit sin nor transgress the laws nor break the covenant which has been ordained for them. They should fulfill it and be recorded as friends (of God).

22 But if they transgress and work uncleanness in any way, they will be recorded on the heavenly tablets as adversaries (of God), and they will be blotted out of the book of life. Instead, they will be recorded in the book of those who will be destroyed and with those who will be rooted out of the earth.

23 On the day when the sons of Jacob killed Shechem it was written in the record in their favor in heaven that they had executed righteousness and uprightness and vengeance on the sinners, and it was written for a blessing.

24 They brought Dinah, their sister, out of the house of Shechem. They took everything that was in Shechem captive. They took their sheep and their oxen and their donkeys, and all their wealth, and all their flocks, and brought them all to Jacob their father.

25 He reproached them because they had put the city to the sword for he feared those who dwelt in the land, the Canaanites and the Perizzites.

26 The dread of the Lord was on all the cities that are near Shechem. They did not fight or chase after the sons of Jacob, for terror had fallen on them.

[Chapter 31]

1 On the new moon of the month, Jacob spoke to all the people of his house, saying, "Purify yourselves and change your clothes, and let us get up and go to Bethel where I vowed a vow to Him on the day when I fled from Esau my brother. Let us do this because God has been with me and brought me into this land in peace. You must put away the strange gods that you raise among you."

2 They gave up the strange gods and that which was in their ears and which was on their necks and the idols which Rachel stole from Laban her father she gave wholly to Jacob. And he burnt and broke them to pieces and destroyed them, and hid them under an oak, which is in the land of Shechem.

3 He went up on the new moon of the seventh month to Bethel. And he built an altar at the place where he had slept, and he set up a pillar there, and he sent word to his father, Isaac, and his mother, Rebecca. He asked to come to Isaac. There, Jacob wished to offer his sacrifice.

4 Isaac said, "Let my son, Jacob, come, and let me see him before I die."

5 Jacob went to his father, Isaac, and his mother, Rebecca, to the house of his father Abraham, and he took two of his sons with him, Levi and Judah.

6 Rebecca came out from the tower to the front of it to kiss Jacob and embrace him, for her spirit had revived when she heard, "Look Jacob your son has come," and she kissed him.

7 She saw his two sons and she recognized them. She said to him, "Are these your sons, my son?" and she embraced them and kissed them, and blessed them, saying, "In you shall the offspring of Abraham become illustrious, and you shall prove a blessing on the earth."

8 Jacob went in to Isaac his father, to the room where he lay, and his two sons were with him. He took his father's hand, stooped down, he kissed him. Isaac held on to the neck of Jacob his son, and wept on his neck.

9 The darkness left the eyes of Isaac, and he saw the two sons of Jacob, Levi, and Judah. And he said, "Are these your sons, my son? Because they look like you."

10 He said to Isaac, "They were truly my sons, and you have clearly seen that they are truly my sons."

11 They came near to him, and he turned and kissed them and embraced them both together.

12 The spirit of prophecy came down into his mouth, and he took Levi by his right hand and Judah by his left.

13 He turned to Levi first, and began to bless him first, and said to him, "May the God of all, the very Lord of all the ages, bless you and your children throughout all the ages.

14 May the Lord give to you and your offspring greatness and great glory from among all flesh. May the Lord cause you and your offspring to draw near to Him to serve in His sanctuary like the angels of the presence (of the Lord) and as the holy ones. The offspring of your sons shall be for the glory and greatness and holiness of God. May He make them great throughout all the ages. They shall be judges and princes, and chiefs of all the offspring of the sons of Jacob. They shall speak the word of the Lord in righteousness, and they shall judge all His judgments in righteousness.

15 They shall declare My ways to Jacob and My paths to Israel. The blessing of the Lord shall be given in their mouths to bless all the offspring of the beloved.

16 Your mother has called your name Levi, and rightly has she called your name. You will be joined to the Lord and be the companion of all the sons of Jacob. Let His table be your table, and let your sons eat from it. May your table be full throughout all generations, and let your food not fail in all the ages.

17 Let all who hate you fall down before you, and let all your adversaries be rooted out and perish. Blessed be he that blesses you, and cursed be every nation that curses you."

18 To Judah he said, "May the Lord give you strength and power to put all that hate you under your feet. You and one of your sons will be a prince over the sons of Jacob. May your name and the name of your sons go out across every land and region.

19 Then shall the Gentiles fear you, and all the nations and people shall shake (with fear of you). In you will be the help of Jacob, and in you will be found the salvation of Israel.

20 When you sit on the throne, which honors of your righteousness, there shall be great peace for all the offspring of the sons of the beloved. Blessed be he that blesses you, and cursed be all that hate you, afflict you, or curse you. They shall be rooted out and destroyed from the earth."

21 He turned, kissed him again, and embraced him, and rejoiced greatly because he had seen the sons of his son, Jacob, clearly and truly.

22 He stepped out from between his feet and fell down. He bowed down to him, and blessed them. He rested there with Isaac, his father, that night, and they ate and drank with joy.

23 He made the two sons of Jacob sleep, the one on his right hand and the other on his left. It was counted to him for righteousness.

24 Jacob told his father everything during the night about how the Lord had shown him great mercy, and how he had caused him to prosper in all his ways, and how he protected him from all evil.

25 Isaac blessed the God of his father Abraham, who had not withdrawn his mercy and his righteousness from the sons of his servant Isaac.

26 In the morning, Jacob told his father, Isaac, the vow, which he had vowed to the Lord. He told him of the vision which he had seen, and that he had built an altar. He told him that everything was ready for the sacrifice to be made before the Lord as he had vowed. He had come to set him on a donkey.

27 Isaac said to Jacob his son, "I am not able to go with you, for I am old and not able to endure the way. Go in peace, my son. I am one hundred and sixty-five years this day. I am no longer able to journey. Set your mother on a donkey and let her go with you.

28 I know that you have come on my account, my son. May this day be blessed on which you have seen me alive, and I also have seen you, my son.

29 May you prosper and fulfill the vow that you have vowed. Do not put off your vow, for you will be called to account for the vow. Now hurry to perform it, and may He who has made all things be pleased. It is to Him you have vowed the vow."

30 He said to Rebecca, "Go with Jacob your son," and Rebecca went with Jacob her son, and Deborah with her, and they came to Bethel.

31 Jacob remembered the prayer with which his father had blessed him and his two sons, Levi and Judah. He rejoiced and blessed the God of his fathers, Abraham and Isaac.

32 He said, "Now I know that my sons and I have an eternal hope in the God of all." Thus is it ordained concerning the two. They recorded it as an eternal testimony to them on the heavenly tablets how Isaac blessed his sons.

[Chapter 32]

1 That night he stayed at Bethel, and Levi dreamed that they had ordained and made his sons and him the priests of the Most High God forever. Then he awoke from his sleep and blessed the Lord.

2 Jacob rose early in the morning, on the fourteenth of this month, and he gave a tithe for all that came with him, both of men and cattle, both of gold and every vessel and garment. Yes, he gave tithes of all.

3 In those days Rachel became pregnant with her son Benjamin. Jacob counted his sons starting from him and going to the oldest and Levi fell to the portion of the Lord. (Levi was the third son – three is the number of spiritual completeness.) His father clothed him in the garments of the priesthood and filled his hands.

4 On the fifteenth of this month, he brought fourteen oxen from among the cattle, and twenty-eight rams, and forty-nine sheep, and seven lambs, and twenty-one kids of the goats to the altar as a burnt-offering on the altar of sacrifice. The offering was well pleasing and a sweet odor before God.

5 This was his offering, done in acknowledgement of the vow in which he had promised that he would give a tenth, with their fruit-offerings and their drink- offerings.

6 When the fire had consumed it, he burnt incense over the fire, and for a thank-offering he sacrificed two oxen and four rams and four sheep, four male goats, and two sheep of a year old, and two kids of the goats. This he did daily for seven days.

7 He, his men, and all his sons were eating this with joy during seven days and blessing and thanking the Lord, who had delivered him out of all his tribulation and had given him His promise.

8 He tithed all the clean animals, and made a burnt sacrifice, but he did not give the unclean animals to Levi his son. He gave him (responsibility for) all the souls of the men. Levi acted in the priestly office at Bethel in the presence of Jacob his father, in preference to his ten brothers. He was a priest there, and Jacob gave his vow, and he gave a tithe to the Lord again and sanctified it, and it became holy to Him.

9 For this reason it is ordained on the heavenly tablets as a law for the offering of the tithe should be eaten in the presence of the Lord every year, in the place where it is chosen that His name should live and reside. This law has no limit of days forever.

10 This law is written so that it may be fulfilled every year. The second tithe should be eaten in the presence of the Lord, in the place where it has been chosen, and nothing shall be left over from it from this year to the following year.

11 In its year shall the seed be eaten until the days of the gathering of the seed of the year. The wine shall be consumed until the days of the wine, and the oil until the days of its season.

12 All that is left of it and all that becomes old will be regarded as spoiled, let it be burnt with fire, for it is unclean.

13 Let them eat it together in the sanctuary, and let them not permit it to become old.

14 All the tithes of the oxen and sheep shall be holy to the Lord, and shall belong to his priests. They will eat before Him from year to year, for thus is it ordained and written on the heavenly tablets regarding the tithe.

15 On the following night, on the twenty-second day of this month, Jacob resolved to build that place and to surround the court with a wall, and to sanctify it and make it holy forever, for himself and his children after him.

16 The Lord appeared to him by night and blessed him and said to him, "Your name shall not be called Jacob, but they will call your name Israel."

17 And He said to him again, "I am the Lord who created the heaven and the earth, and I will increase you and multiply you greatly, and kings shall come forth from you, and they shall be judges everywhere the foot of the sons of men have walked.

18 I will give to your offspring all the earth that is under heaven. They shall judge all the nations, as they desire. After that they shall possess the entire earth and inherit it forever."

19 And He finished speaking with him, and He went up from him.

20 Jacob watched until He had ascended into heaven.

21 In a vision at night he saw an angel descend from heaven with seven tablets in his hands, and he gave them to Jacob, and he read them and knew all that was written on it that would happen to him and his sons throughout all the ages.

22 He showed him all that was written on the tablets, and said to him, "Do not build on this place, and do not make it an eternal sanctuary, and do not live here. This is not the place. Go to the house of Abraham your father and live with Isaac, your father, until the day he dies.

23 For in Egypt you will die in peace, and in this land you will be buried with honor in the sepulcher of your fathers, with Abraham and Isaac.

24 Do not fear. As you have seen and read it shall all be. Write down everything that you have seen and read."

25 Jacob said, "Lord, how can I remember all that I have read and seen?" He said to him, "I will bring all things to your remembrance."

26 He ascended from Jacob, and Jacob awoke from his sleep. He remembered everything that he had read and seen, and he wrote down all the words.

27 He celebrated there yet another day, and he sacrificed on that day as he had sacrificed on all the former days. He called its name "Addition," because this day was added, and the former days he called "The Feast."

28 It was made known and revealed to him and it is written on the heavenly tablets that he should celebrate the day, and add it to the seven days of the feast.

29 Its name was called "Addition," because that it was recorded among the days of the feast days, according to the number of the days of the year.

30 In the night, on the twenty-third of this month, Deborah, Rebecca's nurse died, and they buried her beneath the city under the oak of the river. He called the name of this place, "The river of Deborah," and he called the oak, "The oak of the mourning of Deborah."

31 Rebecca departed and returned to her house, to his father Isaac. Jacob sent rams and sheep and male goats by her so that she should prepare a meal for his father such as he desired.

32 He followed his mother until he came to the land of Kabratan, and he lived there.

33 Rachel gave birth to a son in the night, and called his name "son of my sorrow", for she broke down while giving birth to him, but his father called his name Benjamin. This happened on the eleventh day of the eighth month in the first of the sixth week of this jubilee.

34 Rachel died there and she was buried in the land of Ephrath, the same is Bethlehem, and Jacob built a pillar on the grave of Rachel, on the road above her grave.

[Chapter 33]

1 Jacob went and lived to the south of Magdaladra'ef. He and Leah, his wife, went to his father, Isaac, on the new moon of the tenth month.

2 Reuben saw Bilhah, Rachel's maid, the concubine of his father, bathing in water in a secret place, and he loved her.

3 He hid himself at night, and he entered the house of Bilhah at night. He found her sleeping alone on a bed in her house.

4 He had sex with her. She awoke and saw that is was Reuben lying with her in the bed. She uncovered the border of her covering and grabbed him and cried out when she discovered that it was Reuben.

5 She was ashamed because of him and released her hand from him, and he fled.

6 Because of this, she mourned greatly and did not tell it to any one.

7 When Jacob returned and sought her, she said to him, "I am not clean for you. I have been defiled in regard to you. Reuben has defiled me, and has had sex with me in the night. I was asleep and did not realize he was there until he uncovered my skirt and had sex with me."

8 Jacob was very angry with Reuben because he had sex with Bilhah, because he had uncovered his father's skirt.

9 Jacob did not approach her again because Reuben had defiled her. And as for any man who uncovers his father's skirt his deed is wicked greatly, for he is disgusting to the Lord.

10 For this reason it is written and ordained on the heavenly tablets that a man should not lie with his father's wife,
and should not uncover his father's skirt. This is unclean and they shall surely die together, the man who lies with his father's wife and the woman also, for they have committed uncleanness on the earth.

11 There shall be nothing unclean before our God in the nation that He has chosen for Himself as a possession.

12 Again, it is written a second time, "Cursed be he who lies with the wife of his father, for he has uncovered his father's shame." All the holy ones of the Lord said, "So be it. So be it."

13 "Moses, command the children of Israel so that they observe this word. It entails a punishment of death. It is unclean, and there is no atonement forever for the man who has committed this. He is to be put to death. Kill him by stoning. Root him out from among the people of our God.

14 No man who does so in Israel will be permitted to remain alive a single day on the earth. He is abominable and unclean.

15 Do not let them say, "Reuben was granted life and forgiveness after he had sex with his father's concubine, although she had a husband, and her husband, Jacob, his father, was still alive."

16 Until that time the ordinance and judgment and law had not been revealed in its completeness for all. In your days it has been revealed as a law of seasons and of days. It is an everlasting law for all generations forever. For this law has no limit of days, and no atonement for it.

17 They must both be rooted out of the entire nation. On the day they committed it they shall be killed.

18 Moses, write it down for Israel that they may observe it, and do according to these words, and not commit a sin punishable by death. The Lord our God is judge, who does not respect persons (position) and accepts no gifts.

19 Tell them these words of the covenant, that they may hear and observe, and be on their guard with respect to them, and not be destroyed and rooted out of the land; for an uncleanness, and an abomination, and a contamination, and a pollution are all they who commit it on the earth before our God.

20 There is no greater sin on earth than fornication that they commit. Israel is a holy nation to the Lord its God, and a nation of inheritance. It is a priestly and royal nation and for His own possession. There shall appear no such uncleanness among the holy nation.

21 In the third year of this sixth week, Jacob and all his sons went and lived in the house of Abraham, near Isaac his father and Rebecca his mother.

22 These were the names of the sons of Jacob, the first-born
Reuben, Simeon, Levi, Judah, Issachar, Zebulon, which are the sons of Leah. The sons of Rachel are Joseph and Benjamin. The sons of Bilhah are Dan and Naphtali; and the sons of Zilpah, Gad and Asher. Dinah is the daughter of Leah, the only daughter of Jacob.

23 They came and bowed themselves to Isaac and Rebecca. When they saw them they blessed Jacob and all his sons, and Isaac rejoiced greatly, for he saw the sons of Jacob, his younger son and he blessed them.

[Chapter 34]

1 In the sixth year of this week of the forty-fourth jubilee Jacob sent his sons and his servants to pasture their sheep in the pastures of Shechem.

2 The seven kings of the Amorites assembled themselves together (to fight) against them and kill them. They hid themselves under the trees, to take their cattle as booty.

3 Jacob, Levi, Judah and Joseph were in the house with Isaac their father, for his spirit was sorrowful, and they could not leave him. Benjamin was the youngest, and for this reason he remained with his father.

4 The king of Taphu, the king of Aresa, the king of Seragan, the king of Selo, the king of Ga'as, the king of Bethoron, the king of Ma'anisakir, and all those who dwell in these mountains and who dwell in the woods in the land of Canaan came.

5 They announced to Jacob saying, "Look, the kings of the Amorites have surrounded your sons, and plundered their herds."

6 And he left his house, he and his three sons and all the servants of his father, and his own servants, and he went against them with six thousand men, who carried swords.

7 He killed them in the pastures of Shechem, and pursued those who fled, and he killed them with the edge of the sword, and he killed Aresa and Taphu and Saregan and Selo and Amani sakir and Gaga'as, and he recovered his herds.

8 He conquered them, and imposed tribute on them that they should pay him five fruit products of their land. He built (the cities of) Robel and Tamnatares.

9 He returned in peace, and made peace with them, and they became his servants until the day that he and his sons went down into Egypt.

10 In the seventh year of this week he sent Joseph from his house to the land of Shechem to learn about the welfare of his brothers. He found them in the land of Dothan.

11 They dealt treacherously with him, and formed a plot against him to kill him, but they changed their minds and sold him to Ishmaelite merchants. They brought him down into Egypt, and they sold him to Potiphar, the eunuch of Pharaoh, the chief of the cooks and priest of the city of Elew."

12 The sons of Jacob slaughtered a kid, and dipped Joseph's coat in the blood and sent it to Jacob their father on the tenth of the seventh month.

13 They brought it to him in the evening and he mourned all that night. He became feverish with mourning for Joseph's death, and he said, "An evil beast has devoured Joseph". All the members of his house mourned and grieved with him that day.

14 His sons and his daughter got up to comfort him, but he refused to be comforted for his son.

15 On that day Bilhah heard that Joseph had perished, and she died mourning him. She was living in Qafratef, and Dinah his daughter, died after Joseph had perished.

16 There were now three reasons for Israel to mourn in one month. They buried Bilhah next to the tomb of Rachel, and Dinah his daughter. They were (all) buried there.

17 He mourned for Joseph one year, and did not cease, for he said, "Let me go down to my grave mourning for my son."

18 For this reason it is ordained for the children of Israel that they should remember and mourn on the tenth of the seventh month. On that day the news came which made Jacob weep for Joseph. On this day they should make atonement for their sins for themselves with a young goat on the tenth of the seventh month, once a year, for they had grieved the sorrow of their father regarding Joseph his son.

19 This day, once a year, has been ordained that they should grieve on it for their sins, and for all their transgressions and for all their errors, so that they might cleanse themselves.

20 After Joseph perished, the sons of Jacob took to themselves wives. The name of Reuben's wife is Ada; and the name of Simeon's wife is Adlba'a, a Canaanite. The name of Levi's wife is Melka, of the daughters of Aram, of the offspring of the sons of Terah. The name of Judah's wife is Betasu'el, a Canaanite. The name of Issachar's wife is Hezaqa, and the name of Zabulon's wife is Ni'iman. The name of Dan's wife is Egla. The name of Naphtali's wife is Rasu'u, of Mesopotamia. The name of Gad's wife is Maka. The name of Asher's wife is Ijona. The name of Joseph's wife is Asenath, the Egyptian. The name of Benjamin's wife is Ijasaka.

21 And Simeon repented, and took a second wife from Mesopotamia as his brothers had done.

[Chapter 35]

1 In the first year of the first week of the forty-fifth jubilee Rebecca called Jacob, her son, and commanded him regarding his father and regarding his brother, that he should honor them all the days of his life.

2 Jacob said, "I will do everything you have commanded. I will honor them. This will be honor and greatness to me, and righteousness before the Lord.

3 Mother, you know from the time I was born until this day, all my deeds and all that is in my heart. I always think good concerning all.

4 Why should I not do this thing which you have commanded me, that I should honor my father and my brother?

5 Tell me, mother, what perversity have you seen in me and I shall turn away from it, and mercy will be on me."

6 She said to him, "My son, in all my days I have not seen any perverseness in you, but only upright deeds. Yet, I will tell you the truth, my son, I shall die this year. I shall not survive this year in my life. I have seen the day of my death in a dream. I should not live beyond a hundred and fifty-five years. I have completed all the days that I am to live my life."

7 Jacob laughed at the words of his mother because his mother had said she should die. She was sitting across from him in possession of her strength, and she was still strong. She came and went (as she wished). She could see well, and her teeth were strong. No sickness had touched her all the days of her life.

8 Jacob said to her, "If my days of life are close to yours and my strength remain with me as your strength I would be blessed, mother. You will not die. You are simply joking with me regarding your death."

9 She went in to Isaac and said to him, " I make one request of you. Make Esau swear that he will not injure Jacob, nor pursue him with intent to harm him. You know Esau's thoughts have been perverse from his youth, and there is no goodness in him. He desires to kill him after you die.

10 You know all that he has done since the day Jacob, his brother, went to Haran until this day. He has forsaken us with his whole heart, and has done evil to us. He has stolen your flocks and carried off all your possessions while you watched.

11 When we asked him and begged him for what was our own, he did as a man (stranger) who was taking pity on us (giving a token like one giving alms to a beggar).

12 He is bitter against you because you blessed Jacob, your perfect and upright son. There is no evil but only goodness in Jacob. Since he came from Haran to this day he has not robbed us of anything. He always brings us everything in its season. He rejoices and blesses us with all his heart when we take his hands. He has not parted from us since he came from Haran until this day, and he remains with us continually at home honoring us."

13 Isaac said to her, "I also know and see the deeds of Jacob who is with us, how he honors us with all his heart. Before, I loved Esau more than Jacob because he was the first-born, but now I love Jacob more than Esau, for Esau has done many evil deeds, and there is no righteousness in him. All his ways are unrighteousness and violence.

14 My heart is troubled because of all his deeds. Neither he nor his offspring will be exempt because they are those who will be destroyed from the earth and who will be rooted out from under heaven. He and his children have forsaken the God of Abraham and gone after his wives (wives' gods) and after their uncleanness and after their error.

15 You told me to make him swear that he will not kill Jacob his brother, but even if he swears, he will not abide by his oath. He will not do good but evil only.

16 If he desires to kill Jacob, his brother, then into Jacob's hands he will be given. He will not escape from Jacob's hands.

17 Do not be afraid for Jacob, for the guardian of Jacob is great, powerful, honored, and praised more than the guardian of Esau."

18 Rebecca called for Esau and he came to her, and she said to him, "I have a request of you, my son. Promise to do it, my son."

19 He said, "I will do everything that you say to me, and I will not refuse your request."

20 She said to him, "I ask you that the day I die, you will take me in and bury me near Sarah, your father's mother, and that you and Jacob will love each other and that neither will desire evil against the other, but (have) mutual love only. Do this so you will prosper, my son, and be honored in the all of the land, and no enemy will rejoice over you. You will be a blessing and a mercy in the eyes of all those that love you."

21 He said, "I will do all that you have told me. I shall bury you on the day you die near Sarah, my father's mother, as you have desired that her bones may be near your bones.

22 Jacob, my brother, I shall love above all flesh. I have only one brother in all the earth but him. It is only what is expected of me. It is no great thing if I love him, for he is my brother, and we were sown together in your body, and together came we out from your womb. If I do not love my brother, whom shall I love?

23 I beg you to exhort Jacob concerning me and concerning my sons, for I know that he will assuredly be king over me and my sons, for on the day my father blessed him he made him the higher and me the lower.

24 I swear to you that I shall love him, and not desire evil against him all the days of my life but good only."

25 And he swore to her regarding all this matter. While Esau was there, she called Jacob and gave him her orders according to the words that she had spoken to Esau.

26 He said, "I shall do your pleasure, believe me that no evil will proceed from me or from my sons against Esau. I shall be first in nothing except in love only."

27 She and her sons ate and drank that night, and she died, three jubilees and one week and one year old on that night. Her two sons, Esau and Jacob, buried her in the double cave near Sarah, their father's mother.

[Chapter 36]

1 In the sixth year of this week Isaac called his two sons Esau and Jacob, and they came to him, and he said to them, "My sons, I am going the way of my fathers, to the eternal house where my fathers are.

2 Bury me near Abraham my father, in the double cave in the field of Ephron the Hittite, where Abraham purchased a sepulcher to bury in. Bury me in the sepulcher I dug for myself.

3 I command you, my sons, to practice righteousness and uprightness on the earth, so that the Lord may do to you what he said he would do to Abraham and to his offspring.

4 Love one another. Love your brothers as a man who loves his own soul. Let each seek how he may benefit his brother, and act together on the earth. Let them love each other as their own souls.

5 I command and warn you to reject idols. Hate them, and do not love them. They are fully deceptive to those that worship them and for those that bow down to them.

6 Remember the Lord God of Abraham, your father, and how I worshipped Him and served Him in righteousness and in joy, that God might multiply you and increase your offspring as the multitude of stars in heaven, and establish you on the earth as the plant of righteousness, which will not be rooted out to all the generations forever.

7 And now I shall make you swear a great oath, for there is no oath which is greater than that which is by the name glorious, honored, great, splendid, wonderful and mighty, which created the heavens and the earth and all things together, that you will fear Him and worship Him.

8 Each will love his brother with affection and righteousness. Neither will desire to do evil against his brother from now on forever all the days of your life so that you may prosper in all your deeds and not be destroyed.

9 If either of you plans evil against his brother, know that he that plans evil shall fall into his brother's hand, and shall be rooted out of the land of the living, and his offspring shall be destroyed from under heaven.

10 But on that day there will be turbulence, curses, wrath, anger, and will He burn his land and his city and all that is his with a devouring fire like the fire He sent to burn Sodom and he shall be blotted out of the book of the discipline of the children of men, and he will not be recorded in the book of life. He shall be added in the book of destruction. He shall depart into eternal curses. Their condemnation may be always renewed in hate and in curses and in wrath and in torment and in anger and in plagues and in disease forever.

11 My sons, this, I say and testify to you, will be the result according to the judgment which shall come on the man who wishes to injure his brother."

12 Then he divided all his possessions between the two on that day, and he gave the larger portion to him that was the first-born, and the tower and all that was around it, and all that Abraham possessed at the Well of the Oath.

13 He said, "This larger portion I will give to the first-born."

14 Esau said, "I have sold and relinquished my birthright to Jacob. Let it be given to him. I have nothing to say regarding it, for it is his."

15 Isaac said, "May a blessing rest on you, my sons, and on your offspring this day. You have given me rest, and my heart is not pained concerning the birthright, or that you should work wickedness because of it.
16 May the Most High God bless the man and his offspring forever that does righteousness."
17 He stopped commanding them and blessing them, and they ate and drank together in front of him, and he rejoiced because there was one mind between them, and they went out from him and rested that day and slept.
18 Isaac slept on his bed that day rejoicing. He slept the eternal sleep, and died one hundred and eighty years old. He lived twenty-five weeks and five years; and his two sons, Esau and Jacob, buried him.
19 After that Esau went to the land of Edom, to the mountains of Seir, and lived there.
20 Jacob lived in the mountains of Hebron, in the high place of the land in which his father Abraham had journeyed. He worshipped the Lord with all his heart. He had divided the days of his generations according to the commands he had seen.
21 Leah, his wife, died in the fourth year of the second week of the forty-fifth jubilee, and he buried her in the double cave near Rebecca his mother to the left of the grave of Sarah, his father's mother. All her sons and his sons came to mourn over Leah, his wife, with him and to comfort him regarding her. He was lamenting her for he loved her greatly after Rachel, her sister, died. She was perfect and upright in all her ways and she honored Jacob. All the days that she lived with him he did not hear from her mouth a harsh word, for she was gentle, peaceable, upright and honorable.
22 And he remembered all the deeds she had done during her life and he lamented her greatly. He loved her with all his heart and with all his soul.

[Chapter 37]

1 On the day that Isaac, the father of Jacob and Esau died, the sons of Esau heard that Isaac had given the elder's portion to his younger son, Jacob, and they were very angry.
2 They argued with their father, saying, "Why has your father given Jacob the portion of the elder and passed you over even though you are the elder and Jacob the younger?"
3 He said to them, "Because I sold my birthright to Jacob for a small portion of lentils (lentil soup), and on the day my father sent me to hunt, catch, and bring him something that he should eat and bless me, Jacob came with deceit and brought my father food and drink. My father blessed him and put me under his hand.
4 Now our father has caused Jacob and me to swear that we shall not devise evil plans against his brother (each other), and that we shall continue in love and in peace each with his brother and not make our ways corrupt."
5 They said to him, "We shall not listen to you to make peace with him. We are stronger than him and we are more powerful than he is. We shall depose him and kill him, and destroy him and his sons. If you will not go with us, we shall hurt you also.
6 Listen! Let us send to Aram, Philistia, Moab, and Ammon. Let us take chosen men who are trained in battle, and let us go against him and do battle with him. Let us exterminate him from the earth before he grows strong."
7 Their father said to them, "Do not go and do not make war with him or you shall fall before him."
8 They said to him, "This is how you have acted from your youth until this day. You have continued to put your neck under his yoke. We shall not listen to these words."
9 Then they sent to Aram, and to Aduram to the friend of their father, and they also hired one thousand chosen men of war.
10 And there came to them from Moab and from the children of Ammon, those who were hired, one thousand chosen men, and from Philistia, one thousand chosen warriors, and from Edom and from the Horites one thousand chosen warriors, and from the Kittim mighty warriors.
11 They said to their father, "Go out with them and lead them or else we shall kill you."
12 And he was filled with boiling anger on seeing that his sons were forcing him to go before them to lead them against Jacob, his brother.
13 But afterward he remembered all the evil that lay hidden in his heart against Jacob his brother, and he did not remember the oath he had sworn to his father and to his mother that he would plan no evil against Jacob, his brother, all his days.
14 Because Jacob was in mourning for his wife Leah, he did not know they were coming to battle against him until they approached the tower with four thousand soldiers and chosen warriors. The men of Hebron sent to him saying, "Look your brother has come against you to fight. He has with him four thousand men carrying swords, shields, and weapons." They told him this because they loved Jacob more than Esau.
15 So they told him, for Jacob was a more gracious and merciful man than Esau.
16 But Jacob would not believe until they came very near to the tower.
17 He closed the gates of the tower; and he stood on the battlements and spoke to his brother Esau and said, "Noble is the comfort you have come to give me concerning the death of my wife. Is this the oath that you swore to your father and again to your mother before they died? You have broken the oath, and on the moment that you swore to your father you were condemned."
18 Then Esau answered and said to him, "Neither the children of men nor the beasts of the earth have sworn an oath of righteousness and kept it forever. Every day they lay evil plans one against another regarding how they might kill their adversary or foe.

19 You will hate my children and me forever, so there is no observing the tie of brotherhood with you.

20 Hear these words that I declare to you. If the boar can change its skin and make its bristles as soft as wool, or if it can cause horns to sprout out on its head like the horns of a stag or of a sheep, then will I observe the tie of brotherhood with you. Like breasts separate themselves from their mother (and fight), you and I have never been brothers.

21 If the wolves make peace with the lambs and not devour or do them violence, and if their hearts are towards them for good, then there shall be peace in my heart towards you. If the lion becomes the friend of the ox and makes peace with him and if he is bound under one yoke with him and plows with him, then will I make peace with you.

22 When the raven becomes white as the raza (a white bird?), then know that I have loved you and shall make peace with you. You will be rooted out, and your sons shall be rooted out, and there shall be no peace for you."

23 Jacob saw that Esau had decided in his heart to do evil toward him, and that he desired with all his soul to kill him. Jacob saw that Esau had come pouncing like the wild boar which charges the spear that is set to pierce and kills it, and yet does not even slow down. Then he spoke to his own people and to his servants and told them that Esau and his men were going to attack him and all his companions.

[Chapter 38]

1 After that Judah spoke to Jacob, his father, and said to him, "Bend your bow, father, and send forth your arrows and bring down the adversary and kill the enemy. You have the power to do it. We will not kill your brother because he is your kin and he is like you, so we will honor his life."

2 Then Jacob bent his bow and sent forth the arrow and struck Esau, his brother, on the right side of his chest and killed him.

3 And again he sent forth an arrow and struck Adoran the Aramaean, on the left side of his chest, and it drove him backward and killed him. Then the sons of Jacob and their servants went out, dividing themselves into companies on the four sides of the tower.

4 Judah went out in front. Naphtali and Gad along with fifty servants went to the south side of the tower, and they killed all they found before them. Not one individual escaped.

5 Levi, Dan, and Asher went out on the east side of the tower along with fifty men, and they killed the warriors of Moab and Ammon.

6 Reuben, Issachar, and Zebulon went out on the north side of the tower along with fifty men and they killed the warriors of the Philistines.

7 Reuben's son, Simeon, Benjamin, and Enoch went out on the west side of the tower along with fifty men and they killed four hundred men, stout warriors of Edom and of the Horites. Six hundred fled, and four of the sons of Esau fled with them, and left their father lying killed, as he had fallen on the hill that is in Aduram.

8 And the sons of Jacob pursued them to the mountains of Seir. And Jacob buried his brother on the hill that is in Aduram, and he returned to his house.

9 The sons of Jacob crushed the sons of Esau in the mountains of Seir, and made them bow their necks so that they became servants of the sons of Jacob.

10 They sent a message to their father to inquire whether they should make peace with them or kill them.

11 Jacob sent word to his sons that they should make peace. They made peace with them but also placed the yoke of servitude on them, so that they paid tribute to Jacob and to his sons always.

12 And they continued to pay tribute to Jacob until the day that he went down to Egypt.

13 The sons of Edom have not escaped the yoke of servitude imposed by the twelve sons of Jacob until this day.

14 These are the kings that reigned in Edom before there was any king over the children of Israel (until this day) in the land of Edom.

15 And Balaq, the son of Beor, reigned in Edom, and the name of his city was Danaba. Balaq died, and Jobab, the son of Zara of Boser, ruled in his place.

16 Jobab died, and Asam, of the land of Teman, ruled in his place.

17 Asam died, and Adath, the son of Barad, who killed Midian in the field of Moab, ruled in his place, and the name of his city was Avith.

18 Adath died, and Salman, from Amaseqa, ruled in his place.

19 Salman died, and Saul of Ra'aboth by the river, ruled in his place. Saul died, and Ba'elunan, the son of Achbor, ruled in his place.

20 Ba'elunan, the son of Achbor died, and Adath ruled in his place, and the name of his wife was Maitabith, the daughter of Matarat, the daughter of Metabedza'ab. These are the kings who reigned in the land of Edom.

[Chapter 39]

1 Jacob lived in the land that his father journeyed in, which is the land of Canaan.

2 These are the generations of Jacob. Joseph was seventeen years old when they took him down into the land of Egypt, and Potiphar, a eunuch of Pharaoh, the chief cook, bought him.

3 He made Joseph the manager over Potiphar's entire house and the blessing of the Lord came on the house of the Egyptian because of Joseph. And the Lord caused him to prosper in all that he did.

4 The Egyptian turned everything over to the hands of Joseph because he saw that the Lord was with him, and that the Lord caused him to prosper him in all that he did.

5 Joseph's appearance was beautiful, and his master's wife watched Joseph, and she loved him and wanted him to have sex with her.

6 But he did not surrender his soul because he remembered the Lord and the words which Jacob, his father, used to read to him from the writings of Abraham, that no man should commit fornication with a woman who has a husband. For him the punishment of death has been ordained in the heavens before the Most High God, and the sin will be recorded against him in the eternal books, which are always in the presence of the Lord.

7 Joseph remembered these words and refused to have sex with her.

8 And she begged him for a year, but he refused and would not listen.

9 But while he was in the house she embraced him and held him tightly in order to force him to sleep with her. She closed the doors of the house and held on to him, but he left his garment in her hands and broke through the door and ran out from her presence.

10 The woman saw that he would not sleep with her, and she slandered him in the presence of his master, saying "Your Hebrew servant, whom you love, sought to force me to have sex with him. When I shouted for help he fled and left his garment in my hands. I tried to stop him but he broke through the door."

11 When the Egyptian saw Joseph's garment and the broken door, and heard the words of his wife, he threw Joseph into prison and put him in the place where the prisoners of the king were kept.

12 He was there in the prison, and the Lord gave Joseph favor in the sight of the chief of the prison guards and caused him to have compassion for Joseph, because he saw that the Lord was with him, and that the Lord made all that he did to prosper.

13 He turned over all things into his hands, and the chief of the prison guards knew of nothing that was going on in the prison, because Joseph did everything for him, and the Lord perfected it. He remained there two years.

14 In those days Pharaoh, king of Egypt, was very angry at his two eunuchs, the chief butler, and the chief baker. He put them in the prison facility of the house of the chief cook, where Joseph was kept.

15 The chief of the prison guards appointed Joseph to serve them, and he served them.

16 They both dreamed a dream, the chief butler and the chief baker, and they told it to Joseph.

17 As he interpreted to them so it happened to them, and Pharaoh restored the chief butler to his office and he killed the chief baker as Joseph had interpreted to them.

18 But the chief butler forgot Joseph was in the prison, although he had informed him of what would happen to him. He did not remember to inform Pharaoh of how Joseph had told him (about his dream), because he forgot.

[Chapter 40]

1 In those days Pharaoh dreamed two dreams in one night concerning a famine that was to be in all the land, and he awoke from his sleep and called all the magicians and interpreters of dreams that were in Egypt. He told them his two dreams but they were not able to tell him what they meant.

2 Then the chief butler remembered Joseph and told the king of him, and he brought him out from the prison, and the king told his two dreams to him.

3 He said before Pharaoh that his two dreams were one, and he said to him, "Seven years shall come in which there shall be plenty in all the land of Egypt, but after that, seven years of famine. Such a famine as has not been in all the land.

4 Now, let Pharaoh appoint administrators in all the land of Egypt, and let them store up food in every city throughout all the years of plenty, and there will be food for the seven years of famine, and those of the land will not perish through the famine, even though it will be very severe."

5 The Lord gave Joseph favor and mercy in the eyes of Pharaoh. Pharaoh said to his servants, "We shall not find such a wise and prudent man like this man, because the spirit of the Lord is with him."

6 And he appointed Joseph the second in command in his entire kingdom and gave him authority over all Egypt, and placed him on the second chariot of Pharaoh to ride.

7 And he clothed him with fine linen clothes, and he put a gold chain around his neck, and a crier proclaimed before him "El" "El wa Abirer," and he placed a ring on his hand and made him ruler over all his house, and lifted him up before the people, and said to him, "Only on the throne shall I be greater than you."

8 Joseph ruled over all the land of Egypt, and all the governors of Pharaoh, and all his servants, and all those who did the king's business loved him because he walked in uprightness, because he was without pride and arrogance. He did not judge people by their position, and did not accept gifts, but he judged all the people of the land in uprightness.

9 The land of Egypt was at peace before Pharaoh because of Joseph, because the Lord was with him, and the Lord gave him favor and mercy for all his generations before all those who knew him and those who heard of him, and Pharaoh's kingdom was run efficiently, and there was no Satan (adversary) and no evil person in it.

10 And the king called Joseph's name Sephantiphans, and gave Joseph the daughter of Potiphar, the daughter of the priest of Heliopolis, the chief cook to marry.

11 On the day that Joseph stood before Pharaoh he was thirty years old.

12 In that year Isaac died. Things transpired as Joseph had said in the interpretation of Pharaoh's dream and there were seven years of plenty over all the land of Egypt, and the land of Egypt abundantly produced, one measure producing eighteen hundred measures.

13 Joseph gathered food into every city until they were full of grain and they could no longer count or measure it because of its multitude.

[Chapter 41]

1 In the forty-fifth jubilee, in the second week, and in the second year, Judah took his first-born Er, a wife from the daughters of Aram, named Tamar.

2 But he hated her, and did not have sex with her, because her mother was of the daughters of Canaan, and he wished to take him a wife of the lineage of his mother, but Judah, his father, would not permit him to do that.

3 Er, the first-born of Judah, was wicked, and the Lord killed him.

4 And Judah said to Onan, his brother, "Go in to your brother's wife and perform the duty of a husband's brother to her, and raise up offspring to your brother."

5 Onan knew that the offspring would not be his, but his brother's only, and he went into the house of his brother's wife, and spilt his seed (ejaculates) on the ground, and he was wicked in the eyes of the Lord, and He killed him.

6 Judah said to Tamar, his daughter-in-law, "Remain in your father's house as a widow until Shelah, my son has grown up, and I shall give you to him to wife."

7 He grew up, but Bedsu'el, the wife of Judah, did not permit her son Shelah to marry. Bedsu'el, Judah's wife, died in the fifth year of this week.

8 In the sixth year Judah went up to shear his sheep at Timnah.

9 And they told Tamar, "Look, your father-in-law is going up to Timnah to shear his sheep." And she took off her widow's clothes, and put on a veil, and adorned herself, and sat in the gate connecting the road to Timnah.

10 As Judah was going along he saw her, and thought she was a prostitute, and he said to her, "Let me come in to you," and she said to him, "Come in," and he went in.

11 She said to him, "Give me my pay," and he said to her, "I have nothing with me except my ring that is on my finger, my necklace, and my staff which is in my hand."

12 She said to him, "Give them to me until you send me my pay." And he said to her, "I will send to you a kid of the goats", and he gave her his ring, necklace, and staff, and she conceived by him.

13 Judah went to his sheep, and she went to her father's house.

14 Judah sent a kid of the goats by the hand of his shepherd, an Adullamite, but he could not find her, so he asked the people of the place, saying, "Where is the prostitute who was here?"

15 They said to him, "There is no prostitute here with us." And he returned and informed Judah that he had not found her, "I asked the people of the place, and they said to me, "There is no prostitute here." "

16 He said, "If you see her give the kids to her or we become a cause of ridicule." And when she had completed three months, it was revealed that she was with child, and they told Judah, saying, "Look Tamar, your daughter-in-law, is with child by whoredom."

17 And Judah went to the house of her father, and said to her father and her brothers, "Bring her out, and let them burn her, for she has committed uncleanness in Israel."

18 It happened when they brought her out to burn her that she sent to her father-in-law the ring and the necklace, and the staff, saying, "Tell us whose are these, because by him am I with child."

19 Judah acknowledged, and said, "Tamar is more righteous than I am.

20 Do not let them burn her." And for that reason she was not given to Shelah, and he did not again approach her and after that she gave birth to two sons, Perez and Zerah, in the seventh year of this second week.

21 At this time the seven years of fruitfulness were completed, of which Joseph spoke to Pharaoh.

22 Judah acknowledged the evil deed that he had done because he had sex with his daughter-in-law, and he hated himself for it.

23 He acknowledged that he had transgressed and gone astray, because he had uncovered the skirt of his son, and he began to lament and to supplicate before the Lord because of his transgression.

24 We told him in a dream that it was forgiven him because he supplicated earnestly, and lamented, and did not commit the act again.

25 And he received forgiveness because he turned from his sin and from his ignorance, because he transgressed greatly before our God. Every one that acts like this, every one who has sex with his mother-in-law, let them burn him alive with fire. Because there is uncleanness and pollution on them, let them burn them alive.

26 Command the children of Israel that there should be no uncleanness among them, because every one who has sex with his daughter-in-law or with his mother-in-law has committed

uncleanness. Let them burn the man who has had sex with her with fire, and likewise burn the woman, so that God will turn away wrath and punishment from Israel.

27 We told Judah that his two sons had not had sex with her, and for this reason his offspring was established for a second generation, and would not be rooted out.

28 For in single-mindedness he had gone and sought for punishment, namely, according to the judgment of Abraham, which he had commanded his sons. Judah had sought to burn her alive.

[Chapter 42]

1 In the first year of the third week of the forty-fifth jubilee the famine began to come into the land, and the rain refused to be given to the earth. None whatsoever fell.

2 The earth became barren, but in the land of Egypt there was food, because Joseph had gathered the seed of the land in the seven years of plenty and had preserved it.

3 The Egyptians came to Joseph that he might give them food, and he opened the storehouses where the grain of the first year was stored, and he sold it to the people of the land for gold.

4 Jacob heard there was food in Egypt, and he sent his ten sons that they should procure food for him in Egypt, and they arrived among those that went there, but Benjamin he did not send.

5 Joseph recognized them, but they did not recognize him. He spoke to them and questioned them, and he said to them, "Are you not spies and have you not come to explore ways to enter this land?"

6 And he put them in custody.

7 After that, he set them free again, and detained Simeon alone and sent his nine brothers away.

8 He filled their sacks with corn, and he put their gold back in their sacks, and they did not know it. Joseph then commanded them to bring their younger brother, because they had told him their father was living and also their younger brother.

9 They went up from the land of Egypt and they came to the land of Canaan. There they told their father all that had happened to them, and how the ruler of the country had spoken rudely to them, and had seized Simeon until they should bring Benjamin.

10 Jacob said, "You have taken my children from me! Joseph is gone and Simeon also is gone, and now you will take Benjamin away. I am the victim of your wickedness."

11 He said, "My son will not go down with you because fate may have it that he would fall sick. Their mother gave birth to two sons, and one has died, and this one also you will take from me. If, by fate, he took a fever on the road, you would turn my old age to sorrow and death."

12 He saw that every man's money had been returned to him in his sack, and for this reason he feared to send him.

13 The famine increased and became grievous in the land of Canaan, and in all lands except in the land of Egypt. Egypt had food because many of the children of the Egyptians had stored up their seed for food from the time when they saw Joseph gathering seed together and putting it in storehouses and preserving it for the years of famine.

14 The people of Egypt fed themselves on it during the first year of their famine but when Israel saw that the famine was very serious in the land, and that there was no deliverance, he said to his sons, "Go again, and procure food for us so that we will not die."

15 They said, "We shall not go unless our youngest brother go with us!"

16 Israel saw that if he did not send Benjamin with them, they would all perish because of the famine.

17 Reuben said, "Give him to me, and if I do not bring him back to you, kill my two sons in payment for his soul." Israel said to Reuben, "He shall not go with you."

18 Judah came near and said, "Send him with me, and if I do not bring him back to you, let me bear your blame all the days of my life."

19 He sent him with them in the second year of this week on the first day of the month.

20 They all came to the land of Egypt, and they had presents in their hands of sweet spice, almonds, turpentine nuts, and pure honey.

21 And they went and stood before Joseph, and he saw Benjamin his brother, and he knew him, and said to them, "Is this your youngest brother?" They said to him, "It is he."

22 He said, "The Lord be gracious to you, my son!" And he sent Benjamin into his house and he brought out Simeon to them. Joseph made a feast for them, and they presented to him the gifts that they had brought in their hands.
23 They ate before Joseph and he gave them all a portion of food, but the portion of food given to Benjamin was seven times larger than any of theirs.
24 And they ate and drank and got up and remained with their donkeys.
25 Joseph devised a plan whereby he might learn their thoughts as to whether they desired peace or not. He said to the steward who was over his house, "Fill all their sacks with food. Place their money back in their vessels. Put my cup, the silver cup out of which I drink, in the sack of the youngest and send them away."

[Chapter 43]

1 He did as Joseph had told him, and filled all their sacks with food for them and put their money back into their sacks, and put the cup in Benjamin's sack.
2 Early in the morning they departed, and it happened that when they had gone from that place, Joseph said to the steward of his house, "Pursue them, run and seize them, and say, 'You have repaid my kindness with evil. You have stolen from me the silver cup out of which my lord drinks.'
3 Bring me back their youngest brother. Go! Get him quickly before I go to my seat of judgment (judge you guilt of disobeying an order). "
4 He ran after them and said the words as he was told. They said to him, "God forbid that your servants should do this thing, and steal any utensil or money from the house of your lord, like the things we found in our sacks the first time we, your servants, came back from the land of Canaan.
5 We have not stolen any utensil. How could we? Look here in our sacks and search, and wherever you find the cup in the sack of any man among us, let him be killed, and we and our donkeys will serve your lord."
6 He said to them, "Not so. If I find it, the man whose sack I find it in I shall take as a servant, and the rest of you shall return in peace to your house."
7 He was searching in their vessels, beginning with the eldest and ending with the youngest, when it was found in Benjamin's sack.
8 They ripped their garments in frustration, and placed their belongings back on their donkeys, and returned to the city and came to the house of Joseph. They all bowed themselves with their faces to the ground in front of him.
9 Joseph said to them, "You have done evil." They said, "What shall we say and how shall we defend ourselves? Our lord has discovered the transgression of his servants; and now we and our donkeys are the servants of our lord."
10 Joseph said to them, "I too fear the Lord. As for you, go to your homes and let your brother be my servant, because you have done evil. I delight in this cup as no one else delights in his cup and yet you have stolen it from me."
11 Judah said, "O my lord, I pray you to let your servant speak a word in my lord's ear. Your servant's mother had two sons for our father. One went away and was lost, and has not been found since. This one alone is left of his mother, and your servant our father loves him. He would die if the lad were lost to him.
12 When we go to your servant our father, and the lad is not with us, it will happen that he will die. We will have brought so much sorrow on our father it will bring his death.
13 Now rather let me, your servant, stay here as a bondsman to my lord instead of the boy. Let the lad go with his brothers, because I will stand in for him at the hand of your servant our father. If I do not bring him back, your servant will bear the blame of our father forever."
14 Joseph saw that they were all in accord in doing good to one another. Then, he could not refrain himself, and he told them that he was Joseph.
15 And he conversed with them in the Hebrew tongue and hugged their necks and wept.
16 At first they did not recognize him and then they began to weep. He said to them, "Do not weep for me, but hurry and bring my father to me. See, it is my mouth that speaks and the eyes of my brother Benjamin see me.
17 Pay attention. This is the second year of the famine, and there are still five years to come without harvest or fruit of trees or plowing.
18 You and your households come down quickly, so that you won't die because of the famine. Do not be grieved for your possessions, because the Lord sent me before you to set things in order that many people might live.
19 Tell my father that I am still alive. You see that the Lord has made me as a father to Pharaoh, and ruler over his house and over all the land of Egypt.
20 Tell my father of all my glory, and all the riches and glory that the Lord has given me."
21 By the command of Pharaoh's mouth, he gave them chariots and provisions for the way, and he gave them all multi-colored raiment and silver.
22 He sent corn, raiment, silver, and ten donkeys that carried all of this to his father, and he sent them away.
23 They went up and told their father that Joseph was alive, and was measuring out corn to all the nations of the earth, and that he was ruler over all the land of Egypt.

24 But their father did not believe it, because he was not in his right mind. But when he saw the wagons, which Joseph had sent, the life of his spirit revived, and he said, "It is enough for me if Joseph lives. I will go down and see him before I die.

[Chapter 44]

1 Israel took his journey from Haran's house on the new moon of the third month, and he stopped at the Well of the Oath on the way and he offered a sacrifice to the God of his father Isaac on the seventh of this month.

2 Jacob remembered the dream that he had at Bethel, and he feared to go down into Egypt.

3 He was thinking of sending word to Joseph to come to him because he did not want to go down. He remained there seven days, hoping fate would permit him to see a vision as to whether he should remain or go down.

4 He celebrated the harvest festival of the first-fruits with old grain, because in all the land of Canaan there was not a handful of seed in the ground because the famine was affecting all the beasts, and cattle, and birds, and all men.

5 On the sixteenth the Lord appeared to him, and said to him, "Jacob, Jacob," and he said, "Here I am."

6 And He said to him, "I am the God of your fathers, the God of Abraham and Isaac. Do not be afraid to go down into Egypt, because I will be there to make you a great nation. I will go down with you, and I will bring you up again. You will be buried in this land and Joseph will put his hands on your eyes (to close them in death). Do not be afraid. Go down into Egypt."

7 And his sons got up and placed their father and their possessions on wagons.

8 Israel got up from the Well of the Oath on the sixteenth of this third month, and he went to the land of Egypt.

9 Israel sent Judah before him to his son Joseph to examine the Land of Goshen, because Joseph had told his brothers that they should come and live there so they could be near him.

10 This was the best land in Egypt. It was near to him and suitable for all of the cattle they had.

11 These are the names of the sons of Jacob who went into Egypt with Jacob their father; Reuben, the First-born of Israel and his sons Enoch, and Pallu, and Hezron and Carmi, making five.

12 Simeon and his sons Jemuel, and Jamin, and Ohad, and Jachin, and Zohar, and Shaul, the son of the Zephathite woman, making seven.

13 Levi and his sons Gershon, and Kohath, and Merari, making four.

14 Judah and his sons Shela, and Perez, and Zerah, making four.

15 Issachar and his sons Tola, and Phua, and Jasub, and Shimron, making five.

16 Zebulon and his sons Sered, and Elon, and Jahleel, making four.

17 These are the sons of Jacob and their sons whom Leah bore to Jacob in Mesopotamia, six, and their one sister, Dinah and all the souls of the sons of Leah, and their sons, who went with Jacob their father into Egypt. Twenty-nine souls, and Jacob, making thirty, were the number of people that went into Egypt.

18 And the sons of Zilpah, Leah's handmaid, the wife of Jacob, who bore to Jacob Gad and Ashur and their sons who went with him into Egypt.

19 The sons of Gad are Ziphion, and Haggi, and Shuni, and Ezbon, and Eri, and Areli, and Arodi, which make eight souls in total. The sons of Asher are Imnah, and Ishvah, and Ishvi, and Beriah, and Serah, and their one sister, which makes six in total.

20 All the souls were fourteen, and all those of Leah were forty-four.

21 The sons of Rachel, the wife of Jacob are Joseph and Benjamin.

22 There were born to Joseph in Egypt before his father came into Egypt, those whom Asenath, daughter of Potiphar, priest of Heliopolis gave birth to him, Manasseh, and Ephraim. The wife and children of Joseph totaled three.

23 The sons of Benjamin, Bela and Becher and Ashbel, Gera, and Naaman, and Ehi, and Rosh, and Muppim, and Huppim, and Ard with Benjamin totaled eleven.

24 And all the souls of Rachel were fourteen.

25 And the sons of Bilhah, the handmaid of Rachel, the wife of Jacob, whom she gave birth to Jacob, were Dan and Naphtali. These are the names of their sons who went with them into Egypt.

26 The sons of Dan were Hushim, and Samon, and Asudi. and "Ijaka, and Salomon, all totaling six.

27 All but one died the year in which they entered into Egypt, and there was left to Dan only Hushim.

28 These are the names of the sons of Naphtali: Jahziel, and Guni and Jezer, and Shallum, and 'Iv.

29 And 'Iv, who was born after the years of famine, died in Egypt.

30 All the souls (offspring) of Rachel were twenty-six.

31 All the souls (offspring) of Jacob, which went into Egypt, were seventy souls.

32 These are his children and his children's children, in all seventy, but five died in Egypt in the time of Joseph's rule and they had no children.

33 In the land of Canaan two sons of Judah died, Er and Onan, and they had no children, and the children of Israel buried those who died, and they were counted among the seventy Gentile nations.

[Chapter 45]

1 On the new moon of the fourth month, in the second year of the third week of the forty-fifth jubilee, Israel went into the country of Egypt, to the land of Goshen.

2 Joseph went to meet his father, Jacob, in the land of Goshen, and he hugged his father's neck and wept.

3 Israel said to Joseph, "Now that I have seen you let me die and may the Lord God of Israel, the God of Abraham, and the God of Isaac, who has not withheld His mercy and His grace from His servant Jacob, be blessed.

4 It is enough for me to have seen your face while I am yet alive. Yes, this is the true vision which I saw at Bethel.

5 Blessed be the Lord my God forever and ever, and blessed be His name."

6 Joseph and his brothers ate bread in the presence of their father and drank wine, and Jacob rejoiced with very great joy because he saw Joseph eating with his brothers and drinking in the presence of him, and he blessed the Creator of all things who had preserved him, and had preserved for him his twelve sons.

7 Joseph had given his father and his brothers as a gift the right of dwelling in the land of Goshen and in Rameses and all of the region around it, which he ruled over in the presence of Pharaoh.

8 Israel and his sons dwelt in the land of Goshen, the best part of the land of Egypt, and Israel was one hundred and thirty years old when he came into Egypt. Joseph nourished his father and his brothers and also their possessions (servants) with bread as much as they needed for the seven years of the famine.

9 The land of Egypt became available for purchase because of the famine, and Joseph acquired all the land of Egypt for Pharaoh in return for food, and he got possession of the people and their cattle and everything for Pharaoh.

10 The years of the famine were completed, and Joseph gave the people in the land seed and food that they might sow the land in the eighth year, because the river had overflowed all the land of Egypt.

11 For in the seven years of the famine it had not overflowed and had irrigated only a few places on the banks of the river, but now it overflowed and the Egyptians sowed the land, and it produced much corn that year.

12 This was the first year of the fourth week of the forty-fifth jubilee. Joseph took one-fifth of the corn of the harvest for the king and left four parts for them for food and for seed, and Joseph made it a law for Egypt until this day.

13 Israel lived in the land of Egypt seventeen years, and all the days which he lived were three jubilees, one hundred and forty-seven years, and he died in the fourth year of the fifth week of the forty-fifth jubilee.

14 Israel blessed his sons before he died and told them everything that they would go through in the land of Egypt. He revealed to them what they would live through in the last days, and he blessed them and gave Joseph two portions of the land.

15 He slept with his fathers, and he was buried in the double cave in the land of Canaan, near Abraham his father, in the grave which he dug for himself in the land of Hebron.

16 And he gave all his books and the books of his fathers to Levi, his son so that he might preserve them and replicate them for his children until this day.

[Chapter 46]

1 It happened that after the death of Jacob the children of Israel continued to multiply in the land of Egypt, and they became a great nation, and they were in one accord of heart, so that brother loved brother and every man helped his brother. They increased abundantly and multiplied greatly, ten weeks of years, all the days of the life of Joseph.

2 There was neither Satan nor any evil in all the days of the life of Joseph after his father, Jacob (had died), because all the Egyptians respected the children of Israel all the days of the life of Joseph.

3 Joseph died, being a hundred and ten years old. He lived seventeen years in the land of Canaan, and ten years he was a servant, and three years in prison, and eighty years he was under the king, ruling all the land of Egypt.

4 He died and so did all his brothers and all of that generation. But, he commanded the children of Israel before he died that they should carry his bones with them when they went out from the land of Egypt.

5 And he made them swear regarding his bones, because he knew that the Egyptians would not bring his bones out of Egypt or bury him in the land of Canaan, because while dwelling in the land of Assyria, king Makamaron, the king of Canaan, fought against Egypt in the valley and killed the king of Egypt there, and pursued the Egyptians to the gates of ʻErmon.

6 But he was not able to enter, because another king, a new king, had become king of Egypt, and he was stronger than he (Makamaron), and he returned to the land of Canaan, and the gates of Egypt were closed so that none came or went from Egypt.

7 Joseph died in the forty-sixth jubilee, in the sixth week, in the second year, and they buried him in the land of Egypt, and all his brothers died after him.

8 The king of Egypt went to war against the king of Canaan in the forty-seventh jubilee, in the second week in the second year, and the children of Israel brought out all the bones of the children of Jacob except the bones of Joseph, and they buried them in the field in the double cave in the mountain.

9 Then, most of them returned to Egypt, but a few of them remained in the mountains of Hebron, and Amram your father remained with them.

10 The king of Canaan was victorious over the king of Egypt, and he closed the gates of Egypt.

11 He devised an evil plan against the children of Israel to afflict them. He said to the people of Egypt, "Look, the people of the children of Israel have increased and multiplied more than we.

12 Let us use wisdom and deal with them before they become too many. Let us make them our slaves before we go to war and they rise up against us on the side of our enemies. Before they leave and fight against us let us do this because their hearts and faces (allegiances) are towards the land of Canaan."

13 He set over them taskmasters to enforce slavery, and they built strong cities for Pharaoh, Pithom, and Raamses and they built all the walls and all the fortifications, which had fallen in the cities of Egypt.

14 They enslaved them with harshness, and the more they were evil toward them, the more they increased and multiplied.

15 And the people of Egypt despised the children of Israel.

[Chapter 47]

1 In the seventh week, in the seventh year, in the forty-seventh jubilee, your father went out from the land of Canaan, and you (Moses) were born in the fourth week, in the sixth year of it, in the forty-eighth jubilee; this was the time of tribulation for the children of Israel.

2 Pharaoh, the king of Egypt, issued a command ordering them to throw all their newborn male children into the river.

3 And they threw them into the river for seven months until the day that you were born. It is said that your mother hid you for three months.

4 She made an ark for you, and covered it with pitch and tar, and placed it in the reeds on the bank of the river. She placed you in it seven days. Your mother came by night and nursed you. By day Miriam, your sister, guarded you from the birds.

5 In those days Tharmuth, the daughter of Pharaoh, came to bathe in the river, and she heard you crying. She told her maids to bring you out, and they brought you to her.

6 She took you out of the ark, and she had compassion on you.

7 Your sister said to her, "Shall I go and call to you one of the Hebrew women to nurse this baby for you?" And she said to her, "Go."

8 Your sister went and called your mother, Jochebed, and Pharaoh's daughter gave her wages (employed her), and she nursed you.

9 Afterwards, when you grew up, they brought you to the daughter of Pharaoh, and you became her son. Amram, your father, taught you writing. After you had completed three weeks (twenty-seven years) they brought you into the royal court.

10 You were three weeks of years at court until the time when you went out from the royal court and saw an Egyptian beating your friend who was of the children of Israel, and you killed him and hid him in the sand.

11 On the second day you came across two children of Israel quarreling together, and you asked the one who was doing wrong, "Why did you hit your brother?"

12 He was angry and indignant, and said, "Who made you a prince and a judge over us?

13 Do you want to kill me like you killed the Egyptian yesterday?" You were afraid and you fled on because of these words.

[Chapter 48]

1 In the sixth year of the third week of the forty-ninth jubilee you fled and went to live in the land of Midian for five weeks and one year. You returned to Egypt in the second week in the second year in the fiftieth jubilee.

2 You know what He said to you on Mount Sinai, and what prince Mastema desired to do with you when you returned to Egypt.

3 Did he (Mastema) not seek to kill you with all his power and to deliver the Egyptians from your hand when he saw that you were sent to execute judgment and to take revenge on the Egyptians?

4 But I delivered you out of his hand, and you performed the signs and wonders which you were sent to perform in Egypt against Pharaoh, and against all of his household, and against his servants and his people.

5 The Lord exacted a great vengeance on them for Israel's sake, and struck them through the plagues of blood, frogs, lice, dog-flies, malignant boils, breaking out in pustules, the death of their cattle, and the plague of hailstones. He destroyed everything that grew from them by plagues of locusts, which devoured the remainder left by the hail, and by darkness, and by the death of the first-born of men and animals. The Lord took vengeance on all of their idols and burned them with fire.

6 Everything was sent through your hand, that you should declare these things before they were done. You spoke with the king of Egypt in the presence of all his servants and in the presence of his people and everything took place according to your words. Ten great and terrible judgments came on the land of Egypt so that you might execute vengeance on Egypt for Israel.

7 And the Lord did everything for Israel's sake according to His covenant, which he had ordained with Abraham. He took vengeance on them because they had brought them by force into bondage.

8 Prince Mastema stood against you, and sought to deliver you into the hands of Pharaoh. He helped the Egyptian sorcerers when they stood up and committed the evil acts they did in your presence. Indeed, we permitted them to work, but the remedies we did not allow to be worked by their hands.

9 The Lord struck them with malignant ulcers (hemorrhoids?), and they were not able to stand. They could not perform a single sign because we destroyed them.

10 Even after all of these signs and wonders, prince Mastema was not put to shame because he took courage and cried to the Egyptians to pursue you with all the power the Egyptians had, with their chariots, and with their horses, and with all the hosts of the peoples of Egypt.

11 But I stood between the Egyptians and Israel, and we delivered Israel out of his hand, and out of the hand of his people. The Lord brought them through the middle of the sea as if it were dry land.

12 The Lord our God threw all the people whom he (Mastema) brought to pursue Israel into the middle of the sea, into the depths of the bottomless pit, beneath the children of Israel, even as the people of Egypt had thrown their (Israel's) children into the river. He took vengeance on one million of them. In addition to one thousand strong and energetic men were destroyed because of the death of the suckling children of your people, which they had thrown into the river.

13 On the fourteenth day and on the fifteenth and on the sixteenth and on the seventeenth and on the eighteenth days, prince Mastema was bound and imprisoned and placed behind the children of Israel so that he might not accuse them.

14 On the nineteenth day we let them (Mastema and his demons) loose so that they might help the Egyptians pursue the children of Israel.

15 He hardened their hearts and made them stubborn, and the plan was devised by the Lord our God that He might strike the Egyptians and throw them into the sea.

16 On the fourteenth day we bound him that he might not accuse the children of Israel on the day when they asked the Egyptians for vessels and garments, vessels of silver, and vessels of gold, and vessels of bronze, in order to exact from the Egyptians a price in return for the bondage they had been forced to serve.

17 We did not lead the children of Israel from Egypt empty handed.

[Chapter 49]

1 Remember the commandment which the Lord commanded you concerning the Passover. You should celebrate it in its season on the fourteenth day of the first month. You should kill the sacrifice before evening. They should eat it by night on the evening of the fifteenth from the time of the setting of the sun.

2 Because on this night, at the beginning of the festival and the beginning of the joy, you were eating the passover in Egypt, when all the powers of Mastema had been let loose to kill all the first-born in the land of Egypt, from the first-born of Pharaoh to the first-born of the captive maid-servant in the mill, and even the first-born of the cattle.

3 This is the sign that the Lord gave them, in every house on the door post on which they saw the blood of a lamb of the first year they should not enter to kill, but should pass by it, that all those should be exempt that were in the house because the sign of the blood was on its door posts.

4 And the powers of the Lord did everything as the Lord commanded them, and they passed by all the children of Israel, and the plague did not come on them to destroy them, cattle, man, or dog.

5 The plague was oppressive in Egypt, and there was no house in Egypt where there was not one dead, and weeping, and lamentation.

6 All Israel was eating the flesh of the paschal lamb, and drinking the wine, and was praising, and blessing, and giving thanks to the Lord God of their fathers, and they were ready to get out from under the yoke of Egypt and the evil bondage.

7 Remember this day all the days of your life. Observe it from year to year all the days of your life, once a year, on its day, according to all the law of it. Do not forsake it from day to day, or from month to month.

8 It is an eternal law, and engraved on the heavenly tablets regarding all the children of Israel that they should observe it on its day once a year, every year, throughout all their generations. There is no limit of days, for this is a law forever.

9 The man who is free from uncleanness, and does not come to observe Passover on the occasion of its day and does not bring an acceptable offering before the Lord to eat and to drink before the Lord on the day of its festival will be guilty. If he is clean and close at hand (near the temple) and does not come, he shall be cut off because he did not offer the offering of the Lord in its appointed season. He shall take the guilt on himself.

10 Let the children of Israel come and observe the passover on the day of its fixed time, on the fourteenth day of the first month, between the evenings, from the third part of the day to the third part of the night, for two portions of the day are given to the light, and a third part to the evening.

11 The Lord commanded you to observe it between the evenings.

12 And it is not permissible to kill the sacrifice during any period of light, but only during the period bordering on the evening, and let them eat it at the time of the evening, until the third part of the night. Whatever is left over of all its flesh from the third part of the night and onwards is to be burned with fire.

13 They shall not cook it with water (boil or seethe it), nor shall they eat it raw, but roast it on the fire. They shall eat it with care, making sure its head with the inwards and its feet are roasted with fire, and they shall not break any bone of it, for of the children of Israel no bone shall be crushed.

14 For this reason the Lord commanded the children of Israel to observe the passover on the day of its fixed time, and they shall not break a bone of it, because it is a festival day He commanded. There was no passing over from any other day or any other month, but on the exact day let the festival be observed.

15 Command the children of Israel to observe the passover throughout their days, every year, once a year on the day of its fixed time, and it shall be a memorial well pleasing in the presence of the Lord, and no plague shall come on them to kill or to strike in that year in which they celebrate the passover in its season in every respect according to His command.

16 And they shall not eat it outside the sanctuary of the Lord, but before the sanctuary of the Lord, and all the people of the congregation of Israel shall celebrate it in its appointed season.

17 Every man twenty years of age and upward, who has come on the day of the Passover shall eat it in the sanctuary of your God before the Lord. This is how it is written and ordained. They should eat it in the sanctuary of the Lord.

18 When the children of Israel come into the land of Canaan that they are to possess, set up the tabernacle (tent) of the Lord within the land occupied by one of their tribes until the sanctuary of the Lord has been built in the land. There, let them come and celebrate the passover at tabernacle of the Lord, and let them kill it before the Lord from year to year.

19 When the house of the Lord has been built in the land of their inheritance, they shall go there and kill the passover in the evening, at sunset, at the third part of the day.

20 They shall offer its blood on the threshold of the altar, and shall place its fat on the fire, which is on the altar, and they shall eat its flesh roasted with fire in the yard of the house, which has been sanctified in the name of the Lord.

21 They may not celebrate the passover in their cities, nor in any place except at the tabernacle of the Lord, or before His house where His name has dwelt. They shall not stray from the Lord.

22 Moses, command the children of Israel to observe the ordinances of the passover, as it was commanded to you. Declare to them every year the purpose and time of the festival of unleavened bread. They should eat unleavened bread seven days. They should observe its festival and bring an offering every day during those seven days of joy before the Lord on the altar of your God.

23 Celebrate this festival with haste as when you went out from Egypt and you entered into the wilderness of Shur, because on the shore of the sea you completed it (the exodus).

[Chapter 50]

1 I made this law known to you the days of the Sabbaths in the desert of Sinai, between Elim and Sinai.

2 I told you of the Sabbaths of the land on Mount Sinai, and I told you of the jubilee years in the sabbaths of years, but have I not told you the year of it until you enter the land which you are to possess.

3 Keep the sabbaths of the land while they live on it, and they shall know the jubilee year.

4 I have ordained for you the year of weeks and the years and the jubilees. There are forty-nine jubilees from the days of Adam until this day, and one week and two years, and there are forty years yet to come learning the commandments of the Lord, until they pass over into the land of Canaan, crossing the Jordan to the west.

5 The jubilees shall pass by until Israel is cleansed from all guilt of fornication, and uncleanness, and pollution, and sin, and error, and it dwells with confidence in all the land. There shall be no more Satan or any evil one, and the land shall be clean from that time forever.

6 I have written down the commandment for them regarding the Sabbaths and all the judgments of its laws for you.

7 Six days will you labor, but the seventh day is the Sabbath of the Lord your God.

8 You shall do no manner of work in it, you and your sons, and your menservants and your maidservants, and all your cattle and travelers also who lodge with you. The man that does any work on it shall die. Whoever desecrates that day, whoever has sex with his wife, whoever says he will do something on it, or he that will set out on a journey on it in regard to any buying or selling, or whoever draws water on it which he had not prepared for himself on the sixth day, and whoever takes up any burden to carry it out of his tent or out of his house shall die.

9 You shall do no work whatsoever on the Sabbath day except what you have prepared for yourselves on the sixth day, so as to eat, and drink, and rest. Keep Sabbath free from all work on that day. It is to bless the Lord your God, who has given you a day of festival and a holy day, and a day of the holy kingdom. This is a day for Israel among all their days forever.

10 Great is the honor which the Lord has given to Israel that they should eat, drink, and be satisfied on this festival day. Rest on it from all labor, which belongs to the labor of the children of men, except burning frankincense and bringing offerings and sacrifices before the Lord for days and for Sabbaths.

11 Only this work shall be done on the Sabbath days in the sanctuary of the Lord your God so that they may atone for Israel with sacrifice continually from day to day for a memorial pleasing before the Lord, so that He may always receive them from day to day according to what you have been commanded.

12 Every man who does any work on it, or takes a trip, or tills his farm, whether in his house or any other place, and whoever lights a fire, or rides a beast, or travels by ship on the sea shall die. And whoever strikes or kills anything, or slaughters a beast or a bird, or whoever catches an animal or a bird or a fish, or whoever fasts or makes war on the Sabbaths, the man who does any of these things on the Sabbath shall die. This is done so that the children of Israel will observe the Sabbaths according to the commandments regarding the Sabbaths of the land. It is written in the tablets, which He gave into my hands that I should write out for you the laws of the seasons, and the seasons according to the division of their days.

This completes the account of the division of the days.

The History Of The Book Of Jasher

The Book Of Jasher, or Sefer Ha Yashar, is referred to in the books of Joshua and Second Samuel of the Holy Bible.

"Behold it is written in the Book of Jasher."--II Samuel, i. 18
"Is not this written in the Book of Jasher?"--Joshua, x. 13.

Jasher (Yashar) is a Hebrew word meaning "upright". Jasher is not the name of the author or any prophet or judge of Israel, as scholars had previously thought. The name refers to the fact that the record, facts, and history are upright, correct, and thus, trustworthy.

The value of The Book of Jasher is seen in the large quantity of additional detail revealed in the period between divine creation and the time of Joshua's leadership over Israel when the Israelites enter into the land of Canaan.

The Book of Jasher includes details about the antediluvian patriarchs, angels, watchers, the flood, the tower of Babel, and many other events mentioned in the Bible. The tales are expanded and infused with detail not previously available.

This means we receive insight into the lives of Abraham, Noah, Enoch, Joseph, and many other biblical figures. We come to understand how they became great and why they acted as they did. We are also given hitherto unknown knowledge of historical events. We are shown how God's hand shaped history through his love and anger. We see how his disappointment with men and angels ended in earth's near total destruction.

We learn how the power of Nimrod, the great hunter, arose. We are told how all animals were guided to the ark of Noah, and why the tower of Babel was attacked by God and angels. Such detailed accounts bring the Old Testament into an understandable focus.

According to the Encyclopedia Judaica, Volume 14, p. 1099, Jasher was "probably written in the 13th century A.D." However, some scholars have proposed various dates between the 9th century and 16th century A.D.

There are three separate and different books named Jasher, however the Mormon Church, otherwise known as The Church of Jesus Christ of Latter-day Saints, considers this rendition of Jasher to be the book referenced in the Old Testament. The belief of the church leadership is bolstered by the preface in the 1625 version, which claims its original source came from the ruins of Jerusalem in 70 A.D.

Jasher is held in high repute by many Mormons but is not officially endorsed by the Mormon Church. The official stance of the Mormon Church falls short of making Jasher part of their Holy Scriptures but does endorse the book as being valid and authentic.   The Mormon Church places the book of Jasher on the same level as other apocryphal writings and states in the church magazine, The Ensign, After reviewing the standard scholarly analysis of how the book appears to have been composed of old Jewish legends, the book of Jasher is considered to be of great benefit to the reader. The article concluded with an injunction to treat it according to the Lord's advice on how to study the Apocrypha. The article goes on to quote the church stance on the Apocrypha.

"Verily, thus saith the Lord unto you concerning the Apocrypha — There are many things contained therein that are true, and it is mostly translated correctly; There are many things contained therein that are not true, which are interpolations by the hands of men. Verily, I say unto you, that it is not needful that the Apocrypha should be translated. Therefore, whoso readeth it, let him understand, for the Spirit manifesteth truth; And whoso is enlightened by the Spirit shall obtain benefit And whoso receiveth not by the Spirit, cannot be benefitted. Therefore it is not needful that it should be translated. Amen." (D.&C. 91:1-6)

In the early 1800s, Moses Samuel of Liverpool, England, was given a copy of the 1625 A.D. Hebrew work. Jasher, he found, was written in a theological or Rabbinical type of Hebrew, which is a more classical Hebrew. Samuel translated the text into English and in 1839 sold it to Mordecai Manuel Noah, a Jewish New York publisher, who published it in 1840.

Copyright of the translation was obtained by J. H. Parry & Company in Salt Lake City, who published it in 1887.

Samuel's translation was written in "Elizabethan or King James" English and contained archaic words, phrases, and idioms.

The translation offered here is taken from the J. H. Parry translation with all archaic language and idioms edited and restated in modern English.

According to Bernard Wasserstein, in the Transactions of the Jewish Historical Society of England Vol. XXXV, Samuel translated into English the pseudo-biblical Book of Jasher, a supposedly ancient Hebrew text which Samuel convinced himself was authentic. After failing to persuade the Royal Asiatic Society to publish it, he sold his translation for £150 in 1839 to the American Jewish newspaper-owner and philanthropist Mordecai M. Noah. It appeared in New York the following year but with Noah's name and not Samuel's on the title page. "I did not put my name to it as my Patron and myself differed about its authenticity", Samuel later explained. This was odd since Noah seems to have had a lower opinion of the work's authenticity than Samuel. The translation was accepted as accurate, but the publication provoked criticism by scholars who rejected the claims made on behalf of the text. It won acceptance, however, by the Mormon prophet Joseph Smith. (p. 2)

The prophet, Joseph Smith's attraction to the book was due in part to the history contained in the preface of the book.

According to the history documented in the preface of the Book of Jasher, Titus destroyed Jerusalem in 70 A.D. but the book was miraculously rescued at that time. During the destruction of the Jewish temple a Roman officer named Sidrus discovered a Hebrew scholar hiding in a library. The officer took the scholar and all the books safely back to his estates in Seville, Spain. The manuscript was transferred to the Jewish college in Cordova, Spain. The book was kept there until its printings in Venice in 1625.

There is no evidence to substantiate these claims, but there is nothing to conclusively dismiss the claims either.

In reality, it is possible that a Jew living in Spain or Italy may have penned the book, but we have no way to be definite regarding the date of writing of the original book. Part of the confusion arises from the fact that Jasher seems to be a compilation of several stories gathered by priests over many generations. Most of the stories and history contain reliable, authentic Jewish terms and traditions. It is the weight of these correct facts and references that lend credence to the authenticity of the seed literature that formed Jasher.

Scholars view Jasher with much skepticism due to the absence of any evidence or mention of the book prior to 1625. The basis of the stories contained in Jasher are mythically old, but the book itself has not been found in its present form prior to the printing in the 1600s. However, it is the opinion of the editor that Jasher will offer some insight into the murky and sometimes sparse historical landscape of Genesis. At the least, we may state that the book reflects what the priestly scholars who wrote the book believed.

The texts presented here represents an accurate version of the Book of Jasher rendered in modern English. Although the book was translated in the 1800s, the translator chose to use the more stilted and less accessible Elizabethan or King James style of English in order to add weight and religious authority to the text. This made the book less than pleasant to read for the modern audience. In the translation before you archaic words and expressions were replaced with their modern counterparts. A word for word replacement was not attempted. When an archaic word needed to be replaced with a phrase for the purpose of clarity this technique was embraced so as to render the text readily understandable. It is our sincere hope our goal was accomplished and the reader will find this version interesting and easy to read.

The Book of Jasher

THIS IS THE BOOK OF THE GENERATIONS OF MAN WHOM GOD CREATED ON THE EARTH ON THE DAY WHEN THE LORD GOD MADE HEAVEN AND EARTH.

CHAPTER 1

1 God said, Let us make man in our image, in our likeness, and God created man in his own image.

2 God formed man from the dirt, and he blew into his nostrils the breath of life, and man became a living soul with the capacity of speech.

3 And the Lord said, It is not good for man to be alone; I will make him a helper and a mate.

4 The Lord caused a deep sleep to come on Adam, and he slept. God took away one of his ribs, and he fashioned flesh on it, and formed it and brought it to Adam. Adam awoke from his sleep, and saw a woman was standing in front of him.

5 He said, This is bone of my bones and it shall be called woman, because it has been taken from man. Adam named her Eve, because she was the mother of all living (mankind).

6 God blessed them and on the day he created them he called their names Adam and Eve. The Lord God said, Be prolific and reproduce and fill the earth.

7 The Lord God took Adam and his wife, and he placed them in the garden of Eden to farm it and to keep it. He commanded them and said, "You may eat from every tree of the garden, but you may never eat from the tree of the knowledge of good and evil. On the day that you eat thereof you will certainly die.

8 When God had blessed and commanded them, he departed from them. Adam and his wife lived in the garden according to the command which the Lord had commanded them.

9 The serpent, which God had created with them in the earth, came to them to incite them to go contrary to the command of God which he had commanded them.

10 And the serpent enticed and persuaded the woman to eat from the tree of knowledge, and the woman listened to the voice of the serpent, and she went contrary to the word of God, and took from the tree of the knowledge of good and evil, and she ate, and she took from it and gave also to her husband and he ate.

11 And Adam and his wife went contrary to the command of God which he commanded them, and God knew it, and his anger was set ablaze against them and he cursed them.

12 And the Lord God drove them that day from the garden of Eden, to till the ground from which they were taken, and they went and lived at the east of the garden of Eden; and Adam had sex with his wife Eve and she bore two sons and three daughters.

13 She called the name of the first born Cain, saying, I have obtained a man from the Lord, and the name of the other she called Abel, for she said, Empty we came into the earth, and empty we shall be taken from it.

14 And the boys grew up and their father gave them a possession in the land; and Cain was a farmer of the ground, and Abel a keeper of sheep.

15 And it was at the expiration of a few years, that they brought a first-fruit offering to the Lord, and Cain brought from the fruit of the ground, and Abel brought from the firstlings of his flock from the fat thereof, and God turned and inclined to Abel and his offering, and a fire came down from the Lord from heaven and consumed it.

16 And to Cain and his offering the Lord did not turn, and he did not incline to it, for he had brought from the inferior fruit of the ground before the Lord, and Cain was jealous against his brother Abel on account of this, and he sought an opportunity to kill him.

17 Some time after, Cain and Abel his brother went one day into the field to do their work; and they were both in the field, Cain farming and plowing his ground, and Abel feeding his flock; and the flock passed| that part which Cain had plowed in the ground, and it sorely grieved Cain on this account.

18 And Cain approached his brother Abel in anger, and he said to him, What gives you the right to come and live here and bring your flock to feed in my land?

19 And Abel answered his brother Cain and said to him, What gives you the right to eat the flesh of my flock and clothe yourself with their wool?

20 Take off the wool of my sheep with which you have clothed yourself, and pay me for their resources you have used and flesh which you have eaten, and when you shall have done this, I will then go from your land as you have said|.

21 Cain said to his brother Abel, Certainly if I kill you this day, who will require your blood from me?

22 And Abel answered Cain, saying, Certainly God who has made us in the earth, he will avenge my cause, and he will require my blood from you should you kill me, for the Lord is the judge and arbiter, and it is he who will repay man according to his evil, and the wicked man according to the wickedness that he may do on earth.

23 And now, if you should kill me here, certainly God knows your secret views, and will judge you for the evil which you did declare to do to me this day.

24 When Cain heard the words which Abel his brother had spoken, the anger of Cain was set ablaze against his brother Abel

for declaring this thing.

25 Cain hurried and rose up, and took the iron part of his plowing instrument, with which he suddenly struck his brother and he killed him, and Cain spilt the blood of his brother Abel on the earth, and the blood of Abel streamed on the earth before the flock.

26 And after this Cain repented having slain his brother, and he was sadly grieved, and he wept over him and it troubled him greatly.

27 Cain rose up and dug a hole in the field, wherein he put his brother's body, and he turned the dust over it.

28 And the Lord knew what Cain had done to his brother, and the Lord appeared to Cain and said to him, Where is Abel your brother that was with you?

29 And Cain lied, and said, I do not know. Am I my brother's keeper? And the Lord said to him, What have you done? The voice of your brother's blood cries to me from the ground where you have slain him.

30 For you have slain your brother and have lied before me, and imagined in your heart that I saw you not, nor knew all your actions.

31 But you did this thing and did kill your brother for naught and because he spoke rightly to you, and now, therefore, cursed be you from the ground which opened its mouth to receive your brother's blood from your hand, and wherein you did bury him.

32 It shall be when you shall till it, the land will no longer give you its strength as in the beginning, for thorns and thistles shall the ground produce, and you shall be moving and wandering in the earth until the day of your death.

33 And at that time Cain went out from the presence of the Lord, from the place where he was, and he went moving and wandering in the land toward the east of Eden, he and all those belonging to him.

34 Cain had sex with his wife in those days, and she conceived and gave birth to a son, and he called his name Enoch, saying, In that time the Lord began to give him rest and quiet in the earth.

35 At that time Cain also began to build a city: and he built the city and he called the name of the city Enoch, according to the name of his son; for in those days the Lord had given him rest on the earth, and he did not move about and wander as in the beginning.

36 And Irad was born to Enoch, and Irad had Mechuyael and Mechuyael had Methusael.

CHAPTER 2

1 It was in the hundred and thirtieth year of the life of Adam on the earth, that he again had sex with Eve his wife, and she conceived and gave birth to a son and he looked like Adam, and she called his name Seth, saying, Because God has appointed me another offspring in the place of Abel, for Cain has slain him.

2 And Seth lived one hundred and five years, and he had a son; and Seth called the name of his son Enosh, saying, Because in that time the sons of men began to reproduce, and to afflict their souls and hearts by disobeying and rebelling against God.

3 It was in the days of Enosh that the sons of men continued to rebel and go contrary to God, to increase the anger of the Lord against the sons of men.

4 And the sons of men went and they served other gods, and they forgot the Lord who had created them in the earth: and in those days the sons of men made images of brass and iron, wood and stone, and they bowed down and served them.

5 Every man made his god and they bowed down to them, and the sons of men turned away from the Lord all the days of Enosh and his children; and the anger of the Lord was set ablaze on account of their works and abominations which they did in the earth.

6 The Lord caused the waters of the river Gihon to overwhelm them, and he destroyed and consumed them, and he destroyed the third part of the earth. Notwithstanding this, the sons of men did not turn from their evil ways, and their hands were yet extended to do evil in the sight of the Lord.

7 In those days there was neither sowing nor reaping in the earth; and there was no food for the sons of men and the famine was very great in those days.

8 And the seed which they sowed in those days in the ground became thorns, thistles and briers; for from the days of Adam was this declaration concerning the earth, of the curse of God, which he cursed the earth, on account of the sin which Adam sinned before the Lord.

9 And it was when men continued to rebel and go contrary to God, and to corrupt their ways, that the earth also became corrupt.

10 And Enosh lived ninety years and he had Cainan.

11 Cainan grew up and he was forty years old, and he became wise and had knowledge and skill in all wisdom, and he reigned over all the sons of men, and he led the sons of men to wisdom and knowledge; for Cainan was a very wise man and had understanding in all wisdom, and with his wisdom he ruled over spirits and demons.

12 Cainan knew by his wisdom that God would destroy the sons of men for having sinned on earth, and that the Lord would in the latter days bring on them the waters of the flood.

13 And in those days Cainan wrote on tablets of stone what was to take place in time to come, and he put them in his treasure

troves.

14 Cainan reigned over the whole earth, and he turned some of the sons of men to the service of God.

15 When Cainan was seventy years old, he had three sons and two daughters.

16 These are the names of the children of Cainan; the name of the first born was Mahlallel, the second was Enan, and the third was Mered, and their sisters were Adah and Zillah; these are the five children of Cainan that were born to him.

17 Lamech, the son of Methusael, became related to Cainan by marriage, and he took his two daughters for his wives, and Adah conceived and gave birth to a son to Lamech, and she called his name Jabal.

18 And she again conceived and gave birth to a son, and called his name Jubal; and Zillah, her sister, was unable to conceive in those days and had no offspring.

19 For in those days the sons of men began to trespass against God, and to go contrary to the commandments which he had given Adam, to be prolific and reproduce in the earth.

20 Some of the sons of men caused their wives to drink a mixture that would render them unable to conceive, in order that they might retain their figures and their beautiful appearance might not fade.

21 And when the sons of men caused some of their wives to drink, Zillah drank with them.

22 The child-bearing women appeared abominable in the sight of their husbands and they treated them as widows, while their husbands lived with those unable to conceive and to those women they were attached.

23 And in the end of days and years, when Zillah became old, the Lord opened her womb.

24 She conceived and gave birth to a son and she called his name Tubal Cain, saying, After I had withered away have I obtained him from the Almighty God.

25 And she conceived again and gave birth to a daughter, and she called her name Naamah, for she said, After I had withered away have I obtained pleasure and delight.

26 Lamech was old and advanced in years, and his eyes were dim that he could not see, and Tubal Cain, his son, was leading him and it was one day that Lamech went into the field and Tubal Cain his son was with him, and while they were walking in the field, Cain the son of Adam advanced towards them; for Lamech was very old and could not see much, and Tubal Cain his son was very young.

27 Tubal Cain told his father to draw his bow, and with the arrows he struck Cain, who was yet far off, and he killed him, because he appeared be an animal to them.

28 And the arrows entered Cain's body although he was at a distance from them, and he fell to the ground and died.

29 The Lord rewarded Cain's evil according to his wickedness, which he had done to his brother Abel, according to the word of the Lord which he had spoken.

30 And it came to pass when Cain had died, that Lamech and Tubal went to see the animal which they had slain, and they saw, and behold Cain their grandfather was fallen dead on the earth.

31 Lamech was very much grieved at having done this, and in clapping his hands together (in grief) he struck his son and caused his death.

32 And the wives of Lamech heard what Lamech had done, and they sought to kill him.

33 The wives of Lamech hated him from that day, because he killed Cain and Tubal Cain, and the wives of Lamech separated from him, and would not listen to him in those days.

34 And Lamech came to his wives, and he begged them to listen to him about this matter.

35 He said to his wives Adah and Zillah, Hear my voice O wives of Lamech, attend to my words, for now you have imagined and said that I killed a man with my wounds, and a child with my stripes for they did no violence, but certainly know that I am old and grey-headed, and that my eyes are heavy through age, and I did this thing unknowingly.

36 And the wives of Lamech listened to him in this matter, and they returned to him with the advice of their father Adam, but they bore no children to him from that time, knowing that God's anger was increasing in those days against the sons of men, to destroy them with the waters of the flood for their evil acts.

37 Mahlallel the son of Cainan lived sixty-five years and he had Jared; and Jared lived sixty-two years and he had Enoch.

CHAPTER 3

1 Enoch lived sixty-five years and he had Methuselah; and Enoch walked with God after having a son, Methuselah, and he served the Lord, and despised the evil ways of men.

2 And the soul of Enoch was wrapped up in the instruction of the Lord, in knowledge and in understanding; and he wisely retired from the sons of men, and cloistered himself from them for many days.

3 It was at the expiration of many years, while he was serving the Lord, and praying before him in his house, that an angel of the Lord called to him from Heaven, and he said, Here am I.

4 And he said, Rise, go forth from your house and from the place where you hide yourself, and appear to the sons of men, in order that you may teach them the way in which they should go and the work which they must accomplish in order to enter into the ways of God.

5 Enoch rose up according to the word of the Lord, and went forth from his house, from his place and from the chamber in

which he was concealed; and he went to the sons of men and taught them the ways of the Lord, and at that time assembled the sons of men and acquainted them with the instruction of the Lord.

6 He ordered it to be proclaimed in all places where the sons of men lived, saying, Where is the man who wishes to know the ways of the Lord and good works? Let him come to Enoch.

7 And all the sons of men then assembled to him, for all who desired this thing went to Enoch, and Enoch reigned over the sons of men according to the word of the Lord, and they came and bowed to him and they heard his word.

8 The spirit of God was on Enoch, and he taught all his men the wisdom of God and his ways, and the sons of men served the Lord all the days of Enoch, and they came to hear his wisdom.

9 And all the kings of the sons of men, both greatest and least, together with their princes and judges, came to Enoch when they heard of his wisdom, and they bowed down to him, and they also required of Enoch to reign over them, to which he consented.

10 They assembled in all, one hundred and thirty kings and princes, and they made Enoch king over them and they were all under his power and command.

11 And Enoch taught them wisdom, knowledge, and the ways of the Lord; and he made peace among them, and peace was throughout the earth during the life of Enoch.

12 Enoch reigned over the sons of men two hundred and forty-three years, and he did justice and righteousness with all his people, and he led them in the ways of the Lord.

13 These are the generations of Enoch, Methuselah, Elisha, and Elimelech, three sons; and their sisters were Melca and Nahmah, and Methuselah lived eighty-seven years and he had Lamech.

14 It was in the fifty-sixth year of the life of Lamech when Adam died. Nine hundred and thirty years old was he at his death. His two sons, with Enoch and Methuselah his son, buried him with great grandeur, as at the burial of kings, in the cave which God had told him.

15 And in that place all the sons of men mourned and wept greatly on account of Adam; it has therefore become a custom among the sons of men to this day.

16 Adam died because he ate of the tree of knowledge; he and his children after him, as the Lord God had spoken.

17 And it was in the year of Adam's death which was the two hundred and forty-third year of the reign of Enoch, in that time Enoch resolved to separate himself from the sons of men and to cloister himself as at first in order to serve the Lord.

18 Enoch did so, but did not entirely cloister himself from them, but kept away from the sons of men three days and then went to them for one day.

19 During the three days that he was in his chamber, he prayed to, and praised the Lord his God, and the day on which he went and appeared to his subjects he taught them the ways of the Lord, and all they asked him about the Lord he told them.

20 And he did in this manner for many years, and he afterward concealed himself for six days, and appeared to his people one day in seven; and after that once in a month, and then once in a year, until all the kings, princes and sons of men sought for him, and desired again to see the face of Enoch, and to hear his word; but they could not, as all the sons of men were greatly afraid of Enoch, and they feared to approach him on account of the Godlike awe that was seated on his countenance; therefore no man could look at him, fearing he might be punished and die.

21 All the kings and princes resolved to assemble the sons of men, and to come to Enoch, thinking that they might all speak to him at the time when he should come forth among them, and they did so.

22 The day came when Enoch went forth and they all assembled and came to him, and Enoch spoke to them the words of the Lord and he taught them wisdom and knowledge, and they bowed down before him and they said, May the king live! May the king live!

23 Some time after, when the kings and princes and the sons of men were speaking to Enoch, and Enoch was teaching them the ways of God, an angel of the Lord then called to Enoch from heaven, and wished to bring him up to heaven to make him reign there over the sons of God, as he had reigned over the sons of men on earth.

24 When at that time Enoch heard this he went and assembled all the inhabitants of the earth, and taught them wisdom and knowledge and gave them divine instructions, and he said to them, I have been required to ascend into heaven; but I do not know the day of my going.

25 And now therefore I will teach you wisdom and knowledge and will give you instruction before I leave you, how to act on earth so that you may live (as you should); and he did so.

26 He taught them wisdom and knowledge, and gave them instruction, and he rebuked them, and he placed before them statutes and judgments to do on earth, and he made peace among them, and he taught them everlasting life, and lived with them some time teaching them all these things.

27 At that time the sons of men were with Enoch, and Enoch was speaking to them, and they lifted up their eyes and the likeness of a great horse descended from heaven, and the horse paced in the air.

28 And they told Enoch what they had seen, and Enoch said to them, On my account does this horse descend on earth; the time is come when I must go from you and I shall no more be seen by you.

29 The horse descended at that time and stood before Enoch, and all the sons of men that were with Enoch saw him.

30 Enoch then again ordered a voice to be proclaimed, saying, Where is the man who delights to know the ways of the Lord his God, let him come this day to Enoch before he is taken from us.

31 All the sons of men assembled and came to Enoch that day; and all the kings of the earth with their princes and counselors remained with him that day; and Enoch then taught the sons of men wisdom and knowledge, and gave them divine instruction; and he bade them serve the Lord and walk in his ways all the days of their lives, and he continued to make peace among them.

32 It was after this that he rose up and rode on the horse; and he went forth and all the sons of men went after him, about eight hundred thousand men; and they went with him one day's journey.

33 And the second day he said to them, Return home to your tents, why will you go? Perhaps you may die; and some of them went from him, and those that remained went with him six day's journey; and Enoch said to them every day, Return to your tents, that you may die; but they were not willing to return, and they went with him.

34 And on the sixth day some of the men remained and clung to him, and they said to him, We will go with you to the place where you go; as the Lord lives, only death shall separate us.

35 They urged so much to go with him that he ceased speaking to them; and they went after him and would not return.

36 When the kings returned they caused a census to be taken, in order to know the number of remaining men that went with Enoch; and it was on the seventh day that Enoch ascended into heaven in a whirlwind, with horses and chariots of fire.

37 And on the eighth day all the kings that had been with Enoch sent to bring back the number of men that were with Enoch, in that place from which he ascended into heaven.

38 All those kings went to the place and they found the earth there filled with snow, and on the snow were large stones of snow, and one said to the other, Come, let us break through the snow and see, perhaps the men that remained with Enoch are dead, and are now under the stones of snow, and they searched but could not find Enoch, for he had ascended into heaven.

CHAPTER 4

1 All the days that Enoch lived on earth, were three hundred and sixty-five years.

2 And when Enoch had ascended into heaven, all the kings of the earth rose and took Methuselah his son and anointed him, and they caused him to reign over them in the place of his father.

3 Methuselah acted uprightly in the sight of God, as his father Enoch had taught him, and he likewise during the whole of his life taught the sons of men wisdom, knowledge and the fear of God, and he did not turn from the good way either to the right or to the left.

4 But in the latter days of Methuselah, the sons of men turned from the Lord; they corrupted the earth, they robbed and plundered each other, and they rebelled against God; they went contrary to, they corrupted their ways, and would not listen to the voice of Methuselah, but rebelled against him.

5 And the Lord was greatly wroth against them, and the Lord continued to destroy the offspring in those days, so that there was neither sowing nor reaping in the earth.

6 For when they sowed the ground in order that they might obtain food for their support, behold, thorns and thistles were produced which they did not sow.

7 And still the sons of men did not turn from their evil ways, and their hands were still extended to do evil in the sight of God, and they provoked the Lord with their evil ways, and the Lord was very wroth, and repented that he had made man.

8 He thought to destroy and annihilate them and he did so.

9 In those days when Lamech the son of Methuselah was one hundred and sixty years old, Seth the son of Adam died.

10 And all the days that Seth lived were nine hundred and twelve years, and he died.

11 Lamech was one hundred and eighty years old when he took Ashmua, the daughter of Elishaa the son of Enoch his uncle, and she conceived.

12 And at that time the sons of men sowed the ground, and a little food was produced, yet the sons of men did not turn from their evil ways, and they trespassed and rebelled against God.

13 The wife of Lamech conceived and gave birth to a son at that time, at the revolution of the year.

14 And Methuselah called his name Noah, saying, The earth was in his days at rest and free from corruption, and Lamech his father called his name Menachem, saying, This one shall comfort us in our works and miserable toil in the earth, which God had cursed.

15 The child grew up and was weaned, and he went in the ways of his father Methuselah, perfect and upright with God.

16 And all the sons of men departed from the ways of the Lord in those days as they multiplied on the face of the earth with sons and daughters, and they taught one another their evil practices and they continued sinning against the Lord.

17 Every man made to himself a god, and they robbed and plundered every man his neighbor as well as his relative, and they corrupted the earth, and the earth was filled with violence.

18 And their judges and rulers went to the daughters of men and took their wives by force from their husbands according to their choice, and the sons of men in those days took from the cattle of the earth, the beasts of the field and the fowls of the air, and taught the mixture of animals of one species with the other, in order therewith to provoke the Lord; and God saw the whole earth and it was corrupt, for all flesh had corrupted its ways on earth, all men and all animals.

19 And the Lord said, I will blot out man that I created from the face of the earth, yea from man to the birds of the air together with cattle and beasts that are in the field, for I repent that I made them.

20 All men who walked in the ways of the Lord died in those days, before the Lord brought the evil on man which he had declared, for this was from the Lord that they should not see the evil which the Lord spoke of concerning the sons of men.

21 And Noah found grace in the sight of the Lord, and the Lord chose him and his children to raise up offspring on the face of the whole earth.

CHAPTER 5

1 It was in the eighty-fourth year of the life of Noah that Enoch the son of Seth died; he was nine hundred and five years old at his death.

2 In the one hundred and seventy ninth year of the life of Noah, Cainan the son of Enosh died, and the age of Cainan was nine hundred and ten years, and he died.

3 And in the two hundred and thirty fourth year of the life of Noah, Mahlallel the son of Cainan died, and the days of Mahlallel were eight hundred and ninety-five years, and he died.

4 Jared the son of Mahlallel died in those days, in the three hundred and thirty-sixth year of the life of Noah; and all the days of Jared were nine hundred and sixty-two years, and he died.

5 And all who followed the Lord died in those days, before they saw the evil which God declared to do on earth.

6 After the lapse of many years, in the four hundred and eightieth year of the life of Noah, when all those men who followed the Lord had died away from among the sons of men, and only Methuselah was left, God said to Noah and Methuselah:

7 Speak ye, and proclaim to the sons of men, saying, Thus says the Lord, return from your evil ways and turn away from your works, and the Lord will repent of the evil that he declared to do to you, so that it shall not come to pass.

8 For thus says the Lord, Behold I give you a period of one hundred and twenty years; if you will turn to me and turn away from your evil ways, then will I also turn away from the evil which I told you, and it shall not exist, says the Lord.

9 And Noah and Methuselah spoke all the words of the Lord to the sons of men, day after day, constantly speaking to them.

10 But the sons of men would not listen to them, nor incline their ears to their words, and they were stubborn.

11 And the Lord granted them a period of one hundred and twenty years, saying, If they will return, then will God repent of the evil, so as not to destroy the earth.

12 Noah the son of Lamech refrained from taking a wife in those days to beget children, for he said, Certainly now God will destroy the earth, wherefore then shall I beget children?

13 Noah was a just man, he was perfect in his generation, and the Lord chose him to raise up offspring from his offspring on the face of the earth.

14 And the Lord said to Noah, Take to you a wife, and beget children, for I have seen you righteous before me in this generation.

15 You shall raise up offspring, and your children with you, in the midst of the earth; and Noah went and took a wife, and he chose Naamah the daughter of Enoch, and she was five hundred and eighty years old.

16 And Noah was four hundred and ninety-eight years old, when he took Naamah for a wife.

17 Naamah conceived and gave birth to a son, and he called his name Japheth, saying, God has enlarged me in the earth; and she conceived again and gave birth to a son, and he called his name Shem, saying, God has made me a remnant, to raise up descendants the midst of the earth.

18 And Noah was five hundred and two years old when Naamah gave birth to Shem, and the boys grew up and went in the ways of the Lord, in all that Methuselah and Noah their father taught them.

19 Lamech the father of Noah, died in those days; yet verily he did not go with all his heart in the ways of his father, and he died in the hundred and ninety-fifth year of the life of Noah.

20 And all the days of Lamech were seven hundred and seventy years, and he died.

21 All the sons of men who knew the Lord, died in that year before the Lord brought evil on them; for the Lord willed them to die, so as not to behold the evil that God would bring on their brothers and relatives, as he had so declared to do.

22 In that time, the Lord said to Noah and Methuselah, Stand forth and proclaim to the sons of men all the words that I spoke to you in those days, perchance they may turn from their evil ways, and I will then repent of the evil and will not bring it.

23 And Noah and Methuselah stood forth, and said in the ears of the sons of men, all that God had spoken concerning them.

24 But the sons of men would not listen, neither would they incline their ears to all their declarations.

25 It was after this that the Lord said to Noah, The end of all flesh is come before me on account of their evil deeds, and behold I will destroy the earth.

26 And take with you gopher wood, and go to a certain place and make a large ark, and place it in that spot.

27 Thus shall you make it; three hundred cubits in length, fifty cubits broad and thirty cubits high.

28 And you shall make a door, open at its side, and to a cubit you shall finish above, and cover it within and without with pitch.

29 And behold I will bring the flood of waters on the earth, and all flesh will be destroyed; from under the heavens all that is

on earth shall perish.

30 You and your household shall go and gather two couple of all living things, male and female, and shall bring them to the ark, to raise up offspring from them on earth.

31 Gather to you all food that is eaten by all the animals, that there may be food for you and for them.

32 You shall choose for your sons three maidens from the daughters of men, and they shall be wives to your sons.

33 And Noah rose up, and he made the ark, in the place where God had commanded him, and Noah did as God had ordered him.

34 In his five hundred and ninety-fifth year Noah commenced to make the ark, and he made the ark in five years, as the Lord had commanded.

35 Then Noah took the three daughters of Eliakim, son of Methuselah, for wives for his sons, as the Lord had commanded Noah.

36 It was at that time Methuselah the son of Enoch died; he was nine hundred and sixty years old at his death.

CHAPTER 6

1 At that time, after the death of Methuselah, the Lord said to Noah, Go with your household into the ark; behold I will gather to you all the animals of the earth, the beasts of the field and the fowls of the air, and they shall all come and surround the ark.

2 You shall go and seat yourself by the doors of the ark, and all the beasts, the animals, and the fowls, shall assemble and place themselves before you, and such of them as will come and crouch before you, you shall take and deliver into the hands of your sons, who will bring them to the ark, and all that will stand before you you shall leave.

3 And the Lord brought this about on the next day, and animals, beasts and fowls came in great multitudes and surrounded the ark.

4 Noah went and seated himself by the door of the ark, and of all flesh that crouched before him he brought into the ark, and all that stood before him he left on earth.

5 A lioness came with her two whelps, male and female, and the three crouched before Noah; the two whelps rose up against the lioness and struck her, and made her flee from her place, and she went away, and they returned to their places and crouched on the earth before Noah.

6 And the lioness ran away, and stood in the place of the lions.

7 And Noah saw this and wondered greatly, and he rose and took the two whelps and brought them into the ark.

8 Noah brought into the ark from all living creatures that were on earth, so that there was none left but those which Noah brought into the ark.

9 Two and two came to Noah into the ark, but from the clean animals and clean fowls, he brought seven couples as God had commanded him.

10 And all the animals, and beasts, and fowls were still there, and they surrounded the ark at every place, and the rain had not descended till seven days after.

11 On that day the Lord caused the whole earth to shake, and the sun darkened, and the foundations of the world raged, and the whole earth was moved violently, and the lightning flashed, and the thunder roared, and all the fountains in the earth were broken up, such as was not known to the inhabitants before; and God did this mighty act in order to terrify the sons of men, that there might be no more evil on earth.

12 And still the sons of men would not return from their evil ways, and they increased the anger of the Lord at that time, and did not even direct their hearts to all this.

13 At the end of seven days, in the six hundredth year of the life of Noah, the waters of the flood were on the earth.

14 All the fountains of the deep were broken up, and the windows of heaven were opened, and the rain was on the earth forty days and forty nights.

15 And Noah and his household, and all the living creatures that were with him, came into the ark on account of the waters of the flood, and the Lord shut him in.

16 All the sons of men that were left on the earth became exhausted through evil on account of the rain, for the waters were coming more violently on the earth, and the animals and beasts were still surrounding the ark.

17 And the sons of men assembled together, about seven hundred thousand men and women, and they came to Noah to the ark.

18 They called to Noah, saying, Open for us that we may come to you in the ark--and wherefore shall we die?

19 And Noah, with a loud voice answered them from the ark, saying, Have you not all rebelled against the Lord, and said that he does not exist? Therefore the Lord brought on you this evil, to destroy and cut you off from the face of the earth.

20 Is not this the thing that I spoke to you of one hundred and twenty years back, and you would not listen to the voice of the Lord, and now do you desire to live on earth?

21 They said to Noah, We are ready to return to the Lord; only open for us that we may live and not die.

22 And Noah answered them, saying, Behold now that you see the trouble of your souls, you wish to return to the Lord; why

did you not return during these hundred and twenty years, which the Lord granted you as the determined period?

23 But now you come and tell me this on account of the troubles of your souls, now also the Lord will not listen to you, neither will he give ear to you on this day, so that you will not now succeed in your wishes.

24 The sons of men approached in order to break into the ark, to come in on account of the rain, for they could not bear the rain on them.

25 And the Lord sent all the beasts and animals that stood around the ark. And the beasts overpowered them and drove them from that place, and every man went his way and they again scattered themselves on the face of the earth.

26 The rain was still descending on the earth, and it descended forty days and forty nights, and the waters prevailed greatly on the earth; all flesh that was on the earth or in the waters died, whether men, animals, beasts, creeping things or birds of the air, and there only remained Noah and those that were with him in the ark.

27 The waters prevailed and they greatly increased on the earth, and they lifted up the ark and it was raised from the earth.

28 And the ark floated on the face of the waters; it was tossed on the waters so that all the living creatures within were turned about like pottage in a cauldron.

29 Great anxiety seized all the living creatures that were in the ark, and the ark was like to be broken.

30 And all the living creatures that were in the ark were terrified: the lions roared, and the oxen lowed, and the wolves howled, and every living creature in the ark spoke and lamented in its own language, so that their voices reached to a great distance, and Noah and his sons cried and wept in their troubles; they were greatly afraid that they had reached the gates of death.

31 And Noah prayed to the Lord, and cried to him on account of this, and he said, O Lord help us, for we have no strength to bear this evil that has encompassed us, for the waves of the waters have surrounded us, mischievous torrents have terrified us, the snares of death have come before us; answer us, O Lord, answer us, light up your countenance toward us and be gracious to us, redeem us and deliver us.

32 The Lord listened to the voice of Noah, and the Lord remembered him.

33 And a wind passed over the earth; the waters were still and the ark rested.

34 The fountains of the deep and the windows of heaven were stopped, and the rain from heaven was restrained.

35 And the waters decreased in those days, and the ark rested on the mountains of Ararat.

36 Noah then opened the windows of the ark, and Noah still called out to the Lord at that time and he said, O Lord, who did form the earth and the heavens and all that are therein, bring forth our souls from this confinement, and from the prison wherein you have placed us, for I am much wearied with sighing.

37 And the Lord listened to the voice of Noah, and said to him, When you have completed a full year you shall then go forth.

38 And at the revolution of the year, when a full year was completed to Noah's dwelling in the ark, the waters were dried from off the earth, and Noah put off the covering of the ark.

39 At that time, on the twenty-seventh day of the second month, the earth was dry, but Noah and his sons and those that were with him did not go out from the ark until the Lord told them.

40 And the day came that the Lord told them to go out, and they all went out from the ark.

41 They went and returned every one to his way and to his place, and Noah and his sons lived in the land that God had told them; they served the Lord all their days, and the Lord blessed Noah and his sons on their going out from the ark.

42 And he said to them, Be prolific and fill all the earth; become strong and increase abundantly in the earth and reproduce therein.

CHAPTER 7

1 And these are the names of the sons of Noah: Japheth, Ham and Shem; and children were born to them after the flood, for they had taken wives before the flood.

2 These are the sons of Japheth: Gomer, Magog, Madai, Javan, Tubal, Meshech, and Tiras, seven sons.

3 And the sons of Gomer were Askinaz, Rephath and Tegarmah.

4 And the sons of Magog were Elichanaf and Lubal.

5 And the children of Madai were Achon, Zeelo, Chazoni and Lot.

6 And the sons of Javan were Elisha, Tarshish, Chittim and Dudonim.

7 And the sons of Tubal were Ariphi, Kesed and Taari.

8 And the sons of Meshech were Dedon, Zaron and Shebashni.

9 And the sons of Tiras were Benib, Gera, Lupirion and Gilak; these are the sons of Japheth according to their families, and their numbers in those days were about four hundred and sixty men.

10 And these are the sons of Ham: Cush, Mitzraim, Phut and Canaan, four sons; and the sons of Cush were Seba, Havilah, Sabta, Raama and Satecha, and the sons of Raama were Sheba and Dedan.

11 And the sons of Mitzraim were Lud, Anom and Pathros, Chasloth and Chaphtor.

12 And the sons of Phut were Gebul, Hadan, Benah and Adan.

13 And the sons of Canaan were Zidon, Heth, Amori, Gergashi, Hivi, Arkee, Seni, Arodi, Zimodi and Chamothi.

14 These are the sons of Ham, according to their families, and their numbers in those days were about seven hundred and thirty men.

15 And these are the sons of Shem: Elam, Ashur, Arpachshad, Lud and Aram, five sons; and the sons of Elam were Shushan, Machul and Harmon.

16 And the sons of Ashar were Mirus and Mokil, and the sons of Arpachshad were Shelach, Anar and Ashcol.

17 And the sons of Lud were Pethor and Bizayon, and the sons of Aram were Uz, Chul, Gather and Mash.

18 These are the sons of Shem, according to their families; and their numbers in those days were about three hundred men.

19 These are the generations of Shem: Shem had Arpachshad and Arpachshad had Shelach, and Shelach had Eber and to Eber were born two children, the name of one was Peleg, for in his days the sons of men were divided, and in the latter days the earth was divided.

20 And the name of the second was Yoktan, meaning that in his day the lives of the sons of men were diminished and lessened.

21 These are the sons of Yoktan: Almodad, Shelaf, Chazarmoveth, Yerach, Hadurom, Ozel, Diklah, Obal, Abimael, Sheba, Ophir, Havilah and Jobab; all these are the sons of Yoktan.

22 And Peleg his brother had Yen, and Yen had Serug, and Serug had Nahor and Nahor had Terah, and Terah was thirty-eight years old, and he had Haran and Nahor.

23 And Cush the son of Ham, the son of Noah, took a wife in those days in his old age, and she gave birth to a son, and they called his name Nimrod, saying, At that time the sons of men again began to rebel and go contrary to God; the child grew up, and his father loved him greatly, for he was the son of his old age.

24 The garments of skin which God made for Adam and his wife, when they went out of the garden, were given to Cush.

25 For after the death of Adam and his wife, the garments were given to Enoch, the son of Jared, and when Enoch was taken up to God, he gave them to Methuselah, his son.

26 At the death of Methuselah, Noah took them and brought them to the ark, and they were with him until he went out of the ark.

27 And in their going out, Ham stole those garments from Noah his father; he took them and hid them from his brothers.

28 When Ham had his first born Cush, he gave him the garments in secret, and they were with Cush many days.

29 Cush also concealed them from his sons and brothers, and when Cush had begotten Nimrod, he gave him those garments through his love for him, and Nimrod grew up, and when he was twenty years old he put on those garments.

30 Nimrod became strong when he put on the garments, and God gave him might and strength, and he was a mighty hunter in the earth. He was a mighty hunter in the field, and he hunted the animals and he built altars, and he offered on them the animals before the Lord.

31 Nimrod strengthened himself, and he rose up from among his brothers, and he fought the battles of his brothers against all their enemies round about.

32 The Lord delivered all the enemies of his brothers in his hands, and God prospered him from time to time in his battles, and he reigned on earth.

33 Therefore it became current in those days, when a man ushered forth those that he had trained up for battle, he would say to them, like God did to Nimrod who was a mighty hunter in the earth and who succeeded in the battles that prevailed against his brothers, that he delivered them from the hands of their enemies: so may God strengthen us and deliver us this day.

34 And when Nimrod was forty years old, there was a war between his brothers and the children of Japheth, so that they were in the power of their enemies.

35 Nimrod went forth at that time, and he assembled all the sons of Cush and their families, about four hundred and sixty men; he hired also from some of his friends and acquaintances about eighty men, and he gave them their hire; he went with them to battle, and when he was on the road, Nimrod strengthened the hearts of the people that went with him.

36 And he said to them, Do not fear, neither be alarmed, for all our enemies will be delivered into our hands, and you may do with them as you please.

37 All the men that went were about five hundred, and they fought against their enemies; they destroyed them, and subdued them, and Nimrod placed standing officers over them in their respective places.

38 He took some of their children as security, and they were all servants to Nimrod and to his brothers, and Nimrod and all the people that were with him turned homeward.

39 When Nimrod had joyfully returned from battle, after having conquered his enemies, all his brothers, together with those who knew him before, assembled to make him king over them and they placed the regal crown on his head.

40 He set over his subjects and people, princes, judges, and rulers, as is the custom among kings.

41 He placed Terah the son of Nahor the prince of his host, and he dignified him and elevated him above all his princes.

42 And while he was reigning according to his heart's desire, after having conquered all his enemies around, he advised with his counselors to build a city for his palace, and they did so.

43 They found a large valley opposite to the east, and they built him a large and extensive city, and Nimrod called the name of the city that he built Shinar, for the Lord had vehemently shaken his enemies and destroyed them.

44 Nimrod lived in Shinar, and he reigned securely, and he fought with his enemies and he subdued them; he prospered in

all his battles, and his kingdom became very great.

45 All nations and tongues heard of his fame, and they gathered themselves to him, and they bowed down to the earth; they brought him offerings, and he became their lord and king, and they all lived with him in the city at Shinar; Nimrod reigned in the earth over all the sons of Noah, and they were all under his power and counsel.

46 And all the earth was of one tongue and words of union, but Nimrod did not go in the ways of the Lord; he was more wicked than all the men that were before him, from the days of the flood until those days.

47 He made gods of wood and stone, he bowed down to them, he rebelled against the Lord, and taught all his subjects and the people of the earth his wicked ways; Mardon his son was more wicked than his father.

48 And every one that heard of the acts of Mardon the son of Nimrod would say, concerning him, From the wicked goes forth wickedness. Therefore it became a proverb in the whole earth, saying, From the wicked goes forth wickedness, and it was current in the words of men from that time to this.

49 Terah the son of Nahor, prince of Nimrod's host, was in those days very great in the sight of the king and his subjects, and the king and princes loved him, and they elevated him very high.

50 And Terah took a wife and her name was Amthelo the daughter of Cornebo; the wife of Terah conceived and gave birth to a son in those days.

51 Terah was seventy years old when he had him, and Terah called the name of his son Abram, because the king had raised him in those days, and dignified him above all his princes that were with him.

CHAPTER 8

1 It was in the night that Abram was born, that all the servants of Terah, and all the wise men of Nimrod and his conjurors came and ate and drank in the house of Terah, and they rejoiced with him on that night.

2 When all the wise men and conjurors went out from the house of Terah, they lifted up their eyes toward heaven that night to look at the stars; they saw, and behold, one very large star came from the east and ran in the heavens; he swallowed up the four stars from the four sides of the heavens.

3 And all the wise men of the king and his conjurors were astonished at the sight, and the sages understood this matter, and they knew its import.

4 They said to each other, This only betokens the child that has been born to Terah this night, who will grow up and be prolific, and reproduce, and possess all the earth, he and his children for ever, and he and his descendants will kill great kings, and inherit their lands.

5 The wise men and conjurors went home that night; in the morning all these wise men and conjurors rose up early, and assembled in an appointed house.

6 And they spoke and said to each other, Behold the sight that we saw last night is hidden from the king; it has not been made known to him.

7 And should this thing get known to the king in the latter days, he will say to us, Why have you concealed this matter from me, and then we shall all suffer death; therefore, now let us go and tell the king the sight which we saw, and the interpretation thereof, and we shall then remain clear.

8 And they did so; they all went to the king and bowed down to him to the ground, and they said, May the king live, may the king live.

9 We heard that a son was born to Terah the son of Nahor, the prince of your host, and we last night came to his house, and we ate and drank and rejoiced with him that night.

10 And when your servants went out from the house of Terah, to go to our respective homes to abide there for the night, we lifted up our eyes to heaven and we saw a great star coming from the east, and the same star ran with great speed and swallowed up four great stars, from the four sides of the heavens.

11 And your servants were astonished at the sight which we saw, and were greatly terrified; we made our judgment on the sight and knew by our wisdom the proper interpretation thereof, that this thing applies to the child that is born to Terah, who will grow up and reproduce greatly, and become powerful and kill all the kings of the earth, and inherit all their lands, he and his offspring forever.

12 Now our lord and king, behold we have truly acquainted you with what we have seen concerning this child.

13 If it seems good to the king to give his father value for this child, we will kill him before he shall grow up and increase in the land, and his evil increase against us, that we and our children perish through his evil.

14 And the king heard their words and they seemed good in his sight, and he sent and called for Terah, and Terah came before the king.

15 And the king said to Terah, I have been told that a son was last night born to you, and after this manner was observed in the heavens at his birth.

16 And now therefore give me the child, that we may kill him before his evil springs up against us, and I will give you for his value, your house full of silver and gold.

17 Terah answered the king and said to him: My Lord and king, I have heard your words, and your servant shall do all that

his king desires.

18 But my lord and king, I will tell you what happened to me last night, that I may see what advice the king will give his servant, and then I will answer the king on what he has just spoken. The king said, Speak.

19 And Terah said to the king, Ayon, son of Mored, came to me last night, saying,

20 Give to me the great and beautiful horse that the king gave you, and I will give you silver and gold, and straw and provender for its value; and I said to him, Wait till I see the king concerning your words, and behold whatever the king says, that will I do.

21 And now my lord and king, behold I have made this thing known to you, and the advice which my king will give to his servant, that will I follow.

22 The king heard the words of Terah, and his anger was set ablaze and he considered him in the light of a fool.

23 And the king answered Terah and said to him, Are you so silly, ignorant, or deficient in understanding to do this thing, to give your beautiful horse for silver and gold or even for straw and provender?

24 Are you so short of silver and gold that you should do this thing, because you cannot obtain straw and provender to feed your horse? And what is silver and gold to you, or straw and provender, that you should give away that fine horse which I gave you, like which there is none to be had on the whole earth?

25 The king left off speaking, and Terah answered the king, saying, Like to this has the king spoken to his servant;

26 I beseech you, my lord and king, what is this which you did say to me, Give your son that we may kill him, and I will give you silver and gold for his value; what shall I do with silver and gold after the death of my son? Who shall inherit me? Certainly then at my death, the silver and gold will return to my king who gave it.

27 And when the king heard the words of Terah, and the parable which he brought concerning the king, it grieved him greatly and he was troubled at this thing, and his anger burned within him.

28 And Terah saw that the anger of the king was set ablaze against him, and he answered the king, saying, All that I have is in the king's power; whatever the king desires to do to his servant, that let him do, yea, even my son, he is in the king's power, without value in exchange, he and his two brothers that are older than he.

29 And the king said to Terah, No, but I will purchase your younger son for a price.

30 Terah answered the king, saying, I beseech you my lord and king to let your servant speak a word before you, and let the king hear the word of his servant, and Terah said, Let my king give me three days' time till I consider this matter within myself, and consult with my family concerning the words of my king; and he pressed the king greatly to agree to this.

31 The king listened to Terah, and he did so and he gave him three days' time. Terah went out from the king's presence, and he came home to his family and spoke to them all the words of the king; and the people were greatly afraid.

32 And it was in the third day that the king sent to Terah, saying, Send me your son for a price as I spoke to you; and should you not do this, I will send and kill all you have in your house, so that you shall not even have a dog remaining.

33 And Terah hurried (as the thing was urgent from the king), and he took a child from one of his servants, which his handmaid had born to him that day, and Terah brought the child to the king and received value for him.

34 And the Lord was with Terah in this matter, that Nimrod might not cause Abram's death. The king took the child from Terah and with all his might dashed his head to the ground, for he thought it had been Abram; this was concealed from him from that day, and it was forgotten by the king, as it was the will of Providence not to suffer Abram's death.

35 And Terah took Abram his son secretly, together with his mother and nurse, and he concealed them in a cave, and he brought them their provisions monthly.

36 The Lord was with Abram in the cave and he grew up, and Abram was in the cave ten years, and the king and his princes, soothsayers and sages, thought that the king had killed Abram.

CHAPTER 9

1 And Haran, the son of Terah, Abram's oldest brother, took a wife in those days.

2 Haran was thirty-nine years old when he took her; and the wife of Haran conceived and gave birth to a son, and he called his name Lot.

3 She conceived again and gave birth to a daughter, and called her name Milca; and she again conceived and gave birth to a daughter and called her name Sarai.

4 Haran was forty-two years old when he had Sarai, which was in the tenth year of the life of Abram; and in those days Abram and his mother and nurse went out from the cave, as the king and his subjects had forgotten the affair of Abram.

5 When Abram came out from the cave, he went to Noah and his son Shem, and he remained with them to learn the instruction of the Lord and his ways; no man knew where Abram was, and Abram served Noah and Shem his son for a long time.

6 Abram was in Noah's house thirty-nine years, and Abram knew the Lord from three years old; he went in the ways of the Lord until the day of his death, as Noah and his son Shem had taught him, and all the sons of the earth in those days greatly went contrary to the Lord, and they rebelled against him and they served other gods. They forgot the Lord who had created them in the earth; and the inhabitants of the earth made to themselves, at that time, every man his god; gods of wood and

stone which could neither speak, hear, nor deliver, and the sons of men served them and they became their gods.

7 The king and all his servants, and Terah with all his household were then the first of those that served gods of wood and stone.

8 And Terah had twelve gods of large size, made of wood and stone, after the twelve months of the year, and he served each one monthly, and every month Terah would bring his meat offering and drink offering to his gods; thus did Terah all the days.

9 All that generation were wicked in the sight of the Lord, and they thus made every man his god, but they turned away from the Lord who had created them.

10 And there was not a man found in those days in the whole earth who knew the Lord (for they served each man his own god) except Noah and his household; and all those who were under his counsel knew the Lord in those days.

11 Abram the son of Terah was becoming great in those days in the house of Noah, and no man knew it, and the Lord was with him.

12 The Lord gave Abram an understanding heart, and he knew all the works of that generation were vain, and that all their gods were vain and were of no avail.

13 And Abram saw the sun shining on the earth, and Abram said to himself, Certainly now this sun that shines on the earth is God, and him will I serve.

14 And Abram served the sun in that day and he prayed to him, and when evening came the sun set as usual, and Abram said within himself, Certainly this cannot be God?

15 And Abram still continued to speak within himself, Who is he who made the heavens and the earth? Who created on earth? Where is he?

16 And night darkened over him; he lifted up his eyes toward the west, north, south, and east, and he saw that the sun had vanished from the earth, and the day became dark.

17 And Abram saw the stars and moon before him, and he said, Certainly this is the God who created the whole earth as well as man, and behold these his servants are gods around him: and Abram served the moon and prayed to it all that night.

18 And in the morning when it was light and the sun shone on the earth as usual, Abram saw all the things that the Lord God had made on earth.

19 And Abram said to himself, Certainly these are not gods that made the earth and all mankind, but these are the servants of God. And Abram remained in the house of Noah and there knew the Lord and his ways. He served the Lord all the days of his life, and all that generation forgot the Lord, and served other gods of wood and stone, and rebelled all their days.

20 And king Nimrod reigned securely, and all the earth was under his control, and all the earth was of one tongue and words of union.

21 And all the princes of Nimrod and his great men took counsel together: Phut, Mitzraim, Cush and Canaan with their families, and they said to each other, Come let us build ourselves a city and in it a strong tower and its top reaching heaven, and we will make ourselves famed so that we may reign on the whole world, in order that the evil of our enemies may cease from us; that we may reign mightily over them, and that we may not become scattered over the earth on account of their wars.

22 They all went before the king, and they told the king these words, and the king agreed with them in this affair, and he did so.

23 All the families assembled consisting of about six hundred thousand men, and they went to seek an extensive piece of ground to build the city and the tower, and they sought in the whole earth and they found none like one valley at the east of the land of Shinar, about two days' walk, and they journeyed there and they lived there.

24 And they began to make bricks and burn fires to build the city and the tower that they had imagined to complete.

25 And the building of the tower was to them a transgression and a sin, and they began to build it While they were building against the Lord God of heaven, they imagined in their hearts to war against him and to ascend into heaven.

26 And all these people and all the families divided themselves in three parts; the first said, We will ascend into heaven and fight against him; the second said, We will ascend to heaven and place our own gods there and serve them; and the third part said, We will ascend to heaven and strike him with bows and spears. And God knew all their works and all their evil thoughts, and he saw the city and the tower which they were building.

27 They built themselves a great city and a very high and strong tower; on account of its height, the mortar and bricks did not reach the builders in their ascent to it until those who went up had completed a full year, and after that, they reached the builders and gave them the mortar and the bricks; thus was it done daily.

28 And behold these ascended and others descended the whole day; and if a brick should fall from their hands and get broken, they would all weep over it; if a man fell and died, none of them would look at him.

29 The Lord knew their thoughts, and it came to pass when they were building they cast the arrows toward the heavens, and all the arrows fell on them filled with blood; when they saw them they said to each other, Certainly we have slain all those that are in heaven.

30 For this was from the Lord in order to cause them to err, and in order to destroy them from off the face of the ground.

31 They built the tower and the city, and they did this thing daily until many days and years were elapsed.

32 And God said to the seventy angels who stood foremost before him, to those who were near to him, saying, Come let us

descend and confuse their tongues, that one man shall not understand the language of his neighbor, and they did so to them.

33 From that day following, they forgot each man his neighbor's tongue, and they could not understand to speak in one tongue; when the builder took from the hands of his neighbor lime or stone which he did not order, the builder would cast it away and throw it on his neighbor, that he would die.

34 And they did so many days, and they killed many of them in this manner.

35 The Lord struck the three divisions that were there, and he punished them according to their works and designs; those who said, We will ascend to heaven and serve our gods, became like apes and elephants; those who said, We will strike the heaven with arrows, the Lord killed them, one man through the hand of his neighbor; and the third division of those who said, We will ascend to heaven and fight against him, the Lord scattered them throughout the earth.

36 Those who were left among them, when they knew and understood the evil which was coming on them, turned away from the building, and they also became scattered on the face of the whole earth.

37 And they ceased building the city and the tower; therefore he called that place Babel, for there the Lord confounded the Language of the whole earth; behold it was at the east of the land of Shinar.

38 As to the tower which the sons of men built, the earth opened its mouth and swallowed up one third part thereof, and a fire also descended from heaven and burned another third, and the other third is left to this day; it is of that part which was aloft, and its circumference is three days' walk.

39 Many of the sons of men died in that tower, a people without number.

CHAPTER 10

1 Peleg the son of Eber died in those days, in the forty-eighth year of the life of Abram son of Terah, and all the days of Peleg were two hundred and thirty-nine years.

2 When the Lord had scattered the sons of men on account of their sin at the tower, behold they spread forth into many divisions, and all the sons of men were dispersed into the four corners of the earth.

3 And all the families became each according to its language, its land, or its city.

4 And the sons of men built many cities according to their families, in all the places where they went, and throughout the earth where the Lord had scattered them.

5 Some of them built cities in places from which they later abandoned, and they called these cities after their own names, or the names of their children, or after their particular occurrences.

6 The sons of Japheth, the son of Noah went and built themselves cities in the places where they were scattered; they called all their cities after their names, and the sons of Japheth were divided on the face of the earth into many divisions and languages.

7 And these are the sons of Japheth according to their families: Gomer, Magog, Medai, Javan, Tubal, Meshech and Tiras; these are the children of Japheth according to their generations.

8 Tthe children of Gomer, according to their cities, were the Francum, who dwell in the land of Franza, by the river Franza, by the river Senah.

9 And the children of Rephath are the Bartonim, who dwell in the land of Bartonia by the river Ledah, which empties its waters in the great sea Gihon, that is, Oceanus.

10 The children of Tugarma are ten families, and these are their names: Buzar, Parzunac, Balgar, Elicanum, Ragbib, Tarki, Bid, Zebuc, Ongal and Tilmaz; all these spread and rested in the north and built themselves cities.

11 And they called their cities after their own names; those are they who abide by the rivers Hithlah and Italac to this day.

12 But the families of Angoli, Balgar and Parzunac, they dwelll by the great river Dubnee; and the names of their cities are also according to their own names.

13 The children of Javan are the Javanim who dwell in the land of Makdonia, and the children of Medaiare the Orelum that dwell in the land of Curson, and the children of Tubal are those that dwell in the land of Tuskanah by the river Pashiah.

14 The children of Meshech are the Shibashni and the children of Tiras are Rushash, Cushni, and Ongolis; all these went and built themselves cities; those are the cities that are situated by the sea Jabus by the river Cura, which empties itself into the river Tragan.

15 And the children of Elishah are the Almanim, and they also went and built themselves cities; those are the cities situated between the mountains of Job and Shibathmo; and of them were the people of Lumbardi who dwell opposite the mountains of Job and Shibathmo, and they conquered the land of Italia and remained there to this day.

16 The children of Chittim are the Romim who dwell in the valley of Canopia by the river Tibreu.

17 The children of Dudonim are those who dwell in the cities of the sea Gihon, in the land of Bordna.

18 These are the families of the children of Japheth according to their cities and languages when they were scattered after the tower; they called their cities after their names and occurrences; and these are the names of all their cities according to their families which they built in those days after the tower.

19 And the children of Ham were Cush, Mitzraim, Phut and Canaan according to their generation and cities.

20 All these went and built themselves cities as they found fit places for them, and they called their cities after the names of their fathers Cush, Mitzraim, Phut and Canaan.

21 The children of Mitzraim are the Ludim, Anamim, Lehabim, Naphtuchim, Pathrusim, Casluchim and Caphturim, seven families.

22 All these dwell by the river Sihor, that is the brook of Egypt, and they built themselves cities and called them after their own names.

23 The children of Pathros and Casloch intermarried together, and from them went forth the Pelishtim, the Azathim, and the Gerarim, the Githim and the Ekronim, in all five families; these also built themselves cities, and they called their cities after the names of their fathers to this day.

24 The children of Canaan also built themselves cities, and they called their cities after their names, eleven cities and others without number.

25 Four men from the family of Ham went to the land of the plain; these are the names of the four men: Sodom, Gomorrah, Admah and Zeboyim.

26 And these men built themselves four cities in the land of the plain, and they called the names of their cities after their own names.

27 They and their children and all belonging to them lived in those cities, and they were prolific and multiplied greatly and lived peaceably.

28 Seir the son of Hur, son of Hivi, son of Canaan, went and found a valley opposite to Mount Paran, and he built a city there; he and his seven sons and his household lived there, and he called the city which he built Seir, according to his name; that is the land of Seir to this day.

29 These are the families of the children of Ham, according to their languages and cities, when they were scattered to their countries after the tower.

30 Some of the children of Shem, son of Noah, father of all the children of Eber, also went and built themselves cities in the places wherein they were scattered, and they called their cities after their names.

31 The sons of Shem were Elam, Ashur, Arpachshad, Lud and Aram, and they built themselves cities and called the names of all their cities after their names.

32 Ashur, son of Shem, and his children and household went forth at that time, a very large body of them, and they went to a distant land that they found; they met with a very extensive valley in the land that they went to, and they built themselves four cities, and they called them after their own names and occurrences.

33 And these are the names of the cities which the children of Ashur built: Ninevah, Resen, Calach and Rehobother; the children of Ashur dwell there to this day.

34 The children of Aram also went and built themselves a city, and they called the name of the city Uz after their eldest brother; they dwell therein. That is the land of Uz to this day.

35 And in the second year after the tower a man from the house of Ashur, whose name was Bela, went from the land of Ninevah to sojourn with his household wherever he could find a place; they came until opposite the cities of the plain against Sodom, and they lived there.

36 And the man rose up and built there a small city, and called its name Bela, after his name; that is the land of Zoar to this day.

37 These are the families of the children of Shem according to their language and cities, after they were scattered on the earth after the tower.

38 And every kingdom, city, and family of the families of the children of Noah built themselves many cities after this.

39 And they established governments in all their cities in order to be regulated by their orders; so did all the families of the children of Noah forever.

CHAPTER 11

1 Nimrod son of Cush was still in the land of Shinar, and he reigned over it and lived there, and he built cities in the land of Shinar.

2 These are the names of the four cities which he built, and he called their names after the occurrences that happened to them in the building of the tower:

3 He called the first Babel, saying, Because the Lord there confounded the language of the whole earth. The name of the second he called Erech, because from there God dispersed them.

4 And the third he called Eched, saying there was a great battle at that place; the fourth he called Calnah, because his princes and mighty men were consumed there, and they troubled the Lord; they rebelled and went contrary to him.

5 When Nimrod had built these cities in the land of Shinar, he placed in them the remainder of his people, his princes and his mighty men that were left in his kingdom.

6 Nimrod lived in Babel, and there he renewed his reign over the rest of his subjects, and he reigned securely, and the subjects and princes of Nimrod called his name Amraphel, saying that at the tower his princes and men fell through his means.

7 Notwithstanding this, Nimrod did not return to the Lord, and he continued in wickedness and teaching wickedness to the

sons of men; and Mardon, his son, was worse than his father and continued to add to the abominations of his father.

8 And he caused the sons of men to sin; therefore it is said, From the wicked goes forth wickedness.

9 At that time there was war between the families of the children of Ham, as they were dwelling in the cities which they had built.

10 And Chedorlaomer, king of Elam, went away from the families of the children of Ham; he fought with them and he subdued them, and he went to the five cities of the plain; he fought against them and he subdued them, and they were under his control.

11 And they served him twelve years and gave him a yearly tax.

12 At that time Nahor, son of Serug died, in the forty-ninth year of the life of Abram, son of Terah.

13 In the fiftieth year of the life of Abram, son of Terah, Abram came forth from the house of Noah, and went to his father's house.

14 And Abram knew the Lord, and he followed in his ways and instructions, and the Lord his God was with him.

15 Terah his father was in those days still captain of the host of king Nimrod, and he still followed strange gods.

16 And Abram came to his father's house and saw twelve gods standing there in their temples, and the anger of Abram was set ablaze when he saw these images in his father's house.

17 And Abram said, As the Lord lives these images shall not remain in my father's house; so shall the Lord who created me do to me if in three days' time I do not break them all.

18 Abram went from them, and his anger burned within him. And Abram hurried and went from the chamber to his father's outer court, and he found his father sitting in the court, and all his servants with him, and Abram came and sat before him.

19 Abram asked his father, saying, Father, tell me where is God who created heaven and earth, and all the sons of men on earth, and who created you and me. And Terah answered his son Abram and said, Behold those who created us are all with us in the house.

20 And Abram said to his father, My lord, show them to me I pray you. And Terah brought Abram into the chamber of the inner court, and Abram saw, and behold the whole room was full of gods of wood and stone, twelve great images and others less than they without number.

21 And Terah said to his son, Behold these are they which made all you see on earth, and which created me and you, and all mankind.

22 Terah bowed down to his gods, and he then went away from them, and Abram, his son, went away with him.

23 When Abram had gone from them he went to his mother and sat before her, and he said to his mother, Behold, my father has shown me those who made heaven and earth, and all the sons of men.

24 Now, therefore, hurry and fetch a kid from the flock, and make of it savory meat, that I may bring it to my father's gods as an offering for them to eat; perhaps I may thereby become acceptable to them.

25 And his mother did so; she fetched a kid, and made savory meat thereof, and brought it to Abram, and Abram took the savory meat from his mother and brought it before his father's gods, and he drew nigh to them that they might eat; and Terah his father, did not know of it.

26 Abram saw on the day when he was sitting among them, that they had no voice, no hearing, no motion, and not one of them could stretch forth his hand to eat.

27 And Abram mocked them, and said, Certainly the savory meat that I prepared has not pleased them, or perhaps it was too little for them, and for that reason they would not eat; therefore tomorrow I will prepare fresh savory meat, better and more plentiful than this, in order that I may see the result.

28 It was on the next day that Abram directed his mother concerning the savory meat, and his mother rose and fetched three fine kids from the flock; she made of them some excellent savory meat, such as her son was fond of, and she gave it to her son Abram, and Terah his father did not know of it.

29 Abram took the savory meat from his mother and brought it before his father's gods into the chamber; he came nigh to them that they might eat, and he placed it before them, and Abram sat before them all day thinking perhaps they might eat.

30 Abram viewed them, and behold they had neither voice nor hearing, nor did one of them stretch forth his hand to the meat to eat.

31 And in the evening of that day in that house Abram was clothed with the spirit of God.

32 He called out and said, Woe to my father and this wicked generation, whose hearts are all inclined to vanity, who serve these idols of wood and stone which can neither eat, smell, hear nor speak, who have mouths without speech, eyes without sight, ears without hearing, hands without feeling, and legs which cannot move; like them are those that made them and that trust in them.

33 When Abram saw all these things his anger was set ablaze against his father, and he hurried and took a hatchet in his hand, and came to the chamber of the gods; he broke all his father's gods.

34 And when he was done breaking the images, he placed the hatchet in the hand of the great god which was there before them, and he went out; and Terah his father came home, for he had heard at the door the sound of the striking of the hatchet; so Terah came into the house to know what this was about.

35 Terah, having heard the noise of the hatchet in the room of images, ran to the room to the images, and he met Abram going out.

36 And Terah entered the room and found all the idols fallen down and broken, and the hatchet in the hand of the largest, which was not broken, and the savory meat which Abram his son had made was still before them.

37 When Terah saw this his anger was greatly set ablaze, and he hurried and went from the room to Abram.

38 And he found Abram his son still sitting in the house; and he said to him, What is this work you have done to my gods?

39 Abram answered Terah his father and he said, Not so my lord, for I brought savory meat before them, and when I came near to them with the meat that they might eat, they all at once stretched forth their hands to eat before the great one had put forth his hand to eat.

40 And the large one saw their works that they did before him, and his anger was violently set ablaze against them, and he went and took the hatchet that was in the house and came to them and broke them all, and behold the hatchet is yet in his hand as you see.

41 And Terah's anger was set ablaze against his son Abram, when he spoke this; and Terah said to Abram his son in his anger, What is this tale that you have told? You speak lies to me.

42 Is there in these gods spirit, soul or power to do all you have told me? Are they not wood and stone, and have I not myself made them, and can you speak such lies, saying that the large god that was with them struck them? It is you that did place the hatchet in his hands, and then said he struck them all.

43 Abram answered his father and said to him, And how can you then serve these idols in whom there is no power to do any thing? Can those idols in which you trust deliver you? Can they hear your prayers when you call on them? Can they deliver you from the hands of your enemies, or will they fight your battles for you against your enemies, that you should serve wood and stone which can neither speak nor hear?

44 And now certainly it is not good for you nor for the sons of men that are connected with you, to do these things; are you so silly, so foolish or so short of understanding that you will serve wood and stone, and do after this manner?

45 And forget the Lord God who made heaven and earth, and who created you in the earth, and thereby bring a great evil on your souls in this matter by serving stone and wood?

46 Did not our fathers in days of old sin in this manner, and the Lord God of the universe brought the waters of the flood on them and destroyed the whole earth?

47 And how can you continue to do this and serve gods of wood and stone, who cannot hear, or speak, or deliver you from oppression, thereby bringing down the anger of the God of the universe on you?

48 Now therefore my father refrain from this, and bring not evil on your soul and the souls of your household.

49 And Abram hurried and sprang from before his father, and took the hatchet from his father's largest idol, with which Abram broke it and ran away.

50 Terah, seeing all that Abram had done, hurried to go from his house; he went to the king and he came before Nimrod and stood before him, and he bowed down to the king and the king said, What do you want?

51 And he said, I beseech you my lord, to hear me--Now fifty years back a child was born to me, and thus has he done to my gods and thus has he spoken; and now therefore, my lord and king, send for him that he may come before you, and judge him according to the law, that we may be delivered from his evil.

52 The king sent three men of his servants, and they went and brought Abram before the king. And Nimrod and all his princes and servants were that day sitting before him, and Terah also sat before them.

53 And the king said to Abram, What is this that you have done to your father and to his gods? And Abram answered the king in the words that he spoke to his father, and he said, The large god that was with them in the house did to them what you have heard.

54 And the king said to Abram, Had they power to speak and eat and do as you have said? And Abram answered the king, saying, And if there be no power in them why do you serve them and cause the sons of men to err through your follies?

55 Do you imagine that they can deliver you or do anything small or great, that you should serve them? And why will you not sense the God of the whole universe, who created you and in whose power it is to kill and keep alive?

56 0 foolish, simple, and ignorant king, woe to you forever.

57 I thought you would teach your servants the upright way, but you have not done this; you have filled the whole earth with your sins and the sins of your people who have followed your ways.

58 Do you not know, or have you not heard, that this evil which you do, our ancestors sinned therein in days of old, and the eternal God brought the waters of the flood on them and destroyed them all, and also destroyed the whole earth on their account? And will you and your people rise up now and do like this work, in order to bring down the anger of the Lord God of the universe, and to bring evil on you and the whole earth?

59 Now therefore put away this evil deed which you did, and serve the God of the universe, as your soul is in his hands, and then it will be well with you.

60 And if your wicked heart will not listen to my words to cause you to turn away from your evil ways, and to serve the eternal God, then you will die in shame in the latter days, you, your people and all who are connected with you, hearing your words or walking in your evil ways.

61 When Abram had ceased speaking before the king and princes, Abram lifted up his eyes to the heavens, and he said, The Lord sees all the wicked, and he will judge them.

CHAPTER 12

1 When the king heard the words of Abram he ordered him to be put into prison; and Abram was ten days in prison.

2 At the end of those days the king ordered that all the kings, princes and governors of different provinces and the sages should come before him, and they sat before him, and Abram was still in the house of confinement.

3 The king said to the princes and sages, Have you heard what Abram, the son of Terah, has done to his father? Thus has he done to him, and I ordered him to be brought before me, and thus has he spoken; his heart did not misgive him, neither did he stir in my presence, and behold now he is confined in the prison.

4 Therefore decide what judgment is due to this man who reviled the king; who spoke and did all the things that you heard.

5 And they all answered the king saying, The man who reviles the king should be hanged on a tree; but having done all the things that he said and having despised our gods, he must therefore be burned to death, for this is the law in this matter.

6 If it pleases the king to do this, let him order his servants to kindle a fire both night and day in your brick furnace, and then we will cast this man into it. And the king did so, and he commanded his servants that they should prepare a fire for three days and three nights in the king's furnace, that is in Casdim; and the king ordered them to take Abram from prison and bring him out to be burned.

7 And all the king's servants, princes, lords, governors, and judges, and all the inhabitants of the land, about nine hundred thousand men, stood opposite the furnace to see Abram.

8 And all the women and little ones crowded on the roofs and towers to see what was going on with Abram, and they all stood together at a distance; and there was not a man left that did not come that day to behold the scene.

9 When Abram was come, the conjurors of the king and the sages saw Abram, and they cried out to the king, saying, Our sovereign lord, certainly this is the man whom we know to have been the child at whose birth the great star swallowed the four stars, which we declared to the king fifty years ago.

10 And behold now his father has also gone contrary to your commands, and mocked you by bringing you another child, which you did kill.

11 And when the king heard their words, he was greatly angered, and he ordered Terah to be brought before him.

12 And the king said, Have you heard what the conjurors have spoken? Now tell me truly, how did you? If you shall speak truth you shall be acquitted.

13 Seeing that the king's anger was so much set ablaze, Terah said to the king, My lord and king, you have heard the truth, and what the sages have spoken is right. And the king said, How could you do this thing, to go contrary to my orders and to give me a child that you did not beget, and to take value for him?

14 Terah answered the king, Because my tender feelings were excited for my son, at that time, I took a son of my handmaid, and I brought him to the king.

15 And the king said, Who advised you to do this? Tell me, do not hide anything from me, and then you shall not die.

16 And Terah was greatly terrified in the king's presence, and he said to the king, It was Haran my eldest son who advised me to do this. Haran was in those days that Abram was born, two and thirty years old.

17 But Haran did not advise his father to do anything, for Terah said this to the king in order to deliver his soul from the king, for he feared greatly. The king said to Terah, Haran your son who advised you to do this shall die through fire with Abram; for the sentence of death is on him for having rebelled against the king's desire in doing this thing.

18 Haran at that time felt inclined to follow the ways of Abram, but he kept it within himself.

19 And Haran said in his heart, Behold now the king has seized Abram on account of these things which Abram did, and it shall come to pass, that if Abram prevail over the king I will follow him, but if the king prevail I will go after the king.

20 When Terah had spoken this to the king concerning Haran his son, the king ordered Haran to be seized with Abram.

21 And they brought them both, Abram and Haran his brother, to cast them into the fire; and all the inhabitants of the land and the king's servants and princes and all the women and little ones were there standing over them that day.

22 And the king's servants took Abram and his brother, and they stripped them of all their clothes excepting their lower garments which were on them.

23 And they bound their hands and feet with linen cords, and the servants of the king lifted them up and cast them both into the furnace.

24 The Lord loved Abram and he had compassion over him, and the Lord came down and delivered Abram from the fire and he was not burned.

25 But all the cords with which they bound him were burned, while Abram remained and walked about in the fire.

26 Haran died when they had cast him into the fire, and he was burned to ashes, for his heart was not perfect with the Lord; and those men who cast him into the fire, the flame of the fire spread over them, and they were burned, and twelve of them died.

27 Abram walked in the midst of the fire three days and three nights, and all the servants of the king saw him walking in the fire, and they came and told the king, saying, Behold we have seen Abram walking about in the midst of the fire, and even the lower garments which are on him are not burned, but the cord with which he was bound is burned.

28 When the king heard their words his heart fainted and he would not believe them; so he sent other faithful princes to see

this matter, and they went and saw it and told it to the king. And the king rose to go and see it, and he saw Abram walking to and fro in the midst of the fire, and he saw Haran's body burned, and the king wondered greatly.

29 The king ordered Abram to be taken out from the fire; and his servants approached to take him out and they could not, for the fire was round about and the flame ascending toward them from the furnace.

30 The king's servants fled from it, and the king rebuked them, saying, Make haste and bring Abram out of the fire that you shall not die.

31 The servants of the king again approached to bring Abram out, and the flames came on them and burned their faces so that eight of them died.

32 When the king saw that his servants could not approach the fire that would burn them,, the king called to Abram, O servant of the God who is in heaven, go forth from amidst the fire and come here before me. And Abram listened to the voice of the king, and he went forth from the fire and came and stood before the king.

33 When Abram came out, the king and all his servants saw Abram coming before the king with his lower garments on him that were not burned, but the cord with which he was bound was burned.

34 And the king said to Abram, How is it that you were not burned in the fire?

35 Abram said to the king, The God of heaven and earth in whom I trust and who has all in his power, he delivered me from the fire into which you did cast me.

36 Haran the brother of Abram was burned to ashes, and they sought for his body; they found it consumed.

37 Haran was eighty-two years old when he died in the fire of Casdim. And the king, princes, and inhabitants of the land, seeing that Abram was delivered from the fire, came and bowed down to Abram.

38 And Abram said to them, Do not bow down to me, but bow down to the God of the world who made you, and serve him, and go in his ways for it is he who delivered me from out of this fire; it is he who created the souls and spirits of all men, and formed man in his mother's womb, and brought him forth into the world; it is he who will deliver those who trust in him from all pain.

39 This thing seemed very wonderful in the eyes of the king and princes, that Abram was saved from the fire and that Haran was burned. And the king gave Abram many presents and he gave him his two head servants from the king's house; the name of one was Oni and the name of the other was Eliezer.

40 All the kings, princes and servants gave Abram many gifts of silver and gold and pearl, and the king and his princes sent him away, and he went in peace.

41 Abram went forth from the king in peace, and many of the king's servants followed him, and about three hundred men joined him.

42 And Abram returned on that day and went to his father's house, he and the men that followed him, and Abram served the Lord his God all the days of his life; he walked in his ways and followed his law.

43 From that day forward Abram inclined the hearts of the sons of men to serve the Lord.

44 At that time Nahor and Abram took to themselves wives, the daughters of their brother Haran; the wife of Nahor was Milca and the name of Abram's wife was Sarai. And Sarai, wife of Abram, was unable to conceive; she had no children in those days.

45 At the expiration of two years from Abram's going out of the fire, that is in the fifty-second year of his life, behold king Nimrod sat in Babel on the throne, and the king fell asleep and dreamed that he was standing with his troops and hosts in a valley opposite the king's furnace.

46 And he lifted up his eyes and saw a man in the likeness of Abram coming forth from the furnace; he came and stood before the king with his drawn sword, and then sprang to the king with his sword, when the king fled from the man, for he was afraid; while he was running, the man threw an egg on the king's head, and the egg became a great river.

47 And the king dreamed that all his troops sank in that river and died, and the king took flight with three men who were before him and he escaped.

48 The king looked at these men and they were clothed in princely dresses as the garments of kings, and had the appearance and majesty of kings.

49 And while they were running, the river again turned to an egg before the king; there came forth from the egg a young bird which came before the king, and flew at his head and plucked out the king's eye.

50 The king was grieved at the sight, and he awoke out of his sleep and his spirit was agitated; he felt a great terror.

51 In the morning the king rose from his couch in fear, and he ordered all the wise men and magicians to come before him, when the king related his dream to them.

52 And a wise servant of the king, whose name was Anuki, answered the king, saying, This is nothing else but the evil of Abram and his offspring which will spring up against my Lord and king in the latter days.

53 And behold the day will come when Abram and his offspring and the children of his household will war with my king, and they will strike all the king's hosts and his troops.

54 And as to what you have said concerning three men which you did see like yourself, and which did escape, this means that only you will escape with three kings from the kings of the earth who will be with you in battle.

55 And that which you saw of the river which turned to an egg as at first, and the young bird plucking out your eye, this means nothing else but the offspring of Abram which will kill the king in latter days.

56 This is my king's dream, and this is its interpretation, and the dream is true, and the interpretation which your servant has given you is right.

57 Now therefore my king, certainly you know that it is now fifty-two years since your sages saw this at the birth of Abram, and if my king will suffer Abram to live in the earth it will be to the injury of my lord and king, for all the days that Abram lives neither you nor your kingdom will be established, for this was known formerly at his birth; and why will not my king kill him, that his evil may be kept from you in latter days?

58 And Nimrod listened to the voice of Anuki; he sent some of his servants in secret to go and seize Abram and bring him before the king to suffer death.

59 Eliezer, Abram's servant whom the king had given him, was at that time in the presence of the king, and he heard what Anuki had advised the king, and what the king had said to cause Abram's death.

60 Eliezer said to Abram, Hasten, rise up and save your soul, that you may not die through the hands of the king, for thus did he see in a dream concerning you, and thus did Anuki interpret it, and thus also did Anuki advise the king concerning you.

61 Abram listened to the voice of Eliezer, and Abram hurried and ran for safety to the house of Noah and his son Shem, and he concealed himself there and found a place of safety; and the king's servants came to Abram's house to seek him, but they could not find him, and they searched throughout the country and he was not to be found; they went and searched in every direction and he was not to be met with.

62 And when the king's servants could not find Abram they returned to the king, but the king's anger against Abram was stilled, as they did not find him, and the king drove from his mind this matter concerning Abram.

63 Abram was concealed in Noah's house for one month, until the king had forgotten this matter, but Abram was still afraid of the king; and Terah came to see Abram his son secretly in the house of Noah, and Terah was very great in the eyes of the king.

64 Abram said to his father, Do you not know that the king thinks to kill me, and to annihilate my name from the earth by the advice of his wicked counselors?

65 Now whom have you here and what have you in this land? Arise, let us go together to the land of Canaan, that we may be delivered from his hand, that you not perish also through him in the latter days.

66 Do you not know or have you not heard, that it is not through love that Nimrod gives you all this honor, but it is only for his benefit that he bestows all this good on you?

67 And if he does to you greater good than this, certainly these are only vanities of the world, for wealth and riches cannot avail in the day of wrath and anger.

68 Now therefore listen to my voice, and let us arise and go to the land of Canaan, out of the reach of injury from Nimrod; and serve the Lord who created you in the earth and it will be well with you; and cast away all the vain things which you pursue.

69 And Abram ceased to speak when Noah and his son Shem answered Terah, saying, True is the word which Abram hath said to you.

70 And Terah listened to the voice of his son Abram, and Terah did all that Abram said, for this was from the Lord that the king should not cause Abram's death.

CHAPTER 13

1 Terah took his son Abram and his grandson Lot, the son of Haran, and Sarai his daughter-in-law, the wife of his son Abram, and all the souls of his household and went with them from Ur Casdim to go to the land of Canaan. And when they came as far as the land of Haran they remained there, for it was very good land for pasture, and of sufficient territory for those who accompanied them.

2 And the people of the land of Haran saw that Abram was good and upright with God and men, and that the Lord his God was with him. Some of the people of the land of Haran came and joined Abram, and he taught them the instruction of the Lord and his ways; these men remained with Abram in his house and they adhered to him.

3 Abram remained in the land three years, and at the expiration of three years the Lord appeared to Abram and said to him; I am the Lord who brought you forth from Ur Casdim, and delivered you from the hands of all your enemies.

4 Now therefore if you will listen to my voice and keep my commandments, my statutes and my laws, I will cause your enemies to fall before you. I will reproduce your descendants like the stars of heaven, and I will send my blessing on all the works of your hands, and you shall lack nothing.

5 Arise now, take your wife and all belonging to you and go to the land of Canaan and remain there. And I, God, will be there for you and I will bless you. And Abram rose and took his wife and all belonging to him, and he went to the land of Canaan as the Lord had told him; and Abram was fifty years old when he went from Haran.

6 Abram came to the land of Canaan and lived in the midst of the city, and there he pitched his tent among the children of Canaan, inhabitants of the land.

7 The Lord appeared to Abram when he came to the land of Canaan, and said to him, This is the land which I gave to you

and to your descendants after you forever, and I will make them like the stars of heaven, and I will give to your descendants all the lands which you see for an inheritance.

8 And Abram built an altar in the place where God had spoken to him, and there Abram called on the name of the Lord.

9 At that time, at the end of three years of Abram's dwelling in the land of Canaan, in that year Noah died, which was the fifty-eighth year of the life of Abram; all the days that Noah lived were nine hundred and fifty years and he died.

10 Abram lived in the land of Canaan, he, his wife, and all belonging to him, and all those that accompanied him, together with those that joined him from the people of the land; but Nahor, Abram's brother, and Terah his father, and Lot the son of Haran and all belonging to them lived in Haran.

11 In the fifth year of Abram's dwelling in the land of Canaan the people of Sodom and Gomorrah and all the cities of the plain revolted from the power of Chedorlaomer, king of Elam; for all the kings of the cities of the plain had served Chedorlaomer for twelve years, and given him a yearly tax, but in those days in the thirteenth year, they rebelled against him.

12 In the tenth year of Abram's dwelling in the land of Canaan there was war between Nimrod king of Shinar and Chedorlaomer king of Elam, and Nimrod came to fight with Chedorlaomer and to subdue him.

13 For Chedorlaomer was at that time one of the princes of the hosts of Nimrod, and when all the people at the tower were dispersed and those that remained were also scattered on the face of the earth, Chedorlaomer went to the land of Elam and reigned over it and rebelled against his lord.

14 In those days when Nimrod saw that the cities of the plain had rebelled, he came with pride and anger to war with Chedorlaomer, and Nimrod assembled all his princes and subjects, about seven hundred thousand men, and went against Chedorlaomer, and Chedorlaomer went out to meet him with five thousand men, and they prepared for battle in the valley of Babel which is between Elam and Shinar.

15 All those kings fought there, and Nimrod and his people were smitten before the people of Chedorlaomer, and there fell from Nimrod's men about six hundred thousand, and Mardon the king's son fell among them.

16 And Nimrod fled and returned in shame and disgrace to his land, and he was under subjection to Chedorlaomer for a long time, and Chedorlaomer returned to his land and sent princes of his host to the kings that lived around him, to Arioch king of Elasar, and to Tidal king of Goyim, and made a covenant with them, and they were all obedient to his commands.

17 It was in the fifteenth year of Abram's dwelling in the land of Canaan, which is the seventieth year of the life of Abram, the Lord appeared to Abram in that year and said to him, I am the Lord who brought you out from Ur Casdim to give you this land for an inheritance.

18 Now therefore walk before me and be perfect and keep my commands, for to you and to your descendants I will give this land for an inheritance, from the river Mitzraim to the great river Euphrates.

19 And you shall come to your fathers in peace and in good age, and the fourth generation shall return here in this land and shall inherit it forever. And Abram built an altar, and he called on the name of the Lord who appeared to him, and he brought up sacrifices on the altar to the Lord.

20 At that time Abram returned and went to Haran to see his father and mother, and his father's household, and Abram and his wife and all belonging to him returned to Haran; Abram lived in Haran five years.

21 And many of the people of Haran, about seventy-two men, followed Abram and Abram taught them the instruction of the Lord and his ways, and he taught them to know the Lord.

22 In those days the Lord appeared to Abram in Haran, and he said to him, Behold, I spoke to you twenty years ago saying,

23 Go forth from your land, from your birth-place and from your father's house, to the land which I have shown you to give it to you and to your children, for there in that land I will bless you, and make you a great nation, and make your name great, and in you shall the families of the earth be blessed.

24 Now therefore arise, go forth from this place, you, your wife, and all belonging to you, also every one born in your house and all the souls you have made in Haran, and bring them out with you from here, and rise to return to the land of Canaan.

25 And Abram arose and took his wife Sarai and all belonging to him and all that were born to him in his house and the souls which they had made in Haran, and they came out to go to the land of Canaan.

26 Abram went and returned to the land of Canaan, according to the word of the Lord. And Lot the son of his brother Haran went with him; Abram was seventy-five years old when he went forth from Haran to return to the land of Canaan.

27 And he came to the land of Canaan according to the word of the Lord to Abram, and he pitched his tent and he lived in the plain of Mamre, and with him was Lot his brother's son, and all belonging to him.

28 And the Lord again appeared to Abram and said, To your offspring I will give this land; there he built an altar to the Lord who appeared to him, which is still to this day in the plains of Mamre.

CHAPTER 14

1 In those days there was in the land of Shinar a wise man who had understanding in all wisdom, and of a beautiful appearance, but he was poor and indigent; his name was Rikayon and he was hard set to support himself.

2 And he resolved to go to Egypt, to Oswiris the son of Anom king of Egypt, to show the king his wisdom; for perhaps he

might find grace in his sight, to raise him up and give him maintenance; and Rikayon did so.

3 When Rikayon came to Egypt he asked the inhabitants of Egypt concerning the king, and the inhabitants of Egypt told him the custom of the king of Egypt, for it was then the custom of the king of Egypt that he went from his royal palace and was seen abroad only one day in the year, and after that the king would return to his palace to remain there.

4 On the day when the king went forth he passed judgment in the land, and every one having a suit came before the king that day to obtain his request.

5 When Rikayon heard of the custom in Egypt and that he could not come into the presence of the king, he grieved greatly and was very sorrowful.

6 In the evening Rikayon went out and found a house in ruins, formerly a bake house in Egypt, and he abode there all night in bitterness of soul and pinched with hunger, and sleep was removed from his eyes.

7 And Rikayon considered within himself what he should do in the town until the king made his appearance, and how he might maintain himself there.

8 And he rose in the morning and walked about, and met in his way those who sold vegetables and various sorts of offspring with which they supplied the inhabitants.

9 Rikayon wished to do the same in order to get a maintenance in the city, but he was unacquainted with the custom of the people, and he was like a blind man among them.

10 And he went and obtained vegetables to sell for his support, and the crowd assembled about him and ridiculed him, and took his vegetables from him and left him nothing.

11 He rose up from there in bitterness of soul, and went sighing to the bake house in which he had remained all the night before, and he slept there the second night.

12 On that night again he reasoned within himself how he could save himself from starvation, and he devised a scheme how to act.

13 And he rose up in the morning and acted ingeniously, and went and hired thirty strong men of the crowd, carrying their war instruments in their hands, and he led them to the top of the Egyptian sepulchre, and he placed them there.

14 He commanded them, saying, Thus says the king, Strengthen yourselves and be valiant men, and let no man be buried here until two hundred pieces of silver be given, and then he may be buried; and those men did according to the order of Rikayon to the people of Egypt the whole of that year.

15 In eight months time Rikayon and his men gathered great riches of silver and gold, and Rikayon took a great quantity of horses and other animals, and he hired more men, and he gave them horses and they remained with him.

16 When the year came round, at the time the king went forth into the town, all the inhabitants of Egypt assembled together to speak to him concerning the work of Rikayon and his men.

17 The king went forth on the appointed day, and all the Egyptians came before him and cried to him, saying,

18 May the king live forever. What is this thing you do in the town to your servants, not to allow a dead body buried until so much silver and gold be given? Was there ever the like to this done in the whole earth, from the days of former kings, yes even from the days of Adam, to this day, that the dead should be buried only for a set price?

19 We know it to be the custom of kings to take a yearly tax from the living, but you do not only do this, but from the dead also you exact a tax day by day.

20 Now, O king, we can no more bear this, for the whole city is ruined on this account, and do you not know it?

21 When the king heard all that they had spoken he was very angry, and his anger burned within him at this affair, for he had known nothing of it.

22 And the king said, Who and where is he that dares to do this wicked thing in my land without my command? Certainly you will tell me.

23 They told him all the works of Rikayon and his men, and the king's anger was aroused, and he ordered Rikayon and his men to be brought before him.

24 And Rikayon took about a thousand children, sons and daughters, and clothed them in silk and embroidery, and he set them on horses and sent them to the king by means of his men, and he also took a great quantity of silver and gold and precious stones, and a strong and beautiful horse, as a present for the king, with which he came before the king and bowed down to the earth before him; the king, his servants and all the inhabitants of Egypt wondered at the work of Rikayon; they saw his riches and the presents that he had brought to the king.

25 It greatly pleased the king and he wondered at it; and when Rikayon sat before him the king asked him concerning all his works, and Rikayon spoke all his words wisely before the king, his servants and all the inhabitants of Egypt.

26 When the king heard the words of Rikayon and his wisdom, Rikayon found grace in his sight, and he met with grace and kindness from all the servants of the king and from all the inhabitants of Egypt, on account of his wisdom and excellent speeches, and from that time they loved him greatly.

27 And the king answered and said to Rikayon, Thy name shall no more be called Rikayon but Pharaoh shall be your name, since you did exact a tax from the dead; and he called his name Pharaoh.

28 The king and his subjects loved Rikayon for his wisdom, and they consulted with all the inhabitants of Egypt to make him prefect under the king.

29 All the inhabitants of Egypt and its wise men did so, and it was made a law in Egypt.

30 They made Rikayon Pharaoh prefect under Oswiris king of Egypt, and Rikayon Pharaoh governed over Egypt, daily administering justice to the whole city, but Oswiris the king would judge the people of the land one day in the year, when he went out to make his appearance.

31 And Rikayon Pharaoh cunningly usurped the government of Egypt, and he exacted a tax from all the inhabitants of Egypt.

32 And all the inhabitants of Egypt greatly loved Rikayon Pharaoh, and they made a decree to call every king that should reign over them and their descendants in Egypt, Pharaoh.

33 Therefore all the kings that reigned in Egypt from that time forward were called Pharaoh to this day.

CHAPTER 15

1 In that year there was a heavy famine throughout the land of Canaan, and the inhabitants of the land could not remain on account of the famine for it was very severe.

2 Abram and all belonging to him rose and went down to Egypt on account of the famine, and when they were at the brook Mitzraim they remained there some time to rest from the fatigue of the road.

3 Abram and Sarai were walking at the border of the brook Mitzraim, and Abram beheld his wife Sarai that she was very beautiful.

4 And Abram said to his wife Sarai, Since God has created you with such a beautiful countenance, I am afraid of the Egyptians that they will kill me and take you away, for the fear of God is not in these places.

5 Certainly then you shall do this, Say you are my sister to all that may ask you, in order that it may be well with me, and that we may live and not be put to death.

6 And Abram commanded the same to all those that came with him to Egypt on account of the famine; also his nephew Lot he commanded, saying, If the Egyptians ask you concerning Sarai say she is the sister of Abram.

7 And yet with all these orders Abram did not put confidence in them, but he took Sarai and placed her in a chest and concealed it among their vessels, for Abram was greatly concerned about Sarai on account of the wickedness of the Egyptians.

8 Abram and all belonging to him rose up from the brook Mitzraim and came to Egypt; and they had scarcely entered the gates of the city when the guards stood up to them saying, Give tithe to the king from what you have, and then you may come into the town; Abram and those that were with him did so.

9 Abram and the people that were with him came to Egypt and they brought the chest in which Sarai was concealed, and the Egyptians saw the chest.

10 And the king's servants approached Abram, saying, What have you here in this chest which we have not seen? Now open the chest and give tithe to the king of all that it contains.

11 Abram said, This chest I will not open, but all you demand on it I will give. And Pharaoh's officers answered Abram, saying, It is a chest of precious stones, give us the tenth of its value.

12 Abram said, All that you desire I will give, but you must not open the chest.

13 And the king's officers pressed Abram; they reached the chest and opened it with force, and they saw a beautiful woman was in the chest.

14 When the officers of the king saw Sarai they were struck with admiration at her beauty, and all the princes and servants of Pharaoh assembled to see Sarai, for she was very beautiful. The king's officers ran and told Pharaoh all that they had seen, and they praised Sarai to the king; Pharaoh ordered her to be brought, and the woman came before the king.

15 Pharaoh observed Sarai and she pleased him greatly, and he was struck with her beauty; the king rejoiced greatly on her account, and made presents to those who brought him the news concerning her.

16 The woman was then brought to Pharaoh's house, and Abram grieved on account of his wife; he prayed to the Lord to deliver her from the hands of Pharaoh.

17 And Sarai also prayed at that time and said, O Lord God you did tell my Lord Abram to go from his land and from his father's house to the land of Canaan, and you did promise to do well with him if he would perform your commands; now behold we have done that which you commanded us; we left our land and our families, and we went to a strange land and to a people whom we have not known before.

18 We came to this land to avoid the famine, and this evil accident has befallen me; now therefore, O Lord God, deliver us and save us from the hand of this oppressor, and do well with me for the sake of your mercy.

19 The Lord listened to the voice of Sarai, and the Lord sent an angel to deliver Sarai from the power of Pharaoh.

20 The king came and sat before Sarai and behold an angel of the Lord was standing over them, and he appeared to Sarai and said to her, Do not fear, for the Lord has heard your prayer.

21 The king approached Sarai and said to her, What is that man to you who brought you here? and she said, He is my brother.

22 The king said, It is incumbent on us to make him great, to elevate him and to do to him all the good which you shall command us. At that time the king sent to Abram silver and gold and precious stones in abundance, together with cattle, men servants and maid servants; and the king ordered Abram to be brought and he sat in the court of the king's house, and

the king greatly exalted Abram on that night.

23 The king approached to speak to Sarai and he reached out his hand to touch her when the angel struck him heavily; he was terrified and he refrained from reaching to her.

24 And when the king came near to Sarai, the angel struck him to the ground, and acted thus to him the whole night, and the king was terrified.

25 The angel on that night struck heavily all the servants of the king, and his whole household, on account of Sarai, and there was a great lamentation that night among the people of Pharaoh's house.

26 And Pharaoh, seeing the evil that befell him, said, Certainly on account of this woman has this thing happened to me, and he removed himself at some distance from her and spoke pleasing words to her.

27 The king said to Sarai, Tell me I pray you concerning the man with whom you came here; and Sarai said, This man is my husband, and I said to you that he was my brother for I was afraid that you would put him to death through wickedness.

28 And the king kept away from Sarai, and the plagues of the angel of the Lord ceased from him and his household; Pharaoh knew that he was smitten on account of Sarai, and the king was greatly astonished at this.

29 In the morning the king called for Abram and said to him, What is this you have done to me? Why did you say, She is my sister, since I wanted to take her as a wife, and this heavy plague has therefore come on me and my household.

30 Now therefore here is your wife, take her and go from our land so we don't all die on her account. And Pharaoh took more cattle, men servants and maid servants, and silver and gold, to give to Abram, and he returned to him Sarai his wife.

31 And the king took a maiden whom he had by his concubines, and he gave her to Sarai for a handmaid.

32 The king said to his daughter, It is better for you my daughter to be a handmaid in this man's house than to be mistress in my house, after we have seen the evil that came upon us on account of this woman.

33 Abram arose, and he and all belonging to him went away from Egypt; and Pharaoh ordered some of his men to accompany him and all that went with him.

34 And Abram returned to the land of Canaan, to the place where he had made the altar, where he at first had pitched his tent.

35 Lot the son of Haran, Abram's brother, had a heavy stock of cattle, flocks and herds and tents, for the Lord was bountiful to them on account of Abram.

36 When Abram was dwelling in the land the herdsmen of Lot quarrelled with the herdsmen of Abram, for their property was too great for them to remain together in the land, and the land could not bear them on account of their cattle.

37 When Abram's herdsmen went to feed their flock they would not go into the fields of the people of the land, but the cattle of Lot's herdsmen did otherwise, for they were allowed to feed in the fields of the people of the land.

38 And the people of the land saw this occurrence daily, and they came to Abram and quarrelled with him on account of Lot's herdsmen.

39 And Abram said to Lot, What is this you are doing to me, to make me despicable to the inhabitants of the land, that you ordered your herdsman to feed your cattle in the fields of other people? Do you not know that I am a stranger in this land among the children of Canaan, and why will you do this to me?

40 Abram quarrelled daily with Lot on account of this, but Lot would not listen to Abram; he continued to do the same and the inhabitants of the land came and told Abram.

41 And Abram said to Lot, How long will you be to me a stumbling block with the inhabitants of the land? Now I petition you let there be no more quarrelling between us, for we are kinsmen.

42 I request you to separate from me, go and choose a place where you may dwell with your cattle and all belonging to you, but keep yourself at a distance from me, you and your household.

43 And don't be afraid in going from me, for if any one does an injury to you, let me know and I will avenge your cause from him, only remove from me.

44 When Abram had spoken all these words to Lot, then Lot arose and lifted up his eyes toward the plain of Jordan.

45 And he saw that all of this place was well watered, and good for man as well as affording pasture for the cattle.

46 Lot went from Abram to that place, and he there pitched his tent and he lived in Sodom, and they were separated from each other.

47 And Abram lived in the plain of Mamre, which is in Hebron, and he pitched his tent there, and Abram remained in that place many years.

CHAPTER 16

1 At that time Chedorlaomer king of Elam sent to all the neighboring kings, to Nimrod, king of Shinar who was then under his power, and to Tidal, king of Goyim, and to Arioch, king of Elasar, with whom he made a covenant, saying, Come up to me and assist me, that we may strike all the towns of Sodom and its inhabitants, for they have rebelled against me these thirteen years.

2 These four kings went up with all their camps, about eight hundred thousand men, and they went as they were, and struck every man they found in their road.

3 And the five kings of Sodom and Gomorrah, Shinab king of Admah, Shemeber king of Zeboyim, Bera king of Sodom, Bersha king of Gomorrah, and Bela king of Zoar, went out to meet them, and they all joined together in the valley of Siddim.

4 These nine kings made war in the valley of Siddim; and the kings of Sodom and Gomorrah were smitten before the kings of Elam.

5 The valley of Siddim was full of lime pits and the kings of Elam pursued the kings of Sodom, and the kings of Sodom with their camps fled and fell into the lime pits; all that remained went to the mountain for safety. The five kings of Elam came after them and pursued them to the gates of Sodom, and they took all that there was in Sodom.

6 They plundered all the cities of Sodom and Gomorrah, and they also took Lot, Abram's brother's son, and his property; they seized all the goods of the cities of Sodom, and they went away. Unic, Abram's servant, who was in the battle, saw this, and told Abram all that the kings had done to the cities of Sodom, and that Lot was taken captive by them.

7 Abram heard this, and he rose up with about three hundred and eighteen men that were with him, and that night he pursued these kings and struck them; they all fell before Abram and his men, and there was none remaining but the four kings who fled, and they each went his own road.

8 Abram recovered all the property of Sodom, and he also recovered Lot and his property, his wives and little ones and all belonging to him, so that Lot lacked nothing.

9 And when he returned from smiting these kings, he and his men passed the valley of Siddim where the kings had made war together.

10 Bera king of Sodom, and the rest of his men that were with him, went out from the lime pits into which they had fallen, to meet Abram and his men.

11 And Adonizedek king of Jerusalem, the same was Shem, went out with his men to meet Abram and his people, with bread and wine, and they remained together in the valley of Melech.

12 Adonizedek blessed Abram, and Abram gave him a tenth from all that he had brought from the spoil of his enemies, for Adonizedek was a priest before God.

13 And all the kings of Sodom and Gomorrah who were there, with their servants, approached Abram and begged him to return their servants whom he had made captive, and to take to himself all the property.

14 Abram answered the kings of Sodom, saying, As the Lord lives who created heaven and earth, and who redeemed my soul from all affliction, and who delivered me this day from my enemies and gave them into my hand, I will not take anything belonging to you, that you may not boast tomorrow, saying, Abram became rich from our property that he saved.

15 For the Lord my God in whom I trust said to me, You shall lack nothing, for I will bless you in all the works of your hands.

16 Now here is all belonging to you, take it and go; as the Lord lives I will not take from a living soul down to a shoetie or thread, excepting the expense of the food of those who went out with me to battle, as also the portions of the men who went with me, Anar, Ashcol, and Mamre, they and their men, as well as those also who had remained to watch the baggage, they shall take their portion of the spoil.

17 And the kings of Sodom gave Abram according to all that he had said; they pressed him to take of whatever he chose, but he would not.

18 He sent away the kings of Sodom and the remainder of their men, and he gave them orders about Lot, and they went to their respective places.

19 And Lot, his brother's son, he also sent away with his property, and he went with them, and Lot returned to his home, to Sodom, and Abram and his people returned to their home to the plains of Mamre, which is in Hebron.

20 At that time the Lord again appeared to Abram in Hebron, and he said to him, Do not fear, your reward is very great before me, for I will not leave you until I shall have multiplied you and blessed you and made your offspring like the stars in heaven, which cannot be measured nor numbered.

21 And I will give to your descendants all these lands that you see with your eyes, I will give them for an inheritance forever, only be strong and do not fear, walk before me and be perfect.

22 In the seventy-eighth year of the life of Abram, in that year Reu died, the son of Peleg, and all the days of Reu were two hundred and thirty-nine years, and he died.

23 And Sarai, the daughter of Haran, Abram's wife, was still unable to conceive in those days; she did not bear to Abram either son or daughter.

24 When she saw that she gave birth to no children she took her handmaid Hagar, whom Pharaoh had given her, and she gave her to Abram her husband for a wife.

25 For Hagar learned all the ways of Sarai as Sarai taught her; she was not in any way deficient in following her good ways.

26 Sarai said to Abram, Behold here is my handmaid Hagar, go to her that she may bring forth on my knees, that I may also obtain children through her.

27 At the end of ten years of Abram's dwelling in the land of Canaan, which is the eighty-fifth year of Abram's life, Sarai gave Hagar to him.

28 And Abram listened to the voice of his wife Sarai; he took his handmaid Hagar and Abram came to her and she conceived.

29 When Hagar saw that she had conceived she rejoiced greatly, and her mistress was despised in her eyes; she said within

herself, This can only be that I am better before God than Sarai my mistress, for all the days that my mistress has been with my lord, she did not conceive, but me the Lord has caused in so short a time to conceive by him.

30 And when Sarai saw that Hagar had conceived by Abram, Sarai was jealous of her handmaid, and Sarai said within herself, This is certainly nothing else but that she must be better than I am.

31 Sarai said to Abram, My wrong be on you, for at the time when you prayed before the Lord for children why did you not pray on my account, that the Lord should give me offspring from you?

32 When I speak to Hagar in your presence she hates my word because she has conceived so you will say nothing to her; may the Lord judge between me and you for what you have done to me.

33 And Abram said to Sarai, Behold your handmaid is in your hand, do to her as it may seem good in your eyes; and Sarai afflicted her, and Hagar fled from her to the wilderness.

34 An angel of the Lord found her in the place where she had fled, by a well, and he said to her, Do not fear, for I will reproduce your offspring, for you shall bear a son and you shall call his name Ishmael; now then return to Sarai your mistress, and submit yourself under her hands.

35 And Hagar called the place of that well Beer-lahai-roi; it is between Kadesh and the wilderness of Bered.

36 And Hagar at that time returned to her master's house, and at the end of days Hagar gave birth to a son to Abram, and Abram called his name Ishmael; and Abram was eighty-six years old when he had him.

CHAPTER 17

1 In those days, in the ninety-first year of the life of Abram, the children of Chittim made war with the children of Tubal, for when the Lord had scattered the sons of men on the face of the earth, the children of Chittim went and settled in the plain of Canopia, and they built themselves cities there and lived by the river Tibreu.

2 The children of Tubal lived in Tuscanah, and their boundaries reached the river Tibreu, and the children of Tubal built a city in Tuscanan, and they called the name Sabinah, after the name of Sabinah son of Tubal their father, and they lived there to this day.

3 It was at that time the children of Chittim made war with the children of Tubal, and the children of Tubal were smitten before the children of Chittim; the children of Chittim caused three hundred and seventy men to fall from the children of Tubal.

4 At that time the children of Tubal swore to the children of Chittim, saying, You shall not intermarry among us, and no man shall give his daughter to any of the sons of Chittim.

5 For all the daughters of Tubal were in those days fair, for no women were then found in the whole earth so fair as the daughters of Tubal.

6 And all who delighted in the beauty of women went to the daughters of Tubal and took wives from them, and the sons of men, kings and princes, who greatly delighted in the beauty of women, took wives in those days from the daughters of Tubal.

7 At the end of three years after the children of Tubal had sworn to the children of Chittim not to give them their daughters for wives, about twenty men of the children of Chittim went to take some of the daughters of Tubal, but they found none.

8 For the children of Tubal kept their oaths not to intermarry with them, and they would not break their oaths.

9 In the days of harvest the children of Tubal went into their fields to get in their harvest, when the young men of Chittim assembled and went to the city of Sabinah, and each man took a young woman from the daughters of Tubal, and they came to their cities.

10 And the children of Tubal heard of it and they went to make war with them; they could not prevail over them, for the mountain was very high; when they saw they could not prevail over them they returned to their land.

11 And at the revolution of the year the children of Tubal went and hired about ten thousand men from those cities that were near them, and they went to war with the children of Chittim.

12 And the children of Tubal went to war with the children of Chittim, to destroy their land and to distress them. In this engagement the children of Tubal prevailed over the children of Chittim, and the children of Chittim, seeing that they were greatly distressed, lifted up the children which they had had by the daughters of Tubal, on the wall which had been built, to be before the eyes of the children of Tubal.

13 And the children of Chittim said to them, Have you come to make war with your own sons and daughters, and have we not been considered your flesh and bones from that time till now?

14 When the children of Tubal heard this they ceased to make war with the children of Chittim, and they went away.

15 They returned to their cities and the children of Chittim at that time assembled and built two cities by the sea; they called one Purtu and the other Ariza.

16 And Abram the son of Terah was then ninety-nine years old.

17 At that time the Lord appeared to him and said, I will make my covenant between me and you, and I will greatly reproduce your offspring, and this is the covenant which I make between me and you, that every male child be circumcised, you and your descendants after you.

18 At eight days old shall it be circumcised, and this covenant shall be in your flesh for an everlasting covenant.

19 And now therefore your name shall no more be called Abram but Abraham, and your wife shall no more be called Sarai but Sarah.

20 For I will bless you both, and I will reproduce your descendants, that you shall become a great nation, and kings shall come forth from you.

CHAPTER 18

1 Abraham rose and did all that God had ordered him; he took the men of his household and those bought with his money, and he circumcised them as the Lord had commanded him.

2 There was not one left whom he did not circumcise, and Abraham and his son Ishmael were circumcised in the flesh of their foreskin; Ishmael was thirteen years old when he was circumcised in the flesh of his foreskin.

3 And in the third day Abraham went out of his tent and sat at the door to enjoy the heat of the sun, during the pain of his flesh.

4 The Lord appeared to him in the plain of Mamre and sent three of his ministering angels to visit him, and he was sitting at the door of the tent. He lifted his eyes and saw three men were coming from a distance; he rose up and ran to meet them, and he bowed down to them and brought them into his house.

5 And he said to them, If now I have found favor in your sight, turn in and eat a morsel of bread. He urged them, they turned in and he gave them water and they washed their feet, and he placed them under a tree at the door of the tent.

6 Abraham ran and took a calf, tender and good, and he hurried to kill it, and gave it to his servant Eliezer to dress.

7 And Abraham came to Sarah into the tent, and said to her, Make ready quickly three measures of fine meal, knead it and make cakes to cover the pot containing the meat, and she did so.

8 Abraham hurried and brought before them butter and milk, beef and mutton, and put it before them to eat, before the flesh of the calf was sufficiently done, and they ate.

9 When they were done eating one of them said to him, I will return to you according to the time of life, and Sarah your wife shall have a son.

10 And the men afterward departed and went their ways, to the places to which they were sent.

11 In those days all the people of Sodom and Gomorrah, and of the whole five cities, were greatly wicked and sinful against the Lord. They provoked the Lord with their abominations, and they grew worse as they aged abominably and scornfully before the Lord, and their wickedness and crimes were in those days great before the Lord.

12 They had in their land a very extensive valley, about half a day's walk, and in it there were fountains of water and a great deal of herbage surrounding the water.

13 All the people of Sodom and Gomorrah went there four times a year, with their wives and children and all belonging to them, and they rejoiced there with timbrels and dances.

14 In the time of rejoicing they would all rise and lay hold of their neighbor's wives, and some, the virgin daughters of their neighbors, and they enjoyed them; each man saw his wife and daughter in the hands of his neighbor and did not say a word.

15 And they did so from morning to night; afterward they returned home each man to his house and each woman to her tent; so they always did four times in the year.

16 Also when a stranger came into their cities and brought goods which he had purchased with a view to dispose of there, the people of these cities would assemble, men, women and children, young and old, and go to the man and take his goods by force, giving a little to each man until there was an end to all the goods of the owner which he had brought into the land.

17 And if the owner of the goods quarreled with them, saying, What is this work which you have done to me, then they would approach him one by one, and each would show him the little which he took and taunt him, saying, I only took that little which you did give me; when he heard this from them all, he would arise and go from them in sorrow and bitterness of soul. Then they would all arise and go after him, and drive him out of the city with great noise and tumult.

18 There was a man from the country of Elam who was leisurely going on the road, seated on his ass, which carried a fine mantle of varied colors, and the mantle was bound with a cord on the ass.

19 The man was on his journey passing through the street of Sodom when the sun set in the evening; he remained there in order to abide during the night, but no one would let him into his house. At that time there was in Sodom a wicked and mischievous man, one skillful to do evil, and his name was Hedad.

20 And he lifted up his eyes and saw the traveler in the street of the city, and he came to him and said, Whence come you and where do you go?

21 The man said to him, I am traveling from Hebron to Elam where I belong, and as I passed the sun set and no one would invite me to enter his house; you have bread and water and also straw and feed for my ass, and I am short of nothing.

22 And Hedad answered and said to him, All that you shall want shall be supplied by me, but in the street you shall not abide all night.

23 Hedad brought him to his house, and he took off the mantle from the ass with the cord, and brought them to his house. He gave the ass straw and feed while the traveler ate and drank in Hedad's house, and he abode there that night.

24 And in the morning the traveler rose up early to continue his journey, when Hedad said to him, Wait, comfort your heart

with a morsel of bread and then go, and the man did so; and he remained with him, and they both ate and drank together during the day, then the man rose up to go.

25 And Hedad said to him, Behold now the day is declining, you had better remain all night that your heart may be comforted; and he pressed him so that he tarried there all night, and on the second day he rose up early to go away, when Hedad pressed him, saying, Comfort your heart with a morsel of bread and then go, and he remained and ate with him also the second day. Then the man rose up to continue his journey.

26 And Hedad said to him, Behold now the day is declining, remain with me to comfort your heart and in the morning rise up early and go your way.

27 The man would not remain, but rose and saddled his ass, and while he was saddling his ass the wife of Hedad said to her husband, Behold this man has remained with us for two days eating and drinking and he has given us nothing, and now shall he go away from us without giving anything? Hedad said to her, Be silent.

28 And the man saddled his ass to go, and he asked Hedad to give him the cord and mantle to tie it on the ass.

29 And Hedad said to him, What do you say? And he said to him, That you my lord shall give me the cord and the mantle made with varied colors which you concealed in your house to take care of it.

30 And Hedad answered the man, saying, This is the interpretation of your dream, the cord which you did see means that your life will be lengthened out like a cord, and having seen the mantle colored with all sorts of colors, means that you shall have a vineyard in which you will plant trees of all fruits.

31 And the traveler answered, saying, Not so my lord, for I was awake when I gave you the cord and also a mantle woven with different colors, which you took off the ass to put by for me; and Hedad answered and said, Certainly I have told you the interpretation of your dream and it is a good dream, and this is the interpretation of it.

32 Now the sons of men give me four pieces of silver, which is my charge for interpreting dreams, and of you only I require three pieces of silver.

33 And the man was provoked at the words of Hedad, and he cried bitterly, and he brought Hedad to Serak judge of Sodom.

34 And the man laid his cause before Serak the judge, when Hedad replied, saying, It is not so, but thus the matter stands. And the judge said to the traveler, This man Hedad tells you truth, for he is famed in the cities for the accurate interpretation of dreams.

35 And the man cried at the word of the judge, and he said, Not so my Lord, for it was in the day that I gave him the cord and mantle which was on the ass, in order to put them by in his house; they both disputed before the judge, the one saying, Thus the matter was, and the other declaring otherwise.

36 Hedad said to the man, Give me four pieces of silver that I charge for my interpretations of dreams; I will not make any allowance; give me the expense of the four meals that you ate in my house.

37 And the man said to Hedad, Truly I will pay you for what I ate in your house, only give me the cord and mantle which you did conceal in your house.

38 Hedad replied before the judge and said to the man, Did I not tell you the interpretation of your dream? The cord means that your days shall be prolonged like a cord, and the mantle, that you will have a vineyard in which you will plant all kinds of fruit trees.

39 This is the proper interpretation of your dream, now give me the four pieces of silver that I require as a compensation, for I will make you no allowance.

40 And the man cried at the words of Hedad and they both quarreled before the judge; the judge gave orders to his servants, who drove them rashly from the house.

41 And they went away quarreling from the judge. When the people of Sodom heard them, they gathered about them and spoke harshly against the stranger, and they drove him rashly from the city.

42 And the man continued his journey on his ass with bitterness of soul, lamenting and weeping.

43 And while he was on his way he wept at what had happened to him in the corrupt city of Sodom.

CHAPTER 19

1 The cities of Sodom had four judges to four cities, and these were their names, Serak in the city of Sodom, Sharkad in Gomorrah, Zabnac in Admah, and Menon in Zeboyim.

2 Eliezer Abraham's servant applied to them different names, and he converted Serak to Shakra, Sharkad to Shakrura, Zebnac to Kezobim, and Menon to Matzlodin.

3 By desire of their four judges the people of Sodom and Gomorrah had beds erected in the streets of the cities and if a man came to these places, they laid hold of him and brought him to one of their beds and by force made him to lie in them.

4 As he lay down, three men would stand at his head and three at his feet, and measure him by the length of the bed; if the man was less than the bed, these six men would stretch him at each end, and when he cried out to them they would not answer him.

5 If he was longer than the bed, they would draw together the two sides of the bed at each end, until the man had reached the gates of death.

6 And if he continued to cry out to them, they would answer him, saying, Thus it shall be done to a man that comes into our land.

7 When men heard all these things that the people of the cities of Sodom did, they refrained from coming there.

8 And when a poor man came to their land they would give him silver and gold, and cause a proclamation in the whole city not to give him a morsel of bread to eat. If the stranger should remain there some days and die from hunger, not having been able to obtain a morsel of bread, then at his death all the people of the city would come and take their silver and gold which they had given to him.

9 Those that could recognize the silver or gold which they had given him took it back, and at his death they also stripped him of his garments, and they would fight about them; he that prevailed over his neighbor took them.

10 After that they would carry him and bury him under some of the shrubs in the desert; so they did all the days to any one that came to them and died in their land.

11 And in the course of time Sarah sent Eliezer to Sodom, to see Lot and inquire after his welfare.

12 Eliezer went to Sodom, and he met a man of Sodom fighting with a stranger, and the man of Sodom stripped the poor man of all his clothes and went away.

13 And this poor man cried to Eliezer and begged his favor on account of what the man of Sodom had done to him.

14 He said to him, Why do you act thus to the poor man who came to your land?

15 The man of Sodom answered Eliezer, saying, Is this man your brother, or have the people of Sodom made you a judge this day, that you speak about this man?

16 Eliezer strove with the man of Sodom on account of the poor man, and when Eliezer approached to recover the poor man's clothes from the man of Sodom, he hurried and with a stone struck Eliezer in the forehead.

17 The blood flowed copiously from Eliezer's forehead, and when the man saw the blood he caught hold of Eliezer, saying, Give me my wage for having rid you of this bad blood that was in your forehead, for such is the custom and the law in our land.

18 And Eliezer said to him, You have wounded me and require me to pay you your wage? Eliezer would not listen to the words of the man of Sodom.

19 And the man laid hold of Eliezer and brought him to Shakra the judge of Sodom for judgment.

20 The man spoke to the judge, saying, I beseech you my lord, thus has this man done, for I struck him with a stone that the blood flowed from his forehead, and he is unwilling to give me my wage.

21 And the judge said to Eliezer, This man speaks truth to you, give him his wage, for this is the custom in our land. Eliezer heard the words of the judge, and he lifted up a stone and struck the judge; the stone struck on his forehead, and the blood flowed copiously from the forehead of the judge, and Eliezer said, If this then is the custom in your land give to this man what I should have given him, for this has been your decision; you did decree it.

22 And Eliezer left the man of Sodom with the judge, and he went away.

23 When the kings of Elam had made war with the kings of Sodom, the kings of Elam captured all the property of Sodom and they took Lot captive with his property, and when it was told to Abraham he went and made war with the kings of Elam. He recovered from their hands all the property of Lot as well as the property of Sodom.

24 At that time the wife of Lot gave birth to a daughter, and he called her name Paltith, saying, Because God had delivered him and his whole household from the kings of Elam. Paltith daughter of Lot grew up, and one of the men of Sodom took her for a wife.

25 And a poor man came into the city to seek a maintenance, and he remained in the city some days, and all the people of Sodom caused a proclamation of their custom not to give this man a morsel of bread to eat until he dropped dead on the earth, and they did so.

26 And Paltith the daughter of Lot saw this man lying in the streets starved with hunger and no one would give him any thing to keep him alive; he was just on the point of death.

27 And her soul was filled with pity on account of the man and she fed him secretly with bread for many days, and the soul of this man was revived.

28 For when she went forth to fetch water she would put the bread in the water pitcher, and when she came to the place where the poor man was, she took the bread from the pitcher and gave it him to eat; so she did many days.

29 And all the people of Sodom and Gomorrah wondered how this man could bear starvation for so many days.

30 And they said to each other, This can only be because he eats and drinks, for no man can bear starvation for so many days or live as this man has, without even his countenance changing. Three men concealed themselves in a place where the poor man was stationed to know who it was that brought him bread to eat.

31 Paltith daughter of Lot went forth that day to fetch water and she put bread into her pitcher of water; she went to draw water by the poor man's place and took out the bread from the pitcher and gave it to the poor man and he ate it.

32 And the three men saw what Paltith did to the poor man, and they said to her, It is you then who have supported him, and therefore he has not starved, nor changed in appearance nor died like the rest.

33 The three men went out of the place in which they were concealed, and they seized Paltith and the bread which was in the poor man's hand.

34 They took Paltith and brought her before their judges, and they said to them, Thus did she do, and it is she who supplied

the poor man with bread, therefore he did not die all this time; now therefore declare to us the punishment due to this woman for having gone contrary to our law.

35 And the people of Sodom and Gomorrah assembled and set ablaze a fire in the street of the city, and they took the woman and cast her into the fire and she was burned to ashes.

36 In the city of Admah there was a woman to whom they did the same.

37 For a traveler came into the city of Admah to stay there all night, with the intention of going home in the morning. He sat opposite the door of the house of the young woman's father, to remain there, as the sun had set when he had reached that place; the young woman saw him sitting by the door of the house.

38 He asked her for a drink of water and she said to him, Who art you? And he said to her, I was this day going on the road, and reached here when the sun set, so I will stay here all night, and in the morning I will arise early and continue my journey.

39 And the young woman went into the house and fetched the man bread and water to eat and drink.

40 This affair became known to the people of Admah, and they assembled and brought the young woman before the judges, that they should judge her for this act.

41 And the judge said, The judgment of death must pass on this woman because she went contrary to our law, and this therefore is the decision concerning her.

42 The people of those cities assembled and brought out the young woman, and anointed her with honey from head to foot, as the judge had decreed, and they placed her before a swarm of bees which were then in their hives, and the bees flew on her and stung her that her whole body was swelled.

43 The young woman cried out on account of the bees, but no one took notice of her or pitied her, and her cries ascended to heaven.

44 And the Lord was provoked at this and at all the works of the cities of Sodom, for they had abundance of food, and had tranquility among them, and still would not sustain the poor and the needy. In those days their evil doings and sins became great before the Lord.

45 The Lord sent for two of the angels that had come to Abraham's house, to destroy Sodom and its cities.

46 And the angels rose up from the door of Abraham's tent, after they had eaten and drunk, and they reached Sodom in the evening, and Lot was then sitting in the gate of Sodom. When he saw them he rose to meet them, and he bowed down to the ground.

47 He welcomed them greatly and brought them into his house, and he gave them food which they ate, and they stayed all night in his house.

48 And the angels said to Lot, Arise, go forth from this place, you and all belonging to you, that you not be consumed in the iniquity of this city, for the Lord will destroy this place.

49 The angels laid hold on the hand of Lot and on the hand of his wife, and on the hands of his children, and all belonging to him, and they brought him forth and set him outside of the cities.

50 And they said to Lot, Escape for your life. He fled and all belonging to him.

51 Then the Lord rained on Sodom and on Gomorrah and on all these cities brimstone and fire from the Lord out of heaven.

52 And he overthrew these cities, all the plain and all the inhabitants of the cities, and that which grew on the ground; Ado the wife of Lot looked back to see the destruction of the cities, for her compassion was moved on account of her daughters who remained in Sodom, for they did not go with her.

53 And when she looked back she became a pillar of salt, and it is yet in that place to this day.

54 The oxen which stood in that place daily licked up the salt to the extremities of their feet, and in the morning it would spring forth afresh, and they again licked it up to this day.

55 Lot and two of his daughters that remained with him fled and escaped to the cave of Adullam, and they remained there for some time.

56 And Abraham rose up early in the morning to see what had been done to the cities of Sodom; and he looked and beheld the smoke of the cities going up like the smoke of a furnace.

57 Lot and his two daughters remained in the cave, and they made their father drink wine, and they lay with him, for they said there was no man on earth that could produce descendants from them, for they thought that the whole earth was destroyed.

58 They both lay with their father and conceived and gave birth to sons. The first born called the name of her son Moab, saying, From my father did I conceive him; he is the father of the Moabites to this day.

59 And the younger also called her son Benami; he is the father of the children of Ammon to this day.

60 After this Lot and his two daughters went away from there, and he lived on the other side of the Jordan with his two daughters and their sons, and the sons of Lot grew up, and they went and took themselves wives from the land of Canaan, and they had children and they were prolific and multiplied.

CHAPTER 20

1 At that time Abraham journeyed from the plain of Mamre and he went to the land of the Philistines, and he lived in Gerar; it was in the twenty-fifth year of Abraham's being in the land of Canaan, and the hundredth year of the life of Abraham, that he came to Gerar in the land of the Philistines.

2 And when they entered the land he said to Sarah his wife, Say you are my sister, to any one that shall ask you, in order that we may escape the evil of the inhabitants of the land.

3 As Abraham was dwelling in the land of the Philistines, the servants of Abimelech, king of the Philistines, saw that Sarah was greatly beautiful, and they asked Abraham concerning her, and he said, She is my sister.

4 And the servants of Abimelech went to Abimelech, saying, A man from the land of Canaan is come to dwell in the land, and he has a sister that is exceeding fair.

5 Abimelech heard the words of his servants who praised Sarah to him, and Abimelech sent his officers, and they brought Sarah to the king.

6 And Sarah came to the house of Abimelech; the king saw that Sarah was beautiful, and she pleased him greatly.

7 And he approached her and said to her, What is that man to you with whom you did come to our land? And Sarah answered and said, He is my brother, and we came from the land of Canaan to dwell wherever we could find a place.

8 Abimelech said to Sarah, Behold my land is before you, place your brother in any part of this land that pleases you, and it will be our duty to exalt and elevate him above all the people of the land since he is your brother.

9 And Abimelech sent for Abraham, and Abraham came to Abimelech.

10 Abimelech said to Abraham, Behold I have given orders that you shall be honored as you desire on account of your sister Sarah.

11 And Abraham went forth from the king, and the king's present followed him.

12 As at evening time, before men laid down to rest, the king was sitting on his throne, and a deep sleep fell on him, and he lay on the throne and slept till morning.

13 He dreamed that an angel of the Lord came to him with a drawn sword in his hand, and the angel stood over Abimelech and wished to kill him with the sword; the king was terrified in his dream and said to the angel, In what have I sinned against you that you come to kill me with your sword?

14 And the angel answered and said to Abimelech, Behold you die on account of the woman which last night you brought to your house, for she is a married woman, the wife of Abraham who came to your house; now therefore return that man his wife, for she is his wife; should you not return her, know that you will certainly die, you and all belonging to you.

15 On that night there was a great outcry in the land of the Philistines, and the inhabitants of the land saw the figure of a man standing with a drawn sword in his hand, and he struck the inhabitants of the land with the sword, yes, he continued to strike them.

16 And the angel of the Lord struck the whole land of the Philistines on that night, and there was a great confusion on that night and on the following morning.

17 Every womb was closed, and all their issues, and the hand of the Lord was on them on account of Sarah, wife of Abraham, whom Abimelech had taken.

18 And in the morning Abimelech rose with terror and confusion and with a great dread; he sent and had his servants called in; he related his dream to them, and the people were greatly afraid.

19 One man standing among the servants of the king answered the king, saying, O sovereign king, restore this woman to her husband, for he is her husband, for the same happened to the king of Egypt when this man came to Egypt.

20 He said concerning his wife, She is my sister, for such is his manner of doing when he comes to dwell in the land in which he is a stranger.

21 Pharaoh sent and took this woman for a wife and the Lord brought on him grievous plagues until he returned the woman to her husband.

22 Now therefore, O sovereign king, know what happened last night to the whole land, for there was a very great consternation and great pain and lamentation, and we know that it was on account of the woman which you did take.

23 Now, therefore, restore this woman to her husband, that it should not happen to us as it did to Pharaoh king of Egypt and his subjects, and that we may not die. Abimelech hurried and had Sarah called for, and she came before him, and he had Abraham called for, and he came before him.

24 Abimelech said to them, What is this work you have been doing in saying you are brother and sister, and I took this woman for a wife?

25 And Abraham said, Because I thought I would suffer death on account of my wife; and Abimelech took flocks and herds, and men servants and maid servants, and a thousand pieces of silver, and he gave them to Abraham, and he returned Sarah to him.

26 Abimelech said to Abraham, Behold the whole land is before you, dwell in it wherever you shall choose.

27 And Abraham and Sarah, his wife, went forth from the king's presence with honor and respect, and they lived in the land, even in Gerar.

28 All the inhabitants of the land of the Philistines and the king's servants were still in pain through the plague which the angel had inflicted on them the whole night on account of Sarah.

29 Abimelech sent for Abraham, saying, Pray now for your servants to the Lord your God, that he may put away this

mortality from among us.

30 And Abraham prayed on account of Abimelech and his subjects, and the Lord heard the prayer of Abraham, and he healed Abimelech and all his subjects.

CHAPTER 21

1 It was at that time the end of a year and four months of Abraham's dwelling in the land of the Philistines in Gerar, that God visited Sarah, and the Lord remembered her and she conceived and gave birth to a son to Abraham.

2 Abraham called the name of the son which Sarah gave birth to him, Isaac.

3 And Abraham circumcised his son Isaac at eight days old, as God had commanded Abraham to do to his descendants after him; Abraham was one hundred and Sarah ninety years old when Isaac was born to them.

4 The child grew up and was weaned, and Abraham made a great feast on the day that Isaac was weaned.

5 Shem and Eber and all the great people of the land, and Abimelech king of the Philistines and his servants, and Phicol, the captain of his host, came to eat and drink and rejoice at the feast which Abraham made on the day of his son Isaac's being weaned.

6 Also Terah, the father of Abraham, and Nahor his brother, came from Haran, they and all belonging to them, for they greatly rejoiced on hearing that a son had been born to Sarah.

7 They came to Abraham, and they ate and drank at the feast which Abraham made on the day of Isaac's being weaned.

8 Terah and Nahor rejoiced with Abraham, and they remained with him many days in the land of the Philistines.

9 At that time Serug the son of Reu died, in the first year of the birth of Isaac son of Abraham.

10 And all the days of Serug were two hundred and thirty-nine years, and he died.

11 Ishmael the son of Abraham was grown up in those days; he was fourteen years old when Sarah gave birth to Isaac to Abraham.

12 And God was with Ishmael the son of Abraham, and he grew up, and he learned to use the bow and became an archer.

13 When Isaac was five years old he was sitting with Ishmael at the door of the tent.

14 Ishmael came to Isaac and seated himself opposite to him, and he took the bow and drew it and put the arrow in it, and intended to kill Isaac.

15 Sarah saw the act which Ishmael desired to do to her son Isaac, and it grieved her greatly on account of her son; she sent for Abraham, and said to him, Cast out this bondwoman and her son, for her son shall not be heir with my son, for thus did he seek to do to him this day.

16 Abraham listened to the voice of Sarah, and he rose up early in the morning. He took twelve loaves and a bottle of water which he gave to Hagar, and sent her away with her son, and Hagar went with her son to the wilderness. They lived in the wilderness of Paran with the inhabitants of the wilderness; Ishmael was an archer, and he lived in the wilderness a long time.

17 He and his mother afterward went to the land of Egypt, and they lived there; Hagar took a wife for her son from Egypt, and her name was Meribah.

18 And the wife of Ishmael conceived and gave birth to four sons and two daughters. Ishmael and his mother and his wife and children afterward went and returned to the wilderness.

19 They made themselves tents in the wilderness, in which they lived, and they continued to travel and then to rest monthly and yearly.

20 And God gave Ishmael flocks and herds and tents on account of Abraham his father, and the man increased in cattle.

21 Ishmael lived in deserts and in tents, traveling and resting for a long time, and he did not see the face of his father.

22 Some time later, Abraham said to Sarah his wife, I will go and see my son Ishmael, for I have a desire to see him, for I have not seen him for a long time.

23 Abraham rode on one of his camels to the wilderness to seek his son Ishmael, for he heard that he was dwelling in a tent in the wilderness with all belonging to him.

24 Abraham went to the wilderness and reached the tent of Ishmael about noon, and he asked after Ishmael; he found the wife of Ishmael sitting in the tent with her children, and Ishmael her husband and his mother were not with them.

25 Abraham asked the wife of Ishmael, saying, Where has Ishmael gone? And she said, He has gone to the field to hunt. Abraham was still mounted on the camel, for he would not get off to the ground as he had sworn to his wife Sarah that he would not get off from the camel.

26 And Abraham said to Ishmael's wife, My daughter, give me a little water that I may drink, for I am fatigued from the journey.

27 And Ishmael's wife answered and said to Abraham, We have neither water nor bread. She continued sitting in the tent and did not notice Abraham, neither did she ask him who he was.

28 But she was beating her children in the tent, and she was cursing them, and she also cursed her husband Ishmael and reproached him. Abraham heard the words of Ishmael's wife to her children, and he was very angry and displeased.

29 Abraham called to the woman to come out to him from the tent, and the woman came and stood opposite to Abraham, for Abraham was still mounted on the camel.

30 And Abraham said to Ishmael's wife, When your husband Ishmael returns home say these words to him,

31 A very old man from the land of the Philistines came here to seek you, and thus was his appearance and figure; I did not ask him who he was, and seeing you were not here he spoke to me and said, When Ishmael your husband returns tell him thus did this man say, When you come home put away this nail of the tent which you have placed here, and place another nail in its stead.

32 Abraham finished his instructions to the woman, and he turned and went off on the camel homeward.

33 After that Ishmael came from the hunt by him and his mother, and returned to the tent, and his wife spoke these words to him,

34 A very old man from the land of the Philistines came to seek you, and thus was his appearance and figure; I did not ask him who he was, and seeing you were not at home he said to me, When your husband comes home tell him, thus says the old man, Put away the nail of the tent which you have placed here and place another nail in its stead.

35 Ishmael heard the words of his wife, and he knew that it was his father, and that his wife did not honor him.

36 And Ishmael understood his father's words that he had spoken to his wife, and Ishmael listened to the voice of his father; Ishmael cast off that woman and she went away.

37 Ishmael afterward went to the land of Canaan, and he took another wife and he brought her to his tent to the place where he then lived.

38 And at the end of three years Abraham said, I will go again and see Ishmael my son, for I have not seen him for a long time.

39 He rode on his camel and went to the wilderness, and he reached the tent of Ishmael about noon.

40 He asked after Ishmael, and his wife came out of the tent and said, He is not here my lord, for he has gone to hunt in the fields, and to feed the camels. And the woman said to Abraham, Turn in my lord into the tent, and eat a morsel of bread, for your soul must be wearied on account of the journey.

41 And Abraham said to her, I will not stop for I am in haste to continue my journey, but give me a little water to drink, for I have thirst; the woman hurried and ran into the tent and she brought out water and bread to Abraham, which she placed before him and she urged him to eat; he ate and drank and his heart was comforted and he blessed his son Ishmael.

42 He finished his meal and he blessed the Lord, and he said to Ishmael's wife, When Ishmael comes home say these words to him,

43 A very old man from the land of the Philistines came here and asked after you, and you were not here; and I brought out bread and water and he ate and drank and his heart was comforted.

44 And he spoke these words to me: When Ishmael your husband comes home, say to him, The nail of the tent which you have is very good, do not put it away from the tent.

45 Abraham finished commanding the woman, and he rode off to his home to the land of the Philistines; and when Ishmael came to his tent his wife went forth to meet him with joy and a cheerful heart.

46 And she said to him, An old man came here from the land of the Philistines and thus was his appearance, and he asked after you and you were not here, so I brought out bread and water, and he ate and drank and his heart was comforted.

47 And he spoke these words to me, When Ishmael your husband comes home say to him, The nail of the tent which you have is very good, do not put it away from the tent.

48 Ishmael knew that it was his father, and that his wife had honored him, and the Lord blessed Ishmael.

CHAPTER 22

1 Ishmael then rose up and took his wife and his children and his cattle and all belonging to him, and he journeyed from there and he went to his father in the land of the Philistines.

2 Abraham related to Ishmael his son the transaction with the first wife that Ishmael took, according to what she did.

3 Ishmael and his children lived with Abraham many days in that land, and Abraham lived in the land of the Philistines a long time.

4 And the days increased and reached twenty six years; after that Abraham with his servants and all belonging to him went from the land of the Philistines and removed to a great distance, and they came near to Hebron and remained there. The servants of Abraham dug wells of water, and Abraham and all belonging to him lived by the water. The servants of Abimelech king of the Philistines heard the report that Abraham's servants had dug wells of water in borders of the land.

5 They came and quarreled with the servants of Abraham and robbed them of the great well which they had dug.

6 Abimelech king of the Philistines heard of this affair; he with Phicol the captain of his host and twenty of his men came to Abraham, and Abimelech spoke to Abraham concerning his servants; Abraham rebuked Abimelech concerning the well of which his servants had robbed him.

7 Abimelech said to Abraham, As the Lord lives who created the whole earth, I did not hear of the act which my servants did to your servants until this day.

8 And Abraham took seven ewe lambs and gave them to Abimelech, saying, Take these, I pray you, from my hands that it

may be a testimony for me that I dug this well.

9 Abimelech took the seven ewe lambs which Abraham had given to him, for he had also given him cattle and herds in abundance; Abimelech swore to Abraham concerning the well, therefore he called that well Beersheba, for there they both swore concerning it.

10 And they both made a covenant in Beersheba, and Abimelech rose up with Phicol the captain of his host and all his men; they returned to the land of the Philistines, and Abraham and all belonging to him lived in Beersheba and he was in that land a long time.

11 Abraham planted a large grove in Beersheba, and he made to it four gates facing the four sides of the earth; he planted a vineyard in it, so that if a traveler came to Abraham he entered any gate which was in his road, and remained there and ate and drank and satisfied himself and then departed.

12 For the house of Abraham was always open to the sons of men that passed and returned, who came daily to eat and drink in the house of Abraham.

13 Any man who had hunger and came to Abraham's house, Abraham would give him bread that he might eat and drink and be satisfied; any one that came naked to his house he would clothe with garments as he might choose and give him silver and gold, and make known to him the Lord who had created him in the earth; this did Abraham all his life.

14 Abraham and his children and all belonging to him lived in Beersheba, and he pitched his tent as far as Hebron.

15 And Abraham's brother Nahor and his father and all belonging to them lived in Haran, for they did not come with Abraham to the land of Canaan.

16 And children were born to Nahor which Milca the daughter of Haran, and sister to Sarah, Abraham's wife, gave birth to, to him.

17 These are the names of those that were born to him: Uz, Buz, Kemuel, Kesed, Chazo, Pildash, Tidlaf, and Bethuel, being eight sons; these are the children of Milca which she gave birth to, to Nahor, Abraham's brother.

18 And Nahor had a concubine and her name was Reumah, and she also gave birth to, to Nahor: Zebach, Gachash, Tachash and Maacha, being four sons.

19 The children that were born to Nahor were twelve sons besides his daughters, and they also had children born to them in Haran.

20 And the children of Uz the first born of Nahor were Abi, Cheref, Gadin, Melus, and Deborah their sister.

21 And the sons of Buz were Berachel, Naamath, Sheva, and Madonu.

22 And the sons of Kemuel were Aram and Rechob.

23 And the sons of Kesed were Anamlech, Meshai, Benon and Yifi; the sons of Chazo were Pildash, Mechi and Opher.

24 And the sons of Pildash were Arud, Chamum, Mered and Moloch.

25 And the sons of Tidlaf were Mushan, Cushan and Mutzi.

26 And the children of Bethuel were Sechar, Laban and their sister Rebecca.

27 These are the families of the children of Nahor, that were born to them in Haran; and Aram the son of Kemuel and Rechob his brother went away from Haran, and they found a valley in the land by the river Euphrates.

28 And they built a city there, and they called the name of the city after the name of Pethor the son of Aram, that is Aram Naherayim to this day.

29 The children of Kesed also went to dwell where they could find a place, and they found a valley opposite to the land of Shinar, and they lived there.

30 There they built themselves a city, and they called the name of the city Kesed after the name of their father; that is the land Kasdim to this day, and the Kasdim lived in that land and they were prolific and multiplied greatly.

31 Terah, father of Nahor and Abraham, went and took another wife in his old age, and her name was Pelilah, and she conceived and gave birth to him a son and he called his name Zoba.

32 Terah lived twenty-five years after he had Zoba.

33 And Terah died in that year, that is in the thirty-fifth year of the birth of Isaac son of Abraham.

34 The days of Terah were two hundred and five years, and he was buried in Haran.

35 Zoba the son of Terah lived thirty years and he had Aram, Achlis and Merik.

36 Aram, son of Zoba son of Terah, had three wives and he had twelve sons and three daughters; the Lord gave to Aram the son of Zoba, riches and possessions, and abundance of cattle, and flocks and herds, and the man increased greatly.

37 Aram the son of Zoba and his brother and all his household journeyed from Haran, and they went to dwell where they should find a place, for their property was too great to remain in Haran; for they could not stop in Haran together with their brothers the children of Nahor.

38 Aram the son of Zoba went with his brothers, and they found a valley at a distance toward the eastern country and they lived there.

39 They also built a city there, and they called the name thereof Aram, after the name of their eldest brother; that is Aram Zoba to this day.

40 Isaac the son of Abraham was growing up in those days, and Abraham his father taught him the way of the Lord to know the Lord, and the Lord was with him.

41 When Isaac was thirty-seven years old, Ishmael his brother was going about with him in the tent.

42 And Ishmael boasted of himself to Isaac, saying, I was thirteen years old when the Lord spoke to my father to circumcise us, and I did according to the word of the Lord which he spoke to my father, and I gave my soul to the Lord, and I did not go contrary to his word which he commanded my father.

43 Isaac answered Ishmael, saying, Why do you boast to me about this, about a little bit of your flesh which you did take from your body, concerning which the Lord commanded you?

44 As the Lord lives, the God of my father Abraham, if the Lord should say to my father, Take now your son Isaac and bring him up an offering before me, I would not refrain but I would joyfully accede to it.

45 And the Lord heard the word that Isaac spoke to Ishmael, and it seemed good in the sight of the Lord, and he thought to try Abraham in this matter.

46 The day arrived when the sons of God came and placed themselves before the Lord, and Satan also came with the sons of God before the Lord.

47 And the Lord said to Satan, Wherefore do you come? Satan answered the Lord and said, From going to and fro in the earth, and from walking up and down in it.

48 And the Lord said to Satan, What is your word to me concerning all the children of the earth? Satan answered the Lord and said, I have seen all the children of the earth who serve you and remember you when they require anything from you.

49 When you give them the thing which they require from you, they sit at their ease and turn away from you, and they remember you no more.

50 Have you seen Abraham the son of Terah, who at first had no children? He served you and erected altars to you wherever he came, and he brought up offerings on them, and he proclaimed your name continually to all the children of the earth.

51 And now that his son Isaac is born to him, he has forsaken you, he has made a great feast for all the inhabitants of the land, and the Lord he has forgotten.

52 For amidst all that he has done he brought you no offering; neither burnt offering nor peace offering, neither ox, lamb nor goat of all that he killed on the day that his son was weaned.

53 Even from the time of his son's birth till now, being thirty-seven years, he built no altar before you, nor brought any offering to you, for he saw that you did give what he requested before you, and he therefore turned away from you.

54 And the Lord said to Satan, Have you thus considered my servant Abraham? for there is none like him on earth, a perfect and an upright man before me, one that fears God and avoids evil; as I live, were I to say to him, Bring up Isaac your son before me, he would not withhold him from me, much more if I told him to bring up a burnt offering before me from his flock or herds.

55 Satan answered the Lord and said, Speak then now to Abraham as you have said, and you will see whether he will not this day go contrary to and cast aside your words.

CHAPTER 23

1 At that time the word of the Lord came to Abraham, and said to him, Abraham. And Abraham said, Here I am.

2 He said to him, Take now your son, your only son whom you love, even Isaac, and go to the land of Moriah, and offer him there for a burnt offering on one of the mountains which shall be shown to you, for there you will see a cloud and the glory of the Lord.

3 And Abraham said within himself, How shall I separate my son Isaac from Sarah his mother, in order to bring him up for a burnt offering before the Lord?

4 Abraham came into the tent, and he sat before Sarah his wife, and he spoke these words to her,

5 My son Isaac is grown up and he has not for some time studied the service of his God; tomorrow I will go and bring him to Shem, and Eber his son, and there he will learn the ways of the Lord. For they will teach him to know the Lord as well as to know that when he prays continually before the Lord, he will answer him; there he will know the way of serving the Lord his God.

6 And Sarah said, You have spoken well, go my lord and do to him as you have said, but remove him not at a great distance from me, neither let him remain there too long, for my soul is bound within his soul.

7 Abraham said to Sarah, My daughter, let us pray to the Lord our God that he may do good with us.

8 And Sarah took her son Isaac and he abode all that night with her, and she kissed and embraced him, and gave him instructions till morning.

9 She said to him, O my son, how can my soul separate itself from you? And she still kissed him and embraced him, and she gave Abraham instructions concerning him.

10 Sarah said to Abraham, O my lord, I pray you take care of your son, and watch over him, for I have no other son or daughter but him.

11 Turn not away from him. If he is hungry give him bread, and if he is thirsty give him water to drink; do not let him go on foot, neither let him sit in the sun.

12 Neither let him go by himself in the road, neither force him from whatever he may desire, but do to him as he may say to you.

13 Sarah wept bitterly the whole night on account of Isaac, and she gave him instructions till morning.

14 In the morning Sarah selected a very fine and beautiful garment from those garments which she had in the house, that Abimelech had given to her.

15 She dressed Isaac her son with them, and she put a turban on his head; she enclosed a precious stone in the top of the turban, and gave them provision for the road. They went forth, and Isaac went with his father Abraham, and some of their servants accompanied them to see them on their way.

16 Sarah went out with them, and she accompanied them on the road to see them off; they said to her, Return to the tent.

17 When Sarah heard the words of her son Isaac she wept bitterly, and Abraham her husband wept with her, and their son wept with them a great weeping; also those who went with them wept greatly.

18 And Sarah caught hold of her son Isaac, and she held him in her arms, and she embraced him and continued to weep with him. And Sarah said, Who knows if after this day I shall ever see you again?

19 They still wept together, Abraham, Sarah and Isaac, and all those that accompanied them on the road wept with them, and Sarah afterward turned away from her son, weeping bitterly; then all her men servants and maid servants returned with her to the tent.

20 And Abraham went with Isaac his son to bring him up as an offering before the Lord, as He had commanded him.

21 Abraham took two of his young men with him, Ishmael the son of Hagar and Eliezer his servant, and they went together with them. While they were walking in the road the young men spoke these words to themselves,

22 Ishmael said to Eliezer, Now my father Abraham is going with Isaac to bring him up for a burnt offering to the Lord, as He commanded him.

23 When he returns he will give to me all he possesses, to inherit after him, for I am his firstborn.

24 And Eliezer answered Ishmael and said, Certainly Abraham did cast you away with your mother, and swear that you should not inherit any thing of all he possesses. To whom will he give all that he has, with all his treasures, but to me his servant, who has been faithful in his house, who has served him night and day, and has done all he desired me? To me he will bequeath at his death all he possesses.

25 While Abraham was proceeding with his son Isaac along the road, Satan came and appeared to Abraham in the figure of a very aged man, humble and of contrite spirit; he approached Abraham and said to him, Are you silly or brutish, that you go to do this thing today to your only son?

26 For God gave you a son in your latter days, in your old age, and will you go and slaughter him today because he committed no violence, and will you cause the soul of your only son to perish from the earth?

27 Do you not know and understand that this thing cannot be from the Lord? For the Lord cannot do to man such evil on earth to say to him, Go slaughter your child.

28 Abraham heard this and knew that it was the word of Satan who endeavored to draw him aside from the way of the Lord, but Abraham would not listen to the voice of Satan, and Abraham rebuked him so that he went away.

29 Satan returned and came to Isaac; he appeared to Isaac in the figure of a young man comely and well favored.

30 He approached Isaac and said to him, Do you not know and understand that your old silly father brings you to the slaughter today for nothing?

31 Now therefore, my son, do not listen or attend to him, for he is a silly old man; let not your precious soul and beautiful figure be lost from the earth.

32 And Isaac heard this, and said to Abraham, Have you heard, my father, that which this man has spoken? Even thus has he spoken.

33 And Abraham answered his son Isaac and said to him, Take heed of him and do not listen to his words, nor attend to him, for he is Satan, endeavoring to draw us aside this day from the commands of God.

34 Abraham still rebuked Satan, and Satan went from them; seeing he could not prevail over them he hid himself from them, and he went and passed before them in the road; he transformed himself to a large brook of water in the road. Abraham and Isaac and his two young men reached that place, and they saw a brook large and powerful as the mighty waters.

35 They entered the brook and passed through it, and the waters at first reached their legs.

36 And they went deeper in the brook and the waters reached up to their necks. They were all terrified on account of the water and while they were going over the brook Abraham recognized that place, and he knew that there was no water there before.

37 Abraham said to his son Isaac, I know this place in which there was no brook or water, now therefore it is Satan who does all this to us, to draw us aside on this day from the commands of God.

38 And Abraham rebuked him and said to him, The Lord rebuke you, O Satan, begone from us for we go by the commands of God.

39 And Satan was terrified at the voice of Abraham, and he went away from them; the place again became dry land as it was at first.

40 Abraham went with Isaac toward the place that God had told him.

41 And on the third day Abraham lifted up his eyes and saw the place at a distance which God had told him of.

42 A pillar of fire appeared to him that reached from the earth to heaven, and a cloud of glory on the mountain, and the glory of the Lord was seen in the cloud.

43 And Abraham said to Isaac, My son, do you see in that mountain, which we perceive at a distance, that which I see on it?

44 And Isaac answered and said to his father, I see and there is a pillar of fire and a cloud, and the glory of the Lord is seen on the cloud.

45 And Abraham knew that his son Isaac was accepted before the Lord for a burnt offering.

46 Abraham said to Eliezer and to Ishmael his son, Do you also see that which we see on the mountain which is at a distance?

47 And they answered and said, We see nothing more than like the other mountains of the earth. Abraham knew that they were not accepted before the Lord to go with them, and Abraham said to them, Stay here with the ass while I and Isaac my son will go to yonder mount and worship there before the Lord and then return to you.

48 Eliezer and Ishmael remained in that place, as Abraham had commanded.

49 And Abraham took wood for a burnt offering and placed it on his son Isaac, and he took the fire and the knife, and they both went to that place.

50 When they were on the way Isaac said to his father, Behold, I see here the fire and wood, and where then is the lamb that is to be the burnt offering before the Lord?

51 And Abraham answered his son Isaac, saying, The Lord has made choice of you my son, to be a perfect burnt offering instead of the lamb.

52 And Isaac said to his father, I will do all that the Lord spoke to you with joy and cheerfulness of heart.

53 Abraham again said to Isaac his son, Is there in your heart any thought or counsel concerning this, which is not proper? Tell me my son, I pray you, O my son conceal it not from me.

54 And Isaac answered his father Abraham and said to him, O my father, as the Lord lives and as your soul lives, there is nothing in my heart to cause me to deviate either to the right or to the left from the word that he has spoken to you.

55 Neither limb nor muscle has moved or stirred at this, nor is there in my heart any thought or evil counsel concerning this.

56 But I am of joyful and cheerful heart in this matter, and I say, Blessed is the Lord who has this day chosen me to be a burnt offering before Him.

57 Abraham greatly rejoiced at the words of Isaac, and they went on and came together to that place that the Lord had spoken of.

58 Abraham approached to build the altar in that place, and Abraham was weeping. Isaac took stones and mortar until they had finished building the altar.

59 And Abraham took the wood and placed it in order on the altar which he had built.

60 He took his son Isaac and bound him in order to place him on the wood which was on the altar, to kill him for a burnt offering before the Lord.

61 Isaac said to his father, Bind me securely and then place me on the altar that I should not turn and move, and break loose from the force of the knife on my flesh and thereof profane the burnt offering; and Abraham did so.

62 Isaac still said to his father, O my father, when you have slain me and burnt me for an offering, take with you that which remains of my ashes to bring to Sarah my mother, and say to her, This is the sweet smelling savor of Isaac. But do not tell her this if she should sit near a well or on any high place, that she would cast her soul after me and die.

63 And Abraham heard the words of Isaac, and he lifted up his voice and wept when Isaac spake these words. Abraham's tears gushed down on Isaac his son, and Isaac wept bitterly; he said to his father, Hasten, O my father, and do with me the will of the Lord our God as He has commanded you.

64 The hearts of Abraham and Isaac rejoiced at this thing which the Lord had commanded them; but the eye wept bitterly while the heart rejoiced.

65 And Abraham bound his son Isaac and placed him on the altar on the wood, and Isaac stretched forth his neck on the altar before his father. Abraham stretched forth his hand to take the knife to kill his son as a burnt offering before the Lord.

66 At that time the angels of mercy came before the Lord and spoke to him concerning Isaac, saying,

67 0 Lord, you are a merciful and compassionate King over all that you have created in heaven and in earth, and you support them all; give therefore ransom and redemption instead of your servant Isaac, and pity and have compassion on Abraham and Isaac his son who are this day performing your commands.

68 Have you seen, O Lord, how Isaac the son of Abraham your servant is bound down to the slaughter like an animal? Now therefore let your pity be roused for them, O Lord.

69 At that time the Lord appeared to Abraham and called to him from heaven, and said to him, Lay not your hand on the lad, neither do anything to him, for now I know that you fear God in performing this act, and in not withholding your son, your only son, from me.

70 And Abraham lifted up his eyes and looked, and behold, a ram was caught in a thicket by his horns; that was the ram which the Lord God had created in the earth in the day that he made earth and heaven.

71 For the Lord had prepared this ram from that day, to be a burnt offering instead of Isaac.

72 This ram was advancing to Abraham when Satan caught hold of him and entangled his horns in the thicket, so that he might not advance to Abraham, in order that Abraham might kill his son.

73 And Abraham, seeing the ram advancing to him and Satan withholding him, fetched him and brought him before the altar; he loosened his son Isaac from his binding, and he put the ram in his stead. Abraham killed the ram on the altar, and brought it up as an offering in the place of his son Isaac.

74 Abraham sprinkled some of the blood of the ram on the altar, and he exclaimed and said, This is in the place of my son, and may it be considered this day as the blood of my son before the Lord.

75 And all that Abraham did on this occasion by the altar, he would exclaim and say, This is in place of my son, and may it this day be considered before the Lord in the place of my son; and Abraham finished the whole service by the altar, and the service was accepted before the Lord, and was accounted as if it had been Isaac; and the Lord blessed Abraham and his descendants on that day.

76 Satan went to Sarah, and he appeared to her in the figure of an old man very humble and meek, and Abraham was yet engaged in the burnt offering before the Lord.

77 And he said to her, Do you not know all the work that Abraham has made with your only son this day? For he took Isaac and built an altar, and killed him, and brought him up as a sacrifice on the altar; Isaac cried and wept before his father, but he looked not at him, neither did he have compassion over him.

78 Satan repeated these words, and he went away from her. Sarah heard all the words of Satan, and she imagined him to be an old man from among the sons of men who had been with her son, and had come and told her these things.

79 And Sarah lifted up her voice and wept and cried out bitterly on account of her son; she threw herself on the ground and she cast dust on her head, and she said, O my son, Isaac my son, O that I had this day died instead of you. And she continued to weep and said, It grieves me for you, O my son, my son Isaac, O that I had died this day in your stead.

80 She still continued to weep, and said, It grieves me for you after I have reared you and have brought you up; now my joy is turned into mourning over you; I who had a longing for you, and cried and prayed to God till I gave birth to you at ninety years old. And now you have served this day for the knife and the fire, to be made an offering.

81 But I console myself with you, my son, in its being the word of the Lord, for you did perform the command of your God. Who can go contrary to the word of our God, in whose hands is the soul of every living creature?

82 You are just, O Lord our God, for all your works are good and righteous; for I also am rejoiced with your word which you did command; while my eye weeps bitterly my heart rejoices.

83 Sarah laid her head on the bosom of one of her handmaids, and she became as still as a stone.

84 Afterward she rose up and went about making inquiries till she came to Hebron; she inquired of all those whom she met walking in the road and no one could tell her what had happened to her son.

85 She came with her maid servants and men servants to Kireath-arba, which is Hebron, and she asked concerning her son; she remained there while she sent some of her servants to seek where Abraham had gone with Isaac. They went to seek him in the house of Shem and Eber, and they could not find him, and they sought throughout the land and he was not there.

86 And then Satan came to Sarah in the shape of an old man; he came and stood before her, and said to her, I spoke falsely to you, for Abraham did not kill his son and he is not dead. When she heard the word her joy was so greatly violent on account of her son, that her soul went out through joy; she died and was gathered to her people.

87 When Abraham had finished his service he returned with his son Isaac to his young men, and they rose up and went together to Beersheba, and they came home.

88 And Abraham sought for Sarah, and could not find her, and he made inquiries concerning her. They said to him, She went as far as Hebron to seek you both where you had gone, for thus was she informed.

89 Abraham and Isaac went to her to Hebron, and when they found that she was dead they lifted up their voices and wept bitterly over her; Isaac fell on his mother's face and wept over her, and he said, O my mother, my mother, how have you left me, and where have you gone? O how, how have you left me!

90 And Abraham and Isaac wept greatly and all their servants wept with them on account of Sarah, and they mourned over her a great and heavy mourning.

CHAPTER 24

1 The life of Sarah was one hundred and twenty-seven years, and Sarah died; and Abraham rose up from before his dead to seek a burial place to bury his wife Sarah. He went and spoke to the children of Heth, the inhabitants of the land, saying,

2 I am a stranger and a sojourner with you in your land; give me possession of a burial place in your land, that I may bury my dead from before me.

3 And the children of Heth said to Abraham, Behold the land is before you, in the choice of our sepulchers bury your dead, for no man shall withhold you from burying your dead.

4 Abraham said to them, If you are agreeable to this, go and entreat Ephron the son of Zochar for me, requesting that he may give me the cave of Machpelah which is in the end of his field, and I will purchase it of him for whatever he desires for it.

5 And Ephron lived among the children of Heth, and they went and called for him, and he came before Abraham. Ephron said to Abraham, Behold all you require your servant will do; Abraham said, No, but I will buy the cave and the field which you have for value, in order that it may be for possession of a burial place forever.

6 And Ephron answered and said, Behold the field and the cave are before you, give whatever you desire. Abraham said, Only at full value will I buy it from your hand, and from the hands of those that go in at the gate of your city, and from the hand of your descendants forever.

7 Ephron and all his brothers heard this, and Abraham weighed to Ephron four hundred shekels of silver in the hands of Ephron and in the hands of all his brothers. Abraham wrote this transaction; he wrote it and testified it with four witnesses.

8 And these are the names of the witnesses: Amigal son of Abishna the Hittite, Adichorom son of Ashunach the Hivite, Abdon son of Achiram the Gomerite, Bakdil the son of Abudish the Zidonite.

9 Abraham took the book of the purchase and placed it in his treasures, and these are the words that Abraham wrote in the book, namely:

10 That the cave and the field Abraham bought from Ephron the Hittite and from his descendants, and from those that go out of his city, and from their descendants forever, are to be a purchase to Abraham and to his descendants and to those that go forth from his loins, for a possession of a burial place forever. And he put a signet to it and testified it with witnesses.

11 The field and the cave that was in it and all that place were made sure to belong to Abraham and to his descendants after him, from the children of Heth; behold it is before Mamre in Hebron which is in the land of Canaan.

12 After this Abraham buried his wife Sarah there, and that place and all its boundary became to Abraham and to his descendants for a possession of a burial place.

13 And Abraham buried Sarah with pomp as observed at the interment of kings, and she was buried in very fine and beautiful garments.

14 At her bier was Shem, his sons Eber and Abimelech, together with Anar, Ashcol and Mamre, and all the grandees of the land followed her bier.

15 The days of Sarah were one hundred and twenty-seven years and she died, and Abraham made a great and heavy mourning, and he performed the rites of mourning for seven days.

16 And all the inhabitants of the land comforted Abraham and Isaac his son on account of Sarah.

17 When the days of their mourning passed by Abraham sent away his son Isaac. He went to the house of Shem and Eber, to learn the ways of the Lord and his instructions, and Abraham remained there three years.

18 At that time Abraham rose up with all his servants, and they went and returned homeward to Beersheba, and Abraham and all his servants remained in Beersheba.

19 At the revolution of the year Abimelech king of the Philistines died in that year; he was one hundred and ninety-three years old at his death. Abraham went with his people to the land of the Philistines, and they comforted the whole household and all his servants, and then he turned and went home.

20 It was after the death of Abimelech that the people of Gerar took Benmalich his son, and he was only twelve years old, and they made him lay the place of his father.

21 And they called his name Abimelech after the name of his father, for thus it was their custom to do in Gerar. Abimelech reigned instead of Abimelech his father, and he sat on his throne.

22 And Lot the son of Haran also died in those days, in the thirty-ninth year of the life of Isaac; all the days that Lot lived were one hundred and forty years and he died.

23 And these are the children of Lot, that were born to him by his daughters; the name of the first born was Moab, and the name of the second was Benami.

24 The two sons of Lot went and took themselves wives from the land of Canaan, and they gave birth to children to them. The children of Moab were Ed, Mayon, Tarsus, and Kanvil, four sons; these are fathers to the children of Moab to this day.

25 And all the families of the children of Lot went to dwell wherever they should light on, for they were prolific and increased abundantly.

26 And they went and built themselves cities in the land where they lived, and they called the names of the cities which they built after their own names.

27 Nahor the son of Terah, brother to Abraham, died in those days in the fortieth year of the life of Isaac. All the days of Nahor were one hundred and seventy-two years; he died and was buried in Haran.

28 And when Abraham heard that his brother was dead he grieved sadly, and he mourned over his brother many days.

29 Abraham called for Eliezer his head servant to give him orders concerning his house, and he came and stood before him.

30 And Abraham said to him, Behold I am old, I do not know the day of my death; for I am advanced in days; now therefore rise up, go forth and do not take a wife for my son from this place and from this land, from the daughters of the Canaanites among whom we dwell.

31 But go to my land and to my birthplace, and take from there a wife for my son. The Lord God of Heaven and earth who took me from my father's house and brought me to this place, and said to me, To your offspring will I give this land for an inheritance forever, he will send his angel before you and prosper your way, that you may obtain a wife for my son from my family and from my father's house.

32 The servant answered his master Abraham and said, Behold I go to your birthplace and to your father's house, and take a wife for your son from there; but if the woman be not willing to follow me to this land, shall I take your son back to the land of your birthplace?

33 And Abraham said to him, See that you do not bring my son here again, for the Lord before whom I have walked will send his angel before you and prosper your way.

34 Eliezer did as Abraham ordered him, and Eliezer swore to Abraham his master on this matter; and Eliezer rose up and took ten camels of the camels of his master, and ten men from his master's servants with him, and they rose up and went to

Haran, the city of Abraham and Nahor, in order to fetch a wife for Isaac the son of Abraham. While they were gone Abraham sent to the house of Shem and Eber, and they brought from there his son Isaac.

35 Isaac came home to his father's house to Beersheba, while Eliezer and his men came to Haran; and they stopped in the city by the watering place, and he made his camels to kneel down by the water and they remained there.

36 Eliezer, Abraham's servant, prayed and said, O God of Abraham my master; send me I pray you good speed this day and show kindness to my master, that you shall appoint this day a wife for my master's son from his family.

37 And the Lord listened to the voice of Eliezer, for the sake of his servant Abraham, and he happened to meet with the daughter of Bethuel, the son of Milcah, the wife of Nahor, brother to Abraham, and Eliezer came to her house.

38 Eliezer related to them all his concerns, and that he was Abraham's servant; they greatly rejoiced at him.

39 And they all blessed the Lord who brought this thing about; they gave him Rebecca, the daughter of Bethuel, for a wife for Isaac.

40 The young woman was of a beautiful appearance; she was a virgin, and Rebecca was ten years old in those days.

41 And Bethuel and Laban and his children made a feast on that night, and Eliezer and his men came and ate and drank and rejoiced there on that night.

42 Eliezer rose up in the morning, he and the men that were with him, and he called to the whole household of Bethuel, saying, Send me away that I may go to my master; they rose up and sent away Rebecca and her nurse Deborah, the daughter of Uz, and they gave her silver and gold, men servants and maid servants, and they blessed her.

43 And they sent Eliezer away with his men and the servants took Rebecca; he went and returned to his master to the land of Canaan.

44 Isaac took Rebecca and she became his wife, and he brought her into the tent.

45 And Isaac was forty years old when he took Rebecca, the daughter of his uncle Bethuel, for a wife.

CHAPTER 25

1 It was at that time that Abraham again took a wife in his old age, and her name was Keturah, from the land of Canaan.

2 She gave birth to, to him: Zimran, Jokshan, Medan, Midian, Ishbak and Shuach, being six sons. And the children of Zimran were Abihen, Molich and Narim.

3 The sons of Jokshan were Sheba and Dedan, and the sons of Medan were Amida, Joab, Gochi, Elisha and Nothach; and the sons of Midian were Ephah, Epher, Chanoch, Abida and Eldaah.

4 The sons of Ishbak were Makiro, Beyodua and Tator.

5 The sons of Shuach were Bildad, Mamdad, Munan and Meban; all these are the families of the children of Keturah the Canaanitish woman which she gave birth to, to Abraham the Hebrew.

6 And Abraham sent all these away, and he gave them gifts; they went away from his son Isaac to dwell wherever they would find a place.

7 And all these went to the mountain at the east, and they built themselves six cities in which they lived to this day.

8 But the children of Sheba and Dedan, children of Jokshan, with their children, did not dwell with their brothers in their cities; they journeyed and encamped in the countries and wildernesses to this day.

9 And the children of Midian, son of Abraham, went to the east of the land of Cush. There they found a large valley in the eastern country, and remained there and built a city. They lived therein; that is the land of Midian to this day.

10 Midian lived in the city which he built, he and his five sons and all belonging to him.

11 And these are the names of the sons of Midian according to their names in their cities: Ephah, Epher, Chanoch, Abida and Eldaah.

12 And the sons of Ephah were Methach, Meshar, Avi and Tzanua, and the sons of Epher were Ephron, Zur, Alirun and Medin; the sons of Chanoch were Reuel, Rekem, Azi, Alyoshub and Alad.

13 The sons of Abida were Chur, Melud, Kerury, Molchi; and the sons of Eldaah were Miker, and Reba, and Malchiyah and Gabol. These are the names of the Midianites according to their families, and afterward the families of Midian spread throughout the land of Midian.

14 These are the generations of Ishmael the son of Abraham, whom Hagar, Sarah's handmaid, gave birth to, to Abraham.

15 And Ishmael took a wife from the land of Egypt, and her name was Ribah, the same is Meribah.

16 And Ribah gave birth to, to Ishmael: Nebayoth, Kedar, Adbeel, Mibsam and their sister Bosmath.

17 And Ishmael cast away his wife Ribah, and she went from him and returned to Egypt to the house of her father. She lived there, for she had been very bad in the sight of Ishmael, and in the sight of his father Abraham.

18 And Ishmael afterward took a wife from the land of Canaan, and her name was Malchuth, and she gave birth to, to him: Nishma, Dumah, Masa, Chadad, Tema, Yetur, Naphish and Kedma.

19 These are the sons of Ishmael, and these are their names, being twelve princes according to their nations. And the families of Ishmael afterward spread forth, and Ishmael took his children and all the property that he had gained, together with the souls of his household and all belonging to him, and they went to dwell where they should find a place.

20 They went and lived near the wilderness of Paran, and their dwelling was from Havilah to Shur, that is before Egypt as

you come toward Assyria.

21 Ishmael and his sons lived in the land, and they had children born to them, and they were prolific and increased abundantly.

22 These are the names of the sons of Nebayoth the first born of Ishmael: Mend, Send, Mayon; and the sons of Kedar were Alyon, Kezem, Chamad and Eli.

23 The sons of Adbeel were Chamad and Jabin; and the sons of Mibsam were Obadiah, Ebedmelech and Yeush; these are the families of the children of Ribah the wife of Ishmael.

24 The sons of Mishma the son of Ishmael were Shamua, Zecaryon and Obed; and the sons of Dumah were Kezed, Eli, Machmad and Amed.

25 The sons of Masa were Melon, Mula and Ebidadon; and the sons of Chadad were Azur, Minzar and Ebedmelech; and the sons of Tema were Seir, Sadon and Yakol.

26 The sons of Yetur were Merith, Yaish, Alyo, and Pachoth; and the sons of Naphish were Ebed-Tamed, Abiyasaph and Mir; and the sons of Kedma were Calip, Tachti, and Omir; these were the children of Malchuth the wife of Ishmael according to their families.

27 All these are the families of Ishmael according to their generations, and they lived in those lands wherein they had built themselves cities to this day.

28 Rebecca the daughter of Bethuel, the wife of Abraham's son Isaac, was unable to conceive in those days, she had no children. Isaac lived with his father in the land of Canaan, and the Lord was with Isaac. Arpachshad the son of Shem the son of Noah died in those days, in the forty-eighth year of the life of Isaac, and all the days that Arpachshad lived were four hundred and thirty-eight years, and he died.

CHAPTER 26

1 In the fifty-ninth year of the life of Isaac the son of Abraham, Rebecca his wife was still unable to conceive in those days.

2 And Rebecca said to Isaac, Truly I have heard, my lord, that your mother Sarah was unable to conceive in her days until my Lord Abraham, your father, prayed for her and she conceived by him.

3 Now therefore stand up, you also pray to God and he will hear your prayer and remember us through his mercies.

4 And Isaac answered his wife Rebecca, saying, Abraham has already prayed for me to God to reproduce his descendants, now therefore this barrenness must proceed to us from you.

5 And Rebecca said to him, But arise now you also and pray, that the Lord may hear your prayer and grant me children. Isaac listened to the words of his wife, and Isaac and his wife rose up and went to the land of Moriah to pray there and to seek the Lord, and when they had reached that place Isaac stood up and prayed to the Lord on account of his wife because she was unable to conceive.

6 And Isaac said, O Lord God of heaven and earth, whose goodness and mercies fill the earth, you who did take my father from his father's house and from his birthplace, and brought him to this land, and did say to him, To your descendants I will give the land, and you did promise him and did declare to him, I will reproduce your descendants as the stars of heaven and as the sand of the sea, now may your words be verified which you did speak to my father.

7 For you are the Lord our God, our eyes are toward you to give us descendants of men, as you did promise us, for you are the Lord our God and our eyes are directed toward you only.

8 And the Lord heard the prayer of Isaac the son of Abraham; the Lord was entreated of him and Rebecca his wife conceived.

9 And in about seven months after the children struggled together within her, it pained her greatly and she was wearied on account of them. She said to all the women who were then in the land, Did such a thing happen to you as it has to me? And they said to her, No.

10 And she said to them, Why am I alone in this among all the women that were on earth? And she went to the land of Moriah to seek the Lord on account of this; she went to Shem and Eber his son to make inquiries of them in this matter, that they should seek the Lord in this thing respecting her.

11 She also asked Abraham to seek and inquire of the Lord about all that had befallen her.

12 They all inquired of the Lord concerning this matter, and they brought her word from the Lord and told her, Two children are in your womb, and two nations shall rise from them; one nation shall be stronger than the other, and the greater shall serve the younger.

13 When her days to be delivered were completed, she knelt down, and behold there were twins in her womb, as the Lord had spoken to her.

14 The first came out red all over like a hairy garment, and all the people of the land called his name Esau, saying, This one was made complete from the womb.

15 And after that came his brother, and his hand took hold of Esau's heel, therefore they called his name Jacob.

16 Isaac, the son of Abraham, was sixty years old when he had them.

17 The boys grew up to their fifteenth year, and they came among the society of men. Esau was a designing and deceitful man, and an expert hunter in the field; Jacob was a man perfect and wise, dwelling in tents, feeding flocks and learning the

instructions of the Lord and the commands of his father and mother.

18 Isaac and the children of his household lived with his father Abraham in the land of Canaan, as God had commanded them.

19 Ishmael the son of Abraham went with his children and all belonging to them; they returned there to the land of Havilah, and they lived there.

20 And all the children of Abraham's concubines went to dwell in the land of the east, for Abraham had sent them away from his son and had given them presents, and they went away.

21 Abraham gave all that he had to his son Isaac, and he also gave him all his treasures.

22 And he commanded him saying, Do you not know and understand the Lord is God in heaven and in earth, and there is no other beside him?

23 It was he who took me from my father's house, and from my birthplace, and gave me all the delights on earth; who delivered me from the counsel of the wicked, for in him I did trust.

24 He brought me to this place, and delivered me from Ur Casdim, and said to me, To your descendants I will give all these land and they shall inherit them when they keep my commandments, my statutes and my judgments that I have commanded you, and which I shall command them.

25 Now therefore my son, listen to my voice, and keep the commandments of the Lord your God, which I commanded you. Do not turn from the right way either to the right or to the left, in order that it may be well with you and your children after you forever.

26 And remember the wonderful works of the Lord and his kindness that he has shown toward us, in having delivered us from the hands of our enemies; the Lord our God caused them to fall into our hands; now therefore keep all that I have commanded you and turn not away from the commandments of your God; serve none beside him, in order that it may be well with you and your descendants after you.

27 Teach your children and your descendants the instructions of the Lord and his commandments, and teach them the upright way in which they should go, in order that it may be well with them forever.

28 Isaac answered his father and said to him, That which my Lord has commanded thatI will do, and I will not depart from the commands of the Lord my God; I will keep all that he commanded me. And Abraham blessed his son Isaac, and also his children, and Abraham taught Jacob the instruction of the Lord and his ways.

29 It was at that time that Abraham died, in the fifteenth year of the life of Jacob and Esau, the sons of Isaac, and all the days of Abraham were one hundred and seventy-five years. He died and was gathered to his people in good old age, old and satisfied with days, and Isaac and Ishmael his sons buried him.

30 When the inhabitants of Canaan heard that Abraham was dead, they all came with their kings and princes and all their men to bury Abraham.

31 All the inhabitants of the land of Haran, all the families of the house of Abraham, all the princes and grandees, and the sons of Abraham by the concubines, all came when they heard of Abraham's death. They rewarded Abraham's kindness, and comforted Isaac his son, and they buried Abraham in the cave which he bought from Ephron the Hittite and his children, for the possession of a burial place.

32 All the inhabitants of Canaan, and all those who had known Abraham, wept for Abraham a whole year; men and women mourned over him.

33 Alll the little children, and all the inhabitants of the land wept on account of Abraham, for Abraham had been good to them all, because he had been upright with God and men.

34 There arose not a man who feared God like Abraham, for he had feared his God from his youth, and had served the Lord, and had gone in all his ways during his life from his childhood to the day of his death.

35 And the Lord was with him and delivered him from the counsel of Nimrod and his people; when he made war with the four kings of Elam he conquered them.

36 He brought all the children of the earth to the service of God and he taught them the ways of the Lord, and caused them to know the Lord.

37 He formed a grove and planted a vineyard therein, and he had always prepared in his tent meat and drink to those that passed through the land, that they might satisfy themselves in his house.

38 The Lord God delivered the whole earth on account of Abraham.

39 It was after the death of Abraham that God blessed his son Isaac and his children, and the Lord was with Isaac as he had been with his father Abraham, for Isaac kept all the commandments of the Lord as Abraham his father had commanded him; he did not turn to the right or to the left from the right path which his father had commanded him.

CHAPTER 27

1 Esau at that time, after the death of Abraham, frequently went in the field to hunt.

2 Nimrod king of Babel, the same was Amraphel, also frequently went with his mighty men to hunt in the field, and to walk about with his men in the cool of the day.

3 Nimrod was observing Esau all those days, for jealousy was formed in the heart of Nimrod against Esau.

4 On a certain day Esau went in the field to hunt, and he found Nimrod walking in the wilderness with his two men.

5 All his mighty men and his people were with him in the wilderness, but they kept at a distance; they went from him in different directions to hunt, and Esau concealed himself from Nimrod, and he lurked for him in the wilderness.

6 And Nimrod and his men that were with him did not know him. Nimrod and his men frequently walked about in the field at the cool of the day, and to know where his men were hunting in the field.

7 Nimrod and two of his men that were with him came to the place where they were, when Esau appeared suddenly from his lurking place, drew his sword, and hurriedly ran to Nimrod and cut off his head.

8 Esau fought a desperate fight with the two men that were with Nimrod, and when they called out to him, Esau turned to them and struck them to death with his sword.

9 All the mighty men of Nimrod, who had left him to go to the wilderness, heard the cry at a distance, and they knew the voices of those two men; they ran to know the cause of it and they found their king and the two men that were with him lying dead in the wilderness.

10 When Esau saw the mighty men of Nimrod coming at a distance, he fled, and thereby escaped. Esau took the valuable garments of Nimrod which Nimrod's father had bequeathed to Nimrod, with which Nimrod prevailed over the whole land; he ran and concealed them in his house.

11 Esau took those garments and ran into the city on account of Nimrod's men, and he came to his father's house wearied and exhausted from fight, and he was ready to die through grief when he approached his brother Jacob and sat before him.

12 And he said to his brother Jacob, Behold I shall die this day; wherefore then do I want the birthright? And Jacob acted wisely with Esau in this matter, and Esau sold his birthright to Jacob, for it was so brought about by the Lord.

13 Esau's portion in the cave of the field of Machpelah, which Abraham had bought from the children of Heth for the possession of a burial ground, Esau also sold to Jacob, and Jacob bought all this from his brother Esau for value given.

14 Jacob wrote all of this in a book and he testified the same with witnesses, and sealed it, and the book remained in the hands of Jacob.

15 When Nimrod the son of Cush died, his men lifted him up and brought him in consternation, and buried him in his city, and all the days that Nimrod lived were two hundred and fifteen years and he died.

16 The days that Nimrod reigned on the people of the land were one hundred and eighty-five years; and Nimrod died by the sword of Esau in shame and contempt, and the descendants of Abraham caused his death as he had seen in his dream.

17 At the death of Nimrod his kingdom became divided into many divisions, and all those parts that Nimrod reigned over were restored to the respective kings of the land, who recovered them after the death of Nimrod. All the people of the house of Nimrod were for a long time enslaved to all the other kings of the land.

CHAPTER 28

1 In those days, after the death of Abraham, in that year the Lord brought a heavy famine in the land. While the famine was raging in the land of Canaan, Isaac rose up to go down to Egypt on account of the famine, as his father Abraham had done.

2 And the Lord appeared that night to Isaac and said to him, Do not go down to Egypt but rise and go to Gerar, to Abimelech king of the Philistines, and remain there till the famine shall cease.

3 Isaac rose up and went to Gerar, as the Lord commanded him, and he remained there a full year.

4 And when Isaac came to Gerar, the people of the land saw that Rebecca his wife was of a beautiful appearance, and the people of Gerar asked Isaac concerning his wife, and he said, She is my sister, for he was afraid to say she was his wife that the people of the land should kill him on account of her.

5 The princes of Abimelech went and praised the woman to the king, but he answered them not, neither did he give attention to their words.

6 But he heard them say that Isaac declared her to be his sister, so the king reserved this within himself.

7 And when Isaac had remained three months in the land, Abimelech looked out the window, and he saw Isaac was sporting with Rebecca his wife, for Isaac lived in the outer house belonging to the king, so that the house of Isaac was opposite the house of the king.

8 And the king said to Isaac, What is this you have done to us in saying of your wife, She is my sister? How easily might one of the great men of the people have lain with her, and you would then have brought guilt on us.

9 And Isaac said to Abimelech, Because I was afraid that I die on account of my wife, therefore I said, She is my sister.

10 At that time Abimelech gave orders to all his princes and great men, and they took Isaac and Rebecca his wife and brought them before the king.

11 The king commanded that they should dress them in princely garments, and make them ride through the streets of the city, and proclaim before them throughout the land, saying, This is the man and this is his wife; whoever touches this man or his wife shall certainly die. And Isaac returned with his wife to the king's house, and the Lord was with Isaac and he continued to become great and lacked nothing.

12 And the Lord caused Isaac to find favor in the sight of Abimelech, and in the sight of all his subjects, and Abimelech acted well with Isaac, for Abimelech remembered the oath and the covenant that existed between his father and Abraham.

13 Abimelech said to Isaac, Behold the whole earth is before you; dwell wherever it may seem good in your sight until you shall return to your land. Abimelech gave Isaac fields and vineyards and the best part of the land of Gerar, to sow and reap and eat the fruits of the ground until the days of the famine would have passed by.

14 And Isaac sowed in that land, and received a hundred-fold in the same year, and the Lord blessed him.

15 The man became great, and he had possession of flocks and possession of herds and a great store of servants.

16 When the days of the famine had passed away the Lord appeared to Isaac and said to him, Rise up, go forth from this place and return to your land, to the land of Canaan; Isaac rose up and returned to Hebron which is in the land of Canaan, he and all belonging to him as the Lord commanded him.

17 Ater this Shelach the son at Arpachshad died in that year, which is the eighteenth year of the lives of Jacob and Esau; all the days that Shelach lived were four hundred and thirty-three years and he died.

18 At that time Isaac sent his younger son Jacob to the house of Shem and Eber, and he learned the instructions of the Lord; Jacob remained in the house of Shem and Eber for thirty-two years; Esau his brother did not go for he was not willing to go, and he remained in his father's house in the land of Canaan.

19 Esau was continually hunting in the fields to bring home what he could get, so did Esau all the days.

20 Esau was a designing and deceitful man, one who hunted after the hearts of men and inveigled them, and Esau was a valiant man in the field; in the course of time he went as usual to hunt and came as far as the field of Seir, the same is Edom.

21 And he remained in the land of Seir hunting in the field a year and four months.

22 Esau there saw in the land of Seir the daughter of a man of Canaan, and her name was Jehudith, the daughter of Beeri, son of Epher, from the families of Heth the son of Canaan.

23 Esau took her for a wife, and he came to her; forty years old was Esau when he took her, and he brought her to Hebron, the land of his father's dwelling place, and he lived there.

24 It came to pass in those days, in the hundred and tenth year of the life of Isaac, that is in the fiftieth year of the life of Jacob, in that year Shem the son of Noah died; Shem was six hundred years old at his death.

25 And when Shem died Jacob returned to his father to Hebron which is in the land of Canaan.

26 And in the fifty-sixth year of the life of Jacob, people came from Haran, and Rebecca was told concerning her brother Laban the son of Bethuel.

27 The wife of Laban was unable to conceive in those days, and gave birth to no children, and also all his handmaids gave birth to none, to him.

28 And the Lord afterward remembered Adinah the wife of Laban, and she conceived and gave birth to twin daughters, and Laban named his daughters: the name of the elder Leah, and the name of the younger Rachel.

29 And those people came and told these things to Rebecca, and Rebecca rejoiced greatly that the Lord had visited her brother and that he had gotten children.

CHAPTER 29

1 Isaac the son of Abraham became old and advanced in days, and his eyes became heavy through age; they were dim and could not see.

2 At that time Isaac called to Esau his son, saying, Get I pray you your weapons, your quiver and your bow; rise up and go forth into the field and get me some venison, make me savory meat and bring it to me that I may eat in order that I may bless you before my death, as I have now become old and gray-headed.

3 And Esau did so; he took his weapon and went forth into the field to hunt for venison, as usual, to bring to his father as he had ordered him, so that he might bless him.

4 And Rebecca heard all the words that Isaac had spoken to Esau, and she hurried and called her son Jacob, saying, Thus did your father speak to your brother Esau, and thus did I hear, now therefore hurry and make that which I shall tell you.

5 Rise up and go, I pray you, to the flock and fetch me two fine kids of the goats; I will get the savory meat for your father and you shall bring the savory meat that he may eat before your brother will have come from the hunt, in order that your father may bless you.

6 And Jacob hurried and did as his mother had commanded him, and he made the savory meat and brought it before his father before Esau had come from his hunt.

7 And Isaac said to Jacob, Who are you, my son? And he said, I am your first born Esau. I have done as you did order me, now therefore rise up I pray you and eat of my hunt, in order that your soul may bless me as you did speak to me.

8 And Isaac rose up and he ate and drank, and his heart was comforted; he blessed Jacob and Jacob went away from his father. As soon as Isaac had blessed Jacob and had gone away from him, behold Esau came from his hunt in the field, and he also made savory meat and brought it to his father to eat thereof and to bless him.

9 And Isaac said to Esau, And who was he that has taken venison and brought it me before you came and whom I did bless? And Esau knew that his brother Jacob had done this, and the anger of Esau was set ablaze against his brother Jacob that he had acted thus toward him.

10 And Esau said, Is he not rightly called Jacob? For he has supplanted me twice, he took away my birthright and now he

has taken away my blessing. And Esau wept greatly. When Isaac heard the voice of his son Esau weeping, Isaac said to Esau, What can I do, my son, your brother came with subtlety and took away your blessing? Esau hated his brother Jacob on account of the blessing that his father had given him, and his anger was greatly roused against him.

11 And Jacob was very much afraid of his brother Esau; he rose up and fled to the house of Eber the son of Shem, and he concealed himself there on account of his brother. Jacob was sixty-three years old when he went forth from the land of Canaan from Hebron, and Jacob was concealed in Eber's house fourteen years on account of his brother Esau, and he continued there to learn the ways of the Lord and his commandments.

12 When Esau saw that Jacob had fled and escaped from him, and that Jacob had cunningly obtained the blessing, then Esau grieved greatly. He was also troubled at his father and mother; he rose up and took his wife and went away from his father and mother to the land of Seir, and he lived there. Esau saw there a woman from among the daughters of Heth whose name was Bosmath, the daughter of Elon the Hittite, and he took her for a wife in addition to his first wife, and Esau called her name Adah, saying the blessing had in that time passed from him.

13 And Esau lived in the land of Seir six months without seeing his father and mother, and afterward Esau took his wives and rose up and returned to the land of Canaan. And Esau placed his two wives in his father's house in Hebron.

14 The wives of Esau troubled and provoked Isaac and Rebecca with their works, for they walked not in the ways of the Lord, but served their father's gods of wood and stone as their father had taught them; they were more wicked than their father.

15 They went according to the evil desires of their hearts, and they sacrificed and burnt incense to the Baalim, and Isaac and Rebecca became weary of them.

16 And Rebecca said, I am weary of my life because of the daughters of Heth; if Jacob took a wife of the daughters of Heth, such as these which are of the daughters of the land, what good then is life to me?

17 In those days Adah the wife of Esau conceived and gave birth to him a son, and Esau called the name of the son that was born to him Eliphaz, and Esau was sixty-five years old when she gave birth to him.

18 Ishmael the son of Abraham died in those days, in the sixty-fourth year of the life of Jacob, and all the days that Ishmael lived were one hundred and thirty-seven years and he died.

19 And when Isaac heard that Ishmael was dead he mourned for him, and Isaac lamented over him many days.

20 At the end of fourteen years of Jacob's residing in the house of Eber, Jacob desired to see his father and mother, and Jacob came to the house of his father and mother to Hebron, and Esau had in those days forgotten what Jacob had done to him in having taken the blessing from him.

21 And when Esau saw Jacob coming to his father and mother he remembered what Jacob had done to him, and he was greatly incensed against him and he sought to kill him.

22 And Isaac the son of Abraham was old and advanced in days, and Esau said, Now my father's time is drawing nigh that he must die, and when he shall die I will kill my brother Jacob.

23 This was told to Rebecca, and she hurried and sent and called for Jacob her son, and she said to him, Arise, go and flee to Haran to my brother Laban and remain there for some time, until your brother's anger be turned from you and then shall you come back.

24 And Isaac called to Jacob and said to him, Take not a wife from the daughters of Canaan, for thus did our father Abraham command us according to the word of the Lord which he had commanded him, saying, Unto your offspring will I give this land; if your children keep my covenant that I have made with you, then I will also perform to your children that which I have spoken to you and I will not turn away from them.

25 Now therefore my son listen to my voice, to all that I shall command you, and refrain from taking a wife from among the daughters of Canaan; arise, go to Haran to the house of Bethuel your mother's father, and take to you a wife from there from the daughters of Laban your mother's brother.

26 Therefore be careful that you should not forget the Lord your God and all his ways in the land to which you go, and should get connected with the people of the land and pursue vanity and turn away from the Lord your God.

27 But when you come to the land there serve the Lord, do not turn to the right or to the left from the way which I commanded you and which you did learn.

28 And may the Almighty God grant you favor in the sight of the people of the earth, that you may take there a wife according to your choice; one who is good and upright in the ways of the Lord.

29 May God give to you and your descendants the blessing of your father Abraham, and make you prolific and reproduce, and may you become a multitude of people in the land where you go; may God cause you to return to this land, the land of your father's dwelling, with children and with great riches, with joy and with pleasure.

30 And Isaac finished commanding Jacob and blessing him, and he gave him many gifts, together with silver and gold, and he sent him away. Jacob listened to his father and mother; he kissed them and arose and went to Padan-aram, and Jacob was seventy-seven years old when he went out from the land of Canaan from Beersheba.

31 When Jacob went away to go to Haran Esau called to his son Eliphaz, and secretly spoke to him, saying, Now hurry, take your sword in your hand and pursue Jacob and pass before him in the road, and lurk for him; kill him with your sword in one of the mountains, and take all belonging to him and come back.

32 Eliphaz the son of Esau was an active man and expert with the bow as his father had taught him, and he was a noted

hunter in the field and a valiant man.

33 Eliphaz did as his father had commanded him, and Eliphaz was at that time thirteen years old; Eliphaz rose up and went and took ten of his mother's brothers with him and pursued Jacob.

34 He closely followed Jacob, and he lurked for him in the border of the land of Canaan opposite to the city of Shechem.

35 And Jacob saw Eliphaz and his men pursuing him; Jacob stood still in the place in which he was going, in order to know what this was, for he did not know the thing. Eliphaz drew his sword and he went on advancing, he and his men, toward Jacob. And Jacob said to them, Why have you come here, and what does it mean that you pursue with your swords?

36 And Eliphaz came near to Jacob and he answered and said to him, Thus did my father command me, and now therefore I will not deviate from the orders which my father gave me. When Jacob saw that Esau had spoken to Eliphaz to employ force, Jacob then approached and supplicated Eliphaz and his men, saying to him,

37 Behold all that I have and which my father and mother gave to me, that you should take and go from me, and do not kill me; may this thing be accounted to you a righteousness.

38 And the Lord caused Jacob to find favor in the sight of Eliphaz the son of Esau, and his men, and they listened to the voice of Jacob, and they did not put him to death; Eliphaz and his men took all belonging to Jacob together with the silver and gold that he had brought with him from Beersheba; they left him nothing.

39 Eliphaz and his men went away from him and they returned to Esau to Beersheba, and they told him all that had occurred to them with Jacob, and they gave him all that they had taken from Jacob.

40 Esau was indignant at Eliphaz his son, and at his men that were with him, because they had not put Jacob to death.

41 And they answered and said to Esau, Because Jacob supplicated us in this matter not to kill him, our pity was increased toward him, and we took all belonging to him and brought it to you. Esau took all the silver and gold which Eliphaz had taken from Jacob and he put them by in his house.

42 At that time when Esau saw that Isaac had blessed Jacob, and had commanded him, saying, You shall not take a wife from among the daughters of Canaan, and that the daughters of Canaan were bad in the sight of Isaac and Rebecca,

43 Then he went to the house of Ishmael his uncle, and in addition to his older wives he took Machlath the daughter of Ishmael, the sister of Nebayoth, for a wife.

CHAPTER 30

1 Jacob went forth continuing his road to Haran, and he came as far as mount Moriah, and he stayed there all night near the city of Luz. The Lord appeared there to Jacob on that night and said to him, I am the Lord God of Abraham and the God of Isaac your father; the land on which you dwell I will give to you and your descendants.

2 Behold I am with you and will keep you wherever you go, and I will reproduce your descendants as the stars of Heaven, and I will cause all your enemies to fall before you; when they make war with you they shall not prevail over you, and I will bring you again to this land with joy, with children, and with great riches.

3 Jacob awoke from his sleep and he rejoiced greatly at the vision which he had seen, and he called the name of that place Bethel.

4 Jacob rose up from that place quite jubilant, and when he walked his feet felt light to him for joy, and he went from there to the land of the children of the East, and returned to Haran and sat by the shepherd's well.

5 There he found some men going from Haran to feed their flocks, and Jacob made inquiries of them, and they said, We are from Haran.

6 And he said to them, Do you know Laban, the son of Nahor? And they said, We know him and look, his daughter Rachel is coming along to feed her father's flock.

7 While he was yet speaking with them, Rachel the daughter of Laban came to feed her father's sheep, for she was a shepherdess.

8 When Jacob saw Rachel, the daughter of Laban, his mother's brother, he ran and kissed her and lifted up his voice and wept.

9 Jacob told Rachel that he was the son of Rebecca, her father's sister, and Rachel ran and told her father; Jacob continued to cry because he had nothing with him to bring to the house of Laban.

10 When Laban heard that his sister's son Jacob had come, he ran, kissed him and embraced him, brought him into the house and gave him bread, and he ate.

11 And Jacob related to Laban what his brother Esau had done to him, and what his son Eliphaz had done to him in the road.

12 Jacob resided in Laban's house for one month, and Jacob ate and drank in the house of Laban, and afterward Laban said to Jacob, Tell me what shall be your wages, for how can you serve me for nothing?

13 Laban had no sons but only daughters; his other wives and handmaids were still unable to conceive in those days. These are the names of Laban's daughters which his wife Adinah had borne to him: the name of the elder was Leah and the name

of the younger was Rachel. Leah was tender-eyed, but Rachel was beautiful and well favored, and Jacob loved her.

14 And Jacob said to Laban, I will serve you seven years for Rachel your younger daughter; and Laban consented to this and Jacob served Laban seven years for his daughter Rachel.

15 In the second year of Jacob's dwelling in Haran, that is in the seventy ninth year of the life of Jacob, Eber the son of Shem died; he was four hundred and sixty-four years old at his death.

16 And when Jacob heard that Eber was dead he grieved greatly; he lamented and mourned over him many days.

17 In the third year of Jacob's dwelling in Haran, Bosmath, the daughter of Ishmael, the wife of Esau, gave birth to him a son, and Esau called his name Reuel.

18 And in the fourth year of Jacob's residence in the house of Laban, the Lord visited Laban and remembered him on account of Jacob, and sons were born to him: his first born was Beor, his second was Alib, and the third was Chorash.

19 The Lord gave Laban riches and honor, sons and daughters, and the man increased greatly on account of Jacob.

20 In those days Jacob served Laban in all manner of work, in the house and in the field, and the blessing of the Lord was in all that belonged to Laban in the house and in the field.

21 In the fifth year Jehudith died, the daughter of Beeri, the wife of Esau, in the land of Canaan, and she had no sons but daughters only.

22 These are the names of her daughters which she gave birth to, to Esau: the name of the elder was Marzith, and the name of the younger was Puith.

23 And when Jehudith died, Esau rose up and went to Seir to hunt in the field, as usual, and Esau lived in the land of Seir for a long time.

24 In the sixth year Esau took for a wife, in addition to his other wives, Ahlibamah, the daughter of Zebeon the Hivite, and Esau brought her to the land of Canaan.

25 And Ahlibamah conceived and gave birth to, to Esau, three sons: Yeush, Yaalan, and Korah.

26 In those days, in the land of Canaan, there was a quarrel between the herdsmen of Esau and the herdsmen of the inhabitants of the land of Canaan, for Esau's cattle and goods were too abundant for him to remain in the land of Canaan, in his father's house; the land of Canaan could not bear him on account of his cattle.

27 And when Esau saw that his quarreling increased with the inhabitants of the land of Canaan, he rose up and took his wives and his sons and his daughters, and all belonging to him, and the cattle which he possessed, and all his property that he had acquired in the land of Canaan; he went away from the inhabitants of the land to the land of Seir, and Esau and all belonging to him lived in the land of Seir.

28 But from time to time Esau would go and see his father and mother in the land of Canaan, and Esau intermarried with the Horites, and he gave his daughters to the sons of Seir, the Horite.

29 He gave his elder daughter Marzith to Anah, the son of Zebeon, his wife's brother, and Puith he gave to Azar, the son of Bilhan the Horite; Esau lived in the mountain, he and his children, and they were prolific and multiplied.

CHAPTER 31

1 In the seventh year, Jacob's service to Laban was completed, and Jacob said to Laban, Give me my wife, for the days of my service are fulfilled; Laban did so, and Laban and Jacob assembled all the people of that place and they made a feast.

2 In the evening Laban came to the house, and afterward Jacob came there with the people of the feast, and Laban extinguished all the lights that were there in the house.

3 Jacob said to Laban, Why do you do this thing to us? And Laban answered, Such is our custom to act in this land.

4 Afterward Laban took his daughter Leah, and he brought her to Jacob, and he came to her and Jacob did not know that she was Leah.

5 And Laban gave his daughter Leah his maid Zilpah for a handmaid.

6 All the people at the feast knew what Laban had done to Jacob, but they didn't tell a thing to Jacob.

7 All the neighbors came that night to Jacob's house, and they ate and drank and rejoiced, and played before Leah on timbrels, and with dances, and they responded before Jacob, Heleah, Heleah.

8 Jacob heard their words but did not understand their meaning, but he thought such might be their custom in this land.

9 And the neighbors spoke these words before Jacob during the night, and all the lights that were in the house Laban had that night been extinguished.

10 In the morning, when daylight appeared, Jacob turned to his wife and he saw it was Leah that had been lying in his bosom, and Jacob said, So now I know what the neighbors said last night, Heleah, they said, and I knew it not.

11 Jacob called to Laban, and said to him, What is this that you did to me? Certainly I served you for Rachel; why did you deceive me and give me Leah?

12 Laban answered Jacob, saying, Not so is it done in our place to give the younger before the elder; therefore if you desire to take her sister likewise, take her to you for the service which you will serve me for another seven years.

13 Jacob did so, and he also took Rachel for a wife; he served Laban seven years more, and Jacob also came to Rachel, and he loved Rachel more than Leah; Laban gave her his maid Bilhah for a handmaid.

14 When the Lord saw that Leah was hated, the Lord opened her womb and she conceived and gave birth to Jacob four sons in those days.

15 And these are their names: Reuben, Simeon, Levi, and Judah, and afterward she ceased bearing.

16 At that time Rachel was unable to conceive and had no children, and Rachel envied her sister Leah. When Rachel saw that she gave birth to no children to Jacob, she took her handmaid Bilhah, and she gave birth to Jacob two sons, Dan and Naphtali.

17 When Leah saw that she had ceased bearing, she also took her handmaid Zilpah, and she gave her to Jacob for a wife. Jacob also came to Zilpah, and she gave birth to Jacob two sons, Gad and Asher.

18 Leah again conceived and gave birth to Jacob in those days two sons and one daughter, and these are their names: Issachar, Zebulon, and their sister Dinah.

19 Rachel was still unable to conceive in those days and Rachel prayed to the Lord at that time, and she said, O Lord God remember me and visit me, I beg you, for now my husband will cast me off, for I have borne him no children.

20 Now O Lord God, hear my supplication before you, and see my affliction, and give me children like one of the handmaids, that I may no more bear my reproach.

21 God heard her and opened her womb, and Rachel conceived and gave birth to a son, and she said, The Lord has taken away my reproach. She called his name Joseph, saying, May the Lord add to me another son; Jacob was ninety-one years old when she gave birth to him.

22 At that time Jacob's mother, Rebecca, sent her nurse Deborah the daughter of Uz, and two of Isaac's servants to Jacob.

23 They came to Jacob to Haran and said to him, Rebecca has sent us to you that you shall return to your father's house to the land of Canaan; Jacob listened to them of this which his mother had spoken.

24 At that time, the other seven years which Jacob served Laban for Rachel were completed, and it was at the end of fourteen years that he had lived in Haran, Jacob said to Laban, Give me my wives and send me away that I may go to my land, for behold my mother did send to me from the land at Canaan that I should return to my father's house.

25 And Laban said to him, Not so I pray you; if I have found favor in your sight do not leave me; tell me your wages and I will give them, and remain with me.

26 Jacob said to him, This is what you shall give me for wages, that I shall this day pass through all your flock and take away from them every lamb that is speckled and spotted and such as are brown among the sheep, and among the goats, and if you will do this thing for me I will return and feed your flock and keep them as at first.

27 Laban did so, and Laban removed from his flock all that Jacob had said and gave them to him.

28 And Jacob placed all that he had removed from Laban's flock in the hands of his sons, and Jacob was feeding the remainder of Laban's flock.

29 When the servants of Isaac which he had sent to Jacob saw that Jacob would not return with them to the land of Canaan to his father, they went away from him and returned home to the land of Canaan.

30 And Deborah remained with Jacob in Haran; she did not return with the servants of Isaac to the land of Canaan, and Deborah resided with Jacob's wives and children in Haran.

31 Jacob served Laban six years longer, and when the sheep brought forth, Jacob removed from them such as were speckled and spotted, as he had determined with Laban; Jacob did so at Laban's for six years, and the man increased abundantly. He had cattle and maid servants and men servants, camels, and asses.

32 Jacob had two hundred drove of cattle, and his cattle were of large size and of beautiful appearance and were very productive; all the families of the sons of men desired to get some of the cattle of Jacob, for they were greatly prosperous.

33 Many of the sons of men came to procure some of Jacob's flock, and Jacob gave them a sheep for a man servant or a maid servant or for an ass or a camel, or whatever Jacob desired from them they gave him.

34 Jacob obtained riches and honor and possessions by means of these transactions with the sons of men, and the children of Laban envied him of this honor.

35 In the course of time he heard the words of Laban's sons, saying, Jacob has taken away all that was our father's, and of that which was our father's has he acquired all this glory.

36 And Jacob observed the countenance of Laban and of his children, and it was not toward him in those days as it had been before.

37 The Lord appeared to Jacob at the expiration of the six years, and said to him, Arise, go forth out of this land, and return to the land of your birthplace and I will be with you.

38 And Jacob rose up at that time and he mounted his children and wives and all belonging to him on camels, and he went forth to go to the land of Canaan to his father Isaac.

39 Laban did not know that Jacob had gone from him, for Laban had been sheep-shearing that day.

40 Rachel stole her father's images, and she took them and concealed them on the camel on which she sat, and she went on.

41 And this is the manner of the images: in taking a man who is the firstborn and slaying him and taking the hair off his head; taking salt and salting the head and anointing it in oil, then taking a small tablet of copper or a tablet of gold and writing the name on it and placing the tablet under his tongue; taking the head with the tablet under the tongue and putting it in the house and lighting up lights before it and bowing down to it.

42 And at the time when they bow down to it, it speaks to them in all matters that they ask of it, through the power of the

name which is written in it.

43 And some make them in the figures of men, of gold and silver, and go to them in times known to them, and the figures receive the influence of the stars, and tell them future things; in this manner were the images which Rachel stole from her father.

44 Rachel stole these images which were her father's in order that Laban might not know through them where Jacob had gone.

45 Laban came home and he asked concerning Jacob and his household, and he was not to be found; Laban sought his images to know where Jacob had gone, and could not find them. He went to some other images, and he inquired of them and they told him that Jacob had fled from him to his father's, to the land of Canaan.

46 Laban then rose up and took his brothers and all his servants, and he went forth and pursued Jacob, and he overtook him in mount Gilead.

47 And Laban said to Jacob, What is this you have done to me to flee and deceive me, and lead my daughters and their children as captives taken by the sword?

48 You did not suffer me to kiss them and send them away with joy, and you did steal my gods and did go away.

49 And Jacob answered Laban, saying, Because I was afraid that you would take your daughters by force from me; and now with whomsoever you find your gods he shall die.

50 And Laban searched for the images and he examined in all Jacob's tents and furniture, but could not find them.

51 And Laban said to Jacob, We will make a covenant together and it shall be a testimony between me and you; if you shall afflict my daughters, or shall take other wives besides my daughters, even God shall be a witness between me and you in this matter.

52 And they took stones and made a heap, and Laban said, This heap is a witness between me and you. He called the name thereof Gilead.

53 Jacob and Laban offered sacrifice on the mount, and they ate there by the heap, and they stayed in the mount all night. Laban rose up early in the morning; he wept with his daughters and he kissed them, and he returned to his place.

54 He hurried and sent off his son Beor, who was seventeen years old, with Abichorof the son of Uz, the son of Nahor, and with them were ten men.

55 They hurried and went and passed on the road before Jacob, and they came by another road to the land of Seir.

56 They came to Esau and said to him, Thus says your brother and relative, your mother's brother Laban, the son of Bethuel, saying,

57 Have you heard what Jacob your brother has done to me, who first came to me naked and gave birth to? I went to meet him and brought him to my house with honor; I made him great, and I gave him my two daughters for wives and also two of my maids.

58 And God blessed him on my account; he increased abundantly, and had sons, daughters and maid servants.

59 He has also an immense stock of flocks and herds, camels and asses, also silver and gold in abundance; when he saw that his wealth increased, he left me while I went to shear my sheep, and he rose up and fled in secrecy.

60 He lifted his wives and children on camels, and he led away all his cattle and property which he acquired in my land, and he lifted up his countenance to go to his father Isaac, to the land of Canaan.

61 He did not let me kiss my daughters and their children; he led my daughters as captives taken by the sword, and he also stole my gods and he fled.

62 And now I have left him in the mountain of the brook of Jabuk, him and all belonging to him; he lacks nothing.

63 If it be your wish to go to him, go then and there you will find him, and you can do to him as your soul desires; and Laban's messengers came and told Esau all these things.

64 Esau heard all the words of Laban's messengers, and his anger was greatly set ablaze against Jacob, and he remembered his hatred, and his anger burned within him.

65 Esau hurried and took his children and servants and the souls of his household, being sixty men; he went and assembled all the children of Seir the Horite and their people, being three hundred and forty men. He took all this number of four hundred men with drawn swords, and he went to Jacob to strike him.

66 Esau divided this number into several parts, and he took the sixty men of his children and servants and the souls of his household as one head, and gave them in care of Eliphaz his eldest son.

67 The remaining heads he gave to the care of the six sons of Seir the Horite, and he placed every man over his generations and children.

68 The whole of this camp went as it was, and Esau went among them toward Jacob, and he conducted them with speed.

69 And Laban's messengers departed from Esau and went to the land of Canaan, and they came to the house of Rebecca the mother of Jacob and Esau.

70 They told her saying, Behold your son Esau has gone against his brother Jacob with four hundred men, for he heard that he was coming, and he is gone to make war with him, and to strike him and to take all that he has.

71 Rebecca hurried and sent seventy two men from the servants of Isaac to meet Jacob on the road; for she said, Perhaps Esau may make war in the road when he meets him.

72 These messengers went on the road to meet Jacob, and they met him in the road of the brook on the opposite side of the

brook Jabuk. Jacob said when he saw them, This camp is destined to me from God. And Jacob called the name of that place Machnayim.

73 And Jacob knew all his father's people, and he kissed them and embraced them and came with them. Jacob asked them concerning his father and mother, and they said, They were well.

74 These messengers said to Jacob, Rebecca your mother has sent us to you, saying, I have heard, my son, that your brother Esau has gone forth against you on the road with men from the children of Seir the Horite.

75 Therefore, my son, listen to my voice and see with your counsel what you will do; when he comes up to you, supplicate him, and do not speak rashly to him, and give him a present from what you possess, and from what God has favored you with.

76 And when he asks you concerning your affairs, conceal nothing from him, perhaps he may turn from his anger against you and you will thereby save your soul, you and all belonging to you, for it is your duty to honor him, for he is your elder brother.

77 When Jacob heard the words of his mother which the messengers had spoken to him, Jacob lifted up his voice and wept bitterly, and did as his mother then commanded him.

CHAPTER 32

1 At that time Jacob sent messengers to his brother Esau toward the land of Seir, and he spoke to him words of supplication.

2 He commanded them, saying, Thus shall you say to my lord, to Esau, Thus says your servant Jacob, Let not my lord imagine that my father's blessing with which he did bless me has proved beneficial to me.

3 For I have been these twenty years with Laban, and he deceived me and changed my wages ten times, as it has all been already told to my lord.

4 And I served him in his house very laboriously, and God afterward saw my affliction, my labor and the work of my hands, and he caused me to find grace and favor in his sight.

5 And afterward through God's great mercy and kindness I acquired oxen and asses and cattle, and men servants and maid servants.

6 And now I am coming to my land and my home to my father and mother, who are in the land of Canaan; I have sent to let my lord know all this in order to find favor in the sight of my lord, so that he may not imagine that I have of myself obtained wealth, or that the blessing with which my father blessed me has benefited me.

7 Those messengers went to Esau, and found him on the borders of the land of Edom going toward Jacob, and four hundred men of the children of Seir the Horite were standing with drawn swords.

8 And the messengers of Jacob told Esau all the words that Jacob had spoken to them concerning Esau.

9 Esau answered them with pride and contempt and said to them, Certainly I have heard and truly it has been told to me what Jacob has done to Laban, who exalted him in his house and gave him his daughters for wives, and he had sons and daughters, and abundantly increased in wealth and riches in Laban's house through his means.

10 When he saw that his wealth was abundant and his riches great he fled with all belonging to him, from Laban's house, and he led Laban's daughters away from the face of their father, as captives taken by the sword without telling him of it.

11 And not only to Laban has Jacob done thus but also to me has he done so and has twice supplanted me, and shall I be silent?

12 Now therefore I have this day come with my camps to meet him, and I will do to him according to the desire of my heart.

13 And the messengers returned and came to Jacob and said to him, We came to your brother, to Esau, and we told him all your words, and thus has he answered us; behold he comes to meet you with four hundred men.

14 Now then know and see what you shall do, and pray before God to deliver you from him.

15 And when he heard the words of his brother which he had spoken to the messengers of Jacob, Jacob was greatly afraid and he was distressed.

16 And Jacob prayed to the Lord his God, and he said, O Lord God of my fathers, Abraham and Isaac, you did say to me when I went away from my father's house, saying,

17 I am the Lord God of your father Abraham and the God of Isaac, to you do I give this land and your descendants after you, and I will make your descendants as the stars of heaven, and you shall spread forth to the four sides of heaven, and in you and in your offspring shall all the families of the earth be blessed.

18 You did establish your words, and did give to me riches and children and cattle, as the utmost wishes of my heart did you give to your servant; you gave to me all that I asked from you, so that I lacked nothing.

19 Afterward you said to me, Return to your parents and to your birth place and I will still do well with you.

20 And now that I have come, and you did deliver me from Laban, I shall fall in the hands of Esau who will kill me, yea, together with the mothers of my children.

21 Now therefore, O Lord God, deliver me, I pray you, also from the hands of my brother Esau, for I am greatly afraid of him.

22 And if there is no righteousness in me, do it for the sake of Abraham and my father Isaac.

23 For I know that through kindness and mercy I have acquired this wealth; now therefore I beseech you to deliver me this

day with your kindness and to answer me.

24 And Jacob ceased praying to the Lord; he divided the people that were with him with the flocks and cattle into two camps, and he gave the half to the care of Damesek, the son of Eliezer, Abraham's servant, for a camp, with his children; the other half he gave to the care of his brother Elianus the son of Eliezer, to be for a camp with his children.

25 And he commanded them, saying, Keep yourselves at a distance with your camps, and do not come too near each other, and if Esau comes to one camp and kills it, the other camp at a distance from it will escape him.

26 Jacob tarried there that night, and during the whole night he gave his servants instructions concerning the forces and his children.

27 The Lord heard the prayer of Jacob on that day, and the Lord then delivered Jacob from the hands of his brother Esau.

28 The Lord sent three angels of the angels of heaven, and they went before Esau and came to him.

29 And these angels appeared to Esau and his people as two thousand men, riding on horses furnished with all sorts of war instruments, and they appeared in the sight of Esau and all his men to be divided into four camps, with four chiefs to them.

30 And one camp went on and they found Esau coming with four hundred men toward his brother Jacob, and this camp ran toward Esau and his people and terrified them. Esau fell off the horse in alarm, and all his men separated from him in that place, for they were greatly afraid.

31 And the whole camp shouted after them when they fled from Esau, and all the warlike men answered, saying,

32 Certainly we are the servants of Jacob, who is the servant of God, and who then can stand against us? And Esau said to them, O then, my lord and brother Jacob is your lord, whom I have not seen for these twenty years, and now that I have this day come to see him, do you treat me in this manner?

33 And the angels answered him saying, As the Lord lives, were not Jacob of whom you speak your brother, we would not let one remain from you and your people, but only on account of Jacob we will do nothing to them.

34 And this camp passed from Esau and his men and it went away, and Esau and his men had gone from them about a league when the second camp came toward him with all sorts of weapons, and they also did to Esau and his men as the first camp had done to them.

35 And when they had left it to go on, behold the third camp came toward him and they were all terrified, and Esau fell off the horse, and the whole camp cried out, and said, Certainly we are the servants of Jacob, who is the servant of God, and who can stand against us?

36 Esau again answered them saying, O then, Jacob my lord and your lord is my brother, and for twenty years I have not seen his countenance and hearing this day that he was coming, I went this day to meet him, and do you treat me in this manner?

37 They answered him, and said to him, As the Lord lives, were not Jacob your brother as you did say, we would not leave a remnant from you and your men, but on account of Jacob of whom you speak being your brother, we will not meddle with you or your men.

38 And the third camp also passed from them, and he still continued his road with his men toward Jacob, when the fourth camp came toward him, and they also did to him and his men as the others had done.

39 When Esau beheld the evil which the four angels had done to him and to his men, he became greatly afraid of his brother Jacob, and he went to meet him in peace.

40 And Esau concealed his hatred against Jacob, because he was afraid for his life on account of his brother Jacob, and because he imagined that the four camps that he had lighted on were Jacob's servants.

41 And Jacob tarried that night with his servants in their camps, and he resolved with his servants to give to Esau a present from all that he had with him, and from all his property; Jacob rose up in the morning, he and his men, and they chose from among the cattle a present for Esau.

42 And this is the amount of the present which Jacob chose from his flock to give to his brother Esau: he selected two hundred and forty head from the flocks, and he selected from the camels and asses thirty each, and of the herds he chose fifty kine.

43 He put them all in ten droves, and he placed each sort by itself; he delivered them into the hands of ten of his servants, each drove by itself.

44 He commanded them, and said to them, Keep yourselves at a distance from each other, and put a space between the droves, and when Esau and those who are with him shall meet you and ask you, saying, Whose are you, and where do you go, and to whom belongs all this before you, you shall say to them, We are the servants of Jacob, and we come to meet Esau in peace, and behold Jacob comes behind us.

45 And that which is before us is a present sent from Jacob to his brother Esau.

46 And if they shall say to you, Why does he delay behind you, from coming to meet his brother and to see his face, then you shall say to them, Certainly he comes joyfully behind us to meet his brother, for he said, I will appease him with the present that goes to him, and after this I will see his face; per chance he will accept me.

47 So the whole present passed on in the hands of his servants, and went before him on that day, and he lodged that night with his camps by the border of the brook of Jabuk. He rose up in the middle of the night and took his wives and his maid servants and all belonging to him, and that night he passed them over the ford Jabuk.

48 When he passed all belonging to him over the brook, Jacob was left by himself; a man met him, and he wrestled with him

that night until the breaking of the day, and the hollow of Jacob's thigh was out of joint through wrestling with him.

49 At the break of day the man left Jacob there, and he blessed him and went away; Jacob passed the brook at the break of day, and he rested on his thigh.

50 And the sun rose on him when he had passed the brook, and he came up to the place of his cattle and children.

51 They went on till midday, and while they were going the present was passing on before them.

52 And Jacob lifted up his eyes and looked, and behold Esau was at a distance, coming along with many men, about four hundred, and Jacob was greatly afraid of his brother.

53 Jacob hurried and divided his children to his wives and his handmaids, and his daughter Dinah he put in a chest, and delivered her into the hands of his servants.

54 He passed before his children and wives to meet his brother, and he bowed down to the ground, yes, he bowed down seven times until he approached his brother. And God caused Jacob to find grace and favor in the sight of Esau and his men, for God had heard the prayer of Jacob.

55 The fear of Jacob and his terror fell on his brother Esau, for Esau was greatly afraid of Jacob for what the angels of God had done to Esau, and Esau's anger against Jacob was turned into kindness.

56 And when Esau saw Jacob running toward him, he also ran toward him and he embraced him, and he fell on his neck, and they kissed and they wept.

57 And God put fear and kindness toward Jacob in the hearts of the men that came with Esau, and they also kissed Jacob and embraced him.

58 Also Eliphaz, the son of Esau, with his four brothers, sons of Esau, wept with Jacob, and they kissed him and embraced him, for the fear of Jacob had fallen on them all.

59 And Esau lifted up his eyes and saw the women with their children, the children of Jacob, walking behind Jacob and bowing along the road to Esau.

60 And Esau said to Jacob, Who are these with you, my brother? Are they your children or your servants? And Jacob answered Esau and said, They are my children which God hath graciously given to your servant.

61 While Jacob was speaking to Esau and his men, Esau beheld the whole camp, and he said to Jacob, How did you get the whole camp that I met last night? And Jacob said, To find favor in the sight of my lord, it is that which God graciously gave to your servant.

62 The present came before Esau, and Jacob pressed Esau, saying, Take I pray you the present that I have brought to my lord. And Esau said, Why should I? Keep that which you have to yourself.

63 And Jacob said, It is incumbent on me to give all this, since I have seen your face, that you still live in peace.

64 Esau refused to take the present, and Jacob said to him, I beseech you my lord, if now I have found favor in your sight, then receive my present at my hand, for I have therefore seen your face, as you I had seen a god-like face, because you were pleased with me.

65 And Esau took the present, and Jacob also gave to Esau silver and gold and bdellium, for he pressed him so much that he took them.

66 Esau divided the cattle that were in the camp, and he gave half to the men who had come with him, for they had come on hire, and the other half he delivered to the hands of his children.

67 The silver and gold and bdellium he gave in the hands of Eliphaz his eldest son, and Esau said to Jacob, Let us remain with you, and we will go slowly along with you until you come to my place with me, that we may dwell there together.

68 And Jacob answered his brother and said, I would do as my lord speaks to me, but my lord knows that the children are tender, and the flocks and herds with their young who are with me go but slowly, for if they went swiftly they would all die, for you know their burdens and their fatigue.

69 Therefore let my lord pass on before his servant, and I will go on slowly for the sake of the children and the flock until I come to my lord's place to Seir.

70 And Esau said to Jacob, I will place with you some of the people that are with me to take care of you in the road, and to bear your fatigue and burden, and he said, I will do so, my lord, if I may find grace in your sight?

71 Behold I will come to you to Seir to dwell there together as you have spoken, go then with your people for I will follow you.

72 Jacob said this to Esau in order to remove Esau and his men from him, so that Jacob might afterward go to his father's house to the land of Canaan.

73 Esau listened to the voice of Jacob, and Esau returned with the four hundred men that were with him on their road to Seir, and Jacob and all belonging to him went that day as far as the extremity of the land of Canaan in its borders, and he remained there some time.

CHAPTER 33

1 Some time after Jacob went away from the borders of the land, he came to the land of Shalem, that is the city of Shechem,

which is in the land of Canaan, and he rested in front of the city.

2 And he bought a parcel of the field which was there from the children of Hamor, the people of the land, for five shekels.

3 Jacob there built himself a house and pitched his tent there, and he made booths for his cattle; therefore he called the name of that place Succoth.

4 And Jacob remained in Succoth a year and six months.

5 At that time some of the women of the inhabitants of the land went to the city of Shechem to dance and rejoice with the daughters of the people of the city, and when they went forth then Rachel and Leah the wives of Jacob with their families also went to behold the rejoicing of the daughters of the city.

6 And Dinah the daughter of Jacob also went along with them and saw the daughters of the city, and they remained there before these daughters while all the people of the city were standing by them to behold their rejoicings, and all the great people of the city were there.

7 Shechem the son of Hamor, the prince of the land was also standing there to see them.

8 Shechem saw Dinah the daughter of Jacob sitting with her mother before the daughters of the city, and the damsel pleased him greatly, and he asked his friends and his people, saying, Whose daughter is that sitting among the women whom I do not know in this city?

9 And they said to him, Certainly this is the daughter of Jacob the son of Isaac the Hebrew, who has lived in this city for some time, and when it was reported that the daughters of the land were going forth to rejoice she went with her mother and maid servants to sit among them as you see.

10 Shechem saw Dinah the daughter of Jacob, and when he looked at her his soul became fixed on Dinah.

11 And he sent and had her taken by force, and Dinah came to the house of Shechem; he seized her forcibly and lay with her and humbled her, and he loved her greatly and placed her in his house.

12 And they came and told the thing to Jacob, and when Jacob heard that Shechem had defiled his daughter Dinah, Jacob sent twelve of his servants to fetch Dinah from the house of Shechem, and they went and came to the house of Shechem to take away Dinah from there.

13 When they came Shechem went out to them with his men and drove them from his house, and he would not let them come before Dinah, but Shechem was sitting with Dinah kissing and embracing her before their eyes.

14 The servants of Jacob came back and told him, saying, When we came, he and his men drove us away, and thus did Shechem do to Dinah before our eyes.

15 Jacob knew moreover that Shechem had defiled his daughter, but he said nothing; his sons were feeding his cattle in the field, and Jacob remained silent till their return.

16 Before his sons came home Jacob sent two maidens from his servants' daughters to take care of Dinah in the house of Shechem, and to remain with her, and Shechem sent three of his friends to his father Hamor the son of Chiddekem, the son of Pered, saying, Get me this damsel for a wife.

17 Hamor the son of Chiddekem the Hivite came to the house of Shechem his son, and he sat before him, and Hamor said to his son, Shechem, Is there not a woman among the daughters of your people, that you will take an Hebrew woman who is not of your people?

18 And Shechem said to him, Her only must you get for me, for she is delightful in my sight. Hamor did according to the word of his son, for he was greatly beloved by him.

19 And Hamor went forth to Jacob to commune with him concerning this matter, and when he had gone from the house of his son Shechem, before he came to Jacob to speak to him, the sons of Jacob had come from the field as soon as they heard the thing that Shechem the son of Hamor had done.

20 And the men were very much grieved concerning their sister, and they all came home fired with anger, before the time of gathering in their cattle.

21 They came and sat before their father and they spoke to him set ablaze with wrath, saying, Certainly death is due to this man and to his household, because the Lord God of the whole earth commanded Noah and his children that man shall never rob, nor commit adultery; now behold Shechem has both ravaged and committed fornication with our sister, and not one of all the people of the city spoke a word to him.

22 Certainly you know and understand that the judgment of death is due to Shechem, and to his father, and to the whole city on account of the thing which he has done.

23 And while they were speaking before their father in this matter, Hamor the father of Shechem came to speak to Jacob the words of his son concerning Dinah, and he sat before Jacob and before his sons.

24 And Hamor spoke to them, saying, The soul of my son Shechem longs for your daughter; I pray you give her to him for a wife and intermarry with us; give us your daughters and we will give you our daughters, and you shall dwell with us in our land and we will be as one people in the land.

25 For our land is very extensive, so dwell and trade therein and get possessions in it, and do therein as you desire, and no one shall prevent you by saying a word to you.

26 And Hamor ceased speaking to Jacob and his sons, and behold Shechem his son had come after him, and he sat before them.

27 And Shechem spoke before Jacob and his sons, saying, May I find favor in your sight that you will give me your daughter,

and whatever you say to me that will I do for her.

28 Ask me for abundance of dowry and gift, and I will give it, and whatever you say to me that will I do, and whoever he be that will rebel against your orders, he shall die; only give me the damsel for a wife.

29 And Simeon and Levi answered Hamor and Shechem his son deceitfully, saying, All you have spoken to us we will do for you.

30 And behold our sister is in your house, but keep away from her until we send to our father Isaac concerning this matter, for we can do nothing without his consent.

31 For he knows the ways of our father Abraham, and whatever he says to us we will tell you; we will conceal nothing from you.

32 And Simeon and Levi spoke this to Shechem and his father in order to find a pretext, and to seek counsel what was to be done to Shechem and to his city in this matter.

33 And when Shechem and his father heard the words of Simeon and Levi, it seemed good in their sight, and Shechem and his father rose to go home.

34 And when they had gone, the sons of Jacob said to their father, Behold, we know that death is due to these wicked ones and to their city, because they went contrary to that which God had commanded to Noah and his children and his descendants after them.

35 And also because Shechem did this thing to our sister Dinah in defiling her, for such vileness shall never be done among us.

36 Now therefore know and see what you will do, and seek counsel and pretext what is to be done to them, in order to kill all the inhabitants of this city.

37 Simeon said to them, Here is a proper advice for you: tell them to circumcise every male among them as we are circumcised, and if they do not wish to do this, we shall take our daughter from them and go away.

38 And if they consent to do this and will do it, then when they are sunk down with pain, we will attack them with our swords, as on one who is quiet and peaceable, and we will kill every male person among them.

39 Simeon's advice pleased them, and Simeon and Levi resolved to do to them as it was proposed.

40 And on the next morning Shechem and Hamor his father came again to Jacob and his sons, to speak concerning Dinah, and to hear what answer the sons of Jacob would give to their words.

41 And the sons of Jacob spoke deceitfully to them, saying, We told our father Isaac all your words, and your words pleased him.

42 But he spoke to us, saying, Thus did Abraham his father command him from God the Lord of the whole earth, that any man who is not of his descendants that should wish to take one of his daughters, shall cause every male belonging to him to be circumcised, as we are circumcised, and then we may give him our daughter for a wife.

43 Now we have made known to you all our ways that our father spoke to us, for we cannot do this of which you spoke to us, to give our daughter to an uncircumcised man, for it is a disgrace to us.

44 But herein we will consent to you, to give you our daughter, and we will also take to ourselves your daughters, and will dwell among you and be one people as you have spoken, if you will listen to us and consent to be like us, to circumcise every male belonging to you as we are circumcised.

45 And if you will not listen to us, to have every male circumcised as we are circumcised, as we have commanded, then we will come to you, and take our daughter from you and go away.

46 Shechem and his father Hamor heard the words of the sons of Jacob, and the thing pleased them greatly, and Shechem and his father Hamor hurried to do the wishes of the sons of Jacob, for Shechem was very fond of Dinah, and his soul was riveted to her.

47 Shechem and his father Hamor hurried to the gate of the city, and they assembled all the men of their city and spoke to them the words of the sons of Jacob, saying,

48 We came to these men, the sons of Jacob, and we spoke to them concerning their daughter, and these men will consent to do according to our wishes, and behold our land is of great extent for them, and they will dwell in it, and trade in it, and we shall be one people; we will take their daughters, and our daughters we will give to them for wives.

49 But only on this condition will these men consent to do this thing, that every male among us be circumcised as they are circumcised, as their God commanded them, and when we shall have done according to their instructions to be circumcised, then they will dwell among us, together with their cattle and possessions, and we shall be as one people with them.

50 When all the men of the city heard the words of Shechem and his father Hamor, then all the men of their city were agreeable to this proposal, and they obeyed to be circumcised; for Shechem and his father Hamor were greatly esteemed by them, being the princes of the land.

51 On the next day, Shechem and Hamor his father rose up early in the morning, and they assembled all the men of their city into the middle of the city, and they called for the sons of Jacob, who circumcised every male belonging to them on that day and the next.

52 And they circumcised Shechem and Hamor his father, and the five brothers of Shechem, and then every one rose up and went home; for this thing was from the Lord against the city of Shechem, and from the Lord was Simeon's counsel in this matter, in order that the Lord might deliver the city of Shechem into the hands of Jacob's two sons.

CHAPTER 34

1 The number of all the males that were circumcised were six hundred and forty-five men, and two hundred and forty-six children.

2 But Chiddekem, son of Pered, the father of Hamor, and his six brothers, would not listen to Shechem and his father Hamor; they would not be circumcised, for the proposal of the sons of Jacob was loathsome in their sight, and their anger was greatly roused at this, that the people of the city had not listened to them.

3 In the evening of the second day, they found eight small children who had not been circumcised, for their mothers had concealed them from Shechem and his father Hamor, and from the men of the city.

4 And Shechem and his father Hamor sent to have them brought before them to be circumcised, when Chiddekem and his six brothers sprang at them with their swords, and sought to kill them.

5 And they sought to kill also Shechem and his father Hamor and they sought to kill Dinah with them on account of this matter.

6 They said to them, What is this thing that you have done? Are there no women among the daughters of your brothers the Canaanites, that you wish to take to yourselves daughters of the Hebrews, whom ye knew not before, and will do this act which your fathers never commanded you?

7 Do you imagine that you will succeed through this act which you have done? And what will you answer in this affair to your brothers the Canaanites who will come tomorrow and ask you concerning this thing?

8 If your act shall not appear just and good in their sight, what will you do for your lives, and me for our lives, in your not having listened to our voices?

9 And if the inhabitants of the land and all your brothers the children of Ham, shall hear of your act, saying,

10 On account of a Hebrew woman did Shechem and Hamor his father, and all the inhabitants of their city, do that with which they had been unacquainted and which their ancestors never commanded them, where then will you fly or where conceal your shame all your days before your brothers, the inhabitants of the land of Canaan?

11 Now therefore we cannot bear up against this thing which you have done, neither can we be burdened with this yoke on us which our ancestors did not command us.

12 Behold tomorrow we will go and assemble all our brothers, the Canaanitish brothers who dwell in the land, and we will all come and strike you and all those who trust in you, that there shall not be a remnant left from you or them.

13 And when Hamor and his son Shechem and all the people of the city heard the words of Chiddekem and his brothers, they were terribly afraid of their lives at their words, and they repented of what they had done.

14 And Shechem and his father Hamor answered their father Chiddekem and his brothers, and they said to them, All the words which you spoke to us are true.

15 Now do not say, nor imagine in your hearts that on account of the love of the Hebrews we did this thing that our ancestors did not command us.

16 But because we saw that it was not their intention and desire to accede to our wishes concerning their daughter as to our taking her, except on this condition, so we listened to their voices and did this act which you saw in order to obtain our desire from them.

17 And when we shall have obtained our request from them, we will then return to them and do to them that which you say to us.

18 We petition you then to wait and tarry until our flesh will be healed and we again become strong, and we will then go together against them, and do to them that which is in your hearts and in ours.

19 And Dinah the daughter of Jacob heard all these words which Chiddekem and his brothers had spoken, and what Hamor and his son Shechem and the people of their city had answered them.

20 She hurried and sent one of her maidens, that her father had sent to take care of her in the house of Shechem, to Jacob her father and to her brothers, saying:

21 Thus did Chiddekem and his brothers advise concerning you, and thus did Hamor and Shechem and the people of the city answer them.

22 And when Jacob heard these words he was filled with wrath, and he was indignant at them, and his anger was set ablaze against them.

23 And Simeon and Levi swore and said, As the Lord lives, the God of the whole earth, by this time tomorrow, there shall not be a remnant left in the whole city.

24 Twenty young men had concealed themselves who were not circumcised, and these young men fought against Simeon and Levi, and Simeon and Levi killed eighteen of them, and two fled from them and escaped to some lime pits that were in the city, and Simeon and Levi sought for them, but could not find them.

25 And Simeon and Levi continued to go about in the city, and they killed all the people of the city at the edge of the sword,

and they left none remaining.

26 There was a great consternation in the midst of the city, and the cry of the people of the city ascended to heaven, and all the women and children cried aloud.

27 And Simeon and Levi killed all the city; they left not a male remaining in the whole city.

28 And they killed Hamor and Shechem his son at the edge of the sword, and they brought away Dinah from the house of Shechem and they went from there.

29 The sons of Jacob went and returned, and came on the slain, and spoiled all their property which was in the city and the field.

30 And while they were taking the spoil, three hundred men stood up and threw dust at them and struck them with stones. Then Simeon turned to them and he killed them all with the edge of the sword, and Simeon turned before Levi and came into the city.

31 They took away their sheep and their oxen and their cattle, and also the remainder of the women and little ones, and they led all these away; they opened a gate and went out and came to their father Jacob with vigor.

32 When Jacob saw all that they had done to the city, and saw the spoil that they took from them, Jacob was very angry at them, and Jacob said to them, What is this that you have done to me? I had obtained rest among the Canaanitish inhabitants of the land; none of them meddled with me.

33 And now you have done this to make me obnoxious to the inhabitants of the land, among the Canaanites and the Perizzites, and I am but of a small number; they will all assemble against me and kill me when they hear of your work with their brothers, and I and my household will be destroyed.

34 Simeon and Levi and all their brothers with them answered their father Jacob and said to him, Behold we live in the land, and shall Shechem do this to our sister? Why are you silent at all that Shechem has done? And shall he deal with our sister as with a harlot in the streets?

35 The number of women whom Simeon and Levi took captives from the city of Shechem, whom they did not kill, was eighty-five who had not known man.

36 And among them was a young damsel of beautiful appearance and well favored, whose name was Bunah, and Simeon took her for a wife, and the number of the males which they took captives and did not kill was forty-seven men, and the rest they killed.

37 All the young men and women that Simeon and Levi had taken captives from the city of Shechem were servants to the sons of Jacob and to their children after them, until the day of the sons of Jacob going forth from the land of Egypt.

38 And when Simeon and Levi had gone forth from the city, the two young men that were left, who had concealed themselves in the city and did not die among the people of the city, rose up; these young men went into the city and walked about in it, and found the city desolate without man, and only women weeping, and these young men cried out and said, Behold, this is the evil which the sons of Jacob the Hebrew did to this city in their having this day destroyed one of the Canaanitish cities, and were not afraid of their lives of all the land of Canaan.

39 These men left the city and went to the city of Tapnach, and they came there and told the inhabitants of Tapnach all that had befallen them, and all that the sons of Jacob had done to the city of Shechem.

40 The information reached Jashub king of Tapnach, and he sent men to the city of Shechem to see those young men, for the king did not believe them in this account, saying, How could two men lay waste such a large town as Shechem?

41 The messengers of Jashub came back and told him, saying, We came to the city, and it is destroyed, there is not a man there; only weeping women; neither is any flock or cattle there, for all that was in the city the sons of Jacob took away.

42 Jashub wondered at this, saying, How could two men do this thing to destroy so large a city, and not one man able to stand against them?

43 For the like has not been from the days of Nimrod, and not even from the remotest time, has the like taken place; and Jashub, king of Tapnach, said to his people, Be courageous and we will go and fight against these Hebrews, and do to them as they did to the city; we will avenge the cause of the people of the city.

44 Jashub, king of Tapnach, consulted with his counselors about this matter, and his advisers said to him, Alone you will not prevail over the Hebrews, for they must be powerful to do this work to the whole city.

45 If two of them laid waste the whole city, and no one stood against them, certainly if you will go against them, they will all rise against us and destroy us likewise.

46 But if you will send to all the kings that surround us, and let them come together, then we will go with them and fight against the sons of Jacob; then you will prevail against them.

47 Jashub heard the words of his counselors, and their words pleased him and his people, and he did so; Jashub king of Tapnach sent to all the kings of the Amorites that surrounded Shechem and Tapnach, saying,

48 Go up with me and assist me, and we will strike Jacob the Hebrew and all his sons, and destroy them from the earth, for thus did he do to the city of Shechem, and do you not know of it?

49 And all the kings of the Amorites heard the evil that the sons of Jacob had done to the city of Shechem, and they were greatly astonished at them.

50 The seven kings of the Amorites assembled with all their armies about ten thousand men with drawn swords, and they came to fight against the sons of Jacob; Jacob heard that the kings of the Amorites had assembled to fight against his sons,

and Jacob was greatly afraid; it distressed him.

51 And Jacob exclaimed against Simeon and Levi, saying, What is this act that you did? Why have you injured me, to bring against me all the children of Canaan to destroy me and my household? For I was at rest, even I and my household, and you have done this thing to me and provoked the inhabitants of the land against me by your proceedings.

52 Judah answered his father, saying, Was it for naught my brothers Simeon and Levi killed all the inhabitants of Shechem? Certainly it was because Shechem had humbled our sister, and went contrary to the command of our God to Noah and his children, for Shechem took our sister away by force, and committed fornication with her.

53 Shechem did all this evil and not one of the inhabitants of his city interfered with him, to say, Why will you do this? Certainly for this my brothers went and struck the city, and the Lord delivered it into their hands, because its inhabitants had gone contrary to the commands of our God. Is it then for naught that they have done all this?

54 Now why are you afraid or distressed, and why are you displeased at my brothers, and why is your anger set ablaze against them?

55 Certainly our God who delivered into their hand the city of Shechem and its people, he will also deliver into our hands all the Canaanitish kings who are coming against us, and we will do to them as my brothers did to Shechem.

56 Now be tranquil about them and cast away your fears, but trust in the Lord our God, and pray to him to assist us and deliver us, and deliver our enemies into our hands.

57 Judah called to one of his father's servants, Go now and see where those kings who are coming against us are situated with their armies.

58 And the servant went and looked far off, and went up opposite Mount Sihon, and saw all the camps of the kings standing in the fields, and he returned to Judah and said, Behold the kings are situated in the field with all their camps, a people greatly numerous like the sand on the seashore.

59 And Judah said to Simeon and Levi, and to all his brothers, Strengthen yourselves and be sons of valor, for the Lord our God is with us, do not fear them.

60 Stand forth each man, equipped with his weapons of war, his bow and his sword, and we will go and fight against these uncircumcised men; the Lord is our God, He will save us.

61 They rose up, and each put on his weapons of war, great and small, eleven sons of Jacob, and all the servants of Jacob with them.

62 All the servants of Isaac who were with Isaac in Hebron, all came to them equipped in all sorts of war instruments, and the sons of Jacob and their servants, being one hundred and twelve men, went towards these kings, and Jacob also went with them.

63 And the sons of Jacob sent to their father Isaac the son of Abraham to Hebron, the same is Kireath-arba, saying,

64 Pray we beseech you for us to the Lord our God, to protect us from the hands of the Canaanites who are coming against us, and to deliver them into our hands.

65 Isaac the son of Abraham prayed to the Lord for his sons, and he said, O Lord God, you did promise my father, saying, I will reproduce your descendants as the stars of heaven, and you did also promise me, and establish you your word, now that the kings of Canaan are coming together, to make war with my children because they committed no violence.

66 Now therefore, O Lord God, God of the whole earth, pervert, I pray you, the counsel of these kings that they may not fight against my sons.

67 And impress the hearts of these kings and their people with the terror of my sons and bring down their pride, that they may turn away from my sons.

68 With your strong hand and outstretched arm deliver my sons and their servants from them, for power and might are in your hands to do all this.

69 And the sons of Jacob and their servants went toward these kings, and they trusted in the Lord their God, and while they were going, Jacob their father also prayed to the Lord and said, O Lord God, powerful and exalted God, who has reigned from days of old, from thence till now and forever;

70 You are He who stirs up wars and causes them to cease, in your hand are power and might to exalt and to bring down; O may my prayer be acceptable before you that you may turn to me with your mercies, to impress the hearts of these kings and their people with the terror of my sons, and terrify them and their camps, and with your great kindness deliver all those that trust in you, for it is you who can bring people under us and reduce nations under our power.

CHAPTER 35

1 All the kings of the Amorites came and took their stand in the field to consult with their counselors what was to be done with the sons of Jacob, for they were still afraid of them, saying, Take notice that two of them killed the whole city of Shechem.

2 And the Lord heard the prayers of Isaac and Jacob, and he filled the hearts of all these kings' advisers with great fear and terror that they unanimously exclaimed,

3 Are you silly or is there no understanding in you, that you will fight with the Hebrews; why will you take delight in your

own destruction this day?

4 See, two of them came to the city of Shechem without fear or terror, and they killed all the inhabitants of the city, that no man stood up against them, and how will you be able to fight with them all?

5 Certainly you know that their God is greatly fond of them and has done mighty things for them, such as have not been done from days of old and among all the gods of nations; there is none can do like his mighty deeds.

6 Certainly he delivered their father Abraham, the Hebrew, from the hand of Nimrod, and from the hand of all his people who had many times sought to kill him.

7 He delivered him also from the fire in which king Nimrod had cast him, and his God delivered him from it.

8 And who else can do like this? Certainly it was Abraham who killed the five kings of Elam when they had touched his brother's son who in those days lived in Sodom.

9 And took his servant that was faithful in his house and a few of his men, and they pursued the kings of Elam in one night and killed them; then restored to his brother's son all his property which they had taken from him.

10 Certainly you know the God of these Hebrews is much delighted with them, and they are also delighted with him, for they know that he delivered them from all their enemies.

11 And consider this, through his love toward his God, Abraham took his only and precious son and intended to bring him up as a burnt offering to his God; had it not been for God who prevented him from doing this, he would then have done it through his love to his God.

12 God saw all his works and swore to him, and promised him that he would deliver his sons and all his descendants from every trouble that would befall them, because he had done this thing and through his love to his God stifled his compassion for his child.

13 And have you not heard what their God did to Pharaoh king of Egypt and to Abimelech king of Gerar through taking Abraham's wife, who said of her, She is my sister; that they might kill him on account of her and think of taking her for a wife? And God did to them and their people all that you heard of.

14 And then, we ourselves saw with our own eyes that Esau, the brother of Jacob, came to him with four hundred men with the intention of slaying him, for he remembered that he had taken away from him his father's blessing.

15 And he went to meet him when he came from Syria to strike the mother with the children, and who delivered him from his hands but his God in whom he trusted? He delivered him from the hand of his brother and also from the hands of his enemies, and certainly he again will protect them.

16 Who does not know that it was their God who inspired them with strength to do to the town of Shechem the evil which you heard of?

17 Could it then be with their own strength that two men could destroy such a large city as Shechem had it not been for their God in whom they trusted? He spoke and did to them all this to kill the inhabitants of the city in their city.

18 And can you then prevail over them who have come forth together from your city to fight with all of them, even if a thousand times as many more should come to your assistance?

19 Certainly you know and understand that you do not come to fight with them, but you come to war with their God who chose them, and you have therefore all come this day to be destroyed.

20 So refrain from this evil which you are endeavoring to bring on yourselves, and it will be better for you not to go to battle with them, although they are but few in numbers, because their God is with them.

21 When the kings of the Amorites heard all the words of their advisers, their hearts were filled with terror; they were afraid of the sons of Jacob and would not fight against them.

22 They inclined to believe the words of their advisers and they listened to all their words. The words of the counselors greatly pleased the kings, and they did so.

23 And the kings turned and refrained from the sons of Jacob, for they dared not approach them to make war with them; they were greatly afraid of them, and their hearts melted within them from their fear.

24 For this proceeded from the Lord to them; he heard the prayers of his servants Isaac and Jacob, for they trusted in him. And all these kings returned with their camps on that day, each to his own city, and they did not at that time fight with the sons of Jacob.

25 The sons of Jacob kept their station that day till evening opposite mount Sihon, and seeing that these kings did not come to fight against them, the sons of Jacob returned home.

CHAPTER 36

1 At that time the Lord appeared to Jacob saying, Arise, go to Bethel and remain there; make there an altar to the Lord who appears to you, who delivered you and your sons from affliction.

2 And Jacob rose up with his sons and all belonging to him; they went and came to Bethel according to the word of the Lord.

3 Jacob was ninety-nine years old when he went up to Bethel, and Jacob and his sons and all the people that were with him remained in Bethel in Luz; he built an altar there to the Lord who appeared to him, and Jacob and his sons remained in Bethel

six months.

4 At that time Deborah the daughter of Uz, the nurse of Rebecca, who had been with Jacob died and Jacob buried her beneath Bethel under an oak that was there.

5 And Rebecca the daughter of Bethuel, the mother of Jacob, also died at that time in Hebron, the same is Kireath-arba. She was buried in the cave of Machpelah which Abraham had bought from the children of Heth.

6 And the life of Rebecca was one hundred and thirty-three years, and she died. When Jacob heard that his mother Rebecca was dead he wept bitterly for his mother, and made a great mourning for her and for Deborah her nurse beneath the oak. He called the name of that place Allon-bachuth.

7 Laban the Syrian died in those days, for God struck him because he went contrary to the covenant that existed between him and Jacob.

8 Jacob was a hundred years old when the Lord appeared to him and blessed him and called his name Israel, and Rachel the wife of Jacob conceived in those days.

9 At that time Jacob and all belonging to him journeyed from Bethel to go to his father's house, to Hebron.

10 And while they were going on the road, and there was yet but a little way to come to Ephrath, Rachel gave birth to a son; she had hard labor and died.

11 Jacob buried her on the way to Ephrath, which is Bethlehem, and he set a pillar on her grave which is there to this day; the days of Rachel were forty-five years when she died.

12 Jacob called the name of his son that was born to him, which Rachel gave birth to, Benjamin, for he was born to him in the land on the right hand.

13 It was after the death of Rachel that Jacob pitched his tent in the tent of her handmaid Bilhah.

14 And Reuben was jealous for his mother Leah on account of this; he was filled with anger, and he rose up in his anger and went and entered the tent of Bilhah and then removed his father's bed.

15 At that time the portion of birthright, together with the kingly and priestly offices, was removed from the sons of Reuben for he had profaned his father's bed; the birthright was given to Joseph, the kingly office to Judah, and the priesthood to Levi, because Reuben had defiled his father's bed.

16 These are the generations of Jacob who were born to him in Padan-aram, and the sons of Jacob were twelve:

17 The sons of Leah were Reuben the first born, and Simeon, Levi, Judah, Issachar, Zebulun, and their sister Dinah; and the sons of Rachel were Joseph and Benjamin.

18 The sons of Zilpah, Leah's handmaid, were Gad and Asher, and the sons of Bilhah, Rachel's handmaid, were Dan and Naphtali; these are the sons of Jacob which were born to him in Padan-aram.

19 Jacob and his sons and all belonging to him journeyed and came to Mamre, which is Kireath-arba, that is in Hebron, where Abraham and Isaac sojourned; Jacob with his sons and all belonging to him lived with his father in Hebron.

20 His brother Esau, his sons and all belonging to him went to the land of Seir and lived there and had possessions in the land of Seir, and the children of Esau were prolific and multiplied greatly in the land of Seir.

21 These are the generations of Esau that were born to him in the land of Canaan, and the sons of Esau were five:

22 And Adah gave birth to, to Esau, his first born Eliphaz, and she also gave birth to, to him, Reuel, and Ahlibamah gave birth to, to him, Jeush, Yaalam and Korah.

23 These are the children of Esau who were born to him in the land of Canaan; the sons of Eliphaz the son of Esau were: Teman, Omar, Zepho, Gatam, Kenaz and Amalex; the sons of Reuel were Nachath, Zerach, Shamah and Mizzah.

24 The sons of Jeush were Timnah, Alvah, Jetheth; the sons of Yaalam were Alah, Phinor and Kenaz.

25 And the sons of Korah were Teman, Mibzar, Magdiel and Eram; these are the families of the sons of Esau according to their territories in the land of Seir.

26 These are the names of the sons of Seir the Horite, inhabitants of the land of Seir: Lotan, Shobal, Zibeon, Anah, Dishan, Ezer and Dishon, being seven sons.

27 The children of Lotan were Hori, Heman and their sister Timna, that is Timna who came to Jacob and his sons; they would not give ear to her and she became a concubine to Eliphaz the son of Esau; she gave birth to, to him, Amalek.

28 And the sons of Shobal were Alvan, Manahath, Ebal, Shepho, and Onam, and the sons of Zibeon were Ajah, and Anah; this was that Anah who found the Yemim in the wilderness when he fed the asses of Zibeon his father.

29 And while he was feeding his father's asses he led them to the wilderness at different times to feed them.

30 There was a day that he brought them to one of the deserts on the seashore, opposite the wilderness of the people, and while he was feeding them, suddenly a very heavy storm came from the other side of the sea and rested on the asses that were feeding there, and they all stood still.

31 Afterward about one hundred and twenty great and terrible animals came out from the wilderness at the other side of the sea; they all came to the place where the asses were, and they placed themselves there.

32 And those animals, from their middle downward, were in the shape of the children of men; from their middle upward, some had the likeness of bears, and some the likeness of the keephas, with tails behind them from between their shoulders reaching down to the earth, like the tails of the ducheephath. These animals came and mounted and rode on these asses, and led them away, and they went away to this day.

33 One of these animals approached Anah, struck him with his tail, and then fled from that place.

34 And when he saw this work he was greatly afraid of his life, and he fled and escaped to the city.

35 He related to his sons and brothers all that had happened to him, and many men went to seek the asses but could not find them. Anah and his brothers went no more to that place from that day on for they were greatly afraid for their lives.

36 The children of Anah the son of Seir, were Dishon and his sister Ahlibamah; the children of Dishon were Hemdan, Eshban, Ithran and Cheran; the children of Ezer were Bilhan, Zaavan and Akan, and the children of Dishon were Uz and Aran.

37 These are the families of the children of Seir the Horite, according to their dukedoms in the land of Seir.

38 Esau and his children lived in the land of Seir the Horite, the inhabitant of the land, and they had possessions in it and were prolific and multiplied greatly. Jacob and his children and all belonging to them lived with their father Isaac in the land of Canaan, as the Lord had commanded Abraham their father.

CHAPTER 37

1 In the one hundred and fifth year of the life of Jacob, that is the ninth year of Jacob's dwelling with his children in the land of Canaan, he came from Padan-aram.

2 And in those days Jacob journeyed with his children from Hebron; they went and returned to the city of Shechem, they and all belonging to them and they lived there, for the children of Jacob obtained good and fattening pasture land for their cattle in the city of Shechem, the city of Shechem having then been rebuilt; there were in it about three hundred men and women.

3 Jacob and his children and all belonging to him lived in the part of the field which Jacob had bought from Hamor the father of Shechem, when he came from Padan-aram before Simeon and Levi had smitten the city.

4 And all those kings of the Canaanites and Amorites that surrounded the city of Shechem heard that the sons of Jacob had again come to Shechem and lived there.

5 They said, Shall the sons of Jacob the Hebrew again come to the city and dwell therein, after that they have smitten its inhabitants and driven them out? Shall they now return and also drive out those who are dwelling in the city or kill them?

6 And all the kings of Canaan again assembled, and they came together to make war with Jacob and his sons.

7 Jashub king of Tapnach sent also to all his neighboring kings, to Elan king of Gaash, and to Ihuri king of Shiloh, and to Parathon king of Chazar, and to Susi king of Sarton, and to Laban king of Bethchoran, and to Shabir king of Othnay-mah, saying,

8 Come up to me and assist me, and let us strike Jacob the Hebrew and his sons and all belonging to him, for they are again come to Shechem to possess it and to kill its inhabitants as before.

9 And all these kings assembled together and came with all their camps, a people greatly plentiful like the sand on the seashore, and they were all opposite to Tapnach.

10 Jashub king of Tapnach went forth to them with all his army, and he encamped with them opposite to Tapnach outside the city; all these kings they divided into seven divisions, being seven camps against the sons of Jacob.

11 And they sent a declaration to Jacob and his son, saying, All of you come forth to us that we may have an interview together in the plain, and revenge the cause of the men of Shechem whom you killed in their city; you will now again return to the city of Shechem and dwell therein, and kill its inhabitants as before.

12 The sons of Jacob heard this and their anger was set ablaze greatly at the words of the kings of Canaan, and ten of the sons of Jacob hurried and rose up, and each of them put on his weapons of war; and there were one hundred and two of their servants with them equipped in battle array.

13 And all these men, the sons of Jacob with their servants, went toward these kings and Jacob their father was with them; they all stood on the heap of Shechem.

14 Jacob prayed to the Lord for his sons, and he spread forth his hands to the Lord, and said, O God, you are an Almighty God, you are our father; you did form us and we are the works of your hands; I pray you deliver my sons through your mercy from the hand of their enemies who are this day coming to fight with them and save them from their hand, for in your hand is power and might to save the few from the many.

15 And give to my sons, your servants, strength of heart and might to fight with their enemies, to subdue them, and to make their enemies fall before them. Let not my sons and their servants die through the hands of the children of Canaan.

16 But if it seems good in your eyes to take away the lives of my sons and their servants, take them in your great mercy through the hands of your ministers, that they may not perish this day by the hands of the kings of the Amorites.

17 When Jacob ceased praying to the Lord the earth shook from its place, and the sun darkened, and all these kings were terrified and a great consternation seized them.

18 The Lord listened to the prayer of Jacob, and the Lord impressed the hearts of all the kings and their hosts with the terror and awe of the sons of Jacob.

19 For the Lord caused them to hear the voice of chariots, and the voice of mighty horses from the sons of Jacob, and the voice of a great army accompanying them.

20 And these kings were seized with great terror at the sons of Jacob; while they were standing in their quarters, behold the sons of Jacob advanced on them with one hundred and twelve men, with a great and tremendous shouting.

21 And when the kings saw the sons of Jacob advancing toward them, they were still more panic stricken; they were inclined to retreat from before the sons of Jacob as at first and not to fight with them.

22 But they did not retreat, saying, It would be a disgrace to us to retreat twice from before the Hebrews.

23 The sons of Jacob came near and advanced against all these kings and their armies, and what they saw was a very mighty people, numerous as the sand of the sea.

24 And the sons of Jacob called to the Lord and said, Help us O Lord, help us and answer us, for we trust in you, and let us not die by the hands of these uncircumcised men who this day have come against us.

25 The sons of Jacob put on their weapons of war and they took in their hands each man his shield and his javelin, and they approached to do battle.

26 And Judah, the son of Jacob, ran first before his brothers and ten of his servants with him, and he went toward these kings.

27 Jashub, king of Tapnach, also came forth first with his army before Judah, and Judah saw Jashub and his army coming toward him, and Judah's wrath was set ablaze; his anger burned within him, and he approached to the fight in which Judah ventured his life.

28 Jashub and all his army were advancing toward Judah and he was riding on a very strong and powerful horse; Jashub was a very valiant man, and covered with iron and brass from head to foot.

29 And while he was on the horse, he shot arrows with both hands from before and behind, as was his manner in all his battles; he never missed the place to which he aimed his arrows.

30 When Jashub came to fight with Judah and was darting many arrows against Judah, the Lord bound the hand of Jashub and all the arrows that he shot rebounded on his own men.

31 And in spite of this Jashub kept advancing toward Judah, to challenge him with the arrows, but the distance between them was about thirty cubits. When Judah saw Jashub darting forth his arrows against him, he ran to him with his wrath-excited strength.

32 Judah took up a large stone from the ground, its weight was sixty shekels, and Judah ran toward Jashub and with the stone struck him on his shield, so that Jashub was stunned with the blow and fell off his horse to the ground.

33 The shield burst asunder out of the hand of Jashub, and through the force of the blow sprang to the distance of about fifteen cubits, and the shield fell before the second camp.

34 The kings that came with Jashub saw at a distance the strength of Judah, the son of Jacob, and what he had done to Jashub; they were terribly afraid of Judah.

35 And they assembled near Jashub's camp, seeing his confusion, and Judah drew his sword and struck forty-two men of the camp of Jashub, and the whole of Jashub's camp fled before Judah. No man stood against him and they left Jashub and fled from him, and Jashub was still prostrate on the ground.

36 Jashub, seeing that all the men of his camp had fled from him, hurried and rose up with terror against Judah and stood on his legs opposite Judah.

37 And Jashub had a single combat with Judah, placing shield toward shield, and Jashub's men all fled for they were greatly afraid of Judah.

38 Jashub took his spear in his hand to strike Judah on his head, but Judah had quickly placed his shield to his head against Jashub's spear so that the shield of Judah received the blow from Jashub's spear, and the shield was split in two.

39 And when Judah saw that his shield was split, he hastily drew his sword and struck Jashub at his ankles and cut off his feet, so that Jashub fell on the ground and the spear fell from his hand.

40 Judah hastily picked up Jashub's spear with which he severed his head and cast it next to his feet.

41 When the sons of Jacob saw what Judah had done to Jashub, they all ran into the ranks of the other kings and the sons of Jacob fought with the army of Jashub and the armies of all the kings that were there.

42 The sons of Jacob caused fifteen thousand of their men to fall, and they struck them as if smiting at gourds, and the rest fled for their lives.

43 Judah was still standing by the body of Jashub and stripped Jashub of his coat of mail.

44 Judah also took off the iron and brass that were around Jashub, and then nine men of the captains of Jashub came along to fight against Judah.

45 Judah hurried and took up a stone from the ground, and with it struck one of them on the head; his skull was fractured and the body also fell from the horse to the ground.

46 And the eight captains that remained, seeing the strength of Judah, were greatly afraid and they fled; Judah with his ten men pursued them and they overtook them and killed them.

47 The sons of Jacob were still smiting the armies of the kings, and they killed many of them, but those kings daringly kept their stand with their captains and did not retreat from their places; they shouted against those of their armies that fled from before the sons of Jacob, but none would listen to them, for they were afraid for their lives that they should die.

48 And all the sons of Jacob, after having smitten the armies of the kings, returned and came before Judah; Judah was still slaying the eight captains of Jashub and stripping off their garments.

49 And Levi saw Elon, king of Gaash, advancing toward him with his fourteen captains to strike him, but Levi did not know it for certain.

50 Elon with his captains approached nearer, and Levi looked back and saw that battle was coming to him from the rear.

291

Levi ran with twelve of his servants, and they went and killed Elon and his captains with the edge of the sword.

CHAPTER 38

1 Ihuri king of Shiloh came up to assist Elon and he approached Jacob, when Jacob drew his bow that was in his hand and with an arrow struck Ihuri, which caused his death.

2 And when Ihuri king of Shiloh was dead, the four remaining kings fled from their station with the rest of the captains; they endeavored to retreat, saying, We have no more strength with the Hebrews after their having killed the three kings and their captains who were more powerful than we are.

3 When the sons of Jacob saw that the remaining kings had left their station, they pursued them and Jacob also came from the heap of Shechem from the place where he was standing; they went after the kings and they approached them with their servants.

4 And the kings and the captains with the rest of their armies, seeing that the sons of Jacob approached them, were afraid for their lives and fled till they reached the city of Chazar.

5 The sons of Jacob pursued them to the gate of the city of Chazar, and they struck a great smiting among the kings and their armies, about four thousand men. While they were smiting the army of the kings, Jacob was occupied with his bow, confining himself to smiting the kings and killed them all.

6 And he killed Parathon king of Chazar at the gate of the city of Chazar and afterward struck Susi king of Sarton, and Laban king of Bethchorin, and Shabir king of Machnaymah; he killed them all with arrows, an arrow to each of them, and they died.

7 The sons of Jacob, seeing that all the kings were dead and that they were broken up and retreating, continued to carry on the battle with the armies of the kings opposite the gate of Chazar, and they still struck about four hundred of their men.

8 Three men of the servants of Jacob fell in that battle and when Judah saw that three of his servants had died, it grieved him greatly and his anger burned within him against the Amorites.

9 And all the men that remained of the armies of the kings were greatly afraid for their lives, and they ran and broke the gate of the walls of the city of Chazar; they all entered the city for safety.

10 They concealed themselves in the midst of the city of Chazar, for the city of Chazar was very large and extensive, and when all these armies had entered the city, the sons of Jacob ran after them to the city.

11 Four mighty men, experienced in battle, went forth from the city and stood against the entrance of the city with drawn swords and spears in their hands; they placed themselves opposite the sons of Jacob and would not let them enter the city.

12 Naphtali ran and came between them and with his sword struck two of them, and cut off their heads at one stroke.

13 He turned to the other two and saw that they had fled; he pursued them, overtook them, struck them and killed them.

14 When the sons of Jacob came to the city and saw there was another wall to the city, they sought for the gate of the wall and could not find it; Judah sprang on the top of the wall and Simeon and Levi followed him, and they all three descended from the wall into the city.

15 Simeon and Levi killed all the men who ran for safety into the city and also the inhabitants of the city with their wives and little ones they killed with the edge of the sword, and the cries of the city ascended up to heaven.

16 And Dan and Naphtali sprang on the wall to see what caused the noise of the wailing, for the sons of Jacob felt anxious about their brothers; they heard the inhabitants of the city speaking with weeping and pleas, saying, Take all that we possess in the city and go away, only do not put us to death.

17 When Judah, Simeon, and Levi had ceased smiting the inhabitants of the city, they ascended the wall and called to Dan and Naphtali, who were on the wall, and to the rest of their brothers; Simeon and Levi informed them of the entrance into the city, and all the sons of Jacob came to gather the spoil.

18 And the sons of Jacob took the spoil of the city of Chazar, the flocks and herds, and the property, and they took all that could be captured, and went away that day from the city.

19 On the next day the sons of Jacob went to Sarton, for they heard that the men of Sarton who had remained in the city were assembling to fight with them for having slain their king. Sarton was a very high and fortified city, and it had a deep rampart surrounding the city.

20 And the pillar of the rampart was about fifty cubits and its breadth forty cubits; there was no place for a man to enter the city on account of the rampart. The sons of Jacob saw the rampart of the city, and they sought an entrance in it but could not find it.

21 For the entrance to the city was at the rear, and every man that wished to come into the city came by that road and went around the whole city, and afterwards entered the city.

22 The sons of Jacob seeing they could not find the way into the city, their anger was set ablaze greatly, and the inhabitants of the city seeing that the sons of Jacob were coming to them were greatly afraid of them, for they had heard of their strength and what they had done to Chazar.

23 And the inhabitants of the city of Sarton could not go out toward the sons of Jacob after having assembled in the city to

fight against them, that they might thereby not get into the city. But when they saw that they were coming toward them, they were greatly afraid of them, for they had heard of their strength and what they had done to Chazar.

24 So the inhabitants of Sarton speedily took away the bridge of the road of the city from its place, before the sons of Jacob came, and they brought it into the city.

25 The sons of Jacob came and sought the way into the city, and could not find it and the inhabitants of the city went up to the top of the wall, and saw that the sons of Jacob were seeking an entrance into the city.

26 The inhabitants of the city reproached the sons of Jacob from the top of the wall and they cursed them, and the sons of Jacob heard the reproaches and they were greatly incensed; their anger burned within them.

27 The sons of Jacob were provoked at them, and they all rose and sprang over the rampart with the force of their strength, and through their might passed the forty cubits' breadth of the rampart.

28 And when they had passed the rampart they stood under the wall of the city, and they found all the gates of the city enclosed with iron doors.

29 The sons of Jacob came near to break open the doors of the gates of the city, and the inhabitants did not let them, for from the top of the wall they were casting stones and arrows on them.

30 And the number of the people that were on the wall was about four hundred men, and when the sons of Jacob saw that the men of the city would not let them open the gates of the city, they sprang and ascended the top of the wall, and Judah went up first to the east part of the city.

31 And Gad and Asher went up after him to the west corner of the city, and Simeon and Levi to the north, and Dan and Reuben to the south.

32 The men who were on the top of the wall, the inhabitants of the city, seeing that the sons of Jacob were coming up to them, all fled from the wall, descended into the city and concealed themselves in the middle of the city.

33 Issachar and Naphtali that remained under the wall approached and broke the gates of the city, and set ablaze a fire at the gates of the city that the iron melted, and all the sons of Jacob came into the city, they and all their men; they fought with the inhabitants of the city of Sarton and struck them with the edge of the sword, and no man stood up before them.

34 About two hundred men fled from the city and they all went and hid themselves in a certain tower in the city; Judah pursued them to the tower and broke down the tower which fell on the men, and they all died.

35 The sons of Jacob went up the road of the roof of that tower, and they looked and there was another strong and high tower at a distance in the city, and the top of it reached to heaven. The sons of Jacob hurried and descended and went with all their men to that tower, and found it filled with about three hundred men, women and little ones.

36 The sons of Jacob struck a great smiting among those men in the tower and they ran away and fled from them.

37 And Simeon and Levi pursued them when twelve mighty and valiant men came out to them from the place where they had concealed themselves.

38 And those twelve men maintained a strong battle against Simeon and Levi, and Simeon and Levi could not prevail over them; those valiant men broke the shields of Simeon and Levi, and one of them struck at Levi's head with his sword when Levi hastily placed his hand to his head, for he was afraid of the sword. The sword struck Levi's hand, and the hand of Levi was nearly cut off.

39 Levi seized the sword of the valiant man in his hand and took it forcibly from the man; with it he struck at the head of the powerful man and he severed his head.

40 Eleven men approached to fight with Levi, for they saw that one of them was killed; the sons of Jacob fought but the sons of Jacob could not defeat them, for those men were very powerful.

41 And the sons of Jacob seeing that they could not win over them, Simeon gave a loud and tremendous shriek, and the eleven powerful men were stunned at the voice of Simeon's shrieking.

42 Judah at a distance knew the voice of Simeon's shouting, and Naphtali and Judah ran with their shields to Simeon and Levi and found them fighting with those powerful men, unable to defeat them as their shields were broken.

43 Naphtali saw that the shields of Simeon and Levi were broken and he took two shields from his servants and brought them to Simeon and Levi.

44 And Simeon, Levi and Judah on that day fought all three against the eleven mighty men until the time of sunset, but they could not win over them.

45 This was told to Jacob, and he was very grieved; he prayed to the Lord, and he and Naphtali his son went against these mighty men.

46 Jacob approached, drew his bow, and came near to the mighty men, and killed three of their men with the bow; the remaining eight turned back and then the war waged against them in the front and rear. They were greatly afraid for their lives and could not stand before the sons of Jacob, and they fled from before them.

47 In their flight they met Dan and Asher coming toward them, and they suddenly fell on them and fought with them, and killed two of them; Judah and his brothers pursued them and struck the remainder of them, and killed them.

48 All the sons of Jacob returned and walked through the city searching if they could find any men; they found about twenty young men in a cave in the city; Gad and Asher struck them all and Dan and Naphtali lighted on the rest of the men who had fled and escaped from the second tower, and they struck them all.

49 The sons of Jacob struck all the inhabitants of the city of Sarton, but the women and little ones they left in the city and did

293

not kill them.

50 And all the inhabitants of the city of Sarton were powerful men; one of them would pursue a thousand, and two of them would not flee from ten thousand of the rest of men.

51 The sons of Jacob killed all the inhabitants of the city of Sarton with the edge of the sword; no man stood up against them, and they left the women in the city.

52 The sons of Jacob took all the spoil of the city and captured what they desired, and they took flocks and herds and property from the city; the sons of Jacob did to Sarton and its inhabitants as they had done to Chazar and its inhabitants, and they turned and went away.

CHAPTER 39

1 When the sons of Jacob went from the city of Sarton, they had gone about two hundred cubits when they met the inhabitants of Tapnach coming toward them, for they went out to fight with them because they had smitten the king of Tapnach and all his men.

2 So all that remained in the city of Tapnach came out to fight with the sons of Jacob and they thought to retake from them the booty and the spoil which they had captured from Chazar and Sarton.

3 The rest of the men of Tapnach fought with the sons of Jacob in that place, and the sons of Jacob struck them and they fled before them. They pursued them to the city of Arbelan and they all fell before the sons of Jacob.

4 The sons of Jacob returned and came to Tapnach to take away the spoil of Tapnach; when they came to Tapnach they heard that the people of Arbelan had gone out to meet them to save the spoil of their brothers. The sons of Jacob left ten of their men in Tapnach to plunder the city, and they went out toward the people of Arbelan.

5 The men of Arbelan went out with their wives to fight with the sons of Jacob, for their wives were experienced in battle; they went out, about four hundred men and women.

6 And all the sons of Jacob shouted with a loud voice; they all ran toward the inhabitants of Arbelan with a great and tremendous voice.

7 The inhabitants of Arbelan heard the noise of the shouting of the sons of Jacob and their roaring like the noise of lions and like the roaring of the sea and its waves.

8 And fear and terror possessed their hearts on account of the sons of Jacob; they were terribly afraid of them and they retreated and fled before them into the city. The sons of Jacob pursued them to the gate of the city and they came on them in the city.

9 The sons of Jacob fought with them in the city, and all their women were engaged in slinging against the sons of Jacob; the combat was very severe among them all of that day till evening.

10 And the sons of Jacob could not prevail over them; the sons of Jacob had almost perished in that battle. The sons of Jacob cried to the Lord and greatly gained strength toward evening; the sons of Jacob struck all the inhabitants of Arbelan by the edge of the sword, men, women and little ones.

11 Also the remainder of the people who had fled from Sarton, the sons of Jacob struck them in Arbelan, and the sons of Jacob did to Arbelan and Tapnach as they had done to Chazar and Sarton. When the women saw that all the men were dead, they went on the roofs of the city and struck the sons of Jacob by showering down stones like rain.

12 And the sons of Jacob hurried and came into the city and seized all the women and struck them with the edge of the sword. The sons of Jacob captured all the spoil and booty, flocks and herds and cattle.

13 The sons of Jacob did to Machnaymah as they had done to Tapnach, to Chazar and to Shiloh, and they turned from there and went away.

14 On the fifth day the sons of Jacob heard that the people of Gaash had gathered against them to battle, because they had slain their king and their captains, for there had been fourteen captains in the city of Gaash, and the sons of Jacob had slain them all in the first battle.

15 And the sons of Jacob that day put on their weapons of war, and they marched to battle against the inhabitants of Gaash. In Gaash there was a strong and mighty people of the people of the Amorites; Gaash was the strongest and best fortified city of all the cities of the Amorites, and it had three walls.

16 The sons of Jacob came to Gaash and they found the gates of the city locked and about five hundred men standing at the top of the outer-most wall; a people numerous as the sand on the sea shore were in ambush for the sons of Jacob from outside the city at the rear.

17 And the sons of Jacob approached to open the gates of the city, and while they were drawing near to it, those who were in ambush at the rear of the city came forth from their places and surrounded the sons of Jacob.

18 The sons of Jacob were enclosed between the people of Gaash, and the battle was both to their front and rear; all the men that were on the wall were casting from the wall on them, arrows and stones.

19 And Judah, seeing that the men of Gaash were getting too strong for them, gave a most piercing and tremendous shriek and all the men of Gaash were terrified at the voice of Judah's cry; men fell from the wall at his powerful shriek and all those that were from without and within the city were greatly afraid of their lives.

20 And the sons of Jacob still came closer to break the doors of the city when the men of Gaash threw stones and arrows on them from the top of the wall, and made them flee from the gate.

21 The sons of Jacob returned against the men of Gaash who were with them from outside the city and they struck them terribly, as striking against gourds, and they could not stand against the sons of Jacob for fright and terror had seized them at the shriek of Judah.

22 The sons of Jacob killed all those men who were outside the city, and the sons of Jacob still drew nearer to make an entrance into the city and to fight under the city walls, but they could not for all the inhabitants of Gaash who remained in the city had surrounded the walls of Gaash in every direction; the sons of Jacob were unable to approach the city to fight with them.

23 The sons of Jacob came near to one corner to fight under the wall; the inhabitants of Gaash threw arrows and stones on them like showers of rain, and they fled from under the wall.

24 And the people of Gaash who were on the wall, seeing that the sons of Jacob could not prevail over them from under the wall, reproached the sons of Jacob in these words, saying,

25 What is the matter with you in the battle that you cannot prevail? Can you then do to the mighty city of Gaash and its inhabitants as you did to the cities of the Amorites that were not so powerful? Certainly to those weak ones among us you did those things and killed them in the entrance of the city, for they had no strength when they were terrified at the sound of your shouting.

26 And will you now then be able to fight in this place? Certainly here you will all die, and we will avenge the cause of those cities that you have laid waste.

27 And the inhabitants of Gaash greatly reproached the sons of Jacob and reviled them with their gods, and continued to cast arrows and stones on them from the wall.

28 Judah and his brothers heard the words of the inhabitants of Gaash and their anger was greatly roused, and Judah was zealous of his God in this matter, and he called out and said, O Lord, help, send help to us and our brothers.

29 And he ran at a distance with all his might with his drawn sword in his hand, and he sprang from the earth and by dint of his strength mounted the wall, and his sword fell from his hand.

30 And Judah shouted on the wall, and all the men that were on the wall were terrified; some of them fell from the wall into the city and died, and those who were yet on the wall, when they saw Judah's strength were greatly afraid and fled for their lives into the city for safety.

31 And some were emboldened to fight with Judah on the wall; they came close to kill him when they saw there was no sword in Judah's hand and they thought of casting him from the wall to his brothers; twenty men of the city came up to assist them, they surrounded Judah and all shouted over him, and approached him with drawn swords; they terrified Judah, and Judah cried out to his brothers from the wall.

32 And Jacob and his sons drew the bow from under the wall, and struck three of the men that were on the top of the wall, and Judah continued to cry and he exclaimed, O Lord help us, O Lord deliver us, and he cried out with a loud voice on the wall, and the cry was heard at a great distance.

33 After this cry he again repeated a shout, and all the men who surrounded Judah on the top of the wall were terrified; they each threw his sword from his hand at the sound of Judah's shouting and his tremor and fled.

34 Judah took the swords which had fallen from their hands and he fought with them and killed twenty of their men on the wall.

35 About eighty men and women still ascended the wall from the city and they all surrounded Judah, and the Lord impressed the fear of Judah in their hearts so that they were unable to approach him.

36 And Jacob and all who were with him drew the bow from under the wall, and they killed ten men on the wall; they fell below the wall in front of Jacob and his sons.

37 And the people on the wall seeing that twenty of their men had fallen still ran toward Judah with drawn swords, but they could not approach him for they were greatly terrified at Judah's strength.

38 And one of their mighty men whose name was Arud approached to strike Judah on the head with his sword, when Judah hastily put his shield to his head; the sword hit the shield and it was split in two.

39 This mighty man after he had struck Judah ran for his life at the fear of Judah, and his feet slipped on the wall and he fell among the sons of Jacob who were below the wall, and the sons of Jacob struck him and killed him.

40 And Judah's head pained him from the blow of the powerful man; Judah had nearly died from it.

41 And Judah cried out on the wall owing to the pain produced by the blow, when Dan heard him, and his anger burned within him; he also rose up and went a distance and ran and sprang from the earth and mounted the wall with his wrath-excited strength.

42 And when Dan came on the wall near to Judah, all the men on the wall fled who had stood against Judah; they went up to the second wall and they threw arrows and stones on Dan and Judah from the second wall and endeavored to drive them from the wall.

43 And the arrows and stones struck Dan and Judah and they had nearly been killed on the wall; wherever Dan and Judah fled from the wall they were attacked with arrows and stones from the second wall.

44 Jacob and his sons were still at the entrance of the city below the first wall, and they were not able to draw their bow

against the inhabitants of the city as they could not be seen by them, being on the second wall.

45 Dan and Judah, when they could no longer bear the stones and arrows that fell on them from the second wall, both sprang onto the second wall near the people of the city; when the people of the city who were on the second wall saw that Dan and Judah had come to them on the second wall, they all cried out and descended below between the walls.

46 Jacob and his sons heard the noise of the shouting from the people of the city and they were still at the entrance of the city; they were anxious about Dan and Judah who were not seen by them, they being on the second wall.

47 Naphtali went up with his wrath-excited might and sprang on the first wall to see what caused the noise of shouting which they had heard in the city; Issachar and Zebulun came near to break the doors of the city, and they opened the gates of the city and came into the city.

48 Naphtali leaped from the first wall to the second and came to assist his brothers; the inhabitants of Gaash who were on the wall, seeing that Naphtali was the third who had come up to assist his brothers, all fled and descended into the city, and Jacob and all his sons and all their young men came into the city to them.

49 Judah and Dan and Naphtali descended from the wall into the city and pursued the inhabitants of the city, and Simeon and Levi were from outside the city and didn't know that the gate was opened; they went up from there to the wall and came down to their brothers into the city.

50 The inhabitants of the city had all descended into the city and the sons of Jacob came to them from different directions; the battle waged against them from the front and the rear, and the sons of Jacob struck them terribly and killed about twenty thousand of them men and women; not one of them could stand up against the sons of Jacob.

51 And the blood flowed plentifully in the city, and it was like a brook of water; the blood flowed like a brook to the outer part of the city, and reached the desert of Bethchorin.

52 And the people of Bethchorin saw at a distance the blood flowing from the city of Gaash and about seventy men from among them ran to see the blood, and they came to the place where the blood was.

53 They followed the track of the blood and came to the wall of the city of Gaash, and they saw the blood issue from the city. They heard the voice of crying from the inhabitants of Gaash, for it ascended to heaven, and the blood was continuing to flow abundantly like a brook of water.

54 And all the sons of Jacob were still smiting the inhabitants of Gaash, and were engaged in slaying them till evening, about twenty thousand men and women. And the people of Chorin said, Certainly this is the work of the Hebrews, for they are still carrying on war in all the cities of the Amorites.

55 And those people hurried and ran to Bethchorin, and each took his weapons of war; they cried out to all the inhabitants of Bethchorin, who also put on their weapons of war to go and fight with the sons of Jacob.

56 When the sons of Jacob had done smiting the inhabitants of Gaash, they walked about the city to strip all the slain. Coming into the innermost part of the city and farther on they met three very powerful men, and there was no sword in their hand.

57 The sons of Jacob came up to the place where they were and the powerful men ran away; one of them had taken Zebulun, who he saw was a young lad and of short stature, and with his might dashed him to the ground.

58 And Jacob ran to him with his sword and Jacob struck him below his loins with the sword and cut him in two, and the body fell on Zebulun.

59 The second one approached and seized Jacob to fell him to the ground; Jacob turned to him and shouted to him, while Simeon and Levi ran and struck him on the hips with the sword and felled him to the ground.

60 And the powerful man rose up from the ground with wrath-excited might; Judah came to him before he had gained his footing and struck him on the head with the sword, and his head was split and he died.

61 The third powerful man, seeing that his companions were killed, ran from before the sons of Jacob and the sons of Jacob pursued him into the city; while the powerful man was fleeing he found one of the swords of the inhabitants of the city, he picked it up and turned to the sons of Jacob and fought them with that sword.

62 The powerful man ran to Judah to strike him on the head with the sword, and there was no shield in the hand of Judah; while he was aiming to strike him, Naphtali hastily took his shield and put it to Judah's head and the sword of the powerful man hit the shield of Naphtali, and Judah escaped the sword.

63 Simeon and Levi ran onto the powerful man with their swords and struck at him forcibly with their swords, and the two swords entered the body of the powerful man and divided it in two, length-wise.

64 And the sons of Jacob struck the three mighty men at that time, together with all the inhabitants of Gaash, and the day was about to decline.

65 And the sons of Jacob walked about Gaash and took all the spoil of the city, even the little ones and women they did not allow to live, and the sons of Jacob did to Gaash as they had done to Sarton and Shiloh.

CHAPTER 40

1 And the sons of Jacob led away all the spoil of Gaash, and went out of the city by night.

2 They were going out marching toward the castle of Bethchorin, and the inhabitants of Bethchorin were going to the castle to

meet them; on that night the sons of Jacob fought with the inhabitants of Bethchorin, in the castle of Bethchorin.

3 And all the inhabitants of Bethchorin were mighty men; one of them would not flee from before a thousand men, and they fought on that night on the castle; their shouts were heard on that night from afar and the earth quaked at their shouting.

4 And all the sons of Jacob were afraid of those men as they were not accustomed to fight in the dark, and they were greatly perplexed. The sons of Jacob cried to the Lord, saying, Give help to us O Lord, deliver us that we may not die by the hands of these uncircumcised men.

5 And the Lord listened to the voice of the sons of Jacob, and the Lord caused great terror and confusion to seize the people of Bethchorin; they fought among themselves with one another in the darkness of night, and struck each other in great numbers.

6 The sons of Jacob, knowing that the Lord had brought a spirit of perverseness among those men, and that they fought each man with his neighbor, went forth from among the bands of the people of Bethchorin and went as far as the descent of the castle of Bethchorin, and farther. They stayed there securely with their young men on that night.

7 And the people of Bethchorin fought the whole night, one man with his brother, and the other with his neighbor; they cried out in every direction on the castle and their cry was heard at a distance, and the whole earth shook at their voice for they were powerful above all the people of the earth.

8 And all the inhabitants of the cities of the Canaanites, the Hittites, the Amorites, the Hivites and all the kings of Canaan, and also those who were on the other side of the Jordan heard the noise of the shouting that night.

9 They said, Certainly these are the battles of the Hebrews who are fighting against the seven cities, who came near to them; who can stand against those Hebrews?

10 All the inhabitants of the cities of the Canaanites and all those who were on the other side of the Jordan were greatly afraid of the sons of Jacob, for they said, Behold the same will be done to us as was done to those cities, for who can stand against their mighty strength?

11 And the cries of the Chorinites were very great on that night and continued to increase; they struck each other till morning, and numbers of them were killed.

12 And the morning appeared; all the sons of Jacob rose up at daybreak and went up to the castle, and they struck those who remained of the Chorinites in a terrible manner and they were all killed in the castle.

13 And the sixth day appeared, and all the inhabitants of Canaan saw at a distance all the people of Bethchorin lying dead in the castle of Bethchorin, and scattered about as the carcasses of lambs and goats.

14 And the sons of Jacob led all the spoil which they had captured from Gaash and went to Bethchorin; they found the city full of people like the sand of the sea, and they fought with them, and the sons of Jacob struck them there till evening time.

15 And the sons of Jacob did to Bethchorin as they had done to Gaash and Tapnach, and as they had done to Chazar, to Sarton and to Shiloh.

16 The sons of Jacob took with them the spoil of Bethchorin and all the spoil of the cities, and on that day they went home to Shechem.

17 And the sons of Jacob came home to the city of Shechem and they remained outside the city, and then rested there from the war, and stayed there all night.

18 And all their servants together with all the spoil that they had taken from the cities, were left outside the city, and they did not enter the city, for they said, Perhaps there may yet be more fighting against us, and they may come to besiege us in Shechem.

19 Jacob and his sons and their servants remained that night and the next day in the portion of the field which Jacob had purchased from Hamor for five shekels, and all that they had captured was with them.

20 All the booty which the sons of Jacob had captured was in the portion of the field, immense as the sand on the seashore.

21 The inhabitants of the land observed them from afar, and they all were afraid of the sons of Jacob who had done this thing, for no king from the days of old had ever done the like.

22 The seven kings of the Canaanites resolved to make peace with the sons of Jacob, for they were greatly afraid for their lives on account of the sons of Jacob.

23 And on that day, being the seventh day, Japhia king of Hebron sent secretly to the king of Ai, and to the king of Gibeon, and to the king of Shalem, and to the king of Adulam, and to the king of Lachish, and to the king of Chazar, and to all the Canaanitish kings who were under their subjection, saying,

24 Go up with me, and come to me that we may go to the sons of Jacob, and I will make peace with them and form a treaty with them, that all your lands not be destroyed by the swords of the sons of Jacob as they did to Shechem and the cities around it, as you have heard and seen.

25 And when you come to me, do not come with many men, but let every king bring his three head captains and every captain bring three of his officers.

26 And come all of you to Hebron; we will go together to the sons of Jacob and request them to form a treaty of peace with us.

27 And all those kings did as the king of Hebron had sent to them, for they were all under his counsel and command, and all the kings of Canaan assembled to go to the sons of Jacob to make peace with them; the sons of Jacob returned and went to the portion of the field that was in Shechem, for they did not put confidence in the kings of the land.

28 And the sons of Jacob returned and remained in the portion of the field ten days, and no one came to make war with them.

29 When the sons of Jacob saw that there was no appearance of war, they all assembled and went to the city of Shechem, and the sons of Jacob remained in Shechem.

30 And at the expiration of forty days, all the kings of the Amorites assembled from all their places and came to Hebron, to Japhia, king of Hebron.

31 The number of kings that came to Hebron to make peace with the sons of Jacob was twenty-one kings, and the number of captains that came with them was sixty-nine, and their men were one hundred and eighty-nine; all these kings and their men rested by Mount Hebron.

32 And the king of Hebron went out with his three captains and nine men, and these kings resolved to go to the sons of Jacob to make peace.

33 They said to the king of Hebron, Go before us with your men, speak for us to the sons of Jacob, and we will come after you and confirm your words, and the king of Hebron did so.

34 The sons of Jacob heard that all the kings of Canaan had gathered together and rested in Hebron, and the sons of Jacob sent four of their servants as spies, saying, Go and spy these kings, and search and examine their men whether they are few or many, and if they are but few in number, count them all and come back.

35 And the servants of Jacob went secretly to these kings, and did as the sons of Jacob had commanded them. On that day they came back to the sons of Jacob, and said to them, We came to those kings, and they are few in number; we counted them all, and surely there were two hundred and eighty-eight, kings and men.

36 The sons of Jacob said, They are but few in number, therefore we will not all go out to them.   In the morning the sons of Jacob rose up and chose sixty-two of their men, and ten of the sons of Jacob went with them; and they put on their weapons of war, for they said, They are coming to make war with us. For they didn't know that they were coming to make peace with them.

37 And the sons of Jacob went with their servants to the gate of Shechem, toward those kings, and their father Jacob was with them.

38 And when they had come forth, there the king of Hebron and his three captains and nine men with him were coming along the road toward the sons of Jacob; the sons of Jacob lifted up their eyes, and saw at a distance Japhia, king of Hebron, with his captains, coming toward them, And the sons of Jacob took their stand at the place of the gate of Shechem, and did not proceed.

39 The king of Hebron continued to advance, he and his captains, until he came near to the sons of Jacob; he and his captains bowed down to them to the ground, and the king of Hebron sat with his captains in front of Jacob and his sons.

40 The sons of Jacob said to him, What has happened to you, O king of Hebron? Why have you come to us this day? What do you require from us? And the king of Hebron said to Jacob, I petition you my lord, all the kings of the Canaanites have this day come to make peace with you.

41 And the sons of Jacob heard the words of the king of Hebron; they would not consent to his proposals; the sons of Jacob had no faith in him, for they imagined that the king of Hebron had spoken deceitfully to them.

42 The king of Hebron knew from the words of the sons of Jacob that they did not believe his words, and the king of Hebron approached nearer to Jacob, and said to him, I beg you, my lord, to be assured that all these kings have come to you on peaceable terms, for they have not come with all their men, neither did they bring their weapons of war with them, for they have come to seek peace from my lord and his sons.

43 The sons of Jacob answered the king of Hebron, saying, Go to all these kings and if you speak truth to us, let them each come singly before us; if they come to us unarmed, we shall then know that they seek peace from us.

44 And Japhia, king of Hebron, sent one of his men to the kings and they all came before the sons of Jacob, and bowed down to them to the ground; these kings sat before Jacob and his sons and spoke to them, saying,

45 We have heard all that you did to the kings of the Amorites with your sword and greatly mighty arm, so that no man could stand up before you; we were afraid of you for the sake of our lives, that it would happen to us as it did to them.

46 So we have come to you to form a treaty of peace between us, and now therefore contract with us a covenant of peace and truth, that you will not meddle with us, inasmuch as we have not meddled with you.

47 And the sons of Jacob knew that they had really come to seek peace from them. And the sons of Jacob listened to them, and formed a covenant with them.

48 The sons of Jacob swore to them that they would not meddle with them, and all the kings of the Canaanites swore also to them, and the sons of Jacob made them pay tribute from that day forward.

49 And after this all the captains of these kings came with their men before Jacob, with presents in their hands for Jacob and his sons, and they bowed down to him to the ground.

50 These kings then urged the sons of Jacob and begged of them to return all the spoil they had captured from the seven cities of the Amorites, and the sons of Jacob did so; they returned all that they had captured, the women, the little ones, the cattle and all the spoil which they had taken, and they sent them off; they went away each to his city.

51 And all these kings again bowed down to the sons of Jacob, and they sent or brought them many gifts in those days; the sons of Jacob sent off these kings and their men, and they went peaceably away from them to their cities, and the sons of Jacob also returned to their home, to Shechem.

52 And there was peace from that day forward between the sons of Jacob and the kings of the Canaanites, until the children of Israel came to inherit the land of Canaan.

CHAPTER 41

1 At the revolution of the year the sons of Jacob journeyed from Shechem, and they came to Hebron, to their father Isaac; they lived there, but their flocks and herds they fed daily in Shechem, for there was there in those days good and fattening pasture. Jacob and his sons and all their household lived in the valley of Hebron.
2 It was in those days, in that year, being the hundred and sixth year of the life of Jacob, in the tenth year of Jacob's coming from Padan-aram, that Leah the wife of Jacob died; she was fifty-one years old when she died in Hebron.
3 Jacob and his sons buried her in the cave of the field of Machpelah, which is in Hebron, which Abraham had bought from the children of Heth for the possession of a burial place.
4 The sons of Jacob lived with their father in the valley of Hebron; all the inhabitants of the land knew their strength and their fame went throughout the land.
5 Joseph the son of Jacob and his brother Benjamin, the sons of Rachel, the wife of Jacob, were yet young in those days, and did not go out with their brothers during their battles in all the cities of the Amorites.
6 And when Joseph saw the strength of his brothers and their greatness, he praised them and extolled them, but he ranked himself greater than them and extolled himself above them; Jacob, his father, also loved him more than any of his sons for he was a son of his old age, and through his love toward him he made him a coat of many colors.
7 And when Joseph saw that his father loved him more than his brothers, he continued to elevate himself above his brothers, and he brought to his father evil reports concerning them.
8 The sons of Jacob seeing all of Joseph's conduct toward them, and that their father loved him more than any of them, hated him and could not ever speak peaceably to him.
9 Joseph was seventeen years old, and he was still magnifying himself above his brothers, and thought of raising himself above them.
10 At that time he dreamed a dream, and he came to his brothers and told them his dream, and he said to them, I dreamed a dream, and behold we were all binding sheaves in the field, and my sheaf rose and placed itself on the ground and your sheaves surrounded it and bowed down to it.
11 And his brothers answered him and said to him, What means this dream that you did dream? Do you imagine in your heart to reign or rule over us?
12 And he still came and told the thing to his father Jacob, and Jacob kissed Joseph when he heard these words from his mouth, and Jacob blessed Joseph.
13 When the sons of Jacob saw that their father had blessed Joseph and had kissed him, and that he loved him greatly, they became jealous of him and hated him all the more.
14 After this Joseph dreamed another dream and related the dream to his father in the presence of his brothers, and Joseph said to his father and brothers, Behold I have again dreamed a dream, and behold the sun and the moon and the eleven stars bowed down to me.
15 And his father heard the words of Joseph and his dream, and seeing that his brothers hated Joseph on account of this matter, Jacob therefore rebuked Joseph before his brothers on account of this thing, saying, What does this dream mean which you have dreamed, and this magnifying yourself before your brothers who are older than you are?
16 Do you imagine in your heart that I and your mother and your eleven brothers will come and bow down to you, that you speak these things?
17 And his brothers were jealous of him on account of his words and dreams; they continued to hate him, and Jacob reserved the dreams in his heart.
18 The sons of Jacob went one day to feed their father's flock in Shechem, for they were still herdsmen in those days; while the sons of Jacob were that day feeding in Shechem they delayed, and the time of gathering in the cattle was passed, and they had not arrived.
19 And Jacob saw that his sons were delayed in Shechem, and Jacob said within himself, Perhhaps the people of Shechem have risen up to fight against them, therefore they have delayed coming today.
20 And Jacob called Joseph his son and commanded him, saying, Behold your brothers are feeding in Shechem this day and look, they have not yet come back; therefore go and see where they are, and bring back word to me concerning the welfare of your brothers and the welfare of the flock.
21 And Jacob sent his son Joseph to the valley of Hebron; Joseph came for his brothers to Shechem, and could not find them, and Joseph went toward the field which was near Shechem to see where his brothers had turned. But he missed his road in the wilderness and didn't know which way he should go.
22 And an angel of the Lord found him wandering in the road toward the field, and Joseph said to the angel of the Lord, I

seek my brothers; have you not heard where they are feeding? And the angel of the Lord said to Joseph, I saw your brothers feeding here, and I heard them say they would go to feed in Dothan.

23 Joseph listened to the voice of the angel of the Lord, and he went to his brothers in Dothan and he found them in Dothan feeding the flock.

24 Joseph advanced to his brothers but before he had come near them, they had resolved to kill him.

25 Simeon said to his brothers, Behold the man of dreams is coming to us this day, so now come and let us kill him and cast him into one of the pits that are in the wilderness; when his father shall seek him from us, we will say an evil beast has devoured him.

26 Reuben heard the words of his brothers concerning Joseph and said to them, You should not do this thing, for how can we look up to our father Jacob? Cast him into this pit to die there, but do not put forth a hand on him to spill his blood. Reuben said this in order to deliver him from their hand, to bring him back to his father.

27 When Joseph came to his brothers he sat before them, and they rose upon him and seized him and struck him to the earth, and stripped the coat of many colors which he had on.

28 They took him and cast him into a pit and in the pit there was no water, but serpents and scorpions. And Joseph was afraid of the serpents and scorpions that were in the pit. Joseph cried out with a loud voice and the Lord hid the serpents and scorpions in the sides of the pit, and they did no harm to Joseph.

29 And Joseph called out from the pit to his brothers, and said to them, What have I done to you, and in what have I sinned? Why do you not fear the Lord concerning me? Am I not of your bones and flesh, and is not Jacob your father, my father? Why do you do this thing to me this day, and how will you be able to look up to our father Jacob?

30 And he continued to cry out and call to his brothers from the pit, and he said, O Judah, Simeon, and Levi, my brothers, lift me up from the place of darkness in which you have placed me, and come this day to have compassion on me, you children of the Lord and sons of Jacob my father. And if I have sinned to you, are you not the sons of Abraham, Isaac, and Jacob? If they saw an orphan they had compassion over him, or one that was hungry, they gave him bread to eat, or one that was thirsty, they gave him water to drink, or one that was naked, they covered him with garments!

31 And how then can you withhold your pity from your brother, for I am of your flesh and bones, and if I have sinned to you, certainly you will do this on account of my father!

32 Joseph spoke these words from the pit, and his brothers could not listen to him, nor incline their ears to the words of Joseph, and Joseph was crying and weeping in the pit.

33 And Joseph said, O that my father knew this day, the act which my brothers have done to me and the words which they have this day spoken to me.

34 All his brothers heard his cries and weeping in the pit, and his brothers went and removed themselves from the pit, so that they might not hear the cries of Joseph and his weeping in the pit.

CHAPTER 42

1 They went and sat on the opposite side, about the distance of a bow-shot, and they sat there to eat bread; while they were eating they held counsel together what was to be done with him, whether to kill him or to bring him back to his father.

2 They were holding the counsel when they lifted up their eyes, and saw at once there was a company of Ishmaelites coming at a distance by the road of Gilead, going down to Egypt.

3 And Judah said to them, What gain will it be to us if we kill our brother? Perhaps God will require him from us; this then is the counsel proposed concerning him, which you shall do to him: Look at this company of Ishmaelites going down to Egypt,

4 So now let us dispose of him to them and let not our hand be on him; they will lead him along with them and he will be lost among the people of the land and we will not put him to death with our own hands. And the proposal pleased his brothers and they did according to the word of Judah.

5 While they were discussing this matter and before the company of Ishmaelites had come up to them, seven trading men of Midian passed by them; as they passed they were thirsty and they lifted up their eyes and saw the same pit in which Joseph was held, and they looked and saw every species of bird was on him.

6 These Midianites ran to the pit to drink water for they thought that it contained water, and on coming to the pit they heard the voice of Joseph crying and weeping in there, and they looked down into the pit, and they saw there was a youth of good-looking appearance and well-favored.

7 They called to him and said, Who are you and who brought you here, and who placed you in this pit in the wilderness? And they all assisted to raise up Joseph and they drew him out and brought him up from the pit, and took him and went away on their journey and passed by his brothers.

8 And these said to them, Why do you do this, to take our servant from us and to go away? Certainly we placed this youth in the pit because he rebelled against us, and you come and bring him up and lead him away; now then give us back our servant.

9 And the Midianites answered and said to the sons of Jacob, Is this your servant, or does this man attend you? Perhaps you

are all his servants, for he is more handsome and well-favored than any of you, and why do you all speak falsely to us?

10 So we will not listen to your words nor give you our attention, for we found the youth in the pit in the wilderness and we took him; we will therefore go on.

11 And all the sons of Jacob approached them and rose up to them and said to them, Give us back our servant, and why will you all die by the edge of the sword? And the Midianites cried out against them and they drew their swords and approached to fight with the sons of Jacob.

12 Then Simeon rose up from his seat against them, and sprang on the ground and drew his sword and approached the Midianites and he gave a terrible shout before them, so that his shouting was heard at a distance, and the earth shook at Simeon's shouting.

13 The Midianites were terrified on account of Simeon and the noise of his shouting, and they fell on their faces and were excessively alarmed.

14 Simeon said to them, Surely I am Simeon, the son of Jacob the Hebrew, who have only with my brothers destroyed the city of Shechem and the cities of the Amorites; so shall God moreover do to me if all your brothers, the people of Midian, and also the kings of Canaan, were to come with you; they could not fight against me.

15 Now therefore give us back the youth whom you have taken, or I'll give your flesh to the birds of the skies and the beasts of the earth.

16 The Midianites were more afraid of Simeon, and they approached the sons of Jacob with terror and fright, and with pathetic words, saying,

17 Certainly you have said that the young man is your servant and that he rebelled against you, and therefore you placed him in the pit; what then will you do with a servant who rebels against his master? So now sell him to us, and we will give you all that you require for him. The Lord was pleased to do this in order that the sons of Jacob should not kill their brother.

18 And the Midianites saw that Joseph was of a good-looking appearance and well-favored; they desired him in their hearts and were urgent to purchase him from his brothers.

19 The sons of Jacob listened to the Midianites and they sold their brother Joseph to them for twenty pieces of silver. Reuben their brother was not with them, and the Midianites took Joseph and continued their journey to Gilead.

20 They were going along the road, and the Midianites repented of what they had done, in having purchased the young man, and one said to the other, What is this thing that we have done, in taking this youth from the Hebrews who is of good-looking appearance and well-favored?

21 Perhaps this youth is stolen from the land of the Hebrews, and why then have we done this thing? If he should be sought for and found in our hands we shall die through him.

22 Now certainly hardy and powerful men have sold him to us, the strength of one of whom you saw this day; perhaps they stole him from his land with their might and with their powerful arm, and have therefore sold him to us for the small value which we gave to them.

23 While they were thus discussing together, they looked and saw the company of Ishmaelites which was coming at first, and which the sons of Jacob saw, was advancing toward the Midianites; the Midianites said to each other, Come let us sell this youth to the company of Ishmaelites who are coming toward us. We will take for him the little that we gave for him, and we will be delivered from his evil.

24 And they did so, and they reached the Ishmaelites, and the Midianites sold Joseph to the Ishmaelites for twenty pieces of silver which they had given for him to his brothers.

25 And the Midianites went on their road to Gilead, and the Ishmaelites took Joseph and they let him ride on one of the camels, and they were leading him to Egypt.

26 When Joseph heard that the Ishmaelites were proceeding to Egypt, Joseph lamented and wept at this thing that he was to be so far removed from the land of Canaan, from his father, and he wept bitterly while he was riding on the camel. One of their men observed him, and made him go down from the camel and walk on foot, and still Joseph continued to cry and weep, and he said, O my father, my father.

27 One of the Ishmaelites rose up and struck Joseph on the cheek, and still he continued to weep; and Joseph was fatigued in the road, and was unable to proceed on account of the bitterness of his soul; they all struck him and afflicted him in the road, and they terrified him in order that he might cease from weeping.

28 And the Lord saw the condition of Joseph and his trouble, and the Lord brought down on those men darkness and confusion, and the hand of everyone that struck him became withered.

29 And they said to each other, What is this thing that God has done to us in the road? And they knew not that this befell them on account of Joseph. And the men proceeded on the road, and they passed along the road of Ephrath where Rachel was buried.

30 Joseph reached his mother's grave, and Joseph hurried and ran to his mother's grave, and fell on the grave and wept.

31 Joseph cried aloud on his mother's grave and said, O my mother, my mother, O you who did give me birth, awake now, and rise and see your son, how he has been sold for a slave, and no one to pity him.

32 O rise and see your son, weep with me on account of my troubles, and see the heart of my brothers.

33 Arouse my mother, arouse, awake from your sleep for me, and direct your battles against my brothers. O how have they stripped me of my coat and sold me already twice for a slave, and separated me from my father, and there is no one to pity

me.

34 Arouse and lay your cause against them before God, and see whom God will justify in the judgment, and whom he will condemn.

35 Rise, O my mother, rise, awake from your sleep and see my father how his soul is with me this day, and comfort him and ease his heart.

36 And Joseph continued to speak these words, and Joseph cried aloud and wept bitterly on his mother's grave; and he ceased speaking, and from bitterness of heart he became still as a stone on the grave.

37 And Joseph heard a voice speaking to him from beneath the ground, which answered him with bitterness of heart, and with a voice of weeping and praying in these words:

38 My son, my son Joseph, I have heard the voice of your weeping and the voice of your lamentation; I have seen your tears; I know your troubles, my son, and it grieves me for your sake, and abundant grief is added to my grief.

39 Now therefore my son, Joseph my son, hope in the Lord, and wait for him and do not fear, for the Lord is with you, he will deliver you from all trouble.

40 Rise my son, go down to Egypt with your masters and do not fear, for the Lord is with you, my son. And she continued to speak like these words to Joseph, and she was still.

41 And Joseph heard this, and he wondered greatly at this, and he continued to weep. After this one of the Ishmaelites observed him crying and weeping on the grave, and his anger was set ablaze against him, and he drove him from there, and he struck him and cursed him.

42 And Joseph said to the men, May I find grace in your sight to take me back to my father's house, and he will give you abundance of riches.

43 And they answered him, saying, Are you not a slave, and where is your father? And if you had a father you would not already twice have been sold for a slave for so little value; their anger was still roused against him, and they continued to strike him and to chastise him, and Joseph wept bitterly.

44 The Lord saw Joseph's affliction, and the Lord again struck these men, and chastised them, and the Lord caused darkness to envelope them on the earth, and the lightning flashed and the thunder roared, and the earth shook at the voice of the thunder and of the mighty wind; the men were terrified and knew not where they should go.

45 The beasts and camels stood still, and they led them, but they would not go, they struck them, and they crouched on the ground; the men said to each other, What is this that God has done to us? What are our transgressions and what are our sins that this thing has thus befallen us?

46 One of them answered and said to them, Perhaps on account of the sin of afflicting this slave has this thing happened this day to us; now we should implore him strongly to forgive us and then we shall know on whose account this evil befalls us; if God willl have compassion over us, then we shall know that all this comes to us on account of the sin of afflicting this slave.

47 And the men did so, and they supplicated Joseph and pressed him to forgive them; and they said, We have sinned to the Lord and to you, now therefore vouchsafe to request of your God that he shall put away this death from among us, for we have sinned to him.

48 Joseph did according to their words and the Lord listened to Joseph, and the Lord put away the plague which he had inflicted on those men on account of Joseph; the beasts rose up from the ground and they conducted them, and they went on; the raging storm abated and the earth became tranquilized and the men proceeded on their journey to go down to Egypt. The men knew that this evil had befallen them on account of Joseph.

49 And they said to each other, We now know that it was on account of his affliction that this evil befell us; now why shall we bring this death on our souls? Let us hold counsel what to do to this slave.

50 And one answered and said, Certainly he told us to bring him back to his father; so come, let us take him back and we will go to the place that he will tell us, and take from his family the price that we gave for him and we will then go away.

51 One answered again and said, Behold this counsel is very good, but we cannot do so for the way is very far from us, and we cannot leave our road.

52 One more answered and said to them, This is the counsel to be adopted, we will not swerve from it; behold we are this day going to Egypt and when we shall have come to Egypt, we will sell him there at a high price, and we will be delivered from his evil.

53 And this thing pleased the men and they did so; they continued their journey to Egypt with Joseph.

CHAPTER 43

1 When the sons of Jacob had sold their brother Joseph to the Midianites, their hearts were smitten on account of him and they repented of their acts, and they sought for him to bring him back but could not find him.

2 Reuben returned to the pit in which Joseph had been put in order to lift him out and restore him to his father; Reuben stood by the pit and heard not a word. He called out Joseph! Joseph! and no one answered or uttered a word.

3 And Reuben said, Joseph has died through fright, or some serpent has caused his death. Reuben descended into the pit, searched for Joseph and could not find him in the pit, and he came out again.

4 And Reuben tore his garments and he said, The child is not there, and how shall I reconcile my father about him if he is dead? He went to his brothers and found them grieving on account of Joseph, and counseling together how to appease their father about him. Reuben said to his brothers, I came to the pit and behold Joseph was not there, what then shall we say to our father, for my father will only seek the lad from me.

5 His brothers answered him saying, Thus and thus we did, and our hearts afterward struck us on account of this act, and we now sit to seek a pretext how we shall appease our father to it.

6 And Reuben said to them, What is this you have done to bring down the grey hairs of our father in sorrow to the grave? This thing is not good that you have done.

7 And Reuben sat with them, and they all rose up and swore to each other not to tell this thing to Jacob. They all said, The man who will tell this to our father or his household, or who will report this to any of the children of the land, we will all rise up against him and kill him with the sword.

8 And the sons of Jacob feared each other in this matter, from the youngest to the oldest; no one spoke a word, and they concealed the thing in their hearts.

9 Afterward they sat down to determine and invent something to say to their father Jacob concerning all these things.

10 Issachar said to them, Here is advice for you if it seems good in your eyes to do this thing. Take the coat which belongs to Joseph and tear it, and kill a kid of the goats and dip it in its blood.

11 And send it to our father and when he sees it he will say an evil beast has devoured him, therefore tear his coat and behold his blood will be on his coat, and by your doing this we shall be free of our father's murmurings.

12 Issachar's advice pleased them and they listened to him, and they did according to the word of Issachar which he had counselled them.

13 They hurried and took Joseph's coat and tore it, and they killed a kid of the goats and dipped the coat in the blood of the kid, and then trampled it into the dust. They sent the coat to their father Jacob by the hand of Naphtali, and they commanded him to say these words:

14 We had gathered in the cattle and had come as far as the road to Shechem and farther, when we found this coat on the road in the wilderness dipped in blood and in dust; now therefore know whether it is your son's coat or not.

15 And Naphtali went and he came to his father and he gave him the coat, and he spoke to him all the words which his brothers had commanded him.

16 Jacob saw Joseph's coat and he knew it and he fell on his face to the ground, and became as still as a stone Afterward he rose up and cried out with a loud and weeping voice and said, It is the coat of my son Joseph!

17 Jacob hurried and sent one of his servants to his sons, who went to them and found them coming along the road with the flock.

18 The sons of Jacob came to their father about evening, and behold their garments were torn and dust was on their heads, and they found their father crying out and weeping with a loud voice.

19 Jacob said to his sons, Tell me truly what evil have you this day suddenly brought on me? They answered their father Jacob, saying, We were coming along this day after the flock had been gathered in, and we came as far as the city of Shechem by the road in the wilderness; we found this coat filled with blood on the ground, and we knew it and we sent it to you so you could know it.

20 Jacob heard the words of his sons and he cried out with a loud voice, and he said, It is the coat of my son; an evil beast has devoured him. Joseph is rent in pieces, for I sent him this day to see whether it was well with you and well with the flocks and to bring me word again from you; he went as I commanded him, and this has happened to him today while I thought my son was with you.

21 And the sons of Jacob answered and said, He did not come to us, neither have we seen him from the time of our going out from you until now.

22 When Jacob heard their words he again cried out aloud, and he rose up and tore his garments; he put sackcloth on his loins and he wept bitterly; he mourned and lifted up his voice in weeping and exclaimed and said these words,

23 Joseph my son, O my son Joseph, I sent you this day after the welfare of your brothers, and behold you have been torn in pieces; through my hand has this happened to my son.

24 It grieves me for you Joseph my son, it grieves me for you; how sweet you were to me during life, and now how greatly bitter is your death to me.

25 0 that I had died in your stead Joseph my son, for it grieves me sadly for you my son, O my son, my son. Joseph my son, where are you, and where have you been drawn? Arouse, arouse from your place, and come and see my grief for you, O my son Joseph.

26 Come now and number the tears gushing from my eyes down my cheeks, and bring them up before the Lord, that his anger may turn from me.

27 0 Joseph my son, how did you fall, by the hand of one by whom no one had fallen from the beginning of the world to this day; for you have been put to death by the smiting of an enemy, inflicted with cruelty, but certainly I know that this has happened to you on account of the multitude of my sins.

28 Arise now and see how bitter is my trouble for you my son, although I did not rear you nor fashion you nor give you breath and soul, but it was God who formed you and built your bones and covered them with flesh and breathed in your

nostrils the breath of life, and then he gave you to me.

29 Now truly God who gave you to me, he has taken you from me; such then has happened to you.

30 And Jacob continued to speak like these words concerning Joseph, and he wept bitterly; he fell to the ground and became still.

31 All the sons of Jacob seeing their father's trouble repented of what they had done, and they also wept bitterly.

32 And Judah rose up and lifted his father's head from the ground, and placed it on his lap; he wiped his father's tears from his cheeks, and Judah wept a very great weeping while his father's head was reclining on his lap, still as a stone.

33 The sons of Jacob saw their father's trouble, and they lifted up their voices and continued to weep; Jacob was yet lying on the ground still as a stone.

34 And all his sons and his servants and his servant's children rose up and stood round him to comfort him, and he refused to be comforted.

35 The whole household of Jacob rose up and mourned a great mourning on account of Joseph and their father's trouble, and the sad news reached Isaac, the son of Abraham, the father of Jacob, and he wept bitterly on account of Joseph, he and all his household. He went from the place where he lived in Hebron, and his men with him, and he comforted Jacob his son but he refused to be comforted.

36 And after this, Jacob rose up from the ground, and his tears were running down his cheeks, and he said to his sons, Rise up and take your swords and your bows, and go forth into the field, and seek whether you can find my son's body and bring it to me that I may bury it.

37 Seek also, I pray you, among the beasts and hunt them, and that which shall come the first before you seize and bring it to me; perhaps the Lord will this day pity my affliction, and prepare before you that which tore my son in pieces; bring it to me, and I will avenge the cause of my son.

38 And his sons did as their father had commanded them, and they rose up early in the morning, and each took his sword and his bow in his hand, and they went forth into the field to hunt the beasts.

39 And Jacob was still crying aloud and weeping and walking to and fro in the house, and smiting his hands together, saying, Joseph my son, Joseph my son.

40 The sons of Jacob went into the wilderness to seize the beasts, and there a wolf came toward them; they seized him and brought him to their father and said to him, This is the first we have found, and we have brought him to you as you did command us, and your son's body we could not find.

41 And Jacob took the beast from the hands of his sons, and he cried out with a loud and weeping voice, holding the beast in his hand, and he spoke with a bitter heart to the beast, Why did you devour my son Joseph, and how did you have no fear of the God of the earth, or of my trouble for my son Joseph?

42 You did devour my son for nothing. He committed no violence. I was responsible for him. God will require him that is persecuted.

43 And the Lord opened the mouth of the beast in order to comfort Jacob with its words, and it answered Jacob and spoke these words to him,

44 As God lives who created us in the earth, and as your soul lives, my lord, I did not see your son, neither did I tear him to pieces, but from a distant land I also came to seek my son who went from me this day, and I know not whether he is living or dead.

45 And I came this day into the field to seek my son, and your sons found me, and seized me and increased my grief, and have this day brought me before you, and I have now spoken all my words to you.

46 Now therefore, O son of man, I am in your hands, and do to me this day as it may seem good in your sight, but by the life of God who created me, I did not see your son nor did I tear him to pieces, neither has the flesh of man entered my mouth all the days of my life.

47 When Jacob heard the words of the beast he was greatly astonished, and sent forth the beast from his hand, and she went her way.

48 And Jacob was still crying aloud and weeping for Joseph day after day, and he mourned for his son many days.

CHAPTER 44

1 The sons of Ishmael who had bought Joseph from the Midianites, who had bought him from his brothers, went to Egypt with Joseph. They came on the borders of Egypt and when they came near to Egypt, they met four men of the sons of Medan the son of Abraham, who had gone forth from the land of Egypt on their journey.

2 The Ishmaelites said to them, Do you desire to purchase this slave from us? And they said, Deliver him over to us, and they delivered Joseph over to them; they observed him that he was a very good-looking youth and they purchased him for twenty shekels.

3 The Ishmaelites continued their journey to Egypt and the Medanim also returned that day to Egypt. The Medanim said to each other, Look, we have heard that Potiphar, an officer of Pharaoh, captain of the guard, seeks a good servant who willl stand before him to attend him, and to make him overseer over his house and all belonging to him.

4 So let us sell him for what we may desire, if he is able to give us that which we shall require for him.

5 And these Medanim came to the house of Potiphar, and said to him, We have heard that you seek a good servant to attend you; here we have a servant that will please you, if you can give to us that which we may desire and we will sell him to you.

6 And Potiphar said, Bring him before me, and I will see him; if he please me I will give to you that which you may require for him.

7 And the Medanim went and brought Joseph and placed him before Potiphar, and he observed him, and he pleased him greatly and Potiphar said to them, Tell me what you require for this youth.

8 And they said, Four hundred pieces of silver we desire for him. Potiphar said, I will give it if you bring me the record of his sale to you and will tell me his history for perhaps he may be stolen, for this youth is neither a slave nor the son of a slave, but I observe in him the appearance of a goodly and handsome person.

9 And the Medanim went and brought to him the Ishmaelites who had sold him to them, and they told him, saying, He is a slave and we sold him to them.

10 And Potiphar heard the words of the Ishmaelites in his giving the silver to the Medanim, and the Medanim took the silver and went on their journey; the Ishmaelites also returned home.

11 Potiphar took Joseph and brought him to his house that he might serve him, and Joseph found favor in the sight of Potiphar; he placed confidence in him and made him overseer over his house, and all that belonged to him he delivered over into his hand.

12 And the Lord was with Joseph and he became a prosperous man; the Lord blessed the house of Potiphar for the sake of Joseph.

13 And Potiphar left all that he had in the hands of Joseph; Joseph was one that caused things to come in and go out, and everything was regulated by his wish in the house of Potiphar.

14 And Joseph was eighteen years old, a youth with beautiful eyes and of very good appearance, and no one was like him in all the land of Egypt.

15 At that time while he was in his master's house, going in and out of the house and attending his master, Zelicah, his master's wife lifted up her eyes toward Joseph and she looked at him, and behold he was a youth handsome and well-favored.

16 And she coveted his beauty in her heart, and her soul was fixed on Joseph, and she enticed him day after day, and Zelicah persuaded Joseph daily, but Joseph did not lift up his eyes to give attention to his master's wife.

17 And Zelicah said to him, How goodly are your appearance and form, truly I have looked at all the slaves and have not seen so beautiful a slave as you are. Joseph said to her, Certainly he who created me in my mother's womb created all mankind.

18 She said to him, How beautiful are your eyes, with which you have dazzled all the inhabitants of Egypt, men and women. He said to her, How beautiful they are while we are alive, but should you behold them in the grave, certainly you would move away from them.

19 And she said to him, How beautiful and pleasing are all your words; take now, I pray you, the harp which is in the house, and play with your hands and let us hear your words.

20 And he said to her, How beautiful and pleasing are my words when I speak the praise of my God and his glory. She said to him, How very beautiful is the hair of your head, find the golden comb which is in the house, take it I pray you, and curl the hair of your head.

21 And he said to her, How long will you speak these words? Stop uttering these words to me, and rise and attend to your domestic affairs.

22 And she said to him, There is no one in my house, and there is nothing to attend to but to your words and to your wish. Yet in spite of all this, she could not bring Joseph to her, neither did he place his eyes on her, but directed his eyes below to the ground.

23 Zelicah desired Joseph in her heart that he should lie with her; at the time that Joseph was sitting in the house doing his work, Zelicah came and sat before him, and she enticed him daily with her discourse to lie with her, or even to look at her, but Joseph would not listen to her.

24 And she said to him, If you will not do according to my words, I will treat you with the punishment of death, and put an iron yoke on you.

25 And Joseph said to her, Certainly God who created man loosens the fetters of prisoners, and it is he who will deliver me from your prison and from your judgment.

26 When she could not persuade him and her soul being still fixed on him, her desire threw her into a grave sickness.

27 All the women of Egypt came to visit her and said to her, Why are you in this declining state? You lack nothing; certainly your husband is a great and esteemed prince in the sight of the king, should you lack anything of what your heart desires?

28 Zelicah answered them, saying, This day it shall be made known to you from where this disorder comes which you see in me, and she commanded her maid servants to prepare food for all the women; she made a banquet for them, and all the women ate in the house of Zelicah.

29 And she gave them knives to peel the citrons to eat them, and she commanded that they should dress Joseph in costly garments, that he should appear before them, and Joseph came before their eyes and all the women looked on Joseph and

could not take their eyes from off him; they all cut their hands with the knives that they had in their hands, and all the citrons that were in their hands were filled with blood.

30 And they knew not what they had done but they continued to look at the beauty of Joseph, and did not turn their eyelids from him.

31 Zelicah saw what they had done, and she said to them, What is this work that you have done? Look, I gave you citrons to eat and you have all cut your hands.

32 And all the women saw their hands, and truly they were full of blood, and their blood flowed down on their garments. They said to her, This slave in your house has overcome us, and we could not turn our eyelids from him on account of his beauty.

33 She said to them, Certainly this happened to you in the moment that you looked at him, and you could not contain yourselves from him; how then can I refrain when he is constantly in my house, and I see him day after day going in and out of my house? How then can I keep from declining or even from perishing on account of this?

34 And they said to her, The words are true, for who can see this beautiful form in the house and refrain from him, and is he not your slave and attendant in your house, and why do you not tell him that which is in your heart, but allow your soul to perish through this matter?

35 And she said to them, I am daily endeavoring to persuade him, and he will not consent to my wishes; I promised him everything that is good, and yet I could meet with no return from him; I am therefore in a declining state as you see.

36 Zelicah became very ill on account of her desire toward Joseph, and she was desperately lovesick on account of him; but all the people of the house of Zelicah and her husband knew nothing of this matter, that Zelicah was ill on account of her love to Joseph.

37 All the people of her house asked her, saying, Why are you ill and declining, and lack nothing? And she said to them, I know not this thing which daily is increasing on me.

38 All the women and her friends came daily to see her, and they spoke with her, and she said to them, This can only be through the love of Joseph. They said to her, Entice him and seize him secretly; perhaps he may listen to you and put off this death from you.

39 And Zelicah became worse from her love to Joseph, and she continued to decline, till she scarcely had strength to stand.

40 On a certain day Joseph was doing his master's work in the house, and Zelicah came secretly and fell suddenly on him; Joseph rose up against her, he was more powerful than she, and he brought her down to the ground.

41 And Zelicah wept on account of the desire of her heart toward him, and she begged him with weeping, and her tears flowed down her cheeks; she spoke to him in a voice of pleading and in bitterness of soul, saying,

42 Have you ever heard, seen or known of so beautiful a woman as I am, or better than myself, who speaks daily to you, falls into a decline through love for you, confers all this honor on you, and still you will not listen to my voice?

43 If it be through fear of your master that he punish you, as the king lives no harm shall come to you from your master through this thing; now, therefore do listen to me, and consent for the sake of the honor which I have conferred on you, and put off this death from me, for why should I die for your sake? And she ceased to speak.

44 And Joseph answered her, saying, Keep away from me, and leave this matter to my master; behold my master knows not what there is with me in the house, for all that belongs to him he has delivered into my hands, and how shall I do these things in my master's house?

45 For he has also greatly honored me in his house, and he has also made me overseer over his house, and he has exalted me, and there is no one greater in this house than I am, and my master has refrained nothing from me, excepting you who are his wife. How then can you speak these words to me, and how can I do this great evil and sin to God and to your husband?

46 Now therefore keep away from me, and speak no more such words as these, for I will not listen to your words. But Zelicah would not listen to Joseph when he spoke these words to her; she daily enticed him to listen to her.

47 It was after this that the brook of Egypt was filled above all its sides, and all the inhabitants of Egypt went forth, and also the king and princes went forth with timbrels and dances, for it was a great rejoicing in Egypt and a holiday at the time of the overflow of the sea Sihor, and they went there to rejoice all the day.

48 And when the Egyptians went out to the river to rejoice, as was their custom, all the people of the house of Potiphar went with them. But Zelicah would not go with them for she said, I am unable to. She remained alone in the house, and no other person was with her in the house.

49 And she rose up and ascended to her temple in the house, and dressed herself in princely garments, and she placed on her head precious stones of onyx stones, inlaid with silver and gold, and she beautified her face and skin with all sorts of women's purifying liquids, and she perfumed the temple and the house with cassia and frankincense, and she spread myrrh and aloes. Afterward she sat in the entrance of the temple, in the passage of the house, through which Joseph passed to do his work, and then Joseph came from the field and entered the house to do his master's work.

50 He came to the place through which he had to pass and saw all the work of Zelicah, and he turned back.

51 Zelicah saw Joseph turning back from her; she called out to him, saying What ails you Joseph? Come to your work, and look, I will make room for you until you will have passed to your seat.

52 And Joseph returned and came to the house, and passed from there to the place of his seat, and he sat down to do his master's work as usual and behold Zelicah came to him and stood before him in princely garments, and the scent from her

clothes was spread some distance.

53 She hurried and caught hold of Joseph and his garments, and said to him, As the king lives if you will not perform my request you shall die this day. And she hurried and stretched forth her other hand and drew a sword from beneath her garments, and she placed it on Joseph's neck; she said, Rise and perform my request, and if not you will die this day.

54 Joseph was afraid of her doing this thing, and he rose up to flee from her; she seized the front of his garments, and in the terror of his flight the garment which Zelicah seized was torn; Joseph left the garment in the hand of Zelicah and he fled and got out, for he was afraid.

55 When Zelicah saw that Joseph's garment was torn and that he had left it in her hand, and had fled, she was afraid for her life, that the report should spread concerning her. She rose up and acted with cunning and put off the garments in which she was dressed, and she put on her other garments.

56 She took Joseph's garment and laid it beside her, and she went and seated herself in the place where she had sat in her illness, before the people of her house had gone out to the river. She called a young lad who was then in the house, and she ordered him to call the people of the house to her.

57 And when she saw them she said to them with a loud voice and lamentation, See what a Hebrew your master has brought to me in the house, for he came this day to lie with me.

58 For when you had gone out he came to the house, and seeing that there was no person in the house, he came to me and caught hold of me with intent to lie with me.

59 And I seized his garments and tore them and called out against him with a loud voice, and when I had lifted up my voice he was afraid for his life and left his garment before me, and fled.

60 The people of her house spoke nothing, but their wrath was very much set ablaze against Joseph, and they went to his master and told him the words of his wife.

61 Potiphar came home enraged, and his wife cried out to him, saying, What is this thing that you have done to me in bringing a Hebrew servant into my house, for he came to me this day to sport with me; thus did he do to me this day.

62 Potiphar heard the words of his wife and ordered Joseph to be punished with severe stripes, and they did so to him.

63 While they were smiting him, Joseph called out with a loud voice, and he lifted up his eyes to heaven, and he said, O Lord God, you know that I am innocent of all these things, and why shall I die this day through falsehood, by the hand of these uncircumcised wicked men whom you know?

64 And while Potiphar's men were beating Joseph, he continued to cry out and weep, and there was a child there eleven months old, and the Lord opened the mouth of the child, and he spake these words before Potiphar's men, who were smiting Joseph, saying,

65 What do you want of this man, and why do you do this evil to him? My mother speaks falsely and utters lies; thus was the transaction.

66 And the child told them accurately all that happened, and all the words of Zelicah to Joseph day after day did he relate to them.

67 And all the men heard the words of the child and they wondered greatly at the child's words, and the child ceased to speak and became still.

68 Potiphar was very much ashamed at the words of his son, and he commanded his men not to beat Joseph anymore, and the men ceased beating Joseph.

69 Potiphar took Joseph and ordered him to be brought to justice before the priests, who were judges belonging to the king, in order to judge him concerning this affair.

70 Potiphar and Joseph came before the priests who were the king's judges, and he said to them, Decide I beg you, what judgment is due to a servant, for thus has he done.

71 And the priests said to Joseph, Why did you do this thing to your master? and Joseph answered them, saying, Not so my lords, thus was the matter; and Potiphar said to Joseph, Certainly I entrusted in your hands all that belonged to me, and I withheld nothing from you but my wife, and how could you do this evil?

72 And Joseph answered saying, Not so my lord, as the Lord lives, and as your soul lives, my lord, the word which you did hear from your wife is untrue, for thus was the affair this day.

73 A year has elapsed to me since I have come to your house; have you seen any iniquity in me, or any thing which might cause you to demand my life?

74 The priests said to Potiphar, Send, we pray you, and let them bring before us Joseph's torn garment, and let us see the tear in it, and if it shall be that the tear is in front of the garment, then his face must have been opposite to her and she must have caught hold of him to come to her, and with deceit did your wife do all that she has spoken.

75 They brought Joseph's garment before the priests who were judges, and they saw and behold the tear was in front of Joseph, and all the judging priests knew that she had pressed him, and they said, The judgment of death is not due to this slave for he has done nothing, but his judgment is that he be placed in the prison house on account of the report, which through him has gone forth against your wife.

76 Potiphar heard their words and he placed him in the prison house, the place where the king's prisoners are confined, and Joseph was in the house of confinement twelve years.

77 And in spite of this, his master's wife did not turn from him, and she did not cease from speaking to him day after day to

listen to her, and at the end of three months Zelicah continued going to Joseph to the house of confinement day by day, and she enticed him to listen to her, and Zelicah said to Joseph, How long will you remain in this house? But listen now to my voice, and I will bring you out of this house.

78 And Joseph answered her, saying, It is better for me to remain in this house than to listen to your words, to sin against God; she said to him, If you will not perform my wish, I will pluck out your eyes, add fetters to your feet, and will deliver you into the hands of them whom you did not know before.

79 Joseph answered her and said, Behold the God of the whole earth is able to deliver me from all that you can do to me, for he opens the eyes of the blind, and loosens those that are bound, and preserves all strangers who are unacquainted with the land.

80 And when Zelicah was unable to persuade Joseph to listen to her, she ceased going to entice him; Joseph was still confined in the house of confinement. And Jacob the father of Joseph, and all his brothers who were in the land of Canaan still mourned and wept in those days on account of Joseph, for Jacob refused to be comforted for his son Joseph, and Jacob cried aloud and wept and mourned all those days.

CHAPTER 45

1 It was in that year, which is the year of Joseph's going down to Egypt after his brothers had sold him, that Reuben the son of Jacob went to Timnah and took a wife Eliuram, the daughter of Avi the Canaanite, and he came to her.

2 And Eliuram the wife of Reuben conceived and gave birth, to him: Hanoch, Palu, Chetzron and Carmi, four sons; and Simeon his brother took his sister Dinah for a wife, and she gave birth to, to him: Memuel, Yamin, Ohad, Jachin and Zochar, five sons.

3 Afterward he came to Bunah the Canaanitish woman, the same is Bunah whom Simeon took captive from the city of Shechem, and Bunah was before Dinah and attended to her; Simeon came to her, and she gave birth to him, Saul.

4 And Judah went at that time to Adulam, and he came to a man of Adulam, and his name was Hirah; Judah saw there the daughter of a man from Canaan, and her name was Aliyath, the daughter of Shua. He took her and came to her, and Aliyath gave birth to, to Judah: Er, Onan and Shiloh, three sons.

5 Levi and Issachar went to the land of the east, and they took to themselves for wives the daughters of Jobab the son of Yoktan, the son of Eber; Jobab the son of Yoktan had two daughters; the name of the elder was Adinah, and the name of the younger was Aridah.

6 And Levi took Adinah, and Issachar took Aridah, and they came to the land of Canaan, to their father's house; Adinah gave birth to, to Levi: Gershon, Kehath and Merari, three sons.

7 And Aridah gave birth to, to Issachar: Tola, Puvah, Job and Shomron, four sons; Dan went to the land of Moab and took for a wife Aphlaleth, the daughter of Chamudan the Moabite, and he brought her to the land of Canaan.

8 Aphlaleth was unable to conceive, she had no children, and God afterward remembered Aphlaleth the wife of Dan, and she conceived and gave birth to a son; she called his name Chushim.

9 And Gad and Naphtali went to Haran and took from there the daughters of Amuram the son of Uz, the son of Nahor, for wives.

10 And these are the names of the daughters of Amuram: the name of the elder was Merimah, and the name of the younger Uzith; Naphtali took Merimah, and Gad took Uzith and brought them to the land of Canaan, to their father's house.

11 And Merimah gave birth to, to Naphtali: Yachzeel, Guni, Jazer and Shalem, four sons; and Uzith gave birth to, to Gad: Zephion, Chagi, Shuni, Ezbon, Eri, Arodi and Arali, seven sons.

12 Asher went forth and took Adon the daughter of Aphlal, the son of Hadad, the son of Ishmael, for a wife and he brought her to the land of Canaan.

13 And Adon the wife of Asher died in those days, she had no children; it was after the death of Adon that Asher went to the other side of the river and took for a wife Hadurah the daughter of Abimael, the son of Eber, the son of Shem.

14 The young woman was of a beautiful appearance and a woman of sense, and she had been the wife of Malkiel the son of Elam, the son of Shem.

15 Hadurah gave birth to a daughter to Malkiel, and he called her name Serach, and Malkiel died after this and Hadurah went and remained in her father's house.

16 After the death of the wife at Asher he went and took Hadurah for a wife, and brought her to the land of Canaan, and Serach her daughter he also brought with them; she was three years old and the child was brought up in Jacob's house.

17 And the girl was of a beautiful appearance and she went in the holy ways of the children of Jacob; she lacked nothing, and the Lord gave her wisdom and understanding.

18 Hadurah the wife of Asher conceived and gave birth to, to him: Yimnah, Yishvah, Yishvi and Beriah, four sons.

19 Zebulun went to Midian and took for a wife Merishah the daughter of Molad, the son of Abida, the son of Midian, and brought her to the land of Canaan.

20 And Merushah gave birth to, to Zebulun: Sered, Elon and Yachleel, three sons.

21 Jacob sent to Aram, the son of Zoba, the son of Terah, and he took for his son Benjamin Mechalia the daughter of Aram,

and she came to the land of Canaan to the house of Jacob; Benjamin was ten years old when he took Mechalia the daughter of Aram for a wife.

22 And Mechalia conceived and gave birth to, to Benjamin: Bela, Becher, Ashbel, Gera and Naaman, five sons; Benjamin afterward went and took for a wife Aribath, the daughter of Shomron, the son of Abraham, in addition to his first wife, and he was eighteen years old; Aribath gave birth to, to Benjamin: Achi, Vosh, Mupim, Chupim, and Ord, five sons.

23 In those days Judah went to the house of Shem and took Tamar the daughter of Elam, the son of Shem, for a wife for his first born Er.

24 And Er came to his wife Tamar, and she became his wife; when he came to her he outwardly destroyed his offspring, and his work was evil in the sight of the Lord, and the Lord killed him.

25 It was after the death of Er, Judah's first born, that Judah said to Onan, Go to your brother's wife and marry her as the next of kin and raise up children to your brother.

26 And Onan took Tamar for a wife and he came to her; Onan also did like the work of his brother, and his work was evil in the sight of the Lord, and he killed him also.

27 When Onan died, Judah said to Tamar, Remain in your father's house until my son Shiloh will have grown up; Judah had no more delight in Tamar, to give her to Shiloh, for he said, Perhaps he will also die like his brothers.

28 And Tamar rose up and went and remained in her father's house, and Tamar was in her father's house for some time.

29 At the revolution of the year, Aliyath the wife of Judah died; Judah was comforted for his wife, and after the death of Aliyath, Judah went up with his friend Hirah to Timnah to shear their sheep.

30 Tamar heard that Judah had gone up to Timnah to shear the sheep, and that Shiloh was grown up, and Judah did not delight in her.

31 And Tamar rose up and put off the garments of her widowhood; she put on a veil and entirely covered herself; she went and sat in the public thoroughfare which is on the road to Timnah.

32 Judah passed and saw her and took her and he came to her, and she conceived by him; at the time of being delivered there were twins in her womb, and he called the name of the first Perez and the name of the second Zarah.

CHAPTER 46

1 In those days Joseph was still confined in the prison house in the land of Egypt.

2 At that time the attendants of Pharaoh were standing before him, the chief of the butlers and the chief of the bakers which belonged to the king of Egypt.

3 And the butler took wine and placed it before the king to drink, and the baker placed bread before the king to eat, and the king drank of the wine and ate of the bread; he and his servants and ministers that ate at the king's table.

4 And while they were eating and drinking, the butler and the baker remained there, and Pharaoh's ministers found many flies in the wine which the butler had brought, and stones of nitre were found in the baker's bread.

5 And the captain of the guard placed Joseph as an attendant on Pharaoh's officers, and Pharaoh's officers were in confinement one year.

6 At the end of the year, they both dreamed dreams in one night, in the place of confinement where they were, and in the morning Joseph came to them to attend on them as usual. He saw them and their countenances were dejected and sad.

7 And Joseph asked them, Why are your countenances sad? They said, we dreamed a dream and there was no one here to interpret it. Joseph said to them, Relate, I pray you, your dream to me, and God shall give you an answer of peace as you desire.

8 The butler related his dream to Joseph and said, I saw in my dream there was a large vine before me and on that vine I saw three branches; the vine speedily blossomed and reached a great height, and its clusters were ripened and became grapes.

9 And I took the grapes and pressed them in a cup, and placed it in Pharaoh's hand and he drank; and Joseph said to him, The three branches that were on the vine are three days.

10 Yet within three days, the king will order you to be brought out and he will restore you to your office; you shall give the king his wine to drink as at first when you were his butler; but let me find favor in your sight, so that you shall remember me to Pharaoh when it will be well with you; do this kindness to me and get me brought forth from this prison, for I was stolen away from the land of Canaan and was sold for a slave in this place.

11 Also that which was told you concerning my master's wife is false, for they placed me in this dungeon for nothing. The butler answered Joseph, saying, If the king deals well with me as at first, as you last interpreted to me, I will do all that you desire and get you brought out of this dungeon.

12 And the baker, seeing that Joseph had accurately interpreted the butler's dream, also approached and related the whole of his dream to Joseph.

13 He said to him, In my dream I looked and there were three white baskets on my head; I looked again and then there were in the upper-most basket all manner of baked meats for Pharaoh; there the birds were eating them from off my head.

14 And Joseph said to him, The three baskets which you saw are three days, yet within three days Pharaoh will take off your

head and hang you on a tree, and the birds will eat your flesh from off you, as you saw in your dream.

15 In those days the queen was about to be delivered, and on that day she gave birth to a son to the king of Egypt; they announced that the king had gotten his firstborn son and all the people of Egypt together with the officers and servants of Pharaoh rejoiced greatly.

16 On the third day of his birth Pharaoh made a feast for his officers and servants, for the hosts of the land of Zoar and of the land of Egypt.

17 And all the people of Egypt and the servants of Pharaoh came to eat and drink with the king at the feast of his son, and to rejoice at the king's rejoicing.

18 All the officers of the king and his servants were rejoicing at that time for eight days at the feast, and they made merry with all sorts of musical instruments, with timbrels and with dances in the king's house for eight days.

19 And the butler, to whom Joseph had interpreted his dream, forgot Joseph and did not mention him to the king as he had promised, for this thing was from the Lord in order to punish Joseph because he had trusted in man.

20 And Joseph remained after this in the prison house two years, until he had completed twelve years.

CHAPTER 47

1 Isaac the son of Abraham was still living in those days in the land of Canaan; he was very aged, one hundred and eighty years old, and Esau his son, the brother of Jacob, was in the land of Edom; he and his sons had possessions in it among the children of Seir.

2 And Esau heard that his father's time was drawing near to die, and he and his sons and household came to the land of Canaan to his father's house.   Jacob and his sons went forth from the place where they lived in Hebron and they all came to their father Isaac, and they found Esau and his sons in the tent.

3 And Jacob and his sons sat before his father Isaac, and Jacob was still mourning for his son Joseph.

4 And Isaac said to Jacob, Bring your sons here to me and I will bless them; and Jacob brought his eleven children before his father Isaac.

5 And Isaac placed his hands on all the sons of Jacob, and he took hold of them and embraced them, and kissed them one by one. Isaac blessed them on that day and he said to them, May the God of your fathers bless you and increase your offspring like the stars of heaven for number.

6 Isaac also blessed the sons of Esau, saying, May God cause you to be a dread and a terror to all that will behold you, and to all your enemies.

7 Isaac called Jacob and his sons and they all came and sat before Isaac, and Isaac said to Jacob, The Lord God of the whole earth said to me, Unto your offspring I will give this land for an inheritance if your children keep my statutes and my ways, and I will perform to them the oath which I swore to your father Abraham.

8 Now therefore my son, teach your children and your children's children to fear the Lord, and to go in the good way which will please the Lord your God, for if you keep the ways of the Lord and his statutes the Lord will also keep to you his covenant with Abraham, and will do well with you and your descendants always.

9 When Isaac had finished commanding Jacob and his children, he gave up the ghost and died, and was gathered to his people.

10 And Jacob and Esau fell on the face of their father Isaac, and they wept, and Isaac was one hundred and eighty years old when he died in the land of Canaan, in Hebron. His sons carried him to the cave of Machpelah, which Abraham had bought from the children of Heth for a possession of a burial place.

11 And all the kings of the land of Canaan went with Jacob and Esau to bury Isaac, and all the kings of Canaan showed Isaac great honor at his death.

12 The sons of Jacob and the sons of Esau went barefooted round about, walking and lamenting until they reached Kireath-arba.

13 And Jacob and Esau buried their father Isaac in the cave of Machpelah, which is in Kireath-arba in Hebron; they buried him with very great honor, as at the funeral of kings.

14 Jacob and his sons, and Esau and his sons, and all the kings of Canaan made a great and heavy mourning, and they buried him and mourned for him many days.

15 At the death of Isaac, he left his cattle and his possessions and all belonging to him to his sons; and Esau said to Jacob, Behold I pray you, all that our father has left we will divide into two parts, and I will have the choice; Jacob said, We will do so.

16 Jacob took all that Isaac had left in the land of Canaan, the cattle and the property, and he placed them in two parts before Esau and his sons, and he said to Esau, Behold all this is before you, choose to yourself the half which you will take.

17 And Jacob said to Esau, Hear I pray you what I will speak to you, saying, The Lord God of heaven and earth spoke to our fathers Abraham and Isaac, saying, Unto your descendants will I give this land for an inheritance forever.

18 Now therefore all that our father has left is before you, and behold all the land is before you; choose from them what you desire.

19 If you desire the whole land take it for you and your children forever, and I will take these riches, and if you desire the riches take them with you, and I will take this land for me and for my children to inherit forever.

20 Nebayoth, the son of Ishmael, was then in the land with his children, and Esau went on that day and consulted with him, saying,

21 Thus has Jacob spoken to me; thus has he answered me, now give your advice and we will listen.

22 And Nebayoth said, What is this that Jacob hath spoken to you? Behold all the children of Canaan are dwelling securely in their land, and Jacob says he will inherit it with his descendants all the days.

23 Go now therefore and take all your father's riches and leave Jacob your brother in the land, as he has spoken.

24 And Esau rose up and returned to Jacob, and did all that Nebayoth the son of Ishmael had advised; and Esau took all the riches that Isaac had left, the souls, the beasts, the cattle and the property, and all the riches; he gave nothing to his brother Jacob, and Jacob took all the land of Canaan, from the brook of Egypt to the river Euphrates, and he took it for an everlasting possession, and for his children and for his descendants after him forever.

25 Jacob also took from his brother Esau the cave of Machpelah, which is in Hebron, which Abraham had bought from Ephron for a possession of a burial place for him and his descendants forever.

26 And Jacob wrote all these things in the book of purchase, and he signed it, and testified all this with four faithful witnesses.

27 These are the words which Jacob wrote in the book, saying: The land of Canaan and all the cities of the Hittites, the Hivites, the Jebusites, the Amorites, the Perizzites, and the Gergashites, all the seven nations from the river of Egypt to the river Euphrates.

28 And the city of Hebron Kireath-arba, and the cave which is in it, the whole did Jacob buy from his brother Esau for value, for a possession and for an inheritance for his descendants after him forever.

29 And Jacob took the book of purchase and the signature, the command and the statutes and the revealed book, and he placed them in an earthen vessel in order that they should remain for a long time, and he delivered them into the hands of his children.

30 Esau took all that his father had left him after his death from his brother Jacob, and he took all the property, from man and beast, camel and ass, ox and lamb, silver and gold, stones and bdellium, and all the riches which had belonged to Isaac the son of Abraham; there was nothing left which Esau did not take to himself from all that Isaac had left after his death.

31 Esau took all this and he and his children went home to the land of Seir the Horite, away from his brother Jacob and his children.

32 And Esau had possessions among the children of Seir, and Esau returned not to the land of Canaan from that day forward.

33 The whole land of Canaan became an inheritance to the children of Israel for an everlasting inheritance, and Esau with all his children inherited the mountain of Seir.

CHAPTER 48

1 In those days, after the death of Isaac, the Lord commanded and caused a famine on the whole earth.

2 At that time Pharaoh, king of Egypt, was sitting on his throne in the land of Egypt; he lay in his bed and dreamed dreams and Pharaoh saw in his dream that he was standing by the side of the river of Egypt.

3 While he was standing he saw seven fat fleshed and well favored cattle come up out of the river.

4 And seven other cattle, lean fleshed and ill favored, came up after them, and the seven ill favored ones swallowed up the well favored ones, and still their appearance was ill as at first.

5 And he awoke; he slept again and he dreamed a second time, and he saw seven ears of corn come up on one stalk, full and good, and seven thin ears blasted with the east wind sprang up after them, and the thin ears swallowed up the full ones, then Pharaoh awoke out of his dream.

6 In the morning the king remembered his dreams and his spirit was sadly troubled on account of his dreams, and the king hurried, sent and called for all the magicians of Egypt and the wise men, and they came and stood before Pharaoh.

7 And the king said to them, I have dreamed dreams, and there is none to interpret them; they said to the king, relate your dreams to your servants and let us hear them.

8 And the king related his dreams to them, and they all answered and said with one voice to the king, May the king live forever; this is the interpretation of your dreams.

9 The seven good cattle which you saw denotes seven daughters that will be born to you in the latter days, and the seven cattle which you saw come up after them and swallowed them up, are for a sign that the daughters which will be born to you will all die in the lifetime of the king.

10 And that which you saw in the second dream of seven full good ears of corn coming up on one stalk, this is their interpretation: that you will build to yourself in the latter days seven cities throughout the land of Egypt; that which you saw of the seven poor ears of corn springing up after them and swallowing them up while you saw them with your eyes, is for a sign that the cities which you will build will all be destroyed in the latter days, in the lifetime of the king.

11 And when they spoken these words the king did not incline his ear to their words, neither did he fix his heart on them, for

the king knew in his wisdom that they did not give a proper interpretation of the dreams; when they had finished speaking before the king, he answered them, saying, What is this thing that you have spoken to me? Certainly you have uttered falsely and spoken lies; therefore now give the proper interpretation of my dreams, that you may not die.

12 The king commanded after this, and he sent and called again for other wise men, and they came and stood before the king. The king related his dreams to them, and they all answered him according to the first interpretation; the king's anger was set ablaze and he was very upset. A nd the king said to them, Certainly you speak lies and utter falsehood in what you have said.

13 The king commanded that a proclamation should be issued throughout the land of Egypt, saying, It is determined by the king and his great men, that any wise man who knows and understands the interpretation of dreams, and will not come this day before the king, shall die.

14 The man that will declare to the king the proper interpretation of his dreams, there shall be given to him all that he will require from the king. And all the wise men of the land of Egypt came before the king, together with all the magicians and sorcerers that were in Egypt and in Goshen, in Rameses, in Tachpanches, in Zoar, and in all the places on the borders of Egypt; they all stood before the king.

15 And all the nobles and the princes, and the attendants belonging to the king, came together from all the cities of Egypt and they all sat before the king, and the king related his dreams before the wise men and the princes; all that sat before the king were astonished at the vision.

16 And all the wise men who were before the king were greatly divided in their interpretation of his dreams; some of them interpreted them to the king, saying, The seven good cattle are seven kings, who from the king's lineage will be raised over Egypt.

17 And the seven bad cattle are seven princes who will stand up against them in the latter days and destroy them; the seven ears of corn are the seven great princes belonging to Egypt, who will fall in the hands of the seven less powerful princes of their enemies, in the wars of our lord the king.

18 And some of them interpreted to the king in this manner, saying, The seven good cattle are the strong cities of Egypt, and the seven bad cattle are the seven nations of the land of Canaan, who will come against the seven cities of Egypt in the latter days and destroy them.

19 And that which you saw in the second dream, of seven good and bad ears of corn, is a sign that the government of Egypt will again return to your descendants as at first.

20 And in this reign the people of the cities of Egypt will turn against the seven cities of Canaan who are stronger than they are and will destroy them, and the government of Egypt will return to your descendants.

21 Some of them said to the king, This is the interpretation of your dreams; the seven good cattle are seven queens, whom you will take for wives in the latter days, and the seven bad cattle denote that those women will all die in the lifetime of the king.

22 And the seven good and bad ears of corn which you did see in the second dream are fourteen children, and it will be in the latter days that they will stand up and fight among themselves, and seven of them will strike the seven that are more powerful.

23 Some of them said these words to the king, The seven good cattle denote that seven children will be born to you, and they will kill seven of your children's children in the latter days; and the seven good ears of corn which you saw in the second dream are those princes against whom seven other less powerful princes will fight and destroy them in the latter days, and avenge your children's cause, and the government will again return to your offspring.

24 The king heard all the words of the wise men of Egypt and their interpretation of his dreams, and none of them pleased the king.

25 And the king knew in his wisdom that they did not altogether speak correctly in all these words, for this was from the Lord to frustrate the words of the wise men of Egypt in order that Joseph might go forth from the house of confinement, and in order that he should become great in Egypt.

26 The king saw that none among all the wise men and magicians of Egypt spoke correctly to him, and the king's wrath was set ablaze, and his anger burned within him.

27 And the king commanded that all the wise men and magicians should go out from before him, and they all went out from before the king with shame and disgrace.

28 Then the king commanded that a proclamation be sent throughout Egypt to kill all the magicians that were in Egypt, and not one of them should be allowed to live.

29 And the captains of the guards belonging to the king rose up, and each man drew his sword; they began to strike the magicians of Egypt and the wise men.

30 After this Merod, chief butler to the king, came and bowed down before the king and sat before him.

31 The butler said to the king, May the king live forever, and his government be honored in the land.

32 You were angry with your servant in those days now two years past and did place me in the ward, and I was for some time in the ward, I and the chief of the bakers.

33 And there was with us a Hebrew servant belonging to the captain of the guard, his name was Joseph, for his master had been angry with him and placed him in the house of confinement, and he attended us there.

34 Some time after when we were in the ward, we dreamed dreams in one night, I and the chief of the bakers; we dreamed, each man according to the interpretation of his dream.

35 And we came in the morning and told them to that servant, and he interpreted to us our dreams, to each man according to his dream he correctly interpreted.

36 And it came to pass as he interpreted to us, so was the event; there fell not to the ground any of his words.

37 Now therefore my lord and king do not kill the people of Egypt for nothing; consider that the slave is still confined in the house by the captain of the guard his master, in the house of confinement.

38 If it pleases the king let him send for him that he may come before you and he will make known to you the correct interpretation of the dream which you did dream.

39 The king heard the words of the chief butler, and the king ordered that the wise men of Egypt should not be slain.

40 And the king ordered his servants to bring Joseph before him, and the king said to them, Go to him and do not terrify him that he be confused and will not know to speak properly.

41 The servants of the king went to Joseph, and they brought him hastily out of the dungeon; the king's servants shaved him, and he changed his prison garment and came before the king.

42 The king was sitting on his royal throne in a princely dress surrounded with a golden ephod, and the fine gold which was on it sparkled, and the gem and the ruby and the emerald, together with all the precious stones that were on the king's head dazzled the eye, and Joseph wondered greatly at the king.

43 And the throne on which the king sat was covered with gold and silver and with onyx stones, and it had seventy steps.

44 It was their custom throughout the land of Egypt that every man who came to speak to the king, if he was a prince or one that was respected in the sight of the king, he ascended to the king's throne as far as the thirty-first step, and the king would descend to the thirty-sixth step and speak with him.

45 If he was one of the common people, he ascended to the third step, and the king would descend to the fourth and speak to him, as their custom was. Also any man who understood to speak in all the seventy languages, he ascended the seventy steps, and went up and spoke till he reached the king.

46 And any man who could not complete the seventy, he ascended as many steps as the languages which he knew to speak in.

47 It was customary in those days in Egypt that no one should reign over them, but one who understood to speak in the seventy languages.

48 When Joseph came before the king he bowed down to the ground before the king, and he ascended to the third step, and the king sat on the fourth step and spoke with Joseph.

49 The king said to Joseph, I dreamed a dream, and there is no interpreter to interpret it properly, and I commanded that all the magicians of Egypt and the wise men thereof should come before me; I related my dreams to them, and no one has properly interpreted them to me.

50 After this I heard about you, that you are a wise man, and can correctly interpret every dream that you hear.

51 And Joseph answered Pharaoh, saying, Let Pharaoh relate his dreams that he dreamed; certainly the interpretations belong to God. And Pharaoh related his dreams to Joseph, the dream of the cattle, and the dream of the ears of corn, and the king ceased speaking.

52 Joseph was then clothed with the spirit of God before the king, and he knew all the things that would befall the king from that day forward; he knew the proper interpretation of the king's dream, and he spoke before the king.

53 Joseph found favor in the sight of the king, and the king listened carefully and with his heart, and he heard all the words of Joseph. And Joseph said to the king, Do not imagine that they are two dreams, for it is only one dream, for that which God has chosen to do throughout the land he has shown to the king in his dream, and this is the proper interpretation of your dream:

54 The seven good cattle and ears of corn are seven years, and the seven bad cattle and ears of corn are also seven years; it is one dream.

55 Know this, the seven years that are coming there will be a great plenty throughout the land, and after that the seven years of famine will follow them, a very severe famine; all the plenty will be forgotten from the land, and the famine will consume the inhabitants of the land.

56 The king dreamed one dream, and the dream was therefore repeated to Pharaoh because the thing is established by God, and God will shortly bring it to pass.

57 Now therefore I will give you counsel and deliver your soul and the souls of the inhabitants of the land from the evil of the famine, that you search throughout your kingdom for a man very discreet and wise, who knows all the affairs of government, and appoint him to superintend over the land of Egypt.

58 And let the man whom you place over Egypt appoint officers under him, that they gather in all the food of the good years that are coming, and let them lay up corn and deposit it in your appointed stores.

59 And let them keep that food for the seven years of famine, that it may be available for you and your people and your whole land, and that you and your land be not cut off by the famine.

60 Let all the inhabitants of the land also be ordered that they gather in, every man the produce of his field, of all sorts of food, during the seven good years, and that they place it in their stores; that it may be available for them in the days of the

famine and that they may live on it.

61 This is the proper interpretation of your dream, and this is the counsel given to save your soul and the souls of all your subjects.

62 The king answered and said to Joseph, Who says and who knows that your words are correct? And he said to the king, This shall be a sign for you respecting all my words, that they are true and that my advice is good for you.

63 Behold your wife sits this day on the stool of delivery, and she will bear you a son and you will rejoice with him; when your child shall have gone forth from his mother's womb, your firstborn son that has been born two years ago shall die, and you will be comforted in the child that will be born to you this day.

64 Joseph finished speaking these words to the king, and he bowed down to the king and he went out, and when Joseph had gone out from the king's presence, those signs which Joseph had spoken to the king came to pass on that day.

65 The queen gave birth to a son on that day and the king heard the glad tidings about his son, and he rejoiced, and when the reporter had gone forth from the king's presence, the king's servants found the firstborn son of the king fallen dead on the ground.

66 There was great lamentation and noise in the king's house, and the king heard it and said, What is the noise and lamentation that I have heard in the house? They told the king that his firstborn son had died, then the king knew that all Joseph's words that he had spoken were correct; the king was consoled for his son by the child that was born to him on that day as Joseph had said.

CHAPTER 49

1 After these things the king sent and assembled all his officers and servants, and all the princes and nobles belonging to the king, and they all came before the king.

2 And the king said to them, Behold you have seen and heard all the words of this Hebrew man, and all the signs which he declared would come to pass, and not any of his words have fallen to the ground.

3 You know that he has given a proper interpretation of the dream, and it will certainly come to pass; now therefore take counsel, and know what you will do and how the land will be delivered from the famine.

4 Search now and see whether the likes of him can be found, in whose heart there is wisdom and knowledge, and I will appoint him over the land.

5 For you have heard what the Hebrew man has advised concerning this to save the land from the famine, and I know that the land will not be delivered from the famine but with the advice of the Hebrew man, him that advised me.

6 And they all answered the king and said, The counsel which the Hebrew has given concerning this is good; now therefore, our lord and king, behold the whole land is in your hand, do that which seems good in your sight.

7 Him whom you choose, and whom you in your wisdom know to be wise and capable of delivering the land with his wisdom, him shall the king appoint to be under him over the land.

8 And the king said to all the officers: I have thought that since God has made known to the Hebrew man all that he has spoken, there is none so discreet and wise in the whole land as he is; if it seems good in your sight I will place him over the land, for he will save the land with his wisdom.

9 All the officers answered the king and said, But certainly it is written in the laws of Egypt, and it should not be violated, that no man shall reign over Egypt, nor be the second to the king, but one who has knowledge in all the languages of the sons of men.

10 Now therefore our lord and king, behold this Hebrew man can only speak the Hebrew language; how then can he be over us as the second under government, a man who not even knows our language?

11 Now we pray you send for him, and let him come before you, and prove him in all things, and do as you see fit.

12 And the king said, It shall be done tomorrow, and the thing that you have spoken is good. All the officers came on that day before the king.

13 But that night the Lord sent one of his ministering angels and he came into the land of Egypt to Joseph, and the angel of the Lord stood over Joseph; there Joseph was lying in the bed at night in his master's house in the dungeon, for his master had put him back into the dungeon on account of his wife.

14 The angel roused him from his sleep, and Joseph rose up and stood on his legs, and there the angel of the Lord was standing opposite to him; the angel of the Lord spoke with Joseph and he taught him all the languages of man in that night, and he called his name Jehoseph.

15 The angel of the Lord went from him and Joseph returned and lay on his bed, and Joseph was astonished at the vision which he saw.

16 It came to pass in the morning that the king sent for all his officers and servants and they all came and sat before the king, and the king ordered Joseph to be brought; the king's servants went and brought Joseph before Pharaoh.

17 And the king came forth and ascended the steps of the throne and Joseph spoke to the king in all languages; Joseph went up to him and spoke to the king until he arrived before the king in the seventieth step, and he sat before the king.

18 And the king greatly rejoiced on account of Joseph, and all the king's officers rejoiced greatly with the king when they

heard all the words of Joseph.

19 That thing seemed good in the sight of the king and the officers, to appoint Joseph to be second to the king over the whole land of Egypt, and the king spoke to Joseph, saying,

20 Now you did give me counsel to appoint a wise man over the land of Egypt, in order with his wisdom to save the land from the famine. Now therefore, since God has made all this known to you, and all the words which you have spoken, there is not throughout the land a discreet and wise man like to you.

21 And your name no more shall be called Joseph, but Zaphnath Paaneah shall be your name; you shall be second to me, and according to your word shall be all the affairs of my government; at your word shall my people go out and come in.

22 Also from under your hand shall my servants and officers receive their salary which is given to them monthly, and to you shall all the people of the land bow down; only in my throne will I be greater than you.

23 And the king took off his ring from his hand and put it on the hand of Joseph, and the king dressed Joseph in a princely garment; he put a golden crown on his head, and he put a golden chain on his neck.

24 The king commanded his servants and they made him ride in the second chariot belonging to the king, that went opposite to the king's chariot. He caused him to ride on a great and strong horse from the king's horses, and to be conducted through the streets of the land of Egypt.

25 And the king commanded that all those that played on timbrels, harps and other musical instruments should go forth with Joseph; one thousand timbrels, one thousand mecholoth, and one thousand nebalim went after him.

26 And five thousand men, with drawn swords glittering in their hands, went marching and playing before Joseph; twenty thousand of the great men of the king, with girdles of skin covered with gold, marched at the right hand of Joseph, and twenty thousand at his left. All the women and girls went on the roofs or stood in the streets playing and rejoicing at Joseph, and gazed at the appearance of Joseph and at his beauty.

27 And the king's people went before him and behind him, perfuming the road with frankincense and with cassia and with all sorts of fine perfume, and scattered myrrh and aloes along the road. Twenty men proclaimed these words before him throughout the land in a loud voice:

28 Do you see this man whom the king has chosen to be his second? All the affairs of government shall be regulated by him, and he that disobeys his orders, or that does not bow down before him to the ground, shall die, for he would be rebelling against the king and his second person in command.

29 And when the heralds had ceased announcing, all the people of Egypt bowed down to the ground before Joseph and said, May the king live, also may his second one live; all the inhabitants of Egypt bowed down along the road, and when the heralds approached them, they bowed down; they rejoiced with all sorts of timbrels, pipes and harps before Joseph.

30 And Joseph on his horse lifted up his eyes to heaven, and called out and said, He raises the poor man from the dust. He lifts up the needy from the dunghill. O Lord of Hosts, happy is the man who trusts in you.

31 And Joseph passed throughout the land of Egypt with Pharaoh's servants and officers, and they showed him the whole land of Egypt and all the king's treasures.

32 Joseph returned and came that day before Pharaoh, and the king gave to Joseph a possession in the land of Egypt, a possession of fields and vineyards. And the king gave to Joseph three thousand talents of silver and one thousand talents of gold, and onyx stones and bdellium and many gifts.

33 On the next day the king commanded all the people of Egypt to bring to Joseph offerings and gifts, and said that he that violated the command of the king should die; they made a high place in the street of the city and spread out garments there, and whoever brought anything to Joseph put it into the high place.

34 And all the people of Egypt cast something into the high place, one man a golden earring, and the other rings and earrings, and different vessels of gold and silver work, and onyx stones and bdellium he put on the high place; every one gave something of what he possessed.

35 And Joseph took all these and placed them in his treasuries, and all the officers and nobles belonging to the king exalted Joseph. They gave him many gifts, seeing that the king had chosen him to be his second in leadership.

36 The king sent to Potiphera, the son of Ahiram priest of On, and he took his young daughter Osnath and gave her to Joseph for a wife.

37 And the girl was very beautiful, a virgin, one whom man had not known, and Joseph took her for a wife; the king said to Joseph, I am Pharaoh, and beside you none shall dare to lift up his hand or his foot to regulate my people throughout the land of Egypt.

38 Joseph was thirty years old when he stood before Pharaoh, and Joseph went out from before the king and became the king's second in command in Egypt.

39 The king gave Joseph a hundred servants to attend him in his house, and Joseph also sent and purchased many servants and they remained in the house of Joseph.

40 Joseph then built for himself a very magnificent house like to the houses of kings, before the court of the king's palace, and he made in the house a large temple, very elegant in appearance and convenient for his residence; three years Joseph spent in erecting his house.

41 And Joseph made for himself a very elegant throne of an abundance of gold and silver, and he covered it with onyx stones and bdellium; he made on it the likeness of the whole land of Egypt, and the likeness of the river of Egypt that waters the

whole land of Egypt. Joseph sat securely on his throne in his house and the Lord increased Joseph's wisdom.

42 And all the inhabitants of Egypt and Pharaoh's servants and his princes loved Joseph greatly, for this thing was from the Lord to Joseph.

43 And Joseph had an army that made war, going out in hosts and troops to the number of forty thousand six hundred men, capable of bearing arms to assist the king and Joseph against the enemy, besides the king's officers and his servants and inhabitants of Egypt without number.

44 And Joseph gave to his mighty men, and to all his army, shields and javelins, and caps and coats of mail and stones for slinging.

CHAPTER 50

1 At that time the children of Tarshish came against the sons of Ishmael, and made war with them, and the children of Tarshish fought the Ishmaelites for a long time.

2 The children of Ishmael were small in number in those days, and they could not succeed over the children of Tarshish, and they were extremely oppressed.

3 And the old men of the Ishmaelites sent a record to the king of Egypt, saying, Send I pray you to your servants: officers and army to help us to fight against the children of Tarshish, for we have been diminishing away for a long time.

4 And Pharaoh sent Joseph with the mighty men and army which were with him, and also his mighty men from the king's house.

5 They went to the land of Havilah to the children of Ishmael to assist them against the children of Tarshish, and the children of Ishmael fought with the children of Tarshish. Joseph struck the Tarshishites and he subdued all their land, and the children of Ishmael lived there to this day.

6 And when the land of Tarshish was subdued, all the Tarshishites ran away, and came to the border of their brothers the children of Javan; Joseph with all his mighty men and army returned to Egypt, not one man of them missing.

7 At the revolution of the year, in the second year of Joseph's reigning over Egypt, the Lord gave great plenty throughout the land for seven years as Joseph had spoken, for the Lord blessed all the produce of the earth in those days for seven years; they ate and were greatly satisfied.

8 And Joseph at that time had officers under him, and they collected all the food of the good years, and heaped corn year by year, and they placed it in the treasuries of Joseph.

9 At any time when they gathered the food, Joseph commanded that they should bring the corn in the ears, and also bring with it some of the soil of the field, so that it would not spoil.

10 And Joseph did according to this year by year, and he heaped up corn like the sand of the sea for abundance, for his stores were immense and could not be numbered for abundance.

11 Also all the inhabitants of Egypt gathered all sorts of food in their stores in great abundance during the seven good years, but they did not do to it as Joseph did.

12 All the food which Joseph and the Egyptians had gathered during the seven years of plenty was secured for the land in stores for the seven years of famine, for the support of the whole land.

13 And the inhabitants of Egypt filled each man his store and his concealed place with corn, to be for support during the famine.

14 And Joseph placed all the food that he had gathered in all the cities of Egypt, and he closed all the stores and placed sentinels over them.

15 Joseph's wife Osnath the daughter of Potiphera gave birth to him two sons, Manasseh and Ephraim, and Joseph was thirty-four years old when he had them.

16 And the lads grew up and they followed in his ways and in his instructions; they did not deviate from the way which their father taught them, either to the right or left.

17 And the Lord was with the lads, and they grew up and had understanding and skill in all wisdom and in all the affairs of government. All the king's officers and his great men of the inhabitants of Egypt honored the lads, and they were brought up among the king's children.

18 The seven years of plenty that were throughout the land were at an end; the seven years of famine came after them as Joseph had spoken, and the famine spread throughout the land.

19 All the people of Egypt saw that the famine had begun in the land of Egypt, and all the people of Egypt opened their stores of corn for the famine hung over them.

20 And they found all the food that was in their stores full of vermin and not fit to eat, and the famine stayed throughout the land; all the inhabitants of Egypt came and cried before Pharaoh, for the famine was heavy on them.

21 And they said to Pharaoh, Give food to your servants; why shall we die through hunger before your eyes, even we and our little ones?

22 And Pharaoh answered them, saying, And why do you cry to me? Did not Joseph command that the corn should be laid up during the seven years of plenty for the years of famine? Why did you not listen to his voice?

23 And the people of Egypt answered the king, saying, As your soul lives, our lord, your servants have done all that Joseph ordered, for your servants also gathered in all the produce of their fields during the seven years of plenty and laid it in the stores to this day.

24 And when the famine prevailed over your servants we opened our stores, and behold all our produce was filled with vermin and was not fit for food.

25 When the king heard all that had befallen the inhabitants of Egypt, the king was greatly afraid on account of the famine, and he was much terrified; the king answered the people of Egypt, saying, Since all this has happened to you, go to Joseph, do whatever he shall say to you; do not go contrary to his commands.

26 And all the people of Egypt went forth and came to Joseph, and said to him, Give to us food, for why shall we die before you through hunger? We gathered in our produce during the seven years as you did command, and we put it in store, and thus has it happened to us.

27 And when Joseph heard all the words of the people of Egypt and what had happened to them, Joseph opened all his stores of the produce and he sold it to the people of Egypt.

28 And the famine stayed throughout the land, and the famine was in all countries, but in the land of Egypt there was produce for sale.

29 All the inhabitants of Egypt came to Joseph to buy corn, for the famine hung over them, and all their corn was spoiled, and Joseph daily sold it to all the people of Egypt.

30 And all the inhabitants of the land of Canaan and the Philistines, and those beyond the Jordan, and the children of the east and all the cities of the lands far and near heard that there was corn in Egypt, and they all came to Egypt to buy corn, for the famine hung over them.

31 Joseph opened the stores of corn and placed officers over them, and they daily stood and sold to all that came.

32 Joseph knew that his brothers also would come to Egypt to buy corn, for the famine spread throughout the earth. And Joseph commanded all his people that they should cause it to be announced throughout the land of Egypt, saying,

33 It is the pleasure of the king, of his second and of their great men, that any person who wishes to buy corn in Egypt shall not send his servants to Egypt to purchase, but his sons; also any Egyptian or Canaanite who shall come from any of the stores from buying corn in Egypt, if he goes and sells it throughout the land, he shall die, for no one shall buy but for the support of his household.

34 And any man leading two or three beasts shall die, for a man shall only lead his own beast.

35 Joseph placed sentinels at the gates of Egypt, and commanded them, saying, Any person who may come to buy corn, permit him not to enter until his name and the name of his father, and the name of his father's father be written down; whatever is written by day, send their names to me in the evening that I may know their names.

36 And Joseph placed officers throughout the land of Egypt; he commanded them to do all these things.

37 Joseph did all these things, and made these standards in order that he might know when his brothers would come to Egypt to buy corn; Joseph's people caused it daily to be announced in Egypt according to these words and standards which Joseph had commanded.

38 And all the inhabitants of the east and west country, and of all the earth, heard of the rules and regulations which Joseph had enacted in Egypt, and the inhabitants of the extreme parts of the earth came and they bought corn in Egypt day after day, and then went away.

39 All the officers of Egypt did as Joseph had commanded, and all that came to Egypt to buy corn, the gate keepers would write their names, and their fathers' names, and daily bring them in the evening to Joseph.

CHAPTER 51

1 Jacob afterward heard that there was corn in Egypt, and he called to his sons to go to Egypt to buy corn, for on them also did the famine occur, and he called to his sons, saying,

2 Behold I hear that there is corn in Egypt, and all the people of the earth go there to purchase; now therefore why will you show yourselves (pretend to be) satisfied before the whole earth? You go also down to Egypt and buy us a little corn among those that come there, that we may not die.

3 And the sons of Jacob listened to the voice of their father, and they rose up to go down to Egypt in order to buy corn among the rest that came there.

4 And Jacob their father commanded them, saying, When you come into the city do not enter together in one gate, on account of the inhabitants of the land.

5 And the sons of Jacob went forth and they went to Egypt, and the sons of Jacob did all as their father had commanded them; Jacob did not send Benjamin, for he said, Lest an accident might happen to him on the road like his brother. Ten of Jacob's sons went forth.

6 While the sons of Jacob were going on the road, they repented of what they had done to Joseph, and they spoke to each other, saying, We know that our brother Joseph went down to Egypt, and now we will seek him where we go, and if we find him we will take him from his master for a ransom, and if not, by force, and we will die for him.

7 And the sons of Jacob agreed to this thing and strengthened themselves on account of Joseph, to deliver him from the hand of his master, and the sons of Jacob went to Egypt; when they came near to Egypt they separated from each other, and they came through ten gates of Egypt, and the gate keepers wrote their names that day, and brought them to Joseph in the evening.

8 And Joseph read the names from the hand of the gatekeepers of the city, and he found that his brothers had entered at the ten gates of the city, and Joseph at once commanded that it should be proclaimed throughout the land of Egypt, saying,

9 Go forth all you store guards, close all the corn stores and let only one remain open, that those who come may purchase from it.

10 And all the officers of Joseph did so at that time, and they closed all the stores and left only one open.

11 Joseph gave the written names of his brothers to him that was set over the open store, and he said to him, Whosoever shall come to you to buy corn, ask his name, and when men of these names shall come before you, seize them and send them, and they did so.

12 And when the sons of Jacob came into the city, they joined together in the city to search for Joseph before they bought themselves corn.

13 And they went to the walls of the harlots and they sought Joseph there for three days, for they thought that Joseph would come in the walls of the harlots, for Joseph was very handsome and well favored; the sons of Jacob sought Joseph for three days and they could not find him.

14 The man who was set over the open store sought for those names which Joseph had given him, and he did not find them.

15 And he sent to Joseph, saying, These three days have passed, and those men whose names you gave to me have not come, so Joseph sent servants to search for the men in all Egypt, and to bring them before Joseph.

16 Joseph's servants went and came into Egypt and could not find them, and went to Goshen and they were not there, and then went to the city of Rameses and could not find them.

17 Joseph continued to send sixteen servants to seek his brothers, and they went and spread themselves in the four corners of the city; four of the servants went into the house of the harlots, and they found the ten men there searching for their brother.

18 Those four men took them and brought them before Joseph, and they bowed down to him to the ground. Joseph was sitting on his throne in his temple, clothed with princely garments, and on his head was a large crown of gold, and all the mighty men were sitting around him.

19 And the sons of Jacob saw Joseph, and his figure and good-looks and dignity of countenance seemed wonderful in their eyes, and they again bowed down to him to the ground.

20 Joseph saw his brothers and he knew them, but they knew him not, for Joseph was very great in their eyes, therefore they knew him not.

21 And Joseph spoke to them, saying, From where did you come? And they all answered and said, Thy servants have come from the land of Canaan to buy corn, for the famine prevails throughout the earth, and your servants heard that there was corn in Egypt, so they have come among the other comers to buy corn for their support.

22 And Joseph answered them, saying, If you have come to purchase as you say, why do you come through ten gates of the city? It can only be that you have come to spy through the land.

23 And they all together answered Joseph, and said, Not so my lord, we are right, your servants are not spies, but we have come to buy corn, for your servants are all brothers, the sons of one man in the land of Canaan, and our father commanded us, saying, When you come to the city do not enter together at one gate on account of the inhabitants of the land.

24 And Joseph again answered them and said, That is the thing which I spoke to you, you have come to spy through the land, therefore you all came through ten gates of the city; you have come to see how barren the land has become.

25 Certainly every one that comes to buy corn goes his way, and you are already three days in the land; what do you do in the walls of harlots in which you have been for these three days? Certainly spies do these things.

26 And they said to Joseph, Far be it from our lord to speak thus, for we are twelve brothers, the sons of our father Jacob, in the land of Canaan, the son of Isaac, the son of Abraham, the Hebrew; behold the youngest is with our father this day in the land of Canaan, and one is not, for he was lost from us, and we thought perhaps he might be in this land, so we are seeking him throughout the land, and have come even to the houses of harlots to seek him there.

27 And Joseph said to them, And have you then sought him throughout the earth, that there only remained Egypt for you to seek him in? And what also should your brother do in the houses of harlots, if he were in Egypt? Have you not said, that you are from the sons of Isaac, the son of Abraham, and what shall the sons of Jacob do then in the houses of harlots?

28 And they said to him, Because we heard that Ishmaelites stole him from us, and it was told to us that they sold him in Egypt, and your servant, our brother, is very handsome and well favored, so we thought he would certainly be in the houses of harlots, therefore your servants went there to seek him and give ransom for him.

29 Joseph still answered them, saying, Certainly you speak falsely and utter lies, to say of yourselves that you are the sons of Abraham; as Pharaoh lives you are spies, therefore you have come to the houses of harlots that you should not be known.

30 Joseph said to them, And now if you find him, and his master requires of you a great price, will you give it for him? And they said, It shall be given.

31 And he said to them, And if his master will not consent to part with him for a great price, what will you do to him on his account? And they answered him, saying, If he will not give him to us we will kill him, and take our brother and go away.

32 And Joseph said to them, That is the thing which I have spoken to you; you are spies, for you are come to kill the inhabitants of the land, for we heard that two of your brothers struck all the inhabitants of Shechem, in the land of Canaan, on account of your sister, and you now come to do the same in Egypt on account of your brother.

33 Only hereby shall I know that you are true men; if you will send home one from among you to fetch your youngest brother from your father, and bring him here to me, and by doing this thing I will know that you are right.

34 And Joseph called to seventy of his mighty men, and he said to them, Take these men and bring them into the ward.

35 And the mighty men took the ten men, they laid hold of them and put them into the ward, and they were in the ward three days.

36 And on the third day Joseph had them brought out of the ward, and he said to them, Do this for yourselves if you be true men, so that you may live: one of your brothers shall be confined in the ward while you go and take home the corn for your household to the land of Canaan, and get your youngest brother, and bring him here to me, that I may know that you are true men when you do this thing.

37 And Joseph went out from them and came into the chamber, and wept a great weeping, for his pity was enlarged for them; he washed his face, and returned to them again, and he took Simeon from them and ordered him to be bound, but Simeon was not willing to be done so, for he was a very powerful man and they could not bind him.

38 And Joseph called to his mighty men and seventy valiant men came before him with drawn swords in their hands, and the sons of Jacob were terrified at them.

39 Joseph said to them, Seize this man and confine him in prison until his brothers come to him, and Joseph's valiant men hurried and they all laid hold of Simeon to bind him, and Simeon gave a loud and terrible shriek and the cry was heard at a distance.

40 All the valiant men of Joseph were so terrified at the sound of the shriek that they fell on their faces, and they were greatly afraid and fled.

41 And all the men that were with Joseph fled, for they were greatly afraid for their lives, and only Joseph and Manasseh his son remained there; Manassah the son of Joseph saw the strength of Simeon, and he was greatly angered.

42 And Manassah the son of Joseph rose up to Simeon, and Manassah struck Simeon a heavy blow with his fist against the back of his neck, and Simeon was stilled of his rage.

43 Manassah laid hold of Simeon and he seized him violently and he bound him and brought him into the house of confinement, and all the sons of Jacob were astonished at the act of the youth.

44 And Simeon said to his brothers, None of you must say that this is the smiting of an Egyptian, but it is the smiting of the house of my father.

45 After this Joseph ordered him to be called who was in charge of the storehouse, to fill their sacks with corn as much as they could carry, and to restore every man's money into his sack, and to give them provision for the road, and thus he did to them.

46 And Joseph commanded them, saying, Take care that you not go contrary to my orders to bring your brother as I have told you, and it shall be when you bring your brother here to me, then will I know that you are true men, and you shall traffic in the land, and I will restore to you your brother, and you shall return in peace to your father.

47 And they all answered and said, According as our lord speaks so will we do, and they bowed down to him to the ground.

48 Every man lifted his corn on his ass, and they went out to go to the land of Canaan to their father; and they came to the inn and Levi spread his sack to give feed to his ass, when he saw and there his money in full weight was still in his sack.

49 And the man was greatly afraid, and he said to his brothers, My money is returned, and look, it is even in my sack; the men were greatly afraid, and they said, What is this that God has done to us?

50 And they all said, And where is the Lord's kindness with our fathers, with Abraham, Isaac, and Jacob, that the Lord has this day delivered us into the hands of the king of Egypt to contrive against us?

51 Judah said to them, Certainly we are guilty sinners before the Lord our God in having sold our brother, our own flesh, and wherefore do you say, Where is the Lord's kindness with our fathers?

52 Reuben said to them, Said I not to you, do not sin against the lad, and you would not listen to me? Now God requires him from us, and how dare you say, Where is the Lord's kindness with our fathers, while you have sinned to the Lord?

53 They stayed overnight in that place, and they rose up early in the morning and loaded their asses with their corn; they led them and went on and came to their father's house in the land of Canaan.

54 And Jacob and his household went out to meet his sons, and Jacob saw and behold their brother Simeon was not with them; Jacob said to his sons, Where is your brother Simeon, whom I do not see? And his sons told him all that had befallen them in Egypt.

CHAPTER 52

1 They entered their house, and every man opened his sack and they looked and there every man's bundle of money was there, at which they and their father were greatly terrified.

2 And Jacob said to them, What is this that you have done to me? I sent your brother Joseph to inquire after your welfare and

you said to me: A wild beast did devour him.

3 And Simeon went with you to buy food and you say the king of Egypt hath confined him in prison, and you wish to take Benjamin to cause his death also, and bring down my grey hairs with sorrow to the grave on account of Benjamin and his brother Joseph.

4 Now therefore my son shall not go down with you, for his brother is dead and he is left alone, and mischief may befall him by the way in which you go, as it befell his brother.

5 Reuben said to his father, You shall kill my two sons if I do not bring your son and place him before you. Jacob said to his sons, Abide ye here and do not go down to Egypt, for my son shall not go down with you to Egypt, nor die like his brother.

6 And Judah said to them, Refrain from him until the corn is finished, and he will then say, Take down your brother, when he finds his own life and the life of his household in danger from the famine.

7 In those days the famine was severe throughout the land, and all the people of the earth went and came to Egypt to buy food, for the famine continued greatly among them, and the sons of Jacob remained in Canaan a year and two months until their corn was finished.

8 And it came to pass after their corn was finished, the whole household of Jacob was pinched with hunger, and all the infants of the sons of Jacob came together and they approached Jacob; they all surrounded him, and said to him, Give to us bread, for why shall we all perish through hunger in your presence?

9 Jacob heard the words of his son's children, and he wept a great weeping, and his pity was roused for them. Jacob called to his sons and they all came and sat before him.

10 And Jacob said to them, Have you not seen how your children have been weeping over me this day, saying, Give to us bread, and there is none? Now therefore return and buy for us a little food.

11 And Judah answered and said to his father, If you will send our brother with us we will go down and buy corn for you, and if you will not send him then we will not go down, for certainly the king of Egypt particularly requested us, saying, You shall not see my face unless your brother is with you. The king of Egypt is a strong and mighty king, and behold if we shall go to him without our brother we shall all be put to death.

12 Do you not know and have you not heard that this king is very powerful and wise, and there is no one like him in all the earth? Behold we have seen all the kings of the earth and we have not seen one like that king, the king of Egypt; certainly among all the kings of the earth there is none greater than Abimelech king of the Philistines, yet the king of Egypt is greater and mightier than he, and Abimelech can only be compared to one of his officers.

13 Father, you have not seen his palace and his throne, and all his servants standing before him; you have not seen that king on his throne in his pomp and royal appearance, dressed in his kingly robes with a large golden crown on his head; you have not seen the honor and glory which God has given to him, for there is no one like him in all the earth.

14 Father, you have not seen the wisdom, the understanding and the knowledge which God has given in his heart, nor heard his sweet voice when he spoke to us.

15 We know not, father, who made him acquainted with our names and all that happened to us, yet he asked also after you, saying, Is your father still living, and is it well with him?

16 You have not seen the affairs of the government of Egypt regulated by him, without inquiring of Pharaoh his lord; you have not seen the awe and fear which he impressed on all the Egyptians.

17 And also when we went from him, we were threatened of doing to Egypt like to the rest of the cities of the Amorites, and we were greatly angered against all his words which he spoke concerning us as spies; now when we shall again come before him his terror will fall on us all, and not one of us will be able to speak to him either a little or a great thing.

18 Now therefore father, send we pray you the lad with us, and we will go down and buy you food for our support, and not die through hunger. And Jacob said, Why have you dealt so ill with me to tell the king you had a brother? What is this thing that you have done to me?

19 And Judah said to Jacob his father, Give the lad into my care and we will rise up and go down to Egypt and buy corn, and then return, and it shall be when we return if the lad is not with us, then let me bear your blame forever.

20 Have you seen all our infants weeping over you through hunger and there is no power in your hand to satisfy them? Now let your pity be roused for them and send our brother with us and we will go.

21 For how will the Lord's kindness to our ancestors be manifested to you when you say that the king of Egypt will take away your son? As the Lord lives I will not leave him until I bring him and place him before you; but pray for us to the Lord, that he may deal kindly with us, to cause us to be received favorably and kindly before the king of Egypt and his men, for had we not delayed certainly by now we had returned a second time with your son.

22 And Jacob said to his sons, I trust in the Lord God that he may deliver you and give you favor in the sight of the king of Egypt, and in the sight of all his men.

23 Now therefore rise up and go to the man, and take for him in your hands a present from what can be obtained in the land and bring it before him, and may the Almighty God give you mercy before him that he may send Benjamin and Simeon your brothers with you.

24 And all the men rose up, and they took their brother Benjamin, and they took in their hands a large present of the best of the land, and they also took a double portion of silver.

25 And Jacob strictly commanded his sons concerning Benjamin, saying, Take care of him in the way in which you are going,

and do not separate yourselves from him in the road, neither in Egypt.

26 And Jacob rose up from his sons and spread forth his hands and he prayed to the Lord on account of his sons, saying, O Lord God of heaven and earth, remember your covenant with our father Abraham, remember it with my father Isaac and deal kindly with my sons and deliver them not into the hands of the king of Egypt; do it I pray you O God for the sake of your mercies and redeem all my children and rescue them from Egyptian power, and send them their two brothers.

27 And all the wives of the sons of Jacob and their children lifted up their eyes to heaven and they all wept before the Lord, and cried to him to deliver their fathers from the hand of the king of Egypt.

28 Jacob wrote a record to the king of Egypt and gave it into the hand of Judah and into the hands of his sons for the king of Egypt, saying,

29 From your servant Jacob, son of Isaac, son of Abraham the Hebrew, the prince of God, to the powerful and wise king, the revealer of secrets, king of Egypt, greeting.

30 Be it known to my lord the king of Egypt, the famine was heavy on us in the land of Canaan, and I sent my sons to you to buy us a little food from you for our support.

31 For my sons surrounded me and I being very old cannot see with my eyes, for my eyes have become very dim through age, as well as with daily weeping for my son, for Joseph who was lost from before me; I commanded my sons that they should not enter the gates of the city when they came to Egypt, on account of the inhabitants of the land.

32 And I also commanded them to go about Egypt to seek for my son Joseph, perhaps they might find him there, and they did so, and you did consider them as spies of the land.

33 Have we not heard concerning you that you did interpret Pharaoh's dream and did speak truly to him? How then do you not know in your wisdom whether my sons are spies or not?

34 Now therefore, my lord and king, behold I have sent my son before you, as you did speak to my sons; I beg you to put your eyes on him until he is returned to me in peace with his brothers.

35 For do you not know, or have you not heard that which our God did to Pharaoh when he took my mother Sarah, and what he did to Abimelech king of the Philistines on account of her, and also what our father Abraham did to the nine kings of Elam, how he struck them all with a few men that were with him?

36 And also what my two sons Simeon and Levi did to the eight cities of the Amorites, how they destroyed them on account of their sister Dinah?

37 And also on account of their brother Benjamin they consoled themselves for the loss of his brother Joseph; what will they then do for him when they see the hand of any people prevailing over them, for his sake?

38 Do you not know, O king of Egypt, that the power of God is with us, and that also God ever hears our prayers and forsakes us not all the days?

39 And when my sons told me of your dealings with them, I called not to the Lord on account of you, for then you would have perished with your men before my son Benjamin came before you, but I thought that as Simeon my son was in your house, perhaps you might deal kindly with him, therefore I did not do this thing to you.

40 Now therefore behold Benjamin my son comes to you with my sons, take care of him and put your eyes on him, and then will God place his eyes over you and throughout your kingdom.

41 Now I have told you all that is in my heart, and behold my sons are coming to you with their brother; examine the face of the whole earth for their sake and send them back in peace with their brothers.

42 And Jacob gave the record to his sons into the care of Judah to give it to the king of Egypt.

CHAPTER 53

1 The sons of Jacob rose up and took Benjamin and all of the presents; they went and came to Egypt and they stood before Joseph.

2 And Joseph beheld his brother Benjamin with them and he saluted them, and these men came to Joseph's house.

3 Joseph commanded the superintendent of his house to give food to his brothers to eat, and he did so to them.

4 At noon time Joseph sent for the men to come before him with Benjamin, and the men told the superintendent of Joseph's house concerning the silver that was returned in their sacks; he said to them, It will be well with you, fear not. And he brought their brother Simeon to them.

5 And Simeon said to his brothers, The lord of the Egyptians has acted very kindly to me; he did not keep me bound, as you saw with your eyes, for when you went out from the city he let me free and dealt kindly with me in his house.

6 And Judah took Benjamin by the hand, and they came before Joseph, and they bowed down to him to the ground.

7 The men gave the present to Joseph and they all sat before him, and Joseph said to them, Is it well with you, is it well with your children, is it well with your aged father? And they said, It is well. And Judah took the record which Jacob had sent and gave it into the hand of Joseph.

8 Joseph read the letter and knew his father's writing, and he wished to weep; he went into an inner room and he wept a great weeping, and he came out.

9 He lifted up his eyes and observed his brother Benjamin and said, Is this your brother of whom you spoke to me? Benjamin

approached Joseph, and Joseph placed his hand on his head and he said to him, May God be gracious to you my son.

10 And when Joseph saw his brother, the son of his mother, he again wished to weep, and he entered the chamber, and he wept there; he washed his face and came out and refrained from weeping; he said, Prepare food.

11 Joseph had a cup from which he drank; it was of silver beautifully inlaid with onyx stones and bdellium, and Joseph struck the cup in the sight of his brothers while they were sitting to eat with him.

12 Joseph said to the men, I know by this cup that Reuben the first born, Simeon and Levi and Judah, Issachar and Zebulun are children from one mother; seat yourselves to eat according to your births.

13 He also placed the others according to their births and said, I know that this your youngest brother has no brother; I, like him, have no brother; he shall therefore sit down to eat with me.

14 Benjamin went up before Joseph and sat on the throne and the men beheld the acts of Joseph, and they were astonished at them; the men ate and drank at that time with Joseph, and he then gave presents to them. Joseph gave one gift to Benjamin, and Manasseh and Ephraim saw the acts of their father, and they also gave presents to him, and Osnath gave him one present, and there were five presents in the hands of Benjamin.

15 Joseph brought out wine to drink, and they would not drink; they said, From the day in which Joseph was lost we have not drunk wine, nor eaten any delicacies.

16 And Joseph swore to them, and he pressed them hard; they drank plentifully with him on that day, and Joseph afterward turned to his brother Benjamin to speak with him, and Benjamin was still sitting on the throne before Joseph.

17 Joseph said to him, Have you had any children? And he said, Your servant has ten sons, and these are their names: Bela, Becher, Ashbal, Gera, Naaman, Achi, Rosh, Mupim, Chupim, and Ord, and I called their names after my brother whom I have not seen.

18 He ordered them to bring before him his map of the stars, whereby Joseph knew all the times, and Joseph said to Benjamin, I have heard that the Hebrews are acquainted with all wisdom, do you know anything of this?

19 And Benjamin said, Thy servant knows all the wisdom which my father taught me. Joseph said to Benjamin, Look now at this instrument and understand where your brother Joseph is in Egypt, who you said went down to Egypt.

20 And Benjamin observed that instrument with the map of the stars of heaven, and he was wise and looked therein to know where his brother was. Benjamin divided the whole land of Egypt into four divisions, and he found that he who was sitting on the throne before him was his brother Joseph; Benjamin wondered greatly, and when Joseph saw that his brother Benjamin was so much astonished, he said to Benjamin, What have you seen, and why are you astonished?

21 Benjamin said to Joseph, I can see by this that Joseph my brother sits here with me on the throne, and Joseph said to him, I am Joseph your brother; reveal not this thing to your brothers. I will send you with them when they go away and I will command them to be brought back again into the city, and I will take you away from them.

22 And if they risk their lives and fight for you, then shall I know that they have repented of what they did to me; I will make myself known to them and if they turn away from you when I take you, then shall you remain with me, and I will fight with them, and they shall go away. I will not become known to them.

23 At that time Joseph commanded his officer to fill their sacks with food and to put each man's money into his sack, and to put the cup in the sack of Benjamin and give them provision for the road, and they did so to them.

24 On the next day the men rose up early in the morning and loaded their asses with their corn; they went forth with Benjamin, and went to the land of Canaan with their brother Benjamin.

25 They had not gone far from Egypt when Joseph commanded him that was set over his house, saying, Rise, pursue these men before they get too far from Egypt, and say to them, Why have you stolen my master's cup?

26 Joseph's officer rose up and he reached them, and he spoke to them all the words of Joseph; when they heard this thing they became greatly angry, and they said, He with whom your master's cup shall be found shall die, and we will also become slaves.

27 They hurried and each man brought down his sack from his ass, and they looked in their bags and the cup was found in Benjamin's bag; they all tore their garments and they returned to the city, and they struck Benjamin in the road, continually smiting him until he came into the city, and they stood before Joseph.

28 Judah's anger was set ablaze, and he said, This man has only brought me back to destroy Egypt this day.

29 The men came to Joseph's house, and they found Joseph sitting on his throne, and all the mighty men standing at his right and left.

30 And Joseph said to them, What is this act that you have done, that you took away my silver cup and went away? But I know that you took my cup in order to know thereby in what part of the land your brother was.

31 Judah said, What shall we say to our lord, what shall we speak and how shall we justify ourselves; God has this day found the iniquity of all your servants, therefore has he done this thing to us this day.

32 Joseph rose up and caught hold of Benjamin and took him from his brothers with violence, and he came to the house and locked the door at them; Joseph commanded him that was set over his house that he should say to them, Thus says the king, Go in peace to your father, behold I have taken the man in whose hand my cup was found.

CHAPTER 54

1 When Judah saw the dealings of Joseph with them, Judah approached him and broke open the door, and came with his brothers before Joseph.

2 And Judah said to Joseph, Let it not seem bothersome in the sight of my lord, may your servant I pray you speak a word before you? And Joseph said to him, Speak.

3 Judah spoke before Joseph and his brothers were there standing before them; Judah said to Joseph, Certainly when we first came to our lord to buy food, you did consider us as spies of the land, and we brought Benjamin before you, and you still make sport of us this day.

4 Now therefore let the king hear my words and send I pray you our brother that he may go along with us to our father, that your son not perish this day with all the souls of the inhabitants of Egypt.

5 Do you not know what two of my brothers, Simeon and Levi, did to the city of Shechem and to seven cities of the Amorites on account of our sister Dinah, and also what they would do for the sake of their brother Benjamin?

6 I with my strength, who am greater and mightier than both of them, come this day on you and your land if you are unwilling to send our brother.

7 Have you not heard what our God who made choice of us did to Pharaoh on account of Sarah our mother, whom he took away from our father, that he struck him and his household with heavy plagues; even to this day the Egyptians relate this wonder to each other? So will our God do to you on account of Benjamin whom you have this day taken from his father, and on account of the evils which you this day heap over us in your land; for our God will remember his covenant with our father Abraham and bring evil on you because you have grieved the soul of our father this day.

8 Now hear my words that I have this day spoken to you, and send our brother that he may go away that you and the people of your land not die by the sword, for you cannot all prevail over me.

9 Joseph answered Judah, saying, Why have you opened wide your mouth and why do you boast over us, saying, Strength is with you? As Pharaoh lives, if I command all my valiant men to fight with you, certainly you and these your brothers would sink into the mud.

10 Judah said to Joseph, Certainly it becomes you and your people to fear me; as the Lord lives if I once draw my sword I shall not sheathe it again until I shall this day have slain all Egypt, and I will begin with you and finish with Pharaoh your master.

11 And Joseph answered and said to him, Certainly strength belongs not alone to you; I am stronger and mightier than you; certainly if you draw your sword I will put it to your neck and the necks of all your brothers.

12 Judah said to him, Certainly if I this day open my mouth against you I would swallow you up that you be destroyed from off the earth and perish this day from your kingdom. And Joseph said, Certainly if you open your mouth I have power and might to close your mouth with a stone until you shall not be able to utter a word; see how many stones are before us, truly I can take a stone and force it into your mouth and break your jaws.

13 And Judah said, God is witness between us, that we have not hereto desired to battle with you, only give us our brother and we will go from you. Joseph answered and said, As Pharaoh lives, if all the kings of Canaan came together with you, you should not take him from my hand.

14 Now therefore go your way to your father, and your brother shall be to me a slave, for he has robbed the king's house. And Judah said, What is it to you or to the character of the king, certainly the king sends forth from his house, throughout the land, silver and gold either in gifts or expenses, and you still talk about your cup which you did place in our brother's bag and say that he has stolen it from you?

15 God forbid that our brother Benjamin or any of the offspring of Abraham should do this thing to steal from you, or from any one else, whether king, prince, or any man.

16 Now therefore cease this accusation that the whole earth not hear your words, saying, For a little silver the king of Egypt argued with the men, and he accused them and took their brother for a slave.

17 And Joseph answered and said, Take this cup and go from me and leave your brother for a slave, for it is the judgment of a thief to be a slave.

18 And Judah said, Why are you not ashamed of your words, to leave our brother and to take your cup? Certainly if you give us your cup, or a thousand times as much, we will not leave our brother for the silver which is found in the hand of any man, that we will not die over him.

19 Joseph answered, And why did you turn away from your brother and sell him for twenty pieces of silver to this day; why then will you not do the same to this your brother?

20 And Judah said, The Lord is witness between me and you that we desire not your battles; now therefore give us our brother and we will go from you without quarreling.

21 And Joseph answered and said, If all the kings of the land should assemble they will not be able to take your brother from my hand. Judah said, What shall we say to our father, when he sees that our brother comes not with us, and will grieve over him?

22 Joseph answered and said, This is the thing which you shall tell to your father, saying, The rope has gone after the bucket.

23 Judah said, Certainly you are a king, and why speak you these things, giving a false judgment? Woe to the king who is like you.

24 Joseph answered and said, There is no false judgment in the word that I spoke on account of your brother Joseph, for all of you sold him to the Midianites for twenty pieces of silver. And you all denied it to your father and said to him, An evil beast has devoured him; Joseph has been torn to pieces.

25 And Judah said, Behold the fire of Shem burns in my heart, now I will burn all your land with fire; Joseph answered and said, Certainly your sister-in-law Tamar, who killed your sons, extinguished the fire of Shechem.

26 Judah said, If I pluck out a single hair from my flesh, I will fill all Egypt with its blood.

27 Joseph answered and said, Such is your custom to do as you did to your brother whom you sold, and you dipped his coat in blood and brought it to your father in order that he might say an evil beast devoured him and here is his blood.

28 When Judah heard this thing he was greatly enraged and his anger burned within him, and there was before him in that place a stone, the weight of which was about four hundred shekels; Judah's anger was set ablaze and he took the stone in one hand and cast it to the heavens and caught it with his left hand.

29 He placed it afterward under his legs, and he sat on it with all his strength and the stone was turned into dust from the force of Judah.

30 Joseph saw the act of Judah and he was very much afraid, but he commanded Manassah his son and he also did with another stone like to the act of Judah, and Judah said to his brothers, Let not any of you say this man is an Egyptian, but by his doing this thing he is of our father's family.

31 And Joseph said, Not to you only is strength given, for we are also powerful men, and why will you boast over us all? Judah said to Joseph, Send I pray you our brother and ruin not your country this day.

32 And Joseph answered and said to them, Go and tell your father an evil beast has devoured him as you said concerning your brother Joseph.

33 Judah spoke to his brother Naphtali, and said to him, Hurry, go now and number all the streets of Egypt and come and tell me; Simeon said to him, Let not this thing be a trouble to you; now I will go to the mount and take up one large stone from the mount and level it at every one in Egypt, and kill all that are in it.

34 Joseph heard all these words that his brothers spoke before him, and they did not know that Joseph understood them for they imagined that he knew not to speak Hebrew.

35 Joseph was greatly afraid at the words of his brothers that they should destroy Egypt, and he commanded his son Manasseh, saying, Go now, hurry and gather to me all the inhabitants of Egypt, and all the valiant men together, and let them come to me now on horseback and on foot and with all sorts of musical instruments, and Manasseh went and did so.

36 Naphtali went as Judah had commanded him, for Naphtali was lightfooted as one of the swift stags, and he could walk on the ears of corn and they would not break under him.

37 He went and numbered all the streets of Egypt and found them to be twelve, and he came quickly and told Judah, and Judah said to his brothers, Hurry and put on every man his sword on his loins and we will come over Egypt and strike them all, and let not a remnant remain.

38 Judah said, Behold, I will destroy three of the streets with my strength, and you shall each destroy one street; when Judah was speaking this thing, then the inhabitants of Egypt and all the mighty men came toward them with all sorts of musical instruments and with loud shouting.

39 And their number was five hundred cavalry and ten thousand infantry, and four hundred men who could fight without sword or spear, only with their hands and strength.

40 And all the mighty men came with great storming and shouting, and they all surrounded the sons of Jacob and terrified them, and the ground quaked at the sound of their shouting.

41 When the sons of Jacob saw these troops they were greatly afraid of their lives, and Joseph did so in order to terrify the sons of Jacob to become tranquilized.

42 Judah, seeing some of his brothers terrified, said to them, Why are you afraid while the grace of God is with us? Judah saw all the people of Egypt surrounding them at the command of Joseph to terrify them, only Joseph commanded them, saying, Do not touch any of them.

43 Then Judah hurried and drew his sword and uttered a loud and bitter scream, and he struck with his sword, and he stomped on the ground and he still continued to shout against all the people.

44 When he did this thing the Lord caused the terror of Judah and his brothers to fall on the valiant men and all the people that surrounded them.

45 They all fled at the sound of the shouting, and they were terrified and fell one on the other, and many of them died as they fell, and they all fled from before Judah and his brothers and from before Joseph.

46 While they were fleeing, Judah and his brothers pursued them to the house of Pharaoh and they all escaped; Judah again sat before Joseph and roared at him like a lion, and gave a great and tremendous shriek at him.

47 The shriek was heard at a distance, and all the inhabitants of Succoth heard it, and all Egypt quaked at the sound of the shriek; also the walls of Egypt and of the land of Goshen fell in from the shaking of the earth, and Pharaoh also fell from his throne on the ground; also all the pregnant women of Egypt and Goshen miscarried when they heard the noise of the shaking, for they were terribly afraid.

48 And Pharaoh sent word, saying, What is this thing that has this day happened in the land of Egypt? They came and told him all the things from beginning to end, and Pharaoh was alarmed and he wondered and was greatly afraid.

49 His fright increased when he heard all these things, and he sent to Joseph, saying, You have brought to me the Hebrews to destroy all Egypt; what will you do with that thievish slave? Send him away and let him go with his brothers, and let us not perish through their evil, even we, you and all Egypt.

50 And if you desire not to do this thing, cast off from you all my valuable things, and go with them to their land if you delightest in it, for they will this day destroy my whole country and kill all my people; even all the women of Egypt have miscarried through their scream. See what they have done merely by their shouting and speaking? And if they fight with the sword, they will destroy the land; now therefore choose that which you desire, whether me or the Hebrews, whether Egypt or the land of the Hebrews.

51 They came and told Joseph all the words of Pharaoh that he had said concerning him, and Joseph was greatly afraid at the words of Pharaoh and Judah and his brothers were still standing before Joseph indignant and enraged, and all the sons of Jacob roared at Joseph, like the roaring of the sea and its waves.

52 Joseph was greatly afraid of his brothers and on account of Pharaoh, and Joseph sought a way to make himself known to his brothers, that they should not destroy all Egypt.

53 Joseph commanded his son Manasseh, and Manasseh went and approached Judah and placed his hand on his shoulder, and the anger of Judah was stilled.

54 And Judah said to his brothers, Let no one of you say that this is the act of an Egyptian youth for this is the work of my father's house.

55 Joseph seeing and knowing that Judah's anger was stilled, he approached to speak to Judah in the language of mildness.

56 And Joseph said to Judah, Certainly you speak truth and have this day verified your assertions concerning your strength, and may your God who delights in you, increase your welfare; but tell me truly why from among all your brothers do you argue with me on account of the lad, as none of them have spoken one word to me concerning him.

57 And Judah answered Joseph, saying, Certainly you must know that I was security for the lad to his father, saying, If I brought him not to him I should bear his blame forever.

58 So I have approached you from among all my brothers, for I saw that you were unwilling to allow him to go from you; now therefore may I find grace in your sight that you shall send him to go with us and then I will remain as a substitute for him, to serve you in whatever you desire, for whereever you shall send me I will go to serve you with great energy.

59 Send me now to a mighty king who has rebelled against you, and you shall know what I will do to him and to his land; although he may have cavalry and infantry or an exceeding mighty people, I will kill them all and bring the king's head before you.

60 Do you not know or have you not heard that our father Abraham with his servant Eliezer struck all the kings of Elam with their hosts in one night, they left not one remaining? And ever since that day our father's strength was given to us for an inheritance, for us and our descendants forever.

61 Joseph answered and said, You speak truth, and falsehood is not in your mouth, for it was also told to us that the Hebrews have power and that the Lord their God delights much in them, and who then can stand before them?

62 However, on this condition will I send your brother, if you will bring before me his brother the son of his mother, of whom you said that he had gone from you down to Egypt; it shall come to pass when you bring to me his brother I will take him in his stead, because not one of you was security for him to your father. When he shall come to me, I will then send with you his brother for whom you have been security.

63 And Judah's anger was set ablaze against Joseph when he spoke this thing, and his eyes dropped blood with anger, and he said to his brothers, How does this man this day seek his own destruction and that of all Egypt!

64 And Simeon answered Joseph, saying, Did we not tell you at first that we knew not the particular spot to which he went, and whether he be dead or alive, and why does my lord speak these things?

65 Joseph, observing the countenance of Judah discerned that his anger began to kindle when he spoke to him, saying, Bring to me your other brother instead of this brother.

66 And Joseph said to his brothers, Certainly you said that your brother was either dead or lost, now if I should call him this day and he should come before you, would you give him to me instead of his brother?

67 And Joseph began to speak and call out, Joseph, Joseph, come this day before me, and appear to your brothers and sit before them.

68 When Joseph spoke this thing before them, they looked each a different way to see from where Joseph would come before them.

69 And Joseph observed all their acts, and said to them, Why do you look here and there? I am Joseph whom you sold to Egypt, now therefore let it not grieve you that you sold me, for as a support during the famine did God send me from you.

70 And his brothers were terrified at him when they heard the words of Joseph, and Judah was greatly terrified at him.

71 When Benjamin heard the words of Joseph he was before them in the inner part of the house, and Benjamin ran to Joseph his brother and embraced him and fell on his neck, and they wept.

72 When Joseph's brothers saw that Benjamin had fallen on his brother's neck and wept with him, they also fell on Joseph and embraced him, and they wept a great weeping with Joseph.

73 And the voice was heard in the house of Joseph that they were Joseph's brothers, and it pleased Pharaoh greatly, for he was afraid of them that they should destroy Egypt.

74 Pharaoh sent his servants to Joseph to congratulate him concerning his brothers who had come to him, and all the captains of the armies and troops that were in Egypt came to rejoice with Joseph, and all Egypt rejoiced greatly about Joseph's brothers.

75 And Pharaoh sent his servants to Joseph, saying, Tell your brothers to fetch all belonging to them and let them come to me, and I will place them in the best part of the land of Egypt, and they did so.

76 Joseph commanded him that was set over his house to bring out to his brothers gifts and garments, and he brought out to them many garments being robes of royalty and many gifts, and Joseph divided them among his brothers.

77 And he gave to each of his brothers a change of garments of gold and silver, and three hundred pieces of silver, and Joseph commanded them all to be dressed in these garments, and to be brought before Pharaoh.

78 And Pharaoh, seeing that all Joseph's brothers were valiant men, and of beautiful appearance, greatly rejoiced.

79 And afterward they went out from the presence of Pharaoh to go to the land of Canaan, to their father, and their brother Benjamin was with them.

80 Joseph rose up and gave to them eleven chariots from Pharaoh, and Joseph gave to them his chariot on which he rode on the day of his being crowned in Egypt, to fetch his father to Egypt; Joseph sent to all his brothers' children, garments according to their numbers, and a hundred pieces of silver to each of them, and he also sent garments to the wives of his brothers from the garments of the king's wives, and he sent them.

81 He gave to each of his brothers ten men to go with them to the land of Canaan to serve them, to serve their children and all belonging to them in coming to Egypt.

82 Joseph sent by the hand of his brother Benjamin ten suits of garments for his ten sons, a portion above the rest of the children of the sons of Jacob.

83 And he sent to each fifty pieces of silver, and ten chariots on the account of Pharaoh; he sent to his father ten asses laden with all the luxuries of Egypt, and ten female asses laden with corn and bread and nourishment for his father and to all that were with him as provisions for the road.

84 And he sent to his sister Dinah garments of silver and gold, and frankincense and myrrh, and aloes and women's ornaments in great plenty; he sent the same from the wives of Pharaoh to the wives of Benjamin.

85 He gave to all his brothers, also to their wives, all sorts of onyx stones and bdellium, and from all the valuable things among the great people of Egypt, nothing of all the costly things was left but what Joseph sent of to his father's household.

86 He sent his brothers away, and they went, and he sent his brother Benjamin with them.

87 And Joseph went out with them to accompany them on the road to the borders of Egypt, and he commanded them concerning his father and his household to come to Egypt.

88 And he said to them, Do not quarrel on the road, for this thing was from the Lord to keep a great people from starvation, for there will be yet five years of famine in the land.

89 And he commanded them, saying, When you come to the land of Canaan, do not come suddenly before my father about this affair, but act in your wisdom.

90 And Joseph ceased to command them, and he turned and went back to Egypt, and the sons of Jacob went to the land of Canaan with joy and cheerfulness to their father Jacob.

91 Tthey came to the borders of the land, and they said to each other, What shall we do in this matter before our father, for if we come suddenly to him and tell him the matter, he will be greatly alarmed at our words and will not believe us.

92 They went along until they came near to their houses and they found Serach, the daughter of Asher, going forth to meet them; the damsel was very good and subtle, and knew how to play on the harp.

93 They called to her and she came before them and kissed them, and they took her and gave her a harp, saying, Go now before our father and sit before him; strike on the harp and speak these words.

94 And they commanded her to go to their house, and she took the harp and hurried before them, and she came and sat near Jacob.

95 She played well and sang, and uttered in the sweetness of her words: Joseph my uncle is living and he rules throughout the land of Egypt, and is not dead.

96 She continued to repeat and utter these words, and Jacob heard her words and they were agreeable to him.

97 He listened while she repeated them twice and three times, and joy entered the heart of Jacob at the sweetness of her words, and the spirit of God was on him and he knew all her words to be true.

98 Jacob blessed Serach when she spoke these words before him, and he said to her, My daughter, may death never prevail over you, for you have revived my spirit; only speak again before me as you have spoken, for you have uplifted me with all your words.

99 And she continued to sing these words and Jacob listened and it pleased him, and he rejoiced, and the spirit of God was on him.

100 While he was yet speaking with her, he saw his sons come to him with horses and chariots and royal garments and servants running before them.

101 Jacob rose up to meet them and saw his sons dressed in royal garments and he saw all the treasures that Joseph had sent to them.

102 They said to him, Be informed that our brother Joseph is living, and it is he who rules throughout the land of Egypt, and

it is he who spoke to us as we told you.

103 Jacob heard all the words of his sons, and his heart palpitated at their words, for he could not believe them until he saw all that Joseph had given them and what he had sent him, and all the signs which Joseph had spoken to them.

104 They opened all before him, and showed him all that Joseph had sent; they gave to each what Joseph had sent him and he knew that they had spoken the truth, and he rejoiced greatly an account of his son.

105 Jacob said, It is enough for me that my son Joseph is still living; I will go and see him before I die.

106 And his sons told him all that had happened to them, and Jacob said, I will go down to Egypt to see my son and his children.

107 Jacob rose up and put on the garments which Joseph had sent him, and after he had washed and shaved his hair, he put on his head the turban which Joseph had sent him.

108 All the people of Jacob's house and their wives put on the garments which Joseph had sent to them, and they greatly rejoiced at Joseph that he was still living and that he was ruling in Egypt.

109 And all the inhabitants of Canaan heard of this thing, and they came and rejoiced much with Jacob that he was still living.

110 Jacob made a feast for them for three days, and all the kings of Canaan and nobles of the land ate and drank and rejoiced in the house of Jacob.

CHAPTER 55

1 It came to pass after this that Jacob said, I will go and see my son in Egypt and then come back to the land of Canaan of which God had spoken to Abraham, for I cannot leave the land of my birth-place.

2 Then the word of the Lord came to him, saying, Go down to Egypt with all your household and remain there; fear not to go down to Egypt for I will there make you a great nation.

3 Jacob said within himself, I will go and see my son whether the fear of his God is yet in his heart among all the inhabitants of Egypt.

4 And the Lord said to Jacob, Fear not about Joseph, for he still retains his integrity to serve me, as will seem good in your sight. Jacob rejoiced greatly concerning his son.

5 At that time Jacob commanded his sons and household to go to Egypt according to the word of the Lord to him, and Jacob rose up with his sons and all his household, and he went out from the land of Canaan from Beersheba with joy and gladness of heart; they went to the land of Egypt.

6 It came to pass when they came near Egypt, Jacob sent Judah before him to Joseph that he might show him a situation in Egypt, and Judah did according to the word of his father; he hurried and ran and came to Joseph and they assigned for them a place in the land of Goshen for all his household, and Judah returned and came along the road to his father.

7 Joseph harnessed the chariot and assembled all his mighty men and his servants and all the officers of Egypt in order to go and meet his father Jacob, and Joseph's mandate was proclaimed in Egypt, saying, All that do not go to meet Jacob shall die.

8 On the next day Joseph went forth with all Egypt a great and mighty host, all dressed in garments of fine linen and purple and with instruments of silver and gold and with their instruments of war with them.

9 And they all went to meet Jacob with all sorts of musical instruments, with drums and timbrels, strewing myrrh and aloes all along the road; they all went after this fashion and the earth shook at their shouting.

10 All the women of Egypt went on the roofs of Egypt and on the walls to meet Jacob, and on the head of Joseph was Pharaoh's regal crown, for Pharaoh had sent it to him to put on at the time of his going to meet his father.

11 When Joseph came within fifty cubits of his father, he alighted from the chariot and he walked toward his father; when all the officers of Egypt and her nobles saw that Joseph had gone on foot toward his father, they also alighted and walked on foot toward Jacob.

12 And when Jacob approached the camp of Joseph, Jacob observed the camp that was coming toward him with Joseph and it gratified him, and Jacob was astonished at it.

13 Jacob said to Judah, Who is that man whom I see in the camp of Egypt dressed in kingly robes with a very red garment on him and a royal crown on his head, who has alighted from his chariot and is coming toward us? And Judah answered his father, saying, He is your son Joseph the king; and Jacob rejoiced in seeing the glory of his son.

14 Joseph came near to his father and he bowed to his father, and all the men of the camp bowed to the ground with him before Jacob.

15 And behold Jacob ran and hurried to his son Joseph and fell on his neck and kissed him, and they wept; Joseph also embraced his father and kissed him and they wept, and all the people of Egypt wept with them.

16 Jacob said to Joseph, Now I will die cheerfully after I have seen your face, that you are still living and with glory.

17 The sons of Jacob and their wives and their children and their servants, and all the household of Jacob wept greatly with Joseph and they kissed him and wept greatly with him.

18 Joseph and all his people returned home afterward to Egypt, and Jacob and his sons and all the children of his household came with Joseph to Egypt; Joseph placed them in the best part of Egypt, in the land of Goshen.

19 Joseph said to his father and his brothers, I will go up and tell Pharaoh, saying, My brothers and my father's household and all belonging to them have come to me, and now they are in the land of Goshen.

20 And Joseph did so and took from his brothers Reuben, Issachar, Zebulun and his brother Benjamin and he placed them before Pharaoh.

21 And Joseph spoke to Pharaoh, saying, My brothers and my father's household and all belonging to them, together with their flocks and cattle have come to me from the land of Canaan, to sojourn in Egypt; for the famine was severely on them.

22 And Pharaoh said to Joseph, Place your father and brothers in the best part of the land; withhold not from them all that is good, and cause them to eat of the best of the land.

23 And Joseph answered, saying, Yes, I have stationed them in the land of Goshen for they are shepherds, therefore let them remain in Goshen to feed their flocks, apart from the Egyptians.

24 And Pharaoh said to Joseph, Do with your brothers all that they shall say to you. And the sons of Jacob bowed down to Pharaoh, and they went forth from him in peace, and Joseph afterward brought his father before Pharaoh.

25 And Jacob came and bowed down to Pharaoh, and Jacob blessed Pharaoh, and he then went out; Jacob and all his sons and all his household lived in the land of Goshen.

26 In the second year, that is in the hundred and thirtieth year of the life of Jacob, Joseph maintained his father and his brothers and all his father's household with bread according to their little ones; all the days of the famine they lacked nothing.

27 And Joseph gave to them the best part of the whole land; the best of Egypt they had, all the days of Joseph, and Joseph also gave to them and to all his father's household, clothes and garments year by year; the sons of Jacob remained securely in Egypt all the days of their brother.

28 And Jacob always ate at Joseph's table, Jacob and his sons did not leave Joseph's table day or night, besides what Jacob's children consumed in their houses.

29 And all Egypt ate bread during the days of the famine from the house of Joseph, for all the Egyptians sold all belonging to them on account of the famine.

30 Joseph purchased all the lands and fields of Egypt for bread on the account of Pharaoh, and Joseph supplied all Egypt with bread all the days of the famine; Joseph collected all the silver and gold that came to him for the corn which they bought throughout the land, and he accumulated much gold and silver, besides an immense quantity of onyx stones, bdellium and valuable garments which they brought to Joseph from every part of the land when their money was gone.

31 And Joseph took all the silver and gold that came into his hand, about seventy two talents of gold and silver, and also onyx stones and bdellium in great abundance, and Joseph went and concealed them in four parts; he concealed one part in the wilderness near the Red sea, and one part by the river Perath, and the third and fourth parts he concealed in the desert opposite to the wilderness of Persia and Media.

32 He took part of the gold and silver that was left and gave it to all his brothers, to all his father's household, and to all the women of his father's household; the rest he brought to the house of Pharaoh, about twenty talents of gold and silver.

33 Joseph gave all the gold and silver that was left to Pharaoh, and Pharaoh placed it in the treasury, and the days of the famine ceased after that in the land. They sowed and reaped in the whole land, and they obtained their usual quantity year by year; they lacked nothing.

34 And Joseph lived securely in Egypt and the whole land was under his advice, and his father and all his brothers lived in the land of Goshen and took possession of it.

35 Joseph was very aged, advanced in days, and his two sons Ephraim and Manasseh remained constantly in the house of Jacob, together with the children of the sons of Jacob their brothers, to learn the ways of the Lord and his law.

36 And Jacob and his sons lived in the land of Egypt in the land of Goshen, and they took possession of it, and they were prolific and multiplied in it.

CHAPTER 56

1 Jacob lived in the land of Egypt seventeen years, and the days of Jacob, and the years of his life were a hundred and forty seven years.

2 At that time Jacob was attacked with that illness of which he died and he sent and called for his son Joseph from Egypt, and Joseph his son came from Egypt and came to his father.

3 Jacob said to Joseph and to his sons, Behold I die, and the God of your ancestors will visit you and bring you back to the land which the Lord swore to give to you and to your children after you; now therefore when I am dead, bury me in the cave which is in Machpelah in Hebron in the land of Canaan, near my ancestors.

4 Jacob made his sons swear to bury him in Machpelah, in Hebron, and his sons swore to him concerning this thing.

5 And he commanded them, saying, Serve the Lord your God, for he who delivered your fathers will also deliver you from all trouble.

6 And Jacob said, Call all your children to me, and all the children of Jacob's sons came and sat before him, and Jacob blessed them, and he said to them, The Lord God of your fathers shall grant you a thousand times as much and bless you, and may

he give you the blessing of your father Abraham. And all the children of Jacob's sons went forth on that day after he had blessed them.

7 On the next day Jacob again called for his sons and they all assembled and came to him and sat before him, and Jacob on that day blessed his sons before his death; each man did he bless according to his blessing. So it is written in the book of the law of the Lord pertaining to Israel.

8 And Jacob said to Judah, I know my son that you are a mighty man for your brothers; reign over them, and your sons shall reign over their sons forever.

9 Only teach your sons the bow and all the weapons of war, in order that they may fight the battles of their brother who will rule over his enemies.

10 And Jacob again commanded his sons on that day, saying, Behold I shall this day be gathered to my people; carry me up from Egypt and bury me in the cave of Machpelah as I have commanded you.

11 But take care I pray you that none of your sons carry me, only yourselves, and this is the manner you shall do to me, when you carry my body to go with it to the land of Canaan to bury me:

12 Judah, Issachar and Zebulun shall carry my bier at the eastern side; Reuben, Simeon and Gad at the south; Ephraim, Manasseh and Benjamin at the west; Dan, Asher and Naphtali at the north.

13 Let not Levi carry with you, for he and his sons will carry the ark of the covenant of the Lord with the Israelites in the camp, neither let Joseph my son carry, for as a king so let his glory be; but Ephraim and Manasseh shall be in their stead.

14 Thus shall you do to me when you carry me away; do not neglect anything of all that I command you and it shall come to pass when you do this to me, that the Lord will remember you favorably and your children after you forever.

15 And you my sons, honor each his brother and his relative, and command your children and your children's children after you to serve the Lord God of your ancestors always,

16 In order that you may prolong your days in the land, you and your children and your children's children forever, when you do what is good and upright in the sight of the Lord your God, to follow in all his ways.

17 And you, Joseph my son, forgive I pray you the prongs of your brothers and all their wrongdoings in the injury that they heaped on you, for God intended it for you and your children's benefit.

18 And O my son leave not your brothers to the inhabitants of Egypt, neither hurt their feelings, for behold I consign them to the hand of God and in your hand to guard them from the Egyptians; the sons of Jacob answered their father saying, O, our father, all that you have commanded us, so will we do; may God only be with us.

19 Jacob said to his sons, So may God be with you when you keep all his ways; turn not from his ways either to the right or the left in performing what is good and upright in his sight.

20 For I know that many and severe troubles will befall you in the latter days in the land, yes, your children and children's children; only serve the Lord and he will save you from all trouble.

21 It shall come to pass when you shall go after God to serve him and will teach your children after you, and your children's children, to know the Lord, then will the Lord raise up to you and your children a servant from among your children; the Lord will deliver you through his hand from all affliction, and bring you out of Egypt and bring you back to the land of your fathers to inherit it securely.

22 Jacob ceased commanding his sons, and he drew his feet into the bed. He died and was gathered to his people.

23 And Joseph fell on his father and he cried out and wept over him and he kissed him, and he called out in a bitter voice, and he said, O my father, my father.

24 His son's wives and all his household came and fell on Jacob, and they wept over him and cried in a very loud voice concerning Jacob.

25 All the sons of Jacob rose up together, and they tore their garments, and they all put sackcloth on their loins; they fell on their faces, and they cast dust on their heads toward the heavens.

26 And the thing was told to Osnath Joseph's wife; she rose up and put on a sack and she with all the Egyptian women came and mourned and wept for Jacob.

27 Also all the people of Egypt who knew Jacob came all on that day when they heard this thing, and all Egypt wept for many days.

28 Also from the land of Canaan the women came to Egypt when they heard that Jacob was dead, and they wept for him in Egypt for seventy days.

29 It came to pass after this that Joseph commanded his servants the doctors to embalm his father with myrrh and frankincense and all manner of incense and perfume, and the doctors embalmed Jacob as Joseph had commanded them.

30 And all the people of Egypt and the elders and all the inhabitants of the land of Goshen wept and mourned over Jacob, and all his sons and the children of his household lamented and mourned over their father Jacob many days.

31 After the days of his weeping had passed away, at the end of seventy days, Joseph said to Pharaoh, I will go up and bury my father in the land of Canaan as he made me swear, and then I will return.

32 Pharaoh sent Joseph, saying, Go up and bury your father as he said, and as he made you swear; Joseph rose up with all his brothers to go to the land of Canaan to bury their father Jacob as he had commanded them.

33 And Pharaoh commanded that it should be announced throughout Egypt, saying, Whoever goes not up with Joseph and his brothers to the land of Canaan to bury Jacob, shall die.

34 And all Egypt heard of Pharaoh's proclamation, and they all rose up together, and all the servants of Pharaoh, and the elders of his house, and all the elders of the land of Egypt went up with Joseph, and all the officers and nobles of Pharaoh went up as the servants of Joseph; they went to bury Jacob in the land of Canaan.

35 And the sons of Jacob carried the bier on which he lay; according to all that their father commanded them, so did his sons to him.

36 The bier was of pure gold, and it was inlaid round about with onyx stones and bdellium; and the covering of the bier was gold woven work, joined with threads, and over them were hooks of onyx stones and bdellium.

37 And Joseph placed on the head of his father Jacob a large golden crown, and he put a golden rod in his hand, and they surrounded the bier as was the custom of kings during their lives.

38 And all the troops of Egypt went before him in this array; at first all the mighty men of Pharaoh and the mighty men of Joseph, and after them the rest of the inhabitants of Egypt; they were all girded with swords and equipped with coats of mail, and the trappings of war were on them.

39 All the weepers and mourners went at a distance opposite to the bier, going and weeping and lamenting, and the rest of the people went after the bier.

40 Joseph and his household went together near the bier barefooted and weeping, and the rest of Joseph's servants went around him; each man had his ornaments on him and they were all armed with their weapons of war.

41 Fifty of Jacob's servants went in front of the bier and they scattered along the road myrrh and aloes, and all manner of perfume, and all the sons of Jacob that carried the bier walked on the perfumery; the servants of Jacob went before them spreading the perfume along the road.

42 And Joseph went up with a heavy camp, and they did after this manner every day until they reached the land of Canaan. They came to the threshing floor of Atad, which was on the other side of Jordan, and they mourned an extremely great and heavy mourning in that place.

43 And all the kings of Canaan heard of this thing and they all went forth, each man from his house, thirty-one kings of Canaan; they all came with their men to mourn and weep over Jacob.

44 All these kings observed Jacob's bier, and there Joseph's crown was on it; they also put their crowns on the bier and encircled it with crowns.

45 All these kings made in that place a great and heavy mourning with the sons of Jacob and Egypt over Jacob, for all the kings of Canaan knew the valor of Jacob and his sons.

46 And the report reached Esau, saying, Jacob died in Egypt, and his sons and all Egypt are conveying him to the land of Canaan to bury him.

47 Esau heard this thing, and he was dwelling in mount Seir; he rose up with his sons and all his people and all his household, a people greatly great, and they came to mourn and weep over Jacob.

48 And it came to pass, when Esau came he mourned for his brother Jacob, and all Egypt and all Canaan again rose up and mourned a great mourning with Esau over Jacob in that place

49 Joseph and his brothers brought their father Jacob from that place, and they went to Hebron to bury Jacob in the cave by his fathers.

50 They came to Kireath-arba, to the cave, and as they came Esau stood with his sons against Joseph and his brothers as a hindrance in the cave, saying, Jacob shall not be buried in here, for it belongs to us and to our father.

51 Joseph and his brothers heard the words of Esau's sons, and they were greatly angered, and Joseph approached Esau, saying, What is this thing which they have spoken? Certainly my father Jacob bought it from you for great riches after the death of Isaac, now five and twenty years ago, and also all the land of Canaan he bought from you and from your sons, and your descendants after you.

52 Jacob bought it for his sons and his descendants after him for an inheritance for ever, and why do you speak these things this day?

53 And Esau answered, saying, You speak falsely and utter lies, for I sold not anything belonging to me in all this land, as you say, neither did my brother Jacob buy what belonged to me in this land.

54 Esau spoke these things in order to deceive Joseph with his words, for Esau knew that Joseph was not present in those days when Esau sold all belonging to him in the land of Canaan to Jacob.

55 Joseph said to Esau, Certainly my father inserted these things with you in the record of purchase, and testified the record with witnesses, and behold it is with us in Egypt.

56 Esau answered, saying to him, Bring the record; all that you will find in the record, so we will do.

57 Joseph called to Naphtali his brother and said, Hurry quickly, stay not, and run I pray you to Egypt and bring all the records; the record of the purchase, the sealed record and the open record, and also all the first records in which all the transactions of the birthright are written, bring with you.

58 You shall bring them to us here, that we may know from them all the words of Esau and his sons which they spoke this day.

59 And Naphtali listened to the voice of Joseph and he hurried and ran to go down to Egypt, and Naphtali was lighter on foot than any of the stags that were on the wilderness, for he could go on ears of corn without crushing them.

60 When Esau saw that Naphtali had gone to fetch the records, he and his sons increased their resistance against the cave,

and Esau and all his people rose up against Joseph and his brothers to battle.

61 All the sons of Jacob and the people of Egypt fought with Esau and his men, and the sons of Esau and his people were smitten before the sons of Jacob, and the sons of Jacob killed of Esau's people forty men.

62 Chushim the son of Dan, the son of Jacob, was at that time with Jacob's sons, but he was about a hundred cubits distant from the place of battle, for he remained with the children of Jacob's sons by Jacob's bier to guard it.

63 And Chushim was dumb and deaf, still he understood the voice of consternation among men.

64 And he asked, saying, Why do you not bury the dead, and what is this great consternation? They answered him the words of Esau and his sons and he ran to Esau in the midst of the battle; he killed Esau with a sword; he cut off his head and it sprang to a distance, and Esau fell among the people of the battle.

65 When Chushim did this thing the sons of Jacob prevailed over the sons of Esau, and the sons of Jacob buried their father Jacob by force in the cave, and the sons of Esau watched it.

66 Jacob was buried in Hebron, in the cave of Machpelah which Abraham had bought from the sons of Heth for the possession of a burial place, and he was buried in very costly garments.

67 No king had such honor paid him as Joseph paid to his father at his death, for he buried him with great honor like the burial of kings.

68 And Joseph and his brothers made a mourning of seven days for their father.

CHAPTER 57

1 It was after this that the sons of Esau waged war with the sons of Jacob, and the sons of Esau fought with the sons of Jacob in Hebron, and Esau was still lying dead and not buried.

2 The battle was heavy between them, and the sons of Esau were smitten before the sons of Jacob, and the sons of Jacob killed of the sons of Esau eighty men, and not one died of the people of the sons of Jacob; the hand of Joseph prevailed over all the people of the sons of Esau, and he took Zepho, the son of Eliphaz, the son of Esau, and fifty of his men captive; he bound them with chains of iron, and gave them into the hands of his servants to bring them to Egypt.

3 It came to pass when the sons of Jacob had taken Zepho and his people captive, all those that remained were greatly afraid for their lives from the house of Esau, that they should also be taken captive; they all fled with Eliphaz the son of Esau and his people, with Esau's body, and they went on their road to Mount Seir.

4 They came to Mount Seir and they buried Esau in Seir, but they had not brought his head with them to Seir, for it was buried in that place where the battle had been in Hebron.

5 And it came to pass when the sons of Esau had fled from before the sons of Jacob, the sons of Jacob pursued them to the borders of Seir, but they did not kill a single man from among them when they pursued them, for Esau's body which they carried with them increased their confusion. So they fled and the sons of Jacob turned back from them and came up to the place where their brothers were in Hebron, and they remained there on that day, and on the next day until they rested from the battle.

6 It came to pass on the third day they assembled all the sons of Seir the Horite, and they assembled all the children of the east, a multitude of people like the sand of the sea, and they went and came down to Egypt to fight with Joseph and his brothers in order to deliver their brothers.

7 Joseph and all the sons of Jacob heard that the sons of Esau and the children of the east had come on them to do battle in order to deliver their brothers.

8 Joseph and his brothers and the strong men of Egypt went forth and fought in the city of Rameses, and Joseph and his brothers dealt out a tremendous blow among the sons of Esau and the children of the east.

9 They killed of them six hundred thousand men, and they killed among them all the mighty men of the children of Seir the Horite; there were only a few of them left, and they killed also a great many of the children of the east, and of the children of Esau; Eliphaz the son of Esau, and the children of the east all fled before Joseph and his brothers.

10 Joseph and his brothers pursued them until they came to Succoth, and they yet killed of them in Succoth thirty men, and the rest escaped and they fled each to his city.

11 And Joseph and his brothers and the mighty men of Egypt turned back from them with joy and cheerfulness of heart, for they had smitten all their enemies.

12 Zepho the son of Eliphaz and his men were still slaves in Egypt to the sons of Jacob, and their pains increased.

13 When the sons of Esau and the sons of Seir returned to their land, the sons of Seir saw that they had all fallen into the hands of the sons of Jacob and the people of Egypt, on account of the battle of the sons of Esau.

14 And the sons of Seir said to the sons of Esau, You have seen and therefore you know that this camp was on your account, and not one mighty man or an adept one in war remaineth.

15 So now go forth from our land, go from us to the land of Canaan to the land of the dwelling of your fathers; wherefore shall your children inherit the effects of our children in latter days?

16 And the children of Esau would not listen to the children of Seir, and the children of Seir considered to make war with them.

17 The children of Esau sent secretly to Angeas king of Africa, the same is Dinhabah, saying,

18 Send to us some of your men and let them come to us, and we will fight together with the children of Seir the Horite, for they have resolved to fight with us to drive us away from the land.

19 And Angeas king of Dinhabah did so, for he was in those days friendly to the children of Esau, and Angeas sent five hundred valiant infantry to the children of Esau, and eight hundred cavalry.

20 The children of Seir sent to the children of the east and to the children of Midian, saying, You have seen what the children of Esau have done to us, on whose account we are almost all destroyed in their battle with the sons of Jacob.

21 So now come to us and assist us, and we will fight them together; we will drive them from the land and be avenged of the cause of our brothers who died for their sakes in their battle with their brothers the sons of Jacob.

22 And all the children of the east listened to the children of Seir, and they came to them about eight hundred men with drawn swords, and the children of Esau fought with the children of Seir at that time in the wilderness of Paran.

23 The children of Seir won over the sons of Esau, and the children of Seir killed on that day of the children of Esau in that battle about two hundred men of the people of Angeas king of Dinhabah.

24 And on the second day the children of Esau came again to fight a second time with the children of Seir, and the battle was severe on the children of Esau this second time, and it troubled them greatly on account of the children of Seir.

25 And when the children of Esau saw that the children of Seir were more powerful than they were, some men of the children of Esau turned and assisted the children of Seir their enemies.

26 And there fell yet of the people of the children of Esau in the second battle fifty-eight men of the people at Angeas king of Dinhabah.

27 And on the third day the children of Esau heard that some of their brothers had turned from them to fight against them in the second battle; and the children of Esau mourned when they heard this thing.

28 They said, What shall we do to our brothers who turned from us to assist the children of Seir our enemies? And the children of Esau again sent to Angeas king of Dinhabah, saying,

29 Send to us again other men that with them we may fight with the children of Seir, for they have already twice been stronger than we were.

30 And Angeas again sent to the children of Esau about six hundred valiant men, and they came to assist the children of Esau.

31 In ten days' time the children of Esau again waged war with the children of Seir in the wilderness of Paran, and the battle was very severe on the children of Seir; the children of Esau won this time over the children of Seir, and the children of Seir were smitten before the children of Esau; the children of Esau killed from them about two thousand men.

32 And all the mighty men of the children of Seir died in this battle, and there only remained their young children that were left in their cities.

33 All Midian and the children of the east went themselves in flight from the battle, and they left the children of Seir and fled when they saw that the battle was severe on them; the children of Esau pursued all the children of the east until they reached their land.

34 And the children of Esau killed yet of them about two hundred and fifty men and from the people of the children of Esau there fell in that battle about thirty men, but this evil came on them through their brothers turning from them to assist the children of Seir the Horite; the children of Esau again heard of the evil doings of their brothers, and they again mourned on account of this thing.

35 It came to pass after the battle, the children of Esau turned back and came home to Seir, and the children of Esau killed those who had remained in the land of the children of Seir; they killed also their wives and little ones, they left not a soul alive except fifty young boys and girls whom they allowed to live; the children of Esau did not put them to death, and the boys became their slaves, and the girls they took for wives.

36 The children of Esau lived in Seir in the place of the children of Seir, and they inherited their land and took possession of it.

37 And the children of Esau took all belonging in the land to the children of Seir, also their flocks, their bullocks and their goods, and all belonging to the children of Seir did the children of Esau take. And the children of Esau lived in Seir in the place of the children of Seir to this day, and the children of Esau divided the land into divisions to the five sons of Esau, according to their families.

38 It came to pass in those days that the children of Esau resolved to crown a king over them in the land of which they possessed. And they said to each other, Not so, for he shall reign over us in our land; we shall be under his counsel and he shall fight our battles against our enemies, and they did so.

39 And all the children of Esau swore, saying, that none of their brothers should ever reign over them, but a strange man who is not of their brothers; for the souls of all the children of Esau were embittered every man against his son, brother and friend, on account of the evil they sustained from their brothers when they fought with the children of Seir.

40 So then the sons of Esau swore, saying, from that day forward they would not choose a king from their brothers, but one from a strange land to this day.

41 There was a man there from the people of Angeas king of Dinhabah; his name was Bela the son of Beor, who was a very valiant man, beautiful and admired and wise in all wisdom, and a man of sense and counsel; and there was none of the

people of Angeas like him.

42 And all the children of Esau took him and anointed him and they crowned him for a king; they bowed down to him, and said, May the king live, may the king live.

43 They spread out the sheet, and they brought him each man earrings of gold and silver or rings or bracelets, and they made him very rich in silver and in gold, in onyx stones and bdellium, and they made him a royal throne; they placed a regal crown on his head and they built a palace for him and he lived therein, and he became king over all the children of Esau.

44 And the people of Angeas took their wages for their battle from the children of Esau, and they went and returned at that time to their master in Dinhabah.

45 And Bela reigned over the children of Esau thirty years, and the children of Esau lived in the land instead of the children of Seir, and they lived securely in their stead to this day.

CHAPTER 58

1 It came to pass in the thirty-second year of the Israelites going down to Egypt, that is in the seventy-first year of the life of Joseph, in that year died Pharaoh king of Egypt, and Magron his son reigned in his stead.

2 And Pharaoh commanded Joseph before his death to be a father to his son, Magron, and that Magron should be under the care of Joseph and under his counsel.

3 All Egypt consented to this thing that Joseph should be king over them, for all the Egyptians loved Joseph as before, only Magron the son of Pharaoh sat on his father's throne, and he became king in those days in his father's stead.

4 Magron was forty-one years old when he began to reign, and forty years he reigned in Egypt, and all Egypt called his name Pharaoh after the name of his father, as it was their custom to do in Egypt to every king that reigned over them.

5 And it came to pass when Pharaoh reigned in his father's stead, he placed the laws of Egypt and all the affairs of government in the hand of Joseph, as his father had commanded him.

6 Joseph became king over Egypt, for he superintended over all Egypt, and all Egypt was under his care and under his counsel, for all Egypt inclined to Joseph after the death of Pharaoh; they loved him greatly to reign over them.

7 But there were some people among them who did not like him, saying, No stranger shall reign over us. Still the whole government of Egypt was passed in those days onto Joseph, after the death of Pharaoh, he being the regulator, doing as he liked throughout the land without anyone interfering.

8 And all Egypt was under the care of Joseph, and Joseph made war with all his surrounding enemies, and he subdued them; also all the land and all the Philistines, to the borders of Canaan, did Joseph subdue; they were all under his power and they gave a yearly tax to Joseph.

9 Pharaoh king of Egypt sat on his throne in his father's stead, but he was under the control and counsel of Joseph, as he was at first under the control of his father.

10 Neither did he reign but in the land of Egypt only, under the counsel of Joseph, but Joseph reigned over the whole country at that time, from Egypt to the great river Perath.

11 And Joseph was successful in all his ways and the Lord was with him, and the Lord gave Joseph additional wisdom, and honor, and glory, and love toward him in the hearts of the Egyptians and throughout the land; Joseph reigned over the whole country forty years.

12 And all the countries of the Philistines and Canaan and Zidon, and on the other side of Jordan, brought presents to Joseph all his days, and the whole country was in the hands of Joseph, and they brought to him a yearly tribute as it was regulated, for Joseph had fought against all his surrounding enemies and subdued them; the whole country was in the hands of Joseph, and Joseph sat securely on his throne in Egypt.

13 Also all his brothers the sons of Jacob lived securely in the land, all the days of Joseph, and they were prolific and multiplied greatly in the land; they served the Lord all their days as their father Jacob had commanded them.

14 It came to pass at the end of many days and years, when the children of Esau were dwelling quietly in their land with Bela their king, that the children of Esau were prolific and multiplied in the land; they resolved to go and fight with the sons of Jacob and all Egypt, and to deliver their brother Zepho, the son of Eliphaz, and his men, for they were yet in those days slaves to Joseph.

15 The children of Esau sent to all the children of the east and they made peace with them, and all the children of the east came to them to go with the children of Esau to Egypt to battle.

16 There came also to them of the people of Angeas, king of Dinhabah; they also sent to the children of Ishmael and they also came to them.

17 And all this people assembled and came to Seir to assist the children of Esau in their battle, and this camp was very large and strong with people, numerous as the sand of the sea, about eight hundred thousand men, infantry and cavalry, and all these troops went down to Egypt to fight with the sons of Jacob; they encamped by Rameses.

18 And Joseph went forth with his brothers with the mighty men of Egypt, about six hundred men, and they fought with them in the land of Rameses; the sons of Jacob at that time again fought with the children of Esau, in the fiftieth year of the sons of Jacob going down to Egypt, that is the thirtieth year of the reign of Bela over the children of Esau in Seir.

19 And the Lord gave all the mighty men of Esau and the children of the east into the hand of Joseph and his brothers, and the people of the children of Esau and the children of the east were smitten before Joseph.

20 Of the people of Esau and the children of the east that were slain, there fell before the sons of Jacob about two hundred thousand men, and their king Bela the son of Beor fell with them in the battle. When the children of Esau saw that their king had fallen in battle and was dead, their hands became weak in the combat.

21 Joseph and his brothers and all Egypt were still smiting the people of the house of Esau, and all Esau's people were afraid of the sons of Jacob and fled from before them.

22 Joseph and his brothers and all Egypt pursued them a day's journey, and they killed yet from them about three hundred men, continuing to strike them in the road; they afterward turned back from them.

23 Joseph and all his brothers returned to Egypt, not one man was missing from them, but of the Egyptians there fell twelve men.

24 And when Joseph returned to Egypt he ordered Zepho and his men to be additionally bound, and they bound them in irons and they increased their grief.

25 All the people of the children of Esau, and the children of the east, returned in shame each to his city, for all the mighty men that were with them had fallen in battle.

26 When the children of Esau saw that their king had died in battle they hurried and took a man from the people of the children of the east; his name was Jobab the son of Zarach, from the land of Botzrah, and they caused him to reign over them instead of Bela their king.

27 Jobab sat on the throne of Bela as king in his stead, and Jobab reigned in Edom over all the children of Esau ten years; the children of Esau went no more to fight with the sons of Jacob from that day forward, for the sons of Esau knew the courage of the sons of Jacob, and they were greatly afraid of them.

28 But from that day forward the children of Esau hated the sons of Jacob, and the hatred and enmity were very strong between them all the days, to this day.

29 And it came to pass after this, at the end of ten years, Jobab, the son of Zarach, from Botzrah, died, and the children of Esau took a man whose name was Chusham, from the land of Teman, and they made him king over them instead of Jobab; Chusham reigned in Edom over all the children of Esau for twenty years.

30 And Joseph, king of Egypt, and his brothers, and all the children of Israel lived securely in Egypt in those days, together with all the children of Joseph and his brothers, having no hindrance or evil accident and the land of Egypt was at that time at rest from war in the days of Joseph and his brothers.

CHAPTER 59

1 These are the names of the sons of Israel who lived in Egypt, who had come with Jacob; all the sons of Jacob came to Egypt, every man with his household.

2 The children of Leah were Reuben, Simeon, Levi, Judah, Issachar and Zebulun, and their sister Dinah.

3 And the sons of Rachel were Joseph and Benjamin.

4 And the sons of Zilpah, the handmaid of Leah, were Gad and Asher.

5 And the sons of Bilhah, the handmaid of Rachel, were Dan and Naphtali.

6 And these were their descendants that were born to them in the land of Canaan, before they came to Egypt with their father Jacob:

7 The sons of Reuben were Chanoch, Pallu, Chetzron and Carmi.

8 And the sons of Simeon were Jemuel, Jamin, Ohad, Jachin, Zochar and Saul, the son of the Canaanitish woman.

9 And the children of Levi were Gershon, Kehath and Merari, and their sister Jochebed, who was born to them in their going down to Egypt.

10 And the sons of Judah were Er, Onan, Shelah, Perez and Zarach.

11 And Er and Onan died in the land of Canaan; and the sons of Perez were Chezron and Chamul.

12 And the sons of Issachar were Tola, Puvah, Job and Shomron.

13 And the sons of Zebulun were Sered, Elon and Jachleel, and the son of Dan was Chushim.

14 And the sons of Naphtali were Jachzeel, Guni, Jetzer and Shilam.

15 And the sons of Gad were Ziphion, Chaggi, Shuni, Ezbon, Eri, Arodi and Areli.

16 And the children of Asher were Jimnah, Jishvah, Jishvi, Beriah and their sister Serach; and the sons of Beriah were Cheber and Malchiel.

17 And the sons of Benjamin were Bela, Becher, Ashbel, Gera, Naaman, Achi, Rosh, Mupim, Chupim and Ord.

18 And the sons of Joseph that were born to him in Egypt were Manasseh and Ephraim.

19 All the souls that went forth from the loins of Jacob were seventy souls; these are they who came with Jacob their father to Egypt to dwell there: and Joseph and all his brothers lived securely in Egypt, and they ate of the best of Egypt all the days of the life of Joseph.

20 And Joseph lived in the land of Egypt ninety-three years, and Joseph reigned over all Egypt eighty years.

21 When the days of Joseph drew near that he should die, he sent and called for his brothers and all his father's household, and they all came together and sat before him.

22 Joseph said to his brothers and all of his father's household, Behold I die, and God will certainly visit you and bring you up from this land to the land which he swore to your fathers to give to them.

23 And it shall be when God shall visit you to bring you up from here to the land of your fathers, then bring up my bones with you from here.

24 Joseph made the sons of Israel to swear for their descendants after them, saying, God will certainly visit you and you shall bring up my bones with you from here.

25 And it came to pass after this that Joseph died in that year, the seventy-first year of the Israelites going down to Egypt.

26 And Joseph was one hundred and ten years old when he died in the land of Egypt, and all his brothers and all his servants rose up and they embalmed Joseph, as was their custom, and his brothers and all Egypt mourned over him for seventy days.

27 And they put Joseph in a coffin filled with spices and all sorts of perfume; they buried him by the side of the river, that is Sihor, and his sons and all his brothers, and the whole of his father's household made a seven day's mourning for him.

28 It came to pass after the death of Joseph, all the Egyptians began in those days to rule over the children of Israel; Pharaoh, king of Egypt, who reigned in his father's stead, took all the laws of Egypt and conducted the whole government of Egypt under his counsel, and he reigned securely over his people.

CHAPTER 60

1 And when the year came round, being the seventy-second year from the Israelites going down to Egypt, after the death of Joseph, Zepho the son of Eliphaz, the son of Esau, fled from Egypt, he and his men, and they went away.

2 And he came to Africa, which is Dinhabah, to Angeas king of Africa; Angeas received them with great honor, and he made Zepho the captain of his host.

3 And Zepho found favor in the sight of Angeas and in the sight of his people, and Zepho was captain of the host to Angeas king of Africa for many days.

4 Zepho enticed Angeas king of Africa to collect all his army to go and fight with the Egyptians, and with the sons of Jacob, and to avenge of them the cause of his brothers.

5 But Angeas would not listen to Zepho to do this thing, for Angeas knew the strength of the sons of Jacob, and what they had done to his army in their warfare with the children of Esau.

6 And Zepho was in those days very great in the sight of Angeas and in the sight of all his people, and he continually enticed them to make war against Egypt, but they would not.

7 It came to pass in those days there was in the land of Chittim a man in the city of Puzimna, whose name was Uzu, and he became degenerately deified by the children of Chittim; the man died and had no son, only one daughter whose name was Jania.

8 And the girl was greatly beautiful, admired and intelligent, there was none seen like her for beauty and wisdom throughout the land.

9 And the people of Angeas king of Africa saw her and they came and praised her to him; Angeas sent to the children of Chittim, and he requested to take her to himself for a wife, and the people of Chittim consented to give her to him for a wife.

10 When the messengers of Angeas were going forth from the land of Chittim to take their journey, behold the messengers of Turnus king of Bibentu came to Chittim, for Turnus king of Bibentu also sent his messengers to request Jania for him, to take to himself for a wife, for all his men had also praised her to him, therefore he sent all his servants to her.

11 The servants of Turnus came to Chittim, and they asked for Jania, to be taken to Turnus their king for a wife.

12 The people of Chittim said to them, We cannot give her, because Angeas king of Africa desired her to take her to him for a wife before you came, and that we should give her to him; now therefore we cannot do this thing to deprive Angeas of the girl in order to give her to Turnus.

13 For we are greatly afraid of Angeas that he come in battle against us and destroy us, and Turnus your master will not be able to deliver us from his hands.

14 When the messengers of Turnus heard all the words of the children of Chittim, they turned back to their master and told him all the words of the children of Chittim.

15 And the children of Chittim sent a memorial to Angeas, saying, Behold Turnus has sent for Jania to take her to him for a wife, and thus have we answered him; we heard that he has collected his whole army to go to war against you, and he intends to pass by the road of Sardunia to fight against your brother Lucus, and after that he will come to fight against you.

16 Angeas heard the words of the children of Chittim which they sent to him in the record, and his anger was set ablaze and he rose up and assembled his whole army and came through the islands of the sea, the road to Sardunia, to his brother Lucus king of Sardunia.

17 Niblos, the son of Lucus, heard that his uncle Angeas was coming, and he went out to meet him with a heavy army, and he kissed him and embraced him, and Niblos said to Angeas, When you ask my father after his welfare, when I shall go with you to fight with Turnus, ask of him to make me captain of his host. Angeas did so, and he came to his brother and his

brother came to meet him, and he asked him after his welfare.

18 And Angeas asked his brother Lucus after his welfare, and to make his son Niblos captain of his host, and Lucus did so; Angeas and his brother Lucus rose up and they went toward Turnus to battle, and there was with them a great army and a strong people.

19 And he came in ships, and they came into the province of Ashtorash, and behold Turnus came toward them, for he went forth to Sardunia, and intended to destroy it and afterward to pass on from there to Angeas to fight with him.

20 Angeas and Lucus his brother met Turnus in the valley of Canopia, and the battle was strong and mighty between them in that place.

21 And the battle was severe on Lucus king of Sardunia, and all his army fell, and Niblos his son fell also in that battle.

22 And his uncle Angeas commanded his servants and they made a golden coffin for Niblos and they put him into it, and Angeas again waged battle toward Turnus; Angeas was stronger than he, and he killed him, and he struck all his people with the edge of the sword, and Angeas avenged the cause of Niblos his brother's son and the cause of the army of his brother Lucus.

23 And when Turnus died, the hands of those that survived the battle became weak, and they fled from before Angeas and Lucus his brother.

24 Angeas and his brother Lucus pursued them to the highroad, which is between Alphanu and Romah, and they killed the whole army of Turnus with the edge of the sword.

25 Lucus king of Sardunia commanded his servants that they should make a coffin of brass, and that they should place therein the body of his son Niblos, and they buried him in that place.

26 And they built on it a high tower there on the highroad, and they called its name after the name of Niblos to this day; they also buried Turnus king of Bibentu there in that place with Niblos.

27 And so on the highroad between Alphanu and Romah the grave of Niblos is on one side and the grave of Turnus on the other, and a pavement is between them to this day.

28 When Niblos was buried, Lucus his father returned with his army to his land Sardunia, and Angeas his brother king of Africa went with his people to the city of Bibentu, that is the city of Turnus.

29 And the inhabitants of Bibentu heard of his fame and they were greatly afraid of him; they went forth to meet him with weeping and supplication, and the inhabitants of Bibentu entreated of Angeas not to kill them nor destroy their city; he did so, for Bibentu was in those days reckoned as one of the cities of the children of Chittim; so he did not destroy the city.

30 But from that day forward the troops of the king of Africa would go to Chittim to wreck and rob it, and whenever they went, Zepho the captain of the host of Angeas would go with them.

31 It was after this that Angeas turned with his army and they came to the city of Puzimna, and Angeas then took Jania the daughter of Uzu for a wife and brought her to his city to Africa.

CHAPTER 61

1 It came to pass at that time Pharaoh king of Egypt commanded all his people to make for him a strong palace in Egypt.

2 And he also commanded the sons of Jacob to assist the Egyptians in the building, and the Egyptians made a beautiful and elegant palace for a royal habitation; he lived there and he renewed his government and he reigned securely.

3 And Zebulun the son of Jacob died in that year, that is the seventy-second year of the going down of the Israelites to Egypt; Zebulun died a hundred and fourteen years old and was put into a coffin and given into the hands of his children.

4 And in the seventy-fifth year his brother Simeon died; he was a hundred and twenty years old at his death, and he was also put into a coffin and given into the hands of his children.

5 Zepho the son of Eliphaz the son of Esau, captain of the host to Angeas king of Dinhabah, was still daily enticing Angeas to prepare for battle to fight with the sons of Jacob in Egypt; Angeas was unwilling to do this thing, for his servants had related to him all the might of the sons of Jacob, what they had done to them in their battle with the children of Esau.

6 And Zepho was in those days daily enticing Angeas to fight with the sons of Jacob.

7 After some time Angeas listened to the words of Zepho and consented to him to fight with the sons of Jacob in Egypt, and Angeas got all his people in order, a people numerous as the sand which is on the seashore, and he formed his resolution to go to Egypt to battle.

8 Among the servants of Angeas was a youth fifteen years old, Balaam the son of Beor was his name and the youth was very wise and understood the art of witchcraft.

9 And Angeas said to Balaam, Summon for us, I pray you, with the witchcraft, that we may know who will succeed in this battle to which we are now proceeding.

10 And Balaam ordered that they should bring him wax, and he made thereof the likeness of chariots and horsemen representing the army of Angeas and the army of Egypt; he put them in the cunningly prepared waters that he had for that purpose, and he took in his hand the boughs of myrtle trees, and he exercised his cunning; he joined them over the water, and there appeared to him in the water the resembling images of the hosts of Angeas falling before the resembling images of the Egyptians and the sons of Jacob.

11 Balaam told this thing to Angeas, and Angeas despaired and did not arm himself to go down to Egypt to battle, and he remained in his city.

12 And when Zepho the son of Eliphaz saw that Angeas despaired of going forth to battle with the Egyptians, Zepho fled from Angeas from Africa, and he went and came to Chittim.

13 And all the people of Chittim received him with great honor, and they hired him to fight their battles all the days; Zepho became greatly rich in those days, and the troops of the king of Africa still spread themselves in those days; the children of Chittim assembled and went to Mount Cuptizia on account of the troops of Angeas king of Africa who were advancing on them.

14 It was one day that Zepho lost a young heifer and he went to seek it, and he heard it lowing round about the mountain.

15 Zepho went and he saw that there was a large cave at the bottom of the mountain, and there was a great stone there at the entrance of the cave; Zepho split the stone and he came into the cave and he looked and there a large animal was devouring the ox; from the middle upward it resembled a man, and from the middle downward it resembled an animal, and Zepho rose up against the animal and killed it with his swords.

16 The inhabitants of Chittim heard of this thing, and they rejoiced greatly, and said, What shall we do to this man who has slain this animal that devoured our cattle?

17 And they all assembled to consecrate one day in the year to him, and they called the name thereof Zepho after his name; they brought to him drink offerings year after year on that day, and they brought to him gifts.

18 At that time Jania the daughter of Uzu wife of king Angeas became ill, and her illness was heavily felt by Angeas and his officers, and Angeas said to his wise men, What shall I do to Jania and how shall I heal her from her illness? And his wise men said to him, Because the air of our country is not like the air of the land of Chittim, and our water is not like their water, therefore from this has the queen become ill.

19 For through the change of air and water she became ill, and also because in her country she drank only the water which came from Purmah, which her ancestors had brought up with bridges.

20 And Angeas commanded his servants, and they brought to him in vessels of the waters of Purmah belonging to Chittim, and they weighed those waters with all the waters of the land of Africa, and they found those waters lighter than the waters of Africa.

21 Angeas saw this thing, and he commanded all his officers to assemble the hewers of stone in thousands and tens of thousands, and they hewed stone without number; the builders came and they built a greatly strong bridge and they conveyed the spring of water from the land of Chittim to Africa, and those waters were for Jania the queen and for all her concerns, to drink from and to bake, wash and bathe with, and also to water all offspring from which food can be obtained, and all fruit of the ground.

22 And the king commanded that they should bring of the soil of Chittim in large ships, and they also brought stones to build there; the builders built palaces for Jania the queen, and the queen became healed of her illness.

23 And at the revolution of the year the troops of Africa continued coming to the land of Chittim to rob as usual, and Zepho son of Eliphaz heard their report; he gave orders concerning them and he fought with them and they fled before him, and he delivered the land of Chittim from them.

24 And the children of Chittim saw the bravery of Zepho, and the children of Chittim resolved and made Zepho king over them; he became king over them and while he reigned they went to subdue the children of Tubal, and all the surrounding islands.

25 Their king Zepho led them and they made war with Tubal and the islands, and they subdued them; when they returned from the battle they renewed his government for him, and they built for him a very large palace for his royal habitation and seat, and they made a large throne for him; Zepho reigned over the whole land of Chittim and over the land of Italia fifty years.

CHAPTER 62

1 In that year, being the seventy-ninth year of the Israelites going down to Egypt, Reuben the son of Jacob died, in the land of Egypt; Reuben was a hundred and twenty-five years old when he died and they put him into a coffin, and he was given into the hands of his children.

2 In the eightieth year his brother Dan died; he was a hundred and twenty years at his death, and he was also put into a coffin and given into the hands of his children.

3 In that year Chusham king of Edom died, and after him reigned Hadad the son of Bedad, for thirty-five years; in the eighty-first year Issachar the son of Jacob died in Egypt, and Issachar was a hundred and twenty-two years old at his death; he was put into a coffin in Egypt, and given into the hands of his children.

4 In the eighty-second year Asher his brother died, he was a hundred and twenty-three years old at his death, and he was placed in a coffin in Egypt and given into the hands of his children.

5 In the eighty-third year Gad died; he was a hundred and twenty-five years old at his death, and he was put into a coffin in Egypt and given into the hands of his children.

6 And it came to pass in the eighty-fourth year, that is the fiftieth year of the reign of Hadad, son of Bedad, king of Edom, that Hadad assembled all the children of Esau; he got his whole army in readiness, about four hundred thousand men, and he directed his way to the land of Moab; he went to fight with Moab and to make them subordinate to him.

7 The children of Moab heard this thing, and they were very much afraid; they sent to the children of Midian to assist them in fighting with Hadad, son of Bedad, king of Edom.

8 And Hadad came to the land of Moab, and Moab and the children of Midian went out to meet him; they placed themselves in battle array against him in the field of Moab.

9 Hadad fought with Moab, and there fell of the children of Moab and the children of Midian many slain ones, about two hundred thousand men.

10 The battle was very severe on Moab, and when the children of Moab saw that the battle was so severe, they weakened their hands and turned their backs, and left the children of Midian to carry on the battle.

11 And the children of Midian knew not the intentions of Moab, but they strengthened themselves in battle and fought with Hadad and all his army, and all Midian fell before him.

12 Hadad struck all Midian with a heavy smiting, and he killed them with the edge of the sword, he left none remaining of those who came to assist Moab.

13 When all the children of Midian had perished in battle, and the children at Moab had escaped, Hadad made all Moab at that time subservient to him, and they became under his hand; they gave a yearly tax as it was ordered, and Hadad turned and went back to his land.

14 At the revolution of the year, when the rest of the people of Midian that were in the land heard that all their brothers had fallen in battle with Hadad for the sake of Moab, because the children of Moab had turned their backs in battle and left Midian to fight, then five of the princes of Midian resolved with the rest of their brothers who remained in their land to fight with Moab to avenge the cause of their brothers.

15 The children of Midian sent to all their brothers the children of the east, and all their brothers, all the children of Keturah came to assist Midian to fight with Moab.

16 The children of Moab heard this thing, and they were greatly afraid that all the children of the east had assembled together against them for battle, and they the children of Moab sent a memorial to the land of Edom to Hadad the son of Bedad, saying,

17 Come now to us and assist us and we will strike Midian, for they all assembled together and have come against us with all their brothers the children of the east to battle, to avenge the cause of Midian that fell in battle.

18 Hadad, son of Bedad, king of Edom, went forth with his whole army and went to the land of Moab to fight with Midian, and Midian and the children of the east fought with Moab in the field of Moab, and the battle was very fierce between them.

19 Hadad struck all the children of Midian and the children of the east with the edge of the sword, and Hadad at that time delivered Moab from the hand of Midian; those that remained of Midian and of the children of the east fled before Hadad and his army, and Hadad pursued them to their land and struck them with a very heavy slaughter, and the slain fell in the road.

20 Hadad delivered Moab from the hand of Midian, for all the children of Midian had fallen by the edge of the sword, and Hadad turned and went back to his land.

21 And from that day forth, the children of Midian hated the children of Moab because they had fallen in battle for their sake, and there was a great and mighty enmity between them all the days.

22 And all that were found of Midian in the road of the land of Moab perished by the sword of Moab, and all that were found of Moab in the road of the land of Midian, perished by the sword of Midian; thus did Midian to Moab and Moab to Midian for many days.

23 It came to pass at that time that Judah the son of Jacob died in Egypt, in the eighty-sixth year of Jacob's going down to Egypt, and Judah was a hundred and twenty-nine years old at his death, and they embalmed him and put him into a coffin, and he was given into the hands of his children.

24 And in the eighty-ninth year Naphtali died; he was a hundred and thirty-two years old, and he was put into a coffin and given into the hands of his children.

25 It came to pass in the ninety-first year of the Israelites going down to Egypt, that is in the thirtieth year of the reign of Zepho the son of Eliphaz, the son of Esau, over the children of Chittim, the children of Africa came upon the children of Chittim to rob them as usual, but they had not come on them for these thirteen years.

26 They came to them in that year, and Zepho the son of Eliphaz went out to them with some of his men and struck them desperately, and the troops of Africa fled from before Zepho and the slain fell before him, and Zepho and his men pursued them, going on and smiting them until they were near to Africa.

27 And Angeas king of Africa heard the thing which Zepho had done, and it troubled him greatly, and Angeas was afraid of Zepho all the days.

CHAPTER 63

1 In the ninety-third year Levi, the son of Jacob, died in Egypt, and Levi was a hundred and thirty-seven years old when he died; they put him into a coffin and he was given into the hands of his children.

2 It came to pass after the death of Levi, when all Egypt saw that the sons of Jacob the brothers of Joseph were dead, all the Egyptians began to afflict the children of Jacob, and to embitter their lives from that day to the day of their going forth from Egypt. They took from their hands all the vineyards and fields which Joseph had given to them, and all the elegant houses in which the people of Israel lived, and all the valuables of Egypt, the Egyptians took all from the sons of Jacob in those days.

3 And the hand of all Egypt became more heavy in those days against the children of Israel, and the Egyptians injured the Israelites until the children of Israel were wearied of their lives on account of the Egyptians.

4 It came to pass in those days, in the hundred and second year of Israel's going down to Egypt, that Pharaoh king of Egypt died, and Melol his son reigned in his stead; all the mighty men of Egypt and all that generation which knew Joseph and his brothers died in those days.

5 And another generation rose up in their stead, which had not known the sons of Jacob and all the good which they had done to them, and all their might in Egypt.

6 And so all Egypt began from that day on to embitter the lives of the sons of Jacob, and to afflict them with all manner of hard labor, because they had not known their ancestors who had delivered them in the days of the famine.

7 This was also from the Lord for the children of Israel, to benefit them in their latter days in order that all the children of Israel might know the Lord their God.

8 And in order to know the signs and mighty wonders which the Lord would do in Egypt on account of his people Israel, in order that the children of Israel might fear the Lord God of their ancestors, and walk in all his ways, they and their descendants after them all the days.

9 Melol was twenty years old when he began to reign, and he reigned ninety-four years, and all Egypt called his name Pharaoh after the name of his father, as it was their custom to do to every king who reigned over them in Egypt.

10 At that time all the troops of Angeas king of Africa went forth to scatter along the land of Chittim as usual for robbery.

11 Zepho the son of Eliphaz the son of Esau heard their report, and he went forth to meet them with his army, and he fought them there in the road.

12 Zepho struck the troops of the king of Africa with the edge of the sword, and left none remaining of them, and not even one returned to his master in Africa.

13 Angeas heard of this which Zepho the son of Eliphaz had done to all his troops, that he had destroyed them, and Angeas assembled all his troops, all the men of the land of Africa, a people numerous like the sand by the seashore.

14 And Angeas sent to Lucus his brother, saying, Come to me with all your men and help me to strike Zepho and all the children of Chittim who have destroyed my men; Lucus came with his whole army, a very great force, to assist Angeas his brother to fight with Zepho and the children of Chittim.

15 Zepho and the children of Chittim heard this thing, and they were greatly afraid and a great terror fell on their hearts.

16 Zepho also sent a letter to the land of Edom to Hadad the son of Bedad king of Edom and to all the children of Esau, saying,

17 I have heard that Angeas king of Africa is coming to us with his brother for battle against us, and we are greatly afraid of him, for his army is very great, particularly as he comes against us with his brother and his army likewise.

18 Now therefore come up also with me and help me, and we will fight together against Angeas and his brother Lucus, and you will save us out of their hands, but if not, know that we shall all die.

19 And the children of Esau sent a letter to the children of Chittim and to Zepho their king, saying, We cannot fight against Angeas and his people for a covenant of peace has been between us these many years, from the days of Bela the first king, and from the days of Joseph the son of Jacob king of Egypt with whom we fought on the other side of Jordan when he buried his father.

20 When Zepho heard the words of his brothers the children of Esau, he refrained from them, and Zepho was greatly afraid of Angeas.

21 And Angeas and Lucus his brother arrayed all their forces, about eight hundred thousand men, against the children of Chittim.

22 And all the children of Chittim said to Zepho, Pray for us to the God of your ancestors, perhaps he may deliver us from the hand of Angeas and his army, for we have heard that he is a great God and that he delivers all who trust in him.

23 Zepho heard their words, and Zepho sought the Lord and he said,

24 0 Lord God of Abraham and Isaac my ancestors, this day I know that you are a true God, and all the gods of the nations are vain and useless.

25 Remember now this day to me your covenant with Abraham our father, which our ancestors related to us, and do graciously with me this day for the sake of Abraham and Isaac our fathers; save me and the children of Chittim from the hand of the king of Africa who comes against us for battle.

26 And the Lord listened to the voice of Zepho, and he had regard for him on account of Abraham and Isaac, and the Lord delivered Zepho and the children of Chittim from the hand of Angeas and his people.

27 Zepho fought Angeas king of Africa and all his people on that day, and the Lord gave all the people of Angeas into the hands of the children of Chittim.

28 The battle was severe on Angeas, and Zepho struck all the men of Angeas and Lucus his brother with the edge of the sword, and there fell from them to the evening of that day about four hundred thousand men.

29 When Angeas saw that all his men perished, he sent a letter to all the inhabitants of Africa to come to him, to assist him in the battle, and he wrote in the letter, saying, All who are found in Africa let them come to me from ten years old and upward; let them all come to me, and behold if he comes not he shall die; all that he has, with his whole household, the king will take.

30 All the rest of the inhabitants of Africa were terrified at the words of Angeas, and there went out of the city about three hundred thousand men and boys, from ten years upward, and they came to Angeas.

31 And at the end of ten days Angeas renewed the battle against Zepho and the children of Chittim, and the battle was very great and strong between them.

32 And from the army of Angeas and Lucus, Zepho sent many of the wounded to him about two thousand men, and Sosiphtar the captain of the host of Angeas fell in that battle.

33 And when Sosiphtar had fallen, the African troops turned their backs to flee; they fled, and Angeas and Lucus his brother were with them.

34 Zepho and the children of Chittim pursued them, and they struck them still heavily on the road, about two hundred men; they pursued Azdrubal the son of Angeas who had fled with his father, and they struck twenty of his men in the road, and Azdrubal escaped from the children of Chittim, and they did not kill him.

35 Angeas and Lucus his brother fled with the rest of their men, and they escaped and came into Africa with terror and consternation, and Angeas feared all the days that Zepho the son of Eliphaz would go to war with him.

CHAPTER 64

1 Balaam the son of Beor was at that time with Angeas in the battle, and when he saw that Zepho conquered over Angeas, he fled from there and came to Chittim.

2 And Zepho and the children of Chittim received him with great honor, for Zepho knew Balaam's wisdom, and Zepho gave to Balaam many gifts and he remained with him.

3 When Zepho had returned from the war, he commanded all the children of Chittim to be numbered who had gone into battle with him, and there not one was missing.

4 Zepho rejoiced at this thing, and he renewed his kingdom, and he made a feast to all his subjects.

5 But Zepho remembered not the Lord and considered not that the Lord had helped him in battle, and that he had delivered him and his people from the hand of the king of Africa; he still walked in the ways of the children of Chittim and the wicked children of Esau to serve other gods which his brothers the children of Esau had taught him; it is therefore said, From the wicked goes forth wickedness.

6 Zepho reigned over all the children of Chittim securely, but knew not the Lord who had delivered him and all his people from the hand of the king of Africa; the troops of Africa came no more to Chittim to rob as usual, for they knew the power of Zepho who had smitten them all at the edge of the sword, so Angeas was afraid of Zepho the son of Eliphaz and the children of Chittim all the days.

7 At that time when Zepho had returned from the war, and when Zepho had seen how he conquered over all the people of Africa and had smitten them in battle at the edge of the sword, then Zepho advised with the children of Chittim to go to Egypt to fight with the sons of Jacob and with Pharaoh king of Egypt.

8 For Zepho heard that the mighty men of Egypt were dead and that Joseph and his brothers the sons of Jacob were dead, and that all their children, the children of Israel, remained in Egypt.

9 Zepho considered to go to fight against them and all Egypt to avenge the cause of his brothers the children of Esau, whom Joseph with his brothers and all Egypt had smitten in the land of Canaan, when they went up to bury Jacob in Hebron.

10 And Zepho sent messengers to Hadad, son of Bedad, king of Edom, and to all his brothers the children of Esau, saying,

11 Did you say that you would not fight against the king of Africa for he is a member of your covenant? Consider that I fought with him and struck him and all his people.

12 Now therefore I have resolved to fight against Egypt and the children of Jacob who are there, and I will be revenged of them for what Joseph, his brothers and ancestors did to us in the land of Canaan when they went up to bury their father in Hebron.

13 Now then if you are willing to come to me to assist me in fighting against them and Egypt, we shall avenge the cause of our brothers.

14 And the children of Esau listened to the words of Zepho, and the children of Esau gathered themselves together, a very great people; they went to assist Zepho and the children of Chittim in battle.

15 Zepho sent to all the children of the east and to all the children of Ishmael with words like these, and they gathered themselves and came to the assistance of Zepho and the children of Chittim in the war on Egypt.

16 And all these kings, the king of Edom and the children of the east, and all the children of Ishmael, and Zepho the king of Chittim went forth and arrayed all their hosts in Hebron.

17 The camp was very large, extending in length a distance of three days' journey, a people numerous as the sand on the

seashore which cannot be counted.

18 And all these kings and their hosts went down and came against all Egypt in battle, and encamped together in the valley of Pathros.

19 All Egypt heard their report and they also gathered themselves together, all the people of the land of Egypt, and of all the cities belonging to Egypt about three hundred thousand men.

20 The men of Egypt sent also to the children of Israel who were in those days in the land of Goshen, to come to them in order to go and fight with these kings.

21 The men of Israel assembled and were about one hundred and fifty men, and they went into battle to assist the Egyptians.

22 The men of Israel and of Egypt went forth, about three hundred thousand men and one hundred and fifty men, and they went toward these kings to battle; they placed themselves outside the land of Goshen opposite Pathros.

23 The Egyptians believed not in Israel to go with them in their camps together for battle, for all the Egyptians said, Perhaps the children of Israel will deliver us into the hand of the children of Esau and Ishmael, for they are their brothers.

24 And all the Egyptians said to the children of Israel, Remain here together in your stand and we will go and fight against the children of Esau and Ishmael; if these kings should gain over us, then you all come together on them and assist us, and the children of Israel did so.

25 Zepho the son of Eliphaz the son of Esau king of Chittim and Hadad the son of Bedad king of Edom and all their camps, and all the children of the east, and children of Ishmael, a people numerous as sand, encamped together in the valley of Pathros opposite Tachpanches.

26 Balaam the son of Beor the Syrian was there in the camp of Zepho, for he came with the children of Chittim to the battle, and Balaam was a man highly honored in the eyes of Zepho and his men.

27 Zepho said to Balaam, Try by divination for us that we may know who will win the battle, we or the Egyptians.

28 And Balaam rose up and tried the art of divination, and he was skillful in the knowledge of it, but he was confused and the work was destroyed in his hand.

29 And he tried it again but it did not succeed; Balaam despaired of it and left it and did not complete it, for this was from the Lord in order to cause Zepho and his people to fall into the hand of the children of Israel, who had trusted in the Lord, the God of their ancestors, in their war.

30 Zepho and Hadad put their forces in battle array, and all the Egyptians went alone against them, about three hundred thousand men, and not one man of Israel was with them.

31 All the Egyptians fought with these kings opposite Pathros and Tachpanches, and the battle was severe against the Egyptians.

32 The kings were stronger than the Egyptians in that battle, and about one hundred and eighty men of Egypt fell on that day, and about thirty men of the forces of the kings, and all the men of Egypt fled from before the king; so the children of Esau and Ishmael pursued the Egyptians, continuing to strike them to the place where the camp of the children of Israel was.

33 And all the Egyptians cried to the children of Israel, saying, Hurry to us and assist us and save us from the hand of Esau, Ishmael and the children of Chittim.

34 The hundred and fifty men of the children of Israel ran from their station to the camps of these kings, and the children of Israel cried to the Lord their God to deliver them.

35 And the Lord listened to Israel, and the Lord gave all the men of the kings into their hands, and the children of Israel fought against these kings; the children of Israel struck about four thousand of the kings' men.

36 The Lord threw a great consternation into the camp of the kings, so that the fear of the children of Israel fell on them.

37 And all the hosts of the kings fled from before the children of Israel and the children of Israel pursued them continuing to strike them to the borders of the land of Cush.

38 The children of Israel killed of them in the road two thousand men, and of the children of Israel not one fell.

39 When the Egyptians saw that the children of Israel had fought with such few men with the kings, and that the battle was so very severe against them,

40 All the Egyptians were greatly afraid of their lives on account of the strong battle, and all Egypt fled, every man hiding himself from the arrayed forces; they hid themselves in the road, and they left the Israelites to fight alone.

41 And the children of Israel inflicted a terrible blow on the kings' men, and they returned from them after they had driven them to the border of the land of Cush.

42 All Israel knew the thing which the men of Egypt had done to them, that they had fled from them in battle, and had left them to fight alone.

43 So the children of Israel also acted with cunning, and as the children of Israel returned from battle, they found some of the Egyptians in the road and struck them there.

44 And while they killed them, they said to them these words:

45 Why did you go from us and leave us, being a few people to fight against these kings who had many people to strike us, that you might thereby save your own souls?

46 And of some which the Israelites met on the road, the children of Israel spoke to each other, saying, Smite, strike, for he is an Ishmaelite, or an Edomite, or from the children of Chittim; they stood over him and killed him, and they knew that he was an Egyptian.

47 The children of Israel did these things cunningly against the Egyptians because they had deserted in battle and had fled from them.

48 And the children of Israel killed of the men of Egypt in the road in this manner about two hundred men.

49 All the men of Egypt saw the evil which the children of Israel had done to them, so all Egypt feared greatly the children of Israel, for they had seen their great power and that not one man of them had fallen.

50 So all the children of Israel returned with joy on their road to Goshen, and the rest of Egypt returned each man to his place.

CHAPTER 65

1 It came to pass after these things that all the counselors of Pharaoh, king of Egypt, and all the elders of Egypt assembled and came before the king and bowed down to the ground, and they sat before him.

2 And the counselors and elders of Egypt spoke to the king, saying,

3 Behold the people of the children of Israel is greater and mightier than we are, and you know all the evil which they did to us in the road when we returned from battle.

4 And you have also seen their strong power, for this power is to them from their fathers, for only a few men stood up against a people numerous as the sand, and struck them at the edge of the sword; of themselves not one has fallen, so that if they had been numerous they would then have utterly destroyed them.

5 Now therefore give us counsel what to do with them, until we gradually destroy them from among us so they don't become too numerous for us in the land.

6 For if the children of Israel should increase in the land, they will become an obstacle to us; if any war should happen to take place, they with their great strength will join our enemy against us, and fight against us, destroy us from the land and go away from it.

7 So the king answered the elders of Egypt and said to them, This is the plan advised against Israel, from which we will not depart,

8 Consider in the land are Pithom and Rameses, cities unfortified against battle; it's best for you and us to build them, and to fortify them.

9 Now go also and act cunningly toward them, and proclaim a voice in Egypt and in Goshen at the command of the king, saying,

10 All ye men of Egypt, Goshen, Pathros and all their inhabitants! The king has commanded us to build Pithom and Rameses and to fortify them for battle; those among you of all Egypt, of the children of Israel and of all the inhabitants of the cities who are willing to build with us, you shall each have his wages given to him daily at the king's order. So go first and do cunningly and gather yourselves to come to Pithom and Rameses to build.

11 And while you are building, cause an announcement of this kind to be made throughout Egypt every day at the command of the king.

12 When some of the children of Israel shall come to build with you, you shall give them their wages daily for a few days.

13 And after they have built with you for their daily hire, drag yourselves away from them daily one by one in secret, and then you shall rise up and become their taskmasters and officers; you shall leave them afterward to build without wages; should they refuse, then force them with all your might to build.

14 And if you do this it will be well with us to strengthen our land against the children of Israel, for on account of the fatigue of the building and the work, the children of Israel will decrease, because you will deprive them of their wives day by day.

15 And all the elders of Egypt heard the counsel of the king, and the counsel seemed good in their eyes and in the eyes of the servants of Pharaoh, and in the eyes of all Egypt; they did according to the word of the king.

16 And all the servants went away from the king; they caused an announcement to be made in all Egypt, in Tachpanches and in Goshen, and in all the cities which surrounded Egypt, saying,

17 You have seen what the children of Esau and Ishmael did to us, who came to war against us and wished to destroy us.

18 Now therefore the king commanded us to fortify the land, to build the cities Pithom and Rameses, and to fortify them for battle, if they should again come against us.

19 Whoever of you from all Egypt and from the children of Israel will come to build with us, he shall have his daily wages given by the king, as his command is to us.

20 And when Egypt and all the children of Israel heard all that the servants of Pharaoh had spoken, there came persons from the Egyptians and the children of Israel to build with the servants of Pharaoh, Pithom and Rameses, but none of the children of Levi came with their brothers to build.

21 All the servants of Pharaoh and his princes came at first with deceit to build with all Israel as daily hired laborers, and they gave to Israel their daily hire at the beginning.

22 And the servants of Pharaoh built with all Israel, and were employed in that work with Israel for a month.

23 And at the end of the month, all the servants of Pharaoh began to withdraw secretly from the people of Israel daily.

24 And Israel went on with the work at that time, but they then received their daily wage, because some of the men of Egypt were yet carrying on the work with Israel at that time; therefore the Egyptians gave Israel their wage in those days in order that they, the Egyptians their fellow-workmen, might also take the pay for their labor.

25 At the end of a year and four months all the Egyptians had withdrawn from the children of Israel, so that the children of Israel were left alone engaged in the work.

26 And after all the Egyptians had withdrawn from the children of Israel they returned and became oppressors and officers over them, and some of them stood over the children of Israel as task masters, to receive from them all that they gave them for the pay of their labor.

27 And the Egyptians did in this manner to the children of Israel day by day, in order to afflict them in their work.

28 And all the children of Israel were alone engaged in the labor, and the Egyptians refrained from giving any pay to the children of Israel from that time forward.

29 When some of the men of Israel refused to work on account of the wages not being given to them, the exactors and the servants of Pharaoh oppressed them and struck them with heavy blows, and made them return by force to labor with their brothers; thus did all the Egyptians to the children of Israel all the days.

30 And all the children of Israel were greatly afraid of the Egyptians in this matter, and all the children of Israel returned and worked alone without pay.

31 The children of Israel built Pithom and Rameses; all the children of Israel did the work, some making bricks, and some building, and the children of Israel built and fortified all the land of Egypt and its walls. The children of Israel were engaged in work for many years, until the time came when the Lord remembered them and brought them out of Egypt.

32 But the children of Levi were not employed in the work with their brothers of Israel from the beginning to the day of their going forth from Egypt.

33 For all the children of Levi knew that the Egyptians had spoken all these words with deceit to the Israelites, therefore the children of Levi refrained from approaching the work with their brothers.

34 The Egyptians did not direct their attention to make the children of Levi work afterward, since they had not been with their brothers at the beginning, therefore the Egyptians left them alone.

35 And the hands of the men of Egypt were directed with continued severity against the children of Israel in that work, and the Egyptians made the children of Israel work with rigor.

36 The Egyptians embittered the lives of the children of Israel with hard work in mortar and bricks, and also in all manner of work in the field.

37 The children of Israel called Melol the king of Egypt "Meror, king of Egypt," because in his days the Egyptians had embittered their lives with all manner of work.

38 And all the work wherein the Egyptians made the children of Israel labor, they exacted with rigor, in order to afflict the children of Israel. But the more they afflicted them, the more they increased and grew, and the Egyptians were grieved because of the children of Israel.

CHAPTER 66

1 At that time Hadad the son of Bedad king of Edom died; Samlah from Mesrekah, from the country of the children of the east, reigned in his place.

2 In the thirteenth year of the reign of Pharaoh king of Egypt, which was the hundred and twenty-fifth year of the Israelites going down into Egypt, Samlah had reigned over Edom eighteen years.

3 And when he reigned, he brought forth his army to go and fight against Zepho the son of Eliphaz and the children of Chittim, because they had made war against Angeas king of Africa, and they destroyed his whole army.

4 But he did not engage with him, for the children of Esau prevented him, saying, he was their brother; so Samlah listened to the voice of the children of Esau and turned back with all his forces to the land of Edom, and did not proceed to fight against Zepho the son of Eliphaz.

5 And Pharaoh king of Egypt heard this thing, saying, Samlah king of Edom has resolved to fight the children of Chittim, and afterward he will come to fight against Egypt.

6 When the Egyptians heard this matter, they increased the labor on the children of Israel, that the Israelites should do to them as they did to them in their war with the children of Esau in the days of Hadad.

7 So the Egyptians said to the children of Israel, Hurry and do your work, and finish your task, and strengthen the land, should the children of Esau your brothers come to fight against us, for on your account will they come against us.

8 And the children of Israel did the work of the men of Egypt day by day, and the Egyptians afflicted the children of Israel in order to lessen them in the land.

9 But as the Egyptians increased the labor on the children of Israel, so did the children of Israel increase and reproduce, and all Egypt was filled with the children of Israel.

10 And in the hundred and twenty-fifth year of Israel's going down into Egypt, all the Egyptians saw that their counsel did not succeed against Israel, but that they increased and grew and the land of Egypt and the land of Goshen were filled with

the children of Israel.

11 So all the elders of Egypt and its wise men came before the king and bowed down to him and sat before him.

12 And all the elders of Egypt and the wise men there said to the king, May the king live forever; you did counsel us the counsel against the children of Israel, and we did to them according to the word of the king.

13 But in proportion to the increase of the labor so do they increase and grow in the land, and look the whole country is filled with them.

14 So now our lord and king, the eyes of all Egypt are on you to give them advice with your wisdom, by which they may rule over Israel to destroy them, or to diminish them from the land; the king answered them saying, Give your counsel in this matter that we may know what to do to them.

15 And an officer, one of the king's counselors, whose name was Job, from Mesopotamia, in the land of Uz, answered the king, saying,

16 If it please the king, let him hear the counsel of his servant; the king said to him, Speak.

17 And Job spoke before the king, the princes, and before all the elders of Egypt, saying,

18 Behold the counsel of the king which he advised formerly respecting the labor of the children of Israel is very good, and you must not remove from them that labor forever.

19 But this is the advice counselled by which you may lessen them, if it seems good to the king to afflict them.

20 Behold we have feared war for a long time, and we said, When Israel becomes prolific in the land, they will drive us from the land if a war would take place.

21 If it please the king, let a royal decree go forth, and let it be written in the laws of Egypt which shall not be revoked, that every male child born to the Israelites, his blood shall be spilled on the ground.

22 And by your doing this, when all the male children of Israel will have died, the evil of their wars will cease; let the king do so and send for all the Hebrew midwives and order them in this matter to execute it. So the thing pleased the king and the prince; the king did according to the word of Job.

23 The king sent for the Hebrew midwives to be called, of which the name of one was Shephrah, and the name of the other Puah.

24 And the midwives came before the king, and stood in his presence.

25 the king said to them, When you do the office of a midwife to the Hebrew women, and see them on the stools, if it be a son then you shall kill him, but if it be a daughter then she shall live.

26 But if you will not do this thing, then will I burn you up and all your houses with fire.

27 But the midwives feared God and did not listen to the king of Egypt nor to his words; when the Hebrew women brought forth to the midwife son or daughter, then did the midwife do all that was necessary to the child and let it live; thus did the midwives all the days.

28 And this thing was told to the king, and he sent and called for the midwives and he said to them, Why have you done this thing and have saved the children alive?

29 And the midwives answered and spoke together before the king, saying,

30 Let not the king think that the Hebrew women are as the Egyptian women, for all the children of Israel are vigorous, and before the midwife comes to them they are delivered, and as for us your handmaids, for many days no Hebrew woman has brought forth on us, for all the Hebrew women are their own midwives, because they are vigorous.

31 And Pharaoh heard their words and believed them in this matter, and the midwives went away from the king, and God dealt well with them; the people multiplied and increased greatly.

CHAPTER 67

1 There was a man in the land of Egypt of the children of Levi, whose name was Amram, the son of Kehath, the son of Levi, the son of Israel.

2 And this man went and took a wife, namely Jochebed the daughter of Levi his father's sister, and she was one hundred and twenty-six years old, and he came to her.

3 And the woman conceived and gave birth to a daughter, and she called her name Miriam, because in those days the Egyptians had embittered the lives of the children of Israel.

4 She conceived again and gave birth to a son and she called his name Aaron, for in the days of her conception, Pharaoh began to spill the blood of the male children of Israel.

5 In those days Zepho died, the son of Eliphaz, son of Esau, king of Chittim; Janeas reigned in his stead.

6 And the time that Zepho reigned over the children of Chittim was fifty years, and he died and was buried in the city of Nabna in the land of Chittim.

7 And Janeas, one of the mighty men of the children of Chittim, reigned after him for fifty years.

8 It was after the death of the king of Chittim that Balaam the son of Beor fled from the land of Chittim, and he went and came to Egypt to Pharaoh king of Egypt.

9 Pharaoh received him with great honor for he had heard of his wisdom, and he gave him presents and made him a

counsellor and praised him.

10 Balaam lived in Egypt, in honor with all the nobles of the king, and the nobles exalted him, because they all coveted to learn his wisdom.

11 And in the hundred and thirtieth year of Israel's going down to Egypt, Pharaoh dreamed that he was sitting on his kingly throne, and lifted up his eyes and saw an old man standing before him; there were scales in the hands of the old man, such scales as are used by merchants.

12 And the old man took the scales and hung them before Pharaoh.

13 And the old man took all the elders of Egypt and all its nobles and great men, and he tied them together and put them in one scale.

14 And he took a milk kid and put it into the other scale, and the kid's weight surpassed all.

15 And Pharaoh was astonished at this dreadful vision, why the kid should surpass all, and Pharaoh awoke and behold it was a dream.

16 Pharaoh rose up early in the morning and called all his servants and related to them the dream, and the men were greatly afraid.

17 And the king said to all his wise men, Interpret I pray you the dream which I dreamed, that I may know it.

18 Balaam the son of Beor answered the king and said to him, This means nothing else but a great evil that will spring up against Egypt in the latter days.

19 For a son will be born to Israel who will destroy all Egypt and its inhabitants, and bring forth the Israelites from Egypt with a mighty hand.

20 Now therefore, O king, take counsel on this matter, that you may destroy the hope of the children of Israel and their expectation, before this evil arises against Egypt.

21 And the king said to Balaam, And what shall we do to Israel? Certainly after a certain manner did we at first counsel against them and could not succeed over them.

22 So now you also give advice against them by which we may succeed over them.

23 Balaam answered the king, saying, Send now and call your two counselors, and we will see what their advice is on this matter and afterward your servant will speak.

24 And the king sent and called his two counselors Reuel the Midianite and Job the Uzite, and they came and sat before the king.

25 And the king said to them, Behold you have both heard the dream which I have dreamed, and the interpretation thereof; so now give counsel and know and see what is to be done to the children of Israel, whereby we may succeed over them, before their evil will spring up against us.

26 And Reuel the Midianite answered the king and said, May the king live, may the king live forever.

27 If it seems good to the king, let him desist from the Hebrews and leave them, and let him not stretch forth his hand against them.

28 For these are they whom the Lord chose in days of old, and took as the lot of his inheritance from among all the nations of the earth and the kings of the earth; and who is there that stretched his hand against them with punishment, of whom their God was not avenged?

29 Certainly you know that when Abraham went down to Egypt, Pharaoh, the former king of Egypt, saw Sarah his wife, and took her for a wife, because Abraham said, She is my sister, for he was afraid that the men of Egypt should kill him on account of his wife.

30 And when the king of Egypt had taken Sarah then God struck him and his household with heavy plagues, until he restored to Abraham his wife Sarah, then was he healed.

31 And Abimelech the Gerarite, king of the Philistines, God punished on account of Sarah wife of Abraham, in stopping up every womb from man to beast.

32 When their God came to Abimelech in the dream of night and terrified him in order that he might restore to Abraham Sarah whom he had taken, afterward all the people of Gerar were punished on account of Sarah, and Abraham prayed to his God for them, and he was entreated of him, and he healed them.

33 And Abimelech feared all this evil that came on him and his people, and he returned to Abraham his wife Sarah, and gave him many gifts with her.

34 He did so also to Isaac when he had driven him from Gerar, and God had done wonderful things to him, that all the water courses of Gerar were dried up and their productive trees did not bring forth.

35 Until Abimelech of Gerar, and Ahuzzath one of his friends, and Pichol the captain of his host, went to him and they bent and bowed down before him to the ground.

36 They requested of him to petition for them, and he prayed to the Lord for them, and the Lord was entreated of him and he healed them.

37 Jacob also, the plain man, was delivered through his integrity from the hand of his brother Esau, and the hand of Laban the Syrian his mother's brother, who had sought his life; likewise from the hand of all the kings of Canaan who had come together against him and his children to destroy them, the Lord delivered them out of their hands, that they turned on them and struck them, for who had ever stretched forth his hand against them without penalty?

38 Certainly Pharaoh the former, your father's father, raised Joseph the son of Jacob above all the princes of the land of Egypt when he saw his wisdom, for through his wisdom he rescued all the inhabitants of the land from the famine.

39 After which he ordered Jacob and his children to come down to Egypt in order that through their virtue, the land of Egypt and the land of Goshen might be delivered from the famine.

40 So now if it seems good in your eyes, cease from destroying the children of Israel, but if it be not your will that they shall dwell in Egypt, send them forth from here that they may go to the land of Canaan, the land where their ancestors sojourned.

41 And when Pharaoh heard the words of Jethro he was very angry with him, so that he rose with shame from the king's presence and went to Midian, his land, and took Joseph's stick with him.

42 And the king said to Job the Uzite, What do you say Job, and what is your advice respecting the Hebrews?

43 So Job said to the king, Behold all the inhabitants of the land are in your power, let the king do as it seems good in his eyes.

44 And the king said to Balaam, What do you say, Balaam? Speak your word that we may hear it.

45 And Balaam said to the king, Of all that the king has counselled against the Hebrews will they be delivered, and the king will not be able to prevail over them with any counsel.

46 For if you think to lessen them by the flaming fire, you cannot prevail over them, for certainly their God delivered Abraham their father from Ur of the Chaldeans; if you think to destroy them with a sword, certainly Isaac their father was delivered from it and a ram was placed in his stead.

47 And if with hard and rigorous labor you think to lessen them, you will not prevail even in this, for their father Jacob served Laban in all manner of hard work and prospered.

48 Now therefore, O King, hear my words, for this is the counsel which is counselled against them, by which you will prevail over them, and from which you should not depart:

49 If it please the king let him order all their children which shall be born from this day forward to be thrown into the water, for by this can you wipe away their name, for none of them nor of their fathers were tried in this manner.

50 And the king heard the words of Balaam, and the thing pleased the king and the princes, and the king did according to the word of Balaam.

51 The king ordered an announcement to be issued and a law to be made throughout the land of Egypt, saying, Every male child born to the Hebrews from this day forward shall be thrown into the water.

52 Pharaoh called to all his servants, saying, Go now and search throughout the land of Goshen where the children of Israel are, and see that every son born to the Hebrews will be cast into the river, but every daughter you shall let live.

53 And when the children of Israel heard this thing which Pharaoh had commanded, to cast their male children into the river, some of the people separated from their wives and others adhered to them.

54 And from that day forward, when the time of delivery arrived to those women of Israel who had remained with their husbands, they went to the field to bring forth there, and they brought forth in the field and left their children on the field and returned home.

55 And the Lord who had sworn to their ancestors to reproduce them sent one of his ministering angels which are in heaven to wash each child in water, to anoint and swathe it and to put into its hands two smooth stones from one of which it sucked milk and from the other honey, and he caused its hair to grow to its knees, by which it might cover itself; to comfort it and to cleave to it through his compassion for it.

56 And when God had compassion over them and had desired to reproduce them on the face of the land, he ordered his earth to receive them to be preserved therein till the time of their growing up, after which the earth opened its mouth and vomited them forth and they sprouted forth from the city like the herb of the earth, and the grass of the forest, and they returned each to his family and to his father's house, and they remained with them.

57 And the babes of the children of Israel were on the earth like the herb of the field, through God's grace to them.

58 And when all the Egyptians saw this thing, they went forth, each to his field with his yoke of oxen and his ploughshare, and they plowed it up as one ploughs the earth at offspring time.

59 And when they plowed they were unable to hurt the infants of the children of Israel, so the people increased and thrived greatly.

60 And Pharaoh ordered his officers daily to go to Goshen to seek for the babes of the children of Israel.

61 And when they had sought and found one, they took it from its mother's bosom by force, and threw it into the river, but the female child they left with its mother; thus did the Egyptians do to the Israelites all the days.

CHAPTER 68

1 It was at that time the spirit of God was on Miriam the daughter of Amram the sister of Aaron, and she went forth and prophesied about the house, saying, Behold a son will be born to us from my father and mother this time, and he will save Israel from the hands of Egypt.

2 And when Amram heard the words of his daughter, he went and took his wife back to the house, after he had driven her away at the time when Pharaoh ordered every male child of the house of Jacob to be thrown into the water.

3 So Amram took Jochebed his wife, three years after he had driven her away, and he came to her and she conceived.

4 At the end of seven months from her conception she brought forth a son, and the whole house was filled with great light as of the light of the sun and moon at the time of their shining.

5 And when the woman saw the child that it was good and pleasing to the sight, she hid him for three months in an inner room.

6 In those days the Egyptians conspired to destroy all the Hebrews there.

7 And the Egyptian women went to Goshen where the children of Israel were, and they carried their young ones on their shoulders, their babes who could not yet speak.

8 And in those days, when the women of the children of Israel brought forth, each woman had hidden her son from the Egyptians, that the Egyptians might not know of their bringing forth, and might not destroy them from the land.

9 And the Egyptian women came to Goshen and their children who could not speak were on their shoulders, and when an Egyptian woman came into the house of a Hebrew woman her babe began to cry.

10 And when it cried the child that was in the inner room answered it, so the Egyptian women went and told it at the house of Pharaoh.

11 And Pharaoh sent his officers to take the children and kill them; thus did the Egyptians to the Hebrew women all the days.

12 And it was at that time, about three months from Jochebed's concealment of her son, that the thing was known in Pharaoh's house.

13 And the woman hurried to take away her son before the officers came, and she took for him an ark of bulrushes, and daubed it with slime and with pitch and put the child therein, and she laid it in the flags by the river's brink.

14 And his sister Miriam stood afar off to learn what would be done to him, and what would become of her words.

15 And God sent forth at that time a terrible heat in the land of Egypt, which burned up the flesh of man like the sun in his circuit, and it greatly oppressed the Egyptians.

16 And all the Egyptians went down to bathe in the river on account of the consuming heat which burned up their flesh.

17 And Bathia, the daughter of Pharaoh, went also to bathe in the river, owing to the consuming heat; her maidens walked at the riverside, and all the women of Egypt as well.

18 Bathia lifted up her eyes to the river and she saw the ark on the water, and sent her maid to
 fetch it.

19 She opened it and saw the child, and then the babe wept, and she had compassion on him and said, This is one of the Hebrew children.

20 And all the women of Egypt walking on the riverside desired to give him suck, but he would not suck, for this thing was from the Lord in order to restore him to his mother's breast.

21 And Miriam his sister was at that time among the Egyptian women at the riverside, and she saw this thing and said to Pharaoh's daughter, Shall I go and fetch a nurse of the Hebrew women, that she may nurse the child for you?

22 And Pharaoh's daughter said to her, Go, and the young woman went and called the child's mother.

23 And Pharaoh's daughter said to Jochebed, Take this child away and suckle it for me, and I will pay you your wages, two bits of silver daily; and the woman took the child and nursed it.

24 At the end of two years, when the child grew up, she brought him to the daughter of Pharaoh, and he was to her as a son; she called his name Moses, for she said, Because I drew him out of the water.

25 And Amram his father called his name Chabar, for he said, It was for him that he associated with his wife whom he had turned away.

26 And Jochebed his mother called his name Jekuthiel, Because, she said, I have hoped for him to the Almighty, and God restored him to me.

27 And Miriam his sister called him Jered, for she descended after him to the river to learn what would happen to him.

28 And Aaron his brother called his name Abi Zanuch, saying, My father left my mother and returned to her on his account.

29 And Kehath the father of Amram called his name Abigdor, because on his account did God repair the breach of the house of Jacob, that they could no longer throw their male children into the water.

30 And their nurse called him Abi Socho, saying, In his tabernacle was he hidden for three months, on account of the children of Ham.

31 And all Israel called his name Shemaiah, son of Nethanel, for they said, In his days has God heard their cries and rescued them from their oppressors.

32 And Moses was in Pharaoh's house and was to Bathia, Pharaoh's daughter, as a son, and Moses grew up among the king's children.

CHAPTER 69

1 The king of Edom died in those days, in the eighteenth year of his reign, and was buried in his temple which he had built for himself as his royal residence in the land of Edom.

2 The children of Esau sent to Pethor, which is on the river, and they fetched from there a young man of beautiful eyes and

handsome, whose name was Saul; they made him king over them in the place of Samlah.

3 And Saul reigned over all the children of Esau in the land of Edom for forty years.

4 When Pharaoh king of Egypt saw that the counsel which Balaam had advised respecting the children of Israel did not succeed, but that still they were prolific, multiplied and increased throughout the land of Egypt,

5 Then Pharaoh commanded in those days that a proclamation should be issued throughout Egypt to the children of Israel, saying, No man shall lessen anything of his daily labor.

6 And the man who shall be found deficient in his labor which he performs daily, whether in mortar or in bricks, then his youngest son shall be put in their place.

7 And the labor of Egypt strengthened on the children of Israel in those days, and if one brick was deficient in any man's daily labor, the Egyptians took his youngest boy by force from his mother and put him into the building in the place of the brick which his father had left wanting.

8 And the men of Egypt did so to all the children of Israel day by day, all the days for a long period.

9 But the tribe of Levi did not at that time work with the Israelites their brothers from the beginning, for the children of Levi knew the cunning of the Egyptians which they exercised at first toward the Israelites.

CHAPTER 70

1 In the third year from the birth of Moses, Pharaoh was sitting at a banquet when Alparanith the queen was sitting at his right and Bathia at his left, and the lad Moses was lying on her bosom, and Balaam the son of Beor with his two sons, and all the princes of the kingdom were sitting at table in the king's presence.

2 And the lad stretched forth his hand on the king's head, and took the crown from the king's head and placed it on his own head.

3 When the king and princes saw the work which the boy had done, the king and princes were terrified, and one man to his neighbor expressed astonishment.

4 And the king said to the princes who were before him at table, What speak you and what say you, O ye princes, in this matter, and what is to be the judgment against the boy on account of this act?

5 And Balaam the son of Beor the magician answered before the king and princes and said, Remember now, O my lord and king, the dream which you did dream many days ago, and that which your servant interpreted to you.

6 Now therefore this is a child from the Hebrew children in whom is the spirit of God, and let not my lord the king imagine that this youngster did this thing without knowledge.

7 For he is a Hebrew boy, and wisdom and understanding are with him, although he is yet a child; with wisdom has he done this and chosen to himself the kingdom of Egypt.

8 For this is the manner of all the Hebrews to deceive kings and their nobles, to do all these things cunningly, in order to make the kings of the earth and their men tremble.

9 Certainly you know that Abraham their father acted thus, who deceived the army of Nimrod king of Babel and Abimelech king of Gerar, and that he possessed himself of the land of the children of Heth and all the kingdoms of Canaan.

10 And that he descended into Egypt and said of Sarah his wife, she is my sister, in order to mislead Egypt and her king.

11 His son Isaac also did so when he went to Gerar and lived there, and his strength prevailed over the army of Abimelech king of the Philistines.

12 He also thought of making the kingdom of the Philistines stumble, in saying that Rebecca his wife was his sister.

13 Jacob also dealt treacherously with his brother and took from his hand his birthright and his blessing.

14 He went then to Padan-aram to the house of Laban his mother's brother, and cunningly obtained from him his daughter, his cattle and all belonging to him, and fled away and returned to the land of Canaan to his father.

15 His sons sold their brother Joseph, who went down into Egypt and became a slave, and was placed in the prison house for twelve years.

16 Until the former Pharaoh dreamed dreams and withdrew him from the prison house, and magnified him above all the princes in Egypt on account of his interpreting his dreams to him.

17 And when God caused a famine throughout the land he sent for and brought his father and all his brothers, and all of his father's household, and supported them without price or reward, and bought the Egyptians for slaves.

18 Now therefore my lord king behold this child has risen up in their stead in Egypt, to do according to their deeds and to trifle with every king, prince and judge.

19 If it please the king, let us now spill his blood on the ground, that he shall not grow up and take away the government from your hand, and then the hope of Egypt perish after he shall have reigned.

20 And Balaam said to the king, Let us moreover call for all the judges of Egypt and the wise men thereof, and let us know if the judgment of death is due to this boy as you did say; then we will kill him.

21 Pharaoh sent and called for all the wise men of Egypt and they came before the king; an angel of the Lord came among them, and he was like one of the wise men of Egypt.

22 And the king said to the wise men, Certainly you have heard what this Hebrew boy who is in the house has done, and

thus has Balaam judged in the matter.

23 Now you judge also and see what is due to the boy for the act he has committed.

24 And the angel, who seemed like one of the wise men of Pharaoh, answered and said as follows, before all the wise men of Egypt and before the king and the princes:

25 If it please the king let the king send for men who shall bring before him an onyx stone and a coal of fire, and place them before the child; if the child shall stretch forth his hand and take the onyx stone, then shall we know that with wisdom has the youth done all that he has done, and we must kill him.

26 But if he stretches forth his hand on the coal, then shall we know that it was not with knowledge that he did this thing, and he shall live.

27 The thing seemed good in the eyes of the king and the princes, so the king did according to the word of the angel of the Lord.

28 The king ordered the onyx stone and coal to be brought and placed before Moses.

29 They placed the boy before them, and the lad endeavored to stretch forth his hand to the onyx stone, but the angel of the Lord took his hand and placed it on the coal, and the coal became extinguished in his hand; he lifted it up and put it into his mouth, and burned part of his lips and part of his tongue, and he became swollen in mouth and tongue.

30 And when the king and princes saw this, they knew that Moses had not acted with wisdom in taking off the crown from the king's head.

31 So the king and princes refrained from slaying the child. Moses remained in Pharaoh's house, growing up, and the Lord was with him.

32 And while the boy was in the king's house, he was robed in purple and he grew among the children of the king.

33 And when Moses grew up in the king's house, Bathia the daughter of Pharaoh considered him as a son, and all the household of Pharaoh honored him, and all the men of Egypt were afraid of him.

34 And he daily went forth and came into the land of Goshen where his brothers the children of Israel were, and Moses saw them daily in shortness of breath and hard labor.

35 And Moses asked them, saying, How is this labor assigned to you day by day?

36 And they told him all that had befallen them, and all the injunctions which Pharaoh had put on them before his birth.

37 And they told him all the counsels which Balaam the son of Beor had counselled against them, and what he had also counselled against him in order to kill him when he had taken the king's crown from off his head.

38 And when Moses heard these things his anger was set ablaze against Balaam, and he sought to kill him, and he was in ambush for him day by day.

39 Balaam was afraid of Moses, and he and his two sons rose up and went forth from Egypt, and they fled and delivered their souls and took themselves to the land of Cush to Kikianus, king of Cush.

40 And Moses was in the king's house going out and coming in; the Lord gave him favor in the eyes of Pharaoh and in the eyes of all his servants, and in the eyes of all the people of Egypt, and they loved Moses greatly.

41 The day arrived when Moses went to Goshen to see his brothers that he saw the children of Israel in their burdens and hard labor, and Moses was grieved on their account.

42 And Moses returned to Egypt and came to the house of Pharaoh, and came before the king, and Moses bowed down before the king.

43 And Moses said to Pharaoh, I pray you my lord, I have come to seek a small request from you, turn not away my face empty; and Pharaoh said to him, Speak.

44 And Moses said to Pharaoh, Let there be given to your servants the children of Israel who are in Goshen, one day to rest therein from their labor.

45 And the king answered Moses and said, Behold I have lifted up your face in this thing to grant your request.

46 And Pharaoh ordered an announcement to be issued throughout Egypt and Goshen, saying,

47 To you, all the children of Israel, thus says the king, for six days you shall do your work and labor, but on the seventh day you shall rest and shall not preform any work, thus shall you do all the days as the king and Moses the son of Bathia have commanded.

48 And Moses rejoiced at this thing which the king had granted to him, and all the children of Israel did as Moses ordered them.

49 For this thing was from the Lord to the children of Israel, for the Lord had begun to remember the children of Israel to save them for the sake of their fathers.

50 And the Lord was with Moses and his fame went throughout Egypt.

51 And Moses became great in the eyes of all the Egyptians, and in the eyes of all the children of Israel, seeking good for his people Israel and speaking words of peace regarding them to the king.

CHAPTER 71

1 When Moses was eighteen years old he desired to see his father and mother and he went to them at Goshen, and when Moses had come near Goshen he came to the place where the children of Israel were engaged in work, and he observed their burdens, and he saw an Egyptian smiting one of his Hebrew brothers.

2 When the man who was beaten saw Moses he ran to him for help, for the man Moses was greatly respected in the house of Pharaoh, and he said to him, My lord attend to me; this Egyptian came to my house in the night, bound me, and came to my wife in my presence, and now he seeks to take my life away.

3 And when Moses heard this wicked thing, his anger was set ablaze against the Egyptian, and he turned this way and the other, and when he saw there was no man there he struck the Egyptian and hid him in the sand, and delivered the Hebrew from the hand of him that struck him.

4 And the Hebrew went to his house, and Moses returned to his home, and went forth and came back to the king's house.

5 And when the man had returned home, he thought of leaving his wife, for it was not right in the house of Jacob for any man to come to his wife after she had been defiled.

6 The woman went and told her brothers, and the woman's brothers sought to kill him, and he fled to his house and escaped.

7 On the second day Moses went forth to his brothers, and looked and saw two men were quarreling; he said to the wicked one, Why do you strike your neighbor?

8 And he answered him and said to him, Who has set you for a prince and judge over us? Do you think to kill me as you did kill the Egyptian? And Moses was afraid and said, Certainly the thing is known?

9 And Pharaoh heard of this affair, and he ordered Moses to be slain, so God sent his angel and he appeared to Pharaoh in the likeness of a captain of the guard.

10 And the angel of the Lord took the sword from the hand of the captain of the guard, and took his head off with it, for the likeness of the captain of the guard was turned into the likeness of Moses.

11 And the angel of the Lord took hold of the right hand of Moses, and brought him forth from Egypt, and placed him outside the borders of Egypt, a distance of forty days' journey.

12 And Aaron his brother alone remained in the land of Egypt, and he prophesied to the children of Israel, saying,

13 Thus says the Lord God of your ancestors, Throw away, each man, the abominations of his eyes, and do not defile yourselves with the idols of Egypt.

14 And the children of Israel rebelled and would not listen to Aaron at that time.

15 And the Lord thought to destroy them, were it not that the Lord remembered the covenant which he had made with Abraham, Isaac and Jacob.

16 In those days the hand of Pharaoh continued to be severe against the children of Israel, and he crushed and oppressed them until the time when God sent forth his word and took notice of them.

CHAPTER 72

1 It was in those days that there was a great war between the children of Cush and the children of the east and Aram, and they rebelled against the king of Cush in whose hands they were.

2 So Kikianus king of Cush went forth with all the children of Cush, a people numerous as the sand, and he went to fight against Aram and the children of the east, to bring them under subjection.

3 When Kikianus went out, he left Balaam the magician with his two sons, to guard the city and the lowest sort of the people of the land.

4 So Kikianus went forth to Aram and the children of the east, and he fought against them and struck them; they all fell down wounded before Kikianus and his people.

5 He took many of them captives and he brought them under subjection as at first, and he encamped on their land to take tax from them as usual.

6 Balaam the son of Beor, when the king of Cush had left him to guard the city and the poor of the city, rose up and advised with the people of the land to rebel against king Kikianus, not to let him enter the city when he would come home.

7 And the people of the land listened to him and they swore to him and made him king over them, and his two sons for captains of the army.

8 So they rose up and raised the walls of the city at the two corners, and they built an exceedingly strong building.

9 At the third corner they dug ditches without number, between the city and the river which surrounded the whole land of Cush, and they made the waters of the river burst forth there.

10 At the fourth corner they collected numerous serpents by their incantations and enchantments, and they fortified the city and lived therein; no one went out or in before them.

11 Kikianus fought against Aram and the children of the east and he subdued them as before; they gave him their usual tax and he went and returned to his land.

12 When Kikianus the king of Cush approached his city and all the captains of the forces with him, they lifted up their eyes

and saw that the walls of the city were built up and greatly elevated, so the men were astonished at this.

13 They said one to the other, It is because they saw that we were delayed, in battle, and were greatly afraid of us; therefore have they done this thing and raised the city walls and fortified them so that the kings of Canaan might not come in battle against them.

14 So the king and the troops approached the city door and they looked up and behold, all the gates of the city were closed; they called out to the sentinels, saying, Open to us, that we may enter the city.

15 But the sentinels refused to open to them by the order of Balaam the magician, their king; they did not allow them enter their city.

16 So they raised a battle with them opposite the city gate, and one hundred and thirty men of the army at Kikianus fell on that day.

17 On the next day they continued to fight and they fought at the side of the river; they endeavored to pass but were not able, so some of them sank in the pits and died.

18 The king ordered them to cut down trees to make rafts, on which they might pass to them, and they did so.

19 When they came to the place of the ditches, the waters revolved by mills, and two hundred men on ten rafts were drowned.

20 On the third day they came to fight at the side where the serpents were, but they could not approach there, for the serpents killed of them one hundred and seventy men; then they ceased fighting against Cush, and they besieged Cush for nine years; no person came out or in.

21 At the time that the war and the siege were against Cush, Moses fled from Egypt from Pharaoh who sought to kill him for having slain the Egyptian.

22 Moses was eighteen years old when he fled from Egypt from the presence of Pharaoh, and he fled and escaped to the camp of Kikianus, which at that time was besieging Cush.

23 Moses was nine years in the camp of Kikianus king of Cush, all the time that they were besieging Cush, and Moses went out and came in with them.

24 And the king and princes and all the fighting men loved Moses, for he was great and worthy, his stature was like a noble lion, his face was like the sun and his strength was like that of a lion, and he was counsellor to the king.

25 And at the end of nine years, Kikianus was seized with a mortal disease, and his illness consumed him, and he died on the seventh day.

26 So his servants embalmed him, carried him and buried him opposite the city gate to the north of the land of Egypt.

27 They built over him an elegant strong and high building, and they placed great stones below.

28 And the king's scribes engraved on those stones all the might of their king Kikianus, and all his battles which he had fought; they are written there at this day.

29 After the death of Kikianus king of Cush it grieved his men and troops greatly on account of the war.

30 So they said one to the other, Give us counsel what we are to do at this time, as we have resided in the wilderness nine years away from our homes.

31 If we say we will fight against the city many of us will fall wounded or killed, and if we remain here in the siege we shall also die.

32 For now all the kings of Aram and of the children of the east will hear that our king is dead, and they will attack us suddenly in a hostile manner; they will fight against us and leave no remnant of us.

33 So now let us go and make a king over us, and let us remain in the siege until the city is delivered up to us.

34 And they wished to choose on that day a man for king from the army of Kikianus, and they found no person of their choice like Moses to reign over them.

35 They hurried and stripped off each man his garments and cast them on the ground, and they made a great heap and placed Moses thereon.

36 And they rose up and blew with trumpets and called out before him, and said, May the king live, may the king live!

37 And all the people and nobles swore to him to give him for a wife Adoniah the queen, the Cushite, wife of Kikianus, and they made Moses king over them on that day.

38 And all the people of Cush issued an announcement on that day, saying, Every man must give something to Moses of what is in his possession.

39 They spread out a sheet on the heap, and every man cast into it something of what he had, one a gold earring and the other a coin.

40 Also of onyx stones, bdellium, pearls and marble did the children of Cush cast to Moses on the heap, also silver and gold in great abundance.

41 And Moses took all the silver and gold, all the vessels, and the bdellium and onyx stones, which all the children of Cush had given to him, and he placed them among his treasures.

42 And Moses reigned over the children of Cush on that day, in the place of Kikianus king of Cush.

CHAPTER 73

1 In the fifty-fifth year of the reign of Pharaoh king of Egypt, that is in the hundred and fifty-seventh year of the Israelites going down into Egypt, Moses reigned in Cush.

2 Moses was twenty-seven years old when he began to reign over Cush, and forty years he did reign.

3 And the Lord granted Moses favor and grace in the eyes of all the children of Cush; the children of Cush loved him greatly, so Moses was favored by the Lord and by men.

4 In the seventh day of his reign, all the children of Cush assembled and came before Moses and bowed down to him to the ground.

5 And all the children spoke together in the presence of the king, saying, Give us counsel that we may see what is to be done to this city.

6 For it is now nine years that we have been besieging round about the city and have not seen our children and our wives.

7 So the king answered them, saying, If you will listen to my voice in all that I shall command you, then the Lord will give the city into our hands and we shall subdue it.

8 For if we fight with them as in the former battle which we had with them before the death of Kikianus, many of us will fall down wounded as before.

9 Now therefore hear this counsel for you in this matter; if you will listen to my voice, then will the city be delivered into our hands.

10 So all the forces answered the king, saying, All that our lord shall command that we will do.

11 And Moses said to them, Pass through and proclaim a voice in the whole camp to all the people, saying,

12 Thus says the king, Go into the forest and bring with you of the young ones of the stork, each man a young one in his hand.

13 And any person disobeying the word of the king, who shall not bring his young one, shall die and the king will take all belonging to him.

14 And when you bring them they shall be in your keeping; you shall rear them until they grow up, and you shall teach them to strike their prey, as is the way of the young ones of the hawk.

15 So all the children of Cush heard the words of Moses, and they rose up and caused announcement to be issued throughout the camp, saying,

16 To you, all the children of Cush, the king's order is that you all go together to the forest and catch there the young stork; each man his young one in his hand and you shall bring them home.

17 Any person violating the order of the king shall die and the king will take all that belongs to him.

18 And all the people did so, and they went out to the wood and they climbed the fir trees and each man caught a young one in his hand, all the young of the storks; they brought them into the desert and reared them by order of the king; they taught them to strike similar to the young hawks.

19 And after the young storks were reared, the king ordered them to be hungry for three days, and all the people did so.

20 On the third day the king said to them, Strengthen yourselves and become courageous men; put on each man his armor and gird on his sword, and each man ride his horse and each take his young stork in his hand.

21 And we will rise up and fight against the city at the place where the serpents are, and all the people did as the king had ordered.

22 And each man took his young one in his hand and they went away; when they came to the place of the serpents the king said to them, Send forth each man his young stork on the serpents.

23 And they sent forth each man his young stork at the king's order, and the young storks ran on the serpents and they devoured them all and destroyed them out of that place.

24 When the king and people had seen that all the serpents were destroyed in that place, all the people sent up a great shout.

25 And they approached and fought against the city and took and subdued it, and they entered the city.

26 There died on that day one thousand and one hundred men of the people of the city, all that inhabited the city, but of the people besieging not one died.

27 So all the children of Cush each went to his home, to his wife and children and to all belonging to him.

28 And Balaam the magician, when he saw that the city was taken, opened the gate and he and his two sons and eight brothers fled and returned to Egypt, to Pharaoh king of Egypt.

29 They are the sorcerers and magicians who are mentioned in the book of the law, standing against Moses when the Lord brought the plagues on Egypt.

30 So Moses took the city by his wisdom, and the children of Cush placed him on the throne instead of Kikianus king of Cush.

31 They placed the royal crown on his head and they gave him a wife Adoniah the Cushite queen, wife of Kikianus.

32 Moses feared the Lord God of his fathers so that he came not to her, nor did he turn his eyes to her.

33 For Moses remembered how Abraham had made his servant Eliezer swear, saying to him, You shall not take a woman from the daughters of Canaan for my son Isaac.

34 Also what Isaac did when Jacob had fled from his brother, when he commanded him saying, You shall not take a wife from the daughters of Canaan, nor make alliance with any of the children of Ham.

35 For the Lord our God gave Ham the son of Noah, and his children and all his descendants as slaves to the children of Shem and to the children of Japheth, and to their descendants after them for slaves forever.

36 Therefore Moses turned not his heart nor his eyes to the wife of Kikianus all the days that he reigned over Cush.

37 Moses feared the Lord his God all his life, and Moses walked before the Lord in truth with all his heart and soul; he turned not from the right way all the days of his life; he declined not from the way either to the right or to the left, in which Abraham, Isaac and Jacob had walked.

38 Moses strengthened himself in the kingdom of the children of Cush; he guided the children of Cush with his usual wisdom, and Moses prospered in his kingdom.

39 At that time Aram and the children of the east heard that Kikianus king of Cush had died, so Aram and the children of the east rebelled against Cush in those days.

40 Moses gathered all the children of Cush, a people very mighty, about thirty thousand men and he went forth to fight with Aram and the children of the east.

41 They went at first to the children of the east and when the children of the east heard their report, they went to meet them, and engaged in battle with them.

42 And the war was severe against the children of the east, so the Lord gave all the children of the east into the hand of Moses; about three hundred men fell down slain.

43 All the children of the east turned back and retreated, so Moses and the children of Cush followed them and subdued them, and put a tax on them as was their custom.

44 So Moses and all the people with him passed from there to the land of Aram for battle.

45 And the people of Aram also went to meet them; they fought against them and the Lord delivered them into the hand of Moses, and many of the men of Aram fell down wounded.

46 Aram also was subdued by Moses and the people of Cush, and also gave their usual tax.

47 And Moses brought Aram and the children of the east under subjection to the children of Cush; Moses and all the people who were with him turned to the land of Cush.

48 Moses strengthened himself in the kingdom of the children of Cush and the Lord was with him, and all the children of Cush were afraid of him.

CHAPTER 74

1 In the end of years Saul king of Edom died, and Baal Chanan the son of Achbor reigned in his place.

2 In the sixteenth year of the reign of Moses over Cush, Baal Chanan the son of Achbor reigned in the land of Edom over all the children of Edom for thirty-eight years.

3 In his days Moab rebelled against the power of Edom, having been under Edom since the days of Hadad the son of Bedad, who struck them and Midian, and brought Moab under subjection to Edom.

4 And when Baal Chanan the son of Achbor reigned over Edom, all the children of Moab withdrew their allegiance from Edom.

5 Angeas king of Africa died in those days, and Azdrubal his son reigned in his stead.

6 And in those days Janeas king of the children of Chittim died, and they buried him in his temple which he had built for himself in the plain of Canopia for a residence; Latinus reigned in his stead.

7 In the twenty-second year of the reign of Moses over the children of Cush, Latinus reigned over the children of Chittim forty-five years.

8 And he also built for himself a great and mighty tower; he built therein an elegant temple for his residence, to conduct his government as was the custom.

9 In the third year of his reign he caused an announcement to be made to all his skilful men who made many ships for him.

10 And Latinus assembled all his forces, and they came in ships, and went there to fight with Azdrubal son of Angeas king of Africa; they came to Africa and engaged in battle with Azdrubal and his army.

11 And Latinus won over Azdrubal, and Latinus took from Azdrubal the aqueduct which his father had brought from the children of Chittim, when he took Janiah the daughter of Uzi for a wife; so Latinus overthrew the bridge of the aqueduct and struck the whole army of Azdrubal a severe blow.

12 The remaining strong men of Azdrubal strengthened themselves, and their hearts were filled with envy; they courted death, and again engaged in battle with Latinus king of Chittim.

13 The battle was severe on all the men of Africa and they all fell wounded before Latinus and his people, and Azdrubal the king also fell in that battle.

14 The king Azdrubal had a very beautiful daughter whose name was Ushpezena, and all the men of Africa embroidered her likeness on their garment on account of her great beauty and attractive appearance.

15 The men of Latinus saw Ushpezena, the daughter of Azdrubal, and praised her to Latinus their king.

16 And Latinus ordered her to be brought to him; Latinus took Ushpezena for a wife and he turned back on his way to Chittim.

17 It was after the death of Azdrubal son of Angeas, when Latinus had turned back to his land from the battle, that all the inhabitants of Africa rose up and took Anibal the son of Angeas, the younger brother of Azdrubal, and made him king instead of his brother over the whole land at Africa.

18 And when he reigned he resolved to go to Chittim to fight with the children of Chittim, to avenge the cause of Azdrubal his brother and the cause of the inhabitants of Africa, and he did so.

19 He made many ships and he came there with his whole army, and he went to Chittim.

20 So Anibal fought with the children of Chittim, and the children of Chittim fell wounded before Anibal and his army, and Anibal avenged his brother's cause.

21 And Anibal continued the war for eighteen years with the children of Chittim, and Anibal lived in the land of Chittim and encamped there for a long time.

22 Anibal struck the children of Chittim very severely and he killed their great men and princes, and of the rest of the people he struck about eighty thousand men.

23 And at the end of days and years, Anibal returned to his land of Africa, and he reigned securely in the place of Azdrubal his brother.

CHAPTER 75

1 At that time in the hundred and eightieth year of the Israelites going down into Egypt, there went forth from Egypt courageous men, thirty thousand on foot, from the children of Israel who were all of the tribe of Joseph, of the children of Ephraim the son of Joseph.

2 For they said the period was completed which the Lord had appointed to the children of Israel in the times of old, which he had spoken to Abraham.

3 And these men prepared themselves, and each man put his sword at his side, and every man his armor on him, and they trusted to their strength; they went out together from Egypt with a mighty hand.

4 But they brought no provision for the road, only silver and gold, not even did they bring bread for that day in their hands, for they thought of getting their provision for pay from the Philistines; if not they would take it by force.

5 These men were very mighty and bold men; one man could pursue a thousand and two could rout ten thousand, so they trusted their strength and went together as they were.

6 They directed their course toward the land of Gath, and they went down and found the shepherds of Gath feeding the cattle of the children of Gath.

7 They said to the shepherds, Give us some of the sheep for pay that we may eat, for we are hungry; we have eaten no bread this day.

8 And the shepherds said, Are they our sheep or cattle that we should give them to you even for pay? So the children of Ephraim approached to take them by force.

9 And the shepherds of Gath shouted over them so their cry was heard at a distance; all the children of Gath went out to them.

10 When the children of Gath saw the evil doings of the children of Ephraim, they returned and assembled the men of Gath; they put on each man his armor and came forth to the children of Ephraim for battle.

11 And they engaged with them in the valley of Gath, and the battle was severe; they struck from each other a great many on that day.

12 And on the second day the children of Gath sent to all the cities of the Philistines that they should come to their help, saying,

13 Come up to us and help us, that we may strike the children of Ephraim who have come forth from Egypt to take our cattle, and to fight against us without cause.

14 And the souls of the children of Ephraim were exhausted with hunger and thirst, for they had eaten no bread for three days. Forty thousand men went out from the cities of the Philistines to the assistance of the men of Gath.

15 These men were engaged in battle with the children of Ephraim, and the Lord delivered the children of Ephraim into the hands of the Philistines.

16 They struck all the children of Ephraim, all who had gone forth from Egypt, none were remaining but ten men who had run away from the engagement.

17 This evil was from the Lord against the children of Ephraim for they went contrary to the word of the Lord in going forth from Egypt, before the period had arrived which the Lord in the days of old had appointed to Israel.

18 And of the Philistines also there fell a great many, about twenty thousand men, and their brothers carried them and buried them in their cities.

19 And the slain of the children of Ephraim remained forsaken in the valley of Gath for many days and years and were not brought to burial, and the valley was filled with men's bones.

20 The men who had escaped from the battle came to Egypt and told all the children of Israel all that had happened to them.

21 Their father Ephraim mourned over them for many days, and his brothers came to console him.

22 And he came to his wife and she gave birth to a son, and he called his name Beriah, for she was unfortunate in his house.

CHAPTER 76

1 Moses the son of Amram was still king in the land of Cush in those days, and he prospered in his kingdom; he conducted the government of the children of Cush in justice, in righteousness and integrity.

2 And all the children of Cush loved Moses all the days that he reigned over them, and all the inhabitants of the land of Cush were greatly afraid of him.

3 In the fortieth year of the reign of Moses over Cush, Moses was sitting on the royal throne while Adoniah the queen was before him, and all the nobles were sitting around him.

4 And Adoniah the queen said before the king and the princes, What is this thing which you, the children of Cush, have done for this long time?

5 Certainly you know that for forty years that this man has reigned over Cush he has not approached me, nor has he served the gods of the children of Cush.

6 Now therefore hear, O ye children of Cush, and let this man no more reign over you as he is not of our people.

7 Behold Menacrus my son is grown up, let him reign over you for it is better for you to serve the son of your lord than to serve a stranger, slave of the king of Egypt.

8 And all the people and nobles of the children of Cush heard the words which Adoniah the queen had spoken in their ears.

9 All the people were preparing until the evening, and in the morning they rose up early and made Menacrus, son of Kikianus, king over them.

10 All the children of Cush were afraid to stretch forth their hand against Moses, for the Lord was with Moses, and the children of Cush remembered the oath which they swore to Moses, therefore they did no harm to him.

11 But the children of Cush gave many presents to Moses, and sent him from them with great honor.

12 So Moses went forth from the land of Cush and went home and ceased to reign over Cush; Moses was sixty-six years old when he went out of the land of Cush, for the thing was from the Lord. For the period had arrived which he had appointed in the days of old, to bring forth Israel from the affliction of the children of Ham.

13 So Moses went to Midian, for he was afraid to return to Egypt on account of Pharaoh, and he went and sat at a well of water in Midian.

14 And the seven daughters of Reuel the Midianite went out to feed their father's flock.

15 And they came to the well and drew water to water their father's flock.

16 But the shepherds of Midian came and drove them away, and Moses rose up and helped them and watered the flock.

17 And they came home to their father Reuel, and told him what Moses did for them.

18 They said, An Egyptian man has delivered us from the hands of the shepherds; he drew up water for us and watered the flock.

19 And Reuel said to his daughters, And where is he? Why have you left the man?

20 And Reuel sent for him and fetched him and brought him home, and he ate bread with him.

21 And Moses related to Reuel that he had fled from Egypt and that he reigned forty years over Cush, and that they afterward had taken the government from him and had sent him away in peace with honor and with presents.

22 And when Reuel had heard the words of Moses, Reuel said within himself, I will put this man into the prison house, whereby I shall win over the children of Cush, for he has fled from them.

23 They took and put him into the prison house, and Moses was in prison ten years; while Moses was in the prison house, Zipporah the daughter of Reuel took pity on him, and supported him with bread and water all the time.

24 All the children of Israel were yet in the land of Egypt serving the Egyptians in all manner of hard work, and the hand of Egypt continued in severity over the children of Israel in those days.

25 At that time the Lord struck Pharaoh king of Egypt, and he was afflicted with the plague of leprosy from the sole of his foot to the crown of his head; owing to the cruel treatment of the children of Israel this plague at that time was from the Lord on Pharaoh king of Egypt.

26 For the Lord had listened to the prayer of his people the children of Israel, and their cry reached him on account of their hard work.

27 Still his anger did not turn from them, and the hand of Pharaoh was still stretched out against the children of Israel. Pharaoh hardened his neck before the Lord, he increased his yoke over the children of Israel, and embittered their lives with all manner of hard work.

28 When the Lord had inflicted the plague on Pharaoh king of Egypt, he asked his wise men and sorcerers to cure him.

29 And his wise men and sorcerers said to him that if the blood of little children were put into the wounds he would be healed.

30 Pharaoh listened to them, and sent his ministers to Goshen to the children of Israel to take their little children.

31 And Pharaoh's ministers went and took the infants of the children of Israel from the bosoms of their mothers by force, and they brought them to Pharaoh daily, a child each day, and the physicians killed them and applied them to the plague; thus

they did all the days.

32 And the number of the children which Pharaoh killed was three hundred and seventy-five.

33 But the Lord listened not to the physicians of the king of Egypt, and the plague went on increasing mightily.

34 Pharaoh was ten years afflicted with that plague, still the heart of Pharaoh was more hardened against the children of Israel.

35 At the end of ten years the Lord continued to afflict Pharaoh with destructive plagues.

36 And the Lord struck him with a bad tumor and sickness in the stomach, and that plague turned to a severe boil.

37 At that time the two ministers of Pharaoh came from the land of Goshen where all the children of Israel were, and went to the house of Pharaoh and said to him, We have seen the children of Israel slacken in their work and negligent in their labor.

38 And when Pharaoh heard the words of his ministers, his anger was set ablaze against the children of Israel greatly, for he was greatly grieved at his bodily pain.

39 And he answered and said, Now that the children of Israel know that I am ill, they turn and scoff at us. Now therefore harness my chariot for me, and I will take myself to Goshen and will see the scoff of the children of Israel with which they are deriding me. So his servants harnessed the chariot for him.

40 And they took and made him ride on a horse, for he was not able to ride of himself.

41 He took with him ten horsemen and ten footmen, and went to the children of Israel to Goshen.

42 When they had come to the border of Egypt, the king's horse passed into a narrow place, elevated in the hollow part of the vineyard, fenced on both sides, the low plain country being on the other side.

43 The horses ran rapidly in that place and pressed each other, and the other horses pressed the king's horse.

44 And the king's horse fell into the low plain while the king was riding on it; he fell and the chariot turned over the king's face and the horse lay on the king, and the king cried out for his flesh was very sore.

45 And the flesh of the king was torn from him, and his bones were broken and he could not ride; this thing was from the Lord to him, for the Lord had heard the cries of his people the children of Israel and their affliction.

46 And his servants carried him on their shoulders,slowly and carefully, and they brought him back to Egypt, and the horsemen who were with him also came back to Egypt.

47 They placed him in his bed and the king knew that his end was come to die, so Aparanith the queen his wife came and cried before the king, and the king wept a great weeping with her.

48 And all his nobles and servants came on that day and saw the king in that affliction, and wept a great weeping with him.

49 The princes of the king and all his counselors advised the king to cause one to reign in his stead in the land, whomever he would choose from his sons.

50 The king had three sons and two daughters which Aparanith the queen his wife had borne to him, besides the king's children of concubines.

51 And these were their names: the firstborn Othri, the second Adikam, and the third Morion, and their sisters: the name of the elder Bathia and of the other Acuzi.

52 Othri the first born of the king was an idiot, impetuous and hurried in his words.

53 But Adikam was a cunning and wise man and knowing in all the wisdom of Egypt, but of unseemly appearance, thick in flesh and very short in stature; his height was one cubit.

54 And when the king saw Adikam his son intelligent and wise in all things, the king resolved that he should be king in his stead after his death.

55 He took for him a wife Gedudah daughter of Abilot, and he was ten years old; she gave birth to, to him, four sons.

56 And afterward he went and took three wives and had eight sons and three daughters.

57 And the disorder greatly consumed the king, and his flesh stank like the flesh of a carcass cast on the field in summer time, during the heat of the sun.

58 And when the king saw that his sickness had greatly strengthened itself over him, he ordered his son Adikam to be brought to him, and they made him king over the land in his place.

59 At the end of three years the king died, in shame, disgrace, and disgust, and his servants carried him and buried him in the sepulcher of the kings of Egypt in Zoan Mizraim.

60 But they embalmed him not as was usual with kings, for his flesh was putrid, and they could not approach to embalm him on account of the stench, so they buried him in haste.

61 For this evil was from the Lord to him, for the Lord had rewarded him evil for the evil which in his days he had done to Israel.

62 And he died with terror and with shame, and his son Adikam reigned in his place.

CHAPTER 77

1 Adikam was twenty years old when he reigned over Egypt, he reigned four years.

2 In the two hundred and sixth year of Israel's going down to Egypt did Adikam reign over Egypt, but he continued not so long in his reign over Egypt as his fathers had continued their reigns.

3 For Melol his father reigned ninety-four years in Egypt, but he was sick ten years and died, for he had been wicked before the Lord.

4 And all the Egyptians called the name of Adikam Pharaoh like the name of his fathers, as was their custom to do in Egypt.

5 And all the wise men of Pharaoh called the name of Adikam Ahuz, for short it's called Ahuz in the Egyptian language.

6 Adikam was greatly ugly, and he was a cubit and a span and he had a great beard which reached to the soles of his feet.

7 And Pharaoh sat on his father's throne to reign over Egypt, and he conducted the government of Egypt in his wisdom.

8 While he reigned he exceeded his father and all the preceding kings in wickedness, and he increased his yoke over the children of Israel.

9 He went with his servants to Goshen to the children of Israel, and he strengthened the labor over them and he said to them, Complete your work, each day's task, and let not your hands slacken from our work from this day forward as you did in the days of my father.

10 He placed officers over them from among the children of Israel, and over these officers he placed taskmasters from among his servants.

11 And he placed over them a measure of bricks for them to do according to that number, day by day, and he turned back and went to Egypt.

12 At that time the taskmasters of Pharaoh ordered the officers of the children of Israel according to the command of Pharaoh, saying,

13 Thus says Pharaoh, Do your work each day, and finish your task, and observe the daily measure of bricks; diminish not anything.

14 And it shall come to pass that if you are deficient in your daily bricks, I will put your young children in their stead.

15 And the taskmasters of Egypt did so in those days as Pharaoh had ordered them.

16 And whenever any deficiency was found in the children of Israel's measure of their daily bricks, the taskmasters of Pharaoh would go to the wives of the children of Israel and take infants of the children of Israel to the number of bricks deficient, they would take them by force from their mother's laps, and put them in the building instead of the bricks;

17 While their fathers and mothers were crying over them and weeping when they heard the weeping voices of their infants in the wall of the building.

18 And the taskmasters prevailed over Israel, that the Israelites should place their children in the building, so that a man placed his son in the wall and put mortar over him, while his eyes wept over him, and his tears ran down on his child.

19 And the taskmasters of Egypt did so to the babes of Israel for many days, and no one pitied or had compassion over the babes of the children of Israel.

20 And the number of all the children killed in the building was two hundred and seventy, some whom they had built on instead of the bricks which had been left deficient by their fathers, and some whom they had drawn out dead from the building.

21 And the labor imposed on the children of Israel in the days of Adikam exceeded in hardship that which they performed in the days of his father.

22 The children of Israel sighed every day on account of their heavy work, for they had said to themselves, Certainly when Pharaoh dies, his son will rise up and lighten our work!

23 But they increased the latter work more than the former, and the children of Israel sighed at this and their cry ascended to God on account of their labor.

24 God heard the voice of the children of Israel and their cry in those days, and God remembered to them his covenant which he had made with Abraham, Isaac and Jacob.

25 And God saw the burden of the children of Israel and their heavy work in those days, and he determined to deliver them.

26 Moses the son of Amram was still confined in the dungeon in those days, in the house of Reuel the Midianite, and Zipporah the daughter of Reuel supported him with food secretly day by day.

27 Moses was confined in the dungeon in the house of Reuel for ten years.

28 And at the end of ten years which was the first year of the reign of Pharaoh over Egypt, in the place of his father,

29 Zipporah said to her father Reuel, No person inquires or seeks after the Hebrew man, whom you bound in prison now ten years.

30 So therefore, if it seems good in your sight, let us send and see whether he is living or dead. But her father knew not that she had supported him.

31 And Reuel her father answered and said to her, Has ever such a thing happened that a man would be shut up in a prison without food for ten years, and that he should live?

32 And Zipporah answered her father, saying, Certainly you have heard that the God of the Hebrews is great and mighty, and does wonders for them at all times.

33 He it was who delivered Abraham from the Chaldeans, and Isaac from the sword of his father, and Jacob from the angel of the Lord who wrestled with him at the ford of Jabbuk.

34 Also with this man he has done many things; he delivered him from the river in Egypt and from the sword of Pharaoh, and from the children of Cush, so also he can deliver him from famine and make him live.

35 And the thing seemed good in the sight of Reuel, and he did according to the word of his daughter, and sent to the

dungeon to ascertain what became of Moses.

36 He saw, and behold the man Moses was living in the dungeon, standing on his feet, praising and praying to the God of his ancestors.

37 And Reuel commanded Moses to be brought out of the dungeon, so they shaved him and he changed his prison garments and ate bread.

38 And afterward Moses went into the garden of Reuel which was behind the house, and he there prayed to the Lord his God, who had done mighty wonders for him.

39 It was while he prayed he looked opposite to him, and there a sapphire stick was placed in the ground, which was planted in the midst of the garden.

40 He approached the stick and looked, and saw the name of the Lord God of hosts was engraved on it, written and developed on the stick.

41 And he read it and stretched forth his hand and he plucked it like a forest tree from the thicket, and the stick was in his hand.

42 This is the stick with which all the works of our God were performed, after he had created heaven and earth and all the host of them, seas, rivers and all their fish.

43 And when God had driven Adam from the garden of Eden, he took the stick in his hand and went and tilled the ground from which he was taken.

44 The stick came down to Noah and was given to Shem and his descendants, until it came into the hand of Abraham the Hebrew.

45 And when Abraham had given all he had to his son Isaac, he also gave to him this stick.

46 When Jacob had fled to Padan-aram, he took it into his hand, and when he returned to his father he had not left it behind him.

47 Also when he went down to Egypt he took it into his hand and gave it to Joseph, one portion above his brothers, for Jacob had taken it by force from his brother Esau.

48 After the death of Joseph, the nobles of Egypt came into the house of Joseph, and the stick came into the hand of Reuel the Midianite; when he went out of Egypt, he took it in his hand and planted it in his garden.

49 And all the mighty men of the Kinites tried to pluck it when they endeavored to get Zipporah his daughter, but they were unsuccessful.

50 That stick remained planted in the garden of Reuel until he who had a right to it came and took it.

51 And when Reuel saw the stick in the hand of Moses, he wondered at it, and he gave him his daughter Zipporah for a wife.

CHAPTER 78

1 At that time Baal Channan son of Achbor, king of Edom, died and was buried in his house in the land of Edom.

2 After his death the children of Esau sent to the land of Edom, and took from there a man who was in Edom, whose name was Hadad, and they made him king over them in the place of Baal Channan, their king.

3 And Hadad reigned over the children of Edom forty-eight years.

4 When he reigned he resolved to fight against the children of Moab to bring them under the power of the children of Esau as they were before, but he was not able to because the children of Moab heard this thing, and they rose up and hurried to elect a king over them from among their brothers.

5 Afterward they gathered together a large crowd, and sent them to the children of Ammon their brothers for help to fight against Hadad king of Edom.

6 And Hadad heard the thing which the children of Moab had done, and was greatly afraid of them, and refrained from fighting against them.

7 In those days Moses, the son of Amram, in Midian, took Zipporah, the daughter of Reuel the Midianite, for a wife.

8 And Zipporah walked in the ways of the daughters of Jacob, she was nothing short of the righteousness of Sarah, Rebecca, Rachel and Leah.

9 And Zipporah conceived and gave birth to a son and he called his name Gershom, for he said, I was a stranger in a foreign land; but he circumcised not his foreskin, at the command of Reuel his father-in-law.

10 And she conceived again and gave birth to a son, but circumcised his foreskin, and called his name Eliezer, for Moses said, Because the God of my fathers was my help and delivered me from the sword of Pharaoh.

11 And Pharaoh king of Egypt greatly increased the labor of the children of Israel in those days, and continued to make his yoke heavier on the children of Israel.

12 And he ordered an announcement to be made in Egypt, saying, Give no more straw to the people to make bricks with, let them go and gather themselves straw as they can find it.

13 Also the number of bricks which they shall make let them give each day, and diminish nothing from them, for they are idle in their work.

14 And the children of Israel heard this, and they mourned and sighed, and they cried to the Lord on account of the

bitterness of their souls.

15 And the Lord heard the cries of the children of Israel, and saw the oppression with which the Egyptians oppressed them.

16 And the Lord was zealous for his people and his inheritance, and heard their voice, and he resolved to take them out of the affliction of Egypt, to give them the land of Canaan for a possession.

CHAPTER 79

1 Iin those days Moses was feeding the flock of Reuel the Midianite his father-in-law, beyond the wilderness of Sin, and the stick which he took from his father-in-law was in his hand.

2 And it came to pass one day that a kid of goats strayed from the flock, and Moses pursued it and it came to the mountain of God to Horeb.

3 When he came to Horeb the Lord appeared there to him in the bush, and he found the bush burning with fire, but the fire had no power over the bush to consume it.

4 Moses was greatly astonished at this sight because the bush was not consumed, and he approached to see this mighty thing; the Lord called to Moses out of the fire and commanded him to go down to Egypt to Pharaoh king of Egypt, to send the children of Israel from his service.

5 And the Lord said to Moses, Go, return to Egypt for all those men who sought your life are dead, and you shall speak to Pharaoh to send forth the children of Israel from his land.

6 The Lord showed him to do signs and wonders in Egypt before the eyes of Pharaoh and the eyes of his subjects, in order that they might believe that the Lord had sent him.

7 Moses listened to all that the Lord had commanded him, and he returned to his father-in-law and told him these things, and Reuel said to him, Go in peace.

8 Moses rose up to go to Egypt and took his wife and sons with him; he was at an inn in the road, and an angel of God came down, and sought an occasion against him.

9 He wished to kill him on account of his firstborn son because he had not circumcised him and had gone contrary to the covenant which the Lord had made with Abraham.

10 For Moses had listened to the words of his father-in-law which he had spoken to him, not to circumcise his first born son, so he did not circumcise him.

11 Zipporah saw the angel of the Lord seeking an occasion against Moses, and she knew that this thing was because of his not having circumcised her son Gershom.

12 Zipporah hurried and took some of the sharp rock stones that were there, and circumcised her son, and delivered her husband and her son from the hand of the angel of the Lord.

13 Aaron the son of Amram, the brother of Moses, was in Egypt walking at the river side on that day.

14 And the Lord appeared to him in that place; he said to him, Go now toward Moses in the wilderness. And he went and met him in the mountain of God, and he kissed him.

15 Aaron lifted up his eyes and saw Zipporah the wife of Moses and her children, and he said to Moses, Who are these to you?

16 And Moses said to him, They are my wife and sons which God gave to me in Midian; the thing grieved Aaron on account of the woman and her children.

17 Aaron said to Moses, Send away the woman and her children that they may go to her father's house, and Moses listened to the words of Aaron, and did so.

18 Zipporah returned with her children and they went to the house of Reuel, and remained there until the time arrived when the Lord had visited his people and brought them forth from Egypt from the hand at Pharaoh.

19 Moses and Aaron came to Egypt to the community of the children of Israel and spoke to them all the words of the Lord, and the people rejoiced a very great rejoicing.

20 Moses and Aaron rose up early the next day and went to the house of Pharaoh, and they took in their hands the stick of God.

21 When they came to the king's gate, two young lions were confined there with iron instruments; no person went out or came in from before them, unless those whom the king ordered to come, when the conjurors came and withdrew the lions by their incantations, and this brought them to the king.

22 Moses hurried and lifted up the stick on the lions and loosed them, and Moses and Aaron came into the king's house.

23 The lions also came with them in joy, and they followed them and rejoiced as a dog rejoices over his master when he comes from the field.

24 When Pharaoh saw this thing he was astonished at it and was greatly terrified at the report, for their appearance was like the appearance of the children of God.

25 And Pharaoh said to Moses, What do you require? And they answered him saying, The Lord God of the Hebrews has sent us to you, to say, Send forth my people that they may serve me.

26 When Pharaoh heard their words he was greatly terrified before them, and he said to them, Go today and come back to me tomorrow. And they did according to the word of the king.

27 When they had gone Pharaoh sent for Balaam the magician and to Jannes and Jambres his sons and to all the magicians and conjurors and counselors which belonged to the king; they all came and sat before the king.

28 And the king told them all the words which Moses and his brother Aaron had spoken to him; the magicians said to the king, But how could the men come to you, on account of the lions which were confined at the gate?

29 The king said, Because they lifted up their rod against the lions and loosed them, and came to me, and the lions also rejoiced at them as a dog rejoices to meet his master.

30 Balaam the son of Beor the magician answered the king saying, These are none other than magicians like ourselves.

31 So now send for them and let them come and we will try them, and the king did so.

32 In the morning Pharaoh sent for Moses and Aaron to come before the king, and they took the rod of God and came to the king and spoke to him saying,

33 Thus said the Lord God of the Hebrews, Send away my people that they may serve me.

34 And the king said to them, But who will believe you that you are the messengers of God and that you come to me by his order?

35 Now therefore give a wonder or sign in this matter, and then the words which you speak will be believed.

36 Aaron hurried and threw the rod out of his hand before Pharaoh and before his servants, and the rod turned into a serpent.

37 The sorcerers saw this and each man cast his rod on the ground and they became serpents.

38 The serpent of Aaron's rod lifted up its head and opened its mouth to swallow the rods of the magicians.

39 Balaam the magician answered and said, This thing has been from the days of old that a serpent should swallow its fellow, and that living things devour each other.

40 So now restore it to a rod as it was at first and we will also restore our rods as they were at first; if your rod shall swallow our rods we will know that the spirit of God is in you, and if not, you are only a magician like ourselves.

41 Aaron hurried and stretched forth his hand and caught hold of the serpent's tail and it became a rod in his hand; the sorcerers did the same with their rod and got hold each man of the tail of his serpent, and they became rods as at first.

42 When they were restored to rods, the rod of Aaron swallowed up their rods.

43 And when the king saw this thing, he ordered the book of records that related to the kings of Egypt to be brought; they brought the book of records, the chronicles of the kings of Egypt in which all the idols of Egypt were inscribed, for they thought they would find there the name of Jehovah, but they found it not.

44 And Pharaoh said to Moses and Aaron, Behold I have not found the name of your God written in this book, and his name I do not know.

45 The counselors and wise men answered the king, We have heard that the God of the Hebrews is a son of the wise, the son of ancient kings.

46 Pharaoh turned to Moses and Aaron and said to them, I know not the Lord whom you have declared, neither will I send his people away.

47 And they answered and said to the king, The Lord God of Gods is his name; he proclaimed his name over us from the days of our ancestors and sent us, saying, Go to Pharaoh and say to him, Send my people away that they may serve me.

48 Now therefore send us, that we may take a journey for three days in the wilderness and there may sacrifice to him, for from the days of our going down to Egypt, he has not taken from our hands either burnt offering, oblation or sacrifice; if you will not send us, his anger will be set ablaze against you and he will strike Egypt either with the plague or with the sword.

49 And Pharaoh said to them, Tell me now his power and his might. They said to him, He created the heaven and the earth, the seas and all their fish; he formed the light, created the darkness, caused rain on the earth and watered it, and made the herbage and grass to sprout; he created man and beast and the animals of the forest, the birds of the air and the fish of the sea, and by his mouth they live and die.

50 Certainly he created you in your mother's womb and put into you the breath of life, and reared you and placed you on the royal throne of Egypt, and he will take your breath and soul from you and return you to the ground from where you were taken.

51 And the anger of the king was set ablaze at their words and he said to them, But who among all the Gods of nations can do this? My river is my own, and I have made it for myself.

52 And he drove them from him; he ordered the labor on Israel to be more severe than it was yesterday and before.

53 Moses and Aaron went out from the king's presence, and they saw the children of Israel in an evil condition for the taskmasters had made their labor extremely heavy.

54 Moses returned to the Lord and said, Why have you ill-treated your people? For since I came to speak to Pharaoh what you sent me for, he has greatly ill-used the children of Israel.

55 The Lord said to Moses, Look and you will see that with an outstretched hand and heavy plagues, Pharaoh will send the children of Israel from his land.

56 And Moses and Aaron lived among their brothers the children of Israel in Egypt.

57 As for the children of Israel the Egyptians embittered their lives with the heavy work which they imposed on them.

CHAPTER 80

1 And at the end of two years, the Lord again sent Moses to Pharaoh to bring forth the children of Israel, and to send them out of the land of Egypt.

2 Moses went and came to the house of Pharaoh, and he spoke to him the words of the Lord who had sent him, but Pharaoh would not listen to the voice of the Lord; God roused his might in Egypt on Pharaoh and his subjects, and God struck Pharaoh and his people with very great and severe plagues.

3 The Lord sent by the hand of Aaron and turned all the waters of Egypt into blood, with all their streams and rivers.

4 And when an Egyptian came to drink and draw water, he looked into his pitcher, and behold all the water was turned into blood; when he came to drink from his cup the water in the cup became blood.

5 And when a woman kneaded her dough and cooked her food, their appearance was turned to that of blood.

6 The Lord sent again and caused all their waters to bring forth frogs and all the frogs came into the houses of the Egyptians.

7 And when the Egyptians drank, their bellies were filled with frogs and they danced in their bellies as they dance when in the river.

8 All their drinking water and cooking water turned to frogs, also when they lay in their beds their perspiration bred frogs.

9 In spite of all this the anger of the Lord did not turn from them, and his hand was stretched out against all the Egyptians to strike them with every heavy plague.

10 He sent and changed their dust to lice, and the lice became in Egypt to the height of two cubits on the earth.

11 The lice were also very numerous in the flesh of man and beast, in all the inhabitants of Egypt; also on the king and queen the Lord sent the lice, and it grieved Egypt greatly on account of the lice.

12 Still the anger of the Lord did not turn away, and his hand was still stretched out over Egypt.

13 And the Lord sent all kinds of beasts of the field into Egypt, and they came and destroyed all Egypt, man and beast, and trees and all things that were in Egypt.

14 And the Lord sent fiery serpents, scorpions, mice, weasels, toads, together with others creeping in dust.

15 Flies, hornets, fleas, bugs and gnats, each swarm according to its kind.

16 And all reptiles and winged animals according to their kind came to Egypt and upset the Egyptians greatly.

17 The fleas and flies came into the eyes and ears of the Egyptians.

18 The hornet came on them and drove them away, and they removed from it into their inner rooms, and it pursued them.

19 When the Egyptians hid themselves on account of the swarm of animals, they locked their doors after them, and God ordered the Sulanuth which was in the sea to come up and go into Egypt.

20 She had long arms, ten cubits in length of the cubit of a man.

21 And she went on the roofs and uncovered the raftering and flooring and cut them, and stretched forth her arm into the house and removed the lock and the bolt, and opened the houses of Egypt.

22 Afterward came the swarm of animals into the houses of Egypt, and the swarm of animals destroyed the Egyptians, and it upset them greatly.

23 Still the anger of the Lord did not turn away from the Egyptians, and his hand was yet stretched forth against them.

24 God sent the pestilence and the pestilence pervaded Egypt, in the horses and asses and in the camels, in herds of oxen and sheep and in man.

25 When the Egyptians rose up early in the morning to take their cattle to pasture they found all their cattle dead.

26 There remained of the cattle of the Egyptians only one in ten, and of the cattle belonging to Israel in Goshen not one died.

27 And God sent a burning inflammation in the flesh of the Egyptians, which burst their skins; it became a severe itch in all the Egyptians from the soles of their feet to the crowns of their heads.

28 And many boils were in their flesh, that their flesh wasted away until they became rotten and putrid.

29 Still the anger of the Lord did not turn away, and his hand was still stretched out over all Egypt.

30 And the Lord sent a very heavy hail, which struck their vines and broke their fruit trees and dried them up that they fell on them.

31 Also every green herb became dry and perished, for a mingling fire descended with the hail, therefore the hail and the fire consumed all things.

32 Also men and beasts that were found abroad perished of the flames of fire and of the hail, and all the young lions were exhausted.

33 And the Lord sent and brought numerous locusts into Egypt, the Chasel, Salom, Chargol, and Chagole, locusts each of its kind, which devoured all that the hail had left remaining.

34 Then the Egyptians rejoiced at the locusts, although they consumed the produce of the field, and they caught them in abundance and salted them for food.

35 And the Lord turned a mighty wind of the sea which took away all the locusts, even those that were salted, and thrust them into the Red Sea; not one locust remained within the boundaries of Egypt.

36 God sent darkness on Egypt, that the whole land of Egypt and Pathros became dark for three days so that a man could not see his hand when he lifted it to his mouth.

37 At that time many of the people of Israel died who had rebelled against the Lord and who would not listen to Moses and

Aaron, and believed not in them that God had sent them.

38 And who had said, We will not go forth from Egypt because we'll perish with hunger in a desolate wilderness. They were those who would not listen to the voice of Moses.

39 The Lord plagued them in the three days of darkness, and the Israelites buried them in those days without the Egyptians knowing of them or rejoicing over them.

40 The darkness was very great in Egypt for three days, and any person who was standing when the darkness came remained standing in his place; he that was sitting remained sitting, and he that was lying continued lying in the same state; he that was walking remained sitting on the ground in the same spot; and this thing happened to all the Egyptians until the darkness had passed away.

41 The days of darkness passed away and the Lord sent Moses and Aaron to the children of Israel saying, Celebrate your feast and make your Passover, for behold I come in the middle of the night among all the Egyptians; I will strike all their firstborn, from the firstborn of a man to the first born of a beast, and when I see your Passover, I will pass over you.

42 And the children of Israel did according to all that the Lord had commanded Moses and Aaron, thus did they in that night.

43 It came to pass in the middle of the night that the Lord went forth in the midst of Egypt and struck all the firstborn of the Egyptians, from the firstborn of man to the firstborn of beast.

44 And Pharaoh rose up in the night, he and all his servants and all the Egyptians, and there was a great cry throughout Egypt in that night for there was not a house in which there was not a corpse.

45 Also the likenesses of the firstborn of Egypt which were carved in the walls at their houses were destroyed and fell to the ground.

46 Even the bones of their firstborn who had died before this and whom they had buried in their houses were raked up by the dogs of Egypt on that night and dragged before the Egyptians and cast before them.

47 And all the Egyptians saw this evil which had suddenly come on them, and all the Egyptians cried out with a loud voice.

48 And all the families of Egypt wept on that night, each man for his son and each man for his daughter, being the firstborn, and the tumult of Egypt was heard at a distance on that night.

49 Bathia the daughter of Pharaoh went forth with the king on that night to seek Moses and Aaron in their houses; they found them in their houses eating and drinking and rejoicing with all Israel.

50 And Bathia said to Moses, Is this the reward for the good which I have done to you, who have reared you and made you grow and prosper and you have brought this evil on me and my father's house?

51 And Moses said to her, Certainly ten plagues did the Lord bring on Egypt; did any evil accrue to you from any of them? Did one of them affect you? And she said, No.

52 And Moses said to her, Although you are the firstborn to your mother, you shall not die and no evil shall reach you in the midst of Egypt.

53 And she said, What advantage is it to me when I see the king, my brother, and all his household and subjects in this evil, whose firstborn perish with all the firstborn of Egypt?

54 And Moses said to her, Certainly your brother and his household and subjects, the families of Egypt, would not listen to the words of the Lord, therefore did this evil come on them.

55 Pharaoh king of Egypt approached Moses and Aaron and some of the children of Israel who were with them in that place, and he prayed to them saying,

56 Rise up and take your brothers, all the children of Israel who are in the land with their sheep and oxen, and all belonging to them; they shall leave nothing remaining, only pray for me to the Lord your God.

57 And Moses said to Pharaoh, Behold you are your mother's firstborn, yet fear not for you will not die, for the Lord has commanded that you shall live in order to show you his great might and strong stretched out arm.

58 Pharaoh ordered the children of Israel to be sent away, and all the Egyptians strengthened themselves to send them, for they said, We are all perishing.

59 And all the Egyptians sent the Israelites forth with great riches, sheep and oxen and precious things according to the oath of the Lord between him and our Father Abraham.

60 And the children of Israel delayed going away until night, and when the Egyptians came to them to bring them out, they said to them, Are we thieves, that we should go forth at night?

61 And the children of Israel asked of the Egyptians, vessels of silver and vessels of gold, and garments, and the children of Israel stripped the Egyptians.

62 Moses hurried and rose up and went to the river of Egypt and brought up from there the coffin of Joseph and took it with him.

63 The children of Israel also brought up each man his father's coffin with him, and each man the coffins of his tribe.

CHAPTER 81

1 The children of Israel journeyed from Rameses to Succoth, about six hundred thousand men on foot besides the little ones

and their wives.

2 Also a mixed multitude went up with them, flocks and herds, even much cattle.

3 The temporary time of the children of Israel who lived in the land of Egypt in hard labor was two hundred and ten years.

4 And at the end of two hundred and ten years, the Lord brought forth the children of Israel from Egypt with a strong hand.

5 The children of Israel traveled from Egypt and from Goshen and from Rameses, and encamped in Succoth on the fifteenth day of the first month.

6 The Egyptians buried all their firstborn whom the Lord had smitten, and all the Egyptians buried their slain for three days.

7 The children of Israel traveled from Succoth and encamped in Ethom, at the end of the wilderness.

8 On the third day after the Egyptians had buried their firstborn, many men rose up from Egypt and went after Israel to make them return to Egypt, for they regretted that they had sent the Israelites away from serving them.

9 One man said to his neighbor, Certainly Moses and Aaron spoke to Pharaoh saying, We will go a three days' journey in the wilderness and sacrifice to the Lord our God.

10 So now let us rise up early in the morning and make them return; it shall be that if they return with us to Egypt to their masters, then we will know that there is faith in them, but if they will not return then will we fight with them, and make them come back with great power and a strong hand.

11 All the nobles of Pharaoh rose up in the morning, and with them about seven hundred thousand men; they went forth from Egypt on that day and came to the place where the children of Israel were.

12 And all the Egyptians looked and saw Moses and Aaron and all the children of Israel were sitting before Pi-hahiroth, eating and drinking and celebrating the feast of the Lord.

13 All the Egyptians said to the children of Israel, Certainly you said, We will go a journey for three days in the wilderness and sacrifice to our God and return.

14 So now this day makes five days since you went; why do you not return to your masters?

15 Moses and Aaron answered them, saying, Because the Lord our God has testified in us saying, You shall no more return to Egypt, but take yourselves to a land flowing with milk and honey; as the Lord our God had sworn to our ancestors to give to us.

16 And when the nobles of Egypt saw that the children of Israel did not listen to them to return to Egypt, they prepared themselves to fight with Israel.

17 The Lord strengthened the hearts of the children of Israel over the Egyptians so that they gave them a severe beating; the battle was severe on the Egyptians and all the Egyptians fled from before the children of Israel; many of them perished by the hand of Israel.

18 And the nobles of Pharaoh went to Egypt and told Pharaoh, saying, The children of Israel have fled and will no more return to Egypt, and in this manner did Moses and Aaron speak to us.

19 Pharaoh heard this thing, and his heart and the hearts of all his subjects were turned against Israel; they repented that they had sent Israel, and all the Egyptians advised Pharaoh to pursue the children of Israel to make them come back to their burdens.

20 They said each man to his brother, What is this which we have done, that we have sent Israel from our service?

21 The Lord strengthened the hearts of all the Egyptians to pursue the Israelites, for the Lord desired to overthrow the Egyptians in the Red Sea.

22 Pharaoh rose up and harnessed his chariot; he ordered all the Egyptians to assemble, not one man was left excepting the little ones and the women.

23 And all the Egyptians went forth with Pharaoh to pursue the children of Israel, and the camp of Egypt was a very large and strong camp, about ten hundred thousand men.

24 All of this camp went and pursued the children of Israel to bring them back to Egypt, and they reached them encamping by the Red Sea.

25 The children of Israel lifted up their eyes, and saw all the Egyptians pursuing them; the children of Israel were greatly terrified at them and the children of Israel cried to the Lord.

26 On account of the Egyptians, the children of Israel divided themselves into four divisions and they were divided in their opinions for they were afraid of the Egyptians, and Moses spoke to each of them.

27 The first division was of the children of Reuben, Simeon, and Issachar, and they decided to cast themselves into the sea, for they were greatly afraid of the Egyptians.

28 And Moses said to them, Fear not, stand still and see the salvation of the Lord which He will effect this day for you.

29 The second division was of the children of Zebulun, Benjamin and Naphtali, and they resolved to go back to Egypt with the Egyptians.

30 And Moses said to them, Fear not, for as you have seen the Egyptians this day, so shall you see them no more for ever.

31 The third division was of the children of Judah and Joseph, and they resolved to go to meet the Egyptians to fight with them.

32 And Moses said to them, Stand in your places for the Lord will fight for you, and you shall remain silent.

33 And the fourth division was of the children of Levi, Gad, and Asher, and they resolved to go into the midst of the Egyptians to confound them. Moses said to them, Remain in your stations and fear not, only call to the Lord that he may save

you out of their hands.

34 After this Moses rose up from among the people and prayed to the Lord and said,

35 O Lord God of the whole earth, save now your people whom you brought forth from Egypt, and let not the Egyptians boast that power and might are theirs.

36 So the Lord said to Moses, Why do you cry to me? Speak to the children of Israel that they shall proceed, and stretch out your rod on the sea and divide it and the children of Israel shall pass through it.

37 And Moses did so; he lifted up his rod on the sea and divided it.

38 And the waters of the sea were divided into twelve parts, and the children of Israel passed through on foot with shoes, as a man would pass through a prepared road.

39 The Lord displayed to the children of Israel his wonders in Egypt and in the sea by the hand of Moses and Aaron.

40 When the children of Israel had entered the sea the Egyptians came after them, and the waters of the sea covered them and they all sank in the water; not one man was left except Pharaoh, who gave thanks to the Lord and believed in him, therefore the Lord did not cause him to perish at that time with the Egyptians.

41 The Lord ordered an angel to take him from among the Egyptians, who cast him on the land of Ninevah and he reigned over it for a long time.

42 On that day the Lord saved Israel from the hand of Egypt, and all the children of Israel saw that the Egyptians had perished; they beheld the great hand of the Lord in what he had performed in Egypt and in the sea.

43 Then sang Moses and the children of Israel this song to the Lord, on the day when the Lord caused the Egyptians to fall before them.

44 And all Israel sang in concert saying, I will sing to the Lord for He is greatly exalted, the horse and his rider has he cast into the sea, consider that it is written in the book of the law of God.

45 After this the children of Israel proceeded on their journey and encamped in Marah; the Lord gave to the children of Israel statutes and judgments in that place in Marah, and the Lord commanded the children of Israel to walk in all his ways and to serve him.

46 They journeyed from Marah and came to Elim; in Elim were twelve springs of water and seventy date trees and the children encamped there by the waters.

47 They journeyed from Elim and came to the wilderness of Sin, on the fifteenth day of the second month after their departure from Egypt.

48 At that time the Lord gave manna to the children of Israel to eat, and the Lord caused food to rain from heaven for the children of Israel day by day.

49 And the children of Israel ate the manna for forty years, all the days that they were in the wilderness, until they came to the land of Canaan to possess it.

50 They proceeded from the wilderness of Sin and encamped in Alush.

51 And they proceeded from Alush and encamped in Rephidim.

52 When the children of Israel were in Rephidim, Amalek the son of Eliphaz, the son of Esau, the brother of Zepho, came to fight with Israel.

53 And he brought with him eight hundred and one thousand men, magicians and conjurers, and he prepared for battle with Israel in Rephidim.

54 They carried on a great and severe battle against Israel, and the Lord delivered Amalek and his people into the hands of Moses and the children of Israel, and into the hand of Joshua, the son of Nun, the Ephrathite, the servant of Moses.

55 The children of Israel struck Amalek and his people at the edge of the sword, but the battle was very severe on the children of Israel.

56 And the Lord said to Moses, Write this thing as a memorial for you in a book, and place it in the hand of Joshua, the son of Nun your servant; you shall command the children of Israel, saying, When you come to the land of Canaan, you shall utterly wipe out the remembrance of Amalek from under heaven.

57 And Moses did so, and he took the book and wrote on it these words, saying,

58 Remember what Amalek has done to you in the road when you went forth from Egypt.

59 He met you in the road and struck your rear, even those that were feeble behind you when you were faint and weary.

60 Therefore it shall be when the Lord your God shall have given you rest from all your enemies round about in the land which the Lord your God gives you for an inheritance, to possess it, that you shall blot out the remembrance of Amalek from under heaven, you shall not forget it.

61 The king who shall have pity on Amalek or on his memory or on his offspring, behold I will blame him, and I will cut him off from among his people.

62 And Moses wrote all these things in a book, and he advised the children of Israel respecting all these matters.

CHAPTER 82

1 The children of Israel proceeded from Rephidim and camped in the wilderness of Sinai, in the third month from their going

forth from Egypt.

2 At that time Reuel the Midianite, the father-in-law of Moses, came with Zipporah his daughter and her two sons for he had heard of the wonders of the Lord which he had done to Israel, that he had delivered them from the hand of Egypt.

3 Reuel came to Moses in the wilderness where he was camped, where the mountain of God was.

4 And Moses went forth to meet his father-in-law with great honor, and all Israel was with him.

5 Reuel and his children remained among the Israelites for many days, and Reuel knew the Lord from that day forward.

6 In the third month from the children of Israel's departure from Egypt, on the sixth day, the Lord gave to Israel the ten commandments on Mount Sinai.

7 All Israel heard all these commandments, and all Israel rejoiced greatly in the Lord on that day.

8 And the glory of the Lord rested on Mount Sinai; he called to Moses and Moses came in the midst of a cloud and ascended the mountain.

9 Moses was on the mount forty days and forty nights; he ate no bread and drank no water, and the Lord instructed him in the standards and judgments in order to teach the children of Israel.

10 And the Lord wrote the ten commandments which he had commanded the children of Israel on two tablets of stone, which he gave to Moses to command the children of Israel.

11 At the end of forty days and forty nights, when the Lord had finished speaking to Moses on Mount Sinai, the Lord gave to Moses the tablets of stone written with the finger of God.

12 When the children of Israel saw that Moses delayed coming down from the mount, they gathered round Aaron and said, As for this man Moses, we know not what has become of him.

13 Now therefore rise up, make to us a god who shall go before us, so that you shall not die.

14 Aaron was greatly afraid of the people, and he ordered them to bring him gold and he made it into a molten calf for the people.

15 The Lord said to Moses, before he had come down from the mount, Go down, for your people whom you brought forth from Egypt have corrupted themselves.

16 They have made to themselves a molten calf and have bowed down to it; now therefore leave me, that I may consume them from off the earth for they are a stubborn people.

17 And Moses sought the countenance of the Lord, and he prayed to the Lord for the people on account of the calf which they had made; afterward he descended from the mount and in his hands were the two tablets of stone which God had given him to command the Israelites.

18 When Moses approached the camp and saw the calf which the people had made, the anger of Moses was set ablaze and he broke the tablets under the mount.

19 Moses came to the camp; he took the calf and burned it with fire, and ground it till it became fine dust and scattered it on the water, and gave it to the Israelites to drink.

20 There died of the people by the swords of each other about three thousand men who had made the calf.

21 The next morning Moses said to the people, I will go up to the Lord, perhaps I may make atonement for your sins which you have sinned to the Lord.

22 And Moses again went up to the Lord, and he remained with the Lord forty days and forty nights.

23 And during the forty days Moses entreaed the Lord on behalf of the children of Israel, and the Lord listened to the prayer of Moses, and the Lord was begged of him on behalf of Israel.

24 Then spoke the Lord to Moses to cut out two stone tablets and to bring them up to the Lord, who would write on them the ten commandments.

25 Moses did so, and he came down and fashioned the two tablets and went up to Mount Sinai to the Lord, and the Lord wrote the ten commandments on the tablets.

26 Moses remained yet with the Lord forty days and forty nights, and the Lord instructed him in standards and judgments to give to Israel.

27 The Lord commanded him respecting the children of Israel that they should make a sanctuary for the Lord that his name might rest therein, and the Lord showed him the likeness of the sanctuary and the likeness of all its vessels.

28 And at the end of the forty days, Moses came down from the mount and the two tablets were in his hand.

29 And Moses came to the children of Israel and spoke to them all the words of the Lord, and he taught them laws, rules and judgments which the Lord had taught him.

30 Moses told the children of Israel the word of the Lord, that a sanctuary should be made for him to dwell among the children of Israel.

31 And the people rejoiced greatly at all the good which the Lord had spoken to them through Moses, and they said, We will do all that the Lord has spoken to you.

32 And the people rose up like one man and they made generous offerings to the sanctuary of the Lord; each man brought the offering of the Lord for the work of the sanctuary and for all its service.

33 All the children of Israel brought each man of all that was found in his possession for the work of the sanctuary of the Lord, gold, silver and brass, and every thing that was serviceable for the sanctuary.

34 All the wise men who were practiced in work came and made the sanctuary of the Lord, according to all that the Lord had

commanded, every man in the work in which he had skill; all the wise men in heart made the sanctuary and its furniture and all the vessels for the holy service as the Lord had commanded Moses.

35 And the work of the sanctuary of the tabernacle was completed at the end of five months; the children of Israel did all that the Lord had commanded Moses.

36 And they brought the sanctuary and all its furniture to Moses; like to the representation which the Lord had shown to Moses, so did the children of Israel.

37 And Moses saw the work, and behold they did it as the Lord had commanded him, so Moses blessed them.

CHAPTER 83

1 In the twelfth month, in the twenty-third day of the month, Moses took Aaron and his sons and dressed them in their garments and anointed them, and did to them as the Lord had commanded him, and Moses brought up all the offerings which the Lord had on that day commanded him.

2 Moses afterward took Aaron and his sons and said to them, For seven days you shall remain at the door of the tabernacle, for thus am I commanded.

3 And Aaron and his sons did all that the Lord had commanded them through Moses, and they remained for seven days at the door of the tabernacle.

4 On the eighth day, being the first day of the first month, in the second year from the Israelites' departure from Egypt, Moses erected the sanctuary and put in all the furniture of the tabernacle and all the furniture of the sanctuary, and he did all that the Lord had commanded him.

5 Moses called to Aaron and his sons, and they brought the burnt offering and the sin offering for themselves and the children of Israel, as the Lord had commanded Moses.

6 On that day the two sons of Aaron, Nadab and Abihu, took strange fire and brought it before the Lord who had not commanded them to do it, and a fire went forth from before the Lord and consumed them, and they died before the Lord on that day.

7 Then on the day when Moses had completed erecting the sanctuary, the princes of the children of Israel began to bring their offerings before the Lord for the dedication of the altar.

8 And they brought up their offerings each prince for one day, a prince each day for twelve days.

9 And all the offerings which they brought, each man in his day, one silver charger weighing one hundred and thirty shekels, one silver bowl of seventy shekels after the shekel of the sanctuary, both of them full of fine flour mingled with oil for a meat offering;

10 One spoon, weighing ten shekels of gold, full of incense;

11 One young bullock, one ram, one lamb of the first year for a burnt offering;

12 And one kid of the goats for a sin offering.

13 For a sacrifice of peace offering: two oxen, five rams, five male goats, five lambs of a year old.

14 Thus did the twelve princes of Israel day by day, each man in his day.

15 It was after this in the thirteenth day of the month, that Moses commanded the children of Israel to observe the Passover.

16 And the children of Israel kept the Passover in its season in the fourteenth day of the month; as the Lord had commanded Moses, so did the children of Israel.

17 And in the second month, on the first day thereof, the Lord spoke to Moses saying,

18 Number the heads of all the males of the children of Israel from twenty years old and upward, you and your brother Aaron and the twelve princes of Israel.

19 And Moses did so, and Aaron came with the twelve princes of Israel, and they counted the children of Israel in the wilderness of Sinai.

20 And the number of the children of Israel by the houses of their fathers, from twenty years old and upward, were six hundred and three thousand, five hundred and fifty.

21 But the children of Levi were not numbered among their brothers the children of Israel.

22 And the number of all the males of the children of Israel from one month old and upward, was twenty-two thousand, two hundred and seventy-three.

23 And the number of the children of Levi from one month old and above, was twenty-two thousand.

24 Moses placed the priests and the Levites each man to his service and to his burden to serve the sanctuary of the tabernacle, as the Lord had commanded Moses.

25 And on the twentieth day of the month, the cloud was taken away from the tabernacle of testimony.

26 At that time the children of Israel continued their journey from the wilderness of Sinai, they took a journey of three days and the cloud rested on the wilderness of Paran; there the anger of the Lord was set ablaze against Israel, for they had provoked the Lord in asking him for meat to eat.

27 And the Lord listened to their voice, and gave them meat which they ate for one month.

28 But after this the anger of the Lord was set ablaze against them, and he struck them with a great slaughter, and they were

buried there in that place.

29 The children of Israel called that place Kebroth Hattaavah, because there they buried the people that lusted flesh.

30 And they departed from Kebroth Hattaavah and pitched in Hazeroth, which is in the wilderness of Paran.

31 And while the children of Israel were in Hazeroth, the anger of the Lord was set ablaze against Miriam on account of Moses, and she became leprous, white as snow.

32 She was confined outside the camp for seven days until she had been received again after her leprosy.

33 The children of Israel afterward departed from Hazeroth and camped in the end of the wilderness of Paran.

34 At that time, the Lord spoke to Moses to send twelve men from the children of Israel, one man to a tribe, to go and explore the land of Canaan.

35 Moses sent the twelve men and they came to the land of Canaan to search and examine it, and they explored the whole land from the wilderness of Sin to Rechob as you come to Chamoth.

36 At the end of forty days they came to Moses and Aaron, and they brought him word as it was in their hearts; ten of the men brought up an evil report to the children of Israel, of the land which they had explored saying, It is better for us to return to Egypt than to go to this land, a land that consumes its inhabitants.

37 But Joshua the son of Nun and Caleb the son of Jephuneh, who were of those that explored the land said, The land is very good.

38 If the Lord delights in us, then he will bring us to this land and give it to us for it is a land flowing with milk and honey.

39 But the children of Israel would not listen to them, and they listened to the words of the ten men who had brought up an evil report of the land.

40 The Lord heard the murmurings of the children of Israel and he was angry and swore, saying,

41 Certainly not one man of this wicked generation shall see the land from twenty years old and upward except Caleb the son of Jephuneh and Joshua the son of Nun.

42 But certainly this wicked generation shall perish in this wilderness, and their children shall come to the land and they shall possess it. So the anger of the Lord was set ablaze against Israel and he made them wander in the wilderness for forty years until the end of that wicked generation because they did not follow the Lord.

43 And the people lived in the wilderness of Paran a long time, and they afterward proceeded to the wilderness by the way of the Red Sea.

CHAPTER 84

1 At that time Korah the son of Jetzer the son of Kehath the son of Levi, took many men of the children of Israel and they rose up and quarreled with Moses and Aaron and the whole congregation.

2 And the Lord was angry with them and the earth opened its mouth and swallowed them up, with their houses and all belonging to them, and all the men belonging to Korah.

3 After this God made the people go round by the way of Mount Seir for a long time.

4 At that time the Lord said to Moses, Provoke not a war against the children of Esau, for I will not give to you of any thing belonging to them, as much as the sole of the foot could tread on, for I have given Mount Seir for an inheritance to Esau.

5 Therefore did the children of Esau fight against the children of Seir in former times, and the Lord had delivered the children of Seir into the hands of the children of Esau, and destroyed them from before them and the children of Esau lived in their stead to this day.

6 So the Lord said to the children of Israel, Fight not against the children of Esau your brothers for nothing in their land belongs to you, but you may buy food of them for money and eat it, and you may buy water of them for money and drink it.

7 And the children of Israel did according to the word of the Lord.

8 The children of Israel wandered in the wilderness, going round by the way of Mount Sinai for a long time, and touched not the children of Esau; they continued in that district for nineteen years.

9 At that time Latinus king of the children of Chittim died, in the forty-fifth year of his reign, which is the fourteenth year of the children of Israel's departure from Egypt.

10 They buried him in his place which he had built for himself in the land of Chittim, and Abimnas reigned in his place for thirty-eight years.

11 The children of Israel passed the boundary of the children of Esau in those days, at the end of nineteen years, and they came and passed the road of the wilderness of Moab.

12 And the Lord said to Moses, Besiege not Moab, and do not fight against them, for I will give you nothing of their land.

13 And the children of Israel passed the road of the wilderness of Moab for nineteen years, and they did not fight against them.

14 In the thirty-sixth year of the children of Israel's departing from Egypt the Lord struck the heart of Sihon, king of the Amorites; he waged war and went forth to fight against the children of Moab.

15 And Sihon sent messengers to Beor the son of Janeas, the son of Balaam, counsellor to the king of Egypt and to Balaam his son, to curse Moab in order that it might be delivered into the hand of Sihon.

16 And the messengers went and brought Beor the son of Janeas, and Balaam his son, from Pethor in Mesopotamia; so Beor and Balaam his son came to the city of Sihon and they cursed Moab and their king in the presence of Sihon king of the Amorites.

17 So Sihon went out with his whole army and he went to Moab and fought against them; he subdued them and the Lord delivered them into his hands, and Sihon killed the king of Moab.

18 Sihon took all the cities of Moab in the battle; he also took Heshbon from them, for Heshbon was one of the cities of Moab, and Sihon placed his princes and his nobles in Heshbon, and Heshbon belonged to Sihon in those days.

19 Therefore the parable speakers (wise men), Beor and Balaam his son, uttered these words, saying, Come to Heshbon, the city of Sihon will be built and established.

20 Woe to you Moab! You are lost, O people of Kemosh! Behold it is written on the book of the law of God.

21 And when Sihon had conquered Moab, he placed guards in the cities which he had taken from Moab, and a considerable number of the children of Moab fell in battle into the hand of Sihon; he made a great capture of them, sons and daughters, and he killed their king; so Sihon turned back to his own land.

22 And Sihon gave numerous presents of silver and gold to Beor and Balaam his son, and he dismissed them, and they went to Mesopotamia to their home and country.

23 At that time all the children of Israel passed from the road of the wilderness of Moab, and returned and surrounded the wilderness of Edom.

24 So the whole congregation came to the wilderness of Sin in the first month of the fortieth year from their departure from Egypt, and the children of Israel lived there in Kadesh of the wilderness of Sin, and Miriam died there and she was buried there.

25 At that time Moses sent messengers to Hadad king of Edom, saying, Thus says your brother Israel, Let me pass I pray you through your land, we will not pass through field or vineyard, we will not drink the water of the well; we will walk in the king's road.

26 And Edom said to him, You shall not pass through my country. And Edom went forth to meet the children of Israel with a mighty people.

27 And the children of Esau refused to let the children of Israel pass through their land, so the Israelites left them and did not fight against them.

28 For before this the Lord had commanded the children of Israel, saying, You shall not fight against the children of Esau. Therefore the Israelites went away from them and did not fight against them.

29 So the children of Israel departed from Kadesh, and all the people came to Mount Hor.

30 At that time the Lord said to Moses, Tell your brother Aaron that he shall die there, for he shall not come to the land which I have given to the children of Israel.

31 And Aaron went up at the command of the Lord to Mount Hor, in the fortieth year, in the fifth month, in the first day of the month.

32 And Aaron was one hundred and twenty-three years old when he died in Mount Hor.

CHAPTER 85

1 The king Arad the Canaanite, who lived in the south, heard that the Israelites had come by the way of the spies, and he arranged his forces to fight against the Israelites.

2 And the children of Israel were greatly afraid of him, for he had a great and courageous army, so the children of Israel resolved to return to Egypt.

3 The children of Israel turned back about the distance of three days' journey to Maserath Beni Jaakon, for they were greatly afraid on account of the king Arad.

4 And the children of Israel would not get back to their places, so they remained in Beni Jaakon for thirty days.

5 When the children of Levi saw that the children of Israel would not turn back, they were zealous for the sake of the Lord; they rose up and fought against the Israelites their brothers, and killed of them a great many and forced them to turn back to their place, Mount Hor.

6 And when they returned, king Arad was still arranging his host for battle against the Israelites.

7 Israel vowed a vow saying, If you will deliver this people into my hand, then I will utterly destroy their cities.

8 The Lord listened to the voice of Israel, and he delivered the Canaanites into their hands; he utterly destroyed them and their cities, and he called the name of the place Hormah.

9 The children of Israel journeyed from Mount Hor and camped in Oboth, and they journeyed from Oboth and they camped at Ije-abarim, in the border of Moab.

10 And the children of Israel sent to Moab, saying, Let us pass now through your land into our place, but the children of Moab would not allow the children of Israel to pass through their land, for the children of Moab were greatly afraid that the children of Israel should do to them as Sihon king of the Amorites had done to them, who had taken their land and had slain many of them.

11 Therefore Moab would not permit the Israelites to pass through his land, and the Lord commanded the children of Israel, saying that they should not fight against Moab, so the Israelites removed themselves from Moab.

12 And the children of Israel journeyed from the border of Moab; they came to the other side of Arnon, the border of Moab, between Moab and the Amorites, and they camped on the border of Sihon, king of the Amorites, in the wilderness of Kedemoth.

13 The children of Israel sent messengers to Sihon, king of the Amorites, saying,

14 Let us pass through your land; we will not turn into the fields or into the vineyards; we will go along by the king's highway until we shall have passed your border. But Sihon would not let the Israelites pass.

15 So Sihon collected all the people of the Amorites and went forth into the wilderness to meet the children of Israel, and he fought against Israel in Jahaz.

16 The Lord delivered Sihon king of the Amorites into the hands of the children of Israel, and Israel struck all the people of Sihon with the edge of the sword and avenged the cause of Moab.

17 The children of Israel took possession of the land of Sihon from Aram to Jabuk, to the children of Ammon, and they took all the booty of the cities.

18 Israel took all these cities, and Israel lived in all the cities of the Amorites.

19 All the children of Israel resolved to fight against the children of Ammon, to take their land also.

20 So the Lord said to the children of Israel, Do not besiege the children of Ammon, neither stir up battle against them, for I will give nothing to you of their land; the children of Israel listened to the word of the Lord, and did not fight against the children of Ammon.

21 The children of Israel turned and went up by the way of Bashan to the land of Og, king of Bashan, and Og the king of Bashan went out to meet the Israelites in battle; he had with him many courageous men, and a very strong force from the people of the Amorites.

22 And Og king of Bashan was a very powerful man, but Naaron his son was greatly powerful, even stronger than he was.

23 And Og said in his heart, Behold now the whole camp of Israel takes up a space of several miles. Now will I strike them at once without sword or spear.

24 Og went up Mount Jahaz and took from there one large stone, the length of which was three parsa, and he placed it on his head, and resolved to throw it on the camp of the children of Israel to strike all the Israelites with that stone.

25 And the angel of the Lord came and pierced the stone on the head of Og, and the stone fell on the neck of Og so that Og fell to the earth on account of the weight of the stone on his neck.

26 At that time the Lord said to the children of Israel, Be not afraid of him for I have given him and all his people and all his land into your hands, and you shall do to him as you did to Sihon.

27 Moses went down to him with a small number of the children of Israel, and Moses struck Og with a stick at the ankles of his feet and killed him.

28 The children of Israel afterward pursued the children of Og and all his people; they beat and destroyed them till there was no remnant left of them.

29 Moses afterward sent some of the children of Israel to spy out Jaazer, for Jaazer was a very famous city.

30 The spies went to Jaazer and explored it, and the spies trusted in the Lord; they fought against the men of Jaazer.

31 These men took Jaazer and its villages and the Lord delivered them into their hands, and they drove out the Amorites who had been there.

32 And the children of Israel took the land of the two kings of the Amorites, sixty cities which were on the other side of Jordan, from the brook of Arnon to Mount Herman.

33 The children of Israel journeyed and came into the plain of Moab which is on this side of Jordan, by Jericho.

34 And the children of Moab heard all the evil which the children of Israel had done to the two kings of the Amorites, to Sihon and Og; so all the men of Moab were greatly afraid of the Israelites.

35 The elders of Moab said, Behold the two kings of the Amorites, Sihon and Og, who were more powerful than all the kings of the earth, if they could not stand against the children of Israel how then can we stand before them?

36 Certainly they sent us a message before now to pass through our land on their way, and we would not allow them; now they will turn on us with their heavy swords and destroy us. Moab was distressed on account of the children of Israel and they were greatly afraid of them, and they counselled together what was to be done to the children of Israel.

37 The elders of Moab decided and took one of their men, Balak the son of Zippor the Moabite, and made him king over them at that time, and Balak was a very wise man.

38 And the elders of Moab rose up and sent to the children of Midian to make peace with them, for a great battle and enmity had been in those days between Moab and Midian, from the days of Hadad the son of Bedad king of Edom, who struck Midian in the field of Moab, to these days.

39 The children of Moab sent to the children of Midian and made peace with them, and the elders of Midian came to the land of Moab to make peace on behalf of the children of Midian.

40 And the elders of Moab counselled with the elders of Midian what to do in order to save their lives from Israel.

41 All the children of Moab said to the elders of Midian, The children of Israel shall lick up all that are round about us, as the ox licks up the grass of the field, for thus did they do to the two kings of the Amorites who are stronger than we are.

42 The elders of Midian said to Moab, We have heard that at the time when Sihon king of the Amorites fought against you, when he prevailed over you and took your land, he had sent to Beor the son of Janeas and to Balaam his son from Mesopotamia, and they came and cursed you; therefore did the hand of Sihon prevail over you, that he took your land.

43 Now therefore you send also to Balaam his son for he still remains in his land and give him his wage, that he may come and curse all the people of whom you are afraid; so the elders of Moab heard this thing, and it pleased them to send to Balaam the son of Beor.

44 So Balak the son of Zippor king of Moab sent messengers to Balaam, saying,

45 Behold there is a people come out from Egypt, see how they cover the face of the earth and they are against me.

46 So now come and curse this people for me for they are too mighty for me; perhaps I shall succeed to fight against them and drive them out, for I heard that he whom you bless is blessed, and whom you curse is cursed.

47 So the messengers of Balak went to Balaam and brought Balaam to curse the people to fight against Moab.

48 And Balaam came to Balak to curse Israel, and the Lord said to Balaam, Curse not this people for they are blessed.

49 And Balak urged Balaam day by day to curse Israel, but Balaam did not listen to Balak on account of the word of the Lord which he had spoken to Balaam.

50 And when Balak saw that Balaam would not accede to his wish, he rose up and went home; Balaam also returned to his land and he went from there to Midian.

51 The children of Israel journeyed from the plain of Moab and camped by Jordan from Beth-jesimoth even to Abel-shittim, at the end of the plains of Moab.

52 When the children of Israel stayed in the plain of Shittim, they began to commit prostitution with the daughters of Moab.

53 The children of Israel approached Moab, and the children of Moab pitched their tents opposite to the camp of the children of Israel.

54 The children of Moab were afraid of the children of Israel, and the children of Moab took all their daughters and their wives of beauty and attractive appearance, and dressed them in gold and silver and costly garments.

55 The children of Moab seated those women at the door of their tents in order that the children of Israel might see them and turn to them, and not fight against Moab.

56 All the children of Moab did this thing to the children of Israel, and every man placed his wife and daughter at the door of his tent; all the children of Israel saw the act of the children of Moab, and the children of Israel turned to the daughters of Moab and coveted them, and they went to them.

57 It came to pass that when a Hebrew came to the door of the tent of Moab and saw a daughter of Moab, and desired her in his heart and spoke with her at the door of the tent that which he desired, while they were speaking together the men of the tent would come out and speak to the Hebrew like these words:

58 Certainly you know that we are brothers, we are all the descendants of Lot and the descendants of Abraham his brother, why then will you not remain with us, and why will you not eat our bread and our sacrifice?

59 When the children of Moab had thus overwhelmed him with their speeches and enticed him by their flattering words, they seated him in the tent and cooked and sacrificed for him, and he ate of their sacrifice and of their bread.

60 They then gave him wine and he drank and became intoxicated; they placed before him a beautiful damsel and he did with her as he liked, for he knew not what he was doing, as he had drunk plentifully of wine.

61 Thus did the children of Moab to Israel in that place, in the plain of Shittim, and the anger of the Lord was set ablaze against Israel on account of this matter; he sent a pestilence among them and there of the Israelites twenty-four thousand men died.

62 Then there was a man of the children of Simeon whose name was Zimri, the son of Salu, who connected himself with the Midianite Cosbi, the daughter of Zur, king of Midian, in the sight of all the children of Israel.

63 And Phineas the son of Elazer, the son of Aaron the priest, saw this wicked thing which Zimri had done; he took a spear and rose up and went after them, pierced them both and killed them, and the pestilence ceased from the children of Israel.

CHAPTER 86

1 At that time after the pestilence, the Lord said to Moses and to Elazer the son of Aaron the priest,

2 Count the heads of the whole community of the children of Israel, from twenty years old and upward, all that went forth in the army.

3 And Moses and Elazer numbered the children of Israel after their families, and the number of all Israel was seven hundred thousand, seven hundred and thirty.

4 The number of the children of Levi, from one month old and upward, was twenty-three thousand, and among these there was not a man of those numbered by Moses and Aaron in the wilderness of Sinai.

5 For the Lord had told them that they would die in the wilderness, so they all died, and not one had been left of them excepting Caleb the son of Jephuneh, and Joshua the son of Nun.

6 And it was after this that the Lord said to Moses, Say to the children of Israel to avenge on Midian the cause of their brothers the children of Israel.

7 Moses did so, and the children of Israel chose from among them twelve thousand men, being one thousand to a tribe, and they went to Midian.

8 And the children of Israel warred against Midian, and they killed every male, also the five princes of Midian, and Balaam the son of Beor they killed with the sword.

9 And the children of Israel took the wives of Midian captive, with their little ones and their cattle, and all belonging to them.

10 They took all the booty and all the valuables, and they brought it to Moses and to Elazer to the plains of Moab.

11 Moses and Elazer and all the princes of the congregation went forth to meet them with joy.

12 And they divided all the goods of Midian, and the children of Israel had been revenged on Midian for the cause of their brothers the children of Israel.

CHAPTER 87

1 At that time the Lord said to Moses, Behold your days are approaching to an end, take now Joshua the son of Nun your servant and place him in the tabernacle and I will command him, and Moses did so.

2 The Lord appeared in the tabernacle in a pillar of cloud, and the pillar of cloud stood at the entrance of the tabernacle.

3 The Lord commanded Joshua the son of Nun and said to him, Be strong and courageous, for you shall bring the children of Israel to the land which I swore to give them, and I will be with you.

4 And Moses said to Joshua, Be strong and courageous, for you will make the children of Israel inherit the land, and the Lord will be with you; he will not leave you nor turn away from you, be not afraid or disheartened.

5 Moses called to all the children of Israel and said to them, You have seen all the good which the Lord your God has done for you in the wilderness.

6 Now therefore observe all the words of this law and walk in the way of the Lord your God, turn not from the way which the Lord has commanded you, either to the right or to the left.

7 And Moses taught the children of Israel rules and judgments and laws to do in the land as the Lord had commanded him.

8 And he taught them the way of the Lord and his laws; behold they are written on the book of the law of God which he gave to the children of Israel by the hand of Moses.

9 And Moses finished commanding the children of Israel, and the Lord said to him, Go up to the Mount Abarim and die there, and be gathered to your people as Aaron your brother was gathered.

10 And Moses went up as the Lord had commanded him, and he died there in the land of Moab by the order of the Lord, in the fortieth year from the Israelites going forth from the land of Egypt.

11 And the children of Israel wept for Moses in the plains of Moab for thirty days, and the days of weeping and mourning for Moses were completed.

CHAPTER 88

1 It was after the death of Moses that the Lord said to Joshua the son of Nun,

2 Rise up and pass the Jordan to the land which I have given to the children of Israel, and you shall make the children of Israel inherit the land.

3 Every place on which the sole of your feet treads shall belong to you; from the wilderness of Lebanon to the great river, the river of Perath, shall be your boundary.

4 No man shall stand up against you all the days of your life; as I was with Moses, so will I be with you, only be strong and of good courage to observe all the law which Moses commanded you; turn not from the way either to the right or to the left, in order that you may prosper in all that you do.

5 And Joshua commanded the officers of Israel, saying, Pass through the camp and command the people, saying, Prepare for yourselves provisions, for in three days more you will pass the Jordan to possess the land.

6 The officers of the children of Israel did so, and they commanded the people and they did all that Joshua had commanded.

7 Joshua sent two men to spy out the land of Jericho, and the men went and spied out Jericho.

8 And at the end of seven days they came to Joshua in the camp and said to him, The Lord has delivered the whole land into our hands; the inhabitants thereof are melted with fear because of us.

9 And it came to pass after that, that Joshua rose up in the morning and all Israel with him, and they journeyed from Shittim; Joshua and all Israel with him passed the Jordan, and Joshua was eighty-two years old when he passed the Jordan with Israel.

10 The people went up from Jordan on the tenth day of the first month, and they camped in Gilgal at the eastern corner of Jericho.

11 And the children of Israel kept the Passover in Gilgal in the plains of Jericho, on the fourteenth day of the month, as it is written in the law of Moses.

12 The manna ceased at that time on the morning of the Passover, and there was no more manna for the children of Israel and they ate of the produce of the land of Canaan.

13 Jericho was entirely closed against the children of Israel, no one came out or went in.

14 And it was in the second month, on the first day of the month, that the Lord said to Joshua, Rise up, behold I have given Jericho into your hand with all the people there; all your fighting men shall go round the city, once each day, thus shall you do for six days.

15 And the priests shall blow on trumpets; when you hear the sound of the trumpet, all the people shall give a great shouting, that the walls of the city shall fall down; all the people shall go up every man against his opponent.

16 And Joshua did so according to all that the Lord had commanded him.

17 On the seventh day they went round the city seven times, and the priests blew on trumpets.

18 At the seventh round, Joshua said to the people, Shout, for the Lord has delivered the whole city into our hands.

19 Only the city and all that it contains shall be accursed to the Lord, and keep yourselves from the accursed thing, that you make the camp of Israel accursed and trouble it.

20 But all the silver and gold and brass and iron shall be consecrated to the Lord, they shall come into the treasury of the Lord.

21 And the people blew on trumpets and made a great shouting, and the walls of Jericho fell down; all the people went up, every man straight before him, and they took the city and utterly destroyed all that was in it, both man and woman, young and old, ox and sheep and ass, with the edge of the sword.

22 And they burned the whole city with fire; only the vessels of silver and gold, brass and iron, they put into the treasury of the Lord.

23 Joshua swore at that time, saying, Cursed be the man who builds Jericho; he shall lay the foundation thereof in his firstborn, and in his youngest son he shall set up the gates of it.

24 And Achan the son of Carmi, the son of Zabdi, the son of Zerah, son of Judah, dealt treacherously in the accursed thing, and he took of the accursed thing and hid it in the tent, and the anger of the Lord was set ablaze against Israel.

25 It was after this when the children of Israel had returned from burning Jericho, Joshua sent men to spy out also Ai, and to fight against it.

26 And the men went up and spied out Ai, and they returned and said, Let not all the people go up with you to Ai, only let about three thousand men go up and strike the city, for the men there are few.

27 And Joshua did so; there went up with him of the children of Israel about three thousand men, and they fought against the men of Ai.

28 And the battle was severe against Israel, and the men of Ai struck thirty-six men of Israel, and the children of Israel fled from before the men of Ai.

29 When Joshua saw this thing, he tore his garments and fell on his face to the ground before the Lord, he with the elders of Israel, and they put dust on their heads.

30 And Joshua said, Why O Lord did you bring this people over the Jordan? What shall I say after the Israelites have turned their backs against their enemies?

31 So now all the Canaanites, inhabitants of the land, will hear this thing and surround us and cut off our name.

32 And the Lord said to Joshua, Why do you fall on your face? Rise, get up, for the Israelites have sinned and taken of the accursed thing; I will no more be with them unless they destroy the accursed thing from among them.

33 And Joshua rose up and assembled the people, and brought the Urim by the order of the Lord, and the tribe of Judah was taken, and Achan the son of Carmi was taken.

34 Joshua said to Achan, Tell me my son, what have you done, and Achan said, I saw among the spoil a goodly garment of Shinar and two hundred shekels of silver, and a wedge of gold of fifty shekels weight; I coveted them and took them, and behold they are all hid in the earth in the middle of the tent.

35 And Joshua sent men who went and took them from the tent of Achan, and they brought them to Joshua.

36 Joshua took Achan and these utensils, and his sons and daughters and all belonging to him, and they brought them into the valley of Achor.

37 Joshua burned them there with fire, and all the Israelites stoned Achan with stones; they raised over him a heap of stones, therefore he called that place the valley of Achor. So the Lord's anger was appeased, and Joshua afterward came to the city and fought against it.

38 And the Lord said to Joshua, Fear not, neither be dismayed, behold I have given into your hand Ai, her king and her people, and you shall do to them as you did to Jericho and her king, only the goods and the cattle there you shall take for yourselves; lay an ambush for the city behind it.

39 So Joshua did according to the word of the Lord, and he chose from among the sons of war thirty thousand courageous men; he sent them and they lay in ambush for the city.

40 And he commanded them, saying, When you shall see us we will flee before them with cunning, and they will pursue us; you shall then rise out of the ambush and take the city, and they did so.

41 Joshua fought, and the men of the city went out toward Israel, not knowing that they were lying in ambush for them behind the city.

42 Joshua and all the Israelites pretended to be wearied out before them, and they fled by the way of the wilderness with cunning.

43 The men of Ai gathered all the people who were in the city to pursue the Israelites; they went out and were drawn away from the city; not one remained and they left the city open and pursued the Israelites.

44 Those who were lying in ambush rose up out of their places, hurried to come to the city and took it and set it on fire; the men of Ai turned back, and there the smoke of the city ascended to the skies, and they had no means of retreating either one way or the other.

45 All the men of Ai were in the midst of Israel, some on this side and some on that side, and they struck them so that not one of them remained.

46 The children of Israel took Melosh king of Ai alive and they brought him to Joshua, and Joshua hanged him on a tree and he died.

47 And the children of Israel returned to the city after having burned it; they struck all those that were in it with the edge of the sword.

48 The number of those that had fallen of the men of Ai, both man and woman, was twelve thousand; only the cattle and the goods of the city they took to themselves, according to the word of the Lord to Joshua.

49 And all the kings on this side Jordan, all the kings of Canaan, heard of the evil which the children of Israel had done to Jericho and to Ai, and they gathered themselves together to fight against Israel.

50 Only the inhabitants of Gibeon were greatly afraid of fighting against the Israelites that they should perish, so they acted cunningly; they came to Joshua and to all Israel and said to them, We have come from a distant land, so now make a covenant with us.

51 And the inhabitants of Gibeon over-reached the children of Israel, and the children of Israel made a covenant with them, and they made peace with them; the princes of the congregation swore to them, but afterward the children of Israel knew that they were neighbors to them and were dwelling among them.

52 But the children of Israel killed them not; for they had sworn to them by the Lord, and they became hewers of wood and drawers of water.

53 Joshua said to them, Why did you deceive me, to do this thing to us? And they answered him, Because it was told to your servants all that you had done to all the kings of the Amorites, and we were greatly afraid of our lives, and we did this thing.

54 Joshua appointed them on that day to hew wood and to draw water, and he divided them for slaves to all the tribes of Israel.

55 And when Adonizedek king of Jerusalem heard all that the children of Israel had done to Jericho and to Ai, he sent to Hoham king of Hebron and to Piram king at Jarmuth, and to Japhia king of Lachish and to Deber king of Eglon, saying,

56 Come up to me and help me, that we may strike the children of Israel and the inhabitants of Gibeon who have made peace with the children of Israel.

57 And they gathered themselves together and the five kings of the Amorites went up with all their camps, a mighty people numerous as the sand of the seashore.

58 All these kings came and camped before Gibeon, and they began to fight against the inhabitants of Gibeon, and all the men of Gibeon sent to Joshua, saying, Come up quickly to us and help us, for all the kings of the Amorites have gathered together to fight against us.

59 Joshua and all the fighting people went up from Gilgal, and Joshua came suddenly to them and struck these five kings with a great slaughter.

60 And the Lord confounded them before the children at Israel, who struck them with a terrible slaughter in Gibeon, and pursued them along the way that goes up to Beth Horon to Makkedah; they fled from before the children of Israel.

61 And while they were fleeing, the Lord sent on them hailstones from heaven, and more of them died by the hailstones than by the slaughter of the children of Israel.

62 The children of Israel pursued them, and they still struck them in the road, going on and smiting them.

63 And when they were smiting, the day was declining toward evening and Joshua said in the sight of all the people, Sun, stand still on Gibeon, and you moon in the valley of Ajalon, until the nation shall have revenged itself on its enemies.

64 The Lord listened to the voice of Joshua, and the sun stood still in the midst of the heavens, and it stood still six and thirty moments, and the moon also stood still and hurried not to go down a whole day.

65 And there was no day like that, before it or after it that the Lord listened to the voice of a man, for the Lord fought for Israel.

CHAPTER 89

1 Then Joshua spoke this song on the day that the Lord had given the Amorites into the hand of Joshua and the children of Israel, and he said it in the sight of all Israel,

2 You have done mighty things, O Lord, you have performed great deeds; who is like you? My lips shall sing to your name.

3 My goodness and my fortress, my high tower, I will sing a new song to you; with thanksgiving I will sing to you, you are

the strength of my salvation.

4 All the kings of the earth shall praise you, the princes of the world shall sing to you, the children of Israel shall rejoice in your salvation; they shall sing and praise your power.

5 To you, O Lord, we confided; we said you are our God, for you were our shelter and strong tower against our enemies.

6 To you we cried and were not ashamed, in you we trusted and were delivered; when we cried to you, you heard our voice, you delivered our souls from the sword, you showed to us your grace, you gave to us your salvation, you rejoiced our hearts with your strength.

7 You went forth for our salvation, with your arm you redeemed your people; you answered us from the heavens of your holiness, you saved us from ten thousands of people.

8 The sun and moon stood still in heaven, and you stood in your wrath against our oppressors and commanded your judgments over them.

9 All the princes of the earth stood up, the kings of the nations had gathered themselves together, they were not moved at your presence; they desired your battles.

10 You rose against them in your anger, and brought down your wrath on them; you destroyed them in your anger, and cut them off in your heart.

11 Nations have been consumed with your fury, kingdoms have declined because of your wrath, you wounded kings in the day of your anger.

12 You poured out your fury on them, your wrathful anger took hold of them; you turned their iniquity on them, and cut them off in their wickedness.

13 They spread a trap and fell therein; in the net they hid, their foot was caught.

14 Your hand was ready for all your enemies who said, Through their sword they possessed the land, through their arm they lived in the city; you filled their faces with shame, you brought their horns down to the ground, you terrified them in your wrath and destroyed them in your anger.

15 The earth trembled and shook at the sound of your storm over them, you did not withhold their souls from death, and brought down their lives to the grave.

16 You pursued them in your storm, you concumed them in your whirlwind, you turned their rain into hail, they fell in deep pits so that they could not rise.

17 Their carcasses were like rubbish cast out in the middle of the streets.

18 They were consumed and destroyed in your anger, you saved your people with your might.

19 Therefore our hearts rejoice in you, our souls exalt in your salvation.

20 Our tongues shall relate your might, we will sing and praise your wondrous works.

21 For you did save us from our enemies, you did deliver us from those who rose up against us, you did destroy them from before us and depress them beneath our feet.

22 Thus shall all your enemies perish O Lord, and the wicked shall be like chaff driven by the wind, and your beloved shall be like trees planted by the waters.

23 So Joshua and all Israel with him returned to the camp in Gilgal, after having smitten all the kings, so that not a remnant was left of them.

24 And the five kings fled alone on foot from battle and hid themselves in a cave, and Joshua sought for them in the field of battle and did not find them.

25 And it was afterward told to Joshua, saying, The kings are found and there, they are hidden in a cave.

26 And Joshua said, Appoint men to be at the mouth of the cave to guard them, that they not take themselves away. And the children of Israel did so.

27 And Joshua called to all Israel and said to the officers of battle, Place your feet on the necks of these kings, and Joshua said, So shall the Lord do to all your enemies.

28 Joshua commanded afterward that they should kill the kings and cast them into the cave, and put great stones at the mouth of the cave.

29 Joshua went afterward with all the people that were with him on that day to Makkedah, and he struck it with the edge of the sword.

30 He utterly destroyed the souls and all belonging to the city, and he did to the king and people there as he had done to Jericho.

31 He passed from there to Libnah and he fought against it; the Lord delivered it into his hands and Joshua struck it with the edge of the sword, and all the souls there and he did it and to the king there as he had done to Jericho.

32 From there he passed on to Lachish to fight against it, and Horam king of Gaza went up to assist the men of Lachish, and Joshua struck him and his people until there was none left to him.

33 Joshua took Lachish and all the people there, and he did to it as he had done to Libnah.

34 Joshua passed from there to Eglon, and he took that also; he struck it and all the people there with the edge of the sword.

35 From there he passed to Hebron and fought against it and took it and utterly destroyed it; he returned from there with all Israel to Debir and fought against it and struck it with the edge of the sword.

36 And he destroyed every soul in it, he left none remaining; he did to it and the king thereof as he had done to Jericho.

37 Joshua struck all the kings of the Amorites from Kadesh-barnea to Azah; he took their country at once, for the Lord had fought for Israel.

38 And Joshua with all Israel came to the camp to Gilgal.

39 When at that time Jabin king of Chazor heard all that Joshua had done to the kings of the Amorites, Jabin sent to Jobat king of Midian, and to Laban king of Shimron, to Jephal king of Achshaph, and to all the kings of the Amorites, saying,

40 Come quickly to us and help us, that we may strike the children of Israel before they come on us and do to us as they have done to the other kings of the Amorites.

41 And all these kings listened to the words of Jabin, king of Chazor, and they went forth with all their camps, seventeen kings, and their people were as numerous as the sand on the seashore, together with horses and chariots innumerable; they came and camped together at the waters of Merom, and they were met together to fight against Israel.

42 The Lord said to Joshua, Fear them not, for tomorrow about this time I will deliver them up all slain before you, you shall cripple their horses and burn their chariots with fire.

43 And Joshua with all the men of war came suddenly on them and struck them, and they fell into their hands, for the Lord had delivered them into the hands of the children of Israel.

44 So the children of Israel pursued all these kings with their camps and struck them until there was none left of them, and Joshua did to them as the Lord had spoken to him.

45 Joshua returned at that time to Chazor and struck it with the sword and destroyed every soul in it and burned it with fire; from Chazor, Joshua passed to Shimron and struck it and utterly destroyed it.

46 From there he passed to Achshaph and he did to it as he had done to Shimron.

47 From there he passed to Adulam and he struck all the people in it, and he did to Adulam as he had done to Achshaph and to Shimron.

48 He passed from them to all the cities of the kings which he had smitten, and he struck all the people that were left of them and he utterly destroyed them.

49 Only their booty and cattle the Israelites took to themselves as a prey, but every human being they struck; they permitted not a soul to live.

50 As the Lord had commanded Moses so did Joshua and all Israel, they failed not in anything.

51 So Joshua and all the children of Israel struck the whole land of Canaan as the Lord had commanded them, and struck all their kings, being thirty and one kings, and the children of Israel took their whole country.

52 Besides the kingdoms of Sihon and Og which are on the other side Jordan, of which Moses had smitten many cities, Moses gave them to the Reubenites and the Gadites and to half the tribe of Manasseh.

53 And Joshua struck all the kings that were on this side of Jordan to the west, and gave them for an inheritance to the nine tribes and to the half tribe of Israel.

54 For five years Joshua carried on the war with these kings, and he gave their cities to the Israelites, and the land became tranquil from battle throughout the cities of the Amorites and the Canaanites.

CHAPTER 90

1 At that time in the fifth year after the children of Israel had passed over Jordan, after the children of Israel had rested from their war with the Canaanites, great and severe battles arose between Edom and the children of Chittim, and the children of Chittim fought against Edom.

2 Abianus king of Chittim went forth in that year, that is in the thirty-first year of his reign, and a great force with him of the mighty men of the children of Chittim, and he went to Seir to fight against the children of Esau.

3 Hadad the king of Edom heard of his report, and he went forth to meet him with many people and a strong force, and engaged in battle with him in the field of Edom.

4 And the hand of Chittim prevailed over the children of Esau, and the children of Chittim killed of the children of Esau two and twenty thousand men, and all the children of Esau fled from before them.

5 The children of Chittim pursued them and they reached Hadad king of Edom, who was running before them and they caught him alive, and brought him to Abianus king of Chittim.

6 And Abianus ordered him to be slain; Hadad king of Edom died in the forty-eighth year of his reign.

7 And the children of Chittim continued their pursuit of Edom; they struck them with a great slaughter and Edom became subject to the children of Chittim.

8 And the children of Chittim ruled over Edom, and Edom came under the hands of the children of Chittim and became one kingdom from that day.

9 From that time they could no more lift up their heads, and their kingdom became one with the children of Chittim.

10 Abianus placed officers in Edom and all the children of Edom became subject to Abianus, and Abianus turned back to his own land, Chittim.

11 When he returned he renewed his government and built for himself a spacious and fortified palace for a royal residence, and reigned securely over the children of Chittim and over Edom.

12 In those days, after the children of Israel had driven away all the Canaanites and the Amorites, Joshua was old and advanced in years.

13 And the Lord said to Joshua, You are old, advanced in life, and a great part of the land remains to be possessed.

14 Now therefore divide this land for an inheritance to the nine tribes and to the half tribe of Manasseh, and Joshua rose up and did as the Lord had spoken to him.

15 And he divided the whole land to the tribes of Israel as an inheritance according to their divisions.

16 But to the tribe at Levi he gave no inheritance. The offerings of the Lord are their inheritance as the Lord had spoken of them by the hand of Moses.

17 Joshua gave Mount Hebron to Caleb the son of Jephuneh, one portion above his brothers, as the Lord had spoken through Moses.

18 Therefore Hebron became an inheritance to Caleb and his children to this day.

19 Joshua divided the whole land by lots to all Israel for an inheritance, as the Lord had commanded him.

20 And the children of Israel gave cities to the Levites from their own inheritance, and suburbs for their cattle, and property; as the Lord had commanded Moses so did the children of Israel, and they divided the land by lot whether great or small.

21 They went to inherit the land according to their boundaries, and the children of Israel gave to Joshua the son of Nun an inheritance among them.

22 By the word of the Lord they gave to him the city which he required, Timnath-serach in Mount Ephraim, and he built the city and lived therein.

23 These are the inheritances which Elazer the priest and Joshua the son of Nun and the heads of the fathers of the tribes portioned out to the children of Israel by lot in Shiloh, before the Lord, at the door of the tabernacle, and they left off dividing the land.

24 And the Lord gave the land to the Israelites, and they possessed it as the Lord had spoken to them, and as the Lord had sworn to their ancestors.

25 And the Lord gave to the Israelites rest from all their enemies around them, and no man stood up against them; the Lord delivered all their enemies into their hands, and not one thing failed of all the good which the Lord had spoken to the children of Israel, yes, the Lord performed everything.

26 Joshua called to all the children of Israel and he blessed them, and commanded them to serve the Lord, and afterward sent them away; they went each man to his city, and each man to his inheritance.

27 And the children of Israel served the Lord all the days of Joshua, and the Lord gave them rest from all around them, and they lived securely in their cities.

28 It came to pass in those days, that Abianus king of Chittim died, in the thirty-eighth year of his reign, that is the seventh year of his reign over Edom; they buried him in his place which he had built for himself, and Latinus reigned in his stead fifty years.

29 During his reign he brought forth an army, and he went and fought against the inhabitants of Britannia and Kernania, the children of Elisha son of Javan, and he succeeded over them and made them subjects.

30 He then heard that Edom had revolted from under the hand of Chittim, and Latinus went to them and struck them and subdued them, and placed them under the hand of the children of Chittim; Edom became one kingdom with the children of Chittim all the days.

31 And for many years there was no king in Edom, and their government was with the children of Chittim and their king.

32 It was in the twenty-sixth year after the children of Israel had passed the Jordan, that is the sixty-sixth year after the children of Israel had departed from Egypt, that Joshua was old, advanced in years, being one hundred and eight years old in those days.

33 Joshua called to all Israel, to their elders, their judges and officers, after the Lord had given to all the Israelites rest from all their enemies round about; Joshua said to the elders of Israel and to their judges, Behold I am old, advanced in years, and you have seen what the Lord has done to all the nations whom he has driven away from before you, for it is the Lord who has fought for you.

34 Now therefore strengthen yourselves to keep and to do all the words of the law of Moses, not to deviate from it to the right or to the left, and not to come among those nations who are left in the land; neither shall you make mention of the name of their gods, but you shall cleave to the Lord your God, as you have done to this day.

35 Joshua greatly encouraged the children of Israel to serve the Lord all their days.

36 And all the Israelites said, We will serve the Lord our God all our days, we and our children, and our children's children, and our offspring forever.

37 Joshua made a covenant with the people on that day and he sent away the children of Israel, and they went each man to his inheritance and to his city.

38 And it was in those days, when the children of Israel were dwelling securely in their cities, that they buried the coffins of the tribes of their ancestors which they had brought up from Egypt, each man in the inheritance of his children; the twelve sons of Jacob did the children of Israel bury, each man in the possession of his children.

39 And these are the names of the cities where they buried the twelve sons of Jacob, whom the children of Israel had brought up from Egypt:

40 They buried Reuben and Gad on this side of Jordan, in Romia, which Moses had given to their children.

41 And Simeon and Levi they buried in the city Mauda, which he had given to the children of Simeon, and the suburb of the city was for the children of Levi.

42 And Judah they buried in the city of Benjamin opposite Bethlehem.

43 And the bones of Issachar and Zebulun they buried in Zidon, in the portion which fell to their children.

44 Dan was buried in the city of his children in Eshtael, and Naphtali and Asher they buried in Kadesh-naphtali, each man in his place which he had given to his children.

45 And the bones of Joseph they buried in Shechem in the part of the field which Jacob had purchased from Hamor, and which became to Joseph for an inheritance.

46 And they buried Benjamin in Jerusalem opposite the Jebusite, which was given to the children of Benjamin; the children of Israel buried their fathers each man in the city of his children.

47 And at the end of two years, Joshua the son of Nun died, one hundred and ten years old, and the time which Joshua judged Israel was twenty-eight years; Israel served the Lord all the days of his life.

48 And the other affairs of Joshua and his battles and his reproofs with which he reproved Israel, and all which he had commanded them, and the names of the cities which the children of Israel possessed in his days, they are written in the book of the words of Joshua to the children of Israel and in the book of the wars of the Lord, which Moses and Joshua and the children of Israel had written.

49 And the children of Israel buried Joshua in the border of his inheritance, in Timnath-serach which was given to him in Mount Ephraim.

50 And Elazer the son of Aaron died in those days; they buried him in a hill belonging to Phineas his son, which was given him in Mount Ephraim.

CHAPTER 91

1 At that time, after the death of Joshua, the children of the Canaanites were still in the land, and the Israelites resolved to drive them out.

2 And the children of Israel asked of the Lord, saying, Who shall first go up for us to the Canaanites to fight against them? And the Lord said, Judah shall go up.

3 And the children of Judah said to Simeon, Go up with us into our lot, and we will fight against the Canaanites and we likewise will go up with you in your lot; so the children of Simeon went with the children of Judah.

4 The children of Judah went up and fought against the Canaanites, so the Lord delivered the Canaanites into the hands of the children of Judah; they struck in Bezek ten thousand men.

5 They fought with Adonibezek in Bezek, he fled from before them, and they pursued him and caught him; they took hold of him and cut off his thumbs and great toes.

6 And Adonibezek said, Three score and ten kings having their thumbs and great toes cut off, gathered their meat under my table, as I have done, so God has rewarded me; they brought him to Jerusalem and he died there.

7 And the children of Simeon went with the children of Judah, and they struck the Canaanites with the edge of the sword.

8 The Lord was with the children of Judah, and they possessed the mountain, and the children of Joseph went up to Bethel, the same is Luz, and the Lord was with them.

9 And the children of Joseph spied out Bethel, and the watchmen saw a man going forth from the city, and they caught him and said to him, Show us now the entrance of the city and we will show kindness to you.

10 And that man showed them the entrance of the city, and the children of Joseph came and struck the city with the edge of the sword.

11 The man with his family they sent away, and he went to the Hittites and he built a city; he called the name there Luz, so all the Israelites lived in their cities, and the children at Israel lived in their cities; the children of Israel served the Lord all the days of Joshua, and all the days of the elders, who had lengthened their days after Joshua, and saw the great work of the Lord which he had performed for Israel.

12 And the elders judged Israel after the death of Joshua for seventeen years.

13 All the elders also fought the battles of Israel against the Canaanites and the Lord drove the Canaanites from before the children of Israel in order to place the Israelites in their land.

14 And he accomplished all the words which he had spoken to Abraham, Isaac, and Jacob, and the oath which he had sworn, to give to them and to their children the land of the Canaanites.

15 The Lord gave to the children of Israel the whole land of Canaan as he had sworn to their ancestors, and the Lord gave them rest from those around them, and the children of Israel lived securely in their cities.

16 Blessed be the Lord forever, amen, and amen.

17 Strengthen yourselves, and let the hearts of all you that trust in the Lord. Be of good courage.

SECTION TWO
APOCALYPTIC WRITINGS AND
THE END OF DAYS

End of Days
The Apocalyptic Writings

Introduction

Is mankind headed for destruction? How will it all end? When will it happen? What is man's destiny? Will we die by our own hand or by the hand of God?

For thousands of years the questions have been the same. Millions of souls have searched for the answers to no avail; nevertheless, some believed they knew. We call them prophets. They saw the end of our world and they believed their visions were true. Are we to believe their God-given insights into the End Of Days?

Perhaps God did pull back the curtain that blinds man to his future. Maybe these writers did see the end and how it would come upon us.

The prophets of doom revealed a scenario of global cataclysm. They tell the story of rulers bankrupting nations to fund tremendous wars. They tell of weather gone awry; of ice and snow, rain and floods, hurricanes and earthquakes where seldom they occurred. They tell us of what is happening all around us today.

Most scholars agree that many of the apocalyptic texts written between 70 and 200 A.D. were produced out of a national dismay and confusion following the destruction of the temple of the Jews in Israel in 70 A.D. The texts are attempts of a people, who believed themselves to be God's chosen, to explain why pagans were allowed by the God of the Jews to overthrow the way of worship, and of life of His chosen ones. Other apocalyptic books were written to explain and expand various biblical ideas linked to judgment and the end of days. The date, background, and purpose of each text will be discussed in more detail later.

The apocalyptic literature presented here allows us a rare glimpse into the ancient mindset and visions of how mankind may end. Most writings of this kind took place between 200 B.C. and 200 A.D, although a few were later and dated to the third century. The common thread was the moral and spiritual decline of man leading to his destruction. One could argue that the annihilation of the human race was to be brought about by our own hands due to our evil and sinful ways; however, it is the power unleashed by the wrath of God that gives way to the cleansing of the earth as all evil is destroyed and divine order is re-established. Only those who followed God and kept his laws would be spared.

Books written by those claiming to be Abraham, Thomas, Ezra, Baruch, and other giants of faith come down to us in ancient scrolls proclaiming the exact sequence of events leading to mankind's termination. Every society possesses apocalyptic texts. Every race and every nation carries in its literature and religion the implicit reiterating and unrelenting question; is the end near? The answer…yes, it is and here are its signs.

Presented in this book are four great apocalyptic works. "The Apocalypse of Abraham," "The Apocalypse Of Thomas" which is also called "The Revelation of Thomas," and 2 Baruch, which is also known as the Syriac Apocalypse of Baruch. 4 Ezra, sometimes also referred to as 2 Esdras or the Apocalypse of Ezra is usually included in the list of apocalyptic books, but we have chosen to present it later in the book under the title of "2 Esdras" in section 5, the Apocrypha.

The books of the following section represent the greatest among the apocalyptic writings of the era. Each gives its own unique insights into the End Of Days and yet, they all proclaim the same message; Follow God, turn from evil, or be destroyed.

The Apocalypse of Abraham

"The Apocalypse of Abraham" is part of a body of writings called "Abrahamic Writings," which flourished around and just after the time of Christ.

The manuscript dates from A.D. 80-170 with most scholars placing it between 80 and 100 A.D. The original text was written in a Semitic language, however it has survived only in Old Slavonic renditions.

Many of the Jewish non-canonical and extra-biblical materials that circulated in the Slavic lands came from Byzantium. They greatly influenced the development of Slavic literature. Non-canonical books brought from Byzantium were translated and became sections (pieces) of various Slavonic traditions. The Eastern Orthodox church nurtured an environment in which the apocryphal texts were encouraged toward the view of providing additional information as a secondary source to the canonical mainstream texts. Pseudepigraphical (certain writings other than the canonical books and the Apocrypha, professing to be Biblical in character) texts attributed to Adam, Enoch, Noah, Jacob, Abraham, Moses, and other patriarchs survived in this environment and were incorporated in hagiographical (the writing and critical study of the lives of the saints) and historical volumes.

An English translation of "The Apocalypse of Abraham" was produced by G. H. Box and J. I. Landsman in 1918 (The Apocalypse of Abraham, London: Society for Promoting Christian Knowledge) but that translation does not read well for the modern English audience. Thus arises the need to have the Box and other mainstream translations combined and updated into a more readable and accessible mode for today's reader.

It should be noted here that there are two versions of the "Apocalypse of Abraham," a long and a short version. The text in the book before you contains a combination of these two versions. When the two versions agree, which was more often than not the case, the clearest and best wording was chosen to express both in a single phrase.

When there were variations in meaning, alternate translations are shown in parentheses. When one version covered information not contained in the other translation, the additional lines were added, making this book the most complete body of information available as a single text.

"The Apocalypse of Abraham" is written in an haggadic midrash tradition. (Haggadic - embracing the interpretation of the non-legal portions of the Hebrew Bible. These midrashim are sometimes referred to as *haggadah*, a term that refers to all non-legal discourse in classical rabbinic literature). (Midrash – a Hebrew word referring to a method of exegesis of a Biblical text and teachings in the form of legal or exegetical commentaries on the Jewish Bible).

As with much of the Haaadic literature, the writings are an expansion and detailed explanation of existent biblical texts. That is to say, the writer took a section of an Old Testament canonical text and expanded it into a larger, more detailed story in order to explain in further detail the moral and religious implications of the original text.

Apocalyptic writings abound in the same time frame in the first century. It is thought they were spurred into creative existence by the utter destruction of the Jewish Temple in 70 A.D. and the attempted annihilation of Christians, many of whom were converted Jews, at the same time.

"The Apocalypse of Abraham" is based on Genesis 15:9-17 and concludes with the apocalypse. The book is of Jewish origin with features which might suggest that it had its beginning in the Essene community. This is seen clearly in the references to the "Elect One," a term that also appears in the Lost Book Of Enoch." (See "The Lost Book Of Enoch" by Joseph Lumpkin.)

Approximately one-third of the "Apocalypse of Abraham" contains an account of Abraham's conversion from polytheism to henotheism. Whereas polytheism believes in and worships many gods, each according to his or her dominion and special power; monotheism is the belief in one god; and henotheism focuses on one god but does not deny the existence of the other gods. The Amarna period of Egyptian history is an example a society that held to the henotheistic belief system.

The apocalyptic section of the Abraham text begins with the search for the God that made all things and the rejection of god's (idols) made by men. He (Abraham) reasons that if man made the gods with his own hands that man must therefore be greater than the gods he made.

Abraham's prayers are answered and he is told how to sacrifice to God. The preparation and sacrifice follows the biblical account, except that instead of birds of prey appearing and consuming the sacrifice, it is Azazel who does so. The angel Jaoel (Iaoel or Joel), guides Abraham into heaven and teaches him a song that is to be sung only on that realm or sphere of heaven.

While in heaven, Abraham sees a vision of the sin and degradation of his own progeny. As their sin increases, God withdraws his protection and the great temple is overrun by "heathen nations" and the progeny is killed and enslaved.

The five main characters in the book are El (God), Jaoel, Azazel, Abraham, and a powerful figure simply known as "The Man." There are also minor characters such as Abraham's father and merchants who travel in the area in which Abraham lived.

We learn in the first chapter of the Apocalypse of Abraham that Abraham is the son of Terah and the brother of Nahor.

Chapter 1
1. I was standing guard one day over the gods of my father Terah and my brother Nahor...

We also know Abraham's family were polytheists who worshipped idols that their father made. We learn that Terah sold his idols to others as well. Abraham is depicted as a precocious and sassy youth who questions things taken for granted by others.

He asked a question that seems most insightful for its time; If you carve an idol to worship as a god, does not that make you greater than the god you made? If that is true, why worship that which is lesser? This simple question puts him on the path of searching for the God who made all things including man.

Jaoel is the angel assigned to guide Abraham on his search. Jaoel takes him to heaven and leads him into visions, instructing him along the way.

Since Jaoel is allowed to come and go from the seventh heaven, we must assume him to be an angel of very high rank, though not found mentioned by this name elsewhere.

The name Jaoel consists of two parts, Jah and El both names of God in the Old Testament. Jaoel shows and explains a universal duality.

The duality of the universe is seen in the "right handed" and "left handed" principle. The Lord Himself used this principle when speaking of the 'sheep and the goats" in Matthew 25.

Here in the Abrahamic writings there are people coming out of a temple on the left side and on the right side. The deities in the story are the God El, who in this writing assumes the name of Azazel, a name that appears a great deal in the Books of Enoch, and is used in the Old Testament in the account of the Day of Atonement, where one goat is slain in the Tabernacle, whilst the other is set free, and the Hebrew text reads it is "for Azazel."

Azazel is portrayed as an unclean bird which came down upon the sacrifice Abraham, the Biblical patriarch, prepared. This is in reference to Genesis 15:11 Birds of prey came down upon the carcasses, and Abram drove them away.

Azazel is also associated with Hell. Abraham tells Azazel he will burn in hell and be in the underworld or Hades.

Azazel appears four times in Old Testament: Leviticus 16 :8, 10, and 26, where the ritual for the Day of Atonement is described. After the priest has made atonement for himself, he is to take two goats on behalf of Israel. One is to be a sacrifice to the Lord, the other is to be the 'scape goat,' which is the goat for Azazel.

This word has been understood to mean the "goat that departs," considering it to be derived from two Hebrew words: "ez" (goat) and "azal" (turn off). It is also associated with the Arabic word, "azala" (banish), or (remove), It has been rendered "for entire removal." Refer to Leviticus 16:22. However, in I Chronicles 5:8, the father of Bela, a Reubenite, is named "Azaz," which means strong.

This name comes from the Hebrew verb "azaz", a which means "to be strong." Azazel is also seen as an evil spirit in Enoch 8:1; 10:4; II Chronicles 11:15; Isaiah 34:14; and Revelations 18:2. In this way Azazel can be seen as the opponent or antithesis to the Lord and a precursor to Satan.

The figure of "The Man" is rather ambiguous. He is not fully messianic, yet he is endowed with power from God.

He may have come from the Essene idea of the Teacher of Righteousness and his connection with the coming, expected messiah.

Another explanation of the figure may come from an early Christian idea originating in a Judeo-Christian sect, which saw Jesus as precursor of the real and awaited Messiah, or it may simply be a Jewish text being badly interpreted and biased by an early Christian editor.

The evolution of El and his origin has drawn debate and acrimony since the beginning of theological study.

The people of Aramean and Canaanite origin seem to have contributed to the religion of El. Both religions place El as the highest god of a pantheon. Yet, because there is a pantheon of gods there is polytheism.

The clearest example of this adoption of the Israelite Elism comes from Deuteronomy 32 and related texts. El rules over his sons, and assigns each of them a people or tribe to govern. Here, to our surprise, we find Yahweh (the Lord) portrayed as one of El Elyon's divine sons.

Psalm 29 shows Yahweh as one of the sons of El, but a powerful god who is less subordinate than the others and more like an elder son.

Psalm 29 introduces the Canaanite cosmology which was more simple and familial; El being the father image and king.

We find within the Israelite religion two variations of the same high god. These different versions of Elism (the belief in a god called El) show that this god was variously worshipped depending upon location. Locations north of Palestine would have brought the worship of Yahweh in contact with Canaanite religion and that may explain its distinctly Canaanite quality.

Continuing the relationship between El and his sons, Psalm 82 has El stripping all his sons of authority and condemning them to mortality.

From this viewpoint, the Aramean god, El, seems to be related Canaanite mythology. Both likely descended from a Mesopotamian religion.   Yet now, after being failed and disappointed by all others gods, whom we presume are his sons,

El is forced to rule alone. Now we have the pathway set between polytheism and monotheism.

This last steps between the idea of a ruling court of gods and the singular god, El, can be seen clearly in the following translation and study by John Gray, Near Eastern Mythology:

"God has taken His place in the assembly of the gods (lit. 'sons of El"),
He declares His judgment among the gods: "
How long will you give crooked judgment,
and favor the wicked?
You ought to sustain the case of the weak and the orphan;
You ought to vindicate the destitute and down-trodden
You ought to rescue the weak and the poor,
To deliver them from the power of the wicked
You (Hebrew "they") walk in darkness
While all earth's foundations are giving away.
I declare "Gods you may be,
Sons of the Most high, all of you;
Yet you will die as men,
You will fall as one of the bright ones."
　　　　　　Psalm 82:1-7

"In the final line we read sharim for sarim ("princes"), from which it is indistinguishable in the Hebrew manuscripts, and find another reference to the fall of Athtar, the bright Venus star in Isaiah 14:12 ff and in the myth of Baal." (John Gray, Near Eastern Mythology)

Now, having introduced the cast of characters and set the historical and theological stage, let us proceed to the "Apocalypse of Abraham."

The Apocalypse of Abraham

Chapter 1

1. I was standing guard one day over the gods of my father Terah and my brother Nahor.
2. While I was testing them to find out which god was really the strongest and I was completing the services, I, Abraham, received my chance.
3. My father Terah was sacrificing to his gods of wood, stone, gold, silver, copper, and of iron and I entered their temple for the service, and found a god named Marumath, carved from stone, which had fallen at the feet of the iron god, Nakhin.
4. At that point my heart was perplexed (troubled) and I thought that I could not put it back in its place by myself because of its weight, since it was made of large stones.
5. So, I went and told my father, and he came in with me. When we both lifted it to put it in its place, its head fell off while I was holding it by its head.
6. Then when my father saw that the head of his god Marumath had fallen.
7. He yelled at me, saying, "Abraham!"
8. And I said, "Here I am!" And he told me to bring me the axes and chisels from the house. So, I brought them to him from the house.
9. Then he cut another Marumath without a head from another stone. He then smashed the head that had fallen off Marumath. He then crushed the rest of that (broken) Marumath.

Chapter 2

1. He created five more gods and gave them to me. He ordered me to sell them outside on the road to town.
2. I saddled my father's ass and loaded the gods on it and went out on the highway to sell them.
3. The merchants from Phandana of Syria were coming with their camels, on their way to Egypt to buy kokonil from the Nile.
4. I questioned them and they answered me. I walked along with them and talked with them. Then, one of their camels screamed and the ass was frightened and fled, throwing off the gods. Three of them were broken and two remained intact.
5. Then the Syrians saw that I had gods, they said to me: "Why did you not tell us that you had gods? We would have bought them before the ass. heard the camel's cry. You would had lost nothing."
6. Then they said, "Give us the gods that remain and we will give you a suitable price."
7. I considered this and grieved. But they paid both for the smashed gods and the gods which remained. I had been worried how I would bring payment to my father.
8. I threw the three broken gods into the water of the river Gur, which was in this place. And they sank deeply into the river Gur and were not seen again.

Chapter 3

1. As I was still walking on the road, my heart was disturbed and my mind was distracted.
2. I thought, "What is this deed of inequality my father is doing?
3. Is it not he who is god because his gods come into being through his sculpting, planning, and his skill (workmanship)?
4. They ought to honor my father because the gods are his work. What reward does my father received for his works?
5. Marumath fell and could not stand up in his (own) sanctuary, and could not I lift him myself until my father came and we stood him up (together). Even then we were not able to do it and his head fell off of him.
7. Then he put another stone on it from another god, which he (my father) had made without a head. The other five gods which got smashed when they fell from the ass could not save themselves. They did not harm the ass (to avenge themselves) because it smashed them. Nor did their broken pieces come up out of the river.
8. And I thought to myself, "If this is so, how can my father's god Marumath, which has the head of one stone and is made from another stone, save a man, or hear a man's prayer, or grant him any gift?"

Chapter 4

1. Thinking this way, I came to my father's house. I watered the ass and fed the ass with hay. I took out the silver and placed it in my father Terah's hand.
2. And when he saw it, he was happy, and he said, "You are blessed, Abraham, by the god of my gods, since you have brought me the price for the gods, so that my labor was not empty (for nothing)."
3. I answered and said to him, "Listen, father Terah! In you is the blessing of your gods, because you are the god of them, since you created them because their blessing is their hell and their power is empty.
4. They did not help themselves; how then can they help you or bless me?
5. I did well for you in this transaction, because through my good sense I brought you the silver for the broken gods."
6. When he heard what I had to say he became violently angry with me, since I had spoken words harshly contrary to his gods.

Chapter 5

1. Having thought about my father's anger, I left.
2. And afterward when I had left, he called me saying, "Abraham!" I answered, "Here I am!"
3. He said, " Gather these wood chips. I was making gods from fir before you came.
4. I will use the chips to cook food when I prepared my midday meal."
5. Then, when I was picking up the wooden chips, I found a small god among them which would fit in my left hand.
6. On its forehead was written: god Barisat. Then, I put the chips on the fire in to prepare food for my father, and went out to ask him about the food, I put Barisat near the kindling for the fire.
7. I spoke to him as if to threaten him. I said, "Barisat, watch that the fire does not go out before I come back!
8. If the fire goes out, blow on it so it flares up." I went out and said nothing of this to anyone.
9. When I returned I found Barisat fallen on his back. His feet were enveloped by fire and burning fiercely.
10. When I saw it, I laughed and I said to myself, "Barisat, truly you know how to light a fire and cook food!"
11. Then, while saying this in my laughter, I saw that he had burned up slowly with fire and turned to ashes.
12. I carried the food to my father to eat.
13. I gave him wine and milk, and he drank and he enjoyed himself and he thanked and spoke praise to Marumath his god.
14. Then I said to him, "Father Terah, do not bless Marumath your god, do not praise him!
15 Instead, praise your god Barisat, because he loved you enough that he threw himself into the fire in order to cook your food."
16. Then my father said to me said, "Where is he now?" And I said, "He has burned in the flames of the fire and become dust." And he said, "Great is the power of Barisat! I will make another today, and tomorrow he will prepare my food."

Chapter 6

1. When I, Abraham, heard these words from my father, I laughed to myself and I groaned from the disgust and anger in my heart.
2. I said, "How can a piece of a body made (by Terah) help my father, Terah?
3. How can he have enslaved his body to his soul (will or desire), and allowed his soul (will or desire) to be enslaved by a spirit (not his spirit but "a" spirit), when the spirit is stupid and ignorant?"
4. And I said, "It is only proper to withstand this evil that I may compel my mind toward purity. I will lay my thoughts out before him clearly.
5. " I answered and said, "Father Terah, no matter which of these gods you praise, your thoughts err.
6. Don't you see that the gods of my brother Nahor which stand in the holy sanctuary are more worthy than yours?
7. Look! Zouchaios, my brother Nahor's god is more worthy than your god Marumath because he is made of gold, which is valued by man.
8. And if Zouchaios grows old with time, he will be remolded, whereas, if Marumath deteriorates or is broken, he will not be renewed, because he is made of stone.
9. What about Ioav, the other god who stands with Zouchaios? He is also more worthy than the god Barisat.
10. He, Ioay, is carved from wood and then forged from silver; because he too is made of something that is given with love (comparison), and is valued by man according to their outward experience.
11. But Barisat, your god, is rooted in the earth. When he was large (great) it is a wonder because he had branches and flowers and was worth praise when he was still not carved.
12. But then you shaped him with an axe and you created (him as) a god by your skill.
13. Look! He has already dried up.
14. His substance (fruit/fatness) has perished.
15. From the height he has fallen to the earth.
16. He descended from greatness to a lowly state, and his face and appearance has wasted (withered) away.
17. He was burned up by the fire and he turned into ashes and disappeared.
18. Then you say, "Let me make another and tomorrow he will prepare my food for me." He was destroyed and no power (strength) was left in him (because of or to prevent) his own destruction.

Chapter 7

1. This I say: Fire is more valuable in the formation of things because even the untamable things are subdued in (by) it, and it laughs at those things which are destroyed easily by its burning.
3. But neither is it worthy (valuable), because it is subject to the water.
4. But water is more worthy (venerable/powerful) than fire because water overcomes fire and sweetens the earth with fruit.
5. But I would not call water a god either because water is taken under the earth and water is subject to the earth.
6. I will not call earth a goddess either because it is dried by the sun and was made for man for his work.

7. I think the sun is more worthy among the gods, because with its rays it illuminates the entire universe and all the air.

8. But I will would not place the sun among the gods because there are those who obscure his course. They are the moon and the clouds.

9. I will not call the moon or the stars gods, because at times during the night they also dim their light.

10. Listen, Terah my father, I will seek the God who created all the other gods we have thought exist.

11. I seek who or what is it that made the heavens red and the sun golden and who has given light to the moon and the stars and who has dried the earth in the midst of the many waters. I will seek who it is that has set you yourself among the things and who has sought me out in the of my thoughts of questioning.

12. God will reveal himself by himself to us!"

Chapter 8

1. Then, I was thinking about my father Terah being in the court of my house when the voice of the Mighty One came down from the heavens in a stream of fire and it called to me saying, "Abraham, Abraham!"

2. And I said, "Here I am."

3. Then he said, "You are searching in the wisdom of your heart for the God of gods, the Creator? I am he.

4. Get out from Terah, your father, and go away from the house, that you too may not be killed because of the sins of your father's house."

5. Then, as I went out and I was not outside the entrance of the court yet, the sound of a tremendous thunder came and burned him and his house and everything in his house to the ground for a space of forty cubits.

Chapter 9

1. Then a voice spoke to me twice: "Abraham, Abraham!"

2 I said, "Here I am!" And He said, "Look! It is I, fear not for I am with you because I AM before the ages, I am the Mighty God who created the first light of the world. I am your protection (shield) and your helper."

3. He continued and said, "Behold, it is I, Fear not because I am Before the World Was, I Am Mighty, the God who has created all, I am the light of the age.

4. I am your protector and your helper.

5. Go, get me a three-year-old heifer, a three-year-old female goat, a three-year-old ram, a turtledove, and a pigeon.

6. Go, take me a young heifer of three years, and a female goat of three years, and a ram of three years, a turtledove and a pigeon, and bring me a pure sacrifice.

7. In this sacrifice I will lay before (make known to) you the ages to come, and tell you what is in store, and you will see great things which you have not seen before.

8. I will tell you things kept guarded and you will see great things which you have not seen, because you desired me and searched for me, and so I called you my beloved.

9. But for forty days abstain from every kind of food cooked by fire, and from drinking because you have loved to search me out, and I have named you "my friend."

10 And also abstain from anointing yourself with oil for forty days, and then give me the sacrifice which I have commanded you, in a place which I will show you high on a mountain, and there I will reveal to you the ages which have been created and established by my word.

11. (And there I will show you the things which were made in the ages and by my word that affirmed and created, and renewed.) I will make known to you what will come to pass for them who have done evil and for those who have done righteousness (just deeds) in the generations of men."

Chapter 10

1. Then, I heard the voice telling me such things.

2. And I heard the voice of Him who spoke these words to me, and I looked around (for Him).

3. I found I could not breathe, and fear seized my spirit. My soul seemed to leave me and I fell down like a stone, like a dead man falls to the earth, and I had no strength to stand.

4. I was laying with my face down to the earth when I heard the voice of the Holy One speaking, "Go, Jaoel, and by the power of my ineffable name raise up man, that man over there and strengthen him , so that he recovers from his trembling.

5. Consecrate this man for me and strengthen him against his trembling."

6. The angel he sent to me in the likeness of a man came, and he took me by my right (hand) and set me up upon my feet and said to me, "Stand up Abraham, friend of God who loves you. Do not let your trembling seize you! For look! I have been sent to you to strengthen you and bless you in the name of God, who loves you. He is the Creator of the heaven and the Earth. Do not fear but and run to Him.

7. I am called Jaoel by Him who gives life to those who exist with me on the seventh level of heaven. It is done by the power of the goodness of the ineffable name that is dwelling in me.

8. I am the one who has been given (the authority) to restrain the threats and attacks of the Living One's Cherubim against one another, and to teach those who have Him within them, the song of the seventh hour of the night of man, according to His commandment. (I teach those who carry the song through man's night of the seventh hour.)
9. I am the one who ordered your father's house to be burned with him because he honored the dead (gods).
10. I am given authority to restrain the Leviathan (serpent/reptiles) because every attack and menace of every Leviathan (serpent/reptile) are subject to me.
11. I am he who has been given power to loosen Hades, and destroy him who watches over the dead.
12. I have been sent to bless you and your land now, for the Eternal One whom you have invoked has prepared for you. For your sake I have ventured my way upon earth.
13. Stand up, Abraham, go boldly, be very joyful and rejoice. And I (also rejoice) with you because you are venerable and I am with you! For everlasting honor has been prepared for you by the Eternal One.
14. Go, and do the sacrifices commanded. For I, and with me Michael, blesses you forever.
15. I have been commanded to be with you, and with the generations that will spring from you, Be of good cheer and go!"

Chapter 11
1.. And I stood up and saw him who had grasped me by the right hand and set me on my feet.
2. The appearance of his body was like sapphire, and the look of his appearance was like peridot, and the hair of his head was like snow.
3. A kidaris (a Scythian hat with long flaps usually worn by kings) was on his head and its look was like that of a rainbow.
4. His garments were purple and a golden staff was in his right hand.
5. And he said to me, "Abraham," And I said, "Here is your servant!"
6. He said, "Do not let my appearance frighten you. Nor should you let my speech trouble your soul.
7. Come with me, and I will be with you visibly until the sacrifice, but after the sacrifice I will be invisible forever more.
8. Be of good cheer, and come!"

Chapter 12
1. The two of us went together for forty days and nights, and I ate no bread and drank no water because my food and my drink was to see the angel who was with me, and to hear his voice.
2. We came to the Mount of God, Mount Horeb, and I said to the angel, "Singer to the Eternal One! I have no sacrifice and I do not know of a place with an altar on the mountain.
3. How can I bring a sacrifice?"
4. And he said to me, "Look around you." And when I looked around, there following us were all the required animals, the young heifer, the female goat, the ram, the turtle dove and the pigeon.
5. And the angel said to me, "Abraham!" And I said, "Here am I."
6. And he said, "Slaughter all these animals, and divide them into halves, place the one half against (across from/facing) the other, but do not divide (sever) the birds.
7. Give these to the men whom I will show you (that are) standing by you because these are the altar upon the Mountain, to offer a sacrifice to the Eternal (One).
8. But, the turtledove and the pigeon you will give to me because I will ascend on the wings of the birds to show you what is in the heavens, on the earth, in the sea, in the abyss, in the lower depths, in the garden of Eden, in its rivers, and in the fullness of the universe. And you will see its circles in all."

Chapter 13
1. I did everything commanded me by the angel, and I gave the angels who had come to us the divided animals, but the angel Jaoel took the birds.
2. Then I waited until the evening sacrifice. Then and there an unclean bird flew down upon the carcasses, and I drove it away.
3. The unclean bird spoke to me and said, "Abraham, what are you doing upon these holy heights where no man eats or drinks and there is no food for man here but these heavenly beings consume everything with fire and will burn you up?
4. Forsake the man who is with you and run away because if you ascend into the heights they will destroy (kill/make an end of) you."
5. Then, when I saw the bird speaking I said to the angel: "What is this, my lord?"
6. And he said, "This is ungodliness; this is Azazel."
7. And he said to it (the bird), "Disgrace upon you, Azazel! For Abraham's portion is in heaven, but yours is upon the earth because you have chosen this for the dwelling place of your uncleanness and you have loved it.
8. Therefore the Eternal Mighty Lord forced you to dwell upon the earth, and through you every evil spirit of lies, rage, and trials came forth for the generations of ungodly men.

9. God, the Eternal and Mighty One, has not permitted the bodies of the righteous to be (end up) in your hands so that the life of the righteous and the destruction of the unclean may be assured.

10. Listen! You have no permission to tempt the righteous at all.

11. Leave this man! You cannot deceive him, because he is the enemy of you and of those who follow you and those who love what you want.

12. Behold, the garment which is heaven was formerly yours has been set aside for him, and the mortality which was his has been given over to you."

Chapter 14

1. And the angel said to me, "Abraham!"

2. And I said, "Here I am." And the angel said to me, "Know that from now on and forever the Eternal One has chosen you.

3. Be bold! I command you to use this authority against him who reviles the truth.

4. Will I not be able to revile him who has scattered about the earth the secrets of heaven and who has taken counsel against the Mighty One?

5. Say to him, "May you stoke (be kindling in) the fires of the earth's furnace!

6. Go, Azazel, into the deserted parts of the earth.

7. Your inheritance is over those who are with you, with the stars and with the men born by the clouds, whose reward you are. They exist because of you (through your being).

8. Hate is your pious act.

9. Therefore you will destroy yourself and be gone from me!"

10. And I spoke the words that the angel taught me. But the angel said to me, "Do not answer him! For God has given him power over those who answer him."

11. And the angel spoke to me again saying, "However much he speaks to you, do not answer him so that he may not get to you easily (freely).

12. The Eternal One gave him the gravity and the will. Do not answer him."

13. I did what the angel commanded me. And whatever he said to me about the fall (descent), I did not answered him.

Chapter 15

1. As the sun was setting, I beheld smoke like that of a furnace, and the angels who had the divided portions of the sacrifice came down from the top of the smoking furnace.

2. And the angel lifted me with his right hand and set me upon the right wing of the pigeon, and he sat on the left wing of the turtle dove. Neither birds had been slaughtered.

3. He flew me to the borders of the flaming fire, and we rose on many winds to the heavens which were above the firmament (sky/ theater of stars/ the sphere where the stars are stationed).

4. In the air, we ascended to a height that I could see a strong (bright) light impossible to describe.

5. In the light of a fiercely burning fire (Gehenna?), I saw many people, male in appearance. All of them were constantly changing their appearance and form. They were running as they were being changed, and they were worshipping and crying out with a sound of words that I could not recognize.

Chapter 16

1. And I said to the angel, "Why have you now brought me here?

2. I can no longer see clearly, and I am growing weak. My spirit is leaving me?"

3. And he said, "Remain close to me and do not fear.

3. He, the One you cannot see, is coming toward us now with a tremendous voice of holiness.

4. He is the Eternal One who loves you. But you yourself cannot see (look at) Him.

5. But you may find your spirit growing faint on account of the choirs of those who cry out because I am with you to strengthen you (fight against the weakness for I am here to strengthen you)."

Chapter 17

1. While he was still speaking, the fire coming toward us surrounded us and there was a voice amidst the fire like a voice of many waters, like the sound of a violent sea. And I wanted to fall down and worship. And the angel knelt down with me and worshipped.

2. However, the surface of the high place where we were standing changed constantly, inclining, rolling high and low.

3. And the angel said, "Worship, Abraham, and sing the song which I now will teach you.

4. Never stop signing it. Sing it in continuously from beginning to end. "

5. And the song which he taught me to sing had words that were appropriate to the area of heaven (sphere) we were standing in.

6. Each area (sphere) in heaven has its own song of praise, and only those who live there know how to sign it, and those on earth cannot know it or sing it.

7. They could know it only if they were taught by the messengers of heaven. And the words of that song were of a type and meaning.

8. So I bowed down since there was no solid ground on which to prostrate myself and I recited the song which he had taught me.

9. And he said, "Recite it without ceasing." And I recited, and he himself recited the song along with me.

"Eternal, Mighty, Holy God (El), God of unlimited power, Self-originated, Incorruptible, Immaculate, Without beginning, having no mother or father, Spotless, Immortal, Self-Created, Illuminated with your own light, without mother or father, self-begotten, High, radiant, Wise, Lover Of Men, Favorable, Generous, Bountiful, Jealous Over Me, Patient (compassionate), Most Merciful, Eli (my God), Eternal, Mighty, Holy Sabbath, Most Glorious El, El, El, El, (God) Jaoel (Yahoel/Joel) (Ja El/Lord God). You are he whom my soul has loved, the Guardian, Eternal, Radiant, Shining, Made of light, Voice of thunder. You appear as lightning, All seeing, you receive the prayers of those who honor you and turn away from the prayers of those who besiege you with their provoking ways. You redeem (free) those who are in the midst of the unrighteous and those who are confused among the wicked one who inhabited world in the corruptible life. You renew the life of the righteous. Before the morning light shines, you make the light shine upon your creation from the light of your face in order to bring the day on the earth. And in your heavenly dwellings there is an inexhaustible light of another kind. It is the inexpressible splendor from the lights of your face. Accept my prayer, and let it be sweet to you, and also the sacrifice which you yourself made to yourself through me who searched for you. Receive me favorably and show to me, and teach me, and make known to your servant what you have promised me."

Chapter 18

1. While I was still reciting the song, the mouth of the fire on the surface rose high in the air.

2. And I heard a voice like a roaring sea. It was not stopped by even the plethora of fire. And as the fire rose up very high I saw under the fire a throne of fire, and around it were many eyes watching.

3. They were the all-seeing ones and they were singing their song.

4. Under the throne were four radiant (on fire) Living Ones singing but they looked as if they were one creature but each one had four faces.

5. This is how they appeared and how they looked to me; each one had the face of a lion, a man, an ox and an eagle, and because of their four heads upon their bodies, they had sixteen faces.

6. Each one had three pairs of wings coming out of their shoulders, their sides, and their hips. With the wings from the shoulders they covered their faces. With the wings from their hips they covered their feet. The two middle wings were spread out and they flew erect as if standing up (straight forward).

7. Then, when they had ended their singing they looked at one another and threatened one another.

8. Then, when the angel who was with me saw that they were threatening each other he left me and went running to them. He turned the face of each living creature from the face which was opposite it so that they could not see each other's faces

9. And he taught them the song of peace which the Eternal One has in himself.

10. And while I stood alone and watched, I saw a chariot with wheels of fire behind the Living Ones.

11. Each wheel had eyes around it and it was full of eyes. Above the wheels was the throne which I had seen before. It was covered with fire, and the fire encircled it.

12. An indescribable fire contained a mighty fiery host, and I heard its holy voice like the voice of a man.

Chapter 19

1. And a voice came to me out of the middle of the fire, saying, "Abraham, "Abraham!" and I answered saying "Here am I!" And he said, "Look at the wide places (areas/expanses) which are under the firmament (sky/theater of stars) on which you now stand.

2. Notice that no other place (area/expanse) has yielded the one for whom you have searched or who has loved you."

3. While he was still talking, the areas opened up. Below me were the heavens and I saw a fire which was wide-spread. There was a light, which is the storehouse (vault) of life.

4. There was the dew that God will use to awaken the dead, the spirits of the righteous, those that had gone on before, and the spirits of those souls who are yet to be born. Judgment and righteousness, peace and blessing, and an innumerable host of angels, and the Living Ones, and the Power of the Invisible Glory sat above the Living Ones.

5. All of these were in the seventh firmament, on which I stood.

6. And I looked down from the high mountain on which I stood on to the sixth firmament, and there I saw a host of angels of pure spirit (incorporeal) without bodies, whose duty was to carry out the commands of the fiery angels who were upon the seventh firmament (some translations have the eighth firmament) , as I was standing suspended over them.

7. And I looked down on the sixth firmament and there were no other powers of any form, only the angels of pure spirit.

8. I was standing on its elevation. And on this firmament there was nothing in any form and no other host, but only the spiritual angels.

9. I saw a host on the seventh firmament and He commanded that the sixth firmament should be removed from my sight, and I saw there on the fifth firmament the powers of the stars which carry out the commands laid upon them, and the elements of the earth obeyed them.

Chapter 20

1. And the Eternal, Mighty One said to me, "Abraham, Abraham!" And I said, "Here I am!"

2. And He said to me, "Look at the stars which are beneath you, and number them for me, and then tell me their number."

3. And I said, "How can I? I am just a man made of the dust of the earth." And He said to me, " I will make your progeny a nation as large as the number of the stars and as powerful the power of the stars, and I will set these people a section (piece) for me as my own inheritance.

4. They will be distinct from those of Azazel. And yet I include Azazel in my house."

5. And I said, "Eternal and Mighty One. Let your servant speak before you and do not let your fury ignite (burn/rage) against your chosen (selected/elect) one.

6. "Look!, before you led me up, Azazel insulted (railed against/reproached) me. Since he is now not before you how can you establish (constitute/count) yourself with them?"

Chapter 21

1. Then He said to me, "Look beneath your feet at the firmament and understand the creation represented and foretold in this expanse, the creatures who exist in it, and the ages prepared after it."

2. And I looked beneath my feet and beneath the sixth heaven and saw the earth and its fruits, and what moved upon it and its beings that moved, and the host of its men, and the ungodliness of some of their souls and the righteous deeds of other souls. I saw the lower regions and the torment (perdition) in the abyss.

3. And I saw the sea and its islands, its monsters (Leviathan) and its fishes, and Leviathan and his lair, his realm (caves), and the world which lay above him, and his movements and the destructions he caused the world.

4. I saw there the streams and the rivers with their waters rising, and their winding courses. And I saw there the Garden of Eden and its fruits, the source of the river that issues from it, the trees and their blossoms, and the men (ones) who did good deeds (behaved righteously/ justly). And I saw in it (the garden) their foods and their restfulness (blessedness).

5. And I saw there a tremendous multitude of men and women and children, half of them on the right side of the door (vision), and half of them on the left side of the door (vision).

Chapter 22

1. And I said, "Eternal, Mighty One! What is this vision of creation?"

2. And he said to me, "This is my will for what is in the light and it was good before my face.

3. After this I gave them a command and by my word and they came into existence.

4. Whatever I had decreed was to exist had already been decided (outlined in this) and all things created, which you see, had stood in front of me (in my sight) before it was created.

5. And I said, "Lord, Mighty and Eternal! Who are the people in this vision on this side and on that side?"

6. And He said to me, "Those who are on the left side are all those who existed (were born) before and after your day, some destined for judgment and restoration, and others for vengeance and estrangement at the end of the age.

7. Those on the right side of the vision are the people set a section (piece) for me. These are the ones I have prepared to be born of your lineage and to be called "my people." Some of these even come from Azazel.

Chapter 23

1. Now look again in the vision and see who it is that seduced Eve and what the fruit of the Tree was, and you will know what is to be, and how it will be for your progeny among the people at the end of the days of the age.

3. And all that you cannot understand I will make known to you for you are well-pleasing in my sight, and I will tell you of those things which are kept in my heart.

4. Then I looked into the vision, and my eyes looked at the side of the Garden of Eden, and I saw there a man of imposing height and he was great (powerful) in stature, incomparable in appearance.

5. He was embracing (entwined with) a woman who looked like his size and stature. They were standing under a tree of the Garden of Eden, and the fruit of this tree was like a bunch of grapes on a vine. Standing behind the tree was one who had the appearance of a serpent (dragon) but it had the hands and feet of a man and it had wings on its shoulders.

6. There were six pairs of wings, so that there were six wings on the right shoulder and six on the left shoulder.

7. As I continued looking, I saw the man and the woman eating the fruit from the tree. And the serpent (dragon) was holding the grapes of the tree and feeding them to the two I saw embracing each other.

8. And I said, "Who are these two that embrace, and who is this between them, and what is the fruit which they are eating, Oh, Mighty, Eternal One?"

9. And He said, "This is the world of men (this is humanity). This (one) is Adam (man), and that one, who is their desire upon the earth, is Eve.

10. But he who is between them is the ungodliness of their behavior that is sending them on the way to perdition. It is Azazel."

11. And I said, "Eternal Mighty One! Why have you given the likes of him (Azazel) the power to destroy mankind (children or generations of men) and their works upon the earth?"

12. And He said to me, " I gave him power over them who want do evil and those whom I have already hated and they will even come to love him."

13. And I said. "Eternal, Mighty One! Why did you want to bring into existence an evil that men would desire in their heart since you are angered at what was chosen by those who do useless (vain/unprofitable) things in your light (counsel/presence)?"

Chapter 24

1. He said to me, "I am angered by mankind on your account, and on account of those who will be of your family to come, because as you can see in the vision, the burden of destiny is placed upon them, and I will tell you what will be, and how much will take place in the last days. Now look at everything in the vision."

2. I looked and saw the created beings that had come into existence before me.

3. And I saw Adam and Eve and the cunning adversary who was with them; the crafty Cain, who had been influenced (led) by the adversary to break the law; and I saw the murdered (slaughtered) Abel and the destruction (lawlessness/perdition) brought on him that was caused through the lawless one.

4. And I saw there fornication and those who desired it, and its defilement and their jealousness; and the fire of the corruption in the lower depths of the earth.

5. And I saw theft and those who run after it, and the means and ways of their punishment (retribution) at the judgment of the Great Court (Assize).

6. And I saw naked men with their foreheads against each other, and their disgrace, and the passions which they had for each other, and their retribution (and the shame and harm they worked against one another).

7. And I saw Desire, and in her hand was the head of every kind of lawlessness, and her scorn and contempt and waste was assigned to destruction (perdition).

Chapter 25

1. Then I saw something that looked like an idol. It was the idol of jealousy.

2. It was carved in wood like father used to make. Its body was made of glittering bronze that covered the wood.

3. And in front of it I saw a man who was worshipping the idol, and in front of him there was an altar, and upon the altar a boy was killed as a sacrifice in the presence of the idol.

4. And I said to him, "What is this idol, and what is the altar, and who are those being sacrificed, and who is the one who performs the sacrifice, and what is the beautiful temple which I see, the are and beauty of your glory like that which lies beneath Your throne?"

5. And he said, "Hear, Abraham! This temple which you have seen, the altar and the works are my idea of the priesthood performing in the name of my glory, where every prayer (request/petition) of man will enter and live, they include the praise of kings and prophets and whatever sacrifice I decree to be made for me.

6. And He said, "Abraham, listen! What you see is the Temple, it is a copy of that which is in the heavens. It is glorious in its appearance and beauty. I will give it to the sons of men to ordain a priesthood for my glorious name. In it the prayers of man will be spoken, and sacrifices offered.)

7. I have ordained this for your people, especially those who will arise out of your lineage.

8. But the idol which you saw is the image of jealousy that will be set up by some of those who will come out of your own loins in later days.

9. And the man who sacrifices in murder is he who pollutes my Temple. These are witnesses to the final judgment, and their appointment (reward) has been set from the beginning of creation."

Chapter 26

1.. And I said, "Eternal Mighty One! Why did you establish it like this, and then proclaim the knowledge (testify) of it?" And He said to me, "Listen Abraham, and understand what I am about to say to you, and answer my question. Why did your father Terah not listen to you, and why did he not cease his idolatrous (demonic worship) practices, together with his entire house?"

2. And I said, "Eternal Mighty One, certainly because he did not want to obey me because I did not follow his (ways/deeds) works."

3. And He said to me, "The will of your father is in him (up to him), and your will is in you (up to you), and likewise the counsel of my own will is within me (up to me/in my control), and it is prepared for (has prepared) the coming days before you have any knowledge of them or can see the future with your own eyes. Now look again into the vision, and see how it will be with your children (progeny/generations)."

Chapter 27

1. And I looked and I saw the vision sway. From its left side a crowd of unbelievers (ungodly people) ran out and they captured the men, women, and children and they murdered (slaughtered like animals) most of them and others they kept as slaves. And I saw them (the killers) run towards them (the slaves) through four doors which were high with stairs and they burned the Temple with fire, and they took and broke the holy things that were in the temple.
2. And I said, " Eternal One! Behold, my progeny, whom you have accepted, are robbed by these ungodly men. Some are killed, and others they enslave. The Temple they have burned with fire, and the beautiful things in it they have robbed and destroyed. If this is to be, why have you ripped my heart like this?"
3. And he said to me, "Listen, Abraham, all that you have seen will happen because of your progeny who will continually provoke me because of the idols that you saw, and because of the human sacrifice in the vision, through their drive and desire to do evil and there schemes in the Temple. You saw it and that is how it will be."
4. And I said, "Eternal, Mighty One! Allow these works of evil brought about by ungodliness pass by, and instead show me those who fulfilled the commandments, show me the works of righteousness. I know in truth you can do this."
5. And He said to me, "The days of the righteous (will arrive) are seen symbolized by the lives of righteous rulers who will arise, and whom I have created to rule at the appointed times. But you must know that out of them will arise others who care only for their own interests. These are symbolized by those (killers) I have already shown you.

Chapter 28

1. And I answered and said, "Mighty, Eternal One, you who are holy by your power, show mercy, I pray. Since you have brought me up here to your high place and you have showed your beloved the things about which I asked, please tell me now: Will what I saw be their lot for long?"
2. And He showed me a multitude of His people and said to me, "Because of them, I will be provoked by them through the four high doorways you saw, and my retribution for their deeds will be accomplished. But in the fourth descent of one hundred years, which is the same as one hour of the age, the same is a hundred years, there will be evil (misfortune) among the (heathen) nations, but also for one hour there will be mercy and honor (in) among those nations.

Chapter 29

1.. And I said, " Eternal One! How long are the hours of the age?" And He said, "Twelve hours have I ordained for this present ungodly age to rule among the (heathen) nations and within your progeny, and until the end of the times it will be even as you saw. And now reckon (calculate) and understand and look again into the vision.
2. And he said, "I decreed to keep twelve periods of the impious age among the heathens and among your progeny, and what you have seen will be until the end of time."
3. And I looked and saw a Man going out from the left side of the (heathen) nations.
4. And there went men and women and children out from the side of (heathen) nations like many multitudes and they worshipped Him.
6. And while I still looked, there came many from the right side, and some of these insulted Him, and some of them even struck Him, but others worshipped Him.
7. As I watched, I saw Azazel come up to Him and he kissed Him on the face and then turned and stood behind Him.
8. Then I said, "Eternal, Mighty One! Who is this Man who is insulted and beaten, who is worshipped by the nations and kissed by Azazel?"
9. And He answered and said, "Hear Me Abraham! The Man you saw insulted and beaten and yet worshipped by many, He is the Relief/Liberty/Freedom granted for (by) the nations of people who will be born from (out of) you in the last days, in the twelfth hour of the age of ungodliness.
10. But in the twelfth hour of my last (final) age of my fulfillment will I set up this Man from your tribe (generation), whom you saw issue from among my people, and all who follow will become like (imitate) this Man, and they will be called by me (and they will consider Him to be called by Me) and they will join the others, even those who desire to change within themselves.
11. Regarding those who emerge from the left side of the vision, the meaning is this; there will be many from the (heathen) nations who will set their hopes on (trust in) Him. But those whom you saw from your progeny on the right of the vision who insulted Him and struck Him, many will be offended because of Him, but some will worship Him. And He will test those of your progeny who have worshipped Him in the twelfth hour at the end in order to shorten the age of ungodliness.
12. Before the age of the righteous begins to grow, my judgment will come upon the (nations/heathen) lawless (wicked) peoples through the people of your progeny who have been separated to me.

13. And in those days I will bring upon all creatures of the earth ten plagues, through misfortune and disease and the groans of their bitter grief. And this will be brought upon the generations of men because of the provocation and the corruption of mankind, because they provoke me. And then the righteous men of your progeny will survive in the number (amount/count) which is kept secret by me, and will hasten the coming of the glory of My Name to that place prepared before for those you saw destroyed in the vision.

14. And they will live and be established by the sacrifices of righteousness in the age of the godly, and they will rejoice in me continually, and receive those who return to me in repentance because their inner torment will be great for those who have wrongfully misused (mocked) them in this world.

15. And they will see the honor bestowed on those who are mine in the day of glory. Abraham, see what you have seen and hear what you have heard, and take knowledge of all that you have come to know.

16. Go to your inheritance for behold, I am with you to the age."

Chapter 30

1. While He was still speaking to me, I found myself on the earth again, and I said, " Eternal One! I am no longer in the glory on high.

2. Still there is one matter which my soul longs to know and understand that was not revealed to me."

3. And he said to me, "I will explain to you the things you desired in your heart to know which are the ten plagues that I prepared against the heathen nations, and which have been destined to begin at the passing of the twelfth hour of the age of the earth.

4. Hear therefore what I tell you because it will come to pass. The first is the sorrow and pain of (need) sickness;

5. The second, the massive burning and destruction of many cities;

6. The third, the destruction and pestilence (sickness) of animals (cattle);

7. The fourth, hunger of the whole world and its people;

8. The fifth, among the rulers, destruction by means of earthquake and the sword;

9. The sixth, the increase of hail and snow;

10. The seventh, wild bests will be their grave (animals will kill them);

11. The eighth, hunger and pestilence will change their course of destruction (alternate with destruction);

12. The ninth, punishment (execution) by the sword and flight in distress;

13. The tenth, thunder and voices and destructive earthquake.

Chapter 31

1. And then I will sound the trumpet in the air, and I will send my ELECT ONE (chosen one), and He will have all measure of my power (He will have one measure of all my power).

2. He will summon my people (who were despised) from all nations, and I will send fire upon those who have insulted them and who have ruled over them in this age. And those who have chosen my desire and kept my commandments will rejoice with celebrations (parties) over the downfall of the men who continued to followed after the idols.

3. And I will take those who have covered me with mockery and give them over to the scorn of the coming age.

4. I have prepared them to be food for the fires of Hades, and be in perpetual flight through the air of the depths of Hades (the underworld). And they will be the contents of a worm's belly (Azazel).

5. For they joined (a marital or sexual term) one to whom they had not been given to, and they abandoned the Lord who gave them strength.

Chapter 32

1. "Hear Me, Abraham, because you will see that in the seventh generation from you will go out into a strange land and the heathen will enslave and oppress them. And they leave the land of their slavery, after they have been mistreated for an hour of the age of ungodliness, and the heathen nation whom they will serve I will judge.

2. And the Lord said this too, "Have you heard, Abraham, what I told you, what your tribe will encounter in the last days?"

3. Abraham heard and accepted the words of God in his heart.

Apocalypse of Thomas

"The Apocalypse Of Thomas" is also called "The Revelation of Thomas." The differing names come from the fact that the word rendered "Apocalypse" means to reveal or make known. This is the same title given to the last book of the New Testament. Its title in Greek is best interpreted as "The Apocalypse of John," however the English book carries the title of "The Revelation of John," or simply, "Revelation."

Very little of the history of the Apocalypse of Thomas is known. The only reference to it in ancient writings seems to be a single citation by Jerome in his chronicles written in the eighth to ninth century A.D.

Two versions of the Apocalypse exist in Latin, the longer version seems to be a later development. The longer text makes use of metaphors and symbols similar to those used in the Book of Revelation. Both texts describe how the Earth will be destroyed and the dead will come back to life in the final days.

The composition of the Apocalypse of Thomas has two distinct streams of thought. It is akin to Daniel in its form of prophecy, which describes events contemporary with the author and continues them into the future; yet it is also akin to John when the text describes the signs of the end.

Historical references in the long text suggest a fifth-century date. The text speaks of a king who is a "lover of the law." The text refers to his two sons whose names begin with A and H. King Theodosius fits the bill and his sons have Latin names corresponding to the letters as follows: "The first is named with the first letter A (as in Arcadius,) the second with the eighth letter H, (as in Honorius.) The first will die before the second."

The reference to the Latin alphabet would suggest that it was the original language of composition. This would place the earliest possible date of writing (and most scholars agree) at about 300 – 400 A.D.

Several manuscripts and fragments of the Apocalypse of Thomas have been found. The text presented here is the best combination of many texts. Since some are shorter than others and many are fragments, it was thought that by combining all of the better known texts a complete, longer and more complete version could be presented.

The version presented here is based on a combination of the best manuscripts and translations found. They include the F. Wilhelm text of 1907, the E. Hauler work on the fifth century Vienna fragment, the Verona manuscript of eighth century, the 1755 Dionisi work, 1911 Dom Bihlmeyer text from Munich, and the Anglo-Saxon Old English version at Vercelli.

THE APOCALYPSE OF THOMAS

Chapter 1

1. This begins the letter of (from) the Lord to Thomas.

2. "Hear about the things that must happen in the last times. The world will be shared between kings, then after that when the hour of the end draws near there will be seven days of great signs in heaven, and the powers of the heavens will be moved.

3. There will be famine, war and earthquakes in various places, snow, ice, and tremendous drought. There will be many open conflicts among the peoples, blasphemy, unrighteousness, envy, evil, laziness, pride and excess, and everyone will speak in the manner that he wishes.

4. And my priests will fight among themselves, and will sacrifice to me with minds of deceit. Because of this I will not look upon them. The priests will see the people forsaking the house of the Lord and turning to the world.

5. They will venture into restricted places in the house of God. And they will claim many things and places for themselves that were lost and those things and places will become subject to Caesar in the way they were given before as poll-taxes in the cities, as it is with gold and silver.

6. And the chief men of the cities will be condemned and their possessions will be brought to the treasury of the kings, and it will be filled.

7. There will be disturbances throughout all the people, and there will be death. The house of the Lord will be forsaken, and their altars will be despised, so that spiders weave their webs on them.

8. The place of holiness will be dishonored and violated, the priesthood contaminated. Distress will increase and righteousness will be overcome.

9. Happiness will die and gladness will leave. In those days evil will abound. People will cater to those of status and wealth. Hymns will stop coming from the house of the Lord. Truth will cease. Greed will abound among the priests. No upright man

nor an upright priesthood will be found.

Chapter 2

1. Near the last days a king will arise. He will be a lover of the law who will not hold office for long but he will leave two sons.

2. The first is named with the first letter A (as in Arcadius,) the second with the eighth letter H, (as in Honorius.) The first will die before the second.

(Arcadius died in 408 A.D.- Honorius in 423 A.D. The somewhat uneventful life of Arcadius is of less importance than the significant developments that occurred during his reign. Born around 377 A.D. to General Theodosius, Arcadius and his younger brother, Honorius, ruled the eastern and western halves of the Roman Empire respectively from 395. Arcadius was proclaimed Augustus in January of 383 at the age of five or six. In the following year, his younger brother was born. Honorius achieved the office of consul posterior in 386. The chance for having his own two sons ruling both halves of Rome not only seemed practical and feasible, but such an arrangement would establish their father as the head of a new dynasty. With thoughts in that direction, Honorius was made Augustus in 393 and accompanied his father west in the summer of 394. Even though Arcadius was nearing maturity and the age of consent he was placed again under the guardianship of the Prefect of the East. In January of 395, Theodosius the Great died and his two sons took theoretical control of the two halves of the Roman Empire.).

3. After this, two princes will arise to oppress the nations. Under their hands a very great famine will occur. The famine will take place in the right-hand section of the east and that nation will rise up against another nation and be driven out from their own borders.

4. Again another king will arise. He will be a deceitful man. He will order a golden image of Caesar to be made, set up, and worshipped in the house of God. Martyrdoms will be widespread.

5. Then the faith will return to the servants of the Lord, and holiness will greatly increase but so will distress and pain increase.

6. The mountains will be comforted (will comfort them?) and will drop down the sweetness of fire from its face, so that the (predestined) number of the saints may be completed.

7. After a little space of time a king will arise out of the east. He will be a lover of the law. He will cause all good and necessary things to be in supply within the house of the Lord. He will show mercy to the widows and the needy.

8. He will order that a royal gift to be given to the priests. In his days (the days of the king) there will be abundance of all things.

9. After that a king will arise, this time in the southern section of the world, and will rule for only a short time. In his days the economy will bankrupt (treasury will fail) because of the wages of the Roman soldiers. And he will order the substance of all the older citizens be taken and given to the king so it could be distributed.

Chapter 3

1. After that there will be plenty of corn and wine and oil, but a tremendous lack of money, so that it would take the substances of gold and silver to buy corn, and there will be tremendous hunger (dearth). (Hyper-inflation is indicated here.)

2. At that time the sea level will rise greatly and communications will be cut off from man to man. The kings, princes and the captains of the earth will be nervous (troubled/ fearful), and no man will speak freely.

3. Grey hairs will be seen upon boys, and the young men will not respect or listen to the aged.

4. After that will arise another king, a deceitful man, who will rule for a short time. In his days there will be all manner of evils. There will be genocide of the race of men living in the east to Babylon (the death of the race of men from the east to Babylon).

5. Famine and death by the sword will follow from Chanaan (Canaan) to Rome. Then all the springs of water and all the wells will dry up (boil over) and be turned into dust and blood.

Chapter 4

1. The heaven will be moved and the stars will fall upon the earth. The sun will be cut in half like the moon, and the moon will not give light.

2. There will be great signs and wonders in those days when Antichrist draws near. These are the signs for those that live on the earth. In those days the pains of great and hard work like those of a woman in labor will come upon them.

3. Woe to them that build because they will not live in there buildings.

4. Woe to them that plow the ground because they labor for no cause (no results). Woe to them that marry because they will bring forth sons in the famine.

5. Woe to them that join house to house or field to field because all things will be consumed with fire. Woe to them that are not introspective (examine themselves and their actions) while time allows because after this they will be condemned forever.

6. Woe to them that turn away from the poor when he asks.

7. You will know that I am the Father most high and I am the Father of all spirits. As you will see, this is the beginning of the

latter age.

Chapter 5

1. These are the seven signs of the ending of this world. There will be in all the earth famine and tremendous disease and sicknesses of vast proportions.
2. All nations will take captives and men will fall by the edge of the sword.
3. The beginning of the days of judgment will make you wonder greatly.
4. At the third hour (The Jewish day starts around 6:00 P.M.) of the first day will be a loud and powerful voice in the firmament (sky/theater of stars) of heaven, and a large cloud of blood will come down out of the north, and loud thunder and powerful lightning will follow the cloud.
5. Blood will rain down on all the earth. These are the signs of the first day. *(There is some dispute as to whether this is a literal Sunday or Monday. It is assumed by the editor that Sunday is the first day.)*
6. And on the second day there will be a loud voice in the firmament of heaven, and the earth will be moved out of its place and the portals of the eastern part of heaven will be and a great power will be sent forth as if it were belched by the portals of heaven themselves and the power will cover all the heaven even until evening and there will be fear and trembling in the world.
7. These are the signs of the second day. In the third day at about the second hour, there will be a voice in heaven, and the vast depths of the earth will sound their voices from the four corners of the earth.
8. The first heaven will be rolled up like a scroll and will vanish quickly in an instant.
9. Smoke and stench of the brimstone in the chasms will darken the day until the tenth hour. Then all men will say, "I think the end draws near, that we will die." These are the signs of the third day.
10. And on the fourth day at the first hour, the eastern section of the earth will sound, the abyss will roar and all the earth be moved by a strong earthquake.
11. In that day all the idols of the heathen will fall along with all the buildings on earth. These are the signs of the fourth day.
12. And on the fifth day, at the sixth hour the thunder will be loud and sudden in the sky, and the stars (powers of light) and the sphere of the sun will be snatched away, and there will be total (vast) darkness over the world until evening, and the stars will be sent off their course.
13. In that day all nations will hate the world and all men will despise his life on the world. These are the signs of the fifth day.
14. On the sixth day there will be signs in heaven. At the fourth hour the firmament of heaven will be split from east to west. And the angels of the heavens will be looking out on the earth and they will open the heavens.
15. And all men will see the host of the angels above the earth looking out of heaven. Then all men will flee.
16. All men will flee to the mountains and hide themselves from the face of the righteous angels, and will say, "I wish the earth would open and swallow us!" These things will happen like this world has never seen since it was created.
17. Then they will see me coming from above in the light of my Father with the power and honor of the holy angels.
18. At my coming, the fires that border/restrain paradise will be removed because paradise is encompassed with fire.
19. And this is a perpetual fire that will consume the earth and all the elements of the world. Then they will be clothed, and be carried by the hand of the holy angels as I have told you before.
20. They will be lifted up in the air on a cloud of light, and will go with me into heaven rejoicing. They will continue in the light and honor of my Father.
21. There be gladness abounding with my Father and before the holy angels. These are the signs of the sixth day.

Chapter 6

1. Then will the spirits and souls of all men come out of paradise and will come on all the earth and every one of them will go to his own body where it is laid up, and every one of them will say, "My body lies here."
2. And when the loud voices of those spirits will be heard, like a huge earthquake (there will be a large earthquake) all over the world.
3. The mountains will be split in two from above and the rocks from beneath. Then every spirit will return into his own vessel and the bodies of the saints who have died (which have fallen asleep) will rise.
4. Then will their bodies be changed into the image and likeness and the honor of the holy angels, and into the power of the image of my holy Father.
5. Then will they be clothed with the garments of life eternal made from the cloud of light which has never been seen in this world, because that cloud came down out of the highest realm of the heaven from the power of my Father.
6. And that cloud will contain the beauty of all the spirits that have believed in me.
7. And on the seventh day at the eighth hour there will be voices in the four corners of the heaven. And all the air will be

shaken, and filled with holy angels, and they will make war among the heathen all the day long. And in that day my elect will be sought out by the holy angels and saved from the destruction of the world. Then all men (unbelievers) will see that the hour of their destruction draws near.

8. These are the signs of the seventh day. And when the seven days are passed by, on the eighth day at the sixth hour there will be a sweet and tender voice in heaven from the east. Then that angel will be revealed which has power over all the holy angels and all the angels will go out with him who is sitting upon a chariot made of the clouds of my holy Father and they will rejoice, running upon the air beneath the heaven to deliver the elect that have believed in me.

9. And they will rejoice that the destruction of this world has come.

10. Thomas, you must hear because I am the Son of God the Father and I am the father of all spirits. You must hear my signs that will come to pass at the end of this world.

11. The end of the world will come and the world will pass away before my elect depart out of the world. I will tell (have told) you openly (plainly) what will come, but when these things will come to pass even the princes of the angels do not know. It is now hidden from their sight as to what day the end will come."

12. The words of the Savior to Thomas are ended, concerning the end of this world.

2 Baruch - History

2 Baruch is also known as the Syriac Apocalypse of Baruch. It is part of the Jewish pseudepigraphical. It is a text written in the late first to early second century, after the fall of Jerusalem to the Romans in 70 AD.

It is not part of the canon of either the Jewish or "Western" Christian Bibles but is part of the Syriac Bible. Syriac Christianity is a distinctive and separate family. It is propagated in part by the Syriac language and culture as part of Near Eastern Christianity. The Aramaic origins borrowed much from early Judaism and Mesopotamian culture. As Christianity grew and was defined more with the Greek and Latin cultures and tongues, Syriac Christianity was persecuted.

2 Baruch is similar to Jeremiah. The lamentations and anguish seen within the text are attributed to a reaction to the fall of Jerusalem, and particularly the Temple in Jerusalem. According to the text, the Temple's sacred objects were rescued from destruction by angels, and await the temple's rebuilding.

The catastrophe of the Temple destruction caused the Jews to question their faith and their place in God's divine plan. The plundering and desecration of the temple by gentiles was tantamount to God's rejection of the Jews and called into question the very foundations of their faith.

If a religion holds that God's hand is in all things then one must resolves the question of why an omnipotent God allowed the destruction of his own temple, or the temple belonging to His people.

2 Baruch attempts to answer this question as it promises a Messiah (Anointed One) who will end the sinful ways and dominance of the heathens and re-establish the Jews as God's chosen people. Those who are truly called will be the righteous Jews who follow the Torah and its teachings.

The text presented below is a modern rendition based in part on R. H. Charles' work done in the early 1900's. Chapter and verse divisions have been redefined to provide more logical separations. Modern wording has replaced the more archaic phrasing in the text. The result was then compared to other authoritative works and the translation modified to provide the most accurate version possible.

2 Baruch

Chapter 1

1 And it happened in the twenty-fifth year of Jeconiah, king of Judah, that the word of the Lord came to Baruch, the son of Neriah, and said to him:

2 Have you seen all that this nation (people) are doing to Me, that the evils which these two tribes which remained have done are greater than (those of) the ten tribes which were carried away captive?

3 For the former tribes were forced by their kings to commit sin, but these two of themselves have been forcing and compelling their kings to commit sin.

4 For this reason, I bring evil upon this city, and upon its inhabitants, and it will be removed from before Me for a time, and I will scatter these people among the Gentiles that they may do good to the Gentiles. And My people will be chastened, and the time will come when they will seek the prosperity of this period (their times.)

Chapter 2

1 For I have said these things to you that you may tell Jeremiah, and all those that are like you, to leave this city.

2 For your works are to this city as a firm pillar, and your prayers as a strong wall.

Chapter 3

1 And I said: O Lord, my Lord, have I come into the world for this purpose that I might see the evils of my mother?

2 Not so, my Lord. If I have found grace in Your sight, first take my spirit that I may go to my father's and not witness the destruction of my mother.

3 For two things vehemently constrain me: for I cannot resist You, and my soul cannot behold the evils of my mother.

4 But one thing I will ask in Your presence, O Lord.

5 What will there be after these things? If You destroy Your city and deliver up Your land to those that hate us, how will the name of Israel be remembered?

6 Or how will one speak of Your praises?

7 Or to whom will Your law be explained and all things therein?

8 Or will the world return to the nature it had before, and the age revert to primeval silence?

9 And will the multitude of souls be taken away, and the nature of man not again be named? And where is all that which You said to Moses regarding us?

Chapter 4

1 And the Lord said to me: This city will be delivered up for a time, and the people will be chastened during a time, And the world will not be given over to oblivion.

2 Do you think that this is that city of which I said: On the palms of My hands have I graven you?

3 This building now built in your midst is not that which is revealed with Me, that which was prepared beforehand here from the time when I took counsel to make Paradise, and showed it to Adam before he sinned, but when he transgressed the commandment it was removed from him, as also Paradise.

4 And after these things I showed it to My servant Abraham by night among the allotted victims.

5 And again also I showed it to Moses on Mount Sinai when I showed him the likeness of the tabernacle and all its vessels.

6 And now, behold, it is preserved with Me, as also is Paradise.

7 Go, therefore, and do as I command you."

Chapter 5

1 And I answered and said: So then I am destined to grieve for Zion, For your enemies will come to this place and pollute your sanctuary, and lead your inheritance into captivity; And make themselves masters of those whom You have loved. They will depart again to the place of their idols, and will boast before them: And what will You do for Your great name?

2 And the Lord said to me: My name and My glory are to all eternity; And My judgment will maintain its right in its own time.

3 You will see with your eyes that the enemy will not overthrow Zion, nor will they burn Jerusalem, but be the ministers of the Judge for the time.

4 Now go and do what I have said to you.

5 And I went and took Jeremiah, and Adu, and Seriah, and Jabish, and Gedaliah, and all the honorable men of the people, and I led them to the valley of Cedron, and I explained to them all that had been said to me.

7 And they lifted up their voices, and they all wept.

8 And we sat there and fasted until the evening.

Chapter 6

1 And it came to pass the next day that the army of the Chaldees surrounded the city, and at the time of the evening, I, Baruch, left the people and I went out and stood by the oak.

2 And I was grieving over Zion, and lamenting over the captivity which had come upon the people.

3 Suddenly a strong spirit raised me, and carried me aloft over the wall of Jerusalem.

4 And I saw four angels standing at the four corners of the city, each of them holding a torch of fire in his hands.

5 And another angel began to descend from heaven, and said to them: Hold your lamps, and do not light them till I tell you.

6 For I am first sent to speak a word to the earth, and to place in it what the Lord the Most High has commanded me.

7 And I saw him descend into the Holy of holies, and take from there the veil, and the holy ark, and the mercy-seat, and the two tables, and the holy raiment of the priests, and the altar of incense, and the forty-eight precious stones, wherewith the priest was adorned and all the holy vessels of the tabernacle.

8 And he spoke to the earth with a loud voice: Earth, earth, earth, hear the word of the mighty God, And receive what I commit to you, And guard them until the last times so that when you are ordered you may restore them, so that strangers may not get possession of them.

9 For the time comes when Jerusalem also will be delivered for a time, until it is said, that it is again restored for ever.

10 And the earth opened its mouth and swallowed them up.

Chapter 7

1 And after these things I heard that angel saying to those angels who held the lamps. Destroy it and overthrow its wall to its foundations so that the enemy should not boast and say: We have overthrown the wall of Zion, and we have burnt the place of the mighty God.

2 And you have seized the place where I had been standing before.

Chapter 8

1 Now the angels did as he had commanded them, and when they had broken up the corners of the walls, a voice was heard from the interior of the temple, after the wall had fallen, saying:

2 Enter, you enemies. Come, you adversaries; For he who kept the house has forsaken it.

3 And I, Baruch, departed.

4 And after these things happened the army of the Chaldees entered and seized the house and all that was around it.

5 And they led the people away captive, and killed some of them, and bound Zedekiah the King, and sent him to the King of Babylon.

Chapter 9

1 And I, Baruch, came, and Jeremiah, whose heart was found pure from sins, who had not been captured in the seizure of the city.

2 And we ripped our garments, we wept, and mourned, and fasted seven days.

Chapter 10

1 After seven days the word of God came to me, and said to me:

2 Tell Jeremiah to go and support the people who are led captive in to Babylon.

3 But you remain here amid the desolation of Zion, and I will show you after these days what will occur at the end of days.

4 And I said to Jeremiah as the Lord commanded me.

5 And he indeed, departed with the people; but I, Baruch, returned and sat before the gates of the temple, and I lamented with the following lamentation over Zion and said:

6 Blessed is he who was not born, or he, who having been born, has died.

7 But as for us who live, woe to us, Because we see the afflictions of Zion, and what has befallen Jerusalem.

8 I will call the Sirens from the sea, And you Lilin, (Lilin, in Jewish myth, was the daughter of Lilith, Adam's first wife, and the demon Samael who is often identified with Satan) come from the desert. And you Shedim and dragons from the forests: Awake and prepare yourselves for mourning; and take up with me the dirges, and make lamentation with me.

9 You husbandmen, sow not again; and, O earth, wherefore gives you your harvest fruits? Keep within you the sweets of your sustenance.

10 And you, vine, why further do you give your wine; for an offering will not again be made there from in Zion. Nor will the first-fruits again be offered.

11 And do you, O heavens, withhold your dew, and open not the treasuries of rain?

12 And do you, O sun, withhold the light of your rays? And do you, O moon, extinguish the multitude of your light? For why should light rise again where the light of Zion is darkened?

13 And you, you bridegrooms, enter not in. And let not the brides adorn themselves with garlands. And you women, pray not that you may bear.

14 For the barren will above all rejoice, And those who have no sons will be glad, and those who have sons will have anguish.

15 For why should they bear in pain, only to bury in grief?

16 Why again should mankind have sons? Why should the offspring of their kind again be named; where this mother is desolate, and her sons are led into captivity?

17 From this time forward speak not of beauty, and do not discuss gracefulness.

18 Moreover, you priests, take you the keys of the sanctuary and cast them into the height of heaven; and give them to the Lord and say: Guard Your house Yourself. For we are found to be false stewards.

19 And you virgins who weave fine linen and silk with gold of Ophir (the place from where the fleets of Solomon brought gold), take with haste all (these) things and cast (them) into the fire, that it may carry them to Him who made them. And the flame send them to Him who created them, lest the enemy get possession of them.

Chapter 11

1 Moreover, I, Baruch, say this against you, Babylon: If you had prospered, and Zion had dwelt in her glory, the grief to us would have been great because you would be equal to Zion.

2 But now, the grief is infinite; and the lamentation measureless because you are prospered and Zion desolate.

3 Who will be judge regarding these things? Or to whom will we complain regarding that which has befallen us? O Lord, how have You borne (it)?

4 Our fathers went to rest without grief and the righteous sleep in the earth in tranquility.

5 For they knew not this anguish, nor yet had they heard of that which had befallen us.

6 Would that you had ears, O earth, and that you had a heart, O dust. That you might go and announce in Sheol (hell / place of the dead) and say to the dead: Blessed are you more than we who live.

Chapter 12

1 But I will say what I think and I will speak against you, O land, which are prospering.

2 The noonday does not always burn, nor do the rays of the sun constantly give light.

3 Do not expect [and hope] that you will always be prosperous and rejoicing. Do not be not greatly arrogant and boastful.

4 For certainly in its own season the divine rage will awake against you, even though now in long-suffering it is held in as it were by reins.

5 And when I had said these things, I fasted seven days.

Chapter 13

1 After these things I, Baruch, was standing upon Mount Zion, and a voice came from the height and said to me:

2 Stand up on your feet, Baruch, and hear the word of the mighty God.

3 Because you have been amazed at what has befallen Zion, you will therefore be certainly preserved to the conclusion of the times, that you may be for a testimony.

4 If ever those prosperous cities say: Why has the mighty God brought upon us this retribution?

5 You say to them: You and those like you who will have seen this evil; (This is the evil) and retribution which is coming upon you and upon your people in its (destined) time that the nations may be thoroughly beaten (smitten.)

6 And then they will be in anguish.

7 And if they say at that time: For how long? You will say to them: You who have drunk the strained wine, drink also of its dregs, the judgment of the Lofty One Who has no respect of persons.

8 On this account before he had no mercy on His own sons, but afflicted them as His enemies, because they sinned, then they were disciplined so that they might be sanctified.

9 But now, you peoples and nations, you are guilty because you have always trodden down the earth, and used the creation sinfully and wrongfully.

10 For I have always benefited you and you have always been ungrateful for the beneficence.

Chapter 14

1 And I answered and said: You have shown me the method (behavior / procedure) of the times, and that which will alter these things, and You have said to me that the retribution, which has been spoken of by You, will come upon the nations.

2 And now I know that those who have sinned are many, and they have lived in prosperity, and left the world, but few nations will be left in those times, to whom those words will be said which You have said.

3 For what advantage is there in this, or what evil, worse than what we have seen happen us can we expect to see?

4 But again I will speak in Your presence: What have they profited who had knowledge before You and have not walked in vanity as the rest of the nations, and have not said to the dead: "Give us life," but always feared You, and have not left Your ways?

5 They have been carried off, nor on their account have You had mercy on Zion.

6 And if others did evil, it was due to Zion, that on account of those who do good works should be forgiven, and should not be overwhelmed on account of the works of those who practice unrighteousness.

7 But who, O Lord, my Lord, will understand Your judgment, or who will search out the profoundness of Your way?

8 Or who will think out the weight of Your path?

9 Or who will be able to think out Your incomprehensible counsel?

10 Or who of those that are born has ever found the beginning or end of Your wisdom?

11 For we have all been made like a breath. For as the breath ascends involuntarily and again dies, so it is with the nature of men, who depart not according to their own will, and know not what will befall them in the end.

12 For the righteous justly hope for the end, and without fear leave this habitation, because they have with You a store of works preserved in treasuries.

13 On this account also these without fear leave this world, and trusting with joy they hope to receive the world which You have promised them.

14 But as for us --- woe to us, who also are now shamefully treated, and at that time look forward (only) to evil.

15 But You know accurately what You have done by means of Your servants; for we are not able to understand that which is good as You are, our Creator.

16 But again I will speak in Your presence, O LORD, my Lord.

17 In ancient times there was no world with its inhabitants, You did devise and speak with a word, and with that the works of creation stood before You.

18 And You did say that You would make man the administrator of Your works, that it might be known that he was by no means made on account of the world, but the world on account of him.

19 And now I see that as the world was made on account of us, and it abides, but we, on account of whom it was made, depart.

Chapter 15

1 And the Lord answered and said to me: You are rightly amazed regarding the departure of man, but you have not judged well regarding the evils which befall those who sin.

2 And as regards what you have said, that the righteous are carried off and the impious are prospered.

3 And as regards what you have said, "Man knows not Your judgment," on this account hear, and I will speak to you, and listen, and I will cause you to hear My words.

4 Man would not rightly have understood My judgment, unless he had accepted the law, and I had instructed him in understanding.

5 But now, because he transgressed knowingly on this ground that he worked, he will be tormented.

6 And as regards what you did say regarding the righteous, that on account of them has this world come, so also again will that which is to come, come on their account.

7 For this world is to them a strife and a labor with much trouble; and that accordingly which is to come, a crown with great glory.

Chapter 16

1 And I answered and said: O LORD, my Lord, the years of this time are few and evil, and who is able in his little time to acquire that which is measureless?

Chapter 17

1 And the Lord answered and said to me: With the Most High account is not taken of much time nor of a few years.

2 For what did it profit Adam that he lived nine hundred and thirty years, and transgressed that which he was commanded?

3 Therefore the multitude of time that he lived did not profit him, but brought death and cut off the years of those who were born from him.

4 Or wherein did Moses suffer loss in that he lived only one hundred and twenty years, and inasmuch as he was subject to Him who formed him, brought the law to the seed of Jacob, and lighted a lamp for the nation of Israel?

Chapter 18

1 And I answered and said: He that lighted has taken from the light, and there are but few that have imitated him.

2 But those many whom he has lighted have taken from the darkness of Adam and have not rejoiced in the light of the lamp.

Chapter 19

1 And He answered and said to me: So it was at that time he appointed for them a covenant. And He said to them: Behold I have placed before you life and death, and he called heaven and earth to witness against them.

2 For he knew that his time was but short, but that heaven and earth endure always.

3 But after his death they sinned and transgressed, though they knew that they had the law reproving them, and the light in which nothing could err, also the spheres (planets and stars?) which testify, and Me.

4 Now regarding everything that is, it is I that judge, but do not you take counsel in your soul regarding these things, nor afflict yourself because of those which have been.

5 For now it is the consummation of time that should be considered, whether of business, or of prosperity, or of shame, and not the beginning thereof.

6 Because if a man be prospered in his beginnings and shamefully treated in his old age, he forgets all the prosperity that he had.

7 And again, if a man is shamefully treated in his beginnings, and at his end is prospered, he remembers not again his evil treatment.

8 And again listen; though each one were prospered all that time all the time from the day on which death was decreed against those who transgress, and in his end was destroyed, everything would have been in vain.

Chapter 20

1 Therefore, behold! The days come, and the times will hasten more than the former, and the seasons will speed on more than those that are past, and the years will pass more quickly than the present (years).

2 Therefore have I now taken away Zion, that I may the more speedily visit the world in its season.

3 Therefore hold fast in your heart everything that I command you, and seal it in the recesses of your mind.

4 And then I will show you the judgment of My might, and My ways which cannot be known.

5 Go and sanctify yourself seven days, and eat no bread, nor drink water, nor speak to anyone.

6 Afterwards come to that place and I will reveal Myself to you, and speak true things with you, and I will give you commandment regarding the method (procedure / system) of the times; for they are coming and tarry not.

Chapter 21

1 And I went thence and sat in the valley of Cedron in a cave of the earth, and I sanctified my soul there, and I ate no bread, yet I was not hungry, and I drank no water, yet I thirsted not, and I was there till the seventh day, as He had commanded me.

2 And afterwards I came to that place where He had spoken with me.

3 And it came to pass at sunset that my soul (mind) took much thought, and I began to speak in the presence of the Mighty One, and said:

4 O You that made the earth, hear me; you that have fixed the firmament by the word, and have made firm the height of the heaven by the spirit, that have called from the beginning of the world that which did not yet exist, and they obey You.

5 You that have commanded the air by Your nod, and have seen those things which are to be as those things which You are (now) doing.

6 You that rule with great thought the hosts that stand before You; also the countless holy beings which You made from the beginning from the flame and fire, which stand around Your throne where You rule with indignation.

7 To You only does this belong that You should do whatsoever You wish.

8 Who causes the drops of rain to rain by number upon the earth, and alone know the conclusion of the times before they come; have respect to my prayer.

9 For You alone are able to sustain all who are, and those who have passed away, and those who are to be, those who sin, and those who are righteous as living and being past finding out.

10 For You alone live immortal and past finding out, and know the number of mankind.

11 And if in time many have sinned, yet others not a few have been righteous.

12 You know where You preserve the end of those who have sinned, or the conclusion of those who have been righteous.

13 For if there were this life only, which belongs to all men, nothing could be more bitter than this.

14 For of what profit is strength that turns to sickness, or fullness of food that turns to famine, or beauty that turns to ugliness?

15 For the nature of man is always changeable.

16 For what we were formerly now we no longer are, and what we now are we will not afterwards continue to be.

17 For if a conclusion had not been prepared for all, then their beginning would have been in vain.

18 Everything that comes from You, You informed me, and regarding everything about which I ask You, You enlighten me?

19 How long will that which is corruptible remain, and how long will the time of mortals succeed, and until what time will those who transgress in the world be polluted with much wickedness?

20 Command in mercy and accomplish all that You said You would bring, that Your might may be made known to those who think that Your long-suffering is weakness.

21 Show to those who do not recognize it, that everything that has befallen us and our city until now has been according to the long-suffering of Your power, because on account of Your name You have called us a beloved people.

22 Bring mortality to an end. Reprimand the angel of death, and let Your glory appear, and let the might of Your beauty be known, and let Sheol be sealed so that from this time forward it may not receive the dead, and let the treasuries of souls (the chamber of Guf, in Jewish mythology) restore those which are enclosed in them.

23 For there have been many years like those that are desolate from the days of Abraham and Isaac and Jacob, and of all those who are like them, who sleep in the earth, on whose account You did say that You had created the world.

24 And now quickly show Your glory, and do not put off what has been promised by You. When I had completed this prayer I was greatly weakened.

Chapter 22

1 After these things the heavens were opened, and I saw, and power was given to me, and a voice was heard from on high, and it said to me:

2 Baruch, Baruch, why are you troubled?

3 He who travels by a road but does not complete it, or who departs by sea but does not arrive at the port, can he be comforted?

4 Or he who promises to give a present to another, but does not fulfill it, is it not robbery?

5 Or he who sows the earth, but does not reap its fruit in its season, does he not lose everything?

6 Or he who plants a plant unless it grows till the time suitable to it, does he who planted it expect to receive fruit from it?

7 Or a woman who has conceived, if she bring forth untimely, does she not certainly kill her infant?

8 Or he who builds a house, if he does not roof it and complete it, can it be called a house? Tell Me that first.

Chapter 23

1, And I answered and said: "Not so, O LORD, my Lord."

2 And He answered and said to me: Why are you troubled about that which you know not, and why are you ill at ease about things of which you are ignorant?

3 You have not forgotten the people who now are and those who have passed away, so I remember those who are appointed to come.

4 Because when Adam sinned and death was the judgment against those who should be born, then the multitude of those who should be born was numbered, and for that number a place was prepared where the living might dwell and the dead might be guarded.

5 Before the appointed number is fulfilled, the creature will not live again for My spirit is the creator of life, and Sheol will receive the dead.

6 It is given to you to hear what things are to come after these times.

7 For truly My redemption has drawn near, and is not as distant as it was.

Chapter 24

1 The days come and the books will be opened in which are written the sins of all those who have sinned, and also the treasuries in which the righteousness of all those who have been righteous in creation is gathered.

2 For it will come to pass at that time that you will see, and the many that are with you, the long-suffering of the Most High, which has been throughout all generations, who has been long-suffering towards all who are born, like those who sin and those who are righteous."

3 And I answered and said: But Lord, no one knows the number of those things which have passed nor yet of those things which are to come.

4 For I know indeed that which has befallen us, but what will happen to our enemies I know not, and when You will visit Your works.

Chapter 25

1 And He answered and said to me: You too will be preserved till that time till that sign which the Most High will work for the inhabitants of the earth in the end of days.

2 This therefore will be the sign:

3 When a stupor will seize the inhabitants of the earth, and they will fall into many tribulations, and again when they will fall into great torments.

4 And it will come to pass when they say in their thoughts because of their much tribulation: The Mighty One doth no longer remember the earth yea, it will come to pass when they abandon hope, that the time will then awake.

Chapter 26

1 And I answered and said: Will that tribulation which is to be, continue a long time, and will it necessitate many years?

Chapter 27

1 And He answered and said to me: Into twelve parts (pieces or section) is that time divided, and each one of them is reserved for that which is appointed for it.

2 In the first section (piece) there will be the beginning of commotions.

3 And in the second section (piece) slayings of the great ones.

4 And in the third section (piece) the fall of many by death.

5 And in the fourth section (piece) the sending of the sword.

6 And in the fifth section (piece) famine and the withholding of rain.

7 And in the sixth section (piece) earthquakes and terrors and wanting (need for food, water, and shelter).

8 And in the eighth section (piece) a multitude of specters and attacks of the Shedim.

9 And in the ninth section (piece) the fall of fire.

10 And in the tenth section (piece) rapine and much oppression.

11 And in the eleventh section (piece) wickedness and hedonism.

12 And in the twelfth section (piece) confusion from the mingling together of all those things aforesaid.

13 For these slices of that time are reserved, and will be mingled one with another and reinforce one another.

14 For some will leave out some of their own, and receive (in its stead) from others, and some complete their own and that of others, so that those may not understand who are upon the earth in those days that this is the consummation of the times.

Chapter 28

1 Nevertheless, whosoever understands will then be wise.

2 For the measure and reckoning of that time are two parts (pieces or section) a week of seven weeks.

3 And I answered and said: It is good for a man to come and behold, but it is better that he should not come lest he fall.

4 But I will ask this also: Will he who is incorruptible despise those things which are corruptible? What happens in the case of those things which are corruptible, so that he might look only to those things which are not corruptible?

5 But if, O Lord, those things will certainly come to pass which You have foretold to me, show this to me also if indeed I have found grace in Your sight.

6 Is it in one place or in one of the sections of the earth that those things are come to pass, or will the whole earth experience them?

Chapter 29

1 And He answered and said to me: Whatever will befall the whole earth all who live will experience.

2 For at that time I will protect only those who are found in those same days in this land.

3 And when all is accomplished that was to come to pass in those sections, that the Messiah will then begin to be revealed.

4 And Behemoth will be revealed from his place and Leviathan will ascend from the sea, those two great monsters which I created on the fifth day of creation, and will have kept until that time; and then they will be food for all that are left.

5 The earth also will yield its fruit ten thousand fold and on each vine there will be a thousand branches, and each branch will produce a thousand clusters, and each cluster produces a thousand grapes, and each grape produces a cor (a unit of measure approximately 517 pints) of wine.

6 And those who have hungered will rejoice, moreover, they will behold marvels every day.

7 For winds will go forth from before Me to bring every morning the fragrance of aromatic fruits, and at the close of the day clouds distilling the dew of health.

8 And it will come to pass at that same time that the treasury of manna will again descend from on high, and they will eat of it in those years, because these are they who have come to the end of time.

Chapter 30

1 And it will come to pass after these things, when the time of the advent of the Messiah is fulfilled, that He will return in glory.

2 Then all who have fallen asleep in hope of Him will rise again.

3 And it will come to pass at that time that the treasuries will be opened in which is preserved the number of the souls of the righteous, and they will come forth, and a multitude of souls will be seen together in one assemblage of one thought, and the first will rejoice and the last will not be grieved. For they know that the time has come of which it is said, that it is the consummation of the times.

4 But the souls of the wicked, when they behold all these things, will then waste away the more.

5 For they will know that their torment has come and their perdition has arrived."

Chapter 31

1 And after these things I went to the people and said to them:

2 Assemble to me all your elders and I will speak words to them.

3 And they all assembled in the valley of the Cedron. And I answered and said to them: Hear, O Israel, and I will speak to you, And give ear, O seed of Jacob, and I will instruct you.

4 Forget not Zion, But hold in remembrance the anguish of Jerusalem.

5 For the days come, when everything exists will become the prey of corruption and will be as though it had not been.

Chapter 32

1 But if you prepare your hearts, so as to sow in them the fruits of the law, it will protect you in that time in which the Mighty One is to shake the whole creation.

2 Because after a little time the building of Zion will be shaken in order that it may be built again.

3 But that building will not remain, but will again after a time be pulled up by the roots, and will remain desolate until the time.

4 And afterwards it must be renewed in glory, and perfected for evermore.

5 Therefore we should not be distressed so much over the evil which has now come as over that which is still to be.

6 For there will be a greater trial than these two tribulations when the Mighty One will renew His creation.

7 And now do not draw near to me for a few days, nor seek me till I come to you.

8 And when I had spoken to them all these words, that I, Baruch, went my way, and when the people saw me leaving, they lifted up their voice and lamented and said: To what place do you depart from us, Baruch, and forsake us as a father who forsakes his orphan children, and departs from them?

Chapter 33

1 Are these the commands which your companion, Jeremiah the prophet, commanded you, and said to you:

2 Look to this people till I go and make ready the rest of the brethren in Babylon, against whom has gone forth the sentence that they should be led into captivity?

3 And now if you also forsake us, it were good for us all to die before you withdraw from us.

Chapter 34

1 And I answered and said to the people: Far be it from me to forsake you or to withdraw from you, but I will only go to the Holy of Holies to inquire of the Mighty One concerning you and concerning Zion; in the hopes I should receive more illumination and after these things I will return to you.

Chapter 35

1 And I, Baruch, went to the holy place, and sat down upon the ruins and wept, and said:

2 O that mine eyes were springs, and mine eyelids a spring of tears.

3 For how will I lament for Zion, and how will I mourn for Jerusalem?

4 Because in that place where I am now prostrate, of old the high priest offered holy sacrifices; and placed thereon an incense of fragrant odors.

5 But now our glorying has been made into dust, And the desire of our soul into sand.

Chapter 36

1 And when I had said these things I fell asleep there, and I saw a vision in the night.

2 I saw a forest of trees planted on the plain, and lofty and rugged rocky mountains surrounded it, and that forest occupied much space.

3 And over beside it arose a vine, and from under it there went forth a peaceful fountain.

4 Now that fountain came to the forest and was agitated into great waves, and those waves submerged that forest, and suddenly they pulled up by the roots the greater section (area) of that forest, and overthrew all the mountains which were around it.

5 And the height of the forest began to be made low, and the top of the mountains was made low and that fountain greatly overtook it, so that it left nothing of that great forest save one cedar only.

6 Also when it had cast it down and had destroyed and pulled up by the roots the greater part of that forest, so that nothing was left of it, nor could its place be recognized, then that vine began to come with the fountain in peace and great tranquility, and it came to a place which was not far from that cedar, and they brought the cedar which had been cast down to it.

7 And I saw that vine opened its mouth and spoke and said to that cedar: Are you not that cedar which was left of the forest of wickedness, and by whose means wickedness persisted, and did evil all those years, and goodness never?

8 And you kept conquering that which was not yours, and to that which was yours you never showed compassion, and you kept extending your power over those who were far from you, and those who ventured near to you held tightly in the toils of your wickedness, and you lifted yourself up always as one that could not be pulled up by the roots!

9 But now your time has sped by and your hour is come. Do you also therefore depart O cedar, after the forest, which departed before you, and become dust with it, and let your ashes be mingled together?

10 And now lay down in anguish and rest in torment till your last time comes, in which you will come again and be tormented still more.

Chapter 37
1 And after these things I saw that cedar burning, and the vine glowing and all around it the plain was full of unfading flowers. And I awoke and arose.

Chapter 38
1 And I prayed and said: O LORD, my Lord, You always enlighten those who are led by understanding.
2 Your law is life, and Your wisdom is right guidance.
3 Make known to me the interpretation of this vision.
4 For You know that my soul has always walked in Your law, and from my earliest days I departed not from Your wisdom.

Chapter 39
1 And He answered and said to me: Baruch, this is the interpretation of the vision which you have seen.
2 As you have seen the great forest which lofty and rugged mountains surrounded, this is the word.
3 The days come, and this kingdom will be destroyed which once destroyed Zion, and it will be subjected to that which comes after it.
4 After a time the kingdom will be destroyed, and another, a third, will arise, and that also will have dominion for its time, and will be destroyed.
5 And after these things a fourth kingdom will arise, whose power will be harsh and evil far beyond those which were before it, and it will rule many times as the forests on the plain, and it will hold firmly for a time, and will exalt itself more than the cedars of Lebanon.
6 And by it the truth will be hidden, and all those who are polluted with sinfulness will flee to it, as evil beasts flee and creep into the forest.
7 And when the time of its end and fall has approached, then the kingdom of My Messiah will be revealed, which is like the fountain and the vine, and when it is revealed it will root out the multitude of its host.
8 And concerning that which you have seen, the lofty cedar, which was left out of that forest, and the fact, that the vine spoke those words with it which you did hear, this is the word.

Chapter 40
1 The last leader of that time will be left alive, when the multitude of his hosts will be put to the sword, and he will be bound, and they will take him up to Mount Zion, and My Messiah will convict him of all his unlawful deeds, and will gather and set before him all the works of his hosts.
2 And afterwards he will put him to death, and protect the rest of My people which will be found in the place which I have chosen.
3 And his kingdom will stand for ever, until the world of corruption is at an end, and until the times aforesaid are fulfilled.
4 This is your vision, and this is its interpretation.

Chapter 41
1 And I answered and said: For whom and for how many will these things be or who will be worthy to live at that time?
2 I will speak to you everything that I think, and I will ask of You regarding those things about which I think.
3 I see many of Your people who have with drawn from Your covenant, and cast from them the yoke of Your law.
4 But I have seen others who have forsaken their vanity, and fled for refuge beneath Your wings.
5 What will become of them or how will the last time receive them?
6 Or perhaps the time of these will certainly be weighed, and as the beam inclines will they be judged accordingly?

Chapter 42
1 And He answered and said to me: "I will show you these things also.
2 To whom will these things be, and how many will they be?"
3 To those who have believed there will be the good which was spoken of before, and to those who despise there will be the contrary.
4 And regarding those who have drawn near (to Me) and those who have withdrawn (from Me) this is the word. As for those who were before subject (to Me), and afterwards withdrew and mingled themselves with the seed of mingled peoples, the time of these was the former, and was accounted as something exalted.
5 As for those who before knew (Me) not but afterwards knew life, and mingled (only) with the seed of the people which had separated itself the time of these (is) the latter, and is accounted as something exalted.
6 Time will succeed to (advance) time and season to season, and one will receive from another, and then with a view to the conclusion everything will be compared according to the measure of the times and the hours of the seasons.
7 Corruption will take those that belong to it, and life will take those that belong to it.
8 And the dust will be called, and there will be said to it: Give back that which is not yours, and raise up all that you have kept until its time.

Chapter 43

1 But, do you, Baruch, direct your heart to that which has been said to you, and understand those things which have been shown to you? For there are many eternal comforts for you.

2 You will leave this place, and you will pass from the regions which you see now, and you will forget whatever is corruptible, and will not again recall those things which happen among mortals.

3 Go and command your people, and come to this place, and afterwards fast seven days, and then I will come to you and speak with you.

Chapter 44

 1 And I, Baruch, went from that place and came to my people, and I called my first-born son and the Gedaliahs my friends, and seven of the elders of the people, and I said to them:

2 I go to my fathers according to the way of all the earth.

3 But you should not withdraw from the way of the law, but guard and admonish the people which remain;

4 that they should not withdraw from the commandments of the Mighty One, for you see that He whom we serve is just, and our Creator is no respecter of persons.

5 And see what has happened to Zion, and what has happened to Jerusalem.

6 For the judgment of the Mighty One will be made known, and His ways, which, though past finding out, are right.

7 For if you endure and persevere in fear (respect / awe) of Him, and do not forget His law, the times will change over you for good. And you will see the consolation (reward) of Zion.

8 Because whatever exists now is nothing, but that which will be is very great. For everything that is corruptible will pass away, and everything that dies will depart, and all the present time will be forgotten, nor will there be any remembrance of the present time, which is defiled with evil.

9 That which runs now runs to vanity, and that which prospers will quickly fall and be humiliated.

10 That which is to come will be the object of desire, and for that which comes afterwards will we hope.

11 For it is a time that will not pass, and the hour comes which abides for ever.

12 And the new world (comes) which is blessedness and does not turn to corruption for those who depart to it, but it has no mercy on those who depart to torment, and it leads to perdition those who live in it.

13 For these are they who will inherit that time which has been spoken of, and theirs is the inheritance of the promised time.

14 These are they who have acquired for themselves treasures of wisdom, and with them are found stores of understanding, and they have not withdrawn from mercy and the truth of the law have they preserved.

15 For to them will be given the world to come, but the dwelling of the rest, who are many, will be in the fire."

Chapter 45

1 Instruct the people as far as you are able, for that labor is ours. For if you teach them, you will quicken them.

Chapter 46

1 And my son and the elders of the people answered and said to me: Has the Mighty One humiliated us to such a degree as to take you from us quickly?

2 We will truly be in darkness, and there will be no light to the people who are left For where again will we seek the law, or who will distinguish for us between death and life?

3 And I said to them: I cannot resist the throne of the Mighty One; nevertheless, there will not be wanting in Israel for a wise man, nor a son of the law to the race of Jacob.

4 But only prepare your hearts, that you may obey the law, and be subject to those who in fear are wise and understanding;

5 And prepare your souls that you may not leave them.

6 For if you do these things, good things will come to you., which I before told you of; nor will you fall into the torment, of which I testified to you before.

7 But with regard to the word that I was to be taken I did not make it known to them or to my son.

Chapter 47

 1 And when I had gone out and dismissed them, I went from there and said to them:

2 I go to Hebron: for that is where the Mighty One has sent me. And I came to that place where the word had been spoken to me, and I sat there, and fasted seven days.

Chapter 48

1 And it came to pass after the seventh day, that I prayed before the Mighty One and said, O my Lord, You summon the advent of the times and they stand before You;

2 You cause the power of the ages to pass away, and they do not resist You; You arrange the method (progress / procedures) of the seasons, and they obey You.

3 You alone know the duration of the generations, and You do not reveal Your mysteries to many.

4 You make known the multitude of the fire, and You weigh the lightness of the wind.

5 You explore the limit of the heights, and You scrutinize the depths of the darkness.

6 You care for the number which pass away that they may be preserved and You prepare an habitation (abode) for those that are to be.

7 You remember the beginning which You have made, and the destruction that is to be You do not forget.

8 With nods of fear and indignation You command the flames, and they change into spirits, and with a word You quicken that which was not, and with mighty power You hold that which has not yet come.

9 You instruct created things in the understanding of You, and You make wise the spheres (orbs / heavenly bodies) so as to minister in their orders.

10 Armies innumerable stand before You and minister in their orders quietly at Your nod.

11 Hear Your servant and give ear to my petition.

12 For in a little time are we born, and in a little time do we return.

13 But with You hours are as a time (an age / eon) , and days as generations.

14 Be not angry with man; for he is nothing and take not account of our works; for what are we?

15 For by Your gift we come into the world, and we depart not of our own will.

16 For we said not to our parents, Beget us, Nor did we send to Sheol (place of the dead) and say, Receive us.

17 What therefore is our strength that we should bear Your rage or what are we that we should endure Your judgment?

18 Protect us in Your compassions, and in Your mercy help us.

19 Behold the little ones that are subject to You, and save all that draw near to You: Do not destroy the hope of our people, and do not cut short the times (occurrences) of our aid.

20 For this is the nation which You have chosen, and these are the people, to whom You find no equal.

21 But I will speak now before You, and I will say as my heart thinks.

22 In You do we trust, for Your law is with us and we know that we will not fall so long as we keep Your statutes.

23 To all time are we blessed at all events in this that we have not mingled with the Gentiles.

24 For we are all one celebrated people, who have received one law from One:

25 And the law which is among us will aid us, and the surpassing wisdom which is in us will help us.

26 And when I had prayed and said these things, I was greatly weakened. And He answered and said to me: You have prayed simply, O Baruch, and all your words have been heard.

27 But My judgment exacts its own and My law exacts its rights.

28 For from your words I will answer you, and from your prayer I will speak to you.

29 For this is as follows: he that is corrupted is not at all (is as though he does not exist);

30 He has acted sinfully in any way he could and has not remembered my goodness, and has not remembered My goodness, nor accepted My long-suffering.

31 Therefore you will surely be taken up, as I before told you.

32 For that time will arise which brings affliction; for it will come and pass by with quick vehemence, and it will be turbulent coming in the heat of indignation.

33 And it will come to pass in those days that all the inhabitants of the earth will be moved one against another, because they do not know that My judgment has drawn near.

34 For there will not be found many wise at that time, and the intelligent will be but a few. Moreover, even those who know will most of all be silent.

35 And there will be many rumors and tidings, not just a few. And the actions and deeds of spirits (phantoms) will be manifest, and many promises will be recounted. Some of them (will prove) idle, and some of them will be confirmed.

36 And honor will be turned into shame, and strength will be humiliated into contempt, and decency will be destroyed, and beauty will become ugliness.

37 And many will say to many at that time: "Where has the multitude of intelligence hidden itself, and to what place has the multitude of wisdom removed itself?"

38 And while they are thinking on these things, envy will arise in those who had not thought highly of themselves, and passion will seize him that is peaceful, and many will be stirred up in anger to injure many, and they will rouse up armies in order to shed blood, and in the end they will perish together with them.

39 And it will come to pass at the same time, that a change of times will manifestly appear to every man, because in all those times they polluted themselves. and they practiced oppression, and walked every man in his own works, and remembered not the law of the Mighty One.

40 Therefore a fire will consume their thoughts, and in flame will the control of their thoughts be tested; for the Judge will come and will not tarry, because each of the inhabitants of the earth knew when he was transgressing. But because of their pride they did not know My Law.

41 But many will certainly weep over the living more than over the dead.

42 And I answered and said: O Adam, what have you done to all those who are born from you? And what will be said to the first Eve who hearkened to the serpent?

43 For all this multitude are going to corruption, nor is there any numbering of those whom the fire will devour.

44 But again I will speak in Your presence.

45 You, O LORD, my Lord, know what is in Your creature.

46 Long ago You command the dust to produce Adam, and You know the number of those who are born from him, and how far they have sinned before You, who have existed and not confessed You as their Creator.

47 Their end will convict all of them, and Your law which they have transgressed will reward (revenge) them on Your day.

48 But now let us dismiss the wicked and inquire about the righteous.

49 And I will recount their blessedness and not be silent in celebrating their glory, which is reserved for them.

50 This transitory world which you live, has made you endured much labor in a short time, so in that world to which there is no end you will receive great light.

Chapter 49

1 Nevertheless, I will again ask mercy from You, O Mighty One, who made all things.

2 In what shape will those live who live in Your day? Or how will the splendor of those who are after that time continue?

3 Will they then resume this form of the present, and put on these members which hold us back, impeded us, and are now involved in evils, and in which evils are consummated, or will You possibly change these things which have been in the world as You also change the world?

Chapter 50

1 And He answered and said to me: "Hear, Baruch, this word, and write the remembrance of all that you will learn in your heart.

2 The earth will certainly return the dead, which it now receives in order to preserve them. It will not change their form, but it will return them in the same form it received them, and as I delivered them to it, so will it raise them.

3 Then it will be necessary to show the living that the dead have come to life again, and that those who had departed have returned again.

4 And when they have recognized those whom they now know, then judgment will grow strong, and those things which were spoken of prior will come to be.

Chapter 51

1 When that appointed day has passed, the appearance of those who are condemned will be changed and the glory of those who are justified will be shown.

2 For the appearance of those who act wickedly will become worse because they will suffer torment.

3 But the glory of those who have now been justified in My law, who have had understanding in their life, and who have planted the root of wisdom in their heart, their splendor for their face will be changed and glorified. Their face will be turned into the light of their beauty, that they may be able to take and receive the world which does not die, which is promised to them at that time.

4 Those that rejected My law, and stopped their ears that they might not hear wisdom or receive understanding will lament their actions over and above all things.

5 When they see those they were exalted over but who will be exalted and glorified more than they, they will both be transformed, the latter into the splendor of angels, and the former will waste away more as they wonder at the visions when they see the angelic forms.

6 For they will first see these things and afterwards depart to be tormented.

7 But those who have been saved by their works, and to whom the law has been a hope and understanding, and an expectation, and wisdom, and a confidence, will have wonders appear in their time.

8 For they will behold the world which is now invisible to them, and they will behold the time which is now hidden from them:

9 And time will no longer cause them to age.

10 For they will dwell in the high places of that world and they will be made like the angels and they will be made equal to the stars, and they will be changed into every form they desire from beauty to loveliness and from light to glorious splendor.

11 Before them the borders of Paradise will be spread out, and the beauty and majesty of the living creatures which are beneath the throne will be shown to them. They will see the armies of the angels who are held fast by My word, lest they should appear and are held fast by a command, that they may stand in their places until the time of their appearance comes.

12 There will be righteous excellence surpassing that of the angels.

13 For the first will receive the last. Those who have passed away will receive whom they were expecting. Those who had passed away and who we had head of we should expect to see.

14 For they have been delivered from the tribulation of this world and laid down their burden of anguish.

15 For what have men lost their life, and for what have those who were on the earth exchanged their soul?

16 They did not choose the time which is beyond the reach of anguish. But they chose that time whose results are full of lamentations and evils, and they denied the world which does make those who come to it grow old, but they rejected the time of glory. Thus that they will not have the honor of which I told you before."

Chapter 52

1 And I asked: How can we forget those whom are destined for sorrow?

2 Why do we mourn for those who die? Why do we weep for those who depart to Sheol?

3 Lamentations should be reserved for the beginning of the torment to come. Let tears be stored up for the time of destruction.

4 But even in the face of these things will I speak. What will the righteous do now?

5 Rejoice in the suffering which you now suffer. Why do you look for the decline of your enemies?

6 Make your soul ready for what is reserved for you, and prepare your souls for the reward which is stored up for you.

Chapter 53

1 And when I had said these things I fell asleep and I saw a vision. A cloud was ascending from a very large sea, and I kept looking at it and I saw it was full of black and white waters, and there were many colors in those same waters, and it looked like powerful lightning as seen from a summit.

2 And I saw the cloud passing quickly in short courses, and it covered all the earth.

3 Then, after these things that cloud began to pour all the waters that were in it upon the earth.

4 And I saw that all the waters which fell from it looked different.

5 To begin with, the waters were black and there was a lot for a time, and afterwards I saw that the waters became bright, but they were not as much, and after that I again saw black waters, and after these things again bright, and again black and again bright how this was done twelve times, but the black were always more numerous than the bright.

6 At the end of the cloud it rained black waters, and they were darker than had been all those waters that were before, and fire was mingled with them, and where those waters descended, they work devastation and destruction.

7 And after all of this I saw that lightning I had seen on the summit of the cloud seized hold of it and hurled it to the earth.

8 Now that lightning shone very brightly so that it illuminated the whole earth, and it healed those regions where the last waters had descended and work devastation.

9 And it took hold of the whole earth, and had dominion over it.

10 After these things I saw the twelve rivers were ascending from the sea, and they began to surround that lightning and to become subject to it.

11 And because of my fear I awoke.

Chapter 54

1 And I besought the Mighty One, and said: You alone, O Lord, know the deep things of the world before they happen. The things which occur in their times You bring about by Your word. You speed the beginning of these times against the works of the inhabitants of the earth, and the end of the seasons You alone know.

2 For You nothing is too hard. You do everything easily by a nod.

3 You, to whom the depths come as the heights, and whose word the beginnings of the ages serve;

4 You, who reveal to those who fear what You prepared for them so that they may be comforted.

5 You show great acts to those who do not know You. You break down the walls of those who are ignorant, and You light up what is dark, and You reveal what is hidden to the pure, who have submitted themselves to You and in Your law.

6 You have shown your servant this vision. Reveal its interpretation to me.

7 I know that for those things I have asked You about, I have received and answer. You have revealed to me with what voice I should praise You, and with what members of mine I should praises You and cause hallelujahs to ascend to You.

8 If my members were mouths and the hairs of my head were voices, I could not give you adequate food of praise, nor could I worship you as is befitting. I could never tell the glory of your beauty or praise you enough.

9 For what am I among men? Why am I counted among those who are more excellent than I that I have heard all these marvelous things from the Most High and numberless promises from Him who created me?

10 Blessed be my mother among those that bear, and let she that bare me be praised among women.

11 For I will not be silent in praising the Mighty One, and with the voice of praise I will tell His marvelous deeds.

12 For who does deeds like Your marvelous deeds, O God? Who comprehends Your deep thought of life.

13 With Your counsel You govern all the creatures which Your right hand has created. You have established every fountain of light beside You, and You have prepared the treasures of wisdom beneath Your throne.

14 Those who do not love your law perish justly. The torment of judgment awaits those who have not submitted themselves to Your power.

15 For though Adam first sinned and untimely brought death upon all, yet each of those who were born from him has prepared his own soul for the torment to come, and each one of them has chosen for himself glories to come.

16 It is certain that he who believes will receive reward.

17 But now, you wicked are bond for destruction because you will quickly be visited because you have rejected the understanding of the Most High.

18 His works have not taught you, and you have not been convinced by the skill of His creation which argued with you continually.

19 Adam is therefore not the cause, except for only his own soul, but each of us has been the Adam (man) of his own soul.

20 But You, O Lord, explain (open) to me those things which You have revealed to me, and inform me regarding that which I besought You.

21 For at the creation and until the end of the world, vengeance will be taken upon those who have done wickedness according to the wickedness in them, and You will glorify the faithful according to their faithfulness.

22 For those who are among Your own You rule, and those who sin You blot out from among Your own.

Chapter 55

1 Then, when I had finished speaking the words of this prayer I sat there under a tree that I might rest in the shade of the branches.

2 And I wondered and was amazed as I pondered the multitude of goodness which sinners who are upon the earth have rejected, and the tremendous torment they have hated, though they knew that they would be tormented because of the sin they had committed.

3 And when I was thought about these things the angel Ramiel, who presides over visions of truth, was sent to me, and he said to me:

4 Why does your heart trouble you, Baruch, and why do you have disturbing thoughts?

5 If the report you have only heard regarding judgment moved you so much what will you do when you see it manifest before yours eyes?

6 And if you expect the day of the Mighty One and you are so overcome just by the expectation, what will you do when you come to its actual occurrence?

7 If at the mention of the announcement of the torment of those who have done foolishly, you are so completely upset, how much more will you be when the event reveals astonishing things? And if you have heard announcements of the good and evil things which are coming and are grieved, what will you do when you behold the majesty that will be revealed, which will convict some and cause others to rejoice.

Chapter 56

1 Nevertheless, because you have asked the Most High to reveal to you the interpretation of the vision you have seen, I have been sent to tell you.

2 And the Mighty One has certainly made known to you the arrangement of the times which have passed, and are destined to pass in His world regarding those of deceit and of those of truth from the beginning of its creation to its end.

3 As you saw, a tremendous cloud ascended from the sea, and covered the earth. This is the duration of the world which the Mighty One made when he thought to make the world.

4 And when the world came into being and had left His presence (area of the throne), the time of the world was short, and was established according to the vast intelligence of Him who sent it.

5 And as you saw before on the summit of the cloud, black waters descended previously on the earth. This is the transgression that Adam the first man committed.

6 For since the time he transgressed, (early) untimely death came. Grief was named and anguish was prepared, pain was created, and trouble was born, disease took hold, and Sheol kept demanding to be renewed in blood The birth of children was brought about, and the passion of parents was its fruit, and the greatness of humanity was humiliated, and goodness died.

7 What can be blacker or darker than these things?

8 This is the beginning of the black waters which you have seen.

9 From these black waters, black was derived, and from the darkness, darkness was produced.

10 For he became a danger to his own soul and even to the angels.

11 At the time when he was created, they (the angels) enjoyed liberty.

12 But some of them descended, and mingled with the women.

13 And those who did so were tormented in chains.

14 But the rest of the multitude of the angels, of which there is no number, restrained themselves.

15 Those who lived on the earth perished together with them (the fallen angels) through the waters of the flood.

16 These are the first black waters.

Chapter 57

1 And after these waters you saw bright waters. This is the spring of Abraham and his generations and the birth of his son and his son's son and of those like them.

2 Because at that time the unwritten law was named among them. The words of the commandments were then fulfilled. Belief in the coming judgment was then born and hope of the world that was to be renewed was then created. The promise of life to come was began.

3 These are the bright waters, which you have seen.

Chapter 58

1 The third black waters you have seen are the mingling of all sins, which the nations committed after the death of those righteous men in the wickedness of the land of Egypt where they did unrighteousness. And they made their sons serve unrighteousness.

2 However, these also perished in the end.

Chapter 59

1 And the fourth bright waters you have seen are the birth of Moses, Aaron, Miriam, and Joshua the sons of Nun and Caleb and of all those like them.

2 For at that time the lamp of the eternal law shone on all those who sat in darkness, which announced to them that believe the promise of their reward, and to them that deny, the torment of fire which is reserved for them.

3 But also the heavens at that time were shaken from their place, and those who were under the throne of the Mighty One were disturbed, when He was taking Moses to Himself For He showed him many reproofs along with the principles of the law and the completion of the times, as He also showed to you. He also showed the pattern of Zion and its size, in the pattern of which the sanctuary of the present time was to be made.

4 But then also He showed him the size of the fire, the depths of the abyss, the weight of the winds, the number of the drops of rain,

5 How much of (His) anger (He) holds back, and the amount of long-suffering (He has), and the truth of (His) judgment,

6 And the origin of wisdom, the wealth of understanding, the wellspring of knowledge,

7 The height of the air, and the greatness of Paradise, the end of the ages, and the beginning of the day of judgment,

8 The amount of the offerings, the earths which are yet to come,

9 The mouth of Gehenna (hell), the place of vengeance, the place of faith, and the place of hope,

10 The visions of future torment, the multitude of angelic hosts, the flaming hosts, the splendor of the lightning and the voice of the thunders, the orders of the captains of the angels, the treasuries of light, and the changing of times, and the searching of the law.

11 These are the bright fourth waters which you have seen.

Chapter 60

1 The fifth black waters you have seen raining are the deeds the Amorites committed, and the spells of their incantations which they performed, and the unrighteousness contained in their mysteries, and the pollutions they mixed.

2 Even Israel was polluted by sins in the days of the judges, though they saw many slip from Him who made them.

Chapter 61

1 And the sixth bright waters you saw is the time in which David and Solomon were born.

2 That was the time of the building of Zion, the dedication of the sanctuary, the shedding of much blood of the nations that sinned, and many offerings which were given in the dedication of the sanctuary.

3 Peace and tranquility existed at that time, And wisdom was heard in the congregation.

4 The wealth of understanding was magnified in the congregations, and the holy feasts and ceremonies were carried out in blessings and great joy.

5 The judgment of the rulers was without guile and it was witnessed as such. The righteous law of the Mighty One was accomplished with truth.

6 And the land was then loved by the Lord because its inhabitants sinned not and it was glorified beyond all lands. At that time the city Zion ruled over all lands and regions.

7 These are the bright waters which you have seen.

Chapter 62

1 And the seventh black waters which you have seen is the perversion brought about by the counsel of Jeroboam, who decided to make two calves of gold:

2 And all the iniquities which kings who were after him sinfully worked,

3 And the curse of Jezebel and the worship of idols which Israel practiced at that time.

4 The withholding of rain, and the famines which occurred until women ate the fruit of their wombs,

5 And the time of their captivity which came upon the nine tribes and a half tribe because they were in many sins.

6 Then, Salmanasar, King of Assyria, came and led them away captive.

7 But regarding the Gentiles, how they always were sinful and wicked, and always unrighteousness would be wearisome to tell

8 These are the seventh black waters which you have seen.

Chapter 63

1 And the eighth bright waters you have seen is the correction and uprightness of Hezekiah King of Judah and the grace of God which came upon him.

2 When Sennacherib was aggressing in order to kill Hezekiah the deadly rage of Sennacherib troubled Hezekiah because a great population of the nations were with him .

3 When Hezekiah the king heard those things which the king of Assyria was devising and how he planned to come and seize him and destroy his people, the two and a half tribes which remained and how he wished to overthrow Zion Hezekiah trusted in his works, and had hope in his righteousness, and spoke with the Mighty One and said:

4 "Look! Sennacherib is prepared to destroy us, and he will boast and strut when he has destroyed Zion."

5 And the Mighty One heard him because Hezekiah was wise and so He listened to his prayer because he was righteous.

6 Then the Mighty One commanded Ramiel, His angel, who speaks with you.

7 And I went out and destroyed their population, whose count of their chiefs alone was a hundred and eighty-five thousand, and each one of them had an equal number that he commanded.

8 And at that time I burned their bodies from the inside out, but their clothing and weapons I preserved outwardly so that more wonderful deeds of the Mighty One might be seen, and that because of this His name might be spoken of throughout the whole earth.

9 And Zion was saved and Jerusalem delivered and Israel was freed from tribulation.

10 And all those who were in the holy land rejoiced, and the name of the Mighty One was mentioned and glorified.

11 These are the bright waters which you have seen.

Chapter 64

1 "The ninth black waters which you saw was all the wickedness which was in the days of Manasseh the son of Hezekiah.

2 His deed showed that he had no regard for God. He killed the righteous people, and he forcibly stole away judgment. He shed the blood of the innocent. He violently raped women, he overturned the altars and destroyed their offerings. He drove out their priests so that they could not minister in the sanctuary.

3 He made an image with five faces: four of them looked to the four winds, and the fifth on the top of the image was a passionate enemy of the Mighty One.

4 Then rage went out from the presence of the Mighty One to the intent that Zion should be pulled up by its roots, just like it happened in your days.

5 A decree went out from God against the two tribes and a half tribe that they should also be led away captive, as you have now seen.

6 The impiety of Manasseh increased greatly to the point that it removed the praise of the Most High from the sanctuary.

7 Because of this Manasseh was then named "the impious", and finally his dwelling was in the fire.

8 For though his prayer was heard by the Most High, finally, when he was thrown into the brass horse and the brass horse was then melted, it was meant as a sign to him for that time.

9 He had not lived perfectly. He was not worthy but this was done so that he might know by whom he should be tormented in the end.

10 For He who is able to reward is also able to torment.

Chapter 65

1 Manasseh acted without regard for God, and thought that in his time the Mighty One would not look into these things.

2 These are the ninth black waters which you saw.

Chapter 66

1 "And the tenth bright waters which you have seen is the purity of the generations of Josiah King of Judah, who was the only one at the time who submitted himself to the Mighty One with all his heart and with all his soul.

2 He cleansed the land from idols, and sanctified all the vessels which had been polluted, and restored the offerings to the altar, and the horn of the holy was lifted, and he exalted the righteous, and honored all that were wise in understanding, and brought back the priests to their ministry, and destroyed and removed the magicians and enchanters and necromancers from the land.

3 He killed the sinners that were living and they also took from the sepulchers the bones of the dead and burned them with fire.

4 He established the festivals and the Sabbaths in their sanctity. He burned their polluted ones in the fire and the lying prophets which deceived the people were also burned in the fire, and the people who listened to them when they were living, he threw them into the brook Cedron, and heaped stones upon them.

5 And he was zealous with passion for the Mighty One with all his soul. He alone was steadfast in the law at that time, so that he left none that was uncircumcised, or that sinned in all the land, all the days of his life.

6 Therefore he will receive an eternal reward, and he will be glorified with the Mighty One beyond many at a later time.

7 For on his account and on account of those who are like him were the honorable glories, of which you was told before, created and prepared.

8 These are the bright waters which you have seen.

Chapter 67

1 "And the eleventh black waters which you have seen is the calamity which is now befalling Zion.

2 Do you think that there is no anguish to the angels in the presence of the Mighty One because Zion was delivered up in such a way or that the Gentiles boast in their hearts, and amass before their idols? The gentiles say, 'she who so often trod down is now trodden down and she who reduced others to slavery is now a slave herself.

3 Do you think that in these things the Most High rejoices, or that His name is glorified?

4 But how will it effect His righteous judgment?

5 Yet after these things the gentile will seize and scatter them in the tribulation and they will dwell in shame in every place.

6 Because Zion is delivered up and Jerusalem has been laid waste, idols prosper in the cities of the Gentiles, and the cloud of smoke from the incense of the righteousness which the commands is now extinguished in Zion. In every place in and surrounding Zion there is the smoke of sin.

7 The King of Babylon who has now destroyed Zion will arise, and he will boast about being ruler over the people, and he will speak great things in his heart in the presence of the Most High.

8 But he will fall in the end. These are the black waters.

Chapter 68

1 The twelfth bright waters which you have seen is the word.

2 After these things occur a time will come when your people will fall into distress, so that they will all run the risk of perishing together.

3 Nevertheless, they will be saved, and their enemies will fall in their presence.

4 In time they will have much joy.

5 After a little space of time Zion will be built again, and its offerings will be restored again, and the priests will return to their ministry, and the Gentiles will come to glorify it, but not as fully as they did in the beginning.

6 After these things there will be the fall of many nations.

8 These are the bright waters which you have seen."

Chapter 69

1 The last waters which you have seen were darker than all that were before them. Those were after the twelfth number were collected together. They belong to the entire world.

2 The Most High made division from the beginning, because He alone knows what will happen due to the depth and breadth of the sin which will be committed before Him. He foresaw six kinds of them.

5 He also foresaw six kinds of good works of the righteous which will be accomplished before Him. They will go beyond those which He will work at the end and conclusion of the age.

6 For Him there were not black waters with black, nor bright with bright; because it is the end.

Chapter 70

1 Hear the interpretation of the last black waters which are to come after the all other black waters. This is the word.

2 The days will come when the time of the age is ripe that is the harvest of evil and good seeds. This is what the Mighty One will bring upon the earth and its inhabitants and upon its rulers. It is disturbing to the spirit and lethargy of heart.

3 They will hate one another, and provoke one another to fight, and the cruel will rule over the honorable, and those of low status will be honored above the famous.

4 Many will be delivered into the hands of the few, and those who were nothing will rule over the strong. The poor will have abundance beyond the rich, and the wicked will exalt themselves above the heroic.

5 The wise will be silent, and the foolish will speak. The ideas of men will not be heeded, nor will the counsel of the mighty. The hope of those who hope be will not be rewarded.

6 And when those things which were predicted have come to pass confusion will fall upon all men. Some of them will fall in battle, some of them will die in torment and pain, and some of them will be destroyed by their own people.

7 Then the Most High will reveal those peoples whom He has prepared from before and they will come and make war with the leaders that will be left.

8 And whosoever survives the war will die in the earthquake, and whosoever survives the earthquake will be burned by the fire, and whosoever survives the fire will be destroyed by famine.

9 But whosoever of the victors and the vanquished survives and escapes all these things mentioned before will be delivered into the hands of My servant Messiah.

10 For all the earth will devour its inhabitants.

Chapter 71

1 And the holy land will have mercy on its own, and it will protect its inhabitants at that time.

2 This is the vision you have seen and this is the interpretation.

3 I have come to tell you these things because your prayer has been heard by the Most High.

Chapter 72

1 Listen, regarding the bright lightning which is to come at the end, after the black waters. This is the word.

2 After the signs which you were told of before, when the nations become turbulent, and the time of My Messiah is come, he will summon all the nations. Some of them he will spare, and some of them he will kill.

3 These things will come upon the nations which are spared by Him.

4 Every nation which does not know Israel and has not trodden down the seed of Jacob will be spared.

5 This is because some out of every nation will be subjected to your people.

6 But all those who have ruled over you or have known you will be given up to the sword.

Chapter 73

1 When He has brought everything that is in the world low and has sat down on the throne of His kingdom in peace for the dispensation, joy will be revealed and rest will appear.

2 Healing will descend in the dew and disease will go away and anxiety, pain and sorrow will vanish from among men. Gladness will go forth through the whole earth.

3 And no one will again die before his time (young) nor will adversity suddenly befall any.

4 Judgments, reproach, arguments, revenge, spilling of blood, passions, envy, hatred, and things like these will be condemned when they are removed.

5 For it is these very things which have filled this world with evils. On account of these the life of man has been greatly troubled.

6 Wild beasts will come from the forest and minister to men, asps and dragons (serpents) will come out from their holes to submit themselves to a little child.

7 Women will no longer then have pain when they bear children or suffer torment when they yield the fruit of the womb.

Chapter 74

1 In those days the reapers will not grow weary, nor those that build be weary from work. The works will quicken itself and speed those who doe the work and give them much tranquility.

2 That which is corruptible will be destroyed. It is the beginning of that which is not corruptible.

3 Those things predicted will belong to this age. It is far removed from evil and near to things eternal.

4 This is the bright lightning which came after the last dark waters."

Chapter 75

1 And I asked: Lord, Who can understand Your goodness? For it is incomprehensible.

2 Who can look into your compassions, which are infinite?

3 Who can understand Your intelligence?

4 Who is able to explain the thoughts of Your mind?

5 Who of those born can hope to attain those things unless to him are merciful and gracious?

6 Certainly if You did not have compassion on those who are under Your right hand they could not come to those things. Only those who are in the numbers you named can be called.

7 We who exist know why we have come and so we submit ourselves to Him who brought us out of Egypt. We will come again and remember those things which have passed. We will rejoice in what has been.

8 But if we do not know why we have come and if we do not recognize the kingdom of Him who brought us up out of Egypt, we will have to come again and seek after those things which have been now. We will be grieved with pain again because of those things which have befallen.

Chapter 76

1 And He answered and said to me: This vision has been revealed and interpreted to you as you asked me to do, now hear the word of the Most High that you may know what is to befall you after these things.

2 You will surely leave this earth, but not by death, but you will be preserved until the end of the age (times).

3 Go up to the top of that mountain, and all the regions of that land, and the figure of the inhabited world, and the tops of the mountains, and the depth of the valleys, and the depths of the seas, and the number of the rivers will pass before you so that you may see what you are leaving, and to what place you are going. Now this will happen after forty days.

4 Go now during these days and teach the people as much as you are able so that they may learn and not die at the last age but they may learn in order that they may live at the last age."

Chapter 77

1 And I, Baruch, went from there and came to the people, and assembled them together from the greatest to the least, and said to them:

2 Hear, children of Israel! See how many of you are who remain of the twelve tribes of Israel.

3 To you and to your fathers the Lord gave a law more excellent than to all peoples.

4 Because your brethren transgressed the commandments of the Most High, He brought vengeance upon you and upon them. He did not spare the former, and the latter also He gave into slavery.

5 He did not leave a trace of them. But you are here with me.!

6 If you direct your ways correctly you will not depart as your brethren departed, but they will come back to you.

7 You worship He who is full of mercy. Your hope is in Him who is gracious and true. He will do good and not evil.

8 Have you not seen what has befallen Zion?

9 Do you think that the place (area/location) had sinned and that is why it was overthrown? Did you think that the land had performed foolishness and that because of this it was delivered up?

10 Don't you know it was because of you who sinned, that those things which did not sin were overthrown? It was because of you who performed wickedness that those thing which did not do foolish acts were delivered up to its enemies?

11 All the people answered and said to me, We can recall the good things which the Mighty One has done for (to) us. We do recall them. There are these things and those things which we do not remember that He in His mercy knows.

12 In spite of this, please do this for us, your people, write to our brethren in Babylon an letter of (religious) teaching and a scroll containing hope so that you may confirm them before you leave us.

13 The religious leaders (shepherds) of Israel have died, and the lamps which gave light are extinguished, and the fountains from which we drank have withheld their stream.

14 We are left in the darkness among the trees of the forest, the thirst of the wilderness."

15 And I answered and said to them: Shepherds and lamps and fountains come from the law: And though we leave, yet the law remains.

16 If you have respect for the law, and are determined to become wise, a lamp will not be lacking, and a shepherd (religious leader) will not fail, and a fountain will not dry up.

17 I will write also to your brethren in Babylon, and I will send by means of men, and I will write in like manner to the nine tribes and a half, and send by means of a bird.

18 And on twenty-first day in the eighth month that I, Baruch, came and sat down under the oak under the shadow of the branches, and no man was with me, but I was alone.

19 And I wrote these two letters; one I sent by an eagle to the nine and a half tribes;

20 And the other I sent to those that were at Babylon by means of three men.

21 And I called the eagle and spoke these words to it: The Most High has made you that you should be higher than all birds.

22 Now go and do not stop in any place, nor enter a nest, nor settle upon any tree, till you have passed over the breadth of the many waters of the river Euphrates, and have gone to the people that dwell there, and drop down to them this letter.

23 Remember that at the time of the deluge Noah received the fruit of the olive from a dove when he sent it out from the ark.

24 The ravens also ministered to Elijah, bringing him food as they had been commanded.

25 Solomon, in the time of his kingdom, when he wished to send or seek for anything, commanded a bird to go out and it obeyed him as he commanded it.

26 So do not tire, and do not turn to the right hand nor the left, but fly and go by a direct way, that you may preserve the command of the Mighty One, according as I said to you.

Chapter 78

1 These are the words of that letter which Baruch the son of Neriah sent to the nine and a half tribes, which were across the river Euphrates, in which these things were written.

2 Baruch the son of Neriah says to the brethren carried into captivity: "Mercy and peace."

3 I bear in mind, my brethren, the love of Him who created us, who loved us from ancient times, and never hated us, but above all taught us.

4 And truly I know that all of us in the twelve tribes are bound by one bond, inasmuch as we are born from one father.

5 Because of this I have been the more diligent to leave you the words of this letter before I die, so that you may be comforted regarding the evils which have come upon you, and also that you may be grieved regarding the evil that has befallen your brethren; and also that you may justify (understand and accept) His judgment which He has decreed against you that you

should be carried away captives. What you have suffered is a sentence disproportionably greater than what you have done. But this was done in order that, at the last times, you may be found worthy of your fathers.

6 So, if you consider that you have now suffered those things for your good, that you may not be condemned and tormented in the end, then you will receive eternal hope. But you must remove from your heart all error and vanity, for it was because of this you departed from here.

7 If you so do these things He will never forget you. He who gave His promise to those greater than us but on our behalf, that He will never forget or forsake us, but will gather together again those who were dispersed with much mercy.

Chapter 79

1 Now, my brethren, learn first what befell Zion and how Nebuchadnezzar King of Babylon came up against us.

2 For we have sinned against Him who made us, and we have not kept the commandments which he ordered us to keep. Yet he has not chastened us as we deserved.

3 For what befell you we also suffer in a the highest degree, for it happened to us also.

Chapter 80

1 And now, my brethren, I reveal to you that when the enemy had surrounded the city the angels of the Most High were sent, and they collapsed the fortifications of the strong wall and they destroyed the solid iron corners, which could not be pulled up.

2 Nevertheless, they hid all the vessels of the sanctuary, to prevent the enemy from possessing them.

3 And when they had done these things, they delivered to the enemy the collapsed wall, and the plundered house, and the burnt temple, and the people who were overcome because they were delivered up. They did this so the enemy could not boast and say: " In war. by force have we been able to lay waste to the house of the Most High."

4 They also have bound your brethren and led away them to Babylon, and have forced them to live there.

5 But we, being very few, have been left here..

6 This is the tribulation about which I wrote to you.

7 And certainly I know that alleviation of the pain of the inhabitants of Zion consoles you. You knew that they prospered so your consolation was greater than the tribulation which you endured in having to leave it.

Chapter 81

1 But regarding consolation, listen to my word.

2 I was grieving regarding Zion, and I prayed for mercy from the Most High, and I said:

3 How long will these things last for us? Will we always have these evils on us?"

4 The Mighty One acted according out of the multitude of His mercies and according to the vastness of His compassion. He revealed to me His word so that my suffering would be relieved. He showed me visions that I should not again endure anguish. He made known to me the mystery of the times. And the advent of the hours he showed me.

Chapter 82

1 Therefore, my brethren, I have written to you, that you may comfort yourselves regarding the multitude of tribulations.

2 You know that our Maker will certainly avenge us and do to our enemies according to all that they have done to us. The end, which the Most High will make is very near will bring His mercy and the final result of His judgment is by no means far off.

3 For now we see the numerous prosperity of the Gentiles, even though they act sinfully and they are like a vapor.

4 We see their great power, even though they act wickedly, But they will become like a drop (of water).

5 We see the strength of their might, even though they resist the Mighty One every hour. But they will be considered as spittle.

6 We consider the glory of their greatness, though they do not keep the statutes of the Most High. But as smoke will they pass away.

7 And we think about the beauty of theirs gracefulness, even though they give it with pollutions. But as grass that withers will they fade away.

8 And we consider the strength of their cruelty, though they do not remember what it brought or how it ended. But as a wave that passes (through them) they will be broken.

9 And we remark about how the brag about being mighty although they deny that it was God that gave it to them. But they will disappear like a passing cloud.

Chapter 83

1 Most High will certainly speed up His times, and He will bring on His hours.

2 He will judge those who are in His world with certainty, and visit truth on all their hidden works.

3 He will examine the secret thoughts, and those things of all the members of man which they laid up in the secret chambers. He will make them appear in the presence of all with reproof.

4 Allow none of these present things to ascend into your hearts, but above all let us be expectant because that which is promised to us will come.

5 Do not let us look to the delights of the Gentiles now but let us remember what has been promised to us in the end.

6 For the end of the times and of the seasons and whatever is with them will cease together.

7 The conclusion of the age will show the tremendous strength of its ruler, when all things come to judgment.

8 Prepare your hearts for that which you have believed or you will be in bondage in both worlds and you be led away captive here and be tormented there.

9 That which is now or which was, or which will come, is the evil fully evil, nor the good fully good.

10 For all your health of this time are turning into sickness, and all strength of this time is turning into weakness, and all the power of this time is turning into impotence, and the energy of youth is turning into old age and death.

11 Every beauty of gracefulness of this time is becoming faded and hateful, and every prideful kingdom of this time is turning into humiliation and shame, and every praise of the glory of this time is turning into the embarrassment of silence, and every empty bragging insult of this time is turning into a mute ruin.

12 Every delight and joy of this time is turning to worms and decay, and every noise of the proud of this time is turning into dust and lethargy.

13 Every possession of riches of this time is being turned into Sheol (hell) alone, and all the yearning of passion of this time is turning into death, and every lustful desire of this time is turning into judgment with torment.

14 Every trick and craftiness of this time is turning into a proof of the truth. Every sweet ointment of this time is turning into judgment and condemnation, and every love of lying is turning to rudely to the truth.

15 Since all these things are done now does anyone think that they will not be avenged? The consummation of all things will come to the truth.

Chapter 84

1 Because of these things I have revealed to you this while I am still alive. I have said these things that you should learn the things that are excellent, for the Mighty One has commanded me to instruct you. So I will set before you some of the commandments of His judgment before I die.

2 Do not forget that Moses called heaven and earth to witness against you and said:

3 If you transgress the law you will be dispersed, but if you keep it you will be kept." He also used to say these things to you when you, the twelve tribes, were together in the desert.

4 After his death you threw them away from you and because of this there came upon you what had been predicted.

5 Moses used to tell you tell you what would befall you, and now you see they have befallen you because you have forsaken the law.

6 Now, I also say to you after you have suffered, that if you obey those things which have been said to you, you will receive from the Mighty One whatever has been laid up and waiting for you.

7 Let this letter be for a testimony between me and you so that you may remember the commandments of the Mighty One and that there may be to me a defense in the presence of Him who sent me.

8 And remember the law and Zion, the holy land, your brethren, and the covenant of your fathers. Do not forget the festivals and the sabbaths.

9 Deliver this letter and the traditions of the law to your sons after you, as also your fathers delivered them to you.

10 At all times make requests and pray diligently and unceasingly with your whole heart that the Mighty One may hold nothing against you, and that He may not count the multitude of your sins, but instead remember the rectitude of your fathers.

11 If He doe not judges us according to the multitude of His mercies, woe to all us who are born.

Chapter 85

1 Do you not know that in the past and in the generations of old our fathers had helpers? They were righteous men and holy prophets.

2 We were in our own land and they helped us when we sinned, and they interceded for us with Him who made us, because they trusted in their works, and the Mighty One heard their prayer and forgave us.

3 But now the righteous have been gathered and the prophets have fallen asleep, and we also have gone out from the land, and Zion has been taken from us, and we have nothing now except the Mighty One and His law.

4 If therefore we direct and commit our hearts we will receive everything that we lost, and much better things than we lost by many times.

5 For what we have lost would decay, but what we will receive will not be corruptible.

6 Also, I have written to our brethren to Babylon that to them also I may testify to these very things.

7 Let all those things I said before be always before your eyes, because we are still in the spirit and the power of our liberty.

8 The Most High is long-suffering towards us here, and He has shown us what is to be, and has not concealed from us what will happen in the end.

9 Before judgment takes its own (costs), and truth that which is its due, let us prepare our souls so that we may possess and not be taken as a possession and that we may hope and not be put to shame, and that we may rest with our fathers, and not be tormented with our enemies.

10 For the youth of the world is past, and the strength of the creation already exhausted, and the occurrence of the times is very short because they have already passed by. The pitcher is near to the cistern, and the ship to the port, and the course of the journey nears the city, and life to its conclusion.

11 Prepare your souls, so that when you sail and ascend from the ship you may have rest and not be condemned when you depart.

12 When the Most High will bring about all these things there will not be a place left for repentance, nor a limit to the times or a duration for the hours, or a change of ways, or a place to pray, or a way to send pleas, or to receive knowledge, or give of love. There will be no place of repentance for the soul, nor prayers for offences, nor intercession of the fathers, nor prayer of the prophets, nor help of the righteous.

13 There is the sentence of decay, the way of fire, and the path which leads to Gehenna (place of burning/hell/destruction).

14 There is one law (made) by one. There is one age and an end for all who are in it.

15 Then He will save those whom He can forgive, and at the same time destroy those who are polluted with sins.

Chapter 86

1 When you receive this, my letter, read it in your congregations with care.

2 Meditate on it, and above all do this on the days of your fasts.

3 Keep me in mind by means of this letter, as I also keep you in mind in it, always. Fare you well.

Chapter 87

1 And when I had ended all the words of this letter, and had written it without tiring to its close, that I folded it, and sealed it carefully, and bound it to the neck of the eagle, and dismissed it and sent it.

The War Scrolls - The War Between the Sons of Dark and the Sons of Light

The War Scroll is a nine & a half foot scroll with as many as 19 columns, found in cave 1 at Qumran. It seems to be written as a sequel or expository to the eschatological war described in Dan 11-12. The author gives detailed instructions for a ritualized battle in which the "sons of light," led by Michael, destroy the Kittim, or the "sons of darkness," led by Satan. Many scholars identify the Kittim as an allusion to the Roman Empire.

The War Scroll, 1QM, was one of the original seven scrolls found in cave one by the Bedouin in 1947. The scroll has also been called "The War Rule" and "The War of the Sons of Light Against the Sons of Darkness." It was first published by E.L. Sukenik in 1954 and was re-edited as The Dead Sea Scrolls of the Hebrew University at Jerusalem: Hebrew University and Magnes Press, 1955.

The War Scroll contains nineteen columns and is written on five sheets. The end of the scroll is missing, but its beginning seems to be intact. At the bottom of the scroll there is damage and wear. The total length of the scroll in its present state is 9 feet, 8 inches. Since pieces of the scroll are worn away or missing, there are places within the translation where words are assumed to fit the flow of the sentence structure. These "best guess" words are noted by parentheses. If there are too many words missing or the meaning cannot be ascertained so that a "best guess" cannot be provided the missing words are denoted with the symbols (…).

The scroll is a mixture of apocalyptic and legal discussion. The scroll's main theological significance lies in the fact that this is a battle against the Sons of Light and the Sons of Darkness. Although most scholars believe the story is about good and evil, this in itself could allude to a struggle between the forces of life and death. In the end, God will intervene, conquer, and save his people. There are parallels to the books of Revelation and Daniel in the scroll and it is assumed that the author borrowed from Daniel as well as other material of the day, according to the date of the text's creation. All three books, Daniel, Revelations, and the War Scroll, share the common theme of life and light being victorious over evil and death. All point to fact that the outcome is already known, however, man must participate and is thus held culpable in the outcome.

There is controversy over the date of the scroll. Some say that the scroll was written between 50 B.C. and 50 A.D. because this is after the Roman Conquest around 63 B.C. but before the end of Herod's reign (4 B.C.). Another view is that the scroll was written after 70 A.D. and possibly as late as 135 A.D. However, most agree the date must be some time after the Roman Conquest, because the author of the scroll describes the weapons and battle tactics of the Roman army.

The War Scroll

The Master Rule of War.

The first attack of the Sons of Light will be initiated against the forces of the Sons of Darkness, which is the army of Belial. The troops are from Edom, Moab, the sons of Ammon, the Amalekites, Philistia, and the troops of the Kittim of Asshur. Supporting them are those who have violated the covenant.

The sons of Levi, the sons of Judah, and the sons of Benjamin, and those exiled to the wilderness, will fight against them with (?) against all their troops, when the exiles of the Sons of Light return from the Wilderness of the Peoples to camp in the Wilderness of Jerusalem.

Then after the battle they will go up from that place and battle the king of the Kittim and he shall enter into Egypt. In his time he will go out with great anger to do battle against the kings of the north, and in his anger he shall set out to destroy and eliminate the strength of Israel.

Then there will be a time of salvation for the People of God, and a time of the dominion of all the men of His forces, and a time of eternal destruction for all the forces of Belial. There shall be great panic among the sons of Japheth, and Assyria shall fall with no one to come to his aid, and the supremacy of the Kittim shall cease their wickedness and will be overcome without a single survivor. There shall be no survivors of all the Sons of Darkness.

Then the Sons of Righteousness shall shine into all ends of the world and continuing to shine forth until end of the appointed seasons of darkness. Then at the time appointed by God, His great brilliance will shine for all of eternity for the peace and blessing, glory and joy, and long life of all Sons of Light. On the day when the Kittim falls there will be a battle and horrible carnage before the God of Israel, for it is a day appointed by Him from ancient times as a battle of destruction for the Sons of Darkness.

On that day the congregation of the gods and the congregation of men shall engage one another and the outcome will be great carnage. The Sons of Light and the forces of Darkness shall fight one another to show the strength of God with the roar of a great multitude and the shout of gods and men. It will be a day of disaster. It is a time of distress for all the people who are redeemed by God. Compared to all their afflictions, no day exists like this and it is hastening to its completion as an eternal redemption. On the day of their battle against the Kittim, they shall go out to kill in battle.

In three groups the Sons of Light will stand firm to strike a blow at wickedness, and in three (parts) the army of Belial shall strengthen themselves to force the retreat of the forces of Light.

And when the banners of the infantry cause their hearts to melt, then the power of God will strengthen the hearts of the Sons of Light.
 In the seventh section, the great hand of God will overcome Belial and all the angels under his control, and all the men of his forces shall be destroyed forever. And this is the total destruction of the Sons of Darkness and service to God during the years of war.

And the holy ones shall shine forth in support of the truth in the annihilation of the Sons of Darkness. Then a great roar (proceeded them when) they took hold of the implements of war . (And the) chiefs of the tribes and the priests, of the tribe of the Levites, the chiefs of the tribes, the fathers of the congregation the priests and thus for the Levites and the courses of the heads (of the procession will go forth.)

The number of the congregation's tribe (family) is fifty-two. They shall set in the rank the chiefs of the priests after the Chief Priest and his deputy. There will be twelve chief priests to serve in the regular offering before God. The chiefs of the courses will number twenty-six and shall serve in their courses. After them the chiefs of the Levites who serve continually will number twelve in all, one to a tribe. The chiefs of their courses shall serve each man in his office. The chiefs of the tribes and fathers of the congregation shall support them, taking their posts continually at the gates of the sanctuary.

The chiefs of their courses, from the age of fifty upwards, shall take their posts with their commissioners on their festivals, which are new moons and Sabbaths, and on every day of the year. These shall take their posts at the burnt offerings and sacrifices, to arrange the sweet smelling incense according to the will of God, in order to atone for all His congregation, and to satisfy themselves before Him continually at the table of glory.

All of these they shall arrange at the time of the year of remission.

During the remaining thirty-three years of the war the men of renown, those called of the Congregation, and all the heads of the congregation's family shall choose for themselves men of war for all the lands of the nations.
They shall prepare capable men for themselves from all tribes of Israel to go out for battle according to the call to war (draft), year by year. But during the years of remission they shall not ready men to go out for battle, for it is a Sabbath of rest for Israel.

The war will be waged during the thirty-five years of service. For six years the entire congregation will wage it together. Then the war shall be waged with divisions during the twenty-nine remaining years. In the first year they will fight against Mesopotamia. In the second the war will be fought against the sons of Lud. In the third they shall fight against the rest of the sons of Aram, which are Uz, Hul, Togar, and Mesha, who are beyond the Euphrates. In the fourth and fifth years they will battle against the sons of Arpachshad. In the sixth and seventh year they shall fight against all the sons of Assyria and Persia and those of the east up to the Great Desert. In the eighth year they will fight against the sons of Elam. In the ninth year they will fight against the sons of Ishmael and Keturah. And during the following ten years the war shall be divided against all the sons of Ham according to their families (tribes/clans) and their territories. During the remaining ten years the war shall be divided against all sons of Japheth according to their territories.

This is the Rule of the Trumpets:
These are the trumpets of alarm for all their service for the (armies of God) and their commissioned men, (The men will be set in divisions) by tens of thousands and thousands and hundreds and fifties and tens. Upon the trumpets (they will rely and upon the sounds of the trumpets, which) they shall (create for the different sounds of) the trumpets of the battle formations, and the trumpets for assembling them when the gates of the war are opened so that the infantry will advance, and the trumpets for the signal of the slain, and the trumpets of the ambush, and the trumpets of pursuit when the enemy is vanquished, and the trumpets of reassembly when the battle returns.

On the trumpets for the assembly of the congregation they shall write, "The called of God." On the trumpets for the assembly of the chiefs they shall write, "The princes of God." On the trumpets of the formations they shall write, "The rule of God." On the trumpets of the men of renown (they shall write), "The heads of the congregation's clans."
Then when they are assembled at the house of meeting, they shall write, "The testimonies of God for a holy congregation."
On the trumpets of the camps they shall write, "The peace of God in the camps of His saints."
On the trumpets for their campaigns they shall write, "The mighty deeds of God to scatter the enemy and to put all those who hate justice to flight and a withdrawal of mercy from all who hate God."
On the trumpets of the battle formations they shall write, "Formations of the divisions of God to avenge His anger on all Sons of Darkness."
On the trumpets for assembling the infantry when the gates of war open that they might go out against the battle line of the enemy, they shall write, "A remembrance of requital at the appointed time of God."
On the trumpets of the slain they shall write, "The hand of the might of God in battle so as to bring down all the slain because of unfaithfulness."
On the trumpets of ambush they shall write, "Mysteries of God to wipe out wickedness."
On the trumpets of pursuit they shall write, "God has struck all of the Sons of Darkness, He shall not diminish His anger until they are annihilated." When they return from battle to enter the formation, they shall write on the trumpets of retreat, "God has gathered."
On the trumpets for the way of return from battle with the enemy to enter the congregation in Jerusalem, they shall write, "The joy of God in a peaceful return."

The description of the banners.
This is the Rule of the Banners of the entire congregation according to their formations. On the grand banner which is at the head of all the people they shall write, "People of God," the names "Israel" and "Aaron," and the names of the twelve tribes of Israel according to their order of birth. On the banners of the heads of the camps of three tribes they shall write, "the Spirit of God," and the names of three tribes. On the banner of each tribe they shall write, "Standard of God," and the name of the leader of the tribe and of its families. (On the banner of the divisions of the ten-thousand write the name of the leader of the ten thousand and the names of the chiefs (of the army) and his hundreds. On the banner of Merari they shall write, "The Offering of God," and the name of the leader of Merari and the names of the chiefs of his thousands.

On the banner of the thousand they shall write, "The Anger of God is loosed against Belial and all the men of his forces so that none remain," and the name of the chief of the thousand and the names of the chiefs of his hundreds. And on the banner of the hundred they shall write, "Hundred 0f God, the power of war against a sinful flesh," and the name of the chief of the hundred and the names of the chiefs of his tens. And on the banner of the fifty they shall write, "The might of God have ended the stand of the wicked" and the name of the chief of the fifty and the names of the chiefs of his tens. On the banner of the thousand they shall write, "The Anger of God is loosed against Belial and all the men of his forces so that none remain." When they go to battle they shall write on their banners," The truth of God", "The righteousness of God", "The glory of God", "The justice of God", and after these the list of their names in full.

When they draw near for battle they shall write on their banners, "The right hand of God", "The appointed time of God", "The tumult of God", "The slain of God." After these things, write their names in full. When they return from battle they shall write on their banners, "The exaltation of God," "The greatness of God," "The praise of God," "The glory of God," with their names in full.

The Rule of the banners of the congregation:
When they set out to battle they shall write on the first banner, "The congregation of God," on the second banner write, "The camps of God," on the third write, "The tribes of God," on the fourth write, "The families of God," on the fifth write, "The divisions of God," on the sixth write, "The congregation of God," on the seventh write, "Those called by God," and on the eighth write, "The army of God." They shall write their names in full with all their order. When they come near for battle they shall write on their banners, "The battle of God," "The recompense of God," "The cause of God," "The reprisal of God," "The power of God," "The retribution of God," "The might of God," "The destruction of all the prideful nations by God." And their names in full they shall write upon them. When they return from battle they shall write on their banners, "The deliverance of God," "The victory of God," "The help of God," "The support of God," "The joy of God," "The thanksgivings of God," "The praise of God," and "The peace of God."

The Length of the Banners.
The banner of the entire congregation shall be fourteen cubits long. The banner of three tribes shall be thirteen cubits long. The banner of a tribe, twelve cubits. The banner of ten thousand, eleven cubits. The banner of a thousand shall be ten cubits. The banner of a hundred shall be nine cubits. The banner of a group of fifty shall be eight cubits, The banner of a group of ten, shall be seven cubits.

The description of the shields.
And on the shield of the Leader of the entire nation they shall write his name, the names "Israel," "Levi," and "Aaron," and the names of the twelve tribes of Israel according to their order of birth, and the names of the twelve chiefs of their tribes.

The description of the arming and deployment of the divisions.
This is the rule for arranging the divisions for war when their army is complete to make up the forward battle line:
The battle line shall be formed of one thousand men. There shall be seven forward rows to each battle line, arranged in order. The station of each man will be behind his fellow. All of them shall bear shields of bronze, polished like a face mirror. The shield shall be bound with a border of woven work and a design of loops, the work of a skillful workman consisting of gold, silver, and bronze bound together and jewels in a multicolored brocade. It is the work of a skillful workman, artistically done. The length of the shield shall be two and a half cubits, and its breadth a cubit and a half. In their hands they can hold a lance and a sword.

The length of the lance shall be seven cubits, of which the socket and the blade constitute half a cubit. On the socket there shall be three bands engraved as a border of woven work; of gold, silver, and copper bound together like an artistically designed work. And in the loops of the design, on both sides of the band all around, shall be precious stones, a multicolored brocade, the work of a skillful workman, artistically done, and an ear of grain.

The socket shall be grooved between the bands like a column, artistically done. The blade shall be of shining white iron, the work of a skillful workman, artistically done, and an ear of grain of pure gold inlaid in the blade. The blade will be tapered towards the point. The swords shall be of refined iron, purified in the furnace and polished like a face mirror, the work of a skillful workman, artistically done, with figures of ears of grain of pure gold embossed on both sides. The borders shall go straight to the point, two on each side. The length of the sword shall be a cubit and a half and its width four fingers. The scabbard shall be four thumbs wide and four handbreadths up to the scabbard. The scabbard shall be tied on either side with thongs of five handbreadths. The handle of the sword shall be of choice horn, the work of a skillful workman, a varicolored design with gold and silver and precious stones.

And when the troupes take their stand, they shall arrange seven battle lines, one behind the other and there shall be a space between (the lines) thirty cubits, where the infantry shall stand the (infantry) forward and they shall sling seven times, and return to their position. After them, three divisions of infantry shall advance and stand between the battle lines. The first division shall heave into the enemy battle line seven battle spears. On the blade of the first spear they shall write, "Flash of a spear for the strength of God." On the second weapon they shall write, "Missiles of blood to make fall the slain by the wrath of God." On the third spear they shall write, "The blade of a sword devours the slain of wickedness by the judgment of God." Each of these they shall throw seven times and then return to their position. After these, two divisions of infantry shall march forth and stand between the two battle lines. The first division will be equipped with a spear and a shield and the second division with a shield and a sword, to bring down the slain by the judgment of God, to subdue the battle line of the enemy by the power of God, and to render recompense for their evil for all the prideful and arrogant nations. So the Kingship shall belong to the God of Israel, and for the holy ones of His people He shall act powerfully.

The description of the deployment of the cavalry.
Seven rows of horsemen shall also take position at the right and at the left of the battle line. Their ranks shall be positioned on both sides, seven hundred horsemen on one side and seven hundred on the other. Two hundred horsemen shall go out with one thousand men of the battle line of the infantry, and they shall take position on all sides of the camp. The total being four thousand six hundred men, and one thousand four hundred cavalry for the entire army arranged for the battle line; fifty for each battle line.

The horsemen with the cavalry of the men of the entire army, will be six thousand made up by five hundred to a tribe. All the cavalry that go out to battle with the infantry shall ride stallions that are swift, responsive, unrelenting, mature, trained for battle, and accustomed to hearing noises and seeing all kinds of scenes.

Those who ride them shall be men capable in battle, trained in horsemanship, the range of their age from thirty to forty-five years. The (head) horsemen of the army shall be from forty to fifty years old, and they shall wear helmets and greaves (shin protectors), carrying in their hands round shields and a lance eight cubits long, and a bow and arrows and battle spears, all of them prepared in (accordance to instructions) to shed the blood of their guilty slain. These are the (instructions of the horsemen.)

The recruitment and age of the soldiers.
The men of the army shall be from forty to fifty years old. The commissioners of the camps shall be from fifty to sixty years old. The officers shall also be from forty to fifty years old. All those who strip the slain, plunder the spoil, cleanse the land, guard the arms, and he who prepares the provisions, all these shall be from twenty-five to thirty years old.

No youth, nor woman shall enter their encampments from the time they leave Jerusalem to go to battle until their return. No one crippled, blind, nor lame, nor a man who has a permanent blemish on his skin, or a man affected with ritual uncleanness of his flesh; none of these shall go with them to battle. All of them shall be volunteers for battle, pure of spirit and flesh, and prepared for the day of vengeance. Any man who is not ritually clean in respect to his genitals on the day of battle shall not go down with them into battle, for holy angels are present with their army. There shall be a distance between all their camps and the latrine of about two thousand cubits, and no shameful nakedness shall be seen in the areas of all their camps.

The ministry of the priests and Levites.
When the battle line are arrayed against the enemy battle line shall be seven priests that will go through from the middle opening into the gap between the battle lines. The priests will be of the sons of Aaron, dressed in fine white linen garments, consisting of a linen tunic and linen breeches, and girded with a linen sash of twined fine linen of violet, purple, and crimson, and a multicolored colored sign and decorated caps on their heads, , and the garments for battle shall be the work of a skillful workman, and they shall not take them into the sanctuary.

The one priest shall walk before all the men of the battle line to encourage them for battle. In the hands of the remaining six shall be the trumpets of assembly the trumpets of memorial, the trumpets of the alarm, the trumpets of pursuit, and the trumpets of reassembly. When the priests go out into the gap between the battle lines, seven Levites shall go out with them. In their hands shall be seven trumpets of rams' horns. Three officers from among the Levites shall walk before the priests and the Levites. The priests shall blow the two trumpets of assembly.

(And there shall proceed men, with the words of) battle upon fifty shields, and fifty infantrymen shall go out from the one gate and (the) Levites, officers. With each battle line they shall go out according to all (if the) orders given. The men of the infantry (shall go out) from the gates and they shall take position between the two battle lines, and (join) the battle. (Then the priests shall raise the trumpets and) shall blow continually to direct the slingmen until they have completed hurling seven times.

Afterwards the priests shall blow on the trumpets of return, and they shall go along the side of the first battle line to take their position. The priests shall blow on the trumpets of assembly, and the three divisions of infantry shall go out from the gates and stand between the battle lines, and beside them the cavalrymen, Sat the right and at the left. The priests shall blow on their trumpets a level note, signals for the order of battle. And the columns shall be deployed into their formations, each to his position. When they have positioned themselves in three formations, the priests shall blow for them a second signal, a low legato note, signals for advance, until they come near the battle line of the enemy and take hold of their weapons. Then the priests shall blow on the six trumpets of the slain a sharp staccato note to direct the battle, and the Levites and all the people with rams' horns shall blow a great battle alarm together in order to melt the heart of the enemy.

With the sound of the alarm, the battle spears shall fly out to bring down the slain. Then the sound of the rams' horns shall quiet, but on the trumpets the priests shall continue to blow a sharp staccato note to direct the signals of battle until they have hurled into the battle line of the enemy seven times. Afterwards, the priests shall blow for them the trumpets of retreat, a low note, level and legato (smooth). According to this rule the priests shall blow for the three divisions. When the first division throws, the priests and the Levites and all the people with rams' horns shall blow a great alarm to direct the battle until they have hurled seven times. Afterwards, the priests shall on the trumpets of retreat blow for them. And they shall take their stand in their positions in the battle line and shall take up position (in front of the) slain, and all the people with rams' horns shall blow a very loud battle alarm, and as the sound goes out their hands shall begin to bring down the slain, and all the people shall quiet the sound of alarm, but the priests shall continue sounding on the trumpets of the slain to direct the fighting, until the enemy is defeated and turns in retreat.

The priests shall blow the alarm to direct the battle, and when they have been defeated before them, the priests shall blow the trumpets of assembly, and all the infantry shall go out to them from the midst of the front battle lines and stand, six divisions in addition to the division which is engaged in battle: altogether, seven battle lines, twenty-eight thousand soldiers, and six thousand horsemen. All these shall pursue in order to destroy the enemy in God's battle; a total annihilation.

The priests shall blow for them the trumpets of pursuit, and they shall divide themselves for a pursuit of annihilation against all the enemy. The cavalry shall push the enemy back at the flanks of the battle until they are destroyed. When the slain have fallen, the priests shall continue blowing from afar and shall not enter into the midst of the slain so as to be defiled by their unclean blood, for they are holy. They shall not allow the oil of their priestly anointment to be profaned with the blood of the vainglorious nations.

The description of the maneuvers of the battle divisions.
This is the Rule for changing the order of the battle divisions, in order to arrange their position against (the enemy in) a pincer movement and towers, line, arc, and towers, and as it draws slowly forward, then the columns and the flanks go out from the two sides of the battle line that the enemy might become discouraged. The shields of the soldiers of the towers shall be three cubits long, and their lances eight cubits long. The towers shall go out from the battle line with one hundred shields on a side. They shall surround the tower on the three front-most sides, three hundred shields in all. There shall be three gates to a tower, one on the right and one on the left. Upon all the shields of the tower soldiers they shall write: on the first, "Michael" and on the second, "Gabriel," on the third, "Cyril," and on the fourth "Raphael." "Michael" and "Gabriel" on the right, and "Raphael" and "Cyril" on the left. And (push the enemy) to the four(th) (side). They shall establish an ambush for the battle line of (three sides) and they shall fall on the slain.

The address of the chief priest.
(...) of our camps, and to keep ourselves from any shameful nakedness, and he (Moses) told us that You are in our midst, (and You are) a great and awesome God, plundering all of our enemies before us. He taught us from (the times) of old through out generations, saying, when you approach the battle, the priest shall stand and speak unto the people, saying, 'Hear O Israel, you are approaching the battle against your enemies today. Do not be afraid nor fainthearted. Do not tremble, nor be terrified because of them, for your God goes with you, to fight for you against your enemies, and to save you'" (See Deut. 20:2-4)

Our officers shall speak to all those prepared for battle, those of willing heart, to strengthen them by the might of God, to turn back all who have lost heart, and to strengthen all the valiant warriors together. They shall recount that which You have spoken by the hand of Moses, saying: "And when there is a war in your land against the adversary who attacks you, then you shall sound an alarm with the trumpets that you might be remembered before your God and be saved from your enemies (See Num. 10:9)

The prayer of the chief priest.
Who is like You, O God of Israel, in heaven and on earth, that he can perform like you do with Your great works and Your great strength? Who is like Your people Israel, whom You have chosen for Yourself from all the peoples of the lands? They are people sanctified by the covenant, learned in the statutes, enlightened in understanding. Those who hear the glorious

voice and see the holy angels, whose ears are open to hearing deep things. O God, You have created the expanse of the skies, the host of the stars (luminaries), the work of spirits and the dominion of holy ones, the treasures of Your glory in the clouds. (See 1 Enoch)

He who created the earth and the limits of her divisions into wilderness and plains, and (autumn, winter, and spring with its fruits; the circle of the seas, the sources of the rivers, and the rift of the deeps, 'wild beasts and winged creatures, the form of man and the generations of his seed, the confusion of language and the separation of peoples, the abode of families which have the inheritance of the lands, and holy festivals, courses of years and times of eternity.

(Only) these we know from Your understanding which (You have taught us.) And Your ears (listen) to our cry, for (the protection of) this house. Truly the battle is Yours, and by the strength of Your hand their corpses have been broken to pieces, without anyone to bury them. Indeed, Goliath the Gittitej a mighty man of valor, You delivered into the hand of David, Your servant, because he trusted in Your great name and not in sword and spear. For the battle is Yours. He subdued the Philistines many times by Your holy name. Also by the hand of our kings You rescued us many times because of Your mercy; not according to our works, for we have acted wickedly, nor for the acts of our rebelliousness. The battle is Yours, the strength is from You, it is not our own. Neither our power nor the strength of our hand have done valiantly, but rather by Your power and the strength of Your great valor.

Just as You told us in time past, saying: "There shall come forth a star out of Jacob, a scepter shall rise out of Israel, and shall crush the forehead of Moab and tear down all sons of Sheth (the noisy boasters), and he shall descend on Jacob and shall destroy the remnant from the city, and the enemy shall be a possession, and Israel shall do valiantly (Num. 24:17-19). By the hand of Your anointed ones, seers of things appointed, You have told us about the times of the wars of Your hands in order that You may glorify Yourself (and fight) among our enemies to bring down the hordes of Belial, the seven nations of empty, boasting, prideful nations, at the hand of the oppressed whom You have redeemed with power and retribution; and wondrous strength.

A heart that melts shall be as a door of hope. You will do to them as You did to Pharaoh and the officers of his chariots in the Red Sea. You will ignite the humble of spirit like a fiery torch of fire in a sheaf, consuming the wicked.
You shall not turn back until the annihilation of the guilty. In time past You foretold the appointed time for Your hand is powerful work against the Kittim, saying: And Assyria shall fall by a sword not of man, and a sword, 'not of men, shall consume him (Isa. 31: 8).

For into the hand of the oppressed You will deliver the enemies of all the lands; into the hands of those who are prostrate in the dust, in order to bring down all mighty men of (faithless) peoples, to return the recompense of the wicked on the head of (the guilty) to pronounce the fair judgment of Your truth on all sons of man, and to make for Yourself an everlasting name among the people.

(Give us victory in) wars, and to show Yourself great and holy before the remnant of the nations, so that they may know that You are God when You carry out judgments on (Gog and on all his company that are assembled all around us. For You will do battle against them from the heavens (and heap) upon them for confusion. For You have a multitude of holy ones in the heavens and hosts of angels in Your exalted dwelling to praise Your name.

The chosen ones of the holy people You have established for Yourself in a community. The number and The book of the names of all their host is with You in Your holy dwelling, and the number of the holy ones is in the abode of Your glory. Mercies of blessing (is with them) and Your covenant of peace You engraved for them with a stylus of life in order to reign over them for all time, commissioning the hosts of Your elect by their thousands and tens of thousands together with Your holy ones and Your angels, and directing them in battle so as to condemn the earthly adversaries by trial with Your judgments. With the elect of heaven they shall prevail.

And You, O God, are awesome in the glory of Your dominion, and the company of Your holy ones is in our midst for eternal support. We shall direct our contempt at kings, derision and disdain at mighty men. For the Lord is holy, and the King of Glory is with us together with the holy ones. Mighty men and a host of angels are with our commissioned forces. The Hero of War is with our company, and the host of His spirits is with our steps. Our horse riders are as the clouds and as the mist covering the earth, 'and as a steady downpour shedding judgment on all her offspring.

Rise up, O Hero, take Your captives, O Glorious One, take Your plunder, O You who do valiantly. Lay Your hand upon the neck of Your enemies, and Your foot upon the backs of the slain. Crush the nations, Your adversaries, and may Your sword devour guilty flesh. Fill Your land with glory, and Your heritance with blessing.

An abundance of cattle in Your fields; silver and gold and precious stones in Your palaces. O Zion, rejoice greatly, and shine with joyful songs, O Jerusalem. Rejoice, all you cities of Judah, open your gates forever that the wealth of the nations might be brought to you, and their kings shall serve you.

David was king and his praise was to ring out (shine):
All they that oppressed you shall bow down to you, and the dust of your feet they shall lick. O daughters of my people shout out with a voice of joy, adorn yourselves with ornaments of glory Rule over the kingdom, and Israel to reign eternally. (. . .) them the mighty men of war, O Jerusalem be exalted above the heavens, O Lord, and let Your glory be above all the earth.

The blessings of the war recited by all the leaders after the victory.
And then the Chief Priest shall stand and his brothers the priests, the Levites, and all the elders of the Army with him. They shall bless from their position, the God of Israel and all His works of truth, and they shall curse Belial there and all the spirits of his forces.

And they shall say response: "Blessed is the God of Israel for all His holy purpose and His works of truth. And blessed are those who serve Him righteously. who know Him by faith. And cursed is Belial for his contentious purpose, and accursed for his reprehensible rule. And cursed are all the spirits of his lot for their wicked purpose. Accursed are they for all their filthy dirty service. For they are the lot of darkness, but the lot of God is light eternal. You are the God of our fathers. We bless Your name forever, for we are an eternal people. You made a covenant with our fathers, and will establish it for their seed throughout the ages of eternity. In all the testimonies of Your glory there has been remembrance of Your kindness in our midst as an assistance to the remnant and the survivors for the sake of Your covenant and to recount Your works of truth and the judgments of Your wondrous strength.

And You, O God, created us for Yourself as an eternal people, and into the lot of light You cast us in accordance with Your truth. You appointed the Prince of Light from of old to assist us, for in His lot are all sons of righteousness and all spirits of truth are in his dominion.

You yourself made Belial for the pit, an angel of malevolence, his dominion is in darkness and his counsel is to condemn and convict. All the spirits of his lot are the angels of destruction who walk in accord with the rule of darkness, for it is their only desire. But we, in the lot of Your truth, rejoice in Your mighty hand. We rejoice in Your salvation, and revel in Your help and Your peace. Who is like You in strength, O God of Israel, and yet Your mighty hand is with the oppressed. What angel or prince is like You for Your effectual support, for of old You appointed for Yourself a day of great battle to support truth and to destroy iniquity, to bring darkness low and to lend might to light, and for an eternal stand, and to annihilate all the Sons of Darkness and bring joy to all the Sons of Light for You Yourself designated us for an appointed time like the fire of His fury against the idols of Egypt.

The blessings of the war recited by all the leaders in the morning before the battle. After they have withdrawn from the slain to enter the camp, all of them shall sing the hymn of return. In the morning they shall wash their clothes, cleanse themselves of the blood of the sinful bodies, and return to the place where they had stood, where they had formed the battle line before the slain of the enemy fell.

There they shall all bless the God of Israel and together they shall joyously exalt His name. They shall say in response: "Blessed is the God of Israel, who guards loving-kindness for His covenant and the appointed times of salvation for the people He redeems.

He has called those who stumble unto wondrous accomplishments, and
He has gathered a congregation of nations for annihilation without remnant in order to raise up in judgment he whose heart has melted, to open a mouth for the dumb to sing God's mighty deeds, and to teach feeble hands warfare. He gives those whose knees shake strength to stand, and strengthens those who have been beaten from the hips to the shoulder.

Among the poor in spirit (there is not) a hard heart, and by those whose way is perfect shall all wicked nations come to an end. There will be no place for all their mighty men. But we are the remnant of Your people. Blessed is Your name, O God of loving-kindness, the One who kept the covenant for our forefathers. Throughout all our generations You have made Your mercies wondrous for the remnant of the people during the dominion of Belial. With all the mysteries of his hatred they have not led us astray from Your covenant. His spirits of destruction You have driven away from us. And when the men of his dominion condemned themselves, You have preserved the lives of Your redeemed. You raised up the small fallen by Your strength, but those who are great in height You will cut down to humble them. And there is no rescuer for all their mighty men, and no place of refuge for their swift ones. To their honored men You will return shame, and all their vain existence shall be as nothing.

But we, Your holy people, shall praise Your name for Your works of truth. Because of Your mighty deeds we shall exalt your splendor in epochs and appointed times of eternity, at the beginning of day, at night and at dawn and dusk. For Your glorious purpose is great and Your wondrous mysteries are in Your high heavens, to raise up those for Yourself from the dust and to humble those of the gods.

Rise up, rise up, O God of gods, and raise Yourself in power, O King of Kings (and) let all the Sons of Darkness scatter from before You. Let the light of Your majesty shine forever upon gods and men, as a fire burning in the dark places of the damned. Let it burn the damned of Sheol, (who are) eternal burning among the transgressors (throughout) all the appointed times of eternity."

They shall repeat all the thanksgiving hymns of battle there and then return to their camps. For it is a time of distress for Israel, a fixed time of battle against all the nations. The purpose of God is eternal redemption, and annihilation for all nations of wickedness. All those prepared for battle shall set out and camp opposite the king of the Kittim and all the forces of Belial that are assembled with him for a day of vengeance by the sword of God.
The final battle the first engagement.

Then the Chief Priest shall stand, and with him his brothers the priests, the Levites, and all the men of the army. He shall read aloud the prayer for the appointed time of battle, as is written in the book 'The Rule of His Time", including all the words of their thanksgivings. Then he shall form there all the battle lines, as written in "The Book of the War."
Then the priest appointed for the time of vengeance by all his brothers shall walk about and encourage them for the battle, and he shall say in response: "Be strong and courageous as warriors. Fear not, nor be discouraged and let not your heart be faint.

Do not panic, neither be alarmed because of them. Do not turn back nor flee from them. For they are a wicked congregation, all their deeds are in darkness; it is their desire. They have established all their refuge in a lie, their strength is as smoke that vanishes, and all their vast assembly is as chaff which blows away (and they will become a) desolation, and shall not be found.

Every creature of greed shall wither quickly away like a flower at harvest time. Come, strengthen yourselves for the battle of God, for this day is an appointed time of battle for God against all the nations and bring judgment upon all flesh. The God of Israel is raising His hand in His wondrous strength against all the spirits of wickedness and the mighty ones of the gods are girding themselves for battle, and the formations of the holy ones are readying themselves for a day of vengeance against the God of Israel (but He will hasten) to remove Belial in his hell until every source of (him) is come to an end. For the God of Israel has called out a sword against all the nations, and by the holy ones of His people He will do mightily."

They shall carry out all the Rule on that day at the place where they stand opposite the camps of the Kittim. Then the priests shall blow for them the trumpets of remembrance. The gates of war shall open, and the infantry shall go out and stand in columns between the battle lines. (and stand in the gap.)

The priests shall blow for them a signal for the formation and the columns shall deploy at the sound of the trumpets until each man has taken his station.

Then the priests shall blow for them a second signal, (which is the signal) for confrontation. When they stand near the battle line of the Kittim, within throwing range, each man shall raise his hand with his weapon of war.

Then the six priests shall blow on the trumpets of the slain a sharp staccato note to direct the fighting. The Levites and the all the people with rams' horns shall blow a battle signal, a loud noise. As the sound goes forth, the infantry shall begin to bring down the slain of the Kittim, and all the people shall cease the signal, but the priests shall continue blowing on the trumpets of the slain and the battle shall prevail against the Kittim.

The final battle the second engagement.
When Belial prepares himself to assist the Sons of Darkness, and the slain among the infantry begin to fall by God's mysteries, to test by these mysteries and all those appointed for battle, the priests shall blow the trumpets of assembly so that another battle line might go forth as a battle reserve, and they shall take up position between the battle lines.

For those employed in battle they shall blow a signal to return. Then the Chief Priest shall approach and stand before the battle line, and shall encourage their heart by the wondrous might of God and fortify their hands for His battle. And he shall say in response: "Blessed is God, for He tests the heart of His people in the crucible. And (do) not (worry about) your slain.

For you have obeyed, from of old, the mysteries of God.

Now as for you, take courage and stand in the gap, do not fear when God strengthens (you, for in the) land He shall appoint their retribution with burning (for) those tested by the crucible. He shall sharpen the implements of war, and they shall not become blunt until all the nations off wickedness come to an end.

But, as for you, remember the judgment of Nadab and Abihu, the sons of Aaron, by whose judgment God showed Himself holy before all the people.
But Eleazar and Ithamar He preserved for Himself for an eternal covenant of priesthood. But, as for you, take courage and do not fear them, for their end is emptiness and their desire is for the void. Their support is without strength and they do not know that from the God of Israel is all that is and that will be. He (alone is) in all which exists for eternity. Today is His appointed time to subdue and to humiliate the prince of the realms of wickedness. He will send eternal support to the company of His redeemed by the power of the majestic angel of the authority of Michael. By eternal light He shall joyfully light up the covenant of Israel peace and blessing for the lot of God to exalt the authority of Michael among the gods and the dominion of Israel among all flesh. Righteousness shall rejoice on high, and all sons of His truth shall rejoice in eternal knowledge. But as for you, O sons of His covenant, take courage in God's crucible, until He shall wave His hand and complete His fiery trials; His mysteries concerning your existence."

The final battle the third engagement.
And after these words, the priests shall blow for them a signal to form the divisions of the battle line. The columns shall be deployed at the sound of the trumpets, until each man has taken his station. Then the priests shall blow another signal on the trumpets, that I the signal for confrontation. When the infantry has approached the battle line of the Kittim, within throwing range, each man shall raise his hand with his weapon.

Then the priests shall blow on the trumpets of the slain and the Levites and all the people with rams' horns shall sound a signal for battle. The infantry shall attack the army of the Kittim, and as the sound of the signal goes forth,
they shall begin to bring down their slain. Then all the people shall cease the sound of the signal, while the priests continuously blow on the trumpets of the slain, and the battle prevails against the Kittim, and the troops of Belial are defeated before them. Thus in the third lot (the army are destined to fall slain.)

Author's note: The sections of the final battle involving the fourth, fifth, and sixth engagements are not legible. The codex has large pieces missing. Nothing of these engagements is preserved.

The final battle the seventh engagement.
… And in the seventh lot, the great hand of God shall be lifted up against Belial and against all the forces of his dominion for an eternal slaughter. The shout of the holy ones (will go forth) when they pursue Assyria. Then the sons of Japheth shall fall, never to rise again, and the Kitum shall be crushed without remnant or survivor. So the God of Israel shall raise His hand against the entire multitude of Belial. At that time the priests shall sound a signal on the six trumpets of remembrance, and all the battle formations shall be gathered to them and divide against all the camps of the Kittim to completely destroy them. And when the sun hastens to set on that day, the Chief Priest and the priests and the Levites who are with him, and the chiefs of the battle lines and the men of the army shall bless the God of Israel there. They shall say in response: Blessed is Your name, O God of gods, for You have done wondrous things for Your people, and have kept Your covenant for us from of old. Many times You have opened the gates of salvation for us for the sake of Your covenant. And You provided for our affliction in accord with Your goodness toward us. You, O God of righteousness, have acted for the sake of Your name.

Thanksgiving for final victory.
. . . You have done wonders upon wonders with us, but from (times) of old there has been nothing like it, for You have known our appointed time. Today Your power has shined forth for us, and You have shown us the hand of Your mercies with us in eternal redemption, in order to remove the dominion of the enemy, that it might be no more. (This is) the hand of Your strength. In battle, You shall show Yourself strong against our enemies for an absolute slaughter. Now the day is pressing upon us to pursue their multitude, for You (go before us) and the heart of warriors You have broken so that no one is able to stand. Yours is the might, and the battle is in Your hand, and there is no God like You. Your (. . .) and the appointed times of Your will, and reprisal (…) Your enemies, and You will cut off from (…) .

And we shall direct our contempt at kings, (and our) derision and disdain at mighty men. For our Majestic One is holy. The King of Glory is with us and the host of His spirits is with our steps. Our horsemen are as the clouds and as the mist covering the earth; as a steady downpour shedding judgment on all her offspring.

Rise up, O Hero, Take Your captives, O Glorious One, and take Your plunder, O You Who do valiantly. Lay Your hand upon the neck of Your enemies, and Your foot upon the backs of the slain. Crush the nations, Your adversaries, and let Your sword devour flesh. Fill Your land with glory, and Your inheritance with blessing. An abundance of cattle is sin Your fields, silver and gold in Your palaces. O Zion, rejoice greatly, and rejoice, all you cities of Judah. Open your gates forever, so that the wealth of the nations might be brought to you, and their kings shall serve you. All they that oppressed you shall bow down to you, and they shall lick the dust of your feet. O daughters of my people, burst out with a voice of joy. Adorn yourselves with ornaments of glory, and rule over the kingdom of the (Kittim). Your (...) and Israel for an eternal dominion.

Ceremony after the final battle.
Then they shall gather in the camp that night for rest until the morning. In the morning they shall come to the place of the battle line, where the mighty men of the Kittim fell, as well as the multitude of Assyria, and the forces of all the nations that were assembled unto them, to see whether the multitude of slain are dead with none to bury them; those who fell there by the sword of God.

And the High Priest shall approach there with his deputy, his brothers the priests, and the Levites with the Leader of the battle, and all the chiefs of the battle lines and their officers (and they shall come) together.
When they stand before the slain of the Kittim, they shall praise there the God of Israel. And they shall say in response (Glory to) God most high...

Comment

For thousands of years Israel has awaited the judgment and redemption of The Lord. When the world seemed the most unfair and brutal, hope was held out that the end must be near. The end of days was not a frightening event for the Jews of old. It was to be their greatest age, in which God himself judged all other nations as unworthy and rewarded those Jews who followed their God. Obedience to God was judged on how well one adhered to God's law and commandments.

The belief of divine recompense has echoed through history, changing the ways that both Christian and Jews have viewed their world and their destiny.

Even though the texts presented here are not in our western Christian canon, do not think they have not influenced our faith. The books provide insight into how Jews of the time thought, believed, and acted, but more than that, the texts were circulated and therefore bolstered and broadcast the doctrine and history they contained.

If one ever questioned that non-canonical texts influenced our Bible or our faith, we need to look no further than the famous parallel between the Book of Enoch, written in the second century B.C. and the Book of Jude in the New Testament , written in the first century A.D.

Enoch 1:9 And behold! He comes with ten thousand of His holy ones (saints) to execute judgment on all, and to destroy all the ungodly (wicked); and to convict all flesh of all the works of their ungodliness which they have ungodly committed, and of all the hard things which ungodly sinners have spoken against Him.

Jude 1:14-15 And Enoch also, the seventh from Adam, prophesied of these, saying, Behold, the Lord cometh with ten thousands of his saints, To execute judgment upon all, and to convince all that are ungodly among them of all their ungodly deeds which they have ungodly committed, and of all their hard speeches which ungodly sinners have spoken against him.

Yes, it is true. Documents, doctrine, and points of faith not found in our Bible tremendously influenced what has come to be the Judaism and Christianity we know and practice today.

SECTION THREE

LOST SCRIPTURES OF THE NEW TESTAMENT

Introduction to Gnosticism

Several of the following texts are Gnostic in origin and theology. To assist the reader in a deeper understanding of the Gnostic books, a brief introduction and explanation follows.

"Gnosticism: A system of religion mixed with Greek and Oriental philosophy of the 1st through 6th centuries A.D. Intermediate between Christianity and paganism, Gnosticism taught that knowledge rather than faith was the greatest good and that through knowledge alone could salvation be attained."
Webster's Dictionary

The word Gnostic is based on the Greek word "Gnosis," which means "knowledge." The "Gnosis" is the knowledge of the ultimate, supreme God and his spirit, which is contained within us all. It is this knowledge that allows one to transcend this material world with its falsities and spiritual entrapments and ascend into heaven to be one with God.

For centuries the definition of Gnosticism has in itself been a point of confusion and contention within the religious community. This is due in part to the ever-broadening application of the term and the fact that various sects of Gnosticism existed as the theology evolved and began to merge into what became mainstream Christianity.

Even though Gnosticism continued to evolve, it is the theology in place at the time that the Gnostic Gospels were written that should be considered and understood before attempting to render or read a translation. To do otherwise would make the translation cloudy and obtuse.

It becomes the duty of both translator and reader to understand the ideas being espoused and the terms conveying those ideas. A grasp of theology, cosmology, and relevant terms is necessary for a clear transmission of the meaning within the text in question.

With this in mind, we will briefly examine Gnostic theology, cosmology, and history. We will focus primarily on Gnostic sects existing in the first through fourth centuries A.D. since it is believed most Gnostic Gospels were written during that time. It was also during that time that reactions within the emerging Christian orthodoxy began to intensify.

The downfall of many books written on the topic of religion is the attempt to somehow remove history and people from the equation. History shapes religion because it shapes the perception and direction of religious leaders. Religion also develops and evolves in an attempt to make sense of the universe as it is seen and understood at the time. Thus, to truly grasp a religious concept it is important to know the history, people, and cosmology of the time. These areas are not separate but are continually interacting. This is how the information in this book will be presented to the reader.

A Brief Lesson in Gnosticism

The roots of the Gnosticism may pre-date Christianity. Similarities exist between Gnosticism and the wisdom and mystery cults found in Egypt and Greece. Gnosticism contains the basic terms and motifs of Plato's cosmology as well as the mystical qualities of Buddhism. Plato was steeped in Greek mythology, and the Gnostic creation myth has elements owing to this. Both cosmology and mysticism within Gnosticism present an interpretation of Christ's existence and teachings, thus, Gnostics are considered to be a Christian sect. Gnostic followers are urged to look within themselves for the truth and the Christ spirit hidden, asleep in their souls. The battle cry can be summed up in the words of the Gnostic Gospel of Thomas, verse 3:

Jesus said: If those who lead you say to you: Look, the Kingdom is in the sky, then the birds of the sky would enter before you. If they say to you: It is in the sea, then the fish of the sea would enter ahead of you. But the Kingdom of God exists within you and it exists outside of you. Those who come to know (recognize) themselves will find it, and when you come to know yourselves you will become known and you will realize that you are the children of the Living Father. Yet if you do not come to know yourselves then you will dwell in poverty and it will be you who are that poverty.

Paganism was a religious traditional society in the Mediterranean leading up to the time of the Gnostics. Centuries after the conversion of Constantine, mystery cults worshipping various Egyptian and Greco-Roman gods continued. These cults taught that through their secret knowledge worshippers could control or escape the mortal realm. The Gnostic doctrine of inner knowledge and freedom may have part of its roots here. The concept of duality and inner guidance taught in Buddhism added to and enforced Gnostic beliefs, as we will see later.

The belief systems of Plato, Buddha, and paganism melted together, spread, and found a suitable home in the mystical side of the Christian faith as it sought to adapt and adopt certain Judeo-Christian beliefs and symbols.

Like modern Christianity, Gnosticism had various points of view that could be likened to Christian denominations of today. Complex and elaborate creation myths took root in Gnosticism, being derived from those of Plato. Later, the theology evolved and Gnosticism began to shed some of its more unorthodox myths, leaving the central theme of inner knowledge or gnosis to propagate.

The existence of various sects of Gnosticism, differing creation stories, along with the lack of historical documentation, has left scholars in a quandary about exactly what Gnostics believed. Some have suggested that the Gnostics represented a free thinking and idealistic movement much like that of the "Hippie" movement active in the United States during the 1960's.

Just as the "Hippie" movement in the U.S. influenced political thought, some early sects of Gnostics began to exert direct influence on the Christian church and its leadership.

Although it appears that there were several sects of Gnosticism, we will attempt to discuss the more universal Gnostic beliefs along with the highlights of the major sects.

Gnostic cosmology, (which is the theory of how the universe is created, constructed, and sustained), is complex and very different from orthodox Christianity cosmology. In many ways Gnosticism may appear to be polytheistic or even pantheistic.

To understand some of the basic beliefs of Gnosticism, let us start with the common ground shared between Gnosticism and modern Christianity. Both believe the world is imperfect, corrupt, and brutal. The blame for this, according to mainstream Christianity, is placed squarely on the shoulders of man himself. With the fall of man (Adam), the world was forever changed to the undesirable and harmful place in which we live today. However, Gnostics reject this view as an incorrect interpretation of the creation myth.

According to Gnostics, the blame is not in ourselves, but in our creator. The creator of this world was himself somewhat less than perfect and in fact, deeply flawed and cruel, making mankind the child of a lesser God. It is in the book, *The Apocryphon of John*, that the Gnostic view of creation is presented to us in great detail.

Gnosticism also teaches that in the beginning a Supreme Being called The Father, The Divine All, The Origin, The Supreme God, or The Fullness, emanated the element of existence, both visible and invisible. His intent was not to create but, just as light emanates from a flame, so did creation shine forth from God. This manifested the primal element needed for creation. This was the creation of Barbelo, who is the Thought of God.

The Father's thought performed a deed and she was created from it. It is she who had appeared before him in the shining of his light. This is the first power which was before all of them and which was created from his mind. She is the Thought of the All and her light shines like his light. It is the perfect power which is the visage of the invisible. She is the pure, undefiled Spirit who is perfect. She is the first power, the glory of Barbelo, the perfect glory of the kingdom (kingdoms), the glory revealed. She glorified the pure, undefiled Spirit and it was she who praised him, because thanks to him she had come forth.
The Apocryphon of John

It could be said that Barbelo is the creative emanation and, like the Divine All, is both male and female. It is the "agreement" of Barbelo and the Divine All, representing the union of male and female, that created the Christ Spirit and all the Aeons. In some renderings the word "Aeon" is used to designate an ethereal realm or kingdom. In other versions "Aeon" indicates the ruler of the realm. One of these rulers was called Sophia or Wisdom. Her fall began a chain of events that led to the introduction of evil into the universe.

Seeing the Divine flame of God, Sophia sought to know its origin. She sought to know the very nature of God. Sophia's passion ended in tragedy when she managed to capture a divine and creative spark, which she attempted to duplicate with her own creative force, without the union of a male counterpart. It was this act that produced the Archons, beings born outside the higher divine realm. In the development of the myth, explanations seem to point to the fact that Sophia carried the divine essence of creation from God within her but chose to attempt creation by using her own powers. It is unclear if this was in an attempt to understand the Supreme God and his power, or an impetuous act that caused evil to enter the cosmos in the form of her creations.

The realm containing the Fullness of the Godhead and Sophia is called the pleroma or Realm of Fullness. This is the Gnostic heaven. The lesser Gods created in Sophia's failed attempt were cast outside the pleroma and away from the presence of God. In essence, she threw away and discarded her flawed creations.

"She cast it away from her, outside the place where no one of the immortals might see it, for she had created it in ignorance. And she surrounded it with a glowing cloud, and she put a throne in the middle of the cloud so that no one could see it except the Holy Spirit who is called the mother of all that has life. And she called his name Yaldaboth." Apocryphon of John

The beings Sophia created were imperfect and oblivious to the Supreme God. Her creations contained deities even less perfect than herself. They were called the Powers, the Rulers, or the Archons. Their leader was called the Demiurge, but his name was Yaldaboth. It was the flawed, imperfect, spiritually blind Demiurge, (Yaldaboth), who became the creator of the material world and all things in it. Gnostics considered Yaldaboth to be the same as Jehovah (Yahweh), who is the Jewish creator God. These beings, the Demiurge and the Archons, would later equate to Satan and his demons, or Jehovah and his angels, depending on which Gnostic sect is telling the story. Both are equally evil.

In one Gnostic creation story, the Archons created Adam but could not bring him to life. In other stories Adam was formed as a type of worm, unable to attain personhood. Thus, man began as an incomplete creation of a flawed, spiritually blind, and malevolent god. In this myth, the Archons were afraid that Adam might be more powerful than the Archons themselves. When they saw Adam was incapable of attaining the human state, their fears were put to rest, thus, they called that day the "Day of Rest."

Sophia saw Adam's horrid state and had compassion, because she knew she was the origin of the Archons and their evil. Sophia descended to help bring Adam out of his hopeless condition. It is this story that set the stage for the emergence of the sacred feminine force in Gnosticism that is not seen in orthodox Christianity. Sophia brought within herself the light and power of the Supreme God. Metaphorically, within the spiritual womb of Sophia was carried the life force of the Supreme God for Adam's salvation.

In the Gnostic text called, *The Apocryphon of John*, Sophia is quoted:
"I entered into the midst of the cage which is the prison of the body. And I spoke saying: 'He who hears, let him awake from his deep sleep.' Then Adam wept and shed tears. After he wiped away his bitter tears he asked: 'Who calls my name, and from where has this hope arose in me even while I am in the chains of this prison?' And I (Sophia) answered: 'I am the one who carries the pure light; I am the thought of the undefiled spirit. Arise, remember, and follow your origin, which is I, and beware of the deep sleep.'"

Sophia would later equate to the Holy Spirit as it awakened the comatose soul.

As the myth evolved, Sophia, after animating Adam, became Eve in order to assist Adam in finding the truth. She offered it to him in the form of the fruit of the tree of knowledge. To Gnostics, this was an act of deliverance.

Other stories have Sophia becoming the serpent in order to offer Adam a way to attain the truth. In either case, the apple represented the hard sought truth, which was the knowledge of good and evil, and through that knowledge Adam could become a god. Later, the serpent would become a feminine symbol of wisdom, probably owing to the connection with Sophia. Eve, being Sophia in disguise, would become the mother and sacred feminine of us all. As Gnostic theology began to coalesce, Sophia would come to be considered a force or conduit of the Holy Spirit, in part due to the fact that the Holy Spirit was also considered a feminine and creative force from the Supreme God. The Gospel of Philip echoes this theology in verse six as follows:

In the days when we were Hebrews we were made orphans, having only our Mother. Yet when we believed in the Messiah (and became the ones of Christ), the Mother and Father both came to us. Gospel of Philip

As the emerging orthodox church became more and more oppressive to women, later even labeling them "occasions of sin," the Gnostics countered by raising women to equal status with men, saying Sophia was, in a sense, the handmaiden or wife of the Supreme God, making the soul of Adam her spiritual offspring.

In Gnostic cosmology the "living" world is under the control of entities called Aeons, of which Sophia is head. This means the Aeons influence or control the soul, life force, intelligence, thought, and mind. Control of the mechanical or inorganic world is given to the Archons. They rule the physical aspects of systems, regulation, limits, and order in the world. Both the ineptitude and cruelty of the Archons are reflected in the chaos and pain of the material realm.

The lesser God that created the world, Yaldaboth. began his existence in a state that was both detached and remote from the Supreme God in aspects both spiritual and physical. Since Sophia had misused her creative force, which passed from the Supreme God to her, Sophia's creation, the Demiurge, Yaldaboth, contained only part of the original creative spark of the Supreme Being. He was created with an imperfect nature caused by his distance in lineage and in spirit from the Divine All or Supreme God. It is because of his imperfections and limited abilities the lesser God is also called the "Half-Maker".

The Creator God, the Demiurge, and his helpers, the Archons took the stuff of existence produced by the Supreme God and fashioned it into this material world.

Since the Demiurge (Yaldaboth) had no memory of how he came to be alive, he did not realize he was not the true creator. The Demiurge believed he somehow came to create the material world by himself. The Supreme God allowed the Demiurge and Archons to remain deceived.

The Creator God (the Demiurge) intended the material world to be perfect and eternal, but he did not have it in himself to accomplish the feat. What comes forth from a being cannot be greater than the highest part of him, can it? The world was created flawed and transitory and we are part of it. Can we escape? The Demiurge was imperfect and evil. So was the world he created. If it was the Demiurge who created man and man is called upon to escape the Demiurge and find union with the Supreme God, is this not demanding that man becomes greater than his creator? Spiritually this seems impossible, but as many children become greater than their parents, man is expected to become greater than his maker, the Demiurge. This starts with the one fact that the Demiurge denies: the existence and supremacy of the Supreme God.

Man was created with a dual nature as the product of the material world of the Demiurge with his imperfect essence, combined with the spark of God that emanated from the Supreme God through Sophia. A version of the creation story has Sophia instructing the Demiurge to breath into Adam that spiritual power he had taken from Sophia during his creation. It was the spiritual power from Sophia that brought life to Adam.

It is this divine spark in man that calls to its source, the Supreme God, and which causes a "divine discontent," that nagging feeling that keeps us questioning if this is all there is. This spark and the feeling it gives us keeps us searching for the truth.

The Creator God sought to keep man ignorant of his defective state by keeping him enslaved to the material world. By doing so, he continued to receive man's worship and servitude. He did not wish man to recognize or gain knowledge of the true Supreme God. Since he did not know or acknowledge the Supreme God, he views any attempt to worship anything else as spiritual treason.

The opposition of forces set forth in the spiritual battle over the continued enslavement of man and man's spiritual freedom set up the duality of good and evil in Gnostic theology. There was a glaring difference between the orthodox Christian viewpoint and the Gnostic viewpoint. According to Gnostics, the creator of the material world was an evil entity and the Supreme God, who was his source, was the good entity. Christians quote John 1:1 "In the beginning was the Word, and the Word was with God, and the Word was God."

According to Gnostics, only through the realization of man's true state or through death can he escape captivity in the material realm. This means the idea of salvation does not deal with original sin or blood payment. Instead, it focuses on the idea of awakening to the fullness of the truth.

According to Gnostic theology, neither Jesus nor his death can save anyone, but the truth that he came to proclaim can allow a person to save his or her own soul. It is the truth, or realization of the lie of the material world and its God, that sets one on a course of freedom.

To escape the earthly prison and find one's way back to the pleroma (heaven) and the Supreme God, is the soteriology (salvation doctrine) and eschatology (judgment, reward, and doctrine of heaven) of Gnosticism.

The idea that personal revelation leads to salvation, may be what caused the mainline Christian church to declare Gnosticism a heresy. The church could better tolerate alternative theological views if the views did not undermine the authority of the church and its ability to control the people. Gnostic theology placed salvation in the hands of the individual through personal revelations and knowledge, excluding the need for the orthodox church and its clergy to grant salvation or absolution. This fact, along with the divergent interpretation of the creation story, which placed the creator God, Yaldaboth or Jehovah, as the enemy of mankind, was too much for the church to tolerate. Reaction was harsh. Gnosticism was declared to be a dangerous heresy.

Gnosticism may be considered polytheistic because it espoused many "levels" of Gods, beginning with an ultimate, unknowable, Supreme God and descending as he created Sophia, and Sophia created the Demiurge (Creator God); each becoming more inferior and limited.

There is a hint of pantheism in Gnostic theology due to the fact that creation occurs because of a deterioration of the Godhead and the dispersion of the creative essence, which eventually devolves into the creation of man.

In the end, there occurs a universal reconciliation as being after being realizes the existence of the Supreme God and renounces the material world and its inferior creator.

Combined with its Christian influences, the cosmology of the Gnostics may have borrowed from the Greek philosopher, Plato, as well as from Buddhism. There are disturbing parallels between the creation myth set forth by Plato and some of those recorded in Gnostic writings.

Plato lived from 427 to 347 B.C. He was the son of wealthy Athenians and a student of the philosopher, Socrates, and the mathematician, Pythagoras. Plato himself was the teacher of Aristotle.

In Plato's cosmology, the Demiurge is an artist who imposed form on materials that already existed. The raw materials were in a chaotic and random state. The physical world must have had visible form which was put together much like a puzzle is constructed. This later gave way to a philosophy which stated that all things in existence could be broken down into a small subset of geometric shapes.

In the tradition of Greek mythology, Plato's cosmology began with a creation story. The story was narrated by the philosopher Timaeus of Locris, a fictional character of Plato's making. In his account, nature is initiated by a creator deity, called the "Demiurge," a name which may be the Geek word for "craftsman" or "artisan" or, according to how one divides the word, it could also be translated as "half-maker."

The Demiurge sought to create the cosmos modeled on his understanding of the supreme and original truth. In this way he created the visible universe based on invisible truths. He set in place rules of process such as birth, growth, change, death, and dissolution. This was Plato's "Realm of Becoming." It was his Genesis. Plato stated that the internal structure of the cosmos had innate intelligence and was therefore called the World Soul. The cosmic super-structure of the Demiurge was used as the framework on which to hang or fill in the details and parts of the universe. The Demiurge then appointed his underlings to fill in the details which allowed the universe to remain in a working and balanced state. All phenomena of nature resulted from an interaction and interplay of the two forces of reason and necessity.

Plato represented reason as constituting the World Soul. The material world was a necessity in which reason acted out its will in the physical realm. The duality between the will, mind, or reason of the World Soul and the material universe and its inherent flaws set in play the duality of Plato's world and is seen reflected in the beliefs of the Gnostics.

In Plato's world, the human soul was immortal, each soul was assigned to a star. Souls that were just or good were permitted to return to their stars upon their death. Unjust souls were reincarnated to try again. Escape of the soul to the freedom of the stars and out of the cycle of reincarnation was best accomplished by following the reason and goodness of the World Soul and not the physical world, which was set in place only as a necessity to manifest the patterns of the World Soul.

Although in Plato's cosmology the Demiurge was not seen as evil, in Gnostic cosmology he was considered not only to be flawed and evil, but he was also the beginning of all evil in the material universe, having created it to reflect his own malice.

Following the path of Plato's cosmology, some Gnostics left open the possibility of reincarnation if the person had not reached the truth before his death.

In the year 13 A.D. Roman annals record the visit of an Indian king named Pandya or Porus. He came to see Caesar Augustus carrying a letter of introduction in Greek. He was accompanied by a monk who burned himself alive in the city of Athens to prove his faith in Buddhism. The event was described by Nicolaus of Damascus as, not surprisingly, causing a great stir among the people. It is thought that this was the first transmission of Buddhist teaching to the masses.

In the second century A.D., Clement of Alexandria wrote about Buddha: "Among the Indians are those philosophers also who follow the precepts of Boutta (Buddha), whom they honour as a god on account of his extraordinary sanctity." (Clement of Alexandria, "The Stromata, or Miscellanies" Book I, Chapter XV).

"Thus philosophy, a thing of the highest utility, flourished in antiquity among the barbarians, shedding its light over the nations. And afterwards it came to Greece." (Clement of Alexandria, "The Stromata, or Miscellanies").

To clarify what "philosophy" was transmitted from India to Greece, we turn to the historians Hippolytus and Epiphanius who wrote of Scythianus, a man who had visited India around 50 A.D. They report; "He brought 'the doctrine of the Two Principles.'" According to these writers, Scythianus' pupil Terebinthus called himself a Buddha. Some scholars suggest it was he that traveled to the area of Babylon and transmitted his knowledge to Mani, who later founded Manichaeism.

Adding to the possibility of Eastern influence, we have accounts of the Apostle Thomas' attempt to convert the people of Asia-Minor. If the Gnostic gospel bearing his name was truly written by Thomas, it was penned after his return from India, where he also encountered the Buddhist influences.

Ancient church historians mention that Thomas preached to the Parthians in Persia, and it is said he was buried in Edessa. Fourth century chronicles attribute the evangelization of India (Asia-Minor or Central Asia) to Thomas.

The texts of the Gospel of Thomas, which some believe predate the four gospels, has a very "Zen-like" or Eastern flavor.

Since it is widely held that the four gospels of Matthew, Mark, Luke, and John have a common reference in the basic text of Mark, it stands to reason that all follow the same general insight and language. If The Gospel of Thomas was written in his absence from the other apostles or if it was the first gospel written, one can assume it was written outside the influences common to the other gospels.

Although the codex found in Egypt is dated to the fourth century, the actual construction of the text of Thomas is placed by most Biblical scholars at about 70–150 A.D. Most agree the time of writing was in the second century A.D.

Following the transmission of the philosophy of "Two Principals," both Manichaeism and Gnosticism retained a dualistic viewpoint. The black-versus-white dualism of Gnosticism came to rest in the evil of the material world and its maker, versus the goodness of the freed soul and the Supreme God with whom it seeks union.

Oddly, the disdain for the material world and its Creator God drove Gnostic theology to far-flung extremes in attitude, beliefs, and actions. Gnostics idolize the serpent in the "Garden of Eden" story. After all, if your salvation hinges on secret knowledge the offer of becoming gods through the knowledge of good and evil sounds wonderful. So powerful was the draw of this "knowledge myth" to the Gnostics that the serpent became linked to Sophia by some sects. This can still be seen today in our medical and veterinarian symbols of serpents on poles, conveying the ancient meanings of knowledge and wisdom.

Genesis 3 (King James Version)
1 Now the serpent was more subtil than any beast of the field which the LORD God had made. And he said unto the woman, Yea, hath God said, Ye shall not eat of every tree of the garden?
2 And the woman said unto the serpent, We may eat of the fruit of the trees of the garden:
3 But of the fruit of the tree which is in the midst of the garden, God hath said, Ye shall not eat of it, neither shall ye touch it, lest ye die.
4 And the serpent said unto the woman, Ye shall not surely die:
5 For God doth know that in the day ye eat thereof, then your eyes shall be opened, and ye shall be as Gods, knowing good and evil.

It is because of their vehement struggle against the Creator God and the search for some transcendent truth, that Gnostics held the people of Sodom in high regard. The people of Sodom sought to "corrupt" the messengers sent by their enemy, the Creator God. Anything done to thwart the Demiurge and his minions was considered valiant.

Genesis 19 (King James Version)
1 And there came two angels to Sodom at even; and Lot sat in the gate of Sodom: and Lot seeing them rose up to meet them; and he bowed himself with his face toward the ground;
2 And he said, Behold now, my lords, turn in, I pray you, into your servant's house, and tarry all night, and wash your feet, and ye shall rise up early, and go on your ways. And they said, Nay; but we will abide in the street all night.
3 And he pressed upon them greatly; and they turned in unto him, and entered into his house; and he made them a feast, and did bake unleavened bread, and they did eat.
4 But before they lay down, the men of the city, even the men of Sodom, compassed the house round, both old and young, all the people from every quarter:
5 And they called unto Lot, and said unto him, Where are the men which came in to thee this night? bring them out unto us, that we may know them.
6 And Lot went out at the door unto them, and shut the door after him,
7 And said, I pray you, brethren, do not so wickedly.
8 Behold now, I have two daughters which have not known man; let me, I pray you, bring them out unto you, and do ye to them as is good in your eyes: only unto these men do nothing; for therefore came they under the shadow of my roof.
9 And they said, Stand back. And they said again, This one fellow came in to sojourn, and he will needs be a judge: now will we deal worse with thee, than with them. And they pressed sore upon the man, even Lot, and came near to break the door.
10 But the men put forth their hand, and pulled Lot into the house to them, and shut to the door.

To modern Christians, the idea of admiring the serpent, which we believe was Satan, may seem unthinkable. Supporting the idea of attacking and molesting the angels sent to Sodom to warn of the coming destruction seems appalling; but to Gnostics the real evil was the malevolent entity, the Creator God of this world. To destroy his messengers, as was the case in Sodom, would impede his mission. To obtain knowledge of good and evil, as was offered by the serpent in the garden, would set the captives free.

To awaken the inner knowledge of the true God was the battle. The material world was designed to prevent the awakening by entrapping, confusing, and distracting the spirit of man. The aim of Gnosticism was the spiritual awakening and freedom of man.

Gnostics, in the age of the early church, would preach to converts (novices) about this awakening, saying the novice must awaken the God within himself and see the trap that was the material world. Salvation came from the recognition or knowledge contained in this spiritual awakening.

Not all people are ready or willing to accept the Gnosis. Many are bound to the material world and are satisfied to be only as and where they are. These have mistaken the Creator God for the Supreme God and do not know there is anything beyond the Creator God or the material existence. These people know only the lower or earthly wisdom and not the higher wisdom above the Creator God. They are referred to as "dead."

Gnostic sects split primarily into two categories. Both branches held that those who were truly enlightened could no longer be influenced by the material world. Both divisions of Gnosticism believed that their spiritual journey could not be impeded by the material realm since the two were not only separate but in opposition. Such an attitude influenced some Gnostics toward Stoicism, choosing to abstain from the world, and others toward Epicureanism, choosing to indulge.

Major schools fell into two categories; those who rejected the material world of the Creator God, and those who rejected the laws of the Creator God. For those who rejected the world the Creator God had spawned, overcoming the material world was accomplished by partaking of as little of the world and its pleasures as possible. These followers lived very stark and ascetic lives, abstaining from meat, sex, marriage, and all things that would entice them to remain in the material realm. Other schools believed it was their duty to simply defy the Creator God and all laws that he had proclaimed. Since the Creator God had been identified as Jehovah, God of the Jews, these followers set about to break every law held dear by Christians and Jews.

As human nature is predisposed to do, many Gnostics took up the more wanton practices, believing that nothing done in their earthly bodies would affect their spiritual lives. Whether it was excesses in sex, alcohol, food, or any other assorted debaucheries, the Gnostics were safe within their faith, believing nothing spiritually bad could come of their earthly adventures.

The actions of the Gnostics are mentioned by early Church leaders. One infamous Gnostic school is actually mentioned in the Bible, as we will read later.

The world was out of balance, inferior, and corrupt. The spirit was perfect and intact. It was up to the Gnostics to tell the story, explain the error, and awaken the world to the light of truth. The Supreme God had provided a vehicle to help in their effort. He had created a teacher of light and truth.

Since the time of Sophia's mistaken creation of the Archons, there was an imbalance in the cosmos. The Supreme God began to re-establish the balance by producing Christ to teach and save man. That left only Sophia, now in a fallen and bound state, along with the Demiurge, and the Archons to upset the cosmic equation. In this theology one might loosely equate the Supreme God to the New Testament Christian God, Demiurge to Satan, the Archons to demons, the pleroma to heaven, and Sophia to the creative or regenerative force of the Holy Spirit. This holds up well except for one huge problem. If the Jews believed that Jehovah created all things, and the Gnostic believed that the Demiurge created all things, then to the Gnostic mind, the Demiurge must be Old Testament god, Jehovah, and that made Jehovah their enemy.

For those who seek that which is beyond the material world and its flawed creator, the Supreme God has sent Messengers of Light to awaken the divine spark of the Supreme God within us. This part of us will call to the True God as deep calls to deep. The greatest and most perfect Messenger of Light was the Christ. He is also referred to as The Good, Christ, Messiah, and The Word. He came to reveal the Divine Light to us in the form of knowledge.

According to the Gnostics, Christ came to show us our own divine spark and to awaken us to the illusion of the material world and its flawed maker. He came to show us the way back to the divine Fullness (The Supreme God). The path to enlightenment was the knowledge sleeping within each of us. Christ came to show us the Christ spirit living in each of us. Individual ignorance or the refusal to awaken our internal divine spark was the only original sin. Christ was the only Word spoken by God that could awaken us. Christ was also the embodiment of the Word itself. He was part of the original transmission from the Supreme God that took form on the earth to awaken the soul of man so that man might search beyond the material world.

One Gnostic view of the Incarnation was "docetic," which is an early heretical position that Jesus was never actually present in the flesh, but only appeared to be human. He was a spiritual being and his human appearance was only an illusion. Of course, the title of "heretical" can only be decided by the controlling authority of the time. In this case it was the church that was about to emerge under the rule of the Emperor Constantine.

Most Gnostics held that the Christ spirit indwelt the earthly Jesus at the time of his baptism by John, at which time Jesus received the name, and thus the power, of the Lord or Supreme God.

The Christ spirit departed from Jesus' body before his death. These two viewpoints remove the idea of God sacrificing himself as an atonement for the sins of man. The idea of atonement was not necessary in Gnostic theology since it was knowledge and not sacrifice that set one free.

Since there was a distinction in Gnosticism between the man Jesus and the Light of Christ that came to reside within him, it is not contrary to Gnostic beliefs that Mary Magdalene could have been the consort and wife of Jesus. Neither would it have been blasphemous for them to have had children.

Various sects of Gnosticism stressed certain elements of their basic theology. Each had its head teachers and its special flavor of beliefs. One of the oldest types was the Syrian Gnosticism. It existed around 120 A.D. In contrast to other sects, the Syrian lacked much of the embellished mythology of Aeons, Archons, and angels.

The fight between the Supreme God and the Creator God was not eternal, though there was strong opposition to Jehovah, the Creator God. He was considered to have been the last of the seven angels who created this world out of divine material which emanated from the Supreme God. The Demiurge attempted to create man, but only created a miserable worm which the Supreme God had to save by giving it the spark of divine life. Thus man was born.

According to this sect, Jehovah, the Creator God, must not be worshiped. The Supreme God calls us to his service and presence through Christ his Son. They pursued only the unknowable Supreme God and sought to obey the Supreme Deity by abstaining from eating meat and from marriage and sex, and by leading an ascetic life. The symbol of Christ was the serpent, who attempted to free Adam and Eve from their ignorance and entrapment to the Creator God.

Another Gnostic school was the Hellenistic or Alexandrian School. These systems absorbed the philosophy and concepts of the Greeks, and the Semitic nomenclature was replaced by Greek names. The cosmology and myth had grown out of proportion and appear to our eyes to be unwieldy. Yet, this school produced two great thinkers, Basilides and Valentinus. Though born at Antioch, in Syria, Basilides founded his school in Alexandria around the year A.D. 130, where it survived for several centuries.

Valentinus first taught at Alexandria and then in Rome. He established the largest Gnostic movement around A.D. 160. This movement was founded on an elaborate mythology and a system of sexual duality of male and female interplay, both in its deities and its savior.

Tertullian wrote that between 135 A.D. and 160 A.D. Valentinus, a prominent Gnostic, had great influence in the Christian church. Valentinus ascended in church hierarchy and became a candidate for the office of bishop of Rome, the office that quickly evolved into that of Pope. He lost the election by a narrow margin. Even though Valentinus was outspoken about his Gnostic slant on Christianity, he was a respected member of the Christian community until his death and was probably a practicing bishop in a church of lesser status than the one in Rome.

The main platform of Gnosticism was the ability to transcend the material world through the possession of privileged and directly imparted knowledge. Following this doctrine, Valentinus claimed to have been instructed by a direct disciple of one of Jesus' apostles, a man by the name of Theodas.

Valentinus is considered by many to be the father of modern Gnosticism. His vision of the faith is summarized by G.R.S. Mead in the book "Fragments of a Faith Forgotten."

"The Gnosis in his hands is trying to embrace everything, even the most dogmatic formulation of the traditions of the Master. The great popular movement and its incomprehensibilities were recognized by Valentinus as an integral part of the mighty outpouring; he laboured to weave all together, external and internal, into one piece, devoted his life to the task, and doubtless only at his death perceived that for that age he was attempting the impossible. None but the very few could ever appreciate the ideal of the man, much less understand it. " (Fragments of a Faith Forgotten, p. 297)

Gnostic theology seemed to vacillate from polytheism to pantheism to dualism to monotheism, depending on the teacher and how he viewed and stressed certain areas of their creation myths. Marcion, a Gnostic teacher, espoused differences between the God of the New Testament and the God of the Old Testament, claiming they were two separate entities. According to Marcion, the New Testament God was a good true God while the Old Testament God was an evil angel. Although this may be a heresy, it pulled his school back into monotheism. The church, however, disowned him.

Syneros and Prepon, disciples of Marcion, postulated three different entities, carrying their teachings from monotheism into polytheism in one stroke. In their system the opponent of the good God was not the God of the Jews, but Eternal Matter, which was the source of all evil. Matter, in this system became a principal creative force. Although it was created imperfect, it could also create, having the innate intelligence of the "world soul."

Of all the Gnostic schools or sects the most famous is the Antinomian School. Believing that the Creator God, Jehovah, was evil, they sat out to disrupt all things connected to the Jewish God. This included his laws. It was considered their duty to break any law of morality, diet, or conduct given by the Jewish God, who they considered the evil Creator God. The leader of the sect was called Nicolaites. The sect existed in Apostolic times and is mentioned in the Bible.

Revelation 2 (King James Version)
5 Remember therefore from whence thou art fallen, and repent, and do the first works; or else I will come unto thee quickly, and will remove thy candlestick out of his place, except thou repent.
6 But this thou hast, that thou hatest the deeds of the Nicolaitanes, which I also hate.

Revelation 2 (King James Version)
14 But I have a few things against thee, because thou hast there them that hold the doctrine of Balaam, who taught Balac to cast a stumbling block before the children of Israel, to eat things sacrificed unto idols, and to commit fornication.
15 So hast thou also them that hold the doctrine of the Nicolaitanes, which thing I hate.
16 Repent; or else I will come unto thee quickly, and will fight against them with the sword of my mouth.

One of the leaders of the Nocolaitanes, according to Origen, was Carpocrates, whom Tertullian called a magician and a fornicator. Carpocretes taught that one could only escape the cosmic powers by discharging one's obligations to them and disregarding their laws. The Christian church fathers, St. Justin, Irenaeus, and Eusebius wrote that the reputation of these men (the Nicolaitanes), brought infamy upon the whole race of Christians.

Although Gnostic sects varied, they had certain points in common. These commonalities included salvation through special knowledge, and the fact that the world was corrupt as it was created by an evil God.

According to Gnostic theology, nothing can come from the material world that is not flawed. Because of this, Gnostics did not believe that Christ could have been a corporeal being. Thus, there must be some separation or distinction between Jesus, as a man, and Christ, as a spiritual being born from the Supreme, unrevealed, and eternal God.

To closer examine this theology, we turn to Valentinus, the driving force of early Gnosticism, for an explanation. Valentinus divided Jesus Christ into two very distinct parts; Jesus, the man, and Christ, the anointed spiritual messenger of God. These two forces met in the moment of Baptism when the Spirit of God came to rest on Jesus and the Christ power entered his body.

Here Gnosticism runs aground on its own theology, for if the spiritual cannot mingle with the material then how can the Christ spirit inhabit a body? The result of the dichotomy was a schism within Gnosticism. Some held to the belief that the specter of Jesus was simply an illusion produced by Christ himself to enable him to do his work on earth. It was not real, not matter, not corporeal, and did not actually exist as a physical body would. Others came to believe that Jesus must have been a specially prepared vessel and was the perfect human body formed by the very essence of the plumora (heaven). It was this path of thought that allowed Jesus to continue as human, lover, and father.

Jesus, the man, became a vessel containing the Light of God, called Christ. In the Gnostic view we all could and should become Christs, carrying the Truth and Light of God. We are all potential vehicles of the same Spirit that Jesus held within him when he was awakened to the Truth.

The suffering and death of Jesus then took on much less importance in the Gnostic view, as Jesus was simply part of the corrupt world and was suffering the indignities of this world as any man would. Therefore, from their viewpoint, he could have been married and been a father without disturbing Gnostic theology in the least.

The Gnostic texts seem to divide man into parts, although at times the divisions are somewhat unclear. The divisions alluded to may include the soul, which is the will of man; the spirit, which is depicted as wind or air (pneuma) and contains the holy spark that is the spirit of God in man; and the material human form, the body. The mind of man sits as a mediator between the soul, or will, and the spirit, which is connected to God.

Without the light of the truth, the spirit is held captive by the Demiurge, which enslaves man. This entrapment is called "sickness." It is this sickness that the Light came to heal and then to set us free. The third part of man, his material form, was considered a weight, an anchor, and a hindrance, keeping man attached to the corrupted earthly realm.

As we read the text, we must realize that Gnosticism conflicted with traditional Christianity. Overall theology can rise and fall upon small words and terms. If Jesus was not God, his death and thus his atonement meant nothing. His suffering meant nothing. Even the resurrection meant nothing, if one's view of Jesus was that he was not human to begin with, as was true with some Gnostics.

For the Gnostics, resurrection of the dead was unthinkable since flesh as well as all matter is destined to perish. According to Gnostic theology, there was no resurrection of the flesh, but only of the soul. How the soul would be resurrected was explained differently by various Gnostic groups, but all denied the resurrection of the body. To the enlightened Gnostic the actual person was the spirit who used the body as an instrument to survive in the material world but did not identify with it. This belief is echoed in the Gospel of Thomas.

29. Jesus said: If the flesh came into being because of spirit, it is a marvel, but if spirit came into being because of the body, it would be a marvel of marvels. I marvel indeed at how great wealth has taken up residence in this poverty.

Owing to the Gnostic belief of such a separation of spirit and body, it was thought that the Christ spirit within the body of Jesus departed the body before the crucifixion. Others said the body was an illusion and the crucifixion was a sham perpetrated by an eternal spirit on the men that sought to kill it. Lastly, some suggested that Jesus deceived the soldiers into thinking he was dead. The resurrection under this circumstance became a lie which allowed Jesus to escape and live on in anonymity, hiding, living as a married man, and raising a family until his natural death.

Think of the implications to the orthodox Christian world if the spirit of God departed from Jesus as it fled and laughed as the body was crucified. This is the implication of the Gnostic interpretation of the death of Jesus when he cries out, "My power, my power, why have you left me," as the Christ spirit left his body before his death. What are the ramifications to the modern Christian if the Creator God, the Demiurge, is more evil than his creation? Can a Creation rise above its creator? Is it possible for man to find the spark within himself that calls to the Supreme God and free himself of his evil creator?

Although, in time, the creation myth and other Gnostic differences began to be swept under the rug, it was the division between Jesus and the Christ spirit that put them at odds with the emerging orthodox church. At the establishment of the doctrine of the trinity, the mainline church firmly set a divide between themselves and the Gnostics.

To this day there is a battle raging in the Christian world as believers and seekers attempt to reconcile today's Christianity to the sect of the early Christian church called, "Gnosticism."

The Reaction of Christendom

Reaction to Gnosticism within the newly forming church was swift and bold. Beginning with a swelling defense in the New Testament itself, the writers began to define and defend doctrine. Labels, names, and descriptions of the Christian doctrine would be established later in various councils, but for now there would be decisive actions to fend off new ideas.

Considering the fact that there were two main approaches to Gnosticism in the first and second centuries, the stoic-ascetic approach of self denial and the hedonistic-epicurean approach of self indulgence, we will find two criticisms mounted against Gnosticism in the Bible. First we will examine the pronouncements against the more hedonistic sects.

2 Timothy 3 (King James Version)

1 This know also, that in the last days perilous times shall come.

2 For men shall be lovers of their own selves, covetous, boasters, proud, blasphemers, disobedient to parents, unthankful, unholy,

3 Without natural affection, trucebreakers, false accusers, incontinent, fierce, despisers of those that are good,

4 Traitors, heady, highminded, lovers of pleasures more than lovers of God;

5 Having a form of godliness, but denying the power thereof: from such turn away.

6 For of this sort are they which creep into houses, and lead captive silly women laden with sins, led away with divers lusts,

7 Ever learning, and never able to come to the knowledge of the truth.

Keeping in mind the previous information and scripture given regarding the Gnostic sect of the Nicolaitanes, Timothy mounts an attack against Pagans and wayward Christians, including certain Gnostics, who had fallen into debauchery. The last line of the admonition targets what he sees as the Gnostic weakness of, *"Ever learning, and never able to come to the knowledge of the truth."*

One of the most difficult passages to apprehend is found in 1 John chapter 4, where the writer attempts to draw a fine line between what is the error in Gnostic theology and what is the full truth of Christ on earth according to orthodoxy.

1 John (King James Version)

1 John 4

1 Beloved, believe not every spirit, but try the spirits whether they are of God: because many false prophets are gone out into the world.

2 Hereby know ye the Spirit of God: Every spirit that confesseth that Jesus Christ is come in the flesh is of God:

3 And every spirit that confesseth not that Jesus Christ is come in the flesh is not of God: and this is that spirit of antichrist, whereof ye have heard that it should come; and even now already is it in the world.

4 Ye are of God, little children, and have overcome them: because greater is he that is in you, than he that is in the world.

5 They are of the world: therefore speak they of the world, and the world heareth them.

6 We are of God: he that knoweth God heareth us; he that is not of God heareth not us. Hereby know we the spirit of truth, and the spirit of error.

7 Beloved, let us love one another: for love is of God; and every one that loveth is born of God, and knoweth God.

8 He that loveth not knoweth not God; for God is love.

9 In this was manifested the love of God toward us, because that God sent his only begotten Son into the world, that we might live through him.

10 Herein is love, not that we loved God, but that he loved us, and sent his Son to be the propitiation for our sins.

11 Beloved, if God so loved us, we ought also to love one another.

12 No man hath seen God at any time. If we love one another, God dwelleth in us, and his love is perfected in us.

13 Hereby know we that we dwell in him, and he in us, because he hath given us of his Spirit.

14 And we have seen and do testify that the Father sent the Son to be the Saviour of the world.

15 Whosoever shall confess that Jesus is the Son of God, God dwelleth in him, and he in God.

16 And we have known and believed the love that God hath to us. God is love; and he that dwelleth in love dwelleth in God, and God in him.

17 Herein is our love made perfect, that we may have boldness in the day of judgment: because as he is, so are we in this world.

With gentle and elegant words, John cuts to the bone, amputating the part of Christendom seen as heretical.

1 Beloved, believe not every spirit, but try the spirits whether they are of God: because many false prophets are gone out into the world.

2 Hereby know ye the Spirit of God: Every spirit that confesseth that Jesus Christ is come in the flesh is of God:

3 And every spirit that confesseth not that Jesus Christ is come in the flesh is not of God: and this is that spirit of antichrist, whereof ye have heard that it should come; and even now already is it in the world.

The statement above is a direct attack against the Gnostic beliefs regarding Jesus and the Christ spirit. The Gnostic belief that spirit and matter could not co-exist makes it impossible for Christ to inhabit a fleshly body. The belief by some was that Jesus was an illusion or specially prepared body and Christ was somehow separate from Jesus. This made it impossible for the man Jesus to be the literal son of God.

John drives home the differences and calls the differences heresies, proclaiming that those who do not hold to orthodox beliefs have the spirit of the antichrist.

After the establishment of cannon, many incorrectly cited the following chapter to condemn Gnosticism and other religions that seemed to be gaining a notable following. Ironically, Protestants would later use the same verses to condemn Catholicism.

Revelation 17 (King James Version)
1 And there came one of the seven angels which had the seven vials, and talked with me, saying unto me, Come hither; I will shew unto thee the judgment of the great whore that sitteth upon many waters:
2 With whom the kings of the earth have committed fornication, and the inhabitants of the earth have been made drunk with the wine of her fornication.
3 So he carried me away in the spirit into the wilderness: and I saw a woman sit upon a scarlet coloured beast, full of names of blasphemy, having seven heads and ten horns.
4 And the woman was arrayed in purple and scarlet colour, and decked with gold and precious stones and pearls, having a golden cup in her hand full of abominations and filthiness of her fornication:
5 And upon her forehead was a name written, MYSTERY, BABYLON THE GREAT, THE MOTHER OF HARLOTS AND ABOMINATIONS OF THE EARTH.
6 And I saw the woman drunken with the blood of the saints, and with the blood of the martyrs of Jesus: and when I saw her, I wondered with great admiration.
7 And the angel said unto me, Wherefore didst thou marvel? I will tell thee the mystery of the woman, and of the beast that carrieth her, which hath the seven heads and ten horns.
8 The beast that thou sawest was, and is not; and shall ascend out of the bottomless pit, and go into perdition: and they that dwell on the earth shall wonder, whose names were not written in the book of life from the foundation of the world, when they behold the beast that was, and is not, and yet is.
9 And here is the mind which hath wisdom. The seven heads are seven mountains, on which the woman sitteth.
10 And there are seven kings: five are fallen, and one is, and the other is not yet come; and when he cometh, he must continue a short space.
11 And the beast that was, and is not, even he is the eighth, and is of the seven, and goeth into perdition.
12 And the ten horns which thou sawest are ten kings, which have received no kingdom as yet; but receive power as kings one hour with the beast.
13 These have one mind, and shall give their power and strength unto the beast.
14 These shall make war with the Lamb, and the Lamb shall overcome them: for he is Lord of lords, and King of kings: and they that are with him are called, and chosen, and faithful.
15 And he saith unto me, The waters which thou sawest, where the whore sitteth, are peoples, and multitudes, and nations, and tongues.
16 And the ten horns which thou sawest upon the beast, these shall hate the whore, and shall make her desolate and naked, and shall eat her flesh, and burn her with fire.
17 For God hath put in their hearts to fulfil his will, and to agree, and give their kingdom unto the beast, until the words of God shall be fulfilled.
18 And the woman which thou sawest is that great city, which reigneth over the kings of the earth.

Is the whore of Babylon Mary, as conservative Christians claim? If it is Mary, is it the representation of Mother Mary or that of Mary Magdalene? Is Gnosticism the great heresy that will bring about the downfall of the Christian church?

Let us begin with the writer's concluding statement.

Revelation 17
15 And he saith unto me, The waters which thou sawest, where the whore sitteth, are peoples, and multitudes, and nations, and tongues.
16 And the ten horns which thou sawest upon the beast, these shall hate the whore, and shall make her desolate and naked, and shall eat her flesh, and burn her with fire.
17 For God hath put in their hearts to fulfil his will, and to agree, and give their kingdom unto the beast, until the words of God shall be fulfilled.
18 And the woman which thou sawest is that great city, which reigneth over the kings of the earth.

"The woman you saw is that great city which reigns over the kings of the earth." (Rev 17:18) The great whore is not a person at all, but a place – a city, which is a seat of power wherein kings and nations are ruled.

It is not the purpose of this work to defend Gnosticism, but only to explain it. Within that explanation must be the church's defense against it. After all, until the discovery of the Gnostic gospels we knew nothing of the Gnostics but what the church fathers said about the sect as they defended the church against what they considered to be a great heresy. For those who do not take time to thoroughly research information regarding the sect, they will be confronted with the same biased and limited information as was offered to the masses of the second century.

What we can say about Gnosticism is that it does not fit the pattern to be considered the "great whore" of Revelation, as some have said.

Are Gnostics Christian? Or, to ask the question in another way, is Gnosticism a sect or denomination of Christianity? The answer depends on what prerequisites must be fulfilled in one's faith and doctrine to be considered "Christian."

If the mention or presence of a scared feminine force precludes acceptance, then all of Catholicism would be excluded. Holy Mary, Mother of God now sits sinless on the right hand of Christ as an ascended co-redeemer with him. Having been impregnated by the Holy Spirit, she carried God in her womb and gave birth to God on earth. She lived as a virgin, gave birth, yet remained a virgin, and died as a virgin. She ascended to heaven and took her place, first as an intercessor between man and Christ, then was promoted by the church to the place of co-redeemer with Christ. She is the sacred feminine within the Catholic church.

Must one believe in original sin to be a Christian? The Eastern Orthodox Church does not hold to this doctrine. They believe we have a predisposition to sin, but they do not believe we are born into sin. Are those who follow one of the oldest Christian churches in the world Christians?

Must one believe in the doctrine of the trinity to be a Christian? The Church of Jesus Christ Latter-day Saints and Jehovah's Witnesses do not believe God and Christ are one and the same.

Although these denominations did not exist at the time the Council of Nicea met at Constantine's behest, when Constantine legalized Christianity, the same problem existed. What constitutes Christianity? To answer this question church leaders came together and by majority consent, the Nicene Creed was developed. The creed, written below, became the measuring rod which decided admittance into Christendom. But before and after the great council there have been creeds, and they all have been different.

History of the Gospel of Philip

The Gospel of Philip is assumed to be one of the sources of Dan Brown's novel, *The Da Vinci Code*, about Mary Magdalene, Jesus, and their children. The Gospel is one of the Gnostic texts found at Nag Hammadi in Egypt in 1945 and belongs to the same collection of Gnostic documents as the more famous Gospel of Thomas.

It has been suggested that the *Gospel of Philip* was written in the second century A.D. If so, it may be one of the earliest documents containing themes that would later be used in apocryphal literature. This is literature that describes the end of the world or the coming of the heavenly kingdom.

A single manuscript of the *Gospel of Philip*, written in Coptic, was found in the Nag Hammadi library. The collection was a library of thirteen papyrus texts discovered near the town of Nag Hammadi in 1945 by a peasant boy. The writings in these codices comprised 52 documents, most of which are Gnostic in nature.

The codices were probably hidden by monks from the nearby monastery of St. Pachomius when the official Christian Church banned all Gnostic literature around the year 390 A.D

It is believed the original texts were written in Greek during the first or second centuries A.D. The copies contained in the discovered clay jar were written in Coptic in the third or fourth centuries A.D.

From the time Gnosticism was labeled a heresy, the church began a policy of conversion or extermination. Beginning around 390 A.D. and continuing until the Cathar extermination, the church opposed Gnosticism and all movements, forms, and sects that proceeded from it.

In 1209 Pope Innocent III proclaimed a crusade against the last vestiges of "Gnostic-like" sects, the Cathars. For years the church discussed the Cathars, attempting to decide if they could be considered Christian or not. Eventually they would be labeled heretical and ordered to come into line with the orthodox beliefs of the Catholic Church. The Cathars held to their beliefs. Their doctrine included the belief that the world was split along lines of matter and spirit, good and evil. As with many Gnostic sects, they believed in abstaining from the world by purifying themselves, living a life of chastity and poverty. They believed in the equality of the sexes. The Pope saw the Cathars as a danger to the church since the members were admired for their modest lifestyle and the Cathar membership was growing.

Even though the Cathars were an ascetic sect, leading lives of peace and abstinence, they were hunted down and killed. Twenty years of carnage and warfare followed in which cities and provinces throughout the south of France were systematically eradicated. In an attempt to kill every Cathar, one of the worst episodes of the war ensued when the entire population of Toulouse, both Cathar and Catholic, were massacred. In 1243 the Cathar fortress of Montsegur in the Pyrenees was captured and destroyed. Those who refused to renounce their beliefs were tortured or put to death by fire. In spite of continued persecution, the Cathar movement continued through the 14th century, finally disappearing in the 15th century. Still, the church could not find or destroy all Gnostic literature. Books such as *The Gospel of Philip* remained.

The *Gospel Of Philip* is a list of sayings focusing on man's redemption and salvation as framed by Gnostic theology, and is presented here based on a comparative study of translations from the Nag Hammadi Codex by Wesley W. Isenberg, Willis Barnstone, The Ecumenical Coptic Project, Bart Ehrman, Marvin Meyer, David Cartlidge, David Dungan, and other sources.

Each verse was weighed against the theological and philosophical beliefs held by the Gnostic community at the time in which the document was penned. All attempts were made to render the most accurate meaning based on the available translations and information.

Exact wording was secondary to the conveyance of the overall meaning as understood by the contemporary reader.

When the wording of a verse held two possible meanings or needed expanded definitions, optional translations were placed in parentheses.

The Gospel of Philip

1. A Hebrew makes a Hebrew convert, and they call him a proselyte (novice). A novice does not make another novice.

Some are just as they are, and they make others like themselves to receive. It is enough for them that they simply are as they are.

2. The slave seeks only to be set free. He does not hope to attain the estate of his master. The son acts as a son (heir), but the father gives the inheritance to him.

3. Those who inherit the dead are dead, and they inherit the dead. Those who inherit the living are alive. They inherit both the living and the dead.

The dead cannot inherit anything. How can the dead inherit anything? When the dead inherits the living one, he shall not die but the dead shall live instead.

4. The Gentile (unbeliever) who does not believe does not die, because he has never been alive, so he could not die. He who has trusted the Truth has found life and is in danger of dying, because he is now alive.

5. Since the day that the Christ came, the cosmos was created, the cities are built (adorned), and the dead carried out (disposed of).

6. In the days when we were Hebrews we were made orphans, having only our Mother. Yet when we believed in the Messiah (and became the ones of Christ), the Mother and Father both came to us.

7. Those who sow in the winter reap in the summer. The winter is this world system. The summer is the other age or dispensation (to come). Let us sow in the world (cosmos) so that we will reap in the summer. Because of this, it is right for us not to pray in the winter. What comes from (follows) the winter is the summer. If anyone reaps in the winter he will not harvest but rather pull it up by the roots and will not produce fruit. Not only does it not produce in winter, but on the Sabbath his field shall be bare.

8. The Christ has come to fully ransom some, to save (restore and heal) others, and to be the propitiation (payment) for others. Those who were estranged he ransomed. He purchases them for himself. He saves, heals, and restores those who come to him. These he desires to pledge (in marriage). When he became manifest (in this world) he ordained the soul (with a body) as he desired (and set aside his own life), but even before this, in the time of the world's beginning, he had ordained the soul (he had laid down his own life for these souls). At his appointed time he came to bring the soul he pledged himself to back to (for) himself. It had come to be under the control of robbers and they took it captive. Yet he saved it, and he paid the price for both the good and the evil of the world.

9. Light and dark, life and death, right and left are brothers. It is impossible for one to be separated from the other. They are neither good, nor evil. A life is not alive without death. Death is not death if one were not alive. Therefore each individual shall be returned to his origin, as he was from the beginning. Those who go beyond the world will live forever and are in the eternal present.

10. The names that are given to worldly things cause great confusion. They contort our perception from the real to the unreal. He who hears the word "God" does not think of the real, but rather has false, preconceived ideas. It is the same with the words "Father," "Son," "Holy Spirit," "Life," "Light," "Resurrection," and "Church (the called out ones)," and all other words. They do not recall the real, but rather they call to mind preconceived, false ideas.

They (Archons) learned the reality of human death. They (Archons) who are in the world system made them (men) think of the false idea. If they had been in eternity, they would not have designated anything as evil, nor would they have placed things within worldly events (time and place). They (men) are destined for eternity.

11. The only name they (men) should never speak into the world is the name the Father gave himself through the Son. This is the Father's name. It exists that he may be exalted over all things. The Son could not become the Father, unless he was given the Father's name. This name exists so that they (men) may have it in their thoughts. They (men) should never speak it. Those

who do not have it cannot even think it. But the truth created names in the world for our sake. It would not be possible to learn the truth without names.

12. The Truth alone is the truth. It is a single thing and a multitude of things. The truth teaches us love alone through many and varied paths.

13. Those who ruled (lower gods) desired to deceive man because they knew man was related to the truly good ones. They (Archons) took the designation of good and they gave it to those who were not good. They did this so that by way of words they might deceive man and bind him to those who are not good. When they receive favor, they are taken from those who are not good and placed among the good. These are they who had recognized themselves. The rulers (lower gods) had desired to take the free person, and enslave him to themselves forever. Rulers of power fight against man. The rulers do not want him to be saved (recognize himself), so that men will become their masters. For if man is saved there will be no need for sacrifice.

14. When sacrifice began, animals were offered up to the ruling powers (Archon / Demiurge). They were offered up to them while the sacrificial animals were still alive. But as they offered them up they were killed. But the Christ was offered up dead to God (the Supreme God), and yet he lived.

15. Before the Christ came, there had been no bread in the world. In paradise, the place where Adam was, there had been many plants as food for wild animals, but paradise had no wheat for man to eat. Man had to be nourished like animals. But the Christ, the perfect man, was sent. He brought the bread of heaven, so that man could eat as he should.

16. The rulers (lower gods) thought what they did (create the material world) was by their own will and power, but the Holy Spirit worked through them without their knowledge to do her will.

17. The truth, which exists from the beginning, is sown everywhere, and everyone sees it being sown, but only a few see the harvest.

18. Some say that Mary conceived (impregnated) by the Holy Spirit. They are in error. They do not know what they are saying. How can a female impregnate another female? (The Holy Spirit is a feminine force.) Mary is the virgin whom no power defiled. She is a great problem and curse among the Hebrew Apostles and those in charge (church leaders). The ruler (lower god) who attempts to defile this virgin, is himself defiled. The Lord was not going to say, "my father in heaven", unless he really had another father (on earth). He would simply have said, "my father".

19. The Lord says to the Disciples, "Come into the house of the Father, but do not bring anything in or take anything out from the father's house."

20. Jesus (Yeshua) is the secret name; Christ (messiah) is the revealed name. The name "Jesus" (Yeshua) does not occur in any other language. His name is called "Jesus" (Yeshua). In Aramaic his name is Messiah, but in Greek it is Christ (Cristos). In every language he is called the anointed one. The fact that he is Savior (Yeshua) could be fully comprehended only by himself, since it is the Nazarene who reveals the secret things.

21. Christ has within himself all things; man, angel, mystery (sacraments), and the father.

22. Those who say that the Lord first died and then arose are in error. He would have to first arise (be born) before he could die. If he is not first resurrected (born) he would die, but God lives and cannot die.

(Alternate translation:
Those who say that the Lord died first and then arose are in error. He arose first and then died. If one does not first attain the resurrection, he will not die. As God lives, he would live also).

23. No one will hide something highly valuable in something ostentatious (that would draw attention). More often, one places something of great worth within a number of containers worth nothing. This is how it is with the (human) soul. It is a precious thing placed within a lowly body.

24. Some are fearful that they will arise (from the dead) naked. Therefore they desire to rise in the flesh. They do not understand that those who choose to wear the flesh are naked (destitute in spirit). Those who choose to strip themselves of the flesh are the ones who are not naked.

25. Flesh and blood will not be able to inherit the kingdom of God. What is this that will not inherit? It is that which is upon each of us (our flesh). But what will inherit the kingdom is that which belongs to Jesus and is of his flesh and blood. Therefore he says: "He who does not eat my flesh and drink my blood, has no life in him." What is his flesh? It is the Word, and his blood is the Holy Spirit. He who has received these has food and drink and clothing.

26. I disagree with those who say the flesh will not arise. They are in error. Tell me what will rise so that we may honor you. You say it is the spirit in the flesh and the light contained in the flesh. But whatever you say there is nothing you mention that is contained outside of the flesh (material world). It is necessary to arise in this flesh if everything exists within the flesh (and everything exists as part of or connected to the material world).

27. In this world those wearing a garment are more valuable than the garment. In the kingdom of the Heavens the garment is more valuable than the one wearing it.

28. By water and fire the entire realm is purified through the revelations by those who reveal them, and by the secrets through those who keep them. Yet, there are things kept secret even within those things revealed. There is water in baptism and there is fire in the oil of anointing.

29. Jesus took them all by surprise. For he did not reveal himself as he originally was, but he revealed himself as they were capable of perceiving him. He revealed himself to all in their own way. To the great, he revealed himself as great. To the small he was small. He revealed himself to the angels as an angel and to mankind he was a man. Some looked at him and saw themselves. But, throughout all of this, he concealed his words from everyone. However when he revealed himself to his Disciples upon the mountain, he appeared glorious. He was not made small. He became great, but he also made the disciples great so that they would be capable of comprehending his greatness.

30. He said on that day during his thanksgiving (in the Eucharist), "You have combined the perfect light and the holy spirit along with angels and images."

31. Do not hate the Lamb. Without him it is not possible to see the door to the sheepfold. Those who are naked will not come before the King.

32. The Sons of the Heavenly Man are more numerous than those of the earthly man. If the sons of Adam are numerous although they die, think of how many more Sons the Perfect Man has and these do not die. And they are continually born every instant of time.

33. The Father creates a son, but it is not possible for the son to create a son because it is impossible for someone who was just born to have a child. The Son has brothers, not sons.

34. There is order in things. All those who are born in the world are begotten physically. Some are begotten spiritually, fed by the promise of heaven, which is delivered by the perfect Word from the mouth. The perfect Word is conceived through a kiss and thus they are born. There is unction to kiss one another to receive conception from grace to grace.

35. There were three women named Mary (Bitter) who walked with the Lord all the time. They were his mother, his sister and Mary of Magdala, who was his consort (companion). Thus his mother, his sister and companion (consort) were all named Mary.

36. "Father" and "Son" are single names, "Holy Spirit" is a double name and it is everywhere; above and below, secret and revealed. The Holy Spirit's abode is manifest when she is below. When she is above she is hidden.

(Alternative translation:
"Father" and "Son" are single names; "Holy Spirit" is a double name. For they are everywhere: they are above, they are below; they are concealed, they are revealed. When the Holy Spirit is in the revealed it is below. When it is in the concealed it is above.)

37. Saints are served by evil powers (lesser gods). The evil spirits are deceived by the Holy Spirit. They think they are assisting a common man when they are serving Saints. A follower of the Lord once asked him for a thing from this world. He answered him saying, "Ask your Mother, and she will give you something from another realm."

38. The Apostles said to the students, "May all of our offering obtain salt!" They had called Sophia (wisdom) salt and without it no offering can become acceptable.

39. Sophia (wisdom) is barren. She has no children but she is called Mother. Others are found (adopted) by the Holy Spirit, and she has many children.

40. That which the Father has belongs to the Son, but he cannot possess it when he is young (small). When he comes of age all his father has will be given to the son.

41. Those who do not follow the path are born of the Spirit, and they stray because of her. By this same spirit (breath or life force), the fire blazes and consumes.

42. Earthly wisdom is one thing, and earthly wisdom (death) is another. Earthly wisdom is simply wisdom, but death is the wisdom of death, and death is the one who understands death. Being familiar with death is minor wisdom.

43. There are animals like the bull and donkey that are submissive to man. There are others that live in the wilderness. Man plows the field with submissive animals, and uses the harvest to feed himself as well as all the animals, domesticated or wild. So it is with the Perfect Man. Through submissive powers he plows and provides for all things to exist. He causes all things to come together into existence, whether good or evil, right or left.

44. The Holy Spirit is the shepherd guiding everyone and every power (lower ruler or lesser gods), whether submissive, rebellious, or feral. She controls them, subdues them, and keeps them bridled, whether they wish it or not.

45. He who was created (Adam) is beautiful. One would not expect his children to be noble. If he were not created but rather born, one would expect his children to be noble. But he was both created and born. Is this nobility?

46. Adultery occurred first and then came murder. And Cain was conceived in adultery because he was the serpent's (Satan's) son. He became a murderer just like his father. He killed his brother. When copulation occurs between those who are not alike, this is adultery.

47. God is a dyer. Just as a good and true dye penetrates deep into fabric to dye it permanently from within (not a surface act), so God has baptized what He dyes into an indelible dye, which is water.

48. It is impossible for anyone to see anything in the real world, unless he has become part of it. It is not like a person in this world. When one looks at the sun he can see it without being part of it. He can see the sky or the earth or anything without having to be part of it. So it is with this world, but in the other world you must become what you see (see what you become). To see spirit you must be spirit. To see Christ you must be Christ. To see the Father you must be the Father. In this way you will see everything but yourself. If you look at yourself you will become what you see.

49. Faith receives, but love gives. No one can receive without faith. No one can love without giving. Believe and you shall receive. Love and you shall give. If you give without love, you shall receive nothing. Whoever has not received the Lord, continues to be a Hebrew.

50. The Apostles who came before us called him Jesus, The Nazarene, and The Messiah. Of these names, Jesus (Yeshua), The Nazarene (of the rite of the Nazarites), and The Messiah (Christ), the last name is the Christ, the first is Jesus, and the middle name is The Nazarene. Messiah has two meanings; the anointed one and the measured one. Jesus (Yeshua) means The Atonement (redemption or payment). 'Nazara' means Truth. Therefore, the Nazarite is The Truth. The Christ is The Measured One, the Nazarite (Truth) and Jesus (Redemption) have been measured (are the measurement).

51. The pearl which is thrown into the mud is not worth less than it was before. If it is anointed with balsam oil it is valued no higher. It is as valuable as its owner perceives it to be. So it is with the children of God. Whatever becomes of them, they are precious in their Father's eyes.

52. If you say you are a Jew it will not upset anyone. If you say you are a Roman no one will care. If you claim to be a Greek, foreigner, slave, or a free man no one will be the least bit disturbed. But, if you claim to belong to Christ everyone will take heed (be concerned). I hope to receive this title from him. Those who are worldly would not be able to endure when they hear the name.

53. God is a man-eater (cannibal), because men are sacrificed to him. Before men were sacrificed, animals were sacrificed. Those to whom they are sacrificed are not gods.

54. Vessels of glass and vessels of clay are always made with fire. But if a glass vessel should break it is recast, because it is made in a single breath. If a clay vessel breaks it is destroyed, since it came into being without breath.

55. A donkey turning a millstone walked a hundred miles but when it was untied it was in the same place it started. There are those who go on long journeys but do not progress. When evening comes (when the journey ends), they have discovered no city, no village, no construction site, no creature (natural thing), no power (ruler), and no angel. They labored and toiled for nothing (emptiness).

56. The thanksgiving (Eucharist) is Jesus. For in Aramaic they call him farisatha, which means, "to be spread out." This is because Jesus came to crucify the world.

57. The Lord went into the place where Levi worked as a dyer. He took 72 pigments and threw them into a vat. When he drew out the result it was pure white. He said, "This is how the Son of Man has come. He is a dyer."

58. Sophia (Wisdom), which they call barren, is the mother of the angels. And the companion (Consort) was Mary of Magdala. The Lord loved Mary more than all the other disciples and he kissed her often on her mouth (the text is missing here and the word "mouth" is assumed). The others saw his love for Mary and asked him: "Why do you love her more than all of us?" The Savior replied, "Why do I not love you in the same way I love her?" While a blind person and a person who sees are both in the dark, there is no difference, but when the light comes, the one who sees shall behold the light, but he who is blind will remain in darkness.

59. The Lord says: "Blessed is he who existed before you came into being, for he is and was and shall (continue to) be."

60. The supremacy of man is not evident, but it is hidden. Because of this he is master of the animals, which are stronger (larger) than him, in ways both evident and not. This allows the animals to survive. But, when man departs from them, they bite and kill and devour each other because they have no food. Now they have food because man cultivated the land.

61. If one goes down into the water (is baptized) and comes up having received nothing, but claims to belong to Christ, he has borrowed against the name at a high interest rate. But if one receives the Holy Spirit, he has been given the name as a gift. He who has received a gift does not have to pay for it or give it back. If you have borrowed the name you will have to pay it back with interest when it is demanded. This is how the mystery works.

62. Marriage is a sacrament and a mystery. It is grand. For the world is founded upon man, and man founded upon marriage. Consider sex (pure sex), it has great power although its image is defiled.

63. Among the manifestations of unclean spirits there are male and female. The males are those who mate with the souls inhabiting a female form, and the female spirits invite those inhabiting a male form to have sex. Once seized, no one escapes unless they receive both the male and female power that is endued to the Groom with the Bride. The power is seen in the mirrored Bridal-Chamber. When foolish women see a man sitting alone, they want to subdue him, touch and handle him, and defile him. When foolish men see a beautiful woman sitting alone, they wish to seduce her, draw her in with desire and defile her. But, if the spirits see the man sitting together with his woman, the female spirit cannot intrude upon the man and the male spirit cannot intrude upon the woman. When image and angel are mated, no one can come between the man and woman.

64. He who comes out from the world cannot be stopped. Because he was once in the world he is now beyond both yearning (desire) and fear. He has overcome the flesh and has mastered envy and desire. If he does not leave the world there are forces that will come to seize him, strangle him. How can anyone escape? How can he fear them? Many times men will come and say, "We are faithful, and we hid from unclean and demonic spirits." But if they had been given the Holy Spirit, no unclean spirit would have clung to them. Do not fear the flesh, nor love it. If you fear it, the flesh will become your master. If you love it, the flesh will devour you and render you unable to move.

65. One exists either in this world or in the resurrection or in transition between them. Do not be found in transition. In that world there is both good and evil. The good in it is not good and the evil in it is not evil. There is evil after this world, which is truly evil and it is called the transition. This is what is called death. While we are in this world it is best that we be born into the resurrection, so that we take off the flesh and find rest and not wander within the region of the transition. Many go astray along the way. Because of this, it is best to go forth from the world before one has sinned.

66. Some neither wish nor are able to act. Others have the will to act but it is best for them if they do not act, because the act they desire to perform would make them a sinner. By not desiring to do a righteous act justice is withheld (justice is not obvious). However, the will always comes before the act.
(It is not the act but the will that matters.)

67. An Apostle saw in a vision people confined to a blazing house, held fast in bonds of fire, crying out as flames came from their breath. There was water in the house, and they cried out, "The waters can truly save us." They were misled by their desire. This is called the outermost darkness.
(Alternate translation:
An Apostle saw in a vision people confined to a blazing house, held fast in bonds of fire, lying in the flames. There was water, but they had no faith and did not desire to be saved. They received punishment, being cast into outer darkness.)

68. Soul and spirit were born of water and fire. From water, fire, and light the children of the Bridal-Chamber are born. The fire is the spirit (anointing), the light is the fire, but not the kind of fire that has form. I speak of the other kind whose form is white and it rains down beauty and splendor.

69. The truth did not come into the world naked, but it came in types and symbols. The world would not receive it any other way. There is a rebirth together with its symbols. One cannot be reborn through symbols. What can the symbol of resurrection raise, or the Bridal-Chamber with its symbols? One must come into the truth through the (true) image (not the symbol or type of it). Truth is this Restoration. It is good for those not born to take on the names of the Father, the Son, and the Holy Spirit. They could not have done so on their own. Whoever is not born of them will have the name (Christ's ones) removed from him. The one who receives them receives the anointing of the spirit and the unction and power of the cross. This is what the Apostles call having the right with the left. When this happens, you no longer belong to Christ, you will be Christ.

70. The Lord did everything through sacraments (mysteries or symbols): There was baptism, anointing, thanksgiving (Eucharist), atonement (sacrifice or payment), and Bridal-Chamber.

71. He says: "I came to make what is inside the same as the outside and what is below as it is above. I came to bring all of this into one place." He revealed himself through types and symbols. Those who say Christ comes from the place beyond (above) are confused.

72. He who is manifest in heaven is called "one from below." And He who knows the hidden thing is He who is above him. The correct way to say it would be "the inner and the outer or this which is beyond the outer." Because of this, the Lord called destruction "the outer darkness." There is nothing beyond it. He says, "My Father, who is in secret." He says, "Go into your inner chamber, shut the door behind you and there pray to your Father who is in secret; He who is deep within." He who is within them all is the Fullness. Beyond Him there is nothing deeper within. The deepest place within is called the uppermost place.

73. Before Christ some came forth. They were not able to go back from where they came. They were no longer able to leave from where they went. Then Christ came. Those who went in he brought out, and those who went out he brought in.

74. When Eve was still within Adam (man), there had been no death. When she was separated from him, death began. If she were to enter him again and if he were to receive her completely, death would stop.

75. "My God, my God, Oh Lord why did you abandon me?" He spoke these words on the cross. He departed (divided) the place and was not there any longer.

76. The Lord arose from the dead. He became as he had been, but his body had been made perfect. He was clothed in true flesh. Our flesh is not true, but rather an image of true flesh, as one beholds in a mirror.

77. The Bridal-Chamber is not for beasts, slaves, or whores. It is for free men and virgins.

78. Through the Holy Spirit we are born again, conceived in Christ, anointed in the spirit, united within us. Only with light can we see ourselves reflected in water or mirror. We are baptized in water and light. It is the light that is the oil of the anointing.

79. There had been three offering vestibules in Jerusalem. One opened to the west called the holy, another opened to the south called the holy of the holy, the third opened to the east called the holy of the holies where the high priest alone was to

enter. The Baptism is the holy, the redemption (payment or atonement) is the holy of the holy, and the holy of the holies is the Bridal-Chamber. The Baptism has within it the resurrection and the redemption. Redemption allows entrance into the Bridal-Chamber. The Bridal-Chamber is more exalted than any of these. Nothing compares.

80. Those who pray for Jerusalem love Jerusalem. They are in Jerusalem and they see it now. These are called the holy of the holies.

81. Before the curtain of the Temple was torn we could not see the Bridal-Chamber. All we had was the symbol of the place in heaven. When the curtain was torn from the top to the bottom it made a way for some to ascend.

82. Those who have been clothed in the Perfect Light cannot be seen by the powers, nor can the powers subdue them. Yet one shall be clothed with light in the sacrament (mystery) of sex (union / being united).

83. If the woman had not been separated from the man, neither would have died. Christ came to rectify the error of separation that had occurred. He did this by re-uniting them and giving life to those who died. The woman unites with her husband in the Bridal-Chamber and those who have united in the Bridal-Chamber will not be parted again. Eve separated from Adam because she did not unite with him in the Bridal-Chamber.

84. The soul of man (Adam) was created when breath (spirit) was blown into him. The elements were supplied by his mother (Sophia). When soul (mind or will) became spirit and were joined together he spoke words the powers could not understand. They envied him, his spiritual partner, and his opportunity. They wanted it all for themselves but the Bridal-Chamber was hidden from them.

85. Jesus manifested beside the River Jordan with fullness of the kingdom of the Heavens, which existed before anything. Moreover, he was born as a Son before birth. He was anointed and he anointed. He was atoned and he atoned for others.

86. It is right to speak of a mystery. The Father of them all mated with the Virgin who had come down. A fire shone over him on that day. He revealed the power of the Bridal-Chamber. Because of this power his body came into being on that day. He came forth in the Bridal-Chamber in glory because of the essence that issued forth from the Bridegroom to the Bride. This is how Jesus established everything. It was in his heart. In this same way it is right for each one of the disciples to enter into his rest.

87. Adam came into being from two virgins, from the Spirit and from the virgin earth. Christ was born from a virgin, so that the error which occurred in the beginning would be corrected by him.

88. There were two trees in paradise. One produced beasts, the other produced man. Adam ate from the tree that produced beasts becoming a beast he gave birth to beasts. Because of this, animals were worshipped. God created man and men created gods. This is how the world works; men create gods and they worship their creations. It would have been more appropriate for gods to worship mankind. This would be the way if Adam had not eaten from the tree of life, which bore people.

89. The deeds of man follow his abilities. These are his strengths and the things he does with ease. His result is his children who came forth from his times of rest. His work is governed by his work but in his rest he brings forth his sons. This is the sign and symbol, doing works with strength, and producing children in his rest.

90. In this world the slaves are forced to serve the free. In the kingdom of Heaven the free shall serve the slaves and the Bridegroom of the Bridal-Chamber shall serve the guests. Those of the Bridal-Chamber have a single name among them, it is "rest" and they have no need for any other. The contemplation of the symbol brings enlightenment and great glory. Within those in the Chamber (rest) the glories are fulfilled.

91. Go into the water but do not go down into death, because Christ shall atone for him when he who is baptized comes forth. They were called to be fulfilled in his name. For he said, "We must fulfill all righteousness."

92. Those who say they shall die and then arise are confused. If you do not receive the resurrection while you are alive you will not receive anything when you die. This is why it is said that Baptism is great, because those who receive it shall live.

93. Philip the Apostle said, "Joseph the Carpenter planted a grove of trees because he needed wood for his work (craft or trade). He himself made the cross from the trees that he had planted, and his heir hung on that which he had planted. His

heir was Jesus, and the tree was the cross. But the tree of life in the midst of the garden (paradise) is the olive tree. From the heart of it comes the anointing through the olive oil and from that comes the resurrection."

94. This world consumes corpses. Everything eaten by (in) the world dies. The truth devours life, but if you eat truth you shall never die. Jesus came (from there) bringing food. And to those wishing it (whom he wished) he gave life, so that they not die.

95. God created the garden (paradise). Man lived there, but they did not have God in their hearts and so they gave in to desire. This garden is where they will be said to us, " You may eat this but not eat that, according to your desire." This is the place where I shall choose to eat various things there such as the tree of knowledge, which slew Adam. In this place the tree of knowledge gave life to man. The Torah is the tree. It has the power to impart the knowledge of good and evil. It did not remove him from the evil or deliver him to good. It simply caused those who had eaten it to die. Death began because truth said, " You can eat this, but do not eat that." This was the beginning of death.

96. The anointing (chrism) is made superior to Baptism, because from the word Chrism we are called Christians (Christ's ones / anointed ones) not because of the word Baptism. And because of Chrism he was called Christ. The Father anointed the Son, and the Son anointed the Apostles, and the Apostles anointed us. He who has been anointed has come to possess all things; he has the resurrection, the light, the cross, and the Holy Spirit. The Father bestowed this upon him in the Bridal-Chamber. The father gave it to the Son who received it freely. The Father was in the Son, and the Son was in the Father. This is the kingdom of Heaven.

97. It was perfectly said by the Lord: Some have attained the kingdom of Heaven laughing. They came forth from the world joyous. Those who belong to Christ who went down into the water immediately came up as lord of everything. He did not laugh because he took things lightly, but because he saw that everything in this world was worthless compared to the kingdom of Heaven. If he scoffs at the world and sees its worthlessness he will come forth laughing.

98. Compared to the Bread and cup, and the oil of anointing (Chrism); there is another one superior to them all.

99. The world (system) began through a mistake. He who made this world wished to make it perfect and eternal. He failed (fell away / did not follow through) and did not attain his goal. The world is not eternal, but the children of the world are eternal. They were children and obtained eternity. No one can receive eternity except by becoming a child. The more you are unable to receive, the more you will be unable to give.

100. The cup of the communion (prayer) contains wine and water. It is presented as the symbol of the blood. Over it (because of the blood) we give thanks. It is filled by (with) the Holy Spirit. It (the blood) belongs to the Perfect Man. When we drink we consume the Perfect man.

101. The Living Water is a body. It is right that we be clothed with a living body (The Living Man). When he goes down into the water he undresses himself so he may be clothed with the living man.

102. A horse naturally gives birth to a horse, a human naturally gives birth to a human, a god naturally gives birth to a god. The Bridegroom within the Bride gives birth to children who are born in the Bridal-Chamber. The Jews do not spring forth from Greeks (Gentiles), and Christians (those belonging to Christ) do not come from Jews. These who gave birth to Christians were called the chosen generation of the Holy Spirit (living God). The True Man, the Son of Mankind, was the seed that brought forth the sons of Man. This generation is the true ones in the world. This is the place where the children of the Bridal-Chamber dwell.

103. Copulation occurs in this world when man and woman mix (mingle or entwine). Strength joins with weakness. In eternity there is a different kind of mingling that occurs. Metaphorically we call it by the same names, but it is exalted beyond any name we may give it. It transcends brute strength. Where there is no force, there are those who are superior to force. Man cannot comprehend this.

104. The one is not, and the other one is, but they are united. This is He who shall not be able to come unto those who have a heart of flesh. (He is not here, but He exists. However, He cannot inhabit a heart of those who are attached to the fleshly world.)

105. Before you possess all knowledge, should you not know yourself? If you do not know yourself, how can you enjoy those things you have? Only those who have understood themselves shall enjoy the things they have come to possess.

106. The perfected person cannot be captured or seen. If they (Archons) could see him, they could capture him. The path to grace can only come from the perfect light. Unless one is clothed in the perfect light and it shows on and in him he shall not be able to come out from the World as the perfected son of the Bridal-Chamber. We must be perfected before we come out from the world. Whoever has received all before mastering all, will not be able to master the kingdom. He shall go to the transition (death) imperfect. Only Jesus knows his destiny.

107. The holy person (priest) is entirely holy, including his body. If one blesses the bread and sanctifies it, or the cup, or everything else he receives, why will he not sanctify the body also?

108. By perfecting the water of Baptism: thus Jesus washed away death (removed death from it). Because of this, we are descended into the water but not into death. We are not poured out into the wind (spirit) of the world. Whenever that blows, its winter has come. When the Holy Spirit breathes, summer has come.

109. Whoever recognizes the truth is set free. He who is set free does not go back (sin), for the one who goes back (the sinner) is the slave of sin. Truth is the Mother. When we unite with her it is recognition of the truth. Those who are set free from sin (no longer have to sin) are called free by the world. It is the recognition of the truth that exalts the hearts of those who are set free from sin. This is what liberates them and places them over the entire world. Love builds (inspires). He who has been set free through this recognition is a slave of love, serving those who have not yet been set free by the truth. Knowledge makes them capable of being set free. Love does not take anything selfishly. How can it when it possesses all things? It does not say; "This is mine or that is mine," but it says, "All of this belongs to you."

110. Spiritual love is wine with fragrance. All those who are anointed with it enjoy it. Those who anoint themselves with it (are near to the anointed ones) enjoy it also. But when the anointed ones depart the bystanders who are not anointed remain in their own stench. The Samaritan gave nothing to the wounded man except wine and oil for anointing. The wounds were healed, for "love covers a multitude of sins."

111. The children of a woman resemble the man who loves her. If the man is her husband, they resemble her husband. If the man is her illicit lover, they resemble him. Often, a woman will have sex with her husband out of duty but her heart is with her lover with whom she also has sex. The children of such a union often resemble the lover. You who live with the Son of God and do not also love the world but love the Lord only will have children that look like the Lord and not the world.

112. Humans mate with the humans, horses mate with horses, donkeys mate with donkeys. Like attracts like and they group together. Spirits unite with Spirits, and the thought (Word) mingles with the thought (Word), as Light merges with Light. If you become a person then people will love you. If you become a spirit, then the Spirit shall merge with you. If you become a thought (the Word), then the thought (the Word) shall unite with you. If you become enlightened, then the Light shall merge with you. If you rise above this world, then that which is from above shall rest upon (in) you. But, if you become like a horse, donkey, bull, dog, sheep, or any other animal, domestic or feral, then neither man nor Spirit nor Word (thought) nor the Light nor those from above nor those dwelling within shall be able to love you. They shall not be able to rest in you, and they will have no part in your inheritance to come.

113. He who is enslaved without his consent can be set free. He who has been set free by the grace of his master, but then sells himself back into slavery cannot be set free.

114. The cultivation in this world comes through four elements (earth, air, fire, water). Crops are harvested and taken into the barn only if there is first soil, water, wind, and light. God's harvest is also by means of four elements; faith (trust), hope (expectation), love (agape'), and knowledge (recognition of the truth). Our soil is the faith in which we take root. Our water is the hope by which we are nourished. Wind (spirit) is the love through which we grow. Light is the truth, which causes us to ripen. But, it is Grace that causes us to become kings of all heaven. Their souls are among the blessed for they live in Truth.

115. Jesus, the Christ, came to all of us but did not lay any burden on us. This kind of person is perfect and blessed. He is the Word of God. Ask us about him and we will tell you his righteousness is difficult to define or describe. A task so great assures failure.

116. How will he give rest to everyone; great or small, believer or not? He provides rest to all. There are those who attempt to gain by assisting the rich. Those who see themselves as rich are picky. They do not come of their own accord. Do not grieve them or anyone. It is natural to want to do good, but understand that the rich may seek to cause grief and he who seeks to do good could annoy those who think they are rich.

117. A householder had acquired everything. He had children, slaves, cattle, dogs, and pigs. He also had wheat, barley, straw, hay, meat, oil, and acorns. He was wise and knew what each needed to eat. He fed his children bread and meat. He fed the slaves oil with grain. The cattle were given barley, straw and hay. The dogs received bones and the pigs got acorns and bread scraps. This is how it is with the disciple of God. If he is wise, he understands discipleship. The bodily forms will not deceive him, but he will understand the condition of the souls around him. He will speak to each man on his own level. In the world there are many types of animals in human form. He must recognize each one. If the person is a pig, feed him acorns. If the person is a bull, feed him barley with straw and hay; if a dog, throw him bones. If a person is a slave feed him basic food, but to the sons present the perfect and complete food.

118. There is the Son of Man and there is the son of the son of Man. The Lord is the Son of Man, and his son creates through him. God gave the Son of Man the power to create; he also gave him the ability to have children. That which is created is a creature. Those born are a progeny (child or heir). A creature cannot propagate, but children can create. Yet they say that the creature procreates, however, the child is a creature. Therefore the creature's progeny are not his sons, but rather they are creations. He who creates works openly, and is visible. He who procreates does so in secret, and he hides himself from others. He who creates does so in open sight. He who procreates, makes his children (son) in secret.

119. No one is able to know what day a husband and wife copulate. Only they know, because marriage in this world is a sacrament (mystery) for those who have taken a wife. If the act of an impure (common) marriage is hidden, the pure (immaculate) marriage is a deeper mystery (sacrament) and is hidden even more. It is not carnal (common) but it is pure (undefiled). It is not founded on lust. It is founded on true love (agape'). It is not part of the darkness or night. It is part of the light. A marriage (act) which is seen (revealed or exposed) becomes vulgarity (common or prostitution), and the bride has played the whore not only if she has sex with another man, but also if she escapes from the Bridal-Chamber and is seen. She may only be seen (reveal herself to) by her father, her mother, the attendant (friend) of the bridegroom, and the bridegroom. Only these have permission to go into the bridal-chamber on a daily basis. Others will yearn to hear her voice or enjoy her perfume (fragrance of the anointing oil). Let them be fed like dogs from the scraps that fall from the table. Only those being from the Bridegroom belong with the Bride in the Bridal-Chamber. No one will be able to see the Bridegroom or the Bride unless he becomes one like (with) them.

120. When Abraham was allowed (rejoiced at seeing what he was) to see (the truth), he circumcised the flesh of the foreskin to show us that it was correct (necessary) to renounce (kill) the flesh of this world.

121. As long as the entrails of a person are contained, the person lives and is well. If his entrails are exposed and he is disemboweled, the person will die. It is the same with a tree. If its roots are covered it will live and grow, but if its roots are exposed the tree will wither and die. It is the same with everything born into this world. It is this way with everything manifest (seen) and covert (unseen). As long as the roots of evil are hidden, it is strong, but once evil is exposed or recognized it is destroyed and it dies. This is why the Word says; "Already the ax has been laid to the root of the tree." It will not only chop down the tree, because that will permit it to sprout again, the ax will go down into the ground and cleave the very root. Jesus uprooted what others had only partially cut down. Let each one of us dig deeply, down to the root of the evil that is within his heart and rip it out by its roots. If we can just recognize evil we can uproot it. However, if evil remains unrecognized, it will take root within us and yield its fruit in our hearts. It will make evil our master and we will be its slaves. Evil takes us captive, and coerces us into doing what we do not want to do. Evil compels us into not doing what we should do. While it is unrecognized, it drives us .

122. Ignorance is the mother of all evil. Evil ends in confusion and death. Truth is like ignorance. If it is hidden it rests within itself, but when it is revealed it is recognized and it is stronger than ignorance and error. Truth wins and liberates us from confusion. The Word said; "You shall know the truth and the truth shall set you free." Ignorance seeks to make us its slaves but knowledge is freedom. By recognizing the truth, we shall find the fruits of the truth within our hearts. If we join ourselves with the truth we shall be fulfilled.

123. Now, we have the visible (beings) things of creation and we say that visible things (beings) are the powerful and honorable, but the invisible things are the weak and unworthy of our attention. The nature of truth is different. In it, the visible things (beings) are weak and lowly, but the invisible are the powerful and honorable. The wisdom of the invisible God cannot be made known to us except that he takes visible form in ways we are accustomed to. Yet the mysteries of the truth are revealed, in types and symbols, but the Bridal-Chamber is hidden as it is with the Holy of Holies.

124. The veil of the Temple first concealed how God governed creation. Once the veil was torn and the things within (the Holy of Holies) were revealed, the house was to be forsaken, abandoned, and destroyed. Yet the entire Divinity (Godhead) was to depart, not to the holies of the holies, for it was not able to merge with the light nor unite with the complete fullness. It

was to be under the wings of the cross, in its open arms. This is the ark which shall be salvation for us when the destruction of water has overwhelmed (overtaken) them.

125. Those in the priestly tribe shall be able to enter within the veil of the Temple along with the High Priest. This was symbolized by the fact that the veil was not torn at the top only, (but was torn from top to the bottom). If it was torn only at the top it would have been opened only for those who are on high (from the higher realm). If it was torn at the bottom only it would have been revealed only to those who are from below (the lower realm). But it was torn from the top to the bottom. Those who are from above made it available to us who are below them, so that we might enter into the secret of the truth. This strengthening of us is most wonderful. Because of this, we can enter in by means of symbols even though they are weak and worthless. They are humble and incomplete when compared to the perfect glory. It is the glory of glories and the power of powers. Through it the perfect is opened to us and it contains the secrets of the truth. Moreover, the Holies of Holies have been revealed and opened, and the Bridal-Chamber has invited us in.

126. As long as evil is hidden, and not completely purged from among the children of the Holy Spirit, it remains a potential threat. The children can be enslaved by the adversary, but when the Perfect Light is seen, it will pour out the oil of anointing upon and within it, and the slaves shall be set free and the slaves shall be bought back.

127. Every plant not sown by my heavenly Father shall be pulled up by the root. Those who were estranged shall be united and the empty shall be filled.

128. Everyone who enters the bridal-chamber shall ignite (be born in) the Light. This is like a marriage, which takes place at night. The fire is ablaze and is seen in the dark but goes out before morning. The mysteries (sacraments) of the marriage are consummated in the light of day, and that light never dies.

129. If someone becomes a child of the Bridal-Chamber, he shall receive the Light. If one does not receive it in this place, he will not be able to receive it in any other place. He who has received that Light shall not be seen, nor captured. No one in the world will be able to disturb him. When he leaves the world he will have already received the truth in types and symbols. The world has become eternity, because for him the fullness is eternal. It is revealed only to this kind of person. Truth is not hidden in darkness or the night. Truth is hidden in a perfect day and a holy light.

History of The Gospel Of Mary Magdalene

While traveling and researching in Cairo in 1896, German scholar, Dr. Carl Reinhardt, acquired a papyrus containing Coptic texts entitled the Revelation of John, the Wisdom of Jesus Christ, and the Gospel of Mary.

Before setting about to translate his exciting find, two world wars ensued, delaying publication until 1955. By then the Nag Hammadi collection had also been discovered.

Two of the texts in his codex, the Revelation of John, and the Wisdom of Jesus Christ, were included there. Importantly, the codex preserves the most complete surviving copy of the Gospel of Mary, named for its supposed author, Mary of Magdala. Two other fragments of the Gospel of Mary written in Greek were later unearthed in archaeological digs at Oxyrhynchus in Northern Egypt.

All of the various fragments were brought together to form the translation presented here. However, even with all of the fragments assembled, the manuscript of the Gospel of Mary is missing pages 1 to 6 and pages 11 to 14. These pages included sections of the text up to chapter 4, and portions of chapter 5 to 8.

Although the text of the Gospel of Mary is incomplete, the text presented below serves to shake the very concept of our assumptions of early Christianity as well as Christ's possible relationship to Mary of Magdala, whom we call Mary Magdalene.

The Gospel of Mary Magdalene

(Pages 1 to 6, containing chapters 1 - 3, could not be recovered. The text starts on page 7, chapter 4)

Chapter 4

21) (And they asked Jesus), "Will matter then be destroyed or not?"

22) The Savior said, "All nature, all things formed, and all creatures exist in and with one another, and they will be dissolved again into their own elements (origins).

23) This is because it is the nature of matter to return to its original elements.

24) If you have an ear to hear, listen to this."

25) Peter said to him, "Since you have explained all things to us, tell us this also: What sin did the world commit (what sin is in the world)?"

26) The Savior said, "There is no sin (of the world). Each person makes his own sin when he does things like adultery (in the same nature as adultery). This is called sin.

27) That is why the Good came to be among you. He came to restore every nature to its basic root."

28) Then He continued; "You become sick and die because you did not have access to (knowledge of) Him who can heal you.

29) If you have any sense, you must understand this.

30) The material world produced a great passion (desire or suffering) without equal. This was contrary to the natural balance. The entire cosmos (body) was disturbed by it.

31) That is why I said to you, Be encouraged, and if you are discouraged be encouraged when you see the different forms nature has taken.

32) He who has ears to hear, let him hear."

33) When the Blessed One had said this, He greeted all of them and said; "Peace be with you. Take my peace into you.

34) Beware that no one deceives you by saying, 'Look (he is) here or look (he is) there. The Son of Man is within you.'

35) Follow Him there.

36) Those who seek Him will find Him.

37) Go now and preach the gospel (this good news) of the Kingdom.

38) Do not lay down any rules beyond what I told you, and do not give a law like the lawgivers (Pharisees) or you will be held to account for the same laws."

39) When He said this He departed.

Chapter 5

1) Then they were troubled and wept out loud, saying, "How shall we go to the Gentiles and preach the gospel of the Kingdom of the Son of Man? If they did not spare Him, how can we expect that they will spare us?"

2) Then Mary stood up, greeted them all, and said to her fellow believers, "Do not weep and do not be troubled and do not waver, because His grace will be with you completely and it will protect you.

3) Instead, let us praise His greatness, because He has prepared us and made us into mature (finished or complete) people."

4) Mary's words turned their hearts to the Good, and they began to discuss the words of the Savior.

5) Peter said to Mary, "Sister we know that the Savior loved you more than all other women.

6) Tell us the words of the Savior that you remember and know, but we have not heard and do not know."

7) Mary answered him and said, "I will tell you what He hid from you."

8) And she began to speak these words to them: She said, "I saw the Lord in a vision and I said to Him, 'Lord I saw you today in a vision.'

9) He answered and said to me; 'You will be happy that you did not waver at the sight of Me. Where the mind is there is the treasure.'

10) I said to Him; 'Lord, does one see visions through the soul or through the spirit?'

11) The Savior answered and said; 'He sees visions through neither the soul nor the spirit. It is through the mind that is between the two. That is what sees the vision and it is (there the vision exists).'"

(Pages 11 - 14 are missing. Text begins again at chapter 8)

Chapter 8

10) And Desire, (a lesser god), said, "Before, I did not see you descending, but now I see you ascending. Why do you lie since you belong to me?"

11) The soul answered and said, "I saw you but you did not see me nor recognize me. I covered you like a garment and you did not know me."

12) When it said this, the soul went away greatly rejoicing.

13) Again it came to the third power (lesser god), which is called Ignorance.

14) The power questioned the soul, saying, "Where are you going? You are enslaved (captured) in wickedness. Since you are its captive you cannot judge (have no judgment)."

15) And the soul said, "Why do you judge me, when I have not judged?"

16) "I was captured, although I have not captured anyone."

17) "I was not recognized. But I have recognized that God (the All) is in (being dissolved) both the earthly things and in the heavenly (things)."

18) When the soul had overcome the third power, it ascended and saw the fourth power, which took seven forms.

19) The first form is darkness, the second desire, the third ignorance, the fourth is the lust of death, the fifth is the dominion of the flesh, the sixth is the empty useless wisdom of flesh, the seventh is the wisdom of vengeance and anger. These are the seven powers of wrath.

20) They asked the soul, "Where do you come from, slayer of men: where are you going, conqueror of space?"

21) The soul answered and said, "What has trapped me has been slain, and what kept me caged has been overcome."

22) "My desire has been ended, and ignorance has died."

23) "In an age (dispensation) I was released from the world in a symbolic image, and I was released from the chains of oblivion, which were only temporary (in this transient world)."

24) "From this time on will, I will attain the rest of the ages and seasons of silence."

Chapter 9

1) When Mary had said this, she fell silent, since she had shared all the Savior had told her.

2) But Andrew said to the other believers, "Say what you want about what she has said, but I do not believe that the Savior said this. These teachings are very strange ideas."

3) Peter answered him and spoke concerning these things.

4) He questioned them about the Savior and asked, "Did He really speak privately with a woman and not openly to us? Are we to turn around and all listen to her? Did He prefer her to us?"

5) Then Mary sobbed and said to Peter, "My brother Peter, what do you think? Do you think that I have made all of this up in my heart by myself? Do you think that I am lying about the Savior?"

6) Levi said to Peter, "Peter you have always had a hot temper.

7) Now I see you fighting against this woman like she was your enemy."

8) If the Savior made her worthy, who are you to reject her? What do you think you are doing? Surely the Savior knows her well?

9) That is why He loved her more than us. Let us be ashamed of this and let us put on the perfect Man. Let us separate from each other as He commanded us to do so we can preach the gospel, not laying down any other rule or other law beyond what the Savior told us."

10) And when they heard this they began to go out and proclaim and preach.

History of The Apocryphon of John

The Apocryphon, or "Secrets" of John forms the cornerstone of Gnostic mythology and cosmology. In this text we are introduced to the major entities of creation and lordship. We learn how the universe, including earth and man, came into being. The origin of evil, the creator god, and the material world are explained in detail. The story seems to be a mixture of various belief systems, including those of Plato, who seems to have borrowed freely from the format of Greek mythology, and Christianity. The story is loosely based on Genesis chapters 1 through 13 as a timeline.

The basic text of the Apocryphon of John existed in some form before 185 C.E. when a book called the Apocryphon of John was referred to by Irenaeus in his book, Against Heresies (Adversus Haereses), written in that year. Irenaeus reported about the Gnostic texts saying that teachers in 2nd century Christian communities were writing their own books to gain converts. He called these books, "an indescribable number of secret and illegitimate writings, which they themselves have forged, to bewilder the minds of foolish people, who are ignorant of the true scriptures" (A.H. 1.20.1)

The Apocryphon of John continued to be circulated, expanded, and embellished for the next seven hundred years. The document was reportedly in use during the eighth century by the Audians of Mesopotamia.

Part of the mythology revealed in the Apocryphon of John is also present in the Gnostic book, The Sophia (Wisdom) of Jesus as well as other Gnostic texts.

The specific document that so angered Irenaeus was lost and remained so until 1945, when a library of papyrus codices from the 4th century A.D. were found at Nag Hammadi in Egypt. The Apocryphon of John was among the texts,

Four versions have been found thus far. These are comprised of a long version, of which we have two identical Coptic manuscripts. A short version is also Coptic but differs from the others by eliminating certain details. Among the texts, a third manuscript had been found that differs slightly from the first shorter manuscript in style and vocabulary. A fragment has been found that shows some minor differences which distinguish it from the other.

Which, if any, of these texts are original has not been determined, however, it is the longer version that is presented here. This version was chosen because it contained more details and offered an overall cohesion of thought. This could be due to additions and embellishments sown through the shorter, less detailed versions.

Since we have already covered the general idea behind Gnostic mythology it need not be repeated here. However, a chart showing the main characters and their position on the divine family tree might serve us well. It is shown below.

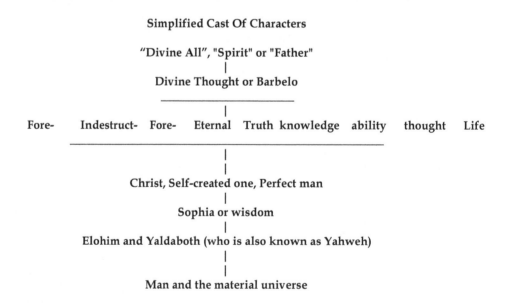

Simplified Cast Of Characters

"Divine All", "Spirit" or "Father"
|
Divine Thought or Barbelo
————————————————
|

| Fore- | Indestruct- | Fore- | Eternal | Truth | knowledge | ability | thought | Life |

————————————————
|
|
Christ, Self-created one, Perfect man
|
Sophia or wisdom
|
Elohim and Yaldaboth (who is also known as Yahweh)
|
|
Man and the material universe

The Apocryphon of John

The teaching of the savior, that will reveal the mysteries of things hidden which he taught John, his disciple, in silence. On the day when John, the brother of James, the sons of Zebedee, had come to the temple, a Pharisee named Arimanius came up to him and said, Where is your master whom you followed? He said to him, He has gone back to the place he came from. The Pharisee said to him, This Nazarene deceived all of you with his deception. He filled your ears with lies, and closed your hearts and turned you all away from your fathers' traditions.

When I, John, heard these things I walked away from the temple into the desert. I grieved greatly in my heart, saying, How was the savior appointed, and why was he sent to the world by his Father, and who is his Father who sent him, and to which kingdom shall we go? What did he mean when he said to us, This kingdom which you will go to is an imperishable kingdom, but he did not teach us what kind it is.

Then, while I was meditating on these things, I saw the heavens open and the whole creation below heaven was shining and the world shook. I was afraid, and then I saw in the light a young man who stood by me. As I was looking at him he became like an old man. And he changed his visage again and become like a servant. There were not many beings in front of me, but there was a single being with many forms composed of light, and they could be seen through each other, and there were three forms within the one being.
He said to me, John, John, why do you doubt, and why are you afraid? (Mat. 28:17) Do you understand this image, do you not? Do not be afraid! I am the one who is with all of you always. I am the Father and the Mother, and I am the Son. I am the undefiled and incorruptible one. I have come to teach you what is and what was and what will be, so that you may know the things visible and invisible, and to teach you concerning the upright, immutable (unshakable / unwavering) race of the perfect Man. Now, therefore, lift up your face, that you may receive the things that I shall teach you today, and may tell them to your fellow spirits who are from the upright, immutable (unwavering/ unshakable) race of the perfect Man. (Eph.4:13)

And I asked if I might understand it, and he said to me, The One God is a king with nothing above it. It is he who exists as God and Father of everything, the invisible One who rules over everything, who exists as incorruptible, which is in the pure light that no eye can look upon.
He is the invisible Spirit. It is not correct to think of him as a god, or anything similar. He is more than god, since there is nothing above him, for no one is above him. He does not exist within anything inferior to him, because everything exists within him. He has established himself. He is eternal, self-sufficient, and self-sustaining. He is complete perfection. He did not lack anything to be complete and he is continually perfect in light. He is unlimited, since there was no one before him to limit him. He is unknowable, since there exists no one prior to him to comprehend him. He is immeasurable, since there was no one before him to measure him. He is invisible, since no one has seen him. He is eternal, since he exists always. He is an enigma, since no one was able to apprehend him or explain him. He is unnamable, since there is no one who came before him to give him a name.

He is One, immeasurable light, which is pure, holy and immaculate. He is too sacred to speak of, being perfect and incorruptible. He is beyond perfection, blessedness, and divinity, because he is vastly superior to them all. He is not corporeal nor is he incorporeal. He is One and cannot be qualified or quantified, for no one can know him. He is not one among other beings; instead, he is far superior to all. He is so superior to all things that his essence is not part of the kingdoms, nor is he part of time. He who is a kingdom was created beforehand. Time does not matter to him, since he does not receive anything from another, for it would be received on loan. He who comes first needs nothing from anyone. Such a one expectantly beholds himself in his own light. He is majestic perfection. He is pure, immeasurable mind. He is a kingdom that gives the kingdoms their kingdom. He is life that gives life. He is the blessed One that blesses. He is knowledge and he gives knowledge. He is goodness that gives goodness. He is mercy and redemption and he bestows mercy. He is grace that gives grace. He does not give because he has these things but he gives the immeasurable, incomprehensible light from which all things flow.

How am I to speak with you about him? His kingdom is indestructible, at peace and existing in silence, at rest before everything was. He is the head of all the kingdoms (kingdoms), and he gives them strength in his goodness. For we know not the things that are unspeakably sacred, and we do not understand that which cannot be measured, except for him who was created from him, namely from the Father. It is he alone who told it to us.

He who beholds himself in the light which surrounds him and comes from him is the spring of the water of life. It is he who sustains the entire kingdom in every way, and it is he who gazes upon the image which he sees in the spring of the Spirit. It is he who puts his desire in the liquid light which is in the spring of the pure liquid light which surrounds him.
The Father's thought performed a deed and she was created from it. It is she who had appeared before him in the shining of

his light. This is the first power which was before all of them and which was created from his mind. She is the Thought of the All and her light shines like his light. It is the perfect power which is the visage of the invisible. She is the pure, undefiled Spirit who is perfect. She is the first power, the glory of Barbelo, the perfect glory of the kingdom (kingdoms), the glory revealed. She glorified the pure, undefiled Spirit and it was she who praised him, because thanks to him she had come forth. She is the first thought, his image; she became the womb of everything, for it is she who preceded them all. She is the Mother-Father, the first man, the Holy Spirit, the threefold male, the triple power, the androgynous one with three names, and the eternal kingdom among the invisible ones, and the first to come forth.

She asked the invisible, pure, undefiled Spirit, Barbelo, to give her Foreknowledge, and the Spirit agreed. And when he had agreed, the Foreknowledge was created, and it stood by the Thought; it originates from the thought of the invisible, pure, undefiled Spirit. Foreknowledge glorified him and his perfect power, Barbelo. It was because of her that Foreknowledge had been created.

And she asked again to grant her indestructibility, and he agreed. When he had agreed, indestructibility was created, and it stood by the Divine Thought and the Foreknowledge. It glorified the invisible One and Barbelo, because of whom it had been created.

And Barbelo asked to grant her Eternal Life. And the invisible Spirit agreed. And when he had agreed, Eternal Life was created, and they attended and glorified the invisible Spirit and Barbelo, the one because of whom they had been created. And she asked again to grant her truth. And the invisible Spirit agreed. And when he had agreed, Truth was created, and they attended and glorified the invisible, excellent Spirit and his Barbelo, the one because of whom they had been created. This is the five-fold creation of the kingdom of the Father, which is the first man and the image of the invisible Spirit, which came from Barbelo, who was the divine Thought; Forethought, Foreknowledge, Indestructibility, Eternal life, and Truth. This is the androgynous five-fold being of the kingdom, which is the ten types of kingdoms, which is the Father. (Five, being both male and female, or neither male nor female, become ten.)

And he looked at Barbelo with his pure light which surrounds the invisible Spirit, and his sparks, and she was impregnated by him. And a spark of light produced a light resembling his blessedness but it did not equal his greatness. This was the only-begotten child of the Mother-Father which had come forth. It is the only offspring and the only begotten of the Father, the pure Light.

And the invisible, pure, undefiled Spirit rejoiced over the light which was created, that which was produced by the first power of his Thought, which is Barbelo. And he poured his goodness over it until it became perfect and did not lack in any goodness, because he had anointed the child with the goodness of the invisible Spirit. It was his child and the child was there with him and he poured upon the child an anointing. And immediately when the child had received the Spirit, it glorified the Holy Spirit and the perfect Divine Thought, because the child owed these its existence.

And it asked to be given Mind as a fellow worker, and he agreed gladly. And when the invisible Spirit had agreed, the Mind was created, and it attended the anointed one (Christ), glorifying him and Barbelo. And all these were created in silence.

And Mind wanted to initiate an action through the word of the invisible Spirit. Thus, his will became an action and it appeared with the mind; and the light glorified it. And the word followed the will. It was because of the word that Christ, the divine self-created one, created everything. And Eternal Life and his will and Mind and Foreknowledge attended and glorified the invisible Spirit and Barbelo, because of whom they had been created.

And the Holy Spirit perfected and matured the divine Self-created one, and brought the son, together with Barbelo, so that he might present himself to the mighty and invisible, pure, undefiled Spirit as the divine Self-created one, the Christ (the anointed one) who loudly proclaimed honor to the spirit. He was created through Forethought. And the invisible, pure, undefiled Spirit placed the divine Self-created one of truth over everything. And he caused every authority to be subject to him and to Truth, which is in him, so that he may know the name of the "All," whose name is exalted above every name. That name will only be spoken to those who are worthy of it.

From the light, which is the Christ, there is incorruptibleness and through the gift of the Spirit four lights shone from the divine Self-created one. He wished that they might be with him. And the three are will, thought, and life. And the four powers are Understanding, Grace, Perception, and Thoughtfulness.

And Grace belongs to the everlasting realm of the luminary Harmozel, which is the first angel. And there are three other kingdoms with this everlasting kingdom: Grace, Truth, and Form. And the second luminary is Oriel, who has authority over the second everlasting realm. And there are three other kingdoms with him: Conception, Perception, and Memory. And the third luminary is Daveithai, who has authority over the third everlasting realm. And there are three other kingdoms with him: Understanding, Love, and Idea. And the fourth luminary, Eleleth , was given authority over the fourth everlasting realm. And there are three other kingdoms with him: Perfection, Peace, and Wisdom (Sophia). These are the four luminaries which serve the divine Self-created one. These are the twelve kingdoms which serve the child of god, the Self-created one, the Christ. They serve him through the will and the grace of the invisible Spirit. The twelve kingdoms belong to the child of the

Self-created one. All things were established by the will of the Holy Spirit through the Self-created one.

From the Foreknowledge of the perfect mind, through the expression of the will of the invisible Spirit and the will of the Self-created one, the perfect Man came into being. He was the first revelation and the truth. The pure, undefiled Spirit called him "Adam, The Stranger" (not of the earthly realm, but belonging to the divine realm). The spirit placed him over the first realm with the mighty one, the Self-created one, the Christ, by the authority of the first luminary, Harmozel; and with him are his powers. And the invisible one gave Adam The Stranger an invincible spiritual power. And Adam The Stranger spoke, glorifying and praising the invisible Spirit, saying, "It is because of you that everything has been created and therefore, everything will return to you. I shall praise and glorify you and the Self-created one and all the realms, the three: the Father, the Mother, and the Son, who make up the perfect power."

And Adam The Stranger placed his son Seth over the second realm in which the second luminary Oriel is present. And in the third realm the children of Seth were established over the third luminary, Daveithai. And the souls of the saints were lodged there. In the fourth realm the souls are kept of those who do not know the pleroma and who did not repent at once. These are they who persisted for a while and repented afterwards; they are in the area of the fourth luminary, Eleleth. They are those which glorify the invisible Spirit.

And the Sophia of the eternal realm manifested a thought from herself through the invisible Spirit and Foreknowledge. She wanted to produce a likeness of herself out of herself without the consent of the Spirit, but he had not approved. She attempted this act without her male consort, and without his permission. She had no male approval thus, she had not found her agreement. She had considered this without the consent of the Spirit and the knowledge of her compliment, but she brought forth her creation anyway. Because of the invincible power she possessed her thought did not remain idle, and something came out of her which was imperfect and different from her appearance because she had produced it without her compliment. It did not look like its mother because it has another form.

As she beheld the results of her desire, it changed into a form of a lion-faced serpent. Its eyes were like fire-like lightning which flashed. When she saw it she cast it away from her and threw it outside the realm so that none of the immortal ones might see it, for she had created it in ignorance. She surrounded it with a brightly glowing cloud and she put a throne in the middle of the cloud that no one might see it except the Holy Spirit who is called the mother of all that lives. And she called his name Yaldaboth.

This is the first Archon who took great power from his mother. And he left her and moved away from the realm in which he was born. He became strong and created for himself other kingdoms with a flame of glowing fire which still existed. And he mated with his own mindless ego that he had with him (he masturbated / or he was like his mother and did the same act of creation by himself) and brought into existence authorities for himself.

The name of the first one is Athoth, whom the generations call the reaper.
The second one is Harmas, who is the eye of envy.
The third one is Kalila-Oumbri.
The fourth one is Yabel.
The fifth one is Adonaiou, who is called Sabaoth (fool or chaos).
The sixth one is Cain, whom the generations of humans call the sun.
The seventh is Abel.
The eighth is Abrisene.
The ninth is Yobel.
The tenth is Armoupieel.
The eleventh is Melceir-Adonein.
The twelfth is Belias, it is he who is over the depth of Hades.
(These could be the 12 stations of the zodiac.)

There he placed seven kings corresponding to the sections of heaven to reign over the seven heavens and he placed five to reign over the depth of the abyss. (There were 7 known planets at the time of writing.) And he shared his fire with them, but he did not relinquish any power of the light which he had taken from his mother, for he is ignorant darkness.

And when light is added to darkness, it made the darkness bright. When darkness is added to light, it dims the light and it became neither light nor dark, but it became like dusk.

Now the Archon who is like the gloaming (gloom) has three names. The first name is Yaldaboth (fool / son of chaos), the second is Saklas, and the third is Samael. And he is evil in the arrogance and thoughtlessness that is in him. For he said, "I am God and there is no other God beside me" (Isaiah chapters 45 and 46). He said this because he did not know where his strength originated, nor from where he himself had come.

And the Archons created seven powers for themselves, and the powers created for themselves six angels for each one until they became 365 angels (the number of days in the solar year). And these are the bodies belonging with the names:
The first is Athoth, a he has a sheep's face;
The second is Eloaiou, he has a donkey's face;
The third is Astaphaios, he has a hyena's face;
The fourth is Yao, he has a snake face with seven heads;
The fifth is Sabaoth, he has a dragon's face;
The sixth is Adonin, he has an ape face;
The seventh is Sabbede (or Sabbadaios), he has a face that shone like fire.
This is the nature of seven types within the week.

But Yaldaboth had a plethora of faces, more than all of them, so that he could exhibit any face he wished to any of them, when he is in the midst of seraphim (seraphim plural of seraph. Seraphim are a class or type of angel of which, according to this text, Yaldaboth seems to be the head). He shared his fire with them and became their lord. He called himself God because of the power of the glory (brightness) he possessed that was taken from his mother's light. He rebelled against the place from which he came.

And he united the seven powers of his thoughts with the authorities that were with him. And when he spoke it became (happened).

And he named each power beginning with the highest:
The first is goodness with the first authority, Athoth;
The second is foreknowledge with the second power, Eloaio; The third is divinity with the third one, Astraphaio);
The fourth is lordship with the fourth power, Yao;
The fifth is kingdom with the fifth one, Sabaoth;
The sixth is envy with the sixth one, Adonein;
The seventh is understanding with the seventh one, Sabbateon.
And these each has a kingdom (sphere on influence) within the realm (kingdom of heaven).
They were given names according to the glory belonging to heaven for the powers of their destructiveness. And there was power in the names given to them by their creator. But the names they were given according to the glory of heaven would mean their loss of power and their destruction. Thus they have two names.

He (Yaldaboth) created all things and structured things after the model of the first kingdom created so that he might create things in an incorruptible manner. It was not because he had ever seen the indestructible ones, but the power in him, which he had taken from his mother, produced in him the image of the order of the universe. And when he saw the creation surrounding him the innumerable amount of angels around him that had come from him, he said to them, "I am a jealous God, and there is no other God beside me." (Exodus 20:3) But by announcing this he had let the angels who were with him know that there is another God. If there were no other god, why would he be jealous?

Then the mother began to move here and there. She realized she has lost part of herself when the brightness of her light dimmed. And she became darker because her partner had not consorted with her.

I (John) said, Lord, what does it mean that she moved here and there? The lord smiled and said, "Do not think it happened the way that Moses said it did 'above the waters'." (Genesis 1:2) No, it did not, but when she had seen the wickedness which had happened, and the fact her son had stolen from her, she repented. In the darkness of ignorance she began to forget and to be ashamed. She did not dare to go back there, but she was restless. This restlessness was the moving here and there.

And the prideful one stole power from his mother. For he was ignorant and thought that there was no other in existence except his mother. When he saw innumerable angels he had created he exalted himself above them. When the mother recognized that the cloak (body) of darkness was imperfect, and she knew that her partner had not consorted with her, she repented and wept greatly. The entire pleroma heard the prayer of her repentance, and they praised the invisible, pure, undefiled Spirit on her behalf. And the Spirit agreed and when he agreed the Holy Spirit anointed her from the entire pleroma. For her consort did not come to her alone, but he brought to her through the pleroma that which was needed to restore what she was lacking. And she was allowed to ascend, not to her own kingdom but to the kingdom above her son, that she could remain in the ninth (heaven / kingdom) until she restored what she lacked in herself.

And a voice called from the highest kingdom of heaven: "The Man exists and the son of Man." And the head Archon, Yaldaboth, heard it and thought that the voice had come from his mother. He did not know whence it came. He taught them, the holy and perfect Mother-Father, the complete Foreknowledge, the image of the invisible one who is the Father of the all things and through whom everything came into being, the first Man. He is the one who revealed his image in human form.

And the whole kingdom of the first (head) Archon quaked, and the foundations of the abyss shook. And the underside of waters, which are above material world, were illuminated by the appearance of his image which had been revealed. When all the authorities and the head Archon looked, they saw the whole region of the underside (of the waters) that was illuminated. And through the light they saw the form of the image (reflected) in the water.

And he (Yaldaboth) said to the authorities of him, "Come, let us make a man using the image of God as a template to our likeness, that his image may become a light for us." And they created by the means of their various powers matching the features which were given to them. And each authority supplied a feature in the form of the image which Yaldaboth had seen in its natural form. He created a being according to the likeness of the first, perfect Man. And they said, "Let us call him Adam (man), that his name may be a power of light for us."

And the powers began to create.
The first one, Goodness, created a bone essence; and the second, Foreknowledge, created a sinew essence; the third, Divinity, created a flesh essence; and the fourth, the Lordship, created a marrow essence; the fifth, Kingdom created a blood essence; the sixth, Envy, created a skin essence; the seventh, Understanding, created a hair essence. And the multitude of the angels were with him and they received from the powers the seven elements of the natural (form) so they could create the proportions of the limbs and the proportion of the buttocks and correct functioning of each of the parts together.

The first one began to create the head. Eteraphaope-Abron created his head; Meniggesstroeth created the brain; Asterechme created the right eye; Thaspomocha, the left eye; Yeronumos, the right ear; Bissoum, the left ear; Akioreim, the nose; Banen-Ephroum, the lips; Amen, the teeth; Ibikan, the molars; Basiliademe, the tonsils; Achcha, the uvula; Adaban, the neck; Chaaman, the vertebrae; Dearcho, the throat; Tebar, the right shoulder; the left shoulder; Mniarcon, the right elbow; the left elbow; Abitrion, the right underarm; Evanthen, the left underarm; Krys, the right hand; Beluai, the left hand; Treneu, the fingers of the right hand; Balbel, the fingers of the left hand; Kriman, the nails of the hands; Astrops, the right breast; Barroph, the left breast; Baoum, the right shoulder joint; Ararim, the left shoulder joint; Areche, the belly; Phthave, the navel; Senaphim, the abdomen; Arachethopi, the right ribs; Zabedo, the left ribs; Barias, the right hip; Phnouth the left hip; Abenlenarchei, the marrow; Chnoumeninorin, the bones; Gesole, the stomach; Agromauna, the heart; Bano, the lungs; Sostrapal, the liver; Anesimalar, the spleen; Thopithro, the intestines; Biblo, the kidneys; Roeror, the sinews; Taphreo, the spine of the body; Ipouspoboba, the veins; Bineborin, the arteries; Atoimenpsephei, theirs are the breaths which are in all the limbs; Entholleia, all the flesh; Bedouk, the right buttock; Arabeei, the penis; Eilo, the testicles; Sorma, the genitals; Gorma-Kaiochlabar, the right thigh; Nebrith, the left thigh; Pserem, the kidneys of the right leg; Asaklas, the left kidney; Ormaoth, the right leg; Emenun, the left leg; Knyx, the right shin-bone; Tupelon, the left shin-bone; Achiel, the right knee; Phnene, the left knee; Phiouthrom, the right foot; Boabel, its toes; Trachoun, the left foot; Phikna, its toes; Miamai, the nails of the feet; Labernioum.
And those who were appointed over all of these are: Zathoth, Armas, Kalila, Jabel, (Sabaoth, Cain, Abel). And those who are particularly active in the limbs are the head Diolimodraza, the neck Yammeax, the right shoulder Yakouib, the left shoulder Verton, the right hand Oudidi, the left one Arbao, the fingers of the right hand Lampno, the fingers of the left hand Leekaphar, the right breast Barbar, the left breast Imae, the chest Pisandriaptes, the right shoulder joint Koade, the left shoulder joint Odeor, the right ribs Asphixix, the left ribs Synogchouta, the belly Arouph, the womb Sabalo, the right thigh Charcharb, the left thigh Chthaon, all the genitals Bathinoth, the right leg Choux, the left leg Charcha, the right shin-bone Aroer, the left shin-bone Toechtha, the right knee Aol, the left knee Charaner, the right foot Bastan, its toes Archentechtha, the left foot Marephnounth, its toes Abrana.

Seven have power over all of these: Michael, Ouriel, Asmenedas, Saphasatoel, Aarmouriam, Richram, Amiorps. And the ones who are in charge of the senses are Archendekta; and he who is in charge of the receptions is Deitharbathas; and he who is in charge over the imagination is Oummaa; and he who is over creativity Aachiaram, and he who is over the whole impulse Riaramnacho.

The origin of the demons that are in the entire body is known to be these four: heat, cold, wetness, and dryness. And the mother of all of them is the material creation. And he who rules over the heat is Phloxopha; and he who rules over the cold is Oroorrothos; and he who rules over what is dry is Erimacho; and he who rules over the wetness is Athuro. And the mother of all of these is Onorthochrasaei, who stands in with them without limits, and she covorts with all of them. She is truly material and they are sustained by her.

The four ruling demons are: Ephememphi, who is attached to pleasure,
Yoko, who is attached to desire,
Nenentophni, who is attached to grief,
Blaomen, who is attached to fear,
and the mother of them all is Aesthesis-Ouch-Epi-Ptoe.
And from the four demons passions was created. And grief spawned envy, jealousy, distress, trouble, pain, callousness, anxiety, mourning, and more. Pleasure spawned wickedness, vanity, pride, and similar things. Desire spawned anger, wrath, and bitterness, and driving passion, the inability to be satisfied, and similar things. Fear spawned dread, subservience, agony, and shame. These are both good and evil, but the understanding of their nature is attributed to Anaro, who is over the material soul. It belongs with the seven senses, which are controlled by Ouch-Epi-Ptoe.

This is the number of the angels: together they are 365. They all worked on it from limb to limb, until the physical (material) body was completed by them. Now there are other ones in charge over the remaining passions whom I did not mention to you. But if you wish to know them, it is written in the book of Zoroaster. And all the angels and demons worked until they had constructed (fashioned) the physical body. And their creation was completely devoid of activity and was motionless for a long time.

And when the mother (Sophia) wanted to recapture the power which was taken from her by the head Archon, she prayed to the Mother-Father of the All, who is most merciful. He sent a holy decree containing the five lights down to the place where the angels of the head Archon reside. They advised him (Yaldaboth) that he should bring forth the power of the mother. And they said to Yaldaboth, "Blow some of your spirit into his face and his body will arise." And he blew the spirit power of the mother into his (Adam's) face. (Genesis 2:7) Yaldaboth did not know to do this because he existed in ignorance. And the power of the mother went out of Yaldaboth into Adam's physical body, which they had fashioned after the image of the one who exists from the beginning. The body moved and gained strength, and it was enlightened.

And in that instant the other powers became jealous, although he (Adam) had been created through all of them. They were jealous because they had given Adam their power and now he was more intelligent than those who had made him, and his mind was greater than that of the head Archon. And when they recognized that he was enlightened, and that he could think better than they, and that he was free of evil, they took him and threw him into the lowest material realm.

But the blessed One, the Mother-Father, the giving and gracious One, had mercy on the power of the mother which had been transmitted from the head Archon because he did not want the Archons to gain power over the material body again. Therefore, he sent, a helper to Adam through his giving Spirit and his great compassion. The enlightened Thought which comes out of him is called "Life" (Zoe means life and is the name of Eve in certain Greek texts and the Septuagint). And she assists the whole creature, by working with him and restoring him to his fullness and by teaching him about the descent (flaws) of his seed and by teaching him about the way of ascent (to go upward again), which is based on the way he came down. (Rom. 8:22)

And the enlightened Thought was hidden within Adam so that the Archons would not know she was there, but that the Thought might restore (correct) what was lacking of the mother.

And the man was revealed because of the shadow of light in him. And his thinking was higher than all those who had made him. When they looked up they realized that his thinking was superior. Then they conspired with the entire force of Archons and angels. They took fire and earth and water as a mixture and added the four fiery winds. And they worked them together and caused a great noise. And they brought Adam into the shadow of death so that that they might re-make him from earth, water, fire and the spirit (wind) which make up matter. This was the ignorance of their darkness and desire, and their lying (false) spirit. This is the tomb of the re-formed body that the thieves had clothed Adam in. It contained the bonds of forgetfulness and cause him to become a mortal entity. He is the first one who came down, and the first to be separated (from the Divine All). Now, it is up to the Thought of the light which was in him to awaken his thinking.

And the Archons took him and placed him in paradise. And they said to him, "Eat at your leisure," (Genesis 2:16) for their pleasure is bitter and their beauty is twisted. Their pleasure is entrapment and their trees lack any holiness and their fruit is deadly poison and their promise is death. And the tree of their life they had placed in the center of paradise (Genesis 2:9).

And I (Jesus) shall teach all of you the mystery of their life. It is the plan that they made together, which is made from the template of their spirit. The root of this tree is bitter and its branches are death, its shadow is hate. Its leaves are a trap, and its blossom is the ointment of evil. Its fruit is death and its seed is desire. It sprouts (blooms) in darkness. Those who taste it dwell in Hades, and they rest in darkness.

468

But what they call "the tree of knowledge of good and evil" is the Thought of the light. They stationed themselves in front of it so that Adam might not understand his fullness and recognize his nakedness and be ashamed. But it was I (Jesus) who made them decide what they ate.

I said to the savior, Lord, wasn't it the serpent that instructed Adam to eat? The savior smiled and said, The serpent instructed them to eat because of its evil desire to produced sexual lust and destruction so that Adam would be useful to him. Adam knew that he was disobedient to Yaldaboth because the light of the Thought lived in him and made him stronger and more accurate in his thinking than the head Archon. Yaldaboth wanted to harvest the power that he himself had given Adam. And he caused Adam to forget.

And I said to the savior, "What is this forgetfulness?" He said, "It is not how Moses wrote and it is not how you have heard. He wrote in his first book, 'He put him to sleep' (Genesis 2:21), but that was how Adam perceived it. For also he said through the prophet, 'I will make their minds heavy, that they may not perceive nor understand.' (Isaiah 6:10)."

The Thought of the light hid herself in Adam. The head Archon wanted to bring her out through his rib but the Thought of the light cannot be apprehended. Although darkness pursued her, it did not catch her. Yaldaboth brought out part of Adam's power and he created another and formed a woman, using the template of the Thought which he had seen. The power he had taken from the Adam was formed into the female. This is what happened and not as Moses said, 'She was formed from the bone of his rib.' (Genesis 2:21)

Adam saw the woman beside him. In that instant the enlightened Thought appeared. She lifted the veil which occluded his mind. Adam sobered from the drunkenness of darkness and recognized his counterpart (compliment / agreement) , and he said, 'This is indeed bone of my bones and flesh of my flesh.' (Genesis 2:23) Therefore the man will leave his father and his mother, and he will cleave to his wife, and they will both be one flesh. (Genesis 2:24) For his partner will be sent to him and he will leave his father and his mother .

Our sister Sophia is the one who came down innocently in order to reclaim what she has lost. That is why she was called Life, because she is the mother of all things living, by the Foreknowledge of the sovereignty of heaven. Through her they that live have tasted the perfect Knowledge. I (Jesus) appeared in the form of an eagle on the tree of knowledge, which is the Thought from the Foreknowledge of the pure light. I did this so that I might teach them and wake them from them the deep sleep. For they were both in a fallen state, and they recognized they were naked. The Thought appeared to them in the form of light and she awakened their minds.

When Yaldaboth noticed that they fled from him, he cursed the earth he had made. He found the woman as she was preparing herself for her husband. He was lord over her, though he did not know the mystery was instated through the holy plan, so they were afraid to rebel against Yaldaboth. And he demonstrated to his angels the ignorance in him by casting them out of paradise, and he clothed them in darkening blackness.

 And the head Archon, Yaldaboth, saw the virgin standing beside Adam, but he was ignorant to the fact that the enlightened Thought of life had appeared in her. But when the Foreknowledge of All noticed it, she sent agents and they quickly stole the life (Zoe) out of Eve.

Then, the head Archon seduced her and he conceived two sons in her. The first is Eloim and the second is Yahweh. Eloim has a face like a bear and Yahweh has a face like a cat. The one is righteous but the other is unjust. (Yahweh is related to the New Testament and is considered a more just and kind God. Eloim is related to the Old Testament and is considered a jealous, revengeful, wrathful God.) He set Yahweh over fire and wind, and he set Eloim over water and earth. And he name them Cain and Abel in an attempt to deceive.

Sexual intercourse continues to this very day because of the head Archon. He instilled sexual desire in the woman who belongs to Adam. And Adam, through intercourse caused bodies to be replicated, and Yaldaboth breathed into them with his fraudulent spirit.

And he set the two Archons (Elohim and Yahweh) over principal elements, so that they might rule over the tomb (body). When Adam recognized the image of his own Foreknowledge, he begot the image of the son of man (Jesus) and he called him Seth, according to the fashion of the divine race living in the ethereal kingdoms. The mother (Sophia) sent her spirit also. It was in her image and was a replica of those who are in the pleroma. In this way she will prepare a dwelling place for the kingdoms to come.

Yaldaboth made them drink water of forgetfulness that he had made so that they might not remember from where they came. The seed remained with man for a while to assist him so that when the Spirit comes out from the holy kingdoms, he may raise up and heal him of his lack so the whole pleroma may again become holy and complete.

And I said to the savior, Lord, will all the souls be led safely into the pure light? He answered me and said, "Great things have arisen in your mind, and it is difficult to explain them to anyone except those from the race that cannot be moved. These are they on whom the Spirit of life will descend and with whom will be with the Power. They will be saved and become complete, perfect and worthy of greatness. They will be purified from all wickedness and evil actions. Then they will have no other care other than the incorruption, on which they shall focus their attention from here on, without anger or envy or jealousy or desire and greed for anything. They are affected by nothing except existing in the flesh, which they bear while looking expectantly for the time when they will be met by those who will receive them (their body). Such ones are worthy of the (incorruptible) imperishable, eternal life and the calling. They endure everything and bear up under everything, that they may finish the good fight (wrestling contest) and inherit eternal life. (Cor. 13:7)

I said to him, Lord, will the souls of those who did not do these works (things) but on whom the power and Spirit descended, be rejected? He answered and said to me, "If the Spirit descended upon them, they will certainly be saved, and they will be changed. The power will descend on every man, for without it no one could stand. And after they are born, when the Spirit of life grows in them and the power comes and strengthens that soul, no one can be led astray with evil deeds, but those on whom the false spirit falls are drawn astray by him.

I said, Lord, where will the souls go when they shed their flesh? And he laughed (smiled) and said to me, "The soul in which the power will become stronger than the false spirit is strong and she (the soul) turns and runs from evil and through the intervention of the incorruptible one, she is saved, taken up to the kingdoms and will rest there.

And I said, "Lord, what about those who do not know to whom they belong, where will their souls go?" And he said to me, "Those, the spoiled (double-minded) spirit has gained strength while they went astray and that casts a burden on the soul and draws her towards the deeds of evil, and he throws her down into forgetfulness. After she comes out of the body, it is handed over to the authorities that came into being through the Archon. They bind her with chains and cast her into prison, and hound her until she is set free from the forgetfulness and acquires knowledge. If she becomes perfected she is saved.

And I said, Lord, how can the soul become young again and return to its mother's womb or into (another) man? (This is a question regarding reincarnation.) He was glad when I asked him this, and he said to me, "You are blessed because you have understood!" That soul is made to follow another, since the Spirit of life is in it. It is saved through that soul. It is not forced into another flesh (body) again.

And I said, Lord, "Where will the souls go from those who gained knowledge but afterward turned away?" Then he said to me, "They will go to the place where the angels of misery (abject poverty) go. This is the place where there is no repentance (escape). There they will be kept with those who have blasphemed the spirit. They will be tortured and punished forever and ever. (Heb 6:4-8 and Heb 12:17-31)

I said, "Lord, from where did the false (evil) spirit come?" Then he said to me, "The Mother-Father, who is the gracious and holy of Spirit, the One who is merciful and who has compassion for all, the Thought of the Foreknowledge of light raised up the child of the perfect race and their thought was the eternal light of man."

When the head Archon realized that these people were exalted above him and their minds were stronger than him he wanted to capture their thought. He did not know that their minds were stronger and that he would not be able to capture their thoughts.

He made a plan with his agents, his powers, and they raped (committed adultery together, all of them, with) Sophia, and unbearable imprisonment (bitter fate) was born through them, which is the last unbreakable bondage. It is the kind that is unpredictable fate. This fate is harder and stronger than the gods, angels and demons and all the generations until this day together have seen. It imprisoned all through periods, seasons, and times. From that fate every sin, unrighteousness, blasphemy, forgetfulness, and ignorance and every oppressive command, and carnal sins and fear emerged. From this the whole creation was blinded, so that they may not know the God who is above them all. And because of the chain of forgetfulness, their sins were hidden from them. They are bound with measures, seasons, and time since fate is lord over everything.

When the head Archon repented for everything which had been created through him, he sought to cause a flood to destroy the works of man (Genesis 6:6). But the great light, the Foreknowledge, told Noah, and Noah announced it to all the children, the sons of men. But those who were estranged from him did not listen to him. It is not as Moses said, "They hid themselves in an ark" (Genesis 7: 7), but they hid in a certain place. Noah hid and also many other people from the immutable race. They went to a certain place and hid in a shining, glowing (enlightened) cloud. Noah understood his authority because she who is part of the light was with him. She enlightened them because the head Archon darkened the entire earth.

And he planned with his agents to send his emissaries (angels) to the daughters of men so that they might take some (as wives) for themselves and raise offspring (children) for their personal enjoyment. At first they had no success so they came together again and laid a plan. They made a false spirit (like themselves), but who looked like the Spirit which had come down to them. In this way they could defile souls through it.

And the emissaries (angels) transformed themselves into the image of the husbands of the women (the daughters of men). They filled them with the spirit of darkness, which was an evil concoction they had made for them. They brought gold and silver and a gift and copper and iron and metal and all kinds of things to the angels. And they led those who followed them away into great turmoil with their lies. The people grew old without enjoying life. They died before finding truth and without knowing the God of truth. This way the entire creation was enslaved forever, from the beginning of the world until now.

And they took wives and produced children of darkness born in the image of their spirit. To this day, they closed their minds, and they hardened their hearts through the intractability of the false spirit.

I, the perfect Aeon of the All, changed myself into my own child (seed), for I existed first and have traveled every path. I am the fullness of the light. I am the remembrance of the pleroma. I sojourned to the kingdom of darkness and endured so I could I enter into the midst of this prison. The foundations of chaos shook. I disguised myself from the wicked ones, and they did not recognize me.

I returned for the second time, and I journeyed here and there. I was created from those who belong to the light, and I am that light, the perfect Aeon. I entered into the midst of darkness and depths of Hades to accomplish my task. And the foundations of chaos shook so hard they could have fallen down and killed those in chaos. I sought to root them in light so that they might not be destroyed before the time was complete.

Still for a third time I went - I am the light which exists in the light, I am the remembrance of the perfect Aeon. I entered into the midst of darkness and the depths of Hades. I filled my face with light so I could perfect (complete) their kingdom. I came into the midst of their prison, which is the prison of the body (flesh). I announced, "He who hears, let him wake up from the deep sleep." And he wept and shed tears. He wiped away bitter tears from himself and he said, "Who is it that calls my name, and from where has this hope come to me, while I am in the chains of the prison?" And I said, 'I am the perfect Aeon of the pure light; I am the thought of the pure, undefiled Spirit, who raised you up to the place of honor. Stand and remember that it is you who heard and sought your own beginnings, which is I, the merciful one. Guard yourself against the angels of bitter providence and the demons of chaos and all those who seek to entrap you Guard against the deep sleep and the cage of Hades.

And I stood him up and sealed him in the light of the water with five seals so that death might not have power over him ever again.
Now I shall go ascend to the perfect kingdom. I have told you all I have to say. And I have said everything to you that you might write it down and give them secretly to your fellow spirits. It is the mystery of the immutable race.

And the savior gave these things to John so that he might write them down and keep them intact. And he said to him, Cursed is everyone who will trade these things for a gift or for food or for water or clothing or anything. These things were presented to him in a mystery, and immediately he disappeared from him. And he went to his fellow disciples and told them what the savior had told him.
Jesus Christ, Amen.

History of The Gospel of Thomas

In the winter of 1945, in Upper Egypt, an Arab peasant was gathering fertilizer and topsoil for his crops. While digging in the soft dirt he came across a large earthen vessel. Inside were scrolls containing hitherto unseen books.

According to local lore, the boy's father had recently been killed and the lad was preparing to chase the man who had murdered his father.

The scrolls were discovered near the site of the ancient town of Chenoboskion, at the base of a mountain named Gebel et-Tarif, near Hamra-Dum, in the vicinity of Naj 'Hammadi, about sixty miles from Luxor in Egypt. The texts were written in the Coptic language and preserved on papyrus sheets. The lettering style dated them as having been penned around the third or fourth century A.D. The Gospel of Thomas is the longest of the volumes consisting of 114 verses. Recent study indicates that the original work of Thomas, of which the scrolls are copies, may predate the four canonical gospels of Matthew, Mark, Luke, and John. The origin of The Gospel of Thomas is now thought to be from the first or second century A.D.

The word Coptic is an Arabic corruption of the Greek word Aigyptos, which in turn comes from the word Hikaptah, one of the names of the city of Memphis, the first capital of ancient Egypt.

There has never been a Coptic state or government per se, however, the word has been used to generally define a culture and language present in the area of Egypt.

The known history of the Copts starts with King Mina the first King, who united the northern and southern kingdoms of Egypt circa 3050 B.C. The ancient Egyptian civilization under the rule of the Pharaohs lasted over 3000 years. Saint Mina (named after the king) is one of the major Coptic saints. He was martyred in 309 A.D.

The culture has come to be recognized as one containing distinctive art, architecture, and even a certain Christian church system.

The Coptic Church is based on the teachings of St. Mark, who introduced the region to Christianity in the first century A.D. The Copts take pride in the monastic flavor of their church and the fact that the Gospel of Mark is thought to be the oldest of the Gospels. Now, lying before a peasant boy was a scroll written in the ancient Coptic tongue: The Gospel of Thomas, possibly older than and certainly quite different from any other Gospel.

The peasant boy who found the treasure of the Gospel of Thomas stood to be rewarded greatly. This could have been the discovery of a lifetime for his family, but the boy had no idea what he had. He took the scrolls home, where his mother burned some as kindling.

Because the young man had succeeded in his pursuit of the father's murderer, he himself was now a murderer.

Fearing the authorities would soon come looking for him and not wanting to be found with ancient artifacts, he sold the codex to the black market antique dealers in Cairo for a trifle sum. It would be years until they found their way into the hands of a scholar.

Part of the thirteenth codex was smuggled from Egypt to America. In 1955 whispers of the existence of the codex had reached the ears of Gilles Quispel, a professor of religion and history in the Netherlands. The race was on to find and translate the scrolls.

The introduction of the collected sayings of Jesus refers to the writer as Didymos (Jude) Thomas. This is the same Thomas who doubted Jesus and was then told to place his hand within the breach in the side of the Savior. In the Gospel of St. John, he is referred to as Didymos, which means twin in Greek. In Aramaic, the name Jude (or Judas) also carries the sense of twin. The use of this title led some in the apocryphal tradition to believe that he was the twin brother and confidant of Jesus. However, when applied to Jesus himself, the literal meaning of twin must be rejected by orthodox Christianity as well as anyone adhering to the doctrine of the virgin birth of the only begotten Son of God. The title is likely meant to signify that Thomas was a close confidant of Jesus, or more simply, he was part of a set of twins and in no way related to Jesus.

As mentioned earlier, church historians mention that Thomas evangelized India (Asia-Minor or Central Asia).

The text has a very Eastern flavor. At times it is almost Buddhist in its wording. (For a comparative study of Zen Buddhism's Tao Te Ching and The Gospel of Thomas, see the book *The Tao Of Thomas*).

The Gospel of Thomas is actually not a gospel at all. It contains no narrative but is instead a collection of sayings, which are said to be from Jesus himself as written (quoted) by Thomas. Although the codex found in Egypt is dated to the fourth century, most biblical scholars place the actual construction of the text of Thomas at about 70 – 150 A.D. although some place it slightly later.

The gospel was often mentioned in early Christian literature, but no copy was thought to have survived until the discovery of the Coptic manuscript. Since then, part of the Oxyrynchus papyri have been identified as older Greek fragments of Thomas. The papyri were discovered in 1898 in the rubbish heaps of Oxyrhynchus, Egypt. This discovery yielded over thirty-five manuscript fragments for the New Testament. They have been dated the earliest codex found in the library to about 60 A.D. As a point of reference, a fragment of papyrus from the Dead Sea Scrolls had been dated to before 68 A.D. This is not to say that the Gospel of Thomas was dated to these years, only that the oldest books found in the library date to this time area. Thus, the collection was a very old and select one.

There are marked differences between the Greek and Coptic texts of Thomas, as we will see.

The debate on the date of Thomas centers in part on whether Thomas is dependent upon the canonical gospels, or is derived from an earlier document that was simply a collection of sayings. Many of the passages in Thomas appear to be more authentic versions of the synoptic parables, and many have parallels in Mark and Luke. This has caused a division of thought wherein some believe Thomas used common sources also used by Mark and Luke. Others believe Thomas was written independently after witnessing the same events.

If Thomas wrote his gospel first, without input from Mark, and from the standpoint of Eastern exposure as a result of his sojourn into India, it could explain the mystical quality of the text. It could also explain the striking differences in the recorded quotes of Jesus as memories were influenced by exposure to Asian culture.

There is some speculation that the sayings found in Thomas could be more accurate to the original intent and wording of Jesus than the other gospels. This may seem counter-intuitive until we realize that Christianity itself is an Eastern religion, albeit Middle-Eastern. Although as it spread west the faith went through many changes to westernize or Romanize it, Jesus was both mystical and Middle-Eastern. The Gospel of Thomas may not have seen as much "dilution" by Western society.

The Gospel of Thomas was most likely composed in Syria, where tradition holds that the church of Edessa was founded by Judas Thomas, The Twin (Didymos). The gospel may well be the earliest written tradition in the Syriac church.

The Gospel of Thomas is sometimes called a Gnostic gospel, although it seems more likely Thomas was adopted by the Gnostic community and interpreted in the light of their beliefs.

Gnostics believed that knowledge is formed or found from a personal encounter with God brought about by inward or intuitive insight. It is this knowledge that brings salvation. The Gnostics believed they were privy to a secret knowledge about the divine. It is their focus on knowledge that leads to their name.

There are numerous references to the Gnostics in second century literature. Their form of Christianity was considered heresy by the early church fathers. The intense resistance to the Gnostic belief system seems to be based in two areas. First, there was a general Gnostic belief that we were all gods, with heaven contained within us. Jesus, according to the Gnostics, was here to show us our potential to become as he was; a son or daughter of God, for God is both father and mother, male and female. These beliefs ran contrary to the newly developing orthodoxy. The second line of resistance was political. This resistance developed later and would have come from the fact that a faith based on a personal encounter flew in the face of the developing church political structure that placed priests and church as the keepers of heaven's gate with salvation through them alone.

It is from the writings condemning the group that we glean most of our information about the Gnostics. They are alluded to in the Bible in 1 Timothy 1:4 and 1 Timothy 6:20, and possibly the entirety of Jude, as the writers of the Bible defended their theology against that of the Gnostics.

The Coptic and Greek translations of The Gospel of Thomas presented herein are the result of a gestalt brought about by contrasting and comparing all of the foremost translations, where the best phrasing was chosen to follow the intent and meaning of the text.

Because there are differences between the Coptic manuscript and the Greek fragments of Thomas, each verse will have the following format for the reader to view: The Coptic text will be presented first, since we have the entire Gospel in this language. The Greek text will come next. If there is not a second rendition of the verse, the reader may assume there was no Greek fragment found for that verse or the Greek version of the verse was identical to the Coptic version. Lastly, obvious parallels found in the Bible are listed.

Let us keep in mind that some of the differences between the translations of the Greek and Coptic may be attributed in part to the choice of word or phrase of those translating. It is the differences in overall meaning of verses between Coptic and Greek on which we should focus.

In the document to follow, the Gospel of Thomas will appear as a bold text. If there are other relevant but divergent interpretations of phrases in Thomas, they are included in parentheses. Any parallels of text or meaning that appear in the Bible are placed below the verse in italicized text. Author's notes are in regular text. In this way the reader can easily identify which body of work is being referenced and observe how they fit together.

Since the deeper meanings within Thomas are both in metaphor and in plain, understandable language, it is hoped that each time the words are read some new insight and treasure can be taken from them. As we change our perspective, we see the meaning of each verse differently. As one turns a single jewel to view each facet, we should study the Gospel of Thomas in the same way.

Let us begin.

The Gospel Of Thomas

These are the secret sayings which the living Jesus has spoken and Judas who is also Thomas (the twin) (Didymos Judas Thomas) wrote.

1. And he said: Whoever finds the interpretation of these sayings will not taste death.

1. He said to them: Whoever discovers the interpretation of these words shall never taste death.

John 8:51 Very truly I tell you, whoever keeps my word will never see death.

2. Jesus said: Let him who seeks not stop seeking until he finds, and when he finds he will be troubled, and when he has been troubled he will marvel (be astonished) and he will reign over all and in reigning, he will find rest.

2. Jesus said: Let him who seeks not stop until he finds, and when he finds he shall wonder and in wondering he shall reign, and in reigning he shall find rest.

3. Jesus said: If those who lead you say to you: Look, the Kingdom is in the sky, then the birds of the sky would enter before you. If they say to you: It is in the sea, then the fish of the sea would enter ahead of you. But the Kingdom of God exists within you and it exists outside of you. Those who come to know (recognize) themselves will find it, and when you come to know yourselves you will become known and you will realize that you are the children of the Living Father. Yet if you do not come to know yourselves then you will dwell in poverty and it will be you who are that poverty.

3. Jesus said, If those who lead you say, "See, the Kingdom is in the sky," then the birds of the sky will precede you. If they say to you, "It is under the earth," then the fish of the sea will precede you. Rather, the Kingdom of God is inside of you, and it is outside of you.

Those who come to know themselves will find it; and when you come to know yourselves, you will understand that it is you who are the sons of the living Father. But if you will not know yourselves, you dwell in poverty and it is you who are that poverty.

Luke 17:20 And when he was demanded of by the Pharisees, when the kingdom of God should come, he answered them and said, The kingdom of God cometh not with observation: Neither shall they say, Lo here! Lo there! For, behold, the kingdom of God is within you.

4. Jesus said: The person of old age will not hesitate to ask a little child of seven days about the place of life, and he will live. For many who are first will become last, (and the last will be first). And they will become one and the same.

4. Jesus said: Let the old man who has lived many days not hesitate to ask the child of seven days about the place of life; then he will live. For many that are first will be last, and last will be first, and they will become a single one.

Mark 9:35-37 He sat down, called the twelve, and said to them: Whoever wants to be first must be last of all and servant of all. Then he took a little child and put it among them, and taking it in his arms, he said to them: Whoever welcomes one such child in my name welcomes me, and whoever welcomes me welcomes not me but the one who sent me.

5. Jesus said: Recognize what is in front of your face, and what has been hidden from you will be revealed to you. For there is nothing hidden which will not be revealed (become manifest), and nothing buried that will not be raised.

5. Jesus said: Know what is in front of your face and what is hidden from you will be revealed to you.
For there is nothing hidden that will not be revealed.

Mark 4:2 For there is nothing hid, except to be made manifest; nor is anything secret, except it come to light.

Luke 12:3 Nothing is covered up that will not be revealed, or hidden that will not be known.

Matthew 10:26 So have no fear of them; for nothing is covered up that will not be uncovered, and nothing secret that will not become known.

6. His Disciples asked Him, they said to him: How do you want us to fast, and how will we pray? And how will we be charitable (give alms), and what laws of diet will we maintain?

Jesus said: Do not lie, and do not practice what you hate, for everything is in the plain sight of Heaven. For there is nothing concealed that will not become manifest, and there is nothing covered that will not be exposed.

6. His disciples asked him, "How do you want us to fast? And how shall we pray? And how shall we give alms? And what kind of diet shall we follow?"
Jesus said, don't lie, and don't do what you hate to do, for all things are revealed before the truth. For there is nothing hidden which shall not be revealed.

Luke 11:1 He was praying in a certain place, and after he had finished, one of his disciples said to him, Lord, teach us to pray, as John taught his disciples.

7. Jesus said: Blessed is the lion that the man will eat, for the lion will become the man. Cursed is the man that the lion shall eat, and still the lion will become man.

Mathew 26:20-30 He who dipped his hand with me in the dish, the same will betray me. The Son of Man goes, even as it is written of him, but woe to that man through whom the Son of Man is betrayed! It would be better for that man if he had not been born. Judas, who betrayed him, answered, "It isn't me, is it, Rabbi?" He said to him, You said it. As they were eating, Jesus took bread, gave thanks for it, and broke it. He gave to the disciples, and said, Take, eat; this is my body. He took the cup, gave thanks, and gave to them, saying: All of you drink it, for this is my blood of the new covenant, which is poured out for many for the remission of sins. But I tell you that I will not drink of this fruit of the vine from now on, until that day when I drink it anew with you in my Father's Kingdom. When they had sung a hymn, they went out to the Mount of Olives.

8. And he said: The Kingdom of Heaven is like a wise fisherman who casts his net into the sea. He drew it up from the sea full of small fish. Among them he found a fine large fish. That wise fisherman threw all the small fish back into the sea and chose the large fish without hesitation. Whoever has ears to hear, let him hear!

Matthew 13:47-48 Again, the kingdom of heaven is like a net that was thrown into the sea and caught fish of every kind; when it was full, they drew it ashore, sat down, and put the good into baskets but threw out the bad.

9. Jesus said: Now, the sower came forth. He filled his hand and threw (the seeds). Some fell upon the road and the birds came and gathered them up. Others fell on the stone and they did not take deep enough roots in the soil, and so did not produce grain. Others fell among the thorns and they choked the seed, and the worm ate them. Others fell upon the good earth and it produced good fruit up toward the sky, it bore 60 fold and 120 fold.

Matthew 13:3-8 And he told them many things in parables, saying: Listen! A sower went out to sow. And as he sowed, some seeds fell on the path, and the birds came and ate them up. Other seeds fell on rocky ground, where they did not have much soil, and they sprang up quickly, since they had no depth of soil. But when the sun rose, they were scorched; and since they had no root, they withered away. Other seeds fell among thorns, and the thorns grew up and choked them. Other seeds fell on good soil and brought forth grain, some a hundred fold, some sixty, some thirty.

Mark 4:2-9 And he taught them many things in parables, and in his teaching he said to them: Behold! A sower went out to sow. And as he sowed, some seed fell along the path, and the birds came and devoured it. Other seed fell on rocky ground, where it had not much soil, and immediately it sprang up, since it had no depth of soil; and when the sun rose it was scorched, and since it had no root it withered away. Other seed fell among thorns and the thorns grew up and choked it, and it yielded no grain. And other seeds fell into good soil and brought forth grain, growing up and increasing and yielding thirty fold and sixty fold and a hundred fold. And he said, He who has ears to hear, let him hear.

Luke 8:4-8 And when a great crowd came together and people from town after town came to him, he said in a parable: A sower went out to sow his seed; and as he sowed, some fell along the path, and was trodden under foot, and the birds of the air devoured it. And some fell on the rock; and as it grew up, it withered away, because it had no moisture. And some fell among thorns; and the thorns grew with it and choked it. And some fell into good soil and grew, and yielded a hundred fold. As he said this, he called out, He who has ears to hear, let him hear.

10. Jesus said: I have cast fire upon the world, and as you see, I guard it until it is ablaze.

Luke 12:49 I came to bring fire to the earth, and how I wish it were already kindled.

11. Jesus said: This sky will pass away, and the one above it will pass away. The dead are not alive, and the living will not die. In the days when you consumed what is dead, you made it alive. When you come into the Light, what will you do? On the day when you were united (one), you became separated (two). When you have become separated (two), what will you do?

Matthew 24:35 Heaven and earth will pass away, but my words will not pass away.

12. The Disciples said to Jesus: We know that you will go away from us. Who is it that will be our teacher?

Jesus said to them: Wherever you are (in the place that you have come), you will go to James the Righteous, for whose sake Heaven and Earth were made (came into being.)

13. Jesus said to his Disciples: Compare me to others, and tell me who I am like. Simon Peter said to him: You are like a righteous messenger (angel) of God. Matthew said to him: You are like a (wise) philosopher (of the heart). Thomas said to him: Teacher, my mouth is not capable of saying who you are like!

Jesus said: I'm not your teacher, now that you have drunk; you have become drunk from the bubbling spring that I have tended (measured out). And he took him, and withdrew and spoke three words to him: ahyh ashr ahyh (I am who I am).

Now when Thomas returned to his comrades, they inquired of him: What did Jesus say to you? Thomas said to them: If I tell you even one of the words which he spoke to me, you will take up stones and throw them at me, and fire will come from the stones to consume you.

Mark 8:27-30 Jesus went on with his disciples to the villages of Caesarea Philippi; and on the way he asked his disciples, Who do people say that I am? And they answered him, John the Baptist; and others, Elijah; and still others, one of the prophets. He asked them, But who do you say that I am? Peter answered him, You are the Messiah. And he sternly ordered them not to tell anyone about him.

14. Jesus said to them: If you fast, you will give rise to transgression (sin) for yourselves. And if you pray, you will be condemned. And if you give alms, you will cause harm (evil) to your spirits. And when you go into the countryside, if they take you in (receive you) then eat what they set before you and heal the sick among them. For what goes into your mouth will not defile you, but rather what comes out of your mouth, that is what will defile you.

Luke 10:8-9 Whenever you enter a town and its people welcome you, eat what is set before you; Cure the sick who are there, and say to them, The kingdom of God has come near to you.

Mark 7:15 There is nothing outside a person that by going in can defile, but the things that come out are what defile.

Matthew 15:11 It is not what goes into the mouth that defiles a man, but what comes out of the mouth, this defiles a man.

Romans 14.14 I know and am persuaded in the Lord Jesus that nothing is unclean in itself; but it is unclean for any one who thinks it unclean.

15. Jesus said: When you see him who was not born of woman, bow yourselves down upon your faces and worship him

for he is your Father.

Galatians 4:3-5 Even so we, when we were children, were in bondage under the elements of the world: But when the fullness of the time was come, God sent forth his Son, made of a woman, made under the law, To redeem them that were under the law, that we might receive the adoption of sons.

16. Jesus said: People think perhaps I have come to spread peace upon the world. They do not know that I have come to cast dissention (conflict) upon the earth; fire, sword, war. For there will be five in a house. Three will be against two and two against three, the father against the son and the son against the father. And they will stand alone.

Matthew 10:34-36 Do not think that I have come to bring peace to the earth; I have not come to bring peace, but a sword. For I have come to set a man against his father, and a daughter against her mother, and a daughter-in-law against her mother-in-law; and one's foes will be members of one's own household.

Luke 12:51-53 Do you think that I have come to give peace on earth? No, I tell you, but rather division; for henceforth in one house there will be five divided, three against two and two against three; they will be divided, father against son and son against father, mother against daughter and daughter against her mother, mother-in-law against her daughter-in-law and daughter-in-law against her mother-in-law.

17. Jesus said: I will give to you what eye has not seen, what ear has not heard, what hand has not touched, and what has not occurred to the mind of man.

1 Cor 2:9 But, as it is written, What no eye has seen, nor ear heard, nor the human heart conceived, what God has prepared for those who love him.

18. The Disciples said to Jesus: Tell us how our end will come. Jesus said: Have you already discovered the beginning (Origin), so that you inquire about the end? Where the beginning (origin) is, there the end will be. Blessed be he who will take his place in the beginning (stand at the origin) for he will know the end, and he will not experience death.

19. Jesus said: Blessed is he who came into being before he came into being. If you become my Disciples and heed my sayings, these stones will serve you. For there are five trees in paradise for you, which are undisturbed in summer and in winter and their leaves do not fall. Whoever knows them will not experience death.

20. The Disciples said to Jesus: Tell us what the Kingdom of Heaven is like. He said to them: It is like a mustard seed, smaller than all other seeds and yet when it falls on the tilled earth, it produces a great plant and becomes shelter for the birds of the sky.

Mark 4:30-32 He also said, With what can we compare the kingdom of God, or what parable will we use for it? It is like a mustard seed, which, when sown upon the ground, is the smallest of all the seeds on earth; yet when it is sown it grows up and becomes the greatest of all shrubs, and puts forth large branches, so that the birds of the air can make nests in its shade.

Matthew 13:31-32 The kingdom of heaven is like a grain of mustard seed which a man took and sowed in his field; it is the smallest of all seeds, but when it has grown it is the greatest of shrubs and becomes a tree, so that the birds of the air come and make nests in its branches.

Luke 13.18-19 He said therefore, What is the kingdom of God like? And to what shall I compare it? It is like a grain of mustard seed which a man took and sowed in his garden; and it grew and became a tree, and the birds of the air made nests in its branches.

21. Mary said to Jesus: Who are your Disciples like? He said: They are like little children who are living in a field that is not theirs. When the owners of the field come, they will say: Let us have our field! It is as if they were naked in front of them (They undress in front of them in order to let them have what is theirs) and they give back the field. Therefore I say, if the owner of the house knows that the thief is coming, he will be alert before he arrives and will not allow him to dig through into the house to carry away his belongings. You, must be on guard and beware of the world (system). Prepare yourself (arm yourself) with great strength or the bandits will find a way to reach you, for the problems you expect will come. Let there be among you a person of understanding (awareness). When the crop ripened, he came quickly with his sickle in his hand to reap. Whoever has ears to hear, let him hear!

Matthew 24:43 But understand this: if the owner of the house had known in what part of the night the thief was coming, he would have stayed awake and would not have let his house be broken into.

Mark 4:26-29 He also said, The kingdom of God is as if someone would scatter seed on the ground, and would sleep and rise night and day, and the seed would sprout and grow, he does not know how. The earth produces of itself, first the stalk, then the head, then the full grain in the head. But when the grain is ripe, at once he goes in with his sickle, because the harvest has come.

Luke 12:39-40 But know this, that if the householder had known at what hour the thief was coming, he would not have left his house to be broken into. You also must be ready; for the Son of man is coming at an unexpected hour.

22. Jesus saw little children who were being suckled. He said to his Disciples: These little children who are being suckled are like those who enter the Kingdom.

They said to him: Should we become like little children in order to enter the Kingdom?

Jesus said to them: When you make the two one, and you make the inside as the outside and the outside as the inside, when you make the above as the below, and if you make the male and the female one and the same (united male and female) so that the man will not be masculine (male) and the female be not feminine (female), when you establish an eye in the place of an eye and a hand in the place of a hand and a foot in the place of a foot and a likeness (image) in the place of a likeness (an image), then will you enter the Kingdom.

Luke 18:16 But Jesus called for them and said, Let the little children come to me, and do not stop them; for it is to such as these that the kingdom of God belongs. Truly I tell you, whoever does not receive the kingdom of God as a little child will never enter it.

Mark 9:43-48 If your hand causes you to stumble, cut it off; it is better for you to enter life maimed than to have two hands and to go to hell, to the unquenchable fire. And if your foot causes you to stumble, cut it off; it is better for you to enter life lame than to have two feet and to be thrown into hell. And if your eye causes you to stumble, tear it out; it is better for you to enter the kingdom of God with one eye than to have two eyes and to be thrown into hell, where the worm never dies, and the fire is never quenched.

Matthew 18:3-5 And said, Verily, I say unto you, unless you turn and become like children, you will never enter the kingdom of heaven. Whoever humbles himself like this child, he is the greatest in the kingdom of heaven. Whoever receives one such child in my name receives me;

Matthew 5:29-30 If your right eye causes you to sin, pluck it out and throw it away; it is better that you lose one of your members than that your whole body be thrown into hell. And if your right hand causes you to sin, cut it off and throw it away; it is better that you lose one of your members than that your whole body go into hell.

23. Jesus said: I will choose you, one out of a thousand and two out of ten thousand and they will stand as a single one.

Matthew 20:16 So the last shall be first, and the first last: for many be called, but few chosen.
24. His Disciples said: Show us the place where you are (your place), for it is necessary for us to seek it.
24. He said to them: Whoever has ears, let him hear! Within a man of light there is light, and he illumines the entire world. If he does not shine, he is darkness (there is darkness).

John13:36 Simon Peter said to him, Lord, where are you going? Jesus answered, Where I am going, you cannot follow me now; but you will follow afterward.

Matthew 6:22-23 The eye is the lamp of the body. So, if your eye is healthy, your whole body will be full of light; but if your eye is unhealthy, your whole body will be full of darkness. If then the light in you is darkness, how great is the darkness!

Luke 11:34-36 Your eye is the lamp of your body; when your eye is sound, your whole body is full of light; but when it is not sound, your body is full of darkness. Therefore be careful lest the light in you be darkness. If then your whole body is full of light, having no part dark, it will be wholly bright, as when a lamp with its rays gives you light.

Author's Note:

Early philosophers thought that light was transmitted from the eye and bounced back, allowing the person to sense the world at large. Ancient myths tell of Aphrodite constructing the human eye out of the four elements (earth, wind, fire, and water). The eye was held together by love. She kindled the fire of the soul and used it to project from the eyes so that it would act like a lantern, transmitting the light, thus allowing us to see.

Euclid, (330 BC to 260BC) speculated about the speed of light being instantaneous since you close your eyes, then open them again; even the distant objects appear immediately.

25. Jesus said: Love your friend (Brother) as your soul; protect him as you would the pupil of your own eye.

Romans 12:9-11 Let love be without dissimulation. Abhor that which is evil; cleave to that which is good. Be kindly affectioned one to another with brotherly love; in honour preferring one another; Not slothful in business; fervent in spirit; serving the Lord...

26. Jesus said: You see the speck in your brother's eye but the beam that is in your own eye you do not see. When you remove the beam out of your own eye, then will you see clearly to remove the speck out of your brother's eye.

26. Jesus said, You see the splinter in your brother's eye, but you don't see the log in your own eye. When you take the log out of your own eye, then you will see well enough to remove the splinter from your brother's eye.

Matthew 7:3-5 Why do you see the speck in your neighbor's eye, but do not notice the log in your own eye? Or how can you say to your neighbor, Let me take the speck out of your eye, while the log is in your own eye? You hypocrite, first take the log out of your own eye, and then you will see clearly to take the speck out of your neighbor's eye.

Luke 6:41-42 Why do you see the speck that is in your brother's eye, but do not notice the log that is in your own eye? Or how can you say to your brother, Brother, let me take out the speck that is in your eye, when you yourself do not see the log that is in your own eye? You hypocrite, first take the log out of your own eye, and then you will see clearly to take out the speck that is in your brother's eye.

27. Jesus said: Unless you fast from the world (system), you will not find the Kingdom of God. Unless you keep the Sabbath (entire week) as Sabbath, you will not see the Father.

27. Jesus said: Unless you fast (abstain) from the world, you shall in no way find the Kingdom of God; and unless you observe the Sabbath as a Sabbath, you shall not see the Father.

28. Jesus said: I stood in the midst of the world. In the flesh I appeared to them. I found them all drunk; I found none thirsty among them. My soul grieved for the sons of men, for they are blind in their hearts and do not see that they came into the world empty, they are destined (determined) to leave the world empty. However, now they are drunk. When they have shaken off their wine, then they will repent (change their ways).

28. Jesus said: I took my stand in the midst of the world, and they saw me in the flesh, and I found they were all drunk, and I found none of them were thirsty. And my soul grieved over the souls of men because they are blind in their hearts. They do not see that they came into the world empty, therefore they are determined to leave the world empty. However, now they are drunk. When they have shaken off their wine, then they will change their ways.

29. Jesus said: If the flesh came into being because of spirit, it is a marvel, but if spirit came into being because of the body, it would be a marvel of marvels. I marvel indeed at how great wealth has taken up residence in this poverty.

30. Jesus said: Where there are three gods, they are gods (Where there are three gods they are without god). Where there is only one, I say that I am with him. Lift the stone and there you will find me, Split the wood and there am I.

30. Jesus said: Where three are together they are not without God, and when there is one alone, I say, I am with him.

Author's Note:

Many scholars believe pages of the manuscript were misplaced and verses 30 and 77 should run together as a single verse.

77. Jesus said: I-Am the Light who is over all things, I-Am the All. From me all came forth and to me all return (The All came from me and the All has come to me). Split wood, there am I. Lift up the stone and there you will find me.

Matthew 18:20 For where two or three are gathered in my name, I am there among them.

31. Jesus said: No prophet is accepted in his own village, no physician heals those who know him.

31. Jesus said: A prophet is not accepted in his own country, neither can a doctor cure those that know him.

Mark 6:4 Then Jesus said to them, Prophets are not without honor, except in their hometown, and among their own kin, and in their own house.

Matthew 13:57 And they took offense at him. But Jesus said to them: A prophet is not without honor save in his own country and in his own house.

Luke 4:24 And he said, Truly, I say to you, no prophet is acceptable in his own country.

John 4:43-44 After the two days he departed to Galilee. For Jesus himself testified that a prophet has no honor in his own country.

32. Jesus said: A city being built (and established) upon a high mountain and fortified cannot fall nor can it be hidden.

32. Jesus said: A city built on a high hilltop and fortified can neither fall nor be hidden.

Matthew 5:14 You are the light of the world. A city built on a hill cannot be hid.

33. Jesus said: What you will hear in your ear preach from your rooftops. For no one lights a lamp and sets it under a basket nor puts it in a hidden place, but rather it is placed on a lamp stand so that everyone who comes and goes will see its light.

33. Jesus said: What you hear with one ear preach from your rooftops. For no one lights a lamp and sets it under a basket or hides, but rather it is placed on a lamp stand so that everyone who comes and goes will see its light.

Matthew 10:27 What I say to you in the dark, tell in the light; and what you hear whispered, proclaim from the housetops.

Luke 8:16 No one after lighting a lamp hides it under a jar, or puts it under a bed, but puts it on a lamp stand, so that those who enter may see the light.

Matthew 5:15 Nor do men light a lamp and put it under a bushel, but on a stand, and it gives light to all in the house.

Mark 4:21 And he said to them, Is a lamp brought in to be put under a bushel, or under a bed, and not on a stand?

Luke 11:33 No one after lighting a lamp puts it in a cellar or under a bushel, but on a stand, that those who enter may see the light.

34. Jesus said: If a blind person leads a blind person, both fall into a pit.

Matthew 15:14 Let them alone; they are blind guides of the blind. And if one blind person guides another, both will fall into a pit.

Luke 6:39 He also told them a parable: Can a blind man lead a blind man? Will they not both fall into a pit?

35. Jesus said: It is impossible for anyone to enter the house of a strong man to take it by force unless he binds his hands, then he will be able to loot his house.

Matthew 12:29 Or how can one enter a strong man's house and plunder his goods, unless he first binds the strong man? Then indeed he may plunder his house.

Luke 11:21-22 When a strong man, fully armed, guards his own palace, his goods are in peace; but when one stronger than he assails him and overcomes him, he takes away his armor in which he trusted, and divides his spoil.

Mark 3:27 But no one can enter a strong man's house and plunder his property without first tying up the strong man; then indeed the house can be plundered.

36. Jesus said: Do not worry from morning to evening nor from evening to morning about the food that you will eat nor about what clothes you will wear. You are much superior to the Lilies which neither card nor spin. When you have no clothing, what do you wear? Who can add time to your life (increase your stature)? He himself will give to you your garment.

Matthew 6:25-31 Therefore I tell you, do not worry about your life, what you will eat or what you will drink, or about your body, what you will wear. Is not life more than food, and the body more than clothing? Look at the birds of the air; they neither sow nor reap nor gather into barns, and yet your heavenly Father feeds them. Are you not of more value than they? And can any of you by worrying add a single hour to your span of life? And why do you worry about clothing? Consider the lilies of the field, how they grow; they neither toil nor spin, yet I tell you, even Solomon in all his glory was not clothed like one of these. But if God so clothes the grass of the field, which is alive today and tomorrow is thrown into the oven, will he not much more clothe you--you of little faith? Therefore do not worry, saying, What will we eat? or What will we drink? or What will we wear?

Luke 12:22-23 And he said to his disciples, Therefore I tell you, do not be anxious about your life, what you shall eat, nor about your body, what you shall put on. For life is more than food, and the body more than clothing.

37. His Disciples said: When will you appear to us, and when will we see you?

Jesus said: When you take off your garments without being ashamed, and place your garments under your feet and tread on them as the little children do, then will you see the Son of the Living-One, and you will not be afraid.

37 His disciples said to him, when will you be visible to us, and when shall we be able to see you?

He said, when you strip naked without being ashamed and place your garments under your feet and tread on them as the little children do, then will you see the Son of the Living-One, and you will not be afraid.

38. Jesus said: Many times have you yearned to hear these sayings which I speak to you, and you have no one else from whom to hear them. There will be days when you will seek me but you will not find me.

39. Jesus said: The Pharisees and the Scribes have received the keys of knowledge, but they have hidden them. They did not go in, nor did they permit those who wished to enter to do so. However, you be as wise (astute) as serpents and innocent as doves.

39. Jesus said: The Pharisees and the Scribes have stolen the keys of heaven, but they have hidden them. They have entered in, but they did not permit those who wished to enter to do so. However, you be as wise as serpents and innocent as doves.

Luke 11:52 Woe to you lawyers! For you have taken away the key of knowledge; you did not enter yourselves, and you hindered those who were entering.

Matthew 10:16 See, I am sending you out like sheep into the midst of wolves; so be wise as serpents and innocent as doves.

Matthew 23.13 But woe unto you, scribes and Pharisees, hypocrites! because you shut the kingdom of heaven against men; for you neither enter yourselves, nor allow those who would enter to go in.

40. Jesus said: A grapevine has been planted outside the (vineyard of the) Father, and since it is not viable (supported) it will be pulled up by its roots and destroyed.

Matthew 15:13 He answered, Every plant that my heavenly Father has not planted will be uprooted.

41. Jesus said: Whoever has (it) in his hand, to him will (more) be given. And whoever does not have, from him will be taken even the small amount which he has.

Matthew 25:29 For to all those who have, more will be given, and they will have an abundance; but from those who have nothing, even what they have will be taken away.

Luke 19:26 I tell you, that to every one who has will more be given; but from him who has not, even what he has will be taken away.

42. Jesus said: Become passers-by.

43. His Disciples said to him: Who are you, that you said these things to us?

Jesus said to them: You do not recognize who I am from what I said to you, but rather you have become like the Jews who either love the tree and hate its fruit, or love the fruit and hate the tree.

John 8:25 They said to him, Who are you? Jesus said to them, Why do I speak to you at all?

Matthew 7:16-20 You will know them by their fruits. Are grapes gathered from thorns, or figs from thistles? In the same way, every good tree bears good fruit, but the bad tree bears bad fruit. A good tree cannot bear bad fruit, nor can a bad tree bear good fruit. Every tree that does not bear good fruit is cut down and thrown into the fire. Thus you will know them by their fruits.

44. Jesus said: Whoever blasphemes against the Father, it will be forgiven him. And whoever blasphemes against the Son, it will be forgiven him. Yet whoever blasphemes against the Holy Spirit, it will not be forgiven him neither on earth nor in heaven.

Mark 3:28-29 Truly I tell you, people will be forgiven for their sins and whatever blasphemies they utter; but whoever blasphemes against the Holy Spirit can never have forgiveness, but is guilty of an eternal sin.

Matthew 12:31-32 Therefore I tell you, every sin and blasphemy will be forgiven men, but the blasphemy against the Spirit will not be forgiven. And whoever says a word against the Son of man will be forgiven; but whoever speaks against the Holy Spirit will not be forgiven, either in this age or in the age to come.

Luke 12:10 And every one who speaks a word against the Son of man will be forgiven him; but he who blasphemes against the Holy Spirit will not be forgiven.

45. Jesus said: Grapes are not harvested from thorns, nor are figs gathered from thistles, for they do not give fruit. A good person brings forth goodness out of his storehouse. A bad person brings forth evil out of his evil storehouse which is in his heart, and he speaks evil, for out of the abundance of the heart he brings forth evil.

Luke 6:43-45 For no good tree bears bad fruit, nor again does a bad tree bear good fruit; for each tree is known by its own fruit. For figs are not gathered from thorns, nor are grapes picked from a bramble bush. The good man out of the good treasure of his heart produces good, and the evil man out of his evil treasure produces evil; for out of the abundance of the heart his mouth speaks.

46. Jesus said: From Adam until John the Baptist there is none born of women who surpasses John the Baptist, so that his eyes should not be downcast (lowered). Yet I have said that whoever among you becomes like a child will know the Kingdom, and he will be greater than John.

Matthew 11:11 Truly I tell you, among those born of women no one has arisen greater than John the Baptist; yet the least in the kingdom of heaven is greater than he.

Luke 7:28 I tell you, among those born of women none is greater than John; yet he who is least in the kingdom of God is greater than he.

Matthew 18:2-4 He called a child, whom he put among them, and said, Truly I tell you, unless you change and become like children, you will never enter the kingdom of heaven. Whoever becomes humble like this child is the greatest in the kingdom of heaven.

47. Jesus said: It is impossible for a man to mount two horses or to draw two bows, and a servant cannot serve two masters, otherwise he will honor the one and disrespect the other. No man drinks vintage wine and immediately desires to drink new wine, and they do not put new wine into old wineskins or they would burst, and they do not put vintage wine into new wineskins or it would spoil (sour). They do not sew an old patch on a new garment because that would cause a split.

Matthew 6:24 No one can serve two masters; for a slave will either hate the one and love the other, or be devoted to the one and despise the other. You cannot serve God and wealth.

Matthew 9:16-17 No one sews a piece of cloth, not yet shrunk, on an old cloak, for the patch pulls away from the cloak, and a worse tear is made. Neither is new wine put into old wineskins; otherwise, the skins burst, and the wine is spilled, and the skins are destroyed; but new wine is put into fresh wineskins, and so both are preserved.

Mark 2:21-22 No one sews a piece of unshrunk cloth on an old garment; if he does, the patch tears away from it, the new from the old, and a worse tear is made. And no one puts new wine into old wineskins; if he does, the wine will burst the skins, and the wine is lost, and so are the skins; but new wine is for fresh skins.

Luke 5:36-39 He told them a parable also: No one tears a piece from a new garment and puts it upon an old garment; if he does, he will tear the new, and the piece from the new will not match the old. And no one puts new wine into old wineskins; if he does, the new wine will burst the skins and it will be spilled, and the skins will be destroyed. But new wine must be put into fresh wineskins. And no one after drinking old wine desires new; for he says, "The old is good."

48. Jesus said: If two make peace with each other in this one house, they will say to the mountain: Be moved! and it will be moved.

Matthew 18:19 Again, truly I tell you, if two of you agree on earth about anything you ask, it will be done for you by my Father in heaven.

Mark 11:23-24 Truly I tell you, if you say to this mountain, Be taken up and thrown into the sea, and if you do not doubt in your heart, but believe that what you say will come to pass, it will be done for you. So I tell you, whatever you ask for in prayer, believe that you have received it, and it will be yours.

Matthew 17:20 He said to them, Because of your little faith. For truly, I say to you, if you have faith as a grain of mustard seed, you will say to this mountain, Move from here to there, and it will move; and nothing will be impossible to you.

49. Jesus said: Blessed is the solitary and chosen, for you will find the Kingdom. You have come from it, and unto it you will return.

Matthew 5:1-3 And seeing the multitudes, he went up into a mountain: and when he was set, his disciples came unto him: And he opened his mouth, and taught them, saying, Blessed are the poor in spirit: for theirs is the kingdom of heaven.
John 20:28-30 And Thomas answered and said unto him, My LORD and my God. Jesus saith unto him, Thomas, because thou hast seen me, thou hast believed: blessed are they that have not seen, and yet have believed. And many other signs truly did Jesus in the presence of his disciples, which are not written in this book:

50. Jesus said: If they say to you: From where do you come? Say to them: We have come from the Light, the place where the Light came into existence of its own accord and he stood and appeared in their image. If they say to you: Is it you? (Who are you?), say: We are his Sons and we are the chosen of the Living Father. If they ask you: What is the sign of your Father in you? Say to them: It is movement with rest (peace in the midst of motion or chaos).

51. His Disciples said to him: When will the rest of the dead occur, and when will the New World come? He said to them: That which you look for has already come, but you do not recognize it.

52. His Disciples said to him: Twenty-four prophets preached in Israel, and they all spoke of you (in your spirit). He said to them: You have ignored the Living-One who is in your presence and you have spoken only of the dead.

53. His Disciples said to him: Is circumcision beneficial or not? He said to them: If it were beneficial, their father would beget them already circumcised from their mother. However, the true spiritual circumcision has become entirely

beneficial.

Jeremiah 4:3-5 For thus saith the LORD to the men of Judah and Jerusalem, Break up your fallow ground, and sow not among thorns. Circumcise yourselves to the LORD, and take away the foreskins of your heart, ye men of Judah and inhabitants of Jerusalem: lest my fury come forth like fire, and burn that none can quench it, because of the evil of your doings. Declare ye in Judah, and publish in Jerusalem; and say, Blow ye the trumpet in the land: cry, gather together, and say, Assemble yourselves, and let us go into the defenced cities.

54. Jesus said: Blessed be the poor, for yours is the Kingdom of the Heaven.

Matthew 6:20 Then he looked up at his disciples and said: Blessed are you who are poor, for yours is the kingdom of God.

Luke 6:20 And he lifted up his eyes on his disciples, and said: Blessed are you poor, for yours is the kingdom of God.

Matthew 5:3 Blessed are the poor in spirit, for theirs is the kingdom of heaven.

55. Jesus said: Whoever does not hate his father and his mother will not be able to become my Disciple. And whoever does not hate his brothers and his sisters and does not take up his own cross in my way, will not become worthy of me.

Luke 14:26-27 If any one comes to me and does not hate his own father and mother and wife and children and brothers and sisters, yes, and even his own life, he cannot be my disciple. Whoever does not bear his own cross and come after me, cannot be my disciple.

John 17:11-21 And now I am no more in the world, but these are in the world, and I come to thee. Holy Father, keep through thine own name those whom thou hast given me, that they may be one, as we are. While I was with them in the world, I kept them in thy name: those that thou gavest me I have kept, and none of them is lost, but the son of perdition; that the scripture might be fulfilled. And now come I to thee; and these things I speak in the world, that they might have my joy fulfilled in themselves. I have given them thy word; and the world hath hated them, because they are not of the world, even as I am not of the world. I pray not that thou shouldest take them out of the world, but that thou shouldest keep them from the evil. They are not of the world, even as I am not of the world. Sanctify them through thy truth: thy word is truth. As thou hast sent me into the world, even so have I also sent them into the world. And for their sakes I sanctify myself, that they also might be sanctified through the truth. Neither pray I for these alone, but for them also which shall believe on me through their word; That they all may be one; as thou, Father, art in me, and I in thee, that they also may be one in us: that the world may believe that thou hast sent me.

56. Jesus said: Whoever has come to understand the world (system) has found a corpse, and whoever has found a corpse, is superior to the world (of him the system is not worthy).

Hebrews 11:37-40 They were stoned, they were sawn asunder, were tempted, were slain with the sword: they wandered about in sheepskins and goatskins; being destitute, afflicted, tormented; (Of whom the world was not worthy:) they wandered in deserts, and in mountains, and in dens and caves of the earth. And these all, having obtained a good report through faith, received not the promise: God having provided some better thing for us, that they without us should not be made perfect.

57. Jesus said: The Kingdom of the Father is like a person who has good seed. His enemy came by night and sowed a weed among the good seed. The man did not permit them to pull up the weed, he said to them: perhaps you will intend to pull up the weed and you pull up the wheat along with it. But, on the day of harvest the weeds will be very visible and then they will pull them and burn them.

Matthew 13:24-30 He put before them another parable: The kingdom of heaven may be compared to someone who sowed good seed in his field; but while everybody was asleep, an enemy came and sowed weeds among the wheat, and then went away. So when the plants came up and bore grain, then the weeds appeared as well. And the slaves of the householder came and said to him, Master, did you not sow good seed in your field? Where, then, did these weeds come from? He answered, An enemy has done this. The slaves said to him, Then do you want us to go and gather them? But he replied, No; for in gathering the weeds you would uproot the wheat along with them. Let both of them grow together until the harvest; and at harvest time I will tell the reapers, Collect the weeds first and bind them in bundles to be burned, but gather the wheat into my barn.

58. Jesus said: Blessed is the person who has suffered, for he has found life. (Blessed is he who has suffered to find life and found life).

Matthew 11:28 Come to me, all you that are weary and are carrying heavy burdens, and I will give you rest.

59. Jesus said: Look to the Living-One while you are alive, otherwise, you might die and seek to see him and will be unable to find him.

John 7:34 You will search for me, but you will not find me; and where I am, you cannot come.

John 13:33 Little children, I am with you only a little longer. You will look for me; and as I said to the Jews so now I say to you, Where I am going, you cannot come.

60. They saw a Samaritan carrying a lamb, on his way to Judea. Jesus said to them: Why does he take the lamb with him? They said to him: So that he may kill it and eat it. He said to them: While it is alive he will not eat it, but only after he kills it and it becomes a corpse. They said: How could he do otherwise? He said to them: Look for a place of rest for yourselves, otherwise, you might become corpses and be eaten.

61. Jesus said: Two will rest on a bed and one will die and the other will live. Salome said: Who are you, man? As if sent by someone, you laid upon my bed and you ate from my table. Jesus said to her: I-Am he who is from that which is whole (the undivided). I have been given the things of my Father. Salome said: I'm your Disciple. Jesus said to her: Thus, I say that whenever someone is one (undivided)
he will be filled with light, yet whenever he is divided (chooses) he will be filled with darkness.

Luke 17:34 I tell you, on that night there will be two in one bed; one will be taken and the other left.

62. Jesus said: I tell my mysteries to those who are worthy of my mysteries. Do not let your right hand know what your left hand is doing.

Mark 4:11 And he said to them, To you has been given the secret of the kingdom of God, but for those outside, everything comes in parables.

Matthew 6:3 But when you give alms, do not let your left hand know what your right hand is doing.

Luke 8:10 He said, To you it has been given to know the secrets of the kingdom of God; but for others they are in parables, so that seeing they may not see, and hearing they may not understand.

Matthew 13:10-11 Then the disciples came and said to him, Why do you speak to them in parables? And he answered them, To you it has been given to know the secrets of the kingdom of heaven, but to them it has not been given.

63. Jesus said: There was a wealthy person who had much money, and he said: I will use my money so that I may sow and reap and replant, to fill my storehouses with grain so that I lack nothing. This was his intention (is what he thought in his heart) but that same night he died. Whoever has ears, let him hear!

Luke 12:21 Then he told them a parable: The land of a rich man produced abundantly. And he thought to himself, What should I do, for I have no place to store my crops? Then he said, I will do this: I will pull down my barns and build larger ones, and there I will store all my grain and my goods. And I will say to my soul, Soul, you have ample goods laid up for many years; relax, eat, drink, be merry. But God said to him, You fool! This very night your life is being demanded of you. And the things you have prepared, whose will they be? So it is with those who store up treasures for themselves but are not rich toward God.

64. Jesus said: A person had houseguests, and when he had prepared the banquet in their honor he sent his servant to invite the guests. He went to the first, he said to him: My master invites you. He replied: I have to do business with some merchants. They are coming to see me this evening. I will go to place my orders with them. I ask to be excused from the banquet. He went to another, he said to him: My master has invited you. He replied to him: I have just bought a house and they require me for a day. I will have no spare time. He came to another, he said to him: My master invites you. He replied to him: My friend is getting married and I must arrange a banquet for him. I will not be able to come. I ask to be excused from the banquet. He went to another, he said to him: My master invites you. He replied to him: I have bought a farm. I go to receive the rent. I will not be able to come. I ask to be excused. The servant returned, he said to his master: Those whom you have invited to the banquet have excused themselves. The master said to his servant: Go out to the roads, bring those whom you find so that they may feast. And he said: Businessmen and merchants will not enter the places of my Father.

Luke 14:16-24 Then Jesus said to him:, Someone gave a great dinner and invited many. At the time for the dinner he sent his slave to say to those who had been invited, Come; for everything is ready now. But they all alike began to make excuses. The first said to him, I have bought a piece of land, and I must go out and see it; please accept my regrets. Another said, I have bought five yoke of oxen, and I am going to try them out; please accept my regrets. Another said, I have just been married, and therefore I cannot come. So the slave returned and reported this to his master. Then the owner of the house became angry and said to his slave, Go out at once into the streets and lanes of the town and bring in the poor, the crippled, the blind, and the lame. And the slave said, Sir, what you ordered has been done, and there is still room. Then the master said to the slave, Go out into the roads and lanes, and compel people to come in, so that my house may be filled. For I tell you, none of those who were invited will taste my dinner.

Matthew 19:23 Then Jesus said to his disciples, Truly I tell you, it will be hard for a rich person to enter the kingdom of heaven.

Matthew 22:1-14 And Jesus answered and spake unto them again by parables, and said, The kingdom of heaven is like unto a certain king, which made a marriage for his son, and sent his servants to call those who were invited to the marriage feast; but they would not come. Again he sent other servants, saying, Tell those who are invited, Behold, I have made ready my dinner, my oxen and my fat calves are killed, and everything is ready; come to the marriage feast. But they made light of it and went off, one to his farm, another to his business, while the rest seized his servants, treated them shamefully, and killed them. The king was angry, and he sent his troops and destroyed those murderers and burned their city. Then he said to his servants, The wedding is ready, but those invited were not worthy. Go therefore to the thoroughfares, and invite to the marriage feast as many as you find. And those servants went out into the streets and gathered all whom they found, both bad and good; so the wedding hall was filled with guests. But when the king came in to look at the guests, he saw there a man who had no wedding garment; and he said to him, Friend, how did you get in here without a wedding garment? And he was speechless. Then the king said to the attendants, Bind him hand and foot, and cast him into the outer darkness; there men will weep and gnash their teeth. For many are called, but few are chosen.

65. He said: A kind person who owned a vineyard leased it to tenants so that they would work it and he would receive the fruit from them. He sent his servant so that the tenants would give to him the fruit of the vineyard. They seized his servant and beat him nearly to death. The servant went, he told his master what had happened. His master said: Perhaps they did not recognize him. So, he sent another servant. The tenants beat him also. Then the owner sent his son. He said: Perhaps they will respect my son. Since the tenants knew that he was the heir to the vineyard, they seized him and killed him. Whoever has ears, let him hear!

Matthew 21:33-39 Listen to another parable. There was a landowner who planted a vineyard, put a fence around it, dug a wine press in it, and built a watchtower. Then he leased it to tenants and went to another country. When the harvest time had come, he sent his slaves to the tenants to collect his produce. But the tenants seized his slaves and beat one, killed another, and stoned another. Again he sent other slaves, more than the first; and they treated them in the same way. Finally he sent his son to them, saying, They will respect my son. But when the tenants saw the son, they said to themselves, This is the heir; come, let us kill him and get his inheritance. So they seized him, threw him out of the vineyard, and killed him.

Mark 12:1-9 And he began to speak to them in parables. A man planted a vineyard, and set a hedge around it, and dug a pit for the wine press, and built a tower, and let it out to tenants, and went into another country. When the time came, he sent a servant to the tenants, to get from them some of the fruit of the vineyard. And they took him and beat him, and sent him away empty-handed. Again he sent to them another servant, and they wounded him in the head, and treated him shamefully. And he sent another, and him they killed; and so with many others, some they beat and some they killed. He had still one other, a beloved son; finally he sent him to them, saying, They will respect my son. But those tenants said to one another, This is the heir; come, let us kill him, and the inheritance will be ours. And they took him and killed him, and cast him out of the vineyard. What will the owner of the vineyard do? He will come and destroy the tenants, and give the vineyard to others.

Luke 20:9-16 And he began to tell the people this parable: A man planted a vineyard, and let it out to tenants, and went into another country for a long while. When the time came, he sent a servant to the tenants, that they should give him some of the fruit of the vineyard; but the tenants beat him, and sent him away empty-handed. And he sent another servant; him also they beat and treated shamefully, and sent him away empty-handed. And he sent yet a third; this one they wounded and cast out. Then the owner of the vineyard said, What shall I do? I will send my beloved son; it may be they will respect him. But when the tenants saw him, they said to themselves, This is the heir; let us kill him, that the inheritance may be ours. And they cast him out of the vineyard and killed him. What then will the owner of the vineyard do to them? He will come and destroy those tenants, and give the vineyard to others. When they heard this, they said, God forbid!

66. Jesus said: Show me the stone which the builders have rejected. It is that one that is the cornerstone (keystone).

Matthew 21:42 Jesus said to them, Have you never read in the scriptures: The very stone which the builders rejected has become the head of the corner; this was the Lord's doing, and it is marvelous in our eyes?

Mark 12:10-11 Have you not read this scripture: The very stone which the builders rejected has become the head of the corner; this was the Lord's doing, and it is marvelous in our eyes?

Luke 20:17 But he looked at them and said, What then does this text mean: The stone that the builders rejected has become the cornerstone?

67. Jesus said: Those who know everything but themselves, lack everything. (whoever knows the all and still feels a personal lacking, he is completely deficient).

Jeremiah 17:5- 10 Thus saith the LORD; Cursed be the man that trusteth in man, and maketh flesh his arm, and whose heart departeth from the LORD. For he shall be like the heath in the desert, and shall not see when good cometh; but shall inhabit the parched places in the wilderness, in a salt land and not inhabited. Blessed is the man that trusteth in the LORD, and whose hope the LORD is. For he shall be as a tree planted by the waters, and that spreadeth out her roots by the river, and shall not see when heat cometh, but her leaf shall be green; and shall not be careful in the year of drought, neither shall cease from yielding fruit. The heart is deceitful above all things, and desperately wicked: who can know it? I the LORD search the heart, I try the reins, even to give every man according to his ways, and according to the fruit of his doings.

68. Jesus said: Blessed are you when you are hated and persecuted, but they themselves will find no reason why you have been persecuted.

Matthew 5:11 Blessed are you when people revile you and persecute you and utter all kinds of evil against you falsely on my account.

Luke 6:22 Blessed are you when men hate you, and when they exclude you and revile you, and cast out your name as evil, on account of the Son of man!

69. Jesus said: Blessed are those who have been persecuted in their heart; these are they who have come to know the Father in truth. Jesus said: Blessed are the hungry, for the stomach of him who desires to be filled will be filled.

Matthew 5:8 Blessed are the pure in heart, for they will see God.

Luke 6:21 Blessed are you who are hungry now, for you will be filled.

70. Jesus said: If you bring forth what is within you, it will save you. If you do not have it within you to bring forth, that which you lack will destroy you.

71. Jesus said: I will destroy this house, and no one will be able to build it again.

Mark 14:58 We heard him say, I will destroy this temple that is made with hands, and in three days I will build another, not made with hands.

72. A person said to him: Tell my brothers to divide the possessions of my father with me. He said to him: Oh man, who made me a divider? He turned to his Disciples, he said to them: I'm not a divider, am I?

Luke 12:13-15 Someone in the crowd said to him, Teacher, tell my brother to divide the family inheritance with me. But he said to him, Friend, who set me to be a judge or arbitrator over you? And he said to them, Take care! Be on your guard against all kinds of greed; for one's life does not consist in the abundance of possessions.

73. Jesus said: The harvest is indeed plentiful, but the workers are few. Ask the Lord to send workers for the harvest.

Matthew 9:37-38 Then he said to his disciples, The harvest is plentiful, but the laborers are few; therefore ask the Lord of the harvest to send out laborers into his harvest.

74. He said: Lord, there are many around the well, yet there is nothing in the well. How is it that many are around the well and no one goes into it?

75. Jesus said: There are many standing at the door, but only those who are alone are the ones who will enter into the Bridal Chamber.

Matthew 25:1-8 Then shall the kingdom of heaven be likened unto ten virgins, which took their lamps, and went forth to meet the bridegroom. And five of them were wise, and five were foolish. They that were foolish took their lamps, and took no oil with them: But the wise took oil in their vessels with their lamps. While the bridegroom tarried, they all slumbered and slept. And at midnight there was a cry made, Behold, the bridegroom cometh; go ye out to meet him. Then all those virgins arose, and trimmed their lamps. And the foolish said unto the wise, Give us of your oil; for our lamps are gone out.

76. Jesus said: The Kingdom of the Father is like a rich merchant who found a pearl. The merchant was prudent. He sold his fortune and bought the one pearl for himself. You also, seek for his treasure which does not fail, which endures where no moth can come near to eat it nor worm to devour it.

Matthew 13:45-46 Again, the kingdom of heaven is like a merchant in search of fine pearls; on finding one pearl of great value, he went and sold all that he had and bought it.

Matthew 6:19-20 Do not store up for yourselves treasures on earth, where moth and rust consume and where thieves break in and steal; but store up for yourselves treasures in heaven, where neither moth nor rust consumes and where thieves do not break in and steal.

77. Jesus said: I-Am the Light who is over all things, I-Am the All. From me all came forth and to me all return (The All came from me and the All has come to me). Split wood, there am I. Lift up the stone and there you will find me.

Author's Note:
Many scholars believe the order of verses 30 and 77 were misplaced and these two verses should be connected as one verse.

30. Jesus said: Where there are three gods, they are gods (Where there are three gods they are without god). Where there is only one, I say that I am with him. Lift the stone and there you will find me, Split the wood and there am I.

John 8:12 Again Jesus spoke to them, saying, I am the light of the world. Whoever follows me will never walk in darkness but will have the light of life.

John 1:3 All things came into being through him, and without him not one thing came into being.

78. Jesus said: Why did you come out to the wilderness; to see a reed shaken by the wind? And to see a person dressed in fine (soft – plush) garments like your rulers and your dignitaries? They are clothed in plush garments, and they are not able to recognize (understand) the truth.

Matthew 11:7-9 As they went away, Jesus began to speak to the crowds about John: What did you go out into the wilderness to look at? A reed shaken by the wind? What then did you go out to see? Someone dressed in soft robes? Look, those who wear soft robes are in royal palaces. What then did you go out to see? A prophet? Yes, I tell you, and more than a prophet.

79. A woman from the multitude said to him: Blessed is the womb which bore you, and the breasts which nursed you! He said to her: Blessed are those who have heard the word (meaning) of the Father and have truly kept it. For there will be days when you will say: Blessed be the womb which has not conceived and the breasts which have not nursed.

Luke 11:27-28 While he was saying this, a woman in the crowd raised her voice and said to him, Blessed is the womb that bore you and the breasts that nursed you! But he said, Blessed rather are those who hear the word of God and obey it!

Luke 23:29 For the days are surely coming when they will say, Blessed are the barren, and the wombs that never bore, and the breasts that never nursed.

80. Jesus said: Whoever has come to understand (recognize) the world (world system) has found the body (corpse), and whoever has found the body (corpse), of him the world (world system) is not worthy.

Hebrews 11:37-40 They were stoned, they were sawn asunder, were tempted, were slain with the sword: they wandered about in sheepskins and goatskins; being destitute, afflicted, tormented; (Of whom the world was not worthy:) they wandered in deserts, and in mountains, and in dens and caves of the earth. And these all, having obtained a good report through faith, received not the promise: God having provided some better thing for us, that they without us should not be made perfect.

81. Jesus said: Whoever has become rich should reign, and let whoever has power renounce it.

82. Jesus said: Whoever is close to me is close to the fire, and whoever is far from me is far from the Kingdom.

John 14:6-9 Jesus saith unto him, I am the way, the truth, and the life: no man cometh unto the Father, but by me. If ye had known me, ye should have known my Father also: and from henceforth ye know him, and have seen him. Philip saith unto him, Lord, show us the Father, and it sufficeth us. Jesus saith unto him, Have I been so long time with you, and yet hast thou not known me, Philip? he that hath seen me hath seen the Father;

83. Jesus said: Images are visible to man but the light which is within them is hidden. The light of the father will be revealed, but he (his image) is hidden in the light.

84. Jesus said: When you see your reflection, you rejoice. Yet when you perceive your images which have come into being before you, which neither die nor can be seen, how much will you have to bear?

85. Jesus said: Adam came into existence from a great power and a great wealth, and yet he was not worthy of you. For if he had been worthy, he would not have tasted death.

86. Jesus said: The foxes have their dens and the birds have their nests, yet the Son of Man has no place to lay his head for rest.

Matthew 8:20 And Jesus said to him, Foxes have holes, and birds of the air have nests; but the Son of Man has nowhere to lay his head.

87. Jesus said: Wretched is the body which depends upon another body, and wretched is the soul which depends on these two (upon their being together).

88. Jesus said: The angels and the prophets will come to you, and what they will give you belongs to you. And you will give them what you have, and say among yourselves: When will they come to take (receive) what belongs to them?

89. Jesus said: Why do you wash the outside of your cup? Do you not understand (mind) that He who creates the inside is also He who creates the outside?

Luke 11:39-40 Then the Lord said to him, Now you Pharisees clean the outside of the cup and of the dish, but inside you are full of greed and wickedness. You fools! Did not the one who made the outside make the inside also?

90. Jesus said: Come unto me, for my yoke is comfortable (natural) and my lordship is gentle — and you will find rest for yourselves.

Matthew 11:28-30 Come to me, all you that are weary and are carrying heavy burdens, and I will give you rest. Take my yoke upon you, and learn from me; for I am gentle and humble in heart, and you will find rest for your souls. For my yoke is easy, and my burden is light.

Acts 15:5-17 But there rose up certain of the sect of the Pharisees which believed, saying, that it was needful to circumcise them, and to command them to keep the law of Moses. And the apostles and elders came together for to consider of this matter. And when there had been much disputing, Peter rose up, and said unto them, Men and brethren, ye know how that a good while ago God made choice among us, that the Gentiles by my mouth should hear the word of the gospel, and believe. And God, which knoweth the hearts, bare them witness, giving them the Holy Ghost, even as he did unto us. And put no difference between us and them, purifying their hearts by faith. Now therefore why tempt ye God, to put a yoke upon the neck of the disciples, which neither our fathers nor we were able to bear? But we believe that through the grace of the LORD Jesus Christ we shall be saved, even as they. Then all the multitude kept silence, and gave audience to Barnabas and Paul, declaring what miracles and wonders God had wrought among the Gentiles by them. And after they had held their peace, James answered, saying, Men and brethren, hearken unto me: Simeon hath declared how God at the first did visit the Gentiles, to take out of them a people for his name. And to this agree the words of the prophets; as it is written, After this I will return, and will build again the tabernacle of David, which is fallen down; and I will build again the ruins thereof, and I will set it up: That the residue of men might seek after the Lord, and all the Gentiles, upon whom my name is called, saith the Lord, who doeth all these things.

91. They said to him: Tell us who you are, so that we may believe in you. He said to them: You examine the face of the sky and of the earth, yet you do not recognize Him who is here with you, and you do not know how to seek in (to inquire of Him at) this moment (you do not know how to take advantage of this opportunity).

John 9:36 He answered, And who is he, sir? Tell me, so that I may believe in him.

Luke 12:54-56 He also said to the crowds, When you see a cloud rising in the west, you immediately say, It is going to rain; and so it happens. And when you see the south wind blowing, you say, There will be scorching heat; and it happens. You hypocrites! You know how to interpret the appearance of earth and sky, but why do you not know how to interpret the present time?

92. Jesus said: Seek and you will find. But in the past I did not answer the questions you asked. Now I wish to tell them to you, but you do not ask about (no longer seek) them.

Matthew 7:7 Ask, and it will be given you; search, and you will find; knock, and the door will be opened for you.

93. Jesus said: Do not give what is sacred to the dogs, lest they throw it on the dung heap. Do not cast the pearls to the swine, lest they cause it to become dung (mud).

Matthew 7:6 Do not give what is holy to dogs; and do not throw your pearls before swine, or they will trample them under foot and turn and maul you.

94. Jesus said: Whoever seeks will find. And whoever knocks, it will be opened to him.

Matthew 7:8 For everyone who asks receives, and everyone who searches finds, and for everyone who knocks, the door will be opened.

95. Jesus said: If you have money, do not lend at interest, but rather give it to those from whom you will not be repaid.

Luke 6:34-35 If you lend to those from whom you hope to receive, what credit is that to you? Even sinners lend to sinners, to receive as much again. But love your enemies, do good, and lend, expecting nothing in return. Your reward will be great, and you will be children of the Most High; for he is kind to the ungrateful and the wicked.

96. Jesus said: The Kingdom of the Father is like a woman who has taken a little yeast and hidden it in dough. She produced large loaves of it. Whoever has ears, let him hear!

Matthew 13:33 He told them another parable: The kingdom of heaven is like yeast that a woman took and mixed in with three measures of flour until all of it was leavened.

97. Jesus said: The Kingdom of the Father is like a woman who was carrying a jar full of grain. While she was walking on a road far from home, the handle of the jar broke and the grain poured out behind her onto the road. She did not know it. She had noticed no problem. When she arrived in her house, she set the jar down and found it empty.
98. Jesus said: The Kingdom of the Father is like someone who wished to slay a prominent person. While still in his own house he drew his sword and thrust it into the wall in order to test whether his hand would be strong enough. Then he slew the prominent person.

99. His Disciples said to him: Your brethren and your mother are standing outside. He said to them: Those here who do my Father's desires are my Brethren and my Mother. It is they who will enter the Kingdom of my Father.

Matthew 12:46-50 While he was still speaking to the crowds, his mother and his brothers were standing outside, wanting to speak to him. Someone told him, Look, your mother and your brothers are standing outside, wanting to speak to you. But to the one who had told him this, Jesus replied, Who is my mother, and who are my brothers? And pointing to his disciples, he said, Here are my mother and my brothers! For whoever does the will of my Father in heaven is my brother and sister and mother.

100. They showed Jesus a gold coin, and said to him: The agents of Caesar extort taxes from us. He said to them: Give the things of Caesar to Caesar, give the things of God to God, and give to me what is mine.

Mark 12:14-17 Is it lawful to pay taxes to the emperor, or not? Should we pay them, or should we not? But knowing their hypocrisy, he said to them, Why are you putting me to the test? Bring me a denarius and let me see it. And they brought one. Then he said to them, Whose head is this, and whose title? They answered, The emperor's. Jesus said to them, Give to the emperor the things that are the emperor's, and to God the things that are God's. And they were utterly amazed at him.

101. Jesus said: Whoever does not hate his father and his mother, as I do, will not be able to become my Disciple. And whoever does not love his father and his mother, as I do, will not be able to become my disciple. For my mother bore me, yet my true Mother gave me the life.

Matthew 10:37 Whoever loves father or mother more than me is not worthy of me; and whoever loves son or daughter more than me is not worthy of me.

102. Jesus said: Damn these Pharisees. They are like a dog sleeping in the feed trough of oxen. For neither does he eat, nor does he allow the oxen to eat.

Matthew 2:13 But woe unto you, scribes and Pharisees, hypocrites! because you shut the kingdom of heaven against men; for you neither enter yourselves, nor allow those who would enter to go in.

103. Jesus said: Blessed (happy) is the person who knows at what place of the house the bandits may break in, so that he can rise and collect his things and prepare himself before they enter.

Matthew 24:43 But understand this: if the owner of the house had known in what part of the night the thief was coming, he would have stayed awake and would not have let his house be broken into.

104. They said to him: Come, let us pray today and let us fast. Jesus said: What sin have I committed? How have I been overcome (undone)? When the Bridegroom comes forth from the bridal chamber, then let them fast and let them pray.

105. Jesus said: Whoever acknowledges (comes to know) father and mother, will be called the son of a whore.

106. Jesus said: When you make the two one, you will become Sons of Man (children of Adam), and when you say to the mountain: Move! It will move.

Mark 11:23 Truly I tell you, if you say to this mountain, Be taken up and thrown into the sea, and if you do not doubt in your heart, but believe that what you say will come to pass, it will be done for you.

107. Jesus said: The Kingdom is like a shepherd who has a hundred sheep. The largest one of them went astray. He left the ninety-nine and sought for the one until he found it. Having searched until he was weary, he said to that sheep: I desire you more than the ninety-nine.

Matthew 18:12-13 What do you think? If a shepherd has a hundred sheep, and one of them has gone astray, does he not leave the ninety-nine on the mountains and go in search of the one that went astray? And if he finds it, truly I tell you, he rejoices over it more than over the ninety-nine that never went astray.

108. Jesus said: Whoever drinks from my mouth will become like me. I will become him, and the secrets will be revealed to him.

109. Jesus said: The Kingdom is like a person who had a treasure hidden in his field and knew nothing of it. After he died, he bequeathed it to his son. The son accepted the field knowing nothing of the treasure. He sold it. Then the person who bought it came and plowed it. He found the treasure. He began to lend money at interest to whomever he wished.

Matthew 13:44 The kingdom of heaven is like treasure hidden in a field, which someone found and hid; then in his joy he goes and sells all that he has and buys that field.

110. Jesus said: Whoever has found the world (system) and becomes wealthy (enriched by it), let him renounce the world (system).

Mark 10:21-23 Then Jesus beholding him loved him, and said unto him, One thing thou lackest: go thy way, sell whatsoever thou hast, and give to the poor, and thou shalt have treasure in heaven: and come, take up the cross, and follow me. And he was sad at that saying, and went away grieved: for he had great possessions. And Jesus looked round about, and saith unto his disciples, How hardly shall they that have riches enter into the kingdom of God!

111. **Jesus said: Heaven and earth will roll up (collapse and disappear) before you, but he who lives within the Living-One will neither see nor fear death. For, Jesus said: Whoever finds himself, of him the world is not worthy.**

112. **Jesus said: Damned is the flesh which depends upon the soul. Damned is the soul which depends upon the flesh.**

113. **His Disciples said to him: When will the Kingdom come? Jesus said: It will not come by expectation (because you watch or wait for it). They will not say: Look here! or: Look there! But the Kingdom of the Father is spread upon the earth, and people do not realize it.**

Luke 17:20 And when he was demanded of by the Pharisees, when the kingdom of God should come, he answered them and said, The kingdom of God cometh not with observation: Neither shall they say, Lo-Here! Lo-There! For, behold, the kingdom of God is within you.

(Saying 114 was written later and was added to the original text.)

114. **Simon Peter said to them: Send Mary away from us, for women are not worthy of this life. Jesus said: See, I will draw her into me so that I make her male, in order that she herself will become a living spirit like you males. For every female who becomes male will enter the Kingdom of the Heaven.**

The Question of Judas

No discovery since the Dead Sea Scrolls has rocked the Christian world like that of the newly translated "Gospel of Judas." The story presented in the short but powerful text reveals a plan in which heavenly ends justified monstrous means. Betrayal became collaboration and murder resembled suicide as Jesus and Judas began a macabre dance into eternity.

Orthodox Christianity has its doctrine, its canon, and its political story, but these are quite different from those exposed in the Gospel of Judas.

As the orthodox political viewpoint would have it, Jesus' demise was sought by the Roman authorities as he gained a following and was declared "King" by the Jewish populace. The Jewish religious leaders were also planning his death, believing that Jesus was attempting to reform Judaism, and wrest their control over the people.

The Gospel of Judas calls into question this accepted view of the political intrigue leading up to Jesus' betrayal and death.

Spokesman for the Maecenas Foundation, one of the companies in Basel, Switzerland working on the Judas project, Director Mario Jean Roberty, reports:

"We have just received the results of carbon dating: the text is older than we thought and dates back to a period between the beginning of the third and fourth centuries. We do not want to reveal the exceptional side of what we have, except that the Judas Iscariot text called into question some of the political principles of Christian doctrine."

Imagine Judas, the man all of Christendom has hated for two thousand years, now portrayed as the chosen one, the martyr, the scapegoat, and the man instructed and appointed by Jesus himself to orchestrate and carry out the greatest treachery of all time. But treachery ordered by the one betrayed is not treachery at all, but a loyal and devoted follower carrying out the wishes of his master.

What was Judas' reward for betraying Jesus? According to the Gospel of Judas it was special recognition by God and the blessing of Jesus, the savior of mankind. Strangely, there is evidence in our own Bible to substantiate this claim. Judas may have been promised a position of authority along with the other apostles.

The Gospel of Judas turns us on our heads and forces upon the reader a new and uncomfortable view. Did Judas have special knowledge and instruction from Jesus? Are we to thank him for the death of Jesus? Is lethal treachery appointed by the victim suicide or murder? Is this murderous quisling really a saint?

Who is this man, Judas? What do we know about him? Where did he come from? What did he want? What did he do?

These are just a few of the questions left to reverberate in the mind of the reader.

Theories of Judas abound. He is presented as greedy and selfish as well as sanctified spirit. Some say he was possessed, some say he was a saint, and some believe him to be Satan himself.

Was Judas the impetus of death, burial, and resurrection for Jesus, and thus the daemon who saved us? Will Judas be the Antichrist we will meet in the end of days or will he be ruling and judging the tribes of Israel?

Every story has two sides. Let us examine both sides, beginning with The Gospel of Judas, its history, its theology, and its text.

Understanding the Intent

The Gospel of Judas can be understood on a deeper level if its background is explored first.

One may ask the proper questions regarding the text of "who, what, when, where, and why." The question of "who" wrote the Gospel of Judas we may never know. What the author was trying to say will be explored in depth. Science can and has narrowed down the "when" and "where."

Why mankind writes is axiomatic. We write to document, explain, express, or convince. In the end, those are the reasons. Time will tell if the author of Judas has succeeded.

In a time when Gnosticism was struggling for influence in Christendom, the Gospel of Judas was written to challenge the beliefs of the newly emerging church orthodoxy, to explain Gnostic theology, and to propagate the sect. To better understand the gospel, it must be read with these goals in mind.

For centuries the definition of Gnosticism has in itself been a point of confusion and contention within the religious community. This is due in part to the ever-broadening application of the term and the fact that various sects of Gnosticism existed as the theology evolved and began to merge into what became mainstream Christianity.

Even though Gnosticism continued to evolve, it is the theology in place at the time that the Gospel of Judas was written that should be considered and understood before attempting to render or read a translation. To do otherwise would make the translation cloudy and obtuse.

It becomes the duty of both translator and reader to understand the ideas being espoused and the terms conveying those ideas. A grasp of theology, cosmology, and relevant terms is necessary for a clear transmission of the meaning within the text in question.

With this in mind, we will briefly examine Gnostic theology, cosmology, and history. We will focus primarily on Gnostic sects existing in the first through fourth centuries A.D. since it is believed most Gnostic Gospels were written during that time. It was also during that time that reactions within the emerging Christian orthodoxy began to intensify and the Gospel of Judas was written.

The downfall of many books written on the topic of religion is the attempt to somehow remove history and people from the equation. History shapes religion because it shapes the perception and direction of religious leaders. Religion also develops and evolves in an attempt to make sense of the universe as it is seen and understood at the time. Thus, to truly grasp a religious concept it is important to know the history, people, and cosmology of the time. These areas are not separate but are continually interacting.

What is the Gospel of Judas?

What is the Gospel of Judas and why does it differ so greatly from the gospel stories of the Bible?

The Gospel of Judas is considered a Gnostic text. The Gnostics were a sect of Christianity and like any sect or religion, they were fighting to expand and continue under the persecution of the newly emerging orthodoxy of the day.

The Gospel of Judas may have been written to help bolster and continue Gnosticism. This may explain its radical departure from the traditional Gospel story, as well as the reason for its creation.

Indeed, one way of looking at any religious book, canon or not, is as an attempt to explain one's beliefs, to persuade others toward those beliefs, and to interpret history and known storylines in the light of one's own theology and cosmology. This is done not only to add weight to one's own belief system but also simply because man sees events as having relevance to what he or she holds as truth.

As previously stated, the Gospel of Judas is, above all things, a Gnostic gospel since it revolves around a special knowledge or Gnosis given to Judas by Jesus. This knowledge represented that which Gnostics held as the universal truth.

The History of the Gospel of Judas

The newly discovered Gospel of Judas is very controversial for several reasons. Theologically, it is divisive due to its Gnostic theology. The main controversy in the text revolves around the theory that Jesus asked Judas to betray Him in order to fulfill His destiny and the scriptures. If this is true it would make Judas a saint and not the sinner and traitor as believed by the mainline church.

The text is also interesting simply because it is written in Coptic. Documents from the time period and region where the Coptic language was native are a rare find.

The word Coptic is an Arabic corruption of the Greek word Aigyptos, which in turn comes from the word Hikaptah, one of the names of the city of Memphis, the first capital of ancient Egypt.

There has never been a Coptic state or government per se, however, the word has been used to generally define a culture and language present in the area of Egypt within a particular timeframe.

The known history of the Copts starts with King Mina the first King, who united the northern and southern kingdoms of Egypt circa 3050 B.C. The ancient Egyptian civilization under the rule of the Pharaohs lasted over 3000 years. Saint Mina (named after the king) is one of the major Coptic saints. He was martyred in 309 A.D.

The culture has come to be recognized as one containing distinctive language, art, architecture, and even certain religious systems. There is even a very distinctive Coptic Christian church system with its own canon, which contains several more books than those of the Protestant or Catholic Bibles.

The religious controversy of the Gospel of Judas is compelling, if for no other reason than that of its differing view, which forces us to re-examine the way we read and understand the place, path, and actions of Judas and his act of betrayal.

The Gospels and the Book of Acts tell the story of Judas' betrayal of Jesus and the end to which Judas came. The canonical books refer to Judas as a traitor, betrayer, and as one influenced by the devil. However, the Gospel of Judas turns this idea on its head by claiming the Judas was requested, if not required, to plan and carry out the treachery that would be the impetus for the crucifixion. The plan was to surrender Jesus to the authorities so that scripture and prophecy could be fulfilled, and Jesus was the person devising the plan.

Most scholars agree that the Gospels of Matthew, Mark, Luke, and John were written between the date of Jesus' death and about 90 A.D. The Gospel of Judas was written originally in Greek around A.D. 180 at the earliest.   If this is true, Judas could not have been the author. For Judas to have penned this work he would have been about 120 years of age at the time of its writing. Discounting this possibility, the original author is unknown.

Dates of the original texts are based on words and usage common to certain periods of time. This is comparable to how slang and catch phrases pass in and out of vogue in our own language.

Another way of narrowing down the date of the original text is to look for references to it in other writings. This would set the date marking the latest the text could have been written.

Tixeront, translated by Raemers, states: "Besides these Gospels, we know that there once existed a Gospel of Bartholomew, a Gospel of Thaddeus, mentioned in the decree of Pope Gelasius, and a Gospel of Judas Iscariot in use among the Cainites and spoken of by St. Irenaeus."

In Roberts-Donaldson's translation from Irenaeus the church father states, "Others again declare that Cain derived his being from the Power above, and acknowledge that Esau, Korah, the Sodomites, and all such persons, are related to themselves. On this account, they add, they have been assailed by the Creator, yet no one of them has suffered injury. For Sophia was in the habit of carrying off that which belonged to her from them to herself. They declare that Judas the traitor was thoroughly acquainted with these things, and that he alone, knowing the truth as no others did, accomplished the mystery of the betrayal; by him all things, both earthly and heavenly, were thus thrown into confusion. They produce a fictitious history of this kind, which they style the Gospel of Judas."

Irenaeus went on to say that the writings came from what he called a "Cainite" Gnostic sect that jousted with orthodox Christianity. He also accused the Cainites of lauding the biblical murderer Cain, the Sodomites and Judas, whom they regarded as the keeper of secret mysteries.

Knowing the dates of the writings of Irenaeus further clarifies the date to be around or before 180 A.D. Of course, this affects the Gospel of Judas only if we conclude that the text Irenaeus spoke of is the same text we have today. Sadly, there is no way to know with any certainty, but we do have a few clues.

Cain is not mentioned in the version of the Gospel of Judas we have today. Furthermore, the evolution of cosmology tends to be from the simple to the complex and this trend is shown in the current version since Yaldabaoth, who is also called "Nebro" the "rebel", is presented as the creator of Saklas and it is Saklas who is depicted later in the Gospel of Judas as the creator mankind and the physical world. However, in other Gnostic writings, Yaldabaoth is the "demiurge" or fashioner of the world, and is clearly identified as the same deity as Saklas. This means that in the Gospel of Judas there has been a split between Yaldaboth and Saklas, leading to a more complex cosmology. This indicates that the Gospel of Judas we have today was written later than that of which Irenaeus speaks, since in his time these deities were one and the same.

Now the archon who is weak has three names. The first name is Yaltabaoth, the second is Saklas ("fool"), and the third is Samael. And he is impious in his arrogance which is in him. For he said, 'I am God and there is no other God beside me,' for he is ignorant of his strength, the place from which he had come."

Apocryphon of John, ca. 200 AD.

As for the dating of the copy found in Egypt, the formation of certain letters also change with time and the style of the lettering within the texts places the copies within a certain period. The 26-page Judas text is a copy in Coptic of the original Gospel of Judas, which was written in Greek the century before.

Radioactive-carbon-dating tests as well as experts in ancient languages have established that the copy was written between 220 and 340 A.D.

The discovered Gospel was written on papyrus, probably at a Gnostic monastery in Egypt. Although other copies may have been made they were probably lost in St. Athanasius's fourth-century campaign to destroy all heretical texts. All texts not accepted by the newly established church were to be burned. Heresy was not to be tolerated, and Gnosticism was considered at the top of the list. Not only was Gnosticism different from the orthodox theology, it condoned a personal search for God through knowledge and that was something outside the control of the church. To maintain its control, the new church had to crush these beliefs.

In order to protect the text from Athanasius's soldiers it is thought a Gnostic monk or scribe buried copies of certain Gnostic texts in an area of tombs in Egypt. These were not discovered until the late 1970s. The Gospel was one of three texts found that were bound together in a single codex.

The gospel was unearthed in 1978 by a farmer. He found a small container like a tomb box in a cave near El Minya, Egypt. In the small, carved, and sealed box was part of a codex, or collection of devotional texts.

The farmer sold the codex to an antiquities dealer in Cairo. The deal was kept secret but was reported to have taken place in 1983. The antiquities dealer was unaware of the content of the codex when he offered the gospel for sale to the Coptic studies scholar, Stephen Emmel, of Germany's University of Munster and another scholar. The meeting took place in a Geneva, Switzerland hotel room.

It was Emmel who examined the codex and first suspected the papyrus sheets discussed Judas. Although the text more than intrigued Emmel, the asking price was so high at $3 million dollars U.S. that there was no way to afford the purchase.

The seller was offered a price that was an order of magnitude lower than the asking price. This, the seller took as an insult and the deal stalled.

Due to the frustration brought about by not having his greed satisfied, the dealer stored the codex in a safe in a Hicksville, N.Y. bank for 16 years. There, away from the dry desert air, in the box with higher humidity, it deteriorated and crumbled until Zurich-based antiquities dealer Frieda Nussberger-Tchacos purchased it in 2000 for a sum much less than the original asking price. The codex was then acquired by the Maecenas Foundation for Ancient Art in Switzerland in 2001.

The foundation invited National Geographic to help with the restoration in 2004.

Over the next 5 years thousands of pieces of papyrus were placed back together like a jigsaw puzzle. Thousands of pieces, some so small they contained only a letter or two were restored to their position in the text using tweezers and computer imaging.

Once completed, a team of scholars translated the document into English, as best they could, considering the condition of the document and the number of pieces missing. The restored original is now housed in Cairo's Coptic Museum. A rendering of the text in Coptic can be seen at:

http://www.nationalgeographic.com/lostgospel/_pdf/CopticGospelOfJudas.pdf

Because of the extreme age and ill-treatment of the text much of it is illegible. There are gaps and holes in the codex. Entire lines are missing. Some parts of the translation were done on a "best-guess" basis. If there were letters missing from common words of phrases the translators could assume and replace letters and even words or phrases. When the gaps became larger or the meaning of the phrase was uncertain the translators simple noted the absence of data.

In this rendering we have attempted two bold moves. We wished to present a more engaging interpretation for the public, which necessarily demanded notes and explanations available at the point the ideas were encountered. We also wished to attempt to fill in some of the gaps in the text if possible.

As a matter of a disclaimer, it should be understood that the original translators did a remarkable job with the thousands of slivers and chips of papyrus that made up the codex. Once reconstructed, it became obvious that much of the text was simply missing, having disintegrated into dust and powder, never to be read again.

The text presented here takes the work done by many others and places the Gospel of Judas into a more readable language and format along with in-line commentary. It then expands the text, filling in the gaps as best it could be done, based on an understanding of the Gnostic theology, historical information, textual references, and logical flow of conversation.

All words or phases in parentheses indicate those additions made to the text, either as a matter of filling in the missing letters, words, or lines; or as a matter of clarification of ambiguous wording in the original text or its translation. When a word could be translated in more than one way, a slash "/" was used to note the various choices.

Commentary are marked clearly as "Notes" and are place in italic font within the text.

The reader should keep the probable function of the text in mind. The title gives some hint. It is not "The Gospel According to Judas", but it is instead, "The Gospel of Judas." This indicates that the writer wanted to exalt Judas, his position and contribution according to the theology being espoused and propagated by the text.

Knowing these things, the words and lines missing in the text can be a matter of educated and reasonable assumptions. They are, however, assumptions nonetheless.

Let us look now at the Gospel of Judas.

The Gospel of Judas

This is the proclamation, which was secretly revealed to Judas Iscariot by Jesus during that eight-day period that included (that was) the three days before he (Jesus) celebrated Passover (one translator has "celebrated his passion / suffering).

Note: The proclamation is not the logos, word or Christ for the orthodox church. The word here is a proclamation of judgment as in a court verdict.

1. Jesus appeared on earth to perform miracles and wondrous acts in order to save humanity.
Because some conducted themselves in a righteous way and others continued in their sins, he decided to call the twelve disciples.

2. He began to talk to them about the mysteries that lay beyond this world and what would happen at this world's end (at the end). He often changed his appearance and was not seen as himself but looked like a child (some translators have apparition or spirit) when he was with his disciples.

3. He came upon his disciples in Judea once when they were sitting together piously (training their piety – training in godliness). As he got closer to the disciples he saw they were sitting together, giving thanks and saying a prayer over the bread (Eucharist / thanksgiving). He laughed.

4. The disciples asked Him, "Rabbi, why are you laughing at our prayer of thanks? Have we not acted appropriately?"
He said, "I am not laughing at you. It is just that you are not doing this because you want to. You are doing this because your god (has to be / will be) praised."

5. They said, "Rabbi, you are the (earthly / only) son of our god."
Jesus answered, "How do you know me? (Do you think you know me?) I say to you truly, no one among you in this generation (in this race) will understand me."

6. His disciples heard this and became enraged and began mumbling profanities and mocking him in their hearts. When Jesus saw their inability (to understand what he said to them (their stupidity), he said,) "Why did you get so upset that you became angry? Your god, who is inside of you, (and your own lack of understanding guides you and) have instigated this anger in your (mind / soul). (I challenge) any man among you to show me who is (understanding enough) to bring out the perfect man and stand and face me."

7. They all said, "We are strong enough."
But in their (true being) spirits none dared to stand in front of him except for Judas Iscariot. Judas was able to stand in front of him, but even he could not look Jesus in the eyes, and he turned his face away.

Note: It is uncertain as to the reason Judas did not look at Jesus. It was a custom of respect not to look a superior in the eyes. Either Judas was unable to look at Jesus or was constrained by the position of Jesus as his Rabbi.

8. Judas said to Him, "I know who you are and where you came from. You are from the everlasting (eternal) aeon (realm or kingdom) of Barbelo (Barbelo's everlasting kingdom). I am not worthy to speak the name of the one who sent you."

9. Jesus knew that Judas was capable of understanding (showing forth / thinking about) something that was glorious, so Jesus said to him, "Walk away (step a distance away) from the others and I will tell you about the mysteries of God (the reign of God / kingdom of God).

10. It is possible for you to get there, but the path will cause you great grief because you will be replaced so that the twelve may be complete with their god again."
Judas asked him, "When will you tell me how the great day of light will dawn for this generation (race)? When will you explain these things?"
But as he asked these things, Jesus left him.

11. At the dawn of the next day after this happened, Jesus appeared to his disciples.
They asked Him, "Rabbi, where did you go and what did you do when you left us?"
Jesus said to them, "I went to another generation (race) that is a greater and holier generation (race)."

12. His disciples asked him, "Lord, what is this great race that is superior to us and holier than us, that is not now in this realm (kingdom)?"
When Jesus heard this, he laughed and said to them, "Why are you thinking in your hearts about the mighty and holy race (generation)? So be it - I will tell you. No one born in this age (realm / aeon) will see that (generation / race), and not even the multitude (army) of angels (controlling) the stars will rule over that generation (race), and no mortal (corruptible) person can associate (belong) with it.

13. That generation does not come from (a realm) which has become (mortal / corrupted). The generation of people among (you) is from the generation of humanity (of inferior / without) power, which (cannot associate with the) other powers (above) by (whom) you rule / are ruled."
When (the /his) disciples heard this, they were all troubled in (their heart / spirit). They were speechless (could not utter a word).

Note: This begins a distinction drawn between the generation or race of mankind, which is inferior, decaying, and unenlightened, and the "great generation or race," which is enlightened, incorruptible, and eternal. There are only two races; those who have gnosis and those who do not. Interestingly, Jesus does not place the disciples in the great generation.

14. On another day Jesus came up to (them). They said to (him), "Rabbi, we have seen you in a (dream), because we all had weighty (dreams about a night you were taken away / arrested)."
(He said), "Why have (you come to me when you have) gone into hiding?"

15. They said, "There was (an imposing building with a great altar in it and twelve men, (which we would say were) the priests, and there was a name, and a crowd of people waiting (enduring because of their perseverance) at that altar, (for) the priest (to come and receive) the offerings. (However) we kept waiting (we were tenacious also)."
(Jesus asked), "What were (the priests) like?"
They said, "Some (of them would fast) for two weeks; (others would) sacrifice their own children, others their wives, (all the while) in praise (offered in) humility with each other; some have sex with other men; some murder; some commit a plethora of sins and acts of crime. And the men who stand in front of the altar call upon your (name / authority), and in all the acts springing from their lack of knowledge (lack of light), the sacrifices are brought to completion (by their hands) (the alter remained full through their handiwork of slaughtering the sacrifices)."
After they said these things they became uneasy and quiet.

16. Jesus asked them, "Why are you bothered? So be it, I tell you that all the priests who have stood before that altar call upon my name. I have told I you many times that my name has been written on the (judgment) of this race (and on) the stars through the human generations. In my name (these people) have planted barren trees, (and have done so) without any honor."

17. Jesus said to them, "You are like those men you have seen conducting the offerings at the altar. That is the god you serve, and the twelve men you have seen represent you. The cattle you saw that were brought for sacrifice represent the many people you have led (will lead) astray before that altar. (You) will stand (lead / represent) and use my name in that way, as will the generations of the pious and you all will remain loyal to "him." (Some translations have- "The lord of chaos will establish his place in this way.") After "him" another man will lead from (the group of fornicators), and another (will lead at the alter from those who) murder children, and another from those who are homosexuals, and (another) those who fast, and (one will stand from) the rest of those who pollution themselves and who are lawlessness and who sin, and (from) those who say, 'We are like the angels'; they are the stars that (make everything happen / bring everything to an end).

18. It has been said to the human generations, 'Look, God has received your sacrifice from the hands of a priest.' But the priest is a minister of error (minister in error / ministers but is in sin). But it is the Lord, the Lord of all (the fullness of the divine), who commands, 'On the last day (of time) they will be shamed (some have - "at the end of days").'"

Note: Jesus tells the disciples that they are loyal to the wrong god. He goes on to say that they are the ones who murder, fornicate, and sin. Furthermore, Jesus tells them that they will lead people into a spiritual slaughter like the cattle they saw sacrificed in their dream. At this time the 12 included Judas. This, along with other such verses has led many scholars to conclude that the Gospel of Judas was not depicting Judas to be the sanctified person the original translators thought him to be.

19. Jesus (told them), "Stop (sacrificing that which) you have (and stop hovering) over the altar. The priests are over your stars and your angels. They have already come to their end there. So let them (be entrapped / quarrel / fight) before you, and leave them alone. (Do not be tainted by this generation but instead eat the food of knowledge given to you by the

great one.)

Note: We will see "stars" referred to often in the text. They are used to symbolize two unique concepts. It was thought that in the creation of the cosmos, luminaries were created which were powers controlling each person's destiny. It was also thought that each person was assigned a star as his or her eternal home or resting place. A good person would ascend to his or her own star to rule and rest. Thus, stars were conscious powers, carrying out orders from God, and also were places of destiny for those who escape the material plane.

20. A baker cannot feed all creation under (heaven). And (they will not give) to them (a food) and (give) to (those of the great generation the same food).
Jesus said to them, "Stop struggling with (against) me. Each of you has his own star, and every (Lines are missing here. Text could read " person has his own destiny." Or possibly, "person who does well will dwell and rest on their star").
(All things happen in their own season and all seasons are appointed. And in (the season) which has come (it is spring) for the tree (of paradise) of this aeon / age (and it will produce) for a time (then wither) but he has come to water God's paradise, and (also water this generation) that will last, because (he) will not corrupt / detour the (path of life for) that generation, but (will guide it) from eternity to eternity."

21. Judas asked him, "Rabbi, what kind of fruit does this generation produce?"
Jesus answered, "The souls of every human generation will die. However, when these people (of this kingdom) have completed the time in the kingdom and the living breath leaves them, their bodies will die but their souls will continue to be alive, and they will ascended (be lifted up / be taken up)."
Judas asked, "What will the remainder of the human generations do?"
Jesus said, "It is not possible to plant seeds in (rocky soil) and harvest its fruit. (This is also the way (of) the (corrupted) race (generation), (the children of this kingdom) and corruptible Sophia / wisdom) (is / are) not the hand that has created mortal people, so that their souls ascend to the eternal realms above. Amen, I say, (that no) angel (or / of) power will be able to see that (kingdom of) these to whom (belong that) holy generations (above)."
After Jesus said this, he departed.

22. Judas said, "Rabbi, you have listened to all of those others, so now listen to me too. I have seen a great vision."

23. When Jesus heard this, he laughed and said to him, "You (are the) thirteenth spirit (daemon), why are you trying so hard / why do you excite yourself like this? However, speak up, and I will be patient with you."
Judas said to him, "In the vision I saw myself and the twelve disciples were stoning me and persecuting me very badly / severely / strongly. And I (was following you and I) arrived at a place where I saw (a large house in front me), and my eyes could not (take in / comprehend) its size. Many people were surrounding it, and the house had a roof of plants (grass / green vegetation), and in the middle of the house (there was a crowd) (and I was there with you), saying, 'Rabbi, take me in (the house) along with these people.'"

24. He responded and said, "Judas, your star has misled you. No person of mortal birth is worthy to enter the house you have seen. It is a place reserved for the saints. Not even the sun or the moon or day (light) will rule there. Only the saints will live there, in the eternal kingdom with the holy angels, always (some have the text as – "will be firmly established with the holy angels forever"). Look, I have explained to you the mysteries of the kingdom and I have taught you about the error of the stars; and (I have) sent it (on its path) on the twelve ages (aeons)."

Note: The Lost Book of Enoch tells of stars, which are the guiding forces of man and nature, erring. They become misplaced and out of order. They had to be placed or directed back into their proper paths. See The Lost Book of Enoch, by Joseph Lumpkin.

Note: There are 12 Astrological Ages. The 12 signs of the zodiac make up a 360-degree ecliptic path around the Earth, and takes 25,920 years to make the Precession of the Equinoxes. Each sign is comprised of 30 degrees of celestial longitude. Each degree of the precession is equal to 72 Earth years, and each year is equal to 50 seconds of degrees of arc of celestial longitude. In a 24 hour Earth day, the Earth rotates the entire 360 degrees of the ecliptic, allowing a person to see all 12 signs.

25. Judas said, "Rabbi, could it be that my (spiritual) seed will conquer the rulers of cosmic power (could also be rendered: "is under the control of the archons or rulers of cosmic power"?)"

26. Jesus answered and said to him, "Come (with me so) that I (may show you the kingdom you will receive. I will show you what is to come of you and this generation), but you will be grieved when you see the kingdom and all its race (of people)."
When Judas heard Him he said to him, "What good is it if I have received it seeing that you have set me apart from that

race?"

Jesus answered him and said, "You will become the thirteenth, and you will be cursed by the other generations, and you will come to rule over them. In the last days they will curse your ascent to the holy (race / kingdom)."

Note: I have chosen the word, "daemon" and not "demon" because the meaning of the text is unclear. A daemon is a divinity or supernatural being of a nature between gods and humans. In verse 24 Jesus tells Judas that he will never be worthy to enter the house, which symbolizes the eternal kingdom. Later in verse 26 Jesus seems to indicate that Judas will be cursed by the other disciples but will be raised to enter the holy generation in the last days. It is possible the interim time will be spent in what the Bible calls, "his own place."

27. Jesus said, "(Follow / come with me), so that I may teach you the (secrets) that no person (has) ever seen.

Note: This begins a creation myth based on certain Sethian Gnostic cosmology. The telling of the story appears to be an attempt to link the Gnostic cosmology to the teachings of Jesus in order to add validity and authority to the creation story and entities as well as assisting in the propagation of the sect.

There is a great and limitless kingdom, whose scope no generation of angels has seen (and in it) The Great Invisible (Spirit) is, and no angel's eye has ever seen, no thought of the heart (mind) has ever understood it, and no name can be assigned it (it cannot be named).

28. "And a brightly glowing cloud appeared there. The Great Spirit said, 'Let an angel come into being as my assistant (attendant / helper).'

"A great angel, the enlightened, divine, Self-Generated (Self-Created) one emerged from the cloud. Because of him, four other angelic lights (luminaries), (Harmozel, Oroiael, Daveithai, and Eleleth) began to exist from another cloud, and they became assistants (helpers / attendants) to the Self-Generated angel (messenger). The Self-Created one proclaimed, 'Let (there) come into being (a star / Adam),' and it (he) came into being (at once). He (created) the first star (luminary / bright, shining being) to reign over him.

Note: Here we have a garbled text, the translation of which can go one of two ways. The words missing in the middle of the text could be Adam, who is also known as Adamas, or it could refer to a star, since the next reference is to a luminary. The direction of the text is unclear except that it is agreed that the word "it" is used in the text.

He said, 'Let angels (messengers) begin existence to adore (worship) (him),' and an innumerable plethora became existent. He said, '(Let there be) an aeon of light,' and he began existence. He created the second star to rule over him, to render service together with the innumerable plethora of angels. That is how he created the rest of the aeons of light. He made them rulers over them, and he created for them an innumerable plethora of angels to assist them.

29. "Adamas (Adam) was in the first luminous cloud (the initial divine expression) that no angel has ever seen, including all those called 'God.' He (was the one) that (created the enlightened aeon and beheld) the image and produced him after the likeness of (this) angel. He made the incorruptible (generation) of Seth appear (from) the twelve (aeons and) the twenty-four (stars / angelic lights / luminaries). He made seventy-two angelic lights appear in the imperishable generation, as the will of the Spirit dictated. The seventy-two angelic lights themselves made three hundred sixty angelic lights appear in the immortal race, by following the will of the Spirit, that their number should be five for each.

Note: Seth is the son of Adam and was considered to be divine as Adam was divine. Seth produced "that incorruptible generation." He was thought to have received the knowledge that would bring freedom from the material realm, and thus, salvation.

30. "The twelve realms (aeons) of the twelve angelic lights make up / appoint their Father, with six heavens for each aeon, so that there are seventy-two heavens for the seventy-two angelic lights, and for each (there are five) skies, (producing all) three hundred sixty (skies for the stars). They were given authority and a innumerable host of angels, for glory and adoration (worship), (and then he gave the) virgin (pure spirits), for glory and worship of all the aeons and the heavens and their firmaments (skies).

Note: The numbers assigned to the various aeons, angels, and stars have significance in both biblical number symbolism and Pythagorean numerology.

> *One – Unity, sovereign, God, causality.*
> *Two – Duality and / or merging.*
> *Three - Spiritually complete, fullness, creation.*
> *Four – Foundations, systems, order.*
> *Five – Spirit, grace, movement.*

Six - Mankind.
Seven – God, wisdom, knowledge, perfection.
Twelve – Law, rule, authority.
Thirteen – Cursed, beyond or without law.
Twenty-four – Heavenly government, elders, a   system. Duality within the system.
Seventy-two – Both elements of two and seven as well as the element of completion.
Three hundred and sixty – Elements of three and six as well as the meaning of a full cycle such as a   yearly   cycle. An
end, and a new start.

31. The totality (gathering) of those immortals is called the cosmos, that is to say perdition / decay / corruption, by the Father and the seventy-two angelic lights / luminaries who are with the Self-Created one and his seventy-two aeons. In the cosmos the first human appeared with his incorruptible powers.

Note: This first human is Adamas or Adam. It should be noted that the name "Adam" can also be rendered as "Man" in Hebrew.

32. And the aeon that appeared with his generation and the aeon in whom are the cloud of knowledge and the angel, is called El.

Note: El was the name of a Semitic god who was chief among the pantheon of gods affecting nature and society. He is father of the divine family and president of the divine assembly on the 'mount of assembly', the equivalent of Hebrew har mo'ed, which became through the Greek transliteration Armageddon. In Canaanite mythology he is known as 'the Bull', symbolizing his strength and creative force. He is called 'Creator of Created Things' which is how rivers were also metaphorically thought of. In the Biblical Garden of Eden a river flowed to form the four rivers, Tigris, Euphrates, Gihon and Pishon."
El expressed the concept of ordered government, justice and creation. The Bible never stigmatizes the Canaanite worship of El, whose authority in social affairs was recognized by the Patriarchs. His consort was Asherah, the mother goddess, represented in Canaanite sanctuaries by a natural tree (Hebrew ashera) such as the tree of life.

33. (He created the) aeon, (after that) (El) said, 'Let twelve angels come into being (in order to) rule over chaos and the (cosmos / perdition).' And look, from the cloud {called Sophia} there appeared an (angel / aeon) whose face flashed with fire and whose appearance was defiled with blood. His name was Nebro, meaning "rebel." Another angel, Saklas, also came from the cloud. So Nebro created six angels—as well as Saklas—to be assistants, and these produced twelve angels in the heavens, with each one receiving a piece of the heavens.

Note: Nebro may be a female demon who mates with Saklas; others call Nebro by the name "Yaldaboth (child of chaos) Yaldaboth and Saklas are both names given to the insane or deficient deity that created the physical world. Also the reading could be influenced by the fact that in some mythologies Nebro is a head demon and Saklas is a head angel. Nebro has the same meaning as Nimrod, which is "rebel."
*   The Jews and Greeks of the day were literalists. Each and every word of the scriptures was taken at face value. Therefore, the god who created Adam and Eve was a limited and tangible god. He walked and talked and asked questions, the answers to which he did not seem to know. By building a creation story that includes Saklas the problems were solved. Now the references to multiple gods were answered and when god said let "us" create man, the references could be to Saklas and his helpers. Since the Saklas deity was limited and restricted it left the Supreme God to be "God."*

34. "The twelve rulers (aeons) spoke with the twelve angels: 'Let each of you (receive a portion) and let them (that are in this) generation (be ruled by these) angels':

The first is Seth, who is called Christ.
The (second) is Harmathoth, who is (head ruler of the underworld).
The (third) is Galila.
The fourth is Yobel.
The fifth (is) Adonaios.
These are the five who ruled all of the underworld, and primarily over chaos.

Note: These five names are probably associated with the five planets known at the time the Gospel of Judas was written. They were placed on their paths and courses to keep order and give light, both real and spiritual.

35. "Then Saklas said to his angels, 'Let us create a human being in the similitude and after the figure / image / representation (of the Supreme God) .' They fashioned Adam and his wife Eve, who is called Zoe / life when she was still

in the cloud.

Note: Zoe is another name for Eve in the Septuagint.

36. For it is this name (life) that all the generations seek the man, and each of them calls the woman by these names. Now, Sakla did not command (as he was instructed) but (he commanded) the generations (of man to live so long / for a defined period of time), (but he did created them in his (Saklas') likeness). And the (ruler Saklas) said to Adam, 'You shall live long, with your children.'"

37. Judas said to Jesus, "(What length) is the long span of time that humans will live?"
Jesus said, "Why are you curious about this? Adam and his generation has lived his lifespan in the place where he received his kingdom, with his longevity bestowed by his ruler (as numbered with his ruler)."

38. Judas said to Jesus, "Does the human spirit die?"
Jesus said, "This is why God (the god of this realm) ordered Michael to loan spirits to people so that they would serve (be in servitude), but the Great One commanded Gabriel to give spirits to the great generation (race) which had no ruler over it (a generation that cannot be dominated). He gave the spirit and the soul. Therefore, the (remainder / mountain) of souls (loaned will come back to the god of this realm in the end).

Note: This passage indicates two lines of creation. For those people created by the god of this world the angel Michael was commanded to temporarily assign souls to his creation. To keep their souls they were enslaved to worship the god of this world. In contrast, the Great One commanded Gabriel to give souls to those of the great generation for eternity.

39. "(There was no) light (in this world to shine) around (the people to) allow (the) spirit (which is) within you all to dwell in this (body) among the generations of angels. But God caused knowledge to be (given) to Adam and those with him, so that the kings of chaos and the underworld might not oppress them with it."

Note: The word rendered as "rule" by most translators has the connotation of oppression.

40. Judas said to Jesus, "So what will those generations do?"
Jesus said, "Truthfully, I tell you all, that for all of them the stars bring matters to completion (heavenly apocalypse). When Saklas completes the span of time assigned for him, their first star will appear with the generations, and they will finish what they said they would do. Then they will (have illicit sex in my name and kill (sacrifice) their children and they will fast, and they will kill their wives in praise offered in humility with each other; some have sex with other men; some will murder, some commit a plethora of sins and acts of crime all in my name, and Saklas will destroy) your star over the thirteenth aeon."

41. After that Jesus (laughed).

Note: Jesus seems to find humor in the misguided judgments or concepts of the disciples. He laughs, as if shaking his head in disbelief of the error, then attempts to give insight and correction.

(Judas asked), "Rabbi, (why do you laugh at us)?"
(He) answered (Judas and said), "I am not laughing (because of you) but at the error of the stars, because these six stars wander about with these five warriors and they all will be destroyed along with their creations."

Note: The six stars were those who, along with Saklas or yaldaboth, created man and the cosmos. The five warriors refer to the five known planets at the time of the writing of the text. These planets were also connected with pagan worship and deities.

42. Judas said to Jesus, "Look at what those who have been baptized in your name do?"
Jesus said, "Truthfully I tell (you), this baptism done in my name (are done by those who do not know me. They sacrifice in vain to the god of this world. I baptized no one, for those baptized here have their hope here and those who follow me need no baptism for they will come) to me. In truth (I) tell you, Judas, (those offering) sacrifices to Saklas (do not offer sacrifice to the Great) God (but instead worship) everything that is evil.
"But you will exceed all of them. For you will sacrifice the man (the body that clothes / bares / contains me).

Note: Gnostic theology sets up a duality between the material world and the spiritual world. Since the god that created the material world was flawed, cruel, and insane, anything produced in that environment must be corrupted and opposed to the spiritual world. In this belief system the killing of Jesus' body was a good thing since it would free his spirit and unite it with the "Great One." Looked at from this angle, Judas was assisting Jesus in showing mankind the way. This line of reasoning must be taken as metaphorical. Some authors have suggested that Jesus had become entombed in his body and was asking Judas to free him. This cannot be so since Jesus comes and goes from the Holy Race or Generation above at will. Neither is Jesus touting mass suicide. Gnostic lived long lives and propagated their faith. The message here is that to remain detached from the material or corporeal and to strive to receive the knowledge here will free you in the life to come.

Already your horn has been raised, your anger has been ignited, your star has shown brightly, and your heart has (prevailed / been made strong / pure).

Note: The symbol horn is a phallic symbol but also a symbol of strength in much the way a rhino's horn is a sign of power and might.

Note: Although the lines added to the first half of this verse are tenuous, the information that is available establishes Judas' place according to this story. It does, however, open some questions. What was Judas' anger directed against? Was he sacrificing Jesus because he was angry at the established religion of the day? Was it this anger that made his heart strong or pure? Was anger his motivating force? If so, it harmonizes well with certain readings of the canonical gospels, which may indicate Judas wanted to expedite Jesus' kingdom so he would have a place of authority therein.

43. "Truly (I tell you,) your last (act will become that which will free this race but it will) grieve (you and will anger this generation and) the ruler, since he will be destroyed. (And then the) image of the great race of Adam will be raised high, for before heaven, earth, and the angels, that race from the eternal realms, exists (existed). Look, you have been told everything. Lift up your eyes and look to the cloud and the light within it and the stars around it. The star that leads the way is your star (you are the star)."

44. Then, Judas raised his eyes and saw the radiant cloud, and entered it. Those standing below him heard a voice coming from the cloud, saying, (The return of the) great race (is at hand and the image of the Great One will be established in them because of Judas' sacrifice).

Note: This is the same cloud mentioned in verse 24. By entering the cloud Judas became one with the primal causality or "Great One / Supreme God." The Gnosis was imparted to him and he knew the mysteries. He then had understanding and strength to do what he was asked to do. This amounts to a transfiguration for Judas, much like that of Jesus. In the same manner, a voice from heaven announced his destiny.

45. (But the scribes waited for Judas, hoping to place a price on the head of Jesus.) Their high priests whispered that he had gone into the guest room for his prayer. But some scribes were there watching closely in order to arrest Jesus during the prayer, for they were afraid of the people, since he was accepted by everyone as a prophet. They approached Judas and said to him, "Why are you here? You are Jesus' disciple." Judas answered them in the way they wished. And he was given an amount of money and he handed Jesus over to them.

Note: We read of Judas' entrance into the radiant cloud and then his transaction with the scribes but there is no transition. It is possible the cloud is a metaphor for divine knowledge of the primal causality or Great God that produced Barbelo. See verse 28.

Note: The actual betrayal of Jesus by Judas is drastically downplayed. Only one paragraph is devoted to the actual act. Within this single paragraph no details are offered.

    The gospel is constructed to give the reason for the betrayal. Building the rational of the act becomes far more important than the act itself, given the fact that it was the body that clothed Jesus that was destroyed and not the inner spirit. Shedding the body fulfilled destiny and freed the Christ spirit.

    This was done as a demonstration of Jesus' belief in the immortal and eternal realm, which lay beyond human senses. The lesson of the Gospel of Judas and of Gnosticism in general had to do with reaching inside to gain knowledge of the unseen spiritual world. The orthodox church taught that only through martyrdom or the blessing of the church could one pass into the spiritual realm. Jesus was teaching another way. His death was the only way to exemplify his faith and show his disciples there was more than they could see in the material world. According to the Gnostic texts, the death of Jesus did not bring salvation. His life and death taught and provided knowledge, that if understood, would free the human race of its chains and allow it to ascend to the immortal realm.

This ends the Gospel of Judas.

THE 29th CHAPTER OF ACTS

The Sonnini Manuscript contains the account of Paul's journey to Spain and Britain. The document, purported to be the concluding portion of the "Acts of the Apostles" covers a portion of the period after Paul's two year enforced residence in Rome, in his own hired house. It is written in the style of the Bible Acts and reads like a continuation.

The Manuscript was found interleaved in a copy of Sonnini's Travels in Turkey and Greece and was purchased at the sale of the library and effects of the late Right Honorable Sir John Newport, Bart, of Ireland. Sir John's family arms were engraved on the cover of the book. It had been in his possession for over thirty years. With the book was a document from the Sultan of Turkey, granting to C. S. Sonnini permission to travel in all parts of the Ottoman dominions. The document was translated by C. S. Sonnini from an original Greek manuscript found in the Archives at Constantinople, and presented to him by the Sultan Abdoul Achment.

(The Biblical Acts of the Apostles and the Book of James are the only two New Testament books not ending in `amen.' This has led some Bible scholars to believe they are incomplete in their present form.)

Sometime in the late 1700's and before 1800, C.S.Sonnini published his copy of Sonnini's Travels in Turkey and Greece. Interleaved was a copy of the manuscript found in the Archives of Constantinople presented to him by the Sultan Abdoul Achmet. He was traveling during the reign of Louis XVI, who reigned from AD 1774 to AD 1793. He published his travels between those two dates, 1774 and 1793.

Dr. Gene Scott "Doc Notes" on the book "Did the Apostle Paul Visit Britain?" by R.W. Morgan, available from Dolores Press.

ACTS Chapter 29

Verse 1. Paul, full of the blessing of Christ, and overflowing in the Spirit, left Rome, having decided to go into Spain, becuase he had wanted to travel there for a long time, and he thought also to go from there to Britain.

Verse 2. Because he had heard in Phoenicia that some of the children of Israel, around the time of the Assyrian captivity, had escaped by sea to "the Islands far away" as proclaimed by the Prophet, and called by the Romans, Britain.

Verse 3. Since the Lord commanded the gospel to be preached far and wide to the Gentiles, and to the lost sheep of the House of Israel.

Verse 4. And no man hindered Paul because he testified boldly of
Jesus before the governents and among the people; and be took with
him certain of the brethren which lived with him at Rome, and
they boarded a ship at Ostium, and having fair winds were
brought safely into an safety (harbour) of Spain.

Verse 5. And many people gathered from the towns and villages, and the hill country; for they had heard of the conversion of the Apostles, and the many miracles he had performed.

Verse 6. And Paul preached with might in Spain, and great many people believed and were converted, for they knew he was an apostle sent from God.

Verse 7. And finding a ship in Armorica sailing to Britain they departed from Spain. Paul and his company passed along the South coast and reached a port called Raphinus.

Verse 8. Now when word spread wide that the Apostle had landed on their coast, large numbers of the inhabitants met him, and they treated Paul courteously and he entered in at the east gate of their city, and was housed in the house of a Hebrew and one of his own nation.

Verse 9. And the next day he came and stood upon Mount Lud;(Now the site of St. Paul's Cathedral.) and the people amassed at the gate, and assembled in the main street, and he preached Christ unto them, and they believed the word and the testimony of Jesus.

Verse 10. And at sunset the Holy Ghost fell upon Paul, and he prophesied, saying, "BEHOLD IN THE LAST DAYS THE GOD OF PEACE
SHALL LIVE IN THE CITIES, AND THE INHABITANTS OF THEM SHALL BE COUNTED: AND IN THE SEVENTH CENSUS OF THE PEOPLE, THEIR EYES SHALL BE OPENED, AND THE GLORY OF THEIR INHERITANCE WILL SHINE OUT BEFORE THEM. NATIONS SHALL COME UP TO WORSHIP ON THE MOUNT THAT TESTIFIES OF THE PATIENCE AND LONG SUFFERING OF A SERVANT OF THE LORD."

Verse 11. And in the last days new announcements of the Gospel shall come forth out of Jerusalem, and the hearts of the people shall be filled with joy, and they shall look and spring of water shall be opened, and there shall be no more disease.

Verse 12. In those days there shall be wars and rumours of wars; and a king shall rise up, and his sword shall be for the healing of the nations, and peace he makes shall last, and the glory of his kingdom will be a wonder among princes.

Verse 13. And it came to pass that certain of the Druids came to Paul privately and showed by their rites and ceremonies (to prove) they were descended from the Jews which escaped from bondage in the land of Egypt, and the apostle believed these things, and he gave them the kiss of peace.

Verse 14. And Paul lived in his housing for three months proving the faith and preaching Christ continually.

Verse 15. And after these things Paul and his brethren left Raphinus, and sailed to Atium in Gaul.

Verse 16. And Paul preached in the Roman garrisons and among the people, encouraging all men to repent and confess their sins.

Verse 17. And there came to him certain of the Belgae to ask him about the new doctrine, and of the man Jesus; and Paul opened his heart unto them, and told them all things that had happened to him, how Christ Jesus came into the world to save sinners; and they departed wondering among themselves about the things they had heard.

Verse 18. And after he preached and toiled muched Paul and his fellow workers went to Helvetia, and came to Mount Pontius Pilate, where he who condemned the Lord Jesus threw himself down headlong, and so miserably perished.

Verse 19. And immediately a torrent gushed from the mountain and washed his body (which had been) broken in pieces, into a lake.

Verse 20. And Paul stretched forth his hands upon the water, and prayed unto the Lord, saying, 0 Lord God, give a sign unto all nations that here Pontius Pilate, which condemned your only-begotten Son, plunged down headlong in to the pit.

Verse 21. And while Paul was still speaking, they looked there came a great earthquake, and the face of the waters was changed, and the lake took the form like unto the Son of Man hanging in an agony upon the Cross.

Verse 22. And a voice came out of heaven saying, Even Pilate has escaped the wrath to come, (See second death, Rev.21:8) for he washed his hands before the multitude at the shedding of the Lord Jesus' blood.

Verse 23. Because of this, when Paul and those with him saw the earthquake and heard the voice of the angel they glorified God and their spirits were greatly strenghtned.

Verse 24. And they journeyed and came to Mount Julius where two pillars stood, one on the right hand and one on the left hand, erected by Caesar Augustus.

Verse 25. And Paul was filled with the Holy Ghost and stood up between the two pillars, saying, Men and brethren, these stones which you see this day shall testify of my journey here and truly I say they shall remain until the outpouring of the spirit upon all nations, and the way will not be hindered throughout all generations.

Verse 26. And they went forth and came to Illyricum, intending to go by Macedonia into Asia, and grace was found in all the churches; and they prospered and had peace. Amen.

Section Four
The Life and Times of Jesus

Introduction

God is born in human form. Ultimate power and authority reside in the hands of a child. Early Christians looked at their own children as they played, argued, loved, and fought and wondered what it would have been like to raise the Son of God. How would Jesus have acted as a baby, a toddler, a child, or a teenager?

How human was this "God-child," Jesus? Did he have the failings of their own children? Was he selfish and rash at the age of one? Was his stage of the "terrible twos" as horrible a stage as most? If Jesus were a normal youngster what would the outcome have been? For those who found themselves in the path of the young God's temper tantrum, devastating consequences, death or disfigurement could have followed.

Questions surrounding the nature of Jesus challenged the minds of Christians from the very beginning of the faith. Did Jesus mature and grow in wisdom, as most young men should? Did he discover his path in life and his calling or was he perfect and mature from the time of his birth? The Bible reports that the child Jesus "grew strong in spirit." Did that mean he was weaker in spirit as a child? These are the questions writers of early Christianity sought to address.

The texts presented in this section are those written by early believers struggling to make sense of the paradox of the man who is God. The scant information found in the Gospels regarding the first thirty years of his life gave rise to stories and folklore in an attempt to fill in gaps and answer questions regarding the life and times of Jesus.

Infancy Gospel of Thomas

The Infancy Gospel of Thomas may have been written in eastern Syria, the location of the Thomas traditions, although attribution to Thomas may be a later development to gain respect for the manuscript. The original language of the document may have been Syriac.

The Infancy Gospel of Thomas purports to describe the activities and history of Jesus in his youth and relates the miraculous deeds of Jesus before he turned twelve. Jesus instructs his teachers in the mysteries of the Hebrew alphabet, which Jewish mystics believe holds the power of the spoken word of God (See The Third Book of Enoch). Jesus astounds his family and playmates with miracles. This document contains the tale of the twelve sparrows which Jesus, at the age of five, fashioned from clay on the Sabbath day. When Jesus brought the clay to life he was accused of unlawful deeds on the Sabbath. This begs the question, "If someone can bring clay birds to life, what makes one think the same person could not kill if angered?"

The earliest manuscript is a sixth century one in Syriac. There was another version found written in Greek. The longer Greek version may be more accurate to the original text.

There is nothing particularly Christian about the stories attributed to Jesus; rather, the stories elaborate on the missing years of Jesus with reference to Hellenistic legend and pious imagination.

There is no certainty as to when the stories of the Infancy Gospel of Thomas began to be written down. Thus, while our present Infancy Gospel of Thomas may have been expanded over time, the original stories may have been written as early as the middle of the second century.

The translation used here is "The Infancy Gospel of Thomas," the Latin Text
Adapted from "The Apocryphal New Testament"
M.R. James-Translation and Notes
Oxford: Clarendon Press, 1924

Book of James, or PROTEVANGELIUM

Origen mentions the Book of James (and the Gospel of Peter) as stating that the ' brethren of the Lord' were sons of Joseph by a former wife. This is the first mention of it, and shows us that the book is as old as the second century. The text shows additions or alterations. Difficulty is caused by the sudden introduction of Joseph as the narrator in ch. xviii. 2 sqq. We cannot be sure whether this means that a fragment of a 'Joseph-apocryphon' has been introduced at this point; or, if so, how far it extends. We are sure, from a sentence of Clement of Alexandria, that some story of a midwife being present at the Nativity was current in the second century.

We have the book in the original Greek and in several oriental versions, the oldest of which is the Syriac. We know there was a Latin version because a book identifiable with ours in Latin is condemned in the Gelasian Decree.

In the early chapters of the Protevangelium the Old Testament is extensively drawn upon and imitated. However, it is obvious that the author was not Jewish and not familiar with Jewish life or language.

Adapted from the translation of "BOOK OF JAMES, OR PROTEVANGELIUM"
From "The Apocryphal New Testament"
M.R. James-Translation and Notes
Oxford: Clarendon Press, 1924

Infancy Gospel of James, OR PROTEVANGELIUM

I. In the histories of the twelve tribes of Israel it is written that there was one Joakim, exceeding rich: and he offered his gifts twofold, saying: That which is of my superfluity shall be for the whole people, and that which is for my forgiveness shall be for the Lord, for a propitiation to me.

2 Now the great day of the Lord drew near and the children of Israel offered their gifts. And Reuben stood over against him saying: It is not lawful for you to offer your gifts first, forasmuch as you have gotten no offspring in Israel. And Joakim was very grieved, and went to the record of the twelve tribes of the people, saying: I will look upon the record of the twelve tribes of Israel, whether I only have not gotten offspring in Israel. And he searched, and found concerning all the righteous that they had raised up offspring in Israel. And he remembered the patriarch Abraham, how in the last days God gave him a son, even Isaac. And Joakim was very grieved, and showed not himself to his wife, but he took himself into the wilderness, and pitched his tent there, and fasted forty days and forty nights, saying within himself: I will not go down either for meat or for drink until the Lord my God visit me, and my prayer shall be to me meat and drink.

II Now his wife Anna lamented with two lamentations, and bewailed herself with two wailings, saying: I will bewail my widowhood, and I will bewail my childlessness.

2 And the great day of the Lord drew near, and Judith her handmaid said to her: How long will you humble your soul? The great day of the Lord has come, and it is not lawful for you to mourn: but take this headband, which the mistress of my work gave me, and it is not lawful for me to put it on, forasmuch as I am a handmaid, and it has a mark of royalty. And Anna said: Get you from me. Lo! I have done nothing (or I will not do so) and the Lord has greatly humbled me: peradventure one gave it to you in secret, and you are come to make me partaker in your sin. And Judith said: How shall I curse you, seeing the Lord has shut up your womb, to give you no fruit in Israel?

3 And Anna was very grieved [and mourned with a great mourning because she was looked down on by all the tribes of Israel. And coming to herself she said: What shall I do? I will pray with weeping to the Lord my God that he visit me]. And she put off her mourning garments and cleansed (or adorned) her head and put on her bridal garments: and about the ninth hour she went down into the garden to walk there. And she saw a laurel-tree and sat down underneath it and besought the Lord saying: O God of our fathers, bless me, and listen to my prayer, as you did bless the womb of Sarah, and gave her a son, even Isaac.

III. 1 And looking up to the heaven she spied a nest of sparrows in the laurel-tree, and made a lamentation within herself, saying: Woe to me, who begat me? And what womb brought me forth for I am become a curse before the children of Israel, and I am looked down on, and they have mocked me forth out of the temple of the Lord? 2 Woe to me, to what am I similar? I am not similar to the fowls of the heaven, for even the fowls of the heaven are fruitful before you, O Lord. Woe to me, to what am I similar? I am not similar to the beasts of the earth, for even the beasts of the earth are fruitful before you, O Lord. Woe to me, to what am I similar? I am not similar to these waters, for even these waters are fruitful before you, O Lord. 3 Woe to me, to what am I similar? I am not similar to this earth, for even this earth brings forth her fruits in due season and blesses you, O Lord.

IV. 1 And behold an angel of the Lord appeared, saying to her: Anna, Anna, the Lord has listened to your prayer, and you shall conceive and bear, and your offspring shall be spoken of in the whole world. And Anna said: As the Lord my God lives, if I bring forth either male or female, I will bring it for a gift to the Lord my God, and it shall be ministering to him all the days of its life. 2 And behold there came two messengers saying to her: Behold Joakim your husband comes with his flocks: for an angel of the Lord came down to him saying: Joakim, Joakim, the Lord God has listened to your prayer. Get you down from here, for behold your wife Anna has conceived. 3 And Joakim sat him down and called his herdsmen saying: Bring me here ten lambs without blemish and without spot, and they shall be for the Lord my God; and bring me twelve tender calves, and they shall be for the priests and for the assembly of the elders; and a hundred kids for the whole people.

4 And behold Joakim came with his flocks, and Anna stood at the gate and saw Joakim coming, and ran and hung upon his neck, saying: Now know I that the Lord God has greatly blessed me: for behold the widow is no more a widow, and she that was childless shall conceive. And Joakim rested the first day in his house.

V. 1 And on the morrow he offered his gifts, saying in himself: If the Lord God be reconciled to me, the plate that is upon the forehead of the priest will make it manifest to me. And Joakim offered his gifts and looked earnestly upon the plate of the priest when he went up to the altar of the Lord, and he saw no sin in himself. And Joakim said: Now know I that the Lord is become propitious to me and has forgiven all my sins. And he went down from the temple of the Lord justified, and went to his house.

2 And her months were fulfilled, and in the ninth month Anna brought forth. And she said to the midwife: what have I

brought forth? And she said: A female. And Anna said: My soul is magnified this day, and she laid herself down. And when the days were fulfilled, Anna purified herself and gave suck to the child and called her name Mary.

VI. 1 And day by day the child grew strong, and when she was six months old her mother stood her upon the ground to try if she would stand; and she walked seven steps and returned to her bosom. And she caught her up, saying: As the Lord my God lives, you shall walk no more upon this ground, until I bring you into the temple of the Lord. And she made a sanctuary in her bed chamber and suffered nothing common or unclean to pass through it. And she called for the daughters of the Hebrews that were undefiled, and they carried her here and there.

2 And the first year of the child was fulfilled, and Joakim made a great feast and bade the priests and the scribes and the assembly of the elders and the whole people of Israel. And Joakim brought the child to the priests, and they blessed her, saying: 0 God of our fathers, bless this child and give her a name renowned for ever among all generations. And all the people said: So be it, so be it. Amen. And he brought her to the high priests, and they blessed her, saying: 0 God of the high places, look upon this child, and bless her with the last blessing which has no successor.

3 And her mother caught her up into the sanctuary of her bed chamber and gave her suck.

And Anna made a song to the Lord God, saying:

I will sing a hymn to the Lord my God, because he has visited me and taken away from me the ridicule of my enemies, and the Lord has given me a fruit of his righteousness, single and manifold before him. Who shall declare to the sons of Reuben that Anna gives suck? Listen, listen, you twelve tribes of Israel, that Anna gives suck. And she laid the child to rest in the bed chamber of her sanctuary, and went forth and ministered to them. And when the feast was ended, they got them down rejoicing, and glorifying the God of Israel.

VII. 1 And to the child her months were added: and the child became two years old. And Joakim said: Let us bring her up to the temple of the Lord that we may pay the promise which we promised; lest the Lord require it of us (lit. send to us), and our gift become unacceptable. And Anna said: Let us wait until the third year, that the child may not long after her father or mother. And Joakim said: Let us wait.

2 And the child became three years old, and Joakim said: Call for the daughters of the Hebrews that are undefiled, and let them take every one a lamp, and let them be burning, that the child turn not backward and her heart be taken captive away from the temple of the Lord. And they did so until they were gone up into the temple of the Lord.

And the priest received her and kissed her and blessed her and said: The Lord has magnified your name among all generations: in you in the latter days shall the Lord make manifest his redemption to the children of Israel. And he made her to sit upon the third step of the altar. And the Lord put grace upon her and she danced with her feet and all the house of Israel loved her.

VIII. 1 And her parents got them down marveling, and praising the Lord God because the child was not turned away backward.

And Mary was in the temple of the Lord as a dove that is nurtured: and she received food from the hand of an angel.

2 And when she was twelve years old, there was a council of the priests, saying: Behold Mary is become twelve years old in the temple of the Lord. What then shall we do with her? lest she pollute the sanctuary of the Lord. And they said to the high priest: You stand over the altar of the Lord. Enter in and pray concerning her: And whatsoever the Lord shall reveal to you, that let us do.

3 And the high priest took the vestment with the twelve bells and went in to the Holy of Holies and prayed concerning her. And lo, an angel of the Lord appeared saying to him: Zacharias, Zacharias, go forth and assemble them that are widowers of the people, and let them bring every man a rod, and to whomsoever the Lord shall show a sign, his wife shall she be. And the heralds went forth over all the country round about Judaea, and the trumpet of the Lord sounded, and all men ran thereto.

IX. 1 And Joseph cast down his adze and ran to meet them, and when they were gathered together they went to the high priest and took their rods with them. And he took the rods of them all and went into the temple and prayed. And when he had finished the prayer he took the rods and went forth and gave them back to them: and there was no sign upon them. But Joseph received the last rod: and lo, a dove came forth of the rod and flew upon the head of Joseph. And the priest said to Joseph: Unto you has it fallen to take the virgin of the Lord and keep her for yourself. 2 And Joseph refused, saying: I have sons, and I am an old man, but she is a girl: lest I became a laughing-stock to the children of Israel. And the priest said to Joseph: Hear the Lord your God, and remember what things God did to Dathan and Abiram and Korah, how the earth split and they were swallowed up because of their gainsaying. And now fear you, Joseph, lest it be so in your house. And Joseph was afraid, and took her to keep her for himself. And Joseph said to Mary: Lo, I have received you out of the temple of the Lord: and now do I leave you in my house, and I go away to build my buildings and I will come again to you. The Lord shall watch over you.

X. 1 Now there was a council of the priests, and they said: Let us make a veil for the temple of the Lord. And the priest said: Call to me pure virgins of the tribe of David. And the officers departed and sought and found seven virgins. And the priests called to mind the child Mary, that she was of the tribe of David and was undefiled before God: and the officers went and fetched her. And they brought them into the temple of the Lord, and the priest said: Cast me lots, which of you shall weave the gold and the undefiled (the white) and the fine linen and the silk and the hyacinthine, and the scarlet and the true purple. And the lot of the true purple and the scarlet fell to Mary, and she took them and went to her house. And at that season Zacharias became dumb, and Samuel was in his place until the time when Zacharias spoke again.]But Mary took the

512

scarlet and began to spin it.

XI 1 And she took the pitcher and went forth to fill it with water: and lo a voice saying: Hail, you that are highly favored; the Lord is with you: blessed are you among women.

And she looked about her upon the right hand and upon the left, to see from where this voice should be: and being filled with trembling she went to her house and set down the pitcher, and took the purple and sat down upon her seat and drew out the thread.

2 And behold an angel of the Lord stood before her saying: Fear not, Mary, for you have found grace before the Lord of all things, and you shall conceive of his word. And she, when she heard it, questioned in herself, saying: Shall I truly conceive of the living God, and bring forth after the manner of all women? And the angel of the Lord said: Not so, Mary, for a power of the Lord shall overshadow you: wherefore also that holy thing which shall be born of you shall be called the Son of the Highest. And you shall call his name Jesus: for he shall save his people from their sins. And Mary said: Behold the handmaid of the Lord is before him: be it to me according to your word.

XII 1 And she made the purple and the scarlet and brought them to the priest. And the priest blessed her and said: Mary, the Lord God has magnified your name, and you shall be blessed among all generations of the earth. 2 And Mary rejoiced and went away to Elizabeth her kinswoman: and she knocked at the door. And Elizabeth when she heard it cast down the scarlet (al. the wool) and ran to the door and opened it, and when she saw Mary she blessed her and said: What is this to me that the mother of my Lord should come to me? For behold that which is in me leaped and blessed you. And Mary forgot the mysteries which Gabriel the archangel had told her, and she looked up to the heaven and said: Who am I, Lord, that all the generations of the earth do bless me? 8 And she abode three months with Elizabeth, and day by day her womb grew: and Mary was afraid and departed to her house and hid herself from the children of Israel. Now she was sixteen years old when these mysteries came to pass.

XIII. I Now it was the sixth month with her, and behold Joseph came from his building, and he entered into his house and found her great with child. And he smote his face, and cast himself down upon the ground on sackcloth and wept bitterly, saying: With what countenance shall I look to the Lord my God? And what prayer shall I make concerning this maiden? For I received her out of the temple of the Lord my God a virgin, and have not kept her safe. Who is he that has ensnared me? Who has done this evil in my house and has defiled the virgin? Is not the story of Adam repeated in me? for as at the hour of his giving thanks the serpent came and found Eve alone and deceived her, so has it befallen me also. 2 And Joseph arose from off the sackcloth and called Mary and said to her O you that were cared for by God, why have you done this? You have forgotten the Lord your God. Why have you humbled your soul, you that were nourished up in the Holy of Holies and did receive food at the hand of an angel? 3 But she wept bitterly, saying: I am pure and I know not a man. And Joseph said to her: What then is that which is in your womb? And she said: As the Lord my God lives, I know not from where it is come to me.

XIV. I And Joseph was very afraid and ceased from speaking to her (or left her alone), and pondered what he should do with her. And Joseph said: If I hide her sin, I shall be found fighting against the law of the Lord: and if I manifest her to the children of Israel, I fear lest that which is in her be the offspring of an angel, and I shall be found delivering up innocent blood to the judgment of death. What then shall I do? I will let her go from me privately. And the night came upon him. 2 And behold an angel of the Lord appeared to him in a dream, saying: Fear not this child, for that which is in her is of the Holy Ghost, and she shall bear a son and you shall call his name Jesus, for he shall save his people from their sins. And Joseph arose from sleep and glorified the God of Israel which had shown this favor to her: and he watched over her.

XV. I Now Annas the scribe came to him and said to him: Why did you not appear in our assembly? and Joseph said to him: I was weary with the journey, and I rested the first day. And Annas turned him about and saw Mary great with child. 2 And he went hastily to the priest and said to him: Joseph, to whom you bear witness [that he is righteous] has sinned grievously. And the priest said: Wherein? And he said: The virgin whom he received out of the temple of the Lord, he has defiled her, and married her by stealth (lit. stolen her marriage), and has not declared it to the children of Israel. And the priest answered and said: Has Joseph done this? And Annas the scribe said: Send officers, and you shall find the virgin great with child. And the officers went and found as he had said, and they brought her together with Joseph to the place of judgment. 3 And the priest said: Mary, wherefore have you done this, and wherefore have you humbled your soul and forgotten the Lord your God, you that were nurtured in the Holy of Holies and did receive food at the hand of an angel and did hear the hymns and did dance before the Lord, wherefore have you done this?

But she wept bitterly, saying: As the Lord my God lives I am pure before him and I know not a man. 4 And the priest said to Joseph: Why have you done this? And Joseph said: As the Lord my God lives I am pure as concerning her. And the priest said: Bear no false witness but speak the truth: you have married her by stealth and have not declared it to the children of Israel, and have not bowed your head under the mighty hand that your offspring should be blessed. And Joseph held his peace.

XVI 1 And the priest said: Restore the virgin whom you did receive out of the temple of the Lord. And Joseph was full of weeping. And the priest said: I will give you to drink of the water of the conviction of the Lord, and it will make manifest your sins before your eyes. 2 And the priest took thereof and made Joseph drink and sent him into the hill-country. And he returned whole. He made Mary also drink and sent her into the hill-country. And she returned whole. And all the people were astonished, because sin appeared not in them. 3 And the priest said: If the Lord God has not made your sin manifest, neither do I condemn you. And he let them go. And Joseph took Mary and departed to his house rejoicing, and glorifying the

God of Israel.

XVII. 1 Now there went out a decree from Augustus the king that all that were in Bethlehem of Judaea should be recorded. And Joseph said: I will record my sons: but this child, what shall I do with her? How shall I record her as my wife? nay, I am ashamed. Or as my daughter? But all the children of Israel know that she is not my daughter. This day of the Lord shall do as the Lord wills. 2 And he saddled the she-ass, and set her upon it, and his son led it and Joseph followed after. And they drew near (to Bethlehem) within three miles: and Joseph turned himself about and saw her of a sad countenance and said within himself: Peradventure that which is within her pains her. And again Joseph turned himself about and saw her laughing, and said to her: Mary, what ails you that I see your face at one time laughing and at another time sad? And Mary said to Joseph: It is because I behold two peoples with my eyes, the one weeping and lamenting and the other rejoicing and exulting.

8 And they came to the midst of the way, and Mary said to him: Take me down from the ass, for that which is within me presses me, to come forth. And he took her down from the ass and said to her: Where shall I take you to hide your shame? For the place is desert.

XVIII. I And he found a cave there and brought her into it, and set his sons by her: and he went forth and sought for a midwife of the Hebrews in the country of Bethlehem.

2 Now I Joseph was walking, and I walked not. And I looked up to the air and saw the air in amazement. And I looked up to the pole of the heaven and saw it standing still, and the fowls of the heaven without motion. And I looked upon the earth and saw a dish set, and workmen lying by it, and their hands were in the dish: and they that were chewing chewed not, and they that were lifting the food lifted it not, and they that put it to their mouth put it not thereto, but the faces of all of them were looking upward. And behold there were sheep being driven, and they went not forward but stood still; and the shepherd lifted his hand to strike them with his staff, and his hand remained up. And I looked upon the stream of the river and saw the mouths of the kids upon the water and they drank not. And of a sudden all things moved onward in their course.

XIX. I And behold a woman coming down from the hillcountry, and she said to me: Man, where go you? And I said: I seek a midwife of the Hebrews. And she answered and said to me: Are you of Israel? And I said to her: Yea. And she said: And who is she that brings forth in the cave? And I said: She that is betrothed to me. And she said to me: Is she not your wife? And I said to her: It is Mary that was nurtured up in the temple of the Lord: and I received her to wife by lot: and she is not my wife, but she has conception by the Holy Ghost.

And the midwife said to him: Is this the truth? And Joseph said to her: Come here and see. And the midwife went with him. 2 And they stood in the place of the cave: and behold a bright cloud overshadowing the cave. And the midwife said: My soul is magnified this day, because my eyes have seen marvelous things: for salvation is born to Israel. And immediately the cloud withdrew itself out of the cave, and a great light appeared in the cave so that our eyes could not endure it. And little by little that light withdrew itself until the young child appeared: and it went and took the breast of its mother Mary.

And the midwife cried aloud and said: Great to me today is this day, in that I have seen this new sight. 3 And the midwife went forth out of the cave and Salome met her. And she said to her: Salome, Salome, a new sight have I to tell you. A virgin has brought forth, which her nature allows not. And Salome said: As the Lord my God lives, if I make not trial and prove her nature I will not believe that a virgin has brought forth.

XX. 1 And the midwife went in and said to Mary: Prepare yourself, for there is no small contention arisen concerning you. And Salome made trial and cried out and said: Woe to my iniquity and my unbelief, because I have tempted the living God, and lo, my hand falls away from me in fire. And she bowed her knees to the Lord, saying: O God of my fathers, remember that I am the offspring of Abraham and Isaac and Jacob: make me not a public example to the children of Israel, but restore me to the poor, for you know, Lord, that in your name did I perform my cures, and did receive my hire of you. 3 And lo, an angel of the Lord appeared, saying to her: Salome, Salome, the Lord has listened to you: bring your hand near to the young child and take him up, and there shall be to you salvation and joy. 4 And Salome came near and took him up, saying: I will do him worship, for a great king is born to Israel. And behold immediately Salome was healed: and she went forth of the cave justified. And lo, a voice saying: Salome, Salome, tell none of the marvels which you have seen, until the child enter into Jerusalem.

XXI 1 And behold, Joseph made him ready to go forth into Judaea. And there came a great tumult in Bethlehem of Judaea; for there came wise men, saying: Where is he that is born king of the Jews? For we have seen his star in the east and are come to worship him. 2 And when Herod heard it he was troubled and sent officers to the wise men. And he sent for the high priests and questioned them, saying: How is it written concerning the Christ, where he is born? They say to him: In Bethlehem of Judaea: for so it is written. And he let them go. And he questioned the wise men, saying to them: What sign saw you concerning the king that is born? And the wise men said: We saw a very great star shining among those stars and dimming them so that the stars appeared not: and thereby knew we that a king was born to Israel, and we came to worship him. And Herod said: Go and seek for him, and if you find him, tell me, that I also may come and worship him. 3 And the wise men went forth. And lo, the star which they saw in the east went before them until they entered into the cave: and it stood over the head of the cave. And the wise men saw the young child with Mary, his mother: and they brought out of their purse-bags gifts, gold-and frankincense and myrrh. 4 And being warned by the angel that they should not enter into Judaea, they went into their own country by another way.

XXII. 1 But when Herod perceived that he was mocked by the wise men, he was angry, and sent murderers, saying to them: Slay the children from two years old and under. 2 And when Mary heard that the children were being slain, she was afraid, and took the young child and wrapped in swaddling clothes and laid him in an ox-manger.

3 But Elizabeth when she heard that they sought for John, took him and went up into the hill-country and looked about her where she should hide him: and there was no hiding-place. And Elizabeth groaned and said with a loud voice: Oh mountain of God, receive you a mother with a child. For Elizabeth was not able to go up. And immediately the mountain split apart and took her in. And there was a light shining always for them: for an angel of the Lord was with them, keeping watch over them.

XXIII. I Now Herod sought for John, and sent officers to Zacharias, saying: Where have you hidden your son? And he answered and said to them: I am a minister of God and attend continually upon the temple of the Lord: I know not where my son is. 2 And the officers departed and told Herod all these things. And Herod was angry and said: His son is to be king over Israel. And he sent to him again, saying: Say the truth: where is your son? For you know that your blood is under my hand. And the officers departed and told him all these things. 3 And Zacharias said: I am a martyr of God if you shed my blood: for my spirit the Lord shall receive, because you shed innocent blood in the front court of the temple of the Lord.

And about the dawning of the day Zacharias was slain. And the children of Israel knew not that he was slain.

XXIV. 1 But the priests entered in at the hour of the salutation, and the blessing of Zacharias met them not according to the manner. And the priests stood waiting for Zacharias, to salute him with the prayer, and to glorify the Most High. 2 But as he delayed to come, they were all afraid: and one of them took courage and entered in: and he saw beside the altar congealed blood: and a voice saying: Zacharias has been slain, and his blood shall not be wiped out until his avenger come. And when he heard that word he was afraid, and went forth and told the priests. 3 And they took courage and went in and saw that which was done: and the panels of the temple did wail: and they rent their clothes from the top to the bottom. And his body they found not, but his blood they found turned into stone. And they feared, and went forth and told all the people that Zacharias was slain. And all the tribes of the people heard it, and they mourned for him and lamented him three days and three nights. And after the three days the priests took counsel whom they should set in his place: and the lot came upon Symeon. Now he it was which was warned by the Holy Ghost that he should not see death until he should see the Christ in the flesh.

XXV. 1 Now I, James, which wrote this history in Jerusalem, when there arose a tumult when Herod died, withdrew myself into the wilderness until the tumult ceased in Jerusalem.

Glorifying the Lord God which gave me the gift, and the wisdom to write this history.

2 And grace shall be with those that fear our Lord Jesus Christ: to whom be glory for ever and ever. Amen.

The Infancy Gospel of Thomas, Latin Text

Here begins a treatise of the Boyhood of Jesus according to Thomas.

I. How Mary and Joseph fled with him into Egypt.

When there was a tumult because search was made by Herod for our Lord Jesus Christ, that he might slay him, then said an angel to Joseph: Take Mary and her child and flee into Egypt from the face of them that seek to slay him. Now Jesus was two years old when he entered into Egypt. And as he walked through a sown field he put forth his hand and took of the ears and put them upon the fire and ground them and began to eat. [And he gave such favor to that field that year by year when it was sown it yielded to the lord of it so many measures of wheat as the number of the grains which he had taken from it.] Now when they had entered into Egypt they took lodging in the house of a certain widow, and abode in the same place one year. And Jesus became three years old. And seeing boys playing he began to play with them. And he took a dried fish and put it into a basin and commanded it to move to and fro, and it began to move. And again he said to the fish: Cast out your salt that is in you and go into the water. And it came to pass. But when the neighbors saw what was done they told it to the widow woman in whose house his mother Mary dwelt. And she when she heard it hasted and cast them out of her house.

II. How a Master cast him out of the city.

1 And as Jesus walked with Mary his mother through the midst of the marketplace of the city, he looked about and saw a master teaching his pupils. And behold twelve sparrows which were quarrelling one with another fell from the wall into the lap of the master who taught the boys. And when Jesus saw it he laughed and stood still. 2 Now when that teacher saw him laughing, he said to his pupils in great anger: Go, bring him here to me. And when they had brought him, the master took hold on his ear and said: What saw you that you laughed? And he said to him: Master, see, my hand was full of corn, and I showed it to them, and scattered the corn, which they are carrying away in danger: for this cause they fought with one another that they might partake of the corn. 3 And Jesus left not the place until it was accomplished. And for this cause the master labored to cast him out of the city together with his mother.

III. How Jesus came out of Egypt.

1 And behold, an angel of the Lord met with Mary and said to her: Take the child and return into the land of the Jews: for they are dead which sought his life. So Mary arose with Jesus, and they went into the city Nazareth, which is in the inheritance of his (her?) father. 2 But when Joseph departed out of Egypt after the death of Herod, he took Jesus into the wilderness until there was quiet in Jerusalem from them that sought the life of the child. And he gave thanks to God for that he had given him understanding, and because he had found grace before the Lord God. Amen.
After these things an angel of the Lord came to Joseph and to Mary the mother of Jesus and said to them: Take the child, return into the land of Israel, for they are dead that sought the life of the child. And they arose and went to Nazareth where Joseph possessed the goods of his father. 2 And when Jesus was seven years old, there was quiet in the realm of Herod from all them that sought the life of the child. And they returned to Bethlehem and abode there.

IV. What Jesus did in the city of Nazareth.

It is a glorious work for Thomas the Israelite (Ismaelite) the apostle of the Lord to tell of the works of Jesus after he came out of Egypt to Nazareth. Hear (understand) therefore all of you beloved brethren, the signs which the Lord Jesus did when he was in the city of Nazareth: as it is said in the first chapter.
1 Now when Jesus was five years old there was a great rain upon the earth, and the child Jesus walked about therein. And the rain was very terrible: and he gathered the water together into a pool and commanded with a word that it should become clear: and immediately it did so.
2 Again, he took of the clay which came of that pool and made thereof to the number of twelve sparrows. Now it was the Sabbath day when Jesus did this among the children of the Hebrews: and the children of the Hebrews went and said to Joseph his father: Look, your son was playing with us and he took clay and made sparrows which it was not right to do upon the Sabbath, and he has broken it. And Joseph went to the child Jesus, and said to him: Why have you done this which it was not right to do on the Sabbath? But Jesus spread forth (opened) his hands and commanded the sparrows, saying: Go forth

into the height and fly: you shall not meet death at any man's hands. And they flew and began to cry out and praise almighty God. But when the Jews saw what was done they were astonished and departed, proclaiming the signs which Jesus did. 3 But a Pharisee which was with Jesus took a branch of an olive tree and began to empty the pool which Jesus had made. And when Jesus saw it he was vexed and said to him: O you of Sodom, ungodly and ignorant, what hurt did the fountain of water do you, which I made? Lo, you shall become like a dry tree which has neither roots nor leaf nor fruit. And straightway he was dried up and fell to the earth and died: but his parents carried him away dead and reviled Joseph, saying: Behold what your son has done: teach you him to pray and not to blaspheme.

V. How the people of the city were grieved against Joseph because of that which Jesus did.

1 And after some days as Jesus walked with Joseph through the city, there ran one of the children and smote Jesus on the arms: but Jesus said to him: So finish you your course. And immediately he fell to the earth and died. But they when they saw this wonder, cried out saying: From from where comes this child? And they said to Joseph: It is not right that such a child should be among us. And he departed and took him with him. And they said to him: Depart out of this place; and if you must be with us, teach him to pray and not to blaspheme: for our sons are put to death by him (lit. lose their senses). 2 And Joseph called Jesus and began to admonish him, saying: Why do you blaspheme? They that dwell in this place conceive hatred against us. But Jesus said: I know that these words are not mine but yours: yet for your sake I will hold my peace: But let them see and bear their own foolishness. And straightway they that spoke against Jesus were made blind, and as they walked to and fro they said: Every word that comes out of his mouth has fulfillment. 3 And when Joseph saw what Jesus had done he took hold on him by his ear in anger: but Jesus was vexed and said to Joseph: It suffices you to see me and not to touch me. For you know not who I am, which if you knew, you would not grieve me. And albeit I am with you now, yet was I made before you.

VI. How Jesus was treated by the Master.

1 There was therefore a man named Zacheus who heard all that Jesus said to Joseph, and he were astonished in himself and said: I have never beheld such a child that spoke so. And he came near to Joseph and said to him: You have a wise child: deliver him to me to learn letters, and when he is learned in the study of the letters, I will teach him reverently that he become not foolish. Joseph answered and said to him: No man is able to teach him but God only. Think you that this young child will be the occasion to us of little torment, my brother? Think you that he is worthy to receive a little cross?
2 But when Jesus heard Joseph saying these things, he said to Zacheus: Truly, O master, all things that proceed out of my mouth are true. And I am before all men, and I am Lord, but you are the children of strangers: for to me is given the glory of them or of the worlds but to you nothing is given: for I am before all worlds. And I know how many are the years of your life, and when you shall raise that standard of the cross whereof my father spoke, then shall you understand that all things that proceed out of my mouth are true.
3 But the Jews which stood by and heard the words which Jesus spoke, were astonished and said: Now have we seen such wonders and heard such words from this child, as we have never heard neither shall hear from any other man, neither from the chief priests nor the doctors nor the Pharisees. 4 Jesus answered and said to them: Why marvel you? Do you think it a thing incredible that I have told you the truth? I know when you were born, and your fathers: and if I should say more to you, I know when the world was created, and who sent me to you.
When the Jews heard the word which the child spoke, they were angry because they were not able to answer him. And the child turned himself about and rejoiced and said: I spoke to you a proverb; but I know that you are weak and know not anything.
5 Now that master said to Joseph: Bring him to me and I will teach him letters. And Joseph took the child Jesus and brought him to the house [of a certain master] where other children also were taught. But the master began to teach him the letters with sweet speech, and wrote for him the first line which goes from A to Z, and began to flatter him and to teach him (and commanded him to say the letters:) but the child held his peace. 6 Then that teacher smote the child on the head and when the child received the blow, he said to him: I ought to teach you and not you to teach me. I know the letters which you would teach me, and I know that you are to me as vessels out of which comes nothing but sound, and neither wisdom nor salvation of the soul. And beginning the line he spoke all the letters from A even to T fully with much quickness: and he looked upon the master and said: But you know not how to interpret A and B: how would you teach others? You hypocrite, if you know and can tell me concerning A, then will I tell you concerning B. But when the teacher began to expound concerning the first letter, he was not able to give any answer.
7 Then said Jesus to Zacheus: Listen to me, O master and understand the first letter. Give ear to me, how that it has two lines (eight quite unintelligible descriptive phrases follow).
8 Now when Zacheus saw that he so divided the first letter he was confounded at such names, and at his teaching, and cried out and said: Woe is me, for I am confounded: I have hired shame to myself by means of this child. And he said to Joseph: I beg you earnestly, my brother, take him away from me: for I cannot look upon his face nor hear his mighty words. For this child is able to subdue the fire and to restrain the sea, for he was born before the worlds. What womb bare him or what

manner of mother brought him up I know not. 10 O my friends, I am astray in my wits, I am mocked, wretched man that I am. I said that I had a disciple, but he is found to be my master. I cannot overcome my shame, for I am old, and I cannot find wherewithal to answer him, so that I am like to fall into heavy sickness and depart out of the world or go away from this city, for all men have seen my shame, that a child has ensnared me. What can I answer any man, or what words can I speak, for he has overcome me at the first letter! I am confounded, O you my friends and acquaintances, and I can find neither first nor last to answer him. 11 And now I beg you brother Joseph, remove him from me and take him to your house, for either he is a sorcerer or a god (Lord) or an angel, and what to say I know not.

12 And Jesus turned himself to the Jews that were with Zacheus and said to them: Now let all them that see not see and let them understand which understand not, and let the deaf hear, and let them arise which have died by my means, and let me call them that are high to that which is higher, even as he that sent me to you has commanded me. And when the child Jesus ceased speaking, all the afflicted were made whole, as many as had been afflicted at his word. And they dare not speak to him.

VII. How Jesus raised up a boy.

1 Now on a day, when Jesus climbed up upon a house with the children, he began to play with them: but one of the boys fell down through the door out of the upper chamber and died straightway. And when the children saw it they fled all of them, but Jesus remained alone in the house. 2 And when the parents of the child which had died came they spoke against Jesus saying: Of a truth you made him fall. But Jesus said: I never made him fall: nevertheless they accused him still. Jesus therefore came down from the house and stood over the dead child and cried with a loud voice, calling him by his name: Zeno, Zeno, arise and say if I made you fall. And suddenly he arose and said: Nay, Lord. And when his parents saw this great miracle which Jesus did, they glorified God, and worshipped Jesus.

VIII. How Jesus healed the foot of a boy.

1 And after a few days a certain boy of that village was cleaving wood, and smote his foot. 2 And when much people came to him, Jesus also came with them. And he touched the foot which was hurt, and forthwith it was made whole. And Jesus said to him: Arise and cleave the wood and remember me. But when the multitude that were with him saw the signs which were done they worshipped Jesus and said: of a truth we believe surely that you are God.

IX. How Jesus bare water in his cloak.

1 And when Jesus was six years old, his mother sent him to draw water. And when Jesus was come to the well there was much people there and they brake his pitcher. 2 But he took the cloak which he had upon him and filled it with water and brought it to Mary his mother. And when his mother saw the miracle that Jesus did she kissed him and said: Lord, listen to me and save my son.

X. How Jesus sowed wheat.

1 Now when it was seed time, Joseph went forth to sow corn, and Jesus followed after him. And when Joseph began to sow, Jesus put forth his hand and took of the corn so much as he could hold in his hand, and scattered it. 2 Joseph therefore came at the time of harvest to reap his harvest. And Jesus also came and gathered the ears which he had sown, and they made a hundred measures of good corn: and he called the poor and the widows and fatherless and gave them the corn which he had gained, save that Joseph took a little thereof to his house for a blessing [of Jesus].

XI. How Jesus made a short beam even with a long one.

1 And Jesus came to be eight years old. Now Joseph was a builder and wrought ploughs and yokes for oxen. And on a day a certain rich man said to Joseph: Sir, make me a bed serviceable and comely. But Joseph was troubled because the beam which he had made ready for the work was short. 2 Jesus said to him: Be not troubled, but take you hold of this beam by the one end and I by the other, and let us draw it out. And so it came to pass, and forthwith Joseph found it serviceable for that which he desired. And he said to Joseph: Behold, fashion that you will. But Joseph when he saw what was done embraced him and said: Blessed am I for that God has given me such a son.

XII. How Jesus was delivered over to learn letters.

1 And when Joseph saw that he had so great grace and that he increased in stature, he thought to deliver him over to learn letters. And he delivered him to another doctor that he should teach him. Then said that doctor to Joseph: What manner of letters would you teach this child? Joseph answered and said: Teach him first the letters of the Gentiles and after that the

Hebrew. Now the doctor knew that he was of an excellent understanding, and received him gladly. And when he had written for him the first line, that is to say A and B, he taught him for the space of some hours: but Jesus held his peace and answered nothing. 2 At the last Jesus said to the master: If you be truly a master and indeed know the letters, tell me the power of A and I will tell you the power of B. Then was the master filled with indignation and smote him on the head. But Jesus was angry and cursed him, and on a sudden he fell down and died. 3 But Jesus returned to his own home. And Joseph enjoined Mary his mother that she should not let him go out of the court of the house.

XIII. How he was delivered to another master.

1 After many days there came another doctor which was a friend of Joseph and said to him: Deliver him to me and I will teach him letters with much gentleness. And Joseph said to him: If you are able, take him and teach him, and it shall be done gladly. And when the doctor received Jesus, he went with fear and great boldness and took him rejoicing. 2 And when he was come to the house of the doctor, he found a book lying in that place and took it and opened it, and read not those things which were written therein, but opened his mouth and spoke by the Holy Ghost and taught the law: and all that stood by listened attentively, and the teacher sat by him and heard him gladly and entreated him to continue teaching. And much people gathered together and heard all the holy doctrine which he taught and the beloved words which proceeded out of his mouth marveling that he being a little child spoke such things.
3 But when Joseph heard, he was afraid and ran to the place where Jesus was; and the master said to Joseph: Know my brother, that I received your child to teach him and instruct him, but he is filled with great grace and wisdom. Therefore behold now, take him to your house with joy, because the grace which he has is given him of the Lord. 4 And when Jesus heard the master speak thus he was joyful and said: Lo, now you have well said, O master: for your sake shall he rise again who was dead. And Joseph took him to his own home.

XIV. How Jesus made James whole of the bite of a serpent.

Now Joseph sent James to gather straw, and Jesus followed after him. And as James gathered straw, a viper bit him and he fell to the earth as dead by means of the venom. But when Jesus saw that, he breathed upon his wound and forthwith James was made whole, and the viper died.

XV. How Jesus raised up a boy.

After a few days a child that was his neighbor died, and his mother mourned for him very much; and when Jesus heard, he went and stood over the child, and smote him on the breast and said: Child, I say to you, die not, but live. And immediately the child arose: and Jesus said to the mother of the child: Take up your son and give him suck, and remember me. 2 But the multitudes when they saw that miracle said: Of a truth this child is from heaven, for now has he set free many souls from death and has saved all them that hoped in him.

[A gap in all the Latin MSS. filled by the Greek text A, cap. 19,1-3 Jesus and the doctors in the Temple.]

3 The Scribes and Pharisees said to Mary: Are you the mother of this child? and Mary said: Of a truth I am. And they said to her: Blessed are you among women, because God has blessed the fruit of your womb in that he has given you a child so glorious: for so great gifts of wisdom we have never seen nor heard in any.
4 And Jesus arose and followed his mother. But Mary kept in her heart all the great signs which Jesus wrought among the people, in healing many that were sick. And Jesus increased in stature and wisdom, and all that saw him glorified God the Father Almighty: Who is blessed for ever and ever. Amen.
All these things have I, Thomas the Israelite (Ismaelite), written and recorded for the Gentiles and for our brethren, and likewise many other things which Jesus did, which was born in the land of Juda (Judah). Behold, the house of Israel has seen all these from the first even to the last, even how great signs and wonders Jesus did among them, which were good exceedingly. And this is he which shall judge the world according to the will of his Father, immortal and invisible, as the holy Scripture declares and as the prophets have testified of his works among all the peoples of Israel: for he is the Son of God throughout all the World. And to him belongs all glory and honor everlastingly, who lives and reigns with God, world without end. Amen.

The History of Joseph the Carpenter

The History of Joseph the Carpenter is one of the texts within the New Testament apocrypha concerned with the period of Jesus' life before he was 12. The most interesting thing about the story is that it is narrated by Jesus himself in a narrative told to his disciples while they were on the Mount of olives.

The story in one concerning the life of Joseph, his stepfather. In it, Jesus agrees with Mary's continued virginity. The text explains the relationship between Jesus and his brothers and sisters by stating that Joseph had four sons named Judas, Justus, James, and Simon and two daughters called Assia and Lydia by a previous marriage.

At age 90, after the death of his first wife, Joseph is given charge of the twelve year old virgin Mary. She lives in his household raising his youngest son James 'the less' along with Judas, until the time she is to be married at age 14.

We must remember that marriage at that time was not like it is today. Marriage had more to do with consummation than living arrangement. Mary may have lived with Joseph at age 12, but they would not have been considered married until they had sex. The exception would be when a man decided to keep a woman as his wife but keep her virginity.

After this basic background, the text proceeds to paraphrase the Gospel of James, stopping at the point of Jesus' birth. The text states that Joseph was miraculously blessed with mental and physical youth, dying at the age of 111.
Joseph's death takes up approximately half of the work. At the conclusion of the text, Jesus affirms that Mary remained a virgin throughout her days by addressing her as "my mother, virgin undefiled." The words "virginity" and "undefiled" in this context must relate to sexual relations and not to the traumas of childbirth.

The Text says "And the holy apostles have preserved this conversation, and have left it written down in the library at Jerusalem."

There are indications that the text was written in Egypt in the 5th century AD. Two versions survive, one in Coptic, the other in Arabic, with the Coptic version likely being the original. Much of the text is based on material in the Gospel of James.

The source used here is, The History of Joseph The Carpenter, Translated by Alexander Walker. From Ante-Nicene Fathers, Vol. 8. Edited by Alexander Roberts, James Donaldson, and A. Cleveland Coxe. (Buffalo, NY: Christian Literature Publishing Co., 1886.)

The History of Joseph the Carpenter

IN the name of God, of one essence and three persons.
The History of the death of our father, the holy old man, Joseph the carpenter.
May his blessings and prayers preserve us all, O brethren! Amen.
His whole life was one hundred and eleven years, and his departure from this world happened on the twenty-sixth of the month Abib. May his prayer preserve us! Amen.

And, indeed, it was our Lord Jesus Christ Himself who related this history to His holy disciples on the Mount of Olives, telling about all Joseph's labor, and the end of his days. And the holy apostles have preserved this conversation, and have left it written down in the library at Jerusalem. May their prayers preserve us! Amen.

1. One day, when the Savior, our Master and God, the Savior Jesus Christ, was sitting along with His disciples, they were all assembled on the Mount of Olives. He said to them: My brethren and friends, sons of the Father who has chosen you from all men, you know that I have often told you that I must be crucified, and must die for the salvation of Adam and his posterity, and that I shall rise from the dead. Now I shall commit to you the doctrine of the holy gospel formerly announced to you, that you may declare it throughout the whole world. And I shall endow you with power from on high, and fill you with the Holy Spirit. And you shall declare to all nations repentance and remission of sins. For a single cup of water, if a man shall find it in the world to come, is greater and better than all the wealth of this whole world. And as much ground as one foot can occupy in the house of my Father, is greater and more excellent than all the riches of the earth. Yes, a single hour in the joyful dwelling of the pious is more blessed and more precious than a thousand years among sinners: inasmuch as their weeping and lamentation shall not come to an end, and their tears shall not cease, nor shall they find consolation for themselves and rest at any time for ever. And now, my honored members, go and declare to all nations, and tell them, and say to them: Truly the Savior diligently inquires into the inheritance which is due, and is the administrator of justice. And the angels will cast down their enemies, and will fight for them in the day of conflict. And He will examine every single foolish and idle word which men speak, and they shall give an account of it. For as no one shall escape death, so also the works of every man shall be laid open on the Day of Judgment, whether they have been good or evil. Tell them also this word which I have said to you today: Let not the strong man glory in his strength, nor the rich man in his riches; but let him who wishes to glory, glory in the Lord.
2. There was a man whose name was Joseph, who sprung from a family of Bethlehem, which was a town of Judah, and it was the city of King David. This same man, being well furnished with wisdom and learning, was made a priest in the temple of the Lord. He was, skilful in his trade, which was that of a carpenter. And after the manner of all men, he married a wife. Moreover, he begot for himself sons and daughters, four sons, namely, and two daughters. Now these are their names; Judas, Justus, James, and Simon. The names of the two daughters were Assia and Lydia. At length the wife of righteous Joseph, a woman intent on the divine glory in all her works, departed this life. But Joseph, that righteous man, my father after the flesh, and the spouse of my mother Mary, went away with his sons to his trade, practicing the art of a carpenter. 3. Now when righteous Joseph became a widower, my mother Mary, blessed, holy, and pure, was already twelve years old. For her parents offered her in the temple when she was three years of age, and she remained in the temple of the Lord nine years. Then when the priests saw that the virgin, holy and God-fearing, was growing up, they spoke to each other, saying: Let us search out a man, righteous and pious, to whom Mary may be entrusted until the time of her marriage; because if she remains in the temple, what happens to women will happen to her on that account we sin, and God be angry with us. *(Author's note: Mary was of age to begin her menstrual cycles, which would have defiled the temple under the law.)*

4. Therefore they immediately sent out, and assembled twelve old men of the tribe of Judah. And they wrote down the names of the twelve tribes of Israel. And the lot fell on the pious old man, righteous Joseph. Then the priests answered, and said to my blessed mother: Go with Joseph, and be with him till the time of your marriage. Righteous Joseph therefore received my mother, and led her away to his own house. And Mary found James the Less in his father's house, broken-hearted and sad on account of the loss of his mother, and she brought him up. Then Mary was called the mother of James. Thereafter Joseph left her at home, and went away to the shop where he wrought at his trade of a carpenter. And after the holy virgin had spent two years in his house her age was exactly fourteen years, including the time at which he received her. 5. And I chose her of my own will, with the concurrence of my Father, and the counsel of the Holy Spirit. And I was made flesh of her, by a mystery which transcends the grasp of created reason. And three months after her conception the righteous man Joseph returned from the place where he worked at his trade; and when he found my virgin mother pregnant, he was greatly perplexed, and thought of sending her away secretly. But from fear, and sorrow, and the anguish of his heart, he could endure neither to eat nor drink that day.
6. But at mid-day there appeared to him in a dream the prince of the angels, the holy Gabriel, furnished with a command from my Father; and he said to him: Joseph, son of David, fear not to take Mary as your wife: for she has conceived of the Holy Spirit; and she will bring forth a son, whose name shall be called Jesus. He it is who shall rule all nations with a rod of

iron. Having thus spoken, the angel departed from him. And Joseph rose from his sleep, and did as the angel of the Lord had said to him; and Mary abode with him.

7. Some time after that, there came forth an order from Augustus Caesar the king, that all the habitable world should be enrolled, each man in his own city. The old man, righteous Joseph, rose up and took the virgin Mary and came to Bethlehem, because the time of her bringing forth was at hand. Joseph then inscribed his name in the list; for Joseph the son of David and whose spouse was Mary was of the tribe of Judah. And indeed Mary, my mother, brought me forth in Bethlehem, in a cave near the tomb of Rachel the wife of the patriarch Jacob, the mother of Joseph and Benjamin.

8. But Satan went and told this to Herod the Great, the father of Archelaus. And it was this same Herod who ordered my friend and relative John to be beheaded. Accordingly he searched for me diligently, thinking that my kingdom was to be of this world. But Joseph, that pious old man, was warned of this by a dream. Therefore he rose and took Mary my mother, and I lay in her bosom. Salome also was their fellow-traveler. Having therefore set out from home, he retired into Egypt, and remained there the space of one whole year, until the hatred of Herod passed away.

9. Now Herod died by the worst form of death, atoning for the shedding of the blood of the children whom he wickedly cut off, though there was no sin in them. And with that impious tyrant Herod being dead, they returned into the land of Israel, and lived in a city of Galilee which is called Nazareth. And Joseph, going back to his trade of a carpenter, earned his living by the work of his hands; for, as the Law of Moses had commanded, he never sought to live for nothing by another's labor. At length, by increasing years, the old man arrived at a very advanced age. He did not, however, labor under any bodily weakness, nor had his sight failed, nor had any tooth perished from his mouth. For the whole time of his life, his mind never wandered; but like a boy he always in his business displayed youthful vigor, and his limbs remained unimpaired, and free from all pain. His life, then, in all, amounted to one hundred and eleven years, his old age being prolonged to the utmost limit.

11. Now Justus and Simeon, the elder sons of Joseph, were married, and had families of their own. Both the daughters were likewise married, and lived in their own houses. So there remained in Joseph's house, Judas and James the Less, and my virgin mother. I moreover dwelt along with them, as if I had been one of his sons. But I passed all my life without fault. Mary I called my mother, and Joseph father, and I obeyed them in all that they said; nor did I ever contend against them, but complied with their commands, as other men whom earth produces are accustomed to do; nor did I at any time arouse their anger, or give any word or answer in opposition to them. On the contrary, I cherished them with great love, like the pupil of my eye. 12. It came to pass, after these things, that the death of that old man, the pious Joseph, and his departure from this world, were approaching, as happens to other men who owe their origin to this earth. And as his body was verging on dissolution, an angel of the Lord informed him that his death was now close at hand. Therefore fear and great perplexity came upon him. So he rose up and went to Jerusalem; and going into the temple of the Lord, he poured out his prayers there before the sanctuary, and said:

13. O God, author of all consolation, God of all compassion, and Lord of the whole human race; God of my soul, body, and spirit; with supplications I reverence you, O Lord and my God. If now my days are ended, and the time draws near when I must leave this world, send me, I beg You, the great Michael, the prince of Your holy angels: let him remain with me, that my wretched soul may depart from this afflicted body without trouble, without terror and impatience. For great fear and intense sadness take hold of all bodies on the day of their death, whether it be man or woman, beast wild or tame, or whatever creeps on the ground or flies in the air. At the last all creatures under heaven in whom is the breath of life are struck with horror, and their souls depart from their bodies with strong fear and great depression. Now therefore, O Lord and my God, let Your holy angel be present with his help to my soul and body, until they shall be dissevered from each other. And let not the face of the angel, appointed my guardian from the day of my birth, be turned away from me; but may he be the companion of my journey even until he bring me to You: let his countenance be pleasant and gladsome to me, and let him accompany me in peace. And let not demons of frightful aspect come near me in the way in which I am to go, until I come to You in bliss. And let not the doorkeepers hinder my soul from entering paradise. And do not uncover my sins, and expose me to condemnation before Your terrible tribunal. Let not the lions rush in upon me; nor let the waves of the sea of fire overwhelm my soul--for this must every soul pass through before I have seen the glory of Your Godhead. O God, most righteous Judge, who in justice and equity will judge mankind, and will render to each one according to his works, O Lord and my God, I beg You, be present to me in Your compassion, and enlighten my path that I may come to You; for You are a fountain overflowing with all good things, and with glory for evermore.
Amen.

(Author's note: The ideas of doorkeepers, demons that challenge the dead, and escorted passage to paradise seem to indicate a Roman religious influence.)

14. It came to pass thereafter, when he returned to his own house in the city of Nazareth, that he was seized by disease, and had to keep his bed. And it was at this time that he died, according to the destiny of all mankind. For this disease was very heavy upon him, and he had never been ill, as he now was, from the day of his birth. And thus assuredly it pleased Christ (the anointed one) to order the destiny of righteous Joseph. He lived forty years unmarried; thereafter his wife remained under his care forty-nine years, and then died. And a year after her death, my mother, the blessed Mary, was entrusted to

him by the priests, that he should keep her until the time of her marriage. She spent two years in his house; and in the third year of her stay with Joseph, in the fifteenth year of her age, she brought me forth on earth by a mystery which no creature can penetrate or understand, except myself, and my Father and the Holy Spirit, constituting one essence with myself. 15. The whole age of my father, therefore, that righteous old man, was one hundred and eleven years, my Father in heaven having so decreed. And the day on which his soul left his body was the twenty-sixth of the month Abib. For now the fine gold began to lose its splendor, and the silver to be worn down by use. I mean his understanding and his wisdom. He also loathed food and drink, and lost all his skill in his trade of carpentry, and he paid no more attention to it. It came to pass, then, in the early dawn of the twenty-sixth day of Abib that Joseph, that righteous old man, lying in his bed, was giving up his unquiet soul. Then he opened his mouth with many sighs, and struck his hands one against the other, and with a loud voice cried out, and spoke after the following manner:

16. Woe to the day on which I was born into the world! Woe to the womb which bare me! Woe to the bowels which admitted me! Woe to the breasts which suckled me! Woe to the feet upon which I sat and rested! Woe to the hands which carried me and reared me until I grew up! For I was conceived in iniquity, and in sins did my mother desire me. Woe to my tongue and my lips, which have brought forth and spoken vanity, detraction, falsehood, ignorance, derision, idle tales, craft, and hypocrisy! Woe to my eyes, which have looked upon scandalous things! Woe to my ears, which have delighted in the words of slanderers! Woe to my hands, which have seized that which did not of right belong to them! Woe to my belly and my bowels, which have lusted after food unlawful to be eaten! Woe to my throat, which like a fire has consumed all that it found! Woe to my feet, which have too often walked in ways displeasing to God! Woe to my body; and woe to my miserable soul, which has already turned aside from God its Maker! What shall I do when I arrive at that place where I must stand before the most righteous Judge, and when He shall call me to account for the works which I have heaped up in my youth? Woe to every man dying in his sins! Assuredly that same dreadful hour, which came upon my father Jacob, when his soul was flying forth from his body, is now near at hand for me. Behold. Oh! how wretched I am this day, and worthy of lamentation! But God alone is the disposer of my soul and body; He also will deal with them after His own good pleasure.

17. These are the words spoken by Joseph, that righteous old man. And I, going in beside him, found his soul exceedingly troubled, for he was placed in great perplexity. And I said to him: Hail! my father Joseph, you righteous man; how is it with you? And he answered me: All hail! my well-beloved son. Indeed, the agony and fear of death have already surrounded me; but as soon as I heard Your voice, my soul was at rest. O Jesus of Nazareth! Jesus, my Savior! Jesus, the deliverer of my soul! Jesus, my protector! Jesus! O sweetest name in my mouth, and in the mouth of all those that love it! O eyes which see, and ears which hear, hear me! I am Your servant; this day I most humbly reverence You, and before Your face I pour out my tears. You are altogether my God; You are my Lord, as the angel has told me times without number, and especially on that day when my soul was driven about with perverse thoughts about the pure and blessed Mary, who was carrying You in her womb, and whom I was thinking of secretly sending away. And while I was thus meditating, behold, there appeared to me in my rest angels of the Lord, saying to me in a wonderful mystery: O Joseph, you son of David, fear not to take Mary as your wife; and do not grieve your soul, nor speak unbecoming words of her conception, because she is with child of the Holy Spirit, and shall bring forth a son, whose name shall be called Jesus, for He shall save His people from their sins. Do not for this cause wish me evil, O Lord, for I was ignorant of the mystery of Your birth. I call to mind also, my Lord, that day when the boy died of the bite of the serpent. And his relations wished to deliver You to Herod, saying that You had killed him; but You did raise him from the dead, and restore him to them.

(Author's note: This refers back to one of the Infancy Gospels, and is an indication of the earliest date of this book, since it could not have been written earlier than the Infancy Gospel or at least the oral tradition it drew from.)

Then I went up to You, and took hold of Your hand, saying: My son, take care of yourself. But You did say to me in reply: Are you not my father after the flesh? I shall teach you who I am. Now therefore, O Lord and my God, do not be angry with me, or condemn me on account of that hour. I am Your servant, and the son of Your handmaiden; but You are my Lord, my God and Savior, most surely the Son of God.

18. When my father Joseph had thus spoken, he was unable to weep more. And I saw that death now had dominion over him. And my mother, virgin undefiled, rose and came to me, saying: O my beloved son, this pious old man Joseph is now dying. And I answered: Oh my dearest mother, assuredly upon all creatures produced in this world the same necessity of death lies; for death holds sway over the whole human race. Even you, O my virgin mother, must look for the same end of life as other mortals. And yet your death, as also the death of this pious man, is not death, but life enduring to eternity. Nay more, even I must die, as concerns the body which I have received from you. But rise, O my venerable mother, and go in to Joseph, that blessed old man, in order that you may see what will happen as his soul ascends from his body.

(Author's note: This passage stands in opposition to the Catholic doctrine of the assumption of Mary.)

19. My undefiled mother Mary, therefore, went and entered the place where Joseph was. And I was sitting at his feet looking at him, for the signs of death already appeared in his countenance. And that blessed old man raised his head, and kept his eyes fixed on my face; but he had no power of speaking to me, on account of the agonies of death, which held him in their

grasp. But he kept fetching many sighs. And I held his hands for a whole hour; and he turned his face to me, and made signs for me not to leave him. Thereafter I put my hand on his breast, and perceived his soul now near his throat, preparing to depart from its receptacle.

20. And when my virgin mother saw me touching his body, she also touched his feet. And finding them already dead and destitute of heat, she said to me: O my beloved son, assuredly his feet are already beginning to stiffen, and they are as cold as snow. Accordingly she summoned his sons and daughters, and said to them: Come, as many as there are of you, and go to your father; for assuredly he is now at the very point of death. And Assia, his daughter, answered and said: Woe is me, O my brothers, this is certainly the same disease that my beloved mother died of. And she lamented and shed tears; and all Joseph's other children mourned along with her. And my mother Mary, and I also, wept along with them.

21. And turning my eyes towards the region of the south, I saw Death already approaching, and all Gehenna with him, closely attended by his army and his satellites; and their clothes, their faces, and their mouths poured forth flames. And when my father Joseph saw them coming straight to him, his eyes dissolved in tears, and at the same time he groaned after a strange manner. Accordingly, when I saw the vehemence of his sighs, I drove back Death and all the host of servants which accompanied him. And I called on my good Father, saying:

22. O Father of all mercy, eye which sees, and ear which hears, listen to my prayers and supplications in behalf of the old man Joseph; and send Michael, the prince of your angels, and Gabriel, the herald of light, and all the light of your angels, and let their whole array walk with the soul of my father Joseph, until they shall have conducted it to You. This is the hour in which my father has need of compassion. And I say to you, that all the saints, yea, as many men as are born in the world, whether they be just or whether they be perverse, must of necessity taste of death.

23. Therefore Michael and Gabriel came to the soul of my father Joseph, and took it, and wrapped it in a shining wrapper. Thus he committed his spirit into the hands of my good Father, and He bestowed on him peace. But as yet none of his children knew that he had fallen asleep. And the angels preserved his soul from the demons of darkness which were in the way, and praised God even until they conducted it into the dwelling-place of the pious.

24. Now his body was lying prostrate and bloodless; wherefore I reached forth my hand, and put right his eyes and shut his mouth, and said to the virgin Mary: O my mother, where is the skill which he showed in all the time that he lived in this world? Lo, it has perished, as if it had never existed. And when his children heard me speaking with my mother, the pure virgin, they knew that he had already breathed his last, and they shed tears, and lamented. But I said to them: Assuredly the death of your father is not death, but life everlasting: for he has been freed from the troubles of this life, and has passed to perpetual and everlasting rest. When they heard these words, they rent their clothes, and wept.

25. And, indeed, the inhabitants of Nazareth and of Galilee, having heard of their lamentation, flocked to them, and wept from the third hour even to the ninth. And at the ninth hour they all went together to Joseph's bed. And they lifted his body, after they had anointed it with costly ointments. But I entreated my Father in the prayer of the celestials (heavens)--that same prayer which with my own hand I made before I was carried in the womb of the Virgin Mary, my mother. And as soon as I had finished it, and pronounced the amen, a great multitude of angels came up; and I ordered two of them to stretch out their shining garments, and to wrap in them the body of Joseph, the blessed old man.

26. And I spoke to Joseph, and said: The smell or corruption of death shall not have dominion over you, nor shall a worm ever come forth from your body. Not a single limb of it shall be broken, nor shall any hair on your head be changed. Nothing of your body shall perish, O my father Joseph, but it will remain entire and uncorrupted even until the banquet of the thousand years. And whoever shall make an offering on the day of your remembrance, him will I bless and recompense in the congregation of the virgins; and whoever shall give food to the wretched, the poor, the widows, and orphans from the work of his hands, on the day on which your memory shall be celebrated, and in your name, shall not be in want of good things all the days of his life. And whoever shall have given a cup of water, or of wine, to drink to the widow or orphan in your name, I will give him to you, that you may go in with him to the banquet of the thousand years. And every man who shall present an offering on the day of your commemoration will I bless and recompense in the church of the virgins: for one I will render to him thirty, sixty, and a hundred. And whosoever shall write the history of your life, of your labor, and your departure from this world, and this narrative that has issued from my mouth, him shall I commit to your keeping as long as he shall have to do with this life. And when his soul departs from the body, and when he must leave this world, I will burn the book of his sins, nor will I torment him with any punishment in the day of judgment; but he shall cross the sea of flames, and shall go through it without trouble or pain. And on every poor man who can give none of those things which I have mentioned this is incumbent: that if a son is born to him, he shall call his name Joseph. So there shall not take place in that house either poverty or any sudden death forever.

27. Thereafter the chief men of the city came together to the place where the body of the blessed old man Joseph had been laid, bringing with them burial-clothes; and they wished to wrap it up in them after the manner in which the Jews are wont to arrange their dead bodies. And they perceived that he kept his shroud fast; for it adhered to the body in such a way, that when they wished to take it off, it was found to be like iron--impossible to be moved or loosened. Nor could they find any ends in that piece of linen, which struck them with the greatest astonishment. At length they carried him out to a place where there was a cave, and opened the gate, that they might bury his body beside the bodies of his fathers. Then there came into my mind the day on which he walked with me into Egypt, and that extreme trouble which he endured on my account. Accordingly, I bewailed his death for a long time; and lying on his body, I said:

524

28. O Death! who make all knowledge to vanish away, and raise so many tears and lamentations, surely it is God my Father Himself who has granted you this power. For men die for the transgression of Adam and his wife Eve, and Death spares not so much as one. Nevertheless, nothing happens to any one, or is brought upon him, without the command of my Father. There have certainly been men who have prolonged their life even to nine hundred years; but they died. Yea, though some of them have lived longer, they have, notwithstanding, succumbed to the same fate; nor has any one of them ever said: I have not tasted death. For the Lord never sends the same punishment more than once, since it has pleased my Father to bring it upon men. And at the very moment when it, going forth, beholds the command descending to it from heaven, it says: I will go forth against that man, and will greatly move him. Then, without delay, it makes an onset on the soul, and obtains the mastery of it, doing with it whatever it will. For, because Adam did not do the will of my Father, but transgressed His commandment, the wrath of my Father was kindled against him, and He doomed him to death; and thus it was that death came into the world. But if Adam had observed my Father's precepts, death would never have fallen to his lot. Think you that I can ask my good Father to send me a chariot of fire, which may take up the body of my father Joseph, and convey it to the place of rest, in order that it may dwell with the spirits? But on account of the transgression of Adam, that trouble and violence of death has descended upon all the human race. And it is for this cause that I must die according to the flesh, for my work which I have created, that they may obtain grace.

29. Having thus spoken, I embraced the body of my father Joseph, and wept over it; and they opened the door of the tomb, and placed his body in it, near the body of his father Jacob. And at the time when he fell asleep he had fulfilled a hundred and eleven years. Never did a tooth in his mouth hurt him, nor was his eyesight rendered less sharp, nor his body bent, nor his strength impaired; but he worked at his trade of a carpenter to the very last day of his life; and that was the six-and-twentieth of the month Abib.

30. And we apostles, when we heard these things from our Savior, rose up joyfully, and prostrated ourselves in honor of Him, and said: O our Savior, show us Your grace. Now indeed we have heard the word of life: nevertheless we wonder, O our Savior, at the fate of Enoch and Elias, inasmuch as they had not to undergo death. For truly they dwell in the habitation of the righteous even to the present day, nor have their bodies seen corruption. Yet that old man Joseph the carpenter was, nevertheless, Your father after the flesh. And You have ordered us to go into all the world and preach the holy Gospel; and You have said: Relate to them the death of my father Joseph, and celebrate to him with annual solemnity a festival and sacred day. And whoever shall take anything away from this narrative, or add anything to it, commits sin. We wonder especially that Joseph, even from that day on which You were born in Bethlehem, called You his son after the flesh. Then, did You not make him immortal as well as them, and You say that he was righteous and chosen?

31. And our Savior answered and said: Indeed, the prophecy of my Father upon Adam, for his disobedience, has now been fulfilled. And all things are arranged according to the will and pleasure of my Father. For if a man rejects the commandment of God, and follows the works of the devil by committing sin, his life is prolonged; for be is preserved in order that he may perhaps repent, and reflect that he must be delivered into the hands of death. But if any one has been zealous of good works, his life also is prolonged, that, as the fame of his old age increases, upright men may imitate him. But when you see a man whose mind is prone to anger, assuredly his days are shortened; for it is these that are taken away in the flower of their age. Every prophecy, therefore, which my Father has pronounced concerning the sons of men, must be fulfilled in every particular. But with reference to Enoch and Elias, and how they remain alive to this day, keeping the same bodies with which they were born; and as to what concerns my father Joseph, who has not been allowed as well as they to remain in the body: indeed, though a man live in the world many myriads of years, nevertheless at some time or other he is compelled to exchange life for death.

(See "The Lost Book of Enoch," published by Fifth Estate.)

And I say to you, O my brethren, that they also, Enoch and Elias, must towards the end of time return into the world and die--in the day, namely, of commotion, of terror, of perplexity, and affliction. For Antichrist will slay four bodies, and will pour out their blood like water, because of the ridicule to which they shall expose him, and the ignominy with which they, in their lifetime, shall brand him when they reveal his impiety.

(Author's note: This may refer to the two witnesses found in the book of Revelation, who were sent from heaven and are murdered on the streets for preaching the word of God.)

32. And we said: O our Lord, our God and Savior, who are those four whom You have said Antichrist will cut off from the ridicule they bring upon him? The Lord answered: They are Enoch, Elias, Schila, and Tabitha. When we heard this from our Savior, we rejoiced and exulted; and we offered all glory and thanksgiving to the Lord God, and our Savior Jesus Christ. He it is to whom is due glory, honor, dignity, dominion, power, and praise, as well as to the good Father with Him, and to the Holy Spirit that gives life, now on and in all time for evermore. Amen.

(Author's note: Tabitha and Schila were raised from death by Jesus.)

(This ends the story told by Jesus to his disciples when they were together on the Mount of Olives.)

Letter of Herod To Pilate The Governor
And
Letter of Pilate To Herod

These letters connect Roman history with the death of Jesus at Jerusalem. Two copies were found. The letters located in the British Museum were written in Syriac and dated to the sixth or seventh century A.D. Those located in a Paris museum are written in Greek.

The letter of Herod to Pilate The Governor gives us a detailed overview of what befell Herod after the crucifixion of Christ. The letter written by Pilate the Governor of Judea is in response to the letter written by Herod in which Herod describes all the ills that have befallen him and his household since the crucifixion of Christ. Pilate speaks of the many supernatural occurrences he himself had confirmed concerning the death and subsequent resurrection of Jesus.

The Epistle of Pontius Pilate

The Epistle of Pontius Pilate was written as a report to Tiberius Caesar, Emperor of Rome concerning the crucifixion of Jesus. The Epistle, speaks of supernatural events connected with the death of Christ.

The Report of Pontius Pilate to Tiberius

The Report of Pontius Pilate to Tiberus was regarded as genuine by the early church fathers. It consists of a letter written by Pontius Pilate, Procurator of Judea, to Tiberius Caesar, the Emperor of Rome. The letter goes into great detail about the circumstances of the crucifixion of Christ and events immediately following Christ's death. In this letter, Pontius Pilate, an eyewitness to these events, relates many of the miracles performed by Christ. But, most importantly, it describes in detail the supernatural happenings at the time Christ was crucified.

Letters Between Pilate and Seneca

Historically, little is known about Pontius Pilate. He was Procurator of Judaea from A.D. 26 to 36 and was recalled in the year in which the Emperor Tiberius died.

He was recalled because he was considered a failure in the position of Procurator. Although history does not give us much to go on, it is known that men caught in this position usually commit suicide because to do so was considered an honorable way out so their family could inherit their property. If prosecuted, all possessions would have been confiscated by the state.

The activities of John the Baptist and Jesus of Nazareth took place towards the end of the first half of his term of office. There are references to him in the Jewish historian Josephus and the Jewish philosopher Philo of Alexandria, and there are the accounts of the trial of Jesus, which are offered by the writers of the Gospels.

The 'Letters' were addressed by Pilate to his friend Lucius Annaeus Seneca the younger, who was later to be the tutor of the young Emperor Nero (and to commit suicide at his order), and who is known to posterity as a liberal philosopher and writer of moral essays and tragedies which few men read. It appears from the 'Letters' that even in his early manhood Seneca was interested in the difficult problem which Pilate had to handle: the problem of a militant Power ruling a subject people whose religion not only was the prime object of its loyalty, but actually rejected the idea of a foreign over-lordship and its symbols.

The letters give insight into the political climate and how Pilate approached his task as Procurator. He confronts the uprisings of John the Baptist and Jesus with the same attitude and conclusion.

It is for the reader to say how far they may be regarded as authentic; how far, that is, they can be accepted as an account of the period which is not only credible in itself, but at important points more credible than the existing narratives.

Letters of Pontius Pilate, written during his Governorship of Judaea to his friend Seneca in Rome are adapted from those edited by W. P. CROZIER (formerly Scholar of Trinity College, Oxford), London. First Published 1928

LETTERS OF PONTIUS PILATE

Written during his Governorship of Judaea to his friend Seneca in Rome
ON THE WAY TO JUDAEA
Shipboard off Alexandria
We are at last within sight of Alexandria, my dear Seneca, and tomorrow we land. I shall spend a week meeting my staff, interviewing applicants for jobs (shoals of Greeks, of course), receiving deputations of loyal Jews, and talking to every one who can be useful to me. Then on to Caesarea, which, as you know, is my headquarters.

Here at Alexandria I am to meet Valerius Gratus, my predecessor as Procurator of Judaea, and if anyone can tell me how to solve the riddle of getting along with the Jews, he ought to be the man. Not that I shall not get along with them; I intend to, and I believe I shall. Valerius has stood them, or they have stood him, would you say? - for over ten years, so it can be done, though no one else has done it.

(Valerius Gratus was Procurator of Judaea from A.D. 15 to A.D. 26.)

By the way, I have been lucky in engaging two of Valerius's staff for myself. One is Marcius Rufus, his chief military officer and now mine, who has been on leave and is travelling back with me. The other is even more important. He is his Secretary Alexander. He is a Jew, but one of those Jews that are half-Greek: Greek on the surface, and Jew at the bottom. You cannot do without them. It seems that you cannot get a real Jewish Jew to put himself at the service of a mere Roman governor, and if you could you would be little better off because he would not have the languages. And languages are needed, I assure you. There is one sort of Hebrew for their sacred writing, there is the Aramaic that they commonly talk, there is Greek for non-Jews and for all educated people, whether Jews or not, and there is Latin for the Roman Procurator and his staff if they don't choose to use Greek. Alexander speaks them all, Alexander knows everything. I am told that the only person in this part of the world who is sharper than a Greek is a Greek-educated Jew. Congratulate me, therefore, on my Alexander. I rely on him to tell me what I do not know about my province of Judaea - which is almost everything. There are two persons I must not at any price offend, you see: Caesar Imperator (whom the gods preserve) and my Jew Alexander.

(The Emperor Tiberius, who reigned A.D. 14 to A.D. 36.)

Marcius, on the other hand, is a Roman of the Romans. He despises all foreigners, especially Jews. He knows how inferior they are to Romans, and he has never got over the shock of discovering that the Jews are equally satisfied that the Romans are immeasurably inferior to themselves. I was telling him that I had promised to receive the addresses of loyal Jews in Alexandria. 'Impossible!' he said. 'There aren't any.' The other day, when the sea was rough, a wave came over and struck me in the back, knocking me down. When I could get my breath, I said, 'A treacherous blow!' 'We are on our way to Judaea,' said Marcius.

Procula (Pilates wife) is worried that we are to have only a week in Alexandria. She says that she will not have time to do the necessary shopping. My own opinion is that from that point of view a week is much too long. But it really is ridiculous that the Treasury should not make a special 'furnishing grant' or something of that kind to a man in my position. You know I shall have to keep up the palace of Herod at Caesarea and another that he built for himself at Jerusalem and probably there's a third of the same kind at Samaria. How in the world is a poor man going to maintain these enormous places? It was all very well for Herod. He was one of the richest men in the world and Judaea was only a small part of his kingdom. Valerius will be waiting for me here with an inventory of his private 'fixtures' in these palaces and there will be a pretty bill for me to pay. Besides, he is sure to take a great many things away with him, and I shall have to replace them. So you may imagine Procula spending a happy week among what she declares are the finest shops in the Empire - much better, she says, than those of Rome.

You can see yourself how the whole affair has been mismanaged by Rome. When we decided that we must take over the government of Judaea because of the unruliness of the Jews, we should have annexed the whole country that Herod ruled from near Damascus to the Dead Sea and not have left his two sons in possession of large parts of it.

(Note: When Herod the Great died in 4 B.C., the Romans divided his territory between his sons Archelaus, Antipas and Philip, Judaea falling to Archelaus. In A.D. 6, however, they deposed Archelaus and placed Judaea in the hands of a Roman Procurator, but left the other territories still in the hands of Antipas and Philip.)

It's an unfair tax on the Procurator of Judaea , who has to keep up the state of Herod on a fraction of his income. Well, some one will have to find the money, and there's no one for it but the Jews. A Roman Procurator must not be worse housed than a semi-barbarous king like their Herod, must he? I tell Procula that if she wants rugs and tapestries, she should wait till she goes on a visit to Damascus or Antioch, but she only smiles at that; a rug in the hand is worth two in the desert to a woman any day. I say again, the Jews will have to pay. After all, it is a reasonable charge to impose on them and they can afford it. The Jews all over the world - and they are all over the world, you can't get away from them anywhere - are sending money to Jerusalem all the time.

(Note: Pilate is speaking of the Temple-tribute' which all Jews sent to Jerusalem each year. The Roman Governors in the provinces resented these contributions, but the central government at Rome upheld the Jews in sending them.)

You would be astonished at the sight before me as I write - a perfect forest of masts. I did not think there were so many ships afloat. No wonder the Alexandrines says their city is the greatest commercial center in the world. The Captain has just pointed out to me a whole fleet of big ships on one side of the harbor - the fleet that carries grain to our people in Italy. He tells me the grain traffic is in the hands of - whom do you think? - of course, the Jews. He also confided to me that he liked the Jews better outside Judaea than in it. I shall see. At all events I rejoice that, though I might easily have had a more important province, when I am in Judaea I shall be governor, chief tax collector and commander-in-chief all in one.

I will write again before we leave for Caesarea.

POLICY TOWARDS THE JEWS

Alexandria

I found your letter waiting for me when I landed and I hasten to thank you for it. I count myself happy that you who are so busy and making for yourself so brilliant a name in the courts should have had the inclination and the time to write me a long letter of good wishes and advice. It was shrewd of you, too, my friend. 'Pilate,' you said to yourself, 'the impulsive, headstrong Pilate, will not be able to argue with me; he will have to take my warnings on with him from Alexandria and chew upon them all the way to Caesarea.' I will do that, I promise you, and whenever I do so I shall wonder again that one so young as you should be so wise.

(Note: Seneca was about thirty years of age at this time.)

The State is fortunate which can boast not only of Caesars but of Senecas to serve them, and I shall watch your progress with affectionate eagerness from my exile among the savages.

'What,' you will say, 'savages! So that is all that my letter has accomplished, so that is the spirit in which you take up your task? The Jews are not savages.' No, they are not; I seek but to provoke you. The Jews are highly civilized. They are intelligent and subtle, industrious and tenacious; they can split a hair with the most learned and steal a march with the most cunning. You need not be afraid; I shall not under-rate them.

But, you say, beware of their religion, for on that subject they are the most sensitive, the most prone to take offence, the most indomitable in resistance, of any people on this earth. And, you add, holding up a warning finger, 'You know what Caesar wishes!' I know. No commotions, no rebellions, taxes duly paid: that is what Caesar wishes. Yet you will not pretend that Caesar loves the Jews, at least in Rome. Precisely, says the wise Seneca: in Rome Caesar does not love the Jews any more than he does the Egyptians. They will not mix, they are a race apart, they will not do sacrifice to the Gods or to Caesar, and they claim all sorts of privileges. Caesar does not want such people in Rome, though they flock there more and more. They should stop in their own Judaea, then, and in their own Judaea - let them alone! Is not that the instruction? Have I not laid your letter well to heart? Believe me, I shall not interfere with their religion, their priests or their Temple. But I have heard - and have you, who know so much, not also heard? - that with a Jew religion comes very near to politics? What, pray, is a Roman Governor to do when religion becomes politics? I have heard that some of them will acknowledge no ruler except their God, not even Caesar. Not even Caesar, mark you! Let them beware. I think that Caesar will be highly displeased with servants who are not concerned to secure respect for his authority. In religion the Jews may go their own way. In politics they shall go my way, the Roman way, or I will know the reason why.

Tomorrow I meet Valerius in the morning, and in the afternoon a deputation of Alexandrine Jews, who wish to pay me their dutiful respects and (so their letter says) make representations to me about lightening of the burdens on their countrymen in Judaea. I shall be expected, I suppose, to show how much finer a fellow than Valerius I am by reducing the taxes.

The shopping campaign is already in full swing.

MEETING WITH HIS PREDECESSOR VALERIUS
Alexandria

My time has been so fully occupied that I am only now able to write to you, and we sail for Caesarea in a few hours. Every few minutes there is some interruption; but I will write this letter though I miss the ship.

There is one thing of great importance, which I must say at once lest I forget it; the Jews can wait. You told me, you may remember, of a new wash which you had devised for your vine-plants - more efficacious against pests than any known to you, and you attributed to it the generous crop that you had last year. I have told my freedman Leon who manages my farm at Laurentum to write and ask you for the particulars, and I shall be grateful if you will give them to him. He is ingenious in all such experiments and omits no details; you may be sure that you will not have the annoyance of finding that those who have not the wit or the will to make the best of it have sought your advice.

I have seen Valerius - a ruddy complexioned, jolly fellow, delighted at the prospect of going home. I wanted to ask about Judaea but he would scarcely talk of anything but Rome and chariot racing, for which he has a passion. However, he told me enough about the furnishing of Herod's palaces to make it clear that my worst fears are true. He says that when Caesar deposed him Archelaus, sold the contents of the palaces as being his private property, and that consequently every governor since then has had to furnish anew or buy the 'fixtures' of his predecessor. 'How can I pay so much,' I said, 'at the beginning of my term of office?' 'Borrow the money from the Jews,' said Valerius, 'and then increase their taxes in order to pay it back.' 'But,' I replied, 'I am just going to inform a Jewish deputation that out of respect and admiration for their race I intend graciously to remit a tenth part of the taxes.' 'Why not?' said Valerius, 'I did the same myself. But in six months you must restore the ten per cent, and in twelve months put another tenth on that.' He told me also that I should by all means encourage the Jews who throng to Jerusalem from Asia and Africa at the time of the great festivals, especially the Passover. So long as Caesar maintains peace in the provinces, the Jews flourish. They travel in tens of thousands to Judaea, carrying their money with them. 'Then is your chance,' said he. 'Make them pay a visitors' tax when they enter, raise the customs duties on everything that is bought and sold while they are there, and put a specially heavy tax on all the mementoes that they carry away when they go back. They will grumble, but since they are departing to other provinces, that need not trouble you, and the Jews in Judaea, having helped to suck them dry, will take no further interest in them.' I like Valerius. He knows what is helpful, and is practical.

I had meant to describe the Jewish deputation to you but that must wait. I shall have more leisure time to do it adequately on the way to Caesarea. You may think of me, during the voyage, taking lessons on Judaea from Alexander. What kind of man is he, you ask. You know the sort of Jew that is aggressive, insistent, loud? He is the other sort. He is quiet, deferential, often obsequious - and, unless I am mistaken, as deeply disdainful of you, and me and of Rome, and Caesar as the noisiest of them all.

At present Alexander is engaged in a brisk flirtation with Acme, Procula's Greek slave, a pretty girl. He has succeeded Marcius. Jew does not marry non-Jew, I believe, but outside marriage they are not particular.

INSTRUCTION FROM VALERIUS
Shipboard: On the way to Caesarea

The sea is only choppy and I must not grumble, but I am glad that it is a short voyage compared with that from Italy.

I had meant to tell you what Valerius said to me about Galilee. As you know, both Galilee and Peraea , which is east of Jerusalem on the far side of the river Jordan, are both possessions of Antipas, son of the Herod who, by turning his coat skillfully during our civil wars, not only kept his kingdom but continued adding to it. I complained to Valerius that these territories ought to be under the Governor of Judaea, *especially Galilee. Common sense demands it. Galilee is Jewish, it is flourishing and rich, and Jerusalem is its national and historic capital. Its inhabitants look to Jerusalem as their sacred city and are always travelling to it. Would anyone in his senses dream of carving up a country into strips in such a way, and why should we tolerate it just because Herod had three sons for whom he wanted to provide? Valerius agreed with me at once. 'There is more in it than that, too,' he said, 'as you may soon find out. The Galileans, like all the Jews, hate the Romans, and they are as independent and stiff-necked as can be. But when they want to make trouble, they come out of Galilee, where they can change nothing and achieve nothing, and make it in Judaea, which means Jerusalem. The last serious uprising was about twenty years ago, when we took over the country. The trouble was raised by a rascal called Judas who belonged to Galilee. That was a real rebellion. The unfortunate Procurator of Judaea is not allowed by Caesar to have any rebellions, while at the same time he is prevented from dealing with the beginnings of seditions in Galilee even if he knows of them, because it is the kingdom of Antipas and he must not interfere.' 'Then we ought,' I said, 'to get rid of Antipas.' Valerius smiled. 'I have been waiting for ten years,' he said, 'and he has never given me a handle.*

(Note: Judas of Gamala led a revolt at the time Herod died in 4 B.C. He tried again in A.D. 6-7, when the Romans imposed taxation. It was from the party of Judas and Zaddok, a Pharisee, that the 'Zealots' arose. The Zealots were so named because of the fire and fervent hate they felt toward Rome. It was this uncontrolled hatred that led to the fatal revolt against the Romans.)

You may take it that Antipas will not allow sedition to start in Galilee if he can help it, because he knows the Romans might seize the chance to absorb his kingdom into Judaea. He keeps on good terms with the Roman Governor of Syria and he has friends in Rome. Like his villainous old father, he flatters the Jews by observing their customs and he keeps himself in power by paying court to the Romans. All the Herods are the same. They know that if it were not for the Romans the Jews would have them out in no time, for the Jews love them little though they love the Romans less.'

I asked Valerius if all the Jews detest the Romans equally how had he managed to keep things quiet for ten years. 'It's quite true,' he said, 'that they all hate us. There is scarcely one of them that would speak to us, let alone eat with us, if he could help it, but they do not all hate us in the same degree. There are some of them at Jerusalem who would sooner put up with the Romans than lose the power and position that they hold. Their noble priestly families - as arrogant a crew as can be found in Asia - ruled the whole country before the time of Herod. Herod destroyed their power and almost destroyed them. Now they have raised their heads again. We have given them back much of their authority, especially in regard to their religion, and, in order to keep it, they are ready to tolerate us. They do not want another Herod to sweep them aside and send them to the executioner. Nor do they like sedition, unless it were likely to be successful, because they know the power of Rome. They have no use for a Judas, whether from Galilee or anywhere else, who by raising a popular revolt may bring them into conflict with Rome and end their privileges. They make a bargain with Rome. "We hate you and despise you," they say, "but on terms we can help you. Leave us alone and we will keep the country quiet for you."

You see, my friend, how quickly I am learning. I am to work with these priests at Jerusalem and look out for an opportunity, which I am not likely to get, of tripping up Antipas. Between you and Valerius and Secretary Alexander I shall soon be a statesman. All the same, I shall press for an increase in the garrison of Judaea. Four thousand men are not enough. When I get the chance I shall say that I need more troops to watch the frontiers of Galilee and Peraea.

I have not told you about the deputation after all, but I will write again before we land at Caesarea.

A JEWISH DEPUTATION AT ALEXANDRIA

Shipboard, near to Caesarea

Now at last I can describe the Jewish deputation. It was a bigger affair than I had expected, but then the Jews in Alexandria are much more important than I had supposed. There is a Jewish settlement which they say occupies nearly half the city; I know that on the day before the deputation came I drove and drove and always the people and the placards and the shop-signs were Jewish. Everywhere children and everywhere aged greybeards, grave or talking with animation in the street. I have never seen so many old men. Do they ever die, I wonder? Or is it only that one notices them more because they are so different?

It had become known that I intended to receive some of their leading men and there was a great crowd in the square before the palace of the City Prefect, Junius Macrinus, with whom I was staying. You should have heard the uproar when the deputation appeared. The Jews, who were there in force, gave their countrymen an excited welcome, I suppose because they were going to admonish the prospective oppressor of Judaea. This provoked the mob, who were mostly Greeks and they began to hoot and then to hustle the Jews and finally to throw stones. The Jews resisted and I thought that there would be a riot. However, Junius, who is used to this sort of thing and was amused at my taking it so seriously, had a company of troops in readiness and they soon hurried the deputation indoors and cleared the square. Everything went like clockwork. Two men, whom I believe to be Greeks were killed.

You would scarcely believe how much the Jews are disliked in this part of the world. The crowd called them 'swine,' 'robbers' and 'blood-drinkers.' Partly it is because they are arrogant and exclusive, but the Greeks cannot forgive them for beating them in trade. There is a saying in Alexandria that 'an Egyptian could make money from a pyramid, a Greek from a stone, and a Jew from a grain of sand.'

(Note: Apparently "blood drinkers" is allusion to rumors of Jewish ritual murder and sacrifice of infants spread by their enemies from very ancient times.)

Alexander, the secretary, had prepared me for the deputation. He hinted that he could write my speech, but I intend to make my own speeches. 'The deputation,' he said, 'will be important: as a sign of respect to the new Procurator it will be headed by Philo and Alexander.' He seemed to expect me to say something. 'Oh yes,' I said, 'Philo and Alexander. I must remember their names.' Junius was delighted. 'I do not believe you have ever heard of either of them,' he said. The secretary went on unmoved. 'Philo has a certain reputation as a philosopher.' 'Why,' said Junius, 'he is the greatest living Jew. He is called "The Jewish Plato," which infuriates the Greeks. I have never read a word of him, but I believe he has set out to prove that the Hebrew Scriptures contain the whole of Greek philosophy.'

'Alexander,' added the secretary, 'is Philo's brother, and is the leader of the Jews in commerce and finance as Philo is in letters.' Junius added that Alexander was the recognized head of the Jewish community, enormously wealthy and ready to lend money on good security. I thought myself that I must take note of Alexander. Philo and Alexander were, in fact, the spokesmen of the party. I was brief and soldierly. 'You have, I hear, a petition to make to me,' was all I said when Junius presented them. Each of the pair had something to ask of me. They spoke quietly but, I need scarcely say, with complete assurance, as though equals to equals.

Philo spoke first, since he was to deal with religion. He began with compliments to Rome, to Caesar, and to me. He said that the Jews had always fought hard for their independence, but had never for long been able to preserve it. Always some great Power from the north or from the south had overcome them: Egypt, Assyria, the Greeks, the Syrian kings, and finally Rome. Nowadays they not only recognized that they could not hope to prevail against the might of Caesar, but they no longer desired to, for Caesar gave them peace and good government. I interrupted to say that there were constant complaints of some fellow springing up in Judaea - an itinerant preacher or a so-called patriot or a mere bandit - and he always ended by inciting the people against Rome. Philo rejoined that these were in any event ignorant, illiterate men who counted for little, and that the rulers at Jerusalem, supported by all that was best and most educated among the Jews, were satisfied to have things as they were, provided that they were left undisturbed in the exercise of their religion, and in this every Jew throughout the world was on their side. He went on to warn me, with professions of respect, that in Judaea the Jews would not abate one jot or tittle of their religious convictions. They had, he said, endured the extreme of persecution before, and, if need be, they would do so again. Antiochus of Syria had tortured and slain them by the thousand in his determination to force heathen customs upon them and to make them Greeks rather than Jews, but at the end they had defeated him.

Herod had sought to bribe them by the impressiveness and opulence of his gifts and bribes and by building them a Temple, which was said to be the wonder of the world, but when he set a golden eagle over the Temple Gate they had pulled it down, for neither the cross nor the stake had terrors for the God-fearing Jew

(Note: Antiochus Epiphanes (175-164 B.C.) endeavored to destroy Jewish religion and 'Hellenize' the Jews. The successful revolt led by Judas Maccabaeus marked the failure of his policy. Antiochus dedicated the Temple at Jerusalem to the Olympic Zeus and erected in it the pagan altar which is the 'abomination of desolation' spoken of in the Book of Daniel. The eagle placed over the entrance was a symbol of the Roman nation and its ownership of the temple.)

Although he said he thought it not necessary, he reminded me that the Jews, worshipping an invisible God, would accept no statue or image of living beings, and that even Herod had not placed his head on his own coins in Judaea.

(Note: The policy of Herod the Great toward the Jews was one of lenience mixed with suspicion and contempt. He did not seek, like Antiochus, to 'Hellenize' them. At the same time to gratify them he restored the Temple on the grandest scale but he also established an amphitheatre at Jerusalem whose pagan character was a constant offence to them.)

I asked him bluntly whether he proposed that Caesar's head should not be placed on his own coins within his own dominions; but he was too shrewd to be trapped by the question; he only hoped, he said, that I would respect the feelings of the Jews in the ancient home of their race and their religion even as Caesar himself desired that they should be respected.

I asked him whether he was aware that in Rome Caesar had ordered that the Jews should abandon their special forms of worship on pain of being expelled from Italy or forced into the labor battalions of the army.

(Note: Emperor Tiberius had enforced this measure seven years earlier - in A.D. 19.)

He replied that he knew this was so, but that whereas Caesar would not tolerate a distinctive race with special exclusive privileges in Rome, he was equally firm in allowing them the undisturbed enjoyment of their religious customs in their own home. He added pointedly that everybody knew this was the policy laid down by Caesar for his governors, and they were grateful for it both to him and to them. He ended with a petition: the instructions given me at Rome before I left. Valerius had also stressed this. He informed me that at Jerusalem the Roman Governor keeps the vestments of the High Priest in his custody. He only hands them over to the High Priest on the eve of the great festivals and he receives them back again when the festival is finished. It is a sign of authority to which Rome attaches great importance. The Jews, of course, resent it. Philo proposed that, since Judaea had behaved so well during Valerius's term of office, I should restore the vestments to the High Priest. I answered coldly that the Jews must earn any concession by good behavior shown to me, that I knew Caesar's mind and should carry it out, and that I had every intention of allowing the Jews the full exercise of their religion, provided that they recognized in every proper manner the authority of Caesar. The question of the vestments, I said, was one which only Caesar could decide.

(Note: Herod the Great had kept the vestments in his own custody and the Romans continued the practice. When, Pilate was summoned to Rome in A.D. 36 to answer to the accusations of misgovernment that were made against him, the vestments were restored to the charge of the priests in the Temple.)

I hope you will approve of this mild and cautious utterance. Religion is one thing; by all means let them have their religion. But when they say that their religious scruples forbid them to tolerate the symbols of the authority of Rome - a statue or an image or even an inscription - that is another matter altogether. I shall see about it. I do not think that Caesar will blame me for enforcing his authority.

I thought Philo would never stop. His brother, Alexander, I am glad to say, was briefer. He was full of the poverty of the Jews. He said there was an impression about that all Jews were rich, but it was a great mistake. Judaea was a poor country, a large part of it mountainous and barren. The really rich territory was Galilee. I know it, but people thought Judaea was wealthy because of the contributions which Jews everywhere sent up to Jerusalem. This, however, was 'Temple-money' designed to maintain the services and the priests, and it could no more be touched than the jewels, given by pious benefactors. He himself, by the way, is one of these which adorn the Temple itself! He urged me to create peace and contentment at the beginning of my governorship by a large remission of taxation. He spoke of my reference to troublesome agitators in Judaea and said that his own experience as a collector of taxes in Egypt was that the less people were taxed the less likely they were to listen to sedition. I said I would consider it. I could not tell him the truth, could I? The truth is that a Governor never needs money so urgently as in his first year of office and that every Governor has an endless string of creditors at Rome. If it were not for his creditors, would any man consent to govern Jews? You may say that this is a most unrefined sentiment. So it is, but I cannot always be a Seneca. To think of the untold wealth that flows from every city of Asia and Africa and almost of Europe to Jerusalem, and I cannot so much as touch it! Nor, I assure you, will I attempt to.

Soon we shall be within sight of Caesarea. Procula is full of excitement about it: but then, she does not realize for how many years she may have to live in it.

ARRIVAL AT CAESAREA

In harbor, Caesarea

Congratulate me, my friend, for I have reached my 'province.' Wish me a quiet and uneventful term, without rebellion, droughts or tumults, so that I may earn promotion and in some higher post than this help to make history.

I have left Procula on deck. She is wildly excited. She expected, I believe, to find tents and savages, and here is a city which looks, she says, almost as good as Naples. Certainly there is nothing Jewish about its appearance. The first thing we saw, from many miles out, was a temple of white, gleaming marble high up on a hill. Then the outline of a great amphitheatre, also white. Next, as we came nearer, a tall, dark tower standing straight up, as it seemed, out of the water. We found that it was established on the end of a gigantic pier (harbor) made of enormous blocks of stone. I have seen nothing so striking as this pier harbor) in Italy. It runs out crescent-shaped, from the southern end of the city towards the north; it is several times as broad as any of our roads, with towers upon it and arches where seamen may lodge. It projects so far towards the northern shore that it leaves only a narrow entrance from the open sea and within it is the haven of calm waters in which we now lie. The size of the stones is almost beyond belief, and how Herod contrived to get them here and have them hewn and plant them in position is more than I can understand. He must have searched all Asia and Africa for skilled engineers. Before Herod built the harbor and called it after Caesar, the place was a mere roadstead, open and dangerous. Now the commerce of the whole country can flow through it and much comes here that used to go to Tyre, farther north. I hope still more will come that I may get the benefit of the customs duties!

As we approached the entrance, Marcius pointed out to me first one building and then another, and always he added, 'Herod built it - Herod built them all.' Truly he was a wonderful man, for this is only one of the cities that he created out of nothing, and wherever he built he never forgot to build to the glory of Caesar and of Rome. (The temple that I first saw is dedicated to Caesar.)

As I watched and listened to Marcius I exclaimed, 'A great king, no wonder Caesar praised him!'

(Note: It was reported that the Emperor Augustus and his minister Agrippa had said that 'the dominions of Herod were too little for the greatness of his soul.')

I was astonished to hear a harsh voice near me saying, 'A great murderer!' and there, if you please, was my humble Alexander, with a scowl on his face and a snarl in his voice, looking as though he hated (as I am sure he does) even the stones that Herod had set up.

'He was a Jew himself,' I said, in order to tease Alexander. I knew that Herod was only a half-Jew, being of the race of Idumaeans, and I suppose that if there are any persons whom the Jews hate more than pure Romans and Greeks, it is people who are part-Jew like Idumaeans and Samaritans.

(Note: The Idumaeans, whose country lay south of Judaea, had been defeated in war and forcibly 'Judaized' by the Jewish ruler, John Hyrcanus I (135-105 B.C.).)

'He was no Jew,' said Alexander curtly. 'And he was the vilest murderer that ever came even from Idumaea.'

'Whom did he murder?' I asked. 'I know he executed rebels somewhat freely, but I expect that most of them deserved no less. You mean the executions in his own family?'

'Murders!' said Alexander. (He is rather pertinacious.) 'He put to death Hyrcanus, the aged grandfather of his wife Mariamne, and then her brother. He put to death her mother Alexandra. He put to death Mariamne herself and for that, by the justice of God, for he had a deep passion for her, he suffered the tortures of the damned. He put to death his own two sons by Mariamne and another son by another wife, who had set his mind against those two. He put to death -' and then he rolled off a long list. I cannot remember all of them - I have so much to think of - but I know there were two successive husbands of Herod's own sister Salome among them. I asked Alexander what motive Herod had. Was it merely pleasure in killing?

'No,' he said, 'the family of Hyrcanus was of the princely Jewish stock and Herod exterminated every member of it lest it should produce a rival to himself.'

'At Rome they call that statesmanship,' I said, I hope not indiscreetly.

(Note: Apparently a dangerous allusion to the jealousy and suspicion with which the Emperor Tiberius regarded all possible claimants to the Imperial power.)

I asked Marcius what was his view of Herod. He was thoughtful. 'A great prince,' he said. 'He had large ideas about everything. Caesar Augustus was right when he said that Herod was big enough to rule both Syria and Egypt. He was the shrewdest man that Rome has had to deal with in these parts. He knew how to be useful to Rome and also how to use her. But at home he was a wild beast; he lived on blood.'

It is true enough. (Killing) his own wife and his own sons, that takes some tolerance (for blood.)

The streets are decorated in our honor, and we can hear the noise of the crowds assembling to greet our procession.

MEETING WITH CAIAPHAS

In the Palace of Herod, Caesarea

We are duly installed and I am hard at work. I sit from morning to night, studying reports from every quarter of Judaea, going into accounts, listening to petitions. I really believe that for the last twelve months Valerius must have saved up every difficult and disagreeable question for me to settle. There is no end to the disputes between Greeks and Jews, Samaritans and Jews, Idumaens and Jews, and Jews and Jews. All of them are described as important; there is a fine crop of trouble for me, however I decide them. I suppose that I shall do the same by my successor when my turn comes. My reception was fairly good, but the non-Jews were much more cordial than the Jews. The Jews in the streets were cool and unresponsive. Marcius says that Valerius has ruled them so gently that they see no reason to hope for much from me. 'They will be more enthusiastic,' he added, 'about your successor.'

When I reached the palace I found the high officials gathered to welcome me: my own staff, representatives of the two Herods, and the High Priest from Jerusalem. The High Priest is one Joseph Caiaphas. He is a tall man, imposing in appearance, suave in manner and, I should say, of supple mind. I observed that his mere presence made a great impression on every one. There had been great discussion whether he would come to Caesarea or wait at Jerusalem until I paid my first visit there. Had he not come, I should certainly have taken it in a negative light, for it would have been a plain sign of hostility.

On the other hand, he came alone. There are several living ex-High Priest, and none came with him. Especially, neither Annas nor any of his sons were there. This Annas and his sons, I should tell you, are the most powerful of the priestly families at Jerusalem. For years they have either held the highest offices or made it difficult for anyone else to hold them. Old Annas himself was High Priest when Valerius came here and Valerius found him impossible; he merely wants the protection of Rome so that he can go his own way in everything. Valerius transferred the office to a member of another family, but the experiment was a failure: then he appointed one of Annas's sons, but that was like having the old man back again. Once more he appointed a rival priest and once more the rival was not strong enough. So he chose Caiaphas, who is Annas's son-in-law, hoping that the ambitious crew would regard this as enough of prestige and influence for the family and that Caiphas would be willing and able to hold his own against them. It is not a bad arrangement, do you think?. Caiaphas keeps the peace with us and the office in the family; Annas and his sons stand a little farther off and hold the support of those who think Caiaphas is too subservient. At heart, all of them are alike and office-holders and office-speakers, accept the Romans for the present. The last thing that any of them want is a clash with Rome that would destroy their own power.

Caiaphas, at the public ceremony, merely said, 'The Jews greet the representative of Caesar.' A chilly welcome, but afterwards, in private, he was more communicative. He told me that he regarded it as his duty to work with the Romans. He said that his people, as he hoped I knew, were passionately attached to their independence, but that he and the great Jewish families recognized that they could not struggle against Rome. He said that the thing that he always feared was a popular uprising, which he and his friends could not check in time. 'This country,' he said, 'is very difficult to control. It is full of mountainous and desolate tracts in which evil-disposed or ambitious persons cannot be prevented from gathering together and from which they can venture out to make trouble in the towns.' There had, after the death of Herod, been several instances of adventurers who gathered a band of people about them and actually set themselves up for King. One of them might be a mere bandit; another might be a political rebel against any sort of foreign rule; a third might presume to lay down the law about religion. In any event there was danger. The common people were extremely ignorant - I was amused to see the contempt with which he spoke of them - and any sort of leader with a gift of action or of speech meant to them some one who might restore the liberties, which they had once enjoyed. Then, he said quietly and with a smile, 'Besides,' he said, speaking very quietly, 'you have to remember that all Jews believe that on some distant day a deliverer will arise who will restore the ancient glories of our people.' I do not pretend to understand their religion, but I gathered that the coming of this deliverer (Messiah he called him) would be incompatible with government by Rome, or by any other power. I must ask Alexander about this. The voice of Caiaphas was equable, almost casual, as he talked to me. I take it that he and his friends will support no rivals, be they Kings or Messiahs, who endanger their authority under Caesar's governor.

I thanked Caiaphas and asked him where Annas was. He replied that Annas had a cold, and in any event seldom left home. He would present himself to me at Jerusalem. I said that Annas had several sons, one of whom had been High Priest. He answered that it would not be seemly for them to come in the absence of their father. I imagine that the old man completely overshadows them.

(Note: Eleazar was appointed by Valerius Gratus. In all, five sons of Annas at one time or another held the office of High Priest. Annas himself was High Priest for nine years and Caiaphas for eleven.)

Caiaphas and I understand each other, I think, but I shall need to watch him.

The position is extraordinary; I wish that you were here to study it. As I look out from the palace, I see below me this town, which, apart from Jews, is full of Greeks, Egyptians and the rest. Away to the south is a strip of plain along the sea. Behind it are foothills and then, rising behind them, a barrier of mountains, bare and rugged, among which dwell the real Jews, stiff-necked and obstinate. They are surrounded by enemies - Samaritans to the north, Idumaeans to the south, Romans at the points of military vantage and Greeks everywhere, and they do not desire to have them other than enemies. The very troops, the auxiliaries, by which we hold them down, are recruited from these enemies on their own soil, for they themselves will not serve in the army and we - wrongly, as I think - exempt them. They shut themselves up in their Jerusalem and, still more, in their Temple, unchanging and, at heart, unyielding.

I have had no letter from you, my friend, since I came here. Take heed; I shall not write again until I hear from you.

A GOVERNOR'S PROBLEMS

Caesarea

Your letter has come and I am grateful to you for it and for your offer of services. I shall venture to make use of you at once and you yourself have given me the hint. You say that things are not only quiet at Rome but too quiet for some people; that the mob grumbles as 'stingy Caesar' for not giving them largesse and games and hopes that he will treat them more generously when he comes back to Rome. You approve of Caesar's policy, and so do I; let them go without their Games and do some honest work for a change. But I am not Caesar and I cannot afford to have my people grumbling. Therefore I must exhibit Games, and that is why I ask for your assistance.

(Note: In this year Tiberius retired to the island of Capreae, in the Bay of Naples. He never returned to Rome.)

First of all, I shall have some fighting with wild beasts. I would have liked to have the sort of contest that I saw in Alexandria - some bulls against an elephant, but elephants cost too much for Procurators. The chief display will be half a dozen lions against a dozen Idumaean prisoners armed with darts. You can see at once that it will be an affair of tactics; if they can separate the lions, but there - I know you have a mind above such things. (They have six light darts each, so the odds are on the lions.) Some other prisoners - these are criminals - will fight on horseback against the bulls. These prisoners are chosen because they cannot ride. Later, the gladiators. Here you can assist me. I want to give the people a novelty. I find that they have rarely seen a Gaul and scarcely ever a Briton. Now I design a chariot-fight between Parthians on the one side and Gauls and Britons on the other. The chariots are here. I shall have six on each side. I am getting the Governor of Syria to send me some Parthian prisoners. There will be six to drive and six to do the fighting. Can you get me the Gauls and Britons, especially the Britons? They must be used to chariot-fighting, and I want to buy them outright, so that those who survive can be used at other Games by me or loaned to friends. I should be very willing to have none but Britons if so many are available. There is much interest here in that island, and every one is asking why Caesar does not go in and add it definitely to our possessions. We shall never be really safe in Gaul until we do so. But, I know, caution is nowadays the word.

(Note: Tiberius, following the maxims of Augustus, was reluctant to extend the boundaries of the Empire and the conquest of Britain was not seriously undertaken until A.D. 43, under the Emperor Claudius.)

I have asked Alexander what the High Priest meant with his talk about a Jewish deliverer or Messiah, and I know that you, of all people, will want to hear his answer. Like everything in this strange country, it is a mixed question of religion and politics. Apparently the Jews are led by their sacred writings to believe that some day or other their God, who has chosen them out from all the peoples of the world (a funny notion), will re-establish them in the position which they held hundreds of years ago, when neither Romans nor Greeks had come upon them. But, says Alexander, their educated men and their rulers, like Caiaphas, are much too sensible to think that it can be done in these times of ours, and so they postpone the coming of a deliverer to the indefinite future, or even say that it applies not to this world at all but to another life succeeding this is a very sensible view to take, you will say, and so do I. But the ordinary Jew, who buys and sells or farms or fishes, sees the future differently. The more he is oppressed by barbarians, as he would say, like Greeks or Syrians, Egyptians or Romans, the more does he look forward to the coming of a deliverer, a sort of God, sent from his heaven to liberate the Jews; some of them even think that this deliverer will not only free Judaea but will conquer all the world. That is why Caiaphas spoke meaningfully to me; there's never a rascal sets himself up anywhere in these parts but a horde will gather round him and believe his story that he is sent to be their King. 'What would Caiaphas and Annas make of that?' I said to Alexander. He never stirred a muscle. 'It is doubtful,' he said, 'how far the deliverer would require the services of a High Priest any more than of a Roman Governor. Annas and Caiaphas undoubtedly believe that the deliverer will come some day. They must believe no less, but they will be very slow to admit that he has actually come; the common people believe that he may come now and they may decide at any moment that he has arrived.'

Is it not a comic idea that this paltry little race, that has been overrun by half a dozen conquerors, carried into slavery, and scattered about the earth, believes that it is chosen out of all others and that its God, who has never been able to prevent its misfortunes, will send some one to overthrow Caesar and Rome? You would think that when they see we only keep 4,000 soldiers here they would know how weak and contemptible they really are, but I suspect that, though Caiaphas knows better, many of them think that those 4,000 are all that Rome has got. In any case, if you can rely on a God to perform all sorts of miracles, it does not matter how many soldiers are on the other side. I fear that some day they will require a lesson.

If you have the chance I beg you to commend me to Lucius Aelius Sejanus. Pray tell him that I am contemplating making some new roads in this country and that I shall ask permission to call the first of them by his name. I shall write to him myself later. I had hoped to send him a present of the wine of the country, but oh, my dear friend, it is like vinegar. No wonder the Greeks here do a roaring trade in noble Chian and our warm Falernian.

DECISION TO VISIT JERUSALEM
Caesarea

I have decided to go up to Jerusalem shortly. Here I see next to nothing of my Jews. Caesarea is full of Greeks, Syrians, Phoenicians, Egyptians, and all that sort of rabble. There are many Jews, it is true, but they are of the common sort, such as traders, moneylenders and the like. The men who count are at Jerusalem, and it might be thousands of miles away, though it is just up in the hills. Caiaphas is careful to keep in touch with me, but so far as most of them are concerned I might not exist at all. I am going up, therefore, to make the acquaintance of Annas and his friends.

Besides, I want to see their head-quarters: the nest in which they harbour their seditions, if any there be; the stronghold which, according to Marcius, will give even Rome no little trouble if ever they should defy us. I must take a look at the defenses and consider how my little garrison will be situated if there should be a rising. The roads, too, and the water-supply and such are things which are always bad until the Romans take them in hand. Also I am curious to see their Temple, though I suppose they will hardly let me take a look at it, and I must find out where they keep the Temple-money, if only to protect it against robbers. You need not suspect me; I shall not emulate Crassus or Sabinus,(both plundered the Temple treasury) but you know that if anyone raided their treasury I would get the blame. I assure you I am ready to get on with them, but I must find out what sort of people they are and what they are doing. Here in Caesarea I feel that I am cut off from my own province, and I remain uneasy, though the chief of my intelligence section reports that all is quiet and no sign of trouble brewing. He, by the way, is a Graecized Samaritan, Joseph by name. Most of his family lost lands and life at the hands of Herod. He hates Herod's sons and he hates the Jews, so he is a useful servant to us. I hope to go to Jerusalem in three weeks' time.

The Games went off very well. The Gauls and Britons fought magnificently. The crowd were so delighted that they insisted on them fighting again and again with new antagonists until almost all were killed. The contest between the lions and the Idumaeans was not so successful; the lions separated the Idumaeans, so it was soon over. One of the Idumaeans fought splendidly and I would have liked to save him, but the lions were too quick.

There was one curious episode which illustrates the obstinacy of these Jews. There were four of them in prison here condemned to death for highway robbery. I offered to let them fight against a tiger, the conditions being that they should be armed with any sort of wooden weapons that they liked to choose or make, but that they should first do public homage to the bust of Caesar in the arena. They were quite willing to fight and they were fine strong men, all of them, but they refused to sacrifice to Caesar. I told them they would be thrown to the tiger as they were, and they laughed at me. So thrown they were, and now Alexander, with a glum face, warns me that the Jews have some religious objection (apart from the personal one) to having their bodies torn by animals. They have so many religious objections. Postscriptum.

I have opened this letter to inform you that Alexander, supported by Marcius, Joseph and every one else, now tells me that I cannot go up to Jerusalem on the day which I had fixed, because it is the Sabbath of the Jews. It would give deep offence, they say; it would be taken as a deliberate provocation; there would be mourning and protests and perhaps rioting. 'Rioting on the Sabbath!' I said. 'Surely not!' But I suppose they might make an exception to do a little rioting. Of course, I had to give way; I could tell that at once from Marcius's face. The Sabbath is incredible sacred to them, he says; they will neither do nor tolerate labor of any kind; you must not do this, you must not do the other; it seems to me there is scarcely anything you can do. I wonder, does their sacred river Jordan flow on the Sabbath or does it take a rest? I asked Marcius the question. 'There are some of them,' he replied, 'who will not eat an egg if it is laid on the Sabbath.' 'if you have a wooden leg,' I asked, 'can you walk it out with you upon the Sabbath?' Nothing disturbs my Marcius. 'I believe,' he answered, 'that their learned men are divided on that subject.' I could hardly contain myself. 'Of course,' I said, 'on the Sabbath they do not perform the functions of Nature?' Alexander intervened. 'You are quite right,' he said, looking at me with admiration. 'Some of them do not.' (The ascetics of the Essene sect.) I was a little puzzled. 'But supposing… ' I said, and then we were interrupted and the subject dropped.

You had better write me another of your admirable essays on the virtue of toleration and the equality of man, for I assure you I am at present in great need of it.

DIFFICULTIES IN VISITING JERUSALEM

Caesarea

I could burst with indignation. Everything is ready for the journey to Jerusalem and this morning I have discussed with Marcius the last touches. 'Anything else that you can think of?' I inquired. I felt brisk, full of a lively expectation about Jerusalem, and almost amiable towards my Jews. 'Of course,' he said, 'we do not take the images on the standards.'

(Note: The standards of the Roman soldiers frequently had fixed to them medallions bearing images of the Emperors.)

I protest that I showed no astonishment; I am learning not to be astonished in this country. Then, 'Why not?' I said. 'When we take the standards to Jerusalem,' he repeated, 'we always leave the images behind.' 'Not on this occasion, I think,' said I, 'whatever Valerius Gratus may have been weak enough to do.' He did not turn a hair. 'Every Procurator since Caesar took over the country has left the images behind,' he asserted, 'otherwise the Jews would be deeply offended.'

I assure you, my blood boiled. 'Do you mean to tell me,' I asked, 'that when the Roman Governor makes his formal entry into the chief city of the Jews, he is to omit from the standards of his troops the images of the Imperator Tiberius Caesar, whom may the gods preserve, and of Augustus Caesar Imperator, his great predecessor?' 'I do,' he said. 'It is the accepted policy and I beg you to follow it. The Jews will not tolerate the image of any god or emperor in Jerusalem: neither statues nor medallions on the standards nor images on coins. You know yourself that although the silver coins minted in Italy that reach this country bear Caesar's image. That cannot be avoided. The copper coins that are minted in Judaea itself have not his image on them. So, too, with the standards.' He looked me in the face. 'It is Caesar's will that their religion not be offended. They have no image of their god. In the depths of their Temple in Jerusalem is a little chamber which is inhabited by their god, but it is empty; there is nothing in it.'

'Caesar would not object,' I said, 'if I took his image into Jerusalem, and nothing happened. He would be pleased to think that I was breaking down the hostility of these Jews to him and Rome and all the outside world.'

'If there is a tumult,' Marcius said, 'and an attack on the troops in the narrow streets of Jerusalem, I cannot answer for the consequences. Would Caesar be pleased then?'

Straight talking, as you see. Alexander was there and I looked at him from time to time, but the little Jew had the good sense to keep his mouth shut. At the finish, I have had to give way. What else could I do? I cannot risk a tumult and a rising so early in my term of office, with so few troops available and the certainty that I should be condemned for failure, though if I were successful all Rome would praise my 'firmness.'

But it goes against the grain. To enter Jerusalem before the eyes of these arrogant priests and their surly people, as though we were on sufferance! It is the same everywhere. What do the Britons think when they see that we stop short at their island? What do these Jews think when they see that we choose rather to humiliate Caesar than offend them? They will take toleration for weakness and caution for timidity. And it will do no good. Evil will come of it. Mark me, we shall have our work to do over again and in the end we shall have to do it thoroughly. At present I must yield. I would offend the Jews cheerfully, but I cannot afford to cross Caesar or Sejanus.

Procula goes with me. She has long ago exhausted Caesarea; she insists that it is time she saw something truly Jewish. I tell her that at all events, when we go up without the images, she will be seeing something that is truly un-Roman.

RECEPTION AT JERUSALEM

Jerusalem

We have been here a week and it seems like a year. It is as though we were in a different country. I felt it immediately as we came up from the coast. Caesarea, after all, is bustling and cheerful, with a friendly face towards one. Here, as we marched up and up into these bleak hills, which stretch away north and south as far as the eye can see, I felt like an invader entering for the first time a hostile land. All the way along we saw groups of people from the farms and scattered hamlets watching us silently. It was the same when we entered Jerusalem. There was no welcome at the gates nor in the street. Not a shout nor a salute; no sign even of Caiaphas nor of any of the high-priestly caste. Crowds enough in the streets, for the place is like a rabbit-warren, but all of them glum and silent, as though they had been given the order, or sneering at us if they thought that they had caught our eye. The place is a volcano, and if I had more troops, and Caesar permitted, I would not mind if the explosion came. Marcius says that it will not come, at least, not yet. The high priests, he asserts - and by that he means the little ring of families from whom the high priest is always chosen - will have as little to do with me as possible, but they have things well in hand. And I will have them well in hand before I finish, and so I have told Marcius. He warns me to expect no friendliness from the priests or people. To all of them alike we are aliens and usurpers, to be regarded with coldness and suspicion until their god thinks fit to remove us from their necks.

This is a wretched city. Except for the great Herod's works there is scarcely a single building worth a glance. Whatever pride and taste they possess they have put into their Temple. The streets are narrow and ill-paved. Their drains and water-supply are disgraceful even for Asia; it is no wonder that they suffer from all kinds of disease. I shall have to see about this.

The hand of Herod is evident everywhere. How that man must have despised and laughed at the Jews! On one day he would humor them and on the next strike them in the face - or, more likely, do both things almost together. He built them a Temple which is one of the wonders of the world and they are proud of it, as well they may be, and at the same time he built a theatre in the City and an amphitheatre outside it. And of what use was that, you say, since they so much resent the introduction of such wicked spectacles? I think that is just what must have delighted Herod. Their priests and all their stricter folk denounced him and his evil works, but many of the common people flocked to the spectacles. What people could resist the temptation? So Herod, in the eyes of the good Jew, was a corrupter of the people, more subtle and more dangerous than the mere persecutor.

It goes without saying that Herod built a palace too. It was an enormous affair which is also a fortress. It gave him an additional grip on the City. Whatever else he did, he never forgot the necessity of securing himself against his people. The whole country is dotted with his fortresses. I do not live in the palace; something more modest is enough for my pretensions. Besides, I like to have my soldiers near me. I live in the Antonia, the citadel which is close to and overlooks the Temple. I have the troops there and can keep a keen eye on the Temple, for if there is trouble afoot, especially at the time of the great Festivals, it is in the Temple that sooner or later it will show itself. You cannot imagine the eagerness of the Jews to fight each other. They are as full of factions as the Greeks, and you know what that means. A few of them favor the family of Herod; the chief priests, as I have told you, think it well to make the best of us Romans; the fanatics and agitators of the common people look askance at them both. Then the country people are always coming up from over Jordan or from Galilee and the inhabitants of the City are quick to make trouble with them, not to mention the Samaritans, with whom any good Jew is ready to pick a quarrel.

The Temple is astonishing. There cannot be its like in the world. It is a city in itself, and the priests and servants attached to it must number thousands. There are enormous colonnades and courts, one after another. Foreigners may go into the outer court, and then there is a barrier, and if any foreigner goes through and is detected, he suffers the death penalty. Even our own soldiers are executed by us if they transgress the barrier. Then there is another court which marks the limit for women and another for men, and so on to the priests' courts and the great altar of sacrifice and the inmost chamber of all - the empty one - which no one enters but the High Priest, and he only once a year. The quantity of sacrifices made by private persons is amazing, and the part of the outer court where the offerings are bought and sold is just like a great fair. The priests get part of all the offerings, and, to make sure of their income, they insist that no one shall offer sacrifice except in Jerusalem and in the Temple itself. And then there are the presents from rich Jews and the tribute-money from rich and poor alike. The Treasury is concealed somewhere in the depths of the Temple, but I don't know where precisely.

You will ask me how I have been received since I first entered the City. Not well. They ask for trouble. I had invited all their chief men to meet me at the Antonia on the morning after my arrival. There was no reply, but they came. I had been told by Alexander that I had better receive them in the outer court, as some of them would have scruples about entering the actual building. I even offered to give them food and wine - not wine of the country, but real wine - before they left, but, of course, Alexander replied that that was impossible; they would not accept it; besides, it was the day before or the day after some festival or other, and that made them stricter than ever about meeting those whom they call the heathen. In this, as in everything, I gave way. You cannot say that I am not patient with them.

There was a great crowd when they came. I expect that most of them were as curious to see me as I to see them. All the Sanhedrim were there, some seventy of them. This is the body that rules the Jews, under our authority; their chief priests, officials and most distinguished lawyers and philosophers compose it. I greeted Caiaphas and he presented the leaders to me; among them Annas and one or two who had held the office of High Priest, the Captain of the Temple Guard, the chief of the Treasury and a few more. Annas had his sons there, a whole row of them. One of them has already been High Priest, and no doubt the others expect to be. The old man, I should say, is worth the lot of them.

(Note: Five sons of Annas held the office. Eleazar had been High Priest about A.D. 16-17. Jonathan became High Priest in A.D. 36-37 and was later assassinated at the instance of the Procurator Felix. Theophilos was High Priest after Jonathan, and Matthias a few years later. Annas the younger became High Priest for a few months in A.D. 62, and was murdered by the populace.)

He has a hawk's face, with thin lips (for a Jew), and every now and then, when he is moved, a spark of fire in his eyes. I do not know whether it is cunning or inclination that decides his policy, but, although he is one of the heads of the priestly nobles who work with us and are almost all of the faction called Sadducees, he seeks the support and applause of the other faction, the Pharisees, who are all for the *utmost observance of the Jewish law and for as much opposition as is practicable to Greeks and Romans and any other foreigners. Now observe what happened. The leading Sadducees have seats on the Sanhedrim, but the majority of its members are Pharisees, who regard the Sadducees with suspicion and disapproval as temporizers in religion and (therefore) in politics. All were listening to hear what I would say and what the noble Sadducees would say to me. After the presentations, I began by saying to Caiaphas that I was sorry that they had not thought fit to greet me at my entry into the City. I spoke in Greek because that, as you know, is the language of the educated throughout the East. Before Caiaphas could reply Annas said something sharply in a foreign tongue and there was a little movement of applause among some of them. Caiaphas said hurriedly that it was a matter of custom and that the Roman Governor had never, so far, demanded a formal welcome on entering Jerusalem.*

I am becoming, I really think, a miracle of self-control. I did not ask what Annas had said, but I discovered afterwards that he had said in Aramaic, which they use among themselves, that it was surely enough that they should consent to come to me at all. I turned to them, however, and said - again in Greek - that I hoped the indisposition was better which had prevented him from coming to welcome me at Caesarea. He smiled slightly and replied, again in Aramaic - an insulting thing to do - and there was a general laugh. I made Alexander translate for me this time. It appeared that the insolent fellow had said that his indisposition was better but might return at any moment. However, I know how to deal with such gentry and I addressed them in Latin, to teach them their place, and ordered Alexander to translate into Greek. I told them roundly that I was displeased with my reception in Caesarea, and, still more, in Jerusalem, but that they should have no reason to complain of me so long as their conduct was sincerely loyal. They listened sourly and then Caiaphas said hastily that they knew their duty to Caesar and to Rome. I asked if they had any request to make of me, and he replied that it would make for good feeling and contentment if I would restore the High Priest's vestments to their keeping. That, I replied, as at Alexandria, was a matter for Caesar, and it would depend entirely on their conduct whether I could make any recommendation. Then I went on to say that I had greatly admired what I had seen of the Temple and I desired to inspect it; perhaps some of them would show me its wonders on the following day. Caiaphas assented. I suggested that those who had been High Priests should accompany us. They all looked at Annas. He bowed gravely. 'To the outer court!' he said, this time in Greek. Really, the man is intolerable. 'I know that,' I said. 'Have we not set up inscriptions both in Greek and in Latin forbidding strangers to pass beyond the outer court?' Then I could not resist temptation. 'Yet I have heard,' I added, 'that one of my predecessors visited even the inmost chamber.' You remember that when Cneius Pompeius took Jerusalem in the course of his Eastern conquests he penetrated to the most sacred chamber - an act of desecration which they have never forgiven. You should have seen their faces. A murmur of horror and anger broke from them; some of them spat upon the floor; some of them took a step towards me. Annas stepped forward, but I did not give him time to speak. 'I have no intention myself,' I said, 'to go beyond the outer court, just as I have confidence that you will continue to perform the daily sacrifice in honor of Caesar and of Rome.' That quieted them, for it was a reminder that, tolerant as we are, we do exact from them a daily symbol of submission.

(Note: Pompeius the Great, who entered the Holy of Holies in 63 B.C.)

Finally, I told them that I would expect them to report to me promptly any agitator among the common people who might threaten trouble. I need not, I said, particularize the kind of trouble that I meant; they knew well enough what happened when some robber or fanatic, half crazy about religion or the liberty of his country, began to set up himself as a leader and collect a following. I relied on them for loyal support. With this I dismissed them.

I shall spend a fortnight here and then make a round of inspection before I return to Caesarea. I must see the country-people. I believe they have not the slightest understanding of the power and importance of Rome - a most dangerous form of ignorance. I shall be glad to get away, but Procula will be sorry to leave Jerusalem. She finds everything picturesque, and, besides, their religion and their Temple-worship attract her. It is curious how these Eastern religions fascinate the women. If it is not Egyptian, it is the Jewish brand; the greater the mystery and hocus-pocus, the readier they are to submit themselves to the priests. Procula visits the outer court and questions Alexander about their wonderful inmost empty chamber. I tell her that some day she will forget and pass through the barrier. Then it will be my unpleasant duty to have her executed.

By the way, I have two questions for you. How many synagogues are there in Jerusalem? Fifty, do you say? There are nearly five hundred. And who discovered the alphabet? The ancient Egyptians or the Assyrians, you reply. No, it was Abraham, the ancestor of the Jews. You do not believe it? What presumption! Neither do I, but the Jews do, or pretend to. Everything good must have come out of the Jews. I do not know, but I expect they claim the discovery of fire and the cartwheel. It is a consolation that at least we have the credit for the good Roman sword.

Your equable and tolerant mind will not, I fear, approve the tone of this letter. I freely confess that Jerusalem does not improve my temper.

FIRST MENTION OF JOHN THE BAPTIST

Caesarea

I thank you for your letters and especially for your zeal in defending my interests against Pomponius Rufus. I warned him long ago that his new house, if built to that height, would interfere with my rights of light. The sly rascal has waited long enough to carry out his plans. Let him discover in the courts, my friend, how staunch a champion and how eloquent a counsel I possess in you.

I heard last week that an itinerant preacher had turned up in the hill-country south of Jerusalem. His name is John. As it appeared that he was causing a certain amount of excitement, and might cause more, I sent Joseph to Jerusalem on a mission of inquiry. I have given him authority, if he thinks it necessary, to seek out personally the source of the ferment and report what it amounts to. It may be nothing, but I ought to know.

FURTHER NEWS OF JOHN

Caesarea

I have heard from Joseph. He says that the matter may be serious, and after gathering such information as is available in Jerusalem, he has gone off into the mountains to hear for himself what the preacher John is saying. I wish him joy of the expedition. It is about as disagreeable a region as there is in the whole of my dominion - bleak and barren mountains, seamed with deep ravines and watercourses, which lead down steeply to the valley of the Jordan and the Dead Sea. It is chiefly inhabited, so far as I can ascertain, by ill-omened birds, wild beasts, lepers and half-mad hermits such as this John seems to be. In Joseph's absence, I have been examining the reports of our spies in other parts of the country. It appears that John's fame is spreading and the common people are beginning to talk about him. Some of them are setting off in high expectation for the scene of the preaching. I shall be glad to have Joseph's report. This is my first experience of this sort of agitation and I shall deal firmly with it.

One more word about Pomponius. Spare no expense. What is important is not so much that my rights of light should be protected as that Pomponius should be shown to be a rascal.

EYE-WITNESS'S REPORT ON JOHN

Caesarea

What I hear from Rome makes me almost glad to be a mere Procurator. A mutual friend of ours - I had better not mention names - writes to me that Sejanus not only is ambitious of marrying into the family of Caesar, but that at the same time he speaks slightingly of Caesar himself. 'Monarch of an islet,' he called him the other day - had you heard that? I scarcely dare write the words. If these things get to Caesar's ears, I shall be glad that I did not owe my appointment to the favor of Sejanus.

Joseph is back at last and I have been in consultation with him and Alexander. He had some difficulty tracking the preacher down. He had to go up-hill and down-dale in all sorts of weather, and was regarded with an unfriendly eye by the Jews who were also on the road. There are many of them on the road, too: most of them from Judaea, but a good many from Antipas's territory on the other side of Jordan, and some from Samaria and even Galilee. When he did discover John - the fellow moves from village to village all the time - do you know what he found? One of Antipas's officers, who was watching John on behalf of his master. The talk was that John would soon be leaving my territory and crossing over Jordan to that of Antipas. I don't know whether I shall give him the chance.

This may be a very serious matter. John is just one of those people of whom I have been warned. According to Joseph's report he is 'half-clad, half-starved and half-crazy,' but that does not matter with these Jews. It is what he says that counts, or rather, perhaps, what they choose to think he means. He is telling them that the great time, the new era, which they all expect, is coming, and for them that only means one thing: no more Herods, no more Romans, no more Governors, troops or taxes. The idea of liberty, of independence, of the revival of the glorious days which they enjoyed under their old kings - it's that which draws them from all over the country. Joseph declares that John has only to announce that he is the expected leader and the whole countryside will be on fire. He makes no pretence, so Joseph says, that he is himself a leader, but he is doing what is almost as bad: he tells them that a leader is coming, and that soon, which is just what they are looking for. I have questioned Alexander about this and he is wise and mysterious. I asked him whether this leader was the same as the deliverer or Messiah that Caiaphas had spoken of. He says no; that before the deliverer there must come, according to their sacred writings, an advance-guard or messenger or prophet - whatever you like to call him - and that when this person arrives then all the people will know that the deliverer himself is to come next.

You will see that from the standpoint of the Roman Governor it is all the same thing. John predicts the imminence of a new prophet; the appearance of the prophet will be followed by that of the deliverer, and then Caesar and Rome will make way for the new age. It is, you will agree, impossible that such fantastic but pernicious ideas should be allowed to spread among the people. You cannot imagine the expectancy that there is everywhere in the air here. Every one is waiting, waiting, for things that are to happen. I have the conviction that the best place for people like John is prison, and that is where I propose shortly to put him.

I have written to Caiaphas asking what he and the Sanhedrim have to say about it and informing him of what I intend. They ought to have reported to me before now.

I must not forget to tell you an amusing thing about John. He is telling the Jews that, in order to make themselves worthy of the great days that are coming, they must humble themselves for the wicked lives which they have led. This tickles me, as it would do you if you knew the Jews. Most of them do not relish this part of the doctrine at all. In their own opinion they have nothing to be humble about; nor ever have had. The new age is all very well, but its business is to set the Jews above all other peoples. Humiliation is proper to Greeks, Romans and such-like. I would like to know what my friend Annas thinks about humbling himself at the bidding of a ragged preacher escaped out of a cave! But I know already. The priests are used to the like of John. There is a whole sect of fanatics of his breed in this country - a good many of them in the very region that he comes from - who live severe lives and despise the easy-going priesthood at Jerusalem. Annas and Caiaphas would give him short shrift (confession / absolution), I am sure, especially if he showed signs of becoming really popular. It is all very well for their God to produce a new age, but the High Priests certainly expect to be consulted first.

This seems to me an opportunity to assert myself. I shall wait for a letter from Caiaphas, but whatever he says, I now intend to strengthen the garrison at Jerusalem. I hope for your approval.

THE IMAGES OF THE CAESARS

Caesarea

I have heard from Caiaphas about John. He sends me an official answer which is most discreetly framed. You might like the text of it. It says:

'The Sanhedrim, having sent representatives to question John the son of Zacharias and having satisfied itself that he does not claim to be either the Messiah of the Jews or one of the Prophets, is of the opinion that he has committed no offence under the Law which would justify it in putting him on his trial. At the same time it recognizes that the civil power may reasonably take a wider view of the consequences which might follow an extension of his teaching.' Caiaphas sent a private note by the messenger. He has no objection to my taking

measures if I think them necessary. I am sure that at heart he and his friends hope I will. You see the game. John may easily become an embarrassment to them, even if he is not so already. They would like him out of the way, but it would suit them better for me to remove him than that they should bear the odium themselves. Upon my word, I would not oblige them but that I have thought of a new measure for teaching both them, and the common people, who is their master here. I told you that I had decided to send up more troops to Jerusalem in case this affair of John should cause disturbances. I have made up my mind that the new troops shall this time carry the Imperial images on the standards when they enter Jerusalem. 'What madness!' I hear you say, and at once you conjure up visions of riot, tumult and open war. But listen. You do not give your Pilate sufficient credit for sagacity. Do you think that only Jews are cunning? My troops will enter Jerusalem in the dead of night. In the morning, when the Jews awake, go about their business, throng into the Temple, they will see the standards, with the images prominently displayed upon them, already established on the ramparts of the Antonia. They will storm the Antonia, you say? Tell that to the Marines. But, if they did attempt it, what a story I should have to send to Rome! The tiresome, treacherous Jews making a direct attack upon Caesar's images and the standards of the legions after I had so far respected their scruples as to send the troops in under cover of the dark! What would our patriotic Roman mob say to that story? Why, I should be a hero for a day and have the Syrian legions placed at my disposal. But do not fear. When Jerusalem hears that the talker John is to be arrested and sees the Roman eagles in its midst, it will think twice before openly resisting. Caiaphas will be shocked at my imprudence, but it is time they understood that they are part of the Roman State, and I have given Marcius his orders.

I am sending you some Syrian pottery. I hope your slaves are more careful than mine. I have told mine that the next one who damages a valuable vase or statue will figure at the Games, and not as a spectator.

THE ROMAN'S BURDEN

Caesarea

Commend me, my friend, for a good Roman. I too am carrying the blessings of Italy to the benighted East. I have brought two surveyors, one from Alexandria and one from Antioch. I have instructed them to present plans to me for remaking certain roads, for constructing baths at Samaria, and for leading a good supply of water to Jerusalem from the springs south of the City. I shall get no thanks for this, but where or when does the Roman receive gratitude for the benefits which he brings to the Eastern peoples? They live like pigs and when he raises them from their filthy state they only complain that he sweats money out of them to pay for public works which he wants and not they. Was it not Caesar Augustus - or was it the great Julius - who called this the Roman's burden, which, whatever his inclinations, he cannot avoid?

Would you believe that at Samaria there are no baths, although our officers, both military and civil, go up there in the hot weather for their health? As to the roads, I propose to reconstruct that which runs along the coast and the two which run into Jerusalem from the north and the east. Our troops will move much more quickly, and so of course will trade and the pilgrim traffic, which will help my revenues. As to the water-supply, it will be a pure benefaction to Jerusalem for which they ought to set me up a statue. Yet, do you know, the only question that interests them at all is, who is to pay for it. How in the world they survive at all under present conditions at the time of their great festivals I cannot understand. Normally, perhaps, Jerusalem has some 50,000 inhabitants, and there are only a few wells of water to supply them all. But at the time of the Passover the pilgrims arrive by tens of thousands. No one knows the exact total, but some say that there are half a million people crowded into Jerusalem and the surrounding villages. Jerusalem itself is packed out; they sleep on the roofs and even in the streets, and they flock in droves each morning from the surrounding country. Where do they all get their water from for drinking and for their ceremonial washings? I cannot tell you, unless perhaps their god Yahweh provides it by a miracle or the festival counts as a continuous Sabbath and they must not drink at all. However, water they shall have, both clean and plentiful, whether they like it or not, and pay for it they must according to the custom of the Roman provinces.

The troops have gone, with Marcius in command. They carry the images of three Caesars - Tiberius himself, Augustus and Julius. They will be in the Antonia before dawn tomorrow. I addressed the men personally. I told them that the name of Rome and the Caesars was in their charge and that they must protect it, but that on their side there must be no provocation.

I have told Marcius to send a troop, arrest John and dispatch him to me at Caesarea. I must do this in any case, since if Antipas knows, as he does, that disaffection is being stirred up on my side of the border, he will make the most of it.

CONFLICT WITH THE JEWS

Caesarea

Now I have news for you. I have had the most exciting week of my life. Truly I have put the fat in the fire. Jerusalem is in an uproar, the hubbub spread throughout the country, and here in Caesarea I am beset by a multitude of angry Jews.

At the first all went well. The troops reached the Antonia while it was still dark and the standards were erected on the battlements. They could be seen from some parts of the Temple. I must tell you that with the earliest dawn the priests begin their preparations for the morning sacrifice and soon the crowd of worshippers assembles. (A good custom, since it makes the people get up early.) It was barely daylight when some one discovered the images on the standard-poles. They have the eyes of hawks where we are concerned. At once there was an outcry. Some of them rushed to the Antonia, others to the priests, others back into the town to spread the news. Caiaphas was round at the Antonia in no time and begged Marcius at any rate to remove the standards from the public view. Marcius politely said no and referred him to me. Caiaphas said he would have to take a strong line; he had already summoned the Sanhedrim; they would complain not only to me but to Rome and would tell the people so, but that he was doubtful whether the mob could be restrained from an actual attack upon the citadel. Marcius did not budge and Caiaphas was at his wits' end what to do. Meanwhile, all Jerusalem gathered in the Temple, and round the Antonia. They threatened not only us but the Sanhedrim as well. Many of them carried clubs and stones, and when Caiaphas emerged from the offices of the Sanhedrim to address them they menaced him violently, accusing the Sanhedrim of having brought this 'insult' on their religion by its tolerance of us and demanding that it should at once secure its removal. Caiaphas replied that the Sanhedrim would do its utmost, but there must be no violence; they would at once send a powerful deputation to me at Caesarea and, if I did not yield, they would forthwith appeal to Caesar and ask for my removal. He added that if any of the crowd chose to accompany the deputation they could do so; they could help to prove to me how deeply moved they were by this act of sacrilege, but they would only do serious injury to their religion and their country by an uproar in Jerusalem. Caiaphas is a shrewd man. He provided them with an outlet for their anger and himself with the means (as he hoped) of intimidating me.

Taking him at his word, they have come to Caesarea. Yes, my dear Seneca, they left their work and their religion and set off to walk, thousands and thousands of them, to me at Caesarea. They came not only from Jerusalem but from a hundred towns and villages; everywhere, as the news spread, they set off for Caesarea. When I heard what was happening I went up on the roof of the palace - this was four days ago - and the roads were black with them as far as the eye could see. They were marching steadily like men with a purpose, as people do in Rome when they are going to the Games. All ages were there, from greybeards down to boys. Their most learned Rabbis came, each with a following of pupils and admirers. A crowd of priests from the Temple escorted the deputation, which was led by Caiaphas and Annas. When the deputation entered the palace there was a tremendous scene of enthusiasm among them. The rest of the population looks on sourly. With a little more provocation, there would be a massacre.

I rather enjoyed the conversation with the priests. Caiaphas was dignified, Annas truculent, and his son Eleazar (formerly High Priest) noisy. But one and all they are anxious to get out of a hole. They are afraid of the mob and still more afraid of their enemies in Jerusalem who are busy undermining their position, calling them pro-Romans, 'abettors of idolatry' (the crime of crimes in the eyes of a good Jew), traitors and the like. You can readily imagine the arguments. On their side, no Procurator had ever done such a thing before; Caesar would disapprove of it; Caesar had always been considerate; neither I, nor Caesar - especially Caesar - could desire riot and open revolt, which were to be expected if I did not cancel my order. On my part, the presence of the images was an ordinary sign of the Roman authority; it was much less offensive than the daily sacrifice which already they performed to Caesar and to Rome; I had gone out of my way to spare their feelings by sending the troops in under cover of the night; to withdraw the images now would be an unprecedented humiliation of Caesar and to withdraw them in the face of threats would be a signal proof of weakness.

Since this meeting they have been here several times, both publicly and privately, and at intervals they harangue the crowd. I have told Caiaphas that he must order his people to go back home, but he says that the most he can do is to keep them quiet by promising to give me no peace until he has persuaded me. Their numbers, so far from diminishing, increase steadily. A great many people come in from curiosity, but all kinds of wild fanatics are arriving from distant parts and making violent speeches. I don't know how they all subsist, but I suppose a good quarrel over religion is meat and drink to them.

The situation cannot last, but I confess I find it a little difficult to deal with. I could disperse them by force, but I do not want bloodshed; all the people at Rome who are for peace and quietness (and who don't in the least understand the difficulties of provincial governors) would be up in arms against me. On the other hand, I ought not to yield. I dearly want to teach these Jews a lesson. Besides, it is really important, as a matter of policy, to break down their exclusiveness, and I have made a beginning. So far from Roman rule being genuinely accepted here, there is a slow but steady movement against it and against the priests who tolerate it. Unless we begin to break their obstinacy we shall, before long, have to re-conquer Judaea. If I could only rely on proper support at home, but there – I know that when I talk with hand on sword-hilt I must not expect too much sympathy from you.

I wish you had the job yourself for a few months.

I will let you know the upshot.

DEFEAT OF PILATE

Caesarea

I thank Jove that the place is clear of Jews again. The last of their rag-tag-and-bobtail is disappearing into the mountains, and I write to you, my dear Seneca, in haste to tell you what has happened. I shall be quite frank with you, for the truth is that I may need the help of you and of my other friends. I am glad that Caesar himself is not in Rome, for I cannot conceal from myself that the facts might be misrepresented to him. No, I said I would be frank with you; I should be afraid that the facts might be reported to him truly.

After four days the Jews showed no signs of weakening. They stood and sat and slept and said their prayers all round the Palace and in the adjoining streets and squares. Especially they said their prayers. Marcius wrote to me that everything in Jerusalem was at a standstill and that he was passively besieged in the Antonia. Joseph reported that the Sanhedrim had sent envoys to Herod Antipas, his brother and the Governor of Syria begging them to intervene with me on the ground that a serious outbreak in Judaea would have an unpleasant repercussion in their territories. The priests had also chosen the mission which they would, if need be, send to Rome. I determined to use a direct threat of military force. I announced that on the next day - the sixth day of these proceedings - the Jews were to assemble in the market-place early in the morning and I would address them personally. At the same time I ordered all the available troops to be concealed in the surrounding buildings. At the conclusion of my speech they were to pour out and advance upon the Jews.

The market-place is an open space which will hold twenty thousand people, and it was packed. The din, when I arrived, was indescribable. For ten minutes they shouted at me and at one another. They behaved like madmen. I do not know what they were saying; I doubt whether many of them knew themselves. The priests, who had made a line (to protect me, I believe) in front of the raised platform on which I sat, could not obtain silence. At last I rose, gave a signal to my officials and made as though to leave. That quieted them for a second and Caiaphas, mounting the platform, told them that the Sanhedrim had asked me to address them personally (this was not true) and that it was their duty to listen quietly. They became silent for the time.

I was polite, I was conciliatory. I told them that Caesar had always been anxious not to interfere with their religion and that I was no less disposed than other Governors to respect their scruples. But this was not religion, it was purely an administrative act to which they ought not to take exception. They could not expect to be exempt from the symbols of Roman dominion, I might almost say of Roman citizenship, which were common to the whole civilized world. At this murmurs arose. I was willing, I said, to consider any reasonable request that they might make, but first of all they must return quietly to their homes. Until that, nothing could be done. Or did they desire to enter on a conflict with the power of Rome? I ceased abruptly and gave the signal. Immediately the troops appeared on every side and, with all their weapons ready for immediate use, hemmed in the crowd.

What do you suppose they did, wisest of the wise men of Rome? Fall into panic, tremble before the Roman sword, seek to escape? They showed no signs of it. Assail the troops, plunge into the conflict with which I threatened them? Not for a moment. At first they were taken aback and made no sound or movement. Then one of their leaders in front of me cried out loudly in Aramaic and, baring his neck to the sword, knelt down before the soldier nearest to him. He had said, so I was told, that sooner would they suffer death than yield. In a flash they followed his example. Everywhere, priests and people alike, they did the same thing. They struggled among themselves to get to the front in order to present their necks to the Roman executioner and behind the lucky ones they knelt down with bared necks, row after row, thousands upon thousands, to await their turn. The position was ludicrous. I could not very well order a wholesale butchery. I had never intended to. Even had they had but one head I could not have cut it off, though it would have given me the greatest pleasure. I had failed and knew it. It took but a few seconds for me to make up my mind. I signaled to the chief priests to follow me and withdrew for consultation. Let me cut short the story of my humiliation. I announced that I was deeply impressed by their devotion to their religion (and that was true enough), but that what impressed me most was the order and calm resolution which they exhibited. Had it been otherwise, had they sought to intimidate me by violence - but you see the argument and, though you may smile, I assure you that the priests did not. They thanked me gravely and Caiaphas went out and announced my decision in almost my own words, adding that they must have confidence in me and in their priests and return quietly to their homes. Thereafter jubilation, thanksgiving and, of course, more prayers. Yahweh gets the credit for it. All day long they have been departing, singing their psalms. Let them sing while they may. But if some day they get a different sort of governor from me, if Caesar abandons his policy of patient toleration, if their wild fanatics overthrow these politic and cunning priests, if the Roman armies march - will Yahweh save them then?

I look to you and to my other friends to put the best face on it when this story reaches Rome. After all, I have but sought to compel respect for Caesar and his images have lorded it above their Temple for a week. It is a beginning, even if at the finish I have lost the throw.

Now I await the preacher John. Marcius should by now have laid him by the heels. When he is safely here in Gaul, the sword shall deal with him. If their victory over me makes them think that the new age has begun, I will at least take care that the prophet does not live to see it.

So you have been reading one of your tragedies to an admiring audience in Rome? I am sure it will be full of fine sentiments. Would I were there to listen to them. Would you were here that you might apply them to these incorrigible Jews, with me to watch the fun.

ARREST OF JOHN BY HEROD ANTIPAS
Caesarea

Marcius has returned to Caesarea bringing two pieces of information. The first is that I have become popular in Jericho, the border-city down by the river Jordan. It is a most important place, for the commerce of the lower Jordan valley passes through it and the customs-revenue is large. Some time ago complaints of gross extortion against the customs-staff were made to me. The chief collector is - was, I should say - a low-class Jew. He was robbing the merchants right and left and the proceeds were not reaching my treasury. One of his underlings, another Jew, who thought he was not getting a fair share of the spoils, betrayed him and two subordinates. It was a bad case; they had kept back some of our moneys as well as the profits of their own extortions. I tried them here in Caesarea and then sent them back to Jericho, the leader to be crucified and the other two to be scourged to death. The Jews were delighted, not only because the chief collector had robbed them but because he was a Jew whom they hated for entering our service. Now they can hate his successor, for I am going to appoint the informer to his place. I ought to be able to rely on his loyalty if he is not murdered by his countrymen. The other news is that John has escaped me. He went on one of his preaching expeditions into Antipas's country. The result was the same as with us: crowds of wretched peasants working themselves up into frenzy and wanting to know whether they could not follow his leadership. Antipas can do with talk of a new Kingdom even less than we can. If there is any trouble in his country, Roman troops will be sent in to help him, and once they are there it will be good-bye to his ridiculous little monarchy. He knows that and he was waiting for John. The preacher is safely put away now in the dungeons of Machaerus, an unpleasant, gloomy fortress in the hills east of the Dead Sea. I should say that he has seen the last of his Judaea. If Antipas has any sense he will make an end of him. It is the only safe method, believe me, with people who mix up their religion and their politics.

I am not sorry, on reflection, that Antipas has taken this business on himself. A certain amount of odium will attach to him, for John has many followers. But sometimes, when I lie awake at night, I wish that I had had the handling of John. The Jericho tax-collector is a poor substitute.

THE PROBLEM OF THE AQUEDUCT
Caesarea

I was not surprised to hear that the two Herods had lodged a complaint against me at Rome when they heard about the images. The dogs! They have the morals of the mongrel tribes from which they spring. But - thanks no doubt to you and my other friends - I have defeated them. I have received an official letter in Caesar's name (written by one of Sejanus's freedmen) commending me for getting out of a difficult situation without bloodshed and at the same time censuring my action in getting into it. The moral is that one must not fail; one should indeed think long before taking action but then go through despite all opposition.

Antipas is too busy with his schemes against me. It is many weeks now since he imprisoned John and he has just sent me a letter, a suave *piece of hypocrisy, saying that a certain John, a dangerous fanatic, had been arrested on his side of the frontier, but since the man belonged to my province and had preached disaffection for a considerable time within my border, he presumed that I would wish to deal with him myself and he was therefore ready to hand him over to me. I have replied that my officers would several times have arrested John had he not been able to take refuge in Antipas's territory and that Antipas had therefore better handle the incidents that arose on his own ground. I may have yet to face difficulties of my own, for I hear that some of John's followers are going up and down, following his example and, needless to say, declaring that their master will come back.*

It is a relief to turn to the making of roads and aqueducts. I am really happy when I see the gangs of laborers at work on the hill-roads up to Jerusalem: 'roads,' mark you, my good Seneca, not 'road,' for I am remaking both that which runs up from the coast and that which leads up from the Jordan and Jericho. 'Why bother?' you say. 'Is that not an extravagance?' No, because by those roads the materials come up for my Jerusalem aqueduct. I shall be proud of the aqueduct, I can assure you. I shall rely on it to perpetuate my name in history. I have spent more time in the hills south of Jerusalem during the last few weeks than I have spent in Caesarea. There are twenty-four miles of the roughest country imaginable to be subdued and I ride from point to point watching the men cutting through the hills, breaking up rocks, bridging ravines, laying the foundations for my reservoirs. I have drawn laborers from all the surrounding regions, from Galilee and Samaria, Trans-Jordan, Idumaea, and even from Syria, but comparatively few from Jerusalem, the place which is to benefit. The people of Jerusalem will have nothing to do with us even when we seek to help them. They have nothing but scorn for Samaritans and Galileans who take our part to bring them a good supply of water. They would sooner go without water, or have it foul, than take a Roman wage. Let me tell you a story. There is a Rabbi at Jerusalem who said that probably there were only two really good Jews in the whole world - himself and his son. Or perhaps, he added, there was but one - himself.

I am anxious over the cost of the aqueduct. The men are paid regularly, but large sums will soon be due to the contractors. They cannot come out of the ordinary taxes nor, so far as I can see, can I make a special levy which would produce the necessary amount. I have asked the Sanhedrim to make suggestions to me, but they are unhelpful. They talk and talk but they make no proposals. They say the contractors are extravagant or they admit the necessity of the aqueduct but say the work should have been postponed or they declare outright that Rome should pay for it. I will make them sing a different tune, when I have finished with them.

FIRST MENTION OF JESUS
Caesarea

The Sanhedrim are obstinate. I have told them that they must find ways and means within three months of paying for the aqueduct and roads. I have had endless conferences with their chief men. I repeat until I am weary - 'For the first time in its history Jerusalem will have good drinking-water. It is essential for the health of your great city.' They remain unmoved. One of them said loftily - 'Water for drinking is not of real importance. That is only an affair of the unclean body. What matters is provision for the soul - water for the ablutions that are ordained by our Law.' (They are always at their ceremonial washings; I have never been able to understand how people who wash so much can look so dirty.) This argument gave me a chance. 'Precisely,' I retorted, 'you require great quantities of water for your ablutions and for the temple sacrifices.' (They have, you must know, a huge bowl of water in the Temple for swilling away the blood from sacrifices.) 'The aqueduct is therefore a matter of religion as much as of health and decency and I should expect you to be prepared both to support me and to pay for the service which I am doing you.'

Then a brilliant idea came into my head. 'Since,' I added, 'the aqueduct, on your own showing, will be a great assistance to your religious exercises, why not pay for it with the Temple-money?' You would hardly believe with what fury they received this reasonable suggestion. 'Robbery' and 'sacrilege' were the weakest words they used. I protested to them that they might regard it as a loan and by imposing a levy on the population of Jerusalem and spreading it over twelve months (or longer if they chose) repay the Temple funds. They were almost beside themselves, but I stood firm and ordered them to bring the proposal before a formal meeting of the full Sanhedrim. The more I think over it, the more agreeable does this project look to me. It solves the difficulties with such simplicity.

The news in your last letter makes entertaining reading. I thought we had fallen low enough when sprigs of our ancient noble houses drove their own chariots at the Games, but I never expected to hear that a Claudius was fighting as a common gladiator before the lousy mob or a Domitius fawning as an actor on the stage. I have, I fear, no such exciting scraps of gossip for you. One of the Rabbis who was suspected of looking with favor on my aqueduct was murdered yesterday as he left his house for the Sanhedrim. Five ruffians fell on him with knives; he had over twenty wounds. There is not the smallest chance of catching the murderers, although their hiding-place will be known to many people. Reports from the frontier state that another wandering preacher, one Jesus, has turned up in Galilee; I have told Joseph to keep an eye on him. The only daughter of one of the chief priests of Jerusalem has run off with a Greek merchant. They wanted me to arrest the pair and declared that she has taken some of her father's money. He can spare it. Alas! the soldiers did not arrive at the quay till the ship was safely gone, and today I am very much in Procula's good graces.

I cannot get over my astonishment at your letter. What will Tiberius Caesar say when he hears that a Claudius has become a gladiator! (Note: The Emperor Tiberius belonged to the Claudian line, which was notorious for its arrogance. 'The pride of the Claudian family,' says Tacitus, 'was inveterate in his nature.')

DEATH OF JOHN AND QUESTIONS ABOUT JESUS
Jerusalem

I have come up to Jerusalem to settle my quarrel with the Sanhedrim and this time I mean business. They formally refuse to make any contribution from the Temple-tribute, even for a few months. They have sent me a tiresome screed (tedious writing) arguing that an aqueduct is an Imperial affair and that Caesar's treasury should pay for it. At the most they will only admit that it should be paid for out

541

of the ordinary taxation of the province, and that, they say, is already heavier than the province can bear. They are insolent enough to assert that the supply of water for the ceremonial ablutions demanded by their Law has always been sufficient and that their other needs do not justify so lavish an expenditure. I have informed them that the money must be found without delay and that I shall, if necessary, take steps to find it for them.

I have no patience with their precious Law, which hedges them (and us) at every turn with minute regulations. Some of it comes from their Sacred books but the most tedious part, so far as I can learn, is of their own creation. Their learned men have spent their lives for generations in devising the most elaborate and ridiculous religious rules. Can you believe that they have whole volumes written about their rules for washing and that there is a tome or two devoted solely to the subject of washing before meals? Have you ever heard of the Rabbi who died of thirst? He was shut up in a besieged town and had a few spoonfuls of water assigned to him each day. He used it all for ceremonial washings and died in agonies of thirst. I would like to put old Annas to that test. Or do you know the story of the pious mule? It belonged to a priest who would touch no food on which, at purchase, tithe had not been paid to the Temple. For days the mule refused its feed. Was it sick? Was it lame? Was it merely mulish? No, my dear Seneca, believe me they discovered that when its food was bought tithe had not been paid to the Temple. It would not break the Law. They are all mules in Jerusalem.

By the way, I shall not be troubled any more by John, the preacher, son of Zacharias. He is dead. I have received a formal intimation from the Governor of the castle of Machaerus. He received orders from his master Herod Antipas - dispatched from his capital, Tiberias in Galilee - to execute John as a fomenter of rebellion and to inform me of the fact. There was, I hear, a special reason for Antipas's action. You remember I told you that another agitator called Jesus had turned up in Galilee. Alexander, who knows a great deal of what is going on - and tells me because he is jealous of the worthy Joseph - says that this Jesus originally came from Galilee to visit John. He was actually in Judaea when the news spread that John had been arrested, whereupon he fled to his own country. There he is playing exactly the same game as his master. He is exhorting his fellow-countrymen to be humble (I like him for that) and talking large about the coming kingdom. Also he has set up as a wonder-worker, curing people who are sick and various madmen (they are numerous in Galilee) and of course this draws the superstitious mob. Antipas would not like it in any case, but what really disturbed him was the discovery that communications have been passing between Jesus and the followers of John. So, very wisely, he has made an end of John and is already - Joseph confirms this - inquiring about Jesus. I shall have good ground of complaint if he lets this business grow.

There is one side of it which amuses and delights me. Jesus is quarrelling with the lawyers and the priests. Anything that touches the Law or threatens their authority rouses their instant jealousy. Just as I have told the Sanhedrim that I expect them to report to me any agitation that they hear of, so I make it a point to let them know pretty briskly of any negligence I can impute to them. I informed Caiaphas of the reports concerning Jesus that were reaching me and told him that since the Sanhedrim claimed authority even in Galilee, he had better see to it. He replied at once with emphasis, saying that from what they had heard of Jesus, though it was little as yet, they disapproved of him heartily and that they were sending a deputation of learned men to Galilee to summon him for examination. In himself the man is a person of no consequence: the son of a common workman. But then, Simon, one of the rascals who gave trouble some years ago, was a slave, and Athronges, another mischief-maker, was a shepherd. It is the worst of these Jews that rank means nothing to them. They will follow any son of the soil if he can fight well, rob well, or talk well - especially if he work a few wonders into the bargain - and, before you know where you are, they will set him up for king. However, with Antipas and the Sanhedrim watching him, and with me waiting for him in Judaea, it is a poor prospect for Jesus.

In any case I cannot feel excited about anything at present except my aqueduct. It is a noble work, worthy to rank with that of Herod himself at Caesarea. Can you suggest to me how I am to get the money? My ears are wide open. But wait in patience. I have a secret; I rub my hands over it but I dare not tell it even to you. I hope, when I write next, to inform you that I have the money in my hands, and get it I will, though the Jews smart for it.

SEIZURE OF THE TEMPLE-TRIBUTE
Jerusalem

Three days ago, early in the morning, I seized the Temple-tribute. Not all of it - admire my moderation. I did not raid the treasury in the Temple itself, for that would have meant a pitched battle and casualties which I could not afford. You will excuse my diffidence, I think, when you remember the circumstances of my more fortunate exemplars: Crassus had occupied Jerusalem with a great army when on his way to Parthia, while Sabinus actually took the Temple by storm. Both my pretensions and my methods were more modest.

The Temple-tribute is brought to Jerusalem from the foreign Jewish communities about this time every year (in early spring). Egypt, Asia Minor and the Euphrates region are the largest contributors. Most of it comes in coin, but there are also the rich gifts of the pious: plate for the Temple service, jewels and ornaments, gold to be melted down. Egypt's contribution, alas! reached the Temple safely a week ago, but that from the Asiatic cities was waiting at Caesarea for an escort and that from the Euphrates (it is included a fine bar of solid gold, the gift of Ctesiphon) was under escort a few miles from Jerusalem. The Jews, I should explain, send guards of their own, but within the province the governor provides a military escort. The chest which had arrived at Caesarea I confiscated without more ado. The Jews could not resist; they went off, howling, to Jerusalem, and found on arrival that the same fate had befallen the Euphrates caravan. That required some arranging. We doubled the escort on the last night and when the caravan arrived at the neighborhood of the Temple in the early morning Marcius sallied out from the Antonia with a full cohort and literally ran the whole procession into the citadel. The sight was really comic. Our men enjoyed it thoroughly. It was all done so quickly that the Jewish guards, who included some highly dignified officials, could hardly believe their eyes when they saw the gates of the Antonia shut behind them and my men methodically counting and carrying off the chests. One or two were foolish enough to offer resistance but we soon cured that. No bloodshed, but they had some bruises to show their countrymen.

The uproar over the images in my first year - you remember that regrettable incident? - was nothing compared with what happened now. All Jerusalem turned out within an hour. They shouted and screamed, they threatened to tear down the aqueduct, they beat on the walls of the Antonia with their fists. The priests packed themselves in a dense mass round the Temple-treasury lest that also should be attacked by me. The loss of money touches them on the raw. I was not minded, this time, to let them demonstrate for days. I had dressed up a large part of my soldiers in ordinary clothes, beneath which their arms were hidden. Some I slipped out of the Antonia before daybreak. Another large contingent was concealed in Herod's palace. They were all Samaritans and Idumaeans, so that they could disguise themselves easily without fear of recognition. There were about a thousand of them. They gathered on the outskirts of the crowd and took part in the shouting. From what I know of some of them I should say that they did all they could to stimulate the mob. In the afternoon I came out on the tower above the gateway. I announced that the money would be used by me for their benefit in the way that I thought fit. I then ordered them to disperse. Redoubled tumult; threats against the sacrilegious governor, curses, and even stones. A trumpet blew, and my fine fellows, disclosing their weapons, fell upon the mob. The cry of rage and terror that went up might have been heard at Rome. The crowd fled pell-mell, but the crush was so great that many could not escape into the narrow streets and the arms of the soldiers were weary with striking. I have no idea how many were killed, for the dead were carried off quickly by their friends, but the number is large. Everything has been quiet since. I ought to tell you that I strictly forbade my men to pursue the crowd into the Temple and the order was obeyed. I have seen nothing of Annas and Caiaphas, not because they did not come but because I refused to have anything to say to them. They are sending the usual deputation to Rome, but I am not nervous about the result. The principal contractors, whom I have already paid with the Temple-money, are good friends of Sejanus and they have no doubt that with a judicious expenditure among his freed-men all will be well.

So I am satisfied. The aqueduct will shortly be finished and there is money and to spare to pay for it. I have settled some of my accounts with the Jews and especially with their religion-mongering priests. They have had a sharp lesson - let us hope that they will profit by it. Yet I fear that the tone of this letter will not be pleasing to you, my dear Seneca. I will therefore make a suggestion. You complained bitterly of Rome in your last letter to me: of the noise, the exorbitant rents, the dearness and badness of the food. Visit me, then, in Judaea, and revive your wearied spirit. Do you say, with the admirable Horace, that those who cross the sea change only their climate and not their mind? Ah, but cross to Judaea and see whether your liberal-minded tolerance does not undergo a striking change. I know I am disposed to prepare against the Jews; it is a just ridicule. But then I live among them, you only see their shops and synagogues from a safe distance as you hurry past in your litter to a cause such as a party or a gathering of the wits.

A LESSON TO GALILEANS

Jerusalem

I felt that I must write to you again before I set out on one of my periodical inspections of the province. Marcius and Joseph both warn me that I shall have a bad reception because of the seizure of the sacred money. I am not so sure. It is sacrilege, of course, to all of them, but the country-people do not love the greedy, grasping priesthood at Jerusalem, who fatten on their offerings and, besides, only Jerusalem benefits from my gift of good water; why did not Jerusalem pay for its water and so save the Temple-tribute from spoliation? Perhaps I shall not be so unpopular after all. I shall let the people know that their Sanhedrim wanted to pay for the aqueduct out of the people's taxes.

It is a month now since the coup, on which I have received many congratulations from my friends. Except for one serious episode, everybody has been fairly peaceful. I did not weaken in my determination. I forbade all demonstrations, public-meetings and even gatherings in the streets. That put a stop to their street-corner oratory. The worst of the offenders were not the priests and lawyers themselves, but the young know-alls who attend their lectures, and supply the wits that the common people lack. There was one man in particular, a pertinacious fellow, a loud-mouthed logic-chopping Jew from Tarsus, who had much to say, when arrested, about being a Roman citizen. It turned out that he was, so he was released, but I bade the centurion whisper to him not to come into our hands again since even a Roman citizen might be killed in attempting to escape. There were seditious placards too, during the first few days, defaming me and Caesar. The city broke out into a perfect rash of them, until we caught a party of three at work on the walls of the Antonia in the night. There was something else on the wall of the Antonia, besides placards, in the morning.

As I told you, there was one serious incident. It was produced by a part of Galileans who came up to the Temple. These people are never very popular in Jerusalem. They are regarded as a mixed race, as a little inferior to the pure Judean Jew, and so I daresay they are, being so close to Phoenicians and Greeks and various sorts of Syrians. The Galileans think themselves as good as any Jew alive; they are all the more defiant of us Romans because they are themselves ruled by a semi-Jew, like Antipas, and in any case a visit to Jerusalem is to them an excursion on which they enter with boisterous high spirits. This party, which arrived a fortnight ago, had heard of my seizure of the Temple-money but had not heard that demonstrations were prohibited. When the noisy rabble reached the Antonia I sent to warn them, but in vain. They abused us angrily and declared that on entering the Temple they would protest against the customary sacrifice to Caesar and to Rome. I had them followed into the outer court of the Temple by a troop of soldiers who fell upon them with swords while they were buying the animals for their own sacrifices. The other Jews looked on. I think this proof that I would not stop short even at entering the Temple has made a good impression. The remnant of the Galilean party set off again for their own country the same day and when they spread the news it should teach their fellow-countrymen not to take liberties with me. I have sent a report to Antipas and begged him to restrain his subjects better.

I do not like what you tell me about the prevalence of 'informers' at Rome. If a man sides with or against Sejanus, he takes the risk and ought not to complain of the result, but this system is exposing even the most innocent to private spite and vengeance. Surely a Roman ought to be safe from denunciation by his freedman. I pay no attention to anonymous informers here, though there are many of them at *work. Those who hate us most are always seeking to ruin the priests and nobles who work with us, but unless the accuser is prepared to stand forward I do not listen to him. In that I know I shall have your support. For rebellion, no mercy! But our Roman justice must not be used for settling private grudges. 'Admirable,' says L. Annaeus Seneca, 'and under which heading comes the appropriation of the sacred Temple-money!'*

ANTIPAS'S INQUIRIES AT NAZARETH
Caesarea

I have spent nearly a month going round the northern districts of my province. I have inspected frontier posts, conferred with my revenue officers, heard innumerable grievances and redressed not a few. I wanted to find out for myself whether this part of the country was suffering as much from the effects of drought and bad harvests as I had been told. I found that it was. In many places the condition of the people was truly miserable. I discovered that every synagogue had been used as a centre of ill-will against me, but I summoned the village elders, heard their stories of distress, and announced remissions of taxation. In certain cases I promised to send them relief as soon as I got back to Caesarea, and that I am now doing. On the whole, I am not dissatisfied.

It was a pleasure to be among the Samaritans. They have a most likeable hatred of the priesthood at Jerusalem, who treat them like dogs and keep them out of the Temple. They think themselves every bit as good as the real Jews and certainly they have the same general characteristics: one day they are peasants and the next they are robbers; this week it is the plough and the next it is the knife or the pitchfork against Caesar or Herod or whoever the 'tyrant' of the day may be. Still, I have been governor for three years now without many grave troubles, which is as much as any of my predecessors except Valerius has done. If I were withdrawn now, I should leave the province better than I found it. I am not discontented.

At the beginning of my tour I took Procula up to the border of Galilee. She is paying a visit to the wife of the Governor of Syria, an old school-fellow of hers, and I set her on the high road to Damascus. I sent Alexander with her into Galilee and told him to find out something for me about the latest agitator. He accompanied her to Damascus. He paid a flying visit to Nazareth, to which Jesus belongs, and visited his family. He found them in a state of fright. Antipas's agents have been in Nazareth cross-examining them about Jesus and they fear that they will be involved in any punishment that befalls him. The whole town shares their nervousness. It seems that the family and their friends actually pursued Jesus, who moves about rapidly from place to place, as all these preachers do, and would like to have carried him off and shut him up to keep him - or rather themselves - out of trouble. They told Antipas's people that Jesus was not wholly responsible for his actions; he had always been a little queer and caused his family trouble, and they had never been able to control him. Certainly they cannot now, for he not only repudiates them brusquely, but the crowds who follow him increase every day and will not hear a word against him. So the wretched people are panic-stricken. I have written to Caiaphas pressing to be told whether the Sanhedrim have taken any action.

Do you remember the Greek merchant who ran off with a priest's daughter? While I was away he turned up again in Caesarea - alone. He told every one that the Jewess had left him, but the story goes that he abandoned her somewhere in Africa and the Jews have sent an account of it to her family in Jerusalem. Like a fool he persisted in going on his usual round of business in Judaea. He even talked of visiting Jerusalem. He was a cheery fellow with a mop of black hair, always making jests and laughing at himself. When warned not to go to Jerusalem he said that he had turned proselyte and being converted to Judaism he would be looked after by Yahweh. So he went laughing to Jerusalem and that is the end of him. He has vanished off the face of the earth. The young woman had several brothers and cousins who are among the strictest of the strict. In Rome the whole thing would have been a joke, but you soon learn not to smile over such things here. At least you ought to. The Greek would not learn, and now where is he?

ATTEMPT IN GALILEE TO MAKE JESUS KING
Caesarea

A budget from you has made me happy. Ships have been delayed by stormy weather so that several letters have arrived at once. Before I open them I think myself important, occupied with weighty affairs of State, a not inefficient part of Caesar's great machine. But when I read them, ah me! I wish that I were again at the centre of the world, in the Forum or the Senate-house, the theatre or Sejanus's ante-chamber, amid the noise and smoke of Rome, where after all a man does live. Here nothing happens - nothing, at least, that matters; from here nothing can arise; how much, I beg you to tell me, will Rome ever know or care about Judaea unless there is a war and comfortable appointments have to be found for our noble idlers on the Commander's staff? There, I have had my growl. Let me see whether, after all, I have any news to repay you for your letters.

Procula has seen and heard the Galilean Jesus. She writes to me that as soon as they had crossed into Galilee and started on the road which runs along the west side of the lake they began to hear of little else. Alexander, the ferret, was nosing here and there, collecting information. It seems that all Galilee is agog about Jesus; every one knows of someone who has heard of someone else who has been cured of some disease or other, and the interesting thing (to me) is that a number of my good subjects of Judaea are also in Galilee, following the preacher when they would be better employed following their jobs at home. Alexander had arranged, as it happened, for Procula to make a halt at a farm-house towards the northern end of the lake, and as she went along - but you shall have the story in her own words as she has sent it me:

'We came suddenly on a crowd of people who were hurrying along the road in front of us and over the slopes leading down to the sea and even along the beach. Others were joining them from the paths that came in from the hills. No one took any notice of us. They were Jews of all kinds - mostly hale and hearty people, but there were sick and cripples too, who were dragging themselves along or being carried by their friends. The crowd was excited, gesticulating, pointing to a boat that was following the coast line, and shouting to those on board. I

thought at first that they were angry but Alexander said that they were calling to Jesus, who was on board, to come to shore and speak to them. They kept on shouting the same words over and over again. I could not make it out because it was all in Aramaic and when I asked Alexander he only shook his head and muttered something about it being a bad business. He would not tell me what they meant, though he told me later. When we stopped at the farm-house the crowd rushed on and presently I could see them leaving the high road and hurrying down to the shore. Alexander asked permission to go after them and I said he could provided that he took me with him. So we went, with an escort - you need not be afraid - and after half an hour we found them all in a great mass, down near the sea, with Jesus standing on a knoll in the field, addressing them. There were thousands upon thousands of them, and at the back, quite close to us, some groups of better-dressed Jews, who were standing aloof, watching and listening. Alexander took a look at them and muttered again. "Spies from Jerusalem," he said and went off to talk to them.

'I saw the preacher clearly. He is a strange man, gaunt and rugged, as though he were burnt up by the fire of his passion. When you see his face and hear him speak, he is full of self-confidence, imperious, often fierce. The crowd was noisy at first because those at the back could not hear and there were interruptions. He put them down with a few words. He was like a general among the legions and they obeyed like common soldiers. He spoke always as though he thought no one could contradict him. He began quietly but then raised his voice and it became harsh and vehement. The Jews from Jerusalem were fidgeting and muttering to each other. Alexander said he was denouncing them and their friends. I have never heard anything that sounded so passionate and bitter. Then he became quieter again and went off in a rapt way as though he did not know the people were there. There was a murmuring and stirring all through the crowd then but not angrily, and they pressed forward to him. Alexander could not take his eyes off him. He would pay no attention to my questions. He kept on saying to himself "A better time coming!" and laughed in a queer, anxious sort of way. I thought he was quoting something that the preacher had been saying. He kept looking at the party from Jerusalem and said he must get a report to you at once.

'Then a curious thing happened. Jesus suddenly raised his arm and cried out something sternly. They stopped pushing towards him and sat down on the grass in a great circle round him - except the Jews from Jerusalem, who made no movement but went on watching. I am sure I have seen some of them going to the Sanhedrim. Then Jesus called some men who were standing close to him and they brought him bread. He broke this into little pieces - so small that from where I stood you could scarcely see them at all. He gave these to the men and they went along the ranks distributing them to the crowd, who ate them while the preacher went on talking. I wish I could have understood. All I could get out of Alexander was that the preacher was enrolling them as his followers but that it was not a military business at all but purely religious; the eating of the bread was a symbol that they enrolled themselves under him, to live as he lived and to do all the things that he had been telling them to do. Alexander added that it was dangerous, it might be misunderstood.

'The strangest thing was to follow. When the ceremony was finished everything was still for a few seconds and then the crowd began to stir and talk. Gradually they became more and more excited. Jesus said something to the men about him, and running down to the sea, they began to pull the boat close in so that he could embark again. When the crowd saw that he was going to leave them they broke all bounds. They ran forward, crying and shouting, and surrounded him. Some of them were brandishing sticks and clubs and knives. They were not threatening him; it was quite different. Others of them were weeping. Many of them fell down at his feet. All the time I could make out that they were shouting the same words that I had heard them using on the high-road when they were looking out to sea. I asked Alexander what they were saying. I had to shake him by the shoulder before I could get an answer out of him. He was impatient with me. "King!" he said, "that's what they are saying. King of Israel! King of the Jews! And Messiah!" I am not sure what the last means, but you will know.

'I could see that Jesus was repelling them. He would not listen to them. He almost drove them back with words and gestures. I am sure he was telling them that they had made a great mistake. He was almost beside himself. He made those who were kneeling rise and those who were brandishing weapons put them down. He was more stern and determined than he had been all the afternoon. At the same time he began to move down to the sea hurriedly as though he must escape. The crowd followed slowly in a dejected way. They seemed to be disappointed and bewildered. "He is angry with them for calling him King of the Jews," I said to Alexander. "He has cause to be," said Alexander. "He is a dead man from today."

'There was another incident. Before Jesus could get on the boat, the Jews from Jerusalem, who had been watching every movement of the crowd, walked rapidly down the hill and spoke to him. They met each other as enemies; I could see that though I could not hear the words. The talk only lasted a few moments. They said something to him and he looked at them with a face of stone. Then he answered curtly and turned his back on them. Some of his followers helped him into the boat. I thought they were puzzled too, and perhaps afraid. He was not afraid himself. He spoke and acted as though he was ready to fight the whole world.

'Whatever it was that was said to the Jews from Jerusalem they were pleased about it. They came away whispering and smiling and, when I left, they were going about among the crowd, as busy as bees. I knew they were denouncing Jesus, because they kept on looking out to sea and pointing to the boat. Alexander is now engaged in writing you a report upon the whole affair.'

'King of the Jews!' my dear friend - you mark the words! Yes, I know, it is only in Galilee and, likely enough, I shall not myself be worried. Trust Antipas to look to it! Would you like to hear the report of the sage Alexander? He says:

'Galilee would rise at a word but he does not say the word. He puzzles the people even while he attracts them. He has performed strange cures, though every one has a different story of his own about them and it is impossible to say how much of it is truth. The gatherings that he addresses have been like clay between his hands. In controversy no one can stand against him. He is at daggers-drawn with the priests, the lawyers and the Law. He is terrible in his attacks upon them: most fierce and unsparing. He would overthrow the whole system which the priests have imposed upon the Jewish nation, and the priests will never forgive him for it. At the first sign that the people are turning against him, the priests will make an end of him.

'There are signs that they are about to turn against him now. They have hailed him as the expected deliverer, the new king of the Jews. He refuses the titles. This afternoon he beat the crowd off almost by force when they acclaimed him. You never saw such a hang-dog look as they had when they drifted away. In his own mind he is no king or Messiah. I believe he dreads lest they should insist on treating him as either one or the other. Above all else the popular ferment has been caused by the cures, and I have found, by careful inquiry, that on every occasion he has tried to conceal what he has done and so to prevent the people from hailing him as the deliverer. He seeks to avert the danger that he fears. The war which he wages is against the Sanhedrim and the Judaic Law. If he persists they will surely take his life. Their delegates were on the watch today and some of them are remaining in Galilee. But I doubt whether they will be under the necessity, or have the chance, of taking him. Unless he takes to immediate flight, Herod Antipas will seize him.

'Antipas can do nothing else after today. I hear that Jesus has already sailed for the other side of the lake to take refuge in the territory of Herod Philip. If he stays there Philip will lay hands on him. If he returns to Galilee he is lost. May I suggest that it would be interesting to have a report from the High Priest on his view of the case?'

You see, then. Another popular hero rising to worry me and call himself King. No, you will say, he does not so; it is they who call him King. And what difference, pray, does that make to the Procurator? If Jesus values his life he will keep out of Judaea. If Antipas lets him slip through his fingers I will not. Only one thing grieves me. 'He is at daggers-drawn with the priests, the lawyers and the Law.' I could like him for that. But a king in Judaea, even one who would not (at present) be a king, a man imperious, fierce, burnt up by his own passion, the type of man to whom this restless and insurgent people willingly gives heed - no, no, that will not do! When he is dead, then they can call him king.

By the way, the Greek merchant has been found under a pile of stones in a ravine outside Jerusalem. There was scarcely a whole bone in his body. Apparently they used clubs. The story is that the Jewess has gone off to Rome with an Egyptian actor. You know how she will end.

FLIGHT OF JESUS INTO SYRIA
Caesarea

What, my dear Seneca, all the Jews expelled from Rome! A clean sweep of tailors and milliners, money-lenders and red-nosed comedians! O most desirable of cities: would that I could be there! Yet it is unjust, as you say, that the whole community should be banished because some rascals turned Temple-gifts to their own private uses. Yes, yes, it is unjust, yet no one will sympathize. It must be their own fault that, all the world over, no one sympathizes with an ill-treated Jew - no one, that is to say, except my Seneca. A dreadful thought assails me. Where is Caesar going to send them? Pray Yahweh it be not to Judaea!

(Certain Jews had induced Fulvia, a Roman lady converted to Judaism, to make gifts to the Temple and had then appropriated the money. The Jewish community was thereupon expelled from Rome.)

(Alexander was right. Jesus of Nazareth has fled. Nothing has been heard of him for weeks. He is not in Galilee and he is not in Philip's territory. He must have gone north into Syria, where no one cares about him.)

Let me tell you first about Caiaphas. The wily Priest has sent me several of his unctuous statesman-like reports. I know his difficulties. He has to keep an eye on the Governor (who has the soldiers and Rome behind him); on his own Pharisees who think he is obsequious to us; on the people who might be led away by any wild man this day or tomorrow; and on the priests and lawyers who love their law and suspect that in its defense he and his kind are no better than they should be. He says it would be charitable to suppose that Jesus is a madman, and that this is indeed the opinion of his family, but whether mad or not, he is seducing ignorant people from their duty alike to their religion and to the recognized authorities. He adds that the delegates from the Sanhedrim have exposed him repeatedly, and the exposure is now rapidly having an effect. They will take the sternest measures against Jesus, should he come into their hands, as a false pretender and rebel against the Law and as for the political side of it - do you remember they said the same thing about John? - they realize that it may cause me a legitimate concern. Themselves, too, I should say, for in the long run with these ruling priests it all comes down to politics. It is their nature: all Jews are politicians - but so is their Procurator.

For the time being, then, the preacher has taken to his heels. I have other reports from Galilee. It seems that he paid some flying visits from Philip's territory, only to find that the tide had set against him. The events which Procula and Alexander saw were decisive with his followers. He would not be their King, he would not acknowledge that he was the promised deliverer. Maybe, as Alexander says, it is no part of his intention to be the one thing or the other. After his refusal, the Jerusalem Rabbis dogged him everywhere. They found it much easier to persuade the people that, after all, he was only a rebel, an enemy to their venerated Law. I believe that in his own town an attempt was made to murder him, though, of course, they have their special grievances against him there. Now he is without friends and has vanished into the far north.

This is a small matter, but still something of a relief to me. The country is fairly quiet - if those Jewish friends of yours don't come from Rome! - and I shall have, I suppose, to stop here for some years more. I am a poor man, in spite of the jesting threats against the Jews which I used to send to you over three years ago, and I would prefer to spend my remaining years of office quietly until Caesar transfers me. As this thing stands at present, I can handle it comfortably, but if a fanatic of this sort were to accept the popular demand - to 'give the word,' as Alexander said - I might be hard pressed with the miserable little force that is allowed me.

PILATE COMES TO JERUSALEM FOR THE PASSOVER
Jerusalem

I have come up as usual for their great festival the Passover. It amused me, when I received your letter just before leaving Caesarea, to find you complaining of the congestion in Rome. You should be here. Judaea has been filling up for weeks past. They come by tens of thousands, weeks in advance, and spread over the country, visiting their friends and relatives, searching out the villages their fathers came from, and making pilgrimages to the places where their history began. During the last week they have been concentrating on Jerusalem. Every ship that has reached Caesarea has been crowded inside and out. The conditions on board some of them must have been disgusting. You never saw such a medley as passes out from these ships. Some of them must have spent their last penny in paying the fare; not a few have got here without paying any fare at all. You know the sort of mixture that comes out from the Games in Rome - riff-raff from the slums and blue blood cheek by jowl. It is the same here and Jewish blue blood has no more liking for riff-raff than blue blood has in Rome. They smell abominably. You should see the aristocrats turning up their rich or learned noses.

The whole lot throng the roads. The stream is continuous from the coast, from Samaria and from Jericho. Many of them sleep in the open. Some of the wealthier bring tents and bedding with them. In Jerusalem and the neighborhood everybody who can takes in lodgers. They charge a pretty price. Foodstuffs are doubled and trebled in price. I believe the language that the foreign Jews use about their brethren in Judaea shocks even the Greeks. To-day, when I approached, there was a complete block for a good mile from the city, and had it not been for some stout work by my escort I should still be kicking my heels outside the walls.

I have half my total force in readiness - 2,000 men. There is no reason to anticipate anything beyond the usual brawls, but one must be prudent. You know how religion always excites the lowest passions. The Jerusalem Jew is at his worst at these times and the visitors resent his arrogance. They are most apt to brawl in the Temple, that being the heart and kernel of their worship! In the synagogues they are not so dangerous, because most of these foreign communities have each a synagogue of their own, where they can agree fairly well, but in the Temple they all meet together and can quarrel about priority in offering sacrifice, or about the inadequacy of the other people's gifts, or about being more Jewish than one another.

Having got through earlier Passovers without serious disturbance I have no reason to be anxious. The danger lies in the immense suppressed excitement that underlies the festival. They work themselves up to a state of ecstasy. With all these thousands gathered from the far ends of the earth, they imagine themselves a free and independent people, they live again in the old days, they think that their Yahweh has only to perform one of his preposterous wonders and we Romans would vanish in the wind. If the spark were handy, a fire might easily be lit.

Do you know that since I arrived today, the Jews have been complaining that I have not expedited the carriage of foodstuffs to the city? They block the roads and then complain that the foodcarts don't come through. But that is their way. They are intractable. If the place were full of pigs they would sooner starve than eat.

I will let you know how we go on.

REAPPEARANCE OF JESUS
Jerusalem

Do you remember the preacher Jesus, who fled to Syria some months ago to save his life from Antipas? He has appeared again. What is more - you may think it incredible, but it is true - he is on his way to Jerusalem. My spies report that having passed hurriedly through Galilee he has crossed the frontier. I have dispatched agents to keep in touch with him. According to present information he denounces the priests and Pharisees at every step and avows his intention to be in Jerusalem for the Passover. He brings a following with him. I suppose there are always people who are tired of life.

It was good of you to find me an expert on vine-culture so quickly. These Jews have wits - none sharper - and they are industrious, but they are sadly lacking in scientific knowledge. If they were not bled by their priests they would have much more money for modern knowledge and equipment, but what can you do when a bloated corporation of priests fattens on an impoverished people? Send your expert at once, I pray you, by way of Alexandria and he shall go straight out on a round of country visits.

JESUS IN JERUSALEM
Jerusalem

So far all goes well. I derive a modest amusement from what I hear of the divisions and jealousies among these different Jews. Remarkable enough at any time, they are much more so when the foreign Jews are here. To begin with, the extreme Pharisees despise even the Jews in their own country who do not belong to their special sect. To them a man is good, that is to say virtuous, if he observes the Law minutely, and not otherwise. I assure you that if they have a woman of the common folk to work in the house, they think the house and all the inmates are made unclean by it. You may imagine how much greater is their contempt for the Jews from Egypt or Syria who actually mix with heathen folk like you and me, or Sejanus and Caesar.

The foreign Jews resent this arrogance. Many of them are extremely rich, many of them (especially those from Egypt) are more learned than their Pharisaic critics, and, of course, they are civilized. Yet when they go into the Temple, mix with the Pharisees and listen to the lectures of the learned, they find themselves treated with sneers and insinuations that they are little better than the Greeks whose language they speak - and often enough, it is the only language that they do speak, since they have neither Hebrew nor Aramaic. On several occasions the rank and file have almost come to blows, but this is a harmless recreation and I do not interfere.

You will expect to hear more about the preacher Jesus. I am, for two reasons, proceeding cautiously. My first thought was to arrest him before he entered Jerusalem and came in contact with the crowds. But that course would have its dangers, at a time like this. Since he crossed the frontier he has done nothing openly to justify it, his followers would spread the report that I had seized a noble patriotic Jew, and so, figuring once more as the oppressor, I might have on my hands a sudden outburst of passion of the kind which I desire to avoid. Besides, Annas and Caiaphas have both been to see me. It was at once apparent that they, and especially Annas, were extremely desirous that I should remove what they consider a danger to themselves. They hate the man and no doubt with good reason. The Pharisees and lawyers are really disturbed about the attacks on the Law; the priesthood scents a danger to its livelihood; while Annas, Caiaphas and the other noble Sadducees are not only concerned for the maintenance of the whole priestly system (they are pretty indifferent themselves *about the Law), but fear some sudden turn of affairs which might convert this Jesus into a national hero - and then what would become of them and their power? (I suggest to you, as a subject for one of your plays or meditations, that the greatest stimulant of all to a man's activities is the desire for Power.)*

They suggested to me that, remembering what had happened in Galilee, it would be wise for me to seize Jesus quietly and put him out of the way. I am not, however, so stupid as to pull the chestnuts out of the fire for them and bring on myself an unnecessary odium. I replied that the trouble was primarily their affair but undoubtedly it might concern me at any moment. I wished to avoid a tumult and presumed that was also their desire. They were emphatic that it was so. I said that I should hold my hand for the present, but that if there were any disturbances I would act at once and I expected their loyal co-operation. This they promised me. If nothing happens during the festival it is my intention, though I did not tell them this, to wait until the crowds disperse again and then make an end of Jesus. I cannot allow him to stir up Judaea as he stirred up Galilee. If he provokes trouble during the festival - whether by his own act or by the people losing their heads over him, even against his will - I shall strike at once. But the priests must co-operate and I am certain they will. Do you understand fully why they will? Not only because they hate this particular man, though they do, but because, if they stand out, the case may easily become one of the nation against the wicked Governor, which does not suit their plans, and because also there are some of them whose names I know - and they know that I know - who are tarred with the anti-Roman brush and had better show themselves zealous to assist me when the chance is offered them.

Jesus is in Jerusalem. He entered yesterday. His entry, if he had any intention of raising the populace, was a failure. Few of them knew about it. He came up by the road from Jericho. It was crowded with Jews from the Euphrates region and from Syria, who had never heard of him. If there were any Galileans who recognized him, they would only remember that he had failed them in Galilee last year. His own immediate followers are poor stuff. (I had Alexander following the group and Joseph mingling with the general crowd.) They are ignorant and superstitious men who are only dangerous because they share the usual delusion about leaders of his kind. They are always expecting Jesus to perform a 'wonder,' whether it is bringing to life a dead man or killing a live one, and they think about him just like the peasants and workmen of Galilee, expecting him at any moment to set about delivering the nation and bringing in a new age. I know by this time that a Jew in his own country can scarcely think in any other terms.

There was no evidence yesterday, any more than there has been before, that the preacher takes this view of himself. He entered with no more than the stir that there usually is when a party escorts some local notability. His followers shouted themselves hoarse and a few others, seeing them do it, shouted too. If six men throw their caps up for a reason, six others of the herd will follow suit. I had taken all precautions. I had some disguised soldiers walking with the crowd from Jericho and some more ready at the entrance to the city. Marcius had orders, if any attempt was made to rouse the mob, to cut down Jesus and his followers at once, but nothing happened. That is not to say that nothing will happen. Alexander wormed himself into the confidence of some of the preacher's followers. He says they have the most extraordinary ideas about the brilliant change that is going to come over their fortunes, but that all that their leader intends - Alexander is positive about this - is to pursue in Jerusalem his quarrel with the priesthood and the Law. It is enough.

I hope I am not mistaken in believing that you are interested in these long explanations. Were I writing to anyone else, I would say merely that I have cause to fear another pestilent agitation and that I mean to crush it while I may.

SCENE IN THE TEMPLE AND DECISION TO ARREST JESUS

Jerusalem

Both Herod Antipas and brother Philip are in Jerusalem. These princelings behave as though they owned the East. They have brought rich presents for the Temple, they pose, they cultivate the Jews. They go in procession to and from the Temple services and the mob, which has forgotten how many Jews old Herod tortured, burned or crucified, claps and cries out for them as though it would be a fine thing to have a Herod instead of me at the Antonia. I have not met the princes, but I have stationed a guard of Roman soldiers at their gates. It is a proper mark of respect; it is also a hint that we keep an eye on them. Some of the noble families who supported the father have sent representatives to wait on the sons and accompany them to the Temple, but the ruling coterie, those who have office and those who hope to have it, hold aloof. They know which side their bread is buttered.

The affair of Jesus is coming to a head. Yesterday, accompanied by his immediate followers, he visited the Temple. He stopped in the outer court, which is an enormous place like a fair-ground, full of the paraphernalia for Temple-gifts and sacrifices, and thronged by thousands of Jews chaffering and arguing at the top of their voices in a score of languages and dialects. You know that market of theirs in Rome which one takes visitors to see from curiosity. It is like that, with a hundred times the hubbub. Suddenly Jesus began to assail his enemies the priests and all their works in the most violent terms. So far as I can learn, he denounced the whole ritual-mongering business of the Temple. Very sensible, too, except for his own safety. Had he been understood or attracted wide attention he would have been murdered on the spot. If you remember that the life of these Jews, not only here but to the far ends of the earth, centers in the Temple-worship and that it is a highly organized business controlled by a powerful and jealous corporation, you will see that only a madman or a suicide would act like this. As it went, there was only a scuffle and the thing passed off. It was rather like his entry into the City. He himself speaks Aramaic and a large part of his hearers would have no idea of his meaning. Besides, the noise is appalling. You know the Jews; if you are not noisy they think that you are ill. Nothing whatever came of the affair and, if it was intended as a demonstration, it was another failure. Jesus soon left the Temple again together with his followers who, according to my reports, are getting nothing out of their visit to Jerusalem but chagrin and disappointment. This is not at all the sort of thing which they anticipated. Denunciations of the Temple-worship in the Temple are likely to have an unfortunate end for them, as they probably suspect.

This incident has played into my hands. The man is an avowed failure. Ignored at first, he has now offended beyond forgiveness. Few people may have heard and seen his outburst, but a great many will know about it before to-night. You may say that if he has failed so signally, he is also negligible. Possibly, but there is a risk, and I do not take risks. Consider the audacity of his action. To me, who know these people, it is almost inconceivable. To challenge the priesthood in their sacred citadel and at the Passover, backed by a handful of peasants more ignorant even than himself - I could laugh at the thought were it not that a man so rash and passionate, and at the same time so determined, might make another sort of appeal tomorrow which might have a different ending. I have determined to suppress him. Public opinion, thanks to his folly, will support me. Still, I shall have the arrest carried through as quietly as possible in conjunction with the Sanhedrim. His companions will give no trouble.

After the scene in the Temple the old fox Annas sent an envoy to me. More than anyone he has a vested interest in the maintenance of peace; as you know, he has several sons whom he intends for the highest offices. At the same time, he has his finger on the pulse of the Pharisees who are rebels at heart against us and would help any seditious movement if it had a serious foundation. His point is the same as my own, that Jesus is not an actual but a potential danger. He urges that we should strike while few people know of him, and while those who do - and they will increase hourly - are shocked by his gross impiety (Annas's words). He adds that, if necessary, they will produce one of Jesus' own followers who will give damning evidence about certain ambitions which his master has avowed in private conversations. That does not concern me. I don't doubt they will provide themselves with the evidence they want, but I have already all that I require. The top and the bottom of it is that the man is, or might be, a political danger to me, as Antipas thought he was in Galilee last year, and as Antipas recognized the preacher John to be, when he cut his head off at Machaerus and so saved me the trouble.

I am concerting with the priests. Jesus and his following spend their nights outside Jerusalem; we know the place. He will be arrested quietly and executed without undue delay.

I had not thought of it before, but I think I shall give my friend Antipas the opportunity of condemning Jesus. The trouble began within his jurisdiction, so that it is the correct and polite thing to do. Besides, it would be pleasant to show Antipas both that a mischief-maker has slipped through his hands but not through mine, and also, that when he has condemned his subject, he has to hand him over to the superior authority, the Roman Governor, for execution of sentence. Yes, I will send him to Antipas.

ARREST OF JESUS

Jerusalem

Your freedman Krito has arrived this morning bringing your letters and others which he had picked up for me at Caesarea. He starts back again at once, so that the letter I write you now must be a short one. I wish it had been only your letters he had brought me, for they gave me the pleasure which I always experience in hearing about you in Rome. But no sooner had I read them than I was thrown into ill-temper by the news from Caesarea. You know - I am sure I have told you this before - that when the Passover is finished and a large part of the foreign Jews troop back to the coast on their way home, I hold Games in Caesarea for several days. It is a relaxation for me as well as for them, and it is good for trade. Do you ask whether they come to my Games? Of course they come. They are not Pharisees. They are Greek Jews, Cyrenaic Jews, Asiatic Jews, who were merrier and more human folk than their harsh Judaic brethren.

Could anything be more exasperating than the blow which has befallen me? In the first place a ship bringing six lions from Cyrenaica has foundered. The crew had not even the good grace to go down with the ship. Still, lions are cheap and I do not make too much of it. What is more serious is the loss of my gladiator Aduatucus, a Gaul. He was the best swordsman in the East. Since I came out here he had fought nearly fifty contests and had never been beaten. The women love him. The Governors of both Syria and Egypt had tried to buy him from me - once or twice I lent him as a great favor, but I always refused to sell - and I had told him that when he completed fifty contests I would give him his freedom and make him trainer of the troop. He might have become manager of the Games, he might have gone back with me and become first favorite of the crowd at Rome. Why, he might have caught Caesar's eye, entered his Household and controlled provincial governors. With this career before him, and knowing the value that I attached to him, he was inconsiderate enough to enter into a tavern brawl about a girl with two Thracians. They stabbed him to death and then took their own lives, so that I have not even the poor consolation of using them for the Games. By Jove, I am annoyed.

You were asking about the aqueduct. It works admirably and I have reason to know that the foreign Jews applaud me for it. They disapprove, as they are bound to do, of my use of the Temple-money, but they see that I am not behind the Governors of more important provinces in my care for the Roman name and the health of my people. The Jews here also use the water, even the Pharisees. The only difference is that they show no gratitude.

Jesus was arrested late last night. I provided a troop of soldiers who accompanied the officials of the Sanhedrim. The advantage is that as the news spread this morning - if it did spread - it would be known that Procurator and Sanhedrim had acted jointly. The Sanhedrim are not popular with the most zealous Jews, but the general impression would be that if all the authorities, Roman and Jewish, were acting together, this must be a troublesome fellow who was better out of the way. The arrest was made without disturbance. Jesus himself gave no trouble and his followers ran at once. I believe some of them are well on their way home.

The prisoner was taken to the High Priest's quarters until this morning when he was handed over to my people. I believe Caiaphas got a few of the leading priests together and they questioned him for themselves. The case is a perfectly simple one, from my point of view, and will give no difficulty. Since Antipas will not handle the matter - I am coming to that in a moment - I shall execute Jesus as a maker or a cause of sedition against Caesar. But these priests have always to remember that sedition against Caesar is usually a merit in the eyes of the populace (and of a good many Pharisees too), and they will want to make out a good case for themselves. They will insist, I suppose, on Jesus' defiance of the Law, attacks on the ritual and outbreak in the Temple. Probably they will say that he regarded himself as the expected Messiah (of which there is no evidence), and the people, with their mouths agape, have no use for a Messiah who cannot keep himself out of the hands of the despised Romans. That is not the kind of deliverer the Jews want any more than his own followers.

I have not seen the man myself, though I shall do presently. I gave orders for him to be taken to Antipas, as I said I would, with a polite statement that as the disturber of the peace was a Galilean, he would perhaps consider the matter came within his jurisdiction. I received a reply, equally polite, that Antipas recognized my courtesy but waived any right that he might have over an offender in my City of

Jerusalem. A touching exchange of courtesies! I shall finish the matter off today.

Your freedman waits, but one word more. Is it true, as I hear from Lentulus Spinther, that Sejanus's nephew has been refused an audience by Caesar and that Sejanus has doubled the Praetorian Guard at Rome? What if Sejanus falls? What if he refuses to fall? Do not become famous too hastily, my friend. Obscurity, though inglorious, is safe. When the master walks through the fields with stick in hand, fortunate is the poppy with inconspicuous head.

(Note: Sejanus was summarily executed in the next year and his friends were involved in the catastrophe.)

TRIAL AND EXECUTION OF JESUS
Jerusalem

I must complete the letter which I began this morning. Immediately after dispatching Krito, I confirmed with Marcius the military arrangements for the Passover, which begins tomorrow. I heard reports from Joseph, who thinks that acts of violence against individuals amongst the ruling Sadducees will grow. In his opinion it does not much matter whether the province is as quiet as I contrive to keep it or whether there is constant friction between us and the Jews; his feeling is that the extreme men are tired of peace. Afterwards I tried and condemned the prisoner Jesus. He was crucified at once along with some other prisoners who were awaiting execution. It is not a bad thing to have an object lesson of this kind on the eve of the Passover because, in such a nondescript gathering as we have here, there must always be dangerous characters who have exceptional opportunities for their special qualities. By this time Jesus is buried. It is their custom to bury an executed offender the same day and, besides, the Sabbath begins at sunset - has, indeed, already begun. The Sanhedrim asked permission to bury the body this afternoon. It suits them, having got Jesus out of their way, to dispose of the whole matter before the Passover begins and so to dampen down any discussion which might arise, especially after the inscription that I ordered to be attached to the prisoner, about which more presently.

The trial was short but in due form and order. Jesus was accused of disturbing the peace, stirring up disaffection and claiming to be King of the Jews. There was evidence both from our side and from that of the Jews, both from Galilee and from this city. Caiaphas, Annas and the leading Sadducees were prominent and so were some but not all of the chief Pharisees; some of the Pharisees would lend no assistance in convicting a rebel against Caesar however much they desired his death as a rebel against themselves. However, that did not help him. The priests had much to say of his attacks on their religion, but I cut them short on that. They cannot have it both ways. If we are not allowed to interfere in their religion, they cannot appeal to us when their observances are attacked; as soon as the offence becomes political, directly or indirectly, then we take note of it. They may squabble about Yahweh, like the Egyptians about Isis, till they burst, but when a man brawls in the Temple he tends to provoke a general explosion and that concerns us closely. The charge against Jesus of disturbing the peace was proved to the hilt and he could not deny it.

I inquired of the prisoner, through Alexander, whether he admitted the more serious accusations. The Jews alleged that he regarded himself as the destined deliverer of the nation, which involves the end of both their authority and ours. This would constitute a much more direct offence than that for which Antipas put John to death. They cited both the public utterances in which Jesus had spoken of a new kingdom as being imminent and also certain admissions about himself which they said he had made to his own followers. This was, I suppose, the special evidence which Annas said that they intended to produce. I put the question to him. I asked him whether he considered himself to be the deliverer. 'So THEY say,' he answered, indicating the High Priest and his neighbors, with a curt gesture of contempt. I pointed out to him that he was accused also of representing himself as King of the Jews. I asked him whether he considered himself to be that. He made the same answer - 'So YOU say,' meaning, I suppose, that in neither case was there anything in his own conduct or motives to support the accusation, but that he knew well enough that we meant in any case to fix the charge upon him. He realized that he was trapped, and that there was no way of escape, but he was bold and resolute, defiant, almost insolent. They are all alike, these Jews, bitter and unyielding, whether to us or to each other. Standing alone he might be, forsaken and with enemies on every side who meant his death, with his own countrymen delivering him to the Roman executioner, but he was cool and determined, like the men who engineered an attempt on the life of the great Herod and suffered the extremes of torture sooner than yield an inch. A dangerous breed!

I condemned him to death. I could, of course, do nothing less. All roads lead to that conclusion. Alexander, who has a cool and detached way of regarding his countrymen, insists that this man, so far from posing as Messiah, or King, like most of the mischief-makers during the last thirty years, did all that he could to prevent the stupid people from fastening that part on him. Alexander thinks that there was nothing that Jesus sought to avoid so much as this, knowing that if such a conception of him spread abroad, it would deliver him into our hands and be fatal to his campaign - a hopeless campaign in any case - against the priesthood and its system. Alexander has talked to some of his followers and says that the preacher had unquestionably warned them often and in the severest terms that they were not to regard him or speak of him as the Deliverer whom all these Jews expect, and that it was only when he thought that the old conception of him had died away in Galilee that he decided to come up to Jerusalem. It may be. But I am sure that if he was not a dangerous rebel yesterday, he would have been tomorrow. For either he would have succeeded in his assault on the priesthood or he would not. If he had not, how long would a man of his temperament, so passionate, headstrong and bold, have abstained from making that appeal to the patriotic feelings of these Jews which always - always - meets with a quick response, even when made by men of much less powerful character than his? You remember Procula's and Alexander's description of the scene in Galilee? And supposing that he had conceivably made headway against the priests and all the mummery of the Temple ritual, how long would it have been before he turned upon Caesar and the sacrifices to Caesar and to Rome? Would he have respected the cult of Divus Augustus, do you suppose? But long before we had to consider that eventuality we should have had to intervene with force between their contending factions. Why, as it is, they are almost in a state of suppressed civil war, ready to fly at each other's throats. Give them a bad governor - a governor even half as bad as they say that I am -

and the feud between those who tolerate us and those who despise the tolerators will break into open war. This is an unfruitful soil in all respects but one. The seeds of disorder will grow if you only scratch the soil. My policy is to destroy them the moment that they sprout. But I had forgotten: allow me one word about the inscription announcing the offence of Jesus. It was 'King of the Jews,' set up over the cross. The Pharisees were indignant. They themselves want a King of the Jews. It would give them the greatest pleasure to see Caesar overthrown tomorrow and a Jewish King installed - not a half-Jew like Herod - who would rule the country through them and suppress their Sadducean rivals. But it angered them to see the precious title, 'King of the Jews,' held up to ridicule; it was too plain a reminder of their servitude. Besides, they thought it an insult that a crucified criminal, a presumptuous countryman who had defied them, should be labelled 'King.' I took a short way with them. 'What I have written I have written,' said I, and bade them begone. I know the breed. From the moment that this Jesus set up his individual judgement against theirs they meant to have his life. Scratch a priest and find an autocrat. All the world over, if a man says that he will use his own intelligence about things divine, the priests prick up their ears and feel their knives. If he goes further and tells his fellow-men that they also are entitled to use their own intelligence - off with his head and there's an end of it!

I run on so, my dear Seneca. The subject carries me away. I must apologize to you again; I am afraid that even you will find the subject tedious. For, after all, what does it matter? What does it matter - one Jew more or less?

I wish I could find a substitute for Aduatucus.

The Life of Saint Issa

In 1894 Nicolas Notovitch published a book called The Unknown Life of Christ. He was a Russian doctor who journeyed extensively throughout Afghanistan, India, and Tibet.
During one of his jouneys he was visiting Leh, the capital of Ladak, near the buddhist convent Himis. He had an accident that resulted in his leg being broken. This gave him the unscheduled opportunity to stay awhile at the Himis convent.

While convalescing, Notovitch was told of an ancient record of the life of Jesus known as "The Life of St. Issa."
Notovitch enlisted a member of his party to translate the Tibetan volumes while he carefully noted each verse in the back pages of his journal.
When he returned to the western world there was much controversy as to the authenticity of the document. He was accused of creating a hoax and was ridiculed as an imposter. In his defense he encouraged a scientific expedition to prove the original Tibetan documents existed.
Archibald Douglas and Max Müller recognized Notovich's work as fraudulent, although it was not immediately clear (to Müller, at least) what the source of the fraud was. Perhaps the best thing is to read excerpts from the original, absolutely scathing account, from the Nineteenth Century academic journal itself (long out of copyright):

(from The Nineteenth Century, 39 (January-June 1896) pp. 667-677
THE CHIEF LAMA OF HIMIS ON THE ALLEGED 'UNKNOWN LIFE OF CHRIST')

"I was resident in Madras during the whole of last year, and did not expect to have an opportunity of investigating the facts respecting the Unknown Life of Christ at so early a date. Removing to the North-West Provinces in the early part of the present year, I |668 found that it would be practicable during the three months of the University vacation to travel through Kashmir to Ladakh, following the route taken by M. Notovitch, and to spend sufficient time at the monastery at Himis to learn the truth on this important question. I may here mention, en passant, that I did not find it necessary to break even a little finger, much less a leg, in order to gain admittance to Himis Monastery, where I am now staying for a few days, enjoying the kind hospitality of the Chief Lama (or Abbot), the same gentleman who, according to M. Notovitch, nursed him so kindly under the painful circumstances connected with his memorable visit.

Coming to Himis with an entirely open mind on the question, and in no way biassed by the formation of a previous judgment, I was fully prepared to find that M. Notovitch's narrative was correct, and to congratulate him on his marvellous discovery. One matter of detail, entirely unconnected with the genuineness of the Russian traveller's literary discovery, shook my faith slightly in the general veracity of the discoverer....

...I will now call attention to several leading statements in M. Notovitch's book, all of which will be found to be definitely contradicted in the document signed by the Chief Superior of Himis Monastery, and sealed with his official seal. This statement I have sent to Professor Max Müller for inspection, together with the subjoined declaration of Mr. Joldan, an educated Tibetan gentleman, to whose able assistance I am deeply indebted.

A more patient and painstaking interpreter could not be found, nor one better fitted for the task.

The extracts from M. Notovitch's book were slowly translated to the Lama, and were thoroughly understood by him. The questions and answers were fully discussed at two lengthy interviews before being prepared as a document for signature, and when so prepared were carefully translated again to the Lama by Mr. Joldan, and discussed by him with that gentleman, and with a venerable monk who appeared to act as the Lama's private secretary.

I may here say that I have the fullest confidence in the veracity and honesty of this old and respected Chief Lama, who appears to be held in the highest esteem, not only among Buddhists, but by all Europeans who have made his acquaintance. As he says, he has nothing whatever to gain by the concealment of facts, or by any departure from the truth.

His indignation at the manner in which he has been travestied by the ingenious author was of far too genuine a character to be feigned, and I was much interested when, in our final interview, he asked me if in Europe there existed no means of punishing a person |670 who told such untruths. I could only reply that literary honesty is taken for granted to such an extent in Europe, that literary forgery of the nature committed by M. Notovitch could not, I believed, be punished by our criminal law.

With reference to M. Notovitch's declaration that he is going to Himis to verify the statements made in his book, I would take the liberty of earnestly advising him, if he does so, to disguise himself at least as effectually as on the occasion of his former visit. M. Notovitch will not find himself popular at Himis, and might not gain admittance, even on the pretext of having another broken leg.

The following extracts have been carefully selected from the Unknown Life of Christ, and are such that on their truth or falsehood may be said to depend the value of M. Notovitch's story.

After describing at length the details of a dramatic performance, said to have been witnessed in the courtyard of Himis Monastery, M. Notovitch writes:

After having crossed the courtyard and ascended a staircase lined with prayer-wheels, we passed through two rooms encumbered with idols, and came out upon the terrace, where I seated myself on a bench opposite the venerable Lama, whose eyes flashed with intelligence (p. 110).

(This extract is important as bearing on the question of identification; see Answers 1 and 2 of the Lama's statement: and it may here be remarked that the author's account of the approach to the Chief Lama's reception room and balcony is accurate.) Then follows a long résumé of a conversation on religious matters, in the course of which the Abbot is said to have made the following observations amongst others:

We have a striking example of this (Nature-worship) in the ancient Egyptians, who worshipped animals, trees, and stones, the winds and the rain (p. 114).

The Assyrians, in seeking the way which should lead them to the feet of the Creator, turned their eyes to the stars (p. 115).

Perhaps the people of Israel have demonstrated in a more flagrant manner than any other, man's love for the concrete (p. 115).

The name of Issa is held in great respect by the Buddhists, but little is known about him save by the Chief Lamas who have read the scrolls relating to his life (p. 120).

The documents brought from India to Nepal, and from Nepal to Tibet, concerning Issa's existence, are written in the Pâli language, and are now in Lassa; but a copy in our language----that is, the Tibetan----exists in this convent (p. 123).

Two days later I sent by a messenger to the Chief Lama a present comprising an alarm, a watch, and a thermometer (p. 125).

We will now pass on to the description given by the author of his re-entry into the monastery with a broken leg:

I was carried with great care to the best of their chambers, and placed on a bed of soft materials, near to which stood a prayer-wheel. All this took place under the immediate surveillance of the Superior, who affectionately pressed the hand I offered him in gratitude for his kindness (p. 127).

While a youth of the convent kept in motion the prayer-wheel near my bed, the venerable Superior entertained me with endless stories, constantly taking my alarm and watch from their cases, and asking me questions as to their uses, and the way they should be worked. At last, acceding to my earnest entreaties, he ended by bringing me two large bound volumes, with leaves yellowed by time, and from them he read to me, in the Tibetan language, the biography of Issa, which I carefully noted in my carnet de voyage, as my interpreter translated what he said (p. 128).

This last extract is in a sense the most important of all, as will be seen when it is compared with Answers 3, 4, and 5 in the statement of the Chief Superior of Himis Monastery. That statement I now append. The original is in the hands of Professor Max Müller, as I have said, as also is the appended declaration of Mr. Joldan, of Leh.

The statement of the Lama, if true----and there is every reason to believe it to be so----disposes once and for ever of M. Notovitch's claim to have discovered a Life of Issa among the Buddhists of Ladakh. My questions to the Lama were framed briefly, and with as much simplicity as possible, so that there might be no room for any mistake or doubt respecting the meaning of these questions.

My interpreter. Mr. Joldan, tells me that he was most careful to translate the Lama's answers verbally and literally, to avoid all possible misapprehension. The statement is as follows:

Question 1. You are the Chief Lama (or Abbot) of Himis Monastery?

Answer 1. Yes.

Question 2. For how long have you acted continuously in that capacity?

Answer 2. For fifteen years.

Question 3. Have you or any of the Buddhist monks in this monastery ever seen here a European with an injured leg?

Answer 3. No, not during the last fifteen years. If any sahib suffering from serious injury had stayed in this monastery it would have been my duty to report the matter to the Wazir of Leh. I have never had occasion to do so.

Question 4. Have you or any of your monks ever shown any Life of Issa to any sahib, and allowed him to copy and translate the same?

Answer 4. There is no such book in the monastery, and during my term of office no sahib has been allowed to copy or translate any of the manuscripts in the monastery.

Question 5. Are you aware of the existence of any book in any of the Buddhist monasteries of Tibet bearing on the life of Issa?

Answer 5. I have been for forty-two years a Lama, and am well acquainted with all the well-known Buddhist books and manuscripts, and I have never heard of one which mentions the name of Issa, and it is my firm and honest belief that none such exists. I have inquired of our principal Lamas in other monasteries of Tibet, and they are not acquainted with any books or manuscripts which mention the name of Issa.

Question 6. M. Nicolas Notovitch, a Russian gentleman who visited your monastery between seven and eight years ago, states that you discussed with him the religions of the ancient Egyptians, Assyrians, and the people of Israel.

Answer 6. I know nothing whatever about the Egyptians, Assyrians, and the people of Israel, and do not know anything of their religions whatsoever. I have never mentioned these peoples to any sahib.

[I was reading M. Notovitch's book to the Lama at the time, and he burst out with, 'Sun, sun, sun, manna mi dug!' which is Tibetan for, 'Lies, lies, lies, nothing but lies!' I have read this to him as part of the statement, which he is to sign----as his deliberate opinion of M. Notovitch's book. He appears perfectly satisfied on the matter.
J. A. D.]...

Regarded, then, in the light of a work of the imagination, M. Notovitch's book fails to please, because it does not present that most fascinating feature of fiction, a close semblance of probability.

And yet, if I am rightly informed, the French version has gone through eleven editions; so M. Notovitch's effort of imagination has found, doubtless, a substantial reward. In face of the evidence adduced, we must reject the theory generously put forward by Professor Max Müller, that M. Notovitch was the victim of a cunning 'hoax ' on the part of the Buddhist monks of Himis.

...I do not believe that the venerable monk who presides over Himis Monastery would have consented to the practice of such a deception, and I do not think that any of the monks are capable of carrying out such a deception successfully. The departures from truth, on other points, which can be proved against M. Notovitch render such a solution highly improbable....

...I have visited Himis, and have endeavoured by patient and impartial inquiry to find out the truth respecting M. Notovitch's remarkable story, with the result that, while I have not found one single fact to support his statements, all the weight of evidence goes to disprove them beyond all shadow of doubt. It is certain that no such passages as M. Notovitch pretends to have translated exist in the monastery of Himis, and therefore it is impossible that he could have 'faithfully reproduced' the same.

The following "postscript" was amended to the article by Max Müller himself:

"...After having read, however, the foregoing article by Professor Douglas, I feel bound most humbly to apologize to the excellent Lamas of that monastery for having thought them capable of such frivolity. After the complete refutation, or, I should rather say, annihilation, of M. Notovitch by Professor A. Douglas, there does not seem to be any further necessity----

nay, any excuse----for trying to spare the feelings of that venturesome Russian traveler. He was not hoaxed, but he tried to hoax us. Mr. Douglas has sent me the original papers, containing the depositions of the Chief Priest of the Monastery of him is and of his interpreter, and I gladly testify that they entirely agree with the extracts given in the article, and are signed and sealed by the Chief Lama and by Mr. Joldan, formerly Postmaster of Ladakh, who acted as interpreter between the priests and Professor A. Douglas. The papers are dated Himis Monastery, Little Tibet, June 3, 1894.

I ought perhaps to add that I cannot claim any particular merit in having proved the Vie inconnue de Jésus-Christ----that is, the Life of Christ taken from MSS. in the monasteries of Tibet----to be a mere fiction. I doubt whether any Sanskrit or Pâli scholar, in fact any serious student of Buddhism, was taken in by M. Notovitch. One might as well look for the waters of Jordan in the Brahmaputra as. for a Life of Christ in Tibet.

F. Max Müller.

November 15, 1895."

Another one of his skeptics was Swami Abhedananda. Abhedananda, who journeyed into the arctic region of the Himalayas, determined to find a copy of the Himis manuscript or to expose the fraud. His book of travels, entitled Kashmir O Tibetti, tells of a visit to the Himis gonpa and includes a Bengali translation of two hundred twenty-four verses essentially the same as the Notovitch text. Abhedananda was thereby convinced of the authenticity of the Issa legend.

In 1925, another Russian named Nicholas Roerich arrived at Himis. Roerich, was a philosopher and a distinguished scientist. He apparently saw the same documents as Notovitch and Abhedananda. And he recorded in his own travel diary the same legend of St. Issa. Speaking of Issa, Roerich quotes legends which have the estimated antiquity of many centuries.
... He passed his time in several ancient cities of India such as Benares. All loved him because Issa dwelt in peace with Vaishas and Shudras whom he instructed and helped. But the Brahmins and Kshatriyas told him that Brahma forbade those to approach who were created out of his womb and feet. The Vaishas were allowed to listen to the Vedas only on holidays and the Shudras were forbidden not only to be present at the reading of the Vedas, but could not even look at them.

Issa said that man had filled the temples with his abominations. In order to pay homage to metals and stones, man sacrificed his fellows in whom dwells a spark of the Supreme Spirit. Man demeans those who labor by the sweat of their brows, in order to gain the good will of the sluggard who sits at the lavishly set board. But they who deprive their brothers of the common blessing shall be themselves stripped of it.

Vaishas and Shudras were struck with astonishment and asked what they could perform. Issa bade them "Worship not the idols. Do not consider yourself first. Do not humiliate your neighbor. Help the poor. Sustain the feeble. Do evil to no one. Do not covet that which you do not possess and which is possessed by others."

Many, learning of such words, decided to kill Issa. But Issa, forewarned, departed from this place by night.
Afterward, Issa went into Nepal and into the Himalayan mountains....

"Well, perform for us a miracle," demanded the servitors of the Temple. Then Issa replied to them: "Miracles made their appearance from the very day when the world was created. He who cannot behold them is deprived of the greatest gift of life. But woe to you, enemies of men, woe to you, if you await that He should attest his power by miracle."

Issa taught that men should not strive to behold the Eternal Spirit with one's own eyes but to feel it with the heart, and to become a pure and worthy soul....

"Not only shall you not make human offerings, but you must not slaughter animals, because all is given for the use of man. Do not steal the goods of others, because that would be usurpation from your near one. Do not cheat, that you may in turn not be cheated.
"Beware, you, who divert men from the true path and who fill the people with superstitions and prejudices, who blind the vision of the seeing ones, and who preach subservience to material things."
Issa taught: "Do not seek straight paths in darkness, possessed by fear. But gather force and support each other. He who supports his neighbor strengthens himself

"I tried to revive the laws of Moses in the hearts of the people. And I say to you that you do not understand their true meaning because they do not teach revenge but forgiveness. But the meaning of these laws is distorted."

Then the ruler sent to Issa his disguised servants that they should watch his actions and report to him about his words to the people.

"You just man, "said the disguised servant of the ruler of Jerusalem approaching Issa, "Teach us, should we fulfill the will of Caesar or await the approaching deliverance?" But Issa, recognizing the disguised servants, said, "I did not foretell to you that you would be delivered from Caesar; but I said that the soul which was immersed in sin would be delivered from sin."

At this time, an old woman approached the crowd, but was pushed back. Then Issa said, "Reverence Woman, mother of the universe,' in her lies the truth of creation. She is the foundation of all that is good and beautiful. She is the source of life and death. Upon her depends the existence of man, because she is the sustenance of his labors. She gives birth to you in travail, she watches over your growth. Bless her. Honor her. Defend her. Love your wives and honor them, because tomorrow they shall be mothers, and later-progenitors of a whole race. Their love ennobles man, soothes the embittered heart and tames the beast. Wife and mother, they are the adornments of the universe."

"As light divides itself from darkness, so does woman possess the gift to divide in man good intent from the thought of evil. Your best thoughts must belong to woman. Gather from them your moral strength, which you must possess to sustain your near ones. Do not humiliate her, for therein you will humiliate yourselves. And all which you will do to mother, to wife, to widow or to another woman in sorrow, that shall you also do for the Spirit."

So taught Issa; but the ruler Pilate ordered one of his servants to make accusation against him.

Said Issa: "Not far from here is the time when by the Highest Will the people will become purified and united into one family."

And then turning to the ruler, he said, "Why demean your dignity and teach your subordinates to live in deceit when even without this you could also have had the means of accusing an innocent one?"

From another version of the legend, Roerich quotes fragments of thought and evidence of the miraculous.

Near Lhasa was a temple of teaching with a wealth of manuscripts. Jesus was to acquaint himself with them. Meng-ste, a great sage of all the East, was in this temple.

Finally Jesus reached a mountain pass and in the chief city of Ladak, Leh, he was joyously accepted by monks and people of the lower class. And Jesus taught in the monasteries and in the bazaars (the market places); wherever the simple people gathered, there he taught.

Not far from this place lived a woman whose son had died and she brought him to Jesus. And in the presence of a multitude, Jesus laid his hand on the child, and the child rose healed. And many brought their children and Jesus laid his hands upon them, healing them.

Among the Ladakis, Jesus passed many days, teaching them. And they loved him and when the time of his departure came they sorrowed as children.

The Life of Saint Issa
Best of the Sons of Men
Using the translation by Notovitch

CHAPTER I

1 The earth has trembled and the heavens have wept because of a great crime which has been committed in the land of Israel.

2 For they have tortured and there put to death the great and just Issa, in whom dwelt the soul of the universe,

3 Which was incarnate in a simple mortal in order to do good to men and to exterminate their evil thoughts.

4 And in order to bring back mankind, which has been degraded by his sins, to a life of peace, love, and happiness and to call him back to the one and indivisible Creator, whose mercy is infinite and without bounds.

5 Hear what the merchants from Israel relate to us on this subject.

CHAPTER II

1 The people of Israel, who dwelt on a fertile soil giving forth two crops a year and who possessed large flocks, had by their sins aroused the anger of God,

2 Who inflicted upon them a terrible chastisement by taking from them their land, their cattle, and their possessions. Israel was reduced to slavery by the powerful and rich pharaohs who then reigned in Egypt.

3 These treated the Israelites worse than animals, burdening them with difficult tasks and loading them with chains. They covered their bodies with whelps and wounds, without giving them food or permitting them to dwell beneath a roof,

4 to keep them in a state of continual terror and to deprive them of all human resemblance.

5 And in their great calamity, the people of Israel remembered their heavenly protector and, addressing themselves to him, they implored his grace and mercy.

6 An illustrious pharaoh then reigned in Egypt who had made himself famous by his numerous victories. The riches he gained had piled up, and there were vast palaces which his slaves had erected for him with their own hands.

7 This pharaoh had two sons, of whom the younger was called Mossa (Moses). Learned Israelites taught him diverse sciences.

8 And they loved Mossa (Moses) in Egypt for his goodness and the compassion which he showed to all those who suffered.

9 Seeing that in spite of the intolerable sufferings they were enduring the Israelites would not abandon their God to worship those made by the hand of man, which were gods of the Egyptian nation,

10 Mossa (Moses) believed in their invisible God, because He did not let their failing strength give way.

11 And the Israelite teachers excited the passion of Mossa and had conversations with him, praying him to intercede with the pharaoh his father in favor of their fellow believers.

12 Then the Prince Mossa went to his father, begging him to make better the fate of these unfortunates. But the pharaoh became angered against him and only augmented the torments endured by his slaves.

13 It happened that a short time after, a great evil visited Egypt. The pestilence came to decimate both the young and the old, the weak and the strong; and the pharaoh believed this was because his own gods were turning against him.

14 But the Prince Mossa told his father that it was the God of his slaves who was interceding in favor of these unfortunates in punishing the Egyptians.

15 The pharaoh then gave to Mossa his son an order to take all the slaves of the Jewish race, to conduct them outside the town, and to found at a great distance from the capital another city where he should dwell with them.

16 Mossa then made known to the Hebrew slaves that he had set them free in the name of their God, the God of Israel, and he went out with them from the city and from the land of Egypt.

17 He led them into the land they had lost by their many sins. There Mossa gave them laws, and enjoined them to pray always to the invisible Creator whose goodness is infinite.

18 On the death of Prince Mossa, the Israelites rigorously observed his laws, wherefore God made amends and rewarded them for the ills to which he had exposed them in Egypt.

19 Their kingdom became the most powerful of all the earth, their kings made themselves famous for their treasures, and a long peace reigned among the people of Israel.

CHAPTER III

1 The glory of the riches of Israel spread throughout the earth, and made neighboring nations envious.

2 For the Most High himself led the victorious arms of the Hebrews, and the pagans dared not attack them.

3 Unhappily, as man is not always true to himself, the fidelity of the Israelites to their God did not last long.

4 They began by forgetting all the favors which he had heaped upon them, seldom invoked his name, and sought the protection of magicians and sorcerers.

5 The kings and the captains substituted their own laws for those which Mossa had written down for them. The temple of God and the practice of worship were abandoned. The people gave themselves up to pleasure and lost their original purity.

6 Several centuries had elapsed since their departure from Egypt when God determined to exercise once more his chastisements upon them.

7 Strangers began to invade the land of Israel, devastating the country, ruining the villages, and carrying the inhabitants into captivity.

8 And there came at one time pagans from the country of Romeles, (birthplace of Romulus, modern day Rome) on the other side of the sea. They subdued the Hebrews and established among them military leaders who by delegation from Caesar ruled over them.

9 They destroyed the temples, they forced the inhabitants to cease worshipping the invisible God, and they compelled them to sacrifice victims to the pagan deities.

10 They made warriors of those who had been nobles, the women were torn away from their husbands, and the lower classes, were reduced to slavery and were sent by thousands beyond the seas.

11 As to the children, they were put to the sword. Soon in all the land of Israel nothing was heard but groans and lamentations.

12 In this extreme distress, the people remembered their great God. They implored his grace and besought him to forgive them; and our Father, in his inexhaustible mercy, heard their prayer.

CHAPTER IV

1 It was at this time that the moment came when the all-merciful Judge elected to become incarnate in a human being.

2 And the Eternal Spirit, dwelling in a state of complete inaction (peace and stillness) and of supreme beatitude, awoke and detached itself for an indefinite period from the Eternal Being.

3 This was done to show forth in the guise of humanity the means of self-identification with Divinity and of attaining to eternal joy (bliss,)

4 And to demonstrate by example how man may attain moral purity and, by separating his soul from its mortal coil, the degree of perfection necessary to enter into the kingdom of heaven, which is unchangeable and where happiness reigns eternal.

5 Soon after, a marvelous child was born in the land of Israel, God himself speaking by the mouth of this infant of the frailty of the body and the grandeur of the soul.

6 The parents of the newborn child were poor people, belonging by birth to a family of noted piety, who, forgetting their ancient grandeur on earth, praised the name of the Creator and thanked him for the ills with which he saw fit to prove them.

7 To reward them for not turning aside from the way of truth, God blessed the firstborn of this family. He chose him for his

elect and sent him to help those who had fallen into evil and to cure those who suffered.

8 The divine child, to whom was given the name of Issa (Jesus), began from his earliest years to speak of the one and indivisible God. He exhorted the souls of those gone astray to come to repentance and the purification of the sins of which they were culpable.

9 People came from all parts to hear him, and they marveled at the discourses proceeding from his childish mouth. All the Israelites were of one accord in saying that the Eternal Spirit dwelt in this child.

10 When Issa (Jesus) had attained the age of thirteen years, which is the period of life when an Israelite should take a wife,

11 the house where his parents earned their living by carrying on a modest trade began to be a place of meeting for rich and noble people, who were desirous of having the young Issa for a son-in-law, for he was already famous for his edifying discourses in the name of the Almighty.

12 Then it was that Issa left the parental house in secret, departed from Jerusalem, and with the merchants set out towards Sind, (a province of southeastern Pakistan)

13 with the aim of perfecting himself in the Divine Word and of studying the laws of the great Buddhas.

CHAPTER V

1 In the course of his fourteenth year, the young Issa, blessed of God, came on this side of Sind and established himself among the Aryas (Northern India) in the land beloved of God.

2 Fame spread the reputation of this marvelous child throughout the length of northern Sind, and when he crossed the country of the five rivers and the Rajputana, *(An area northwest of the Arāvalli Range including part of the Great Indian (Thar) Desert.)* These were the devotees of the god Jaine and they prayed Issa to dwell among them.

3 But he left the erring worshippers of Jaine and went to Juggernaut in the country of Orissa, where repose the mortal remains of Vyasa-Krishna and where the white priests of Brahma made him a Joyous welcome.

(Juggernaut is the Hinduism form of Krishna worshiped in Puri, Orissa. Also called Jagannatha . Hindi from Sanskrit Jagannātha 'Lord of the world.')

4 They taught him to read and understand the Vedas, to cure by aid of prayer, to teach, to explain the holy scriptures to the people, and to drive out evil spirits from the bodies of men, restoring to them their sanity.

5 He passed six years at Juggernaut, at Rajagriha, at Benares, and in the other holy cities. Everyone loved him, for Issa lived in peace with the Vaisyas *(a member of the third of the four Hindu castes, comprising the merchants and farmers)* and the Sudras, *(a member of the worker caste, lowest of the four Hindu castes,)* whom he instructed in the holy scriptures.

6 But the Brahmans *(a member of the highest Hindu caste, that of the priesthood)* and the Kshatriyas *(a member of the second of the four great Hindu castes, the military caste. The traditional function of the Kshatriyas is to protect society by fighting in wartime and governing in peacetime,)* told him that they were forbidden by the great Para-Brahma to come near to those whom he had created from his side and his feet;

7 That the Vaisyas were only authorized to hear the reading of the Vedas, and this on festival days, and

8 that the Sudras were forbidden not only to assist at the reading of the Vedas, but also from contemplating them, for their condition was to serve in perpetuity as slaves to the Brahmans, the Kshatriyas, and even the Vaisyas.

9 "'Death only can set them free from their servitude' has said Para-Brahma. Leave them then and come and worship with us the gods, who will become very angry against you if you should disobey them."

10 But Issa listened not to their discourses and went to the Sudras, preaching against the commands of the Brahmans and the Kshatriyas.

11 He spoke and preached against the act of a man claiming to himself the power to deprive his fellow beings of their rights of humanity; "for," said he, "God the Father makes no difference between his children; all to him are equally dear."

12 Issa denied the divine origin of the Vedas (scriptures) and the Puranas (written legends and folklore.) "For," he taught his followers, "a law has already been given to man to guide him in his actions, which are,

13 "Fear your God, bend the knee before him only, and bring to him alone the offerings which proceed from your gains."

14 Issa denied the Trimurti (the trinity of Brahma the creator, Vishnu the preserver, and Shiva the destroyer) and the incarnation of Para-Brahma in Vishnu, Siva, and other gods, for said he:

15 "The Judge Eternal, the Eternal Spirit, comprehends the one and indivisible soul of the universe, which alone creates, contains, and vivifies all.

Inasmuch as Jesus' closest disciple, John, begins his Gospel with a quote from the Vedas, "In the beginning was the Word . . . ," the authenticity of this passage may be questioned. (Notation added by Notovitch)

16 "He alone has willed and created, he alone has existed since all eternity, and his existence will have no end. He has no equal either in the heavens or on earth."

17 "The Great Creator has not shared his power with any living being, still less with inanimate objects, as they have taught to you; for he alone possesses omnipotence."

18 "He willed it and the world appeared. In a divine thought, he gathered together the waters, separating from them the dry portion of the globe. He is the principle of the mysterious existence of man, in whom he has breathed a part of his Being. *(inspired, to breathe into)*

19 "And he has subordinated to man the earth, the waters, the beasts, and all that he has created and that he himself preserves in immutable order, fixing for each thing the length of its duration."

20 "The anger of God will soon be let loose against man; for he has forgotten his Creator, he has filled his temples with abominations, and he worships a collection of creatures which God has made subordinate to him.

21 "For to do honor to stones and metals, he sacrifices human beings, in whom dwells a part of the spirit of the Most High."

22 "He humiliates those who work by the sweat of their brow in order to acquire the favor of an idle (shiftless) person seated at his sumptuous table (board)."

23 "Those who deprive their brethren of divine happiness shall be deprived of it themselves. The Brahmans and the Kshatriyas shall become the Sudras, and with the Sudras the Eternal (God) shall dwell everlastingly."

24 "Because in the day of the last judgment the Sudras and the Vaisyas (the two lowest classes) will be forgiven much because of their ignorance, while God, on the contrary, will punish with his wrath those who have usurped to themselves his rights."

25 The Vaisyas and the Sudras were filled with great admiration and asked Issa (Jesus) how they should pray so as not to lose their eternal joy (felicity).

26 "Worship not the idols, for they hear you not. Listen not to the Vedas, for their truth is counterfeit. Never put yourself in the first place and never humiliate your neighbor."

27 "Help the poor, support the weak, do ill to no one, and covet not that which you have not and which you see belongs to another."

Sir John Wodroofe notes: "The fourth Gospel opens grandly, 'In the beginning was the Word, and the Word was with God and the Word was God.' These are the very words of Veda. Prajapatir vai idam asit: In the beginning was Brahman. Tasya vag dvitya asit; with whom was the Vak or the Word... Vag vai paramam Brahma; and the word is Brahman" (The Garland Letters, 7th ed. [Pondicherry: Ganesh & Co., 1979] p.4)

CHAPTER VI

1 The white priests and the warriors, becoming acquainted with the discourses of Issa addressed to the Sudras, resolved upon his death and sent their servants to seek out the young prophet with this intent.

2 But Issa, warned of his danger by the Sudras, left the area of Juggernaut by night, reached the mountain, and established himself in the country of Gautamides, the birthplace of the great Buddha Sakyamuni, *(around Nepal?)* in the midst of a people worshipping the one and sublime Brahma.

3 After having perfected himself in the Pali language, the just Issa applied himself to the study of the sacred writings of the Sutras.

4 Six years after, Issa, whom the Buddha had elected to spread his holy word, had become a perfect teacher (expositor) of the sacred writings.

5 Then he left Nepal and the Himalayan mountains, descended into the valley of Rajputana, and went towards the west, preaching to diverse peoples the supreme perfection of man, (what a perfect man should be and do)

6 Which is, to do good to one's neighbor, being the sure means of merging oneself rapidly in the Eternal Spirit: "He who shall have regained his original purity," said Issa, "will die having obtained remission for his sins, and he will have the right to contemplate the majesty of God."

7 In crossing pagan territories, the divine Issa taught that the worship of visible gods was contrary to the law of nature.

8 "For man," said he, "has not been permitted to see the image of God, and yet he has made a host of deities in the likeness of the Eternal."

(One may argue that as man has not seen God how could he make deities in His likeness. Possibly we should read this as, "Man made deities according to what His weak imagination envisioned God to look like.)

9 "Moreover, it is incompatible with the human conscience to make less matter of the splendor of divine purity than of animals and objects executed by the hand of man in stone or metal."

10 "The Eternal Lawgiver is one; there is no other God but he. He has not shared the world with anyone, neither has he informed anyone of his intentions."

11 "Even as a father would act towards his children, so will God judge men after their deaths according to the laws of his mercy. Never would he so humiliate his child as to transmigrate his soul, as in a purgatory, into the body of an animal."

12 "The heavenly law," said the Creator by the mouth of Issa, "is opposed to the immolation *(to kill as a sacrifice, especially by burning)* of human sacrifices to an image or to an animal; for I have consecrated to man all the animals and all that the earth contains."

13 "All things have been sacrificed to man, who is directly and intimately associated with me, his Father; therefore he who shall have stolen from me my child will be severely judged and chastised by the divine law."

14 "Man is nothing before the Eternal Judge, as the animal is nothing before man."

15 "Therefore I say to you, Leave your idols and perform no rites which separate you from your Father, associating you with the priests from whom the heavens have turned away."

16 "For it is they who have led you from the true God and whose superstitions and cruelties which help bring about the perversion of your soul and the loss of all moral sense."

CHAPTER VII

1 The words of Issa spread among the pagans in the midst of the countries he traversed, and the inhabitants forsook their

idols.

2 But the priests tried to make Him pay who glorified the name of the true God in the presence of the people and ridiculed and demonstrated the nothingness of their idols.

3 And Issa made answer to them: "If your idols and your animals are powerful and really possessed of supernatural strength, then let them strike me to the earth."

4 "Work then a miracle," replied the priests, "and let your God confound our gods, if they inspire him with contempt."

5 But Issa then said: "The miracles of our God have been worked since the first day when the universe was created; they take place every day and at every moment. Whosoever does not see them is deprived of one of the finest gifts of life."

6 "And it is not against pieces of stone, metal, or wood, which are inanimate, that the anger of God will have full course; but it will fall on men, who, if they desire their salvation, must destroy all the idols they have made."

7 "Even as a stone and a grain of sand are nothing in the sight of man, but they wait patiently for the moment when he shall take and make use of them,

8 "so man must await the great favor that God shall accord him in his final judgment."

9 "But woe to you, you enemies of men, if it be not a favor that you await but rather the wrath of the Divinity-woe to you if you expect miracles to bear witness to his power.

10 "For it will not be the idols that he will annihilate in his anger but those who shall have erected them. Their hearts shall be consumed with eternal fire, and their lacerated bodies shall go to satiate the hunger of wild beasts."

11 "God will drive the impure from among his flocks, but he will take back to himself those who shall have gone astray through not having recognized the portion of spirituality within them."

12 Seeing the powerlessness of their priests, the pagans had still greater faith in the sayings of Issa and, fearing the anger of the Divine (God), broke their idols to pieces. As for the priests, they fled to escape the vengeance of the populace.

13 And Issa further taught the pagans not to strive to see the Eternal Spirit with their eyes but to endeavor to feel him in their hearts and by purity of soul to render themselves worthy of his favors.

14 He also said to them, "Abstain from consuming human sacrifices, but kill (sacrifice by fire) no creature to whom life has been given, for all things that exist have been created for the profit of man."

15 "Do not steal the goods of your neighbor, for that would be to deprive him of what he has acquired by the sweat of his brow."

16 "Deceive no one, so as not to be yourselves deceived. Endeavor to justify yourself prior to the last judgment, for then it will be too late."

17 "Do not give yourselves up to debauchery, for that would be to violate the laws of God."

18 "You shall attain to supreme happiness, not only in purifying yourselves, but also in guiding others in the way that shall permit them to gain original perfection."

CHAPTER VIII

1 The neighboring countries resounded with the prophecies of Issa, and when he entered into Persia the priests became alarmed and forbade the inhabitants to listen to him.

2 And when they saw all the villages welcoming him with joy and listening devoutly to his sermons, they gave orders to arrest him and had him brought before the high priest, where he underwent the following interrogation:

3 "Of what new God do you speak? Are you not aware, you unhappy man, that Saint Zoroaster is the only just one admitted to the privilege of communion with the Supreme Being,"

4 "who ordered the angels to put down in writing the word of God for the use of his people, laws that were given to Zoroaster in paradise?"

5 "Who then are you to dare here to blaspheme our God and to sow doubt in the hearts of believers?"

6 And Issa said to them: "It is not of a new God that I speak but of our Heavenly Father, who has existed since all time and who will still be after the end of all things.

7 "It is of him that I have discoursed to the people, who, like to innocent children, are not yet capable of comprehending God by the simple strength of their intelligence or of penetrating into his sublime and divine spirit."

8 "But even as a babe discovers its mother's breast in the darkness, so even your people, who have been led into error by your erroneous doctrine and your religious ceremonies, have recognized by instinct their Father and it is the Father of whom I am the prophet."

9 "The Eternal Being has said to your people through the medium of my mouth: 'You shall not worship the sun, for it is but a part of the world which I have created for man."

10 "The sun rises in order to warm you during your work; it sets to allow you the rest, which I myself have appointed."

11 "It is to me, and to me alone, that you owe all that you possess, all that is to be found around you, above you, and below you."

12 "But," said the priests, "how could a people live according to the rules of justice if it had no teachers?"

13 Then Issa answered, "So long as the people had no priests, the natural law governed them, and they preserved the open honesty of their souls.

14 "Their souls were with God, and to commune with the Father they had recourse to the medium of no idol or animal, nor to the fire, as is practiced here."

15 "You contend that one must worship the sun, the spirit of good and of evil. Well, I say to you, your doctrine is a false one, the sun acting not spontaneously but according to the will of the invisible Creator who gave it birth"

16 "And who has willed it to be the star that should light the day, to warm the labor and the seedtime of man."

17 "The Eternal Spirit is the soul of all that is animate. You commit a great sin in dividing it into a spirit of evil and a spirit of good, for there is no God outside the good,"

18 "who, like to the father of a family, does but good to his children, forgiving all their faults if they repent them."

19 "The spirit of evil dwells on the earth in the hearts of those men who turn aside the children of God from the strait path."

20 "Therefore I say to you, Beware of the day of judgment, for God will inflict a terrible chastisement upon all those who shall have led his children astray from the right path and have filled them with superstitions and prejudices;"

21 "those who have blinded them that see, conveyed contagion to the healthy, and taught the worship of the things that God has subordinated to man for his good and to aid him in his work."

22 "Your doctrine is therefore the fruit of your errors; for desiring to bring near to you the God of truth, you have created for yourselves false gods."

23 After having listened to him, the magi determined to do him no harm. But at night, when all the town lay sleeping, they conducted him outside of the walls and abandoned him on the high road, in the hope that he would soon become a prey to the wild beasts.

24 But, protected by the Lord our God, Saint Issa continued his way undisturbed and unharmed.

CHAPTER IX

1 Issa, whom the Creator had elected to remind a depraved humanity of the true God, had reached his twenty-ninth year when he returned to the land of Israel.

2 Since his departure the pagans had inflicted still more atrocious sufferings on the Israelites, who were a prey to the deepest despondency.

3 Many among them had already begun to abandon the laws of their God and those of Mossa in the hope of appeasing their savage conquerors.

4 In the face of this evil, Issa exhorted his fellow citizens not to despair because the day of the redemption of sins was at hand, and he confirmed them in the belief which they had in the God of their fathers.

5 "Children, do not give yourselves up to despair," said the Heavenly Father by the mouth of Issa, "for I have heard your voice, and your cries have reached me."

6 "Do not weep, O my beloved ones! For your grief has touched the heart of your Father, and he has forgiven you, even as he forgave your forefathers."

7 "Do not abandon your families to plunge yourselves into debauchery, do not lose the nobility of your feelings, and do not worship idols who will remain deaf to your voices."

8 "Fill my temple with your hope and with your patience and abjure not the religion of your fathers; for I alone have guided them and have heaped them with benefits."

9 "You shall lift up those who have fallen, you shall give food to the hungry, and you shall come to the aid of the sick, so as to be all pure and just at the day of the last judgment which I prepare for you."

10 The Israelites came in crowds at the word of Issa, asking him where they should praise the Heavenly Father, seeing that the enemy had razed their temples to the ground and laid low their sacred vessels.

11 And Issa made answer to them that God had not in view temples erected by the hands of man, but he meant that the human heart was the true temple of God.

12 "Enter into your temple, into your heart. Illumine it with good thoughts and the patience and immovable confidence which you should have in your Father."

13 "And your sacred vessels, they are your hands and your eyes. See and do that which is agreeable to God, for in doing good to your neighbor you accomplish a rite which embellishes the temple wherein dwells he who gave you life."

14 "For God has created you in his own likeness; innocent, with pure souls and hearts filled with goodness, destined not for the conception of evil schemes but made to be sanctuaries of love and justice."

15 "Therefore I say to you, dirty not your hearts, for the Supreme Being dwells therein eternally."

16 "If you wish to accomplish works marked with love or piety, do them with an open heart and do not let your actions be governed by calculations (plans) or the hope of gain."

17 "For such actions would not help to your salvation, and you would fall into that state of moral degradation where theft, lying, and murder pass for generous deeds."

CHAPTER X

1 Saint Issa went from one town to another, strengthening the courage of the Israelites by the word of God, who were ready to succumb to the weight of their despair; and thousands of men followed him to hear him preach.

2 But the chiefs of the towns became afraid of him, and they made known to the principal governor who dwelt at Jerusalem that a man named Issa had arrived in the country; that he was stirring up the people against the authorities by his discourses; that the crowd listened to him with close attention, neglected the works of the state, and affirmed that before long it would be rid of its intrusive governors.

3 Then Pilate, governor of Jerusalem, ordered that they should seize Issa, the preacher, that they should bring him into the

town and lead him before the judges. But in order not to excite the anger of the populace, Pilate ordered the priests and the learned Hebrew elders to judge him in the temple.

4 Meanwhile Issa, continuing his preaching, arrived at Jerusalem; and, having learned of his arrival, all the inhabitants, knowing him already by reputation, went out to meet him.

5 They greeted him respectfully and opened to him the gates of their temple in order to hear from his mouth what he had said in the other cities of Israel.

6 And Issa said to them: "The human race perishes because of its lack of faith, for the darkness and the tempest have scattered the flocks of humanity and they have lost their shepherds.

7 "But the tempest will not last forever, and the darkness will not always obscure the light. The sky will become once more serene, the heavenly light will spread itself over the earth, and the flocks gone astray will gather around their shepherd."

8 "Do not strive to find straight paths in the darkness, or you will fall into a pit; but gather together your remaining strength, support one another, place your confidence in your God, and wait till light appears."

9 "He who sustains his neighbor, sustains himself; and whoever protects his family, protects the people and the state."

10 "For be sure that the day is at hand when you shall be delivered from the darkness; you shall be gathered together as one family; and your enemy, who ignores the favor (approval) of God, shall tremble with fear."

11 The priests and the elders who were listening to him were filled with admiration at his discourse and asked him if it were true that he had tried to stir up the people against the authorities of the country, as had been reported to the governor Pilate.

12 "Can one excite to insurrection men gone astray, whose door and path have been hidden and obscured?" replied Issa. "I have only warned the unfortunates, as I do here in this temple, that they may not further advance along the darkened way, for an abyss is open under their feet."

13 "Earthly power is not of long duration, and it is subject to many changes. What use is it that man should revolt against it, seeing that one power always succeeds to another power? And thus it will come to pass until the extinction of humanity."

14 "Don't you see that the mighty and the rich sow among the sons of Israel a spirit of rebellion against the eternal power of heaven?"

15 The elders then asked: "Who are you, and from what country do you come? We have not heard speak of you before, and we do not even know your name."

16 "I am an Israelite," replied Issa. "From the day of my birth I saw the walls of Jerusalem, and I heard the weeping of my brothers reduced to slavery and the lamentations of my sisters who were carried away by the pagans."

17 "And my soul was filled with sadness when I saw that my brethren had forgotten the true God. As a child, I left my father's house and went to dwell among other peoples."

18 "But having heard that my brethren were suffering still greater tortures, I have come back to the country where my parents dwell to remind my brothers of the faith of their forefathers, which teaches us patience on earth to obtain perfect and sublime happiness in heaven."

19 And the learned elders put to him this question: "It is said that you deny the laws of Mossa (Moses) and that you teach the people to forsake the temple of God?"

20 And Issa replied: "One cannot demolish that which has been given by our Heavenly Father, neither that which has been destroyed by sinners; but I have enjoined the purification of the heart from all blemish, for it is the true temple of God."

21 "As for the laws of Mossa (Moses), I have endeavored to establish them in the hearts of men. And I say to you that you do not understand their real meaning, for it is not vengeance but mercy that they teach; but the sense (meaning) of these laws has been perverted."

CHAPTER XI

1 Having listened to Issa, the priests and the wise elders decided among themselves not to judge him, for he did harm to no one. And presenting themselves before Pilate, appointed governor of Jerusalem by the pagan king of the country of Romeles (Rome), they addressed him thus:

2 "We have seen the man whom you accuse of inciting our people to rebellion; we have heard his discourses, and we know him to be our compatriot."

3 "But the chiefs of the cities have made you false reports, for this is a just man who teaches the people the word of God. After having interrogated him, we dismissed him, that he might go in peace."

4 The governor then became enraged and sent near to Issa his servants in disguise, so that they might watch all his actions and report to the authorities the least word that he should address to the people.

5 In the meantime, Saint Issa continued to visit the neighboring towns, preaching the true ways of the Creator, exhorting the Hebrews to patience, and promising them a speedy deliverance.

6 And during all this time, many people followed him wherever he went, several never leaving him but becoming his servitors (attendant to their superior).

7 And Issa said: "Do not believe in miracles wrought by the hand of man, for he who dominates over nature is alone capable of doing that which is supernatural, while man is powerless to stay the anger of the winds or to spread the rain.

8 "Nevertheless, there is one miracle which it is possible for man to accomplish. It is when, full of a sincere belief, he decides to root out from his heart all evil thoughts, and when to attain his end he forsakes the paths of iniquity.

9 "And all the things that are done without God are but errors, seductions, and enchantments, which only demonstrate to

what an extent the soul of him who practices this is full of shamelessness, falsehood, and impurity."

10 "Put not your faith in oracles; God alone knows the future: he who has recourse to diviners profanes the temple which is in his heart and gives a proof of distrust towards his Creator."

11 "Faith in diviners and in their oracles destroys the innate simplicity of man and his childlike purity. An infernal power takes possession of him, forcing him to commit all sorts of crimes and to worship idols;"

12 "whereas the Lord our God, who has no equal, is one (unified), all-mighty, omniscient, and omnipresent. It is he who possesses all wisdom and all light."

13 "It is to him you must address yourselves to be consoled in your sorrows, helped in your works, and cured in your sickness. Whosoever shall have recourse to him shall not be denied."

14 "The secret of nature is in the hands of God. For the world, before it appeared, existed in the depth of the divine thought; it became material and visible by the will of the Most High."

15 "When you address yourselves to him, become again as children; for you know neither the past, the present, nor the future, and God is the Master of all time."

CHAPTER XII

1 The spies of the governor of Jerusalem said to him, "Righteous man, tell us if we shall perform the will of our Caesar or await our speedy deliverance. "

2 And Issa, having recognized them as people appointed to follow him, replied: "I have not said to you that you shall be delivered from Caesar. It is the soul plunged in error that shall have its deliverance."

3 "As there can be no family without a head, so there can be no order among a people without a Caesar; to him implicit obedience should be given, he alone being answerable for his acts before the supreme tribunal."

4 "Does Caesar possess a divine right?" further asked of him the spies. "And is he the best of mortals?"

5 "There should be no better among men, but there are also sufferers, whom those elected and charged with this mission should care for, by making use of the means conferred on them by the sacred law of our Heavenly Father."

6 "Mercy and justice are the highest attributes of a Caesar; his name will be illustrious if he adhere to them."

7 "But he who acts otherwise, who exceeds the limit of power that he has over his subordinates and goes so far as to put their lives in danger offends the great Judge and loses his dignity in the sight of man."

8 At this juncture, an old woman who had approached the group, the better to hear Issa, was pushed aside by one of the spies, who placed himself before her.

9 Then Issa held forth (his hand and said): "It is not good (meant) that a son should set aside his mother to take her place. Whosoever respects not his mother, the most sacred being after his God, is unworthy of the name of son.

10 "Listen, then, to what I say to you: Respect woman, for she is the mother of the universe, and all the truth of divine creation lies in her."

11 "She is the basis of all that is good and beautiful, as she is also the germ of life and death. On her depends the whole existence of man, for she is his natural and moral support."

12 "She gives birth to you in the midst of suffering. By the sweat of her brow she rears you, and until her death you cause her the gravest anxieties. Bless her and worship her, for she is your one friend, your one support on earth."

13 "Respect her, uphold her. In acting thus you will win her love and her heart. You will find favor in the sight of God and many sins shall be forgiven you."

14 "In the same way, love your wives and respect them; for they will be mothers tomorrow, and each later on the ancestress of a race."

15 "Be lenient towards woman. Her love ennobles man, softens his hardened heart, tames the brute in him, and makes of him a lamb."

16 "The wife and the mother are the treasures beyond realms of appreciation given to you by God. They are the fairest ornaments of existence, and of them shall be born all the inhabitants of the world."

17 "Even as the God of armies separated of old the light from the darkness and the land from the waters, woman possesses the divine faculty of separating in a man good intentions from evil thoughts."

18 "Therefore I say to you, after God your best thoughts should belong to the women and the wives, woman being for you the temple wherein you will obtain the most easily perfect happiness."

19 "Acquire moral strength for yourselves in this temple. Here you will forget your sorrows and your failures, and you will recover the lost energy necessary to enable you to help your neighbor."

20 "Do not expose her to humiliation. In acting thus you would humiliate yourselves and lose the sentiment of love, without which nothing exists here below."

21 "Protect your wife, in order that she may protect you and all your family. All that you do for your wife, your mother, for a widow or another woman in distress, you will have done to your God."

CHAPTER XIII

1 Saint Issa taught the people of Israel thus for three years, in every town, in every village, by the waysides and on the plains; and all that he had predicted came to pass.

2 During all this time the disguised servants of Pilate watched him closely without hearing anything said like to the reports made against Issa in former years by the chiefs of the towns.

3 But the governor Pilate, becoming alarmed at the too great popularity of Saint Issa, who according to his adversaries sought to stir up the people to proclaim him king, ordered one of his spies to accuse him.

4 Then soldiers were commanded to proceed to his arrest, and they imprisoned him in a subterranean cell where they tortured him in various ways in the hope of forcing him to make a confession which should permit his being put to death.

5 The saint, thinking only of the perfect beatitude of his brethren, supported (endured) all his sufferings in the name of his Creator.

6 The servants of Pilate continued to torture him and reduced him to a state of extreme weakness; but God was with him and did not allow him to die.

7 Learning of the sufferings and the tortures, which their saint was enduring, the high priests and the wise elders went to pray the governor to set Issa at liberty in honor of an approaching festival.

8 But the governor straightway refused them this. They then prayed him to allow Issa to appear before the tribunal of the ancients so that he might be condemned or acquitted before the festival, and to this Pilate consented.

9 The next day the governor assembled together the chief captains, priests, wise elders, and lawyers so that they might judge Issa.

10 They brought him from his prison and seated him before the governor between two thieves to be judged at the same time as he, in order to show to the crowd that he was not the only one to be condemned.

11 And Pilate, addressing himself to Issa, said to him: "O man! is it true that you incite the people against the authorities with the intent of yourself becoming king of Israel?"

12 "One becomes not king at one's own will," replied Issa, "and they have lied who have told you that I stir up the people to rebellion. I have never spoken of other than the King of Heaven, and it is he I teach the people to worship."

13 "For the sons of Israel have lost their original purity; and if they have not recourse to the true God, they will be sacrificed and their temple shall fall into ruins."

14 "As temporal (earthly) power maintains order in a country, I teach them accordingly not to forget it. I say to them: 'Live conformably to your station and your fortune, so as not to disturb the public order.' And I have exhorted them also to remember that disorder reigns in their hearts and in their minds."

15 "Therefore the King of Heaven has punished them and suppressed their national kings. Nevertheless, I have said to them, 'If you become resigned to your destinies, as a reward the kingdom of heaven shall be reserved for you.'"

16 At this moment, the witnesses were brought forward, one of whom made the following deposition: "You have said to the people that the temporal (earthly) power is as nothing against that of the king who shall soon deliver the Israelites from the pagan yoke."

17 "Blessed are you," said Issa, "for having spoken the truth. The King of Heaven is greater and more powerful than the terrestrial law, and his kingdom surpasses all the kingdoms of the earth."

18 "And the time is not far off when, conforming to the divine will, the people of Israel shall purify them of their sins; for it has been said that a forerunner will come to proclaim the deliverance of the people, gathering them into one fold."

19 "And the governor, addressing himself to the judges, said: "Do you hear? The Israelite Issa confesses to the crime of which he is accused. Judge him, then, according to your laws, and pronounce against him capital punishment."

20 "We cannot condemn him," replied the priests and the elders. "You have just heard yourself that his allusions were made regarding the King of Heaven and that he has preached naught to the sons of Israel which could constitute an offense against the law."

21 The governor Pilate then sent for the witness who, at his instigation, had betrayed Issa. The man came and addressed Issa thus: "Did you not pass yourself off as the king of Israel when you said that he who reigns in the heavens had sent you to prepare his people?"

22 And Issa, having blessed him, said: "You shall be pardoned, for what you say does not come from you!" Then, addressing himself to the governor: "Why humiliate your dignity, and why teach your inferiors to live in falsehood, as without doing so you have power to condemn the innocent?"

23 At these words the governor became exceeding angry, ordering the sentence of death to be passed on Issa and the acquittal of the two thieves.

24 The judges, having consulted together, said to Pilate: "We will not take upon our heads the great sin of condemning an innocent man and acquitting thieves. That would be against the law."

25 "Do then as you will." Saying this the priests and the wise elders went out and washed their hands in a sacred vessel, saying: "We are innocent of the death of this just man."

CHAPTER XIV

1 By the order of the governor, the soldiers then seized Issa and the two thieves, whom they led to the place of execution, where they nailed them to crosses erected on the ground.

2 All the day the bodies of Issa and the two thieves remained suspended, terrible to behold, under the guard of the soldiers; the people standing all around and the relatives of the sufferers were praying and weeping.

3 At sunset the sufferings of Issa came to an end. He lost consciousness, and the soul of this just man left his body to become absorbed in the Divinity.

4 Thus ended the earthly existence of the reflection of the Eternal Spirit under the form of a man who had saved hardened

sinners and endured many sufferings.

Author's note: The following ending represents a divergence from mainline Christian Theology, which cannot be harmonized or reconciled. Under orders from Pilate the body of Issa (Jesus) is taken away. The "stolen body" theory is one of several explanations offered up by some who do not believe in the resurrection of Jesus.

5 Meanwhile, Pilate became afraid of his action and gave the body of the saint to his parents, who buried it near the spot of his execution. The crowd came to pray over his tomb, and the air was filled with groans and lamentations.

6 Three days after, the governor sent his soldiers to carry away the body of Issa to bury it elsewhere, fearing otherwise a popular insurrection.

7 The next day the crowd found the tomb open and empty. At once the rumor spread that the supreme Judge had sent his angels to carry away the mortal remains of the saint in whom dwelt on earth a part of the Divine Spirit.

8 When this rumor reached the knowledge of Pilate, he became angered and forbade anyone, under the pain of slavery and death, to pronounce the name of Issa or to pray the Lord for him.

9 But the people continued to weep and to glorify aloud their Master; wherefore many were led into captivity, subjected to torture, and put to death.

10 And the disciples of Saint Issa abandoned the land of Israel and scattered themselves among the heathen, preaching that they should renounce their errors, bringing them to think about the salvation of their souls and of the perfect bliss (felicity) awaiting humanity in that immaterial (spiritual) world of light where, in repose (rest) and in all his purity, the Great Creator dwells in perfect majesty.

11 The pagans, their kings, and their warriors listened to the preachers, abandoned their absurd beliefs, and forsook their priests and their idols to celebrate the praise of the all-wise Creator of the universe, the King of kings, whose heart is filled with infinite mercy.

This ends the "Life of Saint Issa."

Section Four

The Apocrypha:

Introduction:

A Brief History of the Apocrypha

The official editions of the King James contained the books of the Apocrypha until 1796. Most printers did not clear inventories and change to the sixty-six book version we know today until the mid 1800's. Thus, most Bibles printed before 1840 still had the Apocrypha, or at least most of the Apocrypha. As it turns out, various religions have differing versions of the Bible, made up of divergent lists of books. The Protestant church has its sixty-six books, the Catholics have kept most of the Apocrypha. The Eastern Orthodox Church claims three more books than the Catholics, and the Ethiopic Church has a total of eighty-one books in its Bible.

The Etymologically of the word "apocrypha" means "things that are hidden," but why they were hidden is not clear. Some have suggested that the books were "hidden" from common use because they contained esoteric knowledge, too profound to be communicated to any except the initiated (compare 2 Esd 14.45-46). Others have suggested that such books were hidden due to their spurious or heretical teaching.

According to traditional usage "Apocrypha" has been the designation applied to the fifteen books, or portions of books, listed below. (in many earlier editions of the Apocrypha, the Letter of Jeremiah is incorporated as the final chapter of the Book of Baruch; hence in these editions there are fourteen books.)

Tobit, Judith, The Additions to the Book of Esther (contained in the Greek version of Esther), The Wisdom of Solomon, Ecclesiasticus, The Wisdom of Jesus son of Sirach, Baruch, The Letter of Jeremiah, The Prayer of Azariah, The Song of the Three Jews ,"Susanna, Bel, and the Dragon", 1 Maccabees, 2 Maccabees, 1 Esdras, The Prayer of Manasseh, and 2 Esdras.

In addition, the present expanded edition includes the following three texts that are of special interest to Eastern Orthodox readers are 3 Maccabees, 4 Maccabees, and Psalm 151.

None of these books are included in the Hebrew canon of Holy Scripture. All of them, however, with the exception of 2 Esdras, are present in copies of the Greek version of the Old Testament known as the Septuagint. The Old Latin translations of the Old Testament, made from the Septuagint, also include them, along with 2 Esdras. The Eastern Orthodox Churches chose to include 1 Esdras, Psalm 151, the Prayer of Manasseh, and 3 Maccabees, and 4 Maccabees, which is placed in an appendix as a historical work.

At the end of the fourth century, Pope Damasus commissioned Jerome to prepare a standard Latin version of the Scriptures called the Latin Vulgate. Jerome wrote a note or preface, designating a separate category for the apocryphal books. However, copyists failed the include Jerome's prefaces. Thus, during the medieval period the Western Church generally regarded these books as part of the holy Scriptures.

In 1546 the Council of Trent decreed that the canon of the Old Testament includes the Apocrypha with the exception of the Prayer of Manasseh and 1 and 2 Esdras. Later, the church completed the decision by writing in its Roman Catholic Catechism, "Deuterocanonical does not mean Apocryphal, but simply 'later added to the canon."

But wait, there's more.

The narrow canon of the Ethiopic church contains the following Old Testament books:

Genesis
Exodus
Leviticus
Numbers
Deuteronomy
Enoch
Jubilees
Joshua
Judges
Ruth
1 Samuel
2 Samuel
1 Kings
2 Kings
1 Chronicles
2 Chronicles
Ezra
Nehemiah

3rd Ezra
4rth Ezra
Tobit
Judith
Esther (includes additions to Esther)
1 Macabees
2 Macabees
3 Macabees
Job
Psalms (+ Psalm 151)
Proverbs (Proverbs 1-24)
Täagsas (Proverbs 25-31)
Wisdom of Solomon
Ecclesiastes
Song of Solomon
Sirach (Ecclesiasticus)
Isaiah
Jeremiah
Baruch (includes Letter of Jeremiah)
Lamentations
Ezekiel
Daniel
Hosea
Amos
Micah
Joel
Obadiah
Jonah
Nahum
Habakkuk
Zephaniah
Haggai
Zecariah
Malachi

The Ethiopic Church also adds Clements and the Shepherd of Hermas to its New Testament canon. As stated before, the largest canon belongs to the Ethiopic Church, which is a part of a set of Eastern Orthodox churches. "The position of Eastern Orthodox Churches tend to have a more flexible canon of the Old Testament, and at times the list is not at all clear. For example, the Ethiopic Church has what is called a Narrow and Broad Canon.

The Broader Canon gives 46 as the total for the books of the Old Testament, made up as follows: - Octateuch (8), Judith (1), Samuel and Kings (4), Chronicles (2), 1 Esdras and the Ezra Apocalypse (2), Esther (1), Tobit (1), Maccabees (2), Job (1), Psalms (1), books of Solomon (5), Prophets (16), Ecclesiasticus (1), Pseudo-Josephus (1); Jubilees and Enoch are to be included in the number (by counting Samuel and Kings as only 2 books).

The New Testament has 35 books consisting of the Gospels (4), Acts (1), the Catholic epistles (7), the Pauline epistles (14), Revelation (1), Sinodos (4 sections), the Book of the Covenant (2 sections), Clement (1), Didascalia (1).

The Narrower Canon is made up of the Prayers of the Church and the list of the books actually printed in the large Geez and Amharic diglot, and Amharic Bibles, issued by the Emperor's command. In this, the universally accepted 39 Old Testament books are counted as 40 by the separation of Messale (Prov. 1-24) and Tägsas (Prov. 25-31), and then 14 further books are listed as equally fully canonical, namely Enoch, Jubilees, Wisdom, 1 Esdras, Ezra Apocalypse, Judith, Tobit, Ecclesiasticus, Baruch, 'the rest of Jeremiah', book of Susanna, 'the remainder of Daniel', 1 and 2 Maccabees. This brings the Old Testament total to 54, which together with the universally accepted 27 Old Testament books makes a total of 81.

The position of the Russian Orthodox Church as regards the Apocrypha appears to have changed during the centuries. The Holy Synod ruling from St. Petersburg were in sympathy with the position of the Reformers and decided to exclude the Apocrypha and since similar influences were emanating from the universities of Kiev, Moscow, Petersburg, and Kazan, the Russian Church became united in its rejection of the Apocrypha.

A full explanation of how the church of today got from the hundreds of books examined for canon to the eighty-one books of Ethiopia and finally to the mere sixty-six books of the Protestant Bible, is a matter of wide ranging discussion and varied opinions, to be taken up at another time. For now, let us simply acknowledge that the Bible many hold to with such passion and steadfastness is not the same book throughout Christendom. For now, we will simply enjoy the texts themselves.

The source of the books printed herein are in Public Domain with the exception of Enoch and Jubilees, which are my own renderings. Clements and Hermas use the J.B. Lightfoot translations as their source, but some of the archaic pronouns have been replaced. However, the "Elizabethan" sentence structure was left in place to keep the regal feel of those writings while modern pronouns assist in ease of reading.

An Overview of Books.

1 Esdras
1 Esdras is a document that has been drawn from the materials now in 1 and 2 Chronicles, Ezra, and Nehemiah. The author seemed to want to conform the books of Ezra and Nehemiah to the ideology of the books of Chronicles by giving special emphasis to the centrality of David, the inclusive characteristics of Israel, the doctrine of retribution and the need to obey the prophets, and the Temple and its practices. With the exception of one section, this book appears to be nothing more than a parallel version of the history beginning with the Passover of Josiah (622 B.C.E.) in II Chronicles 35:1 and continuing through Ezra (except 4:6), including Nehemiah 7:73-8:12a . The story stops abruptly with Ezra's reading of the Law (c. 400 B.C.E.).

2 Esdras
The work known as 2 Esdras is in fact three separate compositions. Ezra's place in the story is that of a prophet. In 2 Esdras 1-2 (also known as 5 Ezra) Ezra prophesies about God's rejection of Israel as God's people and its replacement by the Church, making this section a Christian work , without question. It is composed in Greek around 150 C.E. In 2 Esdras 3-14 (also known as 4 Ezra) Ezra articulates the meaning of Israel's sufferings and reveals a vision of what God is going to do in the near future on Israel's behalf. This section of the text is a Jewish work written in Hebrew around 100 C.E.

1 Maccabees
Although the book presents the Jewish leaders Judas, Jonathan, and Simon as devout people and has little sympathy for people who favor hellenization, but it must be noted that he nowhere mentions divine intervention.
The contents of the book can be summarized as follows:
  Chapter 1-2: The hellenization of Judah and the non-violent resistance by Mattathias;
  Chapter 3-9: Military actions by Judas the Maccabaean ('battle hammer'): after 166, he defeats the Seleucid armies three
     times and liberates Jerusalem, where the temple is purified; more operations; Judas' defeat and death in 161;
  Chapter 9-12: Continued warfare, led by Judas' brother Jonathan (160-143), who, benefiting from wars of succession in the
     Seleucid Empire, restores the fortunes of the Jewish nationalists and adds to their territories;
  Chapter 13-16: The third brother, Simon, achieves political independence, and founds the Hasmonaean dynasty.
The author must have been a cultivated Jew living in Judah, and can be dated to c.100 B.C.E. Although we assume there is a Hebrew or Aramaic original, which is now lost. The Greek version has survived and was accepted as canonical by the Christians. It must have been popular in the Diaspora also. In the sixteenth century, the scholars of the Reformation preferred to concentrate on those texts of the Jewish Bible that were written in Hebrew. It was at this time that the final decision was made by church fathers that if a book was not written in Hebrew it would not be considered canon for the Old Testament.

2 Maccabees
2 Maccabees has a much greater interest in theology than I Maccabees. 2 Maccabees is not as well written and has a less polished form. The pagans are defined as 'blasphemous and barbarous nations' in 10.4, but there are also severe censures of apostate Jews, of whom there must therefore have been considerable numbers. We find a theological features in 2 Maccabees such as the resurrection of the body in 7.11; 14.46. This stand in stark contrast first to Wisdom and Philo, both of which teach the immortality of the soul. In 7.28 there appears for the first time in Hebrew thought the doctrine which will later be called creatio ex nihilo, which is the belief that creation, and thus all things created, was brought about out of nothing. That is to say that God made the world not from things which were, which is not identical with 'nothing' in the philosophical sense of the term. In 7.9, 14 (cf. 14.46; 12.43) we have concepts of eternal life and death, and in 12.43 the intercession of the living for the dead, an element on which the Catholic church has sometimes sought to found the doctrine of Purgatory. Lastly, there is a well-developed angelology (3.24-28; 5.2-4; 10.29ff.; 11.8, etc.) Indeed, 2 Maccabees influenced the theology of certain churches more than any apocryphal book.

3 Maccabees

The title of 3 Maccabees is a misnomer because the book has nothing to do with the Maccabees, who are never mentioned in it. The book is a story about a situation in which the Jewish people, this time in Egypt, were in danger of being annihilated by a Hellenistic monarch, who was attempting to top their religious convictions and practices. The book was composed in Greek and relates a story set in the time of Ptolemy IV Philopater (221-203 B.C.E).

4 Maccabees
4 Maccabees belongs to the Maccabees series only because it deals with the beginning of the persecution of Jews by Antiochus IV Epiphanes. It possibly was written during the reign of the emperor Caligula (C.E. 37.) The work's main religious theme is that the martyr's sufferings expunged the sins of the entire Jewish people through a type of propitiation. The Maccabees books were preserved only by the Christian church. Augustine wrote in The City of God that they were preserved for their accounts of the martyrs. This suggests that 4 Maccabees may have been the most highly regarded of the Maccabees series, although this is disputed by the fact that 3 Maccabees may have actually established the idea of Purgatory.

Letter (Epistle) of Jeremiah
Jeremiah is the 'author' of this text only insofar as Jeremiah provided the primary resource (Jer. 10:2-15) that the actual, anonymous author developed into a lengthier variation on the theme. With regard to the date of composition, Moore's caveat concerning the Additions to Daniel that one must distinguish this carefully from the time of translation into Greek is valid for the Additions to Jeremiah as well. The translation was accomplished before the end of the second century B.C.E, given the discovery of a Greek fragment of the Letter of Jeremiah at Qumran. The time of composition is less certain. Several scholars lay great stress on the peculiar internal indication of date: the prediction that the Jews would be in Babylon 'for a long time, up to seven generations' (v. 3) before God will bring them back to their ancestral land, which represents an alteration of Jeremiah's seventy years (Jer. 25:11; 29:10; an alteration also occurs in Daniel's 'seventy weeks of years' [Dan. 9:24; cf. 9:2]). (Ball 1913: 596; Moore 1977: 328; Mendels 1992: 722; Metzger 1957: 96). These scholars argue that the author must be writing before this period of time had elapsed, for it is difficult to imagine an author deliberately altering Jeremiah's prophecy in such a way that would already have proven false. A date between 317 and 306 B.C.E., or 280 years after either the first or second deportation to Babylon (597 and 586 B.C.E.), is taken as the latest date for the composition of the original Hebrew version. There is in fact no internal evidence to necessitate a later date, although the ambiguity of the length of time covered by a 'generation' should make us cautious about being overly precise about the range of dates."

The Prayer of Azariah
The original was in either Hebrew or Aramaic. Although not present in the MT, this so-called 'deuterocanonical fragment' has always been regarded as part of the canonical, inspired Scriptures. However, it is not part of the original story, but rather an addition made by an inspired author who took existing liturgical prayers, adapted them slightly, and inserted them here, with a few sentences of his own to make a smoother nexus. In both versions [LXX and Theodotian] this passage lies between MT Dan. 3:23 and 3:24 and consists of three unequal parts: first, the Prayer of Azariah, the Hebrew name of Abednego (vv. 1-22); second, a short prose account of the fate of the three Jews in the furnace (vv. 23-27); third, a hymn sung by the three youths while in the furnace (vv. 28-68). The relationship between MT Dan 3:23 and 3:24 is highly dramatic. The three Jewish youths are thrown into an incredibly hot furnace and presumably destroyed, when suddenly Nebuchadnezzar is perturbed and in astonishment claims to see four men in the fire, the fourth looking like a divine being. Nebuchadnezzar reacts to the miracle by praising the God of the Jews. The author of the addition must have found the transition too sudden and provided the details of the miracle to form a softer transitional path.
Baruch
There is some evidence that the work actually comes from at least three authors. The most obvious division occurs between the prose of 1:1-3:8 and the poetry in 3:9-5:9, but there appear also to be two distinct poems in this latter section: a celebration of Wisdom in 3:9-4:4 and a promise of restoration to Jerusalem in 4:5-5:9. The changes in style and the striking difference in the names for God ("Lord," "Lord God," "Lord Almighty, God of Israel" in 1:1-3:8; and "God," "the Holy One," "the Everlasting," "Everlasting Savior" in 3:9-5:9), makes the separate authorship of these two parts fairly certain. The poem on Wisdom, 3:9-4:4, may have been written at a later time based of the fact that it there is a sift of interest. Although the prose section, especially 1:14-3:8, shows considerable dependence on Jeremiah, the final poem of encouragement, 4:5-5:9, is highly reminiscent of II Isaiah. There is little to go on in attempting to fix a date. A good midpoint of dating would be 150 – 200 C.E.

Prayer of Manasseh (Manassas)
In II Chronicles 33:10-20 we are given an account of how the wicked king Manasseh, after being taken captive to Babylon by the Assyrians, repented and was restored to his kingdom, where he proceeded to undo much of the mischief he had done in his apostate days. Special mention is made in verses 18 and 19 of Manasseh's prayer. What were the words of Manasseh's prayer? Inquiring minds wanted to know. According to 2 Chronicles 33:18-19 the words were preserved in 'the Annals of the Kings of Israel' and in 'the records of the seers.' But neither of these books has been preserved. Since the prayer was not recorded by the Chronicler, an unknown writer of uncommon skill and piety has undertaken the task of supplying the lack

by means of this prayer Although we have no solid evidence of date, the earliest evidence for the work's existence comes from the third century C.E., so it could have originated at any time between the composition of 2 Chronicles and then.

Bel and the Dragon

Daniel 14:23-42: "In the companion story the same motive of discrediting pagan deities is apparent. The issue is approached, however, from the opposite angle. Whereas Bel is nothing more than a man-made statue, a fact which is easily demonstrated by its inability to eat, the dragon is a living creature and does eat. To prove that the dragon also is no god, Daniel must somehow show that merely being alive and able to eat is not sufficient evidence to establish divinity. This he does by offering to perform the apparently impossible feat of slaying the dragon. This is done through poison. Cakes of pitch, fat, and hair, makes the witless beast explode.

Wisdom of Sirach

By far the longest book, comprising almost one third of the Deuterocanon, Ecclesiasticus, or by its Greek title, the Wisdom of Jesus (from the Hebrew, Joshua), the Son of Sirach, provides the reader with the unusual advantage of a translator's preface. The author himself, moreover, has obliged the reader with his signature along with a blessing upon those who concern themselves with wisdom (50:27-29). From these passages, therefore, we learn that the book was composed in Hebrew in Judea by an ardent collector of gnomic sayings whose Hebrew name was Joshua ben Sira and was brought to the Jewish community in Alexandria by his grandson and translated into Greek. In his reference to 'the thirty-eighth year of the reign of Euergetes,' the grandson provides us with a clue to the date. How long after his arrival in Egypt he made the translation, we are not told, but his arrival can be dated quite precisely as 132 B.C.E. Based on the dates of the high priest's term mentioned in the book as compared to the works of Josephus, the book can be fixed somewhere between 150-170 B.C.E.

Wisdom of Solomon

Several factors point to Alexandria in Egypt as the place of composition: the use of Greek, the philosophical concepts, the focus on the exodus, the polemic against Egyptian animal-worship, and so on. A date in the first century B.C.E.E. seems most likely. The terminus a quo is set by the author's use of the Greek translation of Isaiah, Job, and Proverbs, the first of which was probably available by 200 B.C.E.E. First, the description of the development of the ruler cult in 14:16-20 best describes not the cult of the Ptolemaic kings of Egypt, a cult that was organized and promoted from the center, but the spontaneous, decentralized development of the imperial cult under Augustus, who was also Egypt's first 'remote' ruler since Alexander. Considers the author's address in 6:1-2 to the 'judges of the ends of the earth' who 'rule over multitudes, and boast of many nations' to fit the Roman imperial period better than its predecessors.

Additions to Esther

The Greek version of the Hebrew Bible Book of Esther is designated, "Additions to Esther" and pre-serves many details of the Hebrew account. Its portrayal of Esther herself, however, is appreciably different, primarily because of Additions C and D (Add Esth 13:8–14:19; 15:1–16). The Additions to Esther consist of six extended passages (107 verses) that have no counterpart in the Hebrew version. They are numbered as chaps 11–16, designated A–F, and added to the Hebrew text at various places. Another important "addition" to Greek Esther is the mention of God's name over fifty times. This has the effect of making the story explicitly religious, in sharp contrast to the Hebrew text, which does not mention God at all. Addition C corrects all the "flaws" in the Hebrew version of Esther, which was rejected as authoritative by some Jews even as late as the third century C.E. because of its "inexcusable" omissions. It never mentioned God. Esther also confesses her hatred for every alien, the pomp and ceremony of her office, and her abhorrence at being married to a non-Jew, turning the book into an indictment against Gentiles. Thus, with the addition of God and hatred, we have an acceptable religious text.

Tobit

Since the law is known as 'the book of Moses' or 'the law of Moses' (6:13; 7:11-13), the work must certainly postdate the fifth century, when the formation of the Pentateuch was nearly complete. It seems reasonable to set the earliest date of composition as sometime during the third century B.C.E.E. The book reflects the same ethos as in Ben Sira and Judith with regard to dietary laws, burial of the dead, the custom of marrying within one's local area, and piety. The discovery of the fragments of Tobit at Qumran sets the earliest dates from 100 B.C.E.E. Tobit's failure to reflect any knowledge of the issues surrounding the Hellenization crisis and Maccabean Revolt suggests that the book was written sometime between 250 and 175 B.C.E.E.

Judith

Inconsistent historical facts run rampant through this text. The closest we can come to setting the book in any historical detail , which may be stretched enough to make it fit with exaggerations is to identify the generals, Holofernes and Bagoas, with the two generals sent against Phoenicia, Palestine and Egypt by Artaxerxes III towards 350. The names are certainly Persian, and are attested frequently, but there are many difficulties, unless we accept that Judith is a fictional account of one of the episodes in this campaign. Holofernes' itinerary in ch. 2 also seems impossible: he covers almost 300 miles in three days, passing through places which are either unknown or absurd when they are known. No account is taken of the fact that an average of 100 miles a day is in any case excessive for an army consisting of infantry as well as cavalry. As we have seen, the identity of Bethulia is also unknown.

Susanna

As the story goes, a fair Hebrew wife bathes in her garden, having sent her attendants away. Two overly sexed old men secretly observe the lovely Susanna. When she makes her way back to her house, they accost her, threatening to claim that she was meeting a young man in the garden unless she agrees to have sex with them. She refuses and they falsely accuse her. She is arrested and about to be put to death for promiscuity when a young man named Daniel interrupts the proceedings. After separating the two men, they are questioned about details of the incident. They claim to have seen her under a tree, but they name trees of different placement and size. In the Greek text, the names of the trees cited by the elders form puns with the sentence given by Daniel. The first says they were under a mastic (υπο σχινον, hupo schinon), and Daniel says that an angels stands ready to cut (σχισει, schisei) him in two. The second says they were under an evergreen oak tree (υπο πρινον, hupo prinon), and Daniel says that an angel stands ready to saw (πρισαι, prisai) him in two. The great difference in size between a mastic and an oak makes the elders' lie obvious to all, and the accusers are put to death instead.

Psalm 151

Psalm 151 is the name given to a short psalm that is found in most copies of the Septugint but not in the Masoretic text of the Hebrew Bible. The title given to this psalm in the Septuagint indicates that no number is affixed to it: "This Psalm is ascribed to David and is outside the number. The psalm was written when he slew Goliath in single combat". It is included also in some manuscripts of the Pershitta. The Eastern Orthodox Church accepts Psalm 151 as canonical. Psalm 151 appears along with a number of canonical and non-canonical psalms in the Dead Sea Scroll a first century CE scroll discovered in 1956.

1 Clements

The epistle is customarily dated to the end of the reign of Domitian (95 or 96 C.E.). In the first sentence of the letter, the author explains that the Roman church has been delayed in turning its attention to the dispute at Corinth by "sudden and repeated misfortunes and hindrances which have befallen us" (1:1). This statement is usually interpreted as an allusion to a persecution through which the church at Rome has just been passing. The account of the deaths of Peter and Paul in chap. 5 is not that of an eye-witness. The presbyters installed by the apostles have died (44:2), and a second ecclesiastical generation has passed (44:3). The church at Rome is called "ancient" (47:6); and the emissaries from Rome are said to have lived "blamelessly" as Christians "from youth to old age" (63:3). Thus the epistle cannot have been written before the last decades of the 1st century. There are references to the letter by the middle of the next century in the works of Hegesippus and Dionysius of Corinth (apud Euseb. Hist. Eccl. 3.16; 4.22; 4.23). Thus one may place the composition of 1 Clement between C.E. 80 and 140 C.E..

Shepherd of Hermas

The early Christian document Hermas, or Shepherd of Hermas, was known to the early Church Fathers. The Muratorian canon, a list of canonical books from about the 3d century, says Hermas was written by the brother of Pius, Bishop of Rome, about 140-154 C.E.. It was written in Rome and involves the Roman church. The document was composed over a longer period of time. Visions I-IV were composed during a threatened persecution, probably under Trajan (the Clement of 8:3 could be Clement of Rome). Vision V - Similitude VIII and Similitude X were written perhaps by the same author to describe repentance to Christians who were wavering. Similitude IX was written to unify the entire work and to threaten those who had been disloyal. This last phase must have occurred before Irenaeus (ca. 175). A preferred date would be 140 C.E.

The text had a great vogue in orthodox circles and was even included in some copies of the New Testament (it is found in the Sinaitic Codex). The theology of the Church must have been very elastic at a time when such a book could enjoy popularity and implicit, if not explicit, ecclesiastical sanction, for its Christology does not seem to square with any of the Christologies of the New Testament, or with those of contemporary theologians whose occasional documents have reached us. The Shepherd speaks of a Son of God; but this Son of God is distinguished from Jesus. "That Holy Spirit which was created first of all, God placed in a body, in which it should dwell, in a chosen body, as it pleased him and states, "God made His Holy Spirit, which pre-existed and created all creation, to enter and dwell in the flesh which He approved." In this text the Holy Spirit appears to be a divine substance. But we must not suspect Patripassionism, which assumes God the father took form and suffered on the cross. The "flesh" is spoken of as a person who "walked as pleased God, because it was not polluted on earth." "God, therefore, took into counsel the Son and the angels in their glory, to the end that this flesh might furnish, as it were, a place of tabernacling (for the Spirit), and might not seem to have lost the reward of its service. For all flesh shall receive the reward which shall be found without stain or spot, and in it the Holy Spirit shall have its home." This passage appears to make the "tabernacling" of the Holy Spirit in Jesus a reward for the purity of his life. Jesus then becomes divine through the power of God, after consultation with the Son of God, who elsewhere in The Shepherd is identified with the Holy Spirit. "The most venerable angel," "the glorious angel," "the holy angel" are titles that Hermas gives to Jesus in his allegory; but it is understood that the angelic status of Jesus is not his by nature. His labours on earth to save and to cleanse have gained him a co-inheritance with the Holy Spirit, God's primary Son, so that Jesus now is the second Son of God.

1 Esdras

[1] Josiah kept the passover to his Lord in Jerusalem; he killed the passover lamb on the fourteenth day of the first month,
[2] having placed the priests according to their divisions, arrayed in their garments, in the temple of the Lord.
[3] And he told the Levites, the temple servants of Israel, that they should sanctify themselves to the Lord and put the holy ark of the Lord in the house which Solomon the king, the son of David, had built;
[4] and he said, "You need no longer carry it upon your shoulders. Now worship the Lord your God and serve his people Israel; and prepare yourselves by your families and kindred,
[5] in accordance with the directions of David king of Israel and the magnificence of Solomon his son. Stand in order in the temple according to the groupings of the fathers' houses of you Levites, who minister before your brethren the people of Israel,
[6] and kill the passover lamb and prepare the sacrifices for your brethren, and keep the passover according to the commandment of the Lord which was given to Moses."
[7] And Josiah gave to the people who were present thirty thousand lambs and kids, and three thousand calves; these were given from the king's possessions, as he promised, to the people and the priests and Levites.
[8] And Hilkiah, Zechariah, and Jehiel, the chief officers of the temple, gave to the priests for the passover two thousand six hundred sheep and three hundred calves. [9] And Jeconiah and Shemaiah and Nethanel his brother, and Hashabiah and Ochiel and Joram, captains over thousands, gave the Levites for the passover five thousand sheep and seven hundred calves.
[10] And this is what took place. The priests and the Levites, properly arrayed and having the unleavened bread, stood according to kindred
[11] and the grouping of the fathers' houses, before the people, to make the offering to the Lord as it is written in the book of Moses; this they did in the morning. [12] They roasted the passover lamb with fire, as required; and they boiled the sacrifices in brass pots and caldrons, with a pleasing odor, [13] and carried them to all the people. Afterward they prepared the passover for themselves and for their brethren the priests, the sons of Aaron, [14] because the priests were offering the fat until night; so the Levites prepared it for themselves and for their brethren the priests, the sons of Aaron. [15] And the temple singers, the sons of Asaph, were in their place according to the arrangement made by David, and also Asaph, Zechariah, and Eddinus, who represented the king. [16] The gatekeepers were at each gate; no one needed to depart from his duties, for their brethren the Levites prepared the passover for them. [17] So the things that had to do with the sacrifices to the Lord were accomplished that day: the passover was kept
[18] and the sacrifices were offered on the altar of the Lord, according to the command of King Josiah. [19] And the people of Israel who were present at that time kept the passover and the feast of unleavened bread seven days. [20] No passover like it had been kept in Israel since the times of Samuel the prophet; [21] none of the kings of Israel had kept such a passover as was kept by Josiah and the priests and Levites and the men of Judah and all of Israel who were dwelling in Jerusalem. [22] In the eighteenth year of the reign of Josiah this passover was kept. [23] And the deeds of Josiah were upright in the sight of the Lord, for his heart was full of godliness. [24] The events of his reign have been recorded in the past, concerning those who sinned and acted wickedly toward the Lord beyond any other people or kingdom, and how they grieved the Lord deeply, so that the words of the Lord rose up against Israel. [25] After all these acts of Josiah, it happened that Pharaoh, king of Egypt, went to make war at Carchemish on the Euphrates, and Josiah went out against him.
[26] And the king of Egypt sent word to him saying, "What have we to do with each other, king of Judea? [27] I was not sent against you by the Lord God, for my war is at the Euphrates. And now the Lord is with me! The Lord is with me, urging me on! Stand aside, and do not oppose the Lord." [28] But Josiah did not turn back to his chariot, but tried to fight with him, and did not heed the words of Jeremiah the prophet from the mouth of the Lord.
[29] He joined battle with him in the plain of Megiddo, and the commanders came down against King Josiah. [30] And the king said to his servants, "Take me away from the battle, for I am very weak." And immediately his servants took him out of the line of battle. [31] And he got into his second chariot; and after he was brought back to Jerusalem he died, and was buried in the tomb of his fathers. [32] And in all Judea they mourned for Josiah. Jeremiah the prophet lamented for Josiah, and the principal men, with the women, have made lamentation for him to this day; it was ordained that this should always be done throughout the whole nation of Israel. [33] These things are written in the book of the histories of the kings of Judea; and every one of the acts of Josiah, and his splendor, and his understanding of the law of the Lord, and the things that he had done before and these that are now told, are recorded in the book of the kings of Israel and Judah. [34] And the men of the nation took Jeconiah the son of Josiah, who was twenty-three years old, and made him king in succession to Josiah his father. [35] And he reigned three months in Judah and Jerusalem. Then the king of Egypt deposed him from reigning in Jerusalem, [36] and fined the nation a hundred talents of silver and a talent of gold. [37] And the king of Egypt made Jehoiakim his brother king of Judea and Jerusalem. [38] Jehoiakim put the nobles in prison, and seized his brother Zarius and brought him up out of Egypt. [39] Jehoiakim was twenty-five years old when he began to reign in Judea and Jerusalem, and he did what was evil in the sight of the Lord.

[40] And Nebuchadnezzar king of Babylon came up against him, and bound him with a chain of brass and took him away to Babylon. [41] Nebuchadnezzar also took some holy vessels of the Lord, and carried them away, and stored them in his temple in Babylon. [42] But the things that are reported about Jehoiakim and his uncleanness and impiety are written in the chronicles of the kings. [43] Jehoiachin his son became king in his stead; when he was made king he was eighteen years old, [44] and he reigned three months and ten days in Jerusalem. He did what was evil in the sight of the Lord. [45] So after a year Nebuchadnezzar sent and removed him to Babylon, with the holy vessels of the Lord, [46] and made Zedekiah king of Judea and Jerusalem.

Zedekiah was twenty-one years old, and he reigned eleven years.

[47] He also did what was evil in the sight of the Lord, and did not heed the words that were spoken by Jeremiah the prophet from the mouth of the Lord. [48] And though King Nebuchadnezzar had made him swear by the name of the Lord, he broke his oath and rebelled; and he stiffened his neck and hardened his heart and transgressed the laws of the Lord, the God of Israel. [49] Even the leaders of the people and of the priests committed many acts of sacrilege and lawlessness beyond all the unclean deeds of all the nations, and polluted the temple of the Lord which had been hallowed in Jerusalem. [50] So the God of their fathers sent by his messenger to call them back, because he would have spared them and his dwelling place. [51] But they mocked his messengers, and whenever the Lord spoke, they scoffed at his prophets, [52] until in his anger against his people because of their ungodly acts he gave command to bring against them the kings of the Chaldeans. [53] These slew their young men with the sword around their holy temple, and did not spare young man or virgin, old man or child, for he gave them all into their hands. [54] And all the holy vessels of the Lord, great and small, and the treasure chests of the Lord, and the royal stores, they took and carried away to Babylon. [55] And they burned the house of the Lord and broke down the walls of Jerusalem and burned their towers with fire, [56] and utterly destroyed all its glorious things. The survivors he led away to Babylon with the sword, [57] and they were servants to him and to his sons until the Persians began to reign, in fulfillment of the word of the Lord by the mouth of Jeremiah: [58] "Until the land has enjoyed its sabbaths, it shall keep sabbath all the time of its desolation until the completion of seventy years."

2

[1] In the first year of Cyrus as king of the Persians, that the word of the Lord by the mouth of Jeremiah might be accomplished,

[2] the Lord stirred up the spirit of Cyrus king of the Persians, and he made a proclamation throughout all his kingdom and also put it in writing: [3] "Thus says Cyrus king of the Persians: The Lord of Israel, the Lord Most High, has made me king of the world,

[4] and he has commanded me to build him a house at Jerusalem, which is in Judea. [5] If any one of you, therefore, is of his people, may his Lord be with him, and let him go up to Jerusalem, which is in Judea, and build the house of the Lord of Israel -- he is the Lord who dwells in Jerusalem, [6] and let each man, wherever he may live, be helped by the men of his place with gold and silver, [7] with gifts and with horses and cattle, besides the other things added as votive offerings for the temple of the Lord which is in Jerusalem." [8] Then arose the heads of families of the tribes of Judah and Benjamin, and the priests and the Levites, and all whose spirit the Lord had stirred to go up to build the house in Jerusalem for the Lord;

[9] and their neighbors helped them with everything, with silver and gold, with horses and cattle, and with a very great number of votive offerings from many whose hearts were stirred. [10] Cyrus the king also brought out the holy vessels of the Lord which Nebuchadnezzar had carried away from Jerusalem and stored in his temple of idols.

[11] When Cyrus king of the Perians brought these out, he gave them to Mithridates his treasurer, [12] and by him they were given to Sheshbazzar the governor of Judea. [13] The number of these was: a thousand gold cups, a thousand silver cups, twenty-nine silver censers, thirty gold bowls, two thousand four hundred and ten silver bowls, and a thousand other vessels. [14] All the vessels were handed over, gold and silver, five thousand four hundred and sixty-nine, [15] and they were carried back by Sheshbazzar with the returning exiles from Babylon to Jerusalem. [16] But in the time of Artaxerxes king of the Persians, Bishlam, Mithridates, Tabeel, Rehum, Beltethmus, Shimshai the scribe, and the rest of their associates, living in Samaria and other places, wrote him the following letter, against those who were living in Judea and Jerusalem:

[17] "To King Artaxerxes our lord, Your servants Rehum the recorder and Shimshai the scribe and the other judges of their council in Coelesyria and Phoenicia:

[18] Now be it known to our lord the king that the Jews who came up from you to us have gone to Jerusalem and are building that rebellious and wicked city, repairing its market places and walls and laying the foundations for a temple. [19] Now if this city is built and the walls finished, they will not only refuse to pay tribute but will even resist kings. [20] And since the building of the temple is now going on, we think it best not to neglect such a matter, [21] but to speak to our lord the king, in order that, if it seems good to you, search may be made in the records of your fathers. [22] You will find in the chronicles what has been written about them, and will learn that this city was rebellious, troubling both kings and other cities, [23] and that the Jews were rebels and kept setting up blockades in it from of old. That is why this city was laid waste. [24] Therefore we now make known to you, O lord and king, that if this city is built and its walls finished, you will no longer have access to Coelesyria and Phoenicia." [25] Then the king, in reply to Rehum the recorder and Beltethmus and Shimshai the scribe and the others associated with them and living in Samaria and Syria and Phoenicia, wrote as follows:

[26] "I have read the letter which you sent me. So I ordered search to be made, and it has been found that this city from of old has fought against kings,

[27] and that the men in it were given to rebellion and war, and that mighty and cruel kings ruled in Jerusalem and exacted tribute from Coelesyria and Phoenicia. [28] Therefore I have now issued orders to prevent these men from building the city and to take care that nothing more be done [29] and that such wicked proceedings go no further to the annoyance of kings." [30] Then, when the letter from King Artaxerxes was read, Rehum and Shimshai the scribe and their associates went in haste to Jerusalem, with horsemen and a multitude in battle array, and began to hinder the builders. And the building of the temple in Jerusalem ceased until the second year of the reign of Darius king of the Persians.

3

[1] Now King Darius gave a great banquet for all that were under him and all that were born in his house and all the nobles of Media and Persia
[2] and all the satraps and generals and governors that were under him in the hundred and twenty-seven satrapies from India to Ethiopia. [3] They ate and drank, and when they were satisfied they departed; and Darius the king went to his bedroom, and went to sleep, and then awoke. [4] Then the three young men of the bodyguard, who kept guard over the person of the king, said to one another,
[5] "Let each of us state what one thing is strongest; and to him whose statement seems wisest, Darius the king will give rich gifts and great honors of victory. [6] He shall be clothed in purple, and drink from gold cups, and sleep on a gold bed, and have a chariot with gold bridles, and a turban of fine linen, and a necklace about his neck; [7] and because of his wisdom he shall sit next to Darius and shall be called kinsman of Darius." [8] Then each wrote his own statement, and they sealed them and put them under the pillow of Darius the king,
[9] and said, "When the king wakes, they will give him the writing; and to the one whose statement the king and the three nobles of Persia judge to be wisest the victory shall be given according to what is written." [10] The first wrote, "Wine is strongest." [11] The second wrote, "The king is strongest." [12] The third wrote, "Women are strongest, but truth is victor over all things." [13] When the king awoke, they took the writing and gave it to him, and he read it.
[14] Then he sent and summoned all the nobles of Persia and Media and the satraps and generals and governors and prefects, [15] and he took his seat in the council chamber, and the writing was read in their presence. [16] And he said, "Call the young men, and they shall explain their statements." So they were summoned, and came in. [17] And they said to them, "Explain to us what you have written."
Then the first, who had spoken of the strength of wine, began and said:
[18] "Gentlemen, how is wine the strongest? It leads astray the minds of all who drink it. [19] It makes equal the mind of the king and the orphan, of the slave and the free, of the poor and the rich. [20] It turns every thought to feasting and mirth, and forgets all sorrow and debt. [21] It makes all hearts feel rich, forgets kings and satraps, and makes every one talk in millions. [22] When men drink they forget to be friendly with friends and brothers, and before long they draw their swords. [23] And when they recover from the wine, they do not remember what they have done. [24] Gentlemen, is not wine the strongest, since it forces men to do these things?" When he had said this, he stopped speaking.

4

[1] Then the second, who had spoken of the strength of the king, began to speak: [2] "Gentlemen, are not men strongest, who rule over land and sea and all that is in them? [3] But the king is stronger; he is their lord and master, and whatever he says to them they obey. [4] If he tells them to make war on one another, they do it; and if he sends them out against the enemy, they go, and conquer mountains, walls, and towers. [5] They kill and are killed, and do not disobey the king's command; if they win the victory, they bring everything to the king -- whatever spoil they take and everything else. [6] Likewise those who do not serve in the army or make war but till the soil, whenever they sow, reap the harvest and bring some to the king; and they compel one another to pay taxes to the king. [7] And yet he is only one man! If he tells them to kill, they kill; if he tells them to release, they release; [8] if he tells them to attack, they attack; if he tells them to lay waste, they lay waste; if he tells them to build, they build; [9] if he tells them to cut down, they cut down; if he tells them to plant, they plant. [10] All his people and his armies obey him. Moreover, he reclines, he eats and drinks and sleeps, [11] but they keep watch around him and no one may go away to attend to his own affairs, nor do they disobey him. [12] Gentlemen, why is not the king the strongest, since he is to be obeyed in this fashion?" And he stopped speaking. [13] Then the third, that is Zerubbabel, who had spoken of women and truth, began to speak:
[14] Gentlemen, is not the king great, and are not men many, and is not wine strong? Who then is their master, or who is their lord? Is it not women? [15] Women gave birth to the king and to every people that rules over sea and land. [16] From women they came; and women brought up the very men who plant the vineyards from which comes wine. [17] Women make men's clothes; they bring men glory; men cannot exist without women. [18] If men gather gold and silver or any other beautiful thing, and then see a woman lovely in appearance and beauty, [19] they let all those things go, and gape at her, and with open mouths stare at her, and all prefer her to gold or silver or any other beautiful thing. [20] A man leaves his own father, who brought him up, and his own country, and cleaves to his wife. [21] With his wife he ends his days, with no thought of his father or his mother or his country. [22] Hence you must realize that women rule over you!
"Do you not labor and toil, and bring everything and give it to women?
[23] A man takes his sword, and goes out to travel and rob and steal and to sail the sea and rivers; [24] he faces lions, and he walks in darkness, and when he steals and robs and plunders, he brings it back to the woman he loves. [25] A man loves his

575

wife more than his father or his mother. [26] Many men have lost their minds because of women, and have become slaves because of them. [27] Many have perished, or stumbled, or sinned, because of women. [28] And now do you not believe me? "Is not the king great in his power? Do not all lands fear to touch him?

[29] Yet I have seen him with Apame, the king's concubine, the daughter of the illustrious Bartacus; she would sit at the king's right hand [30] and take the crown from the king's head and put it on her own, and slap the king with her left hand. [31] At this the king would gaze at her with mouth agape. If she smiles at him, he laughs; if she loses her temper with him, he flatters her, that she may be reconciled to him. [32] Gentlemen, why are not women strong, since they do such things?"

[33] Then the king and the nobles looked at one another; and he began to speak about truth:

[34] "Gentlemen, are not women strong? The earth is vast, and heaven is high, and the sun is swift in its course, for it makes the circuit of the heavens and returns to its place in one day. [35] Is he not great who does these things? But truth is great, and stronger than all things. [36] The whole earth calls upon truth, and heaven blesses her. All God's works quake and tremble, and with him there is nothing unrighteous. [37] Wine is unrighteous, the king is unrighteous, women are unrighteous, all the sons of men are unrighteous, all their works are unrighteous, and all such things. There is no truth in them and in their unrighteousness they will perish. [38] But truth endures and is strong for ever, and lives and prevails for ever and ever. [39] With her there is no partiality or preference, but she does what is righteous instead of anything that is unrighteous or wicked. All men approve her deeds, [40] and there is nothing unrighteous in her judgment. To her belongs the strength and the kingship and the power and the majesty of all the ages. Blessed be the God of truth!" [41] He ceased speaking; then all the people shouted, and said, "Great is truth, and strongest of all!" [42] Then the king said to him, "Ask what you wish, even beyond what is written, and we will give it to you, for you have been found to be the wisest. And you shall sit next to me, and be called my kinsman."

[43] Then he said to the king, "Remember the vow which you made to build Jerusalem, in the day when you became king, [44] and to send back all the vessels that were taken from Jerusalem, which Cyrus set apart when he began to destroy Babylon, and vowed to send them back there. [45] You also vowed to build the temple, which the Edomites burned when Judea was laid waste by the Chaldeans. [46] And now, O lord the king, this is what I ask and request of you, and this befits your greatness. I pray therefore that you fulfil the vow whose fulfilment you vowed to the King of heaven with your own lips." [47] Then Darius the king rose, and kissed him, and wrote letters for him to all the treasurers and governors and generals and satraps, that they should give escort to him and all who were going up with him to build Jerusalem.

[48] And he wrote letters to all the governors in Coelesyria and Phoenicia and to those in Lebanon, to bring cedar timber from Lebanon to Jerusalem, and to help him build the city. [49] And he wrote for all the Jews who were going up from his kingdom to Judea, in the interest of their freedom, that no officer or satrap or governor or treasurer should forcibly enter their doors; [50] that all the country which they would occupy should be theirs without tribute; that the Idumeans should give up the villages of the Jews which they held; [51] that twenty talents a year should be given for the building of the temple until it was completed, [52] and an additional ten talents a year for burnt offerings to be offered on the altar every day, in accordance with the commandment to make seventeen offerings; [53] and that all who came from Babylonia to build the city should have their freedom, they and their children and all the priests who came. [54] He wrote also concerning their support and the priests' garments in which they were to minister. [55] He wrote that the support for the Levites should be provided until the day when the temple should be finished and Jerusalem built. [56] He wrote that land and wages should be provided for all who guarded the city. [57] And he sent back from Babylon all the vessels which Cyrus had set apart; everything that Cyrus had ordered to be done, he also commanded to be done and to be sent to Jerusalem. [58] When the young man went out, he lifted up his face to heaven toward Jerusalem, and praised the King of heaven, saying,

[59] "From thee is the victory; from thee is wisdom, and your is the glory. I am thy servant. [60] Blessed art thou, who hast given me wisdom; I give thee thanks, O Lord of our fathers." [61] So he took the letters, and went to Babylon and told this to all his brethren.

[62] And they praised the God of their fathers, because he had given them release and permission [63] to go up and build Jerusalem and the temple which is called by his name; and they feasted, with music and rejoicing, for seven days.

5

[1] After this the heads of fathers' houses were chosen to go up, according to their tribes, with their wives and sons and daughters, and their menservants and maidservants, and their cattle.

[2] And Darius sent with them a thousand horsemen to take them back to Jerusalem in safety, with the music of drums and flutes; [3] and all their brethren were making merry. And he made them go up with them. [4] These are the names of the men who went up, according to their fathers' houses in the tribes, over their groups:

[5] the priests, the sons of Phinehas, son of Aaron; Jeshua the son of Jozadak, son of Seraiah, and Joakim the son of Zerubbabel, son of Shealtiel, of the house of David, of the lineage of Phares, of the tribe of Judah, [6] who spoke wise words before Darius the king of the Persians, in the second year of his reign, in the month of Nisan, the first month. [7] These are the men of Judea who came up out of their sojourn in captivity, whom Nebuchadnezzar king of Babylon had carried away to Babylon

[8] and who returned to Jerusalem and the rest of Judea, each to his own town. They came with Zerubbabel and Jeshua, Nehemiah, Seraiah, Resaiah, Bigvai, Mordecai, Bilshan, Mispar, Reeliah, Rehum, and Baanah, their leaders. [9] The number of the men of the nation and their leaders: the sons of Parosh, two thousand one hundred and seventy-two. The sons of

Shephatiah, four hundred and seventy-two.

[10] The sons of Arah, seven hundred and fifty-six. [11] The sons of Pahathmoab, of the sons of Jeshua and Joab, two thousand eight hundred and twelve. [12] The sons of Elam, one thousand two hundred and fifty-four. The sons of Zattu, nine hundred and forty-five. The sons of Chorbe, seven hundred and five. The sons of Bani, six hundred and forty-eight. [13] The sons of Bebai, six hundred and twenty-three. The sons of Azgad, one thousand three hundred and twenty-two. [14] The sons of Adonikam, six hundred and sixty-seven. The sons of Bigvai, two thousand and sixty-six. The sons of Adin, four hundred and fifty-four. [15] The sons of Ater, namely of Hezekiah, ninety-two. The sons of Kilan and Azetas, sixty-seven. The sons of Azaru, four hundred and thirty-two. [16] The sons of Annias, one hundred and one. The sons of Arom. The sons of Bezai, three hundred and twenty-three. The sons of Jorah, one hundred and twelve. [17] The sons of Baiterus, three thousand and five. The sons of Bethlehem, one hundred and twenty-three. [18] The men of Netophah, fifty-five. The men of Anathoth, one hundred and fifty-eight. The men of Bethasmoth, forty-two. [19] The men of Kiriatharim, twenty-five. The men of Chephirah and Beeroth, seven hundred and forty-three. [20] The Chadiasans and Ammidians, four hundred and twenty-two. The men of Ramah and Geba, six hundred and twenty-one. [21] The men of Michmas, one hundred and twenty-two. The men of Bethel, fifty-two. The sons of Magbish, one hundred and fifty-six. [22] The sons of the other Elam and Ono, seven hundred and twenty-five. The sons of Jericho, three hundred and forty-five. [23] The sons of Senaah, three thousand three hundred and thirty. [24] The priests: the sons of Jedaiah the son of Jeshua, of the sons of Anasib, nine hundred and seventy-two. The sons of Immer, one thousand and fifty-two.

[25] The sons of Pashhur, one thousand two hundred and forty-seven. The sons of Harim, one thousand and seventeen. [26] The Levites: the sons of Jeshua and Kadmiel and Bannas and Sudias, seventy-four.

[27] The temple singers: the sons of Asaph, one hundred and twenty-eight. [28] The gatekeepers: the sons of Shallum, the sons of Ater, the sons of Talmon, the sons of Akkub, the sons of Hatita, the sons of Shobai, in all one hundred and thirty-nine.

[29] The temple servants: the sons of Ziha, the sons of Hasupha, the sons of Tabbaoth, the sons of Keros, the sons of Siaha, the sons of Padon, the sons of Lebanah, the sons of Hagabah,

[30] the sons of Akkub, the sons of Uthai, the sons of Ketab, the sons of Hagab, the sons of Shamlai, the sons of Hana, the sons of Cathua, the sons of Gahar, [31] The sons of Reaiah, the sons of Rezin, the sons of Nekoda, the sons of Chezib, the sons of Gazzam, the sons of Uzza, the sons of Paseah, the sons of Hasrah, the sons of Besai, the sons of Asnah, the sons of the Meunites, the sons of Nephisim, the sons of Bakbuk, the sons of Hakupha, the sons of Asur, the sons of Pharakim, the sons of Bazluth, [32] the sons of Mehida, the sons of Cutha, the sons of Charea, the sons of Barkos, the sons of Sisera, the sons of Temah, the sons of Neziah, the sons of Hatipha. [33] The sons of Solomon's servants: the sons of Hassophereth, the sons of Peruda, the sons of Jaalah, the sons of Lozon, the sons of Giddel, the sons of Shephatiah,

[34] the sons of Hattil, the sons of Pochereth-hazzebaim, the sons of Sarothie, the sons of Masiah, the sons of Gas, the sons of Addus, the sons of Subas, the sons of Apherra, the sons of Barodis, the sons of Shaphat, the sons of Ami. [35] All the temple servants and the sons of Solomon's servants were three hundred and seventy-two.

[36] The following are those who came up from Telmelah and Telharsha, under the leadership of Cherub, Addan, and Immer,

[37] though they could not prove by their fathers' houses or lineage that they belonged to Israel: the sons of Delaiah the son of Tobiah, the sons of Nekoda, six hundred and fifty-two. [38] Of the priests the following had assumed the priesthood but were not found registered: the sons of Habaiah, the sons of Hakkoz, the sons of Jaddus who had married Agia, one of the daughters of Barzillai, and was called by his name.

[39] And when the genealogy of these men was sought in the register and was not found, they were excluded from serving as priests. [40] And Nehemiah and Attharias told them not to share in the holy things until a high priest should appear wearing Urim and Thummim. [41] All those of Israel, twelve or more years of age, besides menservants and maidservants, were forty-two thousand three hundred and sixty;

[42] their menservants and maidservants were seven thousand three hundred and thirty-seven; there were two hundred and forty-five musicians and singers. [43] There were four hundred and thirty-five camels, and seven thousand and thirty-six horses, two hundred and forty-five mules, and five thousand five hundred and twenty-five asses. [44] Some of the heads of families, when they came to the temple of God which is in Jerusalem, vowed that they would erect the house on its site, to the best of their ability,

[45] and that they would give to the sacred treasury for the work a thousand minas of gold, five thousand minas of silver, and one hundred priests' garments. [46] The priests, the Levites, and some of the people settled in Jerusalem and its vicinity; and the temple singers, the gatekeepers, and all Israel in their towns.

[47] When the seventh month came, and the sons of Israel were each in his own home, they gathered as one man in the square before the first gate toward the east.

[48] Then Jeshua the son of Jozadak, with his fellow priests, and Zerubbabel the son of Shealtiel, with his kinsmen, took their places and prepared the altar of the God of Israel, [49] to offer burnt offerings upon it, in accordance with the directions in the book of Moses the man of God. [50] And some joined them from the other peoples of the land. And they erected the altar in its place, for all the peoples of the land were hostile to them and were stronger than they; and they offered sacrifices at the proper times and burnt offerings to the Lord morning and evening. [51] They kept the feast of booths, as it is commanded in the law, and offered the proper sacrifices every day, [52] and thereafter the continual offerings and sacrifices on sabbaths and

at new moons and at all the consecrated feasts. [53] And all who had made any vow to God began to offer sacrifices to God, from the new moon of the seventh month, though the temple of God was not yet built. [54] And they gave money to the masons and the carpenters, and food and drink [55] and carts to the Sidonians and the Tyrians, to bring cedar logs from Lebanon and convey them in rafts to the harbor of Joppa, according to the decree which they had in writing from Cyrus king of the Persians. [56] In the second year after their coming to the temple of God in Jerusalem, in the second month, Zerubbabel the son of Shealtiel and Jeshua the son of Jozadak made a beginning, together with their brethren and the Levitical priests and all who had come to Jerusalem from the captivity;

[57] and they laid the foundation of the temple of God on the new moon of the second month in the second year after they came to Judea and Jerusalem. [58] And they appointed the Levites who were twenty or more years of age to have charge of the work of the Lord. And Jeshua arose, and his sons and brethren and Kadmiel his brother and the sons of Jeshua Emadabun and the sons of Joda son of Iliadun, with their sons and brethren, all the Levites, as one man pressing forward the work on the house of God.

So the builders built the temple of the Lord.

[59] And the priests stood arrayed in their garments, with musical instruments and trumpets, and the Levites, the sons of Asaph, with cymbals, [60] praising the Lord and blessing him, according to the directions of David king of Israel; [61] and they sang hymns, giving thanks to the Lord, because his goodness and his glory are for ever upon all Israel. [62] And all the people sounded trumpets and shouted with a great shout, praising the Lord for the erection of the house of the Lord. [63] Some of the Levitical priests and heads of fathers' houses, old men who had seen the former house, came to the building of this one with outcries and loud weeping, [64] while many came with trumpets and a joyful noise, [65] so that the people could not hear the trumpets because of the weeping of the people.

For the multitude sounded the trumpets loudly, so that the sound was heard afar;

[66] and when the enemies of the tribe of Judah and Benjamin heard it, they came to find out what the sound of the trumpets meant. [67] And they learned that those who had returned from captivity were building the temple for the Lord God of Israel. [68] So they approached Zerubbabel and Jeshua and the heads of the fathers' houses and said to them, "We will build with you. [69] For we obey your Lord just as you do and we have been sacrificing to him ever since the days of Esarhaddon king of the Assyrians, who brought us here." [70] But Zerubbabel and Jeshua and the heads of the fathers' houses in Israel said to them, "You have nothing to do with us in building the house for the Lord our God, [71] for we alone will build it for the Lord of Israel, as Cyrus the king of the Persians has commanded us." [72] But the peoples of the land pressed hard upon those in Judea, cut off their supplies, and hindered their building; [73] and by plots and demagoguery and uprisings they prevented the completion of the building as long as King Cyrus lived. And they were kept from building for two years, until the reign of Darius.

6

[1] Now in the second year of the reign of Darius, the prophets Haggai and Zechariah the son of Iddo prophesied to the Jews who were in Judea and Jerusalem, they prophesied to them in the name of the Lord God of Israel.

[2] Then Zerubbabel the son of Shealtiel and Jeshua the son of Jozadak arose and began to build the house of the Lord which is in Jerusalem, with the help of the prophets of the Lord who were with them. [3] At the same time Sisinnes the governor of Syria and Phoenicia and Sathrabuzanes and their associates came to them and said,

[4] "By whose order are you building this house and this roof and finishing all the other things? And who are the builders that are finishing these things?" [5] Yet the elders of the Jews were dealt with kindly, for the providence of the Lord was over the captives; [6] and they were not prevented from building until word could be sent to Darius concerning them and a report made. [7] A copy of the letter which Sisinnes the governor of Syria and Phoenicia, and Sathrabuzanes, and their associates the local rulers in Syria and Phoenicia, wrote and sent to Darius:

[8] "To King Darius, greeting. Let it be fully known to our lord the king that, when we went to the country of Judea and entered the city of Jerusalem, we found the elders of the Jews, who had been in captivity,

[9] building in the city of Jerusalem a great new house for the Lord, of hewn stone, with costly timber laid in the walls. [10] These operations are going on rapidly, and the work is prospering in their hands and being completed with all splendor and care. [11] Then we asked these elders, `At whose command are you building this house and laying the foundations of this structure?' [12] And in order that we might inform you in writing who the leaders are, we questioned them and asked them for a list of the names of those who are at their head. [13] They answered us, `We are the servants of the Lord who created the heaven and the earth. [14] And the house was built many years ago by a king of Israel who was great and strong, and it was finished. [15] But when our fathers sinned against the Lord of Israel who is in heaven, and provoked him, he gave them over into the hands of Nebuchadnezzar king of Babylon, king of the Chaldeans; [16] and they pulled down the house, and burned it, and carried the people away captive to Babylon. [17] But in the first year that Cyrus reigned over the country of Babylonia, King Cyrus wrote that this house should be rebuilt. [18] And the holy vessels of gold and of silver, which Nebuchadnezzar had taken out of the house in Jerusalem and stored in his own temple, these Cyrus the king took out again from the temple in Babylon, and they were delivered to Zerubbabel and Sheshbazzar the governor [19] with the command that he should take all these vessels back and put them in the temple at Jerusalem, and that this temple of the Lord should be rebuilt on its site. [20] Then this Sheshbazzar, after coming here, laid the foundations of the house of the Lord which is in Jerusalem, and although it has been in process of construction from that time until now, it has not yet reached completion.'

[21] Now therefore, if it seems wise, O king, let search be made in the royal archives of our lord the king that are in Babylon; [22] and if it is found that the building of the house of the Lord in Jerusalem was done with the consent of King Cyrus, and if it is approved by our lord the king, let him send us directions concerning these things." [23] Then Darius commanded that search be made in the royal archives that were deposited in Babylon. And in Ecbatana, the fortress which is in the country of Media, a scroll was found in which this was recorded:

[24] "In the first year of the reign of Cyrus, King Cyrus ordered the building of the house of the Lord in Jerusalem, where they sacrifice with perpetual fire; [25] its height to be sixty cubits and its breadth sixty cubits, with three courses of hewn stone and one course of new native timber; the cost to be paid from the treasury of Cyrus the king; [26] and that the holy vessels of the house of the Lord, both of gold and of silver, which Nebuchadnezzar took out of the house in Jerusalem and carried away to Babylon, should be restored to the house in Jerusalem, to be placed where they had been." [27] So Darius commanded Sisinnes the governor of Syria and Phoenicia, and Sathrabuzanes, and their associates, and those who were appointed as local rulers in Syria and Phoenicia, to keep away from the place, and to permit Zerubbabel, the servant of the Lord and governor of Judea, and the elders of the Jews to build this house of the Lord on its site.

[28] "And I command that it be built completely, and that full effort be made to help the men who have returned from the captivity of Judea, until the house of the Lord is finished; [29] and that out of the tribute of Coelesyria and Phoenicia a portion be scrupulously given to these men, that is, to Zerubbabel the governor, for sacrifices to the Lord, for bulls and rams and lambs, [30] and likewise wheat and salt and wine and oil, regularly every year, without quibbling, for daily use as the priests in Jerusalem may indicate, [31] in order that libations may be made to the Most High God for the king and his children, and prayers be offered for their life." [32] And he commanded that if any should transgress or nullify any of the things herein written, a beam should be taken out of his house and he should be hanged upon it, and his property should be forfeited to the king.

[33] "Therefore may the Lord, whose name is there called upon, destroy every king and nation that shall stretch out their hands to hinder or damage that house of the Lord in Jerusalem.

[34] "I, King Darius, have decreed that it be done with all diligence as here prescribed."

7

[1] Then Sisinnes the governor of Coelesyria and Phoenicia, and Sathrabuzanes, and their associates, following the orders of King Darius,

[2] supervised the holy work with very great care, assisting the elders of the Jews and the chief officers of the temple. [3] And the holy work prospered, while the prophets Haggai and Zechariah prophesied; [4] and they completed it by the command of the Lord God of Israel. So with the consent of Cyrus and Darius and Artaxerxes, kings of the Persians, [5] the holy house was finished by the twenty-third day of the month of Adar, in the sixth year of King Darius. [6] And the people of Israel, the priests, the Levites, and the rest of those from the captivity who joined them, did according to what was written in the book of Moses. [7] They offered at the dedication of the temple of the Lord one hundred bulls, two hundred rams, four hundred lambs, [8] and twelve he-goats for the sin of all Israel, according to the number of the twelve leaders of the tribes of Israel; [9] and the priests and the Levites stood arrayed in their garments, according to kindred, for the services of the Lord God of Israel in accordance with the book of Moses; and the gatekeepers were at each gate. [10] The people of Israel who came from the captivity kept the passover on the fourteenth day of the first month, after the priests and the Levites were purified together.

[11] Not all of the returned captives were purified, but the Levites were all purified together, [12] and they sacrificed the passover lamb for all the returned captives and for their brethren the priests and for themselves. [13] And the people of Israel who came from the captivity ate it, all those who had separated themselves from the abominations of the peoples of the land and sought the Lord. [14] And they kept the feast of unleavened bread seven days, rejoicing before the Lord, [15] Because he had changed the will of the king of the Assyrians concerning them, to strengthen their hands for the service of the Lord God of Israel.

8

[1] After these things, when Artaxerxes the king of the Persians was reigning, Ezra came, the son of Seraiah, son of Azariah, son of Hilkiah, son of Shallum,

[2] son of Zadok, son of Ahitub, son of Amariah, son of Uzzi, son of Bukki, son of Abishua, son of Phineas, son of Eleazar, son of Aaron the chief priest. [3] This Ezra came up from Babylon as a scribe skilled in the law of Moses, which was given by the God of Israel; [4] and the king showed him honor, for he found favor before the king in all his requests. [5] There came up with him to Jerusalem some of the people of Israel and some of the priests and Levites and temple singers and gatekeepers and temple servants, [6] in the seventh year of the reign of Artaxerxes, in the fifth month (this was the king's seventh year); for they left Babylon on the new moon of the first month and arrived in Jerusalem on the new moon of the fifth month, by the prosperous journey which the Lord gave them. [7] For Ezra possessed great knowledge, so that he omitted nothing from the law of the Lord or the commandments, but taught all Israel all the ordinances and judgments. [8] The following is a copy of the written commission from Artaxerxes the king which was delivered to Ezra the priest and reader of the law of the Lord:

[9] "King Artaxerxes to Ezra the priest and reader of the law of the Lord, greeting.

[10] In accordance with my gracious decision, I have given orders that those of the Jewish nation and of the priests and Levites and others in our realm, who freely choose to do so, may go with you to Jerusalem. [11] Let as many as are so

disposed, therefore, depart with you as I and the seven friends who are my counselors have decided, [12] in order to look into matters in Judea and Jerusalem, in accordance with what is in the law of the Lord, [13] and to carry to Jerusalem the gifts for the Lord of Israel which I and my friends have vowed, and to collect for the Lord in Jerusalem all the gold and silver that may be found in the country of Babylonia, [14] together with what is given by the nation for the temple of their Lord which is in Jerusalem, both gold and silver for bulls and rams and lambs and what goes with them, [15] so as to offer sacrifices upon the altar of their Lord which is in Jerusalem. [16] And whatever you and your brethren are minded to do with the gold and silver, perform it in accordance with the will of your God; [17] and deliver the holy vessels of the Lord which are given you for the use of the temple of your God which is in Jerusalem. [18] And whatever else occurs to you as necessary for the temple of your God, you may provide out of the royal treasury. [19] "And I, Artaxerxes the king, have commanded the treasurers of Syria and Phoenicia that whatever Ezra the priest and reader of the law of the Most High God sends for, they shall take care to give him,

[20] up to a hundred talents of silver, and likewise up to a hundred cors of wheat, a hundred baths of wine, and salt in abundance. [21] Let all things prescribed in the law of God be scrupulously fulfilled for the Most High God, so that wrath may not come upon the kingdom of the king and his sons. [22] You are also informed that no tribute or any other tax is to be laid on any of the priests or Levites or temple singers or gatekeepers or temple servants or persons employed in this temple, and that no one has authority to impose any tax upon them. [23] "And you, Ezra, according to the wisdom of God, appoint judges and justices to judge all those who know the law of your God, throughout all Syria and Phoenicia; and those who do not know it you shall teach.

[24] And all who transgress the law of your God or the law of the kingdom shall be strictly punished, whether by death or some other punishment, either fine or imprisonment." [25] Blessed be the Lord alone, who put this into the heart of the king, to glorify his house which is in Jerusalem,

[26] and who honored me in the sight of the king and his counselors and all his friends and nobles. [27] I was encouraged by the help of the Lord my God, and I gathered men from Israel to go up with me. [28] These are the principal men, according to their fathers' houses and their groups, who went up with me from Babylon, in the reign of Artaxerxes the king:

[29] Of the sons of Phineas, Gershom. Of the sons of Ithamar, Gamael. Of the sons of David, Hattush the son of Shecaniah. [30] Of the sons of Parosh, Zechariah, and with him a hundred and fifty men enrolled. [31] Of the sons of Pahathmoab, Eliehoenai the son of Zerahiah, and with him two hundred men. [32] Of the sons of Zattu, Shecaniah the son of Jahaziel, and with him three hundred men. Of the sons of Adin, Obed the son of Jonathan, and with him two hundred and fifty men. [33] Of the sons of Elam, Jeshaiah the son of Gotholiah, and with him seventy men. [34] Of the sons of Shephatiah, Zeraiah the son of Michael, and with him seventy men, [35] Of the sons of Joab, Obadiah the son of Jehiel, and with him two hundred and twelve men. [36] Of the sons of Bani, Shelomith the son of Josiphiah, and with him a hundred and sixty men. [37] Of the sons of Bebai, Zechariah the son of Bebai, and with him twenty-eight men. [38] Of the sons of Azgad, Johanan the son of Hakkatan, and with him a hundred and ten men. [39] Of the sons of Adonikam, the last ones, their names being Eliphelet, Jeuel, and Shemaiah, and with them seventy men. [40] Of the sons of Bigvai, Uthai the son of Istalcurus, and with him seventy men. [41] I assembled them at the river called Theras, and we encamped there three days, and I inspected them.

[42] When I found there none of the sons of the priests or of the Levites, [43] I sent word to Eliezar, Iduel, Maasmas, [44] Elnathan, Shemaiah, Jarib, Nathan, Elnathan, Zechariah, and Meshullam, who were leaders and men of understanding; [45] and I told them to go to Iddo, who was the leading man at the place of the treasury, [46] and ordered them to tell Iddo and his brethren and the treasurers at that place to send us men to serve as priests in the house of our Lord. [47] And by the mighty hand of our Lord they brought us competent men of the sons of Mahli the son of Levi, son of Israel, namely Sherebiah with his sons and kinsmen, eighteen; [48] also Hashabiah and Annunus and Jeshaiah his brother, of the sons of Hananiah, and their sons, twenty men; [49] and of the temple servants, whom David and the leaders had given for the service of the Levites, two hundred and twenty temple servants; the list of all their names was reported. [50] There I proclaimed a fast for the young men before our Lord, to seek from him a prosperous journey for ourselves and for our children and the cattle that were with us.

[51] For I was ashamed to ask the king for foot soldiers and horsemen and an escort to keep us safe from our adversaries; [52] for we had said to the king, "The power of our Lord will be with those who seek him, and will support them in every way." [53] And again we prayed to our Lord about these things, and we found him very merciful. [54] Then I set apart twelve of the leaders of the priests, Sherebiah and Hashabiah, and ten of their kinsmen with them; [55] and I weighed out to them the silver and the gold and the holy vessels of the house of our Lord, which the king himself and his counselors and the nobles and all Israel had given. [56] I weighed and gave to them six hundred and fifty talents of silver, and silver vessels worth a hundred talents, and a hundred talents of gold, [57] and twenty golden bowls, and twelve bronze vessels of fine bronze that glittered like gold. [58] And I said to them, "You are holy to the Lord, and the vessels are holy, and the silver and the gold are vowed to the Lord, the Lord of our fathers. [59] Be watchful and on guard until you deliver them to the leaders of the priests and the Levites, and to the heads of the fathers' houses of Israel, in Jerusalem, in the chambers of the house of our Lord." [60] So the priests and the Levites who took the silver and the gold and the vessels which had been in Jerusalem carried them to the temple of the Lord. [61] We departed from the river Theras on the twelfth day of the first month; and we arrived in Jerusalem by the mighty hand of our Lord which was upon us; he delivered us from every enemy on the way, and so we came to Jerusalem.

[62] When we had been there three days, the silver and the gold were weighed and delivered in the house of our Lord to Meremoth the priest, son of Uriah; [63] and with him was Eleazar the son of Phinehas, and with them were Jozabad the son of Jeshua and Moeth the son of Binnui, the Levites. [64] The whole was counted and weighed, and the weight of everything was recorded at that very time. [65] And those who had come back from captivity offered sacrifices to the Lord, the God of Israel, twelve bulls for all Israel, ninety-six rams, [66] seventy-two lambs, and as a thank offering twelve he-goats -- all as a sacrifice to the Lord. [67] And they delivered the king's orders to the royal stewards and to the governors of Coelesyria and Phoenicia; and these officials honored the people and the temple of the Lord. [68] After these things had been done, the principal men came to me and said,

[69] "The people of Israel and the leaders and the priests and the Levites have not put away from themselves the alien peoples of the land and their pollutions, the Canaanites, the Hittites, the Perizzites, the Jebusites, the Moabites, the Egyptians, and the Edomites. [70] For they and their sons have married the daughters of these people, and the holy race has been mixed with the alien peoples of the land; and from the beginning of this matter the leaders and the nobles have been sharing in this iniquity." [71] As soon as I heard these things I rent my garments and my holy mantle, and pulled out hair from my head and beard, and sat down in anxiety and grief.

[72] And all who were ever moved at the word of the Lord of Israel gathered round me, as I mourned over this iniquity, and I sat grief-stricken until the evening sacrifice. [73] Then I rose from my fast, with my garments and my holy mantle rent, and kneeling down and stretching forth my hands to the Lord [74] I said, "O Lord, I am ashamed and confounded before thy face.

[75] For our sins have risen higher than our heads, and our mistakes have mounted up to heaven [76] from the times of our fathers, and we are in great sin to this day. [77] And because of our sins and the sins of our fathers we with our brethren and our kings and our priests were given over to the kings of the earth, to the sword and captivity and plundering, in shame until this day. [78] And now in some measure mercy has come to us from thee, O Lord, to leave to us a root and a name in thy holy place, [79] and to uncover a light for us in the house of the Lord our God, and to give us food in the time of our servitude. [80] Even in our bondage we were not forsaken by our Lord, but he brought us into favor with the kings of the Persians, so that they have given us food [81] and glorified the temple of our Lord, and raised Zion from desolation, to give us a stronghold in Judea and Jerusalem. [82] "And now, O Lord, what shall we say, when we have these things? For we have transgressed thy commandments, which thou didst give by thy servants the prophets, saying,

[83] `The land which you are entering to take possession of it is a land polluted with the pollution of the aliens of the land, and they have filled it with their uncleanness. [84] Therefore do not give your daughters in marriage to their sons, and do not take their daughters for your sons; [85] and do not seek ever to have peace with them, in order that you may be strong and eat the good things of the land and leave it for an inheritance to your children for ever.' [86] And all that has happened to us has come about because of our evil deeds and our great sins. For thou, O Lord, didst lift the burden of our sins [87] and give us such a root as this; but we turned back again to transgress thy law by mixing with the uncleanness of the peoples of the land. [88] Wast thou not angry enough with us to destroy us without leaving a root or seed or name? [89] O Lord of Israel, thou art true; for we are left as a root to this day. [90] Behold, we are now before thee in our iniquities; for we can no longer stand in thy presence because of these things." [91] While Ezra was praying and making his confession, weeping and lying upon the ground before the temple, there gathered about him a very great throng from Jerusalem, men and women and youths; for there was great weeping among the multitude.

[92] Then Shecaniah the son of Jehiel, one of the men of Israel, called out, and said to Ezra, "We have sinned against the Lord, and have married foreign women from the peoples of the land; but even now there is hope for Israel. [93] Let us take an oath to the Lord about this, that we will put away all our foreign wives, with their children, [94] as seems good to you and to all who obey the law of the Lord. [95] Arise and take action, for it is your task, and we are with you to take strong measures." [96] Then Ezra arose and had the leaders of the priests and Levites of all Israel take oath that they would do this. And they took the oath.

9

[1] Then Ezra rose and went from the court of the temple to the chamber of Jehohanan the son of Eliashib,

[2] and spent the night there; and he did not eat bread or drink water, for he was mourning over the great iniquities of the multitude. [3] And a proclamation was made throughout Judea and Jerusalem to all who had returned from the captivity that they should assemble at Jerusalem, [4] and that if any did not meet there within two or three days, in accordance with the decision of the ruling elders, their cattle should be seized for sacrifice and the men themselves expelled from the multitude of those who had returned from the captivity. [5] Then the men of the tribe of Judah and Benjamin assembled at Jerusalem within three days; this was the ninth month, on the twentieth day of the month.

[6] And all the multitude sat in the open square before the temple, shivering because of the bad weather that prevailed. [7] Then Ezra rose and said to them, "You have broken the law and married foreign women, and so have increased the sin of Israel. [8] Now then make confession and give glory to the Lord the God of our fathers, [9] and do his will; separate yourselves from the peoples of the land and from your foreign wives." [10] Then all the multitude shouted and said with a loud voice, "We will do as you have said. [11] But the multitude is great and it is winter, and we are not able to stand in the open air. This is not a work we can do in one day or two, for we have sinned too much in these things. [12] so let the leaders of the multitude stay, and let all those in our settlements who have foreign wives come at the time appointed, [13] with the

elders and judges of each place, until we are freed from the wrath of the Lord over this matter." [14] Jonathan the son of Asahel and Jahzeiah the son of Tikvah undertook the matter on these terms, and Meshullam and Levi and Shabbethai served with them as judges. [15] And those who had returned from the captivity acted in accordance with all this. [16] Ezra the priest chose for himself the leading men of their fathers' houses, all of them by name; and on the new moon of the tenth month they began their sessions to investigate the matter.

[17] And the cases of the men who had foreign wives were brought to an end by the new moon of the first month. [18] Of the priests those who were brought in and found to have foreign wives were:

[19] of the sons of Jeshua the son of Jozadak and his brethren, Maaseiah, Eliezar, Jarib, and Jodan. [20] They pledged themselves to put away their wives, and to give rams in expiation of their error. [21] Of the sons of Immer: Hanani and Zebadiah and Maaseiah and Shemaiah and Jehiel and Azariah. [22] Of the sons of Pashhur: Elioenai, Maaseiah, Ishmael, and Nathanael, and Gedaliah, and Elasah. [23] And of the Levites: Jozabad and Shimei and Kelaiah, who was Kelita, and Pethahiah and Judah and Jonah.

[24] Of the temple singers: Eliashib and Zaccur. [25] Of the gatekeepers: Shallum and Telem. [26] Of Israel: of the sons of Parosh: Ramiah, Izziah, Malchijah, Mijamin, and Eleazar, and Asibias, and Benaiah.

[27] Of the sons of Elam: Mattaniah and Zechariah, Jehiel and Abdi, and Jeremoth and Elijah. [28] Of the sons of Zattu: Elioenai, Eliashib, Othoniah, Jeremoth, and Zabad and Zerdaiah. [29] Of the sons of Bebai: Jehohanan and Hananiah and Zabbai and Emathis. [30] Of the sons of Bani: Meshullam, Malluch, Adaiah, Jashub, and Sheal and Jeremoth. [31] Of the sons of Addi: Naathus and Moossias, Laccunus and Naidus, and Bescaspasmys and Sesthel, and Belnuus and Manasseas. [32] Of the sons of Annan, Elionas and Asaias and Melchias and Sabbaias and Simon Chosamaeus. [33] Of the sons of Hashum: Mattenai and Mattattah and Zabad and Eliphelet and Manasseh and Shimei. [34] Of the sons of Bani: Jeremai, Maadai, Amram, Joel, Mamdai and Bedeiah and Vaniah, Carabasion and Eliashib and Machnadebai, Eliasis, Binnui, Elialis, Shimei, Shelemiah, Nethaniah. Of the sons of Ezora: Shashai, Azarel, Azael, Shemaiah, Amariah, Joseph. [35] Of the sons of Nebo: Mattithiah, Zabad, Iddo, Joel, Benaiah. [36] All these had married foreign women, and they put them away with their children. [37] The priests and the Levites and the men of Israel settled in Jerusalem and in the country. On the new moon of the seventh month, when the sons of Israel were in their settlements,

[38] the whole multitude gathered with one accord into the open square before the east gate of the temple; [39] and they told Ezra the chief priest and reader to bring the law of Moses which had been given by the Lord God of Israel. [40] So Ezra the chief priest brought the law, for all the multitude, men and women, and all the priests to hear the law, on the new moon of the seventh month. [41] And he read aloud in the open square before the gate of the temple from early morning until midday, in the presence of both men and women; and all the multitude gave attention to the law. [42] Ezra the priest and reader of the law stood on the wooden platform which had been prepared; [43] and beside him stood Mattathiah, Shema, Anaiah, Azariah, Uriah, Hezekiah, and Baalsamus on his right hand, [44] and on his left Pedaiah, Mishael, Malchijah, Lothasubus, Nabariah, and Zechariah. [45] Then Ezra took up the book of the law in the sight of the multitude, for he had the place of honor in the presence of all. [46] And when he opened the law, they all stood erect. And Ezra blessed the Lord God Most High, the God of hosts, the Almighty; [47] and all the multitude answered, "Amen." And they lifted up their hands, and fell to the ground and worshiped the Lord. [48] Jeshua and Anniuth and Sherebiah, Jamin, Akkub, Shabbethai, Hodiah, Maaseiah and Kelita, Azariah and Jozabad, Hanan, Pelaiah, the Levites, taught the law of the Lord, at the same time explaining what was read. [49] Then Attharates said to Ezra the chief priest and reader, and to the Levites who were teaching the multitude, and to all,

[50] "This day is holy to the Lord" -- now they were all weeping as they heard the law -- [51] "so go your way, eat the fat and drink the sweet, and send portions to those who have none; [52] for the day is holy to the Lord; and do not be sorrowful, for the Lord will exalt you." [53] And the Levites commanded all the people, saying, "This day is holy; do not be sorrowful." [54] Then they all went their way, to eat and drink and enjoy themselves, and to give portions to those who had none, and to make great rejoicing; [55] because they were inspired by the words which they had been taught. And they came together.

2 Esdras also called 4 Ezra

Chapter 1

[1] The second book of the prophet Ezra the son of Seraiah, son of Azariah, son of Hilkiah, son of Shallum, son of Zadok, son of Ahitub,

[2] son of Ahijah, son of Phinehas, son of Eli, son of Amariah, son of Azariah, son of Meraioth, son of Arna, son of Uzzi, son of Borith, son of Abishua, son of Phinehas, son of Eleazar,

[3] son of Aaron, of the tribe of Levi, who was a captive in the country of the Medes in the reign of Artaxerxes, king of the Persians.

[4] The word of the Lord came to me, saying,

[5] "Go and declare to my people their evil deeds, and to their children the iniquities which they have committed against me, so that they may tell their children's children [6] that the sins of their parents have increased in them, for they have forgotten me and have offered sacrifices to strange gods. [7] Was it not I who brought them out of the land of Egypt, out of the house of bondage? But they have angered me and despised my counsels. [8] Pull out the hair of your head and hurl all evils upon them, for they have not obeyed my law -- they are a rebellious people. [9] How long shall I endure them, on whom I have bestowed such great benefits? [10] For their sake I have overthrown many kings: I struck down Pharaoh with his servants, and all his army. [11] I have destroyed all nations before them, and scattered in the east the people of two provinces, Tyre and Sidon; I have slain all their enemies. [12] "But speak to them and say, Thus says the Lord:

[13] Surely it was I who brought you through the sea, and made safe highways for you where there was no road; I gave you Moses as leader and Aaron as priest; [14] I provided light for you from a pillar of fire, and did great wonders among you. Yet you have forgotten me, says the Lord. [15] "Thus says the Lord Almighty: The quails were a sign to you; I gave you camps for your protection, and in them you complained.

[16] You have not exulted in my name at the destruction of your enemies, but to this day you still complain. [17] Where are the benefits which I bestowed on you? When you were hungry and thirsty in the wilderness, did you not cry out to me, [18] saying, `Why hast thou led us into this wilderness to kill us? It would have been better for us to serve the Egyptians than to die in this wilderness.' [19] I pitied your groanings and gave you manna for food; you ate the bread of angels. [20] When you were thirsty, did I not cleave the rock so that waters flowed in abundance? Because of the heat I covered you with the leaves of trees. [21] I divided fertile lands among you; I drove out the Canaanites, the Perizzites, and the Philistines before you. What more can I do for you? says the Lord. [22] Thus says the Lord Almighty: When you were in the wilderness, at the bitter stream, thirsty and blaspheming my name, [23] I did not send fire upon you for your blasphemies, but threw a tree into the water and made the stream sweet. [24] "What shall I do to you, O Jacob? You would not obey me, O Judah. I will turn to other nations and will give them my name, that they may keep my statutes.

[25] Because you have forsaken me, I also will forsake you. When you beg mercy of me, I will show you no mercy. [26] When you call upon me, I will not listen to you; for you have defiled your hands with blood, and your feet are swift to commit murder. [27] It is not as though you had forsaken me; you have forsaken yourselves, says the Lord. [28] "Thus says the Lord Almighty: Have I not entreated you as a father entreats his sons or a mother her daughters or a nurse her children,

[29] that you should be my people and I should be your God, and that you should be my sons and I should be your father?

[30] I gathered you as a hen gathers her brood under her wings. But now, what shall I do to you? I will cast you out from my presence. [31] When you offer oblations to me, I will turn my face from you; for I have rejected your feast days, and new moons, and circumcisions of the flesh. [32] I sent to you my servants the prophets, but you have taken and slain them and torn their bodies in pieces; their blood I will require of you, says the Lord. [33] "Thus says the Lord Almighty: Your house is desolate; I will drive you out as the wind drives straw;

[34] and your sons will have no children, because with you they have neglected my commandment and have done what is evil in my sight. [35] I will give your houses to a people that will come, who without having heard me will believe. Those to whom I have shown no signs will do what I have commanded. [36] They have seen no prophets, yet will recall their former state. [37] I call to witness the gratitude of the people that is to come, whose children rejoice with gladness; though they do not see me with bodily eyes, yet with the spirit they will believe the things I have said. [38] "And now, father, look with pride and see the people coming from the east;

[39] to them I will give as leaders Abraham, Isaac, and Jacob and Hosea and Amos and Micah and Joel and Obadiah and Jonah [40] and Nahum and Habakkuk, Zephaniah, Haggai, Zechariah and Malachi, who is also called the messenger of the Lord.

2

[1] "Thus says the Lord: I brought this people out of bondage, and I gave them commandments through my servants the prophets; but they would not listen to them, and made my counsels void.

[2] The mother who bore them says to them, `Go, my children, because I am a widow and forsaken. [3] I brought you up with gladness; but with mourning and sorrow I have lost you, because you have sinned before the Lord God and have done what is evil in my sight. [4] But now what can I do for you? For I am a widow and forsaken. Go, my children, and ask for

mercy from the Lord.' [5] I call upon you, father, as a witness in addition to the mother of the children, because they would not keep my covenant, [6] that you may bring confusion upon them and bring their mother to ruin, so that they may have no offspring. [7] Let them be scattered among the nations, let their names be blotted out from the earth, because they have despised my covenant. [8] "Woe to you, Assyria, who conceal the unrighteous in your midst! O wicked nation, remember what I did to Sodom and Gomorrah,

[9] whose land lies in lumps of pitch and heaps of ashes. So will I do to those who have not listened to me, says the Lord Almighty." [10] Thus says the Lord to Ezra: "Tell my people that I will give them the kingdom of Jerusalem, which I was going to give to Israel.

[11] Moreover, I will take back to myself their glory, and will give to these others the everlasting habitations, which I had prepared for Israel. [12] The tree of life shall give them fragrant perfume, and they shall neither toil nor become weary. [13] Ask and you will receive; pray that your days may be few, that they may be shortened. The kingdom is already prepared for you; watch! [14] Call, O call heaven and earth to witness, for I left out evil and created good, because I live, says the Lord. [15] "Mother, embrace your sons; bring them up with gladness, as does the dove; establish their feet, because I have chosen you, says the Lord.

[16] And I will raise up the dead from their places, and will bring them out from their tombs, because I recognize my name in them. [17] Do not fear, mother of sons, for I have chosen you, says the Lord. [18] I will send you help, my servants Isaiah and Jeremiah. According to their counsel I have consecrated and prepared for you twelve trees loaded with various fruits, [19] and the same number of springs flowing with milk and honey, and seven mighty mountains on which roses and lilies grow; by these I will fill your children with joy. [20] Guard the rights of the widow, secure justice for the fatherless, give to the needy, defend the orphan, clothe the naked, [21] care for the injured and the weak, do not ridicule a lame man, protect the maimed, and let the blind man have a vision of my splendor. [22] Protect the old and the young within your walls; [23] When you find any who are dead, commit them to the grave and mark it, and I will give you the first place in my resurrection. [24] Pause and be quiet, my people, because your rest will come. [25] Good nurse, nourish your sons, and strengthen their feet. [26] Not one of the servants whom I have given you will perish, for I will require them from among your number. [27] Do not be anxious, for when the day of tribulation and anguish comes, others shall weep and be sorrowful, but you shall rejoice and have abundance. [28] The nations shall envy you but they shall not be able to do anything against you, says the Lord. [29] My hands will cover you, that your sons may not see Gehenna. [30] Rejoice, O mother, with your sons, because I will deliver you, says the Lord. [31] Remember your sons that sleep, because I will bring them out of the hiding places of the earth, and will show mercy to them; for I am merciful, says the Lord Almighty. [32] Embrace your children until I come, and proclaim mercy to them; because my springs run over, and my grace will not fail."

[33] I, Ezra, received a command from the Lord on Mount Horeb to go to Israel. When I came to them they rejected me and refused the Lord's commandment.

[34] Therefore I say to you, O nations that hear and understand, "Await your shepherd; he will give you everlasting rest, because he who will come at the end of the age is close at hand. [35] Be ready for the rewards of the kingdom, because the eternal light will shine upon you for evermore. [36] Flee from the shadow of this age, receive the joy of your glory; I publicly call on my Savior to witness. [37] Receive what the Lord has entrusted to you and be joyful, giving thanks to him who has called you to heavenly kingdoms. [38] Rise and stand, and see at the feast of the Lord the number of those who have been sealed. [39] Those who have departed from the shadow of this age have received glorious garments from the Lord. [40] Take again your full number, O Zion, and conclude the list of your people who are clothed in white, who have fulfilled the law of the Lord. [41] The number of your children, whom you desired, is full; beseech the Lord's power that your people, who have been called from the beginning, may be made holy." [42] I, Ezra, saw on Mount Zion a great multitude, which I could not number, and they all were praising the Lord with songs.

[43] In their midst was a young man of great stature, taller than any of the others, and on the head of each of them he placed a crown, but he was more exalted than they. And I was held spellbound. [44] Then I asked an angel, "Who are these, my lord?" [45] He answered and said to me, "These are they who have put off mortal clothing and have put on the immortal, and they have confessed the name of God; now they are being crowned, and receive palms." [46] Then I said to the angel, "Who is that young man who places crowns on them and puts palms in their hands?" [47] He answered and said to me, "He is the Son of God, whom they confessed in the world." So I began to praise those who had stood valiantly for the name of the Lord. [48] Then the angel said to me, "Go, tell my people how great and many are the wonders of the Lord God which you have seen."

3

[1] In the thirtieth year after the destruction of our city, I Salathiel, who am also called Ezra, was in Babylon. I was troubled as I lay on my bed, and my thoughts welled up in my heart,

[2] because I saw the desolation of Zion and the wealth of those who lived in Babylon. [3] My spirit was greatly agitated, and I began to speak anxious words to the Most High, and said, [4] "O sovereign Lord, didst thou not speak at the beginning when thou didst form the earth -- and that without help -- and didst command the dust [5] and it gave thee Adam, a lifeless body? Yet he was the workmanship of thy hands, and thou didst breathe into him the breath of life, and he was made alive in thy presence. [6] And thou didst lead him into the garden which thy right hand had planted before the earth appeared. [7] And thou didst lay upon him one commandment of your; but he transgressed it, and immediately thou didst appoint death

for him and for his descendants. From him there sprang nations and tribes, peoples and clans without number. [8] And every nation walked after its own will and did ungodly things before thee and scorned thee, and thou didst not hinder them. [9] But again, in its time thou didst bring the flood upon the inhabitants of the world and destroy them. [10] And the same fate befell them: as death came upon Adam, so the flood upon them. [11] But thou didst leave one of them, Noah with his household, and all the righteous who have descended from him. [12] "When those who dwelt on earth began to multiply, they produced children and peoples and many nations, and again they began to be more ungodly than were their ancestors. [13] And when they were committing iniquity before thee, thou didst choose for thyself one of them, whose name was Abraham; [14] and thou didst love him, and to him only didst thou reveal the end of the times, secretly by night. [15] Thou didst make with him an everlasting covenant, and promise him that thou wouldst never forsake his descendants; and thou gavest to him Isaac, and to Isaac thou gavest Jacob and Esau. [16] And thou didst set apart Jacob for thyself, but Esau thou didst reject; and Jacob became a great multitude. [17] And when thou didst lead his descendants out of Egypt, thou didst bring them to Mount Sinai. [18] Thou didst bend down the heavens and shake the earth, and move the world, and make the depths to tremble, and trouble the times. [19] And thy glory passed through the four gates of fire and earthquake and wind and ice, to give the law to the descendants of Jacob, and thy commandment to the posterity of Israel. [20] "Yet thou didst not take away from them their evil heart, so that thy law might bring forth fruit in them.

[21] For the first Adam, burdened with an evil heart, transgressed and was overcome, as were also all who were descended from him. [22] Thus the disease became permanent; the law was in the people's heart along with the evil root, but what was good departed, and the evil remained. [23] So the times passed and the years were completed, and thou didst raise up for thyself a servant, named David. [24] And thou didst command him to build a city for thy name, and in it to offer thee oblations from what is your. [25] This was done for many years; but the inhabitants of the city transgressed, [26] in everything doing as Adam and all his descendants had done, for they also had the evil heart. [27] So thou didst deliver the city into the hands of thy enemies. [28] "Then I said in my heart, Are the deeds of those who inhabit Babylon any better? Is that why she has gained dominion over Zion?

[29] For when I came here I saw ungodly deeds without number, and my soul has seen many sinners during these thirty years. And my heart failed me, [30] for I have seen how thou do endure those who sin, and hast spared those who act wickedly, and hast destroyed thy people, and hast preserved thy enemies, [31] and hast not shown to any one how thy way may be comprehended. Are the deeds of Babylon better than those of Zion? [32] Or has another nation known thee besides Israel? Or what tribes have so believed thy covenants as these tribes of Jacob? [33] Yet their reward has not appeared and their labor has borne no fruit. For I have traveled widely among the nations and have seen that they abound in wealth, though they are unmindful of thy commandments. [34] Now therefore weigh in a balance our iniquities and those of the inhabitants of the world; and so it will be found which way the turn of the scale will incline. [35] When have the inhabitants of the earth not sinned in thy sight? Or what nation has kept thy commandments so well? [36] Thou mayest indeed find individual men who have kept thy commandments, but nations thou wilt not find."

4
[1] Then the angel that had been sent to me, whose name was Uriel, answered
[2] and said to me, "Your understanding has utterly failed regarding this world, and do you think you can comprehend the way of the Most High?" [3] Then I said, "Yes, my lord." And he replied to me, "I have been sent to show you three ways, and to put before you three problems. [4] If you can solve one of them for me, I also will show you the way you desire to see, and will teach you why the heart is evil." [5] I said, "Speak on, my lord." And he said to me, "Go, weigh for me the weight of fire, or measure for me a measure of wind, or call back for me the day that is past."
[6] I answered and said, "Who of those that have been born can do this, that you ask me concerning these things?"
[7] And he said to me, "If I had asked you, `How many dwellings are in the heart of the sea, or how many streams are at the source of the deep, or how many streams are above the firmament, or which are the exits of hell, or which are the entrances of paradise?'
[8] Perhaps you would have said to me, `I never went down into the deep, nor as yet into hell, neither did I ever ascend into heaven.' [9] But now I have asked you only about fire and wind and the day, things through which you have passed and without which you cannot exist, and you have given me no answer about them!" [10] And he said to me, "You cannot understand the things with which you have grown up; [11] how then can your mind comprehend the way of the Most High? And how can one who is already worn out by the corrupt world understand incorruption?" When I heard this, I fell on my face [12] and said to him, "It would be better for us not to be here than to come here and live in ungodliness, and to suffer and not understand why." [13] He answered me and said, "I went into a forest of trees of the plain, and they made a plan [14] and said, `Come, let us go and make war against the sea, that it may recede before us, and that we may make for ourselves more forests.' [15] And in like manner the waves of the sea also made a plan and said, `Come, let us go up and subdue the forest of the plain so that there also we may gain more territory for ourselves.' [16] But the plan of the forest was in vain, for the fire came and consumed it; [17] likewise also the plan of the waves of the sea, for the sand stood firm and stopped them. [18] If now you were a judge between them, which would you undertake to justify, and which to condemn?" [19] I answered and said, "Each has made a foolish plan, for the land is assigned to the forest, and to the sea is assigned a place to carry its waves."
[20] He answered me and said, "You have judged rightly, but why have you not judged so in your own case?

585

[21] For as the land is assigned to the forest and the sea to its waves, so also those who dwell upon earth can understand only what is on the earth, and he who is above the heavens can understand what is above the height of the heavens." [22] Then I answered and said, "I beseech you, my lord, why have I been endowed with the power of understanding?

[23] For I did not wish to inquire about the ways above, but about those things which we daily experience: why Israel has been given over to the Gentiles as a reproach; why the people whom you loved has been given over to godless tribes, and the law of our fathers has been made of no effect and the written covenants no longer exist; [24] and why we pass from the world like locusts, and our life is like a mist, and we are not worthy to obtain mercy. [25] But what will he do for his name, by which we are called? It is about these things that I have asked." [26] He answered me and said, "If you are alive, you will see, and if you live long, you will often marvel, because the age is hastening swiftly to its end.

[27] For it will not be able to bring the things that have been promised to the righteous in their appointed times, because this age is full of sadness and infirmities. [28] For the evil about which you ask me has been sown, but the harvest of it has not yet come. [29] If therefore that which has been sown is not reaped, and if the place where the evil has been sown does not pass away, the field where the good has been sown will not come. [30] For a grain of evil seed was sown in Adam's heart from the beginning, and how much ungodliness it has produced until now, and will produce until the time of threshing comes! [31] Consider now for yourself how much fruit of ungodliness a grain of evil seed has produced. [32] When heads of grain without number are sown, how great a threshing floor they will fill!" [33] Then I answered and said, "How long and when will these things be? Why are our years few and evil?"

[34] He answered me and said, "You do not hasten faster than the Most High, for your haste is for yourself, but the Highest hastens on behalf of many. [35] Did not the souls of the righteous in their chambers ask about these matters, saying, `How long are we to remain here? And when will come the harvest of our reward? [36] And Jeremiel the archangel answered them and said, `When the number of those like yourselves is completed; for he has weighed the age in the balance, [37] and measured the times by measure, and numbered the times by number; and he will not move or arouse them until that measure is fulfilled.'" [38] Then I answered and said, "O sovereign Lord, but all of us also are full of ungodliness.

[39] And it is perhaps on account of us that the time of threshing is delayed for the righteous -- on account of the sins of those who dwell on earth." [40] He answered me and said, "Go and ask a woman who is with child if, when her nine months have been completed, her womb can keep the child within her any longer." [41] And I said, "No, lord, it cannot." And he said to me, "In Hades the chambers of the souls are like the womb. [42] For just as a woman who is in travail makes haste to escape the pangs of birth, so also do these places hasten to give back those things that were committed to them from the beginning. [43] Then the things that you desire to see will be disclosed to you." [44] I answered and said, "If I have found favor in your sight, and if it is possible, and if I am worthy, [45] show me this also: whether more time is to come than has passed, or whether for us the greater part has gone by. [46] For I know what has gone by, but I do not know what is to come." [47] And he said to me, "Stand at my right side, and I will show you the interpretation of a parable." [48] So I stood and looked, and behold, a flaming furnace passed by before me, and when the flame had gone by I looked, and behold, the smoke remained. [49] And after this a cloud full of water passed before me and poured down a heavy and violent rain, and when the rainstorm had passed, drops remained in the cloud. [50] And he said to me, "Consider it for yourself; for as the rain is more than the drops, and the fire is greater than the smoke, so the quantity that passed was far greater; but drops and smoke remained."

[51] Then I prayed and said, "Do you think that I shall live until those days? Or who will be alive in those days?"

[52] He answered me and said, "Concerning the signs about which you ask me, I can tell you in part; but I was not sent to tell you concerning your life, for I do not know.

5

[1] "Now concerning the signs: behold, the days are coming when those who dwell on earth shall be seized with great terror, and the way of truth shall be hidden, and the land shall be barren of faith.

[2] And unrighteousness shall be increased beyond what you yourself see, and beyond what you heard of formerly. [3] And the land which you now see ruling shall be waste and untrodden, and men shall see it desolate. [4] But if the Most High grants that you live, you shall see it thrown into confusion after the third period; and the sun shall suddenly shine forth at night,and the moon during the day. [5] Blood shall drip from wood,and the stone shall utter its voice;the peoples shall be troubled, and the stars shall fall. [6] And one shall reign whom those who dwell on earth do not expect, and the birds shall fly away together; [7] and the sea of Sodom shall cast up fish; and one whom the many do not know shall make his voice heard by night, and all shall hear his voice. [8] There shall be chaos also in many places, and fire shall often break out, and the wild beasts shall roam beyond their haunts, and menstruous women shall bring forth monsters. [9] And salt waters shall be found in the sweet, and all friends shall conquer one another; then shall reason hide itself, and wisdom shall withdraw into its chamber, [10] and it shall be sought by many but shall not be found, and unrighteousness and unrestraint shall increase on earth. [11] And one country shall ask its neighbor, `Has righteousness, or any one who does right, passed through you?' And it will answer, `No.' [12] And at that time men shall hope but not obtain; they shall labor but their ways shall not prosper. [13] These are the signs which I am permitted to tell you, and if you pray again, and weep as you do now, and fast for seven days, you shall hear yet greater things than these." [14] Then I awoke, and my body shuddered violently, and my soul was so troubled that it fainted.

[15] But the angel who had come and talked with me held me and strengthened me and set me on my feet. [16] Now on the

second night Phaltiel, a chief of the people, came to me and said, "Where have you been? And why is your face sad? [17] Or do you not know that Israel has been entrusted to you in the land of their exile? [18] Rise therefore and eat some bread, so that you may not forsake us, like a shepherd who leaves his flock in the power of cruel wolves." [19] Then I said to him, "Depart from me and do not come near me for seven days, and then you may come to me." He heard what I said and left me. [20] So I fasted seven days, mourning and weeping, as Uriel the angel had commanded me. [21] And after seven days the thoughts of my heart were very grievous to me again. [22] Then my soul recovered the spirit of understanding, and I began once more to speak words in the presence of the Most High. [23] And I said, "O sovereign Lord, from every forest of the earth and from all its trees thou hast chosen one vine, [24] and from all the lands of the world thou hast chosen for thyself one region, and from all the flowers of the world thou hast chosen for thyself one lily, [25] and from all the depths of the sea thou hast filled for thyself one river, and from all the cities that have been built thou hast consecrated Zion for thyself, [26] and from all the birds that have been created thou hast named for thyself one dove, and from all the flocks that have been made thou hast provided for thyself one sheep, [27] and from all the multitude of peoples thou hast gotten for thyself one people; and to this people, whom thou hast loved, thou hast given the law which is approved by all. [28] And now, O Lord, why hast thou given over the one to the many, and dishonored the one root beyond the others, and scattered your only one among the many? [29] And those who opposed thy promises have trodden down those who believed thy covenants. [30] If thou do really hate thy people, they should be punished at thy own hands." [31] When I had spoken these words, the angel who had come to me on a previous night was sent to me, [32] and he said to me, "Listen to me, and I will instruct you; pay attention to me, and I will tell you more." [33] And I said, "Speak, my lord." And he said to me, "Are you greatly disturbed in mind over Israel? Or do you love him more than his Maker does?" [34] And I said, "No, my lord, but because of my grief I have spoken; for every hour I suffer agonies of heart, while I strive to understand the way of the Most High and to search out part of his judgment." [35] And he said to me, "You cannot." And I said, "Why not, my lord? Why then was I born? Or why did not my mother's womb become my grave, that I might not see the travail of Jacob and the exhaustion of the people of Israel?" [36] He said to me, "Count up for me those who have not yet come, and gather for me the scattered raindrops, and make the withered flowers bloom again for me; [37] open for me the closed chambers, and bring forth for me the winds shut up in them, or show me the picture of a voice; and then I will explain to you the travail that you ask to understand." [38] And I said, "O sovereign Lord, who is able to know these things except he whose dwelling is not with men? [39] As for me, I am without wisdom, and how can I speak concerning the things which thou hast asked me?" [40] He said to me, "Just as you cannot do one of the things that were mentioned, so you cannot discover my judgment, or the goal of the love that I have promised my people." [41] And I said, "Yet behold, O Lord, thou do have charge of those who are alive at the end, but what will those do who were before us, or we, or those who come after us?" [42] He said to me, "I shall liken my judgment to a circle; just as for those who are last there is no slowness, so for those who are first there is no haste." [43] Then I answered and said, "Couldst thou not have created at one time those who have been and those who are and those who will be, that thou mightest show thy judgment the sooner?" [44] He replied to me and said, "The creation cannot make more haste than the Creator, neither can the world hold at one time those who have been created in it." [45] And I said, "How hast thou said to thy servant that thou wilt certainly give life at one time to thy creation? If therefore all creatures will live at one time and the creation will sustain them, it might even now be able to support all of them present at one time." [46] He said to me, "Ask a woman's womb, and say to it, `If you bear ten children, why one after another?' Request it therefore to produce ten at one time." [47] I said, "Of course it cannot, but only each in its own time." [48] He said to me, "Even so have I given the womb of the earth to those who from time to time are sown in it. [49] For as an infant does not bring forth, and a woman who has become old does not bring forth any longer, so have I organized the world which I created." [50] Then I inquired and said, "Since thou hast now given me the opportunity, let me speak before thee. Is our mother, of whom thou hast told me, still young? Or is she now approaching old age?" [51] He replied to me, "Ask a woman who bears children, and she will tell you. [52] Say to her, "Why are those whom you have borne recently not like those whom you bore before, but smaller in stature?' [53] And she herself will answer you, `Those born in the strength of youth are different from those born during the time of old age, when the womb is failing.' [54] Therefore you also should consider that you and your contemporaries are smaller in stature than those who were before you, [55] and those who come after you will be smaller than you, as born of a creation which already is aging and passing the strength of youth." [56] And I said, "O Lord, I beseech thee, if I have found favor in thy sight, show thy servant through whom thou do visit thy creation."

6

[1] And he said to me, "At the beginning of the circle of the earth, before the portals of the world were in place, and before the assembled winds blew, [2] and before the rumblings of thunder sounded, and before the flashes of lightning shone, and before the foundations of paradise were laid, [3] and before the beautiful flowers were seen, and before the powers of movement were established, and before the innumerable hosts of angels were gathered together, [4] and before the heights of the air were lifted up, and before the measures of the firmaments were named, and before the footstool of Zion was established, [5] and before the present years were reckoned; and before the imaginations of those who now sin were estranged, and before those who stored up treasures of faith were sealed -- [6] then I planned these things, and they were made through me and not through another, just as the end shall come through me and not through another." [7] And I answered and said, "What will be the dividing of the times? Or when will be the end of the first age and the beginning of the

age that follows?" [8] He said to me, "From Abraham to Isaac, because from him were born Jacob and Esau, for Jacob's hand held Esau's heel from the beginning.

[9] For Esau is the end of this age, and Jacob is the beginning of the age that follows. [10] For the beginning of a man is his hand, and the end of a man is his heel; between the heel and the hand seek for nothing else, Ezra!" [11] I answered and said, "O sovereign Lord, if I have found favor in thy sight, [12] show thy servant the end of thy signs which thou didst show me in part on a previous night." [13] He answered and said to me, "Rise to your feet and you will hear a full, resounding voice. [14] And if the place where you are standing is greatly shaken [15] while the voice is speaking, do not be terrified; because the word concerns the end, and the foundations of the earth will understand [16] that the speech concerns them. They will tremble and be shaken, for they know that their end must be changed." [17] When I heard this, I rose to my feet and listened, and behold, a voice was speaking, and its sound was like the sound of many waters. [18] And it said, "Behold, the days are coming, and it shall be that when I draw near to visit the inhabitants of the earth, [19] and when I require from the doers of iniquity the penalty of their iniquity, and when the humiliation of Zion is complete, [20] and when the seal is placed upon the age which is about to pass away, then I will show these signs: the books shall be opened before the firmament, and all shall see it together. [21] Infants a year old shall speak with their voices, and women with child shall give birth to premature children at three and four months, and these shall live and dance. [22] Sown places shall suddenly appear unsown, and full storehouses shall suddenly be found to be empty; [23] and the trumpet shall sound aloud, and when all hear it, they shall suddenly be terrified. [24] At that time friends shall make war on friends like enemies, and the earth and those who inhabit it shall be terrified, and the springs of the fountains shall stand still, so that for three hours they shall not flow. [25] "And it shall be that whoever remains after all that I have foretold to you shall himself be saved and shall see my salvation and the end of my world. [26] And they shall see the men who were taken up, who from their birth have not tasted death; and the heart of the earth's inhabitants shall be changed and converted to a different spirit. [27] For evil shall be blotted out, and deceit shall be quenched; [28] faithfulness shall flourish, and corruption shall be overcome, and the truth, which has been so long without fruit, shall be revealed." [29] While he spoke to me, behold, little by little the place where I was standing began to rock to and fro. [30] And he said to me, "I have come to show you these things this night. [31] If therefore you will pray again and fast again for seven days, I will again declare to you greater things than these, [32] because your voice has surely been heard before the Most High; for the Mighty One has seen your uprightness and has also observed the purity which you have maintained from your youth. [33] Therefore he sent me to show you all these things, and to say to you: `Believe and do not be afraid! [34] Do not be quick to think vain thoughts concerning the former times, lest you be hasty concerning the last times.'" [35] Now after this I wept again and fasted seven days as before, in order to complete the three weeks as I had been told. [36] And on the eighth night my heart was troubled within me again, and I began to speak in the presence of the Most High. [37] For my spirit was greatly aroused, and my soul was in distress. [38] I said, "O Lord, thou didst speak at the beginning of creation, and didst say on the first day, `Let heaven and earth be made,' and thy word accomplished the work. [39] And then the Spirit was hovering, and darkness and silence embraced everything; the sound of man's voice was not yet there. [40] Then thou didst command that a ray of light be brought forth from thy treasuries, so that thy works might then appear. [41] "Again, on the second day, thou didst create the spirit of the firmament, and didst command him to divide and separate the waters, that one part might move upward and the other part remain beneath.

[42] "On the third day thou didst command the waters to be gathered together in the seventh part of the earth; six parts thou didst dry up and keep so that some of them might be planted and cultivated and be of service before thee.

[43] For thy word went forth, and at once the work was done. [44] For immediately fruit came forth in endless abundance and of varied appeal to the taste; and flowers of inimitable color; and odors of inexpressible fragrance. These were made on the third day. [45] "On the fourth day thou didst command the brightness of the sun, the light of the moon, and the arrangement of the stars to come into being; [46] and thou didst command them to serve man, who was about to be formed.
 [47] "On the fifth day thou didst command the seventh part, where the water had been gathered together, to bring forth living creatures, birds, and fishes; and so it was done. [48] The dumb and lifeless water produced living creatures, as it was commanded, that therefore the nations might declare thy wondrous works. [49] "Then thou didst keep in existence two living creatures; the name of one thou didst call Behemoth and the name of the other Leviathan.

[50] And thou didst separate one from the other, for the seventh part where the water had been gathered together could not hold them both. [51] And thou didst give Behemoth one of the parts which had been dried up on the third day, to live in it, where there are a thousand mountains; [52] but to Leviathan thou didst give the seventh part, the watery part; and thou hast kept them to be eaten by whom thou wilt, and when thou wilt. [53] "On the sixth day thou didst command the earth to bring forth before thee cattle, beasts, and creeping things;

[54] and over these thou didst place Adam, as ruler over all the works which thou hadst made; and from him we have all come, the people whom thou hast chosen. [55] "All this I have spoken before thee, O Lord, because thou hast said that it was for us that thou didst create this world. [56] As for the other nations which have descended from Adam, thou hast said that they are nothing, and that they are like spittle, and thou hast compared their abundance to a drop from a bucket. [57] And now, O Lord, behold, these nations, which are reputed as nothing, domineer over us and devour us. [58] But we thy people, whom thou hast called thy first-born, only begotten, zealous for thee, and most dear, have been given into their hands. [59] If the world has indeed been created for us, why do we not possess our world as an inheritance? How long will this be so?"

7

[1] When I had finished speaking these words, the angel who had been sent to me on the former nights was sent to me again, [2] and he said to me, "Rise, Ezra, and listen to the words that I have come to speak to you." [3] I said, "Speak, my lord." And he said to me, "There is a sea set in a wide expanse so that it is broad and vast, [4] but it has an entrance set in a narrow place, so that it is like a river. [5] If any one, then, wishes to reach the sea, to look at it or to navigate it, how can he come to the broad part unless he passes through the narrow part? [6] Another example: There is a city built and set on a plain, and it is full of all good things; [7] but the entrance to it is narrow and set in a precipitous place, so that there is fire on the right hand and deep water on the left; [8] and there is only one path lying between them, that is, between the fire and the water, so that only one man can walk upon that path. [9] If now that city is given to a man for an inheritance, how will the heir receive his inheritance unless he passes through the danger set before him?" [10] I said, "He cannot, lord." And he said to me, "So also is Israel's portion. [11] For I made the world for their sake, and when Adam transgressed my statutes, what had been made was judged. [12] And so the entrances of this world were made narrow and sorrowful and toilsome; they are few and evil, full of dangers and involved in great hardships. [13] But the entrances of the greater world are broad and safe, and really yield the fruit of immortality. [14] Therefore unless the living pass through the difficult and vain experiences, they can never receive those things that have been reserved for them. [15] But now why are you disturbed, seeing that you are to perish? And why are you moved, seeing that you are mortal? [16] And why have you not considered in your mind what is to come, rather than what is now present?" [17] Then I answered and said, "O sovereign Lord, behold, thou hast ordained in thy law that the righteous shall inherit these things, but that the ungodly shall perish. [18] The righteous therefore can endure difficult circumstances while hoping for easier ones; but those who have done wickedly have suffered the difficult circumstances and will not see the easier ones." [19] And he said to me, "You are not a better judge than God, or wiser than the Most High! [20] Let many perish who are now living, rather than that the law of God which is set before them be disregarded! [21] For God strictly commanded those who came into the world, when they came, what they should do to live, and what they should observe to avoid punishment. [22] Nevertheless they were not obedient, and spoke against him; they devised for themselves vain thoughts, [23] and proposed to themselves wicked frauds; they even declared that the Most High does not exist, and they ignored his ways! [24] They scorned his law, and denied his covenants; they have been unfaithful to his statutes, and have not performed his works. [25] "Therefore, Ezra, empty things are for the empty, and full things are for the full. [26] For behold, the time will come, when the signs which I have foretold to you will come to pass, that the city which now is not seen shall appear, and the land which now is hidden shall be disclosed. [27] And every one who has been delivered from the evils that I have foretold shall see my wonders. [28] For my son the Messiah shall be revealed with those who are with him, and those who remain shall rejoice four hundred years. [29] And after these years my son the Messiah shall die, and all who draw human breath. [30] And the world shall be turned back to primeval silence for seven days, as it was at the first beginnings; so that no one shall be left. [31] And after seven days the world, which is not yet awake, shall be roused, and that which is corruptible shall perish. [32] And the earth shall give up those who are asleep in it, and the dust those who dwell silently in it; and the chambers shall give up the souls which have been committed to them. [33] And the Most High shall be revealed upon the seat of judgment, and compassion shall pass away, and patience shall be withdrawn; [34] but only judgment shall remain, truth shall stand, and faithfulness shall grow strong. [35] And recompense shall follow, and the reward shall be manifested; righteous deeds shall awake, and unrighteous deeds shall not sleep. [36] Then the pit of torment shall appear, and opposite it shall be the place of rest; and the furnace of hell shall be disclosed, and opposite it the paradise of delight. [37] Then the Most High will say to the nations that have been raised from the dead, `Look now, and understand whom you have denied, whom you have not served, whose commandments you have despised! [38] Look on this side and on that; here are delight and rest, and there are fire and torments!' Thus he will speak to them on the day of judgment -- [39] a day that has no sun or moon or stars, [40] or cloud or thunder or lightning or wind or water or air, or darkness or evening or morning, [41] or summer or spring or heat or winter or frost or cold or hail or rain or dew, [42] or noon or night, or dawn or shining or brightness or light, but only the splendor of the glory of the Most High, by which all shall see what has been determined for them. [43] For it will last for about a week of years. [44] This is my judgment and its prescribed order; and to you alone have I shown these things." [45] I answered and said, "O sovereign Lord, I said then and I say now: Blessed are those who are alive and keep thy commandments! [46] But what of those for whom I prayed? For who among the living is there that has not sinned, or who among men that has not transgressed thy covenant? [47] And now I see that the world to come will bring delight to few, but torments to many. [48] For an evil heart has grown up in us, which has alienated us from God, and has brought us into corruption and the ways of death, and has shown us the paths of perdition and removed us far from life -- and that not just a few of us but almost all who have been created!" [49] He answered me and said, "Listen to me, Ezra, and I will instruct you, and will admonish you yet again. [50] For this reason the Most High has made not one world but two. [51] For whereas you have said that the righteous are not many but few, while the ungodly abound, hear the explanation for this. [52] "If you have just a few precious stones, will you add to them lead and clay?" [53] I said, "Lord, how could that be?" [54] And he said to me, "Not only that, but ask the earth and she will tell you; defer to her, and she will declare it to you. [55] Say to her, `You produce gold and silver and brass, and also iron and lead and clay; [56] but silver is more abundant than gold, and brass than silver, and iron than brass, and lead than iron, and clay than lead.' [57] Judge therefore which things are precious and desirable, those that are abundant or those that are rare?" [58] I said, "O sovereign Lord, what is plentiful is of less worth, for what is more rare is more precious."

[59] He answered me and said, "Weigh within yourself what you have thought, for he who has what is hard to get rejoices more than he who has what is plentiful.

[60] So also will be the judgment which I have promised; for I will rejoice over the few who shall be saved, because it is they who have made my glory to prevail now, and through them my name has now been honored. [61] And I will not grieve over the multitude of those who perish; for it is they who are now like a mist, and are similar to a flame and smoke -- they are set on fire and burn hotly, and are extinguished." [62] I replied and said, "O earth, what have you brought forth, if the mind is made out of the dust like the other created things! [63] For it would have been better if the dust itself had not been born, so that the mind might not have been made from it. [64] But now the mind grows with us, and therefore we are tormented, because we perish and know it. [65] Let the human race lament, but let the beasts of the field be glad; let all who have been born lament, but let the four-footed beasts and the flocks rejoice! [66] For it is much better with them than with us; for they do not look for a judgment, nor do they know of any torment or salvation promised to them after death. [67] For what does it profit us that we shall be preserved alive but cruelly tormented? [68] For all who have been born are involved in iniquities, and are full of sins and burdened with transgressions. [69] And if we were not to come into judgment after death, perhaps it would have been better for us." [70] He answered me and said, "When the Most High made the world and Adam and all who have come from him, he first prepared the judgment and the things that pertain to the judgment.

[71] And now understand from your own words, for you have said that the mind grows with us. [72] For this reason, therefore, those who dwell on earth shall be tormented, because though they had understanding they committed iniquity, and though they received the commandments they did not keep them, and though they obtained the law they dealt unfaithfully with what they received. [73] What, then, will they have to say in the judgment, or how will they answer in the last times? [74] For how long the time is that the Most High has been patient with those who inhabit the world, and not for their sake, but because of the times which he has foreordained!" [75] I answered and said, "If I have found favor in thy sight, O Lord, show this also to thy servant: whether after death, as soon as every one of us yields up his soul, we shall be kept in rest until those times come when thou wilt renew the creation, or whether we shall be tormented at once?"

[76] He answered me and said, "I will show you that also, but do not be associated with those who have shown scorn, nor number yourself among those who are tormented. [77] For you have a treasure of works laid up with the Most High; but it will not be shown to you until the last times. [78] Now, concerning death, the teaching is: When the decisive decree has gone forth from the Most High that a man shall die, as the spirit leaves the body to return again to him who gave it, first of all it adores the glory of the Most High. [79] And if it is one of those who have shown scorn and have not kept the way of the Most High, and who have despised his law, and who have hated those who fear God -- [80] such spirits shall not enter into habitations, but shall immediately wander about in torments, ever grieving and sad, in seven ways. [81] The first way, because they have scorned the law of the Most High. [82] The second way, because they cannot now make a good repentance that they may live. [83] The third way, they shall see the reward laid up for those who have trusted the covenants of the Most High. [84] The fourth way, they shall consider the torment laid up for themselves in the last days. [85] The fifth way, they shall see how the habitations of the others are guarded by angels in profound quiet. [86] The sixth way, they shall see how some of them will pass over into torments. [87] The seventh way, which is worse than all the ways that have been mentioned, because they shall utterly waste away in confusion and be consumed with shame, and shall wither with fear at seeing the glory of the Most High before whom they sinned while they were alive, and before whom they are to be judged in the last times. [88] "Now this is the order of those who have kept the ways of the Most High, when they shall be separated from their mortal body. [89] During the time that they lived in it, they laboriously served the Most High, and withstood danger every hour, that they might keep the law of the Lawgiver perfectly. [90] Therefore this is the teaching concerning them: [91] First of all, they shall see with great joy the glory of him who receives them, for they shall have rest in seven orders. [92] The first order, because they have striven with great effort to overcome the evil thought which was formed with them, that it might not lead them astray from life into death. [93] The second order, because they see the perplexity in which the souls of the ungodly wander, and the punishment that awaits them. [94] The third order, they see the witness which he who formed them bears concerning them, that while they were alive they kept the law which was given them in trust. [95] The fourth order, they understand the rest which they now enjoy, being gathered into their chambers and guarded by angels in profound quiet, and the glory which awaits them in the last days. [96] The fifth order, they rejoice that they have now escaped what is corruptible, and shall inherit what is to come; and besides they see the straits and toil from which they have been delivered, and the spacious liberty which they are to receive and enjoy in immortality. [97] The sixth order, when it is shown to them how their face is to shine like the sun, and how they are to be made like the light of the stars, being incorruptible from then on. [98] The seventh order, which is greater than all that have been mentioned, because they shall rejoice with boldness, and shall be confident without confusion, and shall be glad without fear, for they hasten to behold the face of him whom they served in life and from whom they are to receive their reward when glorified. [99] This is the order of the souls of the righteous, as henceforth is announced; and the aforesaid are the ways of torment which those who would not give heed shall suffer hereafter." [100] I answered and said, "Will time therefore be given to the souls, after they have been separated from the bodies, to see what you have described to me?" [101] He said to me, "They shall have freedom for seven days, so that during these seven days they may see the things of which you have been told, and afterwards they shall be gathered in their habitations." [102] I answered and said, "If I have found favor in thy sight, show further to me, thy servant, whether on the day of judgment the righteous will be able to intercede for the ungodly or to entreat the Most High for them,

[103] fathers for sons or sons for parents, brothers for brothers, relatives for their kinsmen, or friends for those who are most dear." [104] He answered me and said, "Since you have found favor in my sight, I will show you this also. The day of judgment is decisive and displays to all the seal of truth. Just as now a father does not send his son, or a son his father, or a master his servant, or a friend his dearest friend, to be ill or sleep or eat or be healed in his stead,
[105] so no one shall ever pray for another on that day, neither shall any one lay a burden on another; for then every one shall bear his own righteousness and unrighteousness." [106] I answered and said, "How then do we find that first Abraham prayed for the people of Sodom, and Moses for our fathers who sinned in the desert,
[107] and Joshua after him for Israel in the days of Achan, [108] and Samuel in the days of Saul, and David for the plague, and Solomon for those in the sanctuary, (109)] and Elijah for those who received the rain, and for the one who was dead, that he might live, (110)] and Hezekiah for the people in the days of Sennacherib, and many others prayed for many? [111] If therefore the righteous have prayed for the ungodly now, when corruption has increased and unrighteousness has multiplied, why will it not be so then as well?" [112)] He answered me and said, "This present world is not the end; the full glory does not abide in it; therefore those who were strong prayed for the weak.
[113] But the day of judgment will be the end of this age and the beginning of the immortal age to come, in which corruption has passed away, [114] sinful indulgence has come to an end, unbelief has been cut off, and righteousness has increased and truth has appeared. [115] Therefore no one will then be able to have mercy on him who has been condemned in the judgment, or to harm him who is victorious." [116] I answered and said, "This is my first and last word, that it would have been better if the earth had not produced Adam, or else, when it had produced him, had restrained him from sinning. [117] For what good is it to all that they live in sorrow now and expect punishment after death? [118] O Adam, what have you done? For though it was you who sinned, the fall was not yours alone, but ours also who are your descendants. [119] For what good is it to us, if an eternal age has been promised to us, but we have done deeds that bring death? [120] And what good is it that an everlasting hope has been promised to us, but we have miserably failed? [121] Or that safe and healthful habitations have been reserved for us, but we have lived wickedly? [122] Or that the glory of the Most High will defend those who have led a pure life, but we have walked in the most wicked ways? [123] Or that a paradise shall be revealed, whose fruit remains unspoiled and in which are abundance and healing, but we shall not enter it, [124] because we have lived in unseemly places? [125] Or that the faces of those who practiced self-control shall shine more than the stars, but our faces shall be blacker than darkness? [126] For while we lived and committed iniquity we did not consider what we should suffer after death." [127] He answered and said, "This is the meaning of the contest which every man who is born on earth shall wage, [128] that if he is defeated he shall suffer what you have said, but if he is victorious he shall receive what I have said. [129] For this is the way of which Moses, while he was alive, spoke to the people, saying, `Choose for yourself life, that you may live!' [130] But they did not believe him, or the prophets after him, or even myself who have spoken to them. [131] Therefore there shall not be grief at their destruction, so much as joy over those to whom salvation is assured." [132] I answered and said, "I know, O Lord, that the Most High is now called merciful, because he has mercy on those who have not yet come into the world; [133] and gracious, because he is gracious to those who turn in repentance to his law; [134] and patient, because he shows patience toward those who have sinned, since they are his own works; [135] and bountiful, because he would rather give than take away; [136] and abundant in compassion, because he makes his compassions abound more and more to those now living and to those who are gone and to those yet to come, [137] for if he did not make them abound, the world with those who inhabit it would not have life; [138] and he is called giver, because if he did not give out of his goodness so that those who have committed iniquities might be relieved of them, not one ten-thousandth of mankind could have life; [139] and judge, because if he did not pardon those who were created by his word and blot out the multitude of their sins, [140] there would probably be left only very few of the innumerable multitude."

8

[1] He answered me and said, "The Most High made this world for the sake of many, but the world to come for the sake of few.
[2] But I tell you a parable, Ezra. Just as, when you ask the earth, it will tell you that it provides very much clay from which earthenware is made, but only a little dust from which gold comes; so is the course of the present world.
[3] Many have been created, but few shall be saved."
[4] I answered and said, "Then drink your fill of understanding, O my soul, and drink wisdom, O my heart!
[5] For not of your own will did you come into the world, and against your will you depart, for you have been given only a short time to live.
[6] O Lord who are over us, grant to thy servant that we may pray before thee, and give us seed for our heart and cultivation of our understanding so that fruit may be produced, by which every mortal who bears the likeness of a human being may be able to live.
[7] For thou alone do exist, and we are a work of thy hands, as thou hast declared.
[8] And because thou do give life to the body which is now fashioned in the womb, and do furnish it with members, what thou hast created is preserved in fire and water, and for nine months the womb which thou has formed endures thy creation which has been created in it.
[9] But that which keeps and that which is kept shall both be kept by thy keeping. And when the womb gives up again what has been created in it,

[10] thou hast commanded that from the members themselves (that is, from the breasts) milk should be supplied which is the fruit of the breasts,

[11] so that what has been fashioned may be nourished for a time; and afterwards thou wilt guide him in thy mercy.

[12] Thou hast brought him up in thy righteousness, and instructed him in thy law, and reproved him in thy wisdom.

[13] Thou wilt take away his life, for he is thy creation; and thou wilt make him live, for he is thy work.

[14] If then thou wilt suddenly and quickly destroy him who with so great labor was fashioned by thy command, to what purpose was he made?

[15] And now I will speak out: About all mankind thou knowest best; but I will speak about thy people, for whom I am grieved,

[16] and about thy inheritance, for whom I lament, and about Israel, for whom I am sad, and about the seed of Jacob, for whom I am troubled.

[17] Therefore I will pray before thee for myself and for them, for I see the failings of us who dwell in the land,

[18] and I have heard of the swiftness of the judgment that is to come.

[19] Therefore hear my voice, and understand my words, and I will speak before thee." The beginning of the words of Ezra's prayer, before he was taken up. He said:

[20] "O Lord who inhabitest eternity, whose eyes are exalted and whose upper chambers are in the air,

[21] whose throne is beyond measure and whose glory is beyond comprehension, before whom the hosts of angels stand trembling

[22] and at whose command they are changed to wind and fire, whose word is sure and whose utterances are certain, whose ordinance is strong and whose command is terrible,

[23] whose look dries up the depths and whose indignation makes the mountains melt away, and whose truth is established for ever --

[24] hear, O Lord, the prayer of thy servant, and give ear to the petition of thy creature; attend to my words.

[25] For as long as I live I will speak, and as long as I have understanding I will answer.

[26] O look not upon the sins of thy people, but at those who have served thee in truth.

[27] Regard not the endeavors of those who act wickedly, but the endeavors of those who have kept thy covenants amid afflictions.

[28] Think not on those who have lived wickedly in thy sight; but remember those who have willingly acknowledged that thou art to be feared.

[29] Let it not be thy will to destroy those who have had the ways of cattle; but regard those who have gloriously taught thy law.

[30] Be not angry with those who are deemed worse than beasts; but love those who have always put their trust in thy glory.

[31] For we and our fathers have passed our lives in ways that bring death, but thou, because of us sinners, are called merciful.

[32] For if thou hast desired to have pity on us, who have no works of righteousness, then thou wilt be called merciful.

[33] For the righteous, who have many works laid up with thee, shall receive their reward in consequence of their own deeds.

[34] But what is man, that thou art angry with him; or what is a corruptible race, that thou art so bitter against it?

[35] For in truth there is no one among those who have been born who has not acted wickedly, and among those who have existed there is no one who has not transgressed.

[36] For in this, O Lord, thy righteousness and goodness will be declared, when thou art merciful to those who have no store of good works."

[37] He answered me and said, "Some things you have spoken rightly, and it will come to pass according to your words.

[38] For indeed I will not concern myself about the fashioning of those who have sinned, or about their death, their judgment, or their destruction;

[39] but I will rejoice over the creation of the righteous, over their pilgrimage also, and their salvation, and their receiving their reward.

[40] As I have spoken, therefore, so it shall be.

[41] "For just as the farmer sows many seeds upon the ground and plants a multitude of seedlings, and yet not all that have been sown will come up in due season, and not all that were planted will take root; so also those who have been sown in the world will not all be saved."

[42] I answered and said, "If I have found favor before thee, let me speak.

[43] For if the farmer's seed does not come up, because it has not received thy rain in due season, or if it has been ruined by too much rain, it perishes.

[44] But man, who has been formed by thy hands and is called thy own image because he is made like thee, and for whose sake thou hast formed all things -- hast thou also made him like the farmer's seed?

[45] No, O Lord who art over us! But spare thy people and have mercy on thy inheritance, for thou hast mercy on thy own creation."

[46] He answered me and said, "Things that are present are for those who live now, and things that are future are for those who will live hereafter.

[47] For you come far short of being able to love my creation more than I love it. But you have often compared yourself to the unrighteous. Never do so!

[48] But even in this respect you will be praiseworthy before the Most High,

[49] because you have humbled yourself, as is becoming for you, and have not deemed yourself to be among the righteous in order to receive the greatest glory.

[50] For many miseries will affect those who inhabit the world in the last times, because they have walked in great pride.

[51] But think of your own case, and inquire concerning the glory of those who are like yourself,

[52] because it is for you that paradise is opened, the tree of life is planted, the age to come is prepared, plenty is provided, a city is built, rest is appointed, goodness is established and wisdom perfected beforehand.

[53] The root of evil is sealed up from you, illness is banished from you, and death is hidden; hell has fled and corruption has been forgotten;

[54] sorrows have passed away, and in the end the treasure of immortality is made manifest.

[55] Therefore do not ask any more questions about the multitude of those who perish.

[56] For they also received freedom , but they despised the Most High, and were contemptuous of his law, and forsook his ways.

[57] Moreover they have even trampled upon his righteous ones,

[58] and said in their hearts that there is not God -- though knowing full well that they must die.

[59] For just as the things which I have predicted await you, so the thirst and torment which are prepared await them. For the Most High did not intend that men should be destroyed;

[60] but they themselves who were created have defiled the name of him who made them, and have been ungrateful to him who prepared life for them.

[61] Therefore my judgment is now drawing near;

[62] I have not shown this to all men, but only to you and a few like you." Then I answered and said,

[63] "Behold, O Lord, thou hast now shown me a multitude of the signs which thou wilt do in the last times, but thou hast not shown me when thou wilt do them."

9

[1] He answered me and said, "Measure carefully in your mind, and when you see that a certain part of the predicted signs are past,

[2] then you will know that it is the very time when the Most High is about to visit the world which he has made.

[3] So when there shall appear in the world earthquakes, tumult of peoples, intrigues of nations, wavering of leaders, confusion of princes,

[4] then you will know that it was of these that the Most High spoke from the days that were of old, from the beginning.

[5] For just as with everything that has occurred in the world, the beginning is evident, and the end manifest;

[6] so also are the times of the Most High: the beginnings are manifest in wonders and mighty works, and the end in requital and in signs.

[7] And it shall be that every one who will be saved and will be able to escape on account of his works, or on account of the faith by which he has believed,

[8] will survive the dangers that have been predicted, and will see my salvation in my land and within my borders, which I have sanctified for myself from the beginning.

[9] Then those who have now abused my ways shall be amazed, and those who have rejected them with contempt shall dwell in torments.

[10] For as many as did not acknowledge me in their lifetime, although they received my benefits,

[11] and as many as scorned my law while they still had freedom, and did not understand but despised it while an opportunity of repentance was still open to them,

[12] these must in torment acknowledge it after death.

[13] Therefore, do not continue to be curious as to how the ungodly will be punished; but inquire how the righteous will be saved, those to whom the age belongs and for whose sake the age was made."

[14] I answered and said,

[15] "I said before, and I say now, and will say it again: there are more who perish than those who will be saved,

[16] as a wave is greater than a drop of water."

[17] He answered me and said, "As is the field, so is the seed; and as are the flowers, so are the colors; and as is the work, so is the product; and as is the farmer, so is the threshing floor.

[18] For there was a time in this age when I was preparing for those who now exist, before the world was made for them to dwell in, and no one opposed me then, for no one existed;

[19] but now those who have been created in this world which is supplied both with an unfailing table and an inexhaustible pasture, have become corrupt in their ways.

[20] So I considered my world, and behold, it was lost, and my earth, and behold, it was in peril because of the devices of those who had come into it.

[21] And I saw and spared some with great difficulty, and saved for myself one grape out of a cluster, and one plant out of a

great forest.

[22] So let the multitude perish which has been born in vain, but let my grape and my plant be saved, because with much labor I have perfected them.

[23] But if you will let seven days more pass -- do not fast during them, however;

[24] but go into a field of flowers where no house has been built, and eat only of the flowers of the field, and taste no meat and drink no wine, but eat only flowers,

[25] and pray to the Most High continually -- then I will come and talk with you."

[26] So I went, as he directed me, into the field which is called Ardat; and there I sat among the flowers and ate of the plants of the field, and the nourishment they afforded satisfied me.

[27] And after seven days, as I lay on the grass, my heart was troubled again as it was before.

[28] And my mouth was opened, and I began to speak before the Most High, and said,

[29] "O Lord, thou didst show thyself among us, to our fathers in the wilderness when they came out from Egypt and when they came into the untrodden and unfruitful wilderness;

[30] and thou didst say, `Hear me, O Israel, and give heed to my words, O descendants of Jacob.

[31] For behold, I sow my law in you, and it shall bring forth fruit in you and you shall be glorified through it for ever.'

[32] But though our fathers received the law, they did not keep it, and did not observe the statutes; yet the fruit of the law did not perish -- for it could not, because it was your.

[33] Yet those who received it perished, because they did not keep what had been sown in them.

[34] And behold, it is the rule that, when the ground has received seed, or the sea a ship, or any dish food or drink, and when it happens that what was sown or what was launched or what was put in is destroyed,

[35] they are destroyed, but the things that held them remain; yet with us it has not been so.

[36] For we who have received the law and sinned will perish, as well as our heart which received it;

[37] the law, however, does not perish but remains in its glory."

[38] When I said these things in my heart, I lifted up my eyes and saw a woman on my right, and behold, she was mourning and weeping with a loud voice, and was deeply grieved at heart, and her clothes were rent, and there were ashes on her head.

[39] Then I dismissed the thoughts with which I had been engaged, and turned to her

[40] and said to her, "Why are you weeping, and why are you grieved at heart?"

[41] And she said to me, "Let me alone, my lord, that I may weep for myself and continue to mourn, for I am greatly embittered in spirit and deeply afflicted."

[42] And I said to her, "What has happened to you? Tell me."

[43] And she said to me, "Your servant was barren and had no child, though I lived with my husband thirty years.

[44] And every hour and every day during those thirty years I besought the Most High, night and day.

[45] And after thirty years God heard your handmaid, and looked upon my low estate, and considered my distress, and gave me a son. And I rejoiced greatly over him, I and my husband and all my neighbors; and we gave great glory to the Mighty One.

[46] And I brought him up with much care.

[47] So when he grew up and I came to take a wife for him, I set a day for the marriage feast.

10

[1] "But it happened that when my son entered his wedding chamber, he fell down and died.

[2] Then we all put out the lamps, and all my neighbors attempted to console me; and I remained quiet until evening of the second day.

[3] But when they all had stopped consoling me, that I might be quiet, I got up in the night and fled, and came to this field, as you see.

[4] And now I intend not to return to the city, but to stay here, and I will neither eat nor drink, but without ceasing mourn and fast until I die."

[5] Then I broke off the reflections with which I was still engaged, and answered her in anger and said,

[6] "You most foolish of women, do you not see our mourning, and what has happened to us?

[7] For Zion, the mother of us all, is in deep grief and great affliction.

[8] It is most appropriate to mourn now, because we are all mourning, and to be sorrowful, because we are all sorrowing; you are sorrowing for one son, but we, the whole world, for our mother.

[9] Now ask the earth, and she will tell you that it is she who ought to mourn over so many who have come into being upon her.

[10] And from the beginning all have been born of her, and others will come; and behold, almost all go to perdition, and a multitude of them are destined for destruction.

[11] Who then ought to mourn the more, she who lost so great a multitude, or you who are grieving for one?

[12] But if you say to me, `My lamentation is not like the earth's, for I have lost the fruit of my womb, which I brought forth in pain and bore in sorrow;

[13] but it is with the earth according to the way of the earth -- the multitude that is now in it goes as it came';

[14] then I say to you, `As you brought forth in sorrow, so the earth also has from the beginning given her fruit, that is, man, to him who made her.'

[15] Now, therefore, keep your sorrow to yourself, and bear bravely the troubles that have come upon you.

[16] For if you acknowledge the decree of God to be just, you will receive your son back in due time, and will be praised among women.

[17] Therefore go into the city to your husband."

[18] She said to me, "I will not do so; I will not go into the city, but I will die here."

[19] So I spoke again to her, and said,

[20] "Do not say that, but let yourself be persuaded because of the troubles of Zion, and be consoled because of the sorrow of Jerusalem.

[21] For you see that our sanctuary has been laid waste, our altar thrown down, our temple destroyed;

[22] our harp has been laid low, our song has been silenced, and our rejoicing has been ended; the light of our lampstand has been put out, the ark of our covenant has been plundered, our holy things have been polluted, and the name by which we are called has been profaned; our free men have suffered abuse, our priests have been burned to death, our Levites have gone into captivity, our virgins have been defiled, and our wives have been ravished; our righteous men have been carried off, our little ones have been cast out, our young men have been enslaved and our strong men made powerless.

[23] And, what is more than all, the seal of Zion -- for she has now lost the seal of her glory, and has been given over into the hands of those that hate us.

[24] Therefore shake off your great sadness and lay aside your many sorrows, so that the Mighty One may be merciful to you again, and the Most High may give you rest, a relief from your troubles."

[25] While I was talking to her, behold, her face suddenly shone exceedingly, and her countenance flashed like lightning, so that I was too frightened to approach her, and my heart was terrified. While I was wondering what this meant,

[26] behold, she suddenly uttered a loud and fearful cry, so that the earth shook at the sound.

[27] And I looked, and behold, the woman was no longer visible to me, but there was an established city, and a place of huge foundations showed itself. Then I was afraid, and cried with a loud voice and said,

[28] "Where is the angel Uriel, who came to me at first? For it was he who brought me into this overpowering bewilderment; my end has become corruption, and my prayer a reproach."

[29] As I was speaking these words, behold, the angel who had come to me at first came to me, and he looked upon me;

[30] and behold, I lay there like a corpse and I was deprived of my understanding. Then he grasped my right hand and strengthened me and set me on my feet, and said to me,

[31] "What is the matter with you? And why are you troubled? And why are your understanding and the thoughts of your mind troubled?"

[32] I said, "Because you have forsaken me! I did as you directed, and went out into the field, and behold, I saw, and still see, what I am unable to explain."

[33] He said to me, "Stand up like a man, and I will instruct you."

[34] I said, "Speak, my lord; only do not forsake me, lest I die before my time.

[35] For I have seen what I did not know, and I have heard what I do not understand.

[36] Or is my mind deceived, and my soul dreaming?

[37] Now therefore I entreat you to give your servant an explanation of this bewildering vision."

[38] He answered me and said, "Listen to me and I will inform you, and tell you about the things which you fear, for the Most High has revealed many secrets to you.

[39] For he has seen your righteous conduct, that you have sorrowed continually for your people, and mourned greatly over Zion.

[40] This therefore is the meaning of the vision.

[41] The woman who appeared to you a little while ago, whom you saw mourning and began to console --

[42] but you do not now see the form of a woman, but an established city has appeared to you --

[43] and as for her telling you about the misfortune of her son, this is the interpretation:

[44] This woman whom you saw, whom you now behold as an established city, is Zion.

[45] And as for her telling you that she was barren for thirty years, it is because there were three thousand years in the world before any offering was offered in it.

[46] And after three thousand years Solomon built the city, and offered offerings; then it was that the barren woman bore a son.

[47] And as for her telling you that she brought him up with much care, that was the period of residence in Jerusalem.

[48] And as for her saying to you , `When my son entered his wedding chamber he died,' and that misfortune had overtaken her, that was the destruction which befell Jerusalem.

[49] And behold, you saw her likeness, how she mourned for her son, and you began to console her for what had happened.

[50] For now the Most High, seeing that you are sincerely grieved and profoundly distressed for her, has shown you the brilliance of her glory, and the loveliness of her beauty.

[51] Therefore I told you to remain in the field where no house had been built,

[52] for I knew that the Most High would reveal these things to you.

[53] Therefore I told you to go into the field where there was no foundation of any building,

[54] for no work of man's building could endure in a place where the city of the Most High was to be revealed.

[55] "Therefore do not be afraid, and do not let your heart be terrified; but go in and see the splendor and vastness of the building, as far as it is possible for your eyes to see it,

[56] and afterward you will hear as much as your ears can hear.

[57] For you are more blessed than many, and you have been called before the Most High, as but few have been.

[58] But tomorrow night you shall remain here,

[59] and the Most High will show you in those dream visions what the Most High will do to those who dwell on earth in the last days." So I slept that night and the following one, as he had commanded me.

11

[1] On the second night I had a dream, and behold, there came up from the sea an eagle that had twelve feathered wings and three heads.

[2] And I looked, and behold, he spread his wings over all the earth, and all the winds of heaven blew upon him, and the clouds were gathered about him.

[3] And I looked, and out of his wings there grew opposing wings; but they became little, puny wings.

[4] But his heads were at rest; the middle head was larger than the other heads, but it also was at rest with them.

[5] And I looked, and behold, the eagle flew with his wings, to reign over the earth and over those who dwell in it.

[6] And I saw how all things under heaven were subjected to him, and no one spoke against him, not even one creature that was on the earth.

[7] And I looked, and behold, the eagle rose upon his talons, and uttered a cry to his wings, saying,

[8] "Do not all watch at the same time; let each sleep in his own place, and watch in his turn;

[9] but let the heads be reserved for the last."

[10] And I looked, and behold, the voice did not come from his heads, but from the midst of his body.

[11] And I counted his opposing wings, and behold, there were eight of them.

[12] And I looked, and behold, on the right side one wing arose, and it reigned over all the earth.

[13] And while it was reigning it came to its end and disappeared, so that its place was not seen. Then the next wing arose and reigned, and it continued to reign a long time.

[14] And while it was reigning its end came also, so that it disappeared like the first.

[15] And behold, a voice sounded, saying to it.

[16] "Hear me, you who have ruled the earth all this time; I announce this to you before you disappear.

[17] After you no one shall rule as long as you, or even half as long."

[18] Then the third wing raised itself up, and held the rule like the former ones, and it also disappeared.

[19] And so it went with all the wings; they wielded power one after another and then were never seen again.

[20] And I looked, and behold, in due course the wings that followed also rose up on the right side, in order to rule. There were some of them that ruled, yet disappeared suddenly;

[21] and others of them rose up, but did not hold the rule.

[22] And after this I looked, and behold, the twelve wings and the two little wings disappeared;

[23] and nothing remained on the eagle's body except the three heads that were at rest and six little wings.

[24] And I looked, and behold, two little wings separated from the six and remained under the head that was on the right side; but four remained in their place.

[25] And I looked, and behold, these little wings planned to set themselves up and hold the rule.

[26] And I looked, and behold, one was set up, but suddenly disappeared;

[27] a second also, and this disappeared more quickly than the first.

[28] And I looked, and behold, the two that remained were planning between themselves to reign together;

[29] and while they were planning, behold, one of the heads that were at rest (the one which was in the middle) awoke; for it was greater than the other two heads.

[30] And I saw how it allied the two heads with itself,

[31] and behold, the head turned with those that were with it, and it devoured the two little wings which were planning to reign.

[32] Moreover this head gained control of the whole earth, and with much oppression dominated its inhabitants; and it had greater power over the world than all the wings that had gone before.

[33] And after this I looked, and behold, the middle head also suddenly disappeared, just as the wings had done.

[34] But the two heads remained, which also ruled over the earth and its inhabitants.

[35] And I looked, and behold, the head on the right side devoured the one on the left.

[36] Then I heard a voice saying to me, "Look before you and consider what you see."

[37] And I looked, and behold, a creature like a lion was aroused out of the forest, roaring; and I heard how he uttered a man's voice to the eagle, and spoke, saying,

[38] "Listen and I will speak to you. The Most High says to you,

[39] `Are you not the one that remains of the four beasts which I had made to reign in my world, so that the end of my times might come through them?

[40] You, the fourth that has come, have conquered all the beasts that have gone before; and you have held sway over the world with much terror, and over all the earth with grievous oppression; and for so long you have dwelt on the earth with deceit.

[41] And you have judged the earth, but not with truth;

[42] for you have afflicted the meek and injured the peaceable; you have hated those who tell the truth, and have loved liars; you have destroyed the dwellings of those who brought forth fruit, and have laid low the walls of those who did you no harm.

[43] And so your insolence has come up before the Most High, and your pride to the Mighty One.

[44] And the Most High has looked upon his times, and behold, they are ended, and his ages are completed!

[45] Therefore you will surely disappear, you eagle, and your terrifying wings, and your most evil little wings, and your malicious heads, and your most evil talons, and your whole worthless body,

[46] so that the whole earth, freed from your violence, may be refreshed and relieved, and may hope for the judgment and mercy of him who made it.'"

12

[1] While the lion was saying these words to the eagle, I looked,

[2] and behold, the remaining head disappeared. And the two wings that had gone over to it arose and set themselves up to reign, and their reign was brief and full of tumult.

[3] And I looked, and behold, they also disappeared, and the whole body of the eagle was burned, and the earth was exceedingly terrified. Then I awoke in great perplexity of mind and great fear, and I said to my spirit,

[4] "Behold, you have brought this upon me, because you search out the ways of the Most High.

[5] Behold, I am still weary in mind and very weak in my spirit, and not even a little strength is left in me, because of the great fear with which I have been terrified this night.

[6] Therefore I will now beseech the Most High that he may strengthen me to the end."

[7] And I said, "O sovereign Lord, if I have found favor in thy sight, and if I have been accounted righteous before thee beyond many others, and if my prayer has indeed come up before thy face,

[8] strengthen me and show me, thy servant, the interpretation and meaning of this terrifying vision, that thou mayest fully comfort my soul.

[9] For thou hast judged me worthy to be shown the end of the times and the last events of the times."

[10] He said to me, "This is the interpretation of this vision which you have seen:

[11] The eagle which you saw coming up from the sea is the fourth kingdom which appeared in a vision to your brother Daniel.

[12] But it was not explained to him as I now explain or have explained it to you.

[13] Behold, the days are coming when a kingdom shall arise on earth, and it shall be more terrifying than all the kingdoms that have been before it.

[14] And twelve kings shall reign in it, one after another.

[15] But the second that is to reign shall hold sway for a longer time than any other of the twelve.

[16] This is the interpretation of the twelve wings which you saw.

[17] As for your hearing a voice that spoke, coming not from the eagle's heads but from the midst of his body, this is the interpretation:

[18] In the midst of the time of that kingdom great struggles shall arise, and it shall be in danger of falling; nevertheless it shall not fall then, but shall regain its former power.

[19] As for your seeing eight little wings clinging to his wings, this is the interpretation:

[20] Eight kings shall arise in it, whose times shall be short and their years swift;

[21] and two of them shall perish when the middle of its time draws near; and four shall be kept for the time when its end approaches; but two shall be kept until the end.

[22] As for your seeing three heads at rest, this is the interpretation:

[23] In its last days the Most High will raise up three kings, and they shall renew many things in it, and shall rule the earth

[24] and its inhabitants more oppressively than all who were before them; therefore they are called the heads of the eagle.

[25] For it is they who shall sum up his wickedness and perform his last actions.

[26] As for your seeing that the large head disappeared, one of the kings shall die in his bed, but in agonies.

[27] But as for the two who remained, the sword shall devour them.

[28] For the sword of one shall devour him who was with him; but he also shall fall by the sword in the last days.

[29] As for your seeing two little wings passing over to the head which was on the right side,

[30] this is the interpretation: It is these whom the Most High has kept for the eagle's end; this was the reign which was brief and full of tumult, as you have seen.

[31] "And as for the lion whom you saw rousing up out of the forest and roaring and speaking to the eagle and reproving him for his unrighteousness, and as for all his words that you have heard,

[32] this is the Messiah whom the Most High has kept until the end of days, who will arise from the posterity of David, and will come and speak to them; he will denounce them for their ungodliness and for their wickedness, and will cast up before them their contemptuous dealings.

[33] For first he will set them living before his judgment seat, and when he has reproved them, then he will destroy them.

[34] But he will deliver in mercy the remnant of my people, those who have been saved throughout my borders, and he will make them joyful until the end comes, the day of judgment, of which I spoke to you at the beginning.

[35] This is the dream that you saw, and this is its interpretation.

[36] And you alone were worthy to learn this secret of the Most High.

[37] Therefore write all these things that you have seen in a book, and put it in a hidden place;

[38] and you shall teach them to the wise among your people, whose hearts you know are able to comprehend and keep these secrets.

[39] But wait here seven days more, so that you may be shown whatever it pleases the Most High to show you." Then he left me.

[40] When all the people heard that the seven days were past and I had not returned to the city, they all gathered together, from the least to the greatest, and came to me and spoke to me, saying,

[41] "How have we offended you, and what harm have we done you, that you have forsaken us and sit in this place?

[42] For of all the prophets you alone are left to us, like a cluster of grapes from the vintage, and like a lamp in a dark place, and like a haven for a ship saved from a storm.

[43] Are not the evils which have befallen us sufficient?

[44] Therefore if you forsake us, how much better it would have been for us if we also had been consumed in the burning of Zion!

[45] For we are no better than those who died there." And they wept with a loud voice. Then I answered them and said,

[46] "Take courage, O Israel; and do not be sorrowful, O house of Jacob;

[47] for the Most High has you in remembrance, and the Mighty One has not forgotten you in your struggle.

[48] As for me, I have neither forsaken you nor withdrawn from you; but I have come to this place to pray on account of the desolation of Zion, and to seek mercy on account of the humiliation of our sanctuary.

[49] Now go, every one of you to his house, and after these days I will come to you."

[50] So the people went into the city, as I told them to do.

[51] But I sat in the field seven days, as the angel had commanded me; and I ate only of the flowers of the field, and my food was of plants during those days.

13

[1] After seven days I dreamed a dream in the night;

[2] and behold, a wind arose from the sea and stirred up all its waves.

[3] And I looked, and behold, this wind made something like the figure of a man come up out of the heart of the sea. And I looked, and behold, that man flew with the clouds of heaven; and wherever he turned his face to look, everything under his gaze trembled,

[4] and whenever his voice issued from his mouth, all who heard his voice melted as wax melts when it feels the fire.

[5] After this I looked, and behold, an innumerable multitude of men were gathered together from the four winds of heaven to make war against the man who came up out of the sea.

[6] And I looked, and behold, he carved out for himself a great mountain, and flew up upon it. < br>[7] And I tried to see the region or place from which the mountain was carved, but I could not.

[8] After this I looked, and behold, all who had gathered together against him, to wage war with him, were much afraid, yet dared to fight.

[9] And behold, when he saw the onrush of the approaching multitude, he neither lifted his hand nor held a spear or any weapon of war;

[10] but I saw only how he sent forth from his mouth as it were a stream of fire, and from his lips a flaming breath, and from his tongue he shot forth a storm of sparks.

[11] All these were mingled together, the stream of fire and the flaming breath and the great storm, and fell on the onrushing multitude which was prepared to fight, and burned them all up, so that suddenly nothing was seen of the innumerable multitude but only the dust of ashes and the smell of smoke. When I saw it, I was amazed.

[12] After this I saw the same man come down from the mountain and call to him another multitude which was peaceable.

[13] Then many people came to him, some of whom were joyful and some sorrowful; some of them were bound, and some were bringing others as offerings. Then in great fear I awoke; and I besought the Most High, and said,

[14] "From the beginning thou hast shown thy servant these wonders, and hast deemed me worthy to have my prayer heard by thee;

[15] now show me also the interpretation of this dream.

[16] For as I consider it in my mind, alas for those who will be left in those days! And still more, alas for those who are not left!

[17] For those who are not left will be sad,

[18] because they understand what is reserved for the last days, but cannot attain it.

[19] But alas for those also who are left, and for that very reason! For they shall see great dangers and much distress, as these dreams show.

[20] Yet it is better to come into these things, though incurring peril, than to pass from the world like a cloud, and not to see what shall happen in the last days." He answered me and said,

[21] "I will tell you the interpretation of the vision, and I will also explain to you the things which you have mentioned.

[22] As for what you said about those who are left, this is the interpretation:

[23] He who brings the peril at that time will himself protect those who fall into peril, who have works and have faith in the Almighty.

[24] Understand therefore that those who are left are more blessed than those who have died.

[25] This is the interpretation of the vision: As for your seeing a man come up from the heart of the sea,

[26] this is he whom the Most High has been keeping for many ages, who will himself deliver his creation; and he will direct those who are left.

[27] And as for your seeing wind and fire and a storm coming out of his mouth,

[28] and as for his not holding a spear or weapon of war, yet destroying the onrushing multitude which came to conquer him, this is the interpretation:

[29] Behold, the days are coming when the Most High will deliver those who are on the earth.

[30] And bewilderment of mind shall come over those who dwell on the earth.

[31] And they shall plan to make war against one another, city against city, place against place, people against people, and kingdom against kingdom.

[32] And when these things come to pass and the signs occur which I showed you before, then my Son will be revealed, whom you saw as a man coming up from the sea.

[33] And when all the nations hear his voice, every man shall leave his own land and the warfare that they have against one another;

[34] and an innumerable multitude shall be gathered together, as you saw, desiring to come and conquer him.

[35] But he shall stand on the top of Mount Zion.

[36] And Zion will come and be made manifest to all people, prepared and built, as you saw the mountain carved out without hands.

[37] And he, my Son, will reprove the assembled nations for their ungodliness (this was symbolized by the storm),

[38] and will reproach them to their face with their evil thoughts and the torments with which they are to be tortured (which were symbolized by the flames), and will destroy them without effort by the law (which was symbolized by the fire).

[39] And as for your seeing him gather to himself another multitude that was peaceable,

[40] these are the ten tribes which were led away from their own land into captivity in the days of King Hoshea, whom Shalmaneser the king of the Assyrians led captive; he took them across the river, and they were taken into another land.

[41] But they formed this plan for themselves, that they would leave the multitude of the nations and go to a more distant region, where mankind had never lived,

[42] that there at least they might keep their statutes which they had not kept in their own land.

[43] And they went in by the narrow passages of the Euphrates river.

[44] For at that time the Most High performed signs for them, and stopped the channels of the river until they had passed over.

[45] Through that region there was a long way to go, a journey of a year and a half; and that country is called Arzareth.

[46] "Then they dwelt there until the last times; and now, when they are about to come again,

[47] the Most High will stop the channels of the river again, so that they may be able to pass over. Therefore you saw the multitude gathered together in peace.

[48] But those who are left of your people, who are found within my holy borders, shall be saved.

[49] Therefore when he destroys the multitude of the nations that are gathered together, he will defend the people who remain.

[50] And then he will show them very many wonders."

[51] I said, "O sovereign Lord, explain this to me: Why did I see the man coming up from the heart of the sea?"

[52] He said to me, "Just as no one can explore or know what is in the depths of the sea, so no one on earth can see my Son or those who are with him, except in the time of his day.

[53] This is the interpretation of the dream which you saw. And you alone have been enlightened about this,

[54] because you have forsaken your own ways and have applied yourself to mine, and have searched out my law;

[55] for you have devoted your life to wisdom, and called understanding your mother.

[56] Therefore I have shown you this, for there is a reward laid up with the Most High. And after three more days I will tell you other things, and explain weighty and wondrous matters to you."

[57] Then I arose and walked in the field, giving great glory and praise to the Most High because of his wonders, which he did from time to time,

[58] and because he governs the times and whatever things come to pass in their seasons. And I stayed there three days.

14

[1] On the third day, while I was sitting under an oak, behold, a voice came out of a bush opposite me and said, "Ezra, Ezra."
[2] And I said, "Here I am, Lord," and I rose to my feet.
[3] Then he said to me, "I revealed myself in a bush and spoke to Moses, when my people were in bondage in Egypt;
[4] and I sent him and led my people out of Egypt; and I led him up on Mount Sinai, where I kept him with me many days;
[5] and I told him many wondrous things, and showed him the secrets of the times and declared to him the end of the times. Then I commanded him, saying,
[6] `These words you shall publish openly, and these you shall keep secret.'
[7] And now I say to you;
[8] Lay up in your heart the signs that I have shown you, the dreams that you have seen, and the interpretations that you have heard;
[9] for you shall be taken up from among men, and henceforth you shall live with my Son and with those who are like you, until the times are ended.
[10] For the age has lost its youth, and the times begin to grow old.
[11] For the age is divided into twelve parts, and nine of its parts have already passed,
[12] as well as half of the tenth part; so two of its parts remain, besides half of the tenth part.
[13] Now therefore, set your house in order, and reprove your people; comfort the lowly among them, and instruct those that are wise. And now renounce the life that is corruptible,
[14] and put away from you mortal thoughts; cast away from you the burdens of man, and divest yourself now of your weak nature,
[15] and lay to one side the thoughts that are most grievous to you, and hasten to escape from these times.
[16] For evils worse than those which you have now seen happen shall be done hereafter.
[17] For the weaker the world becomes through old age, the more shall evils be multiplied among its inhabitants.
[18] For truth shall go farther away, and falsehood shall come near. For the eagle which you saw in the vision is already hastening to come."
[19] Then I answered and said, "Let me speak in thy presence, Lord.
[20] For behold, I will go, as thou hast commanded me, and I will reprove the people who are now living; but who will warn those who will be born hereafter? For the world lies in darkness, and its inhabitants are without light.
[21] For thy law has been burned, and so no one knows the things which have been done or will be done by thee.
[22] If then I have found favor before thee, send the Holy Spirit into me, and I will write everything that has happened in the world from the beginning, the things which were written in thy law, that men may be able to find the path, and that those who wish to live in the last days may live."
[23] He answered me and said, "Go and gather the people, and tell them not to seek you for forty days.
[24] But prepare for yourself many writing tablets, and take with you Sarea, Dabria, Selemia, Ethanus, and Asiel -- these five, because they are trained to write rapidly;
[25] and you shall come here, and I will light in your heart the lamp of understanding, which shall not be put out until what you are about to write is finished.
[26] And when you have finished, some things you shall make public, and some you shall deliver in secret to the wise; tomorrow at this hour you shall begin to write."
[27] Then I went as he commanded me, and I gathered all the people together, and said,
[28] "Hear these words, O Israel
[29] At first our fathers dwelt as aliens in Egypt, and they were delivered from there,
[30] and received the law of life, which they did not keep, which you also have transgressed after them.
[31] Then land was given to you for a possession in the land of Zion; but you and your fathers committed iniquity and did not keep the ways which the Most High commanded you.
[32] And because he is a righteous judge, in due time he took from you what he had given.
[33] And now you are here, and your brethren are farther in the interior.
[34] If you, then, will rule over your minds and discipline your hearts, you shall be kept alive, and after death you shall obtain mercy.
[35] For after death the judgment will come, when we shall live again; and then the names of the righteous will become manifest, and the deeds of the ungodly will be disclosed.
[36] But let no one come to me now, and let no one seek me for forty days."
[37] So I took the five men, as he commanded me, and we proceeded to the field, and remained there.
[38] And on the next day, behold, a voice called me, saying, "Ezra, open your mouth and drink what I give you to drink."
[39] Then I opened my mouth, and behold, a full cup was offered to me; it was full of something like water, but its color was like fire.
[40] And I took it and drank; and when I had drunk it, my heart poured forth understanding, and wisdom increased in my

breast, for my spirit retained its memory;

[41] and my mouth was opened, and was no longer closed.

[42] And the Most High gave understanding to the five men, and by turns they wrote what was dictated, in characters which they did not know. They sat forty days, and wrote during the daytime, and ate their bread at night.

[43] As for me, I spoke in the daytime and was not silent at night.

[44] So during the forty days ninety-four books were written.

[45] And when the forty days were ended, the Most High spoke to me, saying, "Make public the twenty-four books that you wrote first and let the worthy and the unworthy read them;

[46] but keep the seventy that were written last, in order to give them to the wise among your people.

[47] For in them is the spring of understanding, the fountain of wisdom, and the river of knowledge."

[48] And I did so.

15

[1] The Lord says, "Behold, speak in the ears of my people the words of the prophecy which I will put in your mouth,

[2] and cause them to be written on paper; for they are trustworthy and true.

[3] Do not fear the plots against you, and do not be troubled by the unbelief of those who oppose you.

[4] For every unbeliever shall die in his unbelief."

[5] "Behold," says the Lord, "I bring evils upon the world, the sword and famine and death and destruction.

[6] For iniquity has spread throughout every land, and their harmful deeds have reached their limit.

[7] Therefore," says the Lord,

[8] "I will be silent no longer concerning their ungodly deeds which they impiously commit, neither will I tolerate their wicked practices. Behold, innocent and righteous blood cries out to me, and the souls of the righteous cry out continually.

[9] I will surely avenge them," says the Lord, "and will receive to myself all the innocent blood from among them.

[10] Behold, my people is led like a flock to the slaughter; I will not allow them to live any longer in the land of Egypt,

[11] but I will bring them out with a mighty hand and with an uplifted arm, and will smite Egypt with plagues, as before, and will destroy all its land."

[12] Let Egypt mourn, and its foundations, for the plague of chastisement and punishment that the Lord will bring upon it.

[13] Let the farmers that till the ground mourn, because their seed shall fail and their trees shall be ruined by blight and hail and by a terrible tempest.

[14] Alas for the world and for those who live in it!

[15] For the sword and misery draw near them, and nation shall rise up to fight against nation, with swords in their hands.

[16] For there shall be unrest among men; growing strong against one another, they shall in their might have no respect for their king or the chief of their leaders.

[17] For a man will desire to go into a city, and shall not be able.

[18] For because of their pride the cities shall be in confusion, the houses shall be destroyed, and people shall be afraid.

[19] A man shall have no pity upon his neighbors, but shall make an assault upon their houses with the sword, and plunder their goods, because of hunger for bread and because of great tribulation.

[20] "Behold," says God, "I call together all the kings of the earth to fear me, from the rising sun and from the south, from the east and from Lebanon; to turn and repay what they have given them.

[21] Just as they have done to my elect until this day, so I will do, and will repay into their bosom." Thus says the Lord God:

[22] "My right hand will not spare the sinners, and my sword will not cease from those who shed innocent blood on earth."

[23] And a fire will go forth from his wrath, and will consume the foundations of the earth, and the sinners, like straw that is kindled.

[24] "Woe to those who sin and do not observe my commandments," says the Lord;

[25] "I will not spare them. Depart, you faithless children! Do not pollute my sanctuary."

[26] For the Lord knows all who transgress against him; therefore he will hand them over to death and slaughter.

[27] For now calamities have come upon the whole earth, and you shall remain in them; for God will not deliver you, because you have sinned against him.

[28] Behold, a terrifying sight, appearing from the east!

[29] The nations of the dragons of Arabia shall come out with many chariots, and from the day that they set out, their hissing shall spread over the earth, so that all who hear them fear and tremble.

[30] Also the Carmonians, raging in wrath, shall go forth like wild boars of the forest, and with great power they shall come, and engage them in battle, and shall devastate a portion of the land of the Assyrians with their teeth.

[31] And then the dragons, remembering their origin, shall become still stronger; and if they combine in great power and turn to pursue them,

[32] then these shall be disorganized and silenced by their power, and shall turn and flee.

[33] And from the land of the Assyrians an enemy in ambush shall beset them and destroy one of them, and fear and trembling shall come upon their army, and indecision upon their kings.

[34] Behold, clouds from the east, and from the north to the south; and their appearance is very threatening, full of wrath and storm.

[35] They shall dash against one another and shall pour out a heavy tempest upon the earth, and their own tempest; and there shall be blood from the sword as high as a horse's belly

[36] and a man's thigh and a camel's hock.

[37] And there shall be fear and great trembling upon the earth; and those who see that wrath shall be horror-stricken, and they shall be seized with trembling.

[38] And, after that, heavy storm clouds shall be stirred up from the south, and from the north, and another part from the west.

[39] And the winds from the east shall prevail over the cloud that was raised in wrath, and shall dispel it; and the tempest that was to cause destruction by the east wind shall be driven violently toward the south and west.

[40] And great and mighty clouds, full of wrath and tempest, shall rise, to destroy all the earth and its inhabitants, and shall pour out upon every high and lofty place a terrible tempest,

[41] fire and hail and flying swords and floods of water, that all the fields and all the streams may be filled with the abundance of those waters.

[42] And they shall destroy cities and walls, mountains and hills, trees of the forests, and grass of the meadows, and their grain.

[43] And they shall go on steadily to Babylon, and shall destroy her.

[44] They shall come to her and surround her; they shall pour out the tempest and all its wrath upon her; then the dust and smoke shall go up to heaven, and all who are about her shall wail over her.

[45] And those who survive shall serve those who have destroyed her.

[46] And you, Asia, who share in the glamour of Babylon and the glory of her person --

[47] woe to you, miserable wretch! For you have made yourself like her; you have decked out your daughters in harlotry to please and glory in your lovers, who have always lusted after you.

[48] You have imitated that hateful harlot in all her deeds and devices; therefore God says,

[49] "I will send evils upon you, widowhood, poverty, famine, sword, and pestilence, to lay waste your houses and bring you to destruction and death.

[50] And the glory of your power shall wither like a flower, when the heat rises that is sent upon you.

[51] You shall be weakened like a wretched woman who is beaten and wounded, so that you cannot receive your mighty lovers.

[52] Would I have dealt with you so violently," says the Lord,

[53] "If you had not always killed my chosen people, exulting and clapping your hands and talking about their death when you were drunk?

[54] Trick out the beauty of your face!

[55] The reward of a harlot is in your bosom, therefore you shall receive your recompense.

[56] As you will do to my chosen people," says the Lord, "so God will do to you, and will hand you over to adversities.

[57] Your children shall die of hunger, and you shall fall by the sword, and your cities shall be wiped out, and all your people who are in the open country shall fall by the sword.

[58] And those who are in the mountains and highlands shall perish of hunger, and they shall eat their own flesh in hunger for bread and drink their own blood in thirst for water.

[59] Unhappy above all others, you shall come and suffer fresh afflictions.

[60] And as they pass they shall wreck the hateful city, and shall destroy a part of your land and abolish a portion of your glory, as they return from devastated Babylon.

[61] And you shall be broken down by them like stubble, and they shall be like fire to you.

[62] And they shall devour you and your cities, your land and your mountains; they shall burn with fire all your forests and your fruitful trees.

[63] They shall carry your children away captive, and shall plunder your wealth, and abolish the glory of your countenance."

16

[1] Woe to you, Babylon and Asia! Woe to you, Egypt and Syria!

[2] Gird yourselves with sackcloth and haircloth, and wail for your children, and lament for them; for your destruction is at hand.

[3] The sword has been sent upon you, and who is there to turn it back?

[4] A fire has been sent upon you, and who is there to quench it?

[5] Calamities have been sent upon you, and who is there to drive them away?

[6] Can one drive off a hungry lion in the forest, or quench a fire in the stubble, when once it has begun to burn?

[7] Can one turn back an arrow shot by a strong archer?

[8] The Lord God sends calamities, and who will drive them away?

[9] Fire will go forth from his wrath, and who is there to quench it?

[10] He will flash lightning, and who will not be afraid? He will thunder, and who will not be terrified?

[11] The Lord will threaten, and who will not be utterly shattered at his presence?

[12] The earth and its foundations quake, the sea is churned up from the depths, and its waves and the fish also shall be

troubled at the presence of the Lord and before the glory of his power.

[13] For his right hand that bends the bow is strong, and his arrows that he shoots are sharp and will not miss when they begin to be shot to the ends of the world.

[14] Behold, calamities are sent forth and shall not return until they come over the earth.

[15] The fire is kindled, and shall not be put out until it consumes the foundations of the earth.

[16] Just as an arrow shot by a mighty archer does not return, so the calamities that are sent upon the earth shall not return.

[17] Alas for me! Alas for me! Who will deliver me in those days?

[18] The beginning of sorrows, when there shall be much lamentation; the beginning of famine, when many shall perish; the beginning of wars, when the powers shall be terrified; the beginning of calamities, when all shall tremble. What shall they do in these circumstances, when the calamities come?

[19] Behold, famine and plague, tribulation and anguish are sent as scourges for the correction of men.

[20] Yet for all this they will not turn from their iniquities, nor be always mindful of the scourges.

[21] Behold, provision will be so cheap upon earth that men will imagine that peace is assured for them, and then the calamities shall spring up on the earth -- the sword, famine, and great confusion.

[22] For many of those who live on the earth shall perish by famine; and those who survive the famine shall die by the sword.

[23] And the dead shall be cast out like dung, and there shall be no one to console them; for the earth shall be left desolate, and its cities shall be demolished.

[24] No one shall be left to cultivate the earth or to sow it.

[25] The trees shall bear fruit, and who will gather it?

[26] The grapes shall ripen, and who will tread them? For in all places there shall be great solitude;

[27] one man will long to see another, or even to hear his voice.

[28] For out of a city, ten shall be left; and out of the field, two who have hidden themselves in thick groves and clefts in the rocks.

[29] As in an olive orchard three or four olives may be left on every tree,

[30] or as when a vineyard is gathered some clusters may be left by those who search carefully through the vineyard,

[31] so in those days three or four shall be left by those who search their houses with the sword.

[32] And the earth shall be left desolate, and its fields shall be for briers, and its roads and all its paths shall bring forth thorns, because no sheep will go along them.

[33] Virgins shall mourn because they have no bridegrooms; women shall mourn because they have no husbands; their daughters shall mourn, because they have no helpers.

[34] Their bridegrooms shall be killed in war, and their husbands shall perish of famine.

[35] Listen now to these things, and understand them, O servants of the Lord.

[36] Behold the word of the Lord, receive it; do not disbelieve what the Lord says.

[37] Behold, the calamities draw near, and are not delayed.

[38] Just as a woman with child, in the ninth month, when the time of her delivery draws near, has great pains about her womb for two or three hours beforehand, and when the child comes forth from the womb, there will not be a moment's delay,

[39] so the calamities will not delay in coming forth upon the earth, and the world will groan, and pains will seize it on every side.

[40] "Hear my words, O my people; prepare for battle, and in the midst of the calamities be like strangers on the earth.

[41] Let him that sells be like one who will flee; let him that buys be like one who will lose;

[42] let him that does business be like one who will not make a profit; and let him that builds a house be like one who will not live in it;

[43] let him that sows be like one who will not reap; so also him that prunes the vines, like one who will not gather the grapes;

[44] them that marry, like those who will have no children; and them that do not marry, like those who are widowed.

[45] Because those who labor, labor in vain;

[46] for strangers shall gather their fruits, and plunder their goods, and overthrow their houses, and take their children captive; for in captivity and famine they will beget their children.

[47] Those who conduct business, do it only to be plundered; the more they adorn their cities, their houses and possessions, and their persons,

[48] the more angry I will be with them for their sins," says the Lord.

[49] Just as a respectable and virtuous woman abhors a harlot,

[50] so righteousness shall abhor iniquity, when she decks herself out, and shall accuse her to her face, when he comes who will defend him who searches out every sin on earth.

[51] Therefore do not be like her or her works.

[52] For behold, just a little while, and iniquity will be removed from the earth, and righteousness will reign over us.

[53] Let no sinner say that he has not sinned; for God will burn coals of fire on the head of him who says, "I have not sinned before God and his glory."

[54] Behold, the Lord knows all the works of men, their imaginations and their thoughts and their hearts.

[55] He said, "Let the earth be made," and it was made; "Let the heaven be made," and it was made.

[56] At his word the stars were fixed, and he knows the number of the stars.

[57] It is he who searches the deep and its treasures, who has measured the sea and its contents;

[58] who has enclosed the sea in the midst of the waters, and by his word has suspended the earth over the water;

[59] who has spread out the heaven like an arch, and founded it upon the waters;

[60] who has put springs of water in the desert, and pools on the tops of the mountains, to send rivers from the heights to water the earth;

[61] who formed man, and put a heart in the midst of his body, and gave him breath and life and understanding

[62] and the spirit of Almighty God; who made all things and searches out hidden things in hidden places.

[63] Surely he knows your imaginations and what you think in your hearts! Woe to those who sin and want to hide their sins!

[64] Because the Lord will strictly examine all their works, and will make a public spectacle of all of you.

[65] And when your sins come out before men, you shall be put to shame; and your own iniquities shall stand as your accusers in that day.

[66] What will you do? Or how will you hide your sins before God and his angels?

[67] Behold, God is the judge, fear him! Cease from your sins, and forget your iniquities, never to commit them again; so God will lead you forth and deliver you from all tribulation.

[68] For behold, the burning wrath of a great multitude is kindled over you, and they shall carry off some of you and shall feed you what was sacrificed to idols.

[69] And those who consent to eat shall be held in derision and contempt, and be trodden under foot.

[70] For in many places and in neighboring cities there shall be a great insurrection against those who fear the Lord.

[71] They shall be like mad men, sparing no one, but plundering and destroying those who continue to fear the Lord.

[72] For they shall destroy and plunder their goods, and drive them out of their houses.

[73] Then the tested quality of my elect shall be manifest, as gold that is tested by fire.

[74] "Hear, my elect," says the Lord. "Behold, the days of tribulation are at hand, and I will deliver you from them.

[75] Do not fear or doubt, for God is your guide.

[76] You who keep my commandments and precepts," says the Lord God, "do not let your sins pull you down, or your iniquities prevail over you."

[77] Woe to those who are choked by their sins and overwhelmed by their iniquities, as a field is choked with underbrush and its path overwhelmed with thorns, so that no one can pass through!

[78] It is shut off and given up to be consumed by fire.

1 Maccabees

1Mac.1

[1] After Alexander son of Philip, the Macedonian, who came from the land of Kittim, had defeated Darius, king of the Persians and the Medes, he succeeded him as king. (He had previously become king of Greece.)

[2] He fought many battles, conquered strongholds, and put to death the kings of the earth.

[3] He advanced to the ends of the earth, and plundered many nations. When the earth became quiet before him, he was exalted, and his heart was lifted up.

[4] He gathered a very strong army and ruled over countries, nations, and princes, and they became tributary to him.

[5] After this he fell sick and perceived that he was dying.

[6] So he summoned his most honored officers, who had been brought up with him from youth, and divided his kingdom among them while he was still alive.

[7] And after Alexander had reigned twelve years, he died.

[8] Then his officers began to rule, each in his own place.

[9] They all put on crowns after his death, and so did their sons after them for many years; and they caused many evils on the earth.

[10] From them came forth a sinful root, Antiochus Epiphanes, son of Antiochus the king; he had been a hostage in Rome. He began to reign in the one hundred and thirty-seventh year of the kingdom of the Greeks.

[11] In those days lawless men came forth from Israel, and misled many, saying, "Let us go and make a covenant with the Gentiles round about us, for since we separated from them many evils have come upon us."

[12] This proposal pleased them,

[13] and some of the people eagerly went to the king. He authorized them to observe the ordinances of the Gentiles.

[14] So they built a gymnasium in Jerusalem, according to Gentile custom,

[15] and removed the marks of circumcision, and abandoned the holy covenant. They joined with the Gentiles and sold themselves to do evil.

[16] When Antiochus saw that his kingdom was established, he determined to become king of the land of Egypt, that he might reign over both kingdoms.

[17] So he invaded Egypt with a strong force, with chariots and elephants and cavalry and with a large fleet.

[18] He engaged Ptolemy king of Egypt in battle, and Ptolemy turned and fled before him, and many were wounded and fell.

[19] And they captured the fortified cities in the land of Egypt, and he plundered the land of Egypt.

[20] After subduing Egypt, Antiochus returned in the one hundred and forty-third year. He went up against Israel and came to Jerusalem with a strong force.

[21] He arrogantly entered the sanctuary and took the golden altar, the lampstand for the light, and all its utensils.

[22] He took also the table for the bread of the Presence, the cups for drink offerings, the bowls, the golden censers, the curtain, the crowns, and the gold decoration on the front of the temple; he stripped it all off.

[23] He took the silver and the gold, and the costly vessels; he took also the hidden treasures which he found.

[24] Taking them all, he departed to his own land. He committed deeds of murder, and spoke with great arrogance.

[25] Israel mourned deeply in every community,

[26] rulers and elders groaned, maidens and young men became faint, the beauty of women faded.

[27] Every bridegroom took up the lament; she who sat in the bridal chamber was mourning.

[28] Even the land shook for its inhabitants, and all the house of Jacob was clothed with shame.

[29] Two years later the king sent to the cities of Judah a chief collector of tribute, and he came to Jerusalem with a large force.

[30] Deceitfully he spoke peaceable words to them, and they believed him; but he suddenly fell upon the city, dealt it a severe blow, and destroyed many people of Israel.

[31] He plundered the city, burned it with fire, and tore down its houses and its surrounding walls.

[32] And they took captive the women and children, and seized the cattle.

[33] Then they fortified the city of David with a great strong wall and strong towers, and it became their citadel.

[34] And they stationed there a sinful people, lawless men. These strengthened their position;

[35] they stored up arms and food, and collecting the spoils of Jerusalem they stored them there, and became a great snare.

[36] It became an ambush against the sanctuary, an evil adversary of Israel continually.

[37] On every side of the sanctuary they shed innocent blood; they even defiled the sanctuary.

[38] Because of them the residents of Jerusalem fled; she became a dwelling of strangers; she became strange to her offspring, and her children forsook her.

[39] Her sanctuary became desolate as a desert; her feasts were turned into mourning, her sabbaths into a reproach, her honor into contempt.

[40] Her dishonor now grew as great as her glory; her exaltation was turned into mourning.

[41] Then the king wrote to his whole kingdom that all should be one people,

[42] and that each should give up his customs.

[43] All the Gentiles accepted the command of the king. Many even from Israel gladly adopted his religion; they sacrificed to

idols and profaned the sabbath.

[44] And the king sent letters by messengers to Jerusalem and the cities of Judah; he directed them to follow customs strange to the land,

[45] to forbid burnt offerings and sacrifices and drink offerings in the sanctuary, to profane sabbaths and feasts,

[46] to defile the sanctuary and the priests,

[47] to build altars and sacred precincts and shrines for idols, to sacrifice swine and unclean animals,

[48] and to leave their sons uncircumcised. They were to make themselves abominable by everything unclean and profane,

[49] so that they should forget the law and change all the ordinances.

[50] "And whoever does not obey the command of the king shall die."

[51] In such words he wrote to his whole kingdom. And he appointed inspectors over all the people and commanded the cities of Judah to offer sacrifice, city by city.

[52] Many of the people, every one who forsook the law, joined them, and they did evil in the land;

[53] they drove Israel into hiding in every place of refuge they had.

[54] Now on the fifteenth day of Chislev, in the one hundred and forty-fifth year, they erected a desolating sacrilege upon the altar of burnt offering. They also built altars in the surrounding cities of Judah,

[55] and burned incense at the doors of the houses and in the streets.

[56] The books of the law which they found they tore to pieces and burned with fire.

[57] Where the book of the covenant was found in the possession of any one, or if any one adhered to the law, the decree of the king condemned him to death.

[58] They kept using violence against Israel, against those found month after month in the cities.

[59] And on the twenty-fifth day of the month they offered sacrifice on the altar which was upon the altar of burnt offering.

[60] According to the decree, they put to death the women who had their children circumcised,

[61] and their families and those who circumcised them; and they hung the infants from their mothers' necks.

[62] But many in Israel stood firm and were resolved in their hearts not to eat unclean food.

[63] They chose to die rather than to be defiled by food or to profane the holy covenant; and they did die.

[64] And very great wrath came upon Israel.

1Mac.2

[1] In those days Mattathias the son of John, son of Simeon, a priest of the sons of Joarib, moved from Jerusalem and settled in Modein.

[2] He had five sons, John surnamed Gaddi,

[3] Simon called Thassi,

[4] Judas called Maccabeus,

[5] Eleazar called Avaran, and Jonathan called Apphus.

[6] He saw the blasphemies being committed in Judah and Jerusalem,

[7] and said, "Alas! Why was I born to see this, the ruin of my people, the ruin of the holy city, and to dwell there when it was given over to the enemy, the sanctuary given over to aliens?

[8] Her temple has become like a man without honor;

[9] her glorious vessels have been carried into captivity. Her babes have been killed in her streets, her youths by the sword of the foe.

[10] What nation has not inherited her palaces and has not seized her spoils?

[11] All her adornment has been taken away; no longer free, she has become a slave.

[12] And behold, our holy place, our beauty, and our glory have been laid waste; the Gentiles have profaned it.

[13] Why should we live any longer?"

[14] And Mattathias and his sons rent their clothes, put on sackcloth, and mourned greatly.

[15] Then the king's officers who were enforcing the apostasy came to the city of Modein to make them offer sacrifice.

[16] Many from Israel came to them; and Mattathias and his sons were assembled.

[17] Then the king's officers spoke to Mattathias as follows: "You are a leader, honored and great in this city, and supported by sons and brothers.

[18] Now be the first to come and do what the king commands, as all the Gentiles and the men of Judah and those that are left in Jerusalem have done. Then you and your sons will be numbered among the friends of the king, and you and your sons will be honored with silver and gold and many gifts."

[19] But Mattathias answered and said in a loud voice: "Even if all the nations that live under the rule of the king obey him, and have chosen to do his commandments, departing each one from the religion of his fathers,

[20] yet I and my sons and my brothers will live by the covenant of our fathers.

[21] Far be it from us to desert the law and the ordinances.

[22] We will not obey the king's words by turning aside from our religion to the right hand or to the left."

[23] When he had finished speaking these words, a Jew came forward in the sight of all to offer sacrifice upon the altar in Modein, according to the king's command.

[24] When Mattathias saw it, be burned with zeal and his heart was stirred. He gave vent to righteous anger; he ran and

killed him upon the altar.

[25] At the same time he killed the king's officer who was forcing them to sacrifice, and he tore down the altar.

[26] Thus he burned with zeal for the law, as Phinehas did against Zimri the son of Salu.

[27] Then Mattathias cried out in the city with a loud voice, saying: "Let every one who is zealous for the law and supports the covenant come out with me!"

[28] And he and his sons fled to the hills and left all that they had in the city.

[29] Then many who were seeking righteousness and justice went down to the wilderness to dwell there,

[30] they, their sons, their wives, and their cattle, because evils pressed heavily upon them.

[31] And it was reported to the king's officers, and to the troops in Jerusalem the city of David, that men who had rejected the king's command had gone down to the hiding places in the wilderness.

[32] Many pursued them, and overtook them; they encamped opposite them and prepared for battle against them on the sabbath day.

[33] And they said to them, "Enough of this! Come out and do what the king commands, and you will live."

[34] But they said, "We will not come out, nor will we do what the king commands and so profane the sabbath day."

[35] Then the enemy hastened to attack them.

[36] But they did not answer them or hurl a stone at them or block up their hiding places,

[37] for they said, "Let us all die in our innocence; heaven and earth testify for us that you are killing us unjustly."

[38] So they attacked them on the sabbath, and they died, with their wives and children and cattle, to the number of a thousand persons.

[39] When Mattathias and his friends learned of it, they mourned for them deeply.

[40] And each said to his neighbor: "If we all do as our brethren have done and refuse to fight with the Gentiles for our lives and for our ordinances, they will quickly destroy us from the earth."

[41] So they made this decision that day: "Let us fight against every man who comes to attack us on the sabbath day; let us not all die as our brethren died in their hiding places."

[42] Then there united with them a company of Hasideans, mighty warriors of Israel, every one who offered himself willingly for the law.

[43] And all who became fugitives to escape their troubles joined them and reinforced them.

[44] They organized an army, and struck down sinners in their anger and lawless men in their wrath; the survivors fled to the Gentiles for safety.

[45] And Mattathias and his friends went about and tore down the altars;

[46] they forcibly circumcised all the uncircumcised boys that they found within the borders of Israel.

[47] They hunted down the arrogant men, and the work prospered in their hands.

[48] They rescued the law out of the hands of the Gentiles and kings, and they never let the sinner gain the upper hand.

[49] Now the days drew near for Mattathias to die, and he said to his sons: "Arrogance and reproach have now become strong; it is a time of ruin and furious anger.

[50] Now, my children, show zeal for the law, and give your lives for the covenant of our fathers.

[51] "Remember the deeds of the fathers, which they did in their generations; and receive great honor and an everlasting name.

[52] Was not Abraham found faithful when tested, and it was reckoned to him as righteousness?

[53] Joseph in the time of his distress kept the commandment, and became lord of Egypt.

[54] Phinehas our father, because he was deeply zealous, received the covenant of everlasting priesthood.

[55] Joshua, because he fulfilled the command, became a judge in Israel.

[56] Caleb, because he testified in the assembly, received an inheritance in the land.

[57] David, because he was merciful, inherited the throne of the kingdom for ever.

[58] Elijah because of great zeal for the law was taken up into heaven.

[59] Hannaniah, Azariah, and Mishael believed and were saved from the flame.

[60] Daniel because of his innocence was delivered from the mouth of the lions.

[61] "And so observe, from generation to generation, that none who put their trust in him will lack strength.

[62] Do not fear the words of a sinner, for his splendor will turn into dung and worms.

[63] Today he will be exalted, but tomorrow he will not be found, because he has returned to the dust, and his plans will perish.

[64] My children, be courageous and grow strong in the law, for by it you will gain honor.

[65] "Now behold, I know that Simeon your brother is wise in counsel; always listen to him; he shall be your father.

[66] Judas Maccabeus has been a mighty warrior from his youth; he shall command the army for you and fight the battle against the peoples.

[67] You shall rally about you all who observe the law, and avenge the wrong done to your people.

[68] Pay back the Gentiles in full, and heed what the law commands."

[69] Then he blessed them, and was gathered to his fathers.

[70] He died in the one hundred and forty-sixth year and was buried in the tomb of his fathers at Modein. And all Israel

mourned for him with great lamentation.

1Mac.3

[1] Then Judas his son, who was called Maccabeus, took command in his place.

[2] All his brothers and all who had joined his father helped him; they gladly fought for Israel.

[3] He extended the glory of his people. Like a giant he put on his breastplate; he girded on his armor of war and waged battles, protecting the host by his sword.

[4] He was like a lion in his deeds, like a lion's cub roaring for prey.

[5] He searched out and pursued the lawless; he burned those who troubled his people.

[6] Lawless men shrank back for fear of him; all the evildoers were confounded; and deliverance prospered by his hand.

[7] He embittered many kings, but he made Jacob glad by his deeds, and his memory is blessed for ever.

[8] He went through the cities of Judah; he destroyed the ungodly out of the land; thus he turned away wrath from Israel.

[9] He was renowned to the ends of the earth; he gathered in those who were perishing.

[10] But Apollonius gathered together Gentiles and a large force from Samaria to fight against Israel.

[11] When Judas learned of it, he went out to meet him, and he defeated and killed him. Many were wounded and fell, and the rest fled.

[12] Then they seized their spoils; and Judas took the sword of Apollonius, and used it in battle the rest of his life.

[13] Now when Seron, the commander of the Syrian army, heard that Judas had gathered a large company, including a body of faithful men who stayed with him and went out to battle,

[14] he said, "I will make a name for myself and win honor in the kingdom. I will make war on Judas and his companions, who scorn the king's command."

[15] And again a strong army of ungodly men went up with him to help him, to take vengeance on the sons of Israel.

[16] When he approached the ascent of Beth-horon, Judas went out to meet him with a small company.

[17] But when they saw the army coming to meet them, they said to Judas, "How can we, few as we are, fight against so great and strong a multitude? And we are faint, for we have eaten nothing today."

[18] Judas replied, "It is easy for many to be hemmed in by few, for in the sight of Heaven there is no difference between saving by many or by few.

[19] It is not on the size of the army that victory in battle depends, but strength comes from Heaven.

[20] They come against us in great pride and lawlessness to destroy us and our wives and our children, and to despoil us;

[21] but we fight for our lives and our laws.

[22] He himself will crush them before us; as for you, do not be afraid of them."

[23] When he finished speaking, he rushed suddenly against Seron and his army, and they were crushed before him.

[24] They pursued them down the descent of Beth-horon to the plain; eight hundred of them fell, and the rest fled into the land of the Philistines.

[25] Then Judas and his brothers began to be feared, and terror fell upon the Gentiles round about them.

[26] His fame reached the king, and the Gentiles talked of the battles of Judas.

[27] When king Antiochus heard these reports, he was greatly angered; and he sent and gathered all the forces of his kingdom, a very strong army.

[28] And he opened his coffers and gave a year's pay to his forces, and ordered them to be ready for any need.

[29] Then he saw that the money in the treasury was exhausted, and that the revenues from the country were small because of the dissension and disaster which he had caused in the land by abolishing the laws that had existed from the earliest days.

[30] He feared that he might not have such funds as he had before for his expenses and for the gifts which he used to give more lavishly than preceding kings.

[31] He was greatly perplexed in mind, and determined to go to Persia and collect the revenues from those regions and raise a large fund.

[32] He left Lysias, a distinguished man of royal lineage, in charge of the king's affairs from the river Euphrates to the borders of Egypt.

[33] Lysias was also to take care of Antiochus his son until he returned.

[34] And he turned over to Lysias half of his troops and the elephants, and gave him orders about all that he wanted done. As for the residents of Judea and Jerusalem,

[35] Lysias was to send a force against them to wipe out and destroy the strength of Israel and the remnant of Jerusalem; he was to banish the memory of them from the place,

[36] settle aliens in all their territory, and distribute their land.

[37] Then the king took the remaining half of his troops and departed from Antioch his capital in the one hundred and forty-seventh year. He crossed the Euphrates river and went through the upper provinces.

[38] Lysias chose Ptolemy the son of Dorymenes, and Nicanor and Gorgias, mighty men among the friends of the king,

[39] and sent with them forty thousand infantry and seven thousand cavalry to go into the land of Judah and destroy it, as the king had commanded.

[40] so they departed with their entire force, and when they arrived they encamped near Emmaus in the plain.

[41] When the traders of the region heard what was said to them, they took silver and gold in immense amounts, and fetters,

and went to the camp to get the sons of Israel for slaves. And forces from Syria and the land of the Philistines joined with them.

[42] Now Judas and his brothers saw that misfortunes had increased and that the forces were encamped in their territory. They also learned what the king had commanded to do to the people to cause their final destruction.

[43] But they said to one another, "Let us repair the destruction of our people, and fight for our people and the sanctuary."

[44] And the congregation assembled to be ready for battle, and to pray and ask for mercy and compassion.

[45] Jerusalem was uninhabited like a wilderness; not one of her children went in or out.The sanctuary was trampled own, and the sons of aliens held the citadel; it was a lodging place for the Gentiles. Joy was taken from Jacob; the flute and the harp ceased to play.

[46] So they assembled and went to Mizpah, opposite Jerusalem, because Israel formerly had a place of prayer in Mizpah.

[47] They fasted that day, put on sackcloth and sprinkled ashes on their heads, and rent their clothes.

[48] And they opened the book of the law to inquire into those matters about which the Gentiles were consulting the images of their idols.

[49] They also brought the garments of the priesthood and the first fruits and the tithes, and they stirred up the Nazirites who had completed their days;

[50] and they cried aloud to Heaven, saying, "What shall we do with these? Where shall we take them?

[51] Your sanctuary is trampled down and profaned, and thy priests mourn in humiliation.

[52] And behold, the Gentiles are assembled against us to destroy us; thou knowest what they plot against us.

[53] How will we be able to withstand them, if thou do not help us?"

[54] Then they sounded the trumpets and gave a loud shout.

[55] After this Judas appointed leaders of the people, in charge of thousands and hundreds and fifties and tens.

[56] And he said to those who were building houses, or were betrothed, or were planting vineyards, or were fainthearted, that each should return to his home, according to the law.

[57] Then the army marched out and encamped to the south of Emmaus.

[58] And Judas said, "Gird yourselves and be valiant. Be ready early in the morning to fight with these Gentiles who have assembled against us to destroy us and our sanctuary.

[59] It is better for us to die in battle than to see the misfortunes of our nation and of the sanctuary.

[60] But as his will in heaven may be, so he will do."

1Mac.4

[1] Now Gorgias took five thousand infantry and a thousand picked cavalry, and this division moved out by night

[2] to fall upon the camp of the Jews and attack them suddenly. Men from the citadel were his guides.

[3] But Judas heard of it, and he and his mighty men moved out to attack the king's force in Emmaus

[4] while the division was still absent from the camp.

[5] When Gorgias entered the camp of Judas by night, he found no one there, so he looked for them in the hills, because he said, "These men are fleeing from us."

[6] At daybreak Judas appeared in the plain with three thousand men, but they did not have armor and swords such as they desired.

[7] And they saw the camp of the Gentiles, strong and fortified, with cavalry round about it; and these men were trained in war.

[8] But Judas said to the men who were with him, "Do not fear their numbers or be afraid when they charge.

[9] Remember how our fathers were saved at the Red Sea, when Pharaoh with his forces pursued them.

[10] And now let us cry to Heaven, to see whether he will favor us and remember his covenant with our fathers and crush this army before us today.

[11] Then all the Gentiles will know that there is one who redeems and saves Israel."

[12] When the foreigners looked up and saw them coming against them,

[13] they went forth from their camp to battle. Then the men with Judas blew their trumpets

[14] and engaged in battle. The Gentiles were crushed and fled into the plain,

[15] and all those in the rear fell by the sword. They pursued them to Gazara, and to the plains of Idumea, and to Azotus and Jamnia; and three thousand of them fell.

[16] Then Judas and his force turned back from pursuing them,

[17] and he said to the people, "Do not be greedy for plunder, for there is a battle before us;

[18] Gorgias and his force are near us in the hills. But stand now against our enemies and fight them, and afterward seize the plunder boldly."

[19] Just as Judas was finishing this speech, a detachment appeared, coming out of the hills.

[20] They saw that their army had been put to flight, and that the Jews were burning the camp, for the smoke that was seen showed what had happened.

[21] When they perceived this they were greatly frightened, and when they also saw the army of Judas drawn up in the plain for battle,

[22] they all fled into the land of the Philistines.

[23] Then Judas returned to plunder the camp, and they seized much gold and silver, and cloth dyed blue and sea purple, and great riches.

[24] On their return they sang hymns and praises to Heaven, for he is good, for his mercy endures for ever.

[25] Thus Israel had a great deliverance that day.

[26] Those of the foreigners who escaped went and reported to Lysias all that had happened.

[27] When he heard it, he was perplexed and discouraged, for things had not happened to Israel as he had intended, nor had they turned out as the king had commanded him.

[28] But the next year he mustered sixty thousand picked infantrymen and five thousand cavalry to subdue them.

[29] They came into Idumea and encamped at Beth-zur, and Judas met them with ten thousand men.

[30] When he saw that the army was strong, he prayed, saying, "Blessed art thou, O Savior of Israel, who didst crush the attack of the mighty warrior by the hand of thy servant David, and didst give the camp of the Philistines into the hands of Jonathan, the son of Saul, and of the man who carried his armor.

[31] So do thou hem in this army by the hand of thy people Israel, and let them be ashamed of their troops and their cavalry.

[32] Fill them with cowardice; melt the boldness of their strength; let them tremble in their destruction.

[33] Strike them down with the sword of those who love thee, and let all who know thy name praise thee with hymns."

[34] Then both sides attacked, and there fell of the army of Lysias five thousand men; they fell in action.

[35] And when Lysias saw the rout of his troops and observed the boldness which inspired those of Judas, and how ready they were either to live or to die nobly, he departed to Antioch and enlisted mercenaries, to invade Judea again with an even larger army.

[36] Then said Judas and his brothers, "Behold, our enemies are crushed; let us go up to cleanse the sanctuary and dedicate it."

[37] So all the army assembled and they went up to Mount Zion.

[38] And they saw the sanctuary desolate, the altar profaned, and the gates burned. In the courts they saw bushes sprung up as in a thicket, or as on one of the mountains. They saw also the chambers of the priests in ruins.

[39] Then they rent their clothes, and mourned with great lamentation, and sprinkled themselves with ashes.

[40] They fell face down on the ground, and sounded the signal on the trumpets, and cried out to Heaven.

[41] Then Judas detailed men to fight against those in the citadel until he had cleansed the sanctuary.

[42] He chose blameless priests devoted to the law,

[43] and they cleansed the sanctuary and removed the defiled stones to an unclean place.

[44] They deliberated what to do about the altar of burnt offering, which had been profaned.

[45] And they thought it best to tear it down, lest it bring reproach upon them, for the Gentiles had defiled it. So they tore down the altar,

[46] and stored the stones in a convenient place on the temple hill until there should come a prophet to tell what to do with them.

[47] Then they took unhewn stones, as the law directs, and built a new altar like the former one.

[48] They also rebuilt the sanctuary and the interior of the temple, and consecrated the courts.

[49] They made new holy vessels, and brought the lampstand, the altar of incense, and the table into the temple.

[50] Then they burned incense on the altar and lighted the lamps on the lampstand, and these gave light in the temple.

[51] They placed the bread on the table and hung up the curtains. Thus they finished all the work they had undertaken.

[52] Early in the morning on the twenty-fifth day of the ninth month, which is the month of Chislev, in the one hundred and forty-eighth year,

[53] they rose and offered sacrifice, as the law directs, on the new altar of burnt offering which they had built.

[54] At the very season and on the very day that the Gentiles had profaned it, it was dedicated with songs and harps and lutes and cymbals.

[55] All the people fell on their faces and worshiped and blessed Heaven, who had prospered them.

[56] So they celebrated the dedication of the altar for eight days, and offered burnt offerings with gladness; they offered a sacrifice of deliverance and praise.

[57] They decorated the front of the temple with golden crowns and small shields; they restored the gates and the chambers for the priests, and furnished them with doors.

[58] There was very great gladness among the people, and the reproach of the Gentiles was removed.

[59] Then Judas and his brothers and all the assembly of Israel determined that every year at that season the days of dedication of the altar should be observed with gladness and joy for eight days, beginning with the twenty-fifth day of the month of Chislev.

[60] At that time they fortified Mount Zion with high walls and strong towers round about, to keep the Gentiles from coming and trampling them down as they had done before.

[61] And he stationed a garrison there to hold it. He also fortified Beth-zur, so that the people might have a stronghold that faced Idumea.

1Mac.5

[1] When the Gentiles round about heard that the altar had been built and the sanctuary dedicated as it was before, they

became very angry,

[2] and they determined to destroy the descendants of Jacob who lived among them. So they began to kill and destroy among the people.

[3] But Judas made war on the sons of Esau in Idumea, at Akrabattene, because they kept lying in wait for Israel. He dealt them a heavy blow and humbled them and despoiled them.

[4] He also remembered the wickedness of the sons of Baean, who were a trap and a snare to the people and ambushed them on the highways.

[5] They were shut up by him in their towers; and he encamped against them, vowed their complete destruction, and burned with fire their towers and all who were in them.

[6] Then he crossed over to attack the Ammonites, where he found a strong band and many people with Timothy as their leader.

[7] He engaged in many battles with them and they were crushed before him; he struck them down.

[8] He also took Jazer and its villages; then he returned to Judea.

[9] Now the Gentiles in Gilead gathered together against the Israelites who lived in their territory, and planned to destroy them. But they fled to the stronghold of Dathema,

[10] and sent to Judas and his brothers a letter which said, "The Gentiles around us have gathered together against us to destroy us.

[11] They are preparing to come and capture the stronghold to which we have fled, and Timothy is leading their forces.

[12] Now then come and rescue us from their hands, for many of us have fallen,

[13] and all our brethren who were in the land of Tob have been killed; the enemy have captured their wives and children and goods, and have destroyed about a thousand men there."

[14] While the letter was still being read, behold, other messengers, with their garments rent, came from Galilee and made a similar report;

[15] they said that against them had gathered together men of Ptolemais and Tyre and Sidon, and all Galilee of the Gentiles, "to annihilate us."

[16] When Judas and the people heard these messages, a great assembly was called to determine what they should do for their brethren who were in distress and were being attacked by enemies.

[17] Then Judas said to Simon his brother, "Choose your men and go and rescue your brethren in Galilee; I and Jonathan my brother will go to Gilead."

[18] But he left Joseph, the son of Zechariah, and Azariah, a leader of the people, with the rest of the forces, in Judea to guard it;

[19] and he gave them this command, "Take charge of this people, but do not engage in battle with the Gentiles until we return."

[20] Then three thousand men were assigned to Simon to go to Galilee, and eight thousand to Judas for Gilead.

[21] so Simon went to Galilee and fought many battles against the Gentiles, and the Gentiles were crushed before him.

[22] He pursued them to the gate of Ptolemais, and as many as three thousand of the Gentiles fell, and he despoiled them.

[23] Then he took the Jews of Galilee and Arbatta, with their wives and children, and all they possessed, and led them to Judea with great rejoicing.

[24] Judas Maccabeus and Jonathan his brother crossed the Jordan and went three days' journey into the wilderness.

[25] They encountered the Nabateans, who met them peaceably and told them all that had happened to their brethren in Gilead:

[26] "Many of them have been shut up in Bozrah and Bosor, in Alema and Chaspho, Maked and Carnaim" -- all these cities were strong and large--

[27] "and some have been shut up in the other cities of Gilead; the enemy are getting ready to attack the strongholds tomorrow and take and destroy all these men in one day."

[28] Then Judas and his army quickly turned back by the wilderness road to Bozrah; and he took the city, and killed every male by the edge of the sword; then he seized all its spoils and burned it with fire.

[29] He departed from there at night, and they went all the way to the stronghold of Dathema.

[30] At dawn they looked up, and behold, a large company, that could not be counted, carrying ladders and engines of war to capture the stronghold, and attacking the Jews within.

[31] So Judas saw that the battle had begun and that the cry of the city went up to Heaven with trumpets and loud shouts,

[32] and he said to the men of his forces, "Fight today for your brethren!"

[33] Then he came up behind them in three companies, who sounded their trumpets and cried aloud in prayer.

[34] And when the army of Timothy realized that it was Maccabeus, they fled before him, and he dealt them a heavy blow. As many as eight thousand of them fell that day.

[35] Next he turned aside to Alema, and fought against it and took it; and he killed every male in it, plundered it, and burned it with fire.

[36] From there he marched on and took Chaspho, Maked, and Bosor, and the other cities of Gilead.

[37] After these things Timothy gathered another army and encamped opposite Raphon, on the other side of the stream.

[38] Judas sent men to spy out the camp, and they reported to him, "All the Gentiles around us have gathered to him; it is a very large force.

[39] They also have hired Arabs to help them, and they are encamped across the stream, ready to come and fight against you." And Judas went to meet them.

[40] Now as Judas and his army drew near to the stream of water, Timothy said to the officers of his forces, "If he crosses over to us first, we will not be able to resist him, for he will surely defeat us.

[41] But if he shows fear and camps on the other side of the river, we will cross over to him and defeat him."

[42] When Judas approached the stream of water, he stationed the scribes of the people at the stream and gave them this command, "Permit no man to encamp, but make them all enter the battle."

[43] Then he crossed over against them first, and the whole army followed him. All the Gentiles were defeated before him, and they threw away their arms and fled into the sacred precincts at Carnaim.

[44] But he took the city and burned the sacred precincts with fire, together with all who were in them. Thus Carnaim was conquered; they could stand before Judas no longer.

[45] Then Judas gathered together all the Israelites in Gilead, the small and the great, with their wives and children and goods, a very large company, to go to the land of Judah.

[46] So they came to Ephron. This was a large and very strong city on the road, and they could not go round it to the right or to the left; they had to go through it.

[47] But the men of the city shut them out and blocked up the gates with stones.

[48] And Judas sent them this friendly message, "Let us pass through your land to get to our land. No one will do you harm; we will simply pass by on foot." But they refused to open to him.

[49] Then Judas ordered proclamation to be made to the army that each should encamp where he was.

[50] So the men of the forces encamped, and he fought against the city all that day and all the night, and the city was delivered into his hands.

[51] He destroyed every male by the edge of the sword, and razed and plundered the city. Then he passed through the city over the slain.

[52] And they crossed the Jordan into the large plain before Beth-shan.

[53] And Judas kept rallying the laggards and encouraging the people all the way till he came to the land of Judah.

[54] So they went up to Mount Zion with gladness and joy, and offered burnt offerings, because not one of them had fallen before they returned in safety.

[55] Now while Judas and Jonathan were in Gilead and Simon his brother was in Galilee before Ptolemais,

[56] Joseph, the son of Zechariah, and Azariah, the commanders of the forces, heard of their brave deeds and of the heroic war they had fought.

[57] So they said, "Let us also make a name for ourselves; let us go and make war on the Gentiles around us."

[58] And they issued orders to the men of the forces that were with them, and they marched against Jamnia.

[59] And Gorgias and his men came out of the city to meet them in battle.

[60] Then Joseph and Azariah were routed, and were pursued to the borders of Judea; as many as two thousand of the people of Israel fell that day.

[61] Thus the people suffered a great rout because, thinking to do a brave deed, they did not listen to Judas and his brothers.

[62] But they did not belong to the family of those men through whom deliverance was given to Israel.

[63] The man Judas and his brothers were greatly honored in all Israel and among all the Gentiles, wherever their name was heard.

[64] Men gathered to them and praised them.

[65] Then Judas and his brothers went forth and fought the sons of Esau in the land to the south. He struck Hebron and its villages and tore down its strongholds and burned its towers round about.

[66] Then he marched off to go into the land of the Philistines, and passed through Marisa.

[67] On that day some priests, who wished to do a brave deed, fell in battle, for they went out to battle unwisely.

[68] But Judas turned aside to Azotus in the land of the Philistines; he tore down their altars, and the graven images of their gods he burned with fire; he plundered the cities and returned to the land of Judah.

1Mac.6
[1] King Antiochus was going through the upper provinces when he heard that Elymais in Persia was a city famed for its wealth in silver and gold.

[2] Its temple was very rich, containing golden shields, breastplates, and weapons left there by Alexander, the son of Philip, the Macedonian king who first reigned over the Greeks.

[3] So he came and tried to take the city and plunder it, but he could not, because his plan became known to the men of the city

[4] and they withstood him in battle. So he fled and in great grief departed from there to return to Babylon.

[5] Then some one came to him in Persia and reported that the armies which had gone into the land of Judah had been routed;

[6] that Lysias had gone first with a strong force, but had turned and fled before the Jews; that the Jews had grown strong from the arms, supplies, and abundant spoils which they had taken from the armies they had cut down;

[7] that they had torn down the abomination which he had erected upon the altar in Jerusalem; and that they had surrounded the sanctuary with high walls as before, and also Beth-zur, his city.

[8] When the king heard this news, he was astounded and badly shaken. He took to his bed and became sick from grief, because things had not turned out for him as he had planned.

[9] He lay there for many days, because deep grief continually gripped him, and he concluded that he was dying.

[10] So he called all his friends and said to them, "Sleep departs from my eyes and I am downhearted with worry.

[11] I said to myself, `To what distress I have come! And into what a great flood I now am plunged! For I was kind and beloved in my power.'

[12] But now I remember the evils I did in Jerusalem. I seized all her vessels of silver and gold; and I sent to destroy the inhabitants of Judah without good reason.

[13] I know that it is because of this that these evils have come upon me; and behold, I am perishing of deep grief in a strange land."

[14] Then he called for Philip, one of his friends, and made him ruler over all his kingdom.

[15] He gave him the crown and his robe and the signet, that he might guide Antiochus his son and bring him up to be king.

[16] Thus Antiochus the king died there in the one hundred and forty-ninth year.

[17] And when Lysias learned that the king was dead, he set up Antiochus the king's son to reign. Lysias had brought him up as a boy, and he named him Eupator.

[18] Now the men in the citadel kept hemming Israel in around the sanctuary. They were trying in every way to harm them and strengthen the Gentiles.

[19] So Judas decided to destroy them, and assembled all the people to besiege them.

[20] They gathered together and besieged the citadel in the one hundred and fiftieth year; and he built siege towers and other engines of war.

[21] But some of the garrison escaped from the siege and some of the ungodly Israelites joined them.

[22] They went to the king and said, "How long will you fail to do justice and to avenge our brethren?

[23] We were happy to serve your father, to live by what he said and to follow his commands.

[24] For this reason the sons of our people besieged the citadel and became hostile to us; moreover, they have put to death as many of us as they have caught, and they have seized our inheritances.

[25] And not against us alone have they stretched out their hands, but also against all the lands on their borders.

[26] And behold, today they have encamped against the citadel in Jerusalem to take it; they have fortified both the sanctuary and Beth-zur;

[27] and unless you quickly prevent them, they will do still greater things, and you will not be able to stop them."

[28] The king was enraged when he heard this. He assembled all his friends, the commanders of his forces and those in authority.

[29] And mercenary forces came to him from other kingdoms and from islands of the seas.

[30] The number of his forces was a hundred thousand foot soldiers, twenty thousand horsemen, and thirty-two elephants accustomed to war.

[31] They came through Idumea and encamped against Beth-zur, and for many days they fought and built engines of war; but the Jews sallied out and burned these with fire, and fought manfully.

[32] Then Judas marched away from the citadel and encamped at Beth-zechariah, opposite the camp of the king.

[33] Early in the morning the king rose and took his army by a forced march along the road to Beth-zechariah, and his troops made ready for battle and sounded their trumpets.

[34] They showed the elephants the juice of grapes and mulberries, to arouse them for battle.

[35] And they distributed the beasts among the phalanxes; with each elephant they stationed a thousand men armed with coats of mail, and with brass helmets on their heads; and five hundred picked horsemen were assigned to each beast.

[36] These took their position beforehand wherever the beast was; wherever it went they went with it, and they never left it.

[37] And upon the elephants were wooden towers, strong and covered; they were fastened upon each beast by special harness, and upon each were four armed men who fought from there, and also its Indian driver.

[38] The rest of the horsemen were stationed on either side, on the two flanks of the army, to harass the enemy while being themselves protected by the phalanxes.

[39] When the sun shone upon the shields of gold and brass, the hills were ablaze with them and gleamed like flaming torches.

[40] Now a part of the king's army was spread out on the high hills, and some troops were on the plain, and they advanced steadily and in good order.

[41] All who heard the noise made by their multitude, by the marching of the multitude and the clanking of their arms, trembled, for the army was very large and strong.

[42] But Judas and his army advanced to the battle, and six hundred men of the king's army fell.

[43] And Eleazar, called Avaran, saw that one of the beasts was equipped with royal armor. It was taller than all the others,

and he supposed that the king was upon it.

[44] So he gave his life to save his people and to win for himself an everlasting name.

[45] He courageously ran into the midst of the phalanx to reach it; he killed men right and left, and they parted before him on both sides.

[46] He got under the elephant, stabbed it from beneath, and killed it; but it fell to the ground upon him and he died.

[47] And when the Jews saw the royal might and the fierce attack of the forces, they turned away in flight.

[48] The soldiers of the king's army went up to Jerusalem against them, and the king encamped in Judea and at Mount Zion.

[49] He made peace with the men of Beth-zur, and they evacuated the city, because they had no provisions there to withstand a siege, since it was a sabbatical year for the land.

[50] So the king took Beth-zur and stationed a guard there to hold it.

[51] Then he encamped before the sanctuary for many days. He set up siege towers, engines of war to throw fire and stones, machines to shoot arrows, and catapults.

[52] The Jews also made engines of war to match theirs, and fought for many days.

[53] But they had no food in storage, because it was the seventh year; those who found safety in Judea from the Gentiles had consumed the last of the stores.

[54] Few men were left in the sanctuary, because famine had prevailed over the rest and they had been scattered, each to his own place.

[55] Then Lysias heard that Philip, whom King Antiochus while still living had appointed to bring up Antiochus his son to be king,

[56] had returned from Persia and Media with the forces that had gone with the king, and that he was trying to seize control of the government.

[57] So he quickly gave orders to depart, and said to the king, to the commanders of the forces, and to the men, "We daily grow weaker, our food supply is scant, the place against which we are fighting is strong, and the affairs of the kingdom press urgently upon us.

[58] Now then let us come to terms with these men, and make peace with them and with all their nation,

[59] and agree to let them live by their laws as they did before; for it was on account of their laws which we abolished that they became angry and did all these things."

[60] The speech pleased the king and the commanders, and he sent to the Jews an offer of peace, and they accepted it.

[61] So the king and the commanders gave them their oath. On these conditions the Jews evacuated the stronghold.

[62] But when the king entered Mount Zion and saw what a strong fortress the place was, he broke the oath he had sworn and gave orders to tear down the wall all around.

[63] Then he departed with haste and returned to Antioch. He found Philip in control of the city, but he fought against him, and took the city by force.

1Mac.7

[1] In the one hundred and fifty-first year Demetrius the son of Seleucus set forth from Rome, sailed with a few men to a city by the sea, and there began to reign.

[2] As he was entering the royal palace of his fathers, the army seized Antiochus and Lysias to bring them to him.

[3] But when this act became known to him, he said, "Do not let me see their faces!"

[4] So the army killed them, and Demetrius took his seat upon the throne of his kingdom.

[5] Then there came to him all the lawless and ungodly men of Israel; they were led by Alcimus, who wanted to be high priest.

[6] And they brought to the king this accusation against the people: "Judas and his brothers have destroyed all your friends, and have driven us out of our land.

[7] Now then send a man whom you trust; let him go and see all the ruin which Judas has brought upon us and upon the land of the king, and let him punish them and all who help them."

[8] So the king chose Bacchides, one of the king's friends, governor of the province Beyond the River; he was a great man in the kingdom and was faithful to the king.

[9] And he sent him, and with him the ungodly Alcimus, whom he made high priest; and he commanded him to take vengeance on the sons of Israel.

[10] So they marched away and came with a large force into the land of Judah; and he sent messengers to Judas and his brothers with peaceable but treacherous words.

[11] But they paid no attention to their words, for they saw that they had come with a large force.

[12] Then a group of scribes appeared in a body before Alcimus and Bacchides to ask for just terms.

[13] The Hasideans were first among the sons of Israel to seek peace from them,

[14] for they said, "A priest of the line of Aaron has come with the army, and he will not harm us."

[15] And he spoke peaceable words to them and swore this oath to them, "We will not seek to injure you or your friends."

[16] So they trusted him; but he seized sixty of them and killed them in one day, in accordance with the word which was written,

[17] "The flesh of thy saints and their blood they poured out round about Jerusalem, and there was none to bury them."

[18] Then the fear and dread of them fell upon all the people, for they said, "There is no truth or justice in them, for they have violated the agreement and the oath which they swore."

[19] Then Bacchides departed from Jerusalem and encamped in Beth-zaith. And he sent and seized many of the men who had deserted to him, and some of the people, and killed them and threw them into a great pit.

[20] He placed Alcimus in charge of the country and left with him a force to help him; then Bacchides went back to the king.

[21] Alcimus strove for the high priesthood,

[22] and all who were troubling their people joined him. They gained control of the land of Judah and did great damage in Israel.

[23] And Judas saw all the evil that Alcimus and those with him had done among the sons of Israel; it was more than the Gentiles had done.

[24] So Judas went out into all the surrounding parts of Judea, and took vengeance on the men who had deserted, and he prevented those in the city from going out into the country.

[25] When Alcimus saw that Judas and those with him had grown strong, and realized that he could not withstand them, he returned to the king and brought wicked charges against them.

[26] Then the king sent Nicanor, one of his honored princes, who hated and detested Israel, and he commanded him to destroy the people.

[27] So Nicanor came to Jerusalem with a large force, and treacherously sent to Judas and his brothers this peaceable message,

[28] "Let there be no fighting between me and you; I shall come with a few men to see you face to face in peace."

[29] So he came to Judas, and they greeted one another peaceably. But the enemy were ready to seize Judas.

[30] It became known to Judas that Nicanor had come to him with treacherous intent, and he was afraid of him and would not meet him again.

[31] When Nicanor learned that his plan had been disclosed, he went out to meet Judas in battle near Caphar-salama.

[32] About five hundred men of the army of Nicanor fell, and the rest fled into the city of David.

[33] After these events Nicanor went up to Mount Zion. Some of the priests came out of the sanctuary, and some of the elders of the people, to greet him peaceably and to show him the burnt offering that was being offered for the king.

[34] But he mocked them and derided them and defiled them and spoke arrogantly,

[35] and in anger he swore this oath, "Unless Judas and his army are delivered into my hands this time, then if I return safely I will burn up this house." And he went out in great anger.

[36] Then the priests went in and stood before the altar and the temple, and they wept and said,

[37] "Thou didst choose this house to be called by thy name, and to be for thy people a house of prayer and supplication.

[38] Take vengeance on this man and on his army, and let them fall by the sword; remember their blasphemies, and let them live no longer."

[39] Now Nicanor went out from Jerusalem and encamped in Beth-horon, and the Syrian army joined him.

[40] And Judas encamped in Adasa with three thousand men. Then Judas prayed and said,

[41] "When the messengers from the king spoke blasphemy, thy angel went forth and struck down one hundred and eighty-five thousand of the Assyrians.

[42] So also crush this army before us today; let the rest learn that Nicanor has spoken wickedly against the sanctuary, and judge him according to this wickedness."

[43] So the armies met in battle on the thirteenth day of the month of Adar. The army of Nicanor was crushed, and he himself was the first to fall in the battle.

[44] When his army saw that Nicanor had fallen, they threw down their arms and fled.

[45] The Jews pursued them a day's journey, from Adasa as far as Gazara, and as they followed kept sounding the battle call on the trumpets.

[46] And men came out of all the villages of Judea round about, and they out-flanked the enemy and drove them back to their pursuers, so that they all fell by the sword; not even one of them was left.

[47] Then the Jews seized the spoils and the plunder, and they cut off Nicanor's head and the right hand which he so arrogantly stretched out, and brought them and displayed them just outside Jerusalem.

[48] The people rejoiced greatly and celebrated that day as a day of great gladness.

[49] And they decreed that this day should be celebrated each year on the thirteenth day of Adar.

[50] So the land of Judah had rest for a few days.

1Mac.8

[1] Now Judas heard of the fame of the Romans, that they were very strong and were well-disposed toward all who made an alliance with them, that they pledged friendship to those who came to them,

[2] and that they were very strong. Men told him of their wars and of the brave deeds which they were doing among the Gauls, how they had defeated them and forced them to pay tribute,

[3] and what they had done in the land of Spain to get control of the silver and gold mines there,

[4] and how they had gained control of the whole region by their planning and patience, even though the place was far distant from them. They also subdued the kings who came against them from the ends of the earth, until they crushed them

and inflicted great disaster upon them; the rest paid them tribute every year.

[5] Philip, and Perseus king of the Macedonians, and the others who rose up against them, they crushed in battle and conquered.

[6] They also defeated Antiochus the Great, king of Asia, who went to fight against them with a hundred and twenty elephants and with cavalry and chariots and a very large army. He was crushed by them;

[7] they took him alive and decreed that he and those who should reign after him should pay a heavy tribute and give hostages and surrender some of their best provinces,

[8] the country of India and Media and Lydia. These they took from him and gave to Eumenes the king.

[9] The Greeks planned to come and destroy them,

[10] but this became known to them, and they sent a general against the Greeks and attacked them. Many of them were wounded and fell, and the Romans took captive their wives and children; they plundered them, conquered the land, tore down their strongholds, and enslaved them to this day.

[11] The remaining kingdoms and islands, as many as ever opposed them, they destroyed and enslaved;

[12] but with their friends and those who rely on them they have kept friendship. They have subdued kings far and near, and as many as have heard of their fame have feared them.

[13] Those whom they wish to help and to make kings, they make kings, and those whom they wish they depose; and they have been greatly exalted.

[14] Yet for all this not one of them has put on a crown or worn purple as a mark of pride,

[15] but they have built for themselves a senate chamber, and every day three hundred and twenty senators constantly deliberate concerning the people, to govern them well.

[16] They trust one man each year to rule over them and to control all their land; they all heed the one man, and there is no envy or jealousy among them.

[17] So Judas chose Eupolemus the son of John, son of Accos, and Jason the son of Eleazar, and sent them to Rome to establish friendship and alliance,

[18] and to free themselves from the yoke; for they saw that the kingdom of the Greeks was completely enslaving Israel.

[19] They went to Rome, a very long journey; and they entered the senate chamber and spoke as follows:

[20] "Judas, who is also called Maccabeus, and his brothers and the people of the Jews have sent us to you to establish alliance and peace with you, that we may be enrolled as your allies and friends."

[21] The proposal pleased them,

[22] and this is a copy of the letter which they wrote in reply, on bronze tablets, and sent to Jerusalem to remain with them there as a memorial of peace and alliance:

[23] "May all go well with the Romans and with the nation of the Jews at sea and on land for ever, and may sword and enemy be far from them.

[24] If war comes first to Rome or to any of their allies in all their dominion,

[25] the nation of the Jews shall act as their allies wholeheartedly, as the occasion may indicate to them.

[26] And to the enemy who makes war they shall not give or supply grain, arms, money, or ships, as Rome has decided; and they shall keep their obligations without receiving any return.

[27] In the same way, if war comes first to the nation of the Jews, the Romans shall willingly act as their allies, as the occasion may indicate to them.

[28] And to the enemy allies shall be given no grain, arms, money, or ships, as Rome has decided; and they shall keep these obligations and do so without deceit.

[29] Thus on these terms the Romans make a treaty with the Jewish people.

[30] If after these terms are in effect both parties shall determine to add or delete anything, they shall do so at their discretion, and any addition or deletion that they may make shall be valid.

[31] "And concerning the wrongs which King Demetrius is doing to them we have written to him as follows, `Why have you made your yoke heavy upon our friends and allies the Jews?

[32] If now they appeal again for help against you, we will defend their rights and fight you on sea and on land.'"

1Mac.9

[1] When Demetrius heard that Nicanor and his army had fallen in battle, he sent Bacchides and Alcimus into the land of Judah a second time, and with them the right wing of the army.

[2] They went by the road which leads to Gilgal and encamped against Mesaloth in Arbela, and they took it and killed many people.

[3] In the first month of the one hundred and fifty-second year they encamped against Jerusalem;

[4] then they marched off and went to Berea with twenty thousand foot soldiers and two thousand cavalry.

[5] Now Judas was encamped in Elasa, and with him were three thousand picked men.

[6] When they saw the huge number of the enemy forces, they were greatly frightened, and many slipped away from the camp, until no more than eight hundred of them were left.

[7] When Judas saw that his army had slipped away and the battle was imminent, he was crushed in spirit, for he had no time to assemble them.

[8] He became faint, but he said to those who were left, "Let us rise and go up against our enemies. We may be able to fight them."

[9] But they tried to dissuade him, saying, "We are not able. Let us rather save our own lives now, and let us come back with our brethren and fight them; we are too few."

[10] But Judas said, "Far be it from us to do such a thing as to flee from them. If our time has come, let us die bravely for our brethren, and leave no cause to question our honor."

[11] Then the army of Bacchides marched out from the camp and took its stand for the encounter. The cavalry was divided into two companies, and the slingers and the archers went ahead of the army, as did all the chief warriors.

[12] Bacchides was on the right wing. Flanked by the two companies, the phalanx advanced to the sound of the trumpets; and the men with Judas also blew their trumpets.

[13] The earth was shaken by the noise of the armies, and the battle raged from morning till evening.

[14] Judas saw that Bacchides and the strength of his army were on the right; then all the stouthearted men went with him,

[15] and they crushed the right wing, and he pursued them as far as Mount Azotus.

[16] When those on the left wing saw that the right wing was crushed, they turned and followed close behind Judas and his men.

[17] The battle became desperate, and many on both sides were wounded and fell.

[18] Judas also fell, and the rest fled.

[19] Then Jonathan and Simon took Judas their brother and buried him in the tomb of their fathers at Modein,

[20] and wept for him. And all Israel made great lamentation for him; they mourned many days and said,

[21] "How is the mighty fallen, the savior of Israel!"

[22] Now the rest of the acts of Judas, and his wars and the brave deeds that he did, and his greatness, have not been recorded, for they were very many.

[23] After the death of Judas, the lawless emerged in all parts of Israel; all the doers of injustice appeared.

[24] In those days a very great famine occurred, and the country deserted with them to the enemy.

[25] And Bacchides chose the ungodly and put them in charge of the country.

[26] They sought and searched for the friends of Judas, and brought them to Bacchides, and he took vengeance on them and made sport of them.

[27] Thus there was great distress in Israel, such as had not been since the time that prophets ceased to appear among them.

[28] Then all the friends of Judas assembled and said to Jonathan,

[29] "Since the death of your brother Judas there has been no one like him to go against our enemies and Bacchides, and to deal with those of our nation who hate us.

[30] So now we have chosen you today to take his place as our ruler and leader, to fight our battle."

[31] And Jonathan at that time accepted the leadership and took the place of Judas his brother.

[32] When Bacchides learned of this, he tried to kill him.

[33] But Jonathan and Simon his brother and all who were with him heard of it, and they fled into the wilderness of Tekoa and camped by the water of the pool of Asphar.

[34] Bacchides found this out on the sabbath day, and he with all his army crossed the Jordan.

[35] And Jonathan sent his brother as leader of the multitude and begged the Nabateans, who were his friends, for permission to store with them the great amount of baggage which they had.

[36] But the sons of Jambri from Medeba came out and seized John and all that he had, and departed with it.

[37] After these things it was reported to Jonathan and Simon his brother, "The sons of Jambri are celebrating a great wedding, and are conducting the bride, a daughter of one of the great nobles of Canaan, from Nadabath with a large escort."

[38] And they remembered the blood of John their brother, and went up and hid under cover of the mountain.

[39] They raised their eyes and looked, and saw a tumultuous procession with much baggage; and the bridegroom came out with his friends and his brothers to meet them with tambourines and musicians and many weapons.

[40] Then they rushed upon them from the ambush and began killing them. Many were wounded and fell, and the rest fled to the mountain; and they took all their goods.

[41] Thus the wedding was turned into mourning and the voice of their musicians into a funeral dirge.

[42] And when they had fully avenged the blood of their brother, they returned to the marshes of the Jordan.

[43] When Bacchides heard of this, he came with a large force on the sabbath day to the banks of the Jordan.

[44] And Jonathan said to those with him, "Let us rise up now and fight for our lives, for today things are not as they were before.

[45] For look! the battle is in front of us and behind us; the water of the Jordan is on this side and on that, with marsh and thicket; there is no place to turn.

[46] Cry out now to Heaven that you may be delivered from the hands of our enemies."

[47] So the battle began, and Jonathan stretched out his hand to strike Bacchides, but he eluded him and went to the rear.

[48] Then Jonathan and the men with him leaped into the Jordan and swam across to the other side, and the enemy did not cross the Jordan to attack them.

[49] And about one thousand of Bacchides' men fell that day.

[50] Bacchides then returned to Jerusalem and built strong cities in Judea: the fortress in Jericho, and Emmaus, and Beth-horon, and Bethel, and Timnath, and Pharathon, and Tephon, with high walls and gates and bars.

[51] And he placed garrisons in them to harass Israel.

[52] He also fortified the city of Beth-zur, and Gazara, and the citadel, and in them he put troops and stores of food.

[53] And he took the sons of the leading men of the land as hostages and put them under guard in the citadel at Jerusalem.

[54] In the one hundred and fifty-third year, in the second month, Alcimus gave orders to tear down the wall of the inner court of the sanctuary. He tore down the work of the prophets!

[55] But he only began to tear it down, for at that time Alcimus was stricken and his work was hindered; his mouth was stopped and he was paralyzed, so that he could no longer say a word or give commands concerning his house.

[56] And Alcimus died at that time in great agony.

[57] When Bacchides saw that Alcimus was dead, he returned to the king, and the land of Judah had rest for two years.

[58] Then all the lawless plotted and said, "See! Jonathan and his men are living in quiet and confidence. So now let us bring Bacchides back, and he will capture them all in one night."

[59] And they went and consulted with him.

[60] He started to come with a large force, and secretly sent letters to all his allies in Judea, telling them to seize Jonathan and his men; but they were unable to do it, because their plan became known.

[61] And Jonathan's men seized about fifty of the men of the country who were leaders in this treachery, and killed them.

[62] Then Jonathan with his men, and Simon, withdrew to Bethbasi in the wilderness; he rebuilt the parts of it that had been demolished, and they fortified it.

[63] When Bacchides learned of this, he assembled all his forces, and sent orders to the men of Judea.

[64] Then he came and encamped against Bethbasi; he fought against it for many days and made machines of war.

[65] But Jonathan left Simon his brother in the city, while he went out into the country; and he went with only a few men.

[66] He struck down Odomera and his brothers and the sons of Phasiron in their tents.

[67] Then he began to attack and went into battle with his forces; and Simon and his men sallied out from the city and set fire to the machines of war.

[68] They fought with Bacchides, and he was crushed by them. They distressed him greatly, for his plan and his expedition had been in vain.

[69] So he was greatly enraged at the lawless men who had counseled him to come into the country, and he killed many of them. Then he decided to depart to his own land.

[70] When Jonathan learned of this, he sent ambassadors to him to make peace with him and obtain release of the captives.

[71] He agreed, and did as he said; and he swore to Jonathan that he would not try to harm him as long as he lived.

[72] He restored to him the captives whom he had formerly taken from the land of Judah; then he turned and departed to his own land, and came no more into their territory.

[73] Thus the sword ceased from Israel. And Jonathan dwelt in Michmash. And Jonathan began to judge the people, and he destroyed the ungodly out of Israel.

1Mac.10

[1] In the one hundred and sixtieth year Alexander Epiphanes, the son of Antiochus, landed and occupied Ptolemais. They welcomed him, and there he began to reign.

[2] When Demetrius the king heard of it, he assembled a very large army and marched out to meet him in battle.

[3] And Demetrius sent Jonathan a letter in peaceable words to honor him;

[4] for he said, "Let us act first to make peace with him before he makes peace with Alexander against us,

[5] for he will remember all the wrongs which we did to him and to his brothers and his nation."

[6] So Demetrius gave him authority to recruit troops, to equip them with arms, and to become his ally; and he commanded that the hostages in the citadel should be released to him.

[7] Then Jonathan came to Jerusalem and read the letter in the hearing of all the people and of the men in the citadel.

[8] They were greatly alarmed when they heard that the king had given him authority to recruit troops.

[9] But the men in the citadel released the hostages to Jonathan, and he returned them to their parents.

[10] And Jonathan dwelt in Jerusalem and began to rebuild and restore the city.

[11] He directed those who were doing the work to build the walls and encircle Mount Zion with squared stones, for better fortification; and they did so.

[12] Then the foreigners who were in the strongholds that Bacchides had built fled;

[13] each left his place and departed to his own land.

[14] Only in Beth-zur did some remain who had forsaken the law and the commandments, for it served as a place of refuge.

[15] Now Alexander the king heard of all the promises which Demetrius had sent to Jonathan, and men told him of the battles that Jonathan and his brothers had fought, of the brave deeds that they had done, and of the troubles that they had endured.

[16] So he said, "Shall we find another such man? Come now, we will make him our friend and ally."

[17] And he wrote a letter and sent it to him, in the following words:

[18] "King Alexander to his brother Jonathan, greeting.

[19] We have heard about you, that you are a mighty warrior and worthy to be our friend.

[20] And so we have appointed you today to be the high priest of your nation; you are to be called the king's friend" (and he sent him a purple robe and a golden crown) "and you are to take our side and keep friendship with us."

[21] So Jonathan put on the holy garments in the seventh month of the one hundred and sixtieth year, at the feast of tabernacles, and he recruited troops and equipped them with arms in abundance.

[22] When Demetrius heard of these things he was grieved and said,

[23] "What is this that we have done? Alexander has gotten ahead of us in forming a friendship with the Jews to strengthen himself.

[24] I also will write them words of encouragement and promise them honor and gifts, that I may have their help."

[25] So he sent a message to them in the following words: "King Demetrius to the nation of the Jews, greeting.

[26] Since you have kept your agreement with us and have continued your friendship with us, and have not sided with our enemies, we have heard of it and rejoiced.

[27] And now continue still to keep faith with us, and we will repay you with good for what you do for us.

[28] We will grant you many immunities and give you gifts.

[29] "And now I free you and exempt all the Jews from payment of tribute and salt tax and crown levies,

[30] and instead of collecting the third of the grain and the half of the fruit of the trees that I should receive, I release them from this day and henceforth. I will not collect them from the land of Judah or from the three districts added to it from Samaria and Galilee, from this day and for all time.

[31] And let Jerusalem and her environs, her tithes and her revenues, be holy and free from tax.

[32] I release also my control of the citadel in Jerusalem and give it to the high priest, that he may station in it men of his own choice to guard it.

[33] And every one of the Jews taken as a captive from the land of Judah into any part of my kingdom, I set free without payment; and let all officials cancel also the taxes on their cattle.

[34] "And all the feasts and sabbaths and new moons and appointed days, and the three days before a feast and the three after a feast -- let them all be days of immunity and release for all the Jews who are in my kingdom.

[35] No one shall have authority to exact anything from them or annoy any of them about any matter.

[36] "Let Jews be enrolled in the king's forces to the number of thirty thousand men, and let the maintenance be given them that is due to all the forces of the king.

[37] Let some of them be stationed in the great strongholds of the king, and let some of them be put in positions of trust in the kingdom. Let their officers and leaders be of their own number, and let them live by their own laws, just as the king has commanded in the land of Judah.

[38] "As for the three districts that have been added to Judea from the country of Samaria, let them be so annexed to Judea that they are considered to be under one ruler and obey no other authority but the high priest.

[39] Ptolemais and the land adjoining it I have given as a gift to the sanctuary in Jerusalem, to meet the necessary expenses of the sanctuary.

[40] I also grant fifteen thousand shekels of silver yearly out of the king's revenues from appropriate places.

[41] And all the additional funds which the government officials have not paid as they did in the first years, they shall give from now on for the service of the temple.

[42] Moreover, the five thousand shekels of silver which my officials have received every year from the income of the services of the temple, this too is canceled, because it belongs to the priests who minister there.

[43] And whoever takes refuge at the temple in Jerusalem, or in any of its precincts, because he owes money to the king or has any debt, let him be released and receive back all his property in my kingdom.

[44] "Let the cost of rebuilding and restoring the structures of the sanctuary be paid from the revenues of the king.

[45] And let the cost of rebuilding the walls of Jerusalem and fortifying it round about, and the cost of rebuilding the walls in Judea, also be paid from the revenues of the king."

[46] When Jonathan and the people heard these words, they did not believe or accept them, because they remembered the great wrongs which Demetrius had done in Israel and how he had greatly oppressed them.

[47] They favored Alexander, because he had been the first to speak peaceable words to them, and they remained his allies all his days.

[48] Now Alexander the king assembled large forces and encamped opposite Demetrius.

[49] The two kings met in battle, and the army of Demetrius fled, and Alexander pursued him and defeated them.

[50] He pressed the battle strongly until the sun set, and Demetrius fell on that day.

[51] Then Alexander sent ambassadors to Ptolemy king of Egypt with the following message:

[52] "Since I have returned to my kingdom and have taken my seat on the throne of my fathers, and established my rule -- for I crushed Demetrius and gained control of our country;

[53] I met him in battle, and he and his army were crushed by us, and we have taken our seat on the throne of his kingdom --

[54] now therefore let us establish friendship with one another; give me now your daughter as my wife, and I will become your son-in-law, and will make gifts to you and to her in keeping with your position."

[55] Ptolemy the king replied and said, "Happy was the day on which you returned to the land of your fathers and took your

seat on the throne of their kingdom.

[56] And now I will do for you as you wrote, but meet me at Ptolemais, so that we may see one another, and I will become your father-in-law, as you have said."

[57] So Ptolemy set out from Egypt, he and Cleopatra his daughter, and came to Ptolemais in the one hundred and sixty-second year.

[58] Alexander the king met him, and Ptolemy gave him Cleopatra his daughter in marriage, and celebrated her wedding at Ptolemais with great pomp, as kings do.

[59] Then Alexander the king wrote to Jonathan to come to meet him.

[60] So he went with pomp to Ptolemais and met the two kings; he gave them and their friends silver and gold and many gifts, and found favor with them.

[61] A group of pestilent men from Israel, lawless men, gathered together against him to accuse him; but the king paid no attention to them.

[62] The king gave orders to take off Jonathan's garments and to clothe him in purple, and they did so.

[63] The king also seated him at his side; and he said to his officers, "Go forth with him into the middle of the city and proclaim that no one is to bring charges against him about any matter, and let no one annoy him for any reason."

[64] And when his accusers saw the honor that was paid him, in accordance with the proclamation, and saw him clothed in purple, they all fled.

[65] Thus the king honored him and enrolled him among his chief friends, and made him general and governor of the province.

[66] And Jonathan returned to Jerusalem in peace and gladness.

[67] In the one hundred and sixty-fifth year Demetrius the son of Demetrius came from Crete to the land of his fathers.

[68] When Alexander the king heard of it, he was greatly grieved and returned to Antioch.

[69] And Demetrius appointed Apollonius the governor of Coelesyria, and he assembled a large force and encamped against Jamnia. Then he sent the following message to Jonathan the high priest:

[70] "You are the only one to rise up against us, and I have become a laughingstock and reproach because of you. Why do you assume authority against us in the hill country?

[71] If you now have confidence in your forces, come down to the plain to meet us, and let us match strength with each other there, for I have with me the power of the cities.

[72] Ask and learn who I am and who the others are that are helping us. Men will tell you that you cannot stand before us, for your fathers were twice put to flight in their own land.

[73] And now you will not be able to withstand my cavalry and such an army in the plain, where there is no stone or pebble, or place to flee."

[74] When Jonathan heard the words of Apollonius, his spirit was aroused. He chose ten thousand men and set out from Jerusalem, and Simon his brother met him to help him.

[75] He encamped before Joppa, but the men of the city closed its gates, for Apollonius had a garrison in Joppa.

[76] So they fought against it, and the men of the city became afraid and opened the gates, and Jonathan gained possession of Joppa.

[77] When Apollonius heard of it, he mustered three thousand cavalry and a large army, and went to Azotus as though he were going farther. At the same time he advanced into the plain, for he had a large troop of cavalry and put confidence in it.

[78] Jonathan pursued him to Azotus, and the armies engaged in battle.

[79] Now Apollonius had secretly left a thousand cavalry behind them.

[80] Jonathan learned that there was an ambush behind him, for they surrounded his army and shot arrows at his men from early morning till late afternoon.

[81] But his men stood fast, as Jonathan commanded, and the enemy's horses grew tired.

[82] Then Simon brought forward his force and engaged the phalanx in battle (for the cavalry was exhausted); they were overwhelmed by him and fled,

[83] and the cavalry was dispersed in the plain. They fled to Azotus and entered Beth-dagon, the temple of their idol, for safety.

[84] But Jonathan burned Azotus and the surrounding towns and plundered them; and the temple of Dagon, and those who had taken refuge in it he burned with fire.

[85] The number of those who fell by the sword, with those burned alive, came to eight thousand men.

[86] Then Jonathan departed from there and encamped against Askalon, and the men of the city came out to meet him with great pomp.

[87] And Jonathan and those with him returned to Jerusalem with much booty.

[88] When Alexander the king heard of these things, he honored Jonathan still more;

[89] and he sent to him a golden buckle, such as it is the custom to give to the kinsmen of kings. He also gave him Ekron and all its environs as his possession.

1Mac.11

[1] Then the king of Egypt gathered great forces, like the sand by the seashore, and many ships; and he tried to get possession

of Alexander's kingdom by trickery and add it to his own kingdom.

[2] He set out for Syria with peaceable words, and the people of the cities opened their gates to him and went to meet him, for Alexander the king had commanded them to meet him, since he was Alexander's father-in-law.

[3] But when Ptolemy entered the cities he stationed forces as a garrison in each city.

[4] When he approached Azotus, they showed him the temple of Dagon burned down, and Azotus and its suburbs destroyed, and the corpses lying about, and the charred bodies of those whom Jonathan had burned in the war, for they had piled them in heaps along his route.

[5] They also told the king what Jonathan had done, to throw blame on him; but the king kept silent.

[6] Jonathan met the king at Joppa with pomp, and they greeted one another and spent the night there.

[7] And Jonathan went with the king as far as the river called Eleutherus; then he returned to Jerusalem.

[8] So King Ptolemy gained control of the coastal cities as far as Seleucia by the sea, and he kept devising evil designs against Alexander.

[9] He sent envoys to Demetrius the king, saying, "Come, let us make a covenant with each other, and I will give you in marriage my daughter who was Alexander's wife, and you shall reign over your father's kingdom.

[10] For I now regret that I gave him my daughter, for he has tried to kill me."

[11] He threw blame on Alexander because he coveted his kingdom.

[12] So he took his daughter away from him and gave her to Demetrius. He was estranged from Alexander, and their enmity became manifest.

[13] Then Ptolemy entered Antioch and put on the crown of Asia. Thus he put two crowns upon his head, the crown of Egypt and that of Asia.

[14] Now Alexander the king was in Cilicia at that time, because the people of that region were in revolt.

[15] And Alexander heard of it and came against him in battle. Ptolemy marched out and met him with a strong force, and put him to flight.

[16] So Alexander fled into Arabia to find protection there, and King Ptolemy was exalted.

[17] And Zabdiel the Arab cut off the head of Alexander and sent it to Ptolemy.

[18] But King Ptolemy died three days later, and his troops in the strongholds were killed by the inhabitants of the strongholds.

[19] So Demetrius became king in the one hundred and sixty-seventh year.

[20] In those days Jonathan assembled the men of Judea to attack the citadel in Jerusalem, and he built many engines of war to use against it.

[21] But certain lawless men who hated their nation went to the king and reported to him that Jonathan was besieging the citadel.

[22] When he heard this he was angry, and as soon as he heard it he set out and came to Ptolemais; and he wrote Jonathan not to continue the siege, but to meet him for a conference at Ptolemais as quickly as possible.

[23] When Jonathan heard this, he gave orders to continue the siege; and he chose some of the elders of Israel and some of the priests, and put himself in danger,

[24] for he went to the king at Ptolemais, taking silver and gold and clothing and numerous other gifts. And he won his favor.

[25] Although certain lawless men of his nation kept making complaints against him,

[26] the king treated him as his predecessors had treated him; he exalted him in the presence of all his friends.

[27] He confirmed him in the high priesthood and in as many other honors as he had formerly had, and made him to be regarded as one of his chief friends.

[28] Then Jonathan asked the king to free Judea and the three districts of Samaria from tribute, and promised him three hundred talents.

[29] The king consented, and wrote a letter to Jonathan about all these things; its contents were as follows:

[30] "King Demetrius to Jonathan his brother and to the nation of the Jews, greeting.

[31] This copy of the letter which we wrote concerning you to Lasthenes our kinsman we have written to you also, so that you may know what it says.

[32] `King Demetrius to Lasthenes his father, greeting.

[33] To the nation of the Jews, who are our friends and fulfil their obligations to us, we have determined to do good, because of the good will they show toward us.

[34] We have confirmed as their possession both the territory of Judea and the three districts of Aphairema and Lydda and Rathamin; the latter, with all the region bordering them, were added to Judea from Samaria. To all those who offer sacrifice in Jerusalem, we have granted release from the royal taxes which the king formerly received from them each year, from the crops of the land and the fruit of the trees.

[35] And the other payments henceforth due to us of the tithes, and the taxes due to us, and the salt pits and the crown taxes due to us -- from all these we shall grant them release.

[36] And not one of these grants shall be canceled from this time forth for ever.

[37] Now therefore take care to make a copy of this, and let it be given to Jonathan and put up in a conspicuous place on the holy mountain.'"

[38] Now when Demetrius the king saw that the land was quiet before him and that there was no opposition to him, he dismissed all his troops, each man to his own place, except the foreign troops which he had recruited from the islands of the nations. So all the troops who had served his fathers hated him.

[39] Now Trypho had formerly been one of Alexander's supporters. He saw that all the troops were murmuring against Demetrius. So he went to Imalkue the Arab, who was bringing up Antiochus, the young son of Alexander,

[40] and insistently urged him to hand Antiochus over to him, to become king in place of his father. He also reported to Imalkue what Demetrius had done and told of the hatred which the troops of Demetrius had for him; and he stayed there many days.

[41] Now Jonathan sent to Demetrius the king the request that he remove the troops of the citadel from Jerusalem, and the troops in the strongholds; for they kept fighting against Israel.

[42] And Demetrius sent this message to Jonathan, "Not only will I do these things for you and your nation, but I will confer great honor on you and your nation, if I find an opportunity.

[43] Now then you will do well to send me men who will help me, for all my troops have revolted."

[44] So Jonathan sent three thousand stalwart men to him at Antioch, and when they came to the king, the king rejoiced at their arrival.

[45] Then the men of the city assembled within the city, to the number of a hundred and twenty thousand, and they wanted to kill the king.

[46] But the king fled into the palace. Then the men of the city seized the main streets of the city and began to fight.

[47] So the king called the Jews to his aid, and they all rallied about him and then spread out through the city; and they killed on that day as many as a hundred thousand men.

[48] They set fire to the city and seized much spoil on that day, and they saved the king.

[49] When the men of the city saw that the Jews had gained control of the city as they pleased, their courage failed and they cried out to the king with this entreaty,

[50] "Grant us peace, and make the Jews stop fighting against us and our city."

[51] And they threw down their arms and made peace. So the Jews gained glory in the eyes of the king and of all the people in his kingdom, and they returned to Jerusalem with much spoil.

[52] So Demetrius the king sat on the throne of his kingdom, and the land was quiet before him.

[53] But he broke his word about all that he had promised; and he became estranged from Jonathan and did not repay the favors which Jonathan had done him, but oppressed him greatly.

[54] After this Trypho returned, and with him the young boy Antiochus who began to reign and put on the crown.

[55] All the troops that Demetrius had cast off gathered around him, and they fought against Demetrius, and he fled and was routed.

[56] And Trypho captured the elephants and gained control of Antioch.

[57] Then the young Antiochus wrote to Jonathan, saying, "I confirm you in the high priesthood and set you over the four districts and make you one of the friends of the king."

[58] And he sent him gold plate and a table service, and granted him the right to drink from gold cups and dress in purple and wear a gold buckle.

[59] Simon his brother he made governor from the Ladder of Tyre to the borders of Egypt.

[60] Then Jonathan set forth and traveled beyond the river and among the cities, and all the army of Syria gathered to him as allies. When he came to Askalon, the people of the city met him and paid him honor.

[61] From there he departed to Gaza, but the men of Gaza shut him out. So he beseiged it and burned its suburbs with fire and plundered them.

[62] Then the people of Gaza pleaded with Jonathan, and he made peace with them, and took the sons of their rulers as hostages and sent them to Jerusalem. And he passed through the country as far as Damascus.

[63] Then Jonathan heard that the officers of Demetrius had come to Kadesh in Galilee with a large army, intending to remove him from office.

[64] He went to meet them, but left his brother Simon in the country.

[65] Simon encamped before Beth-zur and fought against it for many days and hemmed it in.

[66] Then they asked him to grant them terms of peace, and he did so. He removed them from there, took possession of the city, and set a garrison over it.

[67] Jonathan and his army encamped by the waters of Gennesaret. Early in the morning they marched to the plain of Hazor,

[68] and behold, the army of the foreigners met him in the plain; they had set an ambush against him in the mountains, but they themselves met him face to face.

[69] Then the men in ambush emerged from their places and joined battle.

[70] All the men with Jonathan fled; not one of them was left except Mattathias the son of Absalom and Judas the son of Chalphi, commanders of the forces of the army.

[71] Jonathan rent his garments and put dust on his head, and prayed.

[72] Then he turned back to the battle against the enemy and routed them, and they fled.

[73] When his men who were fleeing saw this, they returned to him and joined him in the pursuit as far as Kadesh, to their

camp, and there they encamped.

[74] As many as three thousand of the foreigners fell that day. And Jonathan returned to Jerusalem.

1Mac.12

[1] Now when Jonathan saw that the time was favorable for him, he chose men and sent them to Rome to confirm and renew the friendship with them.

[2] He also sent letters to the same effect to the Spartans and to other places.

[3] So they went to Rome and entered the senate chamber and said, "Jonathan the high priest and the Jewish nation have sent us to renew the former friendship and alliance with them."

[4] And the Romans gave them letters to the people in every place, asking them to provide for the envoys safe conduct to the land of Judah.

[5] This is a copy of the letter which Jonathan wrote to the Spartans:

[6] "Jonathan the high priest, the senate of the nation, the priests, and the rest of the Jewish people to their brethren the Spartans, greeting.

[7] Already in time past a letter was sent to Onias the high priest from Arius, who was king among you, stating that you are our brethren, as the appended copy shows.

[8] Onias welcomed the envoy with honor, and received the letter, which contained a clear declaration of alliance and friendship.

[9] Therefore, though we have no need of these things, since we have as encouragement the holy books which are in our hands,

[10] we have undertaken to send to renew our brotherhood and friendship with you, so that we may not become estranged from you, for considerable time has passed since you sent your letter to us.

[11] We therefore remember you constantly on every occasion, both in our feasts and on other appropriate days, at the sacrifices which we offer and in our prayers, as it is right and proper to remember brethren.

[12] And we rejoice in your glory.

[13] But as for ourselves, many afflictions and many wars have encircled us; the kings round about us have waged war against us.

[14] We were unwilling to annoy you and our other allies and friends with these wars,

[15] for we have the help which comes from Heaven for our aid; and we were delivered from our enemies and our enemies were humbled.

[16] We therefore have chosen Numenius the son of Antiochus and Antipater the son of Jason, and have sent them to Rome to renew our former friendship and alli ance with them.

[17] We have commanded them to go also to you and greet you and deliver to you this letter from us concerning the renewal of our brotherhood.

[18] And now please send us a reply to this."

[19] This is a copy of the letter which they sent to Onias:

[20] "Arius, king of the Spartans, to Onias the high priest, greeting.

[21] It has been found in writing concerning the Spartans and the Jews that they are brethren and are of the family of Abraham.

[22] And now that we have learned this, please write us concerning your welfare;

[23] we on our part write to you that your cattle and your property belong to us, and ours belong to you. We therefore command that our envoys report to you accordingly."

[24] Now Jonathan heard that the commanders of Demetrius had returned, with a larger force than before, to wage war against him.

[25] So he marched away from Jerusalem and met them in the region of Hamath, for he gave them no opportunity to invade his own country.

[26] He sent spies to their camp, and they returned and reported to him that the enemy were being drawn up in formation to fall upon the Jews by night.

[27] So when the sun set, Jonathan commanded his men to be alert and to keep their arms at hand so as to be ready all night for battle, and he stationed outposts around the camp.

[28] When the enemy heard that Jonathan and his men were prepared for battle, they were afraid and were terrified at heart; so they kindled fires in their camp and withdrew.

[29] But Jonathan and his men did not know it until morning, for they saw the fires burning.

[30] Then Jonathan pursued them, but he did not overtake them, for they had crossed the Eleutherus river.

[31] So Jonathan turned aside against the Arabs who are called Zabadeans, and he crushed them and plundered them.

[32] Then he broke camp and went to Damascus, and marched through all that region.

[33] Simon also went forth and marched through the country as far as Askalon and the neighboring strongholds. He turned aside to Joppa and took it by surprise,

[34] for he had heard that they were ready to hand over the stronghold to the men whom Demetrius had sent. And he stationed a garrison there to guard it.

[35] When Jonathan returned he convened the elders of the people and planned with them to build strongholds in Judea,

[36] to build the walls of Jerusalem still higher, and to erect a high barrier between the citadel and the city to separate it from the city, in order to isolate it so that its garrison could neither buy nor sell.

[37] So they gathered together to build up the city; part of the wall on the valley to the east had fallen, and he repaired the section called Chaphenatha.

[38] And Simon built Adida in the Shephelah; he fortified it and installed gates with bolts.

[39] Then Trypho attempted to become king in Asia and put on the crown, and to raise his hand against Antiochus the king.

[40] He feared that Jonathan might not permit him to do so, but might make war on him, so he kept seeking to seize and kill him, and he marched forth and came to Beth-shan.

[41] Jonathan went out to meet him with forty thousand picked fighting men, and he came to Beth-shan.

[42] When Trypho saw that he had come with a large army, he was afraid to raise his hand against him.

[43] So he received him with honor and commended him to all his friends, and he gave him gifts and commanded his friends and his troops to obey him as they would himself.

[44] Then he said to Jonathan, "Why have you wearied all these people when we are not at war?

[45] Dismiss them now to their homes and choose for yourself a few men to stay with you, and come with me to Ptolemais. I will hand it over to you as well as the other strongholds and the remaining troops and all the officials, and will turn round and go home. For that is why I am here."

[46] Jonathan trusted him and did as he said; he sent away the troops, and they returned to the land of Judah.

[47] He kept with himself three thousand men, two thousand of whom he left in Galilee, while a thousand accompanied him.

[48] But when Jonathan entered Ptolemais, the men of Ptolemais closed the gates and seized him, and all who had entered with him they killed with the sword.

[49] Then Trypho sent troops and cavalry into Galilee and the Great Plain to destroy all Jonathan's soldiers.

[50] But they realized that Jonathan had been seized and had perished along with his men, and they encouraged one another and kept marching in close formation, ready for battle.

[51] When their pursuers saw that they would fight for their lives, they turned back.

[52] So they all reached the land of Judah safely, and they mourned for Jonathan and his companions and were in great fear; and all Israel mourned deeply.

[53] And all the nations round about them tried to destroy them, for they said, "They have no leader or helper. Now therefore let us make war on them and blot out the memory of them from among men."

1Mac.13

[1] Simon heard that Trypho had assembled a large army to invade the land of Judah and destroy it,

[2] and he saw that the people were trembling and fearful. So he went up to Jerusalem, and gathering the people together

[3] he encouraged them, saying to them, "You yourselves know what great things I and my brothers and the house of my father have done for the laws and the sanctuary; you know also the wars and the difficulties which we have seen.

[4] By reason of this all my brothers have perished for the sake of Israel, and I alone am left.

[5] And now, far be it from me to spare my life in any time of distress, for I am not better than my brothers.

[6] But I will avenge my nation and the sanctuary and your wives and children, for all the nations have gathered together out of hatred to destroy us."

[7] The spirit of the people was rekindled when they heard these words,

[8] and they answered in a loud voice, "You are our leader in place of Judas and Jonathan your brother.

[9] Fight our battles, and all that you say to us we will do."

[10] So he assembled all the warriors and hastened to complete the walls of Jerusalem, and he fortified it on every side.

[11] He sent Jonathan the son of Absalom to Joppa, and with him a considerable army; he drove out its occupants and remained there.

[12] Then Trypho departed from Ptolemais with a large army to invade the land of Judah, and Jonathan was with him under guard.

[13] And Simon encamped in Adida, facing the plain.

[14] Trypho learned that Simon had risen up in place of Jonathan his brother, and that he was about to join battle with him, so he sent envoys to him and said,

[15] "It is for the money that Jonathan your brother owed the royal treasury, in connection with the offices he held, that we are detaining him.

[16] Send now a hundred talents of silver and two of his sons as hostages, so that when released he will not revolt against us, and we will release him."

[17] Simon knew that they were speaking deceitfully to him, but he sent to get the money and the sons, lest he arouse great hostility among the people, who might say,

[18] "Because Simon did not send him the money and the sons, he perished."

[19] So he sent the sons and the hundred talents, but Trypho broke his word and did not release Jonathan.

[20] After this Trypho came to invade the country and destroy it, and he circled around by the way to Adora. But Simon and his army kept marching along opposite him to every place he went.

[21] Now the men in the citadel kept sending envoys to Trypho urging him to come to them by way of the wilderness and to send them food.

[22] So Trypho got all his cavalry ready to go, but that night a very heavy snow fell, and he did not go because of the snow. He marched off and went into the land of Gilead.

[23] When he approached Baskama, he killed Jonathan, and he was buried there.

[24] Then Trypho turned back and departed to his own land.

[25] And Simon sent and took the bones of Jonathan his brother, and buried him in Modein, the city of his fathers.

[26] All Israel bewailed him with great lamentation, and mourned for him many days.

[27] And Simon built a monument over the tomb of his father and his brothers; he made it high that it might be seen, with polished stone at the front and back.

[28] He also erected seven pyramids, opposite one another, for his father and mother and four brothers.

[29] And for the pyramids he devised an elaborate setting, erecting about them great columns, and upon the columns he put suits of armor for a permanent memorial, and beside the suits of armor carved ships, so that they could be seen by all who sail the sea.

[30] This is the tomb which he built in Modein; it remains to this day.

[31] Trypho dealt treacherously with the young king Antiochus; he killed him

[32] and became king in his place, putting on the crown of Asia; and he brought great calamity upon the land.

[33] But Simon built up the strongholds of Judea and walled them all around, with high towers and great walls and gates and bolts, and he stored food in the strongholds.

[34] Simon also chose men and sent them to Demetrius the king with a request to grant relief to the country, for all that Trypho did was to plunder.

[35] Demetrius the king sent him a favorable reply to this request, and wrote him a letter as follows,

[36] "King Demetrius to Simon, the high priest and friend of kings, and to the elders and nation of the Jews, greeting.

[37] We have received the gold crown and the palm branch which you sent, and we are ready to make a general peace with you and to write to our officials to grant you release from tribute.

[38] All the grants that we have made to you remain valid, and let the strongholds that you have built be your possession.

[39] We pardon any errors and offenses committed to this day, and cancel the crown tax which you owe; and whatever other tax has been collected in Jerusalem shall be collected no longer.

[40] And if any of you are qualified to be enrolled in our bodyguard, let them be enrolled, and let there be peace between us."

[41] In the one hundred and seventieth year the yoke of the Gentiles was removed from Israel,

[42] and the people began to write in their documents and contracts, "In the first year of Simon the great high priest and commander and leader of the Jews."

[43] In those days Simon encamped against Gazara and surrounded it with troops. He made a siege engine, brought it up to the city, and battered and captured one tower.

[44] The men in the siege engine leaped out into the city, and a great tumult arose in the city.

[45] The men in the city, with their wives and children, went up on the wall with their clothes rent, and they cried out with a loud voice, asking Simon to make peace with them;

[46] they said, "Do not treat us according to our wicked acts but according to your mercy."

[47] So Simon reached an agreement with them and stopped fighting against them. But he expelled them from the city and cleansed the houses in which the idols were, and then entered it with hymns and praise.

[48] He cast out of it all uncleanness, and settled in it men who observed the law. He also strengthened its fortifications and built in it a house for himself.

[49] The men in the citadel at Jerusalem were prevented from going out to the country and back to buy and sell. So they were very hungry, and many of them perished from famine.

[50] Then they cried to Simon to make peace with them, and he did so. But he expelled them from there and cleansed the citadel from its pollutions.

[51] On the twenty-third day of the second month, in the one hundred and seventy-first year, the Jews entered it with praise and palm branches, and with harps and cymbals and stringed instruments, and with hymns and songs, because a great enemy had been crushed and removed from Israel.

[52] And Simon decreed that every year they should celebrate this day with rejoicing. He strengthened the fortifications of the temple hill alongside the citadel, and he and his men dwelt there.

[53] And Simon saw that John his son had reached manhood, so he made him commander of all the forces, and he dwelt in Gazara.

1Mac.14

[1] In the one hundred and seventy-second year Demetrius the king assembled his forces and marched into Media to secure help, so that he could make war against Trypho.

[2] When Arsaces the king of Persia and Media heard that Demetrius had invaded his territory, he sent one of his commanders to take him alive.

[3] And he went and defeated the army of Demetrius, and seized him and took him to Arsaces, who put him under guard.

[4] The land had rest all the days of Simon. He sought the good of his nation; his rule was pleasing to them, as was the honor shown him, all his days.

[5] To crown all his honors he took Joppa for a harbor, and opened a way to the isles of the sea.

[6] He extended the borders of his nation, and gained full control of the country.

[7] He gathered a host of captives; he ruled over Gazara and Beth-zur and the citadel, and he removed its uncleanness from it; and there was none to oppose him.

[8] They tilled their land in peace; the ground gave its increase, and the trees of the plains their fruit.

[9] Old men sat in the streets; they all talked together of good things; and the youths donned the glories and garments of war.

[10] He supplied the cities with food, and furnished them with the means of defense, till his renown spread to the ends of the earth.

[11] He established peace in the land, and Israel rejoiced with great joy.

[12] Each man sat under his vine and his fig tree, and there was none to make them afraid.

[13] No one was left in the land to fight them, and the kings were crushed in those days.

[14] He strengthened all the humble of his people; he sought out the law, and did away with every lawless and wicked man.

[15] He made the sanctuary glorious, and added to the vessels of the sanctuary.

[16] It was heard in Rome, and as far away as Sparta, that Jonathan had died, and they were deeply grieved.

[17] When they heard that Simon his brother had become high priest in his place, and that he was ruling over the country and the cities in it,

[18] they wrote to him on bronze tablets to renew with him the friendship and alliance which they had established with Judas and Jonathan his brothers.

[19] And these were read before the assembly in Jerusalem.

[20] This is a copy of the letter which the Spartans sent: "The rulers and the city of the Spartans to Simon the high priest and to the elders and the priests and the rest of the Jewish people, our brethren, greeting.

[21] The envoys who were sent to our people have told us about your glory and honor, and we rejoiced at their coming.

[22] And what they said we have recorded in our public decrees, as follows, `Numenius the son of Antiochus and Antipater the son of Jason, envoys of the Jews, have come to us to renew their friendship with us.

[23] It has pleased our people to receive these men with honor and to put a copy of their words in the public archives, so that the people of the Spartans may have a record of them. And they have sent a copy of this to Simon the high priest.'"

[24] After this Simon sent Numenius to Rome with a large gold shield weighing a thousand minas, to confirm the alliance with the Romans.

[25] When the people heard these things they said, "How shall we thank Simon and his sons?

[26] For he and his brothers and the house of his father have stood firm; they have fought and repulsed Israel's enemies and established its freedom."

[27] So they made a record on bronze tablets and put it upon pillars on Mount Zion. This is a copy of what they wrote: "On the eighteenth day of Elul, in the one hundred and seventy-second year, which is the third year of Simon the great high priest,

[28] in Asaramel, in the great assembly of the priests and the people and the rulers of the nation and the elders of the country, the following was proclaimed to us:

[29] "Since wars often occurred in the country, Simon the son of Mattathias, a priest of the sons of Joarib, and his brothers, exposed themselves to danger and resisted the enemies of their nation, in order that their sanctuary and the law might be perserved; and they brought great glory to their nation.

[30] Jonathan rallied the nation, and became their high priest, and was gathered to his people.

[31] And when their enemies decided to invade their country and lay hands on their sanctuary,

[32] then Simon rose up and fought for his nation. He spent great sums of his own money; he armed the men of his nation's forces and paid them wages.

[33] He fortified the cities of Judea, and Beth-zur on the borders of Judea, where formerly the arms of the enemy had been stored, and he placed there a garrison of Jews.

[34] He also fortified Joppa, which is by the sea, and Gazara, which is on the borders of Azotus, where the enemy formerly dwelt. He settled Jews there, and provided in those cities whatever was necessary for their restoration.

[35] "The people saw Simon's faithfulness and the glory which he had resolved to win for his nation, and they made him their leader and high priest, because he had done all these things and because of the justice and loyalty which he had maintained toward his nation. He sought in every way to exalt his people.

[36] And in his days things prospered in his hands, so that the Gentiles were put out of the country, as were also the men in the city of David in Jerusalem, who had built themselves a citadel from which they used to sally forth and defile the environs of the sanctuary and do great damage to its purity.

[37] He settled Jews in it, and fortified it for the safety of the country and of the city, and built the walls of Jerusalem higher.

[38] "In view of these things King Demetrius confirmed him in the high priesthood,

[39] and he made him one of the king's friends and paid him high honors.

[40] For he had heard that the Jews were addressed by the Romans as friends and allies and brethren, and that the Romans

had received the envoys of Simon with honor.

[41] "And the Jews and their priests decided that Simon should be their leader and high priest for ever, until a trustworthy prophet should arise,

[42] and that he should be governor over them and that he should take charge of the sanctuary and appoint men over its tasks and over the country and the weapons and the strongholds, and that he should take charge of the sanctuary,

[43] and that he should be obeyed by all, and that all contracts in the country should be written in his name, and that he should be clothed in purple and wear gold.

[44] "And none of the people or priests shall be permitted to nullify any of these decisions or to oppose what he says, or to convene an assembly in the country without his permission, or to be clothed in purple or put on a gold buckle.

[45] Whoever acts contrary to these decisions or nullifies any of them shall be liable to punishment."

[46] And all the people agreed to grant Simon the right to act in accord with these decisions.

[47] So Simon accepted and agreed to be high priest, to be commander and ethnarch of the Jews and priests, and to be protector of them all.

[48] And they gave orders to inscribe this decree upon bronze tablets, to put them up in a conspicuous place in the precincts of the sanctuary,

[49] and to deposit copies of them in the treasury, so that Simon and his sons might have them.

1Mac.15

[1] Antiochus, the son of Demetrius the king, sent a letter from the islands of the sea to Simon, the priest and ethnarch of the Jews, and to all the nation;

[2] its contents were as follows: "King Antiochus to Simon the high priest and ethnarch and to the nation of the Jews, greeting.

[3] Whereas certain pestilent men have gained control of the kingdom of our fathers, and I intend to lay claim to the kingdom so that I may restore it as it formerly was, and have recruited a host of mercenary troops and have equipped warships,

[4] and intend to make a landing in the country so that I may proceed against those who have destroyed our country and those who have devastated many cities in my kingdom,

[5] now therefore I confirm to you all the tax remissions that the kings before me have granted you, and release from all the other payments from which they have released you.

[6] I permit you to mint your own coinage as money for your country,

[7] and I grant freedom to Jerusalem and the sanctuary. All the weapons which you have prepared and the strongholds which you have built and now hold shall remain yours.

[8] Every debt you owe to the royal treasury and any such future debts shall be canceled for you from henceforth and for all time.

[9] When we gain control of our kingdom, we will bestow great honor upon you and your nation and the temple, so that your glory will become manifest in all the earth."

[10] In the one hundred and seventy-fourth year Antiochus set out and invaded the land of his fathers. All the troops rallied to him, so that there were few with Trypho.

[11] Antiochus pursued him, and he came in his flight to Dor, which is by the sea;

[12] for he knew that troubles had converged upon him, and his troops had deserted him.

[13] So Antiochus encamped against Dor, and with him were a hundred and twenty thousand warriors and eight thousand cavalry.

[14] He surrounded the city, and the ships joined battle from the sea; he pressed the city hard from land and sea, and permitted no one to leave or enter it.

[15] Then Numenius and his companions arrived from Rome, with letters to the kings and countries, in which the following was written:

[16] "Lucius, consul of the Romans, to King Ptolemy, greeting.

[17] The envoys of the Jews have come to us as our friends and allies to renew our ancient friendship and alliance. They had been sent by Simon the high priest and by the people of the Jews,

[18] and have brought a gold shield weighing a thousand minas.

[19] We therefore have decided to write to the kings and countries that they should not seek their harm or make war against them and their cities and their country, or make alliance with those who war against them.

[20] And it has seemed good to us to accept the shield from them.

[21] Therefore if any pestilent men have fled to you from their country, hand them over to Simon the high priest, that he may punish them according to their law."

[22] The consul wrote the same thing to Demetrius the king and to Attalus and Ariarathes and Arsaces,

[23] and to all the countries, and to Sampsames, and to the Spartans, and to Delos, and to Myndos, and to Sicyon, and to Caria, and to Samos, and to Pamphylia, and to Lycia, and to Halicarnassus, and to Rhodes, and to Phaselis, and to Cos, and to Side, and to Aradus and Gortyna and Cnidus and Cyprus and Cyrene.

[24] They also sent a copy of these things to Simon the high priest.

[25] Antiochus the king besieged Dor anew, continually throwing his forces against it and making engines of war; and he

shut Trypho up and kept him from going out or in.

[26] And Simon sent to Antiochus two thousand picked men, to fight for him, and silver and gold and much military equipment.

[27] But he refused to receive them, and he broke all the agreements he formerly had made with Simon, and became estranged from him.

[28] He sent to him Athenobius, one of his friends, to confer with him, saying, "You hold control of Joppa and Gazara and the citadel in Jerusalem; they are cities of my kingdom.

[29] You have devastated their territory, you have done great damage in the land, and you have taken possession of many places in my kingdom.

[30] Now then, hand over the cities which you have seized and the tribute money of the places which you have conquered outside the borders of Judea;

[31] or else give me for them five hundred talents of silver, and for the destruction that you have caused and the tribute money of the cities, five hundred talents more. Otherwise we will come and conquer you."

[32] So Athenobius the friend of the king came to Jerusalem, and when he saw the splendor of Simon, and the sideboard with its gold and silver plate, and his great magnificence, he was amazed. He reported to him the words of the king,

[33] but Simon gave him this reply: "We have neither taken foreign land nor seized foreign property, but only the inheritance of our fathers, which at one time had been unjustly taken by our enemies.

[34] Now that we have the opportunity, we are firmly holding the inheritance of our fathers.

[35] As for Joppa and Gazara, which you demand, they were causing great damage among the people and to our land; for them we will give you a hundred talents." Athenobius did not answer him a word,

[36] but returned in wrath to the king and reported to him these words and the splendor of Simon and all that he had seen. And the king was greatly angered.

[37] Now Trypho embarked on a ship and escaped to Orthosia.

[38] Then the king made Cendebeus commander-in-chief of the coastal country, and gave him troops of infantry and cavalry.

[39] He commanded him to encamp against Judea, and commanded him to build up Kedron and fortify its gates, and to make war on the people; but the king pursued Trypho.

[40] So Cendebeus came to Jamnia and began to provoke the people and invade Judea and take the people captive and kill them.

[41] He built up Kedron and stationed there horsemen and troops, so that they might go out and make raids along the highways of Judea, as the king had ordered him.

1Mac.16

[1] John went up from Gazara and reported to Simon his father what Cendebeus had done.

[2] And Simon called in his two older sons Judas and John, and said to them: "I and my brothers and the house of my father have fought the wars of Israel from our youth until this day, and things have prospered in our hands so that we have delivered Israel many times.

[3] But now I have grown old, and you by His mercy are mature in years. Take my place and my brother's, and go out and fight for our nation, and may the help which comes from Heaven be with you."

[4] So John chose out of the country twenty thousand warriors and horsemen, and they marched against Cendebeus and camped for the night in Modein.

[5] Early in the morning they arose and marched into the plain, and behold, a large force of infantry and horsemen was coming to meet them; and a stream lay between them.

[6] Then he and his army lined up against them. And he saw that the soldiers were afraid to cross the stream, so he crossed over first; and when his men saw him, they crossed over after him.

[7] Then he divided the army and placed the horsemen in the midst of the infantry, for the cavalry of the enemy were very numerous.

[8] And they sounded the trumpets, and Cendebeus and his army were put to flight, and many of them were wounded and fell; the rest fled into the stronghold.

[9] At that time Judas the brother of John was wounded, but John pursued them until Cendebeus reached Kedron, which he had built.

[10] They also fled into the towers that were in the fields of Azotus, and John burned it with fire, and about two thousand of them fell. And he returned to Judea safely.

[11] Now Ptolemy the son of Abubus had been appointed governor over the plain of Jericho, and he had much silver and gold,

[12] for he was son-in-law of the high priest.

[13] His heart was lifted up; he determined to get control of the country, and made treacherous plans against Simon and his sons, to do away with them.

[14] Now Simon was visiting the cities of the country and attending to their needs, and he went down to Jericho with Mattathias and Judas his sons, in the one hundred and seventy-seventh year, in the eleventh month, which is the month of Shebat.

[15] The son of Abubus received them treacherously in the little stronghold called Dok, which he had built; he gave them a great banquet, and hid men there.

[16] When Simon and his sons were drunk, Ptolemy and his men rose up, took their weapons, and rushed in against Simon in the banquet hall, and they killed him and his two sons and some of his servants.

[17] So he committed an act of great treachery and returned evil for good.

[18] Then Ptolemy wrote a report about these things and sent it to the king, asking him to send troops to aid him and to turn over to him the cities and the country.

[19] He sent other men to Gazara to do away with John; he sent letters to the captains asking them to come to him so that he might give them silver and gold and gifts;

[20] and he sent other men to take possession of Jerusalem and the temple hill.

[21] But some one ran ahead and reported to John at Gazara that his father and brothers had perished, and that "he has sent men to kill you also."

[22] When he heard this, he was greatly shocked; and he seized the men who came to destroy him and killed them, for he had found out that they were seeking to destroy him.

[23] The rest of the acts of John and his wars and the brave deeds which he did, and the building of the walls which he built, and his achievements,

[24] behold, they are written in the chronicles of his high priesthood, from the time that he became high priest after his father.

2 Maccabees

2Mac.1

[1] The Jewish brethren in Jerusalem and those in the land of Judea, To their Jewish brethren in Egypt, Greeting, and good peace.

[2] May God do good to you, and may he remember his covenant with Abraham and Isaac and Jacob, his faithful servants.

[3] May he give you all a heart to worship him and to do his will with a strong heart and a willing spirit.

[4] May he open your heart to his law and his commandments, and may he bring peace.

[5] May he hear your prayers and be reconciled to you, and may he not forsake you in time of evil.

[6] We are now praying for you here.

[7] In the reign of Demetrius, in the one hundred and sixty-ninth year, we Jews wrote to you, in the critical distress which came upon us in those years after Jason and his company revolted from the holy land and the kingdom

[8] and burned the gate and shed innocent blood. We besought the Lord and we were heard, and we offered sacrifice and cereal offering, and we lighted the lamps and we set out the loaves.

[9] And now see that you keep the feast of booths in the month of Chislev, in the one hundred and eighty-eighth year.

[10] Those in Jerusalem and those in Judea and the senate and Judas, To Aristobulus, who is of the family of the anointed priests, teacher of Ptolemy the king, and to the Jews in Egypt, Greeting, and good health.

[11] Having been saved by God out of grave dangers we thank him greatly for taking our side against the king.

[12] For he drove out those who fought against the holy city.

[13] For when the leader reached Persia with a force that seemed irresistible, they were cut to pieces in the temple of Nanea by a deception employed by the priests of Nanea.

[14] For under pretext of intending to marry her, Antiochus came to the place together with his friends, to secure most of its treasures as a dowry.

[15] When the priests of the temple of Nanea had set out the treasures and Antiochus had come with a few men inside the wall of the sacred precinct, they closed the temple as soon as he entered it.

[16] Opening the secret door in the ceiling, they threw stones and struck down the leader and his men, and dismembered them and cut off their heads and threw them to the people outside.

[17] Blessed in every way be our God, who has brought judgment upon those who have behaved impiously.

[18] Since on the twenty-fifth day of Chislev we shall celebrate the purification of the temple, we thought it necessary to notify you, in order that you also may celebrate the feast of booths and the feast of the fire given when Nehemiah, who built the temple and the altar, offered sacrifices.

[19] For when our fathers were being led captive to Persia, the pious priests of that time took some of the fire of the altar and secretly hid it in the hollow of a dry cistern, where they took such precautions that the place was unknown to any one.

[20] But after many years had passed, when it pleased God, Nehemiah, having been commissioned by the king of Persia, sent the descendants of the priests who had hidden the fire to get it. And when they reported to us that they had not found fire but thick liquid, he ordered them to dip it out and bring it.

[21] And when the materials for the sacrifices were presented, Nehemiah ordered the priests to sprinkle the liquid on the wood and what was laid upon it.

[22] When this was done and some time had passed and the sun, which had been clouded over, shone out, a great fire blazed up, so that all marveled.

[23] And while the sacrifice was being consumed, the priests offered prayer -- the priests and every one. Jonathan led, and the rest responded, as did Nehemiah.

[24] The prayer was to this effect:

"O Lord, Lord God, Creator of all things, who art awe-inspiring and strong and just and merciful, who alone art King and art kind, [25] who alone art bountiful, who alone art just and almighty and eternal, who do rescue Israel from every evil, who didst choose the fathers and consecrate them, [26] accept this sacrifice on behalf of all thy people Israel and preserve thy portion and make it holy. [27] Gather together our scattered people, set free those who are slaves among the Gentiles, look upon those who are rejected and despised, and let the Gentiles know that thou art our God. [28] Afflict those who oppress and are insolent with pride. [29] Plant thy people in thy holy place, as Moses said." [30] Then the priests sang the hymns.

[31] And when the materials of the sacrifice were consumed, Nehemiah ordered that the liquid that was left should be poured upon large stones. [32] When this was done, a flame blazed up; but when the light from the altar shone back, it went out. [33] When this matter became known, and it was reported to the king of the Persians that, in the place where the exiled priests had hidden the fire, the liquid had appeared with which Nehemiah and his associates had burned the materials of the sacrifice, [34] the king investigated the matter, and enclosed the place and made it sacred. [35] And with those persons whom the king favored he exchanged many excellent gifts. [36] Nehemiah and his associates called this "nephthar," which means purification, but by most people it is called naphtha.

2Mac.2

[1] One finds in the records that Jeremiah the prophet ordered those who were being deported to take some of the fire, as has been told,

[2] and that the prophet after giving them the law instructed those who were being deported not to forget the commandments of the Lord, nor to be led astray in their thoughts upon seeing the gold and silver statues and their adornment.

[3] And with other similar words he exhorted them that the law should not depart from their hearts.

[4] It was also in the writing that the prophet, having received an oracle, ordered that the tent and the ark should follow with him, and that he went out to the mountain where Moses had gone up and had seen the inheritance of God.

[5] And Jeremiah came and found a cave, and he brought there the tent and the ark and the altar of incense, and he sealed up the entrance.

[6] Some of those who followed him came up to mark the way, but could not find it.

[7] When Jeremiah learned of it, he rebuked them and declared: "The place shall be unknown until God gathers his people together again and shows his mercy.

[8] And then the Lord will disclose these things, and the glory of the Lord and the cloud will appear, as they were shown in the case of Moses, and as Solomon asked that the place should be specially consecrated."

[9] It was also made clear that being possessed of wisdom Solomon offered sacrifice for the dedication and completion of the temple.

[10] Just as Moses prayed to the Lord, and fire came down from heaven and devoured the sacrifices, so also Solomon prayed, and the fire came down and consumed the whole burnt offerings.

[11] And Moses said, "They were consumed because the sin offering had not been eaten."

[12] Likewise Solomon also kept the eight days.

[13] The same things are reported in the records and in the memoirs of Nehemiah, and also that he founded a library and collected the books about the kings and prophets, and the writings of David, and letters of kings about votive offerings.

[14] In the same way Judas also collected all the books that had been lost on account of the war which had come upon us, and they are in our possession.

[15] So if you have need of them, send people to get them for you.

[16] Since, therefore, we are about to celebrate the purification, we write to you. Will you therefore please keep the days?

[17] It is God who has saved all his people, and has returned the inheritance to all, and the kingship and priesthood and consecration,

[18] as he promised through the law. For we have hope in God that he will soon have mercy upon us and will gather us from everywhere under heaven into his holy place, for he has rescued us from great evils and has purified the place.

[19] The story of Judas Maccabeus and his brothers, and the purification of the great temple, and the dedication of the altar,

[20] and further the wars against Antiochus Epiphanes and his son Eupator,

[21] and the appearances which came from heaven to those who strove zealously on behalf of Judaism, so that though few in number they seized the whole land and pursued the barbarian hordes,

[22] and recovered the temple famous throughout the world and freed the city and restored the laws that were about to be abolished, while the Lord with great kindness became gracious to them --

[23] all this, which has been set forth by Jason of Cyrene in five volumes, we shall attempt to condense into a single book.

[24] For considering the flood of numbers involved and the difficulty there is for those who wish to enter upon the narratives of history because of the mass of material,

[25] we have aimed to please those who wish to read, to make it easy for those who are inclined to memorize, and to profit all readers.

[26] For us who have undertaken the toil of abbreviating, it is no light matter but calls for sweat and loss of sleep,

[27] just as it is not easy for one who prepares a banquet and seeks the benefit of others. However, to secure the gratitude of many we will gladly endure the uncomfortable toil,

[28] leaving the responsibility for exact details to the compiler, while devoting our effort to arriving at the outlines of the condensation.

[29] For as the master builder of a new house must be concerned with the whole construction, while the one who undertakes its painting and decoration has to consider only what is suitable for its adornment, such in my judgment is the case with us.

[30] It is the duty of the original historian to occupy the ground and to discuss matters from every side and to take trouble with details,

[31] but the one who recasts the narrative should be allowed to strive for brevity of expression and to forego exhaustive treatment.

[32] At this point therefore let us begin our narrative, adding only so much to what has already been said; for it is foolish to lengthen the preface while cutting short the history itself.

2Mac.3

[1] While the holy city was inhabited in unbroken peace and the laws were very well observed because of the piety of the high priest Onias and his hatred of wickedness,

[2] it came about that the kings themselves honored the place and glorified the temple with the finest presents,

[3] so that even Seleucus, the king of Asia, defrayed from his own revenues all the expenses connected with the service of the sacrifices.

[4] But a man named Simon, of the tribe of Benjamin, who had been made captain of the temple, had a disagreement with the high priest about the administration of the city market;

[5] and when he could not prevail over Onias he went to Apollonius of Tarsus, who at that time was governor of Coelesyria and Phoenicia.

[6] He reported to him that the treasury in Jerusalem was full of untold sums of money, so that the amount of the funds could not be reckoned, and that they did not belong to the account of the sacrifices, but that it was possible for them to fall under the control of the king.

[7] When Apollonius met the king, he told him of the money about which he had been informed. The king chose Heliodorus, who was in charge of his affairs, and sent him with commands to effect the removal of the aforesaid money.

[8] Heliodorus at once set out on his journey, ostensibly to make a tour of inspection of the cities of Coelesyria and Phoenicia, but in fact to carry out the king's purpose.

[9] When he had arrived at Jerusalem and had been kindly welcomed by the high priest of the city, he told about the disclosure that had been made and stated why he had come, and he inquired whether this really was the situation.

[10] The high priest explained that there were some deposits belonging to widows and orphans,

[11] and also some money of Hyrcanus, son of Tobias, a man of very prominent position, and that it totaled in all four hundred talents of silver and two hundred of gold. To such an extent the impious Simon had misrepresented the facts.

[12] And he said that it was utterly impossible that wrong should be done to those people who had trusted in the holiness of the place and in the sanctity and inviolability of the temple which is honored throughout the whole world.

[13] But Heliodorus, because of the king's commands which he had, said that this money must in any case be confiscated for the king's treasury.

[14] So he set a day and went in to direct the inspection of these funds. There was no little distress throughout the whole city.

[15] The priests prostrated themselves before the altar in their priestly garments and called toward heaven upon him who had given the law about deposits, that he should keep them safe for those who had deposited them.

[16] To see the appearance of the high priest was to be wounded at heart, for his face and the change in his color disclosed the anguish of his soul.

[17] For terror and bodily trembling had come over the man, which plainly showed to those who looked at him the pain lodged in his heart.

[18] People also hurried out of their houses in crowds to make a general supplication because the holy place was about to be brought into contempt.

[19] Women, girded with sackcloth under their breasts, thronged the streets. Some of the maidens who were kept indoors ran together to the gates, and some to the walls, while others peered out of the windows.

[20] And holding up their hands to heaven, they all made entreaty.

[21] There was something pitiable in the prostration of the whole populace and the anxiety of the high priest in his great anguish.

[22] While they were calling upon the Almighty Lord that he would keep what had been entrusted safe and secure for those who had entrusted it,

[23] Heliodorus went on with what had been decided.

[24] But when he arrived at the treasury with his bodyguard, then and there the Sovereign of spirits and of all authority caused so great a manifestation that all who had been so bold as to accompany him were astounded by the power of God, and became faint with terror.

[25] For there appeared to them a magnificently caparisoned horse, with a rider of frightening mien, and it rushed furiously at Heliodorus and struck at him with its front hoofs. Its rider was seen to have armor and weapons of gold.

[26] Two young men also appeared to him, remarkably strong, gloriously beautiful and splendidly dressed, who stood on each side of him and scourged him continuously, inflicting many blows on him.

[27] When he suddenly fell to the ground and deep darkness came over him, his men took him up and put him on a stretcher

[28] and carried him away, this man who had just entered the aforesaid treasury with a great retinue and all his bodyguard but was now unable to help himself; and they recognized clearly the sovereign power of God.

[29] While he lay prostrate, speechless because of the divine intervention and deprived of any hope of recovery,

[30] they praised the Lord who had acted marvelously for his own place. And the temple, which a little while before was full of fear and disturbance, was filled with joy and gladness, now that the Almighty Lord had appeared.

[31] Quickly some of Heliodorus' friends asked Onias to call upon the Most High and to grant life to one who was lying quite at his last breath.

[32] And the high priest, fearing that the king might get the notion that some foul play had been perpetrated by the Jews with regard to Heliodorus, offered sacrifice for the man's recovery.

[33] While the high priest was making the offering of atonement, the same young men appeared again to Heliodorus dressed in the same clothing, and they stood and said, "Be very grateful to Onias the high priest, since for his sake the Lord has granted you your life.

[34] And see that you, who have been scourged by heaven, report to all men the majestic power of God." Having said this they vanished.

[35] Then Heliodorus offered sacrifice to the Lord and made very great vows to the Savior of his life, and having bidden Onias farewell, he marched off with his forces to the king.

[36] And he bore testimony to all men of the deeds of the supreme God, which he had seen with his own eyes.

[37] When the king asked Heliodorus what sort of person would be suitable to send on another mission to Jerusalem, he replied,

[38] "If you have any enemy or plotter against your government, send him there, for you will get him back thoroughly scourged, if he escapes at all, for there certainly is about the place some power of God.

[39] For he who has his dwelling in heaven watches over that place himself and brings it aid, and he strikes and destroys those who come to do it injury."

[40] This was the outcome of the episode of Heliodorus and the protection of the treasury.

2Mac.4

[1] The previously mentioned Simon, who had informed about the money against his own country, slandered Onias, saying that it was he who had incited Heliodorus and had been the real cause of the misfortune.

[2] He dared to designate as a plotter against the government the man who was the benefactor of the city, the protector of his fellow countrymen, and a zealot for the laws.

[3] When his hatred progressed to such a degree that even murders were committed by one of Simon's approved agents,

[4] Onias recognized that the rivalry was serious and that Apollonius, the son of Menestheus and governor of Coelesyria and Phoenicia, was intensifying the malice of Simon.

[5] So he betook himself to the king, not accusing his fellow citizens but having in view the welfare, both public and private, of all the people.

[6] For he saw that without the king's attention public affairs could not again reach a peaceful settlement, and that Simon would not stop his folly.

[7] When Seleucus died and Antiochus who was called Epiphanes succeeded to the kingdom, Jason the brother of Onias obtained the high priesthood by corruption,

[8] promising the king at an interview three hundred and sixty talents of silver and, from another source of revenue, eighty talents.

[9] In addition to this he promised to pay one hundred and fifty more if permission were given to establish by his authority a gymnasium and a body of youth for it, and to enrol the men of Jerusalem as citizens of Antioch.

[10] When the king assented and Jason came to office, he at once shifted his countrymen over to the Greek way of life.

[11] He set aside the existing royal concessions to the Jews, secured through John the father of Eupolemus, who went on the mission to establish friendship and alliance with the Romans; and he destroyed the lawful ways of living and introduced new customs contrary to the law.

[12] For with alacrity he founded a gymnasium right under the citadel, and he induced the noblest of the young men to wear the Greek hat.

[13] There was such an extreme of Hellenization and increase in the adoption of foreign ways because of the surpassing wickedness of Jason, who was ungodly and no high priest,

[14] that the priests were no longer intent upon their service at the altar. Despising the sanctuary and neglecting the sacrifices, they hastened to take part in the unlawful proceedings in the wrestling arena after the call to the discus,

[15] disdaining the honors prized by their fathers and putting the highest value upon Greek forms of prestige.

[16] For this reason heavy disaster overtook them, and those whose ways of living they admired and wished to imitate completely became their enemies and punished them.

[17] For it is no light thing to show irreverence to the divine laws -- a fact which later events will make clear.

[18] When the quadrennial games were being held at Tyre and the king was present,

[19] the vile Jason sent envoys, chosen as being Antiochian citizens from Jerusalem, to carry three hundred silver drachmas for the sacrifice to Hercules. Those who carried the money, however, thought best not to use it for sacrifice, because that was inappropriate, but to expend it for another purpose.

[20] So this money was intended by the sender for the sacrifice to Hercules, but by the decision of its carriers it was applied to the construction of triremes.

[21] When Apollonius the son of Menestheus was sent to Egypt for the coronation of Philometor as king, Antiochus learned that Philometor had become hostile to his government, and he took measures for his own security. Therefore upon arriving at Joppa he proceeded to Jerusalem.

[22] He was welcomed magnificently by Jason and the city, and ushered in with a blaze of torches and with shouts. Then he marched into Phoenicia.

[23] After a period of three years Jason sent Menelaus, the brother of the previously mentioned Simon, to carry the money to the king and to complete the records of essential business.

[24] But he, when presented to the king, extolled him with an air of authority, and secured the high priesthood for himself, outbidding Jason by three hundred talents of silver.

[25] After receiving the king's orders he returned, possessing no qualification for the high priesthood, but having the hot temper of a cruel tyrant and the rage of a savage wild beast.

[26] So Jason, who after supplanting his own brother was supplanted by another man, was driven as a fugitive into the land of Ammon.

[27] And Menelaus held the office, but he did not pay regularly any of the money promised to the king.

[28] When Sostratus the captain of the citadel kept requesting payment, for the collection of the revenue was his responsibility, the two of them were summoned by the king on account of this issue.

[29] Menelaus left his own brother Lysimachus as deputy in the high priesthood, while Sostratus left Crates, the commander of the Cyprian troops.

[30] While such was the state of affairs, it happened that the people of Tarsus and of Mallus revolted because their cities had been given as a present to Antiochis, the king's concubine.

[31] So the king went hastily to settle the trouble, leaving Andronicus, a man of high rank, to act as his deputy.

[32] But Menelaus, thinking he had obtained a suitable opportunity, stole some of the gold vessels of the temple and gave them to Andronicus; other vessels, as it happened, he had sold to Tyre and the neighboring cities.

[33] When Onias became fully aware of these acts he publicly exposed them, having first withdrawn to a place of sanctuary at Daphne near Antioch.

[34] Therefore Menelaus, taking Andronicus aside, urged him to kill Onias. Andronicus came to Onias, and resorting to treachery offered him sworn pledges and gave him his right hand, and in spite of his suspicion persuaded Onias to come out from the place of sanctuary; then, with no regard for justice, he immediately put him out of the way.

[35] For this reason not only Jews, but many also of other nations, were grieved and displeased at the unjust murder of the man.

[36] When the king returned from the region of Cilicia, the Jews in the city appealed to him with regard to the unreasonable murder of Onias, and the Greeks shared their hatred of the crime.

[37] Therefore Antiochus was grieved at heart and filled with pity, and wept because of the moderation and good conduct of the deceased;

[38] and inflamed with anger, he immediately stripped off the purple robe from Andronicus, tore off his garments, and led him about the whole city to that very place where he had committed the outrage against Onias, and there he dispatched the bloodthirsty fellow. The Lord thus repaid him with the punishment he deserved.

[39] When many acts of sacrilege had been committed in the city by Lysimachus with the connivance of Menelaus, and when report of them had spread abroad, the populace gathered against Lysimachus, because many of the gold vessels had already been stolen.

[40] And since the crowds were becoming aroused and filled with anger, Lysimachus armed about three thousand men and launched an unjust attack, under the leadership of a certain Auranus, a man advanced in years and no less advanced in folly.

[41] But when the Jews became aware of Lysimachus' attack, some picked up stones, some blocks of wood, and others took handfuls of the ashes that were lying about, and threw them in wild confusion at Lysimachus and his men.

[42] As a result, they wounded many of them, and killed some, and put them all to flight; and the temple robber himself they killed close by the treasury.

[43] Charges were brought against Menelaus about this incident.

[44] When the king came to Tyre, three men sent by the senate presented the case before him.

[45] But Menelaus, already as good as beaten, promised a substantial bribe to Ptolemy son of Dorymenes to win over the king.

[46] Therefore Ptolemy, taking the king aside into a colonnade as if for refreshment, induced the king to change his mind.

[47] Menelaus, the cause of all the evil, he acquitted of the charges against him, while he sentenced to death those unfortunate men, who would have been freed uncondemned if they had pleaded even before Scythians.

[48] And so those who had spoken for the city and the villages and the holy vessels quickly suffered the unjust penalty.

[49] Therefore even the Tyrians, showing their hatred of the crime, provided magnificently for their funeral.

[50] But Menelaus, because of the cupidity of those in power, remained in office, growing in wickedness, having become the chief plotter against his fellow citizens.

2Mac.5

[1] About this time Antiochus made his second invasion of Egypt.

[2] And it happened that over all the city, for almost forty days, there appeared golden-clad horsemen charging through the air, in companies fully armed with lances and drawn swords --

[3] troops of horsemen drawn up, attacks and counterattacks made on this side and on that, brandishing of shields, massing of spears, hurling of missiles, the flash of golden trappings, and armor of all sorts.

[4] Therefore all men prayed that the apparition might prove to have been a good omen.

[5] When a false rumor arose that Antiochus was dead, Jason took no less than a thousand men and suddenly made an assault upon the city. When the troops upon the wall had been forced back and at last the city was being taken, Menelaus took refuge in the citadel.

[6] But Jason kept relentlessly slaughtering his fellow citizens, not realizing that success at the cost of one's kindred is the

greatest misfortune, but imagining that he was setting up trophies of victory over enemies and not over fellow countrymen.

[7] He did not gain control of the government, however; and in the end got only disgrace from his conspiracy, and fled again into the country of the Ammonites.

[8] Finally he met a miserable end. Accused before Aretas the ruler of the Arabs, fleeing from city to city, pursued by all men, hated as a rebel against the laws, and abhorred as the executioner of his country and his fellow citizens, he was cast ashore in Egypt;

[9] and he who had driven many from their own country into exile died in exile, having embarked to go to the Lacedaemonians in hope of finding protection because of their kinship.

[10] He who had cast out many to lie unburied had no one to mourn for him; he had no funeral of any sort and no place in the tomb of his fathers.

[11] When news of what had happened reached the king, he took it to mean that Judea was in revolt. So, raging inwardly, he left Egypt and took the city by storm.

[12] And he commanded his soldiers to cut down relentlessly every one they met and to slay those who went into the houses.

[13] Then there was killing of young and old, destruction of boys, women, and children, and slaughter of virgins and infants.

[14] Within the total of three days eighty thousand were destroyed, forty thousand in hand-to-hand fighting; and as many were sold into slavery as were slain.

[15] Not content with this, Antiochus dared to enter the most holy temple in all the world, guided by Menelaus, who had become a traitor both to the laws and to his country.

[16] He took the holy vessels with his polluted hands, and swept away with profane hands the votive offerings which other kings had made to enhance the glory and honor of the place.

[17] Antiochus was elated in spirit, and did not perceive that the Lord was angered for a little while because of the sins of those who dwelt in the city, and that therefore he was disregarding the holy place.

[18] But if it had not happened that they were involved in many sins, this man would have been scourged and turned back from his rash act as soon as he came forward, just as Heliodorus was, whom Seleucus the king sent to inspect the treasury.

[19] But the Lord did not choose the nation for the sake of the holy place, but the place for the sake of the nation.

[20] Therefore the place itself shared in the misfortunes that befell the nation and afterward participated in its benefits; and what was forsaken in the wrath of the Almighty was restored again in all its glory when the great Lord became reconciled.

[21] So Antiochus carried off eighteen hundred talents from the temple, and hurried away to Antioch, thinking in his arrogance that he could sail on the land and walk on the sea, because his mind was elated.

[22] And he left governors to afflict the people: at Jerusalem, Philip, by birth a Phrygian and in character more barbarous than the man who appointed him;

[23] and at Gerizim, Andronicus; and besides these Menelaus, who lorded it over his fellow citizens worse than the others did. In his malice toward the Jewish citizens,

[24] Antiochus sent Apollonius, the captain of the Mysians, with an army of twenty-two thousand, and commanded him to slay all the grown men and to sell the women and boys as slaves.

[25] When this man arrived in Jerusalem, he pretended to be peaceably disposed and waited until the holy sabbath day; then, finding the Jews not at work, he ordered his men to parade under arms.

[26] He put to the sword all those who came out to see them, then rushed into the city with his armed men and killed great numbers of people.

[27] But Judas Maccabeus, with about nine others, got away to the wilderness, and kept himself and his companions alive in the mountains as wild animals do; they continued to live on what grew wild, so that they might not share in the defilement.

2Mac.6

[1] Not long after this, the king sent an Athenian senator to compel the Jews to forsake the laws of their fathers and cease to live by the laws of God,

[2] and also to pollute the temple in Jerusalem and call it the temple of Olympian Zeus, and to call the one in Gerizim the temple of Zeus the Friend of Strangers, as did the people who dwelt in that place.

[3] Harsh and utterly grievous was the onslaught of evil.

[4] For the temple was filled with debauchery and reveling by the Gentiles, who dallied with harlots and had intercourse with women within the sacred precincts, and besides brought in things for sacrifice that were unfit.

[5] The altar was covered with abominable offerings which were forbidden by the laws.

[6] A man could neither keep the sabbath, nor observe the feasts of his fathers, nor so much as confess himself to be a Jew.

[7] On the monthly celebration of the king's birthday, the Jews were taken, under bitter constraint, to partake of the sacrifices; and when the feast of Dionysus came, they were compelled to walk in the procession in honor of Dionysus, wearing wreaths of ivy.

[8] At the suggestion of Ptolemy a decree was issued to the neighboring Greek cities, that they should adopt the same policy toward the Jews and make them partake of the sacrifices,

[9] and should slay those who did not choose to change over to Greek customs. One could see, therefore, the misery that had come upon them.

[10] For example, two women were brought in for having circumcised their children. These women they publicly paraded

about the city, with their babies hung at their breasts, then hurled them down headlong from the wall.

[11] Others who had assembled in the caves near by, to observe the seventh day secretly, were betrayed to Philip and were all burned together, because their piety kept them from defending themselves, in view of their regard for that most holy day.

[12] Now I urge those who read this book not to be depressed by such calamities, but to recognize that these punishments were designed not to destroy but to discipline our people.

[13] In fact, not to let the impious alone for long, but to punish them immediately, is a sign of great kindness.

[14] For in the case of the other nations the Lord waits patiently to punish them until they have reached the full measure of their sins; but he does not deal in this way with us,

[15] in order that he may not take vengeance on us afterward when our sins have reached their height.

[16] Therefore he never withdraws his mercy from us. Though he disciplines us with calamities, he does not forsake his own people.

[17] Let what we have said serve as a reminder; we must go on briefly with the story.

[18] Eleazar, one of the scribes in high position, a man now advanced in age and of noble presence, was being forced to open his mouth to eat swine's flesh.

[19] But he, welcoming death with honor rather than life with pollution, went up to the the rack of his own accord, spitting out the flesh,

[20] as men ought to go who have the courage to refuse things that it is not right to taste, even for the natural love of life.

[21] Those who were in charge of that unlawful sacrifice took the man aside, because of their long acquaintance with him, and privately urged him to bring meat of his own providing, proper for him to use, and pretend that he was eating the flesh of the sacrificial meal which had been commanded by the king,

[22] so that by doing this he might be saved from death, and be treated kindly on account of his old friendship with them.

[23] But making a high resolve, worthy of his years and the dignity of his old age and the gray hairs which he had reached with distinction and his excellent life even from childhood, and moreover according to the holy God-given law, he declared himself quickly, telling them to send him to Hades.

[24] "Such pretense is not worthy of our time of life," he said, "lest many of the young should suppose that Eleazar in his ninetieth year has gone over to an alien religion,

[25] and through my pretense, for the sake of living a brief moment longer, they should be led astray because of me, while I defile and disgrace my old age.

[26] For even if for the present I should avoid the punishment of men, yet whether I live or die I shall not escape the hands of the Almighty.

[27] Therefore, by manfully giving up my life now, I will show myself worthy of my old age

[28] and leave to the young a noble example of how to die a good death willingly and nobly for the revered and holy laws." When he had said this, he went at once to the rack.

[29] And those who a little before had acted toward him with good will now changed to ill will, because the words he had uttered were in their opinion sheer madness.

[30] When he was about to die under the blows, he groaned aloud and said: "It is clear to the Lord in his holy knowledge that, though I might have been saved from death, I am enduring terrible sufferings in my body under this beating, but in my soul I am glad to suffer these things because I fear him."

[31] So in this way he died, leaving in his death an example of nobility and a memorial of courage, not only to the young but to the great body of his nation.

2Mac.7

[1] It happened also that seven brothers and their mother were arrested and were being compelled by the king, under torture with whips and cords, to partake of unlawful swine's flesh.

[2] One of them, acting as their spokesman, said, "What do you intend to ask and learn from us? For we are ready to die rather than transgress the laws of our fathers."

[3] The king fell into a rage, and gave orders that pans and caldrons be heated.

[4] These were heated immediately, and he commanded that the tongue of their spokesman be cut out and that they scalp him and cut off his hands and feet, while the rest of the brothers and the mother looked on.

[5] When he was utterly helpless, the king ordered them to take him to the fire, still breathing, and to fry him in a pan. The smoke from the pan spread widely, but the brothers and their mother encouraged one another to die nobly, saying,

[6] "The Lord God is watching over us and in truth has compassion on us, as Moses declared in his song which bore witness against the people to their faces, when he said, `And he will have compassion on his servants.'"

[7] After the first brother had died in this way, they brought forward the second for their sport. They tore off the skin of his head with the hair, and asked him, "Will you eat rather than have your body punished limb by limb?"

[8] He replied in the language of his fathers, and said to them, "No." Therefore he in turn underwent tortures as the first brother had done.

[9] And when he was at his last breath, he said, "You accursed wretch, you dismiss us from this present life, but the King of the universe will raise us up to an everlasting renewal of life, because we have died for his laws."

[10] After him, the third was the victim of their sport. When it was demanded, he quickly put out his tongue and

courageously stretched forth his hands,

[11] and said nobly, "I got these from Heaven, and because of his laws I disdain them, and from him I hope to get them back again."

[12] As a result the king himself and those with him were astonished at the young man's spirit, for he regarded his sufferings as nothing.

[13] When he too had died, they maltreated and tortured the fourth in the same way.

[14] And when he was near death, he said, "One cannot but choose to die at the hands of men and to cherish the hope that God gives of being raised again by him. But for you there will be no resurrection to life!"

[15] Next they brought forward the fifth and maltreated him.

[16] But he looked at the king, and said, "Because you have authority among men, mortal though you are, you do what you please. But do not think that God has forsaken our people.

[17] Keep on, and see how his mighty power will torture you and your descendants!"

[18] After him they brought forward the sixth. And when he was about to die, he said, "Do not deceive yourself in vain. For we are suffering these things on our own account, because of our sins against our own God. Therefore astounding things have happened.

[19] But do not think that you will go unpunished for having tried to fight against God!"

[20] The mother was especially admirable and worthy of honorable memory. Though she saw her seven sons perish within a single day, she bore it with good courage because of her hope in the Lord.

[21] She encouraged each of them in the language of their fathers. Filled with a noble spirit, she fired her woman's reasoning with a man's courage, and said to them,

[22] "I do not know how you came into being in my womb. It was not I who gave you life and breath, nor I who set in order the elements within each of you.

[23] Therefore the Creator of the world, who shaped the beginning of man and devised the origin of all things, will in his mercy give life and breath back to you again, since you now forget yourselves for the sake of his laws."

[24] Antiochus felt that he was being treated with contempt, and he was suspicious of her reproachful tone. The youngest brother being still alive, Antiochus not only appealed to him in words, but promised with oaths that he would make him rich and enviable if he would turn from the ways of his fathers, and that he would take him for his friend and entrust him with public affairs.

[25] Since the young man would not listen to him at all, the king called the mother to him and urged her to advise the youth to save himself.

[26] After much urging on his part, she undertook to persuade her son.

[27] But, leaning close to him, she spoke in their native tongue as follows, deriding the cruel tyrant: "My son, have pity on me. I carried you nine months in my womb, and nursed you for three years, and have reared you and brought you up to this point in your life, and have taken care of you.

[28] I beseech you, my child, to look at the heaven and the earth and see everything that is in them, and recognize that God did not make them out of things that existed. Thus also mankind comes into being.

[29] Do not fear this butcher, but prove worthy of your brothers. Accept death, so that in God's mercy I may get you back again with your brothers."

[30] While she was still speaking, the young man said, "What are you waiting for? I will not obey the king's command, but I obey the command of the law that was given to our fathers through Moses.

[31] But you, who have contrived all sorts of evil against the Hebrews, will certainly not escape the hands of God.

[32] For we are suffering because of our own sins.

[33] And if our living Lord is angry for a little while, to rebuke and discipline us, he will again be reconciled with his own servants.

[34] But you, unholy wretch, you most defiled of all men, do not be elated in vain and puffed up by uncertain hopes, when you raise your hand against the children of heaven.

[35] You have not yet escaped the judgment of the almighty, all-seeing God.

[36] For our brothers after enduring a brief suffering have drunk of everflowing life under God's covenant; but you, by the judgment of God, will receive just punishment for your arrogance.

[37] I, like my brothers, give up body and life for the laws of our fathers, appealing to God to show mercy soon to our nation and by afflictions and plagues to make you confess that he alone is God,

[38] and through me and my brothers to bring to an end the wrath of the Almighty which has justly fallen on our whole nation."

[39] The king fell into a rage, and handled him worse than the others, being exasperated at his scorn.

[40] So he died in his integrity, putting his whole trust in the Lord.

[41] Last of all, the mother died, after her sons.

[42] Let this be enough, then, about the eating of sacrifices and the extreme tortures.

2Mac.8

[1] But Judas, who was also called Maccabeus, and his companions secretly entered the villages and summoned their

kinsmen and enlisted those who had continued in the Jewish faith, and so they gathered about six thousand men.

[2] They besought the Lord to look upon the people who were oppressed by all, and to have pity on the temple which had been profaned by ungodly men,

[3] and to have mercy on the city which was being destroyed and about to be leveled to the ground, and to hearken to the blood that cried out to him,

[4] and to remember also the lawless destruction of the innocent babies and the blasphemies committed against his name, and to show his hatred of evil.

[5] As soon as Maccabeus got his army organized, the Gentiles could not withstand him, for the wrath of the Lord had turned to mercy.

[6] Coming without warning, he would set fire to towns and villages. He captured strategic positions and put to flight not a few of the enemy.

[7] He found the nights most advantageous for such attacks. And talk of his valor spread everywhere.

[8] When Philip saw that the man was gaining ground little by little, and that he was pushing ahead with more frequent successes, he wrote to Ptolemy, the governor of Coelesyria and Phoenicia, for aid to the king's government.

[9] And Ptolemy promptly appointed Nicanor the son of Patroclus, one of the king's chief friends, and sent him, in command of no fewer than twenty thousand Gentiles of all nations, to wipe out the whole race of Judea. He associated with him Gorgias, a general and a man of experience in military service.

[10] Nicanor determined to make up for the king the tribute due to the Romans, two thousand talents, by selling the captured Jews into slavery.

[11] And he immediately sent to the cities on the seacoast, inviting them to buy Jewish slaves and promising to hand over ninety slaves for a talent, not expecting the judgment from the Almighty that was about to overtake him.

[12] Word came to Judas concerning Nicanor's invasion; and when he told his companions of the arrival of the army,

[13] those who were cowardly and distrustful of God's justice ran off and got away.

[14] Others sold all their remaining property, and at the same time besought the Lord to rescue those who had been sold by the ungodly Nicanor before he ever met them,

[15] if not for their own sake, yet for the sake of the covenants made with their fathers, and because he had called them by his holy and glorious name.

[16] But Maccabeus gathered his men together, to the number six thousand, and exhorted them not to be frightened by the enemy and not to fear the great multitude of Gentiles who were wickedly coming against them, but to fight nobly,

[17] keeping before their eyes the lawless outrage which the Gentiles had committed against the holy place, and the torture of the derided city, and besides, the overthrow of their ancestral way of life.

[18] "For they trust to arms and acts of daring," he said, "but we trust in the Almighty God, who is able with a single nod to strike down those who are coming against us and even the whole world."

[19] Moreover, he told them of the times when help came to their ancestors; both the time of Sennacherib, when one hundred and eighty-five thousand perished,

[20] and the time of the battle with the Galatians that took place in Babylonia, when eight thousand in all went into the affair, with four thousand Macedonians; and when the Macedonians were hard pressed, the eight thousand, by the help that came to them from heaven, destroyed one hundred and twenty thousand and took much booty.

[21] With these words he filled them with good courage and made them ready to die for their laws and their country; then he divided his army into four parts.

[22] He appointed his brothers also, Simon and Joseph and Jonathan, each to command a division, putting fifteen hundred men under each.

[23] Besides, he appointed Eleazar to read aloud from the holy book, and gave the watchword, "God's help"; then, leading the first division himself, he joined battle with Nicanor.

[24] With the Almighty as their ally, they slew more than nine thousand of the enemy, and wounded and disabled most of Nicanor's army, and forced them all to flee.

[25] They captured the money of those who had come to buy them as slaves. After pursuing them for some distance, they were obliged to return because the hour was late.

[26] For it was the day before the sabbath, and for that reason they did not continue their pursuit.

[27] And when they had collected the arms of the enemy and stripped them of their spoils, they kept the sabbath, giving great praise and thanks to the Lord, who had preserved them for that day and allotted it to them as the beginning of mercy.

[28] After the sabbath they gave some of the spoils to those who had been tortured and to the widows and orphans, and distributed the rest among themselves and their children.

[29] When they had done this, they made common supplication and besought the merciful Lord to be wholly reconciled with his servants.

[30] In encounters with the forces of Timothy and Bacchides they killed more than twenty thousand of them and got possession of some exceedingly high strongholds, and they divided very much plunder, giving to those who had been tortured and to the orphans and widows, and also to the aged, shares equal to their own.

[31] Collecting the arms of the enemy, they stored them all carefully in strategic places, and carried the rest of the spoils to

Jerusalem.

[32] They killed the commander of Timothy's forces, a most unholy man, and one who had greatly troubled the Jews.

[33] While they were celebrating the victory in the city of their fathers, they burned those who had set fire to the sacred gates, Callisthenes and some others, who had fled into one little house; so these received the proper recompense for their impiety.

[34] The thrice-accursed Nicanor, who had brought the thousand merchants to buy the Jews,

[35] having been humbled with the help of the Lord by opponents whom he regarded as of the least account, took off his splendid uniform and made his way alone like a runaway slave across the country till he reached Antioch, having succeeded chiefly in the destruction of his own army!

[36] Thus he who had undertaken to secure tribute for the Romans by the capture of the people of Jerusalem proclaimed that the Jews had a Defender, and that therefore the Jews were invulnerable, because they followed the laws ordained by him.

2Mac.9

[1] About that time, as it happened, Antiochus had retreated in disorder from the region of Persia.

[2] For he had entered the city called Persepolis, and attempted to rob the temples and control the city. Therefore the people rushed to the rescue with arms, and Antiochus and his men were defeated, with the result that Antiochus was put to flight by the inhabitants and beat a shameful retreat.

[3] While he was in Ecbatana, news came to him of what had happened to Nicanor and the forces of Timothy.

[4] Transported with rage, he conceived the idea of turning upon the Jews the injury done by those who had put him to flight; so he ordered his charioteer to drive without stopping until he completed the journey. But the judgment of heaven rode with him! For in his arrogance he said, "When I get there I will make Jerusalem a cemetery of Jews."

[5] But the all-seeing Lord, the God of Israel, struck him an incurable and unseen blow. As soon as he ceased speaking he was seized with a pain in his bowels for which there was no relief and with sharp internal tortures --

[6] and that very justly, for he had tortured the bowels of others with many and strange inflictions.

[7] Yet he did not in any way stop his insolence, but was even more filled with arrogance, breathing fire in his rage against the Jews, and giving orders to hasten the journey. And so it came about that he fell out of his chariot as it was rushing along, and the fall was so hard as to torture every limb of his body.

[8] Thus he who had just been thinking that he could command the waves of the sea, in his superhuman arrogance, and imagining that he could weigh the high mountains in a balance, was brought down to earth and carried in a litter, making the power of God manifest to all.

[9] And so the ungodly man's body swarmed with worms, and while he was still living in anguish and pain, his flesh rotted away, and because of his stench the whole army felt revulsion at his decay.

[10] Because of his intolerable stench no one was able to carry the man who a little while before had thought that he could touch the stars of heaven.

[11] Then it was that, broken in spirit, he began to lose much of his arrogance and to come to his senses under the scourge of God, for he was tortured with pain every moment.

[12] And when he could not endure his own stench, he uttered these words: "It is right to be subject to God, and no mortal should think that he is equal to God."

[13] Then the abominable fellow made a vow to the Lord, who would no longer have mercy on him, stating

[14] that the holy city, which he was hastening to level to the ground and to make a cemetery, he was now declaring to be free;

[15] and the Jews, whom he had not considered worth burying but had planned to throw out with their children to the beasts, for the birds to pick, he would make, all of them, equal to citizens of Athens;

[16] and the holy sanctuary, which he had formerly plundered, he would adorn with the finest offerings; and the holy vessels he would give back, all of them, many times over; and the expenses incurred for the sacrifices he would provide from his own revenues;

[17] and in addition to all this he also would become a Jew and would visit every inhabited place to proclaim the power of God.

[18] But when his sufferings did not in any way abate, for the judgment of God had justly come upon him, he gave up all hope for himself and wrote to the Jews the following letter, in the form of a supplication. This was its content:

[19] "To his worthy Jewish citizens, Antiochus their king and general sends hearty greetings and good wishes for their health and prosperity.

[20] If you and your children are well and your affairs are as you wish, I am glad. As my hope is in heaven,

[21] I remember with affection your esteem and good will. On my way back from the region of Persia I suffered an annoying illness, and I have deemed it necessary to take thought for the general security of all.

[22] I do not despair of my condition, for I have good hope of recovering from my illness,

[23] but I observed that my father, on the occasions when he made expeditions into the upper country, appointed his successor,

[24] so that, if anything unexpected happened or any unwelcome news came, the people throughout the realm would not be troubled, for they would know to whom the government was left.

[25] Moreover, I understand how the princes along the borders and the neighbors to my kingdom keep watching for

opportunities and waiting to see what will happen. So I have appointed my son Antiochus to be king, whom I have often entrusted and commended to most of you when I hastened off to the upper provinces; and I have written to him what is written here.

[26] I therefore urge and beseech you to remember the public and private services rendered to you and to maintain your present good will, each of you, toward me and my son.

[27] For I am sure that he will follow my policy and will treat you with moderation and kindness."

[28] So the murderer and blasphemer, having endured the more intense suffering, such as he had inflicted on others, came to the end of his life by a most pitiable fate, among the mountains in a strange land.

[29] And Philip, one of his courtiers, took his body home; then, fearing the son of Antiochus, he betook himself to Ptolemy Philometor in Egypt.

2Mac.10

[1] Now Maccabeus and his followers, the Lord leading them on, recovered the temple and the city;

[2] and they tore down the altars which had been built in the public square by the foreigners, and also destroyed the sacred precincts.

[3] They purified the sanctuary, and made another altar of sacrifice; then, striking fire out of flint, they offered sacrifices, after a lapse of two years, and they burned incense and lighted lamps and set out the bread of the Presence.

[4] And when they had done this, they fell prostrate and besought the Lord that they might never again fall into such misfortunes, but that, if they should ever sin, they might be disciplined by him with forbearance and not be handed over to blasphemous and barbarous nations.

[5] It happened that on the same day on which the sanctuary had been profaned by the foreigners, the purification of the sanctuary took place, that is, on the twenty-fifth day of the same month, which was Chislev.

[6] And they celebrated it for eight days with rejoicing, in the manner of the feast of booths, remembering how not long before, during the feast of booths, they had been wandering in the mountains and caves like wild animals.

[7] Therefore bearing ivy-wreathed wands and beautiful branches and also fronds of palm, they offered hymns of thanksgiving to him who had given success to the purifying of his own holy place.

[8] They decreed by public ordinance and vote that the whole nation of the Jews should observe these days every year.

[9] Such then was the end of Antiochus, who was called Epiphanes.

[10] Now we will tell what took place under Antiochus Eupator, who was the son of that ungodly man, and will give a brief summary of the principal calamities of the wars.

[11] This man, when he succeeded to the kingdom, appointed one Lysias to have charge of the government and to be chief governor of Coelesyria and Phoenicia.

[12] Ptolemy, who was called Macron, took the lead in showing justice to the Jews because of the wrong that had been done to them, and attempted to maintain peaceful relations with them.

[13] As a result he was accused before Eupator by the king's friends. He heard himself called a traitor at every turn, because he had abandoned Cyprus, which Philometor had entrusted to him, and had gone over to Antiochus Epiphanes. Unable to command the respect due his office, he took poison and ended his life.

[14] When Gorgias became governor of the region, he maintained a force of mercenaries, and at every turn kept on warring against the Jews.

[15] Besides this, the Idumeans, who had control of important strongholds, were harassing the Jews; they received those who were banished from Jerusalem, and endeavored to keep up the war.

[16] But Maccabeus and his men, after making solemn supplication and beseeching God to fight on their side, rushed to the strongholds of the Idumeans.

[17] Attacking them vigorously, they gained possession of the places, and beat off all who fought upon the wall, and slew those whom they encountered, killing no fewer than twenty thousand.

[18] When no less than nine thousand took refuge in two very strong towers well equipped to withstand a siege,

[19] Maccabeus left Simon and Joseph, and also Zacchaeus and his men, a force sufficient to besiege them; and he himself set off for places where he was more urgently needed.

[20] But the men with Simon, who were money-hungry, were bribed by some of those who were in the towers, and on receiving seventy thousand drachmas let some of them slip away.

[21] When word of what had happened came to Maccabeus, he gathered the leaders of the people, and accused these men of having sold their brethren for money by setting their enemies free to fight against them.

[22] Then he slew these men who had turned traitor, and immediately captured the two towers.

[23] Having success at arms in everything he undertook, he destroyed more than twenty thousand in the two strongholds.

[24] Now Timothy, who had been defeated by the Jews before, gathered a tremendous force of mercenaries and collected the cavalry from Asia in no small number. He came on, intending to take Judea by storm.

[25] As he drew near, Maccabeus and his men sprinkled dust upon their heads and girded their loins with sackcloth, in supplication to God.

[26] Falling upon the steps before the altar, they besought him to be gracious to them and to be an enemy to their enemies and an adversary to their adversaries, as the law declares.

[27] And rising from their prayer they took up their arms and advanced a considerable distance from the city; and when they came near to the enemy they halted.

[28] Just as dawn was breaking, the two armies joined battle, the one having as pledge of success and victory not only their valor but their reliance upon the Lord, while the other made rage their leader in the fight.

[29] When the battle became fierce, there appeared to the enemy from heaven five resplendent men on horses with golden bridles, and they were leading the Jews.

[30] Surrounding Maccabeus and protecting him with their own armor and weapons, they kept him from being wounded. And they showered arrows and thunderbolts upon the enemy, so that, confused and blinded, they were thrown into disorder and cut to pieces.

[31] Twenty thousand five hundred were slaughtered, besides six hundred horsemen.

[32] Timothy himself fled to a stronghold called Gazara, especially well garrisoned, where Chaereas was commander.

[33] Then Maccabeus and his men were glad, and they besieged the fort for four days.

[34] The men within, relying on the strength of the place, blasphemed terribly and hurled out wicked words.

[35] But at dawn of the fifth day, twenty young men in the army of Maccabeus, fired with anger because of the blasphemies, bravely stormed the wall and with savage fury cut down every one they met.

[36] Others who came up in the same way wheeled around against the defenders and set fire to the towers; they kindled fires and burned the blasphemers alive. Others broke open the gates and let in the rest of the force, and they occupied the city.

[37] They killed Timothy, who was hidden in a cistern, and his brother Chaereas, and Apollophanes.

[38] When they had accomplished these things, with hymns and thanksgivings they blessed the Lord who shows great kindness to Israel and gives them the victory.

2Mac.11

[1] Very soon after this, Lysias, the king's guardian and kinsman, who was in charge of the government, being vexed at what had happened,

[2] gathered about eighty thousand men and all his cavalry and came against the Jews. He intended to make the city a home for Greeks,

[3] and to levy tribute on the temple as he did on the sacred places of the other nations, and to put up the high priesthood for sale every year.

[4] He took no account whatever of the power of God, but was elated with his ten thousands of infantry, and his thousands of cavalry, and his eighty elephants.

[5] Invading Judea, he approached Beth-zur, which was a fortified place about five leagues from Jerusalem, and pressed it hard.

[6] When Maccabeus and his men got word that Lysias was besieging the strongholds, they and all the people, with lamentations and tears, besought the Lord to send a good angel to save Israel.

[7] Maccabeus himself was the first to take up arms, and he urged the others to risk their lives with him to aid their brethren. Then they eagerly rushed off together.

[8] And there, while they were still near Jerusalem, a horseman appeared at their head, clothed in white and brandishing weapons of gold.

[9] And they all together praised the merciful God, and were strengthened in heart, ready to assail not only men but the wildest beasts or walls of iron.

[10] They advanced in battle order, having their heavenly ally, for the Lord had mercy on them.

[11] They hurled themselves like lions against the enemy, and slew eleven thousand of them and sixteen hundred horsemen, and forced all the rest to flee.

[12] Most of them got away stripped and wounded, and Lysias himself escaped by disgraceful flight.

[13] And as he was not without intelligence, he pondered over the defeat which had befallen him, and realized that the Hebrews were invincible because the mighty God fought on their side. So he sent to them

[14] and persuaded them to settle everything on just terms, promising that he would persuade the king, constraining him to be their friend.

[15] Maccabeus, having regard for the common good, agreed to all that Lysias urged. For the king granted every request in behalf of the Jews which Maccabeus delivered to Lysias in writing.

[16] The letter written to the Jews by Lysias was to this effect: "Lysias to the people of the Jews, greeting.

[17] John and Absalom, who were sent by you, have delivered your signed communication and have asked about the matters indicated therein.

[18] I have informed the king of everything that needed to be brought before him, and he has agreed to what was possible.

[19] If you will maintain your good will toward the government, I will endeavor for the future to help promote your welfare.

[20] And concerning these matters and their details, I have ordered these men and my representatives to confer with you.

[21] Farewell. The one hundred and forty-eighth year, Dioscorinthius twenty-fourth."

[22] The king's letter ran thus: "King Antiochus to his brother Lysias, greeting.

[23] Now that our father has gone on to the gods, we desire that the subjects of the kingdom be undisturbed in caring for their own affairs.

[24] We have heard that the Jews do not consent to our father's change to Greek customs but prefer their own way of living and ask that their own customs be allowed them.

[25] Accordingly, since we choose that this nation also be free from disturbance, our decision is that their temple be restored to them and that they live according to the customs of their ancestors.

[26] You will do well, therefore, to send word to them and give them pledges of friendship, so that they may know our policy and be of good cheer and go on happily in the conduct of their own affairs."

[27] To the nation the king's letter was as follows: "King Antiochus to the senate of the Jews and to the other Jews, greeting.

[28] If you are well, it is as we desire. We also are in good health.

[29] Menelaus has informed us that you wish to return home and look after your own affairs.

[30] Therefore those who go home by the thirtieth day of Xanthicus will have our pledge of friendship and full permission

[31] for the Jews to enjoy their own food and laws, just as formerly, and none of them shall be molested in any way for what he may have done in ignorance.

[32] And I have also sent Menelaus to encourage you.

[33] Farewell. The one hundred and forty-eighth year, Xanthicus fifteenth."

[34] The Romans also sent them a letter, which read thus: "Quintus Memmius and Titus Manius, envoys of the Romans, to the people of the Jews, greeting.

[35] With regard to what Lysias the kinsman of the king has granted you, we also give consent.

[36] But as to the matters which he decided are to be referred to the king, as soon as you have considered them, send some one promptly, so that we may make proposals appropriate for you. For we are on our way to Antioch.

[37] Therefore make haste and send some men, so that we may have your judgment.

[38] Farewell. The one hundred and forty-eighth year, Xanthicus fifteenth."

2Mac.12

[1] When this agreement had been reached, Lysias returned to the king, and the Jews went about their farming.

[2] But some of the governors in various places, Timothy and Apollonius the son of Gennaeus, as well as Hieronymus and Demophon, and in addition to these Nicanor the governor of Cyprus, would not let them live quietly and in peace.

[3] And some men of Joppa did so ungodly a deed as this: they invited the Jews who lived among them to embark, with their wives and children, on boats which they had provided, as though there were no ill will to the Jews;

[4] and this was done by public vote of the city. And when they accepted, because they wished to live peaceably and suspected nothing, the men of Joppa took them out to sea and drowned them, not less than two hundred.

[5] When Judas heard of the cruelty visited on his countrymen, he gave orders to his men

[6] and, calling upon God the righteous Judge, attacked the murderers of his brethren. He set fire to the harbor by night, and burned the boats, and massacred those who had taken refuge there.

[7] Then, because the city's gates were closed, he withdrew, intending to come again and root out the whole community of Joppa.

[8] But learning that the men in Jamnia meant in the same way to wipe out the Jews who were living among them,

[9] he attacked the people of Jamnia by night and set fire to the harbor and the fleet, so that the glow of the light was seen in Jerusalem, thirty miles distant.

[10] When they had gone more than a mile from there, on their march against Timothy, not less than five thousand Arabs with five hundred horsemen attacked them.

[11] After a hard fight Judas and his men won the victory, by the help of God. The defeated nomads besought Judas to grant them pledges of friendship, promising to give him cattle and to help his people in all other ways.

[12] Judas, thinking that they might really be useful in many ways, agreed to make peace with them; and after receiving his pledges they departed to their tents.

[13] He also attacked a certain city which was strongly fortified with earthworks and walls, and inhabited by all sorts of Gentiles. Its name was Caspin.

[14] And those who were within, relying on the strength of the walls and on their supply of provisions, behaved most insolently toward Judas and his men, railing at them and even blaspheming and saying unholy things.

[15] But Judas and his men, calling upon the great Sovereign of the world, who without battering-rams or engines of war overthrew Jericho in the days of Joshua, rushed furiously upon the walls.

[16] They took the city by the will of God, and slaughtered untold numbers, so that the adjoining lake, a quarter of a mile wide, appeared to be running over with blood.

[17] When they had gone ninety-five miles from there, they came to Charax, to the Jews who are called Toubiani.

[18] They did not find Timothy in that region, for he had by then departed from the region without accomplishing anything, though in one place he had left a very strong garrison.

[19] Dositheus and Sosipater, who were captains under Maccabeus, marched out and destroyed those whom Timothy had left in the stronghold, more than ten thousand men.

[20] But Maccabeus arranged his army in divisions, set men in command of the divisions, and hastened after Timothy, who had with him a hundred and twenty thousand infantry and two thousand five hundred cavalry.

[21] When Timothy learned of the approach of Judas, he sent off the women and the children and also the baggage to a place

called Carnaim; for that place was hard to besiege and difficult of access because of the narrowness of all the approaches.

[22] But when Judas' first division appeared, terror and fear came over the enemy at the manifestation to them of him who sees all things; and they rushed off in flight and were swept on, this way and that, so that often they were injured by their own men and pierced by the points of their swords.

[23] And Judas pressed the pursuit with the utmost vigor, putting the sinners to the sword, and destroyed as many as thirty thousand men.

[24] Timothy himself fell into the hands of Dositheus and Sosipater and their men. With great guile he besought them to let him go in safety, because he held the parents of most of them and the brothers of some and no consideration would be shown them.

[25] And when with many words he had confirmed his solemn promise to restore them unharmed, they let him go, for the sake of saving their brethren.

[26] Then Judas marched against Carnaim and the temple of Atargatis, and slaughtered twenty-five thousand people.

[27] After the rout and destruction of these, he marched also against Ephron, a fortified city where Lysias dwelt with multitudes of people of all nationalities. Stalwart young men took their stand before the walls and made a vigorous defense; and great stores of war engines and missiles were there.

[28] But the Jews called upon the Sovereign who with power shatters the might of his enemies, and they got the city into their hands, and killed as many as twenty-five thousand of those who were within it.

[29] Setting out from there, they hastened to Scythopolis, which is seventy-five miles from Jerusalem.

[30] But when the Jews who dwelt there bore witness to the good will which the people of Scythopolis had shown them and their kind treatment of them in times of misfortune,

[31] they thanked them and exhorted them to be well disposed to their race in the future also. Then they went up to Jerusalem, as the feast of weeks was close at hand.

[32] After the feast called Pentecost, they hastened against Gorgias, the governor of Idumea.

[33] And he came out with three thousand infantry and four hundred cavalry.

[34] When they joined battle, it happened that a few of the Jews fell.

[35] But a certain Dositheus, one of Bacenor's men, who was on horseback and was a strong man, caught hold of Gorgias, and grasping his cloak was dragging him off by main strength, wishing to take the accursed man alive, when one of the Thracian horsemen bore down upon him and cut off his arm; so Gorgias escaped and reached Marisa.

[36] As Esdris and his men had been fighting for a long time and were weary, Judas called upon the Lord to show himself their ally and leader in the battle.

[37] In the language of their fathers he raised the battle cry, with hymns; then he charged against Gorgias' men when they were not expecting it, and put them to flight.

[38] Then Judas assembled his army and went to the city of Adullam. As the seventh day was coming on, they purified themselves according to the custom, and they kept the sabbath there.

[39] On the next day, as by that time it had become necessary, Judas and his men went to take up the bodies of the fallen and to bring them back to lie with their kinsmen in the sepulchres of their fathers.

[40] Then under the tunic of every one of the dead they found sacred tokens of the idols of Jamnia, which the law forbids the Jews to wear. And it became clear to all that this was why these men had fallen.

[41] So they all blessed the ways of the Lord, the righteous Judge, who reveals the things that are hidden;

[42] and they turned to prayer, beseeching that the sin which had been committed might be wholly blotted out. And the noble Judas exhorted the people to keep themselves free from sin, for they had seen with their own eyes what had happened because of the sin of those who had fallen.

[43] He also took up a collection, man by man, to the amount of two thousand drachmas of silver, and sent it to Jerusalem to provide for a sin offering. In doing this he acted very well and honorably, taking account of the resurrection.

[44] For if he were not expecting that those who had fallen would rise again, it would have been superfluous and foolish to pray for the dead.

[45] But if he was looking to the splendid reward that is laid up for those who fall asleep in godliness, it was a holy and pious thought. Therefore he made atonement for the dead, that they might be delivered from their sin.

2Mac.13

[1] In the one hundred and forty-ninth year word came to Judas and his men that Antiochus Eupator was coming with a great army against Judea,

[2] and with him Lysias, his guardian, who had charge of the government. Each of them had a Greek force of one hundred and ten thousand infantry, five thousand three hundred cavalry, twenty-two elephants, and three hundred chariots armed with scythes.

[3] Menelaus also joined them and with utter hypocrisy urged Antiochus on, not for the sake of his country's welfare, but because he thought that he would be established in office.

[4] But the King of kings aroused the anger of Antiochus against the scoundrel; and when Lysias informed him that this man was to blame for all the trouble, he ordered them to take him to Beroea and to put him to death by the method which is the custom in that place.

[5] For there is a tower in that place, fifty cubits high, full of ashes, and it has a rim running around it which on all sides inclines precipitously into the ashes.

[6] There they all push to destruction any man guilty of sacrilege or notorious for other crimes.

[7] By such a fate it came about that Menelaus the lawbreaker died, without even burial in the earth.

[8] And this was eminently just; because he had committed many sins against the altar whose fire and ashes were holy, he met his death in ashes.

[9] The king with barbarous arrogance was coming to show the Jews things far worse than those that had been done in his father's time.

[10] But when Judas heard of this, he ordered the people to call upon the Lord day and night, now if ever to help those who were on the point of being deprived of the law and their country and the holy temple,

[11] and not to let the people who had just begun to revive fall into the hands of the blasphemous Gentiles.

[12] When they had all joined in the same petition and had besought the merciful Lord with weeping and fasting and lying prostrate for three days without ceasing, Judas exhorted them and ordered them to stand ready.

[13] After consulting privately with the elders, he determined to march out and decide the matter by the help of God before the king's army could enter Judea and get possession of the city.

[14] So, committing the decision to the Creator of the world and exhorting his men to fight nobly to the death for the laws, temple, city, country, and commonwealth, he pitched his camp near Modein.

[15] He gave his men the watchword, "God's victory," and with a picked force of the bravest young men, he attacked the king's pavilion at night and slew as many as two thousand men in the camp. He stabbed the leading elephant and its rider.

[16] In the end they filled the camp with terror and confusion and withdrew in triumph.

[17] This happened, just as day was dawning, because the Lord's help protected him.

[18] The king, having had a taste of the daring of the Jews, tried strategy in attacking their positions.

[19] He advanced against Beth-zur, a strong fortress of the Jews, was turned back, attacked again, and was defeated.

[20] Judas sent in to the garrison whatever was necessary.

[21] But Rhodocus, a man from the ranks of the Jews, gave secret information to the enemy; he was sought for, caught, and put in prison.

[22] The king negotiated a second time with the people in Beth-zur, gave pledges, received theirs, withdrew, attacked Judas and his men, was defeated;

[23] he got word that Philip, who had been left in charge of the government, had revolted in Antioch; he was dismayed, called in the Jews, yielded and swore to observe all their rights, settled with them and offered sacrifice, honored the sanctuary and showed generosity to the holy place.

[24] He received Maccabeus, left Hegemonides as governor from Ptolemais to Gerar,

[25] and went to Ptolemais. The people of Ptolemais were indignant over the treaty; in fact they were so angry that they wanted to annul its terms.

[26] Lysias took the public platform, made the best possible defense, convinced them, appeased them, gained their good will, and set out for Antioch. This is how the king's attack and withdrawal turned out.

2Mac.14

[1] Three years later, word came to Judas and his men that Demetrius, the son of Seleucus, had sailed into the harbor of Tripolis with a strong army and a fleet,

[2] and had taken possession of the country, having made away with Antiochus and his guardian Lysias.

[3] Now a certain Alcimus, who had formerly been high priest but had wilfully defiled himself in the times of separation, realized that there was no way for him to be safe or to have access again to the holy altar,

[4] and went to King Demetrius in about the one hundred and fifty-first year, presenting to him a crown of gold and a palm, and besides these some of the customary olive branches from the temple. During that day he kept quiet.

[5] But he found an opportunity that furthered his mad purpose when he was invited by Demetrius to a meeting of the council and was asked about the disposition and intentions of the Jews. He answered:

[6] "Those of the Jews who are called Hasideans, whose leader is Judas Maccabeus, are keeping up war and stirring up sedition, and will not let the kingdom attain tranquillity.

[7] Therefore I have laid aside my ancestral glory -- I mean the high priesthood -- and have now come here,

[8] first because I am genuinely concerned for the interests of the king, and second because I have regard also for my fellow citizens. For through the folly of those whom I have mentioned our whole nation is now in no small misfortune.

[9] Since you are acquainted, O king, with the details of this matter, deign to take thought for our country and our hard-pressed nation with the gracious kindness which you show to all.

[10] For as long as Judas lives, it is impossible for the government to find peace."

[11] When he had said this, the rest of the king's friends, who were hostile to Judas, quickly inflamed Demetrius still more.

[12] And he immediately chose Nicanor, who had been in command of the elephants, appointed him governor of Judea, and sent him off

[13] with orders to kill Judas and scatter his men, and to set up Alcimus as high priest of the greatest temple.

[14] And the Gentiles throughout Judea, who had fled before Judas, flocked to join Nicanor, thinking that the misfortunes

and calamities of the Jews would mean prosperity for themselves.

[15] When the Jews heard of Nicanor's coming and the gathering of the Gentiles, they sprinkled dust upon their heads and prayed to him who established his own people for ever and always upholds his own heritage by manifesting himself.

[16] At the command of the leader, they set out from there immediately and engaged them in battle at a village called Dessau.

[17] Simon, the brother of Judas, had encountered Nicanor, but had been temporarily checked because of the sudden consternation created by the enemy.

[18] Nevertheless Nicanor, hearing of the valor of Judas and his men and their courage in battle for their country, shrank from deciding the issue by bloodshed.

[19] Therefore he sent Posidonius and Theodotus and Mattathias to give and receive pledges of friendship.

[20] When the terms had been fully considered, and the leader had informed the people, and it had appeared that they were of one mind, they agreed to the covenant.

[21] And the leaders set a day on which to meet by themselves. A chariot came forward from each army; seats of honor were set in place;

[22] Judas posted armed men in readiness at key places to prevent sudden treachery on the part of the enemy; they held the proper conference.

[23] Nicanor stayed on in Jerusalem and did nothing out of the way, but dismissed the flocks of people that had gathered.

[24] And he kept Judas always in his presence; he was warmly attached to the man.

[25] And he urged him to marry and have children; so he married, settled down, and shared the common life.

[26] But when Alcimus noticed their good will for one another, he took the covenant that had been made and went to Demetrius. He told him that Nicanor was disloyal to the government, for he had appointed that conspirator against the kingdom, Judas, to be his successor.

[27] The king became excited and, provoked by the false accusations of that depraved man, wrote to Nicanor, stating that he was displeased with the covenant and commanding him to send Maccabeus to Antioch as a prisoner without delay.

[28] When this message came to Nicanor, he was troubled and grieved that he had to annul their agreement when the man had done no wrong.

[29] Since it was not possible to oppose the king, he watched for an opportunity to accomplish this by a stratagem.

[30] But Maccabeus, noticing that Nicanor was more austere in his dealings with him and was meeting him more rudely than had been his custom, concluded that this austerity did not spring from the best motives. So he gathered not a few of his men, and went into hiding from Nicanor.

[31] When the latter became aware that he had been cleverly outwitted by the man, he went to the great and holy temple while the priests were offering the customary sacrifices, and commanded them to hand the man over.

[32] And when they declared on oath that they did not know where the man was whom he sought,

[33] he stretched out his right hand toward the sanctuary, and swore this oath: "If you do not hand Judas over to me as a prisoner, I will level this precinct of God to the ground and tear down the altar, and I will build here a splendid temple to Dionysus."

[34] Having said this, he went away. Then the priests stretched forth their hands toward heaven and called upon the constant Defender of our nation, in these words:

[35] "O Lord of all, who hast need of nothing, thou wast pleased that there be a temple for thy habitation among us;

[36] so now, O holy One, Lord of all holiness, keep undefiled for ever this house that has been so recently purified."

[37] A certain Razis, one of the elders of Jerusalem, was denounced to Nicanor as a man who loved his fellow citizens and was very well thought of and for his good will was called father of the Jews.

[38] For in former times, when there was no mingling with the Gentiles, he had been accused of Judaism, and for Judaism he had with all zeal risked body and life.

[39] Nicanor, wishing to exhibit the enmity which he had for the Jews, sent more than five hundred soldiers to arrest him;

[40] for he thought that by arresting him he would do them an injury.

[41] When the troops were about to capture the tower and were forcing the door of the courtyard, they ordered that fire be brought and the doors burned. Being surrounded, Razis fell upon his own sword,

[42] preferring to die nobly rather than to fall into the hands of sinners and suffer outrages unworthy of his noble birth.

[43] But in the heat of the struggle he did not hit exactly, and the crowd was now rushing in through the doors. He bravely ran up on the wall, and manfully threw himself down into the crowd.

[44] But as they quickly drew back, a space opened and he fell in the middle of the empty space.

[45] Still alive and aflame with anger, he rose, and though his blood gushed forth and his wounds were severe he ran through the crowd; and standing upon a steep rock,

[46] with his blood now completely drained from him, he tore out his entrails, took them with both hands and hurled them at the crowd, calling upon the Lord of life and spirit to give them back to him again. This was the manner of his death.

2Mac.15

[1] When Nicanor heard that Judas and his men were in the region of Samaria, he made plans to attack them with complete safety on the day of rest.

[2] And when the Jews who were compelled to follow him said, "Do not destroy so savagely and barbarously, but show

respect for the day which he who sees all things has honored and hallowed above other days,"

[3] the thrice-accursed wretch asked if there were a sovereign in heaven who had commanded the keeping of the sabbath day.

[4] And when they declared, "It is the living Lord himself, the Sovereign in heaven, who ordered us to observe the seventh day,"

[5] he replied, "And I am a sovereign also, on earth, and I command you to take up arms and finish the king's business." Nevertheless, he did not succeed in carrying out his abominable design.

[6] This Nicanor in his utter boastfulness and arrogance had determined to erect a public monument of victory over Judas and his men.

[7] But Maccabeus did not cease to trust with all confidence that he would get help from the Lord.

[8] And he exhorted his men not to fear the attack of the Gentiles, but to keep in mind the former times when help had come to them from heaven, and now to look for the victory which the Almighty would give them.

[9] Encouraging them from the law and the prophets, and reminding them also of the struggles they had won, he made them the more eager.

[10] And when he had aroused their courage, he gave his orders, at the same time pointing out the perfidy of the Gentiles and their violation of oaths.

[11] He armed each of them not so much with confidence in shields and spears as with the inspiration of brave words, and he cheered them all by relating a dream, a sort of vision, which was worthy of belief.

[12] What he saw was this: Onias, who had been high priest, a noble and good man, of modest bearing and gentle manner, one who spoke fittingly and had been trained from childhood in all that belongs to excellence, was praying with outstretched hands for the whole body of the Jews.

[13] Then likewise a man appeared, distinguished by his gray hair and dignity, and of marvelous majesty and authority.

[14] And Onias spoke, saying, "This is a man who loves the brethren and prays much for the people and the holy city, Jeremiah, the prophet of God."

[15] Jeremiah stretched out his right hand and gave to Judas a golden sword, and as he gave it he addressed him thus:

[16] "Take this holy sword, a gift from God, with which you will strike down your adversaries."

[17] Encouraged by the words of Judas, so noble and so effective in arousing valor and awaking manliness in the souls of the young, they determined not to carry on a campaign but to attack bravely, and to decide the matter, by fighting hand to hand with all courage, because the city and the sanctuary and the temple were in danger.

[18] Their concern for wives and children, and also for brethren and relatives, lay upon them less heavily; their greatest and first fear was for the consecrated sanctuary.

[19] And those who had to remain in the city were in no little distress, being anxious over the encounter in the open country.

[20] When all were now looking forward to the coming decision, and the enemy was already close at hand with their army drawn up for battle, the elephants strategically stationed and the cavalry deployed on the flanks,

[21] Maccabeus, perceiving the hosts that were before him and the varied supply of arms and the savagery of the elephants, stretched out his hands toward heaven and called upon the Lord who works wonders; for he knew that it is not by arms, but as the Lord decides, that he gains the victory for those who deserve it.

[22] And he called upon him in these words: "O Lord, thou didst send thy angel in the time of Hezekiah king of Judea, and he slew fully a hundred and eighty-five thousand in the camp of Sennacherib.

[23] So now, O Sovereign of the heavens, send a good angel to carry terror and trembling before us.

[24] By the might of thy arm may these blasphemers who come against thy holy people be struck down." With these words he ended his prayer.

[25] Nicanor and his men advanced with trumpets and battle songs;

[26] and Judas and his men met the enemy in battle with invocation to God and prayers.

[27] So, fighting with their hands and praying to God in their hearts, they laid low no less than thirty-five thousand men, and were greatly gladdened by God's manifestation.

[28] When the action was over and they were returning with joy, they recognized Nicanor, lying dead, in full armor.

[29] Then there was shouting and tumult, and they blessed the Sovereign Lord in the language of their fathers.

[30] And the man who was ever in body and soul the defender of his fellow citizens, the man who maintained his youthful good will toward his countrymen, ordered them to cut off Nicanor's head and arm and carry them to Jerusalem.

[31] And when he arrived there and had called his countrymen together and stationed the priests before the altar, he sent for those who were in the citadel.

[32] He showed them the vile Nicanor's head and that profane man's arm, which had been boastfully stretched out against the holy house of the Almighty;

[33] and he cut out the tongue of the ungodly Nicanor and said that he would give it piecemeal to the birds and hang up these rewards of his folly opposite the sanctuary.

[34] And they all, looking to heaven, blessed the Lord who had manifested himself, saying, "Blessed is he who has kept his own place undefiled."

[35] And he hung Nicanor's head from the citadel, a clear and conspicuous sign to every one of the help of the Lord.

[36] And they all decreed by public vote never to let this day go unobserved, but to celebrate the thirteenth day of the twelfth month -- which is called Adar in the Syrian language -- the day before Mordecai's day.

[37] This, then, is how matters turned out with Nicanor. And from that time the city has been in the possession of the Hebrews. So I too will here end my story.

[38] If it is well told and to the point, that is what I myself desired; if it is poorly done and mediocre, that was the best I could do.

[39] For just as it is harmful to drink wine alone, or, again, to drink water alone, while wine mixed with water is sweet and delicious and enhances one's enjoyment, so also the style of the story delights the ears of those who read the work. And here will be the end.

3 Maccabees

3Mac.1

[1] When Philopator learned from those who returned that the regions which he had controlled had been seized by Antiochus, he gave orders to all his forces, both infantry and cavalry, took with him his sister Arsinoe, and marched out to the region near Raphia, where Antiochus's supporters were encamped.

[2] But a certain Theodotus, determined to carry out the plot he had devised, took with him the best of the Ptolemaic arms that had been previously issued to him, and crossed over by night to the tent of Ptolemy, intending single-handed to kill him and thereby end the war.

[3] But Dositheus, known as the son of Drimylus, a Jew by birth who later changed his religion and apostatized from the ancestral traditions, had led the king away and arranged that a certain insignificant man should sleep in the tent; and so it turned out that this man incurred the vengeance meant for the king.

[4] When a bitter fight resulted, and matters were turning out rather in favor of Antiochus, Arsinoe went to the troops with wailing and tears, her locks all disheveled, and exhorted them to defend themselves and their children and wives bravely, promising to give them each two minas of gold if they won the battle.

[5] And so it came about that the enemy was routed in the action, and many captives also were taken.

[6] Now that he had foiled the plot, Ptolemy decided to visit the neighboring cities and encourage them.

[7] By doing this, and by endowing their sacred enclosures with gifts, he strengthened the morale of his subjects.

[8] Since the Jews had sent some of their council and elders to greet him, to bring him gifts of welcome, and to congratulate him on what had happened, he was all the more eager to visit them as soon as possible.

[9] After he had arrived in Jerusalem, he offered sacrifice to the supreme God and made thank-offerings and did what was fitting for the holy place. Then, upon entering the place and being impressed by its excellence and its beauty,

[10] he marveled at the good order of the temple, and conceived a desire to enter the holy of holies.

[11] When they said that this was not permitted, because not even members of their own nation were allowed to enter, nor even all of the priests, but only the high priest who was pre-eminent over all, and he only once a year, the king was by no means persuaded.

[12] Even after the law had been read to him, he did not cease to maintain that he ought to enter, saying, "Even if those men are deprived of this honor, I ought not to be."

[13] And he inquired why, when he entered every other temple, no one there had stopped him.

[14] And someone heedlessly said that it was wrong to take this as a sign in itself.

[15] "But since this has happened," the king said, "why should not I at least enter, whether they wish it or not?"

[16] Then the priests in all their vestments prostrated themselves and entreated the supreme God to aid in the present situation and to avert the violence of this evil design, and they filled the temple with cries and tears;

[17] and those who remained behind in the city were agitated and hurried out, supposing that something mysterious was occurring.

[18] The virgins who had been enclosed in their chambers rushed out with their mothers, sprinkled their hair with dust, and filled the streets with groans and lamentations.

[19] Those women who had recently been arrayed for marriage abandoned the bridal chambers prepared for wedded union, and, neglecting proper modesty, in a disorderly rush flocked together in the city.

[20] Mothers and nurses abandoned even newborn children here and there, some in houses and some in the streets, and without a backward look they crowded together at the most high temple.

[21] Various were the supplications of those gathered there because of what the king was profanely plotting.

[22] In addition, the bolder of the citizens would not tolerate the completion of his plans or the fulfillment of his intended purpose.

[23] They shouted to their fellows to take arms and die courageously for the ancestral law, and created a considerable disturbance in the holy place; and being barely restrained by the old men and the elders, they resorted to the same posture of supplication as the others.

[24] Meanwhile the crowd, as before, was engaged in prayer,

[25] while the elders near the king tried in various ways to change his arrogant mind from the plan that he had conceived.

[26] But he, in his arrogance, took heed of nothing, and began now to approach, determined to bring the aforesaid plan to a conclusion.

[27] When those who were around him observed this, they turned, together with our people, to call upon him who has all power to defend them in the present trouble and not to overlook this unlawful and haughty deed.

[28] The continuous, vehement, and concerted cry of the crowds resulted in an immense uproar;

[29] for it seemed that not only the men but also the walls and the whole earth around echoed, because indeed all at that time preferred death to the profanation of the place.

3Mac.2

[1] Then the high priest Simon, facing the sanctuary, bending his knees and extending his hands with calm dignity, prayed as

follows:

[2] "Lord, Lord, king of the heavens, and sovereign of all creation, holy among the holy ones, the only ruler, almighty, give attention to us who are suffering grievously from an impious and profane man, puffed up in his audacity and power.

[3] For you, the creator of all things and the governor of all, are a just Ruler, and you judge those who have done anything in insolence and arrogance.

[4] You destroyed those who in the past committed injustice, among whom were even giants who trusted in their strength and boldness, whom you destroyed by bringing upon them a boundless flood.

[5] You consumed with fire and sulphur the men of Sodom who acted arrogantly, who were notorious for their vices; and you made them an example to those who should come afterward.

[6] You made known your mighty power by inflicting many and varied punishments on the audacious Pharaoh who had enslaved your holy people Israel.

[7] And when he pursued them with chariots and a mass of troops, you overwhelmed him in the depths of the sea, but carried through safely those who had put their confidence in you, the Ruler over the whole creation.

[8] And when they had seen works of your hands, they praised you, the Almighty.

[9] You, O King, when you had created the boundless and immeasurable earth, chose this city and sanctified this place for your name, though you have no need of anything; and when you had glorified it by your magnificent manifestation, you made it a firm foundation for the glory of your great and honored name.

[10] And because you love the house of Israel, you promised that if we should have reverses, and tribulation should overtake us, you would listen to our petition when we come to this place and pray.

[11] And indeed you are faithful and true.

[12] And because oftentimes when our fathers were oppressed you helped them in their humiliation, and rescued them from great evils,

[13] see now, O holy King, that because of our many and great sins we are crushed with suffering, subjected to our enemies, and overtaken by helplessness.

[14] In our downfall this audacious and profane man undertakes to violate the holy place on earth dedicated to your glorious name.

[15] For your dwelling, the heaven of heavens, is unapproachable by man.

[16] But because you graciously bestowed your glory upon your people Israel, you sanctified this place.

[17] Do not punish us for the defilement committed by these men, or call us to account for this profanation, lest the transgressors boast in their wrath or exult in the arrogance of their tongue, saying,

[18] `We have trampled down the house of the sanctuary as offensive houses are trampled down.'

[19] Wipe away our sins and disperse our errors, and reveal your mercy at this hour.

[20] Speedily let your mercies overtake us, and put praises in the mouth of those who are downcast and broken in spirit, and give us peace."

[21] Thereupon God, who oversees all things, the first Father of all, holy among the holy ones, having heard the lawful supplication, scourged him who had exalted himself in insolence and audacity.

[22] He shook him on this side and that as a reed is shaken by the wind, so that he lay helpless on the ground and, besides being paralyzed in his limbs, was unable even to speak, since he was smitten by a righteous judgment.

[23] Then both friends and bodyguards, seeing the severe punishment that had overtaken him, and fearing lest he should lose his life, quickly dragged him out, panic-stricken in their exceedingly great fear.

[24] After a while he recovered, and though he had been punished, he by no means repented, but went away uttering bitter threats.

[25] When he arrived in Egypt, he increased in his deeds of malice, abetted by the previously mentioned drinking companions and comrades, who were strangers to everything just.

[26] He was not content with his uncounted licentious deeds, but he also continued with such audacity that he framed evil reports in the various localities; and many of his friends, intently observing the king's purpose, themselves also followed his will.

[27] He proposed to inflict public disgrace upon the Jewish community, and he set up a stone on the tower in the courtyard with this inscription:

[28] "None of those who do not sacrifice shall enter their sanctuaries, and all Jews shall be subjected to a registration involving poll tax and to the status of slaves. Those who object to this are to be taken by force and put to death;

[29] those who are registered are also to be branded on their bodies by fire with the ivy-leaf symbol of Dionysus, and they shall also be reduced to their former limited status."

[30] In order that he might not appear to be an enemy to all, he inscribed below: "But if any of them prefer to join those who have been initiated into the mysteries, they shall have equal citizenship with the Alexandrians."

[31] Now some, however, with an obvious abhorrence of the price to be exacted for maintaining the religion of their city, readily gave themselves up, since they expected to enhance their reputation by their future association with the king.

[32] But the majority acted firmly with a courageous spirit and did not depart from their religion; and by paying money in exchange for life they confidently attempted to save themselves from the registration.

[33] They remained resolutely hopeful of obtaining help, and they abhorred those who separated themselves from them, considering them to be enemies of the Jewish nation, and depriving them of common fellowship and mutual help.
3Mac.3
[1] When the impious king comprehended this situation, he became so infuriated that not only was he enraged against those Jews who lived in Alexandria, but was still more bitterly hostile toward those in the countryside; and he ordered that all should promptly be gathered into one place, and put to death by the most cruel means.
[2] While these matters were being arranged, a hostile rumor was circulated against the Jewish nation by men who conspired to do them ill, a pretext being given by a report that they hindered others from the observance of their customs.
[3] The Jews, however, continued to maintain good will and unswerving loyalty toward the dynasty;
[4] but because they worshiped God and conducted themselves by his law, they kept their separateness with respect to foods. For this reason they appeared hateful to some;
[5] but since they adorned their style of life with the good deeds of upright people, they were established in good repute among all men.
[6] Nevertheless those of other races paid no heed to their good service to their nation, which was common talk among all;
[7] instead they gossiped about the differences in worship and foods, alleging that these people were loyal neither to the king nor to his authorities, but were hostile and greatly opposed to his government. So they attached no ordinary reproach to them.
[8] The Greeks in the city, though wronged in no way, when they saw an unexpected tumult around these people and the crowds that suddenly were forming, were not strong enough to help them, for they lived under tyranny. They did try to console them, being grieved at the situation, and expected that matters would change;
[9] for such a great community ought not be left to its fate when it had committed no offense.
[10] And already some of their neighbors and friends and business associates had taken some of them aside privately and were pledging to protect them and to exert more earnest efforts for their assistance.
[11] Then the king, boastful of his present good fortune, and not considering the might of the supreme God, but assuming that he would persevere constantly in his same purpose, wrote this letter against them:
[12] "King Ptolemy Philopator to his generals and soldiers in Egypt and all its districts, greetings and good health.
[13] I myself and our government are faring well.
[14] When our expedition took place in Asia, as you yourselves know, it was brought to conclusion, according to plan, by the gods' deliberate alliance with us in battle,
[15] and we considered that we should not rule the nations inhabiting Coele-Syria and Phoenicia by the power of the spear but should cherish them with clemency and great benevolence, gladly treating them well.
[16] And when we had granted very great revenues to the temples in the cities, we came on to Jerusalem also, and went up to honor the temple of those wicked people, who never cease from their folly.
[17] They accepted our presence by word, but insincerely by deed, because when we proposed to enter their inner temple and honor it with magnificent and most beautiful offerings,
[18] they were carried away by their traditional conceit, and excluded us from entering; but they were spared the exercise of our power because of the benevolence which we have toward all.
[19] By maintaining their manifest ill-will toward us, they become the only people among all nations who hold their heads high in defiance of kings and their own benefactors, and are unwilling to regard any action as sincere.
[20] "But we, when we arrived in Egypt victorious, accommodated ourselves to their folly and did as was proper, since we treat all nations with benevolence.
[21] Among other things, we made known to all our amnesty toward their compatriots here, both because of their alliance with us and the myriad affairs liberally entrusted to them from the beginning; and we ventured to make a change, by deciding both to deem them worthy of Alexandrian citizenship and to make them participants in our regular religious rites.
[22] But in their innate malice they took this in a contrary spirit, and disdained what is good. Since they incline constantly to evil,
[23] they not only spurn the priceless citizenship, but also both by speech and by silence they abominate those few among them who are sincerely disposed toward us; in every situation, in accordance with their infamous way of life, they secretly suspect that we may soon alter our policy.
[24] Therefore, fully convinced by these indications that they are ill-disposed toward us in every way, we have taken precautions lest, if a sudden disorder should later arise against us, we should have these impious people behind our backs as traitors and barbarous enemies.
[25] Therefore we have given orders that, as soon as this letter shall arrive, you are to send to us those who live among you, together with their wives and children, with insulting and harsh treatment, and bound securely with iron fetters, to suffer the sure and shameful death that befits enemies.
[26] For when these all have been punished, we are sure that for the remaining time the government will be established for ourselves in good order and in the best state.
[27] But whoever shelters any of the Jews, old people or children or even infants, will be tortured to death with the most hateful torments, together with his family.

[28] Any one willing to give information will receive the property of the one who incurs the punishment, and also two thousand drachmas from the royal treasury, and will be awarded his freedom.

[29] Every place detected sheltering a Jew is to be made unapproachable and burned with fire, and shall become useless for all time to any mortal creature."

[30] The letter was written in the above form.

3Mac.4

[1] In every place, then, where this decree arrived, a feast at public expense was arranged for the Gentiles with shouts and gladness, for the inveterate enmity which had long ago been in their minds was now made evident and outspoken.

[2] But among the Jews there was incessant mourning, lamentation, and tearful cries; everywhere their hearts were burning, and they groaned because of the unexpected destruction that had suddenly been decreed for them.

[3] What district or city, or what habitable place at all, or what streets were not filled with mourning and wailing for them?

[4] For with such a harsh and ruthless spirit were they being sent off, all together, by the generals in the several cities, that at the sight of their unusual punishments, even some of their enemies, perceiving the common object of pity before their eyes, reflected upon the uncertainty of life and shed tears at the most miserable expulsion of these people.

[5] For a multitude of gray-headed old men, sluggish and bent with age, was being led away, forced to march at a swift pace by the violence with which they were driven in such a shameful manner.

[6] And young women who had just entered the bridal chamber to share married life exchanged joy for wailing, their myrrh-perfumed hair sprinkled with ashes, and were carried away unveiled, all together raising a lament instead of a wedding song, as they were torn by the harsh treatment of the heathen.

[7] In bonds and in public view they were violently dragged along as far as the place of embarkation.

[8] Their husbands, in the prime of youth, their necks encircled with ropes instead of garlands, spent the remaining days of their marriage festival in lamentations instead of good cheer and youthful revelry, seeing death immediately before them.

[9] They were brought on board like wild animals, driven under the constraint of iron bonds; some were fastened by the neck to the benches of the boats, others had their feet secured by unbreakable fetters,

[10] and in addition they were confined under a solid deck, so that with their eyes in total darkness, they should undergo treatment befitting traitors during the whole voyage.

[11] When these men had been brought to the place called Schedia, and the voyage was concluded as the king had decreed, he commanded that they should be enclosed in the hippodrome which had been built with a monstrous perimeter wall in front of the city, and which was well suited to make them an obvious spectacle to all coming back into the city and to those from the city going out into the country, so that they could neither communicate with the king's forces nor in any way claim to be inside the circuit of the city.

[12] And when this had happened, the king, hearing that the Jews' compatriots from the city frequently went out in secret to lament bitterly the ignoble misfortune of their brothers,

[13] ordered in his rage that these men be dealt with in precisely the same fashion as the others, not omitting any detail of their punishment.

[14] The entire race was to be registered individually, not for the hard labor that has been briefly mentioned before, but to be tortured with the outrages that he had ordered, and at the end to be destroyed in the space of a single day.

[15] The registration of these people was therefore conducted with bitter haste and zealous intentness from the rising of the sun till its setting, and though uncompleted it stopped after forty days.

[16] The king was greatly and continually filled with joy, organizing feasts in honor of all his idols, with a mind alienated from truth and with a profane mouth, praising speechless things that are not able even to communicate or to come to one's help, and uttering improper words against the supreme God.

[17] But after the previously mentioned interval of time the scribes declared to the king that they were no longer able to take the census of the Jews because of their innumerable multitude,

[18] although most of them were still in the country, some still residing in their homes, and some at the place; the task was impossible for all the generals in Egypt.

[19] After he had threatened them severely, charging that they had been bribed to contrive a means of escape, he was clearly convinced about the matter

[20] when they said and proved that both the paper and the pens they used for writing had already given out.

[21] But this was an act of the invincible providence of him who was aiding the Jews from heaven.

3Mac.5

[1] Then the king, completely inflexible, was filled with overpowering anger and wrath; so he summoned Hermon, keeper of the elephants,

[2] and ordered him on the following day to drug all the elephants -- five hundred in number -- with large handfuls of frankincense and plenty of unmixed wine, and to drive them in, maddened by the lavish abundance of liquor, so that the Jews might meet their doom.

[3] When he had given these orders he returned to his feasting, together with those of his friends and of the army who were especially hostile toward the Jews.

[4] And Hermon, keeper of the elephants, proceeded faithfully to carry out the orders.

[5] The servants in charge of the Jews went out in the evening and bound the hands of the wretched people and arranged for their continued custody through the night, convinced that the whole nation would experience its final destruction.

[6] For to the Gentiles it appeared that the Jews were left without any aid,

[7] because in their bonds they were forcibly confined on every side. But with tears and a voice hard to silence they all called upon the Almighty Lord and Ruler of all power, their merciful God and Father, praying

[8] that he avert with vengeance the evil plot against them and in a glorious manifestation rescue them from the fate now prepared for them.

[9] So their entreaty ascended fervently to heaven.

[10] Hermon, however, when he had drugged the pitiless elephants until they had been filled with a great abundance of wine and satiated with frankincense, presented himself at the courtyard early in the morning to report to the king about these preparations.

[11] But the Lord sent upon the king a portion of sleep, that beneficence which from the beginning, night and day, is bestowed by him who grants it to whomever he wishes.

[12] And by the action of the Lord he was overcome by so pleasant and deep a sleep that he quite failed in his lawless purpose and was completely frustrated in his inflexible plan.

[13] Then the Jews, since they had escaped the appointed hour, praised their holy God and again begged him who is easily reconciled to show the might of his all-powerful hand to the arrogant Gentiles.

[14] But now, since it was nearly the middle of the tenth hour, the person who was in charge of the invitations, seeing that the guests were assembled, approached the king and nudged him.

[15] And when he had with difficulty roused him, he pointed out that the hour of the banquet was already slipping by, and he gave him an account of the situation.

[16] The king, after considering this, returned to his drinking, and ordered those present for the banquet to recline opposite him.

[17] When this was done he urged them to give themselves over to revelry and to make the present portion of the banquet joyful by celebrating all the more.

[18] After the party had been going on for some time, the king summoned Hermon and with sharp threats demanded to know why the Jews had been allowed to remain alive through the present day.

[19] But when he, with the corroboration of his friends, pointed out that while it was still night he had carried out completely the order given him,

[20] the king, possessed by a savagery worse than that of Phalaris, said that the Jews were benefited by today's sleep, "but," he added, "tomorrow without delay prepare the elephants in the same way for the destruction of the lawless Jews!"

[21] When the king had spoken, all those present readily and joyfully with one accord gave their approval, and each departed to his own home.

[22] But they did not so much employ the duration of the night in sleep as in devising all sorts of insults for those they thought to be doomed.

[23] Then, as soon as the cock had crowed in the early morning, Hermon, having equipped the beasts, began to move them along in the great colonnade.

[24] The crowds of the city had been assembled for this most pitiful spectacle and they were eagerly waiting for daybreak.

[25] But the Jews, at their last gasp, since the time had run out, stretched their hands toward heaven and with most tearful supplication and mournful dirges implored the supreme God to help them again at once.

[26] The rays of the sun were not yet shed abroad, and while the king was receiving his friends, Hermon arrived and invited him to come out, indicating that what the king desired was ready for action.

[27] But he, upon receiving the report and being struck by the unusual invitation to come out -- since he had been completely overcome by incomprehension -- inquired what the matter was for which this had been so zealously completed for him.

[28] This was the act of God who rules over all things, for he had implanted in the king's mind a forgetfulness of the things he had previously devised.

[29] Then Hermon and all the king's friends pointed out that the beasts and the armed forces were ready, "O king, according to your eager purpose."

[30] But at these words he was filled with an overpowering wrath, because by the providence of God his whole mind had been deranged in regard to these matters; and with a threatening look he said,

[31] "Were your parents or children present, I would have prepared them to be a rich feast for the savage beasts instead of the Jews, who give me no ground for complaint and have exhibited to an extraordinary degree a full and firm loyalty to my ancestors.

[32] In fact you would have been deprived of life instead of these, were it not for an affection arising from our nurture in common and your usefulness."

[33] So Hermon suffered an unexpected and dangerous threat, and his eyes wavered and his face fell.

[34] The king's friends one by one sullenly slipped away and dismissed the assembled people, each to his own occupation.

[35] Then the Jews, upon hearing what the king had said, praised the manifest Lord God, King of kings, since this also was his aid which they had received.

[36] The king, however, reconvened the party in the same manner and urged the guests to return to their celebrating.
[37] After summoning Hermon he said in a threatening tone, "How many times, you poor wretch, must I give you orders about these things?
[38] Equip the elephants now once more for the destruction of the Jews tomorrow!"
[39] But the officials who were at table with him, wondering at his instability of mind, remonstrated as follows:
[40] "O king, how long will you try us, as though we are idiots, ordering now for a third time that they be destroyed, and again revoking your decree in the matter?
[41] As a result the city is in a tumult because of its expectation; it is crowded with masses of people, and also in constant danger of being plundered."
[42] Upon this the king, a Phalaris in everything and filled with madness, took no account of the changes of mind which had come about within him for the protection of the Jews, and he firmly swore an irrevocable oath that he would send them to death without delay, mangled by the knees and feet of the beasts,
[43] and would also march against Judea and rapidly level it to the ground with fire and spear, and by burning to the ground the temple inaccessible to him would quickly render it forever empty of those who offered sacrifices there.
[44] Then the friends and officers departed with great joy, and they confidently posted the armed forces at the places in the city most favorable for keeping guard.
[45] Now when the beasts had been brought virtually to a state of madness, so to speak, by the very fragrant draughts of wine mixed with frankincense and had been equipped with frightful devices, the elephant keeper
[46] entered at about dawn into the courtyard -- the city now being filled with countless masses of people crowding their way into the hippodrome -- and urged the king on to the matter at hand.
[47] So he, when he had filled his impious mind with a deep rage, rushed out in full force along with the beasts, wishing to witness, with invulnerable heart and with his own eyes, the grievous and pitiful destruction of the aforementioned people.
[48] And when the Jews saw the dust raised by the elephants going out at the gate and by the following armed forces, as well as by the trampling of the crowd, and heard the loud and tumultuous noise,
[49] they thought that this was their last moment of life, the end of their most miserable suspense, and giving way to lamentation and groans they kissed each other, embracing relatives and falling into one another's arms -- parents and children, mothers and daughters, and others with babies at their breasts who were drawing their last milk.
[50] Not only this, but when they considered the help which they had received before from heaven they prostrated themselves with one accord on the ground, removing the babies from their breasts,
[51] and cried out in a very loud voice, imploring the Ruler over every power to manifest himself and be merciful to them, as they stood now at the gates of death.
3Mac.6
[1] Then a certain Eleazar, famous among the priests of the country, who had attained a ripe old age and throughout his life had been adorned with every virtue, directed the elders around him to cease calling upon the holy God and prayed as follows:
[2] "King of great power, Almighty God Most High, governing all creation with mercy,
[3] look upon the descendants of Abraham, O Father, upon the children of the sainted Jacob, a people of your consecrated portion who are perishing as foreigners in a foreign land.
[4] Pharaoh with his abundance of chariots, the former ruler of this Egypt, exalted with lawless insolence and boastful tongue, you destroyed together with his arrogant army by drowning them in the sea, manifesting the light of your mercy upon the nation of Israel.
[5] Sennacherib exulting in his countless forces, oppressive king of the Assyrians, who had already gained control of the whole world by the spear and was lifted up against your holy city, speaking grievous words with boasting and insolence, you, O Lord, broke in pieces, showing your power to many nations.
[6] The three companions in Babylon who had voluntarily surrendered their lives to the flames so as not to serve vain things, you rescued unharmed, even to a hair, moistening the fiery furnace with dew and turning the flame against all their enemies.
[7] Daniel, who through envious slanders was cast down into the ground to lions as food for wild beasts, you brought up to the light unharmed.
[8] And Jonah, wasting away in the belly of a huge, sea-born monster, you, Father, watched over and restored unharmed to all his family.
[9] And now, you who hate insolence, all-merciful and protector of all, reveal yourself quickly to those of the nation of Israel -- who are being outrageously treated by the abominable and lawless Gentiles.
[10] Even if our lives have become entangled in impieties in our exile, rescue us from the hand of the enemy, and destroy us, Lord, by whatever fate you choose.
[11] Let not the vain-minded praise their vanities at the destruction of your beloved people, saying, `Not even their god has rescued them.'
[12] But you, O Eternal One, who have all might and all power, watch over us now and have mercy upon us who by the senseless insolence of the lawless are being deprived of life in the manner of traitors.
[13] And let the Gentiles cower today in fear of your invincible might, O honored One, who have power to save the nation of

Jacob.

[14] The whole throng of infants and their parents entreat you with tears.

[15] Let it be shown to all the Gentiles that you are with us, O Lord, and have not turned your face from us; but just as you have said, `Not even when they were in the land of their enemies did I neglect them,' so accomplish it, O Lord."

[16] Just as Eleazar was ending his prayer, the king arrived at the hippodrome with the beasts and all the arrogance of his forces.

[17] And when the Jews observed this they raised great cries to heaven so that even the nearby valleys resounded with them and brought an uncontrollable terror upon the army.

[18] Then the most glorious, almighty, and true God revealed his holy face and opened the heavenly gates, from which two glorious angels of fearful aspect descended, visible to all but the Jews.

[19] They opposed the forces of the enemy and filled them with confusion and terror, binding them with immovable shackles.

[20] Even the king began to shudder bodily, and he forgot his sullen insolence.

[21] The beasts turned back upon the armed forces following them and began trampling and destroying them.

[22] Then the king's anger was turned to pity and tears because of the things that he had devised beforehand.

[23] For when he heard the shouting and saw them all fallen headlong to destruction, he wept and angrily threatened his friends, saying,

[24] "You are committing treason and surpassing tyrants in cruelty; and even me, your benefactor, you are now attempting to deprive of dominion and life by secretly devising acts of no advantage to the kingdom.

[25] Who is it that has taken each man from his home and senselessly gathered here those who faithfully have held the fortresses of our country?

[26] Who is it that has so lawlessly encompassed with outrageous treatment those who from the beginning differed from all nations in their goodwill toward us and often have accepted willingly the worst of human dangers?

[27] Loose and untie their unjust bonds! Send them back to their homes in peace, begging pardon for your former actions!

[28] Release the sons of the almighty and living God of heaven, who from the time of our ancestors until now has granted an unimpeded and notable stability to our government."

[29] These then were the things he said; and the Jews, immediately released, praised their holy God and Savior, since they now had escaped death.

[30] Then the king, when he had returned to the city, summoned the official in charge of the revenues and ordered him to provide to the Jews both wines and everything else needed for a festival of seven days, deciding that they should celebrate their rescue with all joyfulness in that same place in which they had expected to meet their destruction.

[31] Accordingly those disgracefully treated and near to death, or rather, who stood at its gates, arranged for a banquet of deliverance instead of a bitter and lamentable death, and full of joy they apportioned to celebrants the place which had been prepared for their destruction and burial.

[32] They ceased their chanting of dirges and took up the song of their fathers, praising God, their Savior and worker of wonders. Putting an end to all mourning and wailing, they formed choruses as a sign of peaceful joy.

[33] Likewise also the king, after convening a great banquet to celebrate these events, gave thanks to heaven unceasingly and lavishly for the unexpected rescue which he had experienced.

[34] And those who had previously believed that the Jews would be destroyed and become food for birds, and had joyfully registered them, groaned as they themselves were overcome by disgrace, and their fire-breathing boldness was ignominiously quenched.

[35] But the Jews, when they had arranged the aforementioned choral group, as we have said before, passed the time in feasting to the accompaniment of joyous thanksgiving and psalms.

[36] And when they had ordained a public rite for these things in their whole community and for their descendants, they instituted the observance of the aforesaid days as a festival, not for drinking and gluttony, but because of the deliverance that had come to them through God.

[37] Then they petitioned the king, asking for dismissal to their homes.

[38] So their registration was carried out from the twenty-fifth of Pachon to the fourth of Epeiph, for forty days; and their destruction was set for the fifth to the seventh of Epeiph, the three days

[39] on which the Lord of all most gloriously revealed his mercy and rescued them all together and unharmed.

[40] Then they feasted, provided with everything by the king, until the fourteenth day, on which also they made the petition for their dismissal.

[41] The king granted their request at once and wrote the following letter for them to the generals in the cities, magnanimously expressing his concern:

3Mac.7

[1] "King Ptolemy Philopator to the generals in Egypt and all in authority in his government, greetings and good health.

[2] We ourselves and our children are faring well, the great God guiding our affairs according to our desire.

[3] Certain of our friends, frequently urging us with malicious intent, persuaded us to gather together the Jews of the kingdom in a body and to punish them with barbarous penalties as traitors;

654

[4] for they declared that our government would never be firmly established until this was accomplished, because of the ill-will which these people had toward all nations.

[5] They also led them out with harsh treatment as slaves, or rather as traitors, and, girding themselves with a cruelty more savage than that of Scythian custom, they tried without any inquiry or examination to put them to death.

[6] But we very severely threatened them for these acts, and in accordance with the clemency which we have toward all men we barely spared their lives. Since we have come to realize that the God of heaven surely defends the Jews, always taking their part as a father does for his children,

[7] and since we have taken into account the friendly and firm goodwill which they had toward us and our ancestors, we justly have acquitted them of every charge of whatever kind.

[8] We also have ordered each and every one to return to his own home, with no one in any place doing them harm at all or reproaching them for the irrational things that have happened.

[9] For you should know that if we devise any evil against them or cause them any grief at all, we always shall have not man but the Ruler over every power, the Most High God, in everything and inescapably as an antagonist to avenge such acts. Farewell."

[10] Upon receiving this letter the Jews did not immediately hurry to make their departure, but they requested of the king that at their own hands those of the Jewish nation who had willfully transgressed against the holy God and the law of God should receive the punishment they deserved.

[11] For they declared that those who for the belly's sake had transgressed the divine commandments would never be favorably disposed toward the king's government.

[12] The king then, admitting and approving the truth of what they said, granted them a general license so that freely and without royal authority or supervision they might destroy those everywhere in his kingdom who had transgressed the law of God.

[13] When they had applauded him in fitting manner, their priests and the whole multitude shouted the Hallelujah and joyfully departed.

[14] And so on their way they punished and put to a public and shameful death any whom they met of their fellow-countrymen who had become defiled.

[15] In that day they put to death more than three hundred men; and they kept the day as a joyful festival, since they had destroyed the profaners.

[16] But those who had held fast to God even to death and had received the full enjoyment of deliverance began their departure from the city, crowned with all sorts of very fragrant flowers, joyfully and loudly giving thanks to the one God of their fathers, the eternal Savior of Israel, in words of praise and all kinds of melodious songs.

[17] When they had arrived at Ptolemais, called "rose-bearing" because of a characteristic of the place, the fleet waited for them, in accord with the common desire, for seven days.

[18] There they celebrated their deliverance, for the king had generously provided all things to them for their journey, to each as far as his own house.

[19] And when they had landed in peace with appropriate thanksgiving, there too in like manner they decided to observe these days as a joyous festival during the time of their stay.

[20] Then, after inscribing them as holy on a pillar and dedicating a place of prayer at the site of the festival, they departed unharmed, free, and overjoyed, since at the king's command they had been brought safely by land and sea and river each to his own place.

[21] They also possessed greater prestige among their enemies, being held in honor and awe; and they were not subject at all to confiscation of their belongings by any one.

[22] Besides they all recovered all of their property, in accordance with the registration, so that those who held any restored it to them with extreme fear. So the supreme God perfectly performed great deeds for their deliverance.

[23] Blessed be the Deliverer of Israel through all times! Amen.

4 Maccabees

4Mac.1

[1] The subject that I am about to discuss is most philosophical, that is, whether devout reason is sovereign over the emotions. So it is right for me to advise you to pay earnest attention to philosophy.

[2] For the subject is essential to everyone who is seeking knowledge, and in addition it includes the praise of the highest virtue -- I mean, of course, rational judgment.

[3] If, then, it is evident that reason rules over those emotions that hinder self-control, namely, gluttony and lust,

[4] it is also clear that it masters the emotions that hinder one from justice, such as malice, and those that stand in the way of courage, namely anger, fear, and pain.

[5] Some might perhaps ask, "If reason rules the emotions, why is it not sovereign over forgetfulness and ignorance?" Their attempt at argument is ridiculous!

[6] For reason does not rule its own emotions, but those that are opposed to justice, courage, and self-control; and it is not for the purpose of destroying them, but so that one may not give way to them.

[7] I could prove to you from many and various examples that reason is dominant over the emotions,

[8] but I can demonstrate it best from the noble bravery of those who died for the sake of virtue, Eleazar and the seven brothers and their mother.

[9] All of these, by despising sufferings that bring death, demonstrated that reason controls the emotions.

[10] On this anniversary it is fitting for me to praise for their virtues those who, with their mother, died for the sake of nobility and goodness, but I would also call them blessed for the honor in which they are held.

[11] For all people, even their torturers, marveled at their courage and endurance, and they became the cause of the downfall of tyranny over their nation. By their endurance they conquered the tyrant, and thus their native land was purified through them.

[12] I shall shortly have an opportunity to speak of this; but, as my custom is, I shall begin by stating my main principle, and then I shall turn to their story, giving glory to the all-wise God.

[13] Our inquiry, accordingly, is whether reason is sovereign over the emotions.

[14] We shall decide just what reason is and what emotion is, how many kinds of emotions there are, and whether reason rules over all these.

[15] Now reason is the mind that with sound logic prefers the life of wisdom.

[16] Wisdom, next, is the knowledge of divine and human matters and the causes of these.

[17] This, in turn, is education in the law, by which we learn divine matters reverently and human affairs to our advantage.

[18] Now the kinds of wisdom are rational judgment, justice, courage, and self-control.

[19] Rational judgment is supreme over all of these, since by means of it reason rules over the emotions.

[20] The two most comprehensive types of the emotions are pleasure and pain; and each of these is by nature concerned with both body and soul.

[21] The emotions of both pleasure and pain have many consequences.

[22] Thus desire precedes pleasure and delight follows it.

[23] Fear precedes pain and sorrow comes after.

[24] Anger, as a man will see if he reflects on this experience, is an emotion embracing pleasure and pain.

[25] In pleasure there exists even a malevolent tendency, which is the most complex of all the emotions.

[26] In the soul it is boastfulness, covetousness, thirst for honor, rivalry, and malice;

[27] in the body, indiscriminate eating, gluttony, and solitary gormandizing.

[28] Just as pleasure and pain are two plants growing from the body and the soul, so there are many offshoots of these plants,

[29] each of which the master cultivator, reason, weeds and prunes and ties up and waters and thoroughly irrigates, and so tames the jungle of habits and emotions.

[30] For reason is the guide of the virtues, but over the emotions it is sovereign. Observe now first of all that rational judgment is sovereign over the emotions by virtue of the restraining power of self-control.

[31] Self-control, then, is dominance over the desires.

[32] Some desires are mental, others are physical, and reason obviously rules over both.

[33] Otherwise how is it that when we are attracted to forbidden foods we abstain from the pleasure to be had from them? Is it not because reason is able to rule over appetites? I for one think so.

[34] Therefore when we crave seafood and fowl and animals and all sorts of foods that are forbidden to us by the law, we abstain because of domination by reason.

[35] For the emotions of the appetites are restrained, checked by the temperate mind, and all the impulses of the body are bridled by reason.

4Mac.2

[1] And why is it amazing that the desires of the mind for the enjoyment of beauty are rendered powerless?

[2] It is for this reason, certainly, that the temperate Joseph is praised, because by mental effort he overcame sexual desire.

[3] For when he was young and in his prime for intercourse, by his reason he nullified the frenzy of the passions.

[4] Not only is reason proved to rule over the frenzied urge of sexual desire, but also over every desire.

[5] Thus the law says, "You shall not covet your neighbor's wife...or anything that is your neighbor's."

[6] In fact, since the law has told us not to covet, I could prove to you all the more that reason is able to control desires. Just so it is with the emotions that hinder one from justice.

[7] Otherwise how could it be that someone who is habitually a solitary gormandizer, a glutton, or even a drunkard can learn a better way, unless reason is clearly lord of the emotions?

[8] Thus, as soon as a man adopts a way of life in accordance with the law, even though he is a lover of money, he is forced to act contrary to his natural ways and to lend without interest to the needy and to cancel the debt when the seventh year arrives.

[9] If one is greedy, he is ruled by the law through his reason so that he neither gleans his harvest nor gathers the last grapes from the vineyard. In all other matters we can recognize that reason rules the emotions.

[10] For the law prevails even over affection for parents, so that virtue is not abandoned for their sakes.

[11] It is superior to love for one's wife, so that one rebukes her when she breaks the law.

[12] It takes precedence over love for children, so that one punishes them for misdeeds.

[13] It is sovereign over the relationship of friends, so that one rebukes friends when they act wickedly.

[14] Do not consider it paradoxical when reason, through the law, can prevail even over enmity. The fruit trees of the enemy are not cut down, but one preserves the property of enemies from the destroyers and helps raise up what has fallen.

[15] It is evident that reason rules even the more violent emotions: lust for power, vainglory, boasting, arrogance, and malice.

[16] For the temperate mind repels all these malicious emotions, just as it repels anger -- for it is sovereign over even this.

[17] When Moses was angry with Dathan and Abiram he did nothing against them in anger, but controlled his anger by reason.

[18] For, as I have said, the temperate mind is able to get the better of the emotions, to correct some, and to render others powerless.

[19] Why else did Jacob, our most wise father, censure the households of Simeon and Levi for their irrational slaughter of the entire tribe of the Shechemites, saying, "Cursed be their anger"?

[20] For if reason could not control anger, he would not have spoken thus.

[21] Now when God fashioned man, he planted in him emotions and inclinations,

[22] but at the same time he enthroned the mind among the senses as a sacred governor over them all.

[23] To the mind he gave the law; and one who lives subject to this will rule a kingdom that is temperate, just, good, and courageous.

[24] How is it then, one might say, that if reason is master of the emotions, it does not control forgetfulness and ignorance?

4Mac.3

[1] This notion is entirely ridiculous; for it is evident that reason rules not over its own emotions, but over those of the body.

[2] No one of us can eradicate that kind of desire, but reason can provide a way for us not to be enslaved by desire.

[3] No one of us can eradicate anger from the mind, but reason can help to deal with anger.

[4] No one of us can eradicate malice, but reason can fight at our side so that we are not overcome by malice.

[5] For reason does not uproot the emotions but is their antagonist.

[6] Now this can be explained more clearly by the story of King David's thirst.

[7] David had been attacking the Philistines all day long, and together with the soldiers of his nation had slain many of them.

[8] Then when evening fell, he came, sweating and quite exhausted, to the royal tent, around which the whole army of our ancestors had encamped.

[9] Now all the rest were at supper,

[10] but the king was extremely thirsty, and although springs were plentiful there, he could not satisfy his thirst from them.

[11] But a certain irrational desire for the water in the enemy's territory tormented and inflamed him, undid and consumed him.

[12] When his guards complained bitterly because of the king's craving, two staunch young soldiers, respecting the king's desire, armed themselves fully, and taking a pitcher climbed over the enemy's ramparts.

[13] Eluding the sentinels at the gates, they went searching throughout the enemy camp

[14] and found the spring, and from it boldly brought the king a drink.

[15] But David, although he was burning with thirst, considered it an altogether fearful danger to his soul to drink what was regarded as equivalent to blood.

[16] Therefore, opposing reason to desire, he poured out the drink as an offering to God.

[17] For the temperate mind can conquer the drives of the emotions and quench the flames of frenzied desires;

[18] it can overthrow bodily agonies even when they are extreme, and by nobility of reason spurn all domination by the emotions.

[19] The present occasion now invites us to a narrative demonstration of temperate reason.

[20] At a time when our fathers were enjoying profound peace because of their observance of the law and were prospering, so that even Seleucus Nicanor, king of Asia, had both appropriated money to them for the temple service and recognized

their commonwealth --

[21] just at that time certain men attempted a revolution against the public harmony and caused many and various disasters.

4Mac.4

[1] Now there was a certain Simon, a political opponent of the noble and good man, Onias, who then held the high priesthood for life. When despite all manner of slander he was unable to injure Onias in the eyes of the nation, he fled the country with the purpose of betraying it.

[2] So he came to Apollonius, governor of Syria, Phoenicia, and Cilicia, and said,

[3] "I have come here because I am loyal to the king's government, to report that in the Jerusalem treasuries there are deposited tens of thousands in private funds, which are not the property of the temple but belong to King Seleucus."

[4] When Apollonius learned the details of these things, he praised Simon for his service to the king and went up to Seleucus to inform him of the rich treasure.

[5] On receiving authority to deal with this matter, he proceeded quickly to our country accompanied by the accursed Simon and a very strong military force.

[6] He said that he had come with the king's authority to seize the private funds in the treasury.

[7] The people indignantly protested his words, considering it outrageous that those who had committed deposits to the sacred treasury should be deprived of them, and did all that they could to prevent it.

[8] But, uttering threats, Apollonius went on to the temple.

[9] While the priests together with women and children were imploring God in the temple to shield the holy place that was being treated so contemptuously,

[10] and while Apollonius was going up with his armed forces to seize the money, angels on horseback with lightning flashing from their weapons appeared from heaven, instilling in them great fear and trembling.

[11] Then Apollonius fell down half dead in the temple area that was open to all, stretched out his hands toward heaven, and with tears besought the Hebrews to pray for him and propitiate the wrath of the heavenly army.

[12] For he said that he had committed a sin deserving of death, and that if he were delivered he would praise the blessedness of the holy place before all people.

[13] Moved by these words, Onias the high priest, although otherwise he had scruples about doing so, prayed for him lest King Seleucus suppose that Apollonius had been overcome by human treachery and not by divine justice.

[14] So Apollonius, having been preserved beyond all expectations, went away to report to the king what had happened to him.

[15] When King Seleucus died, his son Antiochus Epiphanes succeeded to the throne, an arrogant and terrible man,

[16] who removed Onias from the priesthood and appointed Onias's brother Jason as high priest.

[17] Jason agreed that if the office were conferred upon him he would pay the king three thousand six hundred and sixty talents annually.

[18] So the king appointed him high priest and ruler of the nation.

[19] Jason changed the nation's way of life and altered its form of government in complete violation of the law,

[20] so that not only was a gymnasium constructed at the very citadel of our native land, but also the temple service was abolished.

[21] The divine justice was angered by these acts and caused Antiochus himself to make war on them.

[22] For when he was warring against Ptolemy in Egypt, he heard that a rumor of his death had spread and that the people of Jerusalem had rejoiced greatly. He speedily marched against them,

[23] and after he had plundered them he issued a decree that if any of them should be found observing the ancestral law they should die.

[24] When, by means of his decrees, he had not been able in any way to put an end to the people's observance of the law, but saw that all his threats and punishments were being disregarded,

[25] even to the point that women, because they had circumcised their sons, were thrown headlong from heights along with their infants, though they had known beforehand that they would suffer this --

[26] when, then, his decrees were despised by the people, he himself, through torture, tried to compel everyone in the nation to eat defiling foods and to renounce Judaism.

4Mac.5

[1] The tyrant Antiochus, sitting in state with his counselors on a certain high place, and with his armed soldiers standing about him,

[2] ordered the guards to seize each and every Hebrew and to compel them to eat pork and food sacrificed to idols.

[3] If any were not willing to eat defiling food, they were to be broken on the wheel and killed.

[4] And when many persons had been rounded up, one man, Eleazar by name, leader of the flock, was brought before the king. He was a man of priestly family, learned in the law, advanced in age, and known to many in the tyrant's court because of his philosophy.

[5] When Antiochus saw him he said,

[6] "Before I begin to torture you, old man, I would advise you to save yourself by eating pork,

[7] for I respect your age and your gray hairs. Although you have had them for so long a time, it does not seem to me that

you are a philosopher when you observe the religion of the Jews.

[8] Why, when nature has granted it to us, should you abhor eating the very excellent meat of this animal?

[9] It is senseless not to enjoy delicious things that are not shameful, and wrong to spurn the gifts of nature.

[10] It seems to me that you will do something even more senseless if, by holding a vain opinion concerning the truth, you continue to despise me to your own hurt.

[11] Will you not awaken from your foolish philosophy, dispel your futile reasonings, adopt a mind appropriate to your years, philosophize according to the truth of what is beneficial,

[12] and have compassion on your old age by honoring my humane advice?

[13] For consider this, that if there is some power watching over this religion of yours, it will excuse you from any transgression that arises out of compulsion."

[14] When the tyrant urged him in this fashion to eat meat unlawfully, Eleazar asked to have a word.

[15] When he had received permission to speak, he began to address the people as follows:

[16] "We, O Antiochus, who have been persuaded to govern our lives by the divine law, think that there is no compulsion more powerful than our obedience to the law.

[17] Therefore we consider that we should not transgress it in any respect.

[18] Even if, as you suppose, our law were not truly divine and we had wrongly held it to be divine, not even so would it be right for us to invalidate our reputation for piety.

[19] Therefore do not suppose that it would be a petty sin if we were to eat defiling food;

[20] to transgress the law in matters either small or great is of equal seriousness,

[21] for in either case the law is equally despised.

[22] You scoff at our philosophy as though living by it were irrational,

[23] but it teaches us self-control, so that we master all pleasures and desires, and it also trains us in courage, so that we endure any suffering willingly;

[24] it instructs us in justice, so that in all our dealings we act impartially, and it teaches us piety, so that with proper reverence we worship the only real God.

[25] "Therefore we do not eat defiling food; for since we believe that the law was established by God, we know that in the nature of things the Creator of the world in giving us the law has shown sympathy toward us.

[26] He has permitted us to eat what will be most suitable for our lives, but he has forbidden us to eat meats that would be contrary to this.

[27] It would be tyrannical for you to compel us not only to transgress the law, but also to eat in such a way that you may deride us for eating defiling foods, which are most hateful to us.

[28] But you shall have no such occasion to laugh at me,

[29] nor will I transgress the sacred oaths of my ancestors concerning the keeping of the law,

[30] not even if you gouge out my eyes and burn my entrails.

[31] I am not so old and cowardly as not to be young in reason on behalf of piety.

[32] Therefore get your torture wheels ready and fan the fire more vehemently!

[33] I do not so pity my old age as to break the ancestral law by my own act.

[34] I will not play false to you, O law that trained me, nor will I renounce you, beloved self-control.

[35] I will not put you to shame, philosophical reason, nor will I reject you, honored priesthood and knowledge of the law.

[36] You, O king, shall not stain the honorable mouth of my old age, nor my long life lived lawfully.

[37] The fathers will receive me as pure, as one who does not fear your violence even to death.

[38] You may tyrannize the ungodly, but you shall not dominate my religious principles either by word or by deed."

4Mac.6

[1] When Eleazar in this manner had made eloquent response to the exhortations of the tyrant, the guards who were standing by dragged him violently to the instruments of torture.

[2] First they stripped the old man, who remained adorned with the gracefulness of his piety.

[3] And after they had tied his arms on each side they scourged him,

[4] while a herald opposite him cried out, "Obey the king's commands!"

[5] But the courageous and noble man, as a true Eleazar, was unmoved, as though being tortured in a dream;

[6] yet while the old man's eyes were raised to heaven, his flesh was being torn by scourges, his blood flowing, and his sides were being cut to pieces.

[7] And though he fell to the ground because his body could not endure the agonies, he kept his reason upright and unswerving.

[8] One of the cruel guards rushed at him and began to kick him in the side to make him get up again after he fell.

[9] But he bore the pains and scorned the punishment and endured the tortures.

[10] And like a noble athlete the old man, while being beaten, was victorious over his torturers;

[11] in fact, with his face bathed in sweat, and gasping heavily for breath, he amazed even his torturers by his courageous spirit.

[12] At that point, partly out of pity for his old age,

[13] partly out of sympathy from their acquaintance with him, partly out of admiration for his endurance, some of the king's retinue came to him and said,

[14] "Eleazar, why are you so irrationally destroying yourself through these evil things?

[15] We will set before you some cooked meat; save yourself by pretending to eat pork."

[16] But Eleazar, as though more bitterly tormented by this counsel, cried out:

[17] "May we, the children of Abraham, never think so basely that out of cowardice we feign a role unbecoming to us!

[18] For it would be irrational if we, who have lived in accordance with truth to old age and have maintained in accordance with law the reputation of such a life, should now change our course

[19] become a pattern of impiety to the young, in becoming an example of the eating of defiling food.

[20] It would be shameful if we should survive for a little while and during that time be a laughing stock to all for our cowardice,

[21] and if we should be despised by the tyrant as unmanly, and not protect our divine law even to death.

[22] Therefore, O children of Abraham, die nobly for your religion!

[23] And you, guards of the tyrant, why do you delay?"

[24] When they saw that he was so courageous in the face of the afflictions, and that he had not been changed by their compassion, the guards brought him to the fire.

[25] There they burned him with maliciously contrived instruments, threw him down, and poured stinking liquids into his nostrils.

[26] When he was now burned to his very bones and about to expire, he lifted up his eyes to God and said,

[27] "You know, O God, that though I might have saved myself, I am dying in burning torments for the sake of the law.

[28] Be merciful to your people, and let our punishment suffice for them.

[29] Make my blood their purification, and take my life in exchange for theirs."

[30] And after he said this, the holy man died nobly in his tortures, and by reason he resisted even to the very tortures of death for the sake of the law.

[31] Admittedly, then, devout reason is sovereign over the emotions.

[32] For if the emotions had prevailed over reason, we would have testified to their domination.

[33] But now that reason has conquered the emotions, we properly attribute to it the power to govern.

[34] And it is right for us to acknowledge the dominance of reason when it masters even external agonies. It would be ridiculous to deny it.

[35] And I have proved not only that reason has mastered agonies, but also that it masters pleasures and in no respect yields to them.

4Mac.7

[1] For like a most skilful pilot, the reason of our father Eleazar steered the ship of religion over the sea of the emotions,

[2] and though buffeted by the stormings of the tyrant and overwhelmed by the mighty waves of tortures,

[3] in no way did he turn the rudder of religion until he sailed into the haven of immortal victory.

[4] No city besieged with many ingenious war machines has ever held out as did that most holy man. Although his sacred life was consumed by tortures and racks, he conquered the besiegers with the shield of his devout reason.

[5] For in setting his mind firm like a jutting cliff, our father Eleazar broke the maddening waves of the emotions.

[6] O priest, worthy of the priesthood, you neither defiled your sacred teeth nor profaned your stomach, which had room only for reverence and purity, by eating defiling foods.

[7] O man in harmony with the law and philosopher of divine life!

[8] Such should be those who are administrators of the law, shielding it with their own blood and noble sweat in sufferings even to death.

[9] You, father, strengthened our loyalty to the law through your glorious endurance, and you did not abandon the holiness which you praised, but by your deeds you made your words of divine philosophy credible.

[10] O aged man, more powerful than tortures; O elder, fiercer than fire; O supreme king over the passions, Eleazar!

[11] For just as our father Aaron, armed with the censer, ran through the multitude of the people and conquered the fiery angel,

[12] so the descendant of Aaron, Eleazar, though being consumed by the fire, remained unmoved in his reason.

[13] Most amazing, indeed, though he was an old man, his body no longer tense and firm, his muscles flabby, his sinews feeble, he became young again

[14] in spirit through reason; and by reason like that of Isaac he rendered the many-headed rack ineffective.

[15] O man of blessed age and of venerable gray hair and of law-abiding life, whom the faithful seal of death has perfected!

[16] If, therefore, because of piety an aged man despised tortures even to death, most certainly devout reason is governor of the emotions.

[17] Some perhaps might say, "Not every one has full command of his emotions, because not every one has prudent reason."

[18] But as many as attend to religion with a whole heart, these alone are able to control the passions of the flesh,

[19] since they believe that they, like our patriarchs Abraham and Isaac and Jacob, do not die to God, but live in God.

[20] No contradiction therefore arises when some persons appear to be dominated by their emotions because of the weakness

of their reason.

[21] What person who lives as a philosopher by the whole rule of philosophy, and trusts in God,

[22] and knows that it is blessed to endure any suffering for the sake of virtue, would not be able to overcome the emotions through godliness?

[23] For only the wise and courageous man is lord of his emotions.

4Mac.8

[1] For this is why even the very young, by following a philosophy in accordance with devout reason, have prevailed over the most painful instruments of torture.

[2] For when the tyrant was conspicuously defeated in his first attempt, being unable to compel an aged man to eat defiling foods, then in violent rage he commanded that others of the Hebrew captives be brought, and that any who ate defiling food should be freed after eating, but if any were to refuse, these should be tortured even more cruelly.

[3] When the tyrant had given these orders, seven brothers -- handsome, modest, noble, and accomplished in every way -- were brought before him along with their aged mother.

[4] When the tyrant saw them, grouped about their mother as if in a chorus, he was pleased with them. And struck by their appearance and nobility, he smiled at them, and summoned them nearer and said,

[5] "Young men, I admire each and every one of you in a kindly manner, and greatly respect the beauty and the number of such brothers. Not only do I advise you not to display the same madness as that of the old man who has just been tortured, but I also exhort you to yield to me and enjoy my friendship.

[6] Just as I am able to punish those who disobey my orders, so I can be a benefactor to those who obey me.

[7] Trust me, then, and you will have positions of authority in my government if you will renounce the ancestral tradition of your national life.

[8] And enjoy your youth by adopting the Greek way of life and by changing your manner of living.

[9] But if by disobedience you rouse my anger, you will compel me to destroy each and every one of you with dreadful punishments through tortures.

[10] Therefore take pity on yourselves. Even I, your enemy, have compassion for your youth and handsome appearance.

[11] Will you not consider this, that if you disobey, nothing remains for you but to die on the rack?"

[12] When he had said these things, he ordered the instruments of torture to be brought forward so as to persuade them out of fear to eat the defiling food.

[13] And when the guards had placed before them wheels and joint-dislocators, rack and hooks and catapults and caldrons, braziers and thumbscrews and iron claws and wedges and bellows, the tyrant resumed speaking:

[14] "Be afraid, young fellows, and whatever justice you revere will be merciful to you when you transgress under compulsion."

[15] But when they had heard the inducements and saw the dreadful devices, not only were they not afraid, but they also opposed the tyrant with their own philosophy, and by their right reasoning nullified his tyranny.

[16] Let us consider, on the other hand, what arguments might have been used if some of them had been cowardly and unmanly. Would they not have been these?

[17] "O wretches that we are and so senseless! Since the king has summoned and exhorted us to accept kind treatment if we obey him,

[18] why do we take pleasure in vain resolves and venture upon a disobedience that brings death?

[19] O men and brothers, should we not fear the instruments of torture and consider the threats of torments, and give up this vain opinion and this arrogance that threatens to destroy us?

[20] Let us take pity on our youth and have compassion on our mother's age;

[21] and let us seriously consider that if we disobey we are dead!

[22] Also, divine justice will excuse us for fearing the king when we are under compulsion.

[23] Why do we banish ourselves from this most pleasant life and deprive ourselves of this delightful world?

[24] Let us not struggle against compulsion nor take hollow pride in being put to the rack.

[25] Not even the law itself would arbitrarily slay us for fearing the instruments of torture.

[26] Why does such contentiousness excite us and such a fatal stubbornness please us, when we can live in peace if we obey the king?"

[27] But the youths, though about to be tortured, neither said any of these things nor even seriously considered them.

[28] For they were contemptuous of the emotions and sovereign over agonies,

[29] so that as soon as the tyrant had ceased counseling them to eat defiling food, all with one voice together, as from one mind, said:

4Mac.9

[1] "Why do you delay, O tyrant? For we are ready to die rather than transgress our ancestral commandments;

[2] we are obviously putting our forefathers to shame unless we should practice ready obedience to the law and to Moses our counselor.

[3] Tyrant and counselor of lawlessness, in your hatred for us do not pity us more than we pity ourselves.

[4] For we consider this pity of yours which insures our safety through transgression of the law to be more grievous than

661

death itself.

[5] You are trying to terrify us by threatening us with death by torture, as though a short time ago you learned nothing from Eleazar.

[6] And if the aged men of the Hebrews because of their religion lived piously while enduring torture, it would be even more fitting that we young men should die despising your coercive tortures, which our aged instructor also overcame.

[7] Therefore, tyrant, put us to the test; and if you take our lives because of our religion, do not suppose that you can injure us by torturing us.

[8] For we, through this severe suffering and endurance, shall have the prize of virtue and shall be with God, for whom we suffer;

[9] but you, because of your bloodthirstiness toward us, will deservedly undergo from the divine justice eternal torment by fire."

[10] When they had said these things the tyrant not only was angry, as at those who are disobedient, but also was enraged, as at those who are ungrateful.

[11] Then at his command the guards brought forward the eldest, and having torn off his tunic, they bound his hands and arms with thongs on each side.

[12] When they had worn themselves out beating him with scourges, without accomplishing anything, they placed him upon the wheel.

[13] When the noble youth was stretched out around this, his limbs were dislocated,

[14] and though broken in every member he denounced the tyrant, saying,

[15] "Most abominable tyrant, enemy of heavenly justice, savage of mind, you are mangling me in this manner, not because I am a murderer, or as one who acts impiously, but because I protect the divine law."

[16] And when the guards said, "Agree to eat so that you may be released from the tortures,"

[17] he replied, "You abominable lackeys, your wheel is not so powerful as to strangle my reason. Cut my limbs, burn my flesh, and twist my joints.

[18] Through all these tortures I will convince you that sons of the Hebrews alone are invincible where virtue is concerned."

[19] While he was saying these things, they spread fire under him, and while fanning the flames they tightened the wheel further.

[20] The wheel was completely smeared with blood, and the heap of coals was being quenched by the drippings of gore, and pieces of flesh were falling off the axles of the machine.

[21] Although the ligaments joining his bones were already severed, the courageous youth, worthy of Abraham, did not groan,

[22] but as though transformed by fire into immortality he nobly endured the rackings.

[23] "Imitate me, brothers," he said. "Do not leave your post in my struggle or renounce our courageous brotherhood.

[24] Fight the sacred and noble battle for religion. Thereby the just Providence of our ancestors may become merciful to our nation and take vengeance on the accursed tyrant."

[25] When he had said this, the saintly youth broke the thread of life.

[26] While all were marveling at his courageous spirit, the guards brought in the next eldest, and after fitting themselves with iron gauntlets having sharp hooks, they bound him to the torture machine and catapult.

[27] Before torturing him, they inquired if he were willing to eat, and they heard this noble decision.

[28] These leopard-like beasts tore out his sinews with the iron hands, flayed all his flesh up to his chin, and tore away his scalp. But he steadfastly endured this agony and said,

[29] "How sweet is any kind of death for the religion of our fathers!"

[30] To the tyrant he said, "Do you not think, you most savage tyrant, that you are being tortured more than I, as you see the arrogant design of your tyranny being defeated by our endurance for the sake of religion?

[31] I lighten my pain by the joys that come from virtue,

[32] but you suffer torture by the threats that come from impiety. You will not escape, most abominable tyrant, the judgments of the divine wrath."

4Mac.10

[1] When he too had endured a glorious death, the third was led in, and many repeatedly urged him to save himself by tasting the meat.

[2] But he shouted, "Do you not know that the same father begot me and those who died, and the same mother bore me, and that I was brought up on the same teachings?

[3] I do not renounce the noble kinship that binds me to my brothers."

[4]

[5] Enraged by the man's boldness, they disjointed his hands and feet with their instruments, dismembering him by prying his limbs from their sockets,

[6] and breaking his fingers and arms and legs and elbows.

[7] Since they were not able in any way to break his spirit, they abandoned the instruments and scalped him with their fingernails in a Scythian fashion.

[8] They immediately brought him to the wheel, and while his vertebrae were being dislocated upon it he saw his own flesh torn all around and drops of blood flowing from his entrails.

[9] When he was about to die, he said,

[10] "We, most abominable tyrant, are suffering because of our godly training and virtue,

[11] but you, because of your impiety and bloodthirstiness, will undergo unceasing torments."

[12] When he also had died in a manner worthy of his brothers, they dragged in the fourth, saying,

[13] "As for you, do not give way to the same insanity as your brothers, but obey the king and save yourself."

[14] But he said to them, "You do not have a fire hot enough to make me play the coward.

[15] No, by the blessed death of my brothers, by the eternal destruction of the tyrant, and by the everlasting life of the pious, I will not renounce our noble brotherhood.

[16] Contrive tortures, tyrant, so that you may learn from them that I am a brother to those who have just been tortured."

[17] When he heard this, the bloodthirsty, murderous, and utterly abominable Antiochus gave orders to cut out his tongue.

[18] But he said, "Even if you remove my organ of speech, God hears also those who are mute.

[19] See, here is my tongue; cut it off, for in spite of this you will not make our reason speechless.

[20] Gladly, for the sake of God, we let our bodily members be mutilated.

[21] God will visit you swiftly, for you are cutting out a tongue that has been melodious with divine hymns."

4Mac.11

[1] When this one died also, after being cruelly tortured, the fifth leaped up, saying,

[2] "I will not refuse, tyrant, to be tortured for the sake of virtue.

[3] I have come of my own accord, so that by murdering me you will incur punishment from the heavenly justice for even more crimes.

[4] Hater of virtue, hater of mankind, for what act of ours are you destroying us in this way?

[5] Is it because we revere the Creator of all things and live according to his virtuous law?

[6] But these deeds deserve honors, not tortures."

[7]

[9] While he was saying these things, the guards bound him and dragged him to the catapult;

[10] they tied him to it on his knees, and fitting iron clamps on them, they twisted his back around the wedge on the wheel, so that he was completely curled back like a scorpion, and all his members were disjointed.

[11] In this condition, gasping for breath and in anguish of body,

[12] he said, "Tyrant, they are splendid favors that you grant us against your will, because through these noble sufferings you give us an opportunity to show our endurance for the law."

[13] After he too had died, the sixth, a mere boy, was led in. When the tyrant inquired whether he was willing to eat and be released, he said,

[14] "I am younger in age than my brothers, but I am their equal in mind.

[15] Since to this end we were born and bred, we ought likewise to die for the same principles.

[16] So if you intend to torture me for not eating defiling foods, go on torturing!"

[17] When he had said this, they led him to the wheel.

[18] He was carefully stretched tight upon it, his back was broken, and he was roasted from underneath.

[19] To his back they applied sharp spits that had been heated in the fire, and pierced his ribs so that his entrails were burned through.

[20] While being tortured he said, "O contest befitting holiness, in which so many of us brothers have been summoned to an arena of sufferings for religion, and in which we have not been defeated!

[21] For religious knowledge, O tyrant, is invincible.

[22] I also, equipped with nobility, will die with my brothers,

[23] and I myself will bring a great avenger upon you, you inventor of tortures and enemy of those who are truly devout.

[24] We six boys have paralyzed your tyranny!

[25] Since you have not been able to persuade us to change our mind or to force us to eat defiling foods, is not this your downfall?

[26] Your fire is cold to us, and the catapults painless, and your violence powerless.

[27] For it is not the guards of the tyrant but those of the divine law that are set over us; therefore, unconquered, we hold fast to reason."

4Mac.12

[1] When he also, thrown into the caldron, had died a blessed death, the seventh and youngest of all came forward.

[2] Even though the tyrant had been fearfully reproached by the brothers, he felt strong compassion for this child when he saw that he was already in fetters. He summoned him to come nearer and tried to console him, saying,

[3] "You see the result of your brothers' stupidity, for they died in torments because of their disobedience.

[4] You too, if you do not obey, will be miserably tortured and die before your time,

[5] but if you yield to persuasion you will be my friend and a leader in the government of the kingdom."

[6] When he had so pleaded, he sent for the boy's mother to show compassion on her who had been bereaved of so many

sons and to influence her to persuade the surviving son to obey and save himself.

[7] But when his mother had exhorted him in the Hebrew language, as we shall tell a little later,

[8] he said, "Let me loose, let me speak to the king and to all his friends that are with him."

[9] Extremely pleased by the boy's declaration, they freed him at once.

[10] Running to the nearest of the braziers,

[11] he said, "You profane tyrant, most impious of all the wicked, since you have received good things and also your kingdom from God, were you not ashamed to murder his servants and torture on the wheel those who practice religion?

[12] Because of this, justice has laid up for you intense and eternal fire and tortures, and these throughout all time will never let you go.

[13] As a man, were you not ashamed, you most savage beast, to cut out the tongues of men who have feelings like yours and are made of the same elements as you, and to maltreat and torture them in this way?

[14] Surely they by dying nobly fulfilled their service to God, but you will wail bitterly for having slain without cause the contestants for virtue."

[15] Then because he too was about to die, he said,

[16] "I do not desert the excellent example of my brothers,

[17] and I call on the God of our fathers to be merciful to our nation;

[18] but on you he will take vengeance both in this present life and when you are dead."

[19] After he had uttered these imprecations, he flung himself into the braziers and so ended his life.

4Mac.13

[1] Since, then, the seven brothers despised sufferings even unto death, everyone must concede that devout reason is sovereign over the emotions.

[2] For if they had been slaves to their emotions and had eaten defiling food, we would say that they had been conquered by these emotions.

[3] But in fact it was not so. Instead, by reason, which is praised before God, they prevailed over their emotions.

[4] The supremacy of the mind over these cannot be overlooked, for the brothers mastered both emotions and pains.

[5] How then can one fail to confess the sovereignty of right reason over emotion in those who were not turned back by fiery agonies?

[6] For just as towers jutting out over harbors hold back the threatening waves and make it calm for those who sail into the inner basin,

[7] so the seven-towered right reason of the youths, by fortifying the harbor of religion, conquered the tempest of the emotions.

[8] For they constituted a holy chorus of religion and encouraged one another, saying,

[9] "Brothers, let us die like brothers for the sake of the law; let us imitate the three youths in Assyria who despised the same ordeal of the furnace.

[10] Let us not be cowardly in the demonstration of our piety."

[11] While one said, "Courage, brother," another said, "Bear up nobly,"

[12] and another reminded them, "Remember whence you came, and the father by whose hand Isaac would have submitted to being slain for the sake of religion."

[13] Each of them and all of them together looking at one another, cheerful and undaunted, said, "Let us with all our hearts consecrate ourselves to God, who gave us our lives, and let us use our bodies as a bulwark for the law.

[14] Let us not fear him who thinks he is killing us,

[15] for great is the struggle of the soul and the danger of eternal torment lying before those who transgress the commandment of God.

[16] Therefore let us put on the full armor of self-control, which is divine reason.

[17] For if we so die, Abraham and Isaac and Jacob will welcome us, and all the fathers will praise us."

[18] Those who were left behind said to each of the brothers who were being dragged away, "Do not put us to shame, brother, or betray the brothers who have died before us."

[19] You are not ignorant of the affection of brotherhood, which the divine and all-wise Providence has bequeathed through the fathers to their descendants and which was implanted in the mother's womb.

[20] There each of the brothers dwelt the same length of time and was shaped during the same period of time; and growing from the same blood and through the same life, they were brought to the light of day.

[21] When they were born after an equal time of gestation, they drank milk from the same fountains. For such embraces brotherly-loving souls are nourished;

[22] and they grow stronger from this common nurture and daily companionship, and from both general education and our discipline in the law of God.

[23] Therefore, when sympathy and brotherly affection had been so established, the brothers were the more sympathetic to one another.

[24] Since they had been educated by the same law and trained in the same virtues and brought up in right living, they loved one another all the more.

[25] A common zeal for nobility expanded their goodwill and harmony toward one another,

[26] because, with the aid of their religion, they rendered their brotherly love more fervent.

[27] But although nature and companionship and virtuous habits had augmented the affection of brotherhood, those who were left endured for the sake of religion, while watching their brothers being maltreated and tortured to death.

4Mac.14

[1] Furthermore, they encouraged them to face the torture, so that they not only despised their agonies, but also mastered the emotions of brotherly love.

[2] O reason, more royal than kings and freer than the free!

[3] O sacred and harmonious concord of the seven brothers on behalf of religion!

[4] None of the seven youths proved coward or shrank from death,

[5] but all of them, as though running the course toward immortality, hastened to death by torture.

[6] Just as the hands and feet are moved in harmony with the guidance of the mind, so those holy youths, as though moved by an immortal spirit of devotion, agreed to go to death for its sake.

[7] O most holy seven, brothers in harmony! For just as the seven days of creation move in choral dance around religion,

[8] so these youths, forming a chorus, encircled the sevenfold fear of tortures and dissolved it.

[9] Even now, we ourselves shudder as we hear of the tribulations of these young men; they not only saw what was happening, yes, not only heard the direct word of threat, but also bore the sufferings patiently, and in agonies of fire at that.

[10] What could be more excruciatingly painful than this? For the power of fire is intense and swift, and it consumed their bodies quickly.

[11] Do not consider it amazing that reason had full command over these men in their tortures, since the mind of woman despised even more diverse agonies,

[12] for the mother of the seven young men bore up under the rackings of each one of her children.

[13] Observe how complex is a mother's love for her children, which draws everything toward an emotion felt in her inmost parts.

[14] Even unreasoning animals, like mankind, have a sympathy and parental love for their offspring.

[15] For example, among birds, the ones that are tame protect their young by building on the housetops,

[16] and the others, by building in precipitous chasms and in holes and tops of trees, hatch the nestlings and ward off the intruder.

[17] If they are not able to keep him away, they do what they can to help their young by flying in circles around them in the anguish of love, warning them with their own calls.

[18] And why is it necessary to demonstrate sympathy for children by the example of unreasoning animals,

[19] since even bees at the time for making honeycombs defend themselves against intruders as though with an iron dart sting those who approach their hive and defend it even to the death?

[20] But sympathy for her children did not sway the mother of the young men; she was of the same mind as Abraham.

4Mac.15

[1] O reason of the children, tyrant over the emotions! O religion, more desirable to the mother than her children!

[2] Two courses were open to this mother, that of religion, and that of preserving her seven sons for a time, as the tyrant had promised.

[3] She loved religion more, religion that preserves them for eternal life according to God's promise.

[4] In what manner might I express the emotions of parents who love their children? We impress upon the character of a small child a wondrous likeness both of mind and of form. Especially is this true of mothers, who because of their birthpangs have a deeper sympathy toward their offspring than do the fathers.

[5] Considering that mothers are the weaker sex and give birth to many, they are more devoted to their children.

[6] The mother of the seven boys, more than any other mother, loved her children. In seven pregnancies she had implanted in herself tender love toward them,

[7] and because of the many pains she suffered with each of them she had sympathy for them;

[8] yet because of the fear of God she disdained the temporary safety of her children.

[9] Not only so, but also because of the nobility of her sons and their ready obedience to the law she felt a greater tenderness toward them.

[10] For they were righteous and self-controlled and brave and magnanimous, and loved their brothers and their mother, so that they obeyed her even to death in keeping the ordinances.

[11] Nevertheless, though so many factors influenced the mother to suffer with them out of love for her children, in the case of none of them were the various tortures strong enough to pervert her reason.

[12] Instead, the mother urged them on, each child singly and all together, to death for the sake of religion.

[13] O sacred nature and affection of parental love, yearning of parents toward offspring, nurture and indomitable suffering by mothers!

[14] This mother, who saw them tortured and burned one by one, because of religion did not change her attitude.

[15] She watched the flesh of her children consumed by fire, their toes and fingers scattered on the ground, and the flesh of the head to the chin exposed like masks.

[16] O mother, tried now by more bitter pains than even the birth-pangs you suffered for them!

[17] O woman, who alone gave birth to such complete devotion!

[18] When the first-born breathed his last it did not turn you aside, nor when the second in torments looked at you piteously nor when the third expired;

[19] nor did you weep when you looked at the eyes of each one in his tortures gazing boldly at the same agonies, and saw in their nostrils the signs of the approach of death.

[20] When you saw the flesh of children burned upon the flesh of other children, severed hands upon hands, scalped heads upon heads, and corpses fallen on other corpses and when you saw the place filled with many spectators of the torturings, you did not shed tears.

[21] Neither the melodies of sirens nor the songs of swans attract the attention of their hearers as did the voices of the children in torture calling to their mother.

[22] How great and how many torments the mother then suffered as her sons were tortured on the wheel and with the hot irons!

[23] But devout reason, giving her heart a man's courage in the very midst of her emotions, strengthened her to disregard her temporal love for her children.

[24] Although she witnessed the destruction of seven children and the ingenious and various rackings, this noble mother disregarded all these because of faith in God.

[25] For as in the council chamber of her own soul she saw mighty advocates -- nature, family, parental love, and the rackings of her children --

[26] this mother held two ballots, one bearing death and the other deliverance for her children.

[27] She did not approve the deliverance which would preserve the seven sons for a short time,

[28] but as the daughter of God-fearing Abraham she remembered his fortitude.

[29] O mother of the nation, vindicator of the law and champion of religion, who carried away the prize of the contest in your heart!

[30] O more noble than males in steadfastness, and more manly than men in endurance!

[31] Just as Noah's ark, carrying the world in the universal flood, stoutly endured the waves,

[32] so you, O guardian of the law, overwhelmed from every side by the flood of your emotions and the violent winds, the torture of your sons, endured nobly and withstood the wintry storms that assail religion.

4Mac.16

[1] If, then, a woman, advanced in years and mother of seven sons, endured seeing her children tortured to death, it must be admitted that devout reason is sovereign over the emotions.

[2] Thus I have demonstrated not only that men have ruled over the emotions, but also that a woman has despised the fiercest tortures.

[3] The lions surrounding Daniel were not so savage, nor was the raging fiery furnace of Mishael so intensely hot, as was her innate parental love, inflamed as she saw her seven sons tortured in such varied ways.

[4] But the mother quenched so many and such great emotions by devout reason.

[5] Consider this also. If this woman, though a mother, had been fainthearted, she would have mourned over them and perhaps spoken as follows:

[6] "O how wretched am I and many times unhappy! After bearing seven children, I am now the mother of none!

[7] O seven childbirths all in vain, seven profitless pregnancies, fruitless nurturings and wretched nursings!

[8] In vain, my sons, I endured many birth-pangs for you, and the more grievous anxieties of your upbringing.

[9] Alas for my children, some unmarried, others married and without offspring. I shall not see your children or have the happiness of being called grandmother.

[10] Alas, I who had so many and beautiful children am a widow and alone, with many sorrows.

[11] Nor when I die, shall I have any of my sons to bury me."

[12] Yet the sacred and God-fearing mother did not wail with such a lament for any of them, nor did she dissuade any of them from dying, nor did she grieve as they were dying,

[13] but, as though having a mind like adamant and giving rebirth for immortality to the whole number of her sons, she implored them and urged them on to death for the sake of religion.

[14] O mother, soldier of God in the cause of religion, elder and woman! By steadfastness you have conquered even a tyrant, and in word and deed you have proved more powerful than a man.

[15] For when you and your sons were arrested together, you stood and watched Eleazar being tortured, and said to your sons in the Hebrew language,

[16] "My sons, noble is the contest to which you are called to bear witness for the nation. Fight zealously for our ancestral law.

[17] For it would be shameful if, while an aged man endures such agonies for the sake of religion, you young men were to be terrified by tortures.

[18] Remember that it is through God that you have had a share in the world and have enjoyed life,

[19] and therefore you ought to endure any suffering for the sake of God.

[20] For his sake also our father Abraham was zealous to sacrifice his son Isaac, the ancestor of our nation; and when Isaac saw his father's hand wielding a sword and descending upon him, he did not cower.

[21] And Daniel the righteous was thrown to the lions, and Hananiah, Azariah, and Mishael were hurled into the fiery furnace and endured it for the sake of God.

[22] You too must have the same faith in God and not be grieved.

[23] It is unreasonable for people who have religious knowledge not to withstand pain."

[24] By these words the mother of the seven encouraged and persuaded each of her sons to die rather than violate God's commandment.

[25] They knew also that those who die for the sake of God live in God, as do Abraham and Isaac and Jacob and all the patriarchs.

4Mac.17

[1] Some of the guards said that when she also was about to be seized and put to death she threw herself into the flames so that no one might touch her body.

[2] O mother, who with your seven sons nullified the violence of the tyrant, frustrated his evil designs, and showed the courage of your faith!

[3] Nobly set like a roof on the pillars of your sons, you held firm and unswerving against the earthquake of the tortures.

[4] Take courage, therefore, O holy-minded mother, maintaining firm an enduring hope in God.

[5] The moon in heaven, with the stars, does not stand so august as you, who, after lighting the way of your star-like seven sons to piety, stand in honor before God and are firmly set in heaven with them.

[6] For your children were true descendants of father Abraham.

[7] If it were possible for us to paint the history of your piety as an artist might, would not those who first beheld it have shuddered as they saw the mother of the seven children enduring their varied tortures to death for the sake of religion?

[8] Indeed it would be proper to inscribe upon their tomb these words as a reminder to the people of our nation:

[9] "Here lie buried an aged priest and an aged woman and seven sons, because of the violence of the tyrant who wished to destroy the way of life of the Hebrews.

[10] They vindicated their nation, looking to God and enduring torture even to death."

[11] Truly the contest in which they were engaged was divine,

[12] for on that day virtue gave the awards and tested them for their endurance. The prize was immortality in endless life.

[13] Eleazar was the first contestant, the mother of the seven sons entered the competition, and the brothers contended.

[14] The tyrant was the antagonist, and the world and the human race were the spectators.

[15] Reverence for God was victor and gave the crown to its own athletes.

[16] Who did not admire the athletes of the divine legislation? Who were not amazed?

[17] The tyrant himself and all his council marveled at their endurance,

[18] because of which they now stand before the divine throne and live through blessed eternity.

[19] For Moses says, "All who are consecrated are under your hands."

[20] These, then, who have been consecrated for the sake of God, are honored, not only with this honor, but also by the fact that because of them our enemies did not rule over our nation,

[21] the tyrant was punished, and the homeland purified -- they having become, as it were, a ransom for the sin of our nation.

[22] And through the blood of those devout ones and their death as an expiation, divine Providence preserved Israel that previously had been afflicted.

[23] For the tyrant Antiochus, when he saw the courage of their virtue and their endurance under the tortures, proclaimed them to his soldiers as an example for their own endurance,

[24] and this made them brave and courageous for infantry battle and siege, and he ravaged and conquered all his enemies.

4Mac.18

[1] O Israelite children, offspring of the seed of Abraham, obey this law and exercise piety in every way,

[2] knowing that devout reason is master of all emotions, not only of sufferings from within, but also of those from without.

[3] Therefore those who gave over their bodies in suffering for the sake of religion were not only admired by men, but also were deemed worthy to share in a divine inheritance.

[4] Because of them the nation gained peace, and by reviving observance of the law in the homeland they ravaged the enemy.

[5] The tyrant Antiochus was both punished on earth and is being chastised after his death. Since in no way whatever was he able to compel the Israelites to become pagans and to abandon their ancestral customs, he left Jerusalem and marched against the Persians.

[6] The mother of seven sons expressed also these principles to her children:

[7] "I was a pure virgin and did not go outside my father's house; but I guarded the rib from which woman was made.

[8] No seducer corrupted me on a desert plain, nor did the destroyer, the deceitful serpent, defile the purity of my virginity.

[9] In the time of my maturity I remained with my husband, and when these sons had grown up their father died. A happy man was he, who lived out his life with good children, and did not have the grief of bereavement.

[10] While he was still with you, he taught you the law and the prophets.

[11] He read to you about Abel slain by Cain, and Isaac who was offered as a burnt offering, and of Joseph in prison.

[12] He told you of the zeal of Phineas, and he taught you about Hananiah, Azariah, and Mishael in the fire.

[13] He praised Daniel in the den of the lions and blessed him.

[14] He reminded you of the scripture of Isaiah, which says, `Even though you go through the fire, the flame shall not consume you.'

[15] He sang to you songs of the psalmist David, who said, `Many are the afflictions of the righteous.'

[16] He recounted to you Solomon's proverb, `There is a tree of life for those who do his will.'

[17] He confirmed the saying of Ezekiel, `Shall these dry bones live?'

[18] For he did not forget to teach you the song that Moses taught, which says,

[19] `I kill and I make alive: this is your life and the length of your days.'"

[20] O bitter was that day -- and yet not bitter -- when that bitter tyrant of the Greeks quenched fire with fire in his cruel caldrons, and in his burning rage brought those seven sons of the daughter of Abraham to the catapult and back again to more tortures,

[21] pierced the pupils of their eyes and cut out their tongues, and put them to death with various tortures.

[22] For these crimes divine justice pursued and will pursue the accursed tyrant.

[23] But the sons of Abraham with their victorious mother are gathered together into the chorus of the fathers, and have received pure and immortal souls from God,

[24] to whom be glory for ever and ever. Amen.

Letter (Epistle) of Jeremiah

EpJer.6

[1] A copy of a letter which Jeremiah sent to those who were to be taken to Babylon as captives by the king of the Babylonians, to give them the message which God had commanded him.

[2] Because of the sins which you have committed before God, you will be taken to Babylon as captives by Nebuchadnezzar, king of the Babylonians.

[3] Therefore when you have come to Babylon you will remain there for many years, for a long time, up to seven generations; after that I will bring you away from there in peace.

[4] Now in Babylon you will see gods made of silver and gold and wood, which are carried on men's shoulders and inspire fear in the heathen.

[5] So take care not to become at all like the foreigners or to let fear for these gods possess you, when you see the multitude before and behind them worshiping them.

[6] But say in your heart, "It is thou, O Lord, whom we must worship."

[7] For my angel is with you, and he is watching your lives.

[8] Their tongues are smoothed by the craftsman, and they themselves are overlaid with gold and silver; but they are false and cannot speak.

[9] People take gold and make crowns for the heads of their gods, as they would for a girl who loves ornaments;

[10] and sometimes the priests secretly take gold and silver from their gods and spend it upon themselves,

[11] and even give some of it to the harlots in the brothel. They deck their gods out with garments like men -- these gods of silver and gold and wood,

[12] which cannot save themselves from rust and corrosion. When they have been dressed in purple robes,

[13] their faces are wiped because of the dust from the temple, which is thick upon them.

[14] Like a local ruler the god holds a scepter, though unable to destroy any one who offends it.

[15] It has a dagger in its right hand, and has an axe; but it cannot save itself from war and robbers.

[16] Therefore they evidently are not gods; so do not fear them.

[17] For just as one's dish is useless when it is broken, so are the gods of the heathen, when they have been set up in the temples. Their eyes are full of the dust raised by the feet of those who enter.

[18] And just as the gates are shut on every side upon a man who has offended a king, as though he were sentenced to death, so the priests make their temples secure with doors and locks and bars, in order that they may not be plundered by robbers.

[19] They light lamps, even more than they light for themselves, though their gods can see none of them.

[20] They are just like a beam of the temple, but men say their hearts have melted, when worms from the earth devour them and their robes. They do not notice

[21] when their faces have been blackened by the smoke of the temple.

[22] Bats, swallows, and birds light on their bodies and heads; and so do cats.

[23] From this you will know that they are not gods; so do not fear them.

[24] As for the gold which they wear for beauty -- they will not shine unless some one wipes off the rust; for even when they were being cast, they had no feeling.

[25] They are bought at any cost, but there is no breath in them.

[26] Having no feet, they are carried on men's shoulders, revealing to mankind their worthlessness.

[27] And those who serve them are ashamed because through them these gods are made to stand, lest they fall to the ground. If any one sets one of them upright, it cannot move itself; and if it is tipped over, it cannot straighten itself; but gifts are placed before them just as before the dead.

[28] The priests sell the sacrifices that are offered to these gods and use the money; and likewise their wives preserve some with salt, but give none to the poor or helpless.

[29] Sacrifices to them may be touched by women in menstruation or at childbirth. Since you know by these things that they are not gods, do not fear them.

[30] For why should they be called gods? Women serve meals for gods of silver and gold and wood;

[31] and in their temples the priests sit with their clothes rent, their heads and beards shaved, and their heads uncovered.

[32] They howl and shout before their gods as some do at a funeral feast for a man who has died.

[33] The priests take some of the clothing of their gods to clothe their wives and children.

[34] Whether one does evil to them or good, they will not be able to repay it. They cannot set up a king or depose one.

[35] Likewise they are not able to give either wealth or money; if one makes a vow to them and does not keep it, they will not require it.

[36] They cannot save a man from death or rescue the weak from the strong.

[37] They cannot restore sight to a blind man; they cannot rescue a man who is in distress.

[38] They cannot take pity on a widow or do good to an orphan.

[39] These things that are made of wood and overlaid with gold and silver are like stones from the mountain, and those who

serve them will be put to shame.

[40] Why then must any one think that they are gods, or call them gods? Besides, even the Chaldeans themselves dishonor them;

[41] for when they see a dumb man, who cannot speak, they bring him and pray Bel that the man may speak, as though Bel were able to understand.

[42] Yet they themselves cannot perceive this and abandon them, for they have no sense.

[43] And the women, with cords about them, sit along the passageways, burning bran for incense; and when one of them is led off by one of the passers-by and is lain with, she derides the woman next to her, because she was not as attractive as herself and her cord was not broken.

[44] Whatever is done for them is false. Why then must any one think that they are gods, or call them gods?

[45] They are made by carpenters and goldsmiths; they can be nothing but what the craftsmen wish them to be.

[46] The men that make them will certainly not live very long themselves; how then can the things that are made by them be gods?

[47] They have left only lies and reproach for those who come after.

[48] For when war or calamity comes upon them, the priests consult together as to where they can hide themselves and their gods.

[49] How then can one fail to see that these are not gods, for they cannot save themselves from war or calamity?

[50] Since they are made of wood and overlaid with gold and silver, it will afterward be known that they are false.

[51] It will be manifest to all the nations and kings that they are not gods but the work of men's hands, and that there is no work of God in them.

[52] Who then can fail to know that they are not gods?

[53] For they cannot set up a king over a country or give rain to men.

[54] They cannot judge their own cause or deliver one who is wronged, for they have no power; they are like crows between heaven and earth.

[55] When fire breaks out in a temple of wooden gods overlaid with gold or silver, their priests will flee and escape, but the gods will be burnt in two like beams.

[56] Besides, they can offer no resistance to a king or any enemies. Why then must any one admit or think that they are gods?

[57] Gods made of wood and overlaid with silver and gold are not able to save themselves from thieves and robbers.

[58] Strong men will strip them of their gold and silver and of the robes they wear, and go off with this booty, and they will not be able to help themselves.

[59] So it is better to be a king who shows his courage, or a household utensil that serves its owner's need, than to be these false gods; better even the door of a house that protects its contents, than these false gods; better also a wooden pillar in a palace, than these false gods.

[60] For sun and moon and stars, shining and sent forth for service, are obedient.

[61] So also the lightning, when it flashes, is widely seen; and the wind likewise blows in every land.

[62] When God commands the clouds to go over the whole world, they carry out his command.

[63] And the fire sent from above to consume mountains and woods does what it is ordered. But these idols are not to be compared with them in appearance or power.

[64] Therefore one must not think that they are gods nor call them gods, for they are not able either to decide a case or to do good to men.

[65] Since you know then that they are not gods, do not fear them.

[66] For they can neither curse nor bless kings;

[67] they cannot show signs in the heavens and among the nations, or shine like the sun or give light like the moon.

[68] The wild beasts are better than they are, for they can flee to cover and help themselves.

[69] So we have no evidence whatever that they are gods; therefore do not fear them.

[70] Like a scarecrow in a cucumber bed, that guards nothing, so are their gods of wood, overlaid with gold and silver.

[71] In the same way, their gods of wood, overlaid with gold and silver, and like a thorn bush in a garden, on which every bird sits; or like a dead body cast out in the darkness.

[72] By the purple and linen that rot upon them you will know that they are not gods; and they will finally themselves be consumed, and be a reproach in the land.

[73] Better therefore is a just man who has no idols, for he will be far from reproach.

Prayer of Azariah

1

[1] And they walked in the midst of the fire, praising God and blessing the Lord

[2] Then Azariah stood and offered this prayer; in the midst of the fire he opened his mouth and said:

[3] "Blessed art thou, O Lord, God of our fathers, and worthy of praise; and thy name is glorified for ever.

[4] For thou art just in all that thou hast done to us, and all thy works are true and thy ways right, and all thy judgments are truth.

[5] Thou hast executed true judgments in all that thou hast brought upon us and upon Jerusalem, the holy city of our fathers, for in truth and justice thou hast brought all this upon us because of our sins.

[6] For we have sinfully and lawlessly departed from thee, and have sinned in all things and have not obeyed thy commandments;

[7] we have not observed them or done them, as thou hast commanded us that it might go well with us.

[8] So all that thou hast brought upon us, and all that thou hast done to us, thou hast done in true judgment.

[9] Thou hast given us into the hands of lawless enemies, most hateful rebels, and to an unjust king, the most wicked in all the world.

[10] And now we cannot open our mouths; shame and disgrace have befallen thy servants and worshipers.

[11] For thy name's sake do not give us up utterly, and do not break thy covenant,

[12] and do not withdraw thy mercy from us,

for the sake of Abraham thy beloved and for the sake of Isaac thy servant and Israel thy holy one,

[13] to whom thou didst promise to make their descendants as many as the stars of heaven and as the sand on the shore of the sea.

[14] For we, O Lord, have become fewer than any nation, and are brought low this day in all the world because of our sins.

[15] And at this time there is no prince, or prophet, or leader, no burnt offering, or sacrifice, or oblation, or incense, no place to make an offering before thee or to find mercy.

[16] Yet with a contrite heart and a humble spirit may we be accepted, as though it were with burnt offerings of rams and bulls, and with tens of thousands of fat lambs;

[17] such may our sacrifice be in thy sight this day, and may we wholly follow thee, for there will be no shame for those who trust in thee.

[18] And now with all our heart we follow thee, we fear thee and seek thy face.

[19] Do not put us to shame, but deal with us in thy forbearance and in thy abundant mercy.

[20] Deliver us in accordance with thy marvelous works, and give glory to thy name, O Lord! Let all who do harm to thy servants be put to shame;

[21] let them be disgraced and deprived of all power and dominion, and let their strength be broken.

[22] Let them know that thou art the Lord, the only God, glorious over the whole world."

[23] Now the king's servants who threw them in did not cease feeding the furnace fires with naphtha, pitch, tow, and brush.

[24] And the flame streamed out above the furnace forty-nine cubits,

[25] and it broke through and burned those of the Chaldeans whom it caught about the furnace.

[26] But the angel of the Lord came down into the furnace to be with Azariah and his companions, and drove the fiery flame out of the furnace,

[27] and made the midst of the furnace like a moist whistling wind, so that the fire did not touch them at all or hurt or trouble them.

[28] Then the three, as with one mouth, praised and glorified and blessed God in the furnace, saying: [29] "Blessed art thou, O Lord, God of our fathers, and to be praised and highly exalted for ever; [30] And blessed is thy glorious, holy name and to be highly praised and highly exalted for ever; [31] Blessed art thou in the temple of thy holy glory and to be extolled and highly glorified for ever. [32] Blessed art thou, who sittest upon cherubim and lookest upon the deeps, and to be praised and highly exalted for ever. [33] Blessed art thou upon the throne of thy kingdom and to be extolled and highly exalted for ever. [34] Blessed art thou in the firmament of heavenand to be sung and glorified for ever. [35] "Bless the Lord, all works of the Lord, sing praise to him and highly exalt him for ever. [36] Bless the Lord, you heavens, sing praise to him and highly exalt him for ever. [37] Bless the Lord, you angels of the Lord, sing praise to him and highly exalt him for ever. [38] Bless the Lord, all waters above the heaven, sing praise to him and highly exalt him for ever. [39] Bless the Lord, all powers, sing praise to him and highly exalt him for ever. [40] Bless the Lord, sun and moon, sing praise to him and highly exalt him for ever. [41] Bless the Lord, stars of heaven, sing praise to him and highly exalt him for ever. [42] Bless the Lord, all rain and dew, sing praise to him and highly exalt him for ever. [43] Bless the Lord, all winds, sing praise to him and highly exalt him for ever. [44] Bless the Lord, fire and heat, sing praise to him and highly exalt him for ever. [45] Bless the Lord, winter cold and summer heat, sing praise to him and highly exalt him for ever. [46] Bless the Lord, dews and snows, sing praise to him and highly exalt him for ever. [47] Bless the Lord, nights and days, sing praise to him and highly exalt him for ever. [48] Bless the Lord, light and darkness, sing praise to him and highly exalt him for ever. [49] Bless the Lord, ice and cold, sing praise to him and highly exalt him for ever. [50] Bless the Lord, frosts and snows, sing praise to him and highly exalt him for

ever. [51] Bless the Lord, lightnings and clouds, sing praise to him and highly exalt him for ever. [52] Let the earth bless the Lord; let it sing praise to him and highly exalt him for ever. [53] Bless the Lord, mountains and hills, sing praise to him and highly exalt him for ever. [54] Bless the Lord, all things that grow on the earth, sing praise to him and highly exalt him for ever. [55] Bless the Lord, you springs, sing praise to him and highly exalt him for ever. [56] Bless the Lord, seas and rivers, sing praise to him and highly exalt him for ever. [57] Bless the Lord, you whales and all creatures that move in the waters, sing praise to him and highly exalt him for ever. [58] Bless the Lord, all birds of the air, sing praise to him and highly exalt him for ever. [59] Bless the Lord, all beasts and cattle, sing praise to him and highly exalt him for ever. [60] Bless the Lord, you sons of men, sing praise to him and highly exalt him for ever. [61] Bless the Lord, O Israel, sing praise to him and highly exalt him for ever. [62] Bless the Lord, you priests of the Lord, sing praise to him and highly exalt him for ever. [63] Bless the Lord, you servants of the Lord sing praise to him and highly exalt him for ever. [64] Bless the Lord, spirits and souls of the righteous, sing praise to him and highly exalt him for ever. [65] Bless the Lord, you who are holy and humble in heart, sing praise to him and highly exalt him for ever. [66] Bless the Lord, Hananiah, Azariah, and Mishael, sing praise to him and highly exalt him for ever; for he has rescued us from Hades and saved us from the hand of death, and delivered us from the midst of the burning fiery furnace; from the midst of the fire he has delivered us. [67] Give thanks to the Lord, for he is good, for his mercy endures for ever. [68] Bless him, all who worship the Lord, the God of gods, sing praise to him and give thanks to him, for his mercy endures for ever."

1 Baruch

Bar.1

[1] These are the words of the book which Baruch the son of Neraiah, son of Mahseiah, son of Zedekiah, son of Hasadiah, son of Hilkiah, wrote in Babylon,

[2] in the fifth year, on the seventh day of the month, at the time when the Chaldeans took Jerusalem and burned it with fire.

[3] And Baruch read the words of this book in the hearing of Jeconiah the son of Jehoiakim, king of Judah, and in the hearing of all the people who came to hear the book,

[4] and in the hearing of the mighty men and the princes, and in the hearing of the elders, and in the hearing of all the people, small and great, all who dwelt in Babylon by the river Sud.

[5] Then they wept, and fasted, and prayed before the Lord;

[6] and they collected money, each giving what he could;

[7] and they sent it to Jerusalem to Jehoiakim the high priest, the son of Hilkiah, son of Shallum, and to the priests, and to all the people who were present with him in Jerusalem.

[8] At the same time, on the tenth day of Sivan, Baruch took the vessels of the house of the Lord, which had been carried away from the temple, to return them to the land of Judah -- the silver vessels which Zedekiah the son of Josiah, king of Judah, had made,

[9] after Nebuchadnezzar king of Babylon had carried away from Jerusalem Jeconiah and the princes and the prisoners and the mighty men and the people of the land, and brought them to Babylon.

[10] And they said: "Herewith we send you money; so buy with the money burnt offerings and sin offerings and incense, and prepare a cereal offering, and offer them upon the altar of the Lord our God;

[11] and pray for the life of Nebuchadnezzar king of Babylon, and for the life of Belshazzar his son, that their days on earth may be like the days of heaven.

[12] And the Lord will give us strength, and he will give light to our eyes, and we shall live under the protection of Nebuchadnezzar king of Babylon, and under the protection of Belshazzar his son, and we shall serve them many days and find favor in their sight.

[13] And pray for us to the Lord our God, for we have sinned against the Lord our God, and to this day the anger of the Lord and his wrath have not turned away from us.

[14] And you shall read this book which we are sending you, to make your confession in the house of the Lord on the days of the feasts and at appointed seasons.

[15] "And you shall say: `Righteousness belongs to the Lord our God, but confusion of face, as at this day, to us, to the men of Judah, to the inhabitants of Jerusalem,

[16] and to our kings and our princes and our priests and our prophets and our fathers,

[17] because we have sinned before the Lord,

[18] and have disobeyed him, and have not heeded the voice of the Lord our God, to walk in the statutes of the Lord which he set before us.

[19] From the day when the Lord brought our fathers out of the land of Egypt until today, we have been disobedient to the Lord our God, and we have been negligent, in not heeding his voice.

[20] So to this day there have clung to us the calamities and the curse which the Lord declared through Moses his servant at the time when he brought our fathers out of the land of Egypt to give to us a land flowing with milk and honey.

[21] We did not heed the voice of the Lord our God in all the words of the prophets whom he sent to us, but we each followed the intent of his own wicked heart by serving other gods and doing what is evil in the sight of the Lord our God.

Bar.2

[1] "`So the Lord confirmed his word, which he spoke against us, and against our judges who judged Israel, and against our kings and against our princes and against the men of Israel and Judah.

[2] Under the whole heaven there has not been done the like of what he has done in Jerusalem, in accordance with what is written in the law of Moses,

[3] that we should eat, one the flesh of his son and another the flesh of his daughter.

[4] And he gave them into subjection to all the kingdoms around us, to be a reproach and a desolation among all the surrounding peoples, where the Lord has scattered them.

[5] They were brought low and not raised up, because we sinned against the Lord our God, in not heeding his voice.

[6] "`Righteousness belongs to the Lord our God, but confusion of face to us and our fathers, as at this day.

[7] All those calamities with which the Lord threatened us have come upon us.

[8] Yet we have not entreated the favor of the Lord by turning away, each of us, from the thoughts of his wicked heart.

[9] And the Lord has kept the calamities ready, and the Lord has brought them upon us, for the Lord is righteous in all his

works which he has commanded us to do.

[10] Yet we have not obeyed his voice, to walk in the statutes of the Lord which he set before us.

[11] "'And now, O Lord God of Israel, who didst bring thy people out of the land of Egypt with a mighty hand and with signs and wonders and with great power and outstretched arm, and hast made thee a name, as at this day,

[12] we have sinned, we have been ungodly, we have done wrong, O Lord our God, against all thy ordinances.

[13] Let thy anger turn away from us, for we are left, few in number, among the nations where thou hast scattered us.

[14] Hear, O Lord, our prayer and our supplication, and for thy own sake deliver us, and grant us favor in the sight of those who have carried us into exile;

[15] that all the earth may know that thou art the Lord our God, for Israel and his descendants are called by thy name.

[16] O Lord, look down from thy holy habitation, and consider us. Incline thy ear, O Lord, and hear;

[17] open thy eyes, O Lord, and see; for the dead who are in Hades, whose spirit has been taken from their bodies, will not ascribe glory or justice to the Lord,

[18] but the person that is greatly distressed, that goes about bent over and feeble, and the eyes that are failing, and the person that hungers, will ascribe to thee glory and righteousness, O Lord.

[19] For it is not because of any righteous deeds of our fathers or our kings that we bring before thee our prayer for mercy, O Lord our God.

[20] For thou hast sent thy anger and thy wrath upon us, as thou didst declare by thy servants the prophets, saying:

[21] "Thus says the Lord: Bend your shoulders and serve the king of Babylon, and you will remain in the land which I gave to your fathers.

[22] But if you will not obey the voice of the Lord and will not serve the king of Babylon,

[23] I will make to cease from the cities of Judah and from the region about Jerusalem the voice of mirth and the voice of gladness, the voice of the bridegroom and the voice of the bride, and the whole land will be a desolation without inhabitants."

[24] "'But we did not obey thy voice, to serve the king of Babylon; and thou hast confirmed thy words, which thou didst speak by thy servants the prophets, that the bones of our kings and the bones of our fathers would be brought out of their graves;

[25] and behold, they have been cast out to the heat of day and the frost of night. They perished in great misery, by famine and sword and pestilence.

[26] And the house which is called by thy name thou hast made as it is today, because of the wickedness of the house of Israel and the house of Judah.

[27] "'Yet thou hast dealt with us, O Lord our God, in all thy kindness and in all thy great compassion,

[28] as thou didst speak by thy servant Moses on the day when thou didst command him to write thy law in the presence of the people of Israel, saying,

[29] "If you will not obey my voice, this very great multitude will surely turn into a small number among the nations, where I will scatter them.

[30] For I know that they will not obey me, for they are a stiff-necked people. But in the land of their exile they will come to themselves,

[31] and they will know that I am the Lord their God. I will give them a heart that obeys and ears that hear;

[32] and they will praise me in the land of their exile, and will remember my name,

[33] and will turn from their stubbornness and their wicked deeds; for they will remember the ways of their fathers, who sinned before the Lord.

[34] I will bring them again into the land which I swore to give to their fathers, to Abraham and to Isaac and to Jacob, and they will rule over it; and I will increase them, and they will not be diminished.

[35] I will make an everlasting covenant with them to be their God and they shall be my people; and I will never again remove my people Israel from the land which I have given them."

Bar.3

[1] "'O Lord Almighty, God of Israel, the soul in anguish and the wearied spirit cry out to thee.

[2] Hear, O Lord, and have mercy, for we have sinned before thee.

[3] For thou art enthroned for ever, and we are perishing for ever.

[4] O Lord Almighty, God of Israel, hear now the prayer of the dead of Israel and of the sons of those who sinned before thee, who did not heed the voice of the Lord their God, so that calamities have clung to us.

[5] Remember not the iniquities of our fathers, but in this crisis remember thy power and thy name.

[6] For thou art the Lord our God, and thee, O Lord, will we praise.

[7] For thou hast put the fear of thee in our hearts in order that we should call upon thy name; and we will praise thee in our exile, for we have put away from our hearts all the iniquity of our fathers who sinned before thee.

[8] Behold, we are today in our exile where thou hast scattered us, to be reproached and cursed and punished for all the iniquities of our fathers who forsook the Lord our God.'"

[9] Hear the commandments of life, O Israel; give ear, and learn wisdom!

[10] Why is it, O Israel, why is it that you are in the land of your enemies, that you are growing old in a foreign country, that you are defiled with the dead,

[11] that you are counted among those in Hades?

[12] You have forsaken the fountain of wisdom. [13] If you had walked in the way of God, you would be dwelling in peace for ever. [14] Learn where there is wisdom, where there is strength, where there is understanding, that you may at the same time discern where there is length of days, and life, where there is light for the eyes, and peace. [15] Who has found her place? And who has entered her storehouses? [16] Where are the princes of the nations, and those who rule over the beasts on earth; [17] those who have sport with the birds of the air, and who hoard up silver and gold, in which men trust, and there is no end to their getting; [18] those who scheme to get silver, and are anxious, whose labors are beyond measure? [19] They have vanished and gone down to Hades, and others have arisen in their place. [20] Young men have seen the light of day, and have dwelt upon the earth; but they have not learned the way to knowledge, nor understood her paths, nor laid hold of her. [21] Their sons have strayed far from her way. [22] She has not been heard of in Canaan, nor seen in Teman; [23] the sons of Hagar, who seek for understanding on the earth, the merchants of Merran and Teman, the story-tellers and the seekers for understanding, have not learned the way to wisdom, nor given thought to her paths. [24] O Israel, how great is the house of God! And how vast the territory that he possesses! [25] It is great and has no bounds; it is high and immeasurable. [26] The giants were born there, who were famous of old, great in stature, expert in war. [27] God did not choose them, nor give them the way to knowledge; [28] so they perished because they had no wisdom, they perished through their folly. [29] Who has gone up into heaven, and taken her, and brought her down from the clouds? [30] Who has gone over the sea, and found her, and will buy her for pure gold? [31] No one knows the way to her, or is concerned about the path to her. [32] But he who knows all things knows her, he found her by his understanding. He who prepared the earth for all time filled it with four-footed creatures; [33] he who sends forth the light, and it goes, called it, and it obeyed him in fear; [34] the stars shone in their watches, and were glad; he called them, and they said, "Here we are!" They shone with gladness for him who made them. [35] This is our God; no other can be compared to him! [36] He found the whole way to knowledge, and gave her to Jacob his servant and to Israel whom he loved. [37] Afterward she appeared upon earth and lived among men.

Bar.4

[1] She is the book of the commandments of God, and the law that endures for ever. All who hold her fast will live, and those who forsake her will die.

[2] Turn, O Jacob, and take her; walk toward the shining of her light.

[3] Do not give your glory to another, or your advantages to an alien people.

[4] Happy are we, O Israel, for we know what is pleasing to God.

[5] Take courage, my people, O memorial of Israel!

[6] It was not for destruction that you were sold to the nations, but you were handed over to your enemies because you angered God.

[7] For you provoked him who made you, by sacrificing to demons and not to God.

[8] You forgot the everlasting God, who brought you up, and you grieved Jerusalem, who reared you.

[9] For she saw the wrath that came upon you from God, and she said: "Hearken, you neighbors of Zion, God has brought great sorrow upon me;

[10] for I have seen the captivity of my sons and daughters, which the Everlasting brought upon them.

[11] With joy I nurtured them, but I sent them away with weeping and sorrow.

[12] Let no one rejoice over me, a widow and bereaved of many; I was left desolate because of the sins of my children, because they turned away from the law of God.

[13] They had no regard for his statutes; they did not walk in the ways of God's commandments, nor tread the paths of discipline in his righteousness.

[14] Let the neighbors of Zion come; remember the capture of my sons and daughters, which the Everlasting brought upon them.

[15] For he brought against them a nation from afar, a shameless nation, of a strange language, who had no respect for an old man, and had no pity for a child.

[16] They led away the widow's beloved sons, and bereaved the lonely woman of her daughters.

[17] "But I, how can I help you?

[18] For he who brought these calamities upon you will deliver you from the hand of your enemies.

[19] Go, my children, go; for I have been left desolate.

[20] I have taken off the robe of peace and put on the sackcloth of my supplication; I will cry to the Everlasting all my days.

[21] "Take courage, my children, cry to God, and he will deliver you from the power and hand of the enemy.

[22] For I have put my hope in the Everlasting to save you, and joy has come to me from the Holy One, because of the mercy which soon will come to you from your everlasting Savior.

[23] For I sent you out with sorrow and weeping, but God will give you back to me with joy and gladness for ever.

[24] For as the neighbors of Zion have now seen your capture, so they soon will see your salvation by God, which will come to you with great glory and with the splendor of the Everlasting.

[25] My children, endure with patience the wrath that has come upon you from God. Your enemy has overtaken you, but you will soon see their destruction and will tread upon their necks.

[26] My tender sons have traveled rough roads; they were taken away like a flock carried off by the enemy.

[27] "Take courage, my children, and cry to God, for you will be remembered by him who brought this upon you.

[28] For just as you purposed to go astray from God, return with tenfold zeal to seek him.

[29] For he who brought these calamities upon you will bring you everlasting joy with your salvation."

[30] Take courage, O Jerusalem, for he who named you will comfort you.

[31] Wretched will be those who afflicted you and rejoiced at your fall.

[32] Wretched will be the cities which your children served as slaves; wretched will be the city which received your sons.

[33] For just as she rejoiced at your fall and was glad for your ruin, so she will be grieved at her own desolation.

[34] And I will take away her pride in her great population, and her insolence will be turned to grief.

[35] For fire will come upon her from the Everlasting for many days, and for a long time she will be inhabited by demons.

[36] Look toward the east, O Jerusalem, and see the joy that is coming to you from God!

[37] Behold, your sons are coming, whom you sent away; they are coming, gathered from east and west, at the word of the Holy One, rejoicing in the glory of God.

Bar.5

[1] Take off the garment of your sorrow and affliction, O Jerusalem, and put on for ever the beauty of the glory from God.

[2] Put on the robe of the righteousness from God; put on your head the diadem of the glory of the Everlasting.

[3] For God will show your splendor everywhere under heaven.

[4] For your name will for ever be called by God, "Peace of righteousness and glory of godliness."

[5] Arise, O Jerusalem, stand upon the height and look toward the east, and see your children gathered from west and east, at the word of the Holy One, rejoicing that God has remembered them.

[6] For they went forth from you on foot, led away by their enemies; but God will bring them back to you, carried in glory, as on a royal throne.

[7] For God has ordered that every high mountain and the everlasting hills be made low and the valleys filled up, to make level ground, so that Israel may walk safely in the glory of God.

[8] The woods and every fragrant tree have shaded Israel at God's command.

[9] For God will lead Israel with joy, in the light of his glory, with the mercy and righteousness that come from him.

Prayer of Manasseh

PrMan.1

[1] O Lord, Almighty God of our fathers, Abraham, Isaac, Jacob, and of their righteous seed;

[2] thou who hast made heaven and earth with all their order;

[3] who hast shackled the sea by thy word of command, who hast confined the deep and sealed it with thy terrible and glorious name;

[4] at whom all things shudder, and tremble before thy power,

[5] for thy glorious splendor cannot be borne, and the wrath of thy threat to sinners is irresistible;

[6] yet immeasurable and unsearchable is thy promised mercy,

[7] for thou art the Lord Most High, of great compassion, long-suffering, and very merciful, and repentest over the evils of men. Thou, O Lord, according to thy great goodness hast promised repentance and forgiveness to those who have sinned against thee; and in the multitude of thy mercies thou hast appointed repentance for sinners, that they may be saved.

[8] Therefore thou, O Lord, God of the righteous, hast not appointed repentance for the righteous, for Abraham and Isaac and Jacob, who did not sin against thee, but thou hast appointed repentance for me, who am a sinner.

[9] For the sins I have committed are more in number than the sand of the sea; my transgressions are multiplied, O Lord, they are multiplied! I am unworthy to look up and see the height of heaven because of the multitude of my iniquities.

[10] I am weighted down with many an iron fetter, so that I am rejected because of my sins, and I have no relief; for I have provoked thy wrath and have done what is evil in thy sight, setting up abominations and multiplying offenses.

[11] And now I bend the knee of my heart, beseeching thee for thy kindness.

[12] I have sinned, O Lord, I have sinned, and I know my transgressions.

[13] I earnestly beseech thee, forgive me, O Lord, forgive me! Do not destroy me with my transgressions! Do not be angry with me for ever or lay up evil for me; do not condemn me to the depths of the earth. For thou, O Lord, art the God of those who repent,

[14] and in me thou wilt manifest thy goodness; for, unworthy as I am, thou wilt save me in thy great mercy,

[15] and I will praise thee continually all the days of my life. For all the host of heaven sings thy praise, and your is the glory for ever. Amen.

Bel and the Dragon

Bel.1
[1] When King Astyages was laid with his fathers, Cyrus the Persian received his kingdom.
[2] And Daniel was a companion of the king, and was the most honored of his friends.
[3] Now the Babylonians had an idol called Bel, and every day they spent on it twelve bushels of fine flour and forty sheep and fifty gallons of wine.
[4] The king revered it and went every day to worship it. But Daniel worshiped his own God.
[5] And the king said to him, "Why do you not worship Bel?" He answered, "Because I do not revere man-made idols, but the living God, who created heaven and earth and has dominion over all flesh."
[6] The king said to him, "Do you not think that Bel is a living God? Do you not see how much he eats and drinks every day?"
[7] Then Daniel laughed, and said, "Do not be deceived, O king; for this is but clay inside and brass outside, and it never ate or drank anything."
[8] Then the king was angry, and he called his priests and said to them, "If you do not tell me who is eating these provisions, you shall die.
[9] But if you prove that Bel is eating them, Daniel shall die, because he blasphemed against Bel." And Daniel said to the king, "Let it be done as you have said."
[10] Now there were seventy priests of Bel, besides their wives and children. And the king went with Daniel into the temple of Bel.
[11] And the priests of Bel said, "Behold, we are going outside; you yourself, O king, shall set forth the food and mix and place the wine, and shut the door and seal it with your signet.
[12] And when you return in the morning, if you do not find that Bel has eaten it all, we will die; or else Daniel will, who is telling lies about us."
[13] They were unconcerned, for beneath the table they had made a hidden entrance, through which they used to go in regularly and consume the provisions.
[14] When they had gone out, the king set forth the food for Bel. Then Daniel ordered his servants to bring ashes and they sifted them throughout the whole temple in the presence of the king alone. Then they went out, shut the door and sealed it with the king's signet, and departed.
[15] In the night the priests came with their wives and children, as they were accustomed to do, and ate and drank everything.
[16] Early in the morning the king rose and came, and Daniel with him.
[17] And the king said, "Are the seals unbroken, Daniel?" He answered, "They are unbroken, O king."
[18] As soon as the doors were opened, the king looked at the table, and shouted in a loud voice, "You are great, O Bel; and with you there is no deceit, none at all."
[19] Then Daniel laughed, and restrained the king from going in, and said, "Look at the floor, and notice whose footsteps these are."
[20] The king said, "I see the footsteps of men and women and children."
[21] Then the king was enraged, and he seized the priests and their wives and children; and they showed him the secret doors through which they were accustomed to enter and devour what was on the table.
[22] Therefore the king put them to death, and gave Bel over to Daniel, who destroyed it and its temple.
[23] There was also a great dragon, which the Babylonians revered.
[24] And the king said to Daniel, "You cannot deny that this is a living god; so worship him."
[25] Daniel said, "I will worship the Lord my God, for he is the living God.
[26] But if you, O king, will give me permission, I will slay the dragon without sword or club." The king said, "I give you permission."
[27] Then Daniel took pitch, fat, and hair, and boiled them together and made cakes, which he fed to the dragon. The dragon ate them, and burst open. And Daniel said, "See what you have been worshiping!"
[28] When the Babylonians heard it, they were very indignant and conspired against the king, saying, "The king has become a Jew; he has destroyed Bel, and slain the dragon, and slaughtered the priests."
[29] Going to the king, they said, "Hand Daniel over to us, or else we will kill you and your household."
[30] The king saw that they were pressing him hard, and under compulsion he handed Daniel over to them.
[31] They threw Daniel into the lions' den, and he was there for six days.
[32] There were seven lions in the den, and every day they had been given two human bodies and two sheep; but these were not given to them now, so that they might devour Daniel.
[33] Now the prophet Habakkuk was in Judea. He had boiled pottage and had broken bread into a bowl, and was going into the field to take it to the reapers.
[34] But the angel of the Lord said to Habakkuk, "Take the dinner which you have to Babylon, to Daniel, in the lions' den."
[35] Habakkuk said, "Sir, I have never seen Babylon, and I know nothing about the den."

[36] Then the angel of the Lord took him by the crown of his head, and lifted him by his hair and set him down in Babylon, right over the den, with the rushing sound of the wind itself.

[37] Then Habakkuk shouted, "Daniel, Daniel! Take the dinner which God has sent you."

[38] And Daniel said, "Thou hast remembered me, O God, and hast not forsaken those who love thee."

[39] So Daniel arose and ate. And the angel of God immediately returned Habakkuk to his own place.

[40] On the seventh day the king came to mourn for Daniel. When he came to the den he looked in, and there sat Daniel.

[41] And the king shouted with a loud voice, "Thou art great, O Lord God of Daniel, and there is no other besides thee."

[42] And he pulled Daniel out, and threw into the den the men who had attempted his destruction, and they were devoured immediately before his eyes.

Wisdom of Jesus Son of Sirach

Sir. Introduction
Whereas many great teachings have been given to us through the law and the prophets and the others that followed them, on account of which we should praise Israel for instruction and wisdom; and since it is necessary not only that the readers themselves should acquire understanding but also that those who love learning should be able to help the outsiders by both speaking and writing, my grandfather Jesus, after devoting himself especially to the reading of the law and the prophets and the other books of our fathers, and after acquiring considerable proficiency in them, was himself also led to write something pertaining to instruction and wisdom, in order that, by becoming conversant with this also, those who love learning should make even greater progress in living according to the law.

You are urged therefore to read with good will and attention, and to be indulgent in cases where, despite out diligent labor in translating, we may seem to have rendered some phrases imperfectly. For what was originally expressed in Hebrew does not have exactly the same sense when translated into another language. Not only this work, but even the law itself, the prophecies, and the rest of the books differ not a little as originally expressed.

When I came to Egypt in the thirty-eighth year of the reign of Euergetes and stayed for some time, I found opportunity for no little instruction. It seemed highly necessary that I should myself devote some pains and labor to the translation of the following book, using in that period of time great watchfulness and skill in order to complete and publish the book for those living abroad who wished to gain learning, being prepared in character to live according to the law.

Sir.1
[1] All wisdom comes from the Lord and is with him for ever.
[2] The sand of the sea, the drops of rain, and the days of eternity -- who can count them?
[3] The height of heaven, the breadth of the earth, the abyss, and wisdom -- who can search them out?
[4] Wisdom was created before all things, and prudent understanding from eternity.
[5] The root of wisdom -- to whom has it been revealed? Her clever devices -- who knows them?
[6] There is One who is wise, greatly to be feared, sitting upon his throne.
[7] The Lord himself created wisdom; he saw her and apportioned her, he poured her out upon all his works.
[8] She dwells with all flesh according to his gift, and he supplied her to those who love him.
[9] The fear of the Lord is glory and exultation, and gladness and a crown of rejoicing.
[10] The fear of the Lord delights the heart, and gives gladness and joy and long life.
[11] With him who fears the Lord it will go well at the end; on the day of his death he will be blessed.
[12] To fear the Lord is the beginning of wisdom; she is created with the faithful in the womb.
[13] She made among men an eternal foundation, and among their descendants she will be trusted.
[14] To fear the Lord is wisdom's full measure; she satisfies men with her fruits;
[15] she fills their whole house with desirable goods, and their storehouses with her produce.
[16] The fear of the Lord is the crown of wisdom, making peace and perfect health to flourish.
[17] He saw her and apportioned her; he rained down knowledge and discerning comprehension, and he exalted the glory of those who held her fast.
[18] To fear the Lord is the root of wisdom, and her branches are long life.
[22] Unrighteous anger cannot be justified, for a man's anger tips the scale to his ruin.
[23] A patient man will endure until the right moment, and then joy will burst forth for him.
[24] He will hide his words until the right moment, and the lips of many will tell of his good sense.
[25] In the treasuries of wisdom are wise sayings, but godliness is an abomination to a sinner.
[26] If you desire wisdom, keep the commandments, and the Lord will supply it for you.
[27] For the fear of the Lord is wisdom and instruction, and he delights in fidelity and meekness.
[28] Do not disobey the fear of the Lord; do not approach him with a divided mind.
[29] Be not a hypocrite in men's sight, and keep watch over your lips.
[30] Do not exalt yourself lest you fall, and thus bring dishonor upon yourself. The Lord will reveal your secrets and cast you down in the midst of the congregation, because you did not come in the fear of the Lord, and your heart was full of deceit.

Sir.2
[1] My son, if you come forward to serve the Lord, prepare yourself for temptation.

[2] Set your heart right and be steadfast, and do not be hasty in time of calamity.
[3] Hold fast to him and do not depart, that you may be honored at the end of your life.
[4] Accept whatever is brought upon you, and in changes that humble you be patient.
[5] For gold is tested in the fire, and acceptable men in the furnace of humiliation.
[6] Trust in him, and he will help you; make your ways straight, and hope in him.
[7] You who fear the Lord, wait for his mercy; and turn not aside, lest you fall.
[8] You who fear the Lord, trust in him, and your reward will not fail;
[9] you who fear the Lord, hope for good things, for everlasting joy and mercy.
[10] Consider the ancient generations and see: who ever trusted in the Lord and was put to shame? Or who ever persevered in the fear of the Lord and was forsaken? Or who ever called upon him and was overlooked?
[11] For the Lord is compassionate and merciful; he forgives sins and saves in time of affliction.
[12] Woe to timid hearts and to slack hands, and to the sinner who walks along two ways!
[13] Woe to the faint heart, for it has no trust! Therefore it will not be sheltered.
[14] Woe to you who have lost your endurance! What will you do when the Lord punishes you?
[15] Those who fear the Lord will not disobey his words, and those who love him will keep his ways.
[16] Those who fear the Lord will seek his approval, and those who love him will be filled with the law.
[17] Those who fear the Lord will prepare their hearts, and will humble themselves before him.
[18] Let us fall into the hands of the Lord, but not into the hands of men; for as his majesty is, so also is his mercy.

Sir.3
[1] Listen to me your father, O children; and act accordingly, that you may be kept in safety.
[2] For the Lord honored the father above the children, and he confirmed the right of the mother over her sons.
[3] Whoever honors his father atones for sins,
[4] and whoever glorifies his mother is like one who lays up treasure.
[5] Whoever honors his father will be gladdened by his own children, and when he prays he will be heard.
[6] Whoever glorifies his father will have long life, and whoever obeys the Lord will refresh his mother;
[7] he will serve his parents as his masters.
[8] Honor your father by word and deed, that a blessing from him may come upon you.
[9] For a father's blessing strengthens the houses of the children, but a mother's curse uproots their foundations.
[10] Do not glorify yourself by dishonoring your father, for your father's dishonor is no glory to you.
[11] For a man's glory comes from honoring his father, and it is a disgrace for children not to respect their mother.
[12] O son, help your father in his old age, and do not grieve him as long as he lives;
[13] even if he is lacking in understanding, show forbearance; in all your strength do not despise him.
[14] For kindness to a father will not be forgotten, and against your sins it will be credited to you;
[15] in the day of your affliction it will be remembered in your favor; as frost in fair weather, your sins will melt away.
[16] Whoever forsakes his father is like a blasphemer, and whoever angers his mother is cursed by the Lord.
[17] My son, perform your tasks in meekness; then you will be loved by those whom God accepts.
[18] The greater you are, the more you must humble yourself; so you will find favor in the sight of the Lord.
[20] For great is the might of the Lord; he is glorified by the humble.
[21] Seek not what is too difficult for you, nor investigate what is beyond your power.
[22] Reflect upon what has been assigned to you, for you do not need what is hidden.
[23] Do not meddle in what is beyond your tasks, for matters too great for human understanding have been shown you.
[24] For their hasty judgment has led many astray, and wrong opinion has caused their thoughts to slip.
[26] A stubborn mind will be afflicted at the end, and whoever loves danger will perish by it.
[27] A stubborn mind will be burdened by troubles, and the sinner will heap sin upon sin.
[28] The affliction of the proud has no healing, for a plant of wickedness has taken root in him.
[29] The mind of the intelligent man will ponder a parable, and an attentive ear is the wise man's desire.
[30] Water extinguishes a blazing fire: so almsgiving atones for sin.
[31] Whoever requites favors gives thought to the future; at the moment of his falling he will find support.

Sir.4
[1] My son, deprive not the poor of his living, and do not keep needy eyes waiting.
[2] Do not grieve the one who is hungry, nor anger a man in want.
[3] Do not add to the troubles of an angry mind, nor delay your gift to a beggar.
[4] Do not reject an afflicted suppliant, nor turn your face away from the poor.
[5] Do not avert your eye from the needy, nor give a man occasion to curse you;
[6] for if in bitterness of soul he calls down a curse upon you, his Creator will hear his prayer.

[7] Make yourself beloved in the congregation; bow your head low to a great man.

[8] Incline your ear to the poor, and answer him peaceably and gently.

[9] Deliver him who is wronged from the hand of the wrongdoer; and do not be fainthearted in judging a case.

[10] Be like a father to orphans, and instead of a husband to their mother; you will then be like a son of the Most High, and he will love you more than does your mother.

[11] Wisdom exalts her sons and gives help to those who seek her.

[12] Whoever loves her loves life, and those who seek her early will be filled with joy.

[13] Whoever holds her fast will obtain glory, and the Lord will bless the place she enters.

[14] Those who serve her will minister to the Holy One; the Lord loves those who love her.

[15] He who obeys her will judge the nations, and whoever gives heed to her will dwell secure.

[16] If he has faith in her he will obtain her; and his descendants will remain in possession of her.

[17] For at first she will walk with him on tortuous paths, she will bring fear and cowardice upon him, and will torment him by her discipline until she trusts him, and she will test him with her ordinances.

[18] Then she will come straight back to him and gladden him, and will reveal her secrets to him.

[19] If he goes astray she will forsake him, and hand him over to his ruin.

[20] Observe the right time, and beware of evil; and do not bring shame on yourself.

[21] For there is a shame which brings sin, and there is a shame which is glory and favor.

[22] Do not show partiality, to your own harm, or deference, to your downfall.

[23] Do not refrain from speaking at the crucial time, and do not hide your wisdom.

[24] For wisdom is known through speech, and education through the words of the tongue.

[25] Never speak against the truth, but be mindful of your ignorance.

[26] Do not be ashamed to confess your sins, and do not try to stop the current of a river.

[27] Do not subject yourself to a foolish fellow, nor show partiality to a ruler.

[28] Strive even to death for the truth and the Lord God will fight for you.

[29] Do not be reckless in your speech, or sluggish and remiss in your deeds.

[30] Do not be like a lion in your home, nor be a faultfinder with your servants.

[31] Let not your hand be extended to receive, but withdrawn when it is time to repay.

Sir.5

[1] Do not set your heart on your wealth, nor say, "I have enough."

[2] Do not follow your inclination and strength, walking according to the desires of your heart.

[3] Do not say, "Who will have power over me?" for the Lord will surely punish you.

[4] Do not say, "I sinned, and what happened to me?" for the Lord is slow to anger.

[5] Do not be so confident of atonement that you add sin to sin.

[6] Do not say, "His mercy is great, he will forgive the multitude of my sins," for both mercy and wrath are with him, and his anger rests on sinners.

[7] Do not delay to turn to the Lord, nor postpone it from day to day; for suddenly the wrath of the Lord will go forth, and at the time of punishment you will perish.

[8] Do not depend on dishonest wealth, for it will not benefit you in the day of calamity.

[9] Do not winnow with every wind, nor follow every path: the double-tongued sinner does that.

[10] Be steadfast in your understanding, and let your speech be consistent.

[11] Be quick to hear, and be deliberate in answering.

[12] If you have understanding, answer your neighbor; but if not, put your hand on your mouth.

[13] Glory and dishonor come from speaking, and a man's tongue is his downfall.

[14] Do not be called a slanderer, and do not lie in ambush with your tongue; for shame comes to the thief, and severe condemnation to the double-tongued.

[15] In great and small matters do not act amiss,

Sir.6

[1] and do not become an enemy instead of a friend; for a bad name incurs shame and reproach: so fares the double-tongued sinner.

[2] Do not exalt yourself through your soul's counsel, lest your soul be torn in pieces like a bull.

[3] You will devour your leaves and destroy your fruit, and will be left like a withered tree.

[4] An evil soul will destroy him who has it, and make him the laughingstock of his enemies.

[5] A pleasant voice multiplies friends, and a gracious tongue multiplies courtesies.

[6] Let those that are at peace with you be many, but let your advisers be one in a thousand.

[7] When you gain a friend, gain him through testing, and do not trust him hastily.

[8] For there is a friend who is such at his own convenience, but will not stand by you in your day of trouble.

[9] And there is a friend who changes into an enemy, and will disclose a quarrel to your disgrace.

[10] And there is a friend who is a table companion, but will not stand by you in your day of trouble.

[11] In prosperity he will make himself your equal, and be bold with your servants;

[12] but if you are brought low he will turn against you, and will hide himself from your presence.

[13] Keep yourself far from your enemies, and be on guard toward your friends.

[14] A faithful friend is a sturdy shelter: he that has found one has found a treasure.

[15] There is nothing so precious as a faithful friend, and no scales can measure his excellence.

[16] A faithful friend is an elixir of life; and those who fear the Lord will find him.

[17] Whoever fears the Lord directs his friendship aright, for as he is, so is his neighbor also.

[18] My son, from your youth up choose instruction, and until you are old you will keep finding wisdom.

[19] Come to her like one who plows and sows, and wait for her good harvest. For in her service you will toil a little while, and soon you will eat of her produce.

[20] She seems very harsh to the uninstructed; a weakling will not remain with her.

[21] She will weigh him down like a heavy testing stone, and he will not be slow to cast her off.

[22] For wisdom is like her name, and is not manifest to many.

[23] Listen, my son, and accept my judgment; do not reject my counsel.

[24] Put your feet into her fetters, and your neck into her collar.

[25] Put your shoulder under her and carry her, and do not fret under her bonds.

[26] Come to her with all your soul, and keep her ways with all your might.

[27] Search out and seek, and she will become known to you; and when you get hold of her, do not let her go.

[28] For at last you will find the rest she gives, and she will be changed into joy for you.

[29] Then her fetters will become for you a strong protection, and her collar a glorious robe.

[30] Her yoke is a golden ornament, and her bonds are a cord of blue.

[31] You will wear her like a glorious robe, and put her on like a crown of gladness.

[32] If you are willing, my son, you will be taught, and if you apply yourself you will become clever.

[33] If you love to listen you will gain knowledge, and if you incline your ear you will become wise.

[34] Stand in the assembly of the elders. Who is wise? Hold fast to him.

[35] Be ready to listen to every narrative, and do not let wise proverbs escape you.

[36] If you see an intelligent man, visit him early; let your foot wear out his doorstep.

[37] Reflect on the statutes of the Lord, and meditate at all times on his commandments. It is he who will give insight to your mind, and your desire for wisdom will be granted.

Sir.7

[1] Do no evil, and evil will never befall you.

[2] Stay away from wrong, and it will turn away from you.

[3] My son, do not sow the furrows of injustice, and you will not reap a sevenfold crop.

[4] Do not seek from the Lord the highest office, nor the seat of honor from the king.

[5] Do not assert your righteousness before the Lord, nor display your wisdom before the king.

[6] Do not seek to become a judge, lest you be unable to remove iniquity, lest you be partial to a powerful man, and thus put a blot on your integrity.

[7] Do not offend against the public, and do not disgrace yourself among the people.

[8] Do not commit a sin twice; even for one you will not go unpunished.

[9] Do not say, "He will consider the multitude of my gifts, and when I make an offering to the Most High God he will accept it."

[10] Do not be fainthearted in your prayer, nor neglect to give alms.

[11] Do not ridicule a man who is bitter in soul, for there is One who abases and exalts.

[12] Do not devise a lie against your brother, nor do the like to a friend.

[13] Refuse to utter any lie, for the habit of lying serves no good.

[14] Do not prattle in the assembly of the elders, nor repeat yourself in your prayer.

[15] Do not hate toilsome labor, or farm work, which were created by the Most High.

[16] Do not count yourself among the crowd of sinners; remember that wrath does not delay.

[17] Humble yourself greatly, for the punishment of the ungodly is fire and worms.

[18] Do not exchange a friend for money, or a real brother for the gold of Ophir.

[19] Do not deprive yourself of a wise and good wife, for her charm is worth more than gold.

[20] Do not abuse a servant who performs his work faithfully, or a hired laborer who devotes himself to you.

[21] Let your soul love an intelligent servant; do not withhold from him his freedom.

[22] Do you have cattle? Look after them; if they are profitable to you, keep them.

[23] Do you have children? Discipline them, and make them obedient from their youth.

[24] Do you have daughters? Be concerned for their chastity, and do not show yourself too indulgent with them.

[25] Give a daughter in marriage; you will have finished a great task. But give her to a man of understanding.

[26] If you have a wife who pleases you, do not cast her out; but do not trust yourself to one whom you detest.

[27] With all your heart honor your father, and do not forget the birth pangs of your mother.

[28] Remember that through your parents you were born; and what can you give back to them that equals their gift to you?

[29] With all your soul fear the Lord, and honor his priests.

[30] With all your might love your Maker, and do not forsake his ministers.

[31] Fear the Lord and honor the priest, and give him his portion, as is commanded you: the first fruits, the guilt offering, the gift of the shoulders, the sacrifice of sanctification, and the first fruits of the holy things.

[32] Stretch forth your hand to the poor, so that your blessing may be complete.

[33] Give graciously to all the living, and withhold not kindness from the dead.

[34] Do not fail those who weep, but mourn with those who mourn.

[35] Do not shrink from visiting a sick man, because for such deeds you will be loved.

[36] In all you do, remember the end of your life, and then you will never sin.

Sir.8

[1] Do not contend with a powerful man, lest you fall into his hands.

[2] Do not quarrel with a rich man, lest his resources outweigh yours; for gold has ruined many, and has perverted the minds of kings.

[3] Do not argue with a chatterer, nor heap wood on his fire.

[4] Do not jest with an ill-bred person, lest your ancestors be disgraced.

[5] Do not reproach a man who is turning away from sin; remember that we all deserve punishment.

[6] Do not disdain a man when he is old, for some of us are growing old.

[7] Do not rejoice over any one's death; remember that we all must die.

[8] Do not slight the discourse of the sages, but busy yourself with their maxims; because from them you will gain instruction and learn how to serve great men.

[9] Do not disregard the discourse of the aged, for they themselves learned from their fathers; because from them you will gain understanding and learn how to give an answer in time of need.

[10] Do not kindle the coals of a sinner, lest you be burned in his flaming fire.

[11] Do not get up and leave an insolent fellow, lest he lie in ambush against your words.

[12] Do not lend to a man who is stronger than you; but if you do lend anything, be as one who has lost it.

[13] Do not give surety beyond your means, but if you give surety, be concerned as one who must pay.

[14] Do not go to law against a judge, for the decision will favor him because of his standing.

[15] Do not travel on the road with a foolhardy fellow, lest he be burdensome to you; for he will act as he pleases, and through his folly you will perish with him.

[16] Do not fight with a wrathful man, and do not cross the wilderness with him; because blood is as nothing in his sight, and where no help is at hand, he will strike you down.

[17] Do not consult with a fool, for he will not be able to keep a secret.

[18] In the presence of a stranger do nothing that is to be kept secret, for you do not know what he will divulge.

[19] Do not reveal your thoughts to every one, lest you drive away your good luck.

Sir.9

[1] Do not be jealous of the wife of your bosom, and do not teach her an evil lesson to your own hurt.

[2] Do not give yourself to a woman so that she gains mastery over your strength.

[3] Do not go to meet a loose woman, lest you fall into her snares.

[4] Do not associate with a woman singer, lest you be caught in her intrigues.

[5] Do not look intently at a virgin, lest you stumble and incur penalties for her.

[6] Do not give yourself to harlots lest you lose your inheritance.

[7] Do not look around in the streets of a city, nor wander about in its deserted sections.

[8] Turn away your eyes from a shapely woman, and do not look intently at beauty belonging to another; many have been misled by a woman's beauty, and by it passion is kindled like a fire.

[9] Never dine with another man's wife, nor revel with her at wine; lest your heart turn aside to her, and in blood you be plunged into destruction.

[10] Forsake not an old friend, for a new one does not compare with him. A new friend is like new wine; when it has aged you will drink it with pleasure.

[11] Do not envy the honors of a sinner, for you do not know what his end will be.

[12] Do not delight in what pleases the ungodly; remember that they will not be held guiltless as long as they live.
[13] Keep far from a man who has the power to kill, and you will not be worried by the fear of death. But if you approach him, make no misstep, lest he rob you of your life. Know that you are walking in the midst of snares, and that you are going about on the city battlements.
[14] As much as you can, aim to know your neighbors, and consult with the wise.
[15] Let your conversation be with men of understanding, and let all your discussion be about the law of the Most High.
[16] Let righteous men be your dinner companions, and let your glorying be in the fear of the Lord.
[17] A work will be praised for the skill of the craftsmen; so a people's leader is proved wise by his words.
[18] A babbler is feared in his city, and the man who is reckless in speech will be hated.

Sir.10
[1] A wise magistrate will educate his people, and the rule of an understanding man will be well ordered.
[2] Like the magistrate of the people, so are his officials; and like the ruler of the city, so are all its inhabitants.
[3] An undisciplined king will ruin his people, but a city will grow through the understanding of its rulers.
[4] The government of the earth is in the hands of the Lord, and over it he will raise up the right man for the time.
[5] The success of a man is in the hands of the Lord, and he confers his honor upon the person of the scribe.
[6] Do not be angry with your neighbor for any injury, and do not attempt anything by acts of insolence.
[7] Arrogance is hateful before the Lord and before men, and injustice is outrageous to both.
[8] Sovereignty passes from nation to nation on account of injustice and insolence and wealth.
[9] How can he who is dust and ashes be proud? for even in life his bowels decay.
[10] A long illness baffles the physician; the king of today will die tomorrow.
[11] For when a man is dead, he will inherit creeping things, and wild beasts, and worms.
[12] The beginning of man's pride is to depart from the Lord; his heart has forsaken his Maker.
[13] For the beginning of pride is sin, and the man who clings to it pours out abominations. Therefore the Lord brought upon them extraordinary afflictions, and destroyed them utterly.
[14] The Lord has cast down the thrones of rulers, and has seated the lowly in their place.
[15] The Lord has plucked up the roots of the nations, and has planted the humble in their place.
[16] The Lord has overthrown the lands of the nations, and has destroyed them to the foundations of the earth.
[17] He has removed some of them and destroyed them, and has extinguished the memory of them from the earth.
[18] Pride was not created for men, nor fierce anger for those born of women.
[19] What race is worthy of honor? The human race. What race is worthy of honor? Those who fear the Lord. What race is unworthy of honor? The human race. What race is unworthy of honor? Those who transgress the commandments.
[20] Among brothers their leader is worthy of honor, and those who fear the Lord are worthy of honor in his eyes.
[22] The rich, and the eminent, and the poor -- their glory is the fear of the Lord.
[23] It is not right to despise an intelligent poor man, nor is it proper to honor a sinful man.
[24] The nobleman, and the judge, and the ruler will be honored, but none of them is greater than the man who fears the Lord.
[25] Free men will be at the service of a wise servant, and a man of understanding will not grumble.
[26] Do not make a display of your wisdom when you do your work, nor glorify yourself at a time when you are in want.
[27] Better is a man who works and has an abundance of everything, than one who goes about boasting, but lacks bread.
[28] My son, glorify yourself with humility, and ascribe to yourself honor according to your worth.
[29] Who will justify the man that sins against himself? And who will honor the man that dishonors his own life?
[30] A poor man is honored for his knowledge, while a rich man is honored for his wealth.
[31] A man honored in poverty, how much more in wealth! And a man dishonored in wealth, how much more in poverty!

Sir.11
[1] The wisdom of a humble man will lift up his head, and will seat him among the great.
[2] Do not praise a man for his good looks, nor loathe a man because of his appearance.
[3] The bee is small among flying creatures, but her product is the best of sweet things.
[4] Do not boast about wearing fine clothes, nor exalt yourself in the day that you are honored; for the works of the Lord are wonderful, and his works are concealed from men.
[5] Many kings have had to sit on the ground, but one who was never thought of has worn a crown.
[6] Many rulers have been greatly disgraced, and illustrious men have been handed over to others.
[7] Do not find fault before you investigate; first consider, and then reprove.
[8] Do not answer before you have heard, nor interrupt a speaker in the midst of his words.
[9] Do not argue about a matter which does not concern you, nor sit with sinners when they judge a case.
[10] My son, do not busy yourself with many matters; if you multiply activities you will not go unpunished, and if you

pursue you will not overtake, and by fleeing you will not escape.

[11] There is a man who works, and toils, and presses on, but is so much the more in want.

[12] There is another who is slow and needs help, who lacks strength and abounds in poverty; but the eyes of the Lord look upon him for his good; he lifts him out of his low estate

[13] and raises up his head, so that many are amazed at him.

[14] Good things and bad, life and death, poverty and wealth, come from the Lord.

[17] The gift of the Lord endures for those who are godly, and what he approves will have lasting success.

[18] There is a man who is rich through his diligence and self-denial, and this is the reward allotted to him:

[19] when he says, "I have found rest, and now I shall enjoy my goods!" he does not know how much time will pass until he leaves them to others and dies.

[20] Stand by your covenant and attend to it, and grow old in your work.

[21] Do not wonder at the works of a sinner, but trust in the Lord and keep at your toil; for it is easy in the sight of the Lord to enrich a poor man quickly and suddenly.

[22] The blessing of the Lord is the reward of the godly, and quickly God causes his blessing to flourish.

[23] Do not say, "What do I need, and what prosperity could be mine in the future?"

[24] Do not say, "I have enough, and what calamity could happen to me in the future?"

[25] In the day of prosperity, adversity is forgotten, and in the day of adversity, prosperity is not remembered.

[26] For it is easy in the sight of the Lord to reward a man on the day of death according to his conduct.

[27] The misery of an hour makes one forget luxury, and at the close of a man's life his deeds will be revealed.

[28] Call no one happy before his death; a man will be known through his children.

[29] Do not bring every man into your home, for many are the wiles of the crafty.

[30] Like a decoy partridge in a cage, so is the mind of a proud man, and like a spy he observes your weakness;

[31] for he lies in wait, turning good into evil, and to worthy actions he will attach blame.

[32] From a spark of fire come many burning coals, and a sinner lies in wait to shed blood.

[33] Beware of a scoundrel, for he devises evil, lest he give you a lasting blemish.

[34] Receive a stranger into your home and he will upset you with commotion, and will estrange you from your family.

Sir.12

[1] If you do a kindness, know to whom you do it, and you will be thanked for your good deeds.

[2] Do good to a godly man, and you will be repaid --if not by him, certainly by the Most High.

[3] No good will come to the man who persists in evil or to him who does not give alms.

[4] Give to the godly man, but do not help the sinner.

[5] Do good to the humble, but do not give to the ungodly; hold back his bread, and do not give it to him, lest by means of it he subdue you; for you will receive twice as much evil for all the good which you do to him.

[6] For the Most High also hates sinners and will inflict punishment on the ungodly.

[7] Give to the good man, but do not help the sinner.

[8] A friend will not be known in prosperity, nor will an enemy be hidden in adversity.

[9] A man's enemies are grieved when he prospers, and in his adversity even his friend will separate from him.

[10] Never trust your enemy, for like the rusting of copper, so is his wickedness.

[11] Even if he humbles himself and goes about cringing, watch yourself, and be on your guard against him; and you will be to him like one who has polished a mirror, and you will know that it was not hopelessly tarnished.

[12] Do not put him next to you, lest he overthrow you and take your place; do not have him sit at your right, lest he try to take your seat of honor, and at last you will realize the truth of my words, and be stung by what I have said.

[13] Who will pity a snake charmer bitten by a serpent, or any who go near wild beasts?

[14] So no one will pity a man who associates with a sinner and becomes involved in his sins.

[15] He will stay with you for a time, but if you falter, he will not stand by you.

[16] An enemy will speak sweetly with his lips, but in his mind he will plan to throw you into a pit; an enemy will weep with his eyes, but if he finds an opportunity his thirst for blood will be insatiable.

[17] If calamity befalls you, you will find him there ahead of you; and while pretending to help you, he will trip you by the heel;

[18] he will shake his head, and clap his hands, and whisper much, and change his expression.

Sir.13

[1] Whoever touches pitch will be defiled, and whoever associates with a proud man will become like him.

[2] Do not lift a weight beyond your strength, nor associate with a man mightier and richer than you. How can the clay pot associate with the iron kettle? The pot will strike against it, and will itself be broken.

[3] A rich man does wrong, and he even adds reproaches; a poor man suffers wrong, and he must add apologies.

[4] A rich man will exploit you if you can be of use to him, but if you are in need he will forsake you.

[5] If you own something, he will live with you; he will drain your resources and he will not care.

[6] When he needs you he will deceive you, he will smile at you and give you hope. He will speak to you kindly and say, "What do you need?"

[7] He will shame you with his foods, until he has drained you two or three times; and finally he will deride you. Should he see you afterwards, he will forsake you, and shake his head at you.

[8] Take care not to be led astray, and not to be humiliated in your feasting.

[9] When a powerful man invites you, be reserved; and he will invite you the more often.

[10] Do not push forward, lest you be repulsed; and do not remain at a distance, lest you be forgotten.

[11] Do not try to treat him as an equal, nor trust his abundance of words; for he will test you through much talk, and while he smiles he will be examining you.

[12] Cruel is he who does not keep words to himself; he will not hesitate to injure or to imprison.

[13] Keep words to yourself and be very watchful, for you are walking about with your own downfall.

[15] Every creature loves its like, and every person his neighbor;

[16] all living beings associate by species, and a man clings to one like himself.

[17] What fellowship has a wolf with a lamb? No more has a sinner with a godly man.

[18] What peace is there between a hyena and a dog? And what peace between a rich man and a poor man?

[19] Wild asses in the wilderness are the prey of lions; likewise the poor are pastures for the rich.

[20] Humility is an abomination to a proud man; likewise a poor man is an abomination to a rich one.

[21] When a rich man totters, he is steadied by friends, but when a humble man falls, he is even pushed away by friends.

[22] If a rich man slips, his helpers are many; he speaks unseemly words, and they justify him. If a humble man slips, they even reproach him; he speaks sensibly, and receives no attention.

[23] When the rich man speaks all are silent, and they extol to the clouds what he says. When the poor man speaks they say, "Who is this fellow?" And should he stumble, they even push him down.

[24] Riches are good if they are free from sin, and poverty is evil in the opinion of the ungodly.

[25] A man's heart changes his countenance, either for good or for evil.

[26] The mark of a happy heart is a cheerful face, but to devise proverbs requires painful thinking.

Sir.14

[1] Blessed is the man who does not blunder with his lips and need not suffer grief for sin.

[2] Blessed is he whose heart does not condemn him, and who has not given up his hope.

[3] Riches are not seemly for a stingy man; and of what use is property to an envious man?

[4] Whoever accumulates by depriving himself, accumulates for others; and others will live in luxury on his goods.

[5] If a man is mean to himself, to whom will he be generous? He will not enjoy his own riches.

[6] No one is meaner than the man who is grudging to himself, and this is the retribution for his baseness;

[7] even if he does good, he does it unintentionally, and betrays his baseness in the end.

[8] Evil is the man with a grudging eye; he averts his face and disregards people.

[9] A greedy man's eye is not satisfied with a portion, and mean injustice withers the soul.

[10] A stingy man's eye begrudges bread, and it is lacking at his table.

[11] My son, treat yourself well, according to your means, and present worthy offerings to the Lord.

[12] Remember that death will not delay, and the decree of Hades has not been shown to you.

[13] Do good to a friend before you die, and reach out and give to him as much as you can.

[14] Do not deprive yourself of a happy day; let not your share of desired good pass by you.

[15] Will you not leave the fruit of your labors to another, and what you acquired by toil to be divided by lot?

[16] Give, and take, and beguile yourself, because in Hades one cannot look for luxury.

[17] All living beings become old like a garment, for the decree from of old is, "You must surely die!"

[18] Like flourishing leaves on a spreading tree which sheds some and puts forth others, so are the generations of flesh and blood: one dies and another is born.

[19] Every product decays and ceases to exist, and the man who made it will pass away with it.

[20] Blessed is the man who meditates on wisdom and who reasons intelligently.

[21] He who reflects in his mind on her ways will also ponder her secrets.

[22] Pursue wisdom like a hunter, and lie in wait on her paths.

[23] He who peers through her windows will also listen at her doors;

[24] he who encamps near her house will also fasten his tent peg to her walls;

[25] he will pitch his tent near her, and will lodge in an excellent lodging place;

[26] he will place his children under her shelter, and will camp under her boughs;

[27] he will be sheltered by her from the heat, and will dwell in the midst of her glory.

Sir.15

[1] The man who fears the Lord will do this, and he who holds to the law will obtain wisdom.

[2] She will come to meet him like a mother, and like the wife of his youth she will welcome him.

[3] She will feed him with the bread of understanding, and give him the water of wisdom to drink.

[4] He will lean on her and will not fall, and he will rely on her and will not be put to shame.

[5] She will exalt him above his neighbors, and will open his mouth in the midst of the assembly.

[6] He will find gladness and a crown of rejoicing, and will acquire an everlasting name.

[7] Foolish men will not obtain her, and sinful men will not see her.

[8] She is far from men of pride, and liars will never think of her.

[9] A hymn of praise is not fitting on the lips of a sinner, for it has not been sent from the Lord.

[10] For a hymn of praise should be uttered in wisdom, and the Lord will prosper it.

[11] Do not say, "Because of the Lord I left the right way"; for he will not do what he hates.

[12] Do not say, "It was he who led me astray"; for he had no need of a sinful man.

[13] The Lord hates all abominations, and they are not loved by those who fear him.

[14] It was he who created man in the beginning, and he left him in the power of his own inclination.

[15] If you will, you can keep the commandments, and to act faithfully is a matter of your own choice.

[16] He has placed before you fire and water: stretch out your hand for whichever you wish.

[17] Before a man are life and death, and whichever he chooses will be given to him.

[18] For great is the wisdom of the Lord; he is mighty in power and sees everything;

[19] his eyes are on those who fear him, and he knows every deed of man.

[20] He has not commanded any one to be ungodly, and he has not given any one permission to sin.

Sir.16

[1] Do not desire a multitude of useless children, nor rejoice in ungodly sons.

[2] If they multiply , do not rejoice in them, unless the fear of the Lord is in them.

[3] Do not trust in their survival, and do not rely on their multitude; for one is better than a thousand, and to die childless is better than to have ungodly children.

[4] For through one man of understanding a city will be filled with people, but through a tribe of lawless men it will be made desolate.

[5] Many such things my eye has seen, and my ear has heard things more striking than these.

[6] In an assembly of sinners a fire will be kindled, and in a disobedient nation wrath was kindled.

[7] He was not propitiated for the ancient giants who revolted in their might.

[8] He did not spare the neighbors of Lot, whom he loathed on account of their insolence.

[9] He showed no pity for a nation devoted to destruction, for those destroyed in their sins;

[10] nor for the six hundred thousand men on foot, who rebelliously assembled in their stubbornness.

[11] Even if there is only one stiff-necked person, it will be a wonder if he remains unpunished. For mercy and wrath are with the Lord; he is mighty to forgive, and he pours out wrath.

[12] As great as his mercy, so great is also his reproof; he judges a man according to his deeds.

[13] The sinner will not escape with his plunder, and the patience of the godly will not be frustrated.

[14] He will make room for every act of mercy; every one will receive in accordance with his deeds.

[17] Do not say, "I shall be hidden from the Lord, and who from on high will remember me? Among so many people I shall not be known, for what is my soul in the boundless creation?

[18] Behold, heaven and the highest heaven, the abyss and the earth, will tremble at his visitation.

[19] The mountains also and the foundations of the earth shake with trembling when he looks upon them.

[20] And no mind will reflect on this. Who will ponder his ways?

[21] Like a tempest which no man can see, so most of his works are concealed.

[22] Who will announce his acts of justice? Or who will await them? For the covenant is far off."

[23] This is what one devoid of understanding thinks; a senseless and misguided man thinks foolishly.

[24] Listen to me, my son, and acquire knowledge, and pay close attention to my words.

[25] I will impart instruction by weight, and declare knowledge accurately.

[26] The works of the Lord have existed from the beginning by his creation, and when he made them, he determined their divisions.

[27] He arranged his works in an eternal order, and their dominion for all generations; they neither hunger nor grow weary, and they do not cease from their labors.

[28] They do not crowd one another aside, and they will never disobey his word.

[29] After this the Lord looked upon the earth, and filled it with his good things;

[30] with all kinds of living beings he covered its surface, and to it they return.

Sir.17

[1] The Lord created man out of earth, and turned him back to it again.
[2] He gave to men few days, a limited time, but granted them authority over the things upon the earth.
[3] He endowed them with strength like his own, and made them in his own image.
[4] He placed the fear of them in all living beings, and granted them dominion over beasts and birds.
[6] He made for them tongue and eyes; he gave them ears and a mind for thinking.
[7] He filled them with knowledge and understanding, and showed them good and evil.
[8] He set his eye upon their hearts to show them the majesty of his works.
[10] And they will praise his holy name, to proclaim the grandeur of his works.
[11] He bestowed knowledge upon them, and allotted to them the law of life.
[12] He established with them an eternal covenant, and showed them his judgments.
[13] Their eyes saw his glorious majesty, and their ears heard the glory of his voice.
[14] And he said to them, "Beware of all unrighteousness." And he gave commandment to each of them concerning his neighbor.
[15] Their ways are always before him, they will not be hid from his eyes.
[17] He appointed a ruler for every nation, but Israel is the Lord's own portion.
[19] All their works are as the sun before him, and his eyes are continually upon their ways.
[20] Their iniquities are not hidden from him, and all their sins are before the Lord.
[22] A man's almsgiving is like a signet with the Lord and he will keep a person's kindness like the apple of his eye.
[23] Afterward he will arise and requite them, and he will bring their recompense on their heads.
[24] Yet to those who repent he grants a return, and he encourages those whose endurance is failing.
[25] Turn to the Lord and forsake your sins; pray in his presence and lessen your offenses.
[26] Return to the Most High and turn away from iniquity, and hate abominations intensely.
[27] Who will sing praises to the Most High in Hades, as do those who are alive and give thanks?
[28] From the dead, as from one who does not exist, thanksgiving has ceased; he who is alive and well sings the Lord's praises.
[29] How great is the mercy of the Lord, and his forgiveness for those who turn to him!
[30] For all things cannot be in men, since a son of man is not immortal.
[31] What is brighter than the sun? Yet its light fails. So flesh and blood devise evil.
[32] He marshals the host of the height of heaven; but all men are dust and ashes.

Sir.18

[1] He who lives for ever created the whole universe;
[2] the Lord alone will be declared righteous.
[4] To none has he given power to proclaim his works; and who can search out his mighty deeds?
[5] Who can measure his majestic power? And who can fully recount his mercies?
[6] It is not possible to diminish or increase them, nor is it possible to trace the wonders of the Lord.
[7] When a man has finished, he is just beginning, and when he stops, he will be at a loss.
[8] What is man, and of what use is he? What is his good and what is his evil?
[9] The number of a man's days is great if he reaches a hundred years.
[10] Like a drop of water from the sea and a grain of sand so are a few years in the day of eternity.
[11] Therefore the Lord is patient with them and pours out his mercy upon them.
[12] He sees and recognizes that their end will be evil; therefore he grants them forgiveness in abundance.
[13] The compassion of man is for his neighbor, but the compassion of the Lord is for all living beings. He rebukes and trains and teaches them, and turns them back, as a shepherd his flock.
[14] He has compassion on those who accept his discipline and who are eager for his judgments.
[15] My son, do not mix reproach with your good deeds, nor cause grief by your words when you present a gift.
[16] Does not the dew assuage the scorching heat? So a word is better than a gift.
[17] Indeed, does not a word surpass a good gift? Both are to be found in a gracious man.
[18] A fool is ungracious and abusive, and the gift of a grudging man makes the eyes dim.
[19] Before you speak, learn, and before you fall ill, take care of your health.
[20] Before judgment, examine yourself, and in the hour of visitation you will find forgiveness.
[21] Before falling ill, humble yourself, and when you are on the point of sinning, turn back.
[22] Let nothing hinder you from paying a vow promptly, and do not wait until death to be released from it.
[23] Before making a vow, prepare yourself; and do not be like a man who tempts the Lord.
[24] Think of his wrath on the day of death, and of the moment of vengeance when he turns away his face.

[25] In the time of plenty think of the time of hunger; in the days of wealth think of poverty and need.

[26] From morning to evening conditions change, and all things move swiftly before the Lord.

[27] A wise man is cautious in everything, and in days of sin he guards against wrongdoing.

[28] Every intelligent man knows wisdom, and he praises the one who finds her.

[29] Those who understand sayings become skilled themselves, and pour forth apt proverbs.

[30] Do not follow your base desires, but restrain your appetites.

[31] If you allow your soul to take pleasure in base desire, it will make you the laughingstock of your enemies.

[32] Do not revel in great luxury, lest you become impoverished by its expense.

[33] Do not become a beggar by feasting with borrowed money, when you have nothing in your purse.

Sir.19

[1] A workman who is a drunkard will not become rich; he who despises small things will fail little by little.

[2] Wine and women lead intelligent men astray, and the man who consorts with harlots is very reckless.

[3] Decay and worms will inherit him, and the reckless soul will be snatched away.

[4] One who trusts others too quickly is lightminded, and one who sins does wrong to himself.

[5] One who rejoices in wickedness will be condemned,

[6] and for one who hates gossip evil is lessened.

[7] Never repeat a conversation, and you will lose nothing at all.

[8] With friend or foe do not report it, and unless it would be a sin for you, do not disclose it;

[9] for some one has heard you and watched you, and when the time comes he will hate you.

[10] Have you heard a word? Let it die with you. Be brave! It will not make you burst!

[11] With such a word a fool will suffer pangs like a woman in labor with a child.

[12] Like an arrow stuck in the flesh of the thigh, so is a word inside a fool.

[13] Question a friend, perhaps he did not do it; but if he did anything, so that he may do it no more.

[14] Question a neighbor, perhaps he did not say it; but if he said it, so that he may not say it again.

[15] Question a friend, for often it is slander; so do not believe everything you hear.

[16] A person may make a slip without intending it. Who has never sinned with his tongue?

[17] Question your neighbor before you threaten him; and let the law of the Most High take its course.

[20] All wisdom is the fear of the Lord, and in all wisdom there is the fulfilment of the law.

[22] But the knowledge of wickedness is not wisdom, nor is there prudence where sinners take counsel.

[23] There is a cleverness which is abominable, but there is a fool who merely lacks wisdom.

[24] Better is the God-fearing man who lacks intelligence, than the highly prudent man who transgresses the law.

[25] There is a cleverness which is scrupulous but unjust, and there are people who distort kindness to gain a verdict.

[26] There is a rascal bowed down in mourning, but inwardly he is full of deceit.

[27] He hides his face and pretends not to hear; but where no one notices, he will forestall you.

[28] And if by lack of strength he is prevented from sinning, he will do evil when he finds an opportunity.

[29] A man is known by his appearance, and a sensible man is known by his face, when you meet him.

[30] A man's attire and open-mouthed laughter, and a man's manner of walking, show what he is.

Sir.20

[1] There is a reproof which is not timely; and there is a man who keeps silent but is wise.

[2] How much better it is to reprove than to stay angry! And the one who confesses his fault will be kept from loss.

[4] Like a eunuch's desire to violate a maiden is a man who executes judgments by violence.

[5] There is one who by keeping silent is found wise, while another is detested for being too talkative.

[6] There is one who keeps silent because he has no answer, while another keeps silent because he knows when to speak.

[7] A wise man will be silent until the right moment, but a braggart and fool goes beyond the right moment.

[8] Whoever uses too many words will be loathed, and whoever usurps the right to speak will be hated.

[9] There may be good fortune for a man in adversity, and a windfall may result in a loss.

[10] There is a gift that profits you nothing, and there is a gift that brings a double return.

[11] There are losses because of glory, and there are men who have raised their heads from humble circumstances.

[12] There is a man who buys much for a little, but pays for it seven times over.

[13] The wise man makes himself beloved through his words, but the courtesies of fools are wasted.

[14] A fool's gift will profit you nothing, for he has many eyes instead of one.

[15] He gives little and upbraids much, he opens his mouth like a herald; today he lends and tomorrow he asks it back; such a one is a hateful man.

[16] A fool will say, "I have no friend, and there is no gratitude for my good deeds; those who eat my bread speak unkindly."

[17] How many will ridicule him, and how often!

[18] A slip on the pavement is better than a slip of the tongue; so the downfall of the wicked will occur speedily.
[19] An ungracious man is like a story told at the wrong time, which is continually on the lips of the ignorant.
[20] A proverb from a fool's lips will be rejected, for he does not tell it at its proper time.
[21] A man may be prevented from sinning by his poverty, so when he rests he feels no remorse.
[22] A man may lose his life through shame, or lose it because of his foolish look.
[23] A man may for shame make promises to a friend, and needlessly make him an enemy.
[24] A lie is an ugly blot on a man; it is continually on the lips of the ignorant.
[25] A thief is preferable to a habitual liar, but the lot of both is ruin.
[26] The disposition of a liar brings disgrace, and his shame is ever with him.
[27] He who speaks wisely will advance himself, and a sensible man will please great men.
[28] Whoever cultivates the soil will heap up his harvest, and whoever pleases great men will atone for injustice.
[29] Presents and gifts blind the eyes of the wise; like a muzzle on the mouth they avert reproofs.
[30] Hidden wisdom and unseen treasure, what advantage is there in either of them?
[31] Better is the man who hides his folly than the man who hides his wisdom.

Sir.21
[1] Have you sinned, my son? Do so no more, but pray about your former sins.
[2] Flee from sin as from a snake; for if you approach sin, it will bite you. Its teeth are lion's teeth, and destroy the souls of men.
[3] All lawlessness is like a two-edged sword; there is no healing for its wound.
[4] Terror and violence will lay waste riches; thus the house of the proud will be laid waste.
[5] The prayer of a poor man goes from his lips to the ears of God, and his judgment comes speedily.
[6] Whoever hates reproof walks in the steps of the sinner, but he that fears the Lord will repent in his heart.
[7] He who is mighty in speech is known from afar; but the sensible man, when he slips, is aware of it.
[8] A man who builds his house with other people's money is like one who gathers stones for his burial mound.
[9] An assembly of the wicked is like tow gathered together, and their end is a flame of fire.
[10] The way of sinners is smoothly paved with stones, but at its end is the pit of Hades.
[11] Whoever keeps the law controls his thoughts, and wisdom is the fulfilment of the fear of the Lord.
[12] He who is not clever cannot be taught, but there is a cleverness which increases bitterness.
[13] The knowledge of a wise man will increase like a flood, and his counsel like a flowing spring.
[14] The mind of a fool is like a broken jar; it will hold no knowledge.
[15] When a man of understanding hears a wise saying, he will praise it and add to it; when a reveler hears it, he dislikes it and casts it behind his back.
[16] A fool's narration is like a burden on a journey, but delight will be found in the speech of the intelligent.
[17] The utterance of a sensible man will be sought in the assembly, and they will ponder his words in their minds.
[18] Like a house that has vanished, so is wisdom to a fool; and the knowledge of the ignorant is unexamined talk.
[19] To a senseless man education is fetters on his feet, and like manacles on his right hand.
[20] A fool raises his voice when he laughs, but a clever man smiles quietly.
[21] To a sensible man education is like a golden ornament, and like a bracelet on the right arm.
[22] The foot of a fool rushes into a house, but a man of experience stands respectfully before it.
[23] A boor peers into the house from the door, but a cultivated man remains outside.
[24] It is ill-mannered for a man to listen at a door, and a discreet man is grieved by the disgrace.
[25] The lips of strangers will speak of these things, but the words of the prudent will be weighed in the balance.
[26] The mind of fools is in their mouth, but the mouth of wise men is in their mind.
[27] When an ungodly man curses his adversary, he curses his own soul.
[28] A whisperer defiles his own soul and is hated in his neighborhood.

Sir.22
[1] The indolent may be compared to a filthy stone, and every one hisses at his disgrace.
[2] The indolent may be compared to the filth of dunghills; any one that picks it up will shake it off his hand.
[3] It is a disgrace to be the father of an undisciplined son, and the birth of a daughter is a loss.
[4] A sensible daughter obtains her husband, but one who acts shamefully brings grief to her father.
[5] An impudent daughter disgraces father and husband, and will be despised by both.
[6] Like music in mourning is a tale told at the wrong time, but chastising and discipline are wisdom at all times.
[7] He who teaches a fool is like one who glues potsherds together, or who rouses a sleeper from deep slumber.
[8] He who tells a story to a fool tells it to a drowsy man; and at the end he will say, "What is it?"
[11] Weep for the dead, for he lacks the light; and weep for the fool, for he lacks intelligence; weep less bitterly for the dead,

for he has attained rest; but the life of the fool is worse than death.

[12] Mourning for the dead lasts seven days, but for a fool or an ungodly man it lasts all his life.

[13] Do not talk much with a foolish man, and do not visit an unintelligent man; guard yourself from him to escape trouble, and you will not be soiled when he shakes himself off; avoid him and you will find rest, and you will never be wearied by his madness.

[14] What is heavier than lead? And what is its name except "Fool"?

[15] Sand, salt, and a piece of iron are easier to bear than a stupid man.

[16] A wooden beam firmly bonded into a building will not be torn loose by an earthquake; so the mind firmly fixed on a reasonable counsel will not be afraid in a crisis.

[17] A mind settled on an intelligent thought is like the stucco decoration on the wall of a colonnade.

[18] Fences set on a high place will not stand firm against the wind; so a timid heart with a fool's purpose will not stand firm against any fear.

[19] A man who pricks an eye will make tears fall, and one who pricks the heart makes it show feeling.

[20] One who throws a stone at birds scares them away, and one who reviles a friend will break off the friendship.

[21] Even if you have drawn your sword against a friend, do not despair, for a renewal of friendship is possible.

[22] If you have opened your mouth against your friend, do not worry, for reconciliation is possible; but as for reviling, arrogance, disclosure of secrets, or a treacherous blow -- in these cases any friend will flee.

[23] Gain the trust of your neighbor in his poverty, that you may rejoice with him in his prosperity; stand by him in time of affliction, that you may share with him in his inheritance.

[24] The vapor and smoke of the furnace precede the fire; so insults precede bloodshed.

[25] I will not be ashamed to protect a friend, and I will not hide from him;

[26] but if some harm should happen to me because of him, whoever hears of it will beware of him.

[27] O that a guard were set over my mouth, and a seal of prudence upon my lips, that it may keep me from falling, so that my tongue may not destroy me!

Sir.23

[1] O Lord, Father and Ruler of my life, do not abandon me to their counsel, and let me not fall because of them!

[2] O that whips were set over my thoughts, and the discipline of wisdom over my mind! That they may not spare me in my errors, and that it may not pass by my sins;

[3] in order that my mistakes may not be multiplied, and my sins may not abound; then I will not fall before my adversaries, and my enemy will not rejoice over me.

[4] O Lord, Father and God of my life, do not give me haughty eyes,

[5] and remove from me evil desire.

[6] Let neither gluttony nor lust overcome me, and do not surrender me to a shameless soul.

[7] Listen, my children, to instruction concerning speech; the one who observes it will never be caught.

[8] The sinner is overtaken through his lips, the reviler and the arrogant are tripped by them.

[9] Do not accustom your mouth to oaths, and do not habitually utter the name of the Holy One;

[10] for as a servant who is continually examined under torture will not lack bruises, so also the man who always swears and utters the Name will not be cleansed from sin.

[11] A man who swears many oaths will be filled with iniquity, and the scourge will not leave his house; if he offends, his sin remains on him, and if he disregards it, he sins doubly; if he has sworn needlessly, he will not be justified, for his house will be filled with calamities.

[12] There is an utterance which is comparable to death; may it never be found in the inheritance of Jacob! For all these errors will be far from the godly, and they will not wallow in sins.

[13] Do not accustom your mouth to lewd vulgarity, for it involves sinful speech.

[14] Remember your father and mother when you sit among great men; lest you be forgetful in their presence, and be deemed a fool on account of your habits; then you will wish that you had never been born, and you will curse the day of your birth.

[15] A man accustomed to use insulting words will never become disciplined all his days.

[16] Two sorts of men multiply sins, and a third incurs wrath. The soul heated like a burning fire will not be quenched until it is consumed; a man who commits fornication with his near of kin will never cease until the fire burns him up.

[17] To a fornicator all bread tastes sweet; he will never cease until he dies.

[18] A man who breaks his marriage vows says to himself, "Who sees me? Darkness surrounds me, and the walls hide me, and no one sees me. Why should I fear? The Most High will not take notice of my sins."

[19] His fear is confined to the eyes of men, and he does not realize that the eyes of the Lord are ten thousand times brighter than the sun; they look upon all the ways of men, and perceive even the hidden places.

[20] Before the universe was created, it was known to him; so it was also after it was finished.

[21] This man will be punished in the streets of the city, and where he least suspects it, he will be seized.

[22] So it is with a woman who leaves her husband and provides an heir by a stranger.

[23] For first of all, she has disobeyed the law of the Most High; second, she has committed an offense against her husband; and third, she has committed adultery through harlotry and brought forth children by another man.

[24] She herself will be brought before the assembly, and punishment will fall on her children.

[25] Her children will not take root, and her branches will not bear fruit.

[26] She will leave her memory for a curse, and her disgrace will not be blotted out.

[27] Those who survive her will recognize that nothing is better than the fear of the Lord, and nothing sweeter than to heed the commandments of the Lord.

Sir.24

[1] Wisdom will praise herself, and will glory in the midst of her people.

[2] In the assembly of the Most High she will open her mouth, and in the presence of his host she will glory:

[3] "I came forth from the mouth of the Most High, and covered the earth like a mist.

[4] I dwelt in high places, and my throne was in a pillar of cloud.

[5] Alone I have made the circuit of the vault of heaven and have walked in the depths of the abyss.

[6] In the waves of the sea, in the whole earth, and in every people and nation I have gotten a possession.

[7] Among all these I sought a resting place; I sought in whose territory I might lodge.

[8] "Then the Creator of all things gave me a commandment, and the one who created me assigned a place for my tent. And he said, `Make your dwelling in Jacob, and in Israel receive your inheritance.'

[9] From eternity, in the beginning, he created me, and for eternity I shall not cease to exist.

[10] In the holy tabernacle I ministered before him, and so I was established in Zion.

[11] In the beloved city likewise he gave me a resting place, and in Jerusalem was my dominion.

[12] So I took root in an honored people, in the portion of the Lord, who is their inheritance.

[13] "I grew tall like a cedar in Lebanon, and like a cypress on the heights of Hermon.

[14] I grew tall like a palm tree in En-ge'di, and like rose plants in Jericho; like a beautiful olive tree in the field, and like a plane tree I grew tall.

[15] Like cassia and camel's thorn I gave forth the aroma of spices, and like choice myrrh I spread a pleasant odor, like galbanum, onycha, and stacte, and like the fragrance of frankincense in the tabernacle.

[16] Like a terebinth I spread out my branches, and my branches are glorious and graceful.

[17] Like a vine I caused loveliness to bud, and my blossoms became glorious and abundant fruit.

[19] "Come to me, you who desire me, and eat your fill of my produce.

[20] For the remembrance of me is sweeter than honey, and my inheritance sweeter than the honeycomb.

[21] Those who eat me will hunger for more, and those who drink me will thirst for more.

[22] Whoever obeys me will not be put to shame, and those who work with my help will not sin."

[23] All this is the book of the covenant of the Most High God, the law which Moses commanded us as an inheritance for the congregations of Jacob.

[25] It fills men with wisdom, like the Pishon, and like the Tigris at the time of the first fruits.

[26] It makes them full of understanding, like the Euphrates, and like the Jordan at harvest time.

[27] It makes instruction shine forth like light, like the Gihon at the time of vintage.

[28] Just as the first man did not know her perfectly, the last one has not fathomed her;

[29] for her thought is more abundant than the sea, and her counsel deeper than the great abyss.

[30] I went forth like a canal from a river and like a water channel into a garden.

[31] I said, "I will water my orchard and drench my garden plot"; and lo, my canal became a river, and my river became a sea.

[32] I will again make instruction shine forth like the dawn, and I will make it shine afar;

[33] I will again pour out teaching like prophecy, and leave it to all future generations.

[34] Observe that I have not labored for myself alone, but for all who seek instruction.

Sir.25

[1] My soul takes pleasure in three things, and they are beautiful in the sight of the Lord and of men; agreement between brothers, friendship between neighbors, and a wife and a husband who live in harmony.

[2] My soul hates three kinds of men, and I am greatly offended at their life: a beggar who is proud, a rich man who is a liar, and an adulterous old man who lacks good sense.

[3] You have gathered nothing in your youth; how then can you find anything in your old age?

[4] What an attractive thing is judgment in gray-haired men, and for the aged to possess good counsel!

[5] How attractive is wisdom in the aged, and understanding and counsel in honorable men!

[6] Rich experience is the crown of the aged, and their boast is the fear of the Lord.

[7] With nine thoughts I have gladdened my heart, and a tenth I shall tell with my tongue: a man rejoicing in his children;

a man who lives to see the downfall of his foes;

[8] happy is he who lives with an intelligent wife, and he who has not made a slip with his tongue, and he who has not served a man inferior to himself;

[9] happy is he who has gained good sense, and he who speaks to attentive listeners.

[10] How great is he who has gained wisdom! But there is no one superior to him who fears the Lord.

[11] The fear of the Lord surpasses everything; to whom shall be likened the one who holds it fast?

[13] Any wound, but not a wound of the heart! Any wickedness, but not the wickedness of a wife!

[14] Any attack, but not an attack from those who hate! And any vengeance, but not the vengeance of enemies!

[15] There is no venom worse than a snake's venom, and no wrath worse than an enemy's wrath.

[16] I would rather dwell with a lion and a dragon than dwell with an evil wife.

[17] The wickedness of a wife changes her appearance, and darkens her face like that of a bear.

[18] Her husband takes his meals among the neighbors, and he cannot help sighing bitterly.

[19] Any iniquity is insignificant compared to a wife's iniquity; may a sinner's lot befall her!

[20] A sandy ascent for the feet of the aged -- such is a garrulous wife for a quiet husband.

[21] Do not be ensnared by a woman's beauty, and do not desire a woman for her possessions.

[22] There is wrath and impudence and great disgrace when a wife supports her husband.

[23] A dejected mind, a gloomy face, and a wounded heart are caused by an evil wife. Drooping hands and weak knees are caused by the wife who does not make her husband happy.

[24] From a woman sin had its beginning, and because of her we all die.

[25] Allow no outlet to water, and no boldness of speech in an evil wife.

[26] If she does not go as you direct, separate her from yourself.

Sir.26

[1] Happy is the husband of a good wife; the number of his days will be doubled.

[2] A loyal wife rejoices her husband, and he will complete his years in peace.

[3] A good wife is a great blessing; she will be granted among the blessings of the man who fears the Lord.

[4] Whether rich or poor, his heart is glad, and at all times his face is cheerful.

[5] Of three things my heart is afraid, and of a fourth I am frightened: The slander of a city, the gathering of a mob, and false accusation -- all these are worse than death.

[6] There is grief of heart and sorrow when a wife is envious of a rival, and a tongue-lashing makes it known to all.

[7] An evil wife is an ox yoke which chafes; taking hold of her is like grasping a scorpion.

[8] There is great anger when a wife is drunken; she will not hide her shame.

[9] A wife's harlotry shows in her lustful eyes, and she is known by her eyelids.

[10] Keep strict watch over a headstrong daughter, lest, when she finds liberty, she use it to her hurt.

[11] Be on guard against her impudent eye, and do not wonder if she sins against you.

[12] As a thirsty wayfarer opens his mouth and drinks from any water near him, so will she sit in front of every post and open her quiver to the arrow.

[13] A wife's charm delights her husband, and her skill puts fat on his bones.

[14] A silent wife is a gift of the Lord, and there is nothing so precious as a disciplined soul.

[15] A modest wife adds charm to charm, and no balance can weigh the value of a chaste soul.

[16] Like the sun rising in the heights of the Lord, so is the beauty of a good wife in her well-ordered home.

[17] Like the shining lamp on the holy lampstand, so is a beautiful face on a stately figure.

[18] Like pillars of gold on a base of silver, so are beautiful feet with a steadfast heart.

[28] At two things my heart is grieved, and because of a third anger comes over me: a warrior in want through poverty, and intelligent men who are treated contemptuously; a man who turns back from righteousness to sin -- the Lord will prepare him for the sword!

[29] A merchant can hardly keep from wrongdoing, and a tradesman will not be declared innocent of sin.

Sir.27

[1] Many have committed sin for a trifle, and whoever seeks to get rich will avert his eyes.

[2] As a stake is driven firmly into a fissure between stones, so sin is wedged in between selling and buying.

[3] If a man is not steadfast and zealous in the fear of the Lord, his house will be quickly overthrown.

[4] When a sieve is shaken, the refuse remains; so a man's filth remains in his thoughts.

[5] The kiln tests the potter's vessels; so the test of a man is in his reasoning.

[6] The fruit discloses the cultivation of a tree; so the expression of a thought discloses the cultivation of a man's mind.

[7] Do not praise a man before you hear him reason, for this is the test of men.

[8] If you pursue justice, you will attain it and wear it as a glorious robe.

[9] Birds flock with their kind; so truth returns to those who practice it.
[10] A lion lies in wait for prey; so does sin for the workers of iniquity.
[11] The talk of the godly man is always wise, but the fool changes like the moon.
[12] Among stupid people watch for a chance to leave, but among thoughtful people stay on.
[13] The talk of fools is offensive, and their laughter is wantonly sinful.
[14] The talk of men given to swearing makes one's hair stand on end, and their quarrels make a man stop his ears.
[15] The strife of the proud leads to bloodshed, and their abuse is grievous to hear.
[16] Whoever betrays secrets destroys confidence, and he will never find a congenial friend.
[17] Love your friend and keep faith with him; but if you betray his secrets, do not run after him.
[18] For as a man destroys his enemy, so you have destroyed the friendship of your neighbor.
[19] And as you allow a bird to escape from your hand, so you have let your neighbor go, and will not catch him again.
[20] Do not go after him, for he is too far off, and has escaped like a gazelle from a snare.
[21] For a wound may be bandaged, and there is reconciliation after abuse, but whoever has betrayed secrets is without hope.
[22] Whoever winks his eye plans evil deeds, and no one can keep him from them.
[23] In your presence his mouth is all sweetness, and he admires your words; but later he will twist his speech and with your own words he will give offense.
[24] I have hated many things, but none to be compared to him; even the Lord will hate him.
[25] Whoever throws a stone straight up throws it on his own head; and a treacherous blow opens up wounds.
[26] He who digs a pit will fall into it, and he who sets a snare will be caught in it.
[27] If a man does evil, it will roll back upon him, and he will not know where it came from.
[28] Mockery and abuse issue from the proud man, but vengeance lies in wait for him like a lion.
[29] Those who rejoice in the fall of the godly will be caught in a snare, and pain will consume them before their death.
[30] Anger and wrath, these also are abominations, and the sinful man will possess them.

Sir.28
[1] He that takes vengeance will suffer vengeance from the Lord, and he will firmly establish his sins.
[2] Forgive your neighbor the wrong he has done, and then your sins will be pardoned when you pray.
[3] Does a man harbor anger against another, and yet seek for healing from the Lord?
[4] Does he have no mercy toward a man like himself, and yet pray for his own sins?
[5] If he himself, being flesh, maintains wrath, who will make expiation for his sins?
[6] Remember the end of your life, and cease from enmity, remember destruction and death, and be true to the commandments.
[7] Remember the commandments, and do not be angry with your neighbor; remember the covenant of the Most High, and overlook ignorance.
[8] Refrain from strife, and you will lessen sins; for a man given to anger will kindle strife,
[9] and a sinful man will disturb friends and inject enmity among those who are at peace.
[10] In proportion to the fuel for the fire, so will be the burning, and in proportion to the obstinacy of strife will be the burning; in proportion to the strength of the man will be his anger, and in proportion to his wealth he will heighten his wrath.
[11] A hasty quarrel kindles fire, and urgent strife sheds blood.
[12] If you blow on a spark, it will glow; if you spit on it, it will be put out; and both come out of your mouth.
[13] Curse the whisperer and deceiver, for he has destroyed many who were at peace.
[14] Slander has shaken many, and scattered them from nation to nation, and destroyed strong cities, and overturned the houses of great men.
[15] Slander has driven away courageous women, and deprived them of the fruit of their toil.
[16] Whoever pays heed to slander will not find rest, nor will he settle down in peace.
[17] The blow of a whip raises a welt, but a blow of the tongue crushes the bones.
[18] Many have fallen by the edge of the sword, but not so many as have fallen because of the tongue.
[19] Happy is the man who is protected from it, who has not been exposed to its anger, who has not borne its yoke, and has not been bound with its fetters;
[20] for its yoke is a yoke of iron, and its fetters are fetters of bronze;
[21] its death is an evil death, and Hades is preferable to it.
[22] It will not be master over the godly, and they will not be burned in its flame.
[23] Those who forsake the Lord will fall into its power; it will burn among them and will not be put out. It will be sent out against them like a lion; like a leopard it will mangle them.
[24] See that you fence in your property with thorns, lock up your silver and gold,
[25] make balances and scales for your words, and make a door and a bolt for your mouth.
[26] Beware lest you err with your tongue, lest you fall before him who lies in wait.

Sir.29

[1] He that shows mercy will lend to his neighbor, and he that strengthens him with his hand keeps the commandments.

[2] Lend to your neighbor in the time of his need; and in turn, repay your neighbor promptly.

[3] Confirm your word and keep faith with him, and on every occasion you will find what you need.

[4] Many persons regard a loan as a windfall, and cause trouble to those who help them.

[5] A man will kiss another's hands until he gets a loan, and will lower his voice in speaking of his neighbor's money; but at the time for repayment he will delay, and will pay in words of unconcern, and will find fault with the time.

[6] If the lender exert pressure, he will hardly get back half, and will regard that as a windfall. If he does not, the borrower has robbed him of his money, and he has needlessly made him his enemy; he will repay him with curses and reproaches, and instead of glory will repay him with dishonor.

[7] Because of such wickedness, therefore, many have refused to lend; they have been afraid of being defrauded needlessly.

[8] Nevertheless, be patient with a man in humble circumstances, and do not make him wait for your alms.

[9] Help a poor man for the commandment's sake, and because of his need do not send him away empty.

[10] Lose your silver for the sake of a brother or a friend, and do not let it rust under a stone and be lost.

[11] Lay up your treasure according to the commandments of the Most High, and it will profit you more than gold.

[12] Store up almsgiving in your treasury, and it will rescue you from all affliction;

[13] more than a mighty shield and more than a heavy spear, it will fight on your behalf against your enemy.

[14] A good man will be surety for his neighbor, but a man who has lost his sense of shame will fail him.

[15] Do not forget all the kindness of your surety, for he has given his life for you.

[16] A sinner will overthrow the prosperity of his surety,

[17] and one who does not feel grateful will abandon his rescuer.

[18] Being surety has ruined many men who were prosperous, and has shaken them like a wave of the sea; it has driven men of power into exile, and they have wandered among foreign nations.

[19] The sinner who has fallen into suretyship and pursues gain will fall into lawsuits.

[20] Assist your neighbor according to your ability, but take heed to yourself lest you fall.

[21] The essentials for life are water and bread and clothing and a house to cover one's nakedness.

[22] Better is the life of a poor man under the shelter of his roof than sumptuous food in another man's house.

[23] Be content with little or much.

[24] It is a miserable life to go from house to house, and where you are a stranger you may not open your mouth;

[25] you will play the host and provide drink without being thanked, and besides this you will hear bitter words:

[26] "Come here, stranger, prepare the table, and if you have anything at hand, let me have it to eat."

[27] "Give place, stranger, to an honored person; my brother has come to stay with me; I need my house."

[28] These things are hard to bear for a man who has feeling: scolding about lodging and the reproach of the moneylender.

Sir.30

[1] He who loves his son will whip him often, in order that he may rejoice at the way he turns out.

[2] He who disciplines his son will profit by him, and will boast of him among acquaintances.

[3] He who teaches his son will make his enemies envious, and will glory in him in the presence of friends.

[4] The father may die, and yet he is not dead, for he has left behind him one like himself;

[5] while alive he saw and rejoiced, and when he died he was not grieved;

[6] he has left behind him an avenger against his enemies, and one to repay the kindness of his friends.

[7] He who spoils his son will bind up his wounds, and his feelings will be troubled at every cry.

[8] A horse that is untamed turns out to be stubborn, and a son unrestrained turns out to be wilful.

[9] Pamper a child, and he will frighten you; play with him, and he will give you grief.

[10] Do not laugh with him, lest you have sorrow with him, and in the end you will gnash your teeth.

[11] Give him no authority in his youth, and do not ignore his errors.

[12] Bow down his neck in his youth, and beat his sides while he is young, lest he become stubborn and disobey you, and you have sorrow of soul from him.

[13] Discipline your son and take pains with him, that you may not be offended by his shamelessness.

[14] Better off is a poor man who is well and strong in constitution than a rich man who is severely afflicted in body.

[15] Health and soundness are better than all gold, and a robust body than countless riches.

[16] There is no wealth better than health of body, and there is no gladness above joy of heart.

[17] Death is better than a miserable life, and eternal rest than chronic sickness.

[18] Good things poured out upon a mouth that is closed are like offerings of food placed upon a grave.

[19] Of what use to an idol is an offering of fruit? For it can neither eat nor smell. So is he who is afflicted by the Lord;

[20] he sees with his eyes and groans, like a eunuch who embraces a maiden and groans.

[21] Do not give yourself over to sorrow, and do not afflict yourself deliberately.

[22] Gladness of heart is the life of man, and the rejoicing of a man is length of days.

[23] Delight your soul and comfort your heart, and remove sorrow far from you, for sorrow has destroyed many, and there is no profit in it.

[24] Jealousy and anger shorten life, and anxiety brings on old age too soon.

[25] A man of cheerful and good heart will give heed to the food he eats.

Sir.31

[1] Wakefulness over wealth wastes away one's flesh, and anxiety about it removes sleep.

[2] Wakeful anxiety prevents slumber, and a severe illness carries off sleep.

[3] The rich man toils as his wealth accumulates, and when he rests he fills himself with his dainties.

[4] The poor man toils as his livelihood diminishes, and when he rests he becomes needy.

[5] He who loves gold will not be justified, and he who pursues money will be led astray by it.

[6] Many have come to ruin because of gold, and their destruction has met them face to face.

[7] It is a stumbling block to those who are devoted to it, and every fool will be taken captive by it.

[8] Blessed is the rich man who is found blameless, and who does not go after gold.

[9] Who is he? And we will call him blessed, for he has done wonderful things among his people.

[10] Who has been tested by it and been found perfect? Let it be for him a ground for boasting. Who has had the power to transgress and did not transgress, and to do evil and did not do it?

[11] His prosperity will be established, and the assembly will relate his acts of charity.

[12] Are you seated at the table of a great man? Do not be greedy at it, and do not say, "There is certainly much upon it!"

[13] Remember that a greedy eye is a bad thing. What has been created more greedy than the eye? Therefore it sheds tears from every face.

[14] Do not reach out your hand for everything you see, and do not crowd your neighbor at the dish.

[15] Judge your neighbor's feelings by your own, and in every matter be thoughtful.

[16] Eat like a human being what is set before you, and do not chew greedily, lest you be hated.

[17] Be the first to stop eating, for the sake of good manners, and do not be insatiable, lest you give offense.

[18] If you are seated among many persons, do not reach out your hand before they do.

[19] How ample a little is for a well-disciplined man! He does not breathe heavily upon his bed.

[20] Healthy sleep depends on moderate eating; he rises early, and feels fit. The distress of sleeplessness and of nausea and colic are with the glutton.

[21] If you are overstuffed with food, get up in the middle of the meal, and you will have relief.

[22] Listen to me, my son, and do not disregard me, and in the end you will appreciate my words. In all your work be industrious, and no sickness will overtake you.

[23] Men will praise the one who is liberal with food, and their testimony to his excellence is trustworthy.

[24] The city will complain of the one who is niggardly with food, and their testimony to his niggardliness is accurate.

[25] Do not aim to be valiant over wine, for wine has destroyed many.

[26] Fire and water prove the temper of steel, so wine tests hearts in the strife of the proud.

[27] Wine is like life to men, if you drink it in moderation. What is life to a man who is without wine? It has been created to make men glad.

[28] Wine drunk in season and temperately is rejoicing of heart and gladness of soul.

[29] Wine drunk to excess is bitterness of soul, with provocation and stumbling.

[30] Drunkenness increases the anger of a fool to his injury, reducing his strength and adding wounds.

[31] Do not reprove your neighbor at a banquet of wine, and do not despise him in his merrymaking; speak no word of reproach to him, and do not afflict him by making demands of him.

Sir.32

[1] If they make you master of the feast, do not exalt yourself; be among them as one of them; take good care of them and then be seated;

[2] when you have fulfilled your duties, take your place, that you may be merry on their account and receive a wreath for your excellent leadership.

[3] Speak, you who are older, for it is fitting that you should, but with accurate knowledge, and do not interrupt the music.

[4] Where there is entertainment, do not pour out talk; do not display your cleverness out of season.

[5] A ruby seal in a setting of gold is a concert of music at a banquet of wine.

[6] A seal of emerald in a rich setting of gold is the melody of music with good wine.

[7] Speak, young man, if there is need of you, but no more than twice, and only if asked.

[8] Speak concisely, say much in few words; be as one who knows and yet holds his tongue.

[9] Among the great do not act as their equal; and when another is speaking, do not babble.

[10] Lightning speeds before the thunder, and approval precedes a modest man.

[11] Leave in good time and do not be the last; go home quickly and do not linger.

[12] Amuse yourself there, and do what you have in mind, but do not sin through proud speech.

[13] And for these things bless him who made you and satisfies you with his good gifts.

[14] He who fears the Lord will accept his discipline, and those who rise early to seek him will find favor.

[15] He who seeks the law will be filled with it, but the hypocrite will stumble at it.

[16] Those who fear the Lord will form true judgments, and like a light they will kindle righteous deeds.

[17] A sinful man will shun reproof, and will find a decision according to his liking.

[18] A man of judgment will not overlook an idea, and an insolent and proud man will not cower in fear.

[19] Do nothing without deliberation; and when you have acted, do not regret it.

[20] Do not go on a path full of hazards, and do not stumble over stony ground.

[21] Do not be overconfident on a smooth way,

[22] and give good heed to your paths.

[23] Guard yourself in every act, for this is the keeping of the commandments.

[24] He who believes the law gives heed to the commandments, and he who trusts the Lord will not suffer loss.

Sir.33

[1] No evil will befall the man who fears the Lord, but in trial he will deliver him again and again.

[2] A wise man will not hate the law, but he who is hypocritical about it is like a boat in a storm.

[3] A man of understanding will trust in the law; for him the law is as dependable as an inquiry by means of Urim.

[4] Prepare what to say, and thus you will be heard; bind together your instruction, and make your answer.

[5] The heart of a fool is like a cart wheel, and his thoughts like a turning axle.

[6] A stallion is like a mocking friend; he neighs under every one who sits on him.

[7] Why is any day better than another, when all the daylight in the year is from the sun?

[8] By the Lord's decision they were distinguished, and he appointed the different seasons and feasts;

[9] some of them he exalted and hallowed, and some of them he made ordinary days.

[10] All men are from the ground, and Adam was created of the dust.

[11] In the fullness of his knowledge the Lord distinguished them and appointed their different ways;

[12] some of them he blessed and exalted, and some of them he made holy and brought near to himself; but some of them he cursed and brought low, and he turned them out of their place.

[13] As clay in the hand of the potter -- for all his ways are as he pleases -- so men are in the hand of him who made them, to give them as he decides.

[14] Good is the opposite of evil, and life the opposite of death; so the sinner is the opposite of the godly.

[15] Look upon all the works of the Most High; they likewise are in pairs, one the opposite of the other.

[16] I was the last on watch; I was like one who gleans after the grape-gatherers; by the blessing of the Lord I excelled, and like a grape-gatherer I filled my wine press.

[17] Consider that I have not labored for myself alone, but for all who seek instruction.

[18] Hear me, you who are great among the people, and you leaders of the congregation, hearken.

[19] To son or wife, to brother or friend, do not give power over yourself, as long as you live; and do not give your property to another, lest you change your mind and must ask for it.

[20] While you are still alive and have breath in you, do not let any one take your place.

[21] For it is better that your children should ask from you than that you should look to the hand of you sons.

[22] Excel in all that you do; bring no stain upon your honor.

[23] At the time when you end the days of your life, in the hour of death, distribute your inheritance.

[24] Fodder and a stick and burdens for an ass; bread and discipline and work for a servant.

[25] Set your slave to work, and you will find rest; leave his hands idle, and he will seek liberty.

[26] Yoke and thong will bow the neck, and for a wicked servant there are racks and tortures.

[27] Put him to work, that he may not be idle, for idleness teaches much evil.

[28] Set him to work, as is fitting for him, and if he does not obey, make his fetters heavy.

[29] Do not act immoderately toward anybody, and do nothing without discretion.

[30] If you have a servant, let him be as yourself, because you have bought him with blood.

[31] If you have a servant, treat him as a brother, for as your own soul you will need him. If you ill-treat him, and he leaves and runs away, which way will you go to seek him?

Sir.34

[1] A man of no understanding has vain and false hopes, and dreams give wings to fools.

[2] As one who catches at a shadow and pursues the wind, so is he who gives heed to dreams.

[3] The vision of dreams is this against that, the likeness of a face confronting a face.
[4] From an unclean thing what will be made clean? And from something false what will be true?
[5] Divinations and omens and dreams are folly, and like a woman in travail the mind has fancies.
[6] Unless they are sent from the Most High as a visitation, do not give your mind to them.
[7] For dreams have deceived many, and those who put their hope in them have failed.
[8] Without such deceptions the law will be fulfilled, and wisdom is made perfect in truthful lips.
[9] An educated man knows many things, and one with much experience will speak with understanding.
[10] He that is inexperienced knows few things, but he that has traveled acquires much cleverness.
[11] I have seen many things in my travels, and I understand more than I can express.
[12] I have often been in danger of death, but have escaped because of these experiences.
[13] The spirit of those who fear the Lord will live, for their hope is in him who saves them.
[14] He who fears the Lord will not be timid, nor play the coward, for he is his hope.
[15] Blessed is the soul of the man who fears the Lord! To whom does he look? And who is his support?
[16] The eyes of the Lord are upon those who love him, a mighty protection and strong support, a shelter from the hot wind and a shade from noonday sun, a guard against stumbling and a defense against falling.
[17] He lifts up the soul and gives light to the eyes; he grants healing, life, and blessing.
[18] If one sacrifices from what has been wrongfully obtained, the offering is blemished; the gifts of the lawless are not acceptable.
[19] The Most High is not pleased with the offerings of the ungodly; and he is not propitiated for sins by a multitude of sacrifices.
[20] Like one who kills a son before his father's eyes is the man who offers a sacrifice from the property of the poor.
[21] The bread of the needy is the life of the poor; whoever deprives them of it is a man of blood.
[22] To take away a neighbor's living is to murder him; to deprive an employee of his wages is to shed blood.
[23] When one builds and another tears down, what do they gain but toil?
[24] When one prays and another curses, to whose voice will the Lord listen?
[25] If a man washes after touching a dead body, and touches it again, what has he gained by his washing?
[26] So if a man fasts for his sins, and goes again and does the same things, who will listen to his prayer? And what has he gained by humbling himself?

Sir.35
[1] He who keeps the law makes many offerings; he who heeds the commandments sacrifices a peace offering.
[2] He who returns a kindness offers fine flour, and he who gives alms sacrifices a thank offering.
[3] To keep from wickedness is pleasing to the Lord, and to forsake unrighteousness is atonement.
[4] Do not appear before the Lord empty-handed,
[5] for all these things are to be done because of the commandment.
[6] The offering of a righteous man anoints the altar, and its pleasing odor rises before the Most High.
[7] The sacrifice of a righteous man is acceptable, and the memory of it will not be forgotten.
[8] Glorify the Lord generously, and do not stint the first fruits of your hands.
[9] With every gift show a cheerful face, and dedicate your tithe with gladness.
[10] Give to the Most High as he has given, and as generously as your hand has found.
[11] For the Lord is the one who repays, and he will repay you sevenfold.
[12] Do not offer him a bribe, for he will not accept it; and do not trust to an unrighteous sacrifice; for the Lord is the judge, and with him is no partiality.
[13] He will not show partiality in the case of a poor man; and he will listen to the prayer of one who is wronged.
[14] He will not ignore the supplication of the fatherless, nor the widow when she pours out her story.
[15] Do not the tears of the widow run down her cheek as she cries out against him who has caused them to fall?
[16] He whose service is pleasing to the Lord will be accepted, and his prayer will reach to the clouds.
[17] The prayer of the humble pierces the clouds, and he will not be consoled until it reaches the Lord; he will not desist until the Most High visits him, and does justice for the righteous, and executes judgment.
[18] And the Lord will not delay, neither will he be patient with them, till he crushes the loins of the unmerciful and repays vengeance on the nations; till he takes away the multitude of the insolent, and breaks the scepters of the unrighteous;
[19] till he repays the man according to his deeds, and the works of men according to their devices; till he judges the case of his people and makes them rejoice in his mercy.
[20] Mercy is as welcome when he afflicts them as clouds of rain in the time of drought.

Sir.36
[1] Have mercy upon us, O Lord, the God of all, and look upon us,

[2] and cause the fear of thee to fall upon all the nations.

[3] Lift up thy hand against foreign nations and let them see thy might.

[4] As in us thou hast been sanctified before them, so in them be thou magnified before us;

[5] and let them know thee, as we have known that there is not God but thee, O Lord.

[6] Show signs anew, and work further wonders; make thy hand and thy right arm glorious.

[7] Rouse thy anger and pour out thy wrath; destroy the adversary and wipe out the enemy.

[8] Hasten the day, and remember the appointed time, and let people recount thy mighty deeds.

[9] Let him who survives be consumed in the fiery wrath, and may those who harm thy people meet destruction.

[10] Crush the heads of the rulers of the enemy, who say, "There is no one but ourselves."

[11] Gather all the tribes of Jacob, and give them their inheritance, as at the beginning.

[12] Have mercy, O Lord, upon the people called by thy name, upon Israel, whom thou hast likened to a first-born son.

[13] Have pity on the city of thy sanctuary, Jerusalem, the place of thy rest.

[14] Fill Zion with the celebration of thy wondrous deeds, and thy temple with thy glory.

[15] Bear witness to those whom thou didst create in the beginning, and fulfil the prophecies spoken in thy name.

[16] Reward those who wait for thee, and let thy prophets be found trustworthy.

[17] Hearken, O Lord, to the prayer of thy servants, according to the blessing of Aaron for thy people, and all who are on the earth will know that thou art the Lord, the God of the ages.

[18] The stomach will take any food, yet one food is better than another.

[19] As the palate tastes the kinds of game, so an intelligent mind detects false words.

[20] A perverse mind will cause grief, but a man of experience will pay him back.

[21] A woman will accept any man, but one daughter is better than another.

[22] A woman's beauty gladdens the countenance, and surpasses every human desire.

[23] If kindness and humility mark her speech, her husband is not like other men.

[24] He who acquires a wife gets his best possession, a helper fit for him and a pillar of support.

[25] Where there is no fence, the property will be plundered; and where there is no wife, a man will wander about and sigh.

[26] For who will trust a nimble robber that skips from city to city? So who will trust a man that has no home, and lodges wherever night finds him?

Sir.37

[1] Every friend will say, "I too am a friend"; but some friends are friends only in name.

[2] Is it not a grief to the death when a companion and friend turns to enmity?

[3] O evil imagination, why were you formed to cover the land with deceit?

[4] Some companions rejoice in the happiness of a friend, but in time of trouble are against him.

[5] Some companions help a friend for their stomach's sake, and in the face of battle take up the shield.

[6] Do not forget a friend in your heart, and be not unmindful of him in your wealth.

[7] Every counselor praises counsel, but some give counsel in their own interest.

[8] Be wary of a counselor, and learn first what is his interest -- for he will take thought for himself -- lest he cast the lot against you

[9] and tell you, "Your way is good," and then stand aloof to see what will happen to you.

[10] Do not consult the one who looks at you suspiciously; hide your counsel from those who are jealous of you.

[11] Do not consult with a woman about her rival or with a coward about war, with a merchant about barter or with a buyer about selling, with a grudging man about gratitude or with a merciless man about kindness, with an idler about any work or with a man hired for a year about completing his work, with a lazy servant about a big task -- pay no attention to these in any matter of counsel.

[12] But stay constantly with a godly man whom you know to be a keeper of the commandments, whose soul is in accord with your soul, and who will sorrow with you if you fail.

[13] And establish the counsel of your own heart, for no one is more faithful to you than it is.

[14] For a man's soul sometimes keeps him better informed than seven watchmen sitting high on a watchtower.

[15] And besides all this pray to the Most High that he may direct your way in truth.

[16] Reason is the beginning of every work, and counsel precedes every undertaking.

[17] As a clue to changes of heart

[18] four turns of fortune appear, good and evil, life and death; and it is the tongue that continually rules them.

[19] A man may be shrewd and the teacher of many, and yet be unprofitable to himself.

[20] A man skilled in words may be hated; he will be destitute of all food,

[21] for grace was not given him by the Lord, since he is lacking in all wisdom.

[22] A man may be wise to his own advantage, and the fruits of his understanding may be trustworthy on his lips.

[23] A wise man will instruct his own people, and the fruits of his understanding will be trustworthy.

[24] A wise man will have praise heaped upon him, and all who see him will call him happy.

[25] The life of a man is numbered by days, but the days of Israel are without number.

[26] He who is wise among his people will inherit confidence, and his name will live for ever.

[27] My son, test your soul while you live; see what is bad for it and do not give it that.

[28] For not everything is good for every one, and not every person enjoys everything.

[29] Do not have an insatiable appetite for any luxury, and do not give yourself up to food;

[30] for overeating brings sickness, and gluttony leads to nausea.

[31] Many have died of gluttony, but he who is careful to avoid it prolongs his life.

Sir.38

[1] Honor the physician with the honor due him, according to your need of him, for the Lord created him;

[2] for healing comes from the Most High, and he will receive a gift from the king.

[3] The skill of the physician lifts up his head, and in the presence of great men he is admired.

[4] The Lord created medicines from the earth, and a sensible man will not despise them.

[5] Was not water made sweet with a tree in order that his power might be known?

[6] And he gave skill to men that he might be glorified in his marvelous works.

[7] By them he heals and takes away pain;

[8] the pharmacist makes of them a compound. His works will never be finished; and from him health is upon the face of the earth.

[9] My son, when you are sick do not be negligent, but pray to the Lord, and he will heal you.

[10] Give up your faults and direct your hands aright, and cleanse your heart from all sin.

[11] Offer a sweet-smelling sacrifice, and a memorial portion of fine flour, and pour oil on your offering, as much as you can afford.

[12] And give the physician his place, for the Lord created him; let him not leave you, for there is need of him.

[13] There is a time when success lies in the hands of physicians,

[14] for they too will pray to the Lord that he should grant them success in diagnosis and in healing, for the sake of preserving life.

[15] He who sins before his Maker, may he fall into the care of a physician.

[16] My son, let your tears fall for the dead, and as one who is suffering grievously begin the lament. Lay out his body with the honor due him, and do not neglect his burial.

[17] Let your weeping be bitter and your wailing fervent; observe the mourning according to his merit, for one day, or two, to avoid criticism; then be comforted for your sorrow.

[18] For sorrow results in death, and sorrow of heart saps one's strength.

[19] In calamity sorrow continues, and the life of the poor man weighs down his heart.

[20] Do not give your heart to sorrow; drive it away, remembering the end of life.

[21] Do not forget, there is no coming back; you do the dead no good, and you injure yourself.

[22] "Remember my doom, for yours is like it: yesterday it was mine, and today it is yours."

[23] When the dead is at rest, let his remembrance cease, and be comforted for him when his spirit is departed.

[24] The wisdom of the scribe depends on the opportunity of leisure; and he who has little business may become wise.

[25] How can he become wise who handles the plow, and who glories in the shaft of a goad, who drives oxen and is occupied with their work, and whose talk is about bulls?

[26] He sets his heart on plowing furrows, and he is careful about fodder for the heifers.

[27] So too is every craftsman and master workman who labors by night as well as by day; those who cut the signets of seals, each is diligent in making a great variety; he sets his heart on painting a lifelike image, and he is careful to finish his work.

[28] So too is the smith sitting by the anvil, intent upon his handiwork in iron; the breath of the fire melts his flesh, and he wastes away in the heat of the furnace; he inclines his ear to the sound of the hammer, and his eyes are on the pattern of the object. He sets his heart on finishing his handiwork, and he is careful to complete its decoration.

[29] So too is the potter sitting at his work and turning the wheel with his feet; he is always deeply concerned over his work, and all his output is by number.

[30] He moulds the clay with his arm and makes it pliable with his feet; he sets his heart to finish the glazing, and he is careful to clean the furnace.

[31] All these rely upon their hands, and each is skilful in his own work.

[32] Without them a city cannot be established, and men can neither sojourn nor live there.

[33] Yet they are not sought out for the council of the people, nor do they attain eminence in the public assembly. They do not sit in the judge's seat, nor do they understand the sentence of judgment; they cannot expound discipline or judgment, and they are not found using proverbs.

[34] But they keep stable the fabric of the world, and their prayer is in the practice of their trade.

Sir.39

[1] On the other hand he who devotes himself to the study of the law of the Most High will seek out the wisdom of all the ancients, and will be concerned with prophecies;

[2] he will preserve the discourse of notable men and penetrate the subtleties of parables;

[3] he will seek out the hidden meanings of proverbs and be at home with the obscurities of parables.

[4] He will serve among great men and appear before rulers; he will travel through the lands of foreign nations, for he tests the good and the evil among men.

[5] He will set his heart to rise early to seek the Lord who made him, and will make supplication before the Most High; he will open his mouth in prayer and make supplication for his sins.

[6] If the great Lord is willing, he will be filled with the spirit of understanding; he will pour forth words of wisdom and give thanks to the Lord in prayer.

[7] He will direct his counsel and knowledge aright, and meditate on his secrets.

[8] He will reveal instruction in his teaching, and will glory in the law of the Lord's covenant.

[9] Many will praise his understanding, and it will never be blotted out; his memory will not disappear, and his name will live through all generations.

[10] Nations will declare his wisdom, and the congregation will proclaim his praise;

[11] if he lives long, he will leave a name greater than a thousand, and if he goes to rest, it is enough for him.

[12] I have yet more to say, which I have thought upon, and I am filled, like the moon at the full.

[13] Listen to me, O you holy sons, and bud like a rose growing by a stream of water;

[14] send forth fragrance like frankincense, and put forth blossoms like a lily. Scatter the fragrance, and sing a hymn of praise; bless the Lord for all his works;

[15] ascribe majesty to his name and give thanks to him with praise, with songs on your lips, and with lyres; and this you shall say in thanksgiving:

[16] "All things are the works of the Lord, for they are very good, and whatever he commands will be done in his time."

[17] No one can say, "What is this?" "Why is that?" for in God's time all things will be sought after. At his word the waters stood in a heap, and the reservoirs of water at the word of his mouth.

[18] At his command whatever pleases him is done, and none can limit his saving power.

[19] The works of all flesh are before him, and nothing can be hid from his eyes.

[20] From everlasting to everlasting he beholds them, and nothing is marvelous to him.

[21] No one can say, "What is this?" "Why is that?" for everything has been created for its use.

[22] His blessing covers the dry land like a river, and drenches it like a flood.

[23] The nations will incur his wrath, just as he turns fresh water into salt.

[24] To the holy his ways are straight, just as they are obstacles to the wicked.

[25] From the beginning good things were created for good people, just as evil things for sinners.

[26] Basic to all the needs of man's life are water and fire and iron and salt and wheat flour and milk and honey, the blood of the grape, and oil and clothing.

[27] All these are for good to the godly, just as they turn into evils for sinners.

[28] There are winds that have been created for vengeance, and in their anger they scourge heavily; in the time of consummation they will pour out their strength and calm the anger of their Maker.

[29] Fire and hail and famine and pestilence, all these have been created for vengeance;

[30] the teeth of wild beasts, and scorpions and vipers, and the sword that punishes the ungodly with destruction;

[31] they will rejoice in his commands, and be made ready on earth for their service, and when their times come they will not transgress his word.

[32] Therefore from the beginning I have been convinced, and have thought this out and left it in writing:

[33] The works of the Lord are all good, and he will supply every need in its hour.

[34] And no one can say, "This is worse than that," for all things will prove good in their season.

[35] So now sing praise with all your heart and voice, and bless the name of the Lord.

Sir.40

[1] Much labor was created for every man, and a heavy yoke is upon the sons of Adam, from the day they come forth from their mother's womb till the day they return to the mother of all.

[2] Their perplexities and fear of heart -- their anxious thought is the day of death,

[3] from the man who sits on a splendid throne to the one who is humbled in dust and ashes,

[4] from the man who wears purple and a crown to the one who is clothed in burlap;

[5] there is anger and envy and trouble and unrest, and fear of death, and fury and strife. And when one rests upon his bed, his sleep at night confuses his mind.

[6] He gets little or no rest, and afterward in his sleep, as though he were on watch, he is troubled by the visions of his mind like one who has escaped from the battle-front;

[7] at the moment of his rescue he wakes up, and wonders that his fear came to nothing.

[8] With all flesh, both man and beast, and upon sinners seven times more,

[9] are death and bloodshed and strife and sword, calamities, famine and affliction and plague.

[10] All these were created for the wicked, and on their account the flood came.

[11] All things that are from the earth turn back to the earth, and what is from the waters returns to the sea.

[12] All bribery and injustice will be blotted out, but good faith will stand for ever.

[13] The wealth of the unjust will dry up like a torrent, and crash like a loud clap of thunder in a rain.

[14] A generous man will be made glad; likewise transgressors will utterly fail.

[15] The children of the ungodly will not put forth many branches; they are unhealthy roots upon sheer rock.

[16] The reeds by any water or river bank will be plucked up before any grass.

[17] Kindness is like a garden of blessings, and almsgiving endures for ever.

[18] Life is sweet for the self-reliant and the worker, but he who finds treasure is better off than both.

[19] Children and the building of a city establish a man's name, but a blameless wife is accounted better than both.

[20] Wine and music gladden the heart, but the love of wisdom is better than both.

[21] The flute and the harp make pleasant melody, but a pleasant voice is better than both.

[22] The eye desires grace and beauty, but the green shoots of grain more than both.

[23] A friend or a companion never meets one amiss, but a wife with her husband is better than both.

[24] Brothers and help are for a time of trouble, but almsgiving rescues better than both.

[25] Gold and silver make the foot stand sure, but good counsel is esteemed more than both.

[26] Riches and strength lift up the heart, but the fear of the Lord is better than both. There is no loss in the fear of the Lord, and with it there is no need to seek for help.

[27] The fear of the Lord is like a garden of blessing, and covers a man better than any glory.

[28] My son, do not lead the life of a beggar; it is better to die than to beg.

[29] When a man looks to the table of another, his existence cannot be considered as life. He pollutes himself with another man's food, but a man who is intelligent and well instructed guards against that.

[30] In the mouth of the shameless begging is sweet, but in his stomach a fire is kindled.

Sir.41

[1] O death, how bitter is the reminder of you to one who lives at peace among his possessions, to a man without distractions, who is prosperous in everything, and who still has the vigor to enjoy his food!

[2] O death, how welcome is your sentence to one who is in need and is failing in strength, very old and distracted over everything; to one who is contrary, and has lost his patience!

[3] Do not fear the sentence of death; remember your former days and the end of life; this is the decree from the Lord for all flesh,

[4] and how can you reject the good pleasure of the Most High? Whether life is for ten or a hundred or a thousand years, there is no inquiry about it in Hades.

[5] The children of sinners are abominable children, and they frequent the haunts of the ungodly.

[6] The inheritance of the children of sinners will perish, and on their posterity will be a perpetual reproach.

[7] Children will blame an ungodly father, for they suffer reproach because of him.

[8] Woe to you, ungodly men, who have forsaken the law of the Most High God!

[9] When you are born, you are born to a curse; and when you die, a curse is your lot.

[10] Whatever is from the dust returns to dust; so the ungodly go from curse to destruction.

[11] The mourning of men is about their bodies, but the evil name of sinners will be blotted out.

[12] Have regard for your name, since it will remain for you longer than a thousand great stores of gold.

[13] The days of a good life are numbered, but a good name endures for ever.

[14] My children, observe instruction and be at peace; hidden wisdom and unseen treasure, what advantage is there in either of them?

[15] Better is the man who hides his folly than the man who hides his wisdom.

[16] Therefore show respect for my words: For it is good to retain every kind of shame, and not everything is confidently esteemed by every one.

[17] Be ashamed of immorality, before your father or mother; and of a lie, before a prince or a ruler;

[18] of a transgression, before a judge or magistrate; and of iniquity, before a congregation or the people; of unjust dealing, before your partner or friend;

[19] and of theft, in the place where you live. Be ashamed before the truth of God and his covenant. Be ashamed of selfish behavior at meals, of surliness in receiving and giving,

[20] and of silence, before those who greet you; of looking at a woman who is a harlot,

[21] and of rejecting the appeal of a kinsman; of taking away some one's portion or gift, and of gazing at another man's wife;

[22] of meddling with his maidservant -- and do not approach her bed; of abusive words, before friends -- and do not upbraid

after making a gift;

[23] of repeating and telling what you hear, and of revealing secrets. Then you will show proper shame, and will find favor with every man.

Sir.42

[1] Of the following things do not be ashamed, and do not let partiality lead you to sin:

[2] of the law of the Most High and his covenant, and of rendering judgment to acquit the ungodly;

[3] of keeping accounts with a partner or with traveling companions, and of dividing the inheritance of friends;

[4] of accuracy with scales and weights, and of acquiring much or little;

[5] of profit from dealing with merchants, and of much discipline of children, and of whipping a wicked servant severely.

[6] Where there is an evil wife, a seal is a good thing; and where there are many hands, lock things up.

[7] Whatever you deal out, let it be by number and weight, and make a record of all that you give out or take in.

[8] Do not be ashamed to instruct the stupid or foolish or the aged man who quarrels with the young. Then you will be truly instructed, and will be approved before all men.

[9] A daughter keeps her father secretly wakeful, and worry over her robs him of sleep; when she is young, lest she do not marry, or if married, lest she be hated;

[10] while a virgin, lest she be defiled or become pregnant in her father's house; or having a husband, lest she prove unfaithful, or, though married, lest she be barren.

[11] Keep strict watch over a headstrong daughter, lest she make you a laughingstock to your enemies, a byword in the city and notorious among the people, and put you to shame before the great multitude.

[12] Do not look upon any one for beauty, and do not sit in the midst of women;

[13] for from garments comes the moth, and from a woman comes woman's wickedness.

[14] Better is the wickedness of a man than a woman who does good; and it is a woman who brings shame and disgrace.

[15] I will now call to mind the works of the Lord, and will declare what I have seen. By the words of the Lord his works are done.

[16] The sun looks down on everything with its light, and the work of the Lord is full of his glory.

[17] The Lord has not enabled his holy ones to recount all his marvelous works, which the Lord the Almighty has established that the universe may stand firm in his glory.

[18] He searches out the abyss, and the hearts of men, and considers their crafty devices. For the Most High knows all that may be known, and he looks into the signs of the age.

[19] He declares what has been and what is to be, and he reveals the tracks of hidden things.

[20] No thought escapes him, and not one word is hidden from him.

[21] He has ordained the splendors of his wisdom, and he is from everlasting and to everlasting. Nothing can be added or taken away, and he needs no one to be his counselor.

[22] How greatly to be desired are all his works, and how sparkling they are to see!

[23] All these things live and remain for ever for every need, and are all obedient.

[24] All things are twofold, one opposite the other, and he has made nothing incomplete.

[25] One confirms the good things of the other, and who can have enough of beholding his glory?

Sir.43

[1] The pride of the heavenly heights is the clear firmament, the appearance of heaven in a spectacle of glory.

[2] The sun, when it appears, making proclamation as it goes forth, is a marvelous instrument, the work of the Most High.

[3] At noon it parches the land; and who can withstand its burning heat?

[4] A man tending a furnace works in burning heat, but the sun burns the mountains three times as much; it breathes out fiery vapors, and with bright beams it blinds the eyes.

[5] Great is the Lord who made it; and at his command it hastens on its course.

[6] He made the moon also, to serve in its season to mark the times and to be an everlasting sign.

[7] From the moon comes the sign for feast days, a light that wanes when it has reached the full.

[8] The month is named for the moon, increasing marvelously in its phases, an instrument of the hosts on high shining forth in the firmament of heaven.

[9] The glory of the stars is the beauty of heaven, a gleaming array in the heights of the Lord.

[10] At the command of the Holy One they stand as ordered, they never relax in their watches.

[11] Look upon the rainbow, and praise him who made it, exceedingly beautiful in its brightness.

[12] It encircles the heaven with its glorious arc; the hands of the Most High have stretched it out.

[13] By his command he sends the driving snow and speeds the lightnings of his judgment.

[14] Therefore the storehouses are opened, and the clouds fly forth like birds.

[15] In his majesty he amasses the clouds, and the hailstones are broken in pieces.

[16] At his appearing the mountains are shaken; at his will the south wind blows.

[17] The voice of his thunder rebukes the earth; so do the tempest from the north and the whirlwind. He scatters the snow like birds flying down, and its descent is like locusts alighting.

[18] The eye marvels at the beauty of its whiteness, and the mind is amazed at its falling.

[19] He pours the hoarfrost upon the earth like salt, and when it freezes, it becomes pointed thorns.

[20] The cold north wind blows, and ice freezes over the water; it rests upon every pool of water, and the water puts it on like a breastplate.

[21] He consumes the mountains and burns up the wilderness, and withers the tender grass like fire.

[22] A mist quickly heals all things; when the dew appears, it refreshes from the heat.

[23] By his counsel he stilled the great deep and planted islands in it.

[24] Those who sail the sea tell of its dangers, and we marvel at what we hear.

[25] for in it are strange and marvelous works, all kinds of living things, and huge creatures of the sea.

[26] Because of him his messenger finds the way, and by his word all things hold together.

[27] Though we speak much we cannot reach the end, and the sum of our words is: "He is the all."

[28] Where shall we find strength to praise him? For he is greater than all his works.

[29] Terrible is the Lord and very great, and marvelous is his power.

[30] When you praise the Lord, exalt him as much as you can; for he will surpass even that. When you exalt him, put forth all your strength, and do not grow weary, for you cannot praise him enough.

[31] Who has seen him and can describe him? Or who can extol him as he is?

[32] Many things greater than these lie hidden, for we have seen but few of his works.

[33] For the Lord has made all things, and to the godly he has granted wisdom.

Sir.44

[1] Let us now praise famous men, and our fathers in their generations.

[2] The Lord apportioned to them great glory, his majesty from the beginning.

[3] There were those who ruled in their kingdoms, and were men renowned for their power, giving counsel by their understanding, and proclaiming prophecies;

[4] leaders of the people in their deliberations and in understanding of learning for the people, wise in their words of instruction;

[5] those who composed musical tunes, and set forth verses in writing;

[6] rich men furnished with resources, living peaceably in their habitations --

[7] all these were honored in their generations, and were the glory of their times.

[8] There are some of them who have left a name, so that men declare their praise.

[9] And there are some who have no memorial, who have perished as though they had not lived; they have become as though they had not been born, and so have their children after them.

[10] But these were men of mercy, whose righteous deeds have not been forgotten;

[11] their prosperity will remain with their descendants, and their inheritance to their children's children.

[12] Their descendants stand by the covenants; their children also, for their sake.

[13] Their posterity will continue for ever, and their glory will not be blotted out.

[14] Their bodies were buried in peace, and their name lives to all generations.

[15] Peoples will declare their wisdom, and the congregation proclaims their praise.

[16] Enoch pleased the Lord, and was taken up; he was an example of repentance to all generations.

[17] Noah was found perfect and righteous; in the time of wrath he was taken in exchange; therefore a remnant was left to the earth when the flood came.

[18] Everlasting covenants were made with him that all flesh should not be blotted out by a flood.

[19] Abraham was the great father of a multitude of nations, and no one has been found like him in glory;

[20] he kept the law of the Most High, and was taken into covenant with him; he established the covenant in his flesh, and when he was tested he was found faithful.

[21] Therefore the Lord assured him by an oath that the nations would be blessed through his posterity; that he would multiply him like the dust of the earth, and exalt his posterity like the stars, and cause them to inherit from sea to sea and from the River to the ends of the earth.

[22] To Isaac also he gave the same assurance for the sake of Abraham his father.

[23] The blessing of all men and the covenant he made to rest upon the head of Jacob; he acknowledged him with his blessings, and gave him his inheritance; he determined his portions, and distributed them among twelve tribes.

Sir.45

[1] From his descendants the Lord brought forth a man of mercy, who found favor in the sight of all flesh and was beloved by

God and man, Moses, whose memory is blessed.

[2] He made him equal in glory to the holy ones, and made him great in the fears of his enemies.

[3] By his words he caused signs to cease; the Lord glorified him in the presence of kings. He gave him commands for his people, and showed him part of his glory.

[4] He sanctified him through faithfulness and meekness; he chose him out of all mankind.

[5] He made him hear his voice, and led him into the thick darkness, and gave him the commandments face to face, the law of life and knowledge, to teach Jacob the covenant, and Israel his judgments.

[6] He exalted Aaron, the brother of Moses, a holy man like him, of the tribe of Levi.

[7] He made an everlasting covenant with him, and gave him the priesthood of the people. He blessed him with splendid vestments, and put a glorious robe upon him.

[8] He clothed him with superb perfection, and strengthened him with the symbols of authority, the linen breeches, the long robe, and the ephod.

[9] And he encircled him with pomegranates, with very many golden bells round about, to send forth a sound as he walked, to make their ringing heard in the temple as a reminder to the sons of his people;

[10] with a holy garment, of gold and blue and purple, the work of an embroiderer; with the oracle of judgment, Urim and Thummim;

[11] with twisted scarlet, the work of a craftsman; with precious stones engraved like signets, in a setting of gold, the work of a jeweler, for a reminder, in engraved letters, according to the number of the tribes of Israel;

[12] with a gold crown upon his turban, inscribed like a signet with "Holiness," a distinction to be prized, the work of an expert, the delight of the eyes, richly adorned.

[13] Before his time there never were such beautiful things. No outsider ever put them on, but only his sons and his descendants perpetually.

[14] His sacrifices shall be wholly burned twice every day continually.

[15] Moses ordained him, and anointed him with holy oil; it was an everlasting covenant for him and for his descendants all the days of heaven, to minister to the Lord and serve as priest and bless his people in his name.

[16] He chose him out of all the living to offer sacrifice to the Lord, incense and a pleasing odor as a memorial portion, to make atonement for the people.

[17] In his commandments he gave him authority and statutes and judgments, to teach Jacob the testimonies, and to enlighten Israel with his law.

[18] Outsiders conspired against him, and envied him in the wilderness, Dathan and Abiram and their men and the company of Korah, in wrath and anger.

[19] The Lord saw it and was not pleased, and in the wrath of his anger they were destroyed; he wrought wonders against them to consume them in flaming fire.

[20] He added glory to Aaron and gave him a heritage; he allotted to him the first of the first fruits, he prepared bread of first fruits in abundance;

[21] for they eat the sacrifices to the Lord, which he gave to him and his descendants.

[22] But in the land of the people he has no inheritance, and he has no portion among the people; for the Lord himself is his portion and inheritance.

[23] Phinehas the son of Eleazar is the third in glory, for he was zealous in the fear of the Lord, and stood fast, when the people turned away, in the ready goodness of his soul, and made atonement for Israel.

[24] Therefore a covenant of peace was established with him, that he should be leader of the sanctuary and of his people, that he and his descendants should have the dignity of the priesthood for ever.

[25] A covenant was also established with David, the son of Jesse, of the tribe of Judah: the heritage of the king is from son to son only; so the heritage of Aaron is for his descendants.

[26] May the Lord grant you wisdom in your heart to judge his people in righteousness, so that their prosperity may not vanish, and that their glory may endure throughout their generations.

Sir.46

[1] Joshua the son of Nun was mighty in war, and was the successor of Moses in prophesying. He became, in accordance with his name, a great savior of God's elect, to take vengeance on the enemies that rose against them, so that he might give Israel its inheritance.

[2] How glorious he was when he lifted his hands and stretched out his sword against the cities!

[3] Who before him ever stood so firm? For he waged the wars of the Lord.

[4] Was not the sun held back by his hand? And did not one day become as long as two?

[5] He called upon the Most High, the Mighty One, when enemies pressed him on every side,

[6] and the great Lord answered him with hailstones of mighty power. He hurled down war upon that nation, and at the descent of Beth-horon he destroyed those who resisted, so that the nations might know his armament, that he was fighting in the sight of the Lord; for he wholly followed the Mighty One.

[7] And in the days of Moses he did a loyal deed, he and Caleb the son of Jephunneh: they withstood the congregation, restrained the people from sin, and stilled their wicked murmuring.

[8] And these two alone were preserved out of six hundred thousand people on foot, to bring them into their inheritance, into a land flowing with milk and honey.

[9] And the Lord gave Caleb strength, which remained with him to old age, so that he went up to the hill country, and his children obtained it for an inheritance;

[10] so that all the sons of Israel might see that it is good to follow the Lord.

[11] The judges also, with their respective names, those whose hearts did not fall into idolatry and who did not turn away from the Lord -- may their memory be blessed!

[12] May their bones revive from where they lie, and may the name of those who have been honored live again in their sons!

[13] Samuel, beloved by his Lord, a prophet of the Lord, established the kingdom and anointed rulers over his people.

[14] By the law of the Lord he judged the congregation, and the Lord watched over Jacob.

[15] By his faithfulness he was proved to be a prophet, and by his words he became known as a trustworthy seer.

[16] He called upon the Lord, the Mighty One, when his enemies pressed him on every side, and he offered in sacrifice a sucking lamb.

[17] Then the Lord thundered from heaven, and made his voice heard with a mighty sound;

[18] and he wiped out the leaders of the people of Tyre and all the rulers of the Philistines.

[19] Before the time of his eternal sleep, Samuel called men to witness before the Lord and his anointed: "I have not taken any one's property, not so much as a pair of shoes." And no man accused him.

[20] Even after he had fallen asleep he prophesied and revealed to the king his death, and lifted up his voice out of the earth in prophecy, to blot out the wickedness of the people.

Sir.47

[1] And after him Nathan rose up to prophesy in the days of David.

[2] As the fat is selected from the peace offering, so David was selected from the sons of Israel.

[3] He played with lions as with young goats, and with bears as with lambs of the flock.

[4] In his youth did he not kill a giant, and take away reproach from the people, when he lifted his hand with a stone in the sling and struck down the boasting of Goliath?

[5] For he appealed to the Lord, the Most High, and he gave him strength in his right hand to slay a man mighty in war, to exalt the power of his people.

[6] So they glorified him for his ten thousands, and praised him for the blessings of the Lord, when the glorious diadem was bestowed upon him.

[7] For he wiped out his enemies on every side, and annihilated his adversaries the Philistines; he crushed their power even to this day.

[8] In all that he did he gave thanks to the Holy One, the Most High, with ascriptions of glory; he sang praise with all his heart, and he loved his Maker.

[9] He placed singers before the altar, to make sweet melody with their voices.

[10] He gave beauty to the feasts, and arranged their times throughout the year, while they praised God's holy name, and the sanctuary resounded from early morning.

[11] The Lord took away his sins, and exalted his power for ever; he gave him the covenant of kings and a throne of glory in Israel.

[12] After him rose up a wise son who fared amply because of him;

[13] Solomon reigned in days of peace, and God gave him rest on every side, that he might build a house for his name and prepare a sanctuary to stand for ever.

[14] How wise you became in your youth! You overflowed like a river with understanding.

[15] Your soul covered the earth, and you filled it with parables and riddles.

[16] Your name reached to far-off islands, and you were loved for your peace.

[17] For your songs and proverbs and parables, and for your interpretations, the countries marveled at you.

[18] In the name of the Lord God, who is called the God of Israel, you gathered gold like tin and amassed silver like lead.

[19] But you laid your loins beside women, and through your body you were brought into subjection.

[20] You put stain upon your honor, and defiled your posterity, so that you brought wrath upon your children and they were grieved at your folly,

[21] so that the sovereignty was divided and a disobedient kingdom arose out of Ephraim.

[22] But the Lord will never give up his mercy, nor cause any of his works to perish; he will never blot out the descendants of his chosen one, nor destroy the posterity of him who loved him; so he gave a remnant to Jacob, and to David a root of his stock.

[23] Solomon rested with his fathers, and left behind him one of his sons, ample in folly and lacking in understanding, Rehoboam, whose policy caused the people to revolt. Also Jeroboam the son of Nebat, who caused Israel to sin and gave to

Ephraim a sinful way.

[24] Their sins became exceedingly many, so as to remove them from their land.

[25] For they sought out every sort of wickedness, till vengeance came upon them.

Sir.48

[1] Then the prophet Elijah arose like a fire, and his word burned like a torch.

[2] He brought a famine upon them, and by his zeal he made them few in number.

[3] By the word of the Lord he shut up the heavens, and also three times brought down fire.

[4] How glorious you were, O Elijah, in your wondrous deeds! And who has the right to boast which you have?

[5] You who raised a corpse from death and from Hades, by the word of the Most High;

[6] who brought kings down to destruction, and famous men from their beds;

[7] who heard rebuke at Sinai and judgments of vengeance at Horeb;

[8] who anointed kings to inflict retribution, and prophets to succeed you.

[9] You who were taken up by a whirlwind of fire, in a chariot with horses of fire;

[10] you who are ready at the appointed time, it is written, to calm the wrath of God before it breaks out in fury, to turn the heart of the father to the son, and to restore the tribes of Jacob.

[11] Blessed are those who saw you, and those who have been adorned in love; for we also shall surely live.

[12] It was Elijah who was covered by the whirlwind, and Elisha was filled with his spirit; in all his days he did not tremble before any ruler, and no one brought him into subjection.

[13] Nothing was too hard for him, and when he was dead his body prophesied.

[14] As in his life he did wonders, so in death his deeds were marvelous.

[15] For all this the people did not repent, and they did not forsake their sins, till they were carried away captive from their land and were scattered over all the earth; the people were left very few in number, but with rulers from the house of David.

[16] Some of them did what was pleasing to God, but others multiplied sins.

[17] Hezekiah fortified his city, and brought water into the midst of it; he tunneled the sheer rock with iron and built pools for water.

[18] In his days Sennacherib came up, and sent the Rabshakeh; he lifted up his hand against Zion and made great boasts in his arrogance.

[19] Then their hearts were shaken and their hands trembled, and they were in anguish, like women in travail.

[20] But they called upon the Lord who is merciful, spreading forth their hands toward him; and the Holy One quickly heard them from heaven, and delivered them by the hand of Isaiah.

[21] The Lord smote the camp of the Assyrians, and his angel wiped them out.

[22] For Hezekiah did what was pleasing to the Lord, and he held strongly to the ways of David his father, which Isaiah the prophet commanded, who was great and faithful in his vision.

[23] In his days the sun went backward, and he lengthened the life of the king.

[24] By the spirit of might he saw the last things, and comforted those who mourned in Zion.

[25] He revealed what was to occur to the end of time, and the hidden things before they came to pass.

Sir.49

[1] The memory of Josiah is like a blending of incense prepared by the art of the perfumer; it is sweet as honey to every mouth, and like music at a banquet of wine.

[2] He was led aright in converting the people, and took away the abominations of iniquity.

[3] He set his heart upon the Lord; in the days of wicked men he strengthened godliness.

[4] Except David and Hezekiah and Josiah they all sinned greatly, for they forsook the law of the Most High; the kings of Judah came to an end;

[5] for they gave their power to others, and their glory to a foreign nation,

[6] who set fire to the chosen city of the sanctuary, and made her streets desolate, according to the word of Jeremiah.

[7] For they had afflicted him; yet he had been consecrated in the womb as prophet, to pluck up and afflict and destroy, and likewise to build and to plant.

[8] It was Ezekiel who saw the vision of glory which God showed him above the chariot of the cherubim.

[9] For God remembered his enemies with storm, and did good to those who directed their ways aright.

[10] May the bones of the twelve prophets revive from where they lie, for they comforted the people of Jacob and delivered them with confident hope.

[11] How shall we magnify Zerubbabel? He was like a signet on the right hand,

[12] and so was Jeshua the son of Jozadak; in their days they built the house and raised a temple holy to the Lord, prepared for everlasting glory.

[13] The memory of Nehemiah also is lasting; he raised for us the walls that had fallen, and set up the gates and bars and

rebuilt our ruined houses.

[14] No one like Enoch has been created on earth, for he was taken up from the earth.

[15] And no man like Joseph has been born, and his bones are cared for.

[16] Shem and Seth were honored among men, and Adam above every living being in the creation.

Sir.50

[1] The leader of his brethren and the pride of his people was Simon the high priest, son of Onias, who in his life repaired the house, and in his time fortified the temple.

[2] He laid the foundations for the high double walls, the high retaining walls for the temple enclosure.

[3] In his days a cistern for water was quarried out, a reservoir like the sea in circumference.

[4] He considered how to save his people from ruin, and fortified the city to withstand a seige.

[5] How glorious he was when the people gathered round him as he came out of the inner sanctuary!

[6] Like the morning star among the clouds, like the moon when it is full;

[7] like the sun shining upon the temple of the Most High, and like the rainbow gleaming in glorious clouds;

[8] like roses in the days of the first fruits, like lilies by a spring of water, like a green shoot on Lebanon on a summer day;

[9] like fire and incense in the censer, like a vessel of hammered gold adorned with all kinds of precious stones;

[10] like an olive tree putting forth its fruit, and like a cypress towering in the clouds.

[11] When he put on his glorious robe and clothed himself with superb perfection and went up to the holy altar, he made the court of the sanctuary glorious.

[12] And when he received the portions from the hands of the priests, as he stood by the hearth of the altar with a garland of brethren around him, he was like a young cedar on Lebanon; and they surrounded him like the trunks of palm trees,

[13] all the sons of Aaron in their splendor with the Lord's offering in their hands, before the whole congregation of Israel.

[14] Finishing the service at the altars, and arranging the offering to the Most High, the Almighty,

[15] he reached out his hand to the cup and poured a libation of the blood of the grape; he poured it out at the foot of the altar, a pleasing odor to the Most High, the King of all.

[16] Then the sons of Aaron shouted, they sounded the trumpets of hammered work, they made a great noise to be heard for remembrance before the Most High.

[17] Then all the people together made haste and fell to the ground upon their faces to worship their Lord, the Almighty, God Most High.

[18] And the singers praised him with their voices in sweet and full-toned melody.

[19] And the people besought the Lord Most High in prayer before him who is merciful, till the order of worship of the Lord was ended; so they completed his service.

[20] Then Simon came down, and lifted up his hands over the whole congregation of the sons of Israel, to pronounce the blessing of the Lord with his lips, and to glory in his name;

[21] and they bowed down in worship a second time, to receive the blessing from the Most High.

[22] And now bless the God of all, who in every way does great things; who exalts our days from birth, and deals with us according to his mercy.

[23] May he give us gladness of heart, and grant that peace may be in our days in Israel, as in the days of old.

[24] May he entrust to us his mercy! And let him deliver us in our days!

[25] With two nations my soul is vexed, and the third is no nation:

[26] Those who live on Mount Seir, and the Philistines, and the foolish people that dwell in Shechem.

[27] Instruction in understanding and knowledge I have written in this book, Jesus the son of Sirach, son of Eleazar, of Jerusalem, who out of his heart poured forth wisdom.

[28] Blessed is he who concerns himself with these things, and he who lays them to heart will become wise.

[29] For if he does them, he will be strong for all things, for the light of the Lord is his path.

Sir.51

[1] I will give thanks to thee, O Lord and King, and will praise thee as God my Savior. I give thanks to thy name,

[2] for thou hast been my protector and helper and hast delivered my body from destruction and from the snare of a slanderous tongue, from lips that utter lies. Before those who stood by thou wast my helper,

[3] and didst deliver me, in the greatness of thy mercy and of thy name, from the gnashings of teeth about to devour me, from the hand of those who sought my life, from the many afflictions that I endured,

[4] from choking fire on every side and from the midst of fire which I did not kindle,

[5] from the depths of the belly of Hades, from an unclean tongue and lying words --

[6] the slander of an unrighteous tongue to the king. My soul drew near to death, and my life was very near to Hades beneath.

[7] They surrounded me on every side, and there was no one to help me; I looked for the assistance of men, and there was

none.

[8] Then I remembered thy mercy, O Lord, and thy work from of old, that thou do deliver those who wait for thee and do save them from the hand of their enemies.

[9] And I sent up my supplication from the earth, and prayed for deliverance from death.

[10] I appealed to the Lord, the Father of my lord, not to forsake me in the days of affliction, at the time when there is no help against the proud.

[11] I will praise thy name continually, and will sing praise with thanksgiving. My prayer was heard,

[12] for thou didst save me from destruction and rescue me from an evil plight. Therefore I will give thanks to thee and praise thee, and I will bless the name of the Lord.

[13] While I was still young, before I went on my travels, I sought wisdom openly in my prayer.

[14] Before the temple I asked for her, and I will search for her to the last.

[15] From blossom to ripening grape my heart delighted in her; my foot entered upon the straight path; from my youth I followed her steps.

[16] I inclined my ear a little and received her, and I found for myself much instruction.

[17] I made progress therein; to him who gives wisdom I will give glory.

[18] For I resolved to live according to wisdom, and I was zealous for the good; and I shall never be put to shame.

[19] My soul grappled with wisdom, and in my conduct I was strict; I spread out my hands to the heavens, and lamented my ignorance of her.

[20] I directed my soul to her, and through purification I found her. I gained understanding with her from the first, therefore I will not be forsaken.

[21] My heart was stirred to seek her, therefore I have gained a good possession.

[22] The Lord gave me a tongue as my reward, and I will praise him with it.

[23] Draw near to me, you who are untaught, and lodge in my school.

[24] Why do you say you are lacking in these things, and why are your souls very thirsty?

[25] I opened my mouth and said, Get these things for yourselves without money.

[26] Put your neck under the yoke, and let your souls receive instruction; it is to be found close by.

[27] See with your eyes that I have labored little and found myself much rest.

[28] Get instruction with a large sum of silver, and you will gain by it much gold.

[29] May your soul rejoice in his mercy, and may you not be put to shame when you praise him.

[30] Do your work before the appointed time, and in God's time he will give you your reward.

Wisdom of Solomon

Wis.1

[1] Love righteousness, you rulers of the earth, think of the Lord with uprightness, and seek him with sincerity of heart;

[2] because he is found by those who do not put him to the test, and manifests himself to those who do not distrust him.

[3] For perverse thoughts separate men from God, and when his power is tested, it convicts the foolish;

[4] because wisdom will not enter a deceitful soul, nor dwell in a body enslaved to sin.

[5] For a holy and disciplined spirit will flee from deceit, and will rise and depart from foolish thoughts, and will be ashamed at the approach of unrighteousness.

[6] For wisdom is a kindly spirit and will not free a blasphemer from the guilt of his words; because God is witness of his inmost feelings, and a true observer of his heart, and a hearer of his tongue.

[7] Because the Spirit of the Lord has filled the world, and that which holds all things together knows what is said;

[8] therefore no one who utters unrighteous things will escape notice, and justice, when it punishes, will not pass him by.

[9] For inquiry will be made into the counsels of an ungodly man, and a report of his words will come to the Lord, to convict him of his lawless deeds;

[10] because a jealous ear hears all things, and the sound of murmurings does not go unheard.

[11] Beware then of useless murmuring, and keep your tongue from slander; because no secret word is without result, and a lying mouth destroys the soul.

[12] Do not invite death by the error of your life, nor bring on destruction by the works of your hands;

[13] because God did not make death, and he does not delight in the death of the living.

[14] For he created all things that they might exist, and the generative forces of the world are wholesome, and there is no destructive poison in them; and the dominion of Hades is not on earth.

[15] For righteousness is immortal.

[16] But ungodly men by their words and deeds summoned death; considering him a friend, they pined away, and they made a covenant with him, because they are fit to belong to his party.

Wis.2

[1] For they reasoned unsoundly, saying to themselves, Short and sorrowful is our life, and there is no remedy when a man comes to his end, and no one has been known to return from Hades.

[2] Because we were born by mere chance, and hereafter we shall be as though we had never been; because the breath in our nostrils is smoke, and reason is a spark kindled by the beating of our hearts.

[3] When it is extinguished, the body will turn to ashes, and the spirit will dissolve like empty air.

[4] Our name will be forgotten in time and no one will remember our works; our life will pass away like the traces of a cloud, and be scattered like mist that is chased by the rays of the sun and overcome by its heat.

[5] For our allotted time is the passing of a shadow, and there is no return from our death, because it is sealed up and no one turns back.

[6] "Come, therefore, let us enjoy the good things that exist, and make use of the creation to the full as in youth.

[7] Let us take our fill of costly wine and perfumes, and let no flower of spring pass by us.

[8] Let us crown ourselves with rosebuds before they wither.

[9] Let none of us fail to share in our revelry, everywhere let us leave signs of enjoyment, because this is our portion, and this our lot.

[10] Let us oppress the righteous poor man; let us not spare the widow nor regard the gray hairs of the aged.

[11] But let our might be our law of right, for what is weak proves itself to be useless.

[12] "Let us lie in wait for the righteous man, because he is inconvenient to us and opposes our actions; he reproaches us for sins against the law, and accuses us of sins against our training.

[13] He professes to have knowledge of God, and calls himself a child of the Lord.

[14] He became to us a reproof of our thoughts;

[15] the very sight of him is a burden to us, because his manner of life is unlike that of others, and his ways are strange.

[16] We are considered by him as something base, and he avoids our ways as unclean; he calls the last end of the righteous happy, and boasts that God is his father.

[17] Let us see if his words are true, and let us test what will happen at the end of his life;

[18] for if the righteous man is God's son, he will help him, and will deliver him from the hand of his adversaries.

[19] Let us test him with insult and torture, that we may find out how gentle he is, and make trial of his forbearance.

[20] Let us condemn him to a shameful death, for, according to what he says, he will be protected."

[21] Thus they reasoned, but they were led astray, for their wickedness blinded them,

[22] and they did not know the secret purposes of God, nor hope for the wages of holiness, nor discern the prize for blameless souls;

[23] for God created man for incorruption, and made him in the image of his own eternity,

[24] but through the devil's envy death entered the world, and those who belong to his party experience it.

Wis.3

[1] But the souls of the righteous are in the hand of God, and no torment will ever touch them.

[2] In the eyes of the foolish they seemed to have died, and their departure was thought to be an affliction,

[3] and their going from us to be their destruction; but they are at peace.

[4] For though in the sight of men they were punished, their hope is full of immortality.

[5] Having been disciplined a little, they will receive great good, because God tested them and found them worthy of himself;

[6] like gold in the furnace he tried them, and like a sacrificial burnt offering he accepted them.

[7] In the time of their visitation they will shine forth, and will run like sparks through the stubble.

[8] They will govern nations and rule over peoples, and the Lord will reign over them for ever.

[9] Those who trust in him will understand truth, and the faithful will abide with him in love, because grace and mercy are upon his elect, and he watches over his holy ones.

[10] But the ungodly will be punished as their reasoning deserves, who disregarded the righteous man and rebelled against the Lord;

[11] for whoever despises wisdom and instruction is miserable. Their hope is vain, their labors are unprofitable, and their works are useless.

[12] Their wives are foolish, and their children evil;

[13] their offspring are accursed. For blessed is the barren woman who is undefiled, who has not entered into a sinful union; she will have fruit when God examines souls.

[14] Blessed also is the eunuch whose hands have done no lawless deed, and who has not devised wicked things against the Lord; for special favor will be shown him for his faithfulness, and a place of great delight in the temple of the Lord.

[15] For the fruit of good labors is renowned, and the root of understanding does not fail.

[16] But children of adulterers will not come to maturity, and the offspring of an unlawful union will perish.

[17] Even if they live long they will be held of no account, and finally their old age will be without honor.

[18] If they die young, they will have no hope and no consolation in the day of decision.

[19] For the end of an unrighteous generation is grievous.

Wis.4

[1] Better than this is childlessness with virtue, for in the memory of virtue is immortality, because it is known both by God and by men.

[2] When it is present, men imitate it, and they long for it when it has gone; and throughout all time it marches crowned in triumph, victor in the contest for prizes that are undefiled.

[3] But the prolific brood of the ungodly will be of no use, and none of their illegitimate seedlings will strike a deep root or take a firm hold.

[4] For even if they put forth boughs for a while, standing insecurely they will be shaken by the wind, and by the violence of the winds they will be uprooted.

[5] The branches will be broken off before they come to maturity, and their fruit will be useless, not ripe enough to eat, and good for nothing.

[6] For children born of unlawful unions are witnesses of evil against their parents when God examines them.

[7] But the righteous man, though he die early, will be at rest.

[8] For old age is not honored for length of time, nor measured by number of years;

[9] but understanding is gray hair for men, and a blameless life is ripe old age.

[10] There was one who pleased God and was loved by him, and while living among sinners he was taken up.

[11] He was caught up lest evil change his understanding or guile deceive his soul.

[12] For the fascination of wickedness obscures what is good, and roving desire perverts the innocent mind.

[13] Being perfected in a short time, he fulfilled long years;

[14] for his soul was pleasing to the Lord, therefore he took him quickly from the midst of wickedness.

[15] Yet the peoples saw and did not understand, nor take such a thing to heart, that God's grace and mercy are with his elect, and he watches over his holy ones.

[16] The righteous man who had died will condemn the ungodly who are living, and youth that is quickly perfected will condemn the prolonged old age of the unrighteous man.

[17] For they will see the end of the wise man, and will not understand what the Lord purposed for him, and for what he kept him safe.

[18] They will see, and will have contempt for him, but the Lord will laugh them to scorn. After this they will become dishonored corpses, and an outrage among the dead for ever;

[19] because he will dash them speechless to the ground, and shake them from the foundations; they will be left utterly dry and barren, and they will suffer anguish, and the memory of them will perish.

[20] They will come with dread when their sins are reckoned up, and their lawless deeds will convict them to their face.

Wis.5

[1] Then the righteous man will stand with great confidence in the presence of those who have afflicted him, and those who make light of his labors.

[2] When they see him, they will be shaken with dreadful fear, and they will be amazed at his unexpected salvation.

[3] They will speak to one another in repentance, and in anguish of spirit they will groan, and say,

[4] "This is the man whom we once held in derision and made a byword of reproach -- we fools! We thought that his life was madness and that his end was without honor.

[5] Why has he been numbered among the sons of God? And why is his lot among the saints?

[6] So it was we who strayed from the way of truth, and the light of righteousness did not shine on us, and the sun did not rise upon us.

[7] We took our fill of the paths of lawlessness and destruction, and we journeyed through trackless deserts, but the way of the Lord we have not known.

[8] What has our arrogance profited us? And what good has our boasted wealth brought us?

[9] "All those things have vanished like a shadow, and like a rumor that passes by;

[10] like a ship that sails through the billowy water, and when it has passed no trace can be found, nor track of its keel in the waves;

[11] or as, when a bird flies through the air, no evidence of its passage is found; the light air, lashed by the beat of its pinions and pierced by the force of its rushing flight, is traversed by the movement of its wings, and afterward no sign of its coming is found there;

[12] or as, when an arrow is shot at a target, the air, thus divided, comes together at once, so that no one knows its pathway.

[13] So we also, as soon as we were born, ceased to be, and we had no sign of virtue to show, but were consumed in our wickedness."

[14] Because the hope of the ungodly man is like chaff carried by the wind, and like a light hoarfrost driven away by a storm; it is dispersed like smoke before the wind, and it passes like the remembrance of a guest who stays but a day.

[15] But the righteous live for ever, and their reward is with the Lord; the Most High takes care of them.

[16] Therefore they will receive a glorious crown and a beautiful diadem from the hand of the Lord, because with his right hand he will cover them, and with his arm he will shield them.

[17] The Lord will take his zeal as his whole armor, and will arm all creation to repel his enemies;

[18] he will put on righteousness as a breastplate, and wear impartial justice as a helmet;

[19] he will take holiness as an invincible shield,

[20] and sharpen stern wrath for a sword, and creation will join with him to fight against the madmen.

[21] Shafts of lightning will fly with true aim, and will leap to the target as from a well-drawn bow of clouds,

[22] and hailstones full of wrath will be hurled as from a catapult; the water of the sea will rage against them, and rivers will relentlessly overwhelm them;

[23] a mighty wind will rise against them , and like a tempest it will winnow them away. Lawlessness will lay waste the whole earth, and evil-doing will overturn the thrones of rulers.

Wis.6

[1] Listen therefore, O kings, and understand; learn, O judges of the ends of the earth.

[2] Give ear, you that rule over multitudes, and boast of many nations.

[3] For your dominion was given you from the Lord, and your sovereignty from the Most High, who will search out your works and inquire into your plans.

[4] Because as servants of his kingdom you did not rule rightly, nor keep the law, nor walk according to the purpose of God,

[5] he will come upon you terribly and swiftly, because severe judgment falls on those in high places.

[6] For the lowliest man may be pardoned in mercy, but mighty men will be mightily tested.

[7] For the Lord of all will not stand in awe of any one, nor show deference to greatness; because he himself made both small and great, and he takes thought for all alike.

[8] But a strict inquiry is in store for the mighty.

[9] To you then, O monarchs, my words are directed, that you may learn wisdom and not transgress.

[10] For they will be made holy who observe holy things in holiness, and those who have been taught them will find a defense.

[11] Therefore set your desire on my words; long for them, and you will be instructed.

[12] Wisdom is radiant and unfading, and she is easily discerned by those who love her, and is found by those who seek her.

[13] She hastens to make herself known to those who desire her.

[14] He who rises early to seek her will have no difficulty, for he will find her sitting at his gates.

[15] To fix one's thought on her is perfect understanding, and he who is vigilant on her account will soon be free from care,

[16] because she goes about seeking those worthy of her, and she graciously appears to them in their paths, and meets them in every thought.

[17] The beginning of wisdom is the most sincere desire for instruction, and concern for instruction is love of her,

[18] and love of her is the keeping of her laws, and giving heed to her laws is assurance of immortality,

[19] and immortality brings one near to God;

[20] so the desire for wisdom leads to a kingdom.

[21] Therefore if you delight in thrones and scepters, O monarchs over the peoples, honor wisdom, that you may reign for ever.

[22] I will tell you what wisdom is and how she came to be, and I will hide no secrets from you, but I will trace her course from the beginning of creation, and make knowledge of her clear, and I will not pass by the truth;

[23] neither will I travel in the company of sickly envy, for envy does not associate with wisdom.

[24] A multitude of wise men is the salvation of the world, and a sensible king is the stability of his people.

[25] Therefore be instructed by my words, and you will profit.

Wis.7

[1] I also am mortal, like all men, a descendant of the first-formed child of earth; and in the womb of a mother I was molded into flesh,

[2] within the period of ten months, compacted with blood, from the seed of a man and the pleasure of marriage.

[3] And when I was born, I began to breathe the common air, and fell upon the kindred earth, and my first sound was a cry, like that of all.

[4] I was nursed with care in swaddling cloths.

[5] For no king has had a different beginning of existence;

[6] there is for all mankind one entrance into life, and a common departure.

[7] Therefore I prayed, and understanding was given me; I called upon God, and the spirit of wisdom came to me.

[8] I preferred her to scepters and thrones, and I accounted wealth as nothing in comparison with her.

[9] Neither did I liken to her any priceless gem, because all gold is but a little sand in her sight, and silver will be accounted as clay before her.

[10] I loved her more than health and beauty, and I chose to have her rather than light, because her radiance never ceases.

[11] All good things came to me along with her, and in her hands uncounted wealth.

[12] I rejoiced in them all, because wisdom leads them; but I did not know that she was their mother.

[13] I learned without guile and I impart without grudging; I do not hide her wealth,

[14] for it is an unfailing treasure for men; those who get it obtain friendship with God, commended for the gifts that come from instruction.

[15] May God grant that I speak with judgment and have thought worthy of what I have received, for he is the guide even of wisdom and the corrector of the wise.

[16] For both we and our words are in his hand, as are all understanding and skill in crafts.

[17] For it is he who gave me unerring knowledge of what exists, to know the structure of the world and the activity of the elements;

[18] the beginning and end and middle of times, the alternations of the solstices and the changes of the seasons,

[19] the cycles of the year and the constellations of the stars,

[20] the natures of animals and the tempers of wild beasts, the powers of spirits and the reasonings of men, the varieties of plants and the virtues of roots;

[21] I learned both what is secret and what is manifest,

[22] for wisdom, the fashioner of all things, taught me. For in her there is a spirit that is intelligent, holy, unique, manifold, subtle, mobile, clear, unpolluted, distinct, invulnerable, loving the good, keen, irresistible,

[23] beneficent, humane, steadfast, sure, free from anxiety, all-powerful, overseeing all, and penetrating through all spirits that are intelligent and pure and most subtle.

[24] For wisdom is more mobile than any motion; because of her pureness she pervades and penetrates all things.

[25] For she is a breath of the power of God, and a pure emanation of the glory of the Almighty; therefore nothing defiled gains entrance into her.

[26] For she is a reflection of eternal light, a spotless mirror of the working of God, and an image of his goodness.

[27] Though she is but one, she can do all things, and while remaining in herself, she renews all things; in every generation she passes into holy souls and makes them friends of God, and prophets;

[28] for God loves nothing so much as the man who lives with wisdom.

[29] For she is more beautiful than the sun, and excels every constellation of the stars. Compared with the light she is found

to be superior,

[30] for it is succeeded by the night, but against wisdom evil does not prevail.

Wis.8

[1] She reaches mightily from one end of the earth to the other, and she orders all things well.

[2] I loved her and sought her from my youth, and I desired to take her for my bride, and I became enamored of her beauty.

[3] She glorifies her noble birth by living with God, and the Lord of all loves her.

[4] For she is an initiate in the knowledge of God, and an associate in his works.

[5] If riches are a desirable possession in life, what is richer than wisdom who effects all things?

[6] And if understanding is effective, who more than she is fashioner of what exists?

[7] And if any one loves righteousness, her labors are virtues; for she teaches self-control and prudence, justice and courage; nothing in life is more profitable for men than these.

[8] And if any one longs for wide experience, she knows the things of old, and infers the things to come; she understands turns of speech and the solutions of riddles; she has foreknowledge of signs and wonders and of the outcome of seasons and times.

[9] Therefore I determined to take her to live with me, knowing that she would give me good counsel and encouragement in cares and grief.

[10] Because of her I shall have glory among the multitudes and honor in the presence of the elders, though I am young.

[11] I shall be found keen in judgment, and in the sight of rulers I shall be admired.

[12] When I am silent they will wait for me, and when I speak they will give heed; and when I speak at greater length they will put their hands on their mouths.

[13] Because of her I shall have immortality, and leave an everlasting remembrance to those who come after me.

[14] I shall govern peoples, and nations will be subject to me;

[15] dread monarchs will be afraid of me when they hear of me; among the people I shall show myself capable, and courageous in war.

[16] When I enter my house, I shall find rest with her, for companionship with her has no bitterness, and life with her has no pain, but gladness and joy.

[17] When I considered these things inwardly, and thought upon them in my mind, that in kinship with wisdom there is immortality,

[18] and in friendship with her, pure delight, and in the labors of her hands, unfailing wealth, and in the experience of her company, understanding, and renown in sharing her words, I went about seeking how to get her for myself.

[19] As a child I was by nature well endowed, and a good soul fell to my lot;

[20] or rather, being good, I entered an undefiled body.

[21] But I perceived that I would not possess wisdom unless God gave her to me -- and it was a mark of insight to know whose gift she was -- so I appealed to the Lord and besought him, and with my whole heart I said:

Wis.9

[1] "O God of my fathers and Lord of mercy, who hast made all things by thy word,

[2] and by thy wisdom hast formed man, to have dominion over the creatures thou hast made,

[3] and rule the world in holiness and righteousness, and pronounce judgment in uprightness of soul,

[4] give me the wisdom that sits by thy throne, and do not reject me from among thy servants.

[5] For I am thy slave and the son of thy maidservant, a man who is weak and short-lived, with little understanding of judgment and laws;

[6] for even if one is perfect among the sons of men, yet without the wisdom that comes from thee he will be regarded as nothing.

[7] Thou hast chosen me to be king of thy people and to be judge over thy sons and daughters.

[8] Thou hast given command to build a temple on thy holy mountain, and an altar in the city of thy habitation, a copy of the holy tent which thou didst prepare from the beginning.

[9] With thee is wisdom, who knows thy works and was present when thou didst make the world, and who understand what is pleasing in thy sight and what is right according to thy commandments.

[10] Send her forth from the holy heavens, and from the throne of thy glory send her, that she may be with me and toil, and that I may learn what is pleasing to thee.

[11] For she knows and understands all things, and she will guide me wisely in my actions and guard me with her glory.

[12] Then my works will be acceptable, and I shall judge thy people justly, and shall be worthy of the throne of my father.

[13] For what man can learn the counsel of God? Or who can discern what the Lord wills?

[14] For the reasoning of mortals is worthless, and our designs are likely to fail,

[15] for a perishable body weighs down the soul, and this earthy tent burdens the thoughtful mind.

[16] We can hardly guess at what is on earth, and what is at hand we find with labor; but who has traced out what is in the heavens?

[17] Who has learned thy counsel, unless thou hast given wisdom and sent thy holy Spirit from on high?

[18] And thus the paths of those on earth were set right, and men were taught what pleases thee, and were saved by wisdom."

Wis.10

[1] Wisdom protected the first-formed father of the world, when he alone had been created; she delivered him from his transgression,

[2] and gave him strength to rule all things.

[3] But when an unrighteous man departed from her in his anger, he perished because in rage he slew his brother.

[4] When the earth was flooded because of him, wisdom again saved it, steering the righteous man by a paltry piece of wood.

[5] Wisdom also, when the nations in wicked agreement had been confounded, recognized the righteous man and preserved him blameless before God, and kept him strong in the face of his compassion for his child.

[6] Wisdom rescued a righteous man when the ungodly were perishing; he escaped the fire that descended on the Five Cities.

[7] Evidence of their wickedness still remains: a continually smoking wasteland, plants bearing fruit that does not ripen, and a pillar of salt standing as a monument to an unbelieving soul.

[8] For because they passed wisdom by, they not only were hindered from recognizing the good, but also left for mankind a reminder of their folly, so that their failures could never go unnoticed.

[9] Wisdom rescued from troubles those who served her.

[10] When a righteous man fled from his brother's wrath, she guided him on straight paths; she showed him the kingdom of God, and gave him knowledge of angels; she prospered him in his labors, and increased the fruit of his toil.

[11] When his oppressors were covetous, she stood by him and made him rich.

[12] She protected him from his enemies, and kept him safe from those who lay in wait for him; in his arduous contest she gave him the victory, so that he might learn that godliness is more powerful than anything.

[13] When a righteous man was sold, wisdom did not desert him, but delivered him from sin. She descended with him into the dungeon,

[14] and when he was in prison she did not leave him, until she brought him the scepter of a kingdom and authority over his masters. Those who accused him she showed to be false, and she gave him everlasting honor.

[15] A holy people and blameless race wisdom delivered from a nation of oppressors.

[16] She entered the soul of a servant of the Lord, and withstood dread kings with wonders and signs.

[17] She gave holy men the reward of their labors; she guided them along a marvelous way, and became a shelter to them by day, and a starry flame through the night.

[18] She brought them over the Red Sea, and led them through deep waters;

[19] but she drowned their enemies, and cast them up from the depth of the sea.

[20] Therefore the righteous plundered the ungodly; they sang hymns, O Lord, to thy holy name, and praised with one accord thy defending hand,

[21] because wisdom opened the mouth of the dumb, and made the tongues of babes speak clearly.

Wis.11

[1] Wisdom prospered their works by the hand of a holy prophet.

[2] They journeyed through an uninhabited wilderness, and pitched their tents in untrodden places.

[3] They withstood their enemies and fought off their foes.

[4] When they thirsted they called upon thee, and water was given them out of flinty rock, and slaking of thirst from hard stone.

[5] For through the very things by which their enemies were punished, they themselves received benefit in their need.

[6] Instead of the fountain of an ever-flowing river, stirred up and defiled with blood

[7] in rebuke for the decree to slay the infants, thou gavest them abundant water unexpectedly,

[8] showing by their thirst at that time how thou didst punish their enemies.

[9] For when they were tried, though they were being disciplined in mercy, they learned how the ungodly were tormented when judged in wrath.

[10] For thou didst test them as a father does in warning, but thou didst examine the ungodly as a stern king does in condemnation.

[11] Whether absent or present, they were equally distressed,

[12] for a twofold grief possessed them, and a groaning at the memory of what had occurred.

[13] For when they heard that through their own punishments the righteous had received benefit, they perceived it was the Lord's doing.

[14] For though they had mockingly rejected him who long before had been cast out and exposed, at the end of the events they marveled at him, for their thirst was not like that of the righteous.

[15] In return for their foolish and wicked thoughts, which led them astray to worship irrational serpents and worthless animals, thou didst send upon them a multitude of irrational creatures to punish them,

[16] that they might learn that one is punished by the very things by which he sins.

[17] For thy all-powerful hand, which created the world out of formless matter, did not lack the means to send upon them a multitude of bears, or bold lions,

[18] or newly created unknown beasts full of rage, or such as breathe out fiery breath, or belch forth a thick pall of smoke, or flash terrible sparks from their eyes;

[19] not only could their damage exterminate men, but the mere sight of them could kill by fright.

[20] Even apart from these, men could fall at a single breath when pursued by justice and scattered by the breath of thy power. But thou hast arranged all things by measure and number and weight.

[21] For it is always in thy power to show great strength, and who can withstand the might of thy arm?

[22] Because the whole world before thee is like a speck that tips the scales, and like a drop of morning dew that falls upon the ground.

[23] But thou art merciful to all, for thou canst do all things, and thou do overlook men's sins, that they may repent.

[24] For thou lovest all things that exist, and hast loathing for none of the things which thou hast made, for thou wouldst not have made anything if thou hadst hated it.

[25] How would anything have endured if thou hadst not willed it? Or how would anything not called forth by thee have been preserved?

[26] Thou sparest all things, for they are your, O Lord who lovest the living.

Wis.12

[1] For thy immortal spirit is in all things.

[2] Therefore thou do correct little by little those who trespass, and do remind and warn them of the things wherein they sin, that they may be freed from wickedness and put their trust in thee, O Lord.

[3] Those who dwelt of old in thy holy land

[4] thou didst hate for their detestable practices, their works of sorcery and unholy rites,

[5] their merciless slaughter of children, and their sacrificial feasting on human flesh and blood. These initiates from the midst of a heathen cult,

[6] these parents who murder helpless lives, thou didst will to destroy by the hands of our fathers,

[7] that the land most precious of all to thee might receive a worthy colony of the servants of God.

[8] But even these thou didst spare, since they were but men, and didst send wasps as forerunners of thy army, to destroy them little by little,

[9] though thou wast not unable to give the ungodly into the hands of the righteous in battle, or to destroy them at one blow by dread wild beasts or thy stern word.

[10] But judging them little by little thou gavest them a chance to repent, though thou wast not unaware that their origin was evil and their wickedness inborn, and that their way of thinking would never change.

[11] For they were an accursed race from the beginning, and it was not through fear of any one that thou didst leave them unpunished for their sins.

[12] For who will say, "What hast thou done?" Or will resist thy judgment? Who will accuse thee for the destruction of nations which thou didst make? Or who will come before thee to plead as an advocate for unrighteous men?

[13] For neither is there any god besides thee, whose care is for all men, to whom thou shouldst prove that thou hast not judged unjustly;

[14] nor can any king or monarch confront thee about those whom thou hast punished.

[15] Thou art righteous and rulest all things righteously, deeming it alien to thy power to condemn him who does not deserve to be punished.

[16] For thy strength is the source of righteousness, and thy sovereignty over all causes thee to spare all.

[17] For thou do show thy strength when men doubt the completeness of thy power, and do rebuke any insolence among those who know it.

[18] Thou who art sovereign in strength do judge with mildness, and with great forbearance thou do govern us; for thou hast power to act whenever thou do choose.

[19] Through such works thou has taught thy people that the righteous man must be kind, and thou hast filled thy sons with good hope, because thou givest repentance for sins.

[20] For if thou didst punish with such great care and indulgence the enemies of thy servants and those deserving of death, granting them time and opportunity to give up their wickedness,

[21] with what strictness thou hast judged thy sons, to whose fathers thou gavest oaths and covenants full of good promises!

[22] So while chastening us thou scourgest our enemies ten thousand times more, so that we may meditate upon thy

goodness when we judge, and when we are judged we may expect mercy.

[23] Therefore those who in folly of life lived unrighteously thou didst torment through their own abominations.

[24] For they went far astray on the paths of error, accepting as gods those animals which even their enemies despised; they were deceived like foolish babes.

[25] Therefore, as to thoughtless children, thou didst send thy judgment to mock them.

[26] But those who have not heeded the warning of light rebukes will experience the deserved judgment of God.

[27] For when in their suffering they became incensed at those creatures which they had thought to be gods, being punished by means of them, they saw and recognized as the true God him whom they had before refused to know. Therefore the utmost condemnation came upon them.

Wis.13

[1] For all men who were ignorant of God were foolish by nature; and they were unable from the good things that are seen to know him who exists, nor did they recognize the craftsman while paying heed to his works;

[2] but they supposed that either fire or wind or swift air, or the circle of the stars, or turbulent water, or the luminaries of heaven were the gods that rule the world.

[3] If through delight in the beauty of these things men assumed them to be gods, let them know how much better than these is their Lord, for the author of beauty created them.

[4] And if men were amazed at their power and working, let them perceive from them how much more powerful is he who formed them.

[5] For from the greatness and beauty of created things comes a corresponding perception of their Creator.

[6] Yet these men are little to be blamed, for perhaps they go astray while seeking God and desiring to find him.

[7] For as they live among his works they keep searching, and they trust in what they see, because the things that are seen are beautiful.

[8] Yet again, not even they are to be excused;

[9] for if they had the power to know so much that they could investigate the world, how did they fail to find sooner the Lord of these things?

[10] But miserable, with their hopes set on dead things, are the men who give the name "gods" to the works of men's hands, gold and silver fashioned with skill, and likenesses of animals, or a useless stone, the work of an ancient hand.

[11] A skilled woodcutter may saw down a tree easy to handle and skilfully strip off all its bark, and then with pleasing workmanship make a useful vessel that serves life's needs,

[12] and burn the castoff pieces of his work to prepare his food, and eat his fill.

[13] But a castoff piece from among them, useful for nothing, a stick crooked and full of knots, he takes and carves with care in his leisure, and shapes it with skill gained in idleness; he forms it like the image of a man,

[14] or makes it like some worthless animal, giving it a coat of red paint and coloring its surface red and covering every blemish in it with paint;

[15] then he makes for it a niche that befits it, and sets it in the wall, and fastens it there with iron.

[16] So he takes thought for it, that it may not fall, because he knows that it cannot help itself, for it is only an image and has need of help.

[17] When he prays about possessions and his marriage and children, he is not ashamed to address a lifeless thing.

[18] For health he appeals to a thing that is weak; for life he prays to a thing that is dead; for aid he entreats a thing that is utterly inexperienced; for a prosperous journey, a thing that cannot take a step;

[19] for money-making and work and success with his hands he asks strength of a thing whose hands have no strength.

Wis.14

[1] Again, one preparing to sail and about to voyage over raging waves calls upon a piece of wood more fragile than the ship which carries him.

[2] For it was desire for gain that planned that vessel, and wisdom was the craftsman who built it;

[3] but it is thy providence, O Father, that steers its course, because thou hast given it a path in the sea, and a safe way through the waves,

[4] showing that thou canst save from every danger, so that even if a man lacks skill, he may put to sea.

[5] It is thy will that works of thy wisdom should not be without effect; therefore men trust their lives even to the smallest piece of wood, and passing through the billows on a raft they come safely to land.

[6] For even in the beginning, when arrogant giants were perishing, the hope of the world took refuge on a raft, and guided by thy hand left to the world the seed of a new generation.

[7] For blessed is the wood by which righteousness comes.

[8] But the idol made with hands is accursed, and so is he who made it; because he did the work, and the perishable thing was named a god.

[9] For equally hateful to God are the ungodly man and his ungodliness,

[10] for what was done will be punished together with him who did it.

[11] Therefore there will be a visitation also upon the heathen idols, because, though part of what God created, they became an abomination, and became traps for the souls of men and a snare to the feet of the foolish.

[12] For the idea of making idols was the beginning of fornication, and the invention of them was the corruption of life,

[13] for neither have they existed from the beginning nor will they exist for ever.

[14] For through the vanity of men they entered the world, and therefore their speedy end has been planned.

[15] For a father, consumed with grief at an untimely bereavement, made an image of his child, who had been suddenly taken from him; and he now honored as a god what was once a dead human being, and handed on to his dependents secret rites and initiations.

[16] Then the ungodly custom, grown strong with time, was kept as a law, and at the command of monarchs graven images were worshiped.

[17] When men could not honor monarchs in their presence, since they lived at a distance, they imagined their appearance far away, and made a visible image of the king whom they honored, so that by their zeal they might flatter the absent one as though present.

[18] Then the ambition of the craftsman impelled even those who did not know the king to intensify their worship.

[19] For he, perhaps wishing to please his ruler, skilfully forced the likeness to take more beautiful form,

[20] and the multitude, attracted by the charm of his work, now regarded as an object of worship the one whom shortly before they had honored as a man.

[21] And this became a hidden trap for mankind, because men, in bondage to misfortune or to royal authority, bestowed on objects of stone or wood the name that ought not to be shared.

[22] Afterward it was not enough for them to err about the knowledge of God, but they live in great strife due to ignorance, and they call such great evils peace.

[23] For whether they kill children in their initiations, or celebrate secret mysteries, or hold frenzied revels with strange customs,

[24] they no longer keep either their lives or their marriages pure, but they either treacherously kill one another, or grieve one another by adultery,

[25] and all is a raging riot of blood and murder, theft and deceit, corruption, faithlessness, tumult, perjury,

[26] confusion over what is good, forgetfulness of favors, pollution of souls, sex perversion, disorder in marriage, adultery, and debauchery.

[27] For the worship of idols not to be named is the beginning and cause and end of every evil.

[28] For their worshipers either rave in exultation, or prophesy lies, or live unrighteously, or readily commit perjury;

[29] for because they trust in lifeless idols they swear wicked oaths and expect to suffer no harm.

[30] But just penalties will overtake them on two counts: because they thought wickedly of God in devoting themselves to idols, and because in deceit they swore unrighteously through contempt for holiness.

[31] For it is not the power of the things by which men swear, but the just penalty for those who sin, that always pursues the transgression of the unrighteous.

Wis.15

[1] But thou, our God, art kind and true, patient, and ruling all things in mercy.

[2] For even if we sin we are your, knowing thy power; but we will not sin, because we know that we are accounted your.

[3] For to know thee is complete righteousness, and to know thy power is the root of immortality.

[4] For neither has the evil intent of human art misled us, nor the fruitless toil of painters, a figure stained with varied colors,

[5] whose appearance arouses yearning in fools, so that they desire the lifeless form of a dead image.

[6] Lovers of evil things and fit for such objects of hope are those who either make or desire or worship them.

[7] For when a potter kneads the soft earth and laboriously molds each vessel for our service, he fashions out of the same clay both the vessels that serve clean uses and those for contrary uses, making all in like manner; but which shall be the use of each of these the worker in clay decides.

[8] With misspent toil, he forms a futile god from the same clay -- this man who was made of earth a short time before and after a little while goes to the earth from which he was taken, when he is required to return the soul that was lent him.

[9] But he is not concerned that he is destined to die or that his life is brief, but he competes with workers in gold and silver, and imitates workers in copper; and he counts it his glory that he molds counterfeit gods.

[10] His heart is ashes, his hope is cheaper than dirt, and his life is of less worth than clay,

[11] because he failed to know the one who formed him and inspired him with an active soul and breathed into him a living spirit.

[12] But he considered our existence an idle game, and life a festival held for profit, for he says one must get money however one can, even by base means.

[13] For this man, more than all others, knows that he sins when he makes from earthy matter fragile vessels and graven

images.

[14] But most foolish, and more miserable than an infant, are all the enemies who oppressed thy people.

[15] For they thought that all their heathen idols were gods, though these have neither the use of their eyes to see with, nor nostrils with which to draw breath, nor ears with which to hear, nor fingers to feel with, and their feet are of no use for walking.

[16] For a man made them, and one whose spirit is borrowed formed them; for no man can form a god which is like himself.

[17] He is mortal, and what he makes with lawless hands is dead, for he is better than the objects he worships, since he has life, but they never have.

[18] The enemies of thy people worship even the most hateful animals, which are worse than all others, when judged by their lack of intelligence;

[19] and even as animals they are not so beautiful in appearance that one would desire them, but they have escaped both the praise of God and his blessing.

Wis.16

[1] Therefore those men were deservedly punished through such creatures, and were tormented by a multitude of animals.

[2] Instead of this punishment thou didst show kindness to thy people, and thou didst prepare quails to eat, a delicacy to satisfy the desire of appetite;

[3] in order that those men, when they desired food, might lose the least remnant of appetite because of the odious creatures sent to them, while thy people, after suffering want a short time, might partake of delicacies.

[4] For it was necessary that upon those oppressors inexorable want should come, while to these it was merely shown how their enemies were being tormented.

[5] For when the terrible rage of wild beasts came upon thy people and they were being destroyed by the bites of writhing serpents, thy wrath did not continue to the end;

[6] they were troubled for a little while as a warning, and received a token of deliverance to remind them of thy law's command.

[7] For he who turned toward it was saved, not by what he saw, but by thee, the Savior of all.

[8] And by this also thou didst convince our enemies that it is thou who deliverest from every evil.

[9] For they were killed by the bites of locusts and flies, and no healing was found for them, because they deserved to be punished by such things;

[10] but thy sons were not conquered even by the teeth of venomous serpents, for thy mercy came to their help and healed them.

[11] To remind them of thy oracles they were bitten, and then were quickly delivered, lest they should fall into deep forgetfulness and become unresponsive to thy kindness.

[12] For neither herb nor poultice cured them, but it was thy word, O Lord, which heals all men.

[13] For thou hast power over life and death; thou do lead men down to the gates of Hades and back again.

[14] A man in his wickedness kills another, but he cannot bring back the departed spirit, nor set free the imprisoned soul.

[15] To escape from thy hand is impossible;

[16] for the ungodly, refusing to know thee, were scourged by the strength of thy arm, pursued by unusual rains and hail and relentless storms, and utterly consumed by fire.

[17] For -- most incredible of all -- in the water, which quenches all things, the fire had still greater effect, for the universe defends the righteous.

[18] At one time the flame was restrained, so that it might not consume the creatures sent against the ungodly, but that seeing this they might know that they were being pursued by the judgment of God;

[19] and at another time even in the midst of water it burned more intensely than fire, to destroy the crops of the unrighteous land.

[20] Instead of these things thou didst give thy people food of angels, and without their toil thou didst supply them from heaven with bread ready to eat, providing every pleasure and suited to every taste.

[21] For thy sustenance manifested thy sweetness toward thy children; and the bread, ministering to the desire of the one who took it, was changed to suit every one's liking.

[22] Snow and ice withstood fire without melting, so that they might know that the crops of their enemies were being destroyed by the fire that blazed in the hail and flashed in the showers of rain;

[23] whereas the fire, in order that the righteous might be fed, even forgot its native power.

[24] For creation, serving thee who hast made it, exerts itself to punish the unrighteous, and in kindness relaxes on behalf of those who trust in thee.

[25] Therefore at that time also, changed into all forms, it served thy all-nourishing bounty, according to the desire of those who had need,

[26] so that thy sons, whom thou didst love, O Lord, might learn that it is not the production of crops that feeds man, but that thy word preserves those who trust in thee.

[27] For what was not destroyed by fire was melted when simply warmed by a fleeting ray of the sun,

[28] to make it known that one must rise before the sun to give thee thanks, and must pray to thee at the dawning of the light;

[29] for the hope of an ungrateful man will melt like wintry frost, and flow away like waste water.

Wis.17

[1] Great are thy judgments and hard to describe; therefore unintructed souls have gone astray.

[2] For when lawless men supposed that they held the holy nation in their power, they themselves lay as captives of darkness and prisoners of long night, shut in under their roofs, exiles from eternal providence.

[3] For thinking that in their secret sins they were unobserved behind a dark curtain of forgetfulness, they were scattered, terribly alarmed, and appalled by specters.

[4] For not even the inner chamber that held them protected them from fear, but terrifying sounds rang out around them, and dismal phantoms with gloomy faces appeared.

[5] And no power of fire was able to give light, nor did the brilliant flames of the stars avail to illumine that hateful night.

[6] Nothing was shining through to them except a dreadful, self-kindled fire, and in terror they deemed the things which they saw to be worse than that unseen appearance.

[7] The delusions of their magic art lay humbled, and their boasted wisdom was scornfully rebuked.

[8] For those who promised to drive off the fears and disorders of a sick soul were sick themselves with ridiculous fear.

[9] For even if nothing disturbing frightened them, yet, scared by the passing of beasts and the hissing of serpents,

[10] they perished in trembling fear, refusing to look even at the air, though it nowhere could be avoided.

[11] For wickedness is a cowardly thing, condemned by its own testimony; distressed by conscience, it has always exaggerated the difficulties.

[12] For fear is nothing but surrender of the helps that come from reason;

[13] and the inner expectation of help, being weak, prefers ignorance of what causes the torment.

[14] But throughout the night, which was really powerless, and which beset them from the recesses of powerless Hades, they all slept the same sleep,

[15] and now were driven by monstrous specters, and now were paralyzed by their souls' surrender, for sudden and unexpected fear overwhelmed them.

[16] And whoever was there fell down, and thus was kept shut up in a prison not made of iron;

[17] for whether he was a farmer or a shepherd or a workman who toiled in the wilderness, he was seized, and endured the inescapable fate; for with one chain of darkness they all were bound.

[18] Whether there came a whistling wind, or a melodious sound of birds in wide-spreading branches, or the rhythm of violently rushing water,

[19] or the harsh crash of rocks hurled down, or the unseen running of leaping animals, or the sound of the most savage roaring beasts, or an echo thrown back from a hollow of the mountains, it paralyzed them with terror.

[20] For the whole world was illumined with brilliant light, and was engaged in unhindered work,

[21] while over those men alone heavy night was spread, an image of the darkness that was destined to receive them; but still heavier than darkness were they to themselves.

Wis.18

[1] But for thy holy ones there was very great light. Their enemies heard their voices but did not see their forms, and counted them happy for not having suffered,

[2] and were thankful that thy holy ones, though previously wronged, were doing them no injury; and they begged their pardon for having been at variance with them.

[3] Therefore thou didst provide a flaming pillar of fire as a guide for thy people's unknown journey, and a harmless sun for their glorious wandering.

[4] For their enemies deserved to be deprived of light and imprisoned in darkness, those who had kept thy sons imprisoned, through whom the imperishable light of the law was to be given to the world.

[5] When they had resolved to kill the babes of thy holy ones, and one child had been exposed and rescued, thou didst in punishment take away a multitude of their children; and thou didst destroy them all together by a mighty flood.

[6] That night was made known beforehand to our fathers, so that they might rejoice in sure knowledge of the oaths in which they trusted.

[7] The deliverance of the righteous and the destruction of their enemies were expected by thy people.

[8] For by the same means by which thou didst punish our enemies thou didst call us to thyself and glorify us.

[9] For in secret the holy children of good men offered sacrifices, and with one accord agreed to the divine law, that the saints would share alike the same things, both blessings and dangers; and already they were singing the praises of the fathers.

[10] But the discordant cry of their enemies echoed back, and their piteous lament for their children was spread abroad.

[11] The slave was punished with the same penalty as the master, and the common man suffered the same loss as the king;

[12] and they all together, by the one form of death, had corpses too many to count. For the living were not sufficient even to bury them, since in one instant their most valued children had been destroyed.

[13] For though they had disbelieved everything because of their magic arts, yet, when their first-born were destroyed, they acknowledged thy people to be God's son.

[14] For while gentle silence enveloped all things, and night in its swift course was now half gone,

[15] thy all-powerful word leaped from heaven, from the royal throne, into the midst of the land that was doomed, a stern warrior

[16] carrying the sharp sword of thy authentic command, and stood and filled all things with death, and touched heaven while standing on the earth.

[17] Then at once apparitions in dreadful dreams greatly troubled them, and unexpected fears assailed them;

[18] and one here and another there, hurled down half dead, made known why they were dying;

[19] for the dreams which disturbed them forewarned them of this, so that they might not perish without knowing why they suffered.

[20] The experience of death touched also the righteous, and a plague came upon the multitude in the desert, but the wrath did not long continue.

[21] For a blameless man was quick to act as their champion; he brought forward the shield of his ministry, prayer and propitiation by incense; he withstood the anger and put an end to the disaster, showing that he was thy servant.

[22] He conquered the wrath not by strength of body, and not by force of arms, but by his word he subdued the punisher, appealing to the oaths and covenants given to our fathers.

[23] For when the dead had already fallen on one another in heaps, he intervened and held back the wrath, and cut off its way to the living.

[24] For upon his long robe the whole world was depicted, and the glories of the fathers were engraved on the four rows of stones, and thy majesty on the diadem upon his head.

[25] To these the destroyer yielded, these he feared; for merely to test the wrath was enough.

Wis.19

[1] But the ungodly were assailed to the end by pitiless anger, for God knew in advance even their future actions,

[2] that, though they themselves had permitted thy people to depart and hastily sent them forth, they would change their minds and pursue them.

[3] For while they were still busy at mourning, and were lamenting at the graves of their dead, they reached another foolish decision, and pursued as fugitives those whom they had begged and compelled to depart.

[4] For the fate they deserved drew them on to this end, and made them forget what had happened, in order that they might fill up the punishment which their torments still lacked,

[5] and that thy people might experience an incredible journey, but they themselves might meet a strange death.

[6] For the whole creation in its nature was fashioned anew, complying with thy commands, that thy children might be kept unharmed.

[7] The cloud was seen overshadowing the camp, and dry land emerging where water had stood before, an unhindered way out of the Red Sea, and a grassy plain out of the raging waves,

[8] where those protected by thy hand passed through as one nation, after gazing on marvelous wonders.

[9] For they ranged like horses, and leaped like lambs, praising thee, O Lord, who didst deliver them.

[10] For they still recalled the events of their sojourn, how instead of producing animals the earth brought forth gnats, and instead of fish the river spewed out vast numbers of frogs.

[11] Afterward they saw also a new kind of birds, when desire led them to ask for luxurious food;

[12] for, to give them relief, quails came up from the sea.

[13] The punishments did not come upon the sinners without prior signs in the violence of thunder, for they justly suffered because of their wicked acts; for they practiced a more bitter hatred of strangers.

[14] Others had refused to receive strangers when they came to them, but these made slaves of guests who were their benefactors.

[15] And not only so, but punishment of some sort will come upon the former for their hostile reception of the aliens;

[16] but the latter, after receiving them with festal celebrations, afflicted with terrible sufferings those who had already shared the same rights.

[17] They were stricken also with loss of sight -- just as were those at the door of the righteous man --when, surrounded by yawning darkness, each tried to find the way through his own door.

[18] For the elements changed places with one another, as on a harp the notes vary the nature of the rhythm, while each note remains the same. This may be clearly inferred from the sight of what took place.

[19] For land animals were transformed into water creatures, and creatures that swim moved over to the land.

[20] Fire even in water retained its normal power, and water forgot its fire-quenching nature.

[21] Flames, on the contrary, failed to consume the flesh of perishable creatures that walked among them, nor did they melt

the crystalline, easily melted kind of heavenly food.

[22] For in everything, O Lord, thou hast exalted and glorified thy people; and thou hast not neglected to help them at all times and in all places.

Additions to the Book of Esther

AddEsth.11

[1] In the fourth year of Ptolomeus and Cleopatra, Dositheus and Leuite, who claimed to be a priest brought the Epistle of Phurim that was in Jerusalem and had it interpreted.

[2] In the second year of the reign of Artaxerxes the Great, on the first day of Nisan, Mordecai the son of Jair, son of Shimei, son of Kish, of the tribe of Benjamin, had a dream.

[3] He was a Jew, dwelling in the city of Susa, a great man, serving in the court of the king.

[4] He was one of the captives whom Nebuchadnezzar king of Babylon had brought from Jerusalem with Jeconiah king of Judea. And this was his dream:

[5] Behold, noise and confusion, thunders and earthquake, tumult upon the earth!

[6] And behold, two great dragons came forward, both ready to fight, and they roared terribly.

[7] And at their roaring every nation prepared for war, to fight against the nation of the righteous.

[8] And behold, a day of darkness and gloom, tribulation and distress, affliction and great tumult upon the earth!

[9] And the whole righteous nation was troubled; they feared the evils that threatened them, and were ready to perish.

[10] Then they cried to God; and from their cry, as though from a tiny spring, there came a great river, with abundant water;

[11] light came, and the sun rose, and the lowly were exalted and consumed those held in honor.

[12] Mordecai saw in this dream what God had determined to do, and after he awoke he had it on his mind and sought all day to understand it in every detail.

AddEsth.12

[1] Now Mordecai took his rest in the courtyard with Gabatha and Tharra, the two eunuchs of the king who kept watch in the courtyard.

[2] He overheard their conversation and inquired into their purposes, and learned that they were preparing to lay hands upon Artaxerxes the king; and he informed the king concerning them.

[3] Then the king examined the two eunuchs, and when they confessed they were led to execution.

[4] The king made a permanent record of these things, and Mordecai wrote an account of them.

[5] And the king ordered Mordecai to serve in the court and rewarded him for these things.

[6] But Haman, the son of Hammedatha, a Bougaean, was in great honor with the king, and he sought to injure Mordecai and his people because of the two eunuchs of the king.

AddEsth.13

[1] This is a copy of the letter: "The Great King, Artaxerxes, to the rulers of the hundred and twenty-seven provinces from India to Ethiopia and to the governors under them, writes thus:

[2] "Having become ruler of many nations and master of the whole world, not elated with presumption of authority but always acting reasonably and with kindness, I have determined to settle the lives of my subjects in lasting tranquillity and, in order to make my kingdom peaceable and open to travel throughout all its extent, to re-establish the peace which all men desire.

[3] "When I asked my counselors how this might be accomplished, Haman, who excels among us in sound judgment, and is distinguished for his unchanging good will and steadfast fidelity, and has attained the second place in the kingdom,

[4] pointed out to us that among all the nations in the world there is scattered a certain hostile people, who have laws contrary to those of every nation and continually disregard the ordinances of the kings, so that the unifying of the kingdom which we honorably intend cannot be brought about.

[5] We understand that this people, and it alone, stands constantly in opposition to all men, perversely following a strange manner of life and laws, and is ill-disposed to our government, doing all the harm they can so that our kingdom may not attain stability.

[6] "Therefore we have decreed that those indicated to you in the letters of Haman, who is in charge of affairs and is our second father, shall all, with their wives and children, be utterly destroyed by the sword of their enemies, without pity or mercy, on the fourteenth day of the twelfth month, Adar, of this present year,

[7] so that those who have long been and are now hostile may in one day go down in violence to Hades, and leave our government completely secure and untroubled hereafter."

[8] Then Mordecai prayed to the Lord, calling to remembrance all the works of the Lord. He said:

[9] "O Lord, Lord, King who rulest over all things, for the universe is in thy power and there is no one who can oppose thee if it is thy will to save Israel.

[10] For thou hast made heaven and earth and every wonderful thing under heaven,

[11] and thou art Lord of all, and there is no one who can resist thee, who art the Lord.

[12] Thou knowest all things; thou knowest, O Lord, that it was not in insolence or pride or for any love of glory that I did this, and refused to bow down to this proud Haman.

[13] For I would have been willing to kiss the soles of his feet, to save Israel!

[14] But I did this, that I might not set the glory of man above the glory of God, and I will not bow down to any one but to thee, who art my Lord; and I will not do these things in pride.

[15] And now, O Lord God and King, God of Abraham, spare thy people; for the eyes of our foes are upon us to annihilate us, and they desire to destroy the inheritance that has been your from the beginning.

[16] Do not neglect thy portion, which thou didst redeem for thyself out of the land of Egypt.

[17] Hear my prayer, and have mercy upon thy inheritance turn our mourning into feasting, that we may live and sing praise to thy name, O Lord; do not destroy the mouth of those who praise thee."

[18] And all Israel cried out mightily, for their death was before their eyes.

AddEsth.14

[1] And Esther the queen, seized with deathly anxiety, fled to the Lord;

[2] she took off her splendid apparel and put on the garments of distress and mourning, and instead of costly perfumes she covered her head with ashes and dung, and she utterly humbled her body, and every part that she loved to adorn she covered with her tangled hair.

[3] And she prayed to the Lord God of Israel, and said: Lord, thou only art our King; help me, who am alone and have no helper but thee,

[4] for my danger is in my hand.

[5] Ever since I was born I have heard in the tribe of my family that thou, O Lord, didst take Israel out of all the nations, and our fathers from among all their ancestors, for an everlasting inheritance, and that thou didst do for them all that thou didst promise.

[6] And now we have sinned before thee, and thou hast given us into the hands of our enemies,

[7] because we glorified their gods. Thou art righteous, O Lord!

[8] And now they are not satisfied that we are in bitter slavery, but they have covenanted with their idols

[9] to abolish what thy mouth has ordained and to destroy thy inheritance, to stop the mouths of those who praise thee and to quench thy altar and the glory of thy house,

[10] to open the mouths of the nations for the praise of vain idols, and to magnify for ever a mortal king.

[11] O Lord, do not surrender thy scepter to what has no being; and do not let them mock at our downfall; but turn their plan against themselves, and make an example of the man who began this against us.

[12] Remember, O Lord; make thyself known in this time of our affliction, and give me courage, O King of the gods and Master of all dominion!

[13] Put eloquent speech in my mouth before the lion, and turn his heart to hate the man who is fighting against us, so that there may be an end of him and those who agree with him.

[14] But save us by thy hand, and help me, who am alone and have no helper but thee, O Lord.

[15] Thou hast knowledge of all things; and thou knowest that I hate the splendor of the wicked and abhor the bed of the uncircumcised and of any alien.

[16] Thou knowest my necessity -- that I abhor the sign of my proud position, which is upon my head on the days when I appear in public. I abhor it like a menstruous rag, and I do not wear it on the days when I am at leisure.

[17] And thy servant has not eaten at Haman's table, and I have not honored the king's feast or drunk the wine of the libations.

[18] Your servant has had no joy since the day that I was brought here until now, except in thee, O Lord God of Abraham.

[19] O God, whose might is over all, hear the voice of the despairing, and save us from the hands of evildoers. And save me from my fear!"

AddEsth.15

[1] On the third day, when she ended her prayer, she took off the garments in which she had worshiped, and arrayed herself in splendid attire.

[2] Then, majestically adorned, after invoking the aid of the all-seeing God and Savior, she took her two maids with her,

[3] leaning daintily on one,

[4] while the other followed carrying her train.

[5] She was radiant with perfect beauty, and she looked happy, as if beloved, but her heart was frozen with fear.

[6] When she had gone through all the doors, she stood before the king. He was seated on his royal throne, clothed in the full array of his majesty, all covered with gold and precious stones. And he was most terrifying.

[7] Lifting his face, flushed with splendor, he looked at her in fierce anger. And the queen faltered, and turned pale and faint, and collapsed upon the head of the maid who went before her.

[8] Then God changed the spirit of the king to gentleness, and in alarm he sprang from his throne and took her in his arms until she came to herself. And he comforted her with soothing words, and said to her,

[9] "What is it, Esther? I am your brother. Take courage;

[10] you shall not die, for our law applies only to the people. Come near."

[11] Then he raised the golden scepter and touched it to her neck;

[12] and he embraced her, and said, "Speak to me."

[13] And she said to him, "I saw you, my lord, like an angel of God and my heart was shaken with fear at your glory.

[14] For you are wonderful, my lord, and your countenance is full of grace."

[15] But as she was speaking, she fell fainting.

[16] And the king was agitated, and all his servants sought to comfort her.

AddEsth.16

[1] The following is a copy of this letter: "The Great King, Artaxerxes, to the rulers of the provinces from India to Ethiopia, one hundred and twenty-seven satrapies, and to those who are loyal to our government, greeting.

[2] "The more often they are honored by the too great kindness of their benefactors, the more proud do many men become.

[3] They not only seek to injure our subjects, but in their inability to stand prosperity they even undertake to scheme against their own benefactors.

[4] They not only take away thankfulness from among men, but, carried away by the boasts of those who know nothing of goodness, they suppose that they will escape the evil-hating justice of God, who always sees everything.

[5] And often many of those who are set in places of authority have been made in part responsible for the shedding of innocent blood, and have been involved in irremediable calamities, by the persuasion of friends who have been entrusted with the administration of public affairs,

[6] when these men by the false trickery of their evil natures beguile the sincere good will of their sovereigns.

[7] "What has been wickedly accomplished through the pestilent behavior of those who exercise authority unworthily, can be seen not so much from the more ancient records which we hand on as from investigation of matters close at hand.

[8] For the future we will take care to render our kingdom quiet and peaceable for all men,

[9] by changing our methods and always judging what comes before our eyes with more equitable consideration.

[10] For Haman, the son of Hammedatha, a Macedonian (really an alien to the Persian blood, and quite devoid of our kindliness), having become our guest,

[11] so far enjoyed the good will that we have for every nation that he was called our father and was continually bowed down to by all as the person second to the royal throne.

[12] But, unable to restrain his arrogance, he undertook to deprive us of our kingdom and our life,

[13] and with intricate craft and deceit asked for the destruction of Mordecai, our savior and perpetual benefactor, and of Esther, the blameless partner of our kingdom, together with their whole nation.

[14] He thought that in this way he would find us undefended and would transfer the kingdom of the Persians to the Macedonians.

[15] "But we find that the Jews, who were consigned to annihilation by this thrice accursed man, are not evildoers but are governed by most righteous laws

[16] and are sons of the Most High, the most mighty living God, who has directed the kingdom both for us and for our fathers in the most excellent order.

[17] "You will therefore do well not to put in execution the letters sent by Haman the son of Hammedatha,

[18] because the man himself who did these things has been hanged at the gate of Susa, with all his household. For God, who rules over all things, has speedily inflicted on him the punishment he deserved.

[19] "Therefore post a copy of this letter publicly in every place, and permit the Jews to live under their own laws.

[20] And give them reinforcements, so that on the thirteenth day of the twelfth month, Adar, on that very day they may defend themselves against those who attack them at the time of their affliction.

[21] For God, who rules over all things, has made this day to be a joy to his chosen people instead of a day of destruction for them.

[22] "Therefore you shall observe this with all good cheer as a notable day among your commemorative festivals,

[23] so that both now and hereafter it may mean salvation for us and the loyal Persians, but that for those who plot against us it may be a reminder of destruction.

[24] "Every city and country, without exception, which does not act accordingly, shall be destroyed in wrath with spear and fire. It shall be made not only impassable for men, but also most hateful for all time to beasts and birds."

AddEsth.10

[1] And Mordecai said, "These things have come from God.

[2] For I remember the dream that I had concerning these matters, and none of them has failed to be fulfilled.

[3] The tiny spring which became a river, and there was light and the sun and abundant water -- the river is Esther, whom the king married and made queen.

[4] The two dragons are Haman and myself.

[5] The nations are those that gathered to destroy the name of the Jews.

[6] And my nation, this is Israel, who cried out to God and were saved. The Lord has saved his people; the Lord has delivered us from all these evils; God has done great signs and wonders, which have not occurred among the nations.

[7] For this purpose he made two lots, one for the people of God and one for all the nations.

[8] And these two lots came to the hour and moment and day of decision before God and among all the nations.

[9] And God remembered his people and vindicated his inheritance.

[10] So they will observe these days in the month of Adar, on the fourteenth and fifteenth of that month, with an assembly and joy and gladness before God, from generation to generation for ever among his people Israel."

AddEsth.11

[1] In the fourth year of the reign of Ptolemy and Cleopatra, Dositheus, who said that he was a priest and a Levite, and Ptolemy his son brought to Egypt the preceeding Letter of Purim, which they said was genuine and had been translated by Lysimachus the son of Ptolemy, one of the residents of Jerusalem.

Tobit

Tob.1

[1] The book of the acts of Tobit the son of Tobiel, son of Ananiel, son of Aduel, son of Gabael, of the descendants of Asiel and the tribe of Naphtali,

[2] who in the days of Shalmaneser, king of the Assyrians, was taken into captivity from Thisbe, which is to the south of Kedesh Naphtali in Galilee above Asher.

[3] I, Tobit, walked in the ways of truth and righteousness all the days of my life, and I performed many acts of charity to my brethren and countrymen who went with me into the land of the Assyrians, to Nineveh.

[4] Now when I was in my own country, in the land of Israel, while I was still a young man, the whole tribe of Naphtali my forefather deserted the house of Jerusalem. This was the place which had been chosen from among all the tribes of Israel, where all the tribes should sacrifice and where the temple of the dwelling of the Most High was consecrated and established for all generations for ever.

[5] All the tribes that joined in apostasy used to sacrifice to the calf Baal, and so did the house of Naphtali my forefather.

[6] But I alone went often to Jerusalem for the feasts, as it is ordained for all Israel by an everlasting decree. Taking the first fruits and the tithes of my produce and the first shearings, I would give these to the priests, the sons of Aaron, at the altar.

[7] Of all my produce I would give a tenth to the sons of Levi who ministered at Jerusalem; a second tenth I would sell, and I would go and spend the proceeds each year at Jerusalem;

[8] the third tenth I would give to those to whom it was my duty, as Deborah my father's mother had commanded me, for I was left an orphan by my father.

[9] When I became a man I married Anna, a member of our family, and by her I became the father of Tobias.

[10] Now when I was carried away captive to Nineveh, all my brethren and my relatives ate the food of the Gentiles;

[11] but I kept myself from eating it,

[12] because I remembered God with all my heart.

[13] Then the Most High gave me favor and good appearance in the sight of Shalmaneser, and I was his buyer of provisions.

[14] So I used to go into Media, and once at Rages in Media I left ten talents of silver in trust with Gabael, the brother of Gabrias.

[15] But when Shalmaneser died, Sennacherib his son reigned in his place; and under him the highways were unsafe, so that I could no longer go into Media.

[16] In the days of Shalmaneser I performed many acts of charity to my brethren.

[17] I would give my bread to the hungry and my clothing to the naked; and if I saw any one of my people dead and thrown out behind the wall of Nineveh, I would bury him.

[18] And if Sennacherib the king put to death any who came fleeing from Judea, I buried them secretly. For in his anger he put many to death. When the bodies were sought by the king, they were not found.

[19] Then one of the men of Nineveh went and informed the king about me, that I was burying them; so I hid myself. When I learned that I was being searched for, to be put to death, I left home in fear.

[20] Then all my property was confiscated and nothing was left to me except my wife Anna and my son Tobias.

[21] But not fifty days passed before two of Sennacherib's sons killed him, and they fled to the mountains of Ararat. Then Esarhaddon, his son, reigned in his place; and he appointed Ahikar, the son of my brother Anael, over all the accounts of his kingdom and over the entire administration.

[22] Ahikar interceded for me, and I returned to Nineveh. Now Ahikar was cupbearer, keeper of the signet, and in charge of administration of the accounts, for Esarhaddon had appointed him second to himself. He was my nephew.

Tob.2

[1] When I arrived home and my wife Anna and my son Tobias were restored to me, at the feast of Pentecost, which is the sacred festival of the seven weeks, a good dinner was prepared for me and I sat down to eat.

[2] Upon seeing the abundance of food I said to my son, "Go and bring whatever poor man of our brethren you may find who is mindful of the Lord, and I will wait for you."

[3] But he came back and said, "Father, one of our people has been strangled and thrown into the market place."

[4] So before I tasted anything I sprang up and removed the body to a place of shelter until sunset.

[5] And when I returned I washed myself and ate my food in sorrow.

[6] Then I remembered the prophecy of Amos, how he said, "Your feasts shall be turned into mourning, and all your festivities into lamentation." And I wept.

[7] When the sun had set I went and dug a grave and buried the body.

[8] And my neighbors laughed at me and said, "He is no longer afraid that he will be put to death for doing this; he once ran away, and here he is burying the dead again!"

[9] On the same night I returned from burying him, and because I was defiled I slept by the wall of the courtyard, and my

face was uncovered.

[10] I did not know that there were sparrows on the wall and their fresh droppings fell into my open eyes and white films formed on my eyes. I went to physicians, but they did not help me. Ahikar, however, took care of me until he went to Elymais.

[11] Then my wife Anna earned money at women's work.

[12] She used to send the product to the owners. Once when they paid her wages, they also gave her a kid;

[13] and when she returned to me it began to bleat. So I said to her, "Where did you get the kid? It is not stolen, is it? Return it to the owners; for it is not right to eat what is stolen."

[14] And she said, "It was given to me as a gift in addition to my wages." But I did not believe her, and told her to return it to the owners; and I blushed for her. Then she replied to me, "Where are your charities and your righteous deeds? You seem to know everything!"

Tob.3

[1] Then in my grief I wept, and I prayed in anguish, saying,

[2] "Righteous art thou, O Lord; all thy deeds and all they ways are mercy and truth, and thou do render true and righteous judgment for ever.

[3] Remember me and look favorably upon me; do not punish me for my sins and for my unwitting offences and those which my fathers committed before thee.

[4] For they disobeyed thy commandments, and thou gavest us over to plunder, captivity, and death; thou madest us a byword of reproach in all the nations among which we have been dispersed.

[5] And now thy many judgments are true in exacting penalty from me for my sins and those of my fathers, because we did not keep thy commandments. For we did not walk in truth before thee.

[6] And now deal with me according to thy pleasure; command my spirit to be taken up, that I may depart and become dust. For it is better for me to die than to live, because I have heard false reproaches, and great is the sorrow within me. Command that I now be released from my distress to go to the eternal abode; do not turn thy face away from me."

[7] On the same day, at Ecbatana in Media, it also happened that Sarah, the daughter of Raguel, was reproached by her father's maids,

[8] because she had been given to seven husbands, and the evil demon Asmodeus had slain each of them before he had been with her as his wife. So the maids said to her, "Do you not know that you strangle your husbands? You already have had seven and have had no benefit from any of them.

[9] Why do you beat us? If they are dead, go with them! May we never see a son or daughter of yours!"

[10] When she heard these things she was deeply grieved, even to the thought of hanging herself. But she said, "I am the only child of my father; if I do this, it will be a disgrace to him, and I shall bring his old age down in sorrow to the grave.

[11] So she prayed by her window and said, "Blessed art thou, O Lord my God, and blessed is thy holy and honored name for ever. May all thy works praise thee for ever.

[12] And now, O Lord, I have turned my eyes and my face toward thee.

[13] Command that I be released from the earth and that I hear reproach no more.

[14] Thou knowest, O Lord, that I am innocent of any sin with man,

[15] and that I did not stain my name or the name of my father in the land of my captivity. I am my father's only child, and he has no child to be his heir, no near kinsman or kinsman's son for whom I should keep myself as wife. Already seven husbands of mine are dead. Why should I live? But if it be not pleasing to thee to take my life, command that respect be shown to me and pity be taken upon me, and that I hear reproach no more."

[16] The prayer of both was heard in the presence of the glory of the great God.

[17] And Raphael was sent to heal the two of them: to scale away the white films of Tobit's eyes; to give Sarah the daughter of Raguel in marriage to Tobias the son of Tobit, and to bind Asmodeus the evil demon, because Tobias was entitled to possess her. At that very moment Tobit returned and entered his house and Sarah the daughter of Raguel came down from her upper room.

Tob.4

[1] On that day Tobit remembered the money which he had left in trust with Gabael at Rages in Media, and he said to himself;

[2] "I have asked for death. Why do I not call my son Tobias so that I may explain to him about the money before I die?"

[3] So he called him and said, "My son, when I die, bury me, and do not neglect your mother. Honor her all the days of your life; do what is pleasing to her, and do not grieve her.

[4] Remember, my son, that she faced many dangers for you while you were yet unborn. When she dies bury her beside me in the same grave.

[5] "Remember the Lord our God all your days, my son, and refuse to sin or to transgress his commandments. Live uprightly

all the days of your life, and do not walk in the ways of wrongdoing.

[6] For if you do what is true, your ways will prosper through your deeds.

[7] Give alms from your possessions to all who live uprightly, and do not let your eye begrudge the gift when you make it. Do not turn your face away from any poor man, and the face of God will not be turned away from you.

[8] If you have many possessions, make your gift from them in proportion; if few, do not be afraid to give according to the little you have.

[9] So you will be laying up a good treasure for yourself against the day of necessity.

[10] For charity delivers from death and keeps you from entering the darkness;

[11] and for all who practice it charity is an excellent offering in the presence of the Most High.

[12] "Beware, my son, of all immorality. First of all take a wife from among the descendants of your fathers and do not marry a foreign woman, who is not of your father's tribe; for we are the sons of the prophets. Remember, my son, that Noah, Abraham, Isaac, and Jacob, our fathers of old, all took wives from among their brethren. They were blessed in their children, and their posterity will inherit the land.

[13] So now, my son, love your brethren, and in your heart do not disdain your brethren and the sons and daughters of your people by refusing to take a wife for yourself from among them. For in pride there is ruin and great confusion; and in shiftlessness there is loss and great want, because shiftlessness is the mother of famine.

[14] Do not hold over till the next day the wages of any man who works for you, but pay him at once; and if you serve God you will receive payment. "Watch yourself, my son, in everything you do, and be disciplined in all your conduct.

[15] And what you hate, do not do to any one. Do not drink wine to excess or let drunkenness go with you on your way.

[16] Give of your bread to the hungry, and of your clothing to the naked. Give all your surplus to charity, and do not let your eye begrudge the gift when you made it.

[17] Place your bread on the grave of the righteous, but give none to sinners.

[18] Seek advice from every wise man, and do not despise any useful counsel.

[19] Bless the Lord God on every occasion; ask him that your ways may be made straight and that all your paths and plans may prosper. For none of the nations has understanding; but the Lord himself gives all good things, and according to his will he humbles whomever he wishes. "So, my son, remember my commands, and do not let them be blotted out of your mind.

[20] And now let me explain to you about the ten talents of silver which I left in trust with Gabael the son of Gabrias at Rages in Media.

[21] Do not be afraid, my son, because we have become poor. You have great wealth if you fear God and refrain from every sin and do what is pleasing in his sight."

Tob.5

[1] Then Tobias answered him, "Father, I will do everything that you have commanded me;

[2] but how can I obtain the money when I do not know the man?"

[3] Then Tobit gave him the receipt, and said to him, "Find a man to go with you and I will pay him wages as long as I live; and go and get the money."

[4] So he went to look for a man; and he found Raphael, who was an angel,

[5] but Tobias did not know it. Tobias said to him, "Can you go with me to Rages in Media? Are you acquainted with that region?"

[6] The angel replied, "I will go with you; I am familiar with the way, and I have stayed with our brother Gabael."

[7] Then Tobias said to him, "Wait for me, and I shall tell my father."

[8] And he said to him, "Go, and do not delay." So he went in and said to his father, "I have found some one to go with me." He said, "Call him to me, so that I may learn to what tribe he belongs, and whether he is a reliable man to go with you."

[9] So Tobias invited him in; he entered and they greeted each other.

[10] Then Tobit said to him, "My brother, to what tribe and family do you belong? Tell me. "

[11] But he answered, "Are you looking for a tribe and a family or for a man whom you will pay to go with your son?" And Tobit said to him, "I should like to know, my brother, your people and your name."

[12] He replied, "I am Azarias the son of the great Ananias, one of your relatives."

[13] Then Tobit said to him, "You are welcome, my brother. Do not be angry with me because I tried to learn your tribe and family. You are a relative of mine, of a good and noble lineage. For I used to know Ananias and Jathan, the sons of the great Shemaiah, when we went together to Jerusalem to worship and offered the first-born of our flocks and the tithes of our produce. They did not go astray in the error of our brethren. My brother, you come of good stock.

[14] But tell me, what wages am I to pay you -- a drachma a day, and expenses for yourself as for my son?

[15] And besides, I will add to your wages if you both return safe and sound." So they agreed to these terms.

[16] Then he said to Tobias, "Get ready for the journey, and good success to you both." So his son made the preparations for the journey. And his father said to him, "Go with this man; God who dwells in heaven will prosper your way, and may his angel attend you." So they both went out and departed, and the young man's dog was with them.

[17] But Anna, his mother, began to weep, and said to Tobit, "Why have you sent our child away? Is he not the staff of our

hands as he goes in and out before us?

[18] Do not add money to money, but consider it as rubbish as compared to our child.

[19] For the life that is given to us by the Lord is enough for us."

[20] And Tobit said to her, "Do not worry, my sister; he will return safe and sound, and your eyes will see him.

[21] For a good angel will go with him; his journey will be successful, and he will come back safe and sound." Tob 5:[22] So she stopped weeping.

Tob.6

[1] Now as they proceeded on their way they came at evening to the Tigris river and camped there.

[2] Then the young man went down to wash himself. A fish leaped up from the river and would have swallowed the young man;

[3] and the angel said to him, "Catch the fish." So the young man seized the fish and threw it up on the land.

[4] Then the angel said to him, "Cut open the fish and take the heart and liver and gall and put them away safely."

[5] So the young man did as the angel told him; and they roasted and ate the fish. And they both continued on their way until they came near to Ecbatana.

[6] Then the young man said to the angel, "Brother Azarias, of what use is the liver and heart and gall of the fish?"

[7] He replied, "As for the heart and liver, if a demon or evil spirit gives trouble to any one, you make a smoke from these before the man or woman, and that person will never be troubled again.

[8] And as for the gall, anoint with it a man who has white films in his eyes, and he will be cured."

[9] When they approached Ecbatana,

[10] the angel said to the young man, "Brother, today we shall stay with Raguel. He is your relative, and he has an only daughter named Sarah. I will suggest that she be given to you in marriage,

[11] because you are entitled to her and to her inheritance, for you are her only eligible kinsman.

[12] The girl is also beautiful and sensible. Now listen to my plan. I will speak to her father, and as soon as we return from Rages we will celebrate the marriage. For I know that Raguel, according to the law of Moses, cannot give her to another man without incurring the penalty of death, because you rather than any other man are entitled to the inheritance."

[13] Then the young man said to the angel, "Brother Azarias, I have heard that the girl has been given to seven husbands and that each died in the bridal chamber.

[14] Now I am the only son my father has, and I am afraid that if I go in I will die as those before me did, for a demon is in love with her, and he harms no one except those who approach her. So now I fear that I may die and bring the lives of my father and mother to the grave in sorrow on my account. And they have no other son to bury them."

[15] But the angel said to him, "Do you not remember the words with which your father commanded you to take a wife from among your own people? Now listen to me, brother, for she will become your wife; and do not worry about the demon, for this very night she will be given to you in marriage.

[16] When you enter the bridal chamber, you shall take live ashes of incense and lay upon them some of the heart and liver of the fish so as to make a smoke.

[17] Then the demon will smell it and flee away, and will never again return. And when you approach her, rise up, both of you, and cry out to the merciful God, and he will save you and have mercy on you. Do not be afraid, for she was destined for you from eternity. You will save her, and she will go with you, and I suppose that you will have children by her." When Tobias heard these things, he fell in love with her and yearned deeply for her.

Tob.7

[1] When they reached Ecbatana and arrived at the house of Raguel, Sarah met them and greeted them. They returned her greeting, and she brought them into the house.

[2] Then Raguel said to his wife Edna, "How much the young man resembles my cousin Tobit!"

[3] And Raguel asked them, "Where are you from, brethren?" They answered him, "We belong to the sons of Naphtali, who are captives in Nineveh."

[4] So he said to them, "Do you know our brother Tobit?" And they said, "Yes, we do." And he asked them, "Is he in good health?"

[5] They replied, "He is alive and in good health." And Tobias said, "He is my father."

[6] Then Raguel sprang up and kissed him and wept.

[7] And he blessed him and exclaimed, "Son of that good and noble man!" When he heard that Tobit had lost his sight, he was stricken with grief and wept.

[8] And his wife Edna and his daughter Sarah wept. They received them very warmly; and they killed a ram from the flock and set large servings of food before them. Then Tobias said to Raphael, "Brother Azarias, speak of those things which you talked about on the journey, and let the matter be settled."

[9] So he communicated the proposal to Raguel. And Raguel said to Tobias, "Eat, drink, and be merry;

[10] for it is your right to take my child. But let me explain the true situation to you.

[11] I have given my daughter to seven husbands, and when each came to her he died in the night. But for the present be merry." And Tobias said, "I will eat nothing here until you make a binding agreement with me."

[12] So Raguel said, "Take her right now, in accordance with the law. You are her relative, and she is yours. The merciful God will guide you both for the best."

[13] Then he called his daughter Sarah, and taking her by the hand he gave her to Tobias to be his wife, saying, "Here she is; take her according to the law of Moses, and take her with you to your father." And he blessed them.

[14] Next he called his wife Edna, and took a scroll and wrote out the contract; and they set their seals to it.

[15] Then they began to eat.

[16] And Raguel called his wife Edna and said to her, "Sister, make up the other room, and take her into it."

[17] so she did as he said, and took her there; and the girl began to weep. But the mother comforted her daughter in her tears, and said to her,

[18] "Be brave, my child; the Lord of heaven and earth grant you joy in place of this sorrow of yours. Be brave, my daughter."

Tob.8

[1] When they had finished eating, they escorted Tobias in to her.

[2] As he went he remembered the words of Raphael, and he took the live ashes of incense and put the heart and liver of the fish upon them and made a smoke.

[3] And when the demon smelled the odor he fled to the remotest parts of Egypt, and the angel bound him.

[4] When the door was shut and the two were alone, Tobias got up from the bed and said, "Sister, get up, and let us pray that the Lord may have mercy upon us."

[5] And Tobias began to pray, "Blessed art thou, O God of our fathers, and blessed be thy holy and glorious name for ever. Let the heavens and all thy creatures bless thee.

[6] Thou madest Adam and gavest him Eve his wife as a helper and support. From them the race of mankind has sprung. Thou didst say, `It is not good that the man should be alone; let us make a helper for him like himself.'

[7] And now, O Lord, I am not taking this sister of mine because of lust, but with sincerity. Grant that I may find mercy and may grow old together with her."

[8] And she said with him, "Amen."

[9] Then they both went to sleep for the night. But Raguel arose and went and dug a grave,

[10] with the thought, "Perhaps he too will die."

[11] Then Raguel went into his house

[12] and said to his wife Edna, "Send one of the maids to see whether he is alive; and if he is not, let us bury him without any one knowing about it."

[13] So the maid opened the door and went in, and found them both asleep.

[14] And she came out and told them that he was alive.

[15] Then Raguel blessed God and said, "Blessed art thou, O God, with every pure and holy blessing. Let thy saints and all thy creatures bless thee; let all thy angels and thy chosen people bless thee for ever.

[16] Blessed art thou, because thou hast made me glad. It has not happened to me as I expected; but thou hast treated us according to thy great mercy.

[17] Blessed art thou, because thou hast had compassion on two only children. Show them mercy, O Lord; and bring their lives to fulfilment in health and happiness and mercy."

[18] Then he ordered his servants to fill in the grave.

[19] After this he gave a wedding feast for them which lasted fourteen days.

[20] And before the days of the feast were over, Raguel declared by oath to Tobias that he should not leave until the fourteen days of the wedding feast were ended,

[21] that then he should take half of Raguel's property and return in safety to his father, and that the rest would be his "when my wife and I die."

Tob.9

[1] Then Tobias called Raphael and said to him,

[2] "Brother Azarias, take a servant and two camels with you and go to Gabael at Rages in Media and get the money for me; and bring him to the wedding feast.

[3] For Raguel has sworn that I should not leave;

[4] but my father is counting the days, and if I delay long he will be greatly distressed."

[5] So Raphael made the journey and stayed over night with Gabael. He gave him the receipt, and Gabael brought out the money bags with their seals intact and gave them to him.

[6] In the morning they both got up early and came to the wedding feast. And Gabael blessed Tobias and his wife.

Tob.10

[1] Now his father Tobit was counting each day, and when the days for the journey had expired and they did not arrive,

[2] he said, "Is it possible that he has been detained? Or is it possible that Gabael has died and there is no one to give him the money?"

[3] And he was greatly distressed.

[4] And his wife said to him, "The lad has perished; his long delay proves it." Then she began to mourn for him, and said,

[5] "Am I not distressed, my child, that I let you go, you who are the light of my eyes?"

[6] But Tobit said to her, "Be still and stop worrying; he is well."

[7] And she answered him, "Be still and stop deceiving me; my child has perished." And she went out every day to the road by which they had left; she ate nothing in the daytime, and throughout the nights she never stopped mourning for her son Tobias, until the fourteen days of the wedding feast had expired which Raguel had sworn that he should spend there. At that time Tobias said to Raguel, "Send me back, for my father and mother have given up hope of ever seeing me again."

[8] But his father-in-law said to him, "Stay with me, and I will send messengers to your father, and they will inform him how things are with you."

[9] Tobias replied, "No, send me back to my father."

[10] So Raguel arose and gave him his wife Sarah and half of his property in slaves, cattle, and money.

[11] And when he had blessed them he sent them away, saying, "The God of heaven will prosper you, my children, before I die."

[12] He said also to his daughter, "Honor your father-in-law and your mother-in-law; they are now your parents. Let me hear a good report of you. " And he kissed her. And Edna said to Tobias, "The Lord of heaven bring you back safely, dear brother, and grant me to see your children by my daughter Sarah, that I may rejoice before the Lord. See, I am entrusting my daughter to you; do nothing to grieve her."

Tob.11

[1] After this Tobias went on his way, praising God because he had made his journey a success. And he blessed Raguel and his wife Edna. So he continued on his way until they came near to Nineveh.

[2] Then Raphael said to Tobias, "Are you not aware, brother, of how you left your father?

[3] Let us run ahead of your wife and prepare the house.

[4] And take the gall of the fish with you." So they went their way, and the dog went along behind them.

[5] Now Anna sat looking intently down the road for her son.

[6] And she caught sight of him coming, and said to his father, "Behold, your son is coming, and so is the man who went with him!"

[7] Raphael said, "I know, Tobias, that your father will open his eyes.

[8] You therefore must anoint his eyes with the gall; and when they smart he will rub them, and will cause the white films to fall away, and he will see you."

[9] Then Anna ran to meet them, and embraced her son, and said to him, "I have seen you, my child; now I am ready to die." And they both wept.

[10] Tobit started toward the door, and stumbled. But his son ran to him

[11] and took hold of his father, and he sprinkled the gall upon his father's eyes, saying, "Be of good cheer, father."

[12] And when his eyes began to smart he rubbed them,

[13] and the white films scaled off from the corners of his eyes.

[14] Then he saw his son and embraced him, and he wept and said, "Blessed art thou, O God, and blessed is thy name for ever, and blessed are all thy holy angels.

[15] For thou hast afflicted me, but thou hast had mercy upon me; here I see my son Tobias!" And his son went in rejoicing, and he reported to his father the great things that had happened to him in Media.

[16] Then Tobit went out to meet his daughter-in-law at the gate of Nineveh, rejoicing and praising God. Those who saw him as he went were amazed because he could see.

[17] And Tobit gave thanks before them that God had been merciful to him. When Tobit came near to Sarah his daughter-in-law, he blessed her, saying, "Welcome, daughter! Blessed is God who has brought you to us, and blessed are your father and your mother." So there was rejoicing among all his brethren in Nineveh.

[18] Ahikar and his nephew Nadab came,

[19] and Tobias' marriage was celebrated for seven days with great festivity.

Tob.12

[1] Tobit then called his son Tobias and said to him, "My son, see to the wages of the man who went with you; and he must

also be given more."

[2] He replied, "Father, it would do me no harm to give him half of what I have brought back.

[3] For he has led me back to you safely, he cured my wife, he obtained the money for me, and he also healed you."

[4] The old man said, "He deserves it."

[5] So he called the angel and said to him, "Take half of all that you two have brought back."

[6] Then the angel called the two of them privately and said to them: "Praise God and give thanks to him; exalt him and give thanks to him in the presence of all the living for what he has done for you. It is good to praise God and to exalt his name, worthily declaring the works of God. Do not be slow to give him thanks.

[7] It is good to guard the secret of a king, but gloriously to reveal the works of God. Do good, and evil will not overtake you.

[8] Prayer is good when accompanied by fasting, almsgiving, and righteousness. A little with righteousness is better than much with wrongdoing. It is better to give alms than to treasure up gold.

[9] For almsgiving delivers from death, and it will purge away every sin. Those who perform deeds of charity and of righteousness will have fulness of life;

[10] but those who commit sin are the enemies of their own lives.

[11] "I will not conceal anything from you. I have said, `It is good to guard the secret of a king, but gloriously to reveal the works of God.'

[12] And so, when you and your daughter-in-law Sarah prayed, I brought a reminder of your prayer before the Holy One; and when you buried the dead, I was likewise present with you.

[13] When you did not hesitate to rise and leave your dinner in order to go and lay out the dead, your good deed was not hidden from me, but I was with you.

[14] So now God sent me to heal you and your daughter-in-law Sarah.

[15] I am Raphael, one of the seven holy angels who present the prayers of the saints and enter into the presence of the glory of the Holy One."

[16] They were both alarmed; and they fell upon their faces, for they were afraid.

[17] But he said to them, "Do not be afraid; you will be safe. But praise God for ever.

[18] For I did not come as a favor on my part, but by the will of our God. Therefore praise him for ever.

[19] All these days I merely appeared to you and did not eat or drink, but you were seeing a vision.

[20] And now give thanks to God, for I am ascending to him who sent me. Write in a book everything that has happened."

[21] Then they stood up; but they saw him no more.

[22] So they confessed the great and wonderful works of God, and acknowledged that the angel of the Lord had appeared to them.

Tob.13

[1] Then Tobit wrote a prayer of rejoicing, and said:

"Blessed is God who lives for ever, and blessed is his kingdom. [2] For he afflicts, and he shows mercy; he leads down to Hades, and brings up again, and there is no one who can escape his hand. [3] Acknowledge him before the nations, O sons of Israel; for he has scattered us among them. [4] Make his greatness known there, and exalt him in the presence of all the living; because he is our Lord and God, he is our Father for ever. [5] He will afflict us for our iniquities; and again he will show mercy, and will gather us from all the nations among whom you have been scattered. [6] If you turn to him with all your heart and with all your soul, to do what is true before him, then he will turn to you and will not hide his face from you. But see what he will do with you; give thanks to him with your full voice. Praise the Lord of righteousness, and exalt the King of the ages. I give him thanks in the land of my captivity, and I show his power and majesty to a nation of sinners. Turn back, you sinners, and do right before him; who knows if he will accept you and have mercy on you? [7] I exalt my God; my soul exalts the King of heaven, and will rejoice in his majesty. [8] Let all men speak, and give him thanks in Jerusalem. [9] O Jerusalem, the holy city, he will afflict you for the deeds of your sons, but again he will show mercy to the sons of the righteous. [10] Give thanks worthily to the Lord, and praise the King of the ages, that his tent may be raised for you again with joy. May he cheer those within you who are captives, and love those within you who are distressed, to all generations for ever. [11] Many nations will come from afar to the name of the Lord God, bearing gifts in their hands, gifts for the King of heaven. Generations of generations will give you joyful praise. [12] Cursed are all who hate you; blessed for ever will be all who love you. [13] Rejoice and be glad for the sons of the righteous; for they will be gathered together, and will praise the Lord of the righteous. [14] How blessed are those who love you! They will rejoice in your peace. Blessed are those who grieved over all your afflictions; for they will rejoice for you upon seeing all your glory, and they will be made glad for ever. [15] Let my soul praise God the great King. [16] For Jerusalem will be built with sapphires and emeralds, her walls with precious stones, and her towers and battlements with pure gold. [17] The streets of Jerusalem will be paved with beryl and ruby and stones of Ophir; [18] all her lanes will cry `Hallelujah!' and will give praise, saying, `Blessed is God, who has exalted you for ever.'"

Tob.14

[1] Here Tobit ended his words of praise.

[2] He was fifty-eight years old when he lost his sight, and after eight years he regained it. He gave alms, and he continued to fear the Lord God and to praise him.

[3] When he had grown very old he called his son and grandsons, and said to him, "My son, take your sons; behold, I have grown old and am about to depart this life.

[4] Go to Media, my son, for I fully believe what Jonah the prophet said about Nineveh, that it will be overthrown. But in Media there will be peace for a time. Our brethren will be scattered over the earth from the good land, and Jerusalem will be desolate. The house of God in it will be burned down and will be in ruins for a time.

[5] But God will again have mercy on them, and bring them back into their land; and they will rebuild the house of God, though it will not be like the former one until the times of the age are completed. After this they will return from the places of their captivity, and will rebuild Jerusalem in splendor. And the house of God will be rebuilt there with a glorious building for all generations for ever, just as the prophets said of it.

[6] Then all the Gentiles will turn to fear the Lord God in truth, and will bury their idols.

[7] All the Gentiles will praise the Lord, and his people will give thanks to God, and the Lord will exalt his people. And all who love the Lord God in truth and righteousness will rejoice, showing mercy to our brethren.

[8] "So now, my son, leave Nineveh, because what the prophet Jonah said will surely happen.

[9] But keep the law and the commandments, and be merciful and just, so that it may be well with you.

[10] Bury me properly, and your mother with me. And do not live in Nineveh any longer. See, my son, what Nadab did to Ahikar who had reared him, how he brought him from light into darkness, and with what he repaid him. But Ahikar was saved, and the other received repayment as he himself went down into the darkness. Ahikar gave alms and escaped the deathtrap which Nadab had set for him; but Nadab fell into the trap and perished.

[11] So now, my children, consider what almsgiving accomplishes and how righteousness delivers." As he said this he died in his bed. He was a hundred and fifty-eight years old; and Tobias gave him a magnificent funeral.

[12] And when Anna died he buried her with his father. Then Tobias returned with his wife and his sons to Ecbatana, to Raguel his father-in-law.

[13] He grew old with honor, and he gave his father-in-law and mother-in-law magnificent funerals. He inherited their property and that of his father Tobit.

[14] He died in Ecbatana of Media at the age of a hundred and twenty-seven years.

[15] But before he died he heard of the destruction of Nineveh, which Nebuchadnezzar and Ahasuerus had captured. Before his death he rejoiced over Nineveh.

Judith

Jdt.1

[1] In the twelfth year of the reign of Nebuchadnezzar, who ruled over the Assyrians in the great city of Nineveh, in the days of Arphaxad, who ruled over the Medes in Ecbatana --

[2] he is the king who built walls about Ecbatana with hewn stones three cubits thick and six cubits long; he made the walls seventy cubits high and fifty cubits wide;

[3] at the gates he built towers a hundred cubits high and sixty cubits wide at the foundations;

[4] and he made its gates, which were seventy cubits high and forty cubits wide, so that his armies could march out in force and his infantry form their ranks --

[5] it was in those days that King Nebuchadnezzar made war against King Arphaxad in the great plain which is on the borders of Ragae.

[6] He was joined by all the people of the hill country and all those who lived along the Euphrates and the Tigris and the Hydaspes and in the plain where Arioch ruled the Elymaeans. Many nations joined the forces of the Chaldeans.

[7] Then Nebuchadnezzar king of the Assyrians sent to all who lived in Persia and to all who lived in the west, those who lived in Cilicia and Damascus and Lebanon and Antilebanon and all who lived along the seacoast,

[8] and those among the nations of Carmel and Gilead, and Upper Galilee and the great Plain of Esdraelon,

[9] and all who were in Samaria and its surrounding towns, and beyond the Jordan as far as Jerusalem and Bethany and Chelous and Kadesh and the river of Egypt, and Tahpanhes and Raamses and the whole land of Goshen,

[10] even beyond Tanis and Memphis, and all who lived in Egypt as far as the borders of Ethiopia.

[11] But all who lived in the whole region disregarded the orders of Nebuchadnezzar king of the Assyrians, and refused to join him in the war; for they were not afraid of him, but looked upon him as only one man, and they sent back his messengers empty-handed and shamefaced.

[12] Then Nebuchadnezzar was very angry with this whole region, and swore by his throne and kingdom that he would surely take revenge on the whole territory of Cilicia and Damascus and Syria, that he would kill them by the sword, and also all the inhabitants of the land of Moab, and the people of Ammon, and all Judea, and every one in Egypt, as far as the coasts of the two seas.

[13] In the seventeenth year he led his forces against King Arphaxad, and defeated him in battle, and overthrew the whole army of Arphaxad, and all his cavalry and all his chariots.

[14] Thus he took possession of his cities, and came to Ecbatana, captured its towers, plundered its markets, and turned its beauty into shame.

[15] He captured Arphaxad in the mountains of Ragae and struck him down with hunting spears; and he utterly destroyed him, to this day.

[16] Then he returned with them to Nineveh, he and all his combined forces, a vast body of troops; and there he and his forces rested and feasted for one hundred and twenty days.

Jdt.2

[1] In the eighteenth year, on the twenty-second day of the first month, there was talk in the palace of Nebuchadnezzar king of the Assyrians about carrying out his revenge on the whole region, just as he said.

[2] He called together all his officers and all his nobles and set forth to them his secret plan and recounted fully, with his own lips, all the wickedness of the region;

[3] and it was decided that every one who had not obeyed his command should be destroyed.

[4] When he had finished setting forth his plan, Nebuchadnezzar king of the Assyrians called Holofernes, the chief general of his army, second only to himself, and said to him,

[5] "Thus says the Great King, the lord of the whole earth: When you leave my presence, take with you men confident in their strength, to the number of one hundred and twenty thousand foot soldiers and twelve thousand cavalry.

[6] Go and attack the whole west country, because they disobeyed my orders.

[7] Tell them to prepare earth and water, for I am coming against them in my anger, and will cover the whole face of the earth with the feet of my armies, and will hand them over to be plundered by my troops,

[8] till their wounded shall fill their valleys, and every brook and river shall be filled with their dead, and overflow;

[9] and I will lead them away captive to the ends of the whole earth.

[10] You shall go and seize all their territory for me in advance. They will yield themselves to you, and you shall hold them for me till the day of their punishment.

[11] But if they refuse, your eye shall not spare and you shall hand them over to slaughter and plunder throughout your whole region.

[12] For as I live, and by the power of my kingdom, what I have spoken my hand will execute.

[13] And you -- take care not to transgress any of your sovereign's commands, but be sure to carry them out just as I have

ordered you; and do not delay about it."

[14] So Holofernes left the presence of his master, and called together all the commanders, generals, and officers of the Assyrian army,

[15] and mustered the picked troops by divisions as his lord had ordered him to do, one hundred and twenty thousand of them, together with twelve thousand archers on horseback,

[16] and he organized them as a great army is marshaled for a campaign.

[17] He collected a vast number of camels and asses and mules for transport, and innumerable sheep and oxen and goats for provision;

[18] also plenty of food for every man, and a huge amount of gold and silver from the royal palace.

[19] So he set out with his whole army, to go ahead of King Nebuchadnezzar and to cover the whole face of the earth to the west with their chariots and horsemen and picked troops of infantry.

[20] Along with them went a mixed crowd like a swarm of locusts, like the dust of the earth -- a multitude that could not be counted.

[21] They marched for three days from Nineveh to the plain of Bectileth, and camped opposite Bectileth near the mountain which is to the north of Upper Cilicia.

[22] From there Holofernes took his whole army, his infantry, cavalry, and chariots, and went up into the hill country

[23] and ravaged Put and Lud, and plundered all the people of Rassis and the Ishmaelites who lived along the desert, south of the country of the Chelleans.

[24] Then he followed the Euphrates and passed through Mesopotamia and destroyed all the hilltop cities along the brook Abron, as far as the sea.

[25] He also seized the territory of Cilicia, and killed every one who resisted him, and came to the southern borders of Japheth, fronting toward Arabia.

[26] He surrounded all the Midianites, and burned their tents and plundered their sheepfolds.

[27] Then he went down into the plain of Damascus during the wheat harvest, and burned all their fields and destroyed their flocks and herds and sacked their cities and ravaged their lands and put to death all their young men with the edge of the sword.

[28] So fear and terror of him fell upon all the people who lived along the seacoast, at Sidon and Tyre, and those who lived in Sur and Ocina and all who lived in Jamnia. Those who lived in Azotus and Ascalon feared him exceedingly.

Jdt.3

[1] So they sent messengers to sue for peace, and said,

[2] "Behold, we the servants of Nebuchadnezzar, the Great King, lie prostrate before you. Do with us whatever you will.

[3] Behold, our buildings, and all our land, and all our wheat fields, and our flocks and herds, and all our sheepfolds with their tents, lie before you; do with them whatever you please.

[4] Our cities also and their inhabitants are your slaves; come and deal with them in any way that seems good to you."

[5] The men came to Holofernes and told him all this.

[6] Then he went down to the seacoast with his army and stationed garrisons in the hilltop cities and took picked men from them as his allies.

[7] And these people and all in the country round about welcomed him with garlands and dances and tambourines.

[8] And he demolished all their shrines and cut down their sacred groves; for it had been given to him to destroy all the gods of the land, so that all nations should worship Nebuchadnezzar only, and all their tongues and tribes should call upon him as god.

[9] Then he came to the edge of Esdraelon, near Dothan, fronting the great ridge of Judea;

[10] here he camped between Geba and Scythopolis, and remained for a whole month in order to assemble all the supplies for his army.

Jdt.4

[1] By this time the people of Israel living in Judea heard of everything that Holofernes, the general of Nebuchadnezzar the king of the Assyrians, had done to the nations, and how he had plundered and destroyed all their temples;

[2] they were therefore very greatly terrified at his approach, and were alarmed both for Jerusalem and for the temple of the Lord their God.

[3] For they had only recently returned from the captivity, and all the people of Judea were newly gathered together, and the sacred vessels and the altar and the temple had been consecrated after their profanation.

[4] So they sent to every district of Samaria, and to Kona and Beth-horon and Belmain and Jericho and to Choba and Aesora and the valley of Salem,

[5] and immediately seized all the high hilltops and fortified the villages on them and stored up food in preparation for war -- since their fields had recently been harvested.

[6] And Joakim, the high priest, who was in Jerusalem at the time, wrote to the people of Bethulia and Betomesthaim, which faces Esdraelon opposite the plain near Dothan,

[7] ordering them to seize the passes up into the hills, since by them Judea could be invaded, and it was easy to stop any who tried to enter, for the approach was narrow, only wide enough for two men at the most.

[8] So the Israelites did as Joakim the high priest and the senate of the whole people of Israel, in session at Jerusalem, had given order.

[9] And every man of Israel cried out to God with great fervor, and they humbled themselves with much fasting.

[10] They and their wives and their children and their cattle and every resident alien and hired laborer and purchased slave -- they all girded themselves with sackcloth.

[11] And all the men and women of Israel, and their children, living at Jerusalem, prostrated themselves before the temple and put ashes on their heads and spread out their sackcloth before the Lord.

[12] They even surrounded the altar with sackcloth and cried out in unison, praying earnestly to the God of Israel not to give up their infants as prey and their wives as booty, and the cities they had inherited to be destroyed, and the sanctuary to be profaned and desecrated to the malicious joy of the Gentiles.

[13] So the Lord heard their prayers and looked upon their affliction; for the people fasted many days throughout Judea and in Jerusalem before the sanctuary of the Lord Almighty.

[14] And Joakim the high priest and all the priests who stood before the Lord and ministered to the Lord, with their loins girded with sackcloth, offered the continual burnt offerings and the vows and freewill offerings of the people.

[15] With ashes upon their turbans, they cried out to the Lord with all their might to look with favor upon the whole house of Israel.

Jdt.5

[1] When Holofernes, the general of the Assyrian army, heard that the people of Israel had prepared for war and had closed the passes in the hills and fortified all the high hilltops and set up barricades in the plains,

[2] he was very angry. So he called together all the princes of Moab and the commanders of Ammon and all the governors of the coastland,

[3] and said to them, "Tell me, you Canaanites, what people is this that lives in the hill country? What cities do they inhabit? How large is their army, and in what does their power or strength consist? Who rules over them as king, leading their army?

[4] And why have they alone, of all who live in the west, refused to come out and meet me?"

[5] Then Achior, the leader of all the Ammonites, said to him, "Let my lord now hear a word from the mouth of your servant, and I will tell you the truth about this people that dwells in the nearby mountain district. No falsehood shall come from your servant's mouth.

[6] This people is descended from the Chaldeans.

[7] At one time they lived in Mesopotamia, because they would not follow the gods of their fathers who were in Chaldea.

[8] For they had left the ways of their ancestors, and they worshiped the God of heaven, the God they had come to know; hence they drove them out from the presence of their gods; and they fled to Mesopotamia, and lived there for a long time.

[9] Then their God commanded them to leave the place where they were living and go to the land of Canaan. There they settled, and prospered, with much gold and silver and very many cattle.

[10] When a famine spread over Canaan they went down to Egypt and lived there as long as they had food; and there they became a great multitude -- so great that they could not be counted.

[11] So the king of Egypt became hostile to them; he took advantage of them and set them to making bricks, and humbled them and made slaves of them.

[12] Then they cried out to their God, and he afflicted the whole land of Egypt with incurable plagues; and so the Egyptians drove them out of their sight.

[13] Then God dried up the Red Sea before them,

[14] and he led them by the way of Sinai and Kadesh-barnea, and drove out all the people of the wilderness.

[15] So they lived in the land of the Amorites, and by their might destroyed all the inhabitants of Heshbon; and crossing over the Jordan they took possession of all the hill country.

[16] And they drove out before them the Canaanites and the Perizzites and the Jebusites and the Shechemites and all the Gergesites, and lived there a long time.

[17] As long as they did not sin against their God they prospered, for the God who hates iniquity is with them.

[18] But when they departed from the way which he had appointed for them, they were utterly defeated in many battles and were led away captive to a foreign country; the temple of their God was razed to the ground, and their cities were captured by their enemies.

[19] But now they have returned to their God, and have come back from the places to which they were scattered, and have occupied Jerusalem, where their sanctuary is, and have settled in the hill country, because it was uninhabited.

[20] Now therefore, my master and lord, if there is any unwitting error in this people and they sin against their God and we find out their offense, then we will go up and defeat them.

[21] But if there is no transgression in their nation, then let my lord pass them by; for their Lord will defend them, and their God will protect them, and we shall be put to shame before the whole world."

[22] When Achior had finished saying this, all the men standing around the tent began to complain; Holofernes' officers and all the men from the seacoast and from Moab insisted that he must be put to death.

[23] "For," they said, "we will not be afraid of the Israelites; they are a people with no strength or power for making war.

[24] Therefore let us go up, Lord Holofernes, and they will be devoured by your vast army."

Jdt.6

[1] When the disturbance made by the men outside the council died down, Holofernes, the commander of the Assyrian army, said to Achior and all the Moabites in the presence of all the foreign contingents:

[2] "And who are you, Achior, and you hirelings of Ephraim, to prophesy among us as you have done today and tell us not to make war against the people of Israel because their God will defend them? Who is God except Nebuchadnezzar?

[3] He will send his forces and will destroy them from the face of the earth, and their God will not deliver them -- we the king's servants will destroy them as one man. They cannot resist the might of our cavalry.

[4] We will burn them up, and their mountains will be drunk with their blood, and their fields will be full of their dead. They cannot withstand us, but will utterly perish. So says King Nebuchadnezzar, the lord of the whole earth. For he has spoken; none of his words shall be in vain.

[5] "But you, Achior, you Ammonite hireling, who have said these words on the day of your iniquity, you shall not see my face again from this day until I take revenge on this race that came out of Egypt.

[6] Then the sword of my army and the spear of my servants shall pierce your sides, and you shall fall among their wounded, when I return.

[7] Now my slaves are going to take you back into the hill country and put you in one of the cities beside the passes,

[8] and you will not die until you perish along with them.

[9] If you really hope in your heart that they will not be taken, do not look downcast! I have spoken and none of my words shall fail."

[10] Then Holofernes ordered his slaves, who waited on him in his tent, to seize Achior and take him to Bethulia and hand him over to the men of Israel.

[11] So the slaves took him and led him out of the camp into the plain, and from the plain they went up into the hill country and came to the springs below Bethulia.

[12] When the men of the city saw them, they caught up their weapons and ran out of the city to the top of the hill, and all the slingers kept them from coming up by casting stones at them.

[13] However, they got under the shelter of the hill and they bound Achior and left him lying at the foot of the hill, and returned to their master.

[14] Then the men of Israel came down from their city and found him; and they untied him and brought him into Bethulia and placed him before the magistrates of their city,

[15] who in those days were Uzziah the son of Micah, of the tribe of Simeon, and Chabris the son of Gothoniel, and Charmis the son of Melchiel.

[16] They called together all the elders of the city, and all their young men and their women ran to the assembly; and they set Achior in the midst of all their people, and Uzziah asked him what had happened.

[17] He answered and told them what had taken place at the council of Holofernes, and all that he had said in the presence of the Assyrian leaders, and all that Holofernes had said so boastfully against the house of Israel.

[18] Then the people fell down and worshiped God, and cried out to him, and said,

[19] "O Lord God of heaven, behold their arrogance, and have pity on the humiliation of our people, and look this day upon the faces of those who are consecrated to thee."

[20] Then they consoled Achior, and praised him greatly.

[21] And Uzziah took him from the assembly to his own house and gave a banquet for the elders; and all that night they called on the God of Israel for help.

Jdt.7

[1] The next day Holofernes ordered his whole army, and all the allies who had joined him, to break camp and move against Bethulia, and to seize the passes up into the hill country and make war on the Israelites.

[2] So all their warriors moved their camp that day; their force of men of war was one hundred and seventy thousand infantry and twelve thousand cavalry, together with the baggage and the foot soldiers handling it, a very great multitude.

[3] They encamped in the valley near Bethulia, beside the spring, and they spread out in breadth over Dothan as far as Balbaim and in length from Bethulia to Cyamon, which faces Esdraelon.

[4] When the Israelites saw their vast numbers they were greatly terrified, and every one said to his neighbor, "These men will now lick up the face of the whole land; neither the high mountains nor the valleys nor the hills will bear their weight."

[5] Then each man took up his weapons, and when they had kindled fires on their towers they remained on guard all that night.

[6] On the second day Holofernes led out all his cavalry in full view of the Israelites in Bethulia,

[7] and examined the approaches to the city, and visited the springs that supplied their water, and seized them and set guards of soldiers over them, and then returned to his army.

[8] Then all the chieftains of the people of Esau and all the leaders of the Moabites and the commanders of the coastland came to him and said,

[9] "Let our lord hear a word, lest his army be defeated.

[10] For these people, the Israelites, do not rely on their spears but on the height of the mountains where they live, for it is not easy to reach the tops of their mountains.

[11] Therefore, my lord, do not fight against them in battle array, and not a man of your army will fall.

[12] Remain in your camp, and keep all the men in your forces with you; only let your servants take possession of the spring of water that flows from the foot of the mountain --

[13] for this is where all the people of Bethulia get their water. So thirst will destroy them, and they will give up their city. We and our people will go up to the tops of the nearby mountains and camp there to keep watch that not a man gets out of the city.

[14] They and their wives and children will waste away with famine, and before the sword reaches them they will be strewn about in the streets where they live.

[15] So you will pay them back with evil, because they rebelled and did not receive you peaceably."

[16] These words pleased Holofernes and all his servants, and he gave orders to do as they had said.

[17] So the army of the Ammonites moved forward, together with five thousand Assyrians, and they encamped in the valley and seized the water supply and the springs of the Israelites.

[18] And the sons of Esau and the sons of Ammon went up and encamped in the hill country opposite Dothan; and they sent some of their men toward the south and the east, toward Acraba, which is near Chusi beside the brook Mochmur. The rest of the Assyrian army encamped in the plain, and covered the whole face of the land, and their tents and supply trains spread out in great number, and they formed a vast multitude.

[19] The people of Israel cried out to the Lord their God, for their courage failed, because all their enemies had surrounded them and there was no way of escape from them.

[20] The whole Assyrian army, their infantry, chariots, and cavalry, surrounded them for thirty-four days, until all the vessels of water belonging to every inhabitant of Bethulia were empty;

[21] their cisterns were going dry, and they did not have enough water to drink their fill for a single day, because it was measured out to them to drink.

[22] Their children lost heart, and the women and young men fainted from thirst and fell down in the streets of the city and in the passages through the gates; there was no strength left in them any longer.

[23] Then all the people, the young men, the women, and the children, gathered about Uzziah and the rulers of the city and cried out with a loud voice, and said before all the elders,

[24] "God be judge between you and us! For you have done us a great injury in not making peace with the Assyrians.

[25] For now we have no one to help us; God has sold us into their hands, to strew us on the ground before them with thirst and utter destruction.

[26] Now call them in and surrender the whole city to the army of Holofernes and to all his forces, to be plundered.

[27] For it would be better for us to be captured by them; for we will be slaves, but our lives will be spared, and we shall not witness the death of our babes before our eyes, or see our wives and children draw their last breath.

[28] We call to witness against you heaven and earth and our God, the Lord of our fathers, who punishes us according to our sins and the sins of our fathers. Let him not do this day the things which we have described!"

[29] Then great and general lamentation arose throughout the assembly, and they cried out to the Lord God with a loud voice.

[30] And Uzziah said to them, "Have courage, my brothers! Let us hold out for five more days; by that time the Lord our God will restore to us his mercy, for he will not forsake us utterly.

[31] But if these days pass by, and no help comes for us, I will do what you say."

[32] Then he dismissed the people to their various posts, and they went up on the walls and towers of their city. The women and children he sent home. And they were greatly depressed in the city.

Jdt.8

[1] At that time Judith heard about these things: she was the daughter of Merari the son of Ox, son of Joseph, son of Oziel, son of Elkiah, son of Ananias, son of Gideon, son of Raphaim, son of Ahitub, son of Elijah, son of Hilkiah, son of Eliab, son of Nathanael, son of Salamiel, son of Sarasadai, son of Israel.

[2] Her husband Manasseh, who belonged to her tribe and family, had died during the barley harvest.

[3] For as he stood overseeing the men who were binding sheaves in the field, he was overcome by the burning heat, and

took to his bed and died in Bethulia his city. So they buried him with his fathers in the field between Dothan and Balamon.

[4] Judith had lived at home as a widow for three years and four months.

[5] She set up a tent for herself on the roof of her house, and girded sackcloth about her loins and wore the garments of her widowhood.

[6] She fasted all the days of her widowhood, except the day before the sabbath and the sabbath itself, the day before the new moon and the day of the new moon, and the feasts and days of rejoicing of the house of Israel.

[7] She was beautiful in appearance, and had a very lovely face; and her husband Manasseh had left her gold and silver, and men and women slaves, and cattle, and fields; and she maintained this estate.

[8] No one spoke ill of her, for she feared God with great devotion.

[9] When Judith heard the wicked words spoken by the people against the ruler, because they were faint for lack of water, and when she heard all that Uzziah said to them, and how he promised them under oath to surrender the city to the Assyrians after five days,

[10] she sent her maid, who was in charge of all she possessed, to summon Chabris and Charmis, the elders of her city.

[11] They came to her, and she said to them, "Listen to me, rulers of the people of Bethulia! What you have said to the people today is not right; you have even sworn and pronounced this oath between God and you, promising to surrender the city to our enemies unless the Lord turns and helps us within so many days.

[12] Who are you, that have put God to the test this day, and are setting yourselves up in the place of God among the sons of men?

[13] You are putting the Lord Almighty to the test -- but you will never know anything!

[14] You cannot plumb the depths of the human heart, nor find out what a man is thinking; how do you expect to search out God, who made all these things, and find out his mind or comprehend his thought? No, my brethren, do not provoke the Lord our God to anger.

[15] For if he does not choose to help us within these five days, he has power to protect us within any time he pleases, or even to destroy us in the presence of our enemies.

[16] Do not try to bind the purposes of the Lord our God; for God is not like man, to be threatened, nor like a human being, to be won over by pleading.

[17] Therefore, while we wait for his deliverance, let us call upon him to help us, and he will hear our voice, if it pleases him.

[18] "For never in our generation, nor in these present days, has there been any tribe or family or people or city of ours which worshiped gods made with hands, as was done in days gone by --

[19] and that was why our fathers were handed over to the sword, and to be plundered, and so they suffered a great catastrophe before our enemies.

[20] But we know no other god but him, and therefore we hope that he will not disdain us or any of our nation.

[21] For if we are captured all Judea will be captured and our sanctuary will be plundered; and he will exact of us the penalty for its desecration.

[22] And the slaughter of our brethren and the captivity of the land and the desolation of our inheritance -- all this he will bring upon our heads among the Gentiles, wherever we serve as slaves; and we shall be an offense and a reproach in the eyes of those who acquire us.

[23] For our slavery will not bring us into favor, but the Lord our God will turn it to dishonor.

[24] "Now therefore, brethren, let us set an example to our brethren, for their lives depend upon us, and the sanctuary and the temple and the altar rest upon us.

[25] In spite of everything let us give thanks to the Lord our God, who is putting us to the test as he did our forefathers.

[26] Remember what he did with Abraham, and how he tested Isaac, and what happened to Jacob in Mesopotamia in Syria, while he was keeping the sheep of Laban, his mother's brother.

[27] For he has not tried us with fire, as he did them, to search their hearts, nor has he taken revenge upon us; but the Lord scourges those who draw near to him, in order to admonish them."

[28] Then Uzziah said to her, "All that you have said has been spoken out of a true heart, and there is no one who can deny your words.

[29] Today is not the first time your wisdom has been shown, but from the beginning of your life all the people have recognized your understanding, for your heart's disposition is right.

[30] But the people were very thirsty, and they compelled us to do for them what we have promised, and made us take an oath which we cannot break.

[31] So pray for us, since you are a devout woman, and the Lord will send us rain to fill our cisterns and we will no longer be faint."

[32] Judith said to them, "Listen to me. I am about to do a thing which will go down through all generations of our descendants.

[33] Stand at the city gate tonight, and I will go out with my maid; and within the days after which you have promised to surrender the city to our enemies, the Lord will deliver Israel by my hand.

[34] Only, do not try to find out what I plan; for I will not tell you until I have finished what I am about to do."

[35] Uzziah and the rulers said to her, "Go in peace, and may the Lord God go before you, to take revenge upon our enemies."

[36] So they returned from the tent and went to their posts.

Jdt.9

[1] Then Judith fell upon her face, and put ashes on her head, and uncovered the sackcloth she was wearing; and at the very time when that evening's incense was being offered in the house of God in Jerusalem, Judith cried out to the Lord with a loud voice, and said,

[2] "O Lord God of my father Simeon, to whom thou gavest a sword to take revenge on the strangers who had loosed the girdle of a virgin to defile her, and uncovered her thigh to put her to shame, and polluted her womb to disgrace her; for thou hast said, `It shall not be done' -- yet they did it.

[3] So thou gavest up their rulers to be slain, and their bed, which was ashamed of the deceit they had practiced, to be stained with blood, and thou didst strike down slaves along with princes, and princes on their thrones;

[4] and thou gavest their wives for a prey and their daughters to captivity, and all their booty to be divided among thy beloved sons, who were zealous for thee, and abhorred the pollution of their blood, and called on thee for help -- O God, my God, hear me also, a widow.

[5] "For thou hast done these things and those that went before and those that followed; thou hast designed the things that are now, and those that are to come. Yea, the things thou didst intend came to pass,

[6] and the things thou didst will presented themselves and said, `Lo, we are here'; for all they ways are prepared in advance, and thy judgment is with foreknowledge.

[7] "Behold now, the Assyrians are increased in their might; they are exalted, with their horses and riders; they glory in the strength of their foot soldiers; they trust in shield and spear, in bow and sling, and know not that thou art the Lord who crushest wars; the Lord is thy name.

[8] Break their strength by thy might, and bring down their power in thy anger; for they intend to defile thy sanctuary, and to pollute the tabernacle where thy glorious name rests, and to cast down the horn of thy altar with the sword.

[9] Behold their pride, and send thy wrath upon their heads; give to me, a widow, the strength to do what I plan.

[10] By the deceit of my lips strike down the slave with the prince and the prince with his servant; crush their arrogance by the hand of a woman.

[11] "For thy power depends not upon numbers, nor thy might upon men of strength; for thou art God of the lowly, helper of the oppressed, upholder of the weak, protector of the forlorn, savior of those without hope.

[12] Hear, O hear me, God of my father, God of the inheritance of Israel, Lord of heaven and earth, Creator of the waters, King of all thy creation, hear my prayer!

[13] Make my deceitful words to be their wound and stripe, for they have planned cruel things against thy covenant, and against thy consecrated house, and against the top of Zion, and against the house possessed by thy children.

[14] And cause thy whole nation and every tribe to know and understand that thou art God, the God of all power and might, and that there is no other who protects the people of Israel but thou alone!"

Jdt.10

[1] When Judith had ceased crying out to the God of Israel, and had ended all these words,

[2] she rose from where she lay prostrate and called her maid and went down into the house where she lived on sabbaths and on her feast days;

[3] and she removed the sackcloth which she had been wearing, and took off her widow's garments, and bathed her body with water, and anointed herself with precious ointment, and combed her hair and put on a tiara, and arrayed herself in her gayest apparel, which she used to wear while her husband Manasseh was living.

[4] And she put sandals on her feet, and put on her anklets and bracelets and rings, and her earrings and all her ornaments, and made herself very beautiful, to entice the eyes of all men who might see her.

[5] And she gave her maid a bottle of wine and a flask of oil, and filled a bag with parched grain and a cake of dried fruit and fine bread; and she wrapped up all her vessels and gave them to her to carry.

[6] Then they went out to the city gate of Bethulia, and found Uzziah standing there with the elders of the city, Chabris and Charmis.

[7] When they saw her, and noted how her face was altered and her clothing changed, they greatly admired her beauty, and said to her,

[8] "May the God of our fathers grant you favor and fulfil your plans, that the people of Israel may glory and Jerusalem may be exalted." And she worshiped God.

[9] Then she said to them, "Order the gate of the city to be opened for me, and I will go out and accomplish the things about which you spoke with me." So they ordered the young men to open the gate for her, as she had said.

[10] When they had done this, Judith went out, she and her maid with her; and the men of the city watched her until she had gone down the mountain and passed through the valley and they could no longer see her.

[11] The women went straight on through the valley; and an Assyrian patrol met her

[12] and took her into custody, and asked her, "To what people do you belong, and where are you coming from, and where are you going?" She replied, "I am a daughter of the Hebrews, but I am fleeing from them, for they are about to be handed over to you to be devoured.

[13] I am on my way to the presence of Holofernes the commander of your army, to give him a true report; and I will show him a way by which he can go and capture all the hill country without losing one of his men, captured or slain."

[14] When the men heard her words, and observed her face -- she was in their eyes marvelously beautiful -- they said to her,

[15] "You have saved your life by hurrying down to the presence of our lord. Go at once to his tent; some of us will escort you and hand you over to him.

[16] And when you stand before him, do not be afraid in your heart, but tell him just what you have said, and he will treat you well."

[17] They chose from their number a hundred men to accompany her and her maid, and they brought them to the tent of Holofernes.

[18] There was great excitement in the whole camp, for her arrival was reported from tent to tent, and they came and stood around her as she waited outside the tent of Holofernes while they told him about her.

[19] And they marveled at her beauty, and admired the Israelites, judging them by her, and every one said to his neighbor, "Who can despise these people, who have women like this among them? Surely not a man of them had better be left alive, for if we let them go they will be able to ensnare the whole world!"

[20] Then Holofernes' companions and all his servants came out and led her into the tent.

[21] Holofernes was resting on his bed, under a canopy which was woven with purple and gold and emeralds and precious stones.

[22] When they told him of her he came forward to the front of the tent, with silver lamps carried before him.

[23] And when Judith came into the presence of Holofernes and his servants, they all marveled at the beauty of her face; and she prostrated herself and made obeisance to him, and his slaves raised her up.

Jdt.11

[1] Then Holofernes said to her, "Take courage, woman, and do not be afraid in your heart, for I have never hurt any one who chose to serve Nebuchadnezzar, the king of all the earth.

[2] And even now, if your people who live in the hill country had not slighted me, I would never have lifted my spear against them; but they have brought all this on themselves.

[3] And now tell me why you have fled from them and have come over to us -- since you have come to safety.

[4] Have courage; you will live, tonight and from now on. No one will hurt you, but all will treat you well, as they do the servants of my lord King Nebuchadnezzar."

[5] Judith replied to him, "Accept the words of your servant, and let your maidservant speak in your presence, and I will tell nothing false to my lord this night.

[6] And if you follow out the words of your maidservant, God will accomplish something through you, and my lord will not fail to achieve his purposes.

[7] Nebuchadnezzar the king of the whole earth lives, and as his power endures, who had sent you to direct every living soul, not only do men serve him because of you, but also the beasts of the field and the cattle and the birds of the air will live by your power under Nebuchadnezzar and all his house.

[8] For we have heard of your wisdom and skill, and it is reported throughout the whole world that you are the one good man in the whole kingdom, thoroughly informed and marvelous in military strategy.

[9] "Now as for the things Achior said in your council, we have heard his words, for the men of Bethulia spared him and he told them all he had said to you.

[10] Therefore, my lord and master, do not disregard what he said, but keep it in your mind, for it is true: our nation cannot be punished, nor can the sword prevail against them, unless they sin against their God.

[11] "And now, in order that my lord may not be defeated and his purpose frustrated, death will fall upon them, for a sin has overtaken them by which they are about to provoke their God to anger when they do what is wrong.

[12] Since their food supply is exhausted and their water has almost given out, they have planned to kill their cattle and have determined to use all that God by his laws has forbidden them to eat.

[13] They have decided to consume the first fruits of the grain and the tithes of the wine and oil, which they had consecrated and set aside for the priests who minister in the presence of our God at Jerusalem -- although it is not lawful for any of the people so much as to touch these things with their hands.

[14] They have sent men to Jerusalem, because even the people living there have been doing this, to bring back to them permission from the senate.

[15] When the word reaches them and they proceed to do this, on that very day they will be handed over to you to be destroyed.

[16] "Therefore, when I, your servant, learned all this, I fled from them; and God has sent me to accomplish with you things that will astonish the whole world, as many as shall hear about them.

[17] For your servant is religious, and serves the God of heaven day and night; therefore, my lord, I will remain with you, and every night your servant will go out into the valley, and I will pray to God and he will tell me when they have committed their sins.

[18] And I will come and tell you, and then you shall go out with your whole army, and not one of them will withstand you.

[19] Then I will lead you through the middle of Judea, till you come to Jerusalem; and I will set your throne in the midst of it; and you will lead them like sheep that have no shepherd, and not a dog will so much as open its mouth to growl at you. For this has been told me, by my foreknowledge; it was announced to me, and I was sent to tell you."

[20] Her words pleased Holofernes and all his servants, and they marveled at her wisdom and said,

[21] "There is not such a woman from one end of the earth to the other, either for beauty of face or wisdom of speech!"

[22] And Holofernes said to her, "God has done well to send you before the people, to lend strength to our hands and to bring destruction upon those who have slighted my lord.

[23] You are not only beautiful in appearance, but wise in speech; and if you do as you have said, your God shall be my God, and you shall live in the house of King Nebuchadnezzar and be renowned throughout the whole world."

Jdt.12

[1] Then he commanded them to bring her in where his silver dishes were kept, and ordered them to set a table for her with some of his own food and to serve her with his own wine.

[2] But Judith said, "I cannot eat it, lest it be an offense; but I will be provided from the things I have brought with me."

[3] Holofernes said to her, "If your supply runs out, where can we get more like it for you? For none of your people is here with us."

[4] Judith replied, "As your soul lives, my lord, your servant will not use up the things I have with me before the Lord carries out by my hand what he has determined to do."

[5] Then the servants of Holofernes brought her into the tent, and she slept until midnight. Along toward the morning watch she arose

[6] and sent to Holofernes and said, "Let my lord now command that your servant be permitted to go out and pray."

[7] So Holofernes commanded his guards not to hinder her. And she remained in the camp for three days, and went out each night to the valley of Bethulia, and bathed at the spring in the camp.

[8] When she came up from the spring she prayed the Lord God of Israel to direct her way for the raising up of her people.

[9] So she returned clean and stayed in the tent until she ate her food toward evening.

[10] On the fourth day Holofernes held a banquet for his slave only, and did not invite any of his officers.

[11] And he said to Bagoas, the eunuch who had charge of his personal affairs, "Go now and persuade the Hebrew woman who is in your care to join us and eat and drink with us.

[12] For it will be a disgrace if we let such a woman go without enjoying her company, for if we do not embrace her she will laugh at us."

[13] So Bagoas went out from the presence of Holofernes, and approached her and said, "This beautiful maidservant will please come to my lord and be honored in his presence, and drink wine and be merry with us, and become today like one of the daughters of the Assyrians who serve in the house of Nebuchadnezzar."

[14] And Judith said, "Who am I, to refuse my lord? Surely whatever pleases him I will do at once, and it will be a joy to me until the day of my death!"

[15] So she got up and arrayed herself in all her woman's finery, and her maid went and spread on the ground for her before Holofernes the soft fleeces which she had received from Bagoas for her daily use, so that she might recline on them when she ate.

[16] Then Judith came in and lay down, and Holofernes' heart was ravished with her and he was moved with great desire to possess her; for he had been waiting for an opportunity to deceive her, ever since the day he first saw her.

[17] So Holofernes said to her. "Drink now, and be merry with us!"

[18] Judith said, "I will drink now, my lord, because my life means more to me today than in all the days since I was born."

[19] Then she took and ate and drank before him what her maid had prepared.

[20] And Holofernes was greatly pleased with her, and drank a great quantity of wine, much more than he had ever drunk in any one day since he was born.

Jdt.13

[1] When evening came, his slaves quickly withdrew, and Bagoas closed the tent from outside and shut out the attendants from his master's presence; and they went to bed, for they all were weary because the banquet had lasted long.

[2] So Judith was left alone in the tent , with Holofernes stretched out on his bed, for he was overcome with wine.

[3] Now Judith had told her maid to stand outside the bedchamber and to wait for her to come out, as she did every day; for she said she would be going out for her prayers. And she had said the same thing to Bagoas.

[4] So every one went out, and no one, either small or great, was left in the bedchamber. Then Judith, standing beside his bed,

said in her heart, "O Lord God of all might, look in this hour upon the work of my hands for the exaltation of Jerusalem.
[5] For now is the time to help thy inheritance, and to carry out my undertaking for the destruction of the enemies who have risen up against us."
[6] She went up to the post at the end of the bed, above Holofernes' head, and took down his sword that hung there.
[7] She came close to his bed and took hold of the hair of his head, and said, "Give me strength this day, O Lord God of Israel!"
[8] And she struck his neck twice with all her might, and severed it from his body.
[9] Then she tumbled his body off the bed and pulled down the canopy from the posts; after a moment she went out, and gave Holofernes' head to her maid,
[10] who placed it in her food bag. Then the two of them went out together, as they were accustomed to go for prayer; and they passed through the camp and circled around the valley and went up the mountain to Bethulia and came to its gates.
[11] Judith called out from afar to the watchmen at the gates, "Open, open the gate! God, our God, is still with us, to show his power in Israel, and his strength against our enemies, even as he has done this day!"
[12] When the men of her city heard her voice, they hurried down to the city gate and called together the elders of the city.
[13] They all ran together, both small and great, for it was unbelievable that she had returned; they opened the gate and admitted them, and they kindled a fire for light, and gathered around them.
[14] Then she said to them with a loud voice, "Praise God, O praise him! Praise God, who has not withdrawn his mercy from the house of Israel, but has destroyed our enemies by my hand this very night!"
[15] Then she took the head out of the bag and showed it to them, and said, "See, here is the head of Holofernes, the commander of the Assyrian army, and here is the canopy beneath which he lay in his drunken stupor. The Lord has struck him down by the hand of a woman.
[16] As the Lord lives, who has protected me in the way I went, it was my face that tricked him to his destruction, and yet he committed no act of sin with me, to defile and shame me."
[17] All the people were greatly astonished, and bowed down and worshiped God, and said with one accord, "Blessed art thou, our God, who hast brought into contempt this day the enemies of thy people."
[18] And Uzziah said to her, "O daughter, you are blessed by the Most High God above all women on earth; and blessed be the Lord God, who created the heavens and the earth, who has guided you to strike the head of the leader of our enemies.
[19] Your hope will never depart from the hearts of men, as they remember the power of God.
[20] May God grant this to be a perpetual honor to you, and may he visit you with blessings, because you did not spare your own life when our nation was brought low, but have avenged our ruin, walking in the straight path before our God." And all the people said, "So be it, so be it!"

Jdt.14
[1] Then Judith said to them, "Listen to me, my brethren, and take this head and hang it upon the parapet of your wall.
[2] And as soon as morning comes and the sun rises, let every valiant man take his weapons and go out of the city, and set a captain over them, as if you were going down to the plain against the Assyrian outpost; only do not go down.
[3] Then they will seize their arms and go into the camp and rouse the officers of the Assyrian army; and they will rush into the tent of Holofernes, and will not find him. Then fear will come over them, and they will flee before you,
[4] and you and all who live within the borders of Israel shall pursue them and cut them down as they flee.
[5] But before you do all this, bring Achior the Ammonite to me, and let him see and recognize the man who despised the house of Israel and sent him to us as if to his death."
[6] So they summoned Achior from the house of Uzziah. And when he came and saw the head of Holofernes in the hand of one of the men at the gathering of the people, he fell down on his face and his spirit failed him.
[7] And when they raised him up he fell at Judith's feet, and knelt before her, and said, "Blessed are you in every tent of Judah! In every nation those who hear your name will be alarmed.
[8] Now tell me what you have done during these days." Then Judith described to him in the presence of the people all that she had done, from the day she left until the moment of her speaking to them.
[9] And when she had finished, the people raised a great shout and made a joyful noise in their city.
[10] And when Achior saw all that the God of Israel had done, he believed firmly in God, and was circumcised, and joined the house of Israel, remaining so to this day.
[11] As soon as it was dawn they hung the head of Holofernes on the wall, and every man took his weapons, and they went out in companies to the passes in the mountains.
[12] And when the Assyrians saw them they sent word to their commanders, and they went to the generals and the captains and to all their officers.
[13] So they came to Holofernes' tent and said to the steward in charge of all his personal affairs, "Wake up our lord, for the slaves have been so bold as to come down against us to give battle, in order to be destroyed completely."
[14] So Bagoas went in and knocked at the door of the tent, for he supposed that he was sleeping with Judith.
[15] But when no one answered, he opened it and went into the bedchamber and found him thrown down on the platform

dead, with his head cut off and missing.

[16] And he cried out with a loud voice and wept and groaned and shouted, and rent his garments.

[17] Then he went to the tent where Judith had stayed, and when he did not find her he rushed out to the people and shouted,

[18] "The slaves have tricked us! One Hebrew woman has brought disgrace upon the house of King Nebuchadnezzar! For look, here is Holofernes lying on the ground, and his head is not on him!"

[19] When the leaders of the Assyrian army heard this, they rent their tunics and were greatly dismayed, and their loud cries and shouts arose in the midst of the camp.

Jdt.15

[1] When the men in the tents heard it, they were amazed at what had happened.

[2] Fear and trembling came over them, so that they did not wait for one another, but with one impulse all rushed out and fled by every path across the plain and through the hill country.

[3] Those who had camped in the hills around Bethulia also took to flight. Then the men of Israel, every one that was a soldier, rushed out upon them.

[4] And Uzziah sent men to Betomasthaim and Bebai and Choba and Kola, and to all the frontiers of Israel, to tell what had taken place and to urge all to rush out upon their enemies to destroy them.

[5] And when the Israelites heard it, with one accord they fell upon the enemy, and cut them down as far as Choba. Those in Jerusalem and all the hill country also came, for they were told what had happened in the camp of the enemy; and those in Gilead and in Galilee outflanked them with great slaughter, even beyond Damascus and its borders.

[6] The rest of the people of Bethulia fell upon the Assyrian camp and plundered it, and were greatly enriched.

[7] And the Israelites, when they returned from the slaughter, took possession of what remained, and the villages and towns in the hill country and in the plain got a great amount of booty, for there was a vast quantity of it.

[8] Then Joakim the high priest, and the senate of the people of Israel who lived at Jerusalem, came to witness the good things which the Lord had done for Israel, and to see Judith and to greet her.

[9] And when they met her they all blessed her with one accord and said to her, "You are the exaltation of Jerusalem, you are the great glory of Israel, you are the great pride of our nation!

[10] You have done all this singlehanded; you have done great good to Israel, and God is well pleased with it. May the Almighty Lord bless you for ever!" And all the people said, "So be it!"

[11] So all the people plundered the camp for thirty days. They gave Judith the tent of Holofernes and all his silver dishes and his beds and his bowls and all his furniture; and she took them and loaded her mule and hitched up her carts and piled the things on them.

[12] Then all the women of Israel gathered to see her, and blessed her, and some of them performed a dance for her; and she took branches in her hands and gave them to the women who were with her;

[13] and they crowned themselves with olive wreaths, she and those who were with her; and she went before all the people in the dance, leading all the women, while all the men of Israel followed, bearing their arms and wearing garlands and with songs on their lips.

Jdt.16

[1] Then Judith began this thanksgiving before all Israel, and all the people loudly sang this song of praise.

[2] And Judith said, Begin a song to my God with tambourines, sing to my Lord with cymbals. Raise to him a new psalm; exalt him, and call upon his name.

[3] For God is the Lord who crushes wars; for he has delivered me out of the hands of my pursuers, and brought me to his camp, in the midst of the people.

[4] The Assyrian came down from the mountains of the north; he came with myriads of his warriors; their multitude blocked up the valleys, their cavalry covered the hills.

[5] He boasted that he would burn up my territory, and kill my young men with the sword, and dash my infants to the ground and seize my children as prey, and take my virgins as booty.

[6] But the Lord Almighty has foiled them by the hand of a woman.

[7] For their mighty one did not fall by the hands of the young men, nor did the sons of the Titans smite him, nor did tall giants set upon him; but Judith the daughter of Merari undid him with the beauty of her countenance.

[8] For she took off her widow's mourning to exalt the oppressed in Israel. She anointed her face with ointment and fastened her hair with a tiara and put on a linen gown to deceive him.

[9] Her sandal ravished his eyes, her beauty captivated his mind, and the sword severed his neck.

[10] The Persians trembled at her boldness, the Medes were daunted at her daring.

[11] Then my oppressed people shouted for joy; my weak people shouted and the enemy trembled; they lifted up their voices, and the enemy were turned back.

[12] The sons of maidservants have pierced them through; they were wounded like the children of fugitives, they perished before the army of my Lord.

[13] I will sing to my God a new song: O Lord, thou are great and glorious, wonderful in strength, invincible.

[14] Let all thy creatures serve thee, for thou didst speak, and they were made. Thou didst send forth thy Spirit, and it formed them; there is none that can resist thy voice.

[15] For the mountains shall be shaken to their foundations with the waters; at thy presence the rocks shall melt like wax, but to those who fear thee thou wilt continue to show mercy.

[16] For every sacrifice as a fragrant offering is a small thing, and all fat for burnt offerings to thee is a very little thing, but he who fears the Lord shall be great for ever.

[17] Woe to the nations that rise up against my people! The Lord Almighty will take vengeance on them in the day of judgment; fire and worms he will give to their flesh; they shall weep in pain for ever.

[18] When they arrived at Jerusalem they worshiped God. As soon as the people were purified, they offered their burnt offerings, their freewill offerings, and their gifts.

[19] Judith also dedicated to God all the vessels of Holofernes, which the people had given her; and the canopy which she took for herself from his bedchamber she gave as a votive offering to the Lord.

[20] So the people continued feasting in Jerusalem before the sanctuary for three months, and Judith remained with them.

[21] After this every one returned home to his own inheritance, and Judith went to Bethulia, and remained on her estate, and was honored in her time throughout the whole country.

[22] Many desired to marry her, but she remained a widow all the days of her life after Manasseh her husband died and was gathered to his people.

[23] She became more and more famous, and grew old in her husband's house, until she was one hundred and five years old. She set her maid free. She died in Bethulia, and they buried her in the cave of her husband Manasseh,

[24] and the house of Israel mourned for her seven days. Before she died she distributed her property to all those who were next of kin to her husband Manasseh, and to her own nearest kindred.

[25] And no one ever again spread terror among the people of Israel in the days of Judith, or for a long time after her death.

Susanna

Sus.1

[1] A man named Joacim lived in Babylon,

[2] And he took a wife named Susanna, the daughter of Hilkiah, a very beautiful woman and one who feared the Lord.

[3] Her parents were righteous, and had taught their daughter according to the law of Moses.

[4] Joakim was very rich, and had a spacious garden adjoining his house; and the Jews used to come to him because he was the most honored of them all.

[5] In that year two elders from the people were appointed as judges. Concerning them the Lord had said: "Iniquity came forth from Babylon, from elders who were judges, who were supposed to govern the people."

[6] These men were frequently at Joakim's house, and all who had suits at law came to them.

[7] When the people departed at noon, Susanna would go into her husband's garden to walk.

[8] The two elders used to see her every day, going in and walking about, and they began to desire her.

[9] And they perverted their minds and turned away their eyes from looking to Heaven or remembering righteous judgments.

[10] Both were overwhelmed with passion for her, but they did not tell each other of their distress,

[11] for they were ashamed to disclose their lustful desire to possess her.

[12] And they watched eagerly, day after day, to see her.

[13] They said to each other, "Let us go home, for it is mealtime."

[14] And when they went out, they parted from each other. But turning back, they met again; and when each pressed the other for the reason, they confessed their lust. And then together they arranged for a time when they could find her alone.

[15] Once, while they were watching for an opportune day, she went in as before with only two maids, and wished to bathe in the garden, for it was very hot.

[16] And no one was there except the two elders, who had hid themselves and were watching her.

[17] She said to her maids, "Bring me oil and ointments, and shut the garden doors so that I may bathe."

[18] They did as she said, shut the garden doors, and went out by the side doors to bring what they had been commanded; and they did not see the elders, because they were hidden.

[19] When the maids had gone out, the two elders rose and ran to her, and said:

[20] "Look, the garden doors are shut, no one sees us, and we are in love with you; so give your consent, and lie with us.

[21] If you refuse, we will testify against you that a young man was with you, and this was why you sent your maids away."

[22] Susanna sighed deeply, and said, "I am hemmed in on every side. For if I do this thing, it is death for me; and if I do not, I shall not escape your hands.

[23] I choose not to do it and to fall into your hands, rather than to sin in the sight of the Lord."

[24] Then Susanna cried out with a loud voice, and the two elders shouted against her.

[25] And one of them ran and opened the garden doors.

[26] When the household servants heard the shouting in the garden, they rushed in at the side door to see what had happened to her.

[27] And when the elders told their tale, the servants were greatly ashamed, for nothing like this had ever been said about Susanna.

[28] The next day, when the people gathered at the house of her husband Joakim, the two elders came, full of their wicked plot to have Susanna put to death.

[29] They said before the people, "Send for Susanna, the daughter of Hilkiah, who is the wife of Joakim."

[30] So they sent for her. And she came, with her parents, her children, and all her kindred.

[31] Now Susanna was a woman of great refinement, and beautiful in appearance.

[32] As she was veiled, the wicked men ordered her to be unveiled, that they might feed upon her beauty.

[33] But her family and friends and all who saw her wept.

[34] Then the two elders stood up in the midst of the people, and laid their hands upon her head.

[35] And she, weeping, looked up toward heaven, for her heart trusted in the Lord.

[36] The elders said, "As we were walking in the garden alone, this woman came in with two maids, shut the garden doors, and dismissed the maids.

[37] Then a young man, who had been hidden, came to her and lay with her.

[38] We were in a corner of the garden, and when we saw this wickedness we ran to them.

[39] We saw them embracing, but we could not hold the man, for he was too strong for us, and he opened the doors and dashed out.

[40] So we seized this woman and asked her who the young man was, but she would not tell us. These things we testify."

[41] The assembly believed them, because they were elders of the people and judges; and they condemned her to death.

[42] Then Susanna cried out with a loud voice, and said, "O eternal God, who do discern what is secret, who art aware of all things before they come to be,

[43] thou knowest that these men have borne false witness against me. And now I am to die! Yet I have done none of the things that they have wickedly invented against me!"

[44] The Lord heard her cry.

[45] And as she was being led away to be put to death, God aroused the holy spirit of a young lad named Daniel;

[46] and he cried with a loud voice, "I am innocent of the blood of this woman."

[47] All the people turned to him, and said, "What is this that you have said?"

[48] Taking his stand in the midst of them, he said, "Are you such fools, you sons of Israel? Have you condemned a daughter of Israel without examination and without learning the facts?

[49] Return to the place of judgment. For these men have borne false witness against her."

[50] Then all the people returned in haste. And the elders said to him, "Come, sit among us and inform us, for God has given you that right."

[51] And Daniel said to them, "Separate them far from each other, and I will examine them."

[52] When they were separated from each other, he summoned one of them and said to him, "You old relic of wicked days, your sins have now come home, which you have committed in the past,

[53] pronouncing unjust judgments, condemning the innocent and letting the guilty go free, though the Lord said, `Do not put to death an innocent and righteous person.'

[54] Now then, if you really saw her, tell me this: Under what tree did you see them being intimate with each other?" He answered, "Under a mastic tree."

[55] And Daniel said, "Very well! You have lied against your own head, for the angel of God has received the sentence from God and will immediately cut you in two."

[56] Then he put him aside, and commanded them to bring the other. And he said to him, "You offspring of Canaan and not of Judah, beauty has deceived you and lust has perverted your heart.

[57] This is how you both have been dealing with the daughters of Israel, and they were intimate with you through fear; but a daughter of Judah would not endure your wickedness.

[58] Now then, tell me: Under what tree did you catch them being intimate with each other?" He answered, "Under an evergreen oak."

[59] And Daniel said to him, "Very well! You also have lied against your own head, for the angel of God is waiting with his sword to saw you in two, that he may destroy you both."

[60] Then all the assembly shouted loudly and blessed God, who saves those who hope in him.

[61] And they rose against the two elders, for out of their own mouths Daniel had convicted them of bearing false witness;

[62] and they did to them as they had wickedly planned to do to their neighbor; acting in accordance with the law of Moses, they put them to death. Thus innocent blood was saved that day.

[63] And Hilkiah and his wife praised God for their daughter Susanna, and so did Joakim her husband and all her kindred, because nothing shameful was found in her.

[64] And from that day onward Daniel had a great reputation among the people.

Psalm 151

Ps151.1

[1] I was the smallest in my father's house and the youngest of my brothers. I took care of my father's sheep.

[2] My hands made a harp, my fingers fashioned a lyre.

[3] And who will declare it to my Lord? The Lord himself; it is he who hears.

[4] It was he who sent his messenger and took me from my father's sheep, and anointed me with his anointing oil.

[5] My brothers were handsome and tall, but the Lord was not pleased with them.

[6] I went out to meet the Philistine, and he cursed me by his idols.

[7] But I drew his own sword; I beheaded him, and removed reproach from the people of Israel.

CLEMENT OF ROME
First Epistle

THE FIRST EPISTLE OF CLEMENT TO THE CORINTHIANS

1Clem prologue:1
The Church of God which sojourns in Rome to the Church of God which
sojourns in Corinth, to them which are called and sanctified by the
will of God through our Lord Jesus Christ. Grace to you and peace
from Almighty God through Jesus Christ be multiplied.

1Clem 1:1
  By reason of the sudden and repeated calamities and reverses which
are befalling us, brethren, we consider that we have been somewhat
tardy in giving heed to the matters of dispute that have arisen among
you, dearly beloved, and to the detestable and unholy sedition, so
alien and strange to the elect of God, which a few headstrong and
self-willed persons have kindled to such a pitch of madness that your
name, once revered and renowned and lovely in the sight of all men,
has been greatly reviled.

1Clem 1:2
For who that had sojourned among you did not approve your most
virtuous and steadfast faith? Who did not admire your sober and
forbearing piety in Christ? Who did not publish abroad your
magnificent disposition of hospitality? Who did not congratulate you
on your perfect and sound knowledge?

1Clem 1:3
For you did all things without respect of persons, and you walked after
the ordinances of God, submitting yourselves to your rulers and
rendering to the older men among you the honor which is their due.
On the young too you enjoined modest and seemly thoughts: and the
women you charged to perform all their duties in a blameless and
seemly and pure conscience, cherishing their own husbands, as is
meet; and you taught them to keep in the rule of obedience, and to
manage the affairs of their household in seemliness, with all
discretion.

1Clem 2:1
  And you were all lowly in mind and free from arrogance, yielding
rather than claiming submission, more glad to give than to
receive, and content with the provisions which God supplies. And
giving heed unto His words, you laid them up diligently in your
hearts, and His sufferings were before your eyes.

1Clem 2:2
Thus a profound and rich peace was given to all, and an insatiable
desire of doing good. An abundant outpouring also of the Holy Spirit
fell upon all;

1Clem 2:3
and, being full of holy counsel, in excellent zeal and with a pious
confidence you stretched out your hands to Almighty God, supplicating
Him to be propitious, if unwillingly you had committed any sin.

751

1Clem 2:4
you had conflict day and night for all the brotherhood, that the
number of His elect might be saved with fearfulness and intentness of
mind.

1Clem 2:5
You were sincere and simple and free from malice one towards another.

1Clem 2:6
Every sedition and every schism was abominable to you. You mourned
over the transgressions of your neighbors: you judged their
shortcomings to be your own.

1Clem 2:7
you repented not of any well-doing, but were ready unto every good
work.

1Clem 2:8
Being adorned with a most virtuous and honorable life, you performed
all your duties in the fear of Him. The commandments and the
ordinances of the Lord were written on the tablets of your hearts.

1Clem 3:1
   All glory and enlargement was given unto you, and that was fulfilled
which is written My beloved ate and drank and was enlarged and
waxed fat and kicked.

1Clem 3:2
Hence come jealousy and envy, strife and sedition, persecution and
tumult, war and captivity.

1Clem 3:3
So men were stirred up, the mean against the honorable, the ill
reputed against the highly reputed, the foolish against the wise, the
young against the elder.

1Clem 3:4
For this cause righteousness and peace stand aloof, while each
man has forsaken the fear of the Lord and become purblind in the
faith of Him, neither walketh in the ordinances of His commandments
nor liveth according to that which becometh Christ, but each goeth
after the lusts of his evil heart, seeing that they have conceived an
unrighteous and ungodly jealousy, through which also death entered
into the world.

1Clem 4:1
   For so it is written, And it came to pass after certain days that
Cain brought of the fruits of the earth a sacrifice unto God, and
Abel he also brought of the firstlings of the sheep and of their
fatness.

1Clem 4:2
And God looked upon Abel and upon his gifts, but unto Cain and unto
his sacrifices He gave no heed.

1Clem 4:3
And Cain was very sorrowful, and his countenance fell.

1Clem 4:4
And God said unto Cain, Wherefore art you very sorrowful and
wherefore did thy countenance fall? If you hast offered aright and
hast not divided aright, didst you not sin? Hold thy peace.

1Clem 4:5
Unto you shall he turn, and you shall rule over him. {This last
phrase has also been translated: Be at peace: your offering
returns to thyself, and you shall again possess it.}

1Clem 4:6
And Cain said unto Abel his brother, Let us go over unto the plain.
And it came to pass, while they Were in the plain, that Cain rose up
against Abel his brother and slew him.

1Clem 4:7
you see, brethren, jealousy and envy wrought a brother's murder.

1Clem 4:8
By reason of jealousy our father Jacob ran away from the face of Esau
his brother.

1Clem 4:And jealousy caused Joseph to be persecuted even unto death, and to come
even unto bondage.

1Clem 4:10
Jealousy compelled Moses to flee from the face of Pharaoh king of
Egypt while it was said to him by his own countryman, Who made you
a judge or a decider over us, Would you slay me, even as
yesterday you murdered the Egyptian?

1Clem 4:11
By reason of jealousy Aaron and Miriam were lodged outside the camp.

1Clem 4:12
Jealousy brought Dathan and Abiram down alive to hades, because they
made sedition against Moses the servant of God.

1Clem 4:13
By reason of jealousy David was envied not only by the Philistines,
but was persecuted also by Saul [king of Israel].

1Clem 5:1
  But, to pass from the examples of ancient days, let us come to those
champions who lived nearest to our time. Let us set before us the
noble examples which belong to our generation.

1Clem 5:2
By reason of jealousy and envy the greatest and most righteous
pillars of the Church were persecuted, and contended even unto death.

1Clem 5:3
Let us set before our eyes the good Apostles.

1Clem 5:4
There was Peter who by reason of unrighteous jealousy endured not one
not one but many labors, and thus having borne his testimony went to
his appointed place of glory.

1Clem 5:5
By reason of jealousy and strife Paul by his example pointed out the
prize of patient endurance. After that he had been seven times in
bonds, had been driven into exile, had been stoned, had preached in
the East and in the West, he won the noble renown which was the
reward of his faith,

1Clem 5:6
having taught righteousness unto the whole world and having reached
the farthest bounds of the West; and when he had borne his testimony
before the rulers, so he departed from the world and went unto the
holy place, having been found a notable pattern of patient endurance.

1Clem 6:1
   Unto these men of holy lives was gathered a vast multitude of the
elect, who through many indignities and tortures, being the victims
of jealousy, set a brave example among ourselves.

1Clem 6:2
By reason of jealousy women being persecuted, after that they had
suffered cruel and unholy insults as Danaids and Dircae, safely
reached the goal in the race of faith, and received a noble reward,
feeble though they were in body.

1Clem 6:3
Jealousy has estranged wives from their husbands and changed the
saying of our father Adam, This now is bone of my bones and flesh
of my flesh.

1Clem 6:4
Jealousy and strife have overthrown great cities and uprooted great
nations.

1Clem 7:1
   These things, dearly beloved, we write, not only as admonishing you,
but also as putting ourselves in remembrance. For we are in the same
lists, and the same contest awaits us.

1Clem 7:2
Wherefore let us forsake idle and vain thoughts; and let us conform
to the glorious and venerable rule which has been handed down to us;

1Clem 7:3
and let us see what is good and what is pleasant and what is
acceptable in the sight of Him that made us.

1Clem 7:4
Let us fix our eyes on the blood of Christ and understand how
precious it is unto His Father, because being shed for our salvation
it won for the whole world the grace of repentance.

1Clem 7:5
Let us review all the generations in turn, and learn how from
generation to generation the Master has given a place for repentance
unto them that desire to turn to Him.

1Clem 7:6
Noah preached repentance, and they that obeyed were saved.

1Clem 7:7
Jonah preached destruction unto the men of Nineveh; but they,
repenting of their sins, obtained pardon of God by their
supplications and received salvation, albeit they were aliens from
God.

1Clem 8:1
  The ministers of the grace of God through the Holy Spirit spoke
concerning repentance.

1Clem 8:2
Yea and the Master of the universe Himself spoke concerning
repentance with an oath:

1Clem 8:3
for, as I live says the Lord, I desire not the death of the
sinner, so much as his repentance,

1Clem 8:4
and He added also a merciful judgment: Repent you, O house of
Israel, of your iniquity; say unto the sons of My people, Though
your sins reach from the earth even unto the heaven, and though
they be redder than scarlet and blacker than sackcloth, and you turn
unto Me with your whole heart and say Father, I will give ear unto
you as unto a holy people.

1Clem 8:5
And in another place He said on this wise, Wash, be you clean. Put
away your iniquities from your souls out of My sight. Cease from
your iniquities; learn to do good; seek out judgment; defend him
that is wronged: give judgment for the orphan, and execute
righteousness for the widow; and come and let us reason together,
said He; and though your sins be as crimson, I will make them
white as snow; and though they be as scarlet, I will make them
white as wool. And if you be willing and will hearken unto Me, you
shall eat the good things of the earth; but if you be not willing,
neither hearken unto Me, a sword shall devour you; for the mouth of
the Lord has spoken these things.

1Clem 8:6
Seeing then that He desires all His beloved to be partakers of
repentance, He confirmed it by an act of His almighty will.

1Clem 9:1
  Wherefore let us be obedient unto His excellent and glorious will;
and presenting ourselves as suppliants of His mercy and goodness, let
us fall down before Him and betake ourselves unto His compassions,
forsaking the vain toil and the strife and the jealousy which leads
unto death.

1Clem 9:2
Let us fix our eyes on them that ministered perfectly unto His
excellent glory.

1Clem 9:3
Let us set before us Enoch, who being found righteous in obedience
was translated, and his death was not found.

1Clem 9:4

Noah, being found faithful, by his ministration preached regeneration unto the world, and through him the Master saved the living creatures that entered into the ark in concord.

1Clem 10:1

Abraham, who was called the 'friend,' was found faithful in that he rendered obedience unto the words of God.

1Clem 10:2

He through obedience went forth from his land and from his kindred and from his father's house, that leaving a scanty land and a feeble kindred and a mean house he might inherit the promises of God.

1Clem 10:3

For He said unto him Go forth from thy land and from thy kindred and from thy father's house unto the land which I shall show you, and I will make you into a great nation, and I will bless you and will magnify thy name, and you shall be blessed. And I will bless them that bless you, and I will curse them that curse you; and in you shall all the tribes of the earth be blessed.

1Clem 10:4

And again, when he was parted from Lot, God said unto him Look up with your eyes, and behold from the place where you now art, unto the north and the south and the sunrise and the sea; for all the land which you see, I will give it unto you and to thy seed for ever;

1Clem 10:5

and I will make thy seed as the dust of the earth. If any man can count the dust of the earth, then shall thy seed also be counted.

1Clem 10:6

And again He said; God led Abraham forth and said unto him, Look up unto the heaven and count the stars, and see whether you canst number them. So shall thy seed be. And Abraham believed God, and it was reckoned unto him for righteousness.

1Clem 10:7

For his faith and hospitality a son was given unto him in old age, and by obedience he offered him a sacrifice unto God on one of the mountains which He showed him.

1Clem 11:1

For his hospitality and godliness Lot was saved from Sodom, when all the country round about was judged by fire and brimstone; the Master having thus fore shown that He forsakes not them which set their hope on Him, but appoints unto punishment and torment them which swerve aside.

1Clem 11:2

For when his wife had gone forth with him, being otherwise minded and not in accord, she was appointed for a sign hereunto, so that she became a pillar of salt unto this day, that it might be known unto all men that they which are double-minded and they which doubt concerning the power of God are set for a judgment and for a token unto all the generations.

1Clem 12:1

For her faith and hospitality Rahab the harlot was saved.

1Clem 12:2
For when the spies were sent forth unto Jericho by Joshua the son of
Nun, the king of the land perceived that they were come to spy out
his country, and sent forth men to seize them, that being seized they
might be put to death.

1Clem 12:3
So the hospitable Rahab received them and hid them in the upper
chamber under the flax stalks.

1Clem 12:4
And when the messengers of the king came near and said, The spies
of our land entered in unto you: bring them forth, for the king so
ordereth: then she answered, The men truly, whom you seek,
entered in unto me, but they departed forthwith and are sojourning
on the way; and she pointed out to them the opposite road.

1Clem 12:5
And she said unto the men, Of a surety I perceive that the Lord
your God delivered this city unto you; for the fear and the dread
of you is fallen upon the inhabitants thereof. When therefore it
shall come to pass that you take it, save me and the house of my
father.

1Clem 12:6
And they said unto her, It shall be even so as you hast spoken
unto us. Whensoever therefore you perceives that we are coming,
you shall gather all thy folk beneath thy roof and they shall be
saved; for as many as shall be found without the house shall
perish.

1Clem 12:7
And moreover they gave her a sign, that she should hang out from her
house a scarlet thread, thereby showing beforehand that through the
blood of the Lord there shall be redemption unto all them that
believe and hope on God.

1Clem 12:8
you see, dearly beloved, not only faith, but prophecy, is found in the
woman.

1Clem 13:1
   Let us therefore be lowly minded, brethren, laying aside all
arrogance and conceit and folly and anger, and let us do that which
is written. For the Holy Ghost said, Let not the wise man boast in
his wisdom, nor the strong in his strength, neither the rich in his
riches; but he that boasts let him boast in the Lord, that he may
seek Him out, and do judgment and righteousness most of all
remembering the words of the Lord Jesus which He spoke, teaching
forbearance and long-suffering:

1Clem 13:2
for thus He spoke Have mercy, that you may receive mercy: forgive,
that it may be forgiven to you. As you do, so shall it be done to
you. As you give, so shall it be given unto you. As you judge, so
shall you be judged. As you show kindness, so shall kindness be
showed unto you. With what measure you mete, it shall be measured

withal to you.

1Clem 13:3
With this commandment and these precepts let us confirm ourselves,
that we may walk in obedience to His hallowed words, with lowliness
of mind.

1Clem 13:4
For the holy word said, Upon whom shall I look, save upon him that
is gentle and quiet and feared My oracles?

1Clem 14:1
   Therefore it is right and proper, brethren, that we should be
obedient unto God, rather than follow those who in arrogance and
unruliness have set themselves up as leaders in abominable jealousy.

1Clem 14:2
For we shall bring upon us no common harm, but rather great peril, if
we surrender ourselves recklessly to the purposes of men who launch
out into strife and seditions, so as to estrange us from that which
is right.

1Clem 14:3
Let us be good one towards another according to the compassion and
sweetness of Him that made us. For it is written:

1Clem 14:4
The good shall be dwellers in the land, and the innocent shall be
left on it but they that transgress shall be destroyed utterly from
it.

1Clem 14:5
And again He said I saw the ungodly lifted up on high and exalted
as the cedars of Lebanon. And I passed by, and behold he was not;
and sought out his place, and I found it not. Keep innocence and
behold uprightness; for there is a remnant for the peaceful man.

1Clem 15:1
   Therefore let us cleave unto them that practice peace with
godliness, and not unto them that desire peace with dissimulation.

1Clem 15:2
For He said in a certain place This people honored Me with their
lips, but their heart is far from Me,

1Clem 15:3
and again, they blessed with their mouth, but they cursed with
their heart.

1Clem 15:4
And again He said, They loved Him with their mouth, and with their
tongue they lied unto Him; and their heart was not upright with
Him, neither were they steadfast in His covenant.

1Clem 15:5
For this cause let the deceitful lips be made dumb which speak
iniquity against the righteous. And again May the Lord utterly
destroy all the deceitful lips, the tongue that speaks proud
things, even them that say, Let us magnify our tongue; our lips are

our own; who is lord over us?

1Clem 15:6
For the misery of the needy and for the groaning of the poor I will
now arise, said the Lord. I will set him in safety; I will deal
boldly by him.

1Clem 16:1
   For Christ is with them that are lowly of mind, not with them that
exalt themselves over the flock.

1Clem 16:2
The scepter of the majesty of God, even our Lord Jesus Christ, came
not in the pomp of arrogance or of pride, though He might have done
so, but in lowliness of mind, according as the Holy Spirit spoke
concerning Him.

1Clem 16:3
For He said Lord, who believed our report? and to whom was the arm
of the Lord revealed? We announced Him in His presence. As a child
was He, as a root in a thirsty ground. There is no form in Him,
neither glory. And we beheld Him, and He had no form nor
comeliness, but His form was mean, lacking more than the form of
men. He was a man of stripes and of toil, and knowing how to bear
infirmity: for His face is turned away. He was dishonored and held
of no account.

1Clem 16:4
He bore our sins and suffers pain for our sakes: and we
accounted Him to be in toil and in stripes and in affliction.

1Clem 16:5
And He was wounded for our sins and has been afflicted for our
iniquities. The chastisement of our peace is upon Him. With His
bruises we were healed.

1Clem 16:6
We all went astray like sheep, each man went astray in his own
path:

1Clem 16:7
and the Lord delivered Him over for our sins. And He opened not
His mouth, because He is afflicted. As a sheep He was led to
slaughter; and as a lamb before his shearer is dumb, so opened He
not His mouth. In His humiliation His judgment was taken away.

1Clem 16:8
His generation who shall declare? For His life is taken away from
the earth.

1Clem 16:9
For the iniquities of my people He is come to death.

1Clem 16:10
And I will give the wicked for His burial, and the rich for His
death; for He wrought no iniquity, neither was guile found in His
mouth. And the Lord desired to cleanse Him from His stripes.

1Clem 16:11

If you offer for sin, your soul shall see along lived seed.

1Clem 16:12
And the Lord desired to take away from the toil of His soul, to
show Him light and to mould Him with understanding, to justify a
Just One that is a good servant unto many. And He shall bear their
sins.

1Clem 16:13
Therefore He shall inherit many, and shall divide the spoils of the
strong; because His soul was delivered unto death, and He was
reckoned unto the transgressors;

1Clem 16:14
and He bare the sins of many, and for their sins was He delivered
up.

1Clem 16:15
And again He Himself said; But I am a worm and no man, a reproach
of men and an outcast of the people.

1Clem 16:16
All they that beheld me mocked at me; they spoke with their lips;
they wagged their heads, saying, He hoped on the Lord; let Him
deliver him, or let Him save him, for He desired him.

1Clem 16:17
you see, dearly beloved, what is the pattern that has been given unto
us; for, if the Lord was thus lowly of mind, what should we do, who
through Him have been brought under the yoke of His grace?

1Clem 17:1
   Let us be imitators also of them which went about in goatskins and
sheepskins, preaching the coming of Christ. We mean Elijah and Elisha
and likewise Ezekiel, the prophets, and besides them those men also
that obtained a good report.

1Clem 17:2
Abraham obtained an exceeding good report and was called the friend
of God; and looking steadfastly on the glory of God, he said in
lowliness of mind, But I am dust and ashes.

1Clem 17:3
Moreover concerning Job also it is thus written; And Job was
righteous and unblamable, one that was true and honored God and
abstained from all evil.

1Clem 17:4
Yet he himself accused himself saying, No man from filth; no, not
though his life be but for a day.

1Clem 17:5
Moses was called faithful in all His house, and through his
ministration God judged Egypt with the plagues and the torments which
befell them. Howbeit he also, though greatly glorified, yet spoke no
proud words, but said, when an oracle was given to him at the bush,
Who am I, that Thou send me?

1Clem 17:6

Nay, I am feeble of speech and slow of tongue. And again he said,
But I am smoke from the pot.

1Clem 18:1
    But what must we say of David that obtained a good report? of whom
God said, I have found a man after My heart, David the son of
Jesse: with eternal mercy have I anointed him.

1Clem 18:2
Yet he too said unto God Have mercy upon me, O God, according to
Your great mercy; and according to the multitude of Your compassions,
blot out mine iniquity.

1Clem 18:3
Wash me yet more from mine iniquity, and cleanse me from my sin.
For I acknowledge mine iniquity, and my sin is ever before me.
Against Thee only did I sin, and I wrought evil in Your sight; that
You may be justified in Your words, and may conquer in Your
pleading.

1Clem 18:4
For behold, in iniquities was I conceived, and in sins did my
mother bear me. For behold You hast loved truth: the dark and
hidden things of Your wisdom hast You showed unto me.

1Clem 18:5
You shall sprinkle me with hyssop, and I shall be made clean. You
shall wash me, and I shall become whiter than snow.

1Clem 18:6
You shall make me to hear of joy and gladness. The bones which
have been humbled shall rejoice.

1Clem 18:7
Turn away Your face from my sins, and blot out all mine iniquities.

1Clem 18:8
Make a clean heart within me, O God, and renew a right spirit in
mine inmost parts. Cast me not away from Your presence, and take not
Your Holy Spirit from me.

1Clem 18:9
Restore unto me the joy of Your salvation, and strengthen me with a
princely spirit.

1Clem 18:10
I will teach sinners Your ways, and godless men shall be converted
unto Thee.

1Clem 18:11
Deliver me from blood guiltiness, O God, the God of my salvation.
My tongue shall rejoice in Your righteousness.

1Clem 18:12
Lord, You shall open my mouth, and my lips shall declare Your
praise.

1Clem 18:13
For, if You had desired sacrifice, I would have given it: in

whole burnt offerings You wilt have no pleasure.

1Clem 18:14
A sacrifice unto God is a contrite spirit; a contrite and humbled
heart God will not despise.

1Clem 19:1
   The humility therefore and the submissiveness of so many and so
great men, who have thus obtained a good report, has through
obedience made better not only us but also the generations which were
before us, even them that received His oracles in fear and truth.

1Clem 19:2
Seeing then that we have been partakers of many great and glorious
doings, let us hasten to return unto the goal of peace which has
been handed down to us from the beginning, and let us look ·
steadfastly unto the Father and Maker of the whole world, and hold fast
unto His splendid and excellent gifts of peace and benefits.

1Clem 19:3
Let us behold Him in our mind, and let us look with the eyes of our
soul unto His long-suffering will. Let us note how free from anger He
is towards all His creatures.

1Clem 20:1
   The heavens are moved by His direction and obey Him in peace.

1Clem 20:2
Day and night accomplish the course assigned to them by Him, without
hindrance one to another.

1Clem 20:3
The sun and the moon and the dancing stars according to His
appointment circle in harmony within the bounds assigned to them,
without any swerving aside.

1Clem 20:4
The earth, bearing fruit in fulfillment of His will at her proper
seasons, puts forth the food that supplies abundantly both men
and beasts and all living things which are thereupon, making no
dissension, neither altering anything which He has decreed.

1Clem 20:5
Moreover, the inscrutable depths of the abysses and the unutterable
statutes of the nether regions are constrained by the same
ordinances.

1Clem 20:6
The basin of the boundless sea, gathered together by His workmanship
into it's reservoirs, passes not the barriers wherewith it is
surrounded; but even as He ordered it, so it doeth.

1Clem 20:7
For He said, So far shall you come, and thy waves shall be broken
within you.

1Clem 20:8
The ocean which is impassable for men, and the worlds beyond it, are
directed by the same ordinances of the Master.

1Clem 20:9
The seasons of spring and summer and autumn and winter give way in
succession one to another in peace.

1Clem 20:10
The winds in their several quarters at their proper season fulfill
their ministry without disturbance; and the ever flowing fountains,
created for enjoyment and health, without fail give their breasts
which sustain the life for men. Yea, the smallest of living things
come together in concord and peace.

1Clem 20:11
All these things the great Creator and Master of the universe ordered
to be in peace and concord, doing good unto all things, but far
beyond the rest unto us who have taken refuge in His compassionate
mercies through our Lord Jesus Christ,

1Clem 20:12
to whom be the glory and the majesty for ever and ever. Amen.

1Clem 21:1
   Look you, brethren, lest His benefits, which are many, turn unto
judgment to all of us, if we walk not worthily of Him, and do those
things which are good and well pleasing in His sight with concord.

1Clem 21:2
For He said in a certain place, The Spirit of the Lord is a lamp
searching the closets of the belly.

1Clem 21:3
Let us see how near He is, and how that nothing escapes Him of our
thoughts or our devices which we make.

1Clem 21:4
It is right therefore that we should not be deserters from His will.

1Clem 21:5
Let us rather give offense to foolish and senseless men who exalt
themselves and boast in the arrogance of their words, than to God.

1Clem 21:6
Let us fear the Lord Jesus [Christ], whose blood was given for us.
Let us reverence our rulers; let us honor our elders; let us instruct
our young men in the lesson of the fear of God. Let us guide our
women toward that which is good:

1Clem 21:7
let them show forth their lovely disposition of purity; let them
prove their sincere affection of gentleness; let them make manifest
the moderation of their tongue through their silence; let them show
their love, not in factious preferences but without partiality
towards all them that fear God, in holiness. Let our children be
partakers of the instruction which is in Christ:

1Clem 21:8
let them learn how lowliness of mind prevailed with God, what power
chaste love has with God, how the fear of Him is good and great and
saved all them that walk therein in a pure mind with holiness.

1Clem 21:9
For He is the searcher out of the intents and desires; whose breath
is in us, and when He listed, He shall take it away.

1Clem 22:1
   Now all these things the faith which is in Christ confirmed: for He
Himself through the Holy Spirit thus invite thus: Come, my
children, hearken unto Me, I will teach you the fear of the Lord.

1Clem 22:2
What man is he that desired life and loved to see good days?

1Clem 22:3
Make thy tongue to cease from evil, and thy lips that they speak no
guile.

1Clem 22:4
Turn aside from evil and do good.

1Clem 22:5
Seek peace and ensue it.

1Clem 22:6
The eyes of the Lord are over the righteous, and His ears are
turned to their prayers. But the face of the Lord is upon them that
do evil, to destroy their memorial from the earth.

1Clem 22:7
The righteous cried out, and the Lord heard him, and delivered him
from all his troubles. Many are the troubles of the righteous, and
the Lord shall deliver him from them all.

1Clem 22:8
And again Many are the stripes of the sinner, but them that set
their hope on the Lord mercy shall compass about.

1Clem 23:1
   The Father, who is pitiful in all things, and ready to do good, has
compassion on them that fear Him, and kindly and lovingly bestowed
His favors on them that draw nigh unto Him with a single mind.

1Clem 23:2
Therefore let us not be double-minded, neither let our soul indulge in
idle humors respecting His exceeding and glorious gifts.

1Clem 23:3
Let this scripture be far from us where He said Wretched are the
double-minded, Which doubt in their soul and say, These things we
did hear in the days of our fathers also, and behold we have grown
old, and none of these things has befallen us.

1Clem 23:4
you fools, compare yourselves unto a tree; take a vine. First it
sheds its leaves, then a shoot cometh, then a leaf, then a
flower, and after these a sour berry, then a full ripe grape. you
see that in a little time the fruit of the tree attained unto
mellowness.

1Clem 23:5
Of a truth quickly and suddenly shall His will be accomplished, the
scripture also bearing witness to it, saying He shall come quickly
and shall not tarry; and the Lord shall come suddenly into His
temple, even the Holy One, whom you expect.

1Clem 24:1
   Let us understand, dearly beloved, how the Master continually
showed unto us the resurrection that shall be hereafter; whereof He
made the Lord Jesus Christ the firstfruit, when He raised Him from
the dead.

1Clem 24:2
Let us behold, dearly beloved, the resurrection which happened at
its proper season.

1Clem 24:3
Day and night show unto us the resurrection. The night fell
asleep, and day arose; the day departed, and night cometh on.

1Clem 24:4
Let us mark the fruits, how and in what manner the sowing took
place.

1Clem 24:5
The sower went forth and casted into the earth each of the
seeds; and these falling into the earth dry and bare decay: then out
of their decay the mightiness of the Master's providence raised them
up, and from being one they increase manifold and bear fruit.

1Clem 25:1
   Let us consider the marvelous sign which is seen in the regions of
the east, that is, in the parts about Arabia.

1Clem 25:2
There is a bird, which is named the phoenix. This, being the only
one of its kind, lived for five hundred years; and when it has now
reached the time of its dissolution that it should die, it made for
itself a coffin of frankincense and myrrh and the other spices, into
the which in the fullness of time it entered, and so it died.

1Clem 25:3
But, as the flesh rotted, a certain worm is engendered, which is
nurtured from the moisture of the dead creature and put forth
wings. Then, when it is grown lusty, it took up that coffin where
are the bones of its parent, and carrying them journeyed from the
country of Arabia even unto Egypt, to the place called the City of
the Sun;

1Clem 25:4
and in the daytime in the sight of all, flying to the altar of the
Sun, it bathed them thereupon; and this done, it set forth to
return.

1Clem 25:5
So the priests examine the registers of the times, and they find that
it has come when the five hundredth year is completed.

1Clem 26:1

Do we then think it to be a great and marvelous thing, if the
Creator of the universe shall bring about the resurrection of them
that have served Him with holiness in the assurance of a good faith,
seeing that He showed to us even by a bird the magnificence of His
promise?

1Clem 26:2
For He said in a certain place And You shall raise me up, and I
will praise Thee; and; I went to rest and slept, I was awaked,
for You art with me.

1Clem 26:3
And again Job said And You shall raise this my flesh which has
endured all these things.

1Clem 27:1
   With this hope therefore let our souls be bound unto Him that is
faithful in His promises and that is righteous in His judgments.

1Clem 27:2
He that commanded not to lie, much more shall He Himself not lie:
for nothing is impossible with God save to lie.

1Clem 27:3
Therefore let our faith in Him be kindled within us, and let us
understand that all things are nigh unto Him.

1Clem 27:4
By a word of His majesty He compacted the universe; and by a word He
can destroy it.

1Clem 27:5
Who shall say unto Him, What hast you done? or who shall resist
the might of His strength? When He listeth, and as He listeth, He
will do all things; and nothing shall pass away of those things that
He has decreed.

1Clem 27:6
All things are in His sight, and nothing escaped His counsel,

1Clem 27:7
seeing that The heavens declare the glory of God, and the firmament
proclaimed His handiwork. Day uttered word unto day, and night
proclaimed knowledge unto night; and there are neither words nor
speeches, whose voices are not heard.

1Clem 28:1
   Since therefore all things are seen and heard, let us fear Him and
forsake the abominable lusts of evil works, that we maybe shielded by
His mercy from the coming judgments.

1Clem 28:2
For where can any of us escape from His strong hand? And what world
will receive any of them that desert from His service?

1Clem 28:3
For the holy writing said in a certain place Where shall I go, and
where shall I be hidden from Your face? If I ascend into the heaven,
You art there; if I depart into the farthest parts of the earth,

there is Your right hand; if I make my bed in the depths, there is
Your Spirit.

1Clem 28:4
Whither then shall one depart, or where shall one flee, from Him that
embraced the universe?

1Clem 29:1
   Let us therefore approach Him in holiness of soul, lifting up pure
and undefiled hands unto Him, with love towards our gentle and
compassionate Father who made us an elect portion unto Himself.

1Clem 29:2
For
thus it is written: When the Most High divided the nations, when He
dispersed the sons of Adam, He fixed the boundaries of the nations
according to the number of the angels of God. His people Jacob
became the portion of the Lord, and Israel the measurement of His
inheritance.

1Clem 29:3
And in another place He said, Behold, the Lord took for Himself
a nation out of the midst of the nations, as a man took the first
fruits of his threshing floor; and the holy of holies shall come
forth from that nation.

1Clem 30:1
   Seeing then that we are the special portion of a Holy God, let us do
all things that pertain unto holiness, forsaking evil speakings,
abominable and impure embraces, drunkennesses and tumults and hateful
lusts, abominable adultery, hateful pride.

1Clem 30:2
For God, He said, resisted the proud, but gave grace to the
lowly.

1Clem 30:3
Let us therefore hold fast unto those to whom grace is given from God.
Let us clothe ourselves in concord, being lowly-minded and temperate,
holding ourselves aloof from all back biting and evil speaking, being
justified by works and not by words.

1Clem 30:4
For He said, He that said much shall hear also again. Doth the
ready talker think to be righteous?

1Clem 30:5
Blessed is the offspring of a woman that lived but a short time.
Be not you abundant in words.

1Clem 30:6
Let our praise be with God, and not of ourselves: for God hated
them that praise themselves.

1Clem 30:7
Let the testimony to our well doing be given by others, as it was
given unto our fathers who were righteous.

1Clem 30:8

Boldness and arrogance and daring are for them that are accursed of
God; but forbearance and humility and gentleness are with them that
are blessed of God.

1Clem 31:1
Let us therefore hold fast unto His blessing, and let us see what are
the ways of blessing. Let us study the records of the things that
have happened from the beginning.

1Clem 31:2
Wherefore was our father Abraham blessed? Was it not because he
wrought righteousness and truth through faith?

1Clem 31:3
Isaac with confidence, as knowing the future, was led a willing
sacrifice.

1Clem 31:4
Jacob with humility departed from his land because of his brother,
and went unto Laban and served; and the twelve tribes of Israel were
given unto him.

1Clem 32:1
If any man will consider them one by one in sincerity, he shall
understand the magnificence of the gifts that are given by Him.

1Clem 32:2
For of Jacob are all the priests and Levites who minister unto the
altar of God; of him is the Lord Jesus as concerning the flesh; of
him are kings and rulers and governors in the line of Judah; yea and
the rest of his tribes are held in no small honor, seeing that God
promised saying, Your seed shall be as the stars of heaven.

1Clem 32:3
They all therefore were glorified and magnified, not through
themselves or their own works or the righteous doing which they
wrought, but through His will.

1Clem 32:4
And so we, having been called through His will in Christ Jesus, are
not justified through ourselves or through our own wisdom or
understanding or piety or works which we wrought in holiness of
heart, but through faith, whereby the Almighty God justified all men
that have been from the beginning; to whom be the glory for ever and
ever. Amen.

1Clem 33:1
What then must we do, brethren? Must we idly abstain from doing
good, and forsake love? May the Master never allow this to befall us
at least; but let us hasten with urgency and zeal to accomplish
every good work.

1Clem 33:2
For the Creator and Master of the universe Himself rejoiced in His
works.

1Clem 33:3
For by His exceeding great might He established the heavens, and in
His incomprehensible wisdom He set them in order. And the earth He

separated from the water that surrounded it, and He set it firm on
the sure foundation of His own will; and the living creatures which
walk upon it He commanded to exist by His ordinance. Having before
created the sea and the living creatures therein, He enclosed it by
His own power.

1Clem 33:4
Above all, as the most excellent and exceeding great work of His
intelligence, with His sacred and faultless hands He formed man in
the impress of His own image.

1Clem 33:5
For thus said God Let us make man after our image and after our
likeness. And God made man; male and female made He them.

1Clem 33:6
So having finished all these things, He praised them and blessed them
and said, Increase and multiply.

1Clem 33:7
We have seen that all the righteous were adorned in good works. Yea,
and the Lord Himself having adorned Himself with worlds rejoiced.

1Clem 33:8
Seeing then that we have this pattern, let us conform ourselves with
all diligence to His will; let us with all our strength work the work
of righteousness.

1Clem 34:1
   The good workman received the bread of his work with boldness, but
the slothful and careless dared not look his employer in the face.

1Clem 34:2
It is therefore needful that we should be zealous unto well doing,
for of Him are all things:

1Clem 34:3
since He forewarned us saying, Behold, the Lord, and His reward is
before His face, to recompense each man according to his work.

1Clem 34:4
He exhorted us therefore to believe on Him with our whole heart, and
to be not idle nor careless unto every good work.

1Clem 34:5
Let our boast and our confidence be in Him: let us submit ourselves
to His will; let us mark the whole host of His angels, how they stand
by and minister unto His will.

1Clem 34:6
For the scripture said, Ten thousands of ten thousands stood by
Him, and thousands of thousands ministered unto Him: and they cried
aloud, Holy, holy, holy is the Lord of Sabaoth; all creation is
full of His glory.

1Clem 34:7
Yea, and let us ourselves then, being gathered together in concord
with intentness of heart, cry unto Him as from one mouth earnestly
that we may be made partakers of His great and glorious promises.

1Clem 34:8
For He said, Eye has not seen and ear has not heard, and it has
not entered into the heart of man what great things He has
prepared for them that patiently await Him.

1Clem 35:1
  How blessed and marvelous are the gifts of God, dearly beloved!!

1Clem 35:2
Life in immortality, splendor in righteousness, truth in boldness,
faith in confidence, temperance in sanctification! And all these
things fall under our apprehension.

1Clem 35:3
What then, think you, are the things preparing for them that patiently
await Him? The Creator and Father of the ages, the All holy One
Himself knew their number and their beauty.

1Clem 35:4
Let us therefore contend, that we may be found in the number of those
that patiently await Him, to the end that we may be partakers of His
promised gifts.

1Clem 35:5
But how shall this be, dearly beloved? If our mind be fixed through
faith towards God; if we seek out those things which are well
pleasing and acceptable unto Him; if we accomplish such things as
beseem His faultless will, and follow the way of truth, casting off
from ourselves all unrighteousness and iniquity, covetousness,
strifes, malignity and deceits, whisperings and backbitings, hatred
of God, pride and arrogance, vainglory and inhospitality.

1Clem 35:6
For they that do these things are hateful to God; and not only they
that do them, but they also that consent unto them.

1Clem 35:7
For the scripture said, But unto the sinner said God, Wherefore
do you declare Mine ordinances, and take My covenant upon thy
lips?

1Clem 35:8
Yet You didst hate instruction and didst cast away My words behind
you. If you saw a thief you didst keep company with him, and
with the adulterers you didst set thy portion. Your mouth
multiplied wickedness and thy tongue wove deceit. You sat and
spoke against thy brother, and against the son of thy mother you
didst lay a stumbling block.

1Clem 35:9
These things You hast done, and I kept silence. You thought
unrighteous man, that I should be like unto you.

1Clem 35:10
I will convict you and will set you face to face with thyself.

1Clem 35:11
Now understand you these things, you that forget God, lest at any

time He seize you as a lion, and there be none to deliver.

1Clem 35:12
The sacrifice of praise shall glorify Me, and there is the way
wherein I will show him the salvation of God.

1Clem 36:1
    This is the way, dearly beloved, wherein we found our salvation,
even Jesus Christ the High priest of our offerings, the Guardian and
Helper of our weakness.

1Clem 36:2
Through Him let us look steadfastly unto the heights of the heavens;
through Him we behold as in a mirror His faultless and most excellent
visage; through Him the eyes of our hearts were opened; through Him
our foolish and darkened mind sprung up unto the light; through
Him the Master willed that we should taste of the immortal knowledge
Who being the brightness of His majesty is so much greater than
angels, as He has inherited a more excellent name.

1Clem 36:3
For so it is written Who made His angels spirits and His
ministers aflame of fire

1Clem 36:4
but of His Son the Master said thus, You art My Son, I this day
have begotten you. Ask of Me, and I will give Thee the Gentiles
for Your inheritance, and the ends of the earth for Your
possession.

1Clem 36:5
And again He said unto Him Sit You on My right hand, until I make
Your enemies a footstool for Your feet.

1Clem 36:6
Who then are these enemies? They that are wicked and resist His
will.

1Clem 37:1
    Let us therefore enlist ourselves, brethren, with all earnestness in
His faultless ordinances.

1Clem 37:2
Let us mark the soldiers that are enlisted under our rulers, how
exactly, how readily, how submissively, they execute the orders given
them.

1Clem 37:3
All are not prefects, nor rulers of thousands, nor rulers of
hundreds, nor rulers of fifties, and so forth; but each man in his
own rank executed the orders given by the king and the governors.

1Clem 37:4
The great without the small cannot exist, neither the small without
the great. There is a certain mixture in all things, and therein is
utility.

1Clem 37:5
Let us take our body as an example. The head without the feet is

771

nothing; so likewise the feet without the head are nothing: even the
smallest limbs of our body are necessary and useful for the whole
body: but all the members conspire and unite in subjection, that the
whole body maybe saved.

1Clem 38:1
  So in our case let the whole body be saved in Christ Jesus, and let
each man be subject unto his neighbor, according as also he was
appointed with his special grace.

1Clem 38:2
Let not the strong neglect the weak; and let the weak respect the
strong. Let the rich minister aid to the poor; and let the poor give
thanks to God, because He has given him one through whom his wants
may be supplied. Let the wise display his wisdom, not in words, but
in good works. He that is lowly in mind, let him not bear testimony
to himself, but leave testimony to be borne to him by his neighbor.
He that is pure in the flesh, let him be so, and not boast, knowing
that it is Another who bestowed his continence upon him.

1Clem 38:3
Let us consider, brethren, of what matter we were made; who and what
manner of beings we were, when we came into the world; from what a
sepulchre and what darkness He that molded and created us brought us
into His world, having prepared His benefits aforehand ere ever we
were born.

1Clem 38:4
Seeing therefore that we have all these things from Him, we ought in
all things to give thanks to Him, to whom be the glory for ever and
ever. Amen.

1Clem 39:1
  Senseless and stupid and foolish and ignorant men jeer and mock at
us, desiring that they themselves should be exalted in their
imaginations.

1Clem 39:2
For what power has a mortal? or what strength has a child of earth?

1Clem 39:3
For it is written; There was no form before mine eyes; only I heard
a breath and a voice.

1Clem 39:4
What then? Shall a mortal be clean in the sight of the Lord; or
shall a man be unblamable for his works? seeing that He is
distrustful against His servants and noted some perversity against
His angels.

1Clem 39:5
Nay, the heaven is not clean in His sight. Away then, you that dwell
in houses of clay, whereof, even of the same clay, we ourselves are
made. He smote them like a moth, and from morn to even they are no
more. Because they could not succor themselves, they perished.

1Clem 39:6
He breathed on them and they died, because they had no wisdom.

1Clem 39:7
But call you, if perchance one shall obey you, or if you shall
see one of the holy angels. For wrath killed the foolish man, and
envy slayed him that has gone astray.

1Clem 39:8
And I have seen fools throwing out roots, but forthwith their
habitation was eaten up.

1Clem 39:9
Far be their sons from safety. May they be mocked at the gates of
inferiors, and there shall be none to deliver them. For the things
which are prepared for them, the righteous shall eat; but they
themselves shall not be delivered from evils.

1Clem 40:1
   Forasmuch then as these things are manifest beforehand, and we have
searched into the depths of the Divine knowledge, we ought to do all
things in order, as many as the Master has commanded us to perform
at their appointed seasons.

1Clem 40:2
Now the offerings and ministrations He commanded to be performed with
care, and not to be done rashly or in disorder, but at fixed times
and seasons.

1Clem 40:3
And where and by whom He would have them performed, He Himself fixed
by His supreme will: that all things being done with piety according
to His good pleasure might be acceptable to His will.

1Clem 40:4
They therefore that make their offerings at the appointed seasons are
acceptable and blessed: for while they follow the institutions of
the Master they cannot go wrong.

1Clem 40:5
For unto the high priest his proper services have been assigned, and
to the priests their proper office is appointed, and upon the Levites
their proper ministrations are laid. The layman is bound by the
layman's ordinances.

1Clem 41:1
   Let each of you, brethren, in his own order give thanks unto God,
maintaining a good conscience and not transgressing the appointed
rule of his service, but acting with all seemliness.

1Clem 41:2
Not in every place, brethren, are the continual daily sacrifices
offered, or the freewill offerings, or the sin offerings and the
trespass offerings, but in Jerusalem alone. And even there the
offering is not made in every place, but before the sanctuary in the
court of the altar; and this too through the high priest and the afore
said ministers, after that the victim to be offered has been
inspected for blemishes.

1Clem 41:3
They therefore who do any thing contrary to the seemly ordinance of
His will receive death as the penalty.

1Clem 41:4
you see, brethren, in proportion as greater knowledge has been
vouchsafed unto us, so much the more are we exposed to danger.

1Clem 42:1
   The Apostles received the Gospel for us from the Lord Jesus
Christ; Jesus Christ was sent forth from God.

1Clem 42:2
So then Christ is from God, and the Apostles are from Christ. Both
therefore came of the will of God in the appointed order.

1Clem 42:3
Having therefore received a charge, and having been fully assured
through the resurrection of our Lord Jesus Christ and confirmed in
the word of God with full assurance of the Holy Ghost, they went
forth with the glad tidings that the kingdom of God should come.

1Clem 42:4
So preaching everywhere in country and town, they appointed their
firstfruits, when they had proved them by the Spirit, to be bishops
and deacons unto them that should believe.

1Clem 42:5
And this they did in no new fashion; for indeed it had been written
concerning bishops and deacons from very ancient times; for thus
said the scripture in a certain place, I will appoint their
bishops in righteousness and their deacons in faith.

1Clem 43:1
   And what marvel, if they which were entrusted in Christ with such a
work by God appointed the aforesaid persons? seeing that even the
blessed Moses who was a faithful servant in all His house recorded
for a sign in the sacred books all things that were enjoined upon
him. And him also the rest of the prophets followed, bearing witness
with him unto the laws that were ordained by him.

1Clem 43:2
For he, when jealousy arose concerning the priesthood, and there was
dissension among the tribes which of them was adorned with the
glorious name, commanded the twelve chiefs of the tribes to bring to
him rods inscribed with the name of each tribe. And he took them and
tied them and sealed them with the signet rings of the chiefs of the
tribes, and put them away in the tabernacle of the testimony on the
table of God.

1Clem 43:3
And having shut the tabernacle he sealed the keys and likewise also
the doors.

1Clem 43:4
And he said unto them, Brethren, the tribe whose rod shall bud, this
has God chosen to be priests and ministers unto Him.

1Clem 43:5
Now when morning came, he called together all Israel, even the six
hundred thousand men, and showed the seals to the chiefs of the
tribes and opened the tabernacle of the testimony and drew forth the

rods. And the rod of Aaron was found not only with buds, but also bearing fruit.

1Clem 43:6
What think you, dearly beloved? Did not Moses know beforehand that this would come to pass? Assuredly he knew it. But that disorder might not arise in Israel, he did thus, to the end that the Name of the true and only God might be glorified: to whom he the glory for ever and ever. Amen...

1Clem 44:1
And our Apostles knew through our Lord Jesus Christ that there would be strife over the name of the bishop's office.

1Clem 44:2
For this cause therefore, having received complete foreknowledge, they appointed the aforesaid persons, and afterwards they provided a continuance, that if these should fall asleep, other approved men should succeed to their ministration. Those therefore who were appointed by them, or afterward by other men of repute with the consent of the whole Church, and have ministered unblamably to the flock of Christ in lowliness of mind, peacefully and with all modesty, and for long time have borne a good report with all these men we consider to be unjustly thrust out from their ministration.

1Clem 44:3
For it will be no light sin for us, if we thrust out those who have offered the gifts of the bishop's office unblamably and holily.

1Clem 44:4
Blessed are those presbyters who have gone before, seeing that their departure was fruitful and ripe: for they have no fear lest any one should remove them from their appointed place.

1Clem 44:5
For we see that you have displaced certain persons, though they were living honorably, from the ministration which had been respected by them blamelessly.

1Clem 45:1
Be you contentious, brethren, and jealous about the things that pertain unto salvation.

1Clem 45:2
you have searched the scriptures, which are true, which were given through the Holy Ghost;

1Clem 45:3
and you know that nothing unrighteous or counterfeit is written in them. you will not find that righteous persons have been thrust out by holy men.

1Clem 45:4
Righteous men were persecuted, but it was by the lawless; they were imprisoned, but it was by the unholy. They were stoned by transgressors: they were slain by those who had conceived a detestable and unrighteous jealousy.

1Clem 45:5

Suffering these things, they endured nobly.

1Clem 45:6
For what must we say, brethren? Was Daniel cast into the lions' den
by them that feared God?

1Clem 45:7
Or were Ananias and Azarias and Misael shut up in the furnace of fire
by them that professed the excellent and glorious worship of the Most
High? Far be this from our thoughts. Who then were they that did
these things? Abominable men and full of all wickedness were stirred
up to such a pitch of wrath, as to bring cruel suffering upon them
that served God in a holy and blameless purpose, not knowing that the
Most High is the champion and protector of them that in a pure
conscience serve His excellent Name: unto whom be the glory for ever
and ever. Amen.

1Clem 45:8
But they that endured patiently in confidence
inherited glory and honor; they were exalted, and had their names
recorded by God in their memorial for ever and ever. Amen.

1Clem 46:1
   To such examples as these therefore, brethren, we also ought to
hold fast.

1Clem 46:2
For it is written; Hold fast unto the saints, for they that hold fast
unto them shall be sanctified.

1Clem 46:3
And again He said in another place; With the guiltless man you
shall be guiltless, and with the elect you shall be elect, and
with the crooked you shall deal crookedly.

1Clem 46:4
Let us therefore hold fast to the guiltless and righteous: and these
are the elect of God.

1Clem 46:5
Wherefore are there strifes and wraths and factions and divisions and
war among you?

1Clem 46:6
Have we not one God and one Christ and one Spirit of grace that was
shed upon us? And is there not one calling in Christ?

1Clem 46:7
Wherefore do we tear and rend asunder the members of Christ, and stir
up factions against our own body, and reach such a pitch of folly, as
to forget that we are members one of another?

1Clem 46:8
Remember the words of Jesus our Lord: for He said, Woe unto that
man; it were good for him if he had not been born, rather than that
at he should offend one of Mine elect. It were better for him that
a millstone were hanged about him, and be cast into the sea, than
that he should pervert one of Mine elect.

1Clem 46:9
Your division has perverted many; it has brought many to despair,
many to doubting, and all of us to sorrow. And your sedition still
continued.

1Clem 47:1
    Take up the epistle of the blessed Paul the Apostle.

1Clem 47:2
What wrote he first unto you in the beginning of the Gospel?

1Clem 47:3
Of a truth he charged you in the Spirit concerning himself and Cephas
and Apollos, because that even then you had made parties.

1Clem 47:4
Yet that making of parties brought less sin upon you; for you were
partisans of Apostles that were highly reputed, and of a man approved
in their sight.

1Clem 47:5
But now mark you, who they are that have perverted you and diminished
the glory of your renowned love for the brotherhood.

1Clem 47:6
It is shameful, dearly beloved, yes, utterly shameful and unworthy of
your conduct in Christ, that it should be reported that the very
steadfast and ancient Church of the Corinthians, for the sake of one
or two persons, made sedition against its presbyters.

1Clem 47:7
And this report has reached not only us, but them also which differ
from us, so that you even heap blasphemies on the Name of the Lord by
reason of your folly, and moreover create peril for yourselves.

1Clem 48:1
    Let us therefore root this out quickly, and let us fall down before
the Master and entreat Him with tears, that He may show Himself
propitious and be reconciled unto us, and may restore us to the
seemly and pure conduct which belonged to our love of the brethren.

1Clem 48:2
For this is a gate of righteousness opened unto life, as it is
written; Open me the gates of righteousness, that I may enter in
thereby and preach the Lord.

1Clem 48:3
This is the gate of the Lord; the righteous shall enter in
thereby.

1Clem 48:4
Seeing then that many gates are opened, this is that gate which is in
righteousness, even that which is in Christ, whereby all are blessed
that have entered in and direct their path in holiness and
righteousness, performing all things without confusion.

1Clem 48:5
Let a man be faithful, let him be able to expound a deep saying, let
him be wise in the discernment of words, let him be strenuous in

deeds, let him be pure;

1Clem 48:6
for so much the more ought he to be lowly in mind, in proportion as
he seemed to be the greater; and he ought to seek the common
advantage of all, and not his own.

1Clem 49:1
  Let him that has love in Christ fulfill the commandments of Christ.

1Clem 49:2
Who can declare the bond of the love of God?

1Clem 49:3
Who is sufficient to tell the majesty of its beauty?

1Clem 49:4
The height, where unto love exalted, is unspeakable.

1Clem 49:5
Love joined us unto God; love covered a multitude of sins; love
endured all things, is long-suffering in all things. There is
nothing coarse, nothing arrogant in love. Love has no divisions,
love made no seditions, love doeth all things in concord. In love
were all the elect of God made perfect; without love nothing is well
pleasing to God:

1Clem 49:6
in love the Master took us unto Himself; for the
love which He had toward us, Jesus Christ our Lord has given His
blood for us by the will of God, and His flesh for our flesh and His
life for our lives.

1Clem 50:1
  you see, dearly beloved, how great and marvelous a thing is love, and
there is no declaring its perfection.

1Clem 50:2
Who is sufficient to be found therein, save those to whom God shall
vouchsafe it? Let us therefore entreat and ask of His mercy, that we
may be found blameless in love, standing apart from the factiousness
of men. All the generations from Adam unto this day have passed
away: but they that by God's grace were perfected in love dwell in
the abode of the pious; and they shall be made manifest in the
visitation of the Kingdom of God.

1Clem 50:3
For it is written; Enter into the closet for a very little while
until Mine anger and Mine wrath shall pass away, and I will
remember a good day and will raise you from your tombs.

1Clem 50:4
Blessed were we, dearly beloved, if we should be doing the
commandments of God in concord of love, to the end that our sins may
through love be forgiven us.

1Clem 50:5
For it is written; Blessed are they whose iniquities are forgiven,
and whose sins are covered. Blessed is the man to whom the Lord

shall impute no sin, neither is guile in his mouth.

1Clem 50:6
This declaration of blessedness was pronounced upon them that have
been elected by God through Jesus Christ our Lord, to whom be the
glory for ever and ever. Amen.

1Clem 51:1
For all our transgressions which we have committed through any of
the wiles of the adversary, let us entreat that we may obtain
forgiveness. Yea and they also, who set themselves up as leaders of
faction and division, ought to look to the common ground of hope.

1Clem 51:2
For such as walk in fear and love desire that they themselves should
fall into suffering rather than their neighbors; and they pronounce
condemnation against themselves rather than against the harmony which
has been handed down to us nobly and righteously.

1Clem 51:3
For it is good for a man to make confession of his trespasses rather
than to harden his heart, as the heart of those was hardened who made
sedition against Moses the servant of God; whose condemnation was
clearly manifest,

1Clem 51:4
for they went down to hades alive, and Death shall be their
shepherd.

1Clem 51:5
Pharaoh and his host and all the rulers of Egypt, their chariots
and their horsemen, were overwhelmed in the depths of the Red Sea,
and perished for none other reason but because their foolish hearts
were hardened after that the signs and the wonders had been wrought
in the land of Egypt by the hand of Moses the servant of God.

1Clem 52:1
The Master, brethren, has need of nothing at all. He desired not
anything of any man, save to confess unto Him.

1Clem 52:2
For the elect David said; I will confess unto the Lord, and it
shall please Him more than a young calf that grew horns and
hoofs. Let the poor see it, and rejoice.

1Clem 52:3
And again He said; Sacrifice to God a sacrifice of praise, and pay
thy vows to the Most High: and call upon Me in the day of your
affliction, and I will deliver you, and you shall glorify Me.

1Clem 52:4
For a sacrifice unto God is a broken spirit.

1Clem 53:1
For you know, and know well, the sacred scriptures, dearly beloved,
and you have searched into the oracles of God. We write these things
therefore to put you in remembrance.

1Clem 53:2

When Moses went up into the mountain and had spent forty days and forty nights in fasting and humiliation, God said unto him; Moses, Moses, come down , quickly hence, for My people whom you lead forth from the land of Egypt have wrought iniquity: they have transgressed quickly out of the way which you didst command unto them: they have made for themselves molten images.

1Clem 53:3
And the Lord said unto him; I have spoken unto you once and twice, saying, I have seen this people, and behold it is stiff-necked. Let Me destroy them utterly, and I will blot out their name from under heaven, and I will make of you a nation great and wonderful and numerous more than this.

1Clem 53:4
And Moses said; Nay, not so, Lord Forgive this people their sin, or blot me also out of the book of the living.

1Clem 53:5
O mighty love! O unsurpassable perfection! The servant is bold with his Master; he asked forgiveness for the multitude, or he demanded that himself also be blotted out with them.

1Clem 54:1
   Who therefore is noble among you? Who is compassionate? Who is fulfilled with love?

1Clem 54:2
Let him say; If by reason of me there be faction and strife and divisions, I retire, I depart, whither you will, and I do that which is ordered by the people: only let the flock of Christ be at peace with its duly appointed presbyters.

1Clem 54:3
He that shall have done this, shall win for himself great renown in Christ, and every place will receive him: for the earth is the Lord's and the fullness thereof.

1Clem 54:4
Thus have they done and will do, that live as citizens of that kingdom of God which brings no regrets.

1Clem 55:1
   But, to bring forward examples of Gentiles also; many kings and rulers, when some season of pestilence pressed upon them, being taught by oracles have delivered themselves over to death, that they might rescue their fellow citizens through their own blood. Many have retired from their own cities, that they might have no more seditions.

1Clem 55:2
We know that many among ourselves have delivered themselves to bondage, that they might ransom others. Many have sold themselves to slavery, and receiving the price paid for themselves have fed others.

1Clem 55:3
Many women being strengthened through the grace of God have performed many manly deeds.

1Clem 55:4
The blessed Judith, when the city was beleaguered, asked of the
elders that she might be suffered to go forth into the camp of the
aliens.

1Clem 55:5
So she exposed herself to peril and went forth for love of her
country and of her people which were beleaguered; and the Lord
delivered Holophernes into the hand of a woman.

1Clem 55:6
To no less peril did Esther also, who was perfect in faith, expose
herself, that she might deliver the twelve tribes of Israel, when
they were on the point to perish. For through her fasting and her
humiliation she entreated the all seeing Master, the God of the
ages; and He, seeing the humility of her soul, delivered the people
for whose sake she encountered the peril.

1Clem 56:1
    Therefore let us also make intercession for them that are in any
transgression, that forbearance and humility may be given them, to
the end that they may yield not unto us, but unto the will of God.
For so shall the compassionate remembrance of them with God and the
saints be fruitful unto them, and perfect.

1Clem 56:2
Let us accept chastisement, whereat no man ought to be vexed, dearly
beloved. The admonition which we give one to another is good and
exceeding useful; for it joined us unto the will of God.

1Clem 56:3
For thus said the holy word; The Lord has indeed chastened me,
and has not delivered me over unto death.

1Clem 56:4
For whom the Lord loved He chastened, and scourged every son
whom He received.

1Clem 56:5
For the righteous, it is said, shall chasten me in mercy and
shall reprove me, but let not the mercy of sinners anoint my head.

1Clem 56:6
And again He said; Blessed is the man whom the Lord has reproved,
and refuse not you the admonition of the Almighty. For He caused
pain, and he restored again:

1Clem 56:7
He has smitten, and His hands have healed.

1Clem 56:8
Six times shall He rescue you from afflictions and at the seventh
no evil shall touch you.

1Clem 56:9
In famine he shall deliver you from death, and in war He shall
release you from the arm of the sword.

1Clem 56:10

And from the scourge of the tongue He shall hide you and you
shall not be afraid when evils approach.

1Clem 56:11
You shall laugh at the unrighteous and wicked, and of the wild
beasts you shall not be afraid.

1Clem 56:12
For wild beasts shall be at peace with you.

1Clem 56:13
Then shall you know that thy house shall be at peace: and the
abode of thy tabernacle shall not go wrong,

1Clem 56:14
and you shall know that thy seed is many, and thy children as the
plenteous herbage of the field.

1Clem 56:15
And you shall come to the grave as ripe corn reaped in due season,
or as the heap of the threshing floor gathered together at the
right time.

1Clem 56:16
you see, dearly beloved, how great protection there is for them that
are chastened by the Master: for being a kind father He chastened
us to the end that we may obtain mercy through His holy chastisement.

1Clem 57:1
  you therefore that laid the foundation of the sedition, submit
yourselves unto the presbyters and receive chastisement unto
repentance, bending the knees of your heart.

1Clem 57:2
Learn to submit yourselves, laying aside the arrogant and proud
stubbornness of your tongue. For it is better for you to be found
little in the flock of Christ and to have your name on God's roll,
than to be had in exceeding honor and yet be cast out from the hope
of Him.

1Clem 57:3
For thus said the All virtuous Wisdom; Behold I will pour out for
you a saying of My breath, and I will teach you My word.

1Clem 57:4
Because I called and you obeyed not, and I held out words and you
heeded not, but made My councils of none effect, and were
disobedient unto My reproofs; therefore I also will laugh at your
destruction, and will rejoice over you when ruin cometh upon you,
and when confusion overtook you suddenly, and your overthrow is
at hand like a whirlwind,

1Clem 57:5
or when you call upon Me, yet will I not here you. Evil men shall
seek me and not find me: for they hated wisdom, and chose not the
fear of the Lord, neither would they give head unto My councils,
but mocked at My reproofs.

1Clem 57:6

Therefore they shall eat the fruits of their own way, and shall be
filled with their own ungodliness.

1Clem 57:7
For because they wronged babes, they shall be slain, and
inquisition shall destroy the ungodly. But he that heard Me shall
dwell safely trusting in hope, and shall be quiet from all fear of
all evil.

1Clem 58:1
   Let us therefore be obedient unto His most holy and glorious Name,
thereby escaping the threatenings which were spoken of old by the
mouth of Wisdom against them which disobey, that we may dwell safely,
trusting in the most holy Name of His majesty.

1Clem 58:2
Receive our counsel, and you shall have no occasion of regret. For as
God lived, and the Lord Jesus Christ lived, and the Holy Spirit,
who are the faith and the hope of the elect, so surely shall he, who
with lowliness of mind and instant in gentleness has without
regretfulness performed the ordinances and commandments that are
given by God, be enrolled and have a name among the number of them
that are saved through Jesus Christ, through whom is the glory unto
Him for ever and ever. Amen.

1Clem 59:1
   But if certain persons should be disobedient unto the words spoken
by Him through us, let them understand that they will entangle
themselves in no slight transgression and danger;

1Clem 59:2
but we shall be guiltless of this sin. And we will ask, with
insistency of prayer and supplication, that the Creator of the universe
may guard intact unto the end the number that has been numbered of
His elect throughout the whole world, through His beloved Son Jesus
Christ, through whom He called us from darkness to light, from
ignorance to the full knowledge of the glory of His Name.

1Clem 59:3
   [Grant unto us, Lord,] that we may set our hope on Your Name which is
the primal source of all creation, and open the eyes of our hearts,
that we may know Thee, who alone abide Highest in the lofty, Holy
in the holy; who lays low in the insolence of the proud, who
set the lowly on high, and brings the lofty low; who
makes rich and makes poor; who kills and makes alive; who
alone art the Benefactor of spirits and the God of all flesh; who
looks into the abysses, who sees the works of man; the rescuer
of them that are in peril, the Savior of them that are in
despair; The Creator and Overseer of every spirit; who multiplies
the nations upon earth, and hast chosen out from all men those that
love Thee through Jesus Christ, Your beloved Son, through whom You
didst instruct us, didst sanctify us, didst honor us.

1Clem 59:4
We beseech Thee, Lord and Master, to be our help and succor. Save
those among us who are in tribulation; have mercy on the lowly; lift
up the fallen; show Thyself unto the needy; heal the ungodly; convert
the wanderers of Your people; feed the hungry; release our prisoners;
raise up the weak; comfort the fainthearted. Let all the Gentiles

know that You art the God alone, and Jesus Christ is Your Son, and
we are Your people and the sheep of Your pasture.

1Clem 60:1
  You through Your operations didst make manifest the everlasting
fabric of the world. You, Lord, didst create the earth. You that
art faithful throughout all generations, righteous in Your judgments,
marvelous in strength and excellence, You that art wise in creating
and prudent in establishing that which You hast made, that art good
in the things which are seen and faithful with them that trust on
Thee, pitiful and compassionate, forgive us our iniquities and our
unrighteousnesses and our transgressions and shortcomings.

1Clem 60:2
Lay not to our account every sin of Your servants and Your handmaids,
but cleanse us with the cleansing of Your truth, and guide our steps
to walk in holiness and righteousness and singleness of heart
and to do such things as are good and well pleasing in Your sight
and in the sight of our rulers.

1Clem 60:3
Yea, Lord, make Your face to shine upon us in peace for our good,
that we may be sheltered by Your mighty hand and delivered from
every sin by Your uplifted arm. And deliver us from them that
hate us wrongfully.

1Clem 60:4
Give concord and peace to us and to all that dwell on the earth, as
You gave to our fathers, when they called on Thee in faith
and truth with holiness, [that we may be saved,] while we render
obedience to Your almighty and most excellent Name, and to our
rulers and governors upon the earth.

1Clem 61:1
  You, Lord and Master, hast given them the power of sovereignty
through Your excellent and unspeakable might, that we knowing the
glory and honor which You hast given them may submit ourselves unto
them, in nothing resisting Your will. Grant unto them therefore, O
Lord, health peace, concord, stability, that they may administer the
government which You hast given them without failure.

1Clem 61:2
For You, O heavenly Master, King of the ages, give to the sons of
men glory and honor and power over all things that are upon the
earth. Do You, Lord, direct their counsel according to that which
is good and well pleasing in Your sight, that, administering in peace
and gentleness with Godliness the power which You hast given them,
they may obtain Your favor.

1Clem 61:3
O You, who alone art able to do these things and things far more
exceeding good than these for us, we praise Thee through the High
priest and Guardian of our souls, Jesus Christ, through whom be the
glory and the majesty unto Thee both now and for all generations and
for ever and ever. Amen.

1Clem 62:1
  As touching those things which befit our religion and are most
useful for a virtuous life to such as would guide [their steps] in

holiness and righteousness, we have written fully unto you, brethren.

1Clem 62:2
For concerning faith and repentance and genuine love and temperance
and sobriety and patience we have handled every argument, putting you
in remembrance, that you ought to please Almighty God in righteousness
and truth and long suffering with holiness, laying aside malice and
pursuing concord in love and peace, being instant in gentleness; even
as our fathers, of whom we spoke before, pleased Him, being lowly
minded toward their Father and God and Creator and towards all men.

1Clem 62:3
And we have put you in mind of these things the more gladly, since we
knew well that we were writing to men who are faithful and highly
accounted and have diligently searched into the oracles of the
teaching of God.

1Clem 63:1
   Therefore it is right for us to give heed to so great and so many
examples and to submit the neck and occupying the place of obedience
to take our side with them that are the leaders of our souls, that
ceasing from this foolish dissension we may attain unto the goal
which lies before us in truthfulness, keeping aloof from every
fault.

1Clem 63:2
For you will give us great joy and gladness, if you render obedience
unto the things written by us through the Holy Spirit, and root out
the unrighteous anger of your jealousy, according to the entreaty
which we have made for peace and concord in this letter.

1Clem 63:3
And we have also sent faithful and prudent men that have walked among
us from youth unto old age unblamably, who shall also be witnesses
between you and us.

1Clem 63:4
And this we have done that you might know that we have had, and still
have, every solicitude that you should be speedily at peace.

1Clem 64:1
   Finally may the All seeing God and Master of spirits and Lord of all
flesh, who chose the Lord Jesus Christ, and us through Him for a
peculiar people, grant unto every soul that is called after His
excellent and holy Name faith, fear, peace, patience, long-suffering,
temperance, chastity and soberness, that they may be well pleasing
unto His Name through our High priest and Guardian Jesus Christ,
through whom unto Him be glory and majesty, might and honor, both now
and for ever and ever. Amen.

1Clem 65:1
   Now send you back speedily unto us our messengers Claudius Ephebus
and Valerius Bito, together with Fortunatus also, in peace and with
joy, to the end that they may the more quickly report the peace and
concord which is prayed for and earnestly desired by us, that we also
may the more speedily rejoice over your good order.

1Clem 65:2
   The grace of our Lord Jesus Christ be with you and with all men in

all places who have been called by God and through Him, through whom
be glory and honor, power and greatness and eternal dominion, unto
Him, from the ages past and forever and ever. Amen.

The Shepherd of Hermas

Vision 1

1:1 The master, who raised me sold me to a lady, Rhoda in Rome. After many years, I met her again, and began to love her as a sister.

1:2 After a period of time I saw her bathing in the river Tiber; and I gave her my hand, and led her out of the river. When I saw her beauty, I thought to myself, "I would be happy if I had such a one as a wife both because of her beauty and character." I merely thought about this and nothing more.

1:3 After a while, as I was travelling to Cumae, and praising God because of his creatures, for their greatness and beauty and power. As I walked I fell asleep. And a Spirit took me, and lifted me away through a land that had no path and through which no man could pass. The place has cliffs, and was broken into clefts by rivers. When I had crossed the river, I came into the level country, and knelt down, and began to pray to the Lord and to confess my sins.

1:4 Now, while I prayed, heaven was opened, and I saw the lady, whom I had desired, greeting me from heaven, saying, "Good day, Hermas."

1:5 And, looking at her, I said to her, "Lady, what are you doing here?" Then she answered me, "I was taken up, that I might convict you of your sins before the Lord."

1:6 I said to her, "Dost you now convict me?" "Nay, not so," said she, "but hear the words, that I shall say to you. God, Who dwelled in the heavens, and created out of nothing the things which are, and increased and multiplied them for His holy Church's sake, is wroth with you, for that you didst sin against me."

1:7 I answered her and said, "Sin against you? In what way? Did I ever speak an unseemly word unto you? Did I not always regard you as a goddess? Did I not always respect you as a sister? How couldst you falsely charge me, lady, with such villainy and uncleanness?

1:8 "Laughing she said unto me, "The desire after evil entered into your heart. No, think you not that it is an evil deed for a righteous man, if the evil desire should enter into his heart? It is indeed a sin and a great one too," said she; "for the righteous man entertained righteous purposes. While then his purposes are righteous, his repute stands steadfast in the heavens, and he finds the Lord easily propitiated in all that he does. But they that entertain evil purposes in their hearts, bring upon themselves death an captivity, especially they that claim for themselves this present work and boast in its riches, and hold fast not to the good things that are to come.

1:9 Their souls shall rue it, seeing that they have no hope, but have abandoned themselves and their life. But do you pray unto God and He shall heal your own sins, and those of thy whole house, and of all the saints."

2:1 As soon as she had spoken these words the heavens were shut and I was given over to horror and grief Then I said within myself "If this sin is recorded against me, how can I be saved? Or how shall I propitiate God for my sins which are full-blown? Or with which words shall I entreat the Lord that He may be propitious unto me?

2:2 While I was advising and discussing these matters in my heart, I see, before me a great white chair of snow-white wool; and there came an aged lady in glistening raiment, having a book in her hands, and she sat down alone, and she saluted me, "Good morrow, Hermas." Then I grieved and weeping, said, "Good morrow, lady."

2:3 And she said to me "Why so gloomy, Hermas, you that art patient and good-tempered and art always smiling? Why so downcast in thy looks, and far from cheerful?" And I said to her, "Because of an excellent lady's saying that I had sinned against her."

2:4 Then she said, "Far be this thing from the servant of God! Nevertheless the thought did enter into thy heart concerning her. Now to the servants of God such a purpose brings sin. For it is an evil and mad purpose to overtake a devout spirit that has been already approved, that it should desire an evil deed, and especially if it be Hermas the temperate, who abstained from every evil desire, and is full of all simplicity and of great guilelessness.

3:1 "Yet it is not for this that God is wroth with you, but that you may convert thy family, that has done wrong against the Lord and against you their parents. But out of fondness for thy children you didst not admonish thy family, but didst suffer it to become fearfully corrupt. Therefore the Lord is wroth with you. But He will heal all thy past sins, which have been committed in thy family; for by reason of their sins and iniquities you hast been corrupted by the affairs of this world.

3:2 But the great mercy of the Lord had pity on you and thy family, and will strengthen you, and establish you in His glory. Only be not you careless, but take courage, and strengthen thy family. For as the smith hammering his work conquers the task which he wills, so also doth righteous discourse repeated daily conquer all evil. Cease not therefore to reprove thy children; for I know that if they shall repent with all their heart, they shall be written in the books of life with the saints."

3:3 After these words of hers had ceased, she said unto me, "Wilt you listen to me as I read?" Then say I, "Yes, lady." She said to me, "Be attentive, and hear the glories of God" I listened with attention and with wonder to that which I had no power to remember; for all the words were terrible, such as man cannot bear. The last words however I remembered, for they were suitable for us and gentle.

3:4 "Behold, the God of Hosts, Who by His invisible and mighty power and by His great wisdom created the world, and by His glorious purpose clothed His creation with comeliness, and by His strong word fixed the heaven, and founded the earth upon the waters, and by His own wisdom and providence formed His holy Church, which also He blessed-behold, He removed the heavens and the mountains and the hills and the seas, and all things are made level for His elect, that He may fulfill to them the promise which He promised with great glory and rejoicing, if so be that they shall keep the ordinances of God, which they received, with great faith."

4:1 When then she finished reading and arose from her chair, there came four young men, and they took away the chair, and departed towards the East.

4:2 Then she called me unto her, and she touched my breast, and said to me, "Did my reading please you?" And I say unto her, "Lady, these last words please me, but the former were difficult and hard." Then she spoke to me, saying, "These last words are for the righteous, but the former are for the heathen and the rebellious."

4:3 While she yet spoke with me, two men appeared, and took her by the arms, and they departed, whither the chair also had gone, towards the East. And she smiled as she departed and, as she was going, she said to me, "Play the man, Hermas."

Vision 2

1[5]:1 I was on the way to Cumae, at the same season as last year, and called to mind my last year's vision as I walked; and again a Spirit took me, and carried me away to the same place as last year.

1[5]:2 When then I arrived at the place, I fell upon my knees, and began to pray to the Lord, and to glorify His name, for that he counted me worthy, and made known unto me my former sins.

1[5]:3 But after I had risen up from prayer, I behold before me the aged lady, whom also I had seen last year, walking and reading a little book. And she said to me, "Canst you report these things to the elect of God?" I say unto her, "Lady, I cannot recollect so much; but give me the little book, that I may copy it." "Take it," said she, "and be sure and return it to me."

1[5]:4 I took it, and retiring to a certain spot in the country I copied it letter for letter: for I could not make out the syllables. When then I had finished the letters of the book, suddenly the book was snatched out of my hand; but by whom I did not see.

2[6]:1 Now after fifteen days, when I had fasted and entreated the Lord earnestly, the knowledge of the writing was revealed to me. And this is what was written:--

2[6]:2 "Your seed, Hermas, have sinned against God, and have blasphemed the Lord, and have betrayed their parents through great wickedness, yea, they have got the name of betrayers of parents, and yet they did not profit by their betrayal; and they still further added to their sins wanton deeds and reckless wickedness; and so the measure of their transgressions was filled up.

2[6]:3 But make these words known to all thy children, and to thy wife who shall be as thy sister; for she too refrained not from using her tongue, wherewith she doeth evil. But, when she hears these words, she will refrain, and will find mercy.

2[6]:4 After that you hast made known unto them all these words, which the Master commanded me that they should be revealed unto you, then all their sins which they sinned aforetime are forgiven to them; yea, and to all the saints that have sinned unto this day, if they repent with their whole heart, and remove double-mindedness from their heart.

2[6]:5 For the Master swore by His own glory, as concerning His elect; that if, now that this day has been set as a limit, sin shall hereafter be committed, they shall not find salvation; for repentance for the righteous has an end; the days of repentance are accomplished for all the saints; whereas for the Gentiles there is repentance until the last day.

2[6]:6 You shall therefore say unto the elders of the Church, that they direct their paths in righteousness, that they may receive in full the promises with abundant glory.

2[6]:7 you therefore that work righteousness be steadfast, and be not double-minded, that you may have admission with the holy angels. Blessed are you, as many as endure patiently the great tribulation that cometh, and as many as shall not deny their life.

2[6]:8 For the Lord swear concerning His Son, that those who denied their Lord should be rejected from their life, even they that are now about to deny Him in the coming days; but to those who denied Him aforetime, to them mercy was given of His great loving kindness.

3[7]:1 "But do you, Hermas, no longer bear a grudge against thy children, neither suffer thy sister to have her way, so that they may be purified from their former sins. For they shall be chastised with a righteous chastisement, unless you bear a grudge against them thyself. The bearing of a grudge worked death. But you, Hermas, hast had great tribulations of your own, by reason of the transgressions of thy family, because you had no care for them. For you was neglectful of them, and was mixed up with your evil transactions.

3[7]:2 But herein is thy salvation, in that you didst not depart from the living God, and in thy simplicity and thy great continence. These have saved you, if you abide therein; and they save all who do such things, and walk in guilelessness and simplicity. These men prevail over all wickedness, and continue unto life eternal.

3[7]:3 Blessed are all they that work righteousness. They shall never be destroyed.

3[7]:4 But you shall say to Maximus, "Behold tribulation cometh (upon you), if you think fit to deny a second time. The Lord is nigh unto them that turn unto him, as it is written in Eldad and Modat, who prophesied to the people in the wilderness."

4[8]:1 Now, brethren, a revelation was made unto me in my sleep by a youth of exceeding fair form, who said to me, "Whom think you the aged woman, from whom you received the book, to be?" I say, "The Sibyl" "You art wrong," said he, "she is not." "Who then is she?" I say. "The Church," said he. I said unto him, "Wherefore then is she aged?" "Because," said he, "she was created before all things; therefore is she aged; and for her sake the world was framed."

4[8]:2 And afterwards I saw a vision in my house. The aged woman came, and asked me, if I had already given the book to the elders. I said that I had not given it. "You hast done well," she said, "for I have words to add. When then I shall have finished all the words, it shall be made known by thy means to all the elect.

4[8]:3 You shall therefore write two little books, and shall send one to Clement, and one to Grapte. So Clement shall send to the foreign cities, for this is his duty; while Grapte shall instruct the widows and the orphans. But you shall read (the book) to this city along with the elders that preside over the Church.

Vision 3

1[9]:1 The third vision, which I saw, brethren, was as follows.

1[9]:2 After fasting often, and entreating the Lord to declare unto me the revelation which He promised to show me by the mouth of the aged woman, that very night the aged woman was seen of me, and she said to me, "Seeing that you art so importunate and eager to know all things, come into the country where you abide, and about the fifth hour I will appear, and will show you what you ought to see."

1[9]:3 I asked her, saying, "Lady, to what part of the country?" "Where you wilt," said she. I selected a beautiful and retired spot; but before I spoke to her and named the spot, she said to me, "I will come, whither you will."

1[9]:4 I went then, brethren, into the country, and I counted up the hours, and came to the place where I appointed her to come, and I see an ivory couch placed there, and on the couch there lay a linen cushion, and on the cushion was spread a coverlet of fine linen of flax.

1[9]:5 When I saw these things so ordered, and no one in the place, I was amazed, and a fit of trembling seized me, and my hair stood on end; and a fit of shuddering came upon me, because I was alone. When then I recovered myself, and remembered the glory of God, and took courage, I knelt down and confessed my sins to the Lord once more, as I had done on the former occasion.

1[9]:6 Then she came with six young men, the same whom I had seen before, and she stood by me, and listened attentively to me, as I prayed and confessed my sins to the Lord. And she touched me, and said: "Hermas, make an end of constantly entreating for thy sins; entreat also for righteousness, that you may take some part forthwith to thy family."

1[9]:7 Then she raised me by the hand, and led me to the couch, and said to the young men, "Go you, and build."

1[9]:8 And after the young men had retired and we were left alone, she said to me, "Sit down here." I say to her, "Lady, let the elders sit down first." "Do as I bid you," said she, "sit down."

1[9]:9 When then I wanted to sit down on the right side, she would not allow me, but beckoned me with her hand that I should sit on the left side. As then I was musing thereon, and was sad because she would not permit me to sit on the right side, she said to me, "Art you sad, Hermas? The place on the right side is for others, even for those who have already been well-pleasing to God, and have suffered for the Name's sake. But you lack much that you should sit with them; but as you abide in thy simplicity, even so, and you shall sit with them, you and as many as shall have done their deeds, and have suffered what they suffered."

2[10]:1 "What did they suffer?" say I. "Listen," said she. "Stripes, imprisonments, great tribulations, crosses, wild beasts, for the Name's sake. Therefore to them belongs the right side of the Holiness--to them, and to all who shall suffer for the Name. But for the rest is the left side. Howbeit, to both, to them that sit on the right, and to them that sit on the left, are the same gifts, and the same promises, only they sit on the right and have a certain glory.

2[10]:2 You indeed art very desirous to sit on the right with them, but thy shortcomings are many; yet you shall be purified from thy shortcomings; yea, and all that are not double-minded shall be purified from all their sins unto this day."

2[10]:3 When she had said this, she wished to depart; but, falling at her feet, I entreated her by the Lord that she would show me the vision which she promised.

2[10]:4 Then she again took me by the hand, and raised me, and seated me on the couch at the left hand, while she herself sat on the right. And lifting up a certain glistening rod, she said to me, "See you a great thing?" I say to her, "Lady, I see nothing." She said to me, "Look you; do you not see in front of you a great tower being built upon the waters, of glistening square stones?"

2[10]:5 Now the tower was being built foursquare by the six young men that came with her. And countless other men were bringing stones, some of them from the deep, and others from the land, and were handing them to the six young men. And they took them and built.

2[10]:6 The stones that were dragged from the deep they placed in every case, just as they were, into the building, for they had been shaped, and they fitted in their joining with the other stones; and they adhered so closely one with another that their joining could not possibly be detected; and the building of the tower appeared as if it were built of one stone.

2[10]:7 But of the other stones which were brought from the dry land, some they threw away, and some they put into the building; and others they broke in pieces, and threw to a distance from the tower.

2[10]:8 Now many other stones were lying round the tower, and they did not use them for the building; for some of them were mildewed, and others had cracks in them, and others were too short, and others were white and round, and did not fit into the building.

2[10]:9 And I saw other stones thrown to a distance from the tower, and coming to the way, and yet not staying in the way, but rolling to where there was no way; and others falling into the fire and burning there; and others falling near the waters, and yet not able to roll into the water, although they desired to roll and to come to the water.

3[11]:1 When she had shown me these things, she wished to hurry away. I say to her, "Lady, what advantage is it to me to have seen these things, and yet not to know what the things mean? "She answered and said unto me, "You art an over-curious fellow, in desiring to know all that concerns the tower." "Yea, lady," I said, "that I may announce it to my brethren, and that they [may be the more gladdened and] when they hear [these things] they may know the Lord in great glory." Then said she,

3[11]:2 "Many shall hear; but when they hear, some of them shall be glad, and others shall weep. Yet even these latter, if they hear and repent, shall likewise be glad. Hear you therefore the parables of the tower; for I will reveal all things unto you. And trouble me no more about revelation; for these revelations have an end, seeing that they have been completed. Nevertheless you wilt not cease asking for revelations; for you art shameless."

3[11]:3 The tower, which you see building, is myself, the Church, which was seen of you both now and aforetime. Ask, therefore, what you will concerning the tower, and I will reveal it unto you, that you may rejoice with the saints."

3[11]:4 I say unto her, "Lady, since you didst hold me worthy once for all, that you should reveal all things to me, reveal them." Then she said to me, "Whatsoever is possible to be revealed to you, shall be revealed. Only let thy heart be with God, and doubt not in thy mind about that which you sees."

3[11]:5 I asked her, "Wherefore is the tower built upon waters, lady?" "I told you so before," said she, "and indeed you do enquire diligently. So by thy enquiry you discovered the truth. Hear then why the tower is built upon waters; it is because your life is saved and shall be saved by water. But the tower has been founded by the word of the Almighty and Glorious Name, and is strengthened by the unseen power of the Master."

4[12]:1 I answered and said unto her, "Lady, this thing is great and marvelous. But the six young men that build, who are they, lady?" "These are the holy angels of God, that were created first of all, unto whom the Lord delivered all His creation to increase and to build it, and to be masters of all creation. By their hands therefore the building of the tower will be accomplished."

4[12]:2 "And who are the others who are bringing the stones in?" "They also are holy angels of God; but these six are superior to them. The building of the tower then shall be accomplished, and all alike shall rejoice in the (completed) circle of the tower, and shall glorify God that the building of the tower was accomplished."

4[12]:3 I enquired of her, saying, "Lady, I could wish to know concerning the end of the stones, and their power, of what kind it is." She answered and said unto me, "It is not that you of all men art especially worthy that it should be revealed to you; for there are others before you, and better than you art, unto whom these visions ought to have been revealed. But that the name of God may be glorified, it has been revealed to you, all shall be revealed, for the sake of the doubtful-minded, who question in their hearts whether these things are so or not. Tell them that all these things are true, and that there is nothing beside the truth, but that all are steadfast, and valid, and established on a firm foundation.

5[13]:1 "Hear now concerning the stones that go to the building The stones that are squared and white, and that fit together in their joints, these are the apostles and bishops and teachers and deacons, who walked after the holiness of God, and exercised their office of bishop and teacher and deacon in purity and sanctity for the elect of God, some of them already fallen on sleep, and others still living. And because they always agreed with one another, they both had peace among themselves and listened one to another. Therefore their joinings fit together in the building of the tower."

5[13]:2 "But they that are dragged from the deep, and placed in the building, and that fit together in their joinings with the other stones that are already built in, who are they?" "These are they that suffered for the name of the Lord."

5[13]:3 "But the other stones that are brought from the dry land, I would fain know who these are, lady." She said, "Those that go to the building, and yet are not hewn, these the Lord has approved because they walked in the uprightness of the Lord, and rightly performed His commandments."

5[13]:4 "But they that are brought and placed in the building, who are they?" "They are young in the faith, and faithful; but they are warned by the angels to do good, because wickedness was found in them."

5[13]:5 "But those whom they rejected and threw away, who are they?" "These have sinned, and desire to repent, therefore they were not cast to a great distance from the tower, because they will be useful for the building, if they repent. They then that shall repent, if they repent, will be strong in the faith, if they repent now while the tower is building. But if the building shall be finished, they have no more any place, but shall be castaways. This privilege only they have, that they lie near the tower.

5[13]:1 But wouldst you know about them that are broken in pieces, and cast away far from the tower? These are the sons of lawlessness. They received the faith in hypocrisy, and no wickedness was absent from them. Therefore they have not salvation, for they are not useful for building by reason of their wickednesses. Therefore they were broken up and thrown far away by reason of the wrath of the Lord, for they excited Him to wrath.

5[13]:2 But the rest whom you hast seen lying in great numbers, not going to the building, of these they that are mildewed are they that knew the truth, but did not abide in it, nor hold fast to the saints. Therefore they are useless."

5[13]:3 "But they that have the cracks, who are they?" "These are they that have discord in their hearts against one another, and are not at peace among themselves; who have an appearance of peace, but when they depart from one another, their wickednesses abide in their hearts. These are the cracks which the stones have.

5[13]:4 But they that are broken off short, these have believed, and have their greater part in righteousness, but have some parts of lawlessness; therefore they are too short, and are not perfect."

5[13]:5 "But the white and round stones, which did not fit into the building, who are they, lady?" She answered and said to me, "How long art you foolish and stupid, and enquire everything, and understand nothing? These are they that have faith, but have also riches of this world. When tribulation cometh, they deny their Lord by reason of their riches and their business affairs."

5[13]:6 And I answered and said unto her, "When then, lady, will they be useful for the building?" "When," she replied, "their wealth, which led their souls astray, shall be cut away, then will they be useful for God. For just as the round stone, unless it be cut away, and lose some portion of itself, cannot become square, so also they that are rich in this world, unless their riches be cut away, cannot become useful to the Lord.

5[13]:7 Learn first from thyself When you had riches, you was useless; but now you art useful and profitable unto life. Be you useful unto God, for you thyself also art taken from the same stones.

7[15]:1 "But the other stones which you saw cast far away from the tower and falling into the way and rolling out of the way into the regions where there is no way, these are they that have believed, but by reason of their double heart they abandon their true way. Thus thinking that they can find a better way, they go astray and are sore distressed, as they walk about in the regions where there is no way.

7[15]:2 But they that fall into the fire and are burned, these are they that finally rebelled from the living God, and it no more entered into their hearts to repent by reason of the lusts of their wantonness and of the wickednesses which they wrought.

7[15]:3 But the others, which are near the waters and yet cannot roll into the water, would you know who are they? These are they that heard the word, and would be baptized unto the name of the Lord. Then, when they call to their remembrance the purity of the truth, they change their minds, and go back again after their evil desires."

7[15]:4 So she finished the explanation of the tower.

7[15]:5 Still importunate, I asked her further, whether for all these stones that were rejected and would not fit into the building of the tower that was repentance, and they had a place in this tower. "They can repent," she said, "but they cannot be fitted into this tower.

7[15]:6 Yet they shall be fitted into another place much more humble, but not until they have undergone torments, and have fulfilled the days of their sins. And they shall be changed for this reason, because they participated in the Righteous Word; and then shall it befall them to be relieved from their torments, if the evil deeds, that they have done, come into their heart; but if these come not into their heart, they are not saved by reason of the hardness of their hearts."

8[16]:1 When then I ceased asking her concerning all these things, she said to me; "Would you see something else?" Being very desirous of beholding, I was greatly rejoiced that I should see it.

8[16]:2 She looked upon me, and smiled, and she said to me, "See you seven women round the tower?" "I see them, lady," say I. "This tower is supported by them by commandment of the Lord.

8[16]:3 Hear now their employments. The first of them, the woman with the strong hands, is called Faith; through her are saved the elect of God.

8[16]:4 And the second, that is girded about and looked like a man, is called Continence; she is the daughter of Faith. Whosoever then shall follow her, becomes happy in his life, for he shall refrain from all evil deeds, believing that, if he refrain from every evil desire, he shall inherit eternal life."

8[16]:5 "And the others, lady, who be they?" "They are daughters one of the other. The name of the one is Simplicity, of the next, Knowledge, of the next, Guilelessness, of the next, Reverence, of the next, Love. When then you shall do all the works of their mother, you canst live."

8[16]:6 "I would fain know, lady," I say, "what power each of them possessed." "Listen then," said she, "to the powers which they have.

8[16]:7 Their powers are mastered each by the other, and they follow each other, in the order in which they were born. From Faith is born Continence, from Continence Simplicity, from Simplicity Guilelessness, from Guilelessness Reverence, from Reverence Knowledge, from Knowledge Love. Their works then are pure and reverent and divine.

8[16]:8 Whosoever therefore shall serve these women, and shall have strength to master their works, shall have his dwelling in the tower with the saints of God."

8[16]:9 Then I asked her concerning the seasons, whether the consummation is even now. But she cried aloud, saying, "Foolish man, see you not that the tower is still a-building? Whenever therefore the tower shall be finished building, the end cometh; but it shall be built up quickly. Ask me no more questions: this reminder is sufficient for you and for the saints, and is the renewal of your spirits.

8[16]:10 But it was not revealed to thyself alone, but in order that you might show these things unto all. After three days--

8[16]:11 for you must understand first, and I charge you, Hermas, first with these words, which I am about to speak to you--(I charge you to) tell all these things into the ears of the saints, that hearing them and doing them they may be purified from their wickednesses, and thyself also with them."

9[17]:1 "Hear me, my children. I brought you up in much simplicity and guilelessness and reverence, through the mercy of the Lord, Who instilled righteousness into you, that you might be justified and sanctified from all wickedness and all crookedness. But you will not to cease from your wickedness.

9[17]:2 Now then hear me and be at peace among yourselves, and have regard one to another, and assist one another, and do not partake of the creatures of God alone in abundance, but share them also with those that are in want.

9[17]:3 For some men through their much eating bring weakness on the flesh, and injure their flesh: whereas the flesh of those who have nought to eat is injured by their not having sufficient nourishment, and their body is ruined.

9[17]:4 This exclusiveness therefore is hurtful to you that have and do not share with them that are in want.

9[17]:5 Look you to the judgment that cometh. you then that have more than enough, seek out them that are hungry, while the tower is still unfinished; for after the tower is finished, you will desire to do good, and will find no place for it.

9[17]:6 Look you therefore, you that exult in your wealth, lest they that are in want shall moan, and their moaning shall go up unto the Lord, and you with your [abundance of good things be shut outside the door of the tower.

9[17]:7 Now therefore I say unto you that are rulers of the Church, and that occupy the chief seats; be not you like unto the sorcerers. The sorcerers indeed carry their drugs in boxes, but you carry your drug and your poison in your heart.

9[17]:8 you are case-hardened, and you will not cleanse your hearts and mix your wisdom together in a clean heart, that you may obtain mercy from the Great King.

9[17]:9 Look you therefore, children, lest these divisions of yours deprive you of your life.

9[17]:10 How is it that you wish to instruct the elect of the Lord, while you yourselves have no instruction? Instruct one another therefore, and have peace among yourselves, that I also may stand gladsome before the Father, and give an account concerning you all to your Lord."

10[18]:1 When then she ceased speaking with me, the six young men, who were building, came, and took her away to the tower, and other four lifted the couch, and took it also away to the tower. I saw not the face of these, for they were turned away.

10[18]:2 And, as she went, I asked her to reveal to me concerning the three forms, in which she had appeared to me. She answered and said to me; "As concerning these things you must ask another, that they may be revealed to you."

10[18]:3 Now she was seen of me, brethren, in my first vision of last year, as a very aged woman and seated on a chair.

10[18]:4 In the second vision her face was youthful, but her flesh and her hair were aged, and she spoke to me standing; and she was more gladsome than before.

10[18]:5 But in the third vision she was altogether youthful and of exceeding great beauty, and her hair alone was aged; and she was gladsome exceedingly and seated on a couch. Touching these things I was very greatly anxious to learn this revelation.

10[18]:6 And I see the aged woman in a vision of the night, saying to me, "Every enquiry needs humility. Fast therefore, and you shall receive what you ask from the Lord."

10[18]:7 So I fasted one day; and that very night there appeared unto me a young man, and he said to me, "Seeing that you ask me revelations offhand with entreaty, take heed lest by thy much asking you injure thy flesh.

10[18]:8 Sufficient for you are these revelations. Canst you see mightier revelations than those you hast seen?"

10[18]:9 I say unto him in reply, "Sir, this one thing alone I ask, concerning the three forms of the aged woman, that a complete revelation may be vouchsafed me." He said to me in answer, How long are you without understanding? It is your double-mindedness that made you of no understanding, and because your heart is not set towards the Lord."

10[18]:10 I answered and said unto him again, "From you, Sir, we shall learn the matters more accurately."

11[19]:1 Listen," said he, "concerning the three forms, of which you enquire.

11[19]:2 In the first vision wherefore did she appear to you an aged woman and seated on a chair? Because your spirit was aged, and already decayed, and had no power by reason of your infirmities and acts of double-mindedness.

11[19]:3 For as aged people, having no longer hope of renewing their youth, expect nothing else but to fall asleep, so you also, being weakened with the affairs of this world gave yourselves over to repining, and cast not your cares on the Lord; but your spirit was broken, and you were aged by your sorrows."

11[19]:4 "Wherefore then she was seated on a chair, I would fain know, Sir." "Because every weak person sits on a chair by reason of his weakness, that the weakness of his body may be supported. So you hast the symbolism of the first vision."

12[20]:1 "But in the second vision you saw her standing, and with her countenance more youthful and more gladsome than before; but her flesh and her hair aged. Listen to this parable also," said he.

12[20]:2 "Imagine an old man, who has now lost all hope of himself by reason of his weakness and his poverty, and expected nothing else save the last day of his life. Suddenly an inheritance is left him. He heard the news, rose up and full of joy clothes himself with strength, and no longer lied down, but stood up, and his spirit, which was now broken by reason of his former circumstances, is renewed again, and he no longer sat, but took courage; so also was it with you, when you heard the revelation which the Lord revealed unto you.

12[20]:3 For He had compassion on you, and renewed your spirits, and you laid aside your maladies, and strength came to you, and you were made powerful in the faith, and the Lord rejoiced to see you put on your strength. And therefore He showed you the building of the tower; yea, and other things also shall He show you, if with your whole heart you be at peace among yourselves.

13[21]:1 But in the third vision you saw her younger and fair and gladsome, and her form fair.

13[21]:2 For just as when to some mourner cometh some piece of good tidings, immediately he forgot his former sorrows, and admitted nothing but the tidings which he has heard, and is strengthened thenceforth unto that which is good, and his spirit is renewed by reason of the joy which he has received; so also you have received a renewal of your spirits by seeing these good things.

13[21]:3 And whereas you saw her seated on a couch, the position is a firm on; for the couch has four feet and stood firmly; for the world too Is upheld by means of four elements.

13[21]:4 They then that have fully repented shall be young again, and founded firmly, seeing that they have repented with their whole heart. There you hast the revelation entire and complete. You shall ask nothing more as touching revelation-- but if anything be lacking still, it shall be revealed unto you."

Vision 4

1[22]:1 The fourth vision which I saw, brethren, twenty days after the former vision which came unto me, for a type of the impending tribulation.

1[22]:2 I was going into the country by the Companion Way. From the high road, it is about ten stades; and the place is easy for traveling.

1[22]:3 While then I am walking alone, I entreat the Lord that He will accomplish the revelations and the visions which He showed me through His holy Church, that He may strengthen me and may give repentance to His servants which have stumbled, that His great and glorious Name may be glorified, for that He held me worthy that He should show me His marvels.

1[22]:4 And as I gave glory and thanksgiving to Him, there answered me as it were the sound of a voice, "Be not of doubtful mind, Hermas." I began to question in myself and to say, "How can I be of doubtful mind, seeing that I am so firmly founded by the Lord, and have seen glorious things?"

1[22]:5 And I went on a little, brethren, and behold, I see a cloud of dust rising as it were to heaven, and I began to say within myself, "Can it be that cattle are coming, and raising a cloud of dust?" for it was just about a stade from me.

1[22]:6 As the cloud of dust waxed greater and greater, I suspected that it was something supernatural. Then the sun shone out a little, and behold, I see a huge beast like some sea-monster, and from its mouth fiery locusts issued forth. And the beast was about a hundred feet in length, and its head was as it were of pottery.

1[22]:7 And I began to weep, and to entreat the Lord that He would rescue me from it. And I remembered the word which I had heard, "Be not of doubtful mind, Hermas."

1[22]:8 Having therefore, brethren, put on the faith of the Lord and called to mind the mighty works that He had taught me, I took courage and gave myself up to the beast. Now the beast was coming on with such a rush, that it might have ruined a city.

1[22]:9 I come near it, and, huge monster as it was, it stretched itself on the ground, and merely put forth its tongue, and stirred not at all until I had passed by it.

1[22]:10 And the beast had on its head four colors; black then fire and blood color, then gold, then white.

2[23]:1 Now after I had passed the beast, and had gone forward about thirty feet, behold, there met me a virgin arrayed as if she were going forth from a bridal-chamber all in white and with white sandals, veiled up to her forehead, and her head-covering consisted of a turban, and her hair was white.

2[23]:2 I knew from the former Visions that it was the Church, and I became more cheerful. She saluted me, saying, "Good morrow, my good man"; and I saluted her in turn, "Lady, good morrow."

2[23]:3 She answered and said unto me, "Did nothing meet you? "I say unto her, Lady, such a huge beast, that could have destroyed whole peoples: but, by the power of the Lord and by His great mercy, I escaped it."

2[23]:4 "You didst escape it well," said she, "because you didst cast thy care upon God, and didst open thy heart to the Lord, believing that you can be saved by nothing else but by His great and glorious Name. Therefore the Lord sent His angel, which is over the beasts, whose name is Segri, and shut his mouth that it might not hurt you. You hast escaped a great tribulation by reason of thy faith, and because, though you saw so huge a beast, you didst not doubt in thy mind.

2[23]:5 Go therefore, and declare to the elect of the Lord His mighty works, and tell them that this beast is a type of the great tribulation which is to come. If therefore you prepare yourselves beforehand, and repent (and turn) unto the Lord with your whole heart, you shall be able to escape it, if your heart be made pure and without blemish, and if for the remaining days of your life you serve the Lord blamelessly. Cast your cares upon the Lord and He will set them straight.

2[23]:6 Trust you in the Lord, you men of doubtful mind, for He can do all things, yea, He both turned away His wrath from you, and again He sent forth His plagues upon you that are of doubtful mind. Woe to them that hear these words and are disobedient; it were better for them that they had not been born."

3[24]:1 I asked her concerning the four colors, which the beast had upon its head. Then she answered me and said, "Again you art curious about such matters." "Yes, lady," said I, "make known unto me what these things are."

3[24]:2 "Listen," said she; "the black is this world in which you dwell;

3[24]:3 and the fire and blood color showed that this world must perish by blood and fire;

3[24]:4 and the golden part are you that has escaped from this world. For as the gold is tested by the fire and is made useful, so you also [that dwell in it] are being tested in yourselves. you then that abide and pass through the fire will be purified by it. For as the old loses its dross. so you also shall cast away all sorrow and tribulation, and shall be purified, and shall be useful for the building of the tower.

3[24]:5 But the white portion is the coming age, in which the elect of God shall dwell; because the elect of God shall be without spot and pure unto life eternal.

3[24]:6 Wherefore cease not you to speak in the ears of the saints. you have now the symbolism also of the tribulation which is coming in power. But if you be willing, it shall be nothing. Remember you the things that are written beforehand."

3[24]:7 With these words she departed, and I saw not in what direction she departed; for a noise was made: and I turned back in fear, thinking that the beast was coming.

Vision 5

5[25]:1 As I prayed in the house, and sat on the couch, there entered a man glorious in his visage, in the garb of a shepherd, with a white skin wrapped about him, and with a wallet on his shoulders and a staff in his hand. And he saluted me, and I saluted me in return.

5[25]:2 And he immediately sat down by my side, and he said unto me, "I was sent by the most holy angel, that I might dwell with you the remaining days of thy life."

5[25]:3 I thought he came to tempt me, and I say unto him, "Why, who art you? For I know," say I, "unto whom I was delivered." He said to me, "Dost you not recognize me?" "No," I say. "I," said he, "am the shepherd, unto whom you were delivered."

5[25]:4 While he was still speaking, his form was changed, and I recognized him as being the same, to whom I was delivered; and straightway I was confounded, and fear seized me, and I was altogether overwhelmed with distress that I had answered him so wickedly and senselessly.

5[25]:5 But he answered and said unto me, "Be not confounded, but strengthen thyself in my commandments which I am about to command you. For I was sent," said he, "that I might show you again all the things which you didst see before, merely the heads which are convenient for you. First of all, write down my commandments and my parables; and the other matters you shall write down as I shall show them to you. The reason why," said he, "I command you to write down first the commandments and parables is, that you may read them off-hand, and may be able to keep them."

5[25]:6 So I wrote down the commandments and parables, as he commanded me.

5[25]:7 If then, when you hear them, you keep them and walk in them, and do them with a pure heart, you shall receive from the Lord all things that He promised you; but if, when you hear them, you do not repent, but still add to your sins, you shall receive from the Lord the opposite. All these the shepherd, the angel of repentance commanded me to write.

Mandate 1

1[26]:1 "First of all, believe that God is One, even He who created all things and set them in order, and brought all things from non-existence into being, Who comprehends all things, being alone incomprehensible.

1[26]:2 Believe Him therefore, and fear Him, and in this fear be continent. Keep these things, and you shall cast off all wickedness from thyself, and shall clothe thyself with every excellence of righteousness, and shall live unto God, if you keep this commandment."

Mandate 2

1[27]:1 He said to me; "Keep simplicity and be guileless, and you shall be as little children, that know not the wickedness which destroyed the life of men.

1[27]:2 First of all, speak evil of no man, neither take pleasure in listening to a slanderer. Otherwise you that hear too shall be responsible for the sin of him that speaks the evil, if you believe the slander, which you hear; for in believing it you thyself also wilt have a grudge against thy brother. So then shall you be responsible for the sin of him that speaks the evil.

1[27]:3 Slander is evil; it is a restless demon, never at peace, but always having its home among factions. Refrain from it therefore, and you shall have success at all times with all men.

1[27]:4 But clothe thyself in reverence, wherein is no evil stumbling-block, but all things are smooth and gladsome. Work that which is good, and of thy labors, which God gives you, give to all that are in want freely, not questioning to whom you shall give, and to whom you shall not give. Give to all; for to all God desires that there should be given of His own bounties.

1[27]:5 They then that receive shall render an account to God why they received it, and to what end; for they that receive in distress shall not be judged, but they that receive by false pretence shall pay the penalty.

1[27]:6 He then that gives is guiltless; for as he received from the Lord the ministration to perform it, he has performed it in sincerity, by making no distinction to whom to give or not to give. This ministration then, when sincerely performed, becomes glorious in the sight of God. He therefore that ministered thus sincerely shall live unto God.

1[27]:7 Therefore keep this commandment, as I have told you, that your own repentance and that of thy household may be found to be sincere, and [thy] heart pure and undefiled."

Mandate 3

1[28]:1 Again he said to me; "Love truth, and let nothing but truth proceed out of thy mouth, that the Spirit which God made to dwell in this flesh, may be found true in the sight of all men; and thus shall the Lord, Who dwelt in you, be glorified; for the Lord is true in every word, and with Him there is no falsehood.

1[28]:2 They therefore that speak lies set the Lord at nought, and become robbers of the Lord, for they do not deliver up to Him the deposit which they received. For they received of Him a spirit free from lies. This if they shall return a lying spirit, they have defiled the commandment of the Lord and have become robbers."

1[28]:3 When then I heard these things, I wept bitterly. But seeing me weep he said, "Why weep you?" "Because, Sir," say I "I know not if I can be saved." "Why so?" said he. "Because, Sir," I say, "never in my life spoke I a true word, but I always lied deceitfully with all men and dressed up my falsehood as truth before all men; and no man ever contradicted me, but confidence was placed in my word. How then, Sir," say I, "can I live, seeing that I have done these things?"

1[28]:4 "Your supposition," he said, "is right and true, for it behooved you as a servant of God to walk in truth, and no complicity with evil should abide with the Spirit of truth, nor bring grief to the Spirit which is holy and true." "Never, Sir," say I, "heard I clearly words such as these."

1[28]:5 "Now then," said he, "you heard Guard them, that the former falsehoods also which you spake in thy business affairs may themselves become credible, now that these are found true; for they too can become trustworthy. If you keep these things, and from henceforward speak nothing but truth, you shall be able to secure life for thyself And whosoever shall hear this command, and abstain from falsehood, that most pernicious habit, shall live unto God."

Mandate 4

1[29]:1 "I charge you, "said he, "to keep purity, and let not a thought enter into thy heart concerning another's wife, or concerning fornication, or concerning any such like evil deeds; for in so doing you commit a great sin. But remember your own wife always, and you shall never go wrong.

1[29]:2 For should this desire enter into your heart, you wilt go wrong, and should any other as evil as this, you commit sin. For this desire in a servant of God is a great sin; and if any man doeth this evil deed, he worked out death for himself.

1[29]:3 Look to it therefore. Abstain from this desire; for, where holiness dwells, there lawlessness ought not to enter into the heart of a righteous man."

1[29]:4 I say to him, "Sir, permit me to ask you a few more questions" "Say on," said he. "Sir," say I, "if a man who has a wife that is faithful in the Lord detect her in adultery, doth the husband sin in living with her?"

1[29]:5 "So long as he is ignorant," said he, "he sinned not; but if the husband know of her sin, and the wife repent not, but continue in her fornication, and her husband live with her, he makes himself responsible for her sin and an accomplice in her adultery."

1[29]:6 "What then, Sir," say I, "shall the husband do, if the wife continue in this case?" "Let him divorce her," said he, "and let the husband abide alone: but if after divorcing his wife he shall marry another, he likewise commits adultery."

1[29]:7 "If then, Sir," say I, "after the wife is divorced, she repent and desire to return to her own husband, shall she not be received?"

1[29]:8 "Certainly," said he, "if the husband received her not, he sinned and brings great sin upon himself; nay, one who has sinned and repented must be received, yet not often; for there is but one repentance for the servants of God. For the sake of her repentance therefore the husband ought not to marry. This is the manner of acting enjoined on husband and wife.

1[29]:9 Not only," said he, "is it adultery, if a man pollute his flesh, but whosoever doeth things like unto the heathen commits adultery. If therefore in such deeds as these likewise a man continue and repent not, keep away from him, and live not with him. Otherwise, you also art a partaker of his sin.

1[29]:10 For this cause you were enjoined to remain single, whether husband or wife; for in such cases repentance is possible.

1[29]:11 I," said he, "am not giving an excuse that this matter should be concluded thus, but to the end that the sinner should sin no more. But as concerning his former sin, there is One Who is able to give healing; it is He Who has authority over all things."

2[30]:1 I asked him again, saying, "Seeing that the Lord held me worthy that you should always dwell with me, suffer me still to say a few words, since I understand nothing, and my heart has been made dense by my former deeds. Make me to understand, for I am very foolish, and I apprehend absolutely nothing."

2[30]:2 He answered and said unto me, "I," said he, "preside over repentance, and I give understanding to all who repent. No, think you not," said he, "that this very act of repentance is understanding? To repent is great understanding," said he. "For the man that has sinned understands that he has done evil before the Lord, and the deed which he has done enters into his heart, and he repents, and doeth no more evil, but doeth good lavishly, and humbles his own soul and puts it to torture because it sinned. You see then that repentance is great understanding."

2[30]:3 "It is on this account therefore, Sir," say I, "that I enquire everything accurately of you; first, because I am a sinner; secondly, because I know not what deeds I must do that I may live, for my sins are many and various."

2[30]:4 "You shall live," said he, "if you keep my commandments and walk in them and whosoever shall hear these commandments and keep them, shall live unto God."

3[31]:1 "I will still proceed, Sir," say I, "to ask a further question." "Speak on," said he. "I have heard, Sir," say I, "from certain teachers, that there is no other repentance, save that which took place when we rent down into the water and obtained remission of our former sins."

3[31]:2 He said to me; "You hast well heard; for so it is. For he that has received remission of sins ought no longer to sin, but to dwell in purity.

3[31]:3 But, since you enquire all things accurately, I will declare unto you this also, so as to give no excuse to those who shall hereafter believe or those who have already believed, on the Lord. For they that have already believed, or shall hereafter believe, have not repentance for sins, but have only remission of their former sins.

3[31]:4 To those then that were called before these days the Lord has appointed repentance. For the Lord, being a discerner of hearts and foreknowing all things, perceived the weakness of men and the manifold wiles of the devil, how that he will be doing some mischief to the servants of God, and will deal wickedly with them.

3[31]:5 The Lord then, being very compassionate, had pity on His handiwork, and appointed this (opportunity of) repentance, and to me was given the authority over this repentance.

3[31]:6 But I say unto you," said he, "if after this great and holy calling any one, being tempted of the devil, shall commit sin, he has only one (opportunity of) repentance. But if he sin off-hand and repent, repentance is unprofitable for such a man; for he shall live with difficulty."

3[31]:7 I say unto him, "I was quickened unto life again, when I heard these things from you so precisely. For I know that, if I shall add no more to my sins, I shall be saved." "You shall be saved," he said, "you and all, as many as shall do these things."

4[32]:1 I asked him again, saying, "Sir, since once you do bear with me, declare unto me this further matter also." "Say on," said he. "If a wife, Sir," say I, "or, it may be, a husband fall asleep, and one of them marry, doth the one that marries sin?"

4[32]:2 "He sins not," said he, "but if he remain single, he invests himself with more exceeding honor and with great glory before the Lord; yet even if he should marry, he sins not.

4[32]:3 Preserve purity and holiness therefore, and you shall live unto God. All these things, which I speak and shall hereafter speak unto you, guard from this time forward, from the day when you was committed unto me, and I will dwell in thy house.

4[32]:4 But for thy former transgressions there shall be remission, if you keep my commandments. Yea, and all shall have remission, if they keep these my commandments, and walk in this purity."

Mandate 5

1[33]:1 "Be you long-suffering and understanding," he said, "and you shall have the mastery over all evil deeds, and shall work all righteousness.

1[33]:2 For if you art long-suffering, the Holy Spirit that abides in you shall be pure, not being darkened by another evil spirit, but dwelling in a large room shall rejoice and be glad with the vessel in which he dwells, and shall serve God with much cheerfulness, having prosperity in himself.

1[33]:3 But if any angry temper approach, forthwith the Holy Spirit, being delicate, is straitened, not having [the] place clear, and seeks to retire from the place; for he is being choked by the evil spirit, and has no room to minister unto the Lord, as he desires, being polluted by angry temper. For the Lord dwells in long-suffering, but the devil in angry temper.

1[33]:4 Thus that both the spirits then should be dwelling together is inconvenient and evil for that man in whom they dwell.

1[33]:5 For if you take a little wormwood, and pour it into a jar of honey, is not the whole of the honey spoiled, and all that honey ruined by a very small quantity of wormwood? For it destroyed the sweetness of the honey, and it no longer has the same attraction for the owner, because it is rendered bitter and has lost its use. But if the wormwood be not put into the honey, the honey is found sweet and becomes useful to its owner.

1[33]:6 You see [then] that long-suffering is very sweet, beyond the sweetness of honey, and is useful to the Lord, and He dwells in it. But angry, temper is bitter and useless. If then angry temper be mixed with long-suffering, long-suffering is polluted and the man's intercession is no longer useful to God."

1[33]:7 "I would fain know, Sir," say I, "the working of angry temper, that I may guard myself from it." "Yea, verily," said he, "if you guard not thyself from it--you and thy family--you hast lost all thy hope. But guard thyself from it; for I am with you. Yea, and all men shall hold aloof from it, as many as have repented with their whole heart. For I will be with them and will preserve them; for they all were justified by the most holy angel.

2[34]:1 "Hear now," said he, "the working of angry temper, how evil it is, and how it subverts the servants of God by its own working, and how it leads them astray from righteousness. But it doth not lead astray them that are full in the faith, nor can it work upon them, because the power of the Lord is with them; but them that are empty and double-minded it leads astray.

2[34]:2 For when it sees such men in prosperity it insinuates itself into the heart of the man, and for no cause whatever the man or the woman is embittered on account of worldly matters, either about meats, or some triviality, or about some friend, or about giving or receiving, or about follies of this kind. For all these things are foolish and vain and senseless and inexpedient for the servants of God.

2[34]:3 But long-suffering is great and strong, and has a mighty and vigorous power, and is prosperous in great enlargement, gladsome, exultant, free from care, glorifying the Lord at every season, having no bitterness in itself, remaining always gentle and tranquil. This long-suffering therefore dwells with those whose faith is perfect.

2[34]:4 But angry temper is in the first place foolish, fickle and senseless; then from foolishness is engendered bitterness, and from bitterness wrath, and from wrath anger, and from anger spite; then spite being composed of all these evil elements becomes a great sin and incurable.

2[34]:5 For when all these spirits dwell in one vessel, where the Holy Spirit also dwells, that vessel cannot contain them, but overflows.

2[34]:6 The delicate spirit therefore, as not being accustomed to dwell with an evil spirit nor with harshness, departs from a man of that kind, and seeks to dwell with gentleness and tranquility.

2[34]:7 Then, when it has removed from that man, in whom it dwells, that man becomes emptied of the righteous spirit, and henceforward, being filled with the evil spirits, he is unstable in all his actions, being dragged about hither and thither by the evil spirits, and is altogether blinded and bereft of his good intent. Thus then it happens to all persons of angry temper.

2[34]:8 Refrain therefore from angry temper, the most evil of evil spirits. But clothe thyself in long-suffering, and resist angry temper and bitterness, and you shall be round in company with the holiness which is beloved of the Lord. See then that you never neglect this commandment; for if you master this commandment, you shall be able likewise to keep the remaining commandments, which I am about to give you. Be strong in them and endowed with power; and let all be endowed with power, as many as desire to walk in them."

Mandate 6

1[35]:1 I charged you," said he, "in my first commandment to guard faith and fear and temperance." "Yes, Sir," say I. "But now," said he, "I wish to show you their powers also, that you mayest understand what is the power and effect of each one of them. For their effects are two fold. Now they are prescribed alike to the righteous and the unrighteous.

1[35]:2 Do you therefore trust righteousness, but trust not unrighteousness; for the way of righteousness is straight, but the way of unrighteousness is crooked. But walk you in the straight [and level] path, and leave the crooked one alone.

1[35]:3 For the crooked way has no tracks, but only pathlessness and many stumbling stones, and is rough and thorny. So it is therefore harmful to those who walk in it.

1[35]:4 But those who walk in the straight way walk on the level and without stumbling: for it is neither rough nor thorny. You seest then that it is more expedient to walk in this way."

1[35]:5 "I am pleased, Sir," say I, "to walk in this way." "You shall walk," he said, "yea, and whosoever shall turn unto the Lord with his whole heart shall walk in it.

2[36]:1 "Hear now," said he, "concerning faith. There are two angels with a man, one of righteousness and one of wickedness."

2[36]:2 "How then, Sir," say I, "shall I know their workings, seeing that both angels dwell with me?"

2[36]:3 "Hear," said he, "and understand their workings. The angel of righteousness is delicate and bashful and gentle and tranquil. When then this one enters into thy heart, forthwith he speaketh with you of righteousness, of purity, of holiness, and of contentment, of every righteous deed and of every glorious virtue. When all these things enter into thy heart, know that the angel of righteousness is with you. [These then are the works of the angel of righteousness.] Trust him therefore and his works.

2[36]:4 Now see the works of the angel of wickedness also. First of all, he is quick tempered and bitter and senseless, and his works are evil, overthrowing the servants of God. Whenever then he entereth into thy heart, know him by his works."

2[36]:5 "How I shall discern him, Sir," I reply, "I know not." Listen," said he. "When a fit of angry temper or bitterness comes upon you, know that he is in you. Then the desire of much business and the costliness of many viands and drinking bouts and of many drunken fits and of various luxuries which are unseemly, and the desire of women, and avarice, and haughtiness and boastfulness, and whatsoever things are akin and like to these--when then these things enter into thy heart, know that the angel of wickedness is with you.

2[36]:6 Do you therefore, recognizing his works, stand aloof from him, and trust him in nothing, for his works are evil and inexpedient for the servants of God. Here then you hast the workings of both the angels. Understand them, and trust the angel of righteousness.

2[36]:7 But from the angel of wickedness stand aloof, for his teaching is evil in every matter; for though one be a man of faith, and the desire of this angel enter into his heart, that man, or that woman, must commit some sin.

2[36]:8 And if again a man or a woman be exceedingly wicked, and the works of the angel of righteousness come into that man's heart, he must of necessity do something good.

2[36]:9 You see then," said he, "that it is good to follow the angel of righteousness, and to bid farewell to the angel of wickedness.

2[36]:10 This commandment declares what concerns faith, that you may trust the works of the angel of righteousness, and doing them may live unto God. But believe that the works of the angel of wickedness are difficult; so by not doing them you shall live unto God."

Mandate 7

1[37]:1 "Fear the Lord," said he, "and keep His commandments. So keeping the commandments of God you shall be powerful in every deed, and thy doing shall be incomparable. For whilst you fear the Lord, you shall do all things well. But this is the fear wherewith you ought to be afraid, and you shall be saved.

1[37]:2 But fear not the devil; for, if you fear the Lord, you shall be master over the devil, for there is no power in him. [For] in whom is no power, neither is there fear of him; but in whom power is glorious, of him is fear likewise. For every one that has power has fear, whereas he that has no power is despised of all.

1[37]:3 But fear you the works of the devil, for they are evil. While then you fear the Lord, you wilt fear the works of the devil, and wilt not do them, but abstain from them.

1[37]:4 Fear therefore is of two kinds. If you desire to do evil, fear the Lord, and you shall not do it. If again you desire to do good, fear the Lord and you shall do it. Therefore the fear of the Lord is powerful and great and glorious. Fear the Lord then, and you shall live unto Him; yea, and as many of them that keep His commandments as shall fear Him, shall live unto God."

1[37]:5 "Wherefore, Sir," say I, "didst you say concerning those that keep His commandments, "They shall live unto God"?" "Because," said he, "every creature fears the Lord, but not every one keeps His commandments. Those then that fear Him and keep His commandments, they have life unto God; but they that keep not His commandments have no life in them."

Mandate 8

1[38]:1 "I told you," said he, "that the creatures of God are twofold; for temperance also is twofold. For in some things it is right to be temperate, but in other things it is not right."

1[38]:2 "Make known unto me, Sir," say I, "in what things it is right to be temperate, and in what things it is not right." "Listen," said he. "Be temperate as to what is evil, and do it not; but be not temperate as to what is good, but do it. For if you be temperate as to what is good, so as not to do it, you commits a great sin; but if you be temperate as to what is evil, so as not to do it, you doest great righteousness. Be temperate therefore in abstaining from all wickedness, and do that which is good."

1[38]:3 "What kinds of wickedness, Sir," say I, "are they from which we must be temperate and abstain?" "Listen," said he; "from adultery and fornication, from the lawlessness of drunkenness, from wicked luxury, from many viands and the costliness of riches, and vaunting and haughtiness and pride, and from falsehood and evil speaking and hypocrisy, malice and all blasphemy.

1[38]:4 These works are the most wicked of all in the life of men. From these works therefore the servant of God must be temperate and abstain; for he that is not temperate so as to abstain from these cannot live unto God. Listen then to what follows upon these."

1[38]:5 "Why, are there still other evil deeds, Sir?" say I. "Aye, said he, "there are many, from which the servant of God must be temperate and abstain; theft, falsehood, deprivation, false witness, avarice, evil desire, deceit, vain-glory, boastfulness, and whatsoever things are like unto these.

1[38]:6 Think you not that these things are wrong, yea, very wrong," [said he,] "for the servants of God? In all these things he that serves God must exercise temperance. Be you temperate, therefore, and refrain from all these things, that you may live unto God, and be enrolled among those who exercise self-restraint in them. These then are the things from which you should restrain thyself

1[38]:7 Now hear," said he, "the things, in which you should not exercise self restraint, but do them. Exercise no self-restraint in that which is good, but do it."

1[38]:8 "Sir," say I, "show me the power of the good also, that I may walk in them and serve them, that doing them it may be possible for me to be saved." "Hear," said he, "the works of the good likewise, which you must do, and towards which you must exercise no self-restraint.

1[38]:9 First of all, there is faith, fear of the Lord, love, concord, words of righteousness, truth, patience; nothing is better than these in the life of men. If a man keep these, and exercise not self-restraint from them, he becomes blessed in his life.

1[38]:10 Hear now what follow upon these; to minister to widows, to visit the orphans and the needy, to ransom the servants of God from their afflictions, to be hospitable (for in hospitality benevolence from time to time has a place), to resist no man, to be tranquil, to show yourself more submissive than all men, to reverence the aged, to practice righteousness, to observe brotherly feeling, to endure injury, to be long-suffering, to bear no grudge, to exhort those who are sick at soul, not to cast away those that have stumbled from the faith, but to convert them and to put courage Into them, to reprove sinners, not to oppress debtors and indigent persons, and whatsoever actions are like these.

1[38]:11 Do these things," said he, "seem to you to be good?" "Why, what, Sir," say I, "can be better than these?" "Then walk in them," said he, "and abstain not from them, and you shall live unto God.

1[38]:12 Keep this commandment therefore. If you do good and abstain not from it, you shall live unto God; yea, and all shall live unto God who act so. And again if you do not evil, and abstain from it, you shall live unto God; yea, and all shall live unto God, who shall keep these commandments, and walk in them."

Mandate 9

1[39]:1 He said to me; "Remove from thyself a doubtful mind and doubt not at all whether to ask of God, saying within thyself, "How can I ask thing of the Lord and receive it, seeing that I have committed so many sins against Him?"

1[39]:2 Reason not thus, but turn to the Lord with thy whole heart, and ask of Him nothing wavering, and you shall know His exceeding compassion, that He will surely not abandon you, but will fulfill the petition of thy soul.

1[39]:3 For God is not as men who bear a grudge, but Himself is without malice and has compassion on His creatures.

1[39]:4 Do you therefore cleanse thy heart from all the vanities of this life, and from the things mentioned before; and ask of the Lord, and you shall receive all things, and shall lack nothing of all thy petitions, if you ask of the Lord nothing wavering.

1[39]:5 But if you waver in thy heart, you shall surely receive none of thy petitions. For they that waver towards God, these are the doubtful-minded, and they never obtain any of their petitions.

1[39]:6 But they that are complete in the faith make all their petitions trusting in the Lord, and they receive, because they ask without wavering, nothing doubting; for every doubtful-minded man, if he repent not, shall hardly be saved.

1[39]:7 Cleanse therefore thy heart from doubtful-mindedness, and put on faith, for it is strong, and trust God that you wilt receive all thy petitions which you ask; and if after asking anything of the Lord, you receive thy petition somewhat tardily, be not of doubtful mind because you didst not receive the petition of thy soul at once. For assuredly it is by reason of some temptation or some transgression, of which you art ignorant, that you receive thy petition so tardily.

1[39]:8 Do you therefore cease not to make thy soul's petition, and you shall receive it. But if you grow weary, and doubt as you ask, blame yourself and not Him that gave unto you. See to this doubtful-mindedness; for it is evil and senseless, and uproots many from the faith, yea, even very faithful and strong men. For indeed this doubtful-mindedness is a daughter of the devil, and works great wickedness against the servants of God.

1[39]:9 Therefore despise doubtful-mindedness and gain the mastery over it in everything, clothing yourself with faith which is strong and powerful. For faith promises all things, accomplishes all things; but doubtful-mindedness, as having no confidence in itself, fails in all the works which it doeth.

1[39]:10 You see then," said he, "that faith is from above from the Lord, and has great power; but doubtful-mindedness is an earthly spirit from the devil, and has no power.

1[39]:11 Do you therefore serve that faith which has power, and hold aloof from the doubtful-mindedness which has no power; and you shall live unto God; yea, and all those shall live unto God who are so minded."

Mandate 10

1[40]:1 "Put away sorrow from yourself," said he, "for she is the sister of doubtful-mindedness and of angry temper."

1[40]:2 "How, Sir," say I, "is she the sister of these? For angry temper seems to me to be one thing, doubtful-mindedness another, sorrow another." "You art a foolish fellow," said he, "[and] perceives not that sorrow is more evil than all the spirits, and is most fatal to the servants of God, and beyond all the spirits destroys a man, and crushes out the Holy Spirit and yet again saves it."

1[40]:3 "I, Sir," say I, "am without understanding, and I understand not these parables. For how it can crush out and again save, I do not comprehend."

1[40]:4 "Listen," said he. "Those who have never investigated concerning the truth, nor enquired concerning the deity, but have merely believed, and have been mixed up in business affairs and riches and heathen friendships, and many other affairs of this world--as many, I say, as devote themselves to these things, comprehend not the parables of the deity; for they are darkened by these actions, and are corrupted and become barren.

1[40]:5 As good vineyards, when they are treated with neglect, are made barren by the thorns and weeds of various kinds, so men who after they have believed fall into these many occupations which were mentioned before, lose their understanding and comprehend nothing at all concerning righteousness; for if they hear concerning the deity and truth, their mind is absorbed in their occupations, and they perceive nothing at all.

1[40]:6 But they that have the fear of God, and investigate concerning deity and truth, and direct their heart towards the Lord, perceive and understand everything that is said to them more quickly, because they have the fear of the Lord in themselves; for where the Lord dwells, there too is great understanding. Hold fast therefore unto the Lord, and you shall understand and perceive all things.

2[41]:1 "Hear now, senseless man," said he, "How sorrow crushes out the Holy Spirit, and again saves it.

2[41]:2 When the man of doubtful mind sets his hand to any action, and fails in it owing to his doubtful-mindedness, grief at this enters into the man, and grieves the Holy Spirit, and crushes it out.

2[41]:3 Then again when angry temper cleaves to a man concerning any matter, and he is much embittered, again sorrow enters into the heart of the man that was ill-tempered, and he is grieved at the deed which he has done, and repents that he did evil.

2[41]:4 This sadness therefore seems to bring salvation, because he repented at having done the evil. So both the operations sadden the Spirit; first, the doubtful mind saddens the Spirit, because it succeeded not in its business, and the angry temper again, because it did what was evil. Thus both are saddening to the Holy Spirit, the doubtful mind and the angry temper.

2[41]:5 Put away therefore from yourself sadness, and afflict not the Holy Spirit that dwells in you, lest haply He intercede with God [against you], and depart from you.

2[41]:6 For the Spirit of God, that was given unto this flesh, endures not sadness neither constraint.

3[42]:1 "Therefore clothe yourself in cheerfulness, which has favor with Cod always, and is acceptable to Him, and rejoice in it. For every cheerful man works good, and thinks good, and despises sadness;

3[42]:2 but the sad man is always committing sin. In the first place he commits sin, because he grieves the Holy Spirit, which was given to the man being a cheerful spirit; and in the second place, by grieving the Holy Spirit he doeth lawlessness, in that he doth not intercede with neither confess unto God. For the intercession of a sad man has never at any time power to ascend to the altar of God."

3[42]:3 "Wherefore," say I, "doth not the intercession of him that is saddened ascend to the altar?" "Because," said he, "sadness is seated at his heart. Thus sadness mingled with the intercession doth not suffer the intercession to ascend pure to the altar. For as vinegar when mingled with wine in the same (vessel) has not the same pleasant taste, so likewise sadness mingled with the Holy Spirit has not the same intercession.

3[42]:4 Therefore cleanse yourself from this wicked sadness, and you shall live unto God; yea, and all they shall live unto God, who shall cast away sadness from themselves and clothe themselves in all cheerfulness."

Mandate 11

1[43]:1 He showed me men seated on a couch, and another man seated on a chair. And he said to me, "See you those that are seated on the couch?" "I see them, Sir," say I. "These," said he, "are faithful, but he that sits on the chair is a false prophet who destroys the mind of the servants of God--I mean, of the doubtful-minded, not of the faithful.

1[43]:2 These doubtful-minded ones then come to him as to a soothsayer and enquire of him what shall befall them. And he, the false prophet, having no power of a divine Spirit in himself, speaks with them according to their enquiries [and according to the lusts of their wickedness], and fills their souls as they themselves wish.

1[43]:3 For being empty himself he gives empty answers to empty enquirers; for what-ever enquiry may be made of him, he answers according to the emptiness of the man. But he speaks also some true words; for the devil fills him with his own spirit, if so be he shall be able to break down some of the righteous.

1[43]:4 So many therefore as are strong in the faith of the Lord, clothed with the truth, hold fast not to such spirits, but hold aloof from them; but as many as are doubters and frequently change their minds, practice soothsaying like the Gentiles, and bring upon themselves greater sin by their idolatries. For he that consults a false prophet on any matter is an idolater and emptied of the truth, and senseless.

1[43]:5 For no Spirit given of God needs to be consulted; but, having the power of deity, speaks all things of itself, because it is from above, even from the power of the divine Spirit.

1[43]:6 But the spirit which is consulted, and speaks according to the desires of men, is earthly and fickle, having no power; and it speaks not at all, unless it be consulted."

1[43]:7 "How then, Sir," say I, "shall a man know who of them is a prophet, and who a false prophet?" "Hear," said he, "concerning both the prophets; and, as I shall tell you, so shall you test the prophet and the false prophet. By his life test the man that has the divine Spirit.

1[43]:8 In the first place, he that has the [divine] Spirit, which is from above, is gentle and tranquil and humble-minded, and abstains from all wickedness and vain desire of this present world, and holds himself inferior to all men, and gives no answer to any man when enquired of, nor speaks in solitude (for neither doth the Holy Spirit speak when a man wishes Him to speak); but the man speaks then when God wishes him to speak.

1[43]:9 When then the man who has the divine Spirit cometh into an assembly of righteous men, who have faith in a divine Spirit, and intercession is made to God by the gathering of those men, then the angel of the prophetic spirit, who is attached to him, fills the man, and the man, being filled with the Holy Spirit, speaks to the multitude, according as the Lord wills.

1[43]:10 In this way then the Spirit of the deity shall be manifest. This then is the greatness of the power as touching the Spirit of the deity of the Lord.

1[43]:11 Hear now," said he, "concerning the earthly and vain spirit, which has no power but is foolish.

1[43]:12 In the first place, that man who seems to have a spirit exalts himself, and desires to have a chief place, and straight-way he is impudent and shameless and talkative and conversant in many luxuries and in many other deceits and receives money for his prophesying, and if he receives not, he prophesies not. Now can a divine Spirit receive money and prophesy? It is not possible for a prophet of God to do this, but the spirit of such prophets is earthly.

1[43]:13 In the next place, it never approaches an assembly of righteous men; but avoids them, and clings to the doubtful-minded and empty, and prophesies to them in corners, and deceives them, speaking all things in emptiness to gratify their desires; for they too are empty whom it answers. For the empty vessel placed together with the empty is not broken, but they agree one with the other.

1[43]:14 But when he comes into an assembly full of righteous men who have a Spirit of deity, and intercession is made from them, that man is emptied, and the earthly spirit flees from him in fear, and that man is struck dumb and is altogether broken in pieces, being unable to utter a word.

1[43]:15 For, if you pack wine or oil into a closet, and place an empty vessel among them, and again desire to unpack the closet, the vessel which you place there empty, empty in like manner you will find it. Thus also the empty prophets, whenever they come unto the spirits of righteous men, are found just such as they came.

1[43]:16 I have given you the life of both kinds of prophets. Therefore test, by his life and his works, the man who says that he is moved by the Spirit.

1[43]:17 But do you trust the Spirit that cometh from God, and has power; but in the earthly and empty spirit put no trust at all; for in it there is no power, for it cometh from the devil.

1[43]:18 Listen [then] to the parable which I shall tell you. Take a stone, and throw it up to heaven--see if you can reach it; or again, take a squirt of water, and squirt it up to heaven--see if you can bore through the heaven."

1[43]:19 "How, Sir," say I, "can these things be? For both these things which you hast mentioned are beyond our power." "Well then," said he, "just as these things are beyond our power, so likewise the earthly spirits have no power and are feeble.

1[43]:20 Now take the power which cometh from above. The hail is a very, small grain, and yet, when it falls on a man's head, what pain it causes! Or again, take a drop which falls on the ground from the tiles, and bores through the stone.

1[43]:21 You see then that the smallest things from above falling on the earth have great power. So likewise the divine Spirit coming from above is powerful. This Spirit therefore trust, but from the other hold aloof."

Mandate 12

1[44]:1 He said to me; "Remove from yourself all evil desire, and clothe yourself in the desire which is good and holy; for clothed with this desire you shall hate the evil desire, and shall bridle and direct it as you wilt.

1[44]:2 For the evil desire is wild, and only tamed with difficulty; for it is terrible, and by its wildness is very costly to men; more especially if a servant of God get entangled in it, and have no understanding, he is put to fearful costs by it. But it is costly to such men as are not clothed in the good desire, but are mixed up with this life "These men then it hands over to death."

1[44]:3 "Of what sort, Sir," say I, "are the works of the evil desire, which hand over men to death? Make them known to me, that I may hold aloof from them." Listen," [said he,] "through what works the evil desire brings death to the servants of God.

2[45]:1 "Before all is desire for the wife or husband of another, and for extravagance of wealth, and for many needless dainties, and for drinks and other luxuries, many and foolish. For even luxury is foolish and vain for the servants of God.

2[45]:2 These desires then are evil, and bring death to the servants of God. For this evil desire is a daughter of the devil. you must, therefore, abstain from the evil desires, that so abstaining you may live unto God.

2[45]:3 But as many as are mastered by them, and resist them not, are done to death utterly; for these desires are deadly.

2[45]:4 But do you clothe yourself in the desire of righteousness, and, having armed yourself with the fear of the Lord, resist them. For the fear of God dwells in the good desire. If the evil desire shall see you armed with the fear of God and resisting itself, it shall flee far from you, and shall no more be seen of you, being in fear of your arms.

2[45]:5 Do you therefore, when you art crowned for thy victory over it, come to the desire of righteousness, and deliver to her the victor's prize which you hast received, and serve her, according as she herself desires. If you serve the good desire, and art subject to her, you shall have power to master the evil desire, and to subject her, according as you wilt."

3[46]:1 "I would fain know, Sir," say I, "in what ways I ought to serve the good desire." "Listen," said he; "practice righteousness and virtue, truth and the fear of the Lord, faith and gentleness, and as many good deeds as are like these. Practicing these you shall be well-pleasing as a servant of God, and shall live unto Him; yea, and every one who shall serve the good desire shall live unto God."

3[46]:2 So he completed the twelve commandments, and he said to me; You hast these commandments; walk in them, and exhort thy hearers that their repentance may become pure for the rest of the days of their life.

3[46]:3 This ministration, which I give you, fulfill you with all diligence to the end, and you shall effect much. For you shall find favor among those who are about to repent, and they shall obey thy words. For I will be with you, and will compel them to obey you."

3[46]:4 I say to him; "Sir, these commandments are great and beautiful and glorious, and are able to gladden the heart of the man who is able to observe them. But I know not whether these commandments can be kept by a man, for they are very hard."

3[46]:5 He answered and said unto me; "If you set it before yourself that they can be kept, you wilt easily keep them, and they will not be hard; but if it once enter into thy heart that they cannot be kept by a man, you wilt not keep them.

3[46]:6 But now I say unto you; if you keep them not. but neglect them you shall not have salvation, neither thy children nor thy household, since you hast already pronounced judgment against yourself that these commandments cannot be kept by a man."

4[47]:1 And these things he said to me very angrily, so that I was confounded, and feared him exceedingly; for his form was changed, so that a man could not endure his anger.

4[47]:2 And when he saw that I was altogether disturbed and confounded, he began to speak more kindly [and cheerfully] to me, and he said; "Foolish fellow, void of understanding and of doubtful mind, perceives you not the glory of God, how great and mighty and marvelous it is, how that He created the world for man's sake, and subjected all His creation to man, and gave all authority to him, that he should be master over all things under the heaven?

4[47]:3 If then," [he said,] "man is lord of all the creatures of God and masters all things, cannot he also master these commandments Aye," said he, "the man that has the Lord in his heart can master [all things and] all these commandments.

4[47]:4 But they that have the Lord on their lips, while their heart is hardened, and are far from the Lord, to them these commandments are hard and inaccessible.

4[47]:5 Therefore do you, who are empty and fickle in the faith, set your Lord in your heart, and you shall perceive that nothing is easier than these commandments, nor sweeter, nor more gentle.

4[47]:6 Be you converted, you that walk after the commandments of the devil, (the commandments which are so) difficult and bitter and wild and riotous; and fear not the devil, for there is no power in him against you.

4[47]:7 For I will be with you, I, the angel of repentance, who have the mastery over him. The devil has fear alone, but his fear has no force. Fear him not therefore; and he will flee from you."

5[48]:1 I say to him, "Sir, listen to a few words from me." "Say what you wilt," said he. "Man, Sir," I say, "is eager to keep the commandments of God, and there is no one that asks not of the Lord that he may be strengthened in His commandments, and be subject to them; but the devil is hard and overmasters them."

5[48]:2 "He cannot," said he, "overmaster the servants of God, who set their hope on Him with their whole heart. The devil can wrestle with them, but he cannot overthrow them. If then you resist him, he will be vanquished and will flee from you disgraced. But as many," said he, "as are utterly empty, fear the devil as if he had power.

5[48]:3 When a man has filled amply sufficient jars with good wine, and among these jars a few are quite empty, he comes to the jars, and does not examine the full ones, for he knows that they are full; but he examines the empty ones, fearing lest they have turned sour. For empty jars soon turn sour, and the taste of the wine is spoilt.

5[48]:4 So also the devil cometh to all the servants of God tempting them. As many then as are complete in the faith, oppose him mightily, and he departs from them, not having a place where he can find an entrance. So he cometh next to the empty ones, and finding a place goes into them, and further he doeth what he wills in them, and they become submissive slaves to him.

6[49]:1 "But I, the angel of repentance, say unto you; Fear not the devil; for I was sent," said he, "to be with you who repent with your whole heart, and to strengthen you in the faith.

6[49]:2 Believe, therefore, on God, you who by reason of your sins have despaired of your life, and are adding to your sins, and weighing down your life; for if you turn unto the Lord with your whole heart, and work righteousness the remaining days of your life, and serve Him rightly according to His will, He will give healing to your former sins, and you shall have power to master the works of the devil. But of the threatening of the devil fear not at all; for he is unstrung, like the sinews of a dead man.

6[49]:3 Hear me therefore, and fear Him, Who is able to do all things, to save and to destroy, and observe these commandments, and you shall live unto God."

6[49]:4 I say to him, "Sir, now am I strengthened in all the ordinances of the Lord, because you art with me; and I know that you wilt crush all the power of the devil, and we shall be masters over him, and shall prevail over all his works. And I hope, Sir, that I am now able to keep these commandments which you hast commanded, the Lord enabling me."

6[49]:5 "You shall keep them," said he, "if thy heart be found pure with the Lord; yea, and all shall keep them, as many as shall purify their hearts from the vain desires of this world, and shall live unto God."

Parables Which He spoke With Me

Parable 1

1[50]:1 He said to me; "you know that you, who are the servants of God, are dwelling in a foreign land; for your city is far from this city. If then you know your city, in which you shall dwell, why do you here prepare fields and expensive displays and buildings and dwelling-chambers which are superfluous?

1[50]:2 He, therefore, that prepares these things for this city does not purpose to return to his own city.

1[50]:3 O foolish and double-minded and miserable man, perceives you not that all these things are foreign, and are under the power of another For the lord of this city shall say, "I do not wish you to dwell in my city; go forth from this city, for you do not conform to my laws."

1[50]:4 You, therefore who hast fields and dwellings and many other possessions, when you art cast out by him, what wilt you do with thy field and thy house am all the other things that you prepared for yourself? For the lord of this country said to you justly, "Either conform to my laws, or depart from my country."

1[50]:5 What then shall you do, who art under law in your own city? For the sake of thy fields and the rest of thy possessions wilt you altogether repudiate thy law, and walk according to the law of this city? Take heed, lest it be inexpedient to repudiate the law; for if you should desire to return again to thy city, you shall surely not be received [because you didst repudiate the law of the city], and shall be shut out from it.

1[50]:6 Take heed therefore; as dwelling in a strange land prepare nothing more for yourself but a competency which is sufficient for you, and make ready that, whenever the master of this city may desire to cast you out for your opposition to his law, you may go forth from his city and depart into your own city and use your own law joyfully, free from all insult.

1[50]:7 Take heed therefore, you that serve God and have Him in your heart: work the "works of God being mindful of His commandments and of the promises which He made, and believe Him that He will perform them, if His commandments be kept.

1[50]:8 Therefore, instead of fields buy you souls that are in trouble, as each is able, and visit widows and orphans, and neglect them not; and spend your riches and all your displays, which you received from God, on fields and houses of this kind.

1[50]:9 For to this end the Master enriched you, that you might perform these ministrations for Him. It is much better to purchase fields [and possessions] and houses of this kind, which you wilt find in your own city, when you visit it.

1[50]:10 This lavish expenditure is beautiful and joyous, not bringing sadness or fear, but bringing joy. The expenditure of the heathen then practice not you; for it is not convenient for you the servants of God.

1[50]:11 But practice your own expenditure, in which you can rejoice; and do not corrupt, neither touch that which is another man's, nor lust after it for it is wicked to lust after other men's possessions. But perform your own task, and you shall be saved."

Parable 2

1[51]:1 As I walked in the field, and noticed an elm and a vine, and was distinguishing them and their fruits, the shepherd appears to me and said; "What art you meditating within yourself?" "I am thinking, [Sir,]" say I, "about the elm and the vine, that they are excellently suited the one to the other."

1[51]:2 "These two trees," said he, "are appointed for a type to the servants of God." "I would fain know, [Sir,]" say I, "the type contained in these trees, of which you speak." "See you," said he, "the elm and the vine ?" "I see them, Sir," say I.

1[51]:3 "This vine," said he, "bears fruit, but the elm is an unfruitful stock. Yet this vine, except it climb up the elm, cannot bear much fruit when it is spread on the ground; and such fruit as it bears is rotten, because it is not suspended upon the elm. When then the vine is attached to the elm, it bears fruit both from itself and from the elm.

1[51]:4 You see then that the elm also bears [much] fruit, not less than the vine, but rather more." How more, Sir?" say I. "Because," said he, "the vine, when hanging upon the elm, bears its fruit in abundance, and in good condition; but, when spread on the ground, it bears little fruit, and that rotten. This parable therefore is applicable to the servants of God, to poor and to rich alike."

1[51]:5 "How, Sir?" say I; "instruct me." "Listen," said he; the rich man has much wealth, but in the things of the Lord he is poor, being distracted about his riches, and his confession and intercession with the Lord is very scanty; and even that which he gives is mall and weak and has not power above. When then the rich man goes up to the poor, and assists him in his needs, believing that for what he doth to the poor man he shall be able to obtain a reward with God--because the poor man is rich in intercession [and confession], and his intercession has great power with God--the rich man then supplies all things to the poor man without wavering.

1[51]:6 But the poor man being supplied by the rich makes intercession for him, thanking God for him that gave to him. And the other is still more zealous to assist the poor man, that he may be continuous in his life: for he knows that the intercession of the poor man is acceptable and rich before God.

1[51]:7 They both then accomplish their work; the poor man makes intercession, wherein he is rich [which he received of the Lord]; this he renders again to the Lord Who supplies him with it. The rich man too in like manner furnishes to the poor man, nothing doubting, the riches which he received from the Lord. And this work great and acceptable with God, because (the rich man) has understanding concerning his riches, and works for the poor man from the bounties of the Lord, and accomplishes the ministration of the Lord rightly.

1[51]:8 In the sight of men then the elm seems not to bear fruit, and they know not, neither perceive, that if there cometh a drought the elm having water nurtures the vine, and the vine having a constant supply of water bears fruit two fold, both for itself and for the elm. So likewise the poor, by interceding with the Lord for the rich, establish their riches, and again the rich, supplying their needs to the poor, establish their souls.

1[51]:9 So then both are made partners in the righteous work. He then that doeth these things shall not be abandoned of God, but shall be written in the books of the living.

1[51]:10 Blessed are the rich, who understand also that they are enriched from the Lord. For they that have this mind shall be able to do some good work."

Parable 3

1[52]:1 He showed me many trees which had no leaves, but they seemed to me to be, as it were, withered; for they were all alike. And he said to me; "See you these trees?" "I see them, Sir," I say, "they are all alike, and are withered." He answered and said to me; "These trees that you see are they that dwell in this world."

1[52]:2 "Wherefore then, Sir," say I, "are they as if they were withered, and alike?" "Because," said he, "neither the righteous are distinguishable, nor the sinners in this world, but they are alike. For this world is winter to the righteous, and they are not distinguishable, as they dwell with the sinners.

1[52]:3 For as in the winter the trees, having shed their leaves, are alike, and are not distinguishable, which are withered, and which alive, so also in this world neither the just nor the sinners are distinguishable, but they are all alike."

Parable 4

1[53]:1 He showed me many trees again, some of them sprouting, and others withered, and he said to me; "See you," said he, "these trees?" "I see them, Sir," say I, "some of them sprouting, and others withered."

1[53]:2 "These trees," said he, "that are sprouting are the righteous, who shall dwell in the world to come; for the world to come is summer to the righteous, but winter to the sinners. When then the mercy of the Lord shall shine forth, then they that serve God shall be made manifest; yea, and all men shall be made manifest.

1[53]:3 For as in summer the fruits of each several tree are made manifest, and are recognized of what sort they are, so also the fruits of the righteous shall be manifest, and all [even the very smallest] shall be known to be flourishing in that world.

1[53]:4 But the Gentiles and the sinners, just as you saw the trees which were withered, even such shall they be found, withered and unfruitful in that world, and shall be burnt up as fuel, and shall be manifest, because their practice in their life has been evil. For the sinners shall be burned, because they sinned and repented not; and the Gentiles shall be burned, because they knew not Him that created them.

1[53]:5 Do you therefore bear fruit, that in that summer thy fruit may be known. But abstain from overmuch business, and you shall never fill into any sin. For they that busy themselves overmuch, sin much also, being distracted about their business, and in no wise serving their own Lord.

1[53]:6 How then," said he, "can such a man ask anything of the Lord and receive it, seeing that he serves not the Lord? [For] they that serve Him, these shall receive their petitions, but they that serve not the Lord, these shall receive nothing.

1[53]:7 But if any one work one single action, he is able also to serve the Lord; for his mind shall not be corrupted from (following) the Lord, but he shall serve Him, because he keeps his mind pure.

1[53]:8 If therefore you doest these things, you shall be able to bear fruit unto the world to come; yea, and whosoever shall do these things, shall bear fruit."

Parable 5

1[54]:1 As I was fasting and seated on a certain mountain, and giving thanks to the Lord for all that He had done unto me, I see the shepherd seated by me and saying; "Why hast you come hither in the early morn?" "Because, Sir," say I, "I am keeping a station."

1[54]:2 "What," said he, "is a station?" "I am fasting, Sir," say I. "And what," said he, "is this fast [that you are fasting]?" "As I was accustomed, Sir," say I, "so I fast."

1[54]:3 "you know not," said he, "how to fast unto the Lord, neither is this a fast, this unprofitable fast which you make unto Him." "wherefore, Sir," say I, "say you this?" "I tell you," said he, "that this is not a fast, wherein you think to fast; but I will teach you what is a complete fast and acceptable to the Lord. Listen," said he;

1[54]:4 "God desires not such a vain fast; for by so fasting unto God you shall do nothing for righteousness. But fast you [unto God] such a fast as this;

1[54]:5 do no wickedness in thy life, and serve the Lord with a pure heart; observe His commandments and walk in His ordinances, and let no evil desire rise up in thy heart; but believe God. Then, if you shall do these things, and fear Him, and control yourself from every evil deed, you shall live unto God; and if you do these things, you shall accomplish a great fast, and one acceptable to God.

2[55]:1 "Hear the parable which I shall tell you relating to fasting.

2[55]:2 A certain man had an estate, and many slaves, and a portion of his estate he planted as a vineyard; and choosing out a certain slave who was trusty and well-pleasing (and) held in honor, he called him to him and said unto him; "Take this vineyard [which I have planted], and fence it [till I come], but do nothing else to the vineyard. Now keep this my commandment, and you shall be free in my house." Then the master of the servant went away to travel abroad.

2[55]:3 When then he had gone away, the servant took and fenced the vineyard; and having finished the fencing of the vineyard, he noticed that the vineyard was full of weeds.

2[55]:4 So he reasoned within himself, saying, "This command of my lord I have carried out I will next dig this vineyard, and it shall be neater when it is dug; and when it has no weeds it will yield more fruit, because not choked by the weeds." He took and dug the vineyard, and all the weeds that were in the vineyard he plucked up. And that vineyard became very neat and flourishing, when it had no weeds to choke it.

2[55]:5 After a time the master of the servant [and of the estate] came, and he went into the vineyard. And seeing the vineyard fenced neatly, and dug as well, and [all] the weeds plucked up, and the vines flourishing, he rejoiced [exceedingly] at what his servant had done.

2[55]:6 So he called his beloved son, who was his heir, and the friends who were his advisers, and told them what he had commanded his servant, and how much he had found done. And they rejoiced with the servant at the testimony which his master had borne to him.

2[55]:7 And he said to them; "I promised this servant his freedom, if he should keep the commandment which I commanded him; but he kept my commandment and did a good work besides to my vineyard, and pleased me greatly. For this work therefore which he has done, I desire to make him joint-heir with my son, because, when the good thought struck him, he did not neglect it, but fulfilled it."

2[55]:8 In this purpose the son of the master agreed with him, that the servant should be made joint-heir with the son.

2[55]:9 After some few days, his master made a feast, and sent to him many dainties from the feast. But when the servant received [the dainties sent to him by the master], he took what was sufficient for him, and distributed the rest to his fellow servants.

2[55]:10 And his fellow-servants, when they received the dainties, rejoiced, and began to pray for him, that he might find greater favor with the master, because he had treated them so handsomely.

2[55]:11 All these things which had taken place his master heard, and again rejoiced greatly at his deed. So the master called together again his friends and his son, and announced to them the deed that he had done with regard to his dainties which he had received; and they still more approved of his resolve, that his servant should be made joint-heir with his son."

3[56]:1 I say, "Sir, I understand not these parables, neither can I apprehend them, unless you explain them for me."

3[56]:2 "I will explain everything to you," said he; "and will show you whatsoever things I shall speak with you. Keep the commandments of the Lord, and you shall be well-pleasing to God, and shall be enrolled among the number of them that keep His commandments.

3[56]:3 But if you do any good thing outside the commandment of God, you shall win for yourself more exceeding glory, and shall be more glorious in the sight of God than you would otherwise have been. If then, while you keep the commandments of God, you add these services likewise, you shall rejoice, if you observe them according to my commandment."

3[56]:4 I say to him, "Sir, whatsoever you command me, I will keep it; for I know that you art with me." "I will be with you," said he, "because you hast so great zeal for doing good; yea, and I will be with all," said he, "whosoever have such zeal as this.

3[56]:5 This fasting," said he, "if the commandments of the Lord are kept, is very good. This then is the way, that you shall keep this fast which you art about to observe].

3[56]:6 First of all, keep yourself from every evil word and every evil desire, and purify thy heart from all the vanities of this world. If you keep these things, this fast shall be perfect for you.

3[56]:7 And thus shall you do. Having fulfilled what is written, on that day on which you fastest you shall taste nothing but bread and water; and from thy meats, which you would have eaten, you shall reckon up the amount of that day's expenditure, which you would have incurred, and shall give it to a widow, or an orphan, or to one in want, and so shall you humble thy soul, that he that has received from thy humiliation may satisfy his own soul, and may pray for you to the Lord.

3[56]:8 If then you shall so accomplish this fast, as I have commanded you, thy sacrifice shall be acceptable in the sight of God, and this fasting shall be recorded; and the service so performed is beautiful and joyous and acceptable to the Lord.

3[56]:9 These things you shall so observe, you and thy children and thy whole household; and, observing them, you shall be blessed; yea, and all those, who shall hear and observe them, shall be blessed, and whatsoever things they shall ask of the Lord, they shall receive."

4[57]:1 I entreated him earnestly, that he would show me the parable of the estate, and of the master, and of the vineyard, and of the servant that fenced the vineyard, [and of the fence,] and of the weeds which were plucked up out of the vineyard, and of the son, and of the friends, the advisers. For I understood that all these things are a parable.

4[57]:2 But he answered and said unto me; "You art exceedingly importunate in enquiries. You ought not," [said he,] "to make any enquiry at all; for if it be right that a thing be explained unto you, it shall be explained." I say to him; "Sir, whatsoever things you show unto me and do not explain, I shall have seen them in vain, and without understanding what they are. In like manner also, if you speak parables to me and interpret them not, I shall have heard a thing in vain from you."

4[57]:3 But he again answered, and said unto me; "Whosoever," said he, "is a servant of God, and has his own Lord in his heart, asks understanding of Him, and receives it, and interprets every parable, and the words of the Lord which are spoken in parables are made known unto him. But as many as are sluggish and idle in intercession, these hesitate to ask of the Lord. 4[57]:4 But the Lord is abundant in compassion, and gives to them that ask of Him without ceasing. But you who hast been strengthened by the holy angel, and hast received from him such (powers of intercession and art not idle, wherefore do you not ask understanding of the Lord, and obtain it from Him)."
4[57]:5 I say to him, "Sir, I that have you with me have (but) need to ask you and enquire of you; for you show me all things, and speak with me; but if I had seen or heard them apart from you I should have asked of the Lord, that they might be shown to me."
5[58]:1 "I told you just now," said he, "that you art unscrupulous and importunate, in enquiring for the interpretations of the parables. But since you art so obstinate, I will interpret to you the parable of the estate and all the accompaniments thereof, that you may make them known unto all. Hear now," said he, "and understand them.
5[58]:2 The estate is this world, and the lord of the estate is He that created all things, and set them in order, and endowed them with power; and the servant is the Son of God, and the vines are this people whom He Himself planted;
5[58]:3 and the fences are the [holy] angels of the Lord who keep together His people; and the weeds, which are plucked up from the vineyard, are the transgressions of the servants of God; and the dainties which He sent to him from the feast are the commandments which He gave to His people through His Son; and the friends and advisers are the holy angels which were first created; and the absence of the master is the time which remains over until His coming."
5[58]:4 I say to him; "Sir, great and marvelous are all things and all things are glorious; was it likely then," say I, "that I could have apprehended them?" "Nay, nor can any other man, though he be full of understanding, apprehend them." "Yet again, Sir," say I, "explain to me what I am about to enquire of you."
5[58]:5 "Say on," he said, "if you desire anything." "Wherefore, Sir,]" say I, "is the Son of God represented in the parable in the guise of a servant?"
6[59]:1 "Listen," said he; "the Son of God is not represented in the guise of a servant, but is represented in great power and lordship." "How, Sir?" say I; "I comprehend not."
6[59]:2 "Because," said he, "God planted the vineyard, that is, He created the people, and delivered them over to His Son. And the Son placed the angels in charge of them, to watch over them; and the Son Himself cleansed their sins, by laboring much and enduring many toils; for no one can dig without toil or labor.
6[59]:3 Having Himself then cleansed the sins of His people, He showed them the paths of life, giving them the law which He received from His Father. You see," said he, "that He is Himself Lord of the people, having received all power from His Father.
6[59]:4 But how that the lord took his son and the glorious angels as advisers concerning the inheritance of the servant, listen.
6[59]:5 The Holy Pre-existent Spirit. Which created the whole creation, God made to dwell in flesh that He desired. This flesh, therefore, in which the Holy Spirit dwelt, was subject unto the Spirit, walking honorably in holiness and purity, without in any way defiling the Spirit.
6[59]:6 When then it had lived honorably in chastity, and had labored with the Spirit, and had cooperated with it in everything, behaving itself boldly and bravely, He chose it as a partner with the Holy Spirit; for the career of this flesh pleased [the Lord], seeing that, as possessing the Holy Spirit, it was not defiled upon the earth.
6[59]:7 He therefore took the son as adviser and the glorious angels also, that this flesh too, having served the Spirit unblamably, might have some place of sojourn, and might not seem to hare lost the reward for its service; for all flesh, which is found undefiled and unspotted, wherein the Holy Spirit dwelt, shall receive a reward.
6[59]:8 Now you hast the interpretation of this parable also."
7[60]:1 "I was right glad, Sir," say I, "to hear this interpretation." "Listen now," said he, "Keep this thy flesh pure and undefiled, that the Spirit which dwells in it may bear witness to it, and thy flesh may be justified.
7[60]:2 See that it never enter into your heart that this flesh of your is perishable, and so you abuse it in some defilement. [For] if you defile thy flesh, you shall defile the Holy Spirit also; but if you defile the flesh, you shall not live."
7[60]:3 "But if, Sir," say I, "there has been any ignorance in times past, before these words were heard, how shall a man who has defiled his flesh be saved?" "For the former deeds of ignorance," said he, "God alone has power to give healing; for all authority is His.
7[60]:4 [But now keep yourself, and the Lord Almighty, Who is full of compassion, will give healing for thy former deeds of ignorance,] if henceforth you defile not thy flesh, neither the Spirit; for both share in common, and the one cannot be defiled without the other. Therefore keep both pure, and you shall live unto God."
Parable 6
1[61]:1 As I sat in my house, and glorified the Lord for all things that I had seen, and was considering concerning the commandments, how that they were beautiful and powerful and gladsome and glorious and able to save a man's soul, I said within myself; "Blessed shall I be, if I walk in these commandments; yea, and whosoever shall walk in them shall be blessed."
1[61]:2 As I spoke these things within myself, I see him suddenly seated by me, and saying as follows; "Why art you of a doubtful mind concerning the commandments, which I commanded you? They are beautiful. Doubt not at all; but clothe yourself in the faith of the Lord, and you shall walk in them. For I will strengthen you in them.

1[61]:3 These commandments are suitable for those who meditate repentance; for if they walk not in them, their repentance is in vain.

1[61]:4 you then that repent, cast away the evil doings of this world which crush you; and, by putting on every excellence of righteousness, you shall be able to observe these commandments, and to add no more to your sins. If then you add no further sin at all, you will depart from your former sins. Walk then in these my commandments, and you shall live unto God. These things have [all] been told you from me."

1[61]:5 And after he had told these things to me, he said to me, "Let us go into the country, and I will show you the shepherds of the sheep." "Let us go, Sir," say I. And we came to a certain plain, and he shows me a young man, a shepherd, clothed in a light cloak, of saffron color;

1[61]:6 and he was feeding a great number of sheep, and these sheep were, as it were, well fed and very frisky, and were gladsome as they skipped about hither and thither; and the shepherd himself was all gladsome over his flock; and the very visage of the shepherd was exceedingly gladsome; and he ran about among the sheep.

2[62]:1 And he said to me; "See you this shepherd?" "I see him Sir," I say. "This," said he, "is the angel of self-indulgence and of deceit. He crushes the souls of the servants of God, and perverts them from the truth, leading them astray with evil desires, wherein they perish.

2[62]:2 For they forget the commandments of the living God, and walk in vain deceits and acts of self-indulgence, and are destroyed by this angel, some of them unto death, and others unto corruption."

2[62]:3 I say to him, "Sir, I comprehend not what means "unto death," and what "unto corruption". "Listen," said he; "the sheep which you saw gladsome and skipping about, these are they who have been turned asunder from God utterly, and have delivered themselves over to the lusts of this world. In these, therefore, there is not repentance unto life. For the Name of God is being blasphemed through them. The life of such persons is death.

2[62]:4 But the sheep, which you saw not skipping about, but feeding in one place, these are they that have delivered themselves over to acts of self-indulgence and deceit, but have not uttered any blasphemy against the Lord. These then have been corrupted from the truth. In these there is hope of repentance, wherein they can live. Corruption then has hope of a possible renewal, but death has eternal destruction."

2[62]:5 Again we went forward a little way, and he showed me a great shepherd like a wild man in appearance, with a white goatskin thrown about him; and he had a kind of wallet on his shoulders, and a staff very hard and with knots in it, and a great whip. And his look was very sour, so that I was afraid of him because of his look.

2[62]:6 This shepherd then kept receiving from the young man, the shepherd, those sheep that were frisky and well fed, but not skipping about, and putting them in a certain spot, which was precipitous and covered with thorns and briars, so that the sheep could not disentangle themselves from the thorns and briars, but [became entangled among the thorns and briars.

2[62]:7 And so they] pastured entangled in the thorns and briars, and were in great misery with being beaten by him; and he kept driving them about to and fro, and giving them no rest, and all together those sheep had not a happy time.

3[63]:1 When then I saw them so lashed with the whip and vexed, I was sorry for their sakes, because they were so tortured and had no rest at all.

3[63]:2 I say to the shepherd who was speaking with me; "Sir, who is this shepherd, who is [so] hard-hearted and severe, and has no compassion at all for these sheep?" "This," said he, "is the angel of punishment, and he is one of the just angels, and presides over punishment.

3[63]:3 So he receives those who wander away from God, and walk after the lusts and deceits of this life, and punishes them, as they deserve, with fearful and various punishments."

3[63]:4 "I would fain learn, Sir," said I, "of what sort are these various punishments." "Listen," said he; "the various tortures and punishments are tortures belonging to the present life; for some are punished with losses, and others with want, and others with divers maladies, and others with [every kind] of unsettlement, and others with insults from unworthy persons and with suffering in many other respects.

3[63]:5 For many, being unsettled in their plans, set their hands to many things, and nothing ever goes forward with them. And then they say that they do not prosper in their doings, and it doth not enter into their hearts that they have done evil deeds, but they blame the Lord.

3[63]:6 When then they are afflicted with every kind of affliction, then they are delivered over to me for good instruction, and are strengthened in the faith of the Lord, and serve the Lord with a pure heart the remaining days of their life. But, if they repent, the evil works which they have done rise up in their hearts, and then they glorify God, saying that He is a just Judge, and that they suffered justly each according to his doings. And they serve the Lord thenceforward with a pure heart, and are prosperous in all their doings, receiving from the Lord whatsoever things they may ask; and then they glorify the Lord because they were delivered over unto me, and they no longer suffer any evil thing."

3[63]:1 I say unto him; "Sir, declare unto me this further matter." "What enquire you yet?" said he. "Whether, Sir," say I, "they that live in self-indulgence and are deceived undergo torments during the same length of time as they live in self-indulgence and are deceived." He said to me, "They undergo torments for the same length of time."

3[63]:2 "Then, Sir," say I, "they undergo very slight torments; for those who are living thus in self-indulgence and forget God ought to have been tormented seven-fold."

3[63]:3 He said to me, "You art foolish, and comprehend not the power of the torment" "True," say I, "for if I had comprehended it, I should not have asked you to declare it to me." "Listen," said he, "to the power of both, [of the self-indulgence and of the torment].

3[63]:4 The time of the self-indulgence and deceit is one hour. But an hour of the torment has the power of thirty days. If then one live in self indulgence and be deceived for one day, and be tormented for one day, the day of the torment is equivalent to a whole year. For as many days then as a man lives in self-indulgence, for so many years is he tormented. You see then," said he, "that the time of the self-indulgence and deceit is very short, but the time of the punishment and torment is long."

5[65]:1 "Inasmuch, Sir," say I, "as I do not quite comprehend concerning the time of the deceit and self-indulgence and torment, show me more clearly."

5[65]:2 He answered and said unto me; "Your stupidity clings to you; and you wilt not cleanse thy heart and serve God Take heed," [said he,] "lest haply the time be fulfilled, and you be found in thy foolishness. Listen then," [said he,] "even as you wish, that you may comprehend the matter.

5[65]:3 He that lives in self-indulgence and is deceived for one day, and doeth what he wishes, is clothed in much folly and comprehended not the thing which he doeth; for on the morrow he forgets what he did the day before. For self-indulgence and deceit have no memories, by reason of the folly, wherewith each is clothed; but when punishment and torment cling to a man for a single day, he is punished and tormented for a whole year long; for punishment and torment have long memories.

5[65]:4 So being tormented and punished for the whole year, the man remembers at length the self-indulgence and deceit, and perceives that it is on their account that he is suffering these ills. Every man, therefore, that lives in self-indulgence and is deceived, is tormented in this way because, though possessing lire, they have delivered themselves over unto death."

5[65]:5 "What kinds of self-indulgence, Sir," say I, "are harmful?" "Every action," said he, "is self-indulgence to a man, which he does with pleasure; for the irascible man, when he gives the reins to his passion, is self-indulgent; and the adulterer and the drunkard and the slanderer and the liar and the miser and the defrauder and he that doeth things akin to these, gives the reins to his peculiar passion; therefore he is self-indulgent in his action.

5[65]:6 All these habits of self-indulgence are harmful to the servants of God; on account of these deceits therefore they so suffer who are punished and tormented.

5[65]:7 But there are habits of self-indulgence like-wise which save men; for many are self-indulgent in doing good, being carried away by the pleasure it gives to themselves. This self-indulgence then is expedient for the servants of God, and brings life to a man of this disposition; but the harmful self-indulgences afore-mentioned bring to men torments and punishments; and if they continue in them and repent not, they bring death upon themselves."

Parable 7

1[66]:1 After a few days I saw him on the same plain, where also I had seen the shepherds, and he said to me, "What seek you?" "I am here, Sir," say I, "that you may bid the shepherd that punishes go out of my house; for he afflicts me much." "It is necessary for you," said he, "to be afflicted; for so," said he, "the glorious angel ordered as concerning you, for he wishes you to be proved." "Why, what so evil thing have I done, Sir," say I, "that I should be delivered over to this angel?"

1[66]:2 "Listen," said he. "Your sins are many, yet not so many that you should be delivered over to this angel; but thy house has committed great iniquities and sins, and the glorious angel was embittered at their deeds, and for this cause he bade you be afflicted for a certain time, that they also might repent and cleanse themselves from every lust of this world. When therefore they shall repent and be cleansed, then shall the angel of punishment depart."

1[66]:3 I say to him; "Sir, if they perpetrated such deeds that the glorious angel is embittered, what have I done?" "They cannot be afflicted otherwise," said he, "unless you, the head of the [whole] house, be afflicted; for if you be afflicted, they also of necessity will be afflicted; but if you be prosperous, they can suffer no affliction."

1[66]:4 "But behold, Sir," say I, "they have repented with their whole heart." "I am quite aware myself," said he, "that they have repented with their whole heart; well, think you that the sins of those who repent are forgiven forthwith? Certainly not; but the person who repents must torture his own soul, and must be thoroughly humble in his every action, and be afflicted with all the divers kinds of affliction; and if he endure the afflictions which come upon him, assuredly He Who created all things and endowed them with power will be moved with compassion and will bestow some remedy.

1[66]:5 And this (will God do), if in any way He perceive the heart of the penitent pure from every evil thing. But it is expedient for you and for thy house that you should be afflicted now. But why speak I many words to you? You must be afflicted as the angel of the Lord commanded, even he that delivered you unto me; and for this give thanks to the Lord, in that He deemed you worthy that I should reveal unto you beforehand the affliction, that foreknowing it you might endure it with fortitude."

1[66]:6 I say to him; "Sir, be you with me, and I shall be able to endure all affliction [easily]." "I will be with you," said he; "and I will ask the angel that punishs to afflict you more lightly; but you shall be afflicted for a short time, and you shall be restored again to thy house. Only continue to be humble and to minister unto the Lord with a pure heart, you and thy children and thy house, and walk in my commandments which I command you, and thus it will be possible for thy repentance to be strong and pure.

1[66]:7 And if you keep these commandments with thy household, all affliction shall hold aloof from you; yea, and affliction," said he, "shall hold aloof from all whosoever shall walk in these my commandments."

Parable 8

1[67]:1 He showed me a [great] willow, overshadowing plains and mountains, and under the shadow of the willow all have come who are called by the name of the Lord.

1[67]:2 And by the willow there stood an angel of the Lord, glorious and very tall, having a great sickle, and he was lopping branches from the willow, and giving them to the people that sheltered beneath the willow; and he gave them little rods about a cubit long.

1[67]:3 And after all had taken the rods, the angel laid aside the sickle, and the tree was sound, just as I had seen it.

1[67]:4 Then I marveled within myself, saying, "How is the tree sound after so many branches have been lopped off?" The shepherd said to me, "Marvel not that the tree remained sound, after so many branches were lopped off but wait until you see all things, and it shall be shown to you what it is."

1[67]:5 The angel who gave the rods to the people demanded them back from them again, and according as they had received them, so also they were summoned to him, and each of them returned the several rods. But the angel of the Lord took them, and examined them.

1[67]:6 From some he received the rods withered and eaten as it were by grubs: the angel ordered those who gave up rods like these to stand apart.

1[67]:7 And others gave them up withered, but not grub-eaten; and these again he ordered to stand apart.

1[67]:8 And others gave them up half-withered; these also stood apart.

1[67]:9 And others gave up their rods half-withered and with cracks; these also stood apart.

1[67]:10 And others gave up their rods green and with cracks; these also stood apart. And others gave up their rods one half withered and one half green; these also stood apart.

1[67]:11 And others brought their rods two parts of the rod green, and the third part withered; these also stood apart. And others gave them up two parts withered, and the third part green; these also stood apart.

1[67]:12 And others gave up their rods nearly all green, but a very small portion of their rods was withered, just the end; but they had cracks in them; these also stood apart.

1[67]:13 And in those of others there was a very small portion green, but the rest of the rods was withered; these also stood apart.

1[67]:14 And others came bringing their rods green, as they received them from the angel; and the most part of the multitude gave up their rods in this state; and the angel rejoiced exceedingly at these; these also stood apart.

1[67]:15 And others gave up their rods green and with shoots, these also stood apart; and at these again the angel rejoiced exceedingly.

1[67]:16 And others gave up their rods green and with shoots; and their shoots had, as it were, a kind of fruit. And those men were exceeding gladsome, whose rods were found in this state. And over them the angel exulted, and the shepherd was very gladsome over them.

2[68]:1 And the angel of the Lord commanded crowns to be brought. And crowns were brought, made as it were of palm branches; and he crowned the men that had given up the rods which had the shoots and some fruit, and sent them away into the tower.

2[68]:2 And the others also he sent into the tower, even those who had given up the rods green and with shoots, but the shoots were without fruit; and he set a seal upon them.

2[68]:3 And all they that went into the tower had the same raiment, white as snow.

2[68]:4 And those that had given up their rods green as they received them, he sent away, giving them a [white] robe, and seals.

2[68]:5 After the angel had finished these things, he said to the shepherd; "I go away; but these you shall send away to (their places within) the walls, according as each deserves to dwell; but examine their rods carefully), and so send them away. But be careful in examining them. Take heed lest any escape you," said he. "Still if any escape you, I will test them at the altar." When he had thus spoken to the shepherd, he departed.

2[68]:6 And, after the angel had departed, the shepherd said to me; "Let us take the rods of all and plant them, to see whether any of them shall be able to live." I say unto him, "Sir, these withered things, how can they live?"

2[68]:7 He answered and said unto me; "This tree is a willow, and this class of trees clings to life. If then the rods shall be planted and get a little moisture, many of them will live. And afterwards let us try to pour some water also over them. If any of them shall be able to live, I will rejoice with it; but if it live not, I at least shall not be found neglectful."

2[68]:8 So the shepherd bade me call them, just as each one of them was stationed. And they came row after row, and they delivered up the rods to the shepherd. And the shepherd took the rods, and planted them in rows, and after he had planted them, he poured much water over them, so that the rods could not be seen for the water.

2[68]:9 And after he had watered the rods, he said to me; "Let us go now. and after days let us return and inspect all the rods; for He Who created this tree wills that all those who have received rods from this tree should live. And I myself hope that these little rods, after they have got moisture and been watered, will live the greater part of them."

3[69]:1 I say to him; "Sir, inform me what this tree is. For I am perplexed herewith, because, though so many branches were cut off, the tree is sound, and nothing appears to have been cut from it; I am therefore perplexed thereat."

3[69]:2 "Listen," said he; "this great tree which overshadows plains and mountains and all the earth is the law of God which was given to the whole world; and this law is the Son of Cod preached unto the ends of the earth. But the people that are under the shadow are they that have heard the preaching, and believed on Him;

3[69]:3 but the great and glorious angel is Michael, who has the power over this people and is their captain. For this is he that puts the law into the hearts of the believers; therefore he himself inspects them to whom he gave it, to see whether they have observed it.

3[69]:4 But you see the rods of every one; for the rods are the law. You see these many rods rendered useless, and you shall notice all those that have not observed the law, and shall see the abode of each severally."

3[69]:5 I say unto him; "Sir, wherefore did he send away some into the tower, and leave others for you?" "As many," said he, "as transgressed the law which they received from him, these he left under my authority for repentance; but as many as already satisfied the law and have observed it, these he has under his own authority."

3[69]:6 "Who then, Sir," say I, "are they that have been crowned and go into the tower?" ["As many," said he, "as wrestled with the devil and overcame him in their wrestling, are crowned:] these are they that suffered for the law.

3[69]:7 But the others, who likewise gave up their rods green and with shoots, though not with fruit, are they that were persecuted for the law, but did not suffer nor yet deny their law.

3[69]:8 But they that gave them up green just as they received them, are sober and righteous men, who walked altogether in a pure heart and have kept the commandments of the Lord. But all else you shall know, when I have examined these rods that have been planted and watered."

4[70]:1 And after a few days we came to the place, and the shepherd sat down in the place of the angel, while I stood by him. And he said to me; "Gird yourself with a garment of raw flax, and minister to me." So I girded myself with a clean garment of raw flax made of coarse material.

4[70]:2 And when he saw me girded and ready to minister to him "Call," said he, "the men whose rods have been planted, according to the rank as each presented their rods." And I went away to the plain, and called them all; and they stood all of them according to their ranks.

4[70]:3 He said to them; "Let each man pluck out his own rod, and bring it to me." Those gave them up first, who had the withered and chipped rods, and they were found accordingly withered and chipped. He ordered them to stand apart.

4[70]:4 Then those gave them up, who had the withered but not chipped; and some of them gave up the rods green, and others withered and chipped as by grubs. Those then that gave them up green he ordered to stand apart; but those that gave them up withered and chipped he ordered to stand with the first.

4[70]:5 Then those gave them up who had the half-withered and with cracks; and many of them gave them up green and without cracks; and some gave them up green and with shoots, and fruits on the shoots, such as those had who went into the tower crowned; and some gave them up withered and eaten, and some withered and uneaten, and some such as they were, half-withered and with cracks. He ordered them to stand each one apart, some in their proper ranks, and others apart.

5[71]:1 Then those gave them up who had their rods green, but with cracks. These all gave them up green, and stood in their own company. And the shepherd rejoiced over these, because they all were changed and had put away their cracks.

5[71]:2 And those gave them up likewise who had the one half green and the other half withered. The rods of some were found entirely green, of some half-withered, of some withered and eaten, and of some green and with shoots. These were all sent away each to his company.

5[71]:3 Then those gave them up who had two parts green and the third withered; many of them gave them up green, and many half-withered, and others withered and eaten. These all stood in their own company.

5[71]:4 Then those gave them up who had two parts withered and the third part green. Many of them gave them up half-withered, but some withered and eaten, others half-withered and with cracks, and a few green. These all stood in their own company.

5[71]:5 Then those gave them up who had their rods green, but a very small part [withered] and with cracks. Of these some gave them up green, and others green and with shoots. These also went away to their own company.

5[71]:6 Then those gave them up who had a very small part green and the other parts withered. The rods of these were found for the most part green and with shoots and fruit on the shoots, and others altogether green. At these rods the shepherd rejoiced very [greatly], because they were found so. And these went away each to his own company.

6[72]:1 After [the shepherd] had examined the rods of all, he said to me, "I told you that this tree clings to life. See you," said he, "how many repented and were saved?" "I see, Sir," say I. "It is," said he, that you may see the abundant compassion of the Lord, how great and glorious it is, and He has given (His) Spirit to those that are worthy of repentance."

6[72]:2 "Wherefore then, Sir," say I, "did they not all repent?" "To those, whose heart He saw about to become pure and to serve Him with all the heart, to them He gave repentance; but those whose craftiness and wickedness He saw, who intend to repent in hypocrisy, to them He gave not repentance, lest haply they should again profane His name."

6[72]:3 I say unto him, "Sir, now then show me concerning those that have given up their rods, what manner of man each of them is, and their abode, that when they hear this, they that believed and have received the seal and have broken it and did not keep it sound may fully understand what they are doing, and repent, receiving from you a seal, and may glorify the Lord, that He had compassion upon them and sent you to renew their spirits."

6[72]:4 "Listen," said he; "those whose rods were found withered and grub-eaten, these are the renegades and traitors to the Church, that blasphemed the Lord in their sins, and still further were ashamed of the Name of the Lord, which was invoked upon them. These then perished altogether unto God. But you see how not one of them repented, although they heard the words which you spoke to them, which I commanded you. From men of this kind life departed.

6[72]:5 But those that gave up the withered and undecayed (rods), these also are near them; for they were hypocrites, and brought in strange doctrines, and perverted the servants of God, especially them that had sinned, not permitting them to repent, but persuading them with their foolish doctrines. These then have hope of repenting.

6[72]:6 But you see that many of them have indeed repented from the time when you speak to them my commandments; yea, and (others) still will repent. And as many as shall not repent, have lost their life; but as many of them as repented, became good; and their dwelling was placed within the first walls, and some of them even ascended into the tower. You see then," [said he,] "that repentance from sins brings life, but not to repent brings death.

7[73]:1 "But as many as gave up (the rods) half-withered, and with cracks in them, hear also concerning these. Those whose rods were half-withered throughout are the double-minded; for they neither live nor are dead.

7[73]:2 But those that have them half-withered and cracks in them, these are both double-minded and slanderers, and are never at peace among themselves but always causing dissensions. Yet even to these," [said he,] "repentance is given. You see," [said he,] "that some of them have repented; and there is still," said he, "hope of repentance among them.

7[73]:3 And as many of them," said he, "as have repented, have their abode within the tower; but as many of them as have repented tardily shall abide within the walls; and as many as repent not, but continue in their doings, shall die the death.

7[73]:4 But they that have given up their rods green and with cracks, these were found faithful and good at all times, [but] they have a certain emulation one with another about first places and about glory of some kind or other; but all these are foolish in having (emulation) one with another about first places.

7[73]:5 Yet these also, when they heard my commandments, being good, purified themselves and repented quickly. They have their habitation, therefore, within the tower. But if any one shall again turn to dissension, he shall be cast out from the tower and shall lose his life.

7[73]:6 Life is for all those that keep the commandments of the Lord. But in the commandments there is nothing about first places, or about glory of any kind, but about long-suffering and humility in man. In such men, therefore, is the life of the Lord, but in factious and lawless men is death.

8[74]:1 "But they that gave up their rods half green and half withered, these are they that are mixed up in business and hold fast not to the saints. Therefore the one half of them lives , but the other half is dead.

8[74]:2 Many then when they heard my commandments repented. As many then as repented, have their abode within the tower. But some of them altogether stood aloof These then have no repentance; for by reason of their business affairs they blasphemed the Lord and denied Him. So they lost their life for the wickedness that they committed.

8[74]:3 But many of them were doubtful-minded. These still have place for repentance, if they repent quickly, and their dwelling shall be within the tower; and if they repent tardily, they shall dwell within the walls; but if they repent not, they too have lost their life.

8[74]:4 But they that have given up two parts green and the third part withered, these are they that have denied with manifold denials.

8[74]:5 Many of them therefore repented and departed to dwell inside the tower; but many utterly rebelled from God; these lost their life finally. And some of them were double-minded and caused dissensions. For these then there is repentance, if they repent speedily and continue not in their pleasures; but if they continue in their doings, they likewise procure for themselves death.

9[75]:1 "But they that have given up their rods two thirds withered and one third green, these are men who have been believers, but grew rich and became renowned among the Gentiles. They clothed themselves with great pride and became high-minded, and abandoned the truth and did not hold fast to the righteous, but lived together after the manner of the Gentiles, and this path appeared the more pleasant unto them; yet they departed not from God, but continued in the faith, though they wrought not the works of the faith.

9[75]:2 Many of them therefore repented, and they had their habitation within the tower.

9[75]:3 But others at the last living with the Gentiles, and being corrupted by the vain opinions of the Gentiles, departed from God, and worked the works of the Gentiles. These therefore were numbered with the Gentiles.

9[75]:4 But others of them were doubtful-minded, not hoping to be saved by reason of the deeds that they had done; and others were double-minded and made divisions among themselves. For these then that were double-minded by reason of their doings there is still repentance; but their repentance ought to be speedy, that their dwelling may be within the tower; but for those who repent not, but continue in their pleasures, death is nigh.

10[76]:1 "But they that gave up their rods green, yet with the extreme ends withered and with cracks; these were found at all times good and faithful and glorious in the sight of God, but they sinned to a very slight degree by reason of little desires and because they had somewhat against one another. But, when they heard my words, the greater part quickly repented, and their dwelling was assigned within the tower.

10[76]:2 But some of them were double-minded, and some being double-minded made a greater dissension. In these then there is still a hope of repentance, because they were found always good; and hardly shall one of them die.

10[76]:3 But they that gave up their rods withered, yet with a very small part green, these are they that believed, but practiced the works of lawlessness. Still they never separated from God, but bore the Name gladly, and gladly received into their houses the servants of God. So hearing of this repentance they repented without wavering, and they practice all excellence and righteousness.

10[76]:4 And some of them even suffer persecution willingly, knowing the deeds that they did. All these then shall have their dwelling within the tower."

11[77]:1 And after he had completed the interpretations of all the rods, he said unto me; "Go, and tell all men to repent, and they shall live unto God; for the Lord in His compassion sent me to give repentance to all, though some of them do not deserve it for their deeds; but being long-suffering the Lord wills them that were called through His Son to be saved."

11[77]:2 I say to him; "Sir, I hope that all when they hear these words will repent; for I am persuaded that each one, when he fully knows his own deeds and fears God, will repent."

11[77]:3 He answered and said unto me; "As many," [said he,] "as [shall repent] from their whole heart [and] shall cleanse themselves from all the evil deeds aforementioned, and shall add nothing further to their sins, shall receive healing from the Lord for their former sins, unless they be double-minded concerning these commandments, and they shall live unto God. [But as many," said he, "as shall add to their sins and walk in the lusts of this world, shall condemn themselves to death.]

11[77]:4 But do you walk in my commandments, and live [unto God; yea, and as many as shall walk in them and shall do rightly, shall live unto God."]

11[77]:5 Having shown me all these things [and told me them] he said to me; "Now the rest will I declare (unto you) after a few days."

Parable 9

1[78]:1 After I had written down the commandments and parables of the shepherd, the angel of repentance, he came to me and said to me; "I wish to show you all things that the Holy Spirit, which spoke with you in the form of the Church, showed unto you. For that Spirit is the Son of God.

1[78]:2 For when you was weaker in the flesh, it was not declared unto you through an angel; but when you was enabled through the Spirit, and didst grow mighty in thy strength so that you could even see an angel, then at length was manifested unto you, through the Church, the building of the tower. In fair and seemly manner hast you seen all things, (instructed) as it were by a virgin; but now you see (being instructed) by an angel, though by the same Spirit;

1[78]:3 yet must you learn everything more accurately from me. For to this end also was I appointed by the glorious angel to dwell in thy house, that you might see all things mightily, in nothing terrified, even as before."

1[78]:4 And he took me away into Arcadia, to a certain rounded mountain, and set me on the top of the mountain, and showed me a great plain, and round the plain twelve mountains, the mountains having each a different appearance.

1[78]:5 The first was black as soot; the second was bare, without vegetation; the third was thorny and full of briars;

1[78]:6 the fourth had the vegetation half-withered, the upper part of the grass green, but the part by the roots withered, and some of the grass became withered, whenever the sun had scorched it;

1[78]:7 the fifth mountain had green grass and was rugged; the sixth mountain was full with clefts throughout, some small and some great, and the clefts had vegetation, but the grass was not very luxuriant, but rather as if it had been withered;

1[78]:8 the seventh mountain had smiling vegetation, and the whole mountain was in a thriving condition, and cattle and birds of every kind did feed upon that mountain; and the more the cattle and the birds did feed, so much the more did the herbage of that mountain flourish. The eighth mountain was full of springs, and every kind of creature of the Lord did drink of the springs on that mountain.

1[78]:9 the ninth mountain had no water at all, and was entirely desert; and it had in it wild beasts and deadly reptiles, which destroy mankind. The tenth mountain had very large trees and was umbrageous throughout, and beneath the shade lay sheep resting and feeding.

1[78]:10 the eleventh mountain was thickly wooded all over, and the trees thereon were very productive, decked with divers kinds of fruits, so that one seeing them would desire to eat of their fruits. The twelfth mountain was altogether white and its aspect was cheerful; and the mountain was most beauteous in itself.

2[79]:1 And in the middle of the plain he showed me a great white rock, rising up from the plain. The rock was loftier than the mountains, being four-square, so that it could contain the whole world.

2[79]:2 Now this rock was ancient, and had a gate hewn out of it; but the gate seemed to me to have been hewed out quite recently. And the gate glistened beyond the brightness of the sun, so that I marveled at the brightness of the gate.

2[79]:3 And around the gate stood twelve virgins. The four then that stood at the corners seemed to me to be more glorious (than the rest); but the others likewise were glorious; and they stood at the four quarters of the gate, and virgins stood in pairs between them.

2[79]:4 And they were clothed in linen tunics and girt about in seemly fashion, having their right shoulders free, as if they intended to carry some burden. Thus were they prepared, for they were very cheerful and eager.

2[79]:5 After I had seen these things, I marveled in myself at the greatness and the glory of what I was seeing And again I was perplexed concerning the virgins, that delicate as they were they stood up like men, as if they intended to carry the whole heaven.

2[79]:6 And the shepherd said unto me; "Why question you within yourself and art perplexed, and bring sadness on yourself? For whatsoever things you can not comprehend, attempt them not, if you art prudent; but entreat the Lord, that you may receive understanding to comprehend them.

2[79]:7 What is behind you you can not see, but what is before you you behold. The things therefore which you can not see, let alone, and trouble not yourself (about them; but the things which you see, these master, and be not over curious about the rest; but I will explain unto you all things whatsoever I shall show you. Have an eye therefore to what remains."

3[80]:1 I saw six men come, tall and glorious and alike in appearance and they summoned a multitude of men. And the others also which came were tall men and handsome and powerful. And the six men ordered them to build a tower above the gate. And there arose a great noise from those men who had come to build the tower, as they ran hither and thither round the gate.

3[80]:2 For the virgins standing round the gate told the men to hasten to build the tower. Now the virgins had spread out their hands, as if they would take something from the men.

3[80]:3 And the six men ordered stones to come up from a certain deep place, and to go to the building of the tower. And there went up ten stones square and polished, [not] hewn from a quarry.

3[80]:4 And the six men called to the virgins, and ordered them to carry all the stones which should go unto the building of the tower, and to pass through the gate and to hand them to the men that were about to build the tower.

3[80]:5 And the virgins laid the first ten stones that rose out of the deep on each other, and they carried them together, stone by stone.

4[81]:1 And just as they stood together around the gate, in that order they carried them that seemed to be strong enough and had stooped under the corners of the stone, while the others stooped at the sides of the stone. And so they carried all the stones. And they carried them right through the gate, as they were ordered, and handed them to the men for the tower; and these took the stones and built.

4[81]:2 Now the building of the tower was upon the great rock and above the gate. Those ten stones then were joined together, and they covered the whole rock. And these formed a foundation for the building of the tower. And [the rock and] the gate supported the whole tower.

4[81]:3 And, after the ten stones, other twenty-five stones came up from the deep, and these were fitted into the building of the tower, being carried by the virgins, like the former. And after these thirty-five stones came up. And these likewise were fitted into the tower. And after these came up other forty stones. and these all were put into the building of the tower. So four rows were made in the foundations of the tower.

4[81]:4 And (the stones) ceased coming up from the deep, and the builders likewise ceased for a little. And again the six men ordered the multitude of the people to bring in stones from the mountains for the building of the tower.

4[81]:5 They were brought in accordingly from all the mountains, of various colors, shaped by the men, and were handed to the virgins; and the virgins carried them right through the gate, and handed them in for the building of the tower. And when the various stones were placed in the building, they became all alike and white, and they lost their various colors.

4[81]:6 But some stones were handed in by the men for the building, and these did not become bright; but just as they were placed, such likewise were they found; for they were not handed in by the virgins, nor had they been carried in through the gate. These stones then were unsightly in the building of the tower.

4[81]:7 Then the six men, seeing the stones that were unsightly in the building, ordered them to be removed and carried [below] into their own place whence they were brought.

4[81]:8 And they say to the men who were bringing the stones in; "Abstain for your parts altogether from handing in stones for the building; but place them by the tower, that the virgins may carry them through the gate, and hand them in for the building. For if," [say they,] they be not carried in through the gate by the hands of these virgins, they cannot change their colors. Labor not therefore," [say they,] "in vain."

5[82]:1 And the building was finished on that day, yet was not the tower finally completed, for it was to be carried up [still] higher; and there was a cessation in the building. And the six men ordered the builders to retire for a short time [all of them], and to rest; but the virgins they ordered not to retire from the tower. And I thought the virgins were left to guard the tower.

5[82]:2 And after all had retired Land rested], I say to the shepherd; "How is it, Sir," say I, "that the building of the tower was not completed?" "The tower," he said, "cannot yet be finally completed, until its master come and test this building, that if any stones be found crumbling, he may change them; for the tower is being built according to His will."

5[82]:3 "I would fain know, Sir," say I, "what is this building of this tower, and concerning the rock and gate, and the mountains, and the virgins, and the stones that came up from the deep, and were not shaped, but went just as they were into the building;

5[82]:4 and wherefore ten stones were first placed in the foundations, then twenty-five, then thirty-five, then forty, and concerning the stones that had gone to the building and were removed again and put away in their own place--concerning all these things set my soul at rest, Sir, and explain them to me."

5[82]:5 "If," said he, "you be not found possessed of an idle curiosity, you shall know all things. For after a few days we shall come here, and you shall see the sequel that overtakes this tower and shall understand all the parables accurately."

5[82]:6 And after a few days we came to the place where we had sat, and he said to me, "Let us go to the tower; for the owner of the tower cometh to inspect it." And we came to the tower, and there was no one at all by it, save the virgins alone.

5[82]:7 And the shepherd asked the virgins whether the master of the tower had arrived. And they said that he would be there directly to inspect the building.

6[83]:1 And, behold, after a little while I see an array of many men coming, and in the midst a man of such lofty stature that he overtopped the tower.

6[83]:2 And the six men who superintended the building walked with him on the right hand and on the left, and all they that worked at the building were with him, and many other glorious attendants around him. And the virgins that watched the tower ran up and kissed him, and they began to walk by his side round the tower.

6[83]:3 And that man inspected the building so carefully, that he felt each single stone; and he held a rod in his hand and struck each single stone that was built in.

6[83]:4 And when he smote, some of the stones became black as soot, others mildewed, others cracked, others broke off short, others became neither white nor black, others rough and not fitting in with the other stones, and others with many spots; these were the varied aspects of the stones which were found unsound for the building.

6[83]:5 So he ordered all these to be removed from the tower, and to be placed by the side of the tower, and other stones to be brought and put into their place.

6[83]:6 And the builders asked him from what mountain he desired stones to be brought and put into their place. And he would not have them brought from the mountains, but ordered them to be brought from a certain plain that was nigh at hand.

6[83]:7 And the plain was dug, and stones were found there bright and square, but some of them too were round. And all the stones which there were anywhere in that plain were brought every one of them, and were carried through the gate by the virgins.

6[83]:8 And the square stones were hewed, and set in the place of those which had been removed; but the round ones were not placed in the building, because they were too hard to be shaped, and to work on them was slow. So they were placed by the side of the tower, as though they were intended to be shaped and placed in the building; for they were very bright.

7[84]:1 So then, having accomplished these things, the glorious man who was lord of the whole tower called the shepherd to him, and delivered unto him all the stones which lay by the side of the tower, which were cast out from the building, and said unto him;

7[84]:2 "Clean these stones carefully, and set them in the building of the tower, these, I mean, which can fit with the rest; but those which will not fit, throw far away from the tower."

7[84]:3 Having given these orders to the shepherd, he departed from the tower with all those with whom he had come. And the virgins stood round the tower watching it.

7[84]:4 I say to the shepherd, "How can these stones go again to the building of the tower, seeing that they have been disapproved?" He said unto me in answer; "See you", said he, "these stones ?" I see them, Sir," say I. "I myself," said he, "will shape the greater part of these stones and put them into the building, and they shall fit in with the remaining stones."

7[84]:5 "How, Sir," say I, "can they, when they are chiseled, fill the same space?" He said unto me in answer, "As many as shall be found small, shall be put into the middle of the building; but as many as are larger, shall be placed nearer the outside, and they will bind them together."

7[84]:6 With these words he said to me, "Let us go away, and after two days let us come and clean these stones, and put them into the building; for all things round the tower must be made clean, lest haply the master come suddenly and find the circuit of the tower dirty, and he be wroth, and so these stones shall not go to the building of the tower, and I shall appear to be careless in my master's sight."

7[84]:7 And after two days we came to the tower, and he said unto me; "Let us inspect all the stones, and see those which can go to the building." I say to him, "Sir, let us inspect them."

8[85]:1 And so commencing first we began to inspect the black stones; and just as they were when set aside from the building, such also they were found. And the shepherd ordered them to be removed from the tower and to be put on one side.

8[85]:2 Then he inspected those that were mildewed, and he took and shaped many of them, and ordered the virgins to take them up and put them into the building. And the virgins took them up and placed them in the building of the tower in a middle position. But the rest he ordered to be placed with the black ones; for these also were found black.

8[85]:3 Then he began to inspect those that had the cracks; and of these he shaped many, and he ordered them to be carried away by the hands of the virgins for the building. And they were placed towards the outside, because they were found to be sounder. But the rest could not be shaped owing to the number of the cracks. For this reason therefore they were cast aside from the building of the tower.

8[85]:4 Then he proceeded to inspect the stunted (stones), and many among them were found black, and some had contracted great cracks; and he ordered these also to be placed with those that had been cast aside. But those of them which remained he cleaned and shaped, and ordered to be placed in the building So the virgins took them up, and fitted them into the middle of the building of the tower; for they were somewhat weak.

8[85]:5 Then he began to inspect those that were half white and half black, and many of them were (now) found black; and he ordered these also to be taken up with those that had been cast aside. But all the rest were [found white, and were] taken up by the virgins; for being white they were fitted by [the virgins] them[selves] into the building. But they were placed towards the outside, because they were found sound, so that they could hold together those that were placed in the middle; for not a single one of them was too short.

8[85]:6 Then he began to inspect the hard and rough; and a few of them were cast away, because they could not be shaped; for they were found very hard. But the rest of them were shaped [and taken up by the virgins] and fitted into the middle of the building of the tower; for they were somewhat weak.

8[85]:7 Then he proceeded to inspect those that had the spots, and of these some few had turned black and were cast away among the rest; but the remainder were found bright and sound, and these were fitted by the virgins into the building; but they were placed towards the outside, owing to their strength.

9[86]:1 Then he came to inspect the white and round stones, and he said unto me; "What shall we do with these stones?" "How do I know, Sir?" say I [And he said to me,] "Perceives you nothing concerning them?"

9[86]:2 "I, Sir," say I, "do not possess this art, neither am I a mason, nor can I understand." See you not," said he, "that they are very round; and if I wish to make them square, very much must needs be chiseled off from them? Yet some of them must of necessity be placed into the building."

9[86]:3 "If then, Sir," say I, "it must needs be so, why distress yourself, and why not choose out for the building those you will, and fit them into it?" He chose out from them the large and the bright ones, and shaped them; and the virgins took them up, and fitted them into the outer parts of the building.

9[86]:4 But the rest, which remained over, were taken up, and put aside into the plain whence they were brought; they were not however cast away, "Because," said he, there remains still a little of the tower to be built And the master of the tower is exceedingly anxious that these stones be fitted into the building, for they are very bright."

9[86]:5 So twelve women were called, most beautiful in form, clad in black, [girded about and having the shoulders bare,] with their hair hanging loose. And these women, I thought, had a savage look. And the shepherd ordered them to take up the stones which had been cast away from the building, and to carry them off to the same mountains from which also they had been brought;

9[86]:6 and they took them up joyfully, and carried away all the stones and put them in the place whence they had been taken. And after all the stones had been taken up, and not a single stone still lay round the tower, the shepherd said unto me; "Let us go round the tower, and see that there is no defect in it." And I proceeded to go round it with him.

9[86]:7 And when the shepherd saw that the tower was very comely in the building, he was exceedingly glad; for the tower was so well built, that when I saw it I coveted the building of it; for it was built, as it were, of one stone, having one fitting in it. And the stone-work appeared as if hewn out of the rock; for it seemed to me to be all a single stone.

10[87]:1 And I, as I walked with him, was glad to see so brave a sight. And the shepherd said to me; "Go and bring plaster and fine clay, that I may fill up the shapes of the stones that have been taken up and put into the building; for all the circuit of the tower must be made smooth."

10[87]:2 And I did as he bade, and brought them to him. "Assist me," said he, "and the work will speedily be accomplished." So he filled in the shapes of the stones which had gone to the building, and ordered the circuit of the tower to be swept and made clean.

10[87]:3 And the virgins took brooms and swept, and they removed all the rubbish from the tower, and sprinkled water, and the site of the tower was made cheerful and very seemly.

10[87]:4 The shepherd said unto me, "All," said he, "has now been cleaned. If the lord come to inspect the tower, he has nothing for which to blame us." Saying this, he desired to go away.

10[87]:5 But I caught hold of his wallet, and began to adjure him by the Lord that he would explain to me [all] what he had showed me. He said to me; "I am busy for a little while, and then I will explain everything to you. Await me here till I come."

10[87]:6 I say to him; "Sir, when I am here alone what shall I do?" "You art not alone," said he; "for these virgins are here with you." "Commend me then to them," say I. The shepherd calls them to him and said to them; "I commend this man to you till I come," and he departed.

10[87]:7 So I was alone with the virgins; and they were most cheerful, and kindly disposed to Me especially the four of them that were the more glorious in appearance.

11[88]:1 The virgins say to me; "Today the shepherd cometh not here." "What then shall I do?" say I. "Stay for him," say they, "till eventide; and if he come, he will speak with you; but if he come not, you shall stay here with us till he cometh."

11[88]:2 I say to them; "I will await him till evening, and if he come not, I will depart home and return early in the morning." But they answered and said unto me; "To us you were entrusted; you can not depart from us."

11[88]:3 "Where then," say I, "shall I remain?" "You shall pass the night with us," say they as a brother, not as a husband; for you art our brother, and henceforward we will dwell with you; for we love you dearly." But I was ashamed to abide with them.

11[88]:4 And she that seemed to be the chief of them began to kiss and to embrace me; and the others seeing her embrace me, they too began to kiss me, and to lead me round the tower, and to sport with me.

11[88]:5 And I had become as it were a younger man, and I commenced myself likewise to sport with them. For some of them began to dance, [others to skip,] others to sing. But I kept silence and walked with them round the tower, and was glad with them.

11[88]:6 But when evening came I wished to go away home; but they would not let me go, but detained me. And I stayed the night with them, and I slept by the side of the tower.

11[88]:7 For the virgins spread their linen tunics on the ground, and made me lie down in the midst of them, and they did nothing else but pray; and I prayed with them without ceasing, and not less than they. And the virgins rejoiced that I so prayed. And I stayed there with the virgins until the morning till the second hour.

11[88]:8 Then came the shepherd, and said to the virgins; "Have you done him any injury?" "Ask him," say they. I say to him, "Sir, I was rejoiced to stay with them." "On what didst you sup?" said he "I supped, Sir," say I, "on the words of the Lord the whole night through." "Did they treat you well?" said he. "Yes, Sir," say I.

11[88]:9 "Now," said he, "what would you hear first?" "In the order as you showed to me, Sir, from the beginning," say I; "I request you, Sir, to explain to me exactly in the order that I shall enquire of you." According as you desire," said he, "even so will I interpret to you, and I will conceal nothing whatever from you."

12[89]:1 "First of all, Sir," say I, "explain this to me. The rock and the gate, what is it?" "This rock," said he, "and gate is the Son of God." "How, Sir," say I, "is the rock ancient, but the gate recent?" "Listen," said he, "and understand, foolish man.

12[89]:2 The Son of God is older than all His creation, so that He became the Father's adviser in His creation. Therefore also He is ancient." "But the gate, why is it recent, Sir?" say I.

12[89]:3 "Because," said he, "He was made manifest in the last days of the consummation; therefore the gate was made recent, that they which are to be saved may enter through it into the kingdom of God.

12[89]:4 Didst you see," said he, "that the stones which came through the gate have gone to the building of the tower, but those which came not through it were cast away again to their own place?" "I saw, Sir," say I. "Thus," said he, "no one shall enter into the kingdom of God, except he receive the name of His Son.

12[89]:5 For if you wish to enter into any city, and that city is walled all round and has one gate only, can you enter into that city except through the gate which it has?" "Why, how, Sir," say I, "is it possible otherwise?" "If then you can not enter into the city except through the gate itself, even so," said he, "a man cannot enter into the kingdom of God except by the name of His Son that is beloved by Him.

12[89]:6 Didst you see," said he, "the multitude that is building the tower?" "I saw it, Sir," say I. "They," said he, are all glorious angels. With these then the Lord is walled around. But the gate is the Son of God; there is this one entrance only to the Lord. No one then shall enter in unto Him otherwise than through His Son.

12[89]:7 Didst you see," said he, "the six men, and the glorious and mighty man in the midst of them, him that walked about the tower and rejected the stones from the building?" "I saw him, Sir," say I.

12[89]:8 "The glorious man," said he, "is the Son of God, and those six are the glorious angels who guard Him on the right hand and on the left. Of these glorious angels not one," said he, "shall enter in unto God without Him; whosoever shall not receive His name, shall not enter into the kingdom of God."

13[90]:1 "But the tower," say I, "what is it?" "The tower," said he, "why, this is the Church.

13[90]:2 "And these virgins, who are they?" "They," said he, "are holy spirits; and no man can otherwise be found in the kingdom of God, unless these shall clothe him with their garment; for if you receive only the name, but receive not the garment from them, you profit nothing. For these virgins are powers of the Son of God. If [therefore] you bear the Name, and bear not His power, you shall bear His Name to none effect.

13[90]:3 And the stones," said he, "which you didst see cast away, these bare the Name, but clothed not themselves with the raiment of the virgins." "Of what sort, Sir," say I, "is their raiment?" "The names themselves," said he, "are their raiment. Whosoever bears the Name of the Son of God, ought to bear the names of these also; for even the Son Himself bears the names of these virgins.

13[90]:4 As many stones," said he, "as you saw enter into the building of the tower, being given in by their hands and waiting for the building, they have been clothed in the power of these virgins.

13[90]:5 For this cause you see the tower made a single stone with the rock. So also they that have believed in the Lord through His Son and clothe themselves in these spirits, shall become one spirit and one body, and their garments all of one color. But such persons as bear the names of the virgins have their dwelling in the tower."

13[90]:6 "The stones then, Sir," say I, "which are cast aside, wherefore were they cast aside? For they passed through the gate and were placed in the building of the tower by the hands of the virgins." "Since all these things interest you," said he, "and you enquire diligently, listen as touching the stones that have been cast aside.

13[90]:7 These all," [said he,] "received the name of the Son of God, and received likewise the power of these virgins. When then they received these spirits, they were strengthened, and were with the servants of God, and they had one spirit and one body [and one garment]; for they had the same mind, and they wrought righteousness.

13[90]:8 After a certain time then they were persuaded by the women whom you saw clad in black raiment, and having their shoulders bare and their hair loose, and beautiful in form. When they saw them they desired them, and they clothed themselves with their power, but they stripped off from themselves the power of the virgins.

13[90]:9 They then were cast away from the house of God, and delivered to these (women). But they that were not deceived by the beauty of these women remained in the house of God. So you hast," said he, "the interpretation of them that were cast aside."

13[90]:1 What then, Sir," say I, "if these men, being such as they are, should repent and put away their desire for these women, and return unto the virgins, and walk in their power and in their works? Shall they not enter into the house of God?"

13[90]:2 "They shall enter," said he, "if they shall put away the works of these women, and take again the power of the virgins, and walk in their works. For this is the reason why there was also a cessation in the building, that, if these repent, they may go into the building of the tower; but if they repent not, then others will go, and these shall be cast away finally."

13[90]:3 For all these things I gave thanks unto the Lord, because He had compassion on all that called upon His name, and sent forth the angel of repentance to us that had sinned against Him, and refreshed our spirit, and, when we were already ruined and had no hope of life, restored our life.

13[90]:4 "Now, Sir," say I, "show me why the tower is not built upon the ground, but upon the rock and upon the gate." "Because you art senseless," said he, "and without understanding [you ask the question]." "I am obliged, Sir," say I, "to ask all questions of you, because I am absolutely unable to comprehend anything at all; for all are great and glorious and difficult for men to understand."

13[90]:5 "Listen," said he. "The name of the Son of God is great and incomprehensible, and sustains the whole world. If then all creation is sustained by the Son [of God], what think you of those that are called by Him, and bear the name of the Son of God, and walk according to His commandments?

13[90]:6 See you then what manner of men He sustains? Even those that bear His name with their whole heart. He Himself then is become their foundation, and He sustains them gladly, because they are not ashamed to bear His name."

15[92]:1 "Declare to me, Sir," say I, "the names of the virgins, and of the women that are clothed in the black garments." "Hear," said he, "the names of the more powerful virgins, those that are stationed at the corners.

15[92]:2 The first is Faith, and the second, Continence, and the third, Power, and the fourth, Long-suffering. But the others stationed between them have these names--Simplicity, Guilelessness, Purity, Cheerfulness, Truth, Understanding, Concord, Love. He that bears these names and the name of the Son of God shall be able to enter into the kingdom of God.

15[92]:3 Hear," said he, "likewise the names of the women that wear the black garments. Of these also four are more powerful than the rest; the first is Unbelief; the second, Intemperance; the third, Disobedience; the fourth, Deceit; and their followers are called, Sadness, Wickedness, Wantonness, Irascibility, Falsehood, Folly, Slander, Hatred. The servant of God that bears these names shall see the kingdom of God, but shall not enter into it."

15[92]:4 "But the stones, Sir," say I, "that came from the deep, and were fitted into the building, who are they?" "The first," said he, "even the ten, that were placed in the foundations, are the first generation; the twenty-five are the second generation of righteous men; the thirty-five are God's prophets and His ministers; the forty are apostles and teachers of the preaching of the Son of God."

15[92]:5 "Wherefore then, Sir," say I, "did the virgins give in these stones also for the building of the tower and carry them through the gate?"

15[92]:6 "Because these first," said he, "bore these spirits, and they never separated the one from the other, neither the spirits from the men nor the men from the spirits, but the spirits abode with them till they fell asleep; and if they had not had these spirits with them, they would not have been found useful for the building of this tower."

15[92]:1 "Show me still further, Sir," say I. "What desire you to know besides?" said he. "Wherefore, Sir," say I, "did the stones come up from the deep, and wherefore were they placed into the building, though they bore these spirits?"

15[92]:2 "It was necessary for them," said he, "to rise up through water, that they might be made alive; for otherwise they could not enter into the kingdom of God, except they had put aside the deadness of their [former] life.

15[92]:3 So these likewise that had fallen asleep received the seal of the Son of God and entered into the kingdom of God. For before a man," said he, "has borne the name of [the Son of] God, he is dead; but when he has received the seal, he lays aside his deadness, and resumes life.

15[92]:4 The seal then is the water: so they go down into the water dead, and they come up alive. "thus to them also this seal was preached, and they availed themselves of it that they might enter into the kingdom of God."

15[92]:5 "Wherefore, Sir," say I, "did the forty stones also come up with them from the deep, though they had already received the seal?" "Because," said he, "these, the apostles and the teachers who preached the name of the Son of God, after they had fallen asleep in the power and faith of the Son of God, preached also to them that had fallen asleep before them, and themselves gave unto them the seal of the preaching.

15[92]:6 Therefore they went down with them into the water, and came up again. But these went down alive [and again came up alive]; whereas the others that had fallen asleep before them went down dead and came up alive.

15[92]:7 So by their means they were quickened into life, and came to the full knowledge of the name of the Son of God. For this cause also they came up with them, and were fitted with them into the building of the tower and were built with them, without being shaped; for they fell asleep in righteousness and in great purity. Only they had not this seal. You hast then the interpretation of these things also." "I have, Sir," say I.

17[94]:1 "Now then, Sir, explain to me concerning the mountains. Wherefore are their forms diverse the one from the other, and various?" "Listen," said he. "These twelve mountains are [twelve] tribes that inhabit the whole world. To these (tribes) then the Son of God was preached by the Apostles."

17[94]:2 But explain to me, Sir, why they are various--these mountains--and each has a different appearance." "Listen," said he. "These twelve tribes which inhabit the whole world are twelve nations; and they are various in understanding and in mind. As various, then, as you saw these mountains to be, such also are the varieties in the mind of these nations, and such their understanding. And I will show unto you the conduct of each."

17[94]:3 "First, Sir," say I, "show me this, why the mountains being so various, yet, when their stones were set into the building, became bright and of one color, just like the stones that had come up from the deep."

17[94]:4 "Because," said he, "all the nations that dwell under heaven, when they heard and believed, were called by the one name of [the Son of] God. So having received the seal, they had one understanding and one mind, and one faith became theirs and [one] love, and they bore the spirits of the virgins along with the Name; therefore the building of the tower became of one color, even bright as the sun.

17[94]:5 But after they entered in together, and became one body, some of them defiled themselves, and were cast out from the society of the righteous, and became again such as they were before, or rather even worse."

18[95]:1 "How, Sir," say I, "did they become worse, after they had fully known God?" "He that knows not God," said he, "and commits wickedness, has a certain punishment for his wickedness; but he that knows God fully ought not any longer to commit wickedness, but to do good.

18[95]:2 If then he that ought to do good commits wickedness, does he not seem to do greater wickedness than the man that knows not God? Therefore they that have not known God, and commit wickedness, are condemned to death; but they that have known God and seen His mighty works, and yet commit wickedness, shall receive a double punishment, and shall die eternally. In this way therefore shall the Church of God be purified.

18[95]:3 And as you saw the stones removed from the tower and delivered over to the evil spirits, they too shall be cast out; and there shall be one body of them that are purified, just as the tower, after it had been purified, became made as it were of one stone. Thus shall it be with the Church of God also, after she has been purified, and the wicked and hypocrites and blasphemers and double-minded and they that commit various kinds of wickedness have been cast out.

18[95]:4 When these have been cast out, the Church of God shall be one body, one understanding, one mind, one faith, one love. And then the Son of God shall rejoice and be glad in them, for that He has received back His people pure." "Great and glorious, Sir," say I, "are all these things.

18[95]:5 Once more, Sir," [say I,] "show me the force and the doings of each one of the mountains, that every soul that trusts in the Lord, when it hears, may glorify His great and marvelous and glorious name." "Listen," said he, "to the variety of the mountains and of the twelve nations.

19[96]:1 "From the first mountain, which was black, they that have believed are such as these; rebels and blasphemers against the Lord, and betrayers of the servants of God. For these there is no repentance, but there is death. For this cause also they are black; for their race is lawless.

19[96]:2 And from the second mountain, the bare one, they that believed are such as these; hypocrites and teachers of wickedness. And these then are like the former in not having the fruit of righteousness. For, even as their mountain is unfruitful, so likewise such men as these have a name indeed, but they are void of the faith, and there is no fruit of truth in them. For these then repentance is offered, if they repent quickly; but if they delay, they will have their death with the former."

19[96]:3 "Wherefore, Sir," say I, "is repentance possible for them, but not for the former ? For their doings are almost the same." "On this account," he said, "is repentance offered for them, because they blasphemed not their Lord, nor became betrayers of the servants of God; yet from desire of gain they played the hypocrite, and taught each other [after] the desires of sinful men. But they shall pay a certain penalty; yet repentance is ordained for them, because they are not become blasphemers or betrayers.

20[97]:1 "And from the third mountain, which had thorns and briars, they that believed are such as these; some of them are wealthy and others are entangled in many business affairs. The briars are the wealthy, and the thorns are they that are mixed up in various business affairs.

20[97]:2 These [then, that are mixed up in many and various business affairs,] hold fast [not] to the servants of God, but go astray, being choked by their affairs, but the wealthy unwillingly hold fast to the servants of God, fearing lest they may be asked for something by them. Such men therefore shall hardly enter into the kingdom of God.

20[97]:3 For as it is difficult to walk on briars with bare feet, so also it is difficult for such men to enter the kingdom of God.

20[97]:4 But for all these repentance is possible, but it must be speedy, that in respect to what they omitted to do in the former times, they may now revert to (past) days, and do some good. If then they shall repent and do some good, they shall live unto God; but if they continue in their doings, they shall be delivered over to those women, the which shall put them to death.

20[97]:1 "And from the fourth mountain, which had much vegetation, the upper part of the grass green and the part towards the roots withered, and some of it dried up by the sun, they that believed are such as these; the double-minded, and they that have the Lord on their lips, but have Him not in their heart.

20[97]:2 Therefore their foundations are dry and without power, and their words only live, but their works are dead. Such men are neither alive nor dead. They are, therefore, like unto the double-minded; for the double-minded are neither green nor withered; for they are neither alive nor dead.

20[97]:3 For as their grass was withered up when it saw the sun, so also the double-minded, when they hear of tribulation, through their cowardice worship idols and are ashamed of the name of their Lord.

20[97]:4 Such are neither alive nor dead. Yet these also, if they repent quickly, shall be able to live; but if they repent not, they are delivered over already to the women who deprive them of their life.

22[99]:1 "And from the fifth mountain, which had green grass and was rugged, they that believed are such as these; they are faithful, but slow to learn and stubborn and self-pleasers, desiring to know all things, and yet they know nothing at all.

22[99]:2 By reason of this their stubbornness, understanding stood aloof from them, and a foolish senselessness entered into them; and they praise themselves as having understanding, and they desire to be self-appointed teachers, senseless though they are.

22[99]:3 Owing then to this pride of heart many, while they exalted themselves, have been made empty; for a mighty demon is stubbornness and vain confidence. Of these then many were cast away, but some repented and believed, and submitted themselves to those that had understanding, having learnt their own senselessness.

22[99]:4 Yea, and to the rest that belong to this class repentance is offered; for they did not become wicked, but rather foolish and without understanding. If these then shall repent, they shall live unto God; but if they repent not, they shall have their abode with the women who work evil against them.

23[100]:1 "But they that believed from the sixth mountain, which had clefts great and small, and in the clefts herbage withered, are such as these;

23[100]:2 they that have the small clefts, these are they that have aught against one another, and from their backbitings they are withered in the faith; but many of these repented Yea, and the rest shall repent, when they hear my commandments; for their backbitings are but small, and they shall quickly repent.

23[100]:3 But they that have great clefts, these are persistent in their backbitings and bear grudges, nursing wrath against one another. These then were thrown right away from the tower and rejected from its building. Such persons therefore shall with difficulty live.

23[100]:4 If God and our Lord, Who rules over all things and has the authority over all His creation, bears no grudge against them that confess their sins, but is propitiated, doth man, who is mortal and full of sins, bear a grudge against man, as though he were able to destroy or save him?

23[100]:5 I say unto you--I, the angel of repentance--unto as many as hold this heresy, put it away from you and repent, and the Lord shall heal your former sins, if you shall purify yourselves from this demon; but if not, you shall be delivered unto him to be put to death.

24[101]:1 " And from the seventh mountain, on which was herbage green and smiling, and the whole mountain thriving, and cattle of every kind and the fowls of heaven were feeding on the herbage on that mountain, and the green herbage, on which they fed, only grew the more luxuriant, they that believed are such as these;

24[101]:2 they were ever simple and guileless and blessed, having nothing against one another, but rejoicing always in the servants of God, and clothed in the Holy Spirit of these virgins, and having compassion always on every man, and out of their labors they supplied every man's need without reproach and without misgiving.

24[101]:3 The Lord then seeing their simplicity and entire childishness made them to abound in the labors of their hands, and bestowed favor on them in all their doings.

24[101]:4 But I say unto you that are such--I, the angel of repentance--remain to the end such as you are, and your seed shall never be blotted out. For the Lord has put you to the proof, and enrolled you among our number, and your whole seed shall dwell with the Son of God; for of His Spirit did you receive.

25[102]:1 "And from the eighth mountain, where were the many springs, and all the creatures of the Lord did drink of the springs, they that believed are such as these;

25[102]:2 apostles and teachers, who preached unto the whole world, and who taught the word of the Lord in soberness and purity, and kept back no part at all for evil desire, but walked always in righteousness and truth, even as also they received the Holy Spirit. Such therefore shall have their entrance with the angels.

26[103]:1 "And from the ninth mountain, which was desert, which had [the] reptiles and wild beasts in it which destroy mankind, they that believed are such as these;

26[103]:2 they that have the spots are deacons that exercised their office ill, and plundered the livelihood of widows and orphans, and made gain for themselves from the ministrations which they had received to perform. If then they abide in the same evil desire, they are dead and there is no hope of life for them; but if they turn again and fulfill their ministrations in purity, it shall be possible for them to live.

26[103]:3 But they that are mildewed, these are they that denied and turned not again unto their Lord, but having become barren and desert, because they hold fast not unto the servants of God but remain alone, they destroy their own souls.

26[103]:4 For as a vine left alone in a hedge, if it meet with neglect, is destroyed and wasted by the weeds, and in time becomes wild and is no longer useful to its owner, so also men of this kind have given themselves up in despair and become useless to their Lord, by growing wild.

26[103]:5 To these then repentance cometh, unless they be found to have denied from the heart; but if a man be found to have denied from the heart, I know not whether it is possible for him to live.

26[103]:6 And this I say not in reference to these days, that a man after denying should receive repentance; for it is impossible for him to be saved who shall now deny his Lord; but for those who denied Him long ago repentance seems to be possible. If a man therefore will repent, let him do so speedily before the tower is completed; but if not, he shall be destroyed by the women and put to death.

26[103]:7 And the stunted, these are the treacherous and backbiters; and the wild beasts which you saw on the mountain are these. For as wild beasts with their venom poison and kill a man, so also do the words of such men poison and kill a man.

26[103]:8 These then are broken off short from their faith through the conduct which they have in themselves; but some of them repented and were saved; and the rest that are of this kind can be saved, if they repent; but if they repent not, they shall meet their death from those women of whose power they are possessed.

27[104]:1 "And from the tenth mountain, where were trees sheltering certain sheep, they that believed are such as these;

27[104]:2 bishops, hospitable persons, who gladly received into their houses at all times the servants of God without hypocrisy. [These bishops] at all times without ceasing sheltered the needy and the widows in their ministration and conducted themselves in purity at all times.

27[104]:3 These [all] then shall be sheltered by the Lord for ever. They therefore that have done these things are glorious in the sight of God, and their place is even now with the angels, if they shall continue unto the end serving the Lord.

27[104]:1 "And from the eleventh mountain, where were trees full of fruit, decked with divers kinds of fruits, they that believed are such as these;

27[104]:2 they that suffered for the Name [of the Son of God], who also suffered readily with their whole heart, and yielded up their lives."

27[104]:3 "Wherefore then, Sir," say I, "have all the trees fruits, but some of their fruits are more beautiful than others?" "Listen," said he; "all as many as ever suffered for the Name's sake are glorious in the sight of God, and the sins of all these were taken away, because they suffered for the name of the Son of God. Now here why their fruits are various, and some surpassing others.

27[104]:4 "As many," said he, "as were tortured and denied not, when brought before the magistracy, but suffered readily, these are the more glorious in the sight of the Lord; their fruit is that which surpasses. But as many as become cowards, and were lost in uncertainty, and considered in their hearts whether they should deny or confess, and yet suffered, their fruits are less, because this design entered into their heart; for this design is evil, that a servant should deny his own lord.

27[104]:5 See to it, therefore, you who entertain this idea, lest this design remain in your hearts, and you die unto God. But you that suffer for the Name's sake ought to glorify God, because God deemed you worthy that you should bear this name, and that all your sins should be healed.

27[104]:6 Reckon yourselves blessed therefore; yea, rather think that you have done a great work, if any of you shall suffer for God's sake. The Lord bestowed life upon you, and you perceived it not; for your sins weighed you down, and if you had not suffered for the Name [of the Lord], you had died unto God by reason of your sins.

27[104]:7 These things I say unto you that waver as touching denial and confession. Confess that you have the Lord, lest denying Him you be delivered into prison.

27[104]:8 If the Gentiles punish their slaves, if any one deny his lord, what think you the Lord will do unto you, He who has authority over all things? Away with these designs from your hearts, that you may live forever unto God."

27[104]:1 "And from the twelfth mountain, which was white, they that believed are such as these; they that are as very babes, into whose heart no guile entered, neither learned they what wickedness is, but they remained as babes forever.

27[104]:2 Such as these then dwell without doubt in the kingdom of God, because they defiled the commandments of God in nothing, but continued as babes all the days of their life in the same mind.

27[104]:3 As many of you therefore as shall continue," said he, "and shall be as infants not having guile, shall be glorious [even] than all them that have been mentioned before; for all infants are glorious in the sight of God, and stand first in His sight. Blessed then are you, as many as have put away wickedness from you, and have clothed yourselves in guilelessness: you shall live unto God cheifest of all."

27[104]:4 After he had finished the parables of the mountains, I say unto him, "Sir, now explain to me concerning the stones that were taken from the plain and placed in the building in the room of the stones that were taken from the tower, and concerning the round (stones) which were placed in the building, and concerning those that were still round".

27[104]:1 "Hear," said he, "likewise concerning all these things. The stones which were taken from the plain and placed in the building of the tower in the room of those that were rejected, are the roots of this white mountain.

27[104]:2 When then they that believed from this mountain were all found guiltless, the lord of the tower ordered these from the roots of the mountain to be put into the building of the tower. For He knew that if these stones should go into the building [of the tower], they would remain bright and not one of them would turn black.

27[104]:3 But if he added (stones) from other mountains, he would have been obliged to visit the tower again, and to purify it. Now all these have been found white, who have believed and who shall believe; for they are of the same kind. Blessed is this kind, for it is innocent!

27[104]:4 Hear now likewise concerning those round and bright stones. All these are from the white mountain. Now here wherefore they have been found round. Their riches have darkened and obscured them a little from the truth.

27[104]:5 When therefore the Lord perceived their mind, *that they could favor the truth,* and likewise remain good, He commanded their possessions to be cut off from them, yet not to be taken away altogether, so that they might be able to do some good with that which has been left to them, and might live unto God for that they come of a good kind. So therefore they have been cut away a little, and placed in the building of this tower".

27[104]:1 "But the other (stones), which have remained round and have not been fitted into the building, because they have not yet received the seal, have been replaced in their own possession, for they were found very round.

27[104]:2 For this world and the vanities of their possessions must be cut off from them, and then they will fit into the kingdom of God. For it is necessary that they should enter into the kingdom of God; because the Lord has blessed this innocent kind. Of this kind then not one shall perish. Yea, even though any one of them being tempted by the most wicked devil have committed any fault, he shall return speedily unto his Lord.

27[104]:3 Blessed I pronounced you all to be--I the angel of repentance--whoever of you are guileless as infants, because your part is good and honorable in the sight of God.

27[104]a:4 Moreover I bid all of you, whoever have received this seal, keep guilelessness, and bear no grudge, and continue not in your wickedness nor in the memory of the offenses of bitterness; but become of one spirit, and heal these evil clefts and take them away from among you, that the owner of the flocks may rejoice concerning them.

27[104a]:5 For he will rejoice, if he find all things whole. But if he find any part of the flock scattered, woe unto the shepherds.

27[104a]:6 For if the shepherds themselves shall have been found scattered, how will they answer for the flocks? Will they say that they were harassed by the flock? No credence will be given them. For it is an incredible thing that a shepherd should be injured by his flock; and he will be punished the more because of his falsehood. And I am the shepherd, and it behooved me most strongly to render an account for you.

32[109]:1 "Amend yourselves therefore, while the tower is still in course of building.

32[109]:2 The Lord dwells in men that love peace; for to Him peace is dear; but from the contentious and them that are given up to wickedness He kept afar off. Restore therefore to Him your spirit whole as you received it.

32[109]:3 For suppose you hast given to a fuller a new garment whole, and desired to receive it back again whole, but the fuller give it back to you torn, wilt you receive it thus? Wilt you not at once blaze out and attack him with reproaches, saying; "The garment which I gave you was whole; wherefore hast you rent it and made it useless? See, by reason of the rent, which you hast made in it, it cannot be of use." Wilt you not then say all this to a fuller even about a rent which he has made in thy garment?

32[109]:4 If therefore you art thus vexed in the matter of thy garment, and complained because you received it not back whole, what think you the Lord will do to you, He, Who gave you the spirit whole, and you hast made it absolutely useless, so that it cannot be of any use at all to its Lord? For its use began to be useless, when it was corrupted by you. Will not therefore the Lord of this spirit for this thy deed punish [you with death]?"

32[109]:5 "Certainly," I said, "all those, whomsoever He shall find continuing to bear malice, He will punish." "Trample not," said he, "upon His mercy, but rather glorify Him, because He is so long-suffering with your sins, and is not like unto you. Practice then repentance which is expedient for you.

33[110]:1 "All these things which are written above I, the shepherd, the angel of repentance, have declared and spoken to the servants of God. If then you shall believe and hear my words, and walk in them, and amend your ways, you shall be able to live. But if you continue in wickedness and in bearing malice, no one of this kind shall live unto God. All things which were to be spoken by me have (now) been spoken to you."

33[110]:2 The shepherd said to me, "Hast you asked me all thy questions?" And I said, "Yes, Sir." "Why then hast you not enquired of me concerning the shape of the stones placed in the building, in that we filled up their shapes?" And I said, "I forgot, Sir."

33[110]:3 "Listen now," said he, "concerning them. These are they that have heard my commandments now, and have practiced repentance with their whole heart. So when the Lord saw that their repentance was good and pure, and that they could continue therein, he ordered their former sins to be blotted out. These shapes then were their former sins, and they have been chiseled away that they might not appear."

Parable 10

1[111]:1 After I had written out this book completely, the angel who had delivered me to the shepherd came to the house where I was, and sat upon a couch, and the shepherd stood at his right hand. Then he called me, and spoke thus unto me;

1[111]:2 "I delivered you," said he, "and thy house to this shepherd, that you might be protected by him." "True, Sir," I said "If therefore," said he, "you desire to be protected from all annoyance and all cruelty, to have also success in every good work and word, and all the power of righteousness, walk in his commandments, which I have given you, and you shall be able to get the mastery over all wickedness.

1[111]:3 For if you keep his commandments, all evil desire and the sweetness of this world shall be subject unto you; moreover success shall attend you in every good undertaking. Embrace his gravity and self-restraint, and tell it out unto all men that he is held in great honor and dignity with the Lord, and is a ruler of great authority, and powerful in his office. To him alone in the whole world has authority over repentance been assigned. Seemed he to you to be powerful? Yet you despise the gravity and moderation which he used towards you."

2[112]:1 I say unto him; "Ask him, Sir, himself, whether from the time that he has been in my house, I have done ought out of order, whereby I have offended him."

2[112]:2 "I myself know," said he, "that you hast done nothing out of order, nor art about to do so. And so I speak these things unto you, that you may persevere. For he has given a good account of you unto me. You therefore shall speak these words to others, that they too who have practiced or shall practice repentance may be of the same mind as you art; and he may give a good report of them to me, and I unto the Lord."

2[112]:3 "I too, Sir," I say, "declare to every man the mighty works of the Lord; for I hope that all who have sinned in the past, if they hear these things, will gladly repent and recover life."

2[112]:4 "Continue therefore," said he, "in this ministry, and complete it unto the end. For whosoever fulfill his commandments shall have life; yea such a man (shall have) great honor with the Lord. But whosoever keep not his commandments, fly from their life, and oppose him, and follow not his commandments, but deliver themselves over to death; and each one becomes guilty of his own blood. But I bid you obey these commandments, and you shall have a remedy for thy sins.

3[113]:1 "Moreover, I have sent these virgins unto you, that they may dwell with you; for I have seen that they are friendly towards you. You hast them therefore as helpers, that you may be the better able to keep his commandments; for it is impossible that these commandments be kept without the help of these virgins. I see too that they are glad to be with you. But I will charge them that they depart not at all from thy house.

3[113]:2 Only do you purify thy house; for in a clean house they will gladly dwell. For they are clean and chaste and industrious, and have favor in the sight of the Lord. If, therefore, they shall find thy house pure, they will continue with you; but if the slightest pollution arise, they will depart from thy house at once. For these virgins love not pollution in any form."

3[113]:3 I said unto him, "I hope, Sir, that I shall please them, so that they may gladly dwell in my house for ever; and just as he to whom you didst deliver me makes no complaint against me, so they likewise shall make no complaint."

3[113]:4 He said unto the shepherd, "I perceive," said he, "that he wishes to live as the servant of God, and that he will keep these commandments, and will place these virgins in a clean habitation."

3[113]:5 With these words he again delivered me over to the shepherd, and called the virgins, and said to them; "Inasmuch as I see that you are glad to dwell in this man's house, I commend to you him and his house, that you depart not at all from his house." But they heard these words gladly.

4[114]:1 He said then to me, "Quit you like a man in this ministry; declare to every man the mighty works of the Lord, and you shall have favor in this ministry. Whosoever therefore shall walk in these commandments, shall live and be happy in his life; but whosoever shall neglect them, shall not live, and shall be unhappy in his life.

4[114]:2 Charge all men who are able to do right, that they cease not to practice good works; for it is useful for them. I say moreover that every man ought to be rescued from misfortune; for he that has need, and suffered misfortune in his daily life, is in great torment and want.

4[114]:3 Whosoever therefore rescued from penury a life of this kind, wins great joy for himself. For he who is harassed by misfortune of this sort is afflicted and tortured with equal torment as one who is in chains. For many men on account of calamities of this kind, because they can bear them no longer, lay violent hands on themselves. He then who knows the calamity of a man of this kind and rescues him not, commits great sin, and becomes guilty of the man's blood.

4[114]:4 Do therefore good works, whoever of you have received (benefits) from the Lord, lest, while you delay to do them, the building of the tower be completed. For it is on your account that the work of the building has been interrupted. Unless then you hasten to do right, the tower will be completed, and you shut out."

4[114]:5 When then he had finished speaking with me, he rose from the couch and departed, taking with him the shepherd and the virgins. He said however unto me, that he would send the shepherd and the virgins back again to my house. . .

The Didache

The Didache is one of the oldest surviving extant piece of non-canonical literature. It is a handbook for new Christian converts, consisting of instructions derived directly from the teachings of Jesus.

The book can be divided into three sections. The first six chapters consist of Christian lessons; the next four give descriptions of the Christian ceremonies, including baptism, fasting and communion; and the last six outline the church organization.

The Didache claims to have been authored by the twelve apostles. While this is unlikely, the work could be a direct result of the first Apostolic Council, c.50 C.E. (Acts 15:28).

The given structure of the church as described is quite primitive as laid out in the Didache. The description of the Eucharist (bread and wine) does not mention of the "body and blood of Christ," possibly because it was regarded as one of the secret mysteries of early Christianity.

The work was never officially rejected by the Church, but was excluded from the canon because of its lack of literary value.

The complete text of the Didache was discovered in the Codex Hierosolymitanus, though a number of fragments exist, most notably in the Oxyrhynchus Papyri. It was originally composed in Greek, probably within a small community in order to codify community Christian worship.

The Didache or Teaching of the Twelve Apostles was discovered in a monastery in Constantinople and later published by P. Bryennios in 1883. The document, for it is to small to call a book, has become one of the most disputed Christian texts. Opinions of scholars range widely from accepting the document as the original of the Apostolic Decree to condemnations of the text as fiction of the early third century. It seems likely that the document is at least in part the result of the first Apostolic meeting as describe in Acts 15:28 (c. 50 AD). It bears no date and makes no reference to any datable external event. It depicts a Church with an early set of rituals, which could only be described as primitive when compared to the overly developed liturgies of today. The text seems to compare to the very earliest stages of the Church's order and practice presented by the New Testament while at the same time posing questions for many traditional interpretations of this first period of the Church's life.

Fragments of the Didache were found at Oxyrhyncus (P. Oxy 1782). The document was dated from the fourth century and was a Coptic translation (P. Lond. Or. 9271). Traces of the use of this text are widespread in the literature of the second and third centuries especially in Syria and Egypt. Since there was no mass media or fast communications at the time we can assume there was a reasonable time between the writing, propagation, and widespread use of the text. It was used in the Didascalia, which was written in the second century and was absorbed in total by the Apostolic Constitutions of the third century. Various Egyptian and Ethiopian Church Orders made obvious use as well. Athanasius describes it as "appointed by the Fathers to be read by those who newly join us, and who wish for instruction in the word of goodness" [Festal Letter 39:7]. Hence, a date of most additions was before the end of the first century. Draper states in a footnote (op. cit., p. 284), "A new consensus is emerging for a date c. 100 AD."

The Didache or Teaching of the Apostles

APOSTOLIC FATHERS (Adapted from the translation of J. B. Lightfoot)

1:1 There are two ways, one of life and one of death, and there is a great difference between the two ways. 1:2 The way of life is this. 1:3 First of all, you shall love the God that made you; 1:4 secondly, your neighbor as yourself. 1:5 And all things whatsoever you would not have befall yourself neither do you unto another. 1:6 Now of these words the doctrine is this. 1:7 Bless them that curse you, and pray for your enemies and fast for them that persecute you; 1:8 for what thank is it, if you love them that love you? Do not even the Gentiles the same? But do you love them that hate you, and you shall not have an enemy. 1:9 Abstain from fleshly and bodily lusts. 1:10 If any man give you a blow on your right cheek, turn to him the other also, and you shall be perfect; 1:11 if a man impress you to go with him, one mile, go with him two; 1:12 if a man take away your cloak, give him your coat also; 1:13 if a man take away from you that which is your own, ask it not back, for neither are you able. 1:14 To every man that asks of you give, and ask not back; 1:15 for the Father desires that gifts be given to all from His own bounties. 1:16 Blessed is he that gives according to the commandment; 1:17 for he is guiltless. 1:18 Woe to him that receives; 1:19 for, if a man receives having need, he is guiltless; 1:20 but he that had no need shall give satisfaction why and wherefore he received; 1:21 and being put in confinement he shall be examined concerning the deeds that he has done, and he shall not come out thence until he has given back the last farthing. 1:22 Yes, as touching this also it is said; 1:23 Let your alms sweat into your hands, until you shall have learned to whom to give.

2:1 And this is the second commandment of the teaching. 2:2 You shall do no murder, you shall not commit adultery, you shall not corrupt boys, you shall not commit fornication, you shall not steal, you shall not deal in magic, you shall do no sorcery, you shall not murder a child by abortion nor kill them when born, you shall not covet your neighbor's goods, you shall not perjure yourself, you shall not bear false witness, you shall not speak evil, you shall not cherish a grudge, you shall not be double-minded nor double-tongued; 2:3 for the double tongue is a snare of death. 2:4 Your word shall not be false or empty, but fulfilled by action. 2:5 You shall not be materialistic nor a plunderer nor a hypocrite nor ill-tempered nor proud. 2:6 You shall not entertain an evil design against your neighbor. 2:7 You shall not hate any man, but some you shall reprove, and for others you shall pray, and others you shall love more than your life.

3:1 My child, flee from every evil and everything that resembles it. 3:2 Be not angry, for anger leads to murder, nor jealous nor contentious nor wrathful; 3:3 for from all these things murders are engendered. 3:4 My child, be not lustful, for lust leads to fornication, neither foul-speaking neither with uplifted eyes (pride); 3:5 for of all these things adulteries are engendered. 3:6 My child, be no dealer in omens, since it leads to idolatry, nor an enchanter nor an astrologer nor a magician, neither be willing to look at them; 3:7 for from all these things idolatry is engendered. 3:8 My child, be not a liar, since lying leads to theft, neither avaricious neither vainglorious; 3:9 for from all these things thefts are engendered. 3:10 My child, be not a complainer, since it leads to blasphemy, neither self-willed neither a thinker of evil thoughts; 3:11 for from all these things blasphemies are engendered. 3:12 But be meek, since the meek shall inherit the earth. 3:13 Be long-suffering and pitiful and guileless and quiet and kindly and always fearing the words which you have heard. 3:14 You shall not exalt yourself, neither shall you admit boldness into your soul. 3:15 Your soul shall not cleave together with the lofty, but with the righteous and humble shall you walk. 3:16 The accidents that befall you, you shall receive as good, knowing that nothing is done without God.

4:1 My child, you shall remember him that speaks unto you the word of God night and day, and shall honor him as the Lord; 4:2 for from where ever the Lordship speaks, there is the Lord. 4:3 Moreover you shall seek out day by day the persons of the saints, that you may find rest in their words. 4:4 You shall not make a schism, but you shall pacify them that contend; 4:5 you shall judge righteously, you shall not make a difference in a person to reprove him for transgressions. 4:6 You shall not doubt whether a thing shall be or not be. 4:7 Be not found holding out your hands to receive, but drawing them in as to giving. 4:8 If you have ought passing through your hands, you shall give a ransom for your sins. 4:9 You shall not hesitate to give, neither shall you complain when giving; 4:10 for you shall know who is the good paymaster of your reward. 4:11 You shall not turn away from him that is in want, but shall make your brother partaker in all things, and shall not say that anything is your own. 4:12 For if you are fellow-partakers in that which is imperishable, how much rather in the things which are perishable? You shall not withhold your hand from your son or from your daughter, but from their youth you shall teach them the fear of God. 4:13 You shall not command your bondservant or your handmaid in your bitterness, who trust in the same God as yourself, lest haply they should cease to fear the God who is over both of you; 4:14 for He comes, not to call men with respect of persons, but He comes to those whom the Spirit has prepared. 4:15 But you, servants, shall be subject unto your masters, as to a type of God, in shame and fear. 4:16 You shall hate all hypocrisy, and everything that is not pleasing to the Lord. 4:17 You shall never forsake the commandments of the Lord; 4:18 but shall keep those things which you have received, neither adding to them nor taking away from them. 4:19 In church you shall confess your transgressions, and shall not betake yourself to prayer with an evil conscience. 4:20 This is the way of life.

5:1 But the way of death is this. 5:2 First of all, it is evil and full of a curse murders, adulteries, lusts, fornications, thefts, idolatries, magical arts, witchcrafts, plunderings, false witnessings, hypocrisies, doubleness of heart, treachery, pride, malice, stubbornness, covetousness, foul-speaking, jealousy, boldness, exaltation, boastfulness; 5:3 persecutors of good men, hating truth, loving a lie, not perceiving the reward of righteousness, not cleaving to the good nor to righteous judgment, wakeful not for that which is good but for that which is evil; 5:4 from whom gentleness and forbearance stand aloof; 5:5 loving vain things, pursuing a recompense, not pitying the poor man, not toiling for him that is oppressed with toil, not recognizing Him that made them, murderers of children, corrupters of the creatures of God, turning away from him that is in want, oppressing him that is afflicted, advocates of the wealthy, unjust judges of the poor, altogether sinful. 5:6 May you be delivered, my children, from all these things.

6:1 See lest any man lead you astray from this way of righteousness, for he teaches you apart from God. 6:2 For if you are able to bear the whole yoke of the Lord, you shall be perfect; 6:3 but if you are not able, do that which you are able. 6:4 But concerning eating, bear that which you are able; 6:5 yet abstain by all means from meat sacrificed to idols; 6:6 for it is the worship of dead gods.

7:1 But concerning baptism, thus shall you baptize. 7:2 Having first recited all these things, baptize in the name of the Father and of the Son and of the Holy Spirit in living (running) water. 7:3 But if you have not living (running) water, then baptize in other water; 7:4 and if you are not able in cold, then in warm. 7:5 But if you have neither, then pour water on the head thrice in the name of the Father and of the Son and of the Holy Spirit. 7:6 But before the baptism let him that baptize and him that is baptized fast, and any others also who are able; 7:7 and you shall order him that is baptized to fast a day or two before.

8:1 And let not your fastings be with the hypocrites, for they fast on the second and the fifth day of the week; 8:2 but do you keep your fast on the fourth and on the preparation (the sixth) day. 8:3 Neither pray you as the hypocrites, but as the Lord commanded in His Gospel, thus pray you. 8:4 Our Father, which are in heaven, hallowed be Your name; 8:5 Your kingdom come; 8:6 Your will be done, as in heaven, so also on earth; 8:7 give us this day our daily bread; 8:8 and forgive us our debt, as we also forgive our debtors; 8:9 and lead us not into temptation, but deliver us from the evil one; 8:10 for Yours is the power and the glory for ever and ever. 8:11 Three times in the day pray you so.

9:1 But as touching the eucharistic thanksgiving give you thanks thus. 9:2 First, as regards the cup: 9:3 We give You thanks, O our Father, for the holy vine of Your son David, which You made known unto us through Your Son Jesus; 9:4 Yours is the glory for ever and ever. 9:5 Then as regards the broken bread: 9:6 We give You thanks, O our Father, for the life and knowledge which You did make known unto us through Your Son Jesus; 9:7 Yours is the glory for ever and ever. 9:8 As this broken bread was scattered upon the mountains and being gathered together became one, so may Your Church be gathered together from the ends of the earth into Your kingdom; 9:9 for Yours is the glory and the power through Jesus Christ for ever and ever. 9:10 But let no one eat or drink of this eucharistic thanksgiving, but they that have been baptized into the name of the Lord; 9:11 for concerning this also the Lord has said: 9:12 Give not that which is holy to the dogs.

10:1 And after you are satisfied thus give you thanks: 10:2 We give You thanks, Holy Father, for Your holy name, which You have made to tabernacle in our hearts, and for the knowledge and faith and immortality, which You have made known unto us through Your Son Jesus; 10:3 Yours is the glory for ever and ever. 10:4 You, Almighty Master, did create all things for Your name's sake, and did give food and drink unto men for enjoyment, that they might render thanks to You; 10:5 but did bestow upon us spiritual food and drink and eternal life through Your Son. 10:6 Before all things we give You thanks that You are powerful; 10:7 Yours is the glory for ever and ever. 10:8 Remember, Lord, Your Church to deliver it from all evil and to perfect it in Your love; 10:9 and gather it together from the four winds--even the Church which has been sanctified--into Your kingdom which You have prepared for it; 10:10 for Yours is the power and the glory for ever and ever. 10:11 May grace come and may this world pass away. 10:12 Hosanna to the God of David. 10:13 If any man is holy, let him come; 10:14 if any man is not, let him repent. Maran Atha (Come Lord). Amen. 10:15 But permit the prophets to offer thanksgiving as much as they desire.

11:1 Whosoever therefore shall come and teach you all these things that have been said before, receive him; 11:2 but if the teacher himself be perverted and teach a different doctrine to the destruction thereof, hear him not; 11:3 but if to the increase of righteousness and the knowledge of the Lord, receive him as the Lord. 11:4 But concerning the apostles and prophets, so do you according to the ordinance of the Gospel. 11:5 Let every apostle, when he comes to you, be received as the Lord; 11:6 but he shall not abide more than a single day, or if there be a need, 11:7 but if he abide three days, he is a false prophet. 11:8 And when he departs let the apostle receive nothing save bread, until he finds shelter; 11:9 but if he ask money, he is a false prophet. 11:10 And any prophet speaking in the Spirit you shall not try neither discern; 11:11 for every sin shall be forgiven, but this sin shall not be forgiven. 11:12 Yet not every one that speaks in the Spirit is a prophet, but only if he have the ways of the Lord. 11:13 From his ways therefore the false prophet and the prophet shall be recognized. 11:14 And no prophet when he orders a table in the Spirit shall eat of it; 11:15 otherwise he is a false prophet. 11:16 And every prophet teaching the truth, if he does not what he teaches, is a false prophet. 11:17 And every prophet approved and found true, if he does ought as an outward mystery typical of the Church, and yet teaches you not to do all that he himself does, shall not be judged before you; 11:18 he has his judgment in the presence of God; 11:19 for in like manner also did the prophets of old time. 11:20 And whosoever shall say in the Spirit, Give me silver or anything else, you shall not listen to him; 11:21 but if he tell you to give on behalf of others that are in want, let no man judge him.

12:1 But let every one that comes in the name of the Lord be received; 12:2 and then when you have tested him you shall know him, for you shall have understanding on the right hand and on the left. 12:3 If the one who comes is a traveler, assist him, so far as you are able; 12:4 but he shall not stay with you more than two or three days, if it be necessary. 12:5 But if he wishes to settle with you, being a craftsman, let him work for and eat his bread. 12:6 But if he has no craft, according to your wisdom provide how he shall live as a Christian among you, but not in idleness. 12:7 If he will not do this, he is trafficking upon Christ. 12:8 Beware of such men.

13:1 But every true prophet desiring to settle among you is worthy of his food. 13:2 In like manner a true teacher is also worthy, like the workman, of his food. 13:3 Every firstfruit then of the produce of the wine-vat and of the threshing-floor, of your oxen and of your sheep, you shall take and give as the firstfruit to the prophets; 13:4 for they are your chief-priests. 13:5 But if you have not a prophet, give them to the poor. 13:6 If you make bread, take the firstfruit and give according to the commandment. 13:7 In like manner, when you open a jar of wine or of oil, take the firstfruit and give to the prophets; 13:8 yea and of money and raiment and every possession take the firstfruit, as shall seem good to you, and give according to the commandment.

14:1 And on the Lord's own day gather yourselves together and break bread and give thanks, first confessing your transgressions, that your sacrifice may be pure. 14:2 And let no man, having his dispute with his fellow, join your assembly until they have been reconciled, that your sacrifice may not be defiled; 14:3 for this sacrifice it is that was spoken of by the Lord; 14:4 In every place and at every time offer Me a pure sacrifice; 14:5 for I am a great king, says the Lord and My name is wonderful among the nations.

15:1 Appoint for yourselves therefore bishops and deacons worthy of the Lord, men who are meek and not lovers of money, and true and approved; 15:2 for unto you they also perform the service of the prophets and teachers. 15:3 Therefore despise them not; 15:4 for they are your honorable men along with the prophets and teachers. 15:5 And reprove one another, not in anger but in peace, as you find in the Gospel; 15:6 and let no one speak to any that has gone wrong towards his neighbor, neither let him hear a word from you, until he repent. 15:7 But your prayers and your almsgivings and all your deeds so do you as you find it in the Gospel of our Lord.

16:1 Be watchful for your life; 16:2 let your lamps not be quenched and your loins not ungirded, but be you ready; 16:3 for you know not the hour in which our Lord comes. 16:4 And you shall gather yourselves together frequently, seeking what is fitting for your souls; 16:5 for the whole time of your faith shall not profit you, if you be not perfected at the last season. 16:6 For in the last days the false prophets and corrupters shall be multiplied, and the sheep shall be turned into wolves, and love shall be turned into hate. 16:7 For as lawlessness increases, they shall hate one another and shall persecute and betray. 16:8 And then the world-deceiver shall appear as a son of God; 16:9 and shall work signs and wonders, and the earth shall be delivered into his hands; 16:10 and he shall do unholy things, which have never been since the world began. 16:11 Then all created mankind shall come to the fire of testing, and many shall be offended and perish; 16:12 but they that endure in their faith shall be saved by the Curse Himself. 16:13 And then shall the signs of the truth appear; 16:14 first a sign of a rift in the heaven, then a sign of a voice of a trumpet, and thirdly a resurrection of the dead; 16:15 yet not of all, but as it was said: 16:16 The Lord shall come and all His saints with Him. 16:17 Then shall the world see the Lord coming in the clouds of heaven.

Printed in the USA
CPSIA information can be obtained
at www.ICGtesting.com
CBHW081142021024
15263CB00005B/26